Second Edition

With chapters by

R. DEAN CODDINGTON, M.D.

Professor, Departments of Psychiatry and Pediatrics
Ohio State University College of Medicine

JOHN O. KANGAS, Ph.D.

Associate Professor, Departments of Psychiatry and Psychology
Ohio State University

PHILIP A. MARKS, Ph.D.

Professor, Departments of Psychiatry and Psychology
Ohio State University

CHARLES A. ROBERTS, M.D.

Associate Professor, Departments of Psychiatry and Public Health
University of Toronto

BURTRUM C. SCHIELE, M.D.

Professor, Department of Psychiatry and Neurology
University of Minnesota Medical School

Fundamentals of
PSYCHIATRY

IAN GREGORY, M.D.

Professor and Chairman, Department
of Psychiatry, Ohio State University
College of Medicine

1968   W. B. SAUNDERS COMPANY
PHILADELPHIA · LONDON · TORONTO

W. B. Saunders Company: West Washington Square
Philadelphia, Pa. 19105

12 Dyott Street
London W.C.1

1835 Yonge Street
Toronto 7, Ontario

Fundamentals of Psychiatry

To
Jean, Robert, Mary, Heather, and Roderick

PREFACE

It is a thing of no great difficulty to raise objections against another man's oration—nay, it is a very easy matter; but to produce a better in its place is a work extremely troublesome.

Of Hearing by Plutarch

Let us settle the facts first and fight about the moral tendencies afterwards.

The Way of All Flesh by Samuel Butler

Life is the art of drawing sufficient conclusions from insufficient premises.

Note-books. Lord, What Is Man? by Samuel Butler

The first edition of this book was published in 1961, and was intended to serve as an introduction to clinical psychiatry for medical students as well as a concise but comprehensive summary of scientific information for physicians in other fields. By that time I had studied, practiced, and taught psychiatry for thirteen years, and was emerging from a developmental stage of skepticism in which the more I learned the less I knew. Existing textbooks of psychiatry appeared unduly committed to some arbitrary theoretical position, and to involve repetitive elaboration of observational data and reductionistic interpretations.

In view of the clinical clerkship in psychiatry that was already required in many medical schools, I assumed that it was no longer desirable to include extensive illustrative case history material in a textbook that was intended to integrate scientific information concerning etiology and treatment. Physicians, medical students, and their instructors, however, are concerned primarily with patients and with accurate evaluation and effective therapeutic intervention. Recognition of these goals has led to radical revision in both content and organization of the present volume.

During the first half of the present century, psychiatry progressed from a preoccupation with description and classification toward a dynamic understanding of intra-psychic and interpersonal forces influencing human motivation and behavior. The past two decades have wit-nessed the acquisition of scientific information relevant to psychiatry by research in various disciplines that include genetics, physiology, biochemistry, psychology, sociology, and anthropology. Unfortunately, the rapid advances in each field of specialization have been accompanied by some degree of isolation from scientists working in related areas. Psychiatry, psychoanalysis, and psychology are all accumulating extensive literature, and effective communication between members of various disciplines is essential for the rapid integration of new concepts and findings. This fact was particularly brought home to me during the course of a fruitful collaboration with a psy-chologist, resulting in the 1965 publication of our textbook of abnormal psychology. It was during this time that the format and method of presentation employed in the present volume gradually took shape.

The first half of this book contains general principles of psychopathology and their application in clinical psy-chiatry. A historical introduction is followed by chapters on definition, description, and classification; dynamics, development, and etiology; psychiatric and psychological evaluation; psychosocial and organic therapies; and pre-ventive and legal aspects of psychiatry. The second half of the book is then devoted to a more detailed considera-tion of various psychiatric syndromes confronting the physician—neurotic and psychophysiological disorders, functional psychotic and behavior disorders, organic brain disorders, mental retardation, and disorders of childhood. Various forms of illustration have been employed for pur-poses of clarification, including tables, figures, and many case histories. The latter are drawn from all age groups and walks of life, and are intended to illustrate the applica-tion of various treatments, as well as description, dynamics, and multiple factors in etiology.

The main goal of the present volume is to meet the needs of the medical student and physician for a practical and systematic summary of fundamental knowledge in psy-chopathology and clinical psychiatry. The theoretical orientation with which I approach this task may be de-scribed as eclectic, holistic, and pragmatic. Since various interpretations may be placed upon these terms, however, they merit some elaboration.

In ancient times, the eclectics were a group of Greek philosophers who selected such doctrines as pleased them from the philosophies advanced by others. In more recent times, eclecticism has been viewed as a transitional attempt to resolve conflicting viewpoints when the truth is not certain. Such an approach may lead to two major kinds of difficulty. On the one hand there may be an uncritical acceptance of contradictory views, on the dubious assumption that there is a little bit of good (or truth) in everything. On the other hand, the selectiveness inherent in the definition may be arbitrary, as in the outright rejection of psychoanalytic theory and therapy by a number of psychiatrists who have claimed to be eclectic. In the present context, however, eclecticism is interpreted as meaning selective on the basis of scientific merit; the breadth of scientific disciplines contributing relevant knowledge to psychiatry has already been indicated.

The term holistic has been applied to schools of philosophy and psychology that emphasize the unity of mind and body. In a modern conception of psychiatry, however, it may be employed to emphasize both the interaction between somatic and psychosocial forces and the integration of relevant information concerning etiology, treatment, and prevention. The term pragmatic is particularly applicable to techniques of therapy employed, since the latter are to some extent empirical and not necessarily based upon certain etiologic knowledge. The same is true in other fields of medicine, but there is now much more accurate information available concerning personality development than was true a generation ago. We may confidently anticipate that further advances in knowledge will lead to continuing improvement in specific techniques of therapy and prevention.

Even within the field of psychiatry there is an increasing tendency for specialization, and I have found it necessary to call upon colleagues to contribute several chapters in the present volume. I am most grateful to Doctor Dean Coddington, who has written a chapter on disorders of childhood, to Doctors John Kangas and Philip Marks, who have contributed a chapter on psychological tests in diagnosis, to Doctor Charles Roberts, who has provided a chapter on preventive psychiatry, and to Doctor Burtrum Schiele, who has written the general chapter on organic therapies employed in psychiatry. I wish to express my sincere appreciation to Mrs. Regina Doll, Mrs. Thelma Hager, and Mrs. Julie Smith for their invaluable secretarial assistance. I am also indebted to various authors and publishers who kindly consented to the reproduction of tables, figures, and excerpts from published material and who receive individual acknowledgment in the text.

IAN GREGORY

CONTENTS

No man is an Iland, intire of itselfe; every man is a peece of the Continent, a part of the maine.

Devotions by John Donne

The mind is its own place, and in itself
Can make a heaven of hell, a hell of heaven.

From "Paradise Lost" by John Milton

Historical Introduction

PSYCHIATRY, PSYCHOANALYSIS, AND PSYCHOLOGY

PSYCHIATRY

Psychiatry is the medical specialty concerned with the study, diagnosis, treatment, and prevention of mental, emotional, and behavior disorders. The term is derived from Greek roots meaning mind-healing, and was widely adopted during the latter part of the nineteenth century, as reflecting appropriate medical concern and responsibility for the care and treatment of patients with mental disorders. The psychiatrist is therefore a physician with special training and experience in the evaluation and treatment of patients with psychiatric disorders. These disorders may affect persons of all ages, and may involve predominantly intellectual or emotional processes, verbal or nonverbal behavior. They may result mainly from disturbances in biological function, or from the adverse influence of psychological or sociocultural factors. They may be treated exclusively by psychosocial techniques of therapy, or sometimes by drugs or other somatic therapies.

Every psychiatrist employs certain techniques known as psychotherapy, a generic term for various forms of treatment based primarily upon verbal or nonverbal communication with the patient, in contrast to the use of drugs or physical measures such as electroshock. The relative emphasis on different techniques of psychotherapy, however, varies with the interests and training of the psychiatrist, as well as with the nature of the problems presented by the patient. The majority of psychiatrists agree with other physicians in regarding intensive psychotherapy as a medical responsibility, but similar techniques may be employed by psychologists or other professional personnel who also work with psychiatric patients.

The different interests and training of psychiatrists sometimes set them apart from other physicians, and various nonmedical definitions of psychiatry have been proposed. Sullivan conceived of psychiatry as the study of processes that involve or go on between people—interpersonal human relationships. Masserman defined psychiatry as the science of human behavior. Such definitions, however, are unduly broad and conflict with modern concepts of the behavioral and social sciences. Berelson and Steiner pointed out that the *social sciences* usually include six disciplines: anthropology, economics, history, political science, psychology,

1

and sociology. They defined the *behavioral sciences* as being the disciplines of anthropology, psychology, and sociology, minus and plus: *minus* certain specialized sectors as physiological psychology, archaeology, technical linguistics, and most of physical anthropology; *plus* social geography, some psychiatry, and the behavioral parts of economics, political science, and law.

With such considerations in mind, one may agree with Redlich and Freedman that psychiatry is an applied science dealing with abnormal human behavior. Psychiatrists are primarily scientifically informed medical practitioners whose task is to help people with certain kinds of difficulties. They therefore require training in all relevant basic biological and behavioral sciences. It has also been increasingly recognized that *all* physicians require some training in behavioral sciences as well as clinical psychiatry. In many medical schools psychiatry has become one of the five major clinical specialties in which medical students have a required clerkship. Increasing emphasis on psychiatry in general medical training is reflected not only in curriculum time but also in its independent representation in the examinations of the National Board of Medical Examiners.

At the present time there are approximately a quarter of a million physicians in the United States, and roughly 15,000 of these physicians are members of the American Psychiatric Association. The latter organization had its origin in 1844 as the Association of Medical Superintendents of American Institutions for the Insane. In 1892 the name of this organization was changed to the American Medico-Psychological Association, and this was changed to its present name in 1921. It was not until 1934, however, that the American Board of Psychiatry and Neurology was established jointly by action of the American Medical Association, the American Neurological Association, and the American Psychiatric Association,

to determine the competence of specialists in psychiatry and in neurology.

Neurology is the medical specialty devoted to the study, diagnosis, treatment, and prevention of organic diseases of the nervous system. Formerly, many specialists were certified by the American Board as competent to practice both neurology and psychiatry. The close relationship between these two specialties is still recognized in the training requirements and examinations of the American Board, about one-third of the examination for specialist certification in psychiatry being devoted to neurology and its basic sciences (and vice versa). Psychiatry and neurology are still divisions of the same department in a number of medical schools, whereas in others neurology is an independent department or division of the department of internal medicine. The trend toward increasing specialization, and requirements involving additional residency training for those seeking certification in both specialties, have led to a diminishing proportion of individuals with competence in both fields.

Among the requirements for admission to the American Board examinations for specialist certification in psychiatry or neurology are the following: graduation from an approved medical school, a legal license to practice medicine, one year of approved internship, three years of approved residency training in the United States or Canada, and two additional years of experience in the specialty in one of these two countries. Admission to the examinations for specialist certification in psychiatry or neurology therefore requires a minimum of six years following graduation from an approved medical school.

It is specified that residency training in general psychiatry should include clinical work with neurotic and psychotic patients, combined with the study of the basic psychiatric sciences, medical and social psychology, psychopathology, psychotherapy, and the physiological and pharmacological therapies, including a basic knowledge of the form, function, and pertinent pathology of the nervous system. This training should include instruction in psychiatric aspects of general medical and surgical conditions, and the behavior disorders of children and adolescents, sufficient to develop practical ability to direct the treatment of such conditions. It should also include collaborative work with social workers, clinical psychologists, courts, and other social agencies.

In 1959 the American Board of Psychiatry and Neurology established a committee on certification in child psychiatry. In addition to other requirements already mentioned, admission to the examinations in child psychiatry requires previous certification as a specialist in general psychiatry, and one additional year of residency training — two of the required four years being in general psychiatry, and two being in child psychiatry. At the present time, approximately one half of the members of the American Psychiatric Association are certified as specialists in general psychiatry, roughly five percent as specialists in neurology, and about two percent as specialists in child psychiatry.

PSYCHOANALYSIS

Psychoanalysis is the term applied by Sigmund Freud (1896) to the theory and practice of his method of treating psychiatric disorders. At least three aspects of psychoanalysis are frequently distinguished from one another: a psychological theory of human development and behavior; a method research; and Freud's system of psychotherapy, whereby free association and dream interpretation are employed to trace emotions and behavior to repressed instinctive drives and unconscious defenses against them. Psychoanalytic treatment seeks to

eliminate or diminish the undesirable effects of unconscious conflicts by bringing into conscious awareness their existence, origin, and inappropriate expression in current emotions and behavior. Psychoanalytic therapy has received most widespread application in the treatment of neuroses, but Freud and others have believed that its longterm contributions to the basic sciences of human behavior would be more significant than its contributions as a form of treatment. The latter are limited partly by the length of time and expense involved, which in turn restrict the numbers of trained psychoanalysts and their availability to treat patients with psychiatric disorder.

Because of its origins in the genius of one man, the early survival of psychoanalysis as an independent discipline involved intolerance of deviation in theory or techniques of therapy. This led to the establishment of Jung's separate system of analytic psychology, Adler's system of individual psychology, and other related systems. None of these deviant groups attracted as many practitioners as psychoanalysis, nor contributed as much to the theory and practice of psychiatry, and to the behavioral and social sciences. The intensive longterm study of small numbers of individuals by means of psychoanalysis provides information that is complemented by means of experimental manipulation and extensive studies involving large numbers of individuals. Psychoanalysis may thus be regarded as one of the relevant basic sciences of human behavior. While psychoanalytic concepts are integrated throughout the present volume, there will be further discussion of Freud's contributions later in the present chapter, of dynamics and development in Chapter 3, and of psychoanalytic therapy in Chapter 11.

Freud was in favor of training nonmedical psychoanalysts but many of his students opposed this, particularly in the United States, where economic and philosophical factors combined to favor the development of psychoanalysis and a closer relationship with psychiatry and medical education than in other countries. The American Psychoanalytic Association was founded in 1911 and accepts only physicians with some residency training in psychiatry for formal psychoanalytic training and membership in the association. The American Psychoanalytic Association has 26 affiliate societies and 19 approved training institutes, among which are some that accept nonphysicians as associate or affiliate members. The combined membership of the American Psychoanalytic Association and its affiliate societies numbers approximately 1500, and there are not more than about 2000 psychoanalysts in the world.

Psychoanalytic training in most American institutes consists of a didactic analysis of the student by an approved training analyst, the supervision or "control" of several therapeutic psychoanalyses carried out by the student, four or five years of didactic courses, and sometimes a thesis. The didactic analysis usually lasts for hundreds of hours over a period of several years, and full psychoanalytic training is likely to require at least six years, costing the student up to $25,000. Many psychiatric residents who do *not* enter formal psychoanalytic training, however, undergo a more limited period of personal analysis or psychotherapy, with the goal of learning more about themselves and psychopathology, and learning techniques of psychotherapy applicable in treating their patients.

PSYCHOLOGY

Psychology has been successively defined as the study of the soul or mind, the study of conscious experience, and as the science of behavior. Until the late nineteenth century, philosophy, based on speculation and logic, and physiology, based on experimental observations, were the only two approaches to what has since become the field of psychology. In 1879 Wilhelm Wundt founded the first laboratory dedicated to the experimental study of conscious experience. His structural approach to psychology was followed in this country by the functional approach of John Dewey and others, who redefined psychology as the study of man's adjustment to his environment. Other psychologists influenced by the work of Pavlov emphasized the study of overt behavior, and the Gestalt school emphasized complex patterns or configurations of behavior and experience. During the present century, many psychologists have been strongly influenced by psychoanalytic formulations regarding unconscious mental processes, and psychologists are now less distinguishable from one another by adherence to some particular school of thought than by their field of professional activity.

Psychology has therefore been defined as an academic discipline, a profession, and a science dealing with the study of mental processes and behavior in man and animal. The American Psychological Association was founded in 1892, and now has about 25,000 members including most of the qualified psychologists in the country. The minimum standard for election to full membership is receipt of the doctoral degree, based in part upon a psychological dissertation and conferred by a graduate school of recognized standing. In order to qualify as an associate member, an applicant must have completed two years of graduate work in psychology, or have received the master's degree in psychology from a recognized graduate school and also completed one full year of professional work in psychology. In order to give recognition to the specialized interests of different psychologists, the American Psychological Association includes 24 divisions, among which are clinical, consulting, industrial, educational, and counseling psychology. Psychologists working in close collaborative relationships with psychiatrists are most likely to be members of the division of clinical psychology, which includes more than 3000 fellows and full members. Almost half of these clinical psychologists have obtained the additional diploma qualification which are awarded by the American Board of Examiners in Professional Psychology.

The fully qualified clinical psychologist has therefore undergone long and arduous training in the evaluation and psychotherapy of clients or patients with certain varieties of mental, emotional, or behavior disorder. Traditionally, the psychologist's training has been more academic and research-oriented than that of the psychiatrist, but a number of psychologists have introduced new techniques or approaches in psychotherapy, which will be discussed in Chapter 11. Because of their interest in counseling or psychotherapy, psychologists have sometimes come into conflict with those psychiatrists or other members of the medical profession who regard *all* treatment of patients, including psychotherapy, as a medical responsibility and prerogative. In many instances, excellent collaborative relationships between the professions have already been firmly established. It may be appropriate here however to reproduce brief passages from official statements made by the American Psychiatric Association (endorsing an earlier position taken by the American Medical Association), and by the American Psychological Association. The statement by the American Psychiatric Association (1964) included the following:

. . . An objective evaluation of the medical profession's present relations with other health professions has convinced the committee that physicians must initiate and develop more effective interprofessional relationships . . . .

. . . To place the most critical aspect of the problem under specific discussion in its proper perspective, namely the professional need for cooperatively defining and respecting the areas of activity and responsibility for scientists who participate in the care of the patient, it must be fully realized that physicians have the ultimate responsibility for patient care, and that they, and they alone, are trained to assume this responsibility. . . .

The statement by the American Psychological Association included the following passage:

. . . The profession of psychology approves the practice of psychotherapy by psychologists only if it meets conditions of genuine collaboration with physicians most qualified to deal with the borderline problems which arise (e.g.) differential diagnosis, intercurrent disease, psychosomatic problems. Such collaboration is not necessarily indicated in remedial teaching or vocational and educational counselling.

Members of professions other than psychology have made major contributions to our knowledge of psychopathology and to the effective treatment of patients with psychiatric disorders, and their work continues. A number of contributions by biological, behavioral, and social scientists are discussed in Chapters 5 through 8; some specific functions of other mental health professions such as psychiatric social work and nursing are discussed in Chapters 9 and 11. The important contributions made by such other members of the mental health professions are also implicit in other information presented throughout this volume. The present section however has been concerned with defining psychiatry, psychoanalysis, and psychology, and relationships between these disciplines. In the remainder of the present chapter, we shall review the main historical trends in psychiatric theory and practice from antiquity to the present.

PRIMITIVE ANIMISM AND GRECO-ROMAN ENLIGHTENMENT

Primitive man was confronted with many events and experiences beyond his comprehension, to which he may have attributed a magical or supernatural origin. Favorable or pleasurable events were apt to be regarded as blessings from the gods, and painful or unfavorable events as punishments invoked by gods or devils, or by other human beings in league with them. Such evil visitations and punishments may have been regarded as just or unjust, and led man to search for post hoc supernatural explanations of why he should have been subjected to flood or famine, plague or pestilence, madness or melancholy.

As primitive man searched for explanations of human thought and actions, he frequently concluded that there are two independent agencies involved: his body and an internal animating principle or soul. Mental retardation, insanity, and evil behavior might then be attributed to such agencies as possession of the owner's body by a god or evil spirit, or alternatively to absence of the owner's soul on travels elsewhere. Such interpretations tended to be correlated with the treatment accorded the mentally deranged individual by his fellow man. If the prevailing belief was that of possession by a god, he may have been revered and treated kindly. If his body were thought to be possessed by a devil, it may have been made a very unpleasant place for that devil to live by means of exorcism, torture, and sometimes death. The missing-soul hypothesis may also have provided rationalization and sanction for killing the body so that it might rejoin the wandering soul.

Even in those primitive societies where the mentally deranged were treated kindly, superstition generally led them to be regarded with fear and awe, and they were rarely liked, admired, or given high social status. More frequently they were regarded as outcasts, suffering just retribution for their own imagined sins or those of their parents, and subjected to social ostracism or physical abuse. Three major trends, however, appear to be associated with changes in concepts of mental disorder and the treatment of affected individuals throughout recorded history. The first of these is the growth of *naturalism*, involving attempts to explain all phenomena and account for all values by means of strictly natural (as opposed to supernatural) agencies. This led to the interpretation of mental disorder in terms of organic brain disease or of reactions to environmental experiences.

A second related trend has involved the growth of *empiricism*, a term originally applied to a sect of physicians who based their practice on experience—i.e., on observation and experiment alone. Once a derogatory term for quackery, empiricism came to be applied to the experimental analysis of observational data, contributing in turn to the development of scientific determinism. The third major trend evident over the centuries has been the growth of *humanitarianism*, emphasizing the rights to humane treatment of all individuals, including the mentally deranged. While the preceding trends may be partially interrelated, there has been no uniform progression, and there was indeed a prolonged period of regression during the Dark Ages preceding the Renaissance.

In ancient Greece, the word psyche meant breath and hence life, soul, or spirit, as distinct from body. In Greek mythology, Psyche was the personification of the human soul. She was so beautiful that Eros (Cupid), the god of love, took her to an isolated castle, but forbade her to look at him since he was a god. When she disobeyed, he abandoned her, but she searched for him and performed many difficult tasks, until at last she was reunited with Eros forever and made immortal, their marriage representing a union between soul and love. Modern usage of the term psyche to mean "mind" apparently dates back to the seventeenth century.

Ancient Greek poetry and mythology record episodes of frenzy affecting the heroes, and early Egyptian papyri contain some references to mental distubances. More specific accounts of mental disorder are contained in the books of the Old Testament, Saul, David, and Nebuchadnezzar being cited as examples. Epileptic convulsions were long recognized and known as the "sacred disease," but Hippocrates (460-377 B.C.) remarked that epilepsy appeared to him in no way more divine or sacred than other diseases, but that it had a natural cause. "If you cut open the head," he remarked, "you will find the brain humid, full of sweat and smelling badly. And in this way you may see that it is not a god which injures the body, but disease." Hippocrates is generally regarded as the father of medicine, which he attempted to place on a scientific plane based on objective observation and critical deductive reasoning. He followed the current belief that disease resulted from an imbalance of the four bodily humors, but maintained that the disturbance was influenced by outside forces, and that the humors were glandular secretions. He ascribed various forms of mental disorder to bodily causes, and interpreted hysteria as due to the wandering of the uterus (hystera), for which his therapeutic recommendation was marriage — not far removed from the "prescription" of a nineteenth-century gynecologist cited by Freud, "Penis normalis dosim, repetatur," or from Freud's own dictum that with a normal sex life, no neurosis is possible.

The maxim "Know thyself" was attributed to Thales (C.636-C.546 B.C.) but later became attached to the name of Socrates (469-399 B.C. who also advised military surgeons that they ought to attempt to treat the soul as well as the body of their patients, a theme that was elaborated by his pupil Plato (C.427-C.347 B.C.). Plato's chief contribution to psychological thought was his conception of the soul as being divided into three parts: logic associated with the brain, courage or will associated with the chest, and appetitive instincts associated with the abdomen. Plato argued for the independent reality of ideas as the only guarantee of ethical standards

and of objective scientific knowledge. His idealism was followed by the realism of Aristotle (384-322 B.C.), who emphasized the direct observation of nature and taught that theory must follow fact. While he formulated rules of logic and causation that endured for two millennia, Aristotle still erred in locating the soul, as the origin of thought, in the heart.

Asclepiades (C.124-40 B.C.) was a Greek physician who founded an influential school of medicine in Rome. He believed that disease is caused by disturbances in the movement of the atoms or particles of which he thought the body was composed, but he distinguished between delirium and mental disorders caused by emotional disturbances, and he pioneered in the humane treatment of the insane using baths, massage, exercises, and diet. Other physicians of this era were able to distinguish between certain forms of mental disorder; Aretaeus (C.30-90 A.D.) suggested that mania and melancholia were two expressions of the same illness. He also appears to have been the first to become interested in the prepsychotic personality of patients who developed mental disorder. He regarded melancholia as developing from a tendency to sadness, and mania from proneness to irritability, violence, and childish impulsiveness — thus the concept that abnormality may represent only a quantitative exaggeration of normal characteristics.

Many physicians of the time advocated treating the mentally ill with emetics, purgatives, bloodletting, alcohol, opium, darkness, fasting, whipping, music, or sexual love. The humanitarian approach of Asclepiades however was also advocated by Soranus (second century A.D.), a Greek physician who practiced in Alexandria and Rome. He asked how intoxication with alcohol or other drugs could be expected to dispel mental states that frequently resembled the confusion and irrationality of gross intoxication. He suggested placing maniacs in a moderately lighted room, using much tact and discretion, and avoiding shock or the careless application of restraining bands that would increase or produce fury or agitation. The writings of Soranus were translated into Latin by Caelius Aurelianus, who also recommended humane measures that would not aggravate the mental disorder for which they were administered.

Toward the end of the Greco-Roman era, major scientific contributions to anatomy and medicine were made by Galen (c.130-200 A.D.), a physician born of Greek parents, who practiced in Rome. Through dissection and experiment he searched for anatomical bases of function and pathology. He regarded the central nervous system as the center for sensation, mobility, and mental functions, and he considered mental disorders as being disorders of the brain. He viewed symptoms as having multiple origins or causes, and elaborated the humoral theory of body types and temperamental characteristics. He was the most influential medical writer after Hippocrates, and some of his observations and speculations survived as dogma throughout the Middle Ages.

MEDIEVAL REGRESSION AND HUMANE REFORM

Before the death of Galen, Rome had already been stricken with hedonistic self-indulgence, internal conflict, intrigue, and political instability. Her frequently changing rulers made it their business to crush all science, and slaughtered many scholars. In the year 313 A.D. Constantine and his fellow emperor, Licinius, issued the Edict of Milan, stating that Christianity would be tolerated throughout the Roman Empire. This did not, as is sometimes stated, make Christianity the official state religion, and Constantine continued to tolerate paganism, but it was not long before the study of Plato and Aristotle was banned. As Christianity spread, priests and monks, who were often the only literate people in the community, took over the function of caring for the sick, particularly the mentally ill. Through ignorance, madness was once more attributed to supernatural causes. Religious fanatics now viewed insanity as the work of the devil, the result of sinful communion between the madman and demons, frequently including sexual relations.

As superstition spread, bodily illness as well as mental disorder was regarded as divine punishment, coming under the jurisdiction of theology. The clergy took over the functions of physicians, interceding on behalf of the presumed sinners, prescribing prayers and penance, and administering drugs with religious or astrological implications. Such magical concoctions contain some fantastic ingredients, as in the following prescription:

"Take a testicle of a goat that has been killed on a Tuesday midnight during the first quarter of the moon, and the heart of a dog, mixed with the excrement of a new born babe, and after pulverizing, take an amount equivalent to half an olive twice a day." This "dung pharmacopoeia" was supplemented by incantations such as that described by Zilboorg and Henry as being invoked in the tenth century treatment of a young woman with hysteria:

. . . I conjure thee, O womb, in the name of the Holy Trinity, to come back to the place from which thou shouldst neither move nor turn away, without further molestation, and to return without anger, to the place where the Lord has put thee originally. . . .I conjure thee not to harm that maid of God, N., not to occupy her head, throat, neck, chest, ears, teeth, eyes, nostrils, shoulder blades, arms, hands, heart, stomach, spleen, kidneys, back, sides, joints, navel, intestines, bladder, thighs, shins, heels, nails, but to lie down quietly in the place where God chose for thee, so that this maid of God, N., be restored to health.

Fear and hostility led increasingly to the assumption that the mentally ill were witches or sorcerers possessed by the devil. To be in league with the devil was the worst crime imaginable, and the Old Testament decreed that no sorcerer or witch should be allowed to live. Convinced, however, that those possessed by the devil would deny this or even be unaware of it, various tests were devised to diagnose and ferret out those who were so possessed. Birth marks and deformities, hyperesthesia or anesthesia, or failure to bleed when pricked were among the characteristics assumed to be stigmata of demoniacal possession. Those suspected of such possession were subject to inquisition involving interrogation and torture, and ultimate sentence of death. In a patriarchal society the women were scapegoats, and it has been estimated that 50 women were convicted as witches for every man who was convicted as a sorcerer. Thousands were executed, many of them after receiving abusive treatment such as being brought to trial naked with their heads shaved, and not facing the judges lest the women bewitch them.

The rationalization of such brutality was undertaken by two Dominican monks, Heinrich Kramer and Johann Sprenger, who wrote the notorious book entitled *Malleus Maleficarum (Hammer of the Witches)*. This volume became the bible of all witch hunters, and in 1484 its authors received the approval of the Pope to act as inquisitors in the task of eradicating the evil. Roback remarked that these Dominican "Dogs of the Lord" (Canes Domini), as they styled themselves, were wolves on the prowl, serpents insidiously pouncing on their prey; and the deadly effect of their poisonous fangs penetrated all Christendom.

"All witchcraft," said the *Malleus*, "comes from carnal lust, which is in women insatiable. . . wherefore for the sake of fulfilling their lusts they consort even with devils." The volume included detailed documentation of such hypothetical sexual relationships, as well as the various manifestations of witchcraft, and the procedures to be adopted in apprehending, trying, convicting, and executing the witches. The latter included the following passage:

And while she is being questioned about each several point, let her be often and frequently exposed to torture beginning with the more gentle of them; for the Judge should not be too hasty to proceed to the graver kind. And while this is being done, let the Notary write all down how she is tortured and what questions are asked and how she answers.

Although there were others who did not believe in witchcraft or the methods of persecution in current vogue, it was not until 1563 that Johann Weyer published his two-volume work entitled *De Praestigiis Daemonum (On the Delusions about Demons)*. This was a learned refutation of witchcraft, in which the author was cautious about expressing religious convictions. Weyer was the first physician to document mental illness in such detail, and maintained that most witches were mentally disordered persons innocent of the accusations brought against them. "I show that those illnesses the origin of which is attributed to witches come from natural causes," he wrote. In addition to describing various symptoms of psychosis, and demonstrating the fantastic nature of various old wives' tales, he also attacked the inquisitors and convicting judges for their lack of common sense and their brutality.

It is not surprising that others should subsequently attack Weyer, or be led to defend him. A lawyer by the name of Jean Bodin attempted to refute Weyer's position in his *Demonomanie des Sorciers*, published in 1580. On the other hand, an English layman by the name of Reginald Scot wrote 16 volumes in support of Weyer's humane and enlightened views, and published them in 1584 under the title *Discoverie of Witchcraft*. Widespread belief in witchcraft persisted, however; King James I both ordered the burning of Scot's book and was moved to write his own book entitled *Daemonologie*, which was published in 1597.

Demonology persisted throughout the seventeenth century, and witches were still being sentenced to death in Poland, Mexico, and Switzerland until almost 1800. Nevertheless, the seventeenth century witnessed an increasing emphasis on naturalistic explanations of mental disorder, and an awakening of medical interest in such problems. Robert Burton, an English clergyman whose well-known work *The Anatomy of Melancholy* was published in 1621, attempted to explore the causes and manifestations of melancholy. Thomas Sydenham was a physician who recognized hysterical and hypochondriacal reactions as widespread and complex. Thomas Willis described general paresis (identified much later as central nervous system syphilis), and differentiated mental deficiency from deteriorating mental illness of later onset. The Scottish physician George Cheyne described neurosis under the term "The English Malady," which he believed to be responsible for about one-third of all consulting of physicians by patients. Georg Ernst Stahl regarded the relationships between body and mind as being interactional, and originated the distinction between the organic ("sympathetic") and functional ("pathetic") mental disorders which still exists. In spite of such medical advances, however, improvements in the treatment and investigation of psychiatric disorders awaited the humanitarian reforms of later generations.

The first asylums or mental hospitals appeared in Europe about the twelfth century, and the first place in England to care for the insane was the priory of St. Mary of Bethlehem in London (later known as "Bedlam") where six lunatics were confined in the year 1403. It remained a priory until 1546, and it was not until 1632 that a medical man (Crookes) was appointed governor.

Similar developments took place in other countries; the first asylum in the New World was founded by Bernardino Alvarez in 1566 at San Hippolito, Mexico.

During the seventeenth century, early settlers in the American colonies frequently held the prevailing belief that the distraught or insane were possessed by demons, and treated them accordingly. Hollingshead and Redlich gave the following account of the care accorded to the mentally ill at that time.

Often they created civil disturbances and were driven from their homes and towns or jailed along with beggars and criminals. The family of any person mentally ill was legally responsible for his care. Where a family was able to keep a deranged member at home, the sick person was locked and often chained in a barred room. When the family would not or could not care for its "insane" member, he was placed under the control of the King's Peace Officers. When the King's Officers were forced to intervene, the individual was taken to jail. If witchcraft was suspected, torture and occasionally hanging followed.

During the eighteenth century it became generally recognized that "idiots" and "distraught persons" were different from delinquents or criminals. Those without family, friends, or money became a charge upon the community of birth or residence, which tried to avoid such responsibility in two ways: either by abandoning the insane person in another town (usually at night) or by sale of the person at an annual auction to the lowest bidder (who tried to use him as labor on his farm). During the latter part of the eighteenth century, the indigent insane began to be admitted to the workhouse, which was a combination "poor house" and jail operated by the city and designed to accommodate a variety of persons such as the following: ". . . rogues, disorderly persons, all runaway stubborn servants and children, night workers, pilferers; all persons who neglect their callings, misspend earnings and do not provide for their families; and all persons under distraction, unfit to be at large and not cared for by their friends or relatives." The overseer of the workhouse was empowered to "punish with fetters and shackles and by whipping on the naked body not more than ten strikes at a time, or with close confinement without food or drink" those who did not follow his orders.

Humane reform and the abolition of restraint are generally credited to the Frenchman Philippe Pinel (1745-1826), although physicians and reformers in other countries were also influential in this movement. Pinel was Professor of Hygiene and Internal Medicine at the University of Paris, as well as being director of the Bicêtre Asylum and the Women's Hospital known as La Salpêtrière. In 1793, Pinel obtained permission from the Revolutionary Commune to remove the chains from his charges at the Bicêtre and gradually liberated more than 50 patients, some of whom had been in chains for 30 years. He believed that the chained patients had become unmanageable because of the treatment they had received, and his view was borne out by the improved behavior of those released. His book *Traité médico-philosophique sur l'aliénation mentale* was published in 1801, and was influential in promoting humane reform in other countries. Esquirol (1772-1840) succeeded Pinel and made further extensive reforms in the housing and management of the mentally ill throughout France.

An English Quaker by the name of William Tuke (1732-1822) had been so disgusted with the abuse of the mentally disturbed in the York asylum that he enlisted the help of fellow members of the Society of Friends and established the York Retreat in 1792. During the next three decades he continued to devote his efforts to reforming the treatment of mental patients, so that the York Retreat became a model for similar institutions in England and the United States.

Figure 1-1. Philippe Pinel (1745–1826). (Courtesy of National Library of Medicine.)

In this country the Quakers of Philadelphia had set aside special cells for housing the mentally ill in the cellar of the Pennsylvania Hospital, which was opened in 1756. Twenty years later the Virginia legislature became the first in the United States to vote public funds to help in building a hospital devoted exclusively to the insane. The second hospital in the United States built especially for the mentally ill was the Friends Asylum at Frankford, Pennsylvania, which was opened in 1817 by the Philadelphia Society of Friends. Other mental hospitals were built, and in 1841 the Pennsylvania Hospital became the first general hospital in the United States to erect a wing for the care of the mentally ill. However, during the first half of the nineteenth century many people continued to associate insanity with pauperism, and the mentally ill frequently continued to be confined in poor houses under unfortunate conditions.

Early reforms in the care of the mentally ill in the United States are often associated with the name of Benjamin Rush (1745-1813), who has been called the Father of American Psychiatry, and whose silhouette appears on the seal of the American Psychiatric Association. A Quaker who was influenced by William Tuke, Rush was one of the signers of the Declaration of Independence, and was the first real teacher of psychiatry in the United States. He not only worked for humane reforms of mental institutions, but also opposed slavery and the death sentence. In contrast with Pinel, however, he appears to have believed exclusively in somatic etiology of mental disorder, and to have relied heavily on old therapeutic techniques such as bleeding and purging.

Another motive force behind many reforms in both America and Europe was a retired schoolteacher from Boston, Dorothea Lynde Dix (1802-1887). She became shocked by what she had seen of the neglect and maltreatment of mental patients, and succeeded in stimulating governmental agencies in the United States and elsewhere to provide new and improved facilities for the care of the mentally ill. She has been credited with having been directly responsible for creating or extending the facilities of a total of 32 hospitals. By the middle of the nineteenth century, therefore, it was widely recognized that the mentally ill should be treated humanely, and that physicians should provide leadership in the study, evaluation, and treatment of psychiatric disorders. The stage was now set for scientific advances in definition and description, the recognition of biological and psychosocial factors in etiology, and the development of psychosocial and somatic techniques of treatment.

DESCRIPTIVE AND BIOLOGICAL APPROACHES

A Swedish botanist and physician, Carolus Linnaeus (1707-1778), published the first edition of his *Systema Na-* *turae* in 1735. In this volume he presented his systematic classification of plants, animals, and minerals. Despite deficiencies in his premises, his system remained the basis for a modern taxonomy and nomenclature in biology. Linnaeus also published a classification of diseases in 1763, but it is not surprising that the latter was of less enduring significance. His better known contributions paved the way for a French naturalist, Jean Baptiste Lamarck (1744-1829), who is noted for his study and classification of invertebrates and for his introduction of evolutionary theories. Lamarck asserted that all life forms have arisen by a continuous process of gradual modification throughout geologic history, and attempted to explain this process through the transmission of acquired characteristics from an organism to its offspring. The latter concept is not compatible with modern knowledge of hereditary transmission, but the process of evolution was extensively documented by Charles Darwin (1809-1882) in his *Origin of Species,* published in 1859.

The cellular structure of plants and animals was observed by the botanist Schleiden and the zoologist Schwann in the years 1838-1839. Experimental studies of physiological function were undertaken, and the French physiologist Claude Bernard (1813-1878) is generally regarded as the founder of experimental medicine. During the latter part of the nineteenth century, impetus was also given by Francis Galton (1822-1911), a cousin of Charles Darwin, to the study of individual differences, family resemblances, and statistical techniques that were later applied in both genetics and behavioral sciences.

During this period a talented English neurologist, John Hughlings Jackson (1835-1911), adapted the scientific concerns of his day to the formulation of functional relationships within the nervous system. He viewed the nervous system as organized in hierarchical fashion, with the most complex functions (associated with the cerebral cortex) being the most recently acquired from an evolutionary point of view, and also being the most vulnerable to dissolution under conditions of trauma, fatigue, or stress. Under such adverse conditions, Jackson postulated a regression of neural function to lower and more primitive levels, since he recognized that higher centers may be concerned with inhibiting the functions of lower centers, which would then act unopposed when the functions of the higher centers were disrupted. In analyzing the effects of brain damage, he therefore distinguished between negative symptoms due to loss of function (loss of "government") and positive symptoms due to release from inhibition ("the anarchy of the now uncontrolled people"). For every mental state there was a correlative physical state in the brain, and the observable symptoms and signs of neurological and psychiatric disorder were due to a combination of positive with negative symptoms.

Jackson's principle of the dissolution of complex functions and his concepts of dynamic interaction within the nervous system are of particular relevance in the manifestations of organic brain syndromes (Chapter 24), and were also employed by Freud in his formulations on unconscious intrapsychic dynamic processes. Other contributions to neuropsychiatry came from the studies of brain pathologists such as Franz Nissl (1860-1919) and Constantin von Economo (1876-1931), but such information on structural brain pathology is of relevance mainly to the organic brain syndromes rather than the functional psychiatric disorders.

Ernst von Feuchtersleben (1806-1849), Dean of the Medical School at the University of Vienna, gave articulate expression to the principle of a mind-body unity. He has been spoken of as the founder of psychosomatic medicine, but he died at the age of 43 and his approach tended to be submerged by concern with the problems of adult psychotic patients in mental hospitals. Wilhelm Griesinger (1817-1869), however, made a distinction between psychotic and neurotic patients and professed an interest in both. On accepting his appointment as Professor of Psychiatry and Medicine at the University of Berlin, he stipulated that he be given a clinic for the neurotic as well as responsibility for the care of psychotic patients. His textbook *Mental Pathology and Therapeutics,* however, emphasized organic rather than psychological factors in etiology. He regarded psychic disorders as brain diseases, with a great variety of manifestations related to the premorbid personality. Although he did not believe in a clear differentiation of normal from abnormal processes, and recognized the possible significance of multiple etiological factors, he still felt that there was only one psychosis (with a variety of symptoms) and relied heavily on drugs such as cathartics and emetics in treatment.

In addition to emphasis on biological etiology and somatic therapy, nineteenth century psychiatry demonstrated the same concern with description and classification as other developing biological sciences. The French psychiatrist Jean-Pierre Falret (1794-1870) studied under Esquirol and continued the tradition of his predecessors at La Salpêtrière. He introduced the term "mental alienation" in place of "dementia" and "furor," and considered both mania and depression as different phases of the same disorder, which he termed "La Folie Circulaire." Benedict Morel (1809-1873), born in Germany and educated in France, was for a time assistant and secretary to Falret. Morel wrote a survey of psychiatry in half a dozen European countries and the United States, and a large volume entitled *Études médico-psychologiques sur l'aliénation mentale,* in which he considered somatic, psychological, and sociological aspects of mental disorder. He introduced the term *demence précoce* for certain disorders later known as dementia praecox or schizophrenia, but he may be best remembered for his notion that mental disorder was the result of progressive degenerative processes. The latter theme was subsequently elaborated by the Italian criminologist and physician Cesare Lombroso (1835-1909). Lombroso's anthropometric studies of criminals in turn stimulated the morphological studies of psychiatric patients by Ernst Kretschmer (1888-) and concepts of constitutional predisposition still held in various parts of the world. In the United States, relationships between somatotype and temperamental characteristics have been explored by William Sheldon; this line of research will be reviewed in Chapter 6.

During the second half of the nineteenth century, German psychiatrists described a number of syndromes that have been retained in more recent classifications. Karl Kahlbaum (1828-1899) identified catatonia and paraphrenia while Ewald Hecker (1843-1909) described hebephrenia. It remained for Emil Kraepelin (1856-1928) to introduce a systematic descriptive classification of psychiatric disorder that was widely accepted. Kraepelin studied under the neuroanatomist Paul Flechsig and the psychologist Wilhelm Wundt, worked in several mental hospitals, and was Professor of Psychiatry at the Universities of Dorpat, Heidelberg, and Munich. He based his classification in part on the natural history and prognosis of psychiatric disorders, making a distinction between various types of dementia praecox and manic-depressive psychoses. His well-known textbook *Psychiatrie—Ein Lehrbuch* first appeared in 1883 and remained influential throughout eight editions. In it he emphasized the etiological importance of heredity and constitution, and recommended largely somatic methods of treatment, although he was essentially nihilistic in his evaluation of the results of therapy.

By contrast, the Swiss psychiatrist

Figure 1-2. Emil Kraepelin (1856–1926). (Courtesy of National Library of Medicine.)

Eugen Bleuler (1857-1939) stressed the importance of psychological factors in etiology and therapy. He was much more optimistic than Kraepelin regarding the natural outcome and effects of therapy in psychosis, and he advocated replacing the term dementia praecox with the more modern concept of the group of schizophrenias—emphasizing the split between various psychological functions, their multiple manifestations and etiology, and the facts that they did not necessarily progress to irrecoverable dementia or have an insidious onset during adolescence. Bleuler introduced the well-known terms *ambivalence, autism,* and *depth psychology,* and he had a lasting influence on both European and American psychiatry.

Adolf Meyer (1866-1950) was also born in Switzerland but came to the United States in 1892, after studying at Zurich, Paris, London, Edinburgh, and Berlin. He was director of research at various hospitals and taught psychiatry at Cornell University prior to serving as Professor of Psychiatry at Johns

Figure 1–3. Eugen Bleuler (1857–1939). (Courtesy of National Library of Medicine.)

Hopkins from 1910 to 1941. Meyer has sometimes been regarded as antagonistic to psychoanalysis, but he was influential in helping this discipline to become established in the United States. His system of psychobiology was truly eclectic and dynamic in its emphasis on biological and psychological factors operative throughout the life history of the individual. His system of classification did not survive the test of time and his views were transmitted to others mainly through his students; but many of the latter assumed positions of leadership so that Meyer exerted a profound influence on the development of psychiatry in the United States during the present century. Other men such as Morton Prince (1854-1929) and William Alanson White (1870-1937) were also influential in fostering the development of dynamic psychiatry in this country.

DYNAMIC AND PSYCHOLOGICAL APPROACHES

The dynamic concepts of neural function introduced by Hughlings Jackson have already been outlined in the preceding section. During the nineteenth century, other neurologists were confronted with patients whose bodily symptoms could not be attributed to anatomical lesions in the nervous system. Such patients with conversion hysteria and other neuroses appeared relatively intact in intellectual, emotional, and behavioral function, and were frequently seen as clinic out patients or general hospital in patients, rather than as residents of mental hospitals. The main stimulus to psychological treatment and understanding of such patients came from the therapeutic application of hypnosis.

Franz Anton Mesmer (c.1733-1815) was a German physician who claimed to cure all illnesses by the touch of a rod, thereby equalizing a magnetic field that was assumed to fill the universe. Disease was attributed to the uneven distri-

Figure 1–4. Adolf Meyer (1866–1950). (From American Journal of Psychiatry *123*, 320 [1966]. Courtesy of the American Psychiatric Association and Fabian Bachrach.)

bution of animal magnetism, but Mesmer's views were discredited by the French Academy of Sciences, and he was forced to retire from his fashionable practice in Paris. A British surgeon, James Braid (1795-1860), rejected Mesmer's theories but became interested in the phenomenon which he termed hypnosis ("nervous sleep"). It has been considered likely that the application of hypnosis to produce anesthesia for surgery was prevented only by the discovery of nitrous oxide, ether, and chloroform.

A French physician by the name of Ambroise Liébeault (1823-1904) became interested in hypnotism after listening to a report of Braid's work before the French Academy of Sciences, and applied the technique in the treatment of hysterical patients at Nancy. In 1883, Hippolyte Bernheim (1840-1919), a Jewish physician in charge of the Nancy Asylum, referred a patient suffering from sciatica to Liébeault and was amazed to find the patient cured. Bernheim in turn became an exponent of hypnotism, which he regarded as merely an exaggerated form of suggestion, and only quantitatively different from phenomena of normal mental function. He also investigated posthypnotic suggestion or "latent memory" by "implanting" suggestions during the hypnotic trance, which the patient later performed without any subsequent recollection of the suggestion or its source. Bernheim was among the first to use the term psychoneurosis, but did not consider that suggestion and posthypnotic amnesia were restricted to neurotic patients.

By contrast, the more famous French physician Jean-Martin Charcot (1825-1893), regarded hysteria as a disease of the internal capsule and hypnotic phenomena as unique to hysterical patients. Charcot took charge of La Salpêtrière in 1866, attained widespread renown, and attracted many students who witnessed his dramatic demonstration of hypnosis in hysterical patients. One of his students, Pierre Janet

(1859-1947), studied many other neurotic manifestations including phobias, anxiety, obsessions, various abnormal impulses, and tics. He introduced the terms neurasthenia and psychasthenia, but is better remembered for his report (1889) that some neurotic patients recalled traumatic memories under hypnosis and became well after such ideas were consciously expressed. While he corroborated Freud's early findings on the clinical significance of unconscious processes and the therapeutic effects of catharsis, Janet's methods of treatment, however, were directed more toward conscious and emotional re-education.

The man who was destined to become the best-known student of Charcot and Bernheim was Sigmund Freud (1856-1939), the development of whose ideas and techniques has been portrayed in the detailed biography by his student and colleague Ernest Jones. Freud's contributions have influenced psychiatry in this country more than those of any other single man, and have also had a major impact on other disciplines throughout the western world. Since much of his thinking has now pervaded the entire conceptual framework of psychiatry, it has also been integrated with other information throughout the present volume. In many instances, separate acknowledgment is therefore not possible, but the specific contributions of Freud are most clearly recognizable in the summary description of psychoanalysis in the present chapter, in his formulations on unconscious psychodynamics and personality development (Chapter 3), and in his approach to psychotherapy (Chapter 11).

Freud was born in Freiberg, a small town in Moravia which was then part of Austria. His father was a Jewish merchant who moved his family to Vienna when Freud was a child. The latter continued to live there until 1938, when the political situation forced him to take refuge in London, where he died the following year. Freud was a brilliant

Figure 1-5. Sigmund Freud (1856–1939). (Courtesy of National Library of Medicine.)

student and experienced some conflict between his theoretical interests or scientific curiosity and the practical necessity of earning a living as a physician. For six years he worked in Ernst Brucke's physiological laboratory and studied the histology of the nervous system. He graduated from medical school in 1881 and the following year he transferred to the general hospital where he continued studying the anatomy of the brain and organic diseases of the nervous system. In 1885 he went to Paris for a year to study under Charcot; the following year he married and opened a neurological practice in Vienna.

Neurological practice involved many neurotic patients, and Freud was dissatisfied with current techniques of hydrotherapy, electrotherapy, massage, rest, and diet. From Charcot he had learned that hysteria could occur in men as well as women and that hypnosis could produce hysterical symptoms as well as remove them. From Bernheim he learned that private patients could not be hypnotized as readily as the charity patients in the clinic, and that suggestion alone (in a waking state) might be as effective as suggestion performed while the patient was under hypnosis.

After his visit to Bernheim in 1889, Freud collaborated with Josef Breuer, who had previously used hypnosis in the prolonged treatment of a hysterical girl (from 1880 to 1882). Under hypnosis this patient had recalled previously forgotten and highly emotional experiences from which specific symptoms could be dated. After talking over such emotional experiences with Breuer under hypnosis, she had been relieved of the symptom that had dated from these experiences. Freud confirmed these observations and published with Breuer their results in their *Studies in Hysteria* (1893-1895). They postulated that events having unpleasant emotional significance may be repressed from consciousness, that under hypnosis such events may be recalled, and that some detail of the traumatic experience may be shown to have identity with some aspect of the hysterical symptom. They termed the transformation of an emotional impulse into an abnormal bodily function *conversion,* their method of treatment *emotional catharsis,* and the emotional release that took place *abreaction.*

Freud encountered various problems in the application of hypnosis and suggestion to patients. Not all patients could be hypnotized, and symptoms removed during hypnosis were apt to be replaced by other symptoms before long. Moreover, hypnosis had no effect on the repressive forces responsible for excluding traumatic memories from consciousness. However, he found that repressed material could sometimes be recalled with difficulty in the waking state by means of free association, involving uninhibited verbal reporting of all conscious thought regardless of apparent irrelevancy. He soon found that these free associations were not really free, and concluded that they were determined by unconscious material that had to be analyzed and interpreted.

He therefore termed his new technique *psychoanalysis* (1896).

He also noted that when patients associated freely, dreams of the night before or of many years previous might occur to them. Free associations to each fragment of a dream often led more quickly to the disclosure of unconscious memories and fantasies than free associations to other subjects, and he concluded that dreams represented symbolic or disguised forms of wish fulfillment. He termed the image recalled on awakening *the manifest content*, and the true underlying motive *the latent content*. He postulated that the symbols represented in dreams are derived not only from the experiences of the individual, but also from a widespread tendency of people in a given culture to represent certain unconscious thoughts (particularly sexual ones) by characteristic symbols. Thus the human body might be represented by a house; the male genital by snakes, sticks, weapons, or trees; and the female genital by boxes, caves, other containers or doorways.

In 1900 Freud published the *Interpretation of Dreams*, and the following year the *Psychopathology of Everyday Life*. By applying methods of free association and dream analysis he was able to help patients recall forgotten emotional experiences, and this process was frequently accompanied by relief from neurotic symptoms. However, these patients often returned before long with somewhat different symptoms, and he concluded that this was because he had not analyzed emotional experiences far enough back in the patient's life. For a while he believed that the neurosis had originated in some isolated emotional shock that the patient had undergone, and he probed further back into the patient's childhood and even infancy. Frequently his female patients reported having been seduced or sexually attacked by fathers, brothers, or other relatives, but a number of these recollections were found to have no basis in fact. Freud considered that these spurious memories represented fantasies of later childhood arising from unfulfilled wishes of early childhood. Since it was impossible to achieve anything like complete intellectual recall of the events of early childhood, he was led to believe that cure of the neurosis might be accomplished by revival of the emotional attitude of early childhood, and the reliving of earlier experiences through the transference relationship with the psychoanalyst, who represented the parental and authority figure of early childhood.

The three successive goals toward which Freud directed his efforts in psychoanalysis may be summarized as follows: (1) understanding the patient's unconscious emotions or conflicts and interpreting them to the patient at the right time; (2) forcing the patient to confirm such interpretations through his own recall, by enabling the patient to understand the resistances that prevented their recall; and (3) enabling the patient to relive repressed emotional situations in the form of a current experience. The main theories arising out of these efforts to help patients may also be divided into three broad groups: (1) economic concepts, (2) dynamic concepts, and (3) topographic concepts, later developing into his structural theory of personality.

The *economic concepts* of Freud's theories concerned the fundamental modes of operation and distribution of psychic energies. The energy of the sex instinct is termed libido, and some authors have termed the energy of the aggressive instinct destrudo. Freud conceived of dammed up psychic energy as causing pain and tension, and the release of energy as producing pleasure. The basic tendency to seek pleasure and avoid pain was termed the "pleasure principle," which was modified during the course of the individual's development by the "reality principle," involving the postponement of impulse gratification in accordance with demands of the environment. An even more basic tendency than the pleasure principle was termed by Freud the repetition compulsion, which involved the tendency to repeat emotional situations and experiences regardless of their apparent pleasurable or painful consequences.

Freud's *dynamic concepts* dealt with the interaction of forces leading to conflict or overt behavior. Originally he divided all instincts into the sex drive (serving the pleasure principle) and self-preservative drives (serving the reality principle). Subsequently he combined these into the concept of Eros, which he now considered opposed by Thanatos, consisting of the aggressive instincts and drives toward death, destruction, and dissolution. The most significant factor involving each of these drives was the object toward which it was directed, and Freud postulated simultaneous direction of opposing drives toward the same object or person. In exploring infantile and childhood sexuality, he further postulated a universal sequence of psychosexual development, which will be outlined further in Chapter 3. He also introduced the concepts of fixation at, or regression to, immature levels of psychosexual development, consequent upon either undue gratification or excessive frustration and conflict. His *structural concepts* of personality, divisible into id, ego, and superego, are also widely known and will be discussed further in Chapter 3, together with the various ego-defense mechanisms against conscious anxiety, as formulated by Freud and elaborated by his daughter Anna.

Freud was about 40 years old at the time he began his major work with psychoanalysis, and throughout the remainder of his life he remained extremely productive in spite of personal handicaps which included a painful carcinoma of the jaw. He viewed himself as a discoverer rather than a genius, and was sensitive to the rejection of his ideas by the medical profession (particularly in Vienna), as well as by some of his early colleagues whose conflicting views led to their separation from the psychoanalytic movement. His dissatisfaction with medicine as a career and with members of this profession found

expression in his advocating "lay" psychoanalysis by nonphysicians. He also retained a strong preference for the Old World over the New, but his theories and methods have found greater acceptance among physicians in the United States than in other countries.

A strong personality like that of Freud may first attract and then repel other strong personalities. Two such men were Alfred Adler (1870-1937) and Carl Gustav Jung (1875-1961). While Adler was intimately associated with Freud in Vienna and was the first to break away from the inner circle, Jung was located in Zurich, Switzerland, but nevertheless became for a while Freud's heir apparent. Jung's ideas were closer to those of Freud than were Adler's in that Jung emphasized biophysical concepts of energy conservation and motivation, and his contributions will therefore be considered before those of Adler, whose position bears many similarities to those of subsequent "neo-Freudians" such as Horney, Fromm, and Sullivan.

Carl Gustav Jung (1875-1961) was an assistant of Eugen Bleuler, read Freud's *Interpretation of Dreams* soon after its publication, and sought to prove the

Figure 1-6. Carl Gustav Jung (1875–1961.) (Courtesy of National Library of Medicine.)

validity of some of Freud's hypotheses. In 1906 he began a regular correspondence with Freud and the following year paid his first visit to Vienna. The two men admired each other; Jung became the first president of the *International Psychoanalytic Association*, which was founded in 1910. Three years later, however, Jung's position had become so conflicting with that of Freud that they terminated their correspondence. The following year Jung withdrew from membership in the Psychoanalytic Association and pursued his own theories and methods of therapy, which became known as the School of *Analytical Psychology.*

One of the precipitating reasons for the breach between these two men was Jung's rejection of Freud's emphasis on sexual motivation. Jung widened the concept of libido to include the whole range of human motivation and energy, roughly equivalent to Schopenhauer's will to live, to Bergson s élan vital or to Freud's later concept of Eros or life instincts. Jung was the originator of word association tests, introduced the term *complex*, and elaborated the well-known concepts of introverted versus extroverted personality characteristics. While he started with an objective and experimental approach, however, he subsequently became the least empirical of all the analysts, and pursued the study of ancient or primitive myths and art forms, by which he expected to clarify the deep images of the unconscious. His therapy was directed increasingly toward helping persons in the second half of life who were oppressed by a sense of emptiness and futility. Analysis of the individual s personal unconscious was followed by analysis of the racial or collective unconscious, which he conceived as being inherited from our primitive ancestors. He encouraged his patients to develop an interest in religion and mythology, and to focus largely on their future.

Alfred Adler (1870-1937) received his medical degree from the University of Vienna in 1895, and became one of the

Figure 1–7. Alfred Adler (1870–1937). (Courtesy of Dr. Alexandria Adler.)

charter members of the Vienna Psychoanalytic Society and later its president. By 1908, however, Adler had reached the conclusion that aggression was a more important motivational force than sexuality. Very soon he placed specific emphasis on the "will to power" or dominance, which he regarded as a masculine characteristic. It was at this time (about 1910) that he put forward the idea of the "masculine protest" as a form of overcompensation adopted by both men and women as a defense against feelings of inadequacy and inferiority. He subsequently emphasized the "striving for superiority," so that Hall and Lindzey identified three stages in Adler's thinking regarding the final goal of man: to be aggressive, to be powerful, and then to be superior. His views were so at variance with those of Freud and other members of the Vienna Psychoanalytic Society that he met with vehement criticism and denunciation. In 1911 he resigned the presidency of the Society, and soon terminated his connections altogether to found the School of Individual Psychology.

Adler's emphasis on individual differences in personality and conscious motivation has been regarded as superficial by the majority of psychoanalysts. However, his emphasis on social and interpersonal factors in personality function, and his practical interests in child rearing and guidance, were attractive to large numbers of teachers, physicians, and criminologists, as well as to the man on the street. Ansbacher and Ansbacher took the position that Adler had so much in common with later neo-Freudian analysts that the latter might be termed neo-Adlerian with equal validity. So many of his specific formulations became part of the common stock of ideas or cliches, however, that he was not regarded as their originator. Occasional reference is still made to Adler's notions regarding the significance of ordinal position within the family of orientation, and it may be noted in passing that he attributed some of the differences between Freud and himself to this factor (Freud being an eldest child while Adler himself was second born). However, his dogmatic assertions were based upon clinical impressions and were sometimes contradictory, so that he is better remembered for his consistent emphasis on interpersonal relationships and early life experiences. He regarded the most important relationship of childhood as that with the mother, but commented that the so-called Oedipus complex was not a "fundamental fact" but simply an unnatural result of maternal overindulgence. The entire family situation with which the child was confronted in his early years stimulated him to develop a certain "style of life," and the neurotic individual was one whose "style of life" lacked proper balance between the individualistic and social drives. Treatment by Adler's method involved a comprehensive analysis of the patient's behavior traits and a direct conversational approach, leading the patient to see how he had been trying to achieve superiority "on the useless side of life" while missing opportunities "on the useful side."

Otto Rank (1844-1949) was one of Freud's first students and one of the major contributors to psychoanalytic theory until shortly before 1923, at which time he published a book entitled *The Trauma of Birth and Its Importance in Psychoanalytic Therapy.* He speculated that expulsion from the womb and separation of the infant from the mother was the most painfully anxious experience that man undergoes during his life. He believed that everyone required the entire period of childhood to overcome the birth trauma, and that neurotics were people who had failed to do so. This theory concerning birth trauma is the concept for which he is best known, but he was also one of the first to suggest that psychoanalysts should be concerned not only with the past, but also with the present situation.

Many orthodox psychoanalysts have disagreed with Freud on certain points of theory such as the polarity of life and death instincts. A large group, however, preferred to differentiate their theories and therapeutic techniques quite clearly from those proposed by Freud, and have often been referred to as neo-Freudian. Among the better known exponents of such views are Franz Alexander, Thomas French, Erich Fromm, Frieda Fromm-Reichmann, Karen Horney, Abram Kardiner, and Harry Stack Sullivan. While their positions have differed somewhat from one another, their emphasis tended to be on social relationships rather than biological factors, the ego rather than the id and superego, the striving for self-actualization rather than the sex instinct, and the present situation rather than early experiences.

The sociocultural viewpoint was presented by both Abram Kardiner and Erich Fromm. The latter expressed his belief that man is primarily a social being, and not as Freud assumed primarily self-sufficient and only secondarily in need of others to satisfy his instinctual needs. Freud interpreted neurosis and the Oedipus complex as resulting from the conflict between the irrational passions of the child and "reality" as represented by parents and society. Fromm pointed out that the rivalry between father and son was not found in societies lacking strong patriarchal authority, and regarded both the Oedipus complex and neurosis as expressions of a conflict between man's legitimate strivings for freedom and independence, and those social arrangements that frustrated man's striving for self-fulfillment, happiness, and independence.

Karen Horney (1885-1952) took issue with Freud's concepts of the libido and the death instinct and his unflattering concept of the feminine personality. She concluded that sexual difficulties were the effect rather than the cause of the neurotic character structure, and that the ultimate motive force was native responsiveness to environmental conditions, rather than instinctual energy seeking outlet. She distinguished between character neurosis and situation neurosis, and concluded that hostile impulses of various kinds were the main source from which neurotic anxiety arose. She postulated that the basic causation of a character neurosis was invariably a lack of genuine warmth and affection during childhood, the main reason for which was the incapacity of the parents to give warmth and affection on account of their own neuroses. The child's helplessness, fear, need of love, and feelings of guilt all combined to bring about a repression of hostility resulting in basic anxiety. She concluded that the goals of therapy should not be unearthing the repressed desires of early childhood, but enabling the patient to see his conflicting character trends, and to mobilize his constructive desires for a more adequate personality and relationships. Nevertheless, she retained the following convictions, which she regarded as the fundamentals of psychoanalytic theory

Figure 1–8. Harry Stack Sullivan (1892–1949). (Courtesy of the William Alanson White Psychiatric Foundation.)

and practice: (1) psychic determinism, (2) the importance of emotional forces, (3) unconscious motivation, (4) repression and resistance and the importance of analyzing resistances during therapy, (5) inner conflicts, (6) the persistent influence of childhood experiences, and (7) the essential techniques of free association, dream interpretation, and the utilization of transference.

Harry Stack Sullivan (1892-1949) made his main contributions in emphasizing the etiologic and therapeutic significance of interpersonal relationships, and applied modified analytic techniques in the treatment of young hospitalized schizophrenic patients. His definition of psychiatry as the study of interpersonal relations is unduly restrictive but led to increased concern with communication processes and interpersonal transactions that has had a major impact on American psychiatry, and will be discussed further in Chapters 3 and 11. For Sullivan the process of becoming a human being was synonymous with the process of acculturation or socialization, determined by the significant interpersonal relationships from infancy onward. He postulated that all human motivation involves the pursuit of satisfactions (such as sleep and rest, food and drink, and sexual fulfillment), and the pursuit of security through habit patterns arising from the disappointments and frustrations of early infancy. He attached fundamental importance to the role of the parents (especially mother or her substitute during infancy and early childhood)—but he did not consider this role a sexual one and stated that a parent's "feeling of familiarity" toward children of the same sex leads to an authoritarian attitude that may produce resentment and hostility in the child. While the interpersonal relationships of early childhood are vitally important, he considered that their effects may be modified by all subsequent interpersonal relationships, including that provided during the course of psychotherapy.

TWENTIETH CENTURY PSYCHIATRY

The historical trends that have been reviewed in the three preceding sections of this chapter were neither consecutive nor isolated from one another but were closely interrelated. Sequential presentation has necessitated identifying individuals with one or another major trend, but some of these distinctions may be somewhat arbitrary. Adolf Meyer, for example, made both humanistic and dynamic contributions. Moreover, none of these trends in psychiatric theory or practice terminated with the contributions last mentioned in each of the three preceding sections. Humanitarian concern and social action, descriptive and biological approaches to psychiatry as well as dynamic and psychotherapeutic approaches have not only persisted but constantly expanded their scope during the course of the present century. While

there has been rapid expansion of both population and knowledge in many areas, however, the first half of the present century witnessed particularly rapid development in the newer sciences of psychology, sociology, and anthropology.

Technological advances, stimulated further by two world wars, resulted in new somatic therapies and increasing applications of learning and communication theories in a variety of psychosocial therapies. The former isolation of psychiatrist, whether in hospital practice with in patients or in out patient treatment of neurotic adults, gave way to increased communication and collaboration with members of the medical and other professions as well as with the general public. Increasing recognition of the widespread nature of psychopathology was also reflected in the provision of diversified treatment services, and increased emphasis on psychiatric training in medical schools as well as following graduation. Diversification of both theory and therapy, however, has been a bane as well as a blessing, and the effective integration of scientific knowledge with practical experience continues to confront psychiatry with a major challenge at the present time. In the remainder of the present chapter, an attempt will be made to summarize some of the developments of the present century, proceeding from social concern through therapeutic innovations to theoretical integration.

Two forerunners of current mental health associations were founded during the nineteenth century. A Society for Improving the Conditions of the Insane was organized in London in 1842, and an American group known as the National Association for the Protection of the Insane and Prevention of Insanity was active in this country during the years from 1872 to 1886. It was during the first decade of the twentieth century, however, that citizens became concerned with improving a variety of medical care programs and founded numerous voluntary health organizations. As a result of his experiences as a patient in three mental hospitals, Clifford Beers (1876-1943) wrote his well-known book entitled *A Mind That Found Itself*, published in 1908. Beers was subsequently successful in founding the Connecticut Society for Mental Hygiene and the National Committee for Mental Hygiene, which later became one of the parent bodies for the current National Association for Mental Health. At about the same time, the Child Study Association of America and the American Social Hygiene Association were also founded.

A clinic and school for children had been established in Philadelphia in 1897 by the psychologist Lightner Witmer. Newly developed intelligence tests were introduced soon afterward, and by 1908 psychiatrists such as William Healy had also begun to work with children. The mental hygiene movement was material in helping to establish clinics for the outpatient treatment of adults and children with psychiatric problems. Before long such clinics were established in connection with juvenile courts, institutions for delinquents, jails, mental hospitals, and general hospitals. The main method of treatment employed in these facilities was psychotherapy; some psychologists were involved in testing or in directing clinics, but it was not until much later that the team approach (involving psychiatrists, psychologists, and social workers) was developed. The American Orthopsychiatric Association was founded in 1924, and promoted interest in mental hygiene clinics and in child psychiatry. The first textbook in the latter field, however, did not appear until 1926 when Homburger published his "Lectures on the Psychopathology of Childhood."

Each of the two world wars drew attention to psychiatry, both through the high frequency of psychiatric casualties and through high rates of rejection at induction centers on account of intellectual, emotional, or behavioral disorders. These rates were among the factors involved in the passage of the National Mental Health Act in 1946, which led to a dramatic increase in funding for service, research, and training in psychiatry and related disciplines. Between 1945 and 1950 the number of appointments available for residency training in psychiatry alone increased from 632 to 1754. Greatly increased numbers of physicians were attracted into this specialty, and sought more comprehensive training in theory and therapy. In recent years there has also been increased emphasis on reasonable self-determination by patients (such as voluntary admission and discharge, open doors in hospitals), on continuity of patient care in outpatient and inpatient settings, and on the community or social approach to psychiatric disorder, its treatment and prevention.

During the first half of the present century, medical, pharmacological, and surgical advances were accompanied by the widespread empirical application of *somatic treatments for psychiatric disorders.* Weir Mitchell (1829-1914) had previously developed a program of total rest accompanied by diet, massage, and electrostimulation in the treatment of neurotic battle casualties of the Civil War, and subsequently of other neurotic patients. In the early years of the present century, the increasing availability of sedative drugs, which could be administered in accurate doses, let to the introduction of prolonged or continuous sleep therapy, which was further developed after 1922 when Klaesi in Switzerland started using barbiturates for this purpose. The treatment was not without danger, due to pneumonia and other complications, particularly before the advent of antibiotics. It became progressively less frequently used in western countries, but has persisted in Russia (e.g., Andreev, 1960) where psychiatry has been dominated by Pavlovian concepts of partial inhibition.

Various forms of fever therapy were

developed during the earlier part of the present century, and Julius von Wagner-Jauregg (1857-1940) earned a Nobel Prize for his introduction of malaria therapy in the treatment of general paresis. Manfred Sakel (1900-1957) developed the insulin coma therapy of schizophrenia, which was used most extensively for about 20 years. L. von Meduna (1896-1964) introduced chemical convulsive therapy in 1933, which was modified by Cerletti and Bini in 1937 into the widely used electroconvulsive therapies. Lobotomy had been tried in 1888 by the Swiss psychiatrist Burkhardt, but was abandoned until 1935 when it was again introduced by Egaz Moniz and Almeida Lima. Many forms of psychosurgery were developed and undertaken in this country and elsewhere during the next 20 years, but all the preceding somatic therapies declined in frequency following the introduction of the major phenothiazine drugs in France by Delay and Deniker (1952) and in North America by Heinz Lehmann. Various other tranquilizing and antidepressive drugs have since been developed and will be reviewed in Chapter 12.

The goals of various *psychosocial therapies* include reduction in symptoms and changes in behavior or personality. It has long been recognized that such changes involve processes of learning and unlearning, but it is only during the present century that experimental studies have helped to elucidate some of the major principles of learning (which will be reviewed in Chapters 7 and 11). The Russian neurologist and physiologist Ivan Sechenov (1859-1905) had formulated some ideas on psychic stimulation and action, which was studied experimentally by Ivan Petrovich Pavlov (1849-1936). In his early work as a physiologist Pavlov explored circulation and innervation of the heart. By the time he received a Nobel Prize in 1904, however, he had already turned his attention to a new line of investigation, announced in a

Figure 1-9. Ivan Petrovich Pavlov (1849-1936). (Courtesy of National Library of Medicine.)

lecture on "Experimental Psychology and Psychopathology in Animals." His work on the classical (respondent) conditioning of salivary responses was followed by studies on perceptual discrimination and the experimental induction of neurotic behavior in animals. His experimental studies have since been elaborated by many investigators in Russia and western countries, but his theoretical formulations regarding human psychopathology have found only limited acceptance and application outside of his own country.

Experimental studies of learning in this country were initiated by Edward Lee Thorndike (1874-1949), whose "law of effect" was discovered about 1898, some four years prior to Pavlov's "law of reinforcement." The trial-and-error learning from favorable consequences, as studied by Thorndike and many others, subsequently became known as instrumental or operant learning because the behavioral response was instrumental in attaining desirable goals or operated on the environment to

Figure 1–10. Edward Lee Thorndike (1874–1949). (From *Psychological Review* 56 No. 5, 1949. Courtesy of the American Psychological Association.)

generate favorable consequences. Various schedules of reinforcement leading to the learning or extinction of behavior were studied by B. F. Skinner and other experimental psychologists. Escape and avoidance learning was conceptualized as a combination of classical conditioning with instrumental learning. A number of forms of perceptual learning have been recognized, as has the significant role of imitation in the learning of social behavior patterns. Principles of learning theory have been deliberately applied in some of the psychosocial therapies, but sometimes the techniques involved remain intuitive rather than rational. Nevertheless, the past two decades have witnessed increasing application of information derived from the behavioral sciences to current psychiatric theory and practice.

An extensive study of social class and mental illness was undertaken by a team of Yale University sociologists and psychiatrists, and the results were published by Hollingshead, Redlich, and their associates. An attempt was made to identify all patients from the city of New Haven, Connecticut, receiving active psychiatric treatment or custodial care during the year 1950. Members of different social classes were found to differ from one another in a variety of ways, including the frequency and form of psychopathology, their childhood and adult experiences, and the nature of psychiatric treatment in which they became involved. Some of the findings of this well-known study will be reviewed in Chapter 8. Meanwhile it may be noted that the investigators also examined in detail the main characteristics of the psychiatrists caring for these patients. On the basis of two criteria—the *principal method of therapy* employed and the *training for such therapy*—they distinguished between two major groups of psychiatrists: those with an *analytic and psychological orientation* (termed the A-P group), and those with a *directive and organic orientation* (termed the D-O group). The main characteristics of these two groups were summarized by MacIver and Redlich (1959) as follows:

In the A-P Group, composed of psychoanalysts and practitioners trained and influenced by psychoanalysts, the therapeutic approach is almost entirely psychological and non-directive. The emphasis is on the gaining and application of insight. Whenever physical examinations or organic treatments are necessary, even within the field of psychiatry, patients are referred to another specialist.

The approach of the D-O practitioners is quite different and consists in changing patient attitudes and behavior by means of directive methods (such as suggestion, reassurance, advice, and reproof) and organic therapeutic measures. The latter include medical and neurological examination, the prescribing of drugs such as barbiturates and ataraxics, and shock treatments. The D-O practitioners have little or no interest or training in psychoanalytic theory.

These authors also recognized a third group of truly *eclectic psychiatrists* (as contrasted with members of the D-O group to whom the term was often applied) but regarded them as extremely rare. In their study, the university psychiatrists were all members of the A-P group, the state hospital psychiatrists were all in the D-O group, and those in private practice contained representatives of both groups. The A-P private practitioners saw about seven patients per day, for a standard session of 45 to 50 minutes, on an average of almost three times a week, for an average duration of 18 months. The D-O private practitioners saw from 10 to 12 patients each day, for a period of 15 to 40 minutes, on an average of once a week for an average duration of about six months. Among patients seen by the A-P groups, the most common diagnosis received was character neurosis; among those seen by D-O private practitioners, anxiety state and depression; and among those seen by the state hospital psychiatrists, schizophrenia.

When asked about the rewarding and disappointing aspects of psychiatric practice and of their own motivation in becoming psychiatrists, the A-P group almost invariably gave intellectual or self-oriented replies, whereas the replies of the D-O group indicated conformity with the general medical ideals of helping their patients to improve. There were also interesting differences between social and cultural backgrounds and characteristics of the two groups of psychiatrists in this study. In a later study of psychiatrists in a midwestern metropolitan community, Malmquist (1964) reported statistically significant differences between ordinal position in the family of orientation among two similarly contrasting groups, with the A-P psychiatrists including a high proportion of youngest children, while the D-O group contained a high proportion of eldest children.

Another study of psychiatrists, conducted by Ehrlich and Sabshin (1964), was based on questionnaire data obtained from 338 psychiatrists selected to represent *three* major orientations in the profession. Apart from the predominantly psychotherapeutic and somatotherapeutic positions already outlined, these authors identified a separate third group of psychiatrists with a *predominantly sociotherapeutic orientation.* As a group the latter tended to ascribe significant therapeutic value to a wide range of interpersonal and situational interactions; to encourage changes in current social and physical features of the treatment setting; to be critical of stringent institutional restrictions; and to have a pronounced lack of sympathy for traditional authority lines in the total treatment process. This third group also displayed greater readiness to regard other professional groups as competent and to collaborate with them. The psychiatrists with this sociotherapeutic orientation tended to have had administrative experience, to have been actively involved in research (both psychiatric and nonpsychiatric), and to have had some teaching experience, in spite of the fact that they were somewhat younger than members of the other two groups. Proportionally more of the sociotherapeutic group had also attended medical schools ranking high nationally, but had taken their internship in public hospitals such as city, county, state, or federal institutions. While their varied experiences might well have led to the development of their interest in sociotherapy, however, the authors recognized that psychiatrists attracted to more experimental and pragmatic orientations would also tend to expose temselves to a variety of professional experiences.

Different orientations toward psychiatric treatment are correlated not only with different types of training experience, but also with convictions regarding the significance of various biological, psychological, or sociocultural factors in etiology, and hence also with the individual's knowledge of scientific literature in each of these diverse areas. Rapidly expanding knowledge in these disciplines makes it increasingly difficult to maintain a broad competence in all relevant scientific areas. Nevertheless, the truly eclectic psychiatrist attempts to select information on the basis of objective scientific criteria rather than subjective preference. During the past two decades there has been considerable rapprochement between extremist viewpoints. The well-trained physician of today tends to have a much more balanced orientation than his predecessor toward the relative contributions of biological, psychological, and sociocultural factors in both etiology and therapy. The task remains, however, for him to integrate new information with old and to search for specificity in causation, treatment, and prevention.

SELECTED REFERENCES

Ackerknecht. E. H. 1959. *A Short History of Psychiatry*, tr. S. Wolff. New York, Hafner Pub. Co., Inc.

Adler, A. 1924. *The Practice and Theory of Individual Psychology*. New York, Harcourt, Brace & World, Inc.

Allen, C. 1949. *Modern Discoveries in Medical Psychology*, 2nd edition. London, The Macmillan Co.

American Medical Association. 1967. *Directory of Approved Internships and Residencies*. Chicago, American Medical Association.

American Psychiatric Association. 1944. *One Hundred Years of American Psychiatry*. Washington, D.C., American Psychiatric Association.

American Psychiatric Association. 1952. *Psychiatry and Medical Education*. Washington, D.C., American Psychiatric Association.

American Psychiatric Association. 1953. *The Psychiatrist: His Training and Development*. Washington, D.C., American Psychiatric Association.

American Psychiatric Association. 1963. *Training the Psychiatrist to Meet Changing Needs*. Washington, D.C., American Psychiatric Association.

American Psychiatric Association. 1964. *Principles Underlying Interdisciplinary Relations between the Professions of Psychiatry and Psychology*. Washington, D.C., American Psychiatric Association.

American Psychiatric Association. 1964. *A Psychiatric Glossary*, 2nd edition. Washington, D. C., American Psychiatric Association.

American Psychiatric Association. 1967. *Membership Directory*. Washington, D.C., American Psychiatric Association.

American Psychoanalytic Association. 1967. *Roster of the American Psychoanalytic Association, Inc.* New York, American Psychoanalytic Association.

American Psychological Association. 1967. *Directory*. Washington, D.C., American Psychological Association.

Andreev, B. V. 1960. *Sleep Therapy in the Neuroses*, tr. B. Haigh. The International Behavioral Sciences Series, ed. J. Wortis. New York, Consultants Bureau.

Ansbacher, H., and Ansbacher, R. 1956. *The Individual Psychology of Alfred Adler*. New York, Basic Books, Inc.

Arieti, S., ed. 1959. *American Handbook of Psychiatry*, Vol. 1 and 2. New York, Basic Books, Inc.

Arieti, S., ed 1966. *American Handbook of Psychiatry*, Vol. 3. New York, Basic Books, Inc.

Beers, C. W. 1908. *A Mind That Found Itself*. New York, Longmans, Green & Co., Inc.

Berelson, B., and Steiner, G. A. 1964. *Human Behavior: An Inventory of Scientific Findings*. New York, Harcourt, Brace & World, Inc.

Bleuler, E. 1950. *Dementia Praecox or the Group of Schizophrenias*. New York, International Universities Press, Inc.

Breuer, J., and Freud, S. 1893-95. *Studies on Hysteria*. New York, Basic Books, Inc., 1957.

Burnham, J. C. 1966. *The Relationship between Psychoanalysis and American Medicine before 1918*. New York, International Universities Press, Inc.

Deutsch, A. 1949. *The Mentally Ill in America*, 2nd edition. New York, Columbia University Press.

Dollard, J., and Miller, N. E. 1950. *Personality and Psychotherapy*. New York, McGraw-Hill Book Co., Inc.

Ehrlich, D., and Sabshin, M. 1964. A study of sociotherapeutically oriented psychiatrists. American Journal of Orthopsychiatry *34*, 469-480.

Esquirol, J. E. D. 1845. *Mental Maladies: A Treatise on Insanity*, tr. E. K. Hunt. Philadelphia, Lea and Blanchard.

Fenichel, O. 1945. *The Psychoanalytic Theory of Neurosis*. New York, W. W. Norton & Co., Inc.

Freud, A. 1937. *The Ego and the Mechanisms of Defence*. London, Hogarth Press.

Freud, S. 1914. *On the History of the Psychoanalytic Movement*. Standard edition, Vol. 14. London, Hogarth Press, 1959.

Freud, S. 1954. *Origins of Psycho-Analysis*, ed. M. M. Bonaparte, A. Freud, and E. Kris. New York, Basic Books, Inc.

Fromm, E. 1941. *Escape from Freedom*. New York, Rinehart & Co., Inc.

Group for the Advancement of Psychiatry. 1960. *The Psychiatrist and His Roles in a Mental Health Association*. New York, Group for the Advancement of Psychiatry Report No. 44.

Group for the Advancement of Psychiatry. 1964. *Pavlovian Conditioning and American Psychiatry*. New York, Group for the Advancement of Psychiatry, Symposium No. 9.

Griesinger, W. 1882. *Mental Pathology and Thera-*

peutics, translated from German 2nd edition. New York. Wood's Library of Standard Medical Authors.

Hall, C. S., and Lindzey, G. 1957. *Theories of Personality.* New York, John Wiley & Sons, Inc.

Hartmann, H. 1958. *Ego Psychology and the Problem of Adaptation.* New York, International Universities Press, Inc.

Hollingshead, A. B., and Redlich, F. C. 1958. *Social Class and Mental Illness.* New York, John Wiley & Sons, Inc.

Holt, R. R., and Luborsky, L. 1958. *Personality Patterns of Psychiatrists.* New York, Basic Books, Inc.

Horney, K. 1950. *Neurosis and Human Growth.* New York, W. W. Norton & Co., Inc.

Jackson, J. H. 1884. Croonian lectures on the evolution and dissolution of the nervous system. Lancet *1,* 555.

Jones, E. 1953-57. *The Life and Work of Sigmund Freud.* Vol. 1-3. New York, Basic Books, Inc.

Jung, C. G. 1928. *Contributions to Analytic Psychology* New York, Harcourt, Brace & World, Inc.

Kardiner, A. 1945. *The Psychological Frontiers of Society.* New York, Columbia University Press.

Kiev, A. 1966. Prescientific psychiatry. In *American Handbook of Psychiatry.* New York, Basic Books, Inc., Vol. 3, ch. 12.

Kluckhohn, C., Murray, H. A., and Schneider, D. M. 1953. *Personality: In Nature, Society and Culture.* 2nd edition. New York, Alfred A. Knopf, Inc.

Kraepelin, E. 1921. *Clinical Psychiatry: A Text-Book for Students and Physicians,* tr. and adapted from the 7th German edition by A. R. Deifendorf. New York, The Macmillan Co.

Kruse, H. D., ed. 1957. *Integrating the Approaches to Mental Disease.* New York, Hoeber Medical Division, Harper & Row, Publishers, Inc.

Lewin, B. D., and Ross, H. 1960. *Psychoanalytic Education in the United States.* New York, W. W. Norton & Co., Inc.

Lewis, N. D. C. 1959. American psychiatry from its beginnings to World War II. In *American Handbook of Psychiatry.* New York, Basic Books, Inc., Vol. 1, ch. 1.

Linton, R. 1946. *Culture and Mental Disorders.* Springfield, Illinois. Charles C Thomas, Publisher.

MacIver, J., and Redlich, F. C. 1959. Patterns of psychiatric practice. American Journal of Psychiatry *115,* 692-697.

Malmquist, C. P. 1964. Psychiatry in a midwestern metropolitan community. Mental Hygiene *48,* 55-65.

Meyer, A. 1951. *Collected Papers of Adolf Meyer,* ed.

E. E. Winters, Vol. I-III. Baltimore, The Johns Hopkins Press.

Mora, G. 1959. Recent American psychiatric developments (since 1939). In *American Handbook of Psychiatry.* New York, Basic Books, Inc., Vol. 1, ch. 2.

Munroe, R. L. 1955. *Schools of Psychoanalytic Thought.* New York, The Dryden Press.

Murphy, G. 1949. *Historical Introduction to Modern Psychology.* New York, Harcourt, Brace & World, Inc.

Pavlov, I. P. 1941. *Lectures on Conditioned Reflexes,* tr. and ed. W. H. Gantt. New York, International Publishers Co., Inc., 2 volumes.

Rank, O. 1952. *The Trauma of Birth* New York, Basic Books, Inc.

Redlich, F. C., and Freedman, D. X. 1966. *The Theory and Practice of Psychiatry.* New York, Basic Books, Inc.

Roback, A. A. 1961. *History of Psychology and Psychiatry.* New York, Philosophical Library.

Rosen, E., and Gregory, I. 1965. *Abnormal Psychology.* Philadelphia, W. B. Saunders Co., ch. 2 and 4.

Shipley, T., ed. 1961. *Classics in Psychology.* New York, Philosophical Library.

Skinner, B. F. 1953. *Science and Human Behavior.* New York, The Macmillan Co.

Stengel, E. 1963. Hughlings Jackson's influence in psychiatry. British Journal of Psychiatry *109,* 348.

Sullivan, H. S. 1947. *Conceptions of Modern Psychiatry.* Washington, D.C., William Alanson White Psychiatric Foundation.

Sullivan, H. S. 1953. *The Interpersonal Theory of Psychiatry.* New York, W. W. Norton & Co., Inc.

Szasz, T. S. 1959. Psychiatry, psychotherapy, and psychology. AMA Archives of General Psychiatry *1,* 455-463.

Szasz, T. S., and Nemiroff, R. A. 1963. A questionnaire study of psychoanalytic practices and opinions. Journal of Nervous and Mental Disease *137,* 209-221.

Thorndike, E. I. 1905. *The Elements of Psychology.* New York, A. G. Seiler.

Thorndike, E. L. 1931. *Human Learning,* New York, Century Co.

Woodworth, R. S. 1948. *Contemporary Schools of Psychology.* New York, The Ronald Press Co.

World Health Organization. 1961. Teaching of Psychiatry and Mental Health. Geneva, World Health Organization, Public Health Papers No. 9.

Zilboorg, G., and Henry, G. W. 1941. *A History of Medical Psychology.* New York, W. W. Norton & Co., Inc.

Definition, Description, and Classification

RELATIVITY IN DEFINING ABNORMALITY

If a person were observed wearing sunglasses after dark, under conditions of low light intensity, by other persons who were not themselves wearing sunglasses, at least some of these other persons might notice the wearer and regard his behavior as unusual, eccentric, inappropriate, or abnormal. Whether these other persons notice the wearer, and whether they judge his behavior as abnormal, may depend on a number of factors of which they are partly or completely unaware. These will include their perception of the *reality situation* (the light intensity), the conditions under which they themselves are in the habit of wearing sunglasses, and their accumulated knowledge of the reasons and conditions under which other people may wear sunglasses.

Curiosity may lead the observers to consider reasons why the wearer is behaving in what they consider an unusual manner. If they find reasons that satisfy them, then they may conclude that the behavior is rational. Otherwise they may conclude that the wearer is eccentric or abnormal, and this conclusion itself will render their perception of other abnormality more likely. Some alternative explanations for the wearing of sunglasses under conditions of low light intensity will be considered in the next chapter, as a model for the analysis of multiple factors in causation. In the present context, however, the behavior itself illustrates several problems confronting society in defining and recognizing abnormality in its members.

Firstly, the *behavioral response may be part of a discrete, or of a continuous, distribution*. Discrete distributions have an all-or-nothing quality about them and provide a marked contrast, as between black and white. The distinction between categories is often viewed as qualitative rather than quantitative, as in the example of wearing sunglasses or not, at a given point in time. However, distributions that first appear to be discrete may well turn out to be simply the extreme values of a continuous distribution. Between black and white there are innumerable shades of gray. Between genius and mental retardation are the majority of individuals whose intelligence falls within the average range. Moreover, as soon as we start counting the frequency or duration for which an individual wears sunglasses under conditions of low light intensity, this distribution also becomes continuous rather than discrete. A great

30

many human characteristics (bodily, intellectual, or temperamental) are in fact distributed in the population in a frequency that corresponds closely with the normal or Gaussian curve, which is reproduced in Figure 2-1. Sometimes the continuous distribution curve is bimodal, having two peaks that may either reflect mainly quantitative differences as with skin color (Negro or white), or alternatively a combination of observations from two discrete groups such as males and females or widely separated age groups.

A second major difficulty in the analysis of abnormality is in the *variable nature of the reality situation, stimulus, or provocation under which specified behavioral responses are likely to occur.* While the wearing of sunglasses at a point in time may be a discrete all-or-nothing response, the light intensity at that time may be easily seen to vary along a wide continuum. Similarly the admission of a patient to a mental hospital or a specific psychiatric diagnosis such as schizophrenia may be taken as a pseudo-objective criterion of abnormality, but the antecedent stress or deprivation leading to this eventuality may vary along a number of recognized as well as unknown continua. Whether fear or anger or misery is viewed as normal or pathological depends partly upon the observer's evaluation of the circumstances or provocation under which they occur.

A third area of relativity in defining abnormality involves *the position of the observer along the continuum of characteristics, responses, or stimuli that he is attempting to evaluate.* A person with medium-brown hair may be described as fair-haired by another person whose own hair is darker, or as dark-haired by another person whose own hair is lighter in color. An individual who is unusually shy and introverted may regard another of average sociability as being extroverted and outgoing. A woman who is unusually uninterested in sexual relations may claim that her husband is a "sex maniac" when he desires normal intercourse with average frequency. A genius may regard another person of above average intelligence as mediocre or stupid. A poor man may be unable to understand how another can become severely depressed over financial losses, when the latter still remains wealthy by comparison with himself. This same problem of relativity may affect the judgment of the physician or the psychologist in his evaluation of a patient's problems, unless he is consciously aware of the differences in perspective from which he views these problems.

It is not, however, the judgment of the psychiatrist or psychologist alone

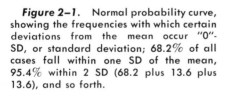

Figure 2-1. Normal probability curve, showing the frequencies with which certain deviations from the mean occur "0"-SD, or standard deviation; 68.2% of all cases fall within one SD of the mean, 95.4% within 2 SD (68.2 plus 13.6 plus 13.6), and so forth.

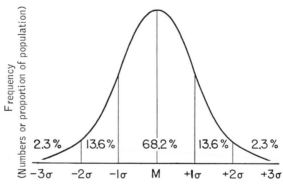

Extent of deviation from mean value for criterion (e.g., height, intelligence).

that determines whether a given behavior or constellation of behaviors is to be looked upon as abnormal or pathological. While professionals have a major voice in influencing the judgment of society, it is the collective judgment of the larger social group that determines whether its members are to be viewed as sick or criminal, eccentric or immoral. This collective judgment may be observed to undergo transition over a period of time, as in the general trend toward viewing alcoholism as sickness rather than criminality. At a given point in time, social judgment of what constitutes abnormality will still vary widely from one place to another, and in a given locality it will vary according to the smaller social group, or even to the individual, making the judgment.

While there are many factors involved in determining this collective social judgment of abnormality, Anastasi correctly recognized three distinct concepts that are frequently involved. The first or *antinormative* view regards any deviation from the ideal or perfect condition as abnormal. According to this view, normality would be the exception rather than the rule, and the majority of the population would be abnormal at least sometime during their lives—for example, when they consulted the dentist about their cavities or a physician about any form of bodily or emotional ailment. The second view identifies abnormality with *pathological* or dangerous conditions (either to the individual or society), which are present in a relatively small proportion of the population at a given point in time. Both of the preceding views involve arbitrary standards or judgments, whereas the third or *statistical* concept of abnormality is more objective and empirical. According to the latter view, individuals would be regarded as abnormal if they deviated from the mean value for the population by more than about two standard deviations in either direction. As applied to tested intelligence, this would mean that approximately two and a half per cent of the population with superior intelligence (an intelligence quotient of 130 or more) would be regarded as no less abnormal than the corresponding proportion of the population with mental retardation (having a tested intelligence quotient of 70 or less). Other difficulties in adopting the purely statistical concept of abnormality are the reliability of any such test instrument, and the variability in individuals or their characteristics over a period of time.

The statistical concept of abnormality may be extended to include hypothetical constructs about the ability of the individual to tolerate and adapt successfully to varying degrees of frustration, stress, or deprivation. In practice, however, the clinician's pragmatic need for empirical criteria that will assist in diagnosis, prognosis, and therapy leads to varying reliance on the different concepts of abnormality we have considered.

One further problem may be mentioned at this point, and this is the matter of recognizing and counting the frequency of abnormality in the population once definition has been accepted. Suppose it is agreed that the wearing of sunglasses with a specified frequency and duration, under specified conditions of light intensity, is to be regarded as abnormal. We would still be confronted with an extremely difficult task in estimating its frequency in the general population, since there might be some individuals who only behaved in this manner at home and not in public. The latter would become more likely if there was social disapproval attached to the behavior. In this particular example, however, the behavior is not generally considered to be harmful to the individual or to society, and is therefore unlikely to arouse the same kind of concern as other behavioral manifestations that will now be considered.

SYMPTOMS OF PSYCHIATRIC DISORDER

In the field of medicine as a whole, the term *symptom* has been used to describe the subjective complaints of the patient about disordered bodily functions indicative of illness, in contrast with the physical *signs* of illness discovered by the physician on objective examination. In psychiatry this distinction between signs and symptoms has not usually been preserved, and a symptom has been defined as "a specific manifestation of an illness, objective, subjective, or both." The term *syndrome* on the other hand has generally been applied to a group or combination of symptoms or signs that may be consistently associated with a certain category of abnormality or illness. In the present section, the most frequent symptoms and signs of psychopathology will be defined, preparatory to reviewing the main syndromes and their classification.

DISORDERED SENSORY PERCEPTION

A wide variety of stimuli originating in the outside world and within our own bodies impinge upon a number of specialized sense organs leading to the transmission of impulses along sensory nerves to the brain, where the integration of these impulses results in perception. Stimuli transmitted along different specialized nervous pathways and integrated in different parts of the brain are perceived by us as sensations of vision, hearing, smell, taste, pain, touch, heat or cold, or orientation in space, for example. Disturbances in sensory input or in our perceptions of various stimuli lead to modifications in our thinking, emotions, and behavior

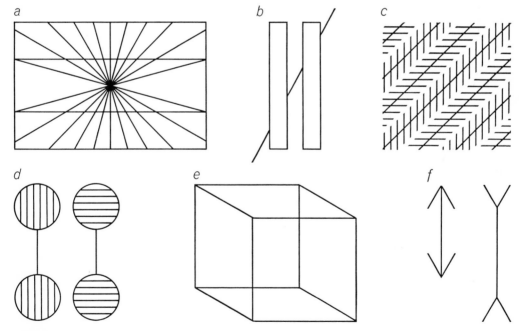

Figure 2-2. Visual illusions involve erroneous sensory reports. None of the figures is what it seems to be. In *a* the horizontal lines are parallel; in *b* the diagonal line is not staggered; in *c* the diagonal lines are parallel, and the appearance of a steplike arrangement is also illusory; in *d* the two pairs of circles are equally bright and the lines within them are equally sharp, as is evident if one turns the page 90 degrees; in *e* the cube changes perspective as one stares at it; in *f* the vertical lines are equal. (From Kolers, P. A. The illusion of movement. Scientific American 211:100 [Oct.]. Copyright © 1964 by Scientific American, Inc. All right reserved.)

that may sometimes be described as abnormal.

Disturbances of sensation following normal stimulation may involve its diminution (*hypoesthesia*), or absense (*anesthesia*), increase (*hyperesthesia*), or distortion (*paresthesia*). These terms are usually applied to disturbances in peripheral bodily sensations such as pain, touch, and temperature; whereas visual anesthesia is described as blindness, and auditory anesthesia as deafness. Any of these disorders of sensation may result either from bodily disease or from emotional disorder in the absence of somatic pathology (e.g., conversion hysteria).

When we turn from peripheral sensation to central integration, two common types of disordered perception must be distinguished from one another. An *illusion* consists of the misinterpretation of real sensory experience arising from a stimulus outside the body. A *hallucination* on the other hand is a false sensory perception arising in the absence of any external stimulus. Both illusions and hallucinations may involve any of the senses and may therefore be referred to as visual, auditory, olfactory, gustatory, or tactile (the last variety sometimes being known as haptic).

Visual illusions concerning the size and shape of objects can readily be produced in normal persons, and several of these are reproduced in Figure 2-2. Visual hallucinations, on the other hand, only occur in normal individuals in the form of dreams during sleep, or occasionally in the hypnogogic state, intermediate between waking and sleeping. Both illusions and hallucinations may be present during the course of the same psychiatric disorder, which may be either an organic brain syndrome or a "functional" disorder (without known bodily pathology) such as schizophrenia. However, visual illusions are particularly common in acute reversible organic brain syndromes, whereas auditory hallucinations are particularly common in schizophrenia.

DISORDERED INTELLECTUAL FUNCTIONS

Intelligence may be defined as the ability of an individual to comprehend, learn, remember, integrate, and mobilize information in solving new problems. The complex nature of intelligence is apparent in this definition, in the various tests that have been devised to measure intelligence, and in the extensive literature on the subject. Since the beginning of the present century, however, considerable progress has been made in the study and measurement of intellectual functions. It is known that these functions increase progressively throughout childhood and adolescence up to the age of about 16 years, and the intelligence quotient (IQ) constitutes a numerical comparison between the individual's intellectual performance at a given point in time and the statistical norm for other individuals of the same age. During childhood the IQ is obtained as a percentage of the mental age (MA) divided by the chronological age (CA). The distribution of intelligence quotients in the general population corresponds approximately with the normal curve, having a mean of 100 and a standard deviation of approximately 15 (Figure 2-3). This means that approximately 68 percent of the population will have IQ's between 85 and 115 (one standard deviation above or below the mean) while approximately 95 percent of the population will have IQ's between 70 and 130 (two standard deviations above or below the mean).

The *intellectual capacity* of an individual may be regarded as his theoretical maximum potential, determined at the time of conception and attainable only under the most nearly ideal environmental circumstances. His *intellectual function* at any given time is that which is measured by intelligence tests, and ordinarily shows considerable stability throughout life, except when it is impaired by certain forms of psychopathology. When this intellectual function is consistently much lower than the average for persons of his age group (two or more standard deviations below the mean, corresponding with an IQ of less than 70) from the time of birth onward, the person is said to have *mental retardation*, also known as *mental deficiency, intellectual subnormality, amentia,* or *oligophrenia.* These terms are all associated with diminished potentiality for understanding, learning, remembering, and problem solving.

Intellectual impairment consists of a reduction in various intellectual abilities commencing at any time after birth, and sometimes not until old age. Such impairment of intellectual functions may result from a wide variety of acute reversible or chronic irreversible brain disorders, or alternatively from some "functional" disorders such as schizophrenia or severe depression.

Among the intellectual functions that may be most severely affected is memory, and *amnesia* or pathological loss of memory may again be found in either organic brain syndromes or "functional" disorders, such as hysterical dissociative reactions. Amnesia may be *anterograde* (forward in time) or *retrograde* (backward in time) from a given event such as a head injury. Such loss of memory is usually accompanied by *disorientation*, which involves loss of awareness of the self in relationship to time, place, or other persons. The latter is often associated with perplexity or *confusion*, and there may also be accompanying clouding of consciousness sufficiently severe to amount to *stupor* or *coma. In severe confusion there is often perseveration,* resulting in a stereotyped repetition of the same ideas or replies to unrelated questions. There may also be *confabulation*, involving an attempt to compensate for memory defects by reporting imaginary experiences.

The repetitive and persistent intrusion into consciousness of an unwanted thought, desire, or impulse constitutes an obsession. Usually the recurrent thought is unpleasant to the person concerned, and when it is associated with a persistent unrealistic affect of fear, the latter is known as a *phobia.* According to psychodynamic theory, the phobia arises through displacement of fear, resulting from unconscious conflict, onto an external object sym-

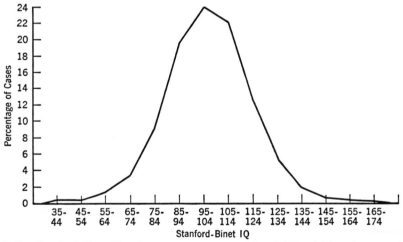

Figure 2–3. Stanford-Binet IQs of a representative sample of 2904 children between the ages of 2 and 18. (From Terman, L. M., and Merrill, M. A., 1937. *Measuring Intelligence.* Boston, Houghton Mifflin, p. 37.)

bolically related to the conflict. A large number of specific names for different varieties of phobia have been derived from Greek roots (e.g., acrophobia, a fear of heights; agoraphobia, fear of open spaces; and claustrophobia, fear of closed spaces), but these terms are much less commonly used than formerly.

Concrete thinking involves literal interpretations of events, and is observed in young children as well as in any variety of intellectual subnormality or impairment (for example in mental retardation, organic brain syndromes, or schizophrenia). *Autistic thinking*, also known as *dereistic, magical, paralogical*, or *prelogical* thinking, on the other hand, involves reasoning peculiar to the self or individual, and is characteristic of schizophrenia. The difference between concrete and autistic thinking may be illustrated by the responses of patients when asked to interpret simple proverbs. When asked what is usually meant by the saying, "A stitch in time saves nine," a concrete or literal response would be, "If you had a tear in your clothing and sewed it up right away, you'd be saving time." Two autistic responses to the same question given by schizophrenic patients are the following: "If I would take a stitch ahead of time, I would know nine times better how to do another stitch," and from another patient, "I could do something and it would help everyone else."

Primitive forms of thinking associated with distorted interpretations of reality, such as occur in dreaming or in schizophrenic patients who are awake, may be referred to as *primary process thinking*, in contrast with *secondary process thinking* that is based on an accurate perception and evaluation of reality. Prolonged misinterpretation of reality is associated with delusional beliefs.

A *delusion* may be defined as a fixed false belief that is out of keeping with the individual's level of knowledge and cultural group, and that is maintained despite objective evidence and logical argument to the contrary. Delusions are found in various types of psychosis and may be associated with disordered perception (illusions and hallucinations), impairment of memory, autistic thinking, or disorders of mood. The main categories of delusion are the following:

Delusions of *reference* involve the incorrect assumption that coincidental or unrelated events (usually the remarks or behavior of other persons) have particular reference, meaning, or application to the individual concerned.

Delusions of *influence* involve magical ("telepathic") communication and control of one person's thoughts or behavior by another. In delusions of *active* influence, the patient has the grandiose notion that he can control other people in this matter, whereas in delusions of *passive* influence he believes that he is being controlled, and usually persecuted, in this way.

Delusions of *persecution* involve the false belief that other people are hostile, discriminating against the individual, and singling him out for unwelcome attention or persecution. Delusions of reference, influence, and persecution are prominent symptoms in paranoid schizophrenia and related paranoid psychoses.

Delusions of *grandeur* consist of unrealistic beliefs in one's importance or identity: wealth, fame, power, knowledge. They are characteristically associated with euphoria (a mood of abnormal well-being found in hypomanic or manic states) but are also found in various paranoid reactions including those associated with organic brain disease (such as general paresis).

Delusions of *guilt self-accusation, worthlessness*, and *hopelessness* are characteristic of patients who are severely depressed, whether this mood is the most obvious abnormality present (as in "affective psychoses") or is associated with schizophrenia, paranoid reacions, or organic brain syndromes.

Somatic delusions are any fixed false

beliefs concerning the structural function of the patient's own body, and are commonly associated with depressive psychosis or schizophrenia. *Nihilistic* delusions are a special variety of somatic delusion in which the patient believes that a part or all of himself is nonexistent.

There are several related anomalies in which there is misinterpretation of reality, which may or may not be of delusional intensity depending upon the fixity of conviction accompanying the belief. These include *depersonalization*, in which the person feels that he has lost his identity; *misidentification*, in which he misidentifies other people around him (family, doctors, nurses, or complete strangers); and *déja vu*, a subjective feeling that an experience which is occurring for the first time has actually happened before. The last is related to *déjà entendu*, the feeling that a new auditory perception has been experienced before, and to *déjà éprouvé*, the feeling that an intended action has been accomplished.

DISORDERED AFFECT OR MOOD

In the newborn infant, emotional responses are undifferentiated. Any strong stimulation results in *excitement*, but it is not long before the latter can readily be distinguished as either *distress* or *delight*. The former is the prototype for all subsequently developed *dysphoric* emotions, such as anger, fear, disgust, or misery; whereas the latter constitutes the earliest manifestation of *euphoria*, elation, or joy.

There is disagreement as to the total number of emotions that can appropriately be distinguished in adults and their sequence of development in the young child, which appears to differ considerably from one individual to another, depending at least in part upon the variety of experience to which he is exposed. The following six main classes of human emotions were proposed by Krech and Crutchfield:

1. *Primary emotion*, e.g., joy, fear, anger, grief
2. Emotions pertaining to *sensory stimulation*, e.g., pain, disgust, horror, delight
3. Emotions pertaining to *self-appraisal*, e.g., shame, pride, guilt
4. Emotions pertaining to *other people;* e.g., love, hate, pity
5. *Appreciative emotions*, e.g., humor, beauty, wonder
6. *Moods*, e.g., sadness, anxiety, elation

From the point of view of the clinician, such profusion is frequently accompanied by confusion, and he is mainly concerned with the exaggerated or distorted manifestations of the *four primary emotions*: one euphoric (joy or elation) and three dysphoric (fear, fury, or futility—otherwise described as fear, anger, and grief). These affects or emotions may deviate from normal in four general ways: by being increased or decreased in intensity, variability, or duration, and by being inappropriate to the external situation.

Normal *joy* implies the attainment of a desired goal with approach and gratification. In *euphoria* however there is an exaggerated feeling of well-being, with diminished perception of physical pain and of control by conscience, so that there is reckless behavior with disregard of consequences. The mood is out of proportion to any objective evidence of goal attainment and not infrequently appears to be an inappropriate or paradoxical reaction to circumstances that would normally provoke anger or grief. Moreover, it is frequently accompanied by erratic and unpredictable variations in mood, with temporary episodes of misery or anger and violence.

Normal *anger* implies a blocking of goal attainment (frustration), with consequent approach, attack, and attempts to destroy the obstruction. Learned controls over behavior ordinarily lead to the modification of violent aggressive impulses, and their expression in acceptable or substitute forms. Manifestations of anger or hostility, however, may be pathological in intensity, and either generalized or focused upon specific objects or persons that may be inappropriate to the original source of frustration.

Normal *grief* or sorrow implies the loss or withdrawal of a desired goal or love-object. In pathological *depression* there is morbid sadness, dejection, and melancholia, together with an exaggerated perception of physical pain and of conscience, with inappropriate feelings of guilt and remorse. Individuals vulnerable to depression often react in this manner under conditions of frustration to which others would respond with externally directed anger and aggression.

Fear implies impending danger or disaster with consequent avoidance and escape. Fear is focused on a consciously recognized external threat or danger, although in the case of a *phobia* the fear is irrational and focused on some object other than the original source. In *anxiety* on the other hand there is apprehension, tension, or uneasiness associated with the anticipation of danger or future disaster the nature of which is largely unrecognized (i.e., vague, non-specific, objectless, or "free-floating.") In patients, anxiety frequently appears to represent fear of impulses, emotions, and behavior that are socially unacceptable and consciously intolerable to the patient, such as sexual and aggressive impulses.

Ambivalence refers to the coexistence of two opposing emotions toward the same object (person or goal), either or both of which may remain largely unconscious—e.g., coexisting love and hate toward the same person.

In addition to the preceding abnormalities in the *predominant mood or emotional tone*, there may be increased or decreased variability in the *emotional reaction or response* within a short space of time. There is usually a characteristic pattern of association between emotional tone on the one hand and response on the other, four variations in this overall pattern being illustrated in Figure 2-4. A prevailing mood within normal limits is usually associated with moderate variations in response. A mood of euphoria is usually associated with an excessive variability or *lability* of affect. In psychotic depression on the

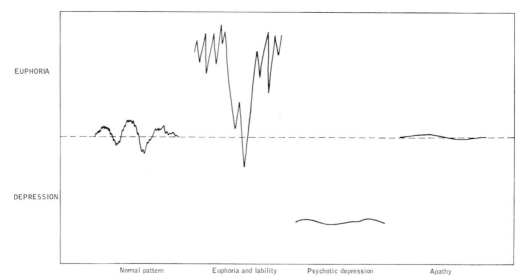

Figure 2–4. Four patterns of affective tone and variability.

EUPHORIA

DEPRESSION

Normal pattern   Euphoria and lability   Psychotic depression   Apathy

other hand there is usually diminished variability or coarctation, whereas in *apathy* the mood is within normal limits but the response is inadequate, shallow, flattened, or coarcted. Clinically, apathy is most commonly seen in some patients with organic brain syndromes or severe schizophrenia. The diminished range of affective response in some varieties of schizophrenia has been regarded by some investigators as of primary significance, and Rado has used the term *anhedonia* to describe their inability to experience pleasure.

An *inappropriate emotional* response consists of a display of affect that is qualitatively different from what would be experienced by the majority of people in similar circumstances: for example, laughter in situations in which most people would feel grief or anger, or vice versa. The inappropriate response is most characteristic of certain patients with schizophrenia, and represents one form of incongruity between their ideation, emotion, and behavior.

DISORDERED MOTIVATION

There is widespread interest in understanding the reasons and motive forces underlying our own behavior and that of other human beings, and we apply such knowledge in our daily conscious choice of action and predictions of other persons' reactions. Generations of philosophers, authors, and psychologists have analyzed the motives of mankind and have offered various interpretations: some idealistic, others materialistic and deterministic in nature. Man has been viewed as the pawn of fates, the passive instrument or victim of supernatural forces outside himself, or alternatively as the rational master of his destiny, as in the words of Henley, "I am the captain of my fate, I am the master of my soul."

Aristotle described man as a "political animal" but many have continued to regard him as predominantly animal, while others have preferred to emphasize the political or social aspects of his behavior. During the past half century, psychoanalytic insights have led to increased emphasis on unconscious motivation, and the next chapter will be devoted to further exploration of the dynamics and development of psychopathology.

Some psychologists have tended to view man as a machine whose behavior can be interpreted in terms of stimulus and response, with little attention being paid to intelligence, emotion, and motivation. Those concerned with motivational drives have tended to make distinctions between primary physiological drives and secondary drives involving a large element of learning. Distinctions have also been made between *deficiency motivation* directed toward the aims of survival and security, and *abundancy motivation* directed toward the aims of satisfaction and stimulation. Attempts have been made to measure the relative strength of different drives in experimental animals, and to explore conscious motivation in human subjects.

Perhaps the most significant finding of such studies involves the tremendous differences that are found to exist in motivational patterns between different individuals of the same age and sex, let alone within the same individual during the course of his lifetime. One man's meat is indeed another man's poison. The predominant goals of the infant, the school child prior to puberty, the postpubertal adolescent, the parent of young children, and the elderly person all differ from each other in many respects. Conscience, attitudes, and beliefs are frequently rationalizations of unconscious motives, as may be illustrated by a frequent change in attitudes toward premarital chastity between a young bachelor and the same man when he is the middle-aged father of a teen-age daughter. Such changes may occur within much shorter periods of time, even when they are not associated with obvious evidence of psychopathology.

The individual s goals, ideas, and behavior are related to his conscience or internal control system (superego); this aspect of personality development will be considered further in the next chapter. In the presence of various forms of psychopathology, however, there may be considerable variation in motivation and controls over behavior. Unpleasant hallucinations may be associated with impulsive aggressive behavior, and intellectual impairment may also result in diminished behavioral controls. A persistent mood of depression is associated with self-blame and excessive inhibition, while euphoria tends to be accompanied by diminished conscience and controls. Misinterpretation of reality may lead to some extreme manifestations of aggression, inwardly directed as in suicide or outwardly directed as in the murder of imagined persecutors.

In addition to the preceding situations, however, in which the disturbance in judgment appears secondary to other disturbances in mental function, there are also forms of abnormal behavior in which the primary defect appears to be in the area of values, conscience, and internal controls. Such defects are likely to lead to disorders of personality or character in which the most obvious symptoms are various forms of impulsive antisocial behavior.

DISORDERED BEHAVIOR

Various forms of complex behavior may be regarded as disorders because they fail to conform with what is acceptable to the society in which the individual lives. These include antisocial or delinquent behavior, a wide variety of sexual practices that deviate from the cultural norm, and addiction to alcohol or various other drugs. Apart from this socially unacceptable behavior, such persons may appear in other respects to be fairly well integrated. The same applies to patients with symptoms of neurosis whose behavior may incon-venience the patient more than other persons around him. Thus, the patient with a neurotic *compulsion* must repeatedly carry out some act or ritual, such as continually washing his hands, that is frequently related to a recurrent obsessional thought or phobia, the compulsive behavior representing a symbolic form of his undoing or atonement.

In addition to such disorders of behavior in otherwise well-integrated individuals, there are various forms of regressive or grossly abnormal behavior that are commonly associated with severe disorders of perception, thinking, and affect. There may be generalized *retardation* of movement, sometimes amounting to stupor; or alternatively extreme motor *restlessness*, *agitation*, or *excitement*. Either of these two phases may occur in organic brain disorders, in affective disorders, or in catatonic schizophrenia. The term *catalepsy* refers to an increase in muscle tone with fixity of posture, which may occur in either severe hysterical or schizophrenic states. The term *cataplexy* means a sudden transient attack of muscular weakness, with or without loss of consciousness. *Automatism* is a form of mechanical, repetitious, apparently undirected behavior, which may occur in fugue states (hysterical or epileptic) or in schizophrenia. Various other forms of unusual behavior usually associated with a diagnosis of schizophrenia include prolonged *posturing*, stereotyped repetition of certain movements such as facial grimaces or bodily mannerisms, *negativism* (doing the opposite of what is required), or *echopraxia* (imitating the movements of another person).

Speech may be regarded simply as verbal behavior, so that disorders of speech frequently parallel those of other motor behavior. In the neuroses and disorders of character or personality the main abnormality to be found is in the *content*. Other speech anomalies likely to be associated with neurosis include *stuttering* or *stammering*, or some degree of *emotional blocking* which results in interruption of train of thought or speech. Severe blocking may result in complete *mutism* and is found in the depressive or schizophrenic psychoses in which there is retardation. When the latter disorders are accompanied by increased psychomotor activity, on the other hand, there tends to be *logorrhea* (excessive speech), with *flight of ideas* from one subject to another that is only tangentially related. In euphoria it is usually possible to recognize the association underlying the flight of ideas, whereas in schizophrenia the *fragmentation of thinking* often makes it impossible to recognize any logical association. Other disorders of speech that may be found in euphoria include *rhyming*, *punning*, and *clang associations*, in which associations between consecutive words or phrases involve their sound alone. Other speech disorders observed in schizophrenia include *neologisms* (new words), *verbigeration* (stereotyped repetition of words or sentences), *echolalia* (a repetition of what has been said by someone else), and *word salad* (an unintelligible mixture of words and phrases).

SYNDROMES OF PSYCHIATRIC DISORDER

Society has long been able to distinguish between the delinquent, the defective, and the distraught. In other words, society has long been able to recognize that different kinds of action may be appropriate and necessary—(1) to eradicate antisocial behavior, such as offenses against other persons or property (delinquency), (2) to protect and provide for the care of individuals who can never learn to look after themselves (those who are mentally retarded from birth), and (3) to protect society and/or provide help and recovery for those who appeared to develop normally but subsequently became insane (the distraught). Although such distinctions are centuries old, they were at times ignored by our ancestors, and all such categories of the socially deviant were often segregated in a single type of institution prior to the humanitarian reforms of the early nineteenth century.

Under the concept of "moral insanity" Prichard described a group of criminals characterized by impulsive antisocial behavior that would conform with the more recent concepts of *psychopathic* or *sociopathic personality*. Another distinction that has persisted over the years is that between *psychoneuroses* (or neurotic disorders) that are relatively mild in degree, and *psychoses* that involve severe distortion of reality and correspond roughly with the legal concept of insanity. In general the neurotic patient has tended to recognize himself as sick (though he has not necessarily recognized the nature of his sickness) and to seek help voluntarily as an outpatient. By contrast, the psychotic patient (with severe distortions of perception, intellectual functions, or affect) has typically failed to recognize his sickness, and treatment traditionally involved other persons' arranging for his involuntary commitment to an institution. This distinction on the basis of reality distortion is epitomized in the statement, "A psychotic thinks that two and two make five; whereas a neurotic knows that two and two make four, but it makes him nervous." A similar epigram has it that "the neurotic builds castles in the air; the psychotic lives in them—and the psychiatrist charges him rent."

During the latter part of the nineteenth century, the search for bodily causes of insanity led to a distinction being made between *organic psychoses*, consistently associated with some form of brain lesion, and "functional" psychoses, in which no such brain pathology could be discovered. During the present century there has also been a great deal of psychiatric interest and investigation of a group of diverse bodily disorders frequently associated with emotional pathology, and currently described as *psycho-physiologic* disorders. There has also been increasing interest in various other forms of abnormal behavior such as sexual deviation, alcoholism, and drug addiction, and in spite of their heterogeneity the latter forms of abnormal behavior have tended to be looked upon as closely related to psychopathic or *sociopathic personality.*

At the present time *six major groups of psychiatric disorders* may be recognized, mainly on the basis of clinical symptoms but also partly on the basis of established causation. (1) *Organic brain disorders* may be divided into those that are acute and reversible, and those that are chronic and irreversible. (2) *Mental deficiency or retardation* may be subdivided according to the presence or absence of recognizable brain pathology into "subcultural" (usually mild) and "pathological" (usually severe) categories. (3) The major "*functional psychoses*" include the affective disorders, the schizophrenias, and paranoid reactions. (4) The *psychophysiologic disorders* involve disordered bodily functions, particularly those mediated by the autonomic nervous system, and are related in varying degrees to emotional stress. (5) The *neurotic disorders* are characterized by unresolved emotional conflict and anxiety, with various attempts at restitution. (6) The *disorders of personality, character, or behavior* are usually subdivided into personality pattern or trait disturbances, sociopathic personality disturbances, sexual deviation, and addiction to alcohol or other drugs.

In a monograph on the classification of mental disorders published by the World Health Organization, Stengel listed eleven official, semiofficial or national classifications, and 27 other schemes of diagnostic classification proposed mostly by individuals. Such profusion indicates the variety of opinions that exist, but in the present volume it is only necessary to elaborate on the classification in most widespread use in the United States, which is known as the Standard Nomenclature. The following is an outline of this classification, together with some explanatory comments.

Standard Nomenclature of Psychiatric Disorders

I. *ORGANIC BRAIN DISORDERS.* Disorders caused by or associated with impairment of brain tissue function.
  A. Acute Brain Syndromes
    Temporary and reversible changes in brain cell functions. Due to a wide variety of of infections, intoxications with drugs or poisons, physical trauma, disturbances of blood circulation or metabolism, and other bodily illness. Impairment of intellectual functions, memory, and orientation, frequently accompanied by illusions, hallucinations, and delusions.
  B. Chronic Brain Syndromes
    Permanent irreversible damage to brain structure. May result from any of the same pathological processes as acute reversible disorders, and also frequently from insidious localized disease of the brain. Impairment of intellectual functions, memory, and orientation, with or without secondary manifestations of psychosis, neurosis, or personality disorder.
II. *MENTAL DEFICIENCY*
    Primarily a defective intelligence existing since birth, without demonstrated organic brain disease or known prenatal cause. According to this classification, this category includes only those cases of intellectual subnormality formerly known as familial or "idiopathic" mental deficiency, since the group with known brain pathology are classified with the chronic brain syndromes. Traditionally, the term

Standard Nomenclature of Psychiatric Disorders *(Continued)*

mental deficiency has been reserved for persons with an intelligence quotient (IQ) of less than 70 (involving less than 3 percent of the general population). A more comprehensive classification has been published by the American Association on Mental Deficiency.

III. *FUNCTIONAL DISORDERS.* Disorders of psychogenic origin, or without clearly defined physical cause or structural change in the brain.

   A. Psychotic Disorders ("functional psychoses")

   Involve marked distortion of socially accepted interpretations of reality. Frequently accompanied by severe distortions of perception, intellectual functioning, affect, motivation, and behavior. Personality decompensation and regression. Patients usually lack insight into the nature and severity of the disturbance, and admission to hospital was traditionally accomplished by involuntary commitment.

     1. Involutional psychotic reaction—severe depression or paranoid ideation during the involutional period, with no history of previous psychosis.

     2. Affective reactions—exaggerations of mood with related disturbances of thinking and behavior.

       a. Manic depressive reaction—recurrent episodes of elation or depression, or alternation between these extremes.

       b. Psychotic depressive reaction—severe depression with no previous history of psychosis.

     3. Schizophrenic reactions (formerly known as dementia praecox)—a group of psychotic reactions with disturbances in reality relationships and variable disturbances in perception, intellectual functions, affect, and behavior.

       a. Simple type—apathy, lack of initiative and social withdrawal, without conspicuous hallucinations, delusions, or intellectual impairment.

       b. Hebephrenic type—shallow and inappropriate affect with hallucinations, delusions, mannerisms, and silly and regressive behavior.

       c. Catatonic type—conspicuous disturbances in motor behavior, with generalized inhibition and stupor, or alternatively excessive activity and excitement.

       d. Paranoid type—poorly systematized delusions, usually accompanied by hallucinations and hostility, sometimes by aggressive behavior.

       e. Acute undifferentiated type—sudden onset of schizophrenic symptoms which may resolve rapidly or develop into another definable type.

       f. Chronic and undifferentiated type—schizophrenic symptoms of prolonged duration, not predominantly those of any other single type.

       g. Schizo-affective type—mixture of schizophrenic and affective reactions.

       h. Childhood type—schizophrenic reactions occurring before puberty.

       i. Residual type—mild residual symptoms following more severe episode.

     4. Paranoid reactions—well systematized delusions, usually without hallucinations. Intelligence well preserved. Affect and behavior consistent with delusions.

       a. Paranoia—logical elaboration of a single delusion (monomania). Extremely rare, and of interest only as theoretical construct.

       b. Paranoid state—delusional system intermediate between the bizarre fragmentation of paranoid schizophrenia and the logical validity of true paranoia.

   B. Psychophysiologic Autonomic and Visceral Disorders

   Sometimes referred to as psychosomatic disorders, somatization reactions, or organ neuroses. A diverse group of disorders in bodily function and structure, often associated with emotional conflict and stress. Frequently interpreted as resulting from exaggerated physiological expression of emotion, which is repressed and discharged through the viscera.

     1. Skin reaction—such as neurodermatitis or some varieties of eczema.

     2. Musculoskeletal reactions—as in some types of backache or tension headache.

     3. Respiratory reaction—as in some kinds of asthma.

Standard Nomenclature of Psychiatric Disorders *(Continued)*

4. Cardiovascular reaction—as in some cases of hypertension or migraine head-ache.
5. Hemic or lymphatic reaction—involving changes in blood or lymphatic systems.
6. Gastrointestinal reaction—as in some cases of peptic ulcer, ulcerative colitis, constipation, vomiting, and anorexia nervosa.
7. Genitourinary reaction—as in some types of impotence, frigidity, menstrual disturbances, and frequency of urination.
8. Endocrine reaction—as in some cases of hyperthyroidism.
9. Nervous system reaction—as in some cases of fatigue or "neurasthenia."
10. Reactions of organs of special sense—such as the eye or ear.

C. Psychoneurotic Disorders (neuroses)
The chief characteristic is anxiety which may be consciously experienced or un-consciously controlled by means of various psychological defense mechanisms. There is no gross distortion of reality or disorganization of personality. Such persons usually seek help voluntarily as outpatients.
1. Anxiety reaction—diffuse or "free-floating" anxiety and apprehension, often accompanied by overactivity of certain physiological functions (e.g., sweating, palpitation of the heart).
2. Dissociative reaction—such as amnesia, fugue, sleep-walking, multiple per-sonality.
3. Conversion reaction—loss of sensory or motor functions (i.e., anesthesia or paralysis) or alternatively sensory hyperacuity or motor hyperactivity (tic, tremor, or epileptic-like seizures).
4. Phobic reaction—specific neurotic fears that persist despite the individual's realization that they are irrational.
5. Obsessive-compulsive reaction—persistent, unwanted obsessional thoughts, and/or compulsions to perform repetitive actions.
6. Depressive reaction—depression that is intermediate in intensity between normal grief and psychotic depression. Usually an unduly severe reaction to loss, in an individual with other neurotic characteristics or symptoms.
7. Psychoneurotic reaction—other.

D. Personality Disorders (character disorders)
Developmental defects or pathological trends in personality structure with minimal objective anxiety and little or no sense of distress. Usually manifested by a lifelong pattern of action or behavior rather than by disorders of perception, intellectual functions, or affect.
1. Personality pattern disturbance—long-standing personality types that can rarely be altered much by therapy, and which tend to decompensate to psy-chosis under stress (inadequate personality, schizoid personality, cyclothymic personality, paranoid personality).
2. Personality trait disturbance—emotional immaturity with inability to maintain emotional equilibrium and independence under even minor stress (emo-tionally unstable personality, passive-aggressive personality, compulsive per-sonality, other personality trait disturbance).
3. Sociopathic personality disturbance—characterized by behavior that fails to conform with prevailing social and ethical standards.
   a. Antisocial reaction—impulsive, hedonistic, and egocentric, having no real loyalties to any person, group, or code.
   b. Dyssocial reaction—antisocial individuals reared in an abnormal moral environment and capable of loyalty to their own predatory, criminal, or other social group.
   c. Sexual deviation—characterized by consistent preference for any variety of sexual behavior that is regarded by this society as deviant.
   d. Addiction—alcoholism and drug addiction.
4. Special symptom reactions—disturbances where a specific symptom is the single outstanding expression of the psychopathology. These reactions are often

found in childhood: for example, learning disturbance, speech disturbance (e.g. stuttering), enuresis (bed wetting), and somnambulism (sleep-walking).

E. Transient Situational Personality Disorders

These are acute and temporary reactions which develop in response to an overwhelming situation in persons with basically stable personalities.

1. Gross stress reaction — reactions to combat or to civilian catastrophes.
2. Adult situational reactions — brief maladaptive behavior appearing in response to a difficult situation.
3. Adjustment reaction of infancy — temporary apathy, excitability, feeding or sleeping difficulties in response to environmental situations.
4. Adjustment reaction of childhood — temporary habit disturbances (such as nail biting, thumb sucking, enuresis, masturbation, temper tantrums); conduct disturbances (such as truancy, stealing, destructiveness, cruelty, sexual offenses, or use of alcohol); or neurotic traits (such as tics, habit spasms, somnambulism, stammering, overactivity, or phobias). A more comprehensive classification has been published by the Group for the Advancement of Psychiatry.
5. Adjustment reaction of adolescence — temporary disturbances in otherwise normal individuals.
6. Adjustment reaction of late life — temporary responses to changed environmental situations.

THE RELIABILITY OF PSYCHIATRIC DIAGNOSES

When the main clinical diagnoses were introduced in psychiatry toward the end of the nineteenth century, there was a tendency to regard them as separate and mutually exclusive diseases which remained essentially static and unchanging over prolonged periods of time. The major "functional" diagnostic categories were viewed as manifestations of specific hereditary or constitutional vulnerability and, though the symptoms might vary in intensity from time to time, the diagnostic category should remain unchanged throughout the remainder of the patient's lifetime. It was soon recognized, however, that some patients showed symptoms typical of more than one major diagnostic category, either simultaneously at a given moment in time, or else when they were observed over a prolonged period of time.

The main clinical diagnoses are in fact largely descriptive rather than etiologic, and are in no way more mutually exclusive than any of a wide variety of bodily illnesses. There is no reason, for example, why a single individual should not be born mentally defective, develop symptoms of neurosis or sociopathic behavior, become psychotically depressed or schizophrenic, and also develop one of the many varieties of organic brain disorder. At any given time, the diagnosis is apt to be made in terms of the predominant symptom pattern or syndrome present at that time. However, differences in the conceptual frameworks of different psychiatrists and changing patterns of psychopathology within the same individual may combine to produce conflicting diagnoses in the same patient.

There have been some interesting comparisons between clinical diagnoses on the same patient admitted to different mental hospitals in close geographical proximity and within a short period of time. Elkind and Doering (1928) compared the diagnoses received by a group of patients in the Boston Psychopathic hospital from 1925 to 1926 with the diagnoses received by the same patients in various state hospitals, and their data are reproduced in Table 2-1. It may be seen that approximately

Table 2-1. Diagnosis on Patients Admitted to Boston Psychopathic Hospital and Massachusetts State Hospitals†

STATE HOSPITAL DIAGNOSIS	BOSTON PSYCHOPATHIC HOSPITAL, 1925-1926																				Total
	(1) Dementia Praecox°	(2) Manic-Depressive	(3) Alcoholic Group	(4) Paranoid Condition	(5) Involutional Melancholia	(6) Undiagnosed	(7) Cerebral Arteriosclerosis	(8) General Paralysis	(9) Psychosis With Other Brain and Nerve Dis.	(10) Psychosis with other Somatic Diseases	(11) Mental Deficiency	(12) Senile	(13) Cerebral Syphilis	(14) Epileptic Psychosis	(15) Not Insane	(16) Psychopathic Personality	(17) Psychoneurosis	(18) Traumatic Psychosis	(19) Psychosis Due to Drugs, etc.	(20) Brain Tumor	
1. Dementia Praecox°	230	44	6	21	1	36	2	1	6	4	3	—	1	—	—	3	—	—	—	—	358
2. Manic-Depressive	26	153	1	5	15	23	2	1	3	6	1	2	1	—	—	1	2	1	—	—	243
3. Alcoholic Group	9	1	58	4	—	11	1	—	1	—	—	—	—	—	—	1	—	1	—	—	87
4. Paranoid Condition	17	4	—	23	2	7	—	—	—	—	—	—	—	—	—	1	—	—	—	—	54
5. Involutional Melancholia	1	4	1	—	9	3	—	—	—	1	—	—	—	—	—	—	—	—	—	—	19
6. Undiagnosed	14	7	1	7	3	20	—	—	—	—	—	—	—	—	—	3	2	—	—	—	57
7. Cerebral Arteriosclerosis	2	5	2	—	1	5	26	2	4	1	—	6	1	—	—	—	—	—	—	—	55
8. General Paralysis	1	—	2	—	—	6	2	82	2	—	—	—	—	—	—	—	—	—	—	—	95
9. Psychosis With Other Brain and Nerve Disease	1	—	2	—	—	2	2	1	9	—	—	1	—	—	—	—	—	—	—	—	18
10. Psychosis With Other Somatic Diseases	2	1	2	—	—	3	1	—	1	12	1	1	—	—	1	—	—	—	—	—	25
11. Mental Deficiency	11	4	1	2	—	5	—	—	—	1	24	1	—	—	—	—	—	—	—	—	49
12. Senile	1	2	—	—	—	3	—	1	—	—	—	14	3	—	—	—	—	—	—	—	24
13. Cerebral Syphilis	—	—	—	—	—	—	—	2	—	—	—	—	3	—	—	—	—	—	—	—	5
14. Epileptic Psychosis	—	—	—	—	—	—	—	—	—	—	3	—	—	6	—	—	—	—	—	—	9
15. Not Insane	1	3	3	4	—	6	4	2	6	—	1	1	—	—	4	—	—	—	—	—	35
16. Psychopathic Personality	2	5	—	—	—	5	—	—	2	3	—	—	—	—	1	3	—	—	—	—	21
17. Psychoneurosis	4	3	—	—	—	3	—	—	—	—	—	—	—	—	—	1	3	1	—	—	15
18. Traumatic Psychosis	—	1	—	—	—	—	—	—	—	—	—	—	—	—	—	—	—	3	—	—	4
19. Psychosis Due to Drugs, etc.	1	1	—	—	—	—	—	—	—	—	—	—	—	—	—	—	—	—	—	—	2
20. Brain Tumor	—	—	—	—	—	—	—	—	—	—	—	—	—	—	—	—	—	—	—	2	2
TOTAL	323	238	79	68	31	138	40	92	33	28	33	26	9	6	6	13	7	5	—	2	1,177

*N.B. Diagnoses "Dementia Praecox" and "Schizophrenia" are treated as the same.

†Adapted from Gruenberg, E. M. 1950. In *Epidemiology of Mental Disorder.* New York, Milbank Memorial Fund, pp. 42-43.

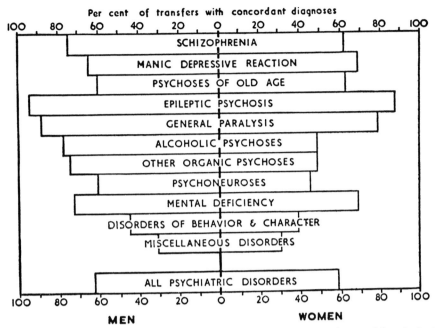

Figure 2–5. Consistency of diagnosis between observation units and mental hospitals, London, England, 1947–1949. (From Norris, V., 1959. *Mental Illness in London.* Maudsley Monograph No. 6, Institute of Psychiatry. London, Oxford University Press.)

30 per cent of the diagnoses differed from one hospital to another; Gruenberg (1950) pointed out that this was about the same discrepancy as Cabot found between clinical diagnosis in medicine and autopsy findings. A similar degree of diagnostic inconsistency was found by Norris (1959) for patients admitted to observation units and mental hospitals in the London area between 1947 and 1949 (see Figure 2-5). However, Norris pointed out that the observation units were very similar in respect to the proportion of concordant diagnoses, as were the ultimate diagnoses of persons with initially discordant diagnoses. She concluded that the discordance was due less to different diagnostic practices between psychiatrists than to different clinical features' becoming more prominent at different stages of certain psychiatric disorders.

In a different type of study, Lewis and Pietrowski (1954) followed up 122 patients, all of whom had been admitted to the New York State Psychiatric Institute, and had discharge diagnoses of either manic depressive psychosis or psychoneurosis. They were diagnosed by Lewis at least three years and not more than 20 years after discharge on the basis of historical information and of a personal examination, except in the case of patients hospitalized elsewhere at the time of the study. In over 90 per cent of these patients, the follow-up interval was at least seven years. Out of 70 patients earlier considered manic depressive, 38 (i.e., 54 per cent) were subsequently diagnosed as schizophrenic, and out of 52 patients initially considered psychoneurotic, 24 (i.e., 46 per cent) were later thought to have developed clearcut signs of schizophrenia. This tendency to revise diagnoses in the direction of schizophrenia has been noted empirically in other hospitals in North America and may be related to three factors: (1) a tendency for more severe or typical signs of schizophrenia to develop over a period of time; (2) a concept of schizophrenia which has been enlarged to include schizo-affective psychosis (often formerly diagnosed as manic depressive), and "pseudo-neurotic" and "pseudo-psychopathic" schizophrenias; (3) a tendency on the part of some psychiatrists to diagnose schizophrenia simply on the basis of chronicity.

Some workers have concluded that it is pointless to distinguish between different clinical syndromes on the basis of the overt symptoms of abnormality, and that all mental illness represents a single abnormality, the external manifestations of which (1) vary quantitatively rather than qualitatively, (2) are all likely to be helped by the same kind of treatment, and (3) do not differ essentially in their causation. Karl Menninger et al. (1958) advocated a *unitary concept of mental illness* along the following lines: ". . . we believe that the natural 'class' in psychiatry must be either the disturbed individual or all mankind in trouble. There are no natural mental disease entities. An ordering of clinical phenomena on the basis of the economics of adaptation such as we have proposed does justice to the essential unity of sickness and health; at the same time, it leaves room for recognizing the latent potential of every individual." This notion is by no means new, and the latter authors quoted Heinrich Neumann as having written in 1859 ". . . We consider any classification of mental illness to be artificial, and therefore unsatisfactory, (and) we do not believe that one can make progress in psychiatry until one has resolved to throw over-board all classifications and to declare with us: there is only one kind of mental illness. . . ."

The contrary viewpoint is that this is comparable to regarding all blindness, all deafness, or possibly all bodily illness as qualitatively identical, whereas accurate knowledge of specific causation, useful for effective treatment and logical preventive measures, should be based on clarity of diagnostic criteria. This traditional medical viewpoint is summarized in the following lines from the introduction to the International Statistical Classification: "Classification is fundamental to the quantitative study of any phenomenon. It is recognized as the basis of all scientific generalizations and is therefore an essential element in statistical methodology." While a descriptive approach may be necessary in the early development of a science, advances lead to increasing concern with dynamic and causal relationships, which will be elaborated in the next six chapters.

SELECTED REFERENCES

American Association on Mental Deficiency. 1961. *A Manual on Terminology and Classification in Mental Retardation.* 2nd edition. Prepared by R. Heber. Monograph Supplement to American Journal of Mental Deficiency.

American Psychiatric Association. 1952. *Diagnostic and Statistical Manual for Mental Disorders.* Washington, D.C., American Psychiatric Association.

American Psychiatric Association. 1964. *A Psychiatric Glossary,* 2nd edition. Washington, D.C., American Psychiatric Association.

Anastasi, A. 1958. *Differential Psychology,* 3rd edition. New York, The Macmillan Co.

Beck, A. T. 1962. Reliability of psychiatric diagnoses: 1. A critique of systematic studies. American Journal of Psychiatry *119*, 210-216.

Beck, A. T., Ward, C. H., Mendelson, M., Mock, J. E., and Erbaugh, J. K. 1962. Reliability of psychiatric diagnoses: 2. A study of consistency of clinical judgments and ratings. American Journal of Psychiatry *119*, 351-357.

Elkind, H. B., and Doering, C. G. 1928. Epidemiology of mental disease; further studies, I. Variation in diagnosis. Reprint No. 5 in Schizophrenia. Statistical studies from the Boston Psychopathic Hospital (1925-1934).

Engel, G. L. 1962. *Psychological Development in Health and Disease.* Philadelphia, W. B. Saunders Co., ch. 29.

Gauron, E. F., and Dickinson, J. K. 1966. Diagnostic decision making psychiatry. A.M.A. Archives of Psychiatry *14*, 225-237.

Goldfarb, A. 1959. Reliability of diagnostic judgments made by psychologists. Journal of Clinical Psychology *15*, 392-396.

Group for the Advancement of Psychiatry. 1966.

Psychopathological Disorders in Childhood: Theoretical Considerations and a Proposed Classification. New York, Group for the Advancement of Psychiatry, Vol. VI, Report No. 62.

Hart, B. 1957. *The Psychology of Insanity*, 5th edition. London, Cambridge University Press.

Hoch, P., and Zubin, J. 1953. *Current Problems in Psychiatric Diagnosis.* New York, Grune & Stratton, Inc.

Kline, N. S., and Gerard, D. L. 1953. Taxonomy of mental disease. Journal of General Psychology *49*, 201.

Krech, D., and Crutchfield, R. S. 1959. *Elements of Psychology.* New York, Alfred A. Knopf, Inc.

Kreitman, N. 1961. The reliability of psychiatric diagnosis. Journal of Mental Science *107*,876-886.

Kreitman, N., Sainsbury, P., Morrisey, J., Towers, J., and Scrivener, J. 1961. The reliability of psychiatric assessment: an analysis. Journal of Mental Science *107*, 887-908.

Lewis, N. D. C., and Pietrowski, Z. A. 1954. In *Depression*, P. Hoch and J. Zubin. New York, Grune & Stratton, Inc., p. 28.

Loftus, T. A. 1960. *Meaning and Methods of Diagnosis in Clinical Psychiatry.* Philadelphia, Lea & Febiger.

Menninger, K., Ellenberger, H., Pruyser, P., and Mayman, M. 1958. The unitary concept of mental illness. Bulletin of the Menninger Clinic *22*,4-12.

Morgan, C. T. 1961. *Introduction to Psychology*, 2nd edition. New York, McGraw-Hill Book Co.

Norris, V. 1959. *Mental Illness in London*, Maudsley Monograph No. 6. London, Oxford University Press, pp. 51-53.

Scott, W. A. 1958. Research definitions of mental health and mental illness. The Psychological Bulletin *55*, No. 1.

Stengel, E. 1960. Classification of mental disorders. Bulletin of the World Health Organization *21*, 601-663.

Szasz, T. 1961. *The Myth of Mental Illness.* New York, Hoeber Medical Division, Harper & Row, Publishers, Inc.

Ward, C. H., Beck, A. T., Mendelson, M., Mock, J. E., and Erbaugh, J. K. 1962. The psychiatric nomenclature: reasons for diagnostic disagreement. Archives of General Psychiatry *7*, 198-205.

West, L. J. 1962. Hallucinations. New York, Grune & Stratton, Inc.

Zigler, E., and Phillips, L. 1961. Psychiatric diagnosis and symptomatology. Journal of Abnormal and Social Psychology *63*, 69-75.

Zigler, E., and Phillips, L. 1961. Psychiatric diagnosis: a critique. Journal of Abnormal and Social Psychology *63*, 607-618.

CHAPTER 3

The childhood shows the man,
As morning shows the day.

From "Paradise Regained" by John Milton

A man will sometimes rage at his wife when in reality his mistress has offended him, and a lady complain of the cruelty of her husband when she has no other enemy than bad cards.

Samuel Johnson

Dynamics, Development, and Communication

DEPTH PSYCHOLOGY

Psychopathology has been defined in the glossary of the American Psychiatric Association as "the study of the significant causes and processes in the development of mental illness. In general, synonymous with psychogenesis." In the same publication *psychogenesis* was defined as "production or causation of a symptom or illness by mental or psychic factors as opposed to organic ones."

While there is general agreement on the latter concept of psychogenesis, the preceding definition of psychopathology would be regarded by many psychiatrists as unduly narrow and restrictive. There are indeed four distinct, although interrelated, types of data that are of legitimate concern to students of psychopathology: (1) *description*, based upon observation and study of readily observable external factors (as already discussed in the preceding chapter); (2) *dynamics*, or the study of mental forces in action, particularly emotion and motivation, and various intrapsychic defense mechan-

isms; (2) *development*, which involves interaction between (a) intrinsic biological maturation and (b) adaptation to extrinsic circumstances through learning, and hence the study of interpersonal relationships as well as intrapsychic dynamics; (4) *etiology*, or the analysis of causation, which includes the entire range of biological, psychological, and sociocultural factors that are relevant in determining development and dynamics, as well as descriptive manifestations of psychopathology.

It will be recognized that the term *genesis* has been used in several ways that may or may not imply ultimate causation. Fenichel for example regarded a dynamic explanation of intrapsychic processes as also being a genetic one, whereas Levine and others have made distinctions between clinical diagnosis, dynamic diagnosis, and genetic diagnosis. The field of genetic psychology is generally regarded as synonymous with developmental psychology, which may be observational or etiologic. The science of genetics on the other hand may be defined as the scientific study of biological inheritance. However, it is necessary to consider other forms of biogenesis as well as psychogenesis or sociogenesis. The present chapter will focus on dynamics and development as intermediate steps in analyzing the causation as well as the meaning of psychopathology. We shall then return to the further analysis of psychological determinants (such as learning, frustration, and conflict) in one of the five succeeding chapters (Chapter 7), all of which are concerned with etiologic research.

It has been remarked facetiously that psychology first lost its soul, and then its consciousness, and finally its mind. Early philosophical preoccupations with the soul were indeed replaced first with the introspective analysis of conscious mental processes, then with widespread interest in unconscious processes that has persisted to the present time. Only in some quarters was there abandonment of interest in mental processes in favor of the mechanistic study of behavior and its analysis in terms of stimulus and response.

Schopenhauer recognized the force of unconscious will in influencing conscious thought and action, and Nietzsche considered conscious motives as rationalizations of underlying unconscious forces. Other philosophers and a few early experimental psychologists also attributed considerable significance to motivating forces of which the individual was unaware, but it remained for Freud to analyze and theorize about such forces in detail.

Most rational behavior had hitherto been explained through conscious motivation that could be established by introspection or verbal communication. Freud proposed that many of the psychological functions of everyday life such as fantasy and dreaming, as well as neurotic and psychotic symptoms, became intelligible only when the underlying unconscious motivation was reconstructed or made conscious. By definition, the content and functions of the *unconscious* part of the mind are *not*

subject to voluntary recall and only rarely enter conscious awareness, frequently in disguised or symbolic form. Information that is not in immediate awareness, but that can be recalled by a conscious effort, is referred to as *preconscious.* By contrast, the unconscious mind is a repository for data (a) that have never been conscious due to primary repression, or (b) that may have become conscious briefly and then have become unconscious through secondary repression.

In his early studies with Breuer, Freud discovered that information not subject to voluntary recall might be remembered and reported in vivid detail when the patient (Anna O.) was placed in a hypnotic trance. Freud's initial enthusiasm for the therapeutic effectiveness of arousing painful memories and feelings under hypnosis was dampened, however, when it failed to work in other patients with different neurotic manifestations. He turned then to the technique of free association (the reporting of all thoughts as they become spontaneously conscious), and the analysis of dreams, which he came to regard as "the royal road to the unconscious."

Continuing investigations by Freud and his colleagues led to the enumeration of numerous defensive processes, operating in normal as well as neurotic or psychotic individuals, by which the conscious mind was protected from the awareness of unacceptable or intolerable impulses, wishes, or emotions. It has become commonplace to compare mental processes with an iceberg, only the conscious and preconscious aspects being above the surface of voluntary recall, while the majority of processes and intrapsychic energies remain beneath the surface. Dynamically oriented psychologists refer to the accessibility of various levels of the psyche by means of different tests that will be described in Chapter 10. According to such a schema, self-reporting inventories such as the Minnesota Multiphasic Personality Inventory would be concerned with more superficial aspects of mental function than projective tests. Among the latter, the Thematic Apperception Test, based on the patient's stories about cards including human figures, would give information about more superficial functions than the Rorschach Ink Blot Test, or the even *less* structured test in which the individual is asked to draw a house, a tree, and a person of each sex. The term *depth psychology* has been applied to any psychological approach to the study of unconscious mental processes, but by far the majority of the concepts involved come from the field of *psychoanalysis* developed by Freud (and outlined in Chapter 1).

Freud was concerned with tracing back the origins of dynamic processes observed in adults to their biological roots in infancy and early childhood. Some of his findings and interpretations were bound by the culture in which he and his analytic subjects themselves developed and lived, as was the rejection of some of his valid insights by his medical colleagues of that era. Subsequent generations have been more receptive to his proposition that much of the dysphoric affect or anxiety against which normal individuals and psychiatric patients develop unconscious defenses originates in conflicts over forbidden, unacceptable, and consciously intolerable impulses. The most significant of these forbidden impulses involve sexual behavior and aggression, and the most primitive and unacceptable of these impulses were perceived as being directed by the infant or young child toward his own parents. While Freud emphasized the role of psychosexual development and its root in infancy, however, neo-Freudian analysts placed increasing emphasis on the role of aggression in interpersonal relationships, and on variations from one society or culture to another.

In his later writings Freud formulated his concept of personality structure and its differentiation into id, ego, and superego. The id represents the unorganized source of primitive instinctual impulses as summarized in the phrase "it wants." The ego was initially viewed as the seat of the conscious, intellectual, and self-preservative functions, as summarized in the phrase "I will, or I will not." The superego represents intrapsychic prohibitions and ideals including conscience, which are largely automatic and unconscious, as summarized in the phrase "thou shalt, or thou shalt not."

In current psychoanalytic theory, the ego is regarded as the integrative and executive portion of the personality, adapting constantly to the forces and pressures exerted by the id, the superego, and the external reality situation. The defense mechanisms that follow are therefore viewed as functions of the ego in its efforts to maintain the integrity of the individual, whether this individual is currently considered normal, neurotic, or psychotic. The same defense mechanism may involve varying degrees of reality distortion, may meet with varying success in assisting the overall efforts of the individual toward adaptation, and may be used with varying frequency by different individuals. It is these latter factors that determine the extent to which a given defense mechanism should be regarded as abnormal or maladaptive.

DEFENSE MECHANISMS

Repression is the common denominator and unconscious precursor of all other defense mechanisms. It involves the involuntary relegation of unbearable ideas and impulses into the unconscious, whence they are not ordinarily subject to voluntary recall, but may emerge in disguised form through utilization of other mental mechanisms. Repression may involve keeping out of conscious awareness information or impulses that have never been conscious, or alternatively may involve a form of purposeful forgetting. Pathological loss of memory, or amnesia, may of course result from organic brain disease as well as emotional conflict, but even organic damage to the brain may result in *selective* amnesia associated with repression of painful thoughts or impulses. Repression needs to be distinguished from *suppression*, which is not an unconscious defense, but a conscious effort to control and conceal unacceptable impulses, thoughts, feelings, or acts.

The term *denial* was used in early psychoanalytic theory to refer to the denial of intolerable external reality. This mechanism has been compared with the action of the ostrich in burying his head in the sand, with the implication that what cannot be perceived does not exist and cannot therefore be painful. The patient dying of cancer may deny his impending death and make elaborate plans for his future, even though he may be a physician who has been informed of his somatic pathology and his life expectancy. Similarly, the loss or death of a loved person may be denied, so that the individual believes and acts as though the lost loved one was still present or would soon return. The latter convictions and behavior may, of course, involve psychotic distortion of reality. In milder degrees there may be excessive preoccupation with inner fantasy, which is at least temporarily more satisfying than the painful external reality. In modern usage, the term denial is also applied to the rejection of intolerable thoughts, feelings, or wishes. Neurotic patients frequently deny the reality of sexual or hostile impulses in themselves or others. The hysterical girl may thus act in a seductive and provocative manner without recognizing the implications of her behavior, and may then be surprised and "hurt" when her boyfriend reacts by making sexual advances. The denial of dysphoric affect may be observed in the manic patient who may

become euphoric following the loss of a loved person or other circumstances that would normally result in grief.

The latter example may also be used as an illustration of *reaction formation*, in which attitudes and behavior are adopted that are the opposites of impulses to which the individual is reacting. The mother who unconsciously hates an unwanted child may react toward this child by overprotection and overindulgence ("smother love"). The individual with strong unconscious hostility toward other human beings may react against this by extreme concern for the welfare of animals and lead an antivivisection campaign. A person with strongly repressed sexual impulses may deplore the ready availability of salacious literature, and take an active part in a campaign for censorship of reading materials or movies—frequently assuming the role of one of the censors, so that he is exposed to the pornographic material from which others are to be protected.

The term *overcompensation* has sometimes been applied to the mechanism of reaction formation, but is more often applied to any conscious or unconscious process in which a real or fancied physical or psychological deficit inspires exaggerated correction. Congenital or acquired bodily defects sometimes lead to prodigious efforts to overcome them, so that a few such handicapped individuals have become world renowned athletes. Similarly the stutterer may succeed in becoming a fluent public speaker, or the shy introverted individual may strive to become adept in social situations.

Rationalization involves unconscious efforts through which an individual justifies and makes consciously tolerable those feelings, behaviors, and motives that would otherwise be intolerable to him. Hostile, punitive, and sadistic behavior toward children may be rationalized as having been provoked by them, or motivated through concern for their welfare ("spare the rod and spoil the child"). The unacceptable tendencies remain repressed and hidden from the individual concerned, although not necessarily from those around him. A special example of this mechanism consists of the sour-grapes maneuver, whereby failure becomes less painful through disparaging the goal. Similarly, the sweet-lemon maneuver permits the individual to convince himself that an unsatisfactory reality is not only tolerable but pleasant.

In *projection*, emotions, motivation, and behavior that are ego-alien and consciously unacceptable are not only denied but also attributed and projected onto other individuals. While this process may be considered relatively normal in the infant or young child, in adult persons it is apt to involve profound distortion of reality associated with paranoid delusions. In place of the intolerable impulse toward sexual relations with a man other than her husband, a paranoid woman may project onto her husband the belief that he is unfaithful to her, or onto another man the wish to have sexual relations with her. Similarly a man with unacceptable latent homosexual feelings toward another man may first deny love while admitting hate, and then project this hate onto the other man who is perceived as a persecutor.

Identification is an unconscious process by which an individual models his attitudes and behavior after another person. It is viewed as one of the most important mechanisms involved in personality development, with respect to both psychosexual development and the development of the superego or internal control system. This form of identification has also been spoken of as *internalization*, since it involves taking into one's self the instructions, prohibitions, and attitudes of the individual with whom the identification is made. The term *introjection* has also been applied to the symbolic taking into one's self of other individuals, but has been discarded as inaccurate and unsatis-factory by a number of analysts. Similarly, the concept of *incorporation* refers mainly to the infant's taking certain attributes into his own body through his mouth, and does not refer to the more mature process of identification. The mechanism of *identification* is not restricted to personality development, however, and may become a defensive measure when an individual identifies with an aggressor or powerful enemy.

The *displacement of affect or emotion* is a process whereby an emotion is displaced or redirected from the original object or person onto a more acceptable or less dangerous substitute. This mechanism is of great importance in daily living, in personality development, in manifestations of psychiatric disorder, and in the treatment of psychiatric patients. Its daily significance may be observed in the transfer of dangerous hostility, which may be aroused by an employer or business associates, onto members of the individual's family (see Figure 3-1), opponents in sporting events, minority social groups or "scapegoats," or people in foreign countries who are perceived as "enemies." The developmental significance involves sexual or hostile feelings toward parents, deeply ingrained through childhood experiences repeated over many years, which are displaced onto others of the same sex as the parent or onto representatives of authority encountered through adult life. Examples of displacement in the development of psychiatric symptoms may be seen in the case of sexual deviation, from adult individuals of the opposite sex onto various less dangerous substitutes; or in the redirection of fear resulting in the development of various phobias. During psychiatric treatment, the unconscious displacement of affect constitutes the basis of *transference*, the patient's irrational feelings and behavior toward his therapist based on earlier interpersonal relationships, and also of *counter-transference* consisting of the therapist's

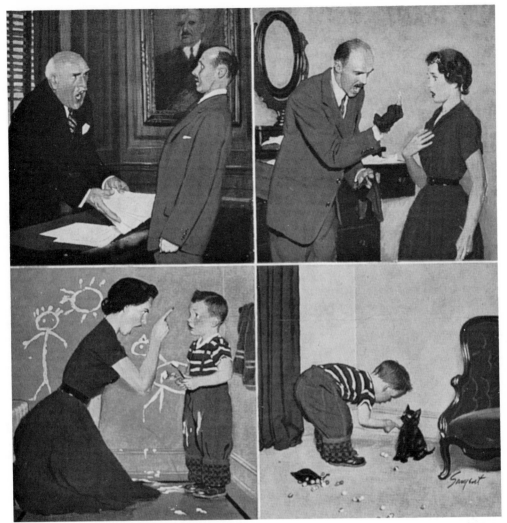

Figure 3–1. Displacement of affect or emotion. (Reprinted by courtesy of Dick Sargent and The Saturday Evening Post. Copyright © 1954, The Curtis Publishing Company.)

unconscious emotional reaction toward his patient.

Substitution is similar to displacement, but involves the substitution of a more acceptable form of activity in place of the emotion's being displaced onto another individual. By means of substitution, a murderous impulse may be replaced by a minor aggression or released in some impersonal destructive act such as chopping wood or striking a punching bag. Such substitutive activity is sometimes considered to have therapeutic as well as dynamic significance.

Sublimation is the defense considered most important to society as a whole, since it consists of diverting unacceptable instinctual drives (particularly sexual and aggressive) into personally and socially acceptable channels such as various forms of creative activity. The term sublimation should *not* be used to refer to "platonic" love from which the sensual element has been excluded, which was referred to by Freud as "aim-inhibited love."

Turning feelings toward one's self, sometimes known as *retroflexion,* is another defense against intolerable impulses such as hostility. In this instance, the consequence is lowered self-esteem, self-accusation, and depression, but the defense may also involve turning sexual feelings back upon the self, resulting in narcissistic self-love.

Regression involves the partial or symbolic reversion under stress to earlier patterns of behavior and gratification that may be more typical of the normal infant or young child. Regression is implied by the turning inward of sexual feelings and return to self-love, to which reference has just been made, but it may also involve many other forms of immature behavior. It occurs under a wide variety of circumstances such as normal sleep, play activities, severe physical illness, and in neurotic or psychotic disorders (see Figure 3-2). Regression under conditions of stress or frustration should be distinguished from *fixation,* involving a premature arrest in development, which is generally considered to be due either to excessive frustration or to excessive gratification at some specific stage of development.

Conversion is the mechanism by which unconscious conflicts are given symbolic external expression in the form of various bodily symptoms such as loss of sensation, loss of movement, or involuntary movements. Conversion is one of the main mechanisms used in hysterical neuroses, the other being *dissociation,* which involves a psychological separation or splitting off of emotion from an ideal, situation, or object. The latter results in a variety of manifestations such as loss of memory, fugue (loss of memory with physical flight), somnambulism or sleep walking, and multiple personality.

Isolation is a technique that is largely restricted to compulsive neuroses, in which an unacceptable impulse idea or act is separated from its original memory source. This then becomes the basis of many compulsive rituals such as touching or repeated washing. The latter rituals may also constitute forms of *undoing,* whereby an attempt is made to alleviate guilt for unacceptable past behavior by actions of symbolic atonement. Thus repeated washing of the hands may be a symbolic atonement for various activities (real or imagined) including masturbation, theft, and murder.

Acting out involves the behavioral expression of unconscious emotional conflicts or feelings of hostility or love in actions that the individual does not consciously know are related to such conflicts or feelings. One interpretation of delinquent behavior is that it represents a defense against conscious anxiety through the acting out of such unconscious conflicts or impulses.

DEVELOPMENTAL DYNAMICS

In her book *The Ego and the Mechanisms of Defence,* Anna Freud wrote as follows:

The considerations which determine the ego's choice of mechanism remain uncertain. Perhaps repression is pre-eminently of value in combating sexual wishes, while other methods can more readily be employed against instinctual forces of a different kind, in particular, against aggressive impulses. Or it may be that these other methods have only to complete what repression has left undone or to deal with such prohibited ideas as return to consciousness when repression fails. Or possibly each defence-mechanism is first evolved in order to master some specific instinctual urge and so is associated with a particular phase of infantile development.

What determines the choice of specific defense mechanisms remains as uncertain today as when the preceding sentences were written. To some extent therefore it may be concluded that the

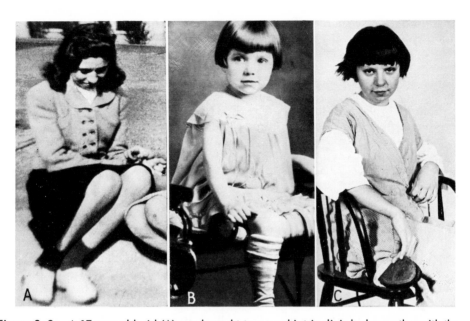

Figure 3–2. A 17-year-old girl (A) was brought to a psychiatric clinic by her mother with the complaint that for the preceding five months her behavior had become increasingly irrational and destructive. The history revealed that after the patient was about four years old her parents had begun to quarrel violently, making her early environment extremely contentious and unstable. At about this age she first developed various neurotic traits: nail-biting, temper-tantrums, enuresis, and numerous phobias. When the patient was seven the mother refused further sexual relations with the father and left the marital bed, but the patient continued to sleep with the father until she was 13. At this time the mother suspected that the patient was being incestuously seduced, obtained legal custody of the girl, and moved away with her to a separate home. The patient resented this, quarreled frequently with her mother, became a disciplinary problem at home and at school, and acquired a police record for various delinquencies. Three years later, at the patient's insistence, she and her mother paid an unexpected visit to the father, and found him living with another girl in questionable circumstances. In a violent scene, the mother denounced the father for unfaithfulness and, again contrary to the patient's wishes, took her home. There the patient refused to attend school and rapidly became sullen, withdrawn, and noncommunicative. During her mother's absence at work she would keep the house in disorder, destroy clothes her mother had made for her, and throw her mother's effects out of the window. During one of these forays she discovered a photograph of herself at the age of five (B), which, incidentally, was so poorly lighted and faded that, for one detail, it did not show her eyebrows. Using this as a pattern, she shaved off her own eyebrows, cut her hair to the same baby bob, and began to affect the facial expression and sitting posture of the pictured child (C). When brought to the hospital her general behavior was correspondingly childish; she was untidy and enuretic, giggled incessantly or spoke in simple monosyllabic sentences, spent most of her time on the floor playing with blocks or paper dolls, and had to be fed, cleaned, and supervised as though she were an infant. In effect, she appeared to have regressed to a relatively desirable period in life antedating disruptive jealousies and other conflicts; moreover, she acted out this regression in unconsciously determined but strikingly symbolic patterns of eliminating the mother as a rival and regaining the father she had lost in her childhood.

Thanks are due to Dr. John Romano, Professor of Psychiatry, University of Rochester, and to Dr. Richard Renneker for providing the photographs and data. (From Masserman, J. H. 1961. *Principles of Dynamic Psychiatry*, 2nd ed. Philadelphia, W. B. Saunders Co.)

study of these intrapsychic forces is descriptive rather than etiologic. Past behavior however may be the best predictor of future behavior, and analysts have continued to search for the childhood roots of adult personality, with both theoretical and therapeutic intent.

Maturation and involution refer to biological processes of growth and decline that are relatively independent of the environment. *Development* refers to interactions between these biological processes and various environmental influences involving learning or adaptation. The primary interpersonal environment of the child is ordinarily created by his natural parents, however, who transmit to the individual the patterns of the culture in which they live. Biological, psychological, and sociocultural influences upon personality development therefore become closely interwoven, and it may be impossible to assign relative significance to each type of factor. However, developmental studies may permit some valid generalizations.

In psychoanalytic theory, one of the most important of these generalizations concerns the *repetition compulsion,* which consists of the impulse to reenact earlier emotional experiences, regardless of the consequences for the individual in terms of pain or pleasure. Freud considered the repetition compulsion even more fundamental than the *pleasure principle,* according to which man instinctively seeks to avoid pain and discomfort, and strives for gratification and pleasure. In the structural concept of personality, the pleasure principle is therefore the servant of the id, which seeks immediate gratification of primitive impulses regardless of future consequences. As the child develops however, the ego modifies or postpones the gratification of these impulses in conformity with the *reality principle,* which takes into account the inescapable demands and requirements of the external world. The reality principle does not deny and oppose the demands of the pleasure principle completely, but involves compromises in the nature of gratification and allows for its postponement to a more appropriate time.

In the preceding section, *identification* was mentioned as one of the most important of mechanisms involved in personality development, and its significance relates both to superego development and psychosexual differentiation. The child is not born with a superego, conscience, or internal control system capable of producing intrapsychic guilt or remorse for unacceptable thoughts or behavior. In his initial conflicts with authority and external reality, the child conforms with various instructions and prohibitions through fear of punishment or withdrawal of affection and approval. Early in life the child formulates a conscious *ego-ideal* which represents a picture of the sort of child he would have to be in order to be assured of the parent's love and to avoid their disapproval or punishment. The superego then develops, ordinarily by the age of five or six years, through the internalization and automatization of these positive strivings represented by the ego-ideal, as well as the various negative parental prohibitions. Since the latter involves 'nonverbal as well as verbal communications, the superego may be regarded as developing on the basis of instruction, prohibition, and example. In adult psychiatric patients with neurosis and depression there is evidence of an unduly strong, harsh, punitive, and critical superego, whereas in other patients characterized by impulsive antisocial or sociopathic behavior there is evidence of inadequate superego development and internal controls. It has been remarked that the neurotic feels guilty for *thinking* what the sociopathic individual does *not* feel guilty for *doing.*

In addition to the development of superego, the process of identification is also responsible for the adult individual's predominant psychosexual orientation. Since identification ordinarily occurs with parents and other individuals of both sexes, the attitudes, interests, and behavior of adults of both sexes are distributed continuously along various scales from extremes of masculinity to extremes of femininity. This conforms with Freud's concept that every individual is bisexual, but in fact these continuous distributions are bimodal, and the majority of males are distributed toward the masculine end of the continuum while the majority of females are distributed toward the feminine end of the continuum. By an early age the majority of children have made their decisive identification with the parent or other significant individuals of the same sex. When the latter is absent or represents a relatively unsatisfactory model, however, the child may be led to make his decisive identification with the parent of the opposite sex, resulting in psychosexual inversion, which is frequently though not invariably accompanied by a persistent preference for overt homosexual behavior during adult life (see Chapter 20).

Another intrapsychic mechanism of great importance for personality development is the *displacement of affect.* The significance of this mechanism for adult personality, behavior, and psychopathology results from the unconscious displacement of predominant affects aroused by parents onto other representatives of authority or other individuals of the same sex as the parent (e.g., a husband or wife) throughout adult life. The word predominant may be emphasized, since love and hate, anger and fear may be aroused by the same individual at different times. The loved parent may be temporarily hated when he or she frustrates the child; this coexistence of opposing affects toward the same person is termed *ambivalence,* which Freud regarded as universal. While hostility or sexual love may be consciously unacceptable, however, they

may still be displaced onto other objects or persons and find devious forms of expression at a much later date.

Another important aspect of unconscious dynamic factors in personality development involves the *sequence of psychosexual development.* Analysts do not attribute to infants or children the complex pattern of adult sexuality, but maintain that the roots of the ultimate sexual pattern are to be found in the child in the form that foreshadows but does not completely define the ultimate pattern.

The earliest phase of infantile psychosexual development is known as the *oral stage,* lasting throughout the first year of life. It is usually divided into two successive phases: the oral erotic, related to the pleasurable sensations of sucking; and the oral sadistic, associated with aggressive biting. Both are normally preserved as partial aims in later life, and may appear in disguised and sublimated forms, associated with personality traits that are characterized largely by extreme dependency. Under conditions of overgratification or undue frustration there may be fixation at, or regression to, this level of development, as is hypothesized in certain functional psychoses, in alcoholism, and in drug addiction.

Our society chooses the second year of life as the appropriate time for toilet training, and the child derives conscious pleasure from his excretory functions and his ability to control them. This *anal stage* of development implies the ability to give or to withhold, and involves learning to make compromises between his primitive wishes and the rewards to be obtained by conforming with the demands and expectations of significant adults responsible for his care. "Anal" traits persisting in adults include excessive orderliness, miserliness, and obstinacy; if present in excessive degree they may be associated with the development of obsessive-compulsive neurosis. The latter has frequently been attributed to early exposure of the child to harsh and compulsive toilet training practices. A direct cause and effect relationship remains highly questionable, however, and toilet training may be only one example of many restrictive child rearing practices that precede the onset of such neurotic symptoms.

The next period of psychosexual development lasts from the age of about two and a half to six years, and is known as the *phallic stage* since children may display considerable sexual interest and curiosity focused upon the penis or the clitoris. The observed difference between male and female genitals may lead to the childhood fantasy that female genitals result from loss of a penis. According to psychoanalytic theory, the boy then develops a *castration complex*, fearing castration at the hands of his father for his forbidden Oedipal strivings to possess his mother. At this age the girl, on the other hand, is assumed to have Oedipal conflict (formerly sometimes referred to as an Electra conflict or complex) over her forbidden longings to replace her mother in the affections of her father. Much of the girl's behavior at this age has been interpreted as due to *penis envy*, which may be generalized or persist as a female wish for male attributes, positions, or advantages. According to psychoanalytic theory, hysteria is the form of neurosis resulting from unsatisfactory resolution of the Oedipal conflict. Various forms of sexual deviations in the male are also viewed as having their origins in this stage as unconscious defenses against anxiety over castration.

Burton and Whiting have advanced a more general *status-envy hypothesis* for both sexes, to the effect that identification consists of the covert practice of the role of an envied status. According to this hypothesis, a child maximally identifies with people who consume resources in his presence but who do not give him any. He does not identify with the people he loves unless they withhold from him something he wants.

These authors then viewed the Oedipal conflict in each sex as only one particular instance of this more general phenomenon.

The next stage in development lasts from the age of about six years until puberty and is regarded as one of sexual *latency.* Hopefully, the child has now resolved his Oedipal conflict, made his decisive identification with the parent of the same sex, and developed an adequate superego or internal control system. The intrafamilial relationships of the preschool years constitute the nucleus of his knowledge of the human race, which is now expanded in school and play activities, in relationships with other adults, and in collaborative or competitive activities with his peers. Old techniques of adaptation will be repeated and reinforced, or extinguished and replaced by newer techniques that are found more rewarding. Maladaptive patterns of behavior, however, may well be perpetuated by continuation of the conditions under which they developed or lack of motivation for change.

Puberty and adolescence lead to a reawakening of sexual interest, which is now conscious, verbalized, and acted upon in accordance with the mores of the peer group. During this period there is increasing desire to be freed from infantile dependency and to achieve adult status. This results in rejection of the standards and validity of the demands imposed by parents and other adults, with a tendency for uncritical acceptance of the philosophy of the peer group. In this process, there are often partial identifications with others of the same sex who are just a little older than the individual himself and who are admired by his peer group. The gradual emancipation from parental controls is hopefully accompanied by increasing responsibility and mature genitality based on mutual respect. The preceding history of psychosexual development was summarized in a table by Fenichel which is reproduced herewith (Table 3-1).

TABLE 3–1.*

Stages of Libidinal Organization	Stages in Development of Object Love	Dominant Point of Fixation in
1. Early oral (sucking) stage	Autoeroticism (no object, preambivalent)	Certain types of schizophrenia (stupor)
2. Late oral-sadistic (cannibalistic) stage	Narcissism: total incorporation of the object	Manic-depressive disorders (addiction, morbid impulses)
3. Early anal-sadistic stage	Partial love with incorporation	Paranoia, certain pregenital conversion neuroses
4. Late anal-sadistic stage	Partial love	Compulsion neurosis, other pregenital conversion neuroses
5. Early genital (phallic) stage	Object love, limited by the predominant castration complex	Hysteria
6. Final genital stage	Love (postambivalent)	Normality

(Stages 2–5 bracketed as "Ambivalent")

*Reprinted from Fenichel, O. *The Psychoanalytic Theory of Neurosis*, p. 101. By permission of W. W. Norton & Company, Inc. Copyright 1945 by W. W. Norton & Company, Inc., p. 101.

INTERPERSONAL DYNAMICS — COMMUNICATION OF AFFECT AND ROLE-EXPECTATION

The concepts outlined in the three preceding sections of this chapter have met with varying degrees of acceptance and rejection by psychiatrists, psychologists, and other members of society. In general, the sequence in which they have been presented corresponds roughly with the extent of their utilization in psychiatric theory and practice, but all of these ideas have received widespread attention and investigation.

There are other psychoanalytic formulations that have been generally regarded as far less credible or probable. Among these are Otto Rank's theories on birth trauma, according to which anxiety and neurosis are related to the inevitable psychic shock of being born. Many other such interpretations have been advanced, however, as adequate explanations of observed phenomena or reported fantasy, but without any supporting evidence as to their probable causal significance.

In a report on psychiatry and medical education published by the American Psychiatric Association, it was remarked that the formulation of psychodynamic principles in psychiatry for teaching purposes has tended to outrun the validation process, and many of the bolder dynamic hypotheses have not been of a character that made feasible prompt scientific validation or rejection. In a highly critical article, Cleckley and Thigpen added the following: "Were these bold hypotheses presented modestly as hypotheses, there would be little reason for objection. When presented to the medical student or the reading public as scientific fact established by evidence, they can be misleading and detrimental." One of the discussants of this paper suggested that part of the problem lay in not recognizing the difference between dynamics and description, in mistaking motivation for etiology, in not taking into account the role of biochemical and physiological factors in dynamics, as well as in equating psychodynamics with dynamics.

While psychodynamics focuses on the role of unconscious motivation in human behavior, it should be recognized that a great deal of significance is also attributed to the role of dynamic interpersonal relationships both in determining current behavior and in influencing personality development. Indeed, Harry Stack Sullivan defined psychiatry as the study of interpersonal processes, and other neo-Freudians have emphasized the significance of nonverbal communication in therapy as well as in the development of psychopathology. Some analysts have emphasized the importance of the "corrective emotional experience" within the transference relationship, as being of greater potential benefit than the interpretation of hitherto unconscious material.

Types of learning that may be relevant to therapy as well as etiology will be discussed further in Chapter 7, but the remainder of the present chapter will be concerned with certain aspects of communication, particularly those involving emotions and role-expectation.

Communication deals with the transmission of information from one individual to another, and of recent years this process has been extensively studied in both animals and humans. In an excellent review of animal studies, Frings discussed briefly the available *channels of communication* and elaborated more fully on the *nature of information*

communicated by animals. In man the eyes and ears are the most familiar channels of communication, but in many animals there is much greater dependence on touch and the chemical senses of taste and smell. The honeybee has the most highly developed system of tactile signals currently known, but even in man much of the traditional language of love is tactile. In the words of a song from the musical comedy *My Fair Lady* (based on the play *Pygmalion* by George Bernard Shaw):

Don't talk of stars burning above; if you're in love, show me.

Tell me no dreams filled with desire; if you're on fire, show me. . . .

Sing me no song, read me no rhyme, don't waste my time, show me.

Don't talk of June, don't talk of fall; don't talk at all, show me.

Signals transmitted through the sense of smell have an advantage over tactile signals in that they may be transmitted over greater distances, but have the disadvantage that they are persistent. In general, odors are most frequently used to enable species identification and sexual identification or stimulation. Vision and hearing, on the other hand, are used to convey a variety of information rapidly over considerable distances. Many species of birds have six or seven different calls that enable species identification, ensure the maintenance of distance by members of the same species, convey information about sources of food or the presence of possible enemies, and attract or stimulate members of the opposite sex for mating.

Scott pointed out that animal systems of communication possess in rudimentary form most of the basic characteristics of human language. Thus, many birds and mammals employ some sort of vocal communication, convey information about objects or situations in the environment, and may affect the behavior of other animals. Animal signals transmitted by smell may also be so persistent that they influence the behavior of other animals at distant periods in time. Scott concluded that the one unique characteristic of human language is the fact that it is largely independent of heredity.

Communication between human beings, however, does not take place through the medium of language alone, and many extremely important interpersonal communications between individuals of all ages are *nonverbal* in nature. Ruesch and Bateson described an *interpersonal event* as being characterized by "(a) the presence of expressive acts on the part of one or more persons; (b) the conscious or unconscious perception of such expressive actions by other persons; (c) the return observation that such expressive actions were perceived by others. The perception of having been perceived is a fact which deeply influences and changes human behavior." Communications may thus be received by any of the sense organs and may be transmitted through any of the effector organs. Ruesch also remarked that "man uses his communication system: (a) to receive and transmit messages and to retain information; (b) to perform operations with the existing information for the purpose of deriving new conclusions which were not directly perceived, and for reconstructing past and anticipated future events; (c) to initiate and modify physiological processes within his body; (d) to influence and direct other people and external events."

In a subsequent book on *nonverbal communication*, Ruesch and Kees presented many photographic illustrations of information regarding human relationships perceived visually. Of recent years, a number of scientists have also been investigating other channels of nonverbal communication, and the content of what is communicated, independently of any words that may be used in the process of communication. It has long been known that actions speak louder than words, and psychotherapists are acutely aware that what is said may frequently be less signi-

ficant than the manner in which it is said, or alternatively that which is left unsaid.

This does not apply only in psychotherapy, however, but also in current everyday interpersonal relationships and in the early childhood relationships which contribute significantly to personality development. In all such situations it appears that from a practical point of view we should consider *two basic categories of information that is communicated*: (1) the communication of affect or emotional tone; (2) the communication of expectations regarding acceptable behavior.

The communication of affect or emotion may take place directly or indirectly. When we associate with someone who is happy or miserable, particularly if we have a strong positive affection for him, we tend to identify with him and some of his mood is apt to rub off on us. ("A joy shared is a joy doubled, and a trouble shared is a trouble halved.") If, on the other hand, a person is angry for whatever reasons, some of his anger is apt to be generalized and displaced onto others with whom he comes in contact (as in the illustration earlier in this chapter). Similarly, fear may be transmitted either by repeated warnings or by example, particularly when the cautious or frightened individual is perceived as someone powerful who would not be afraid of trivialities. This is precisely the way in which the child perceives his parent, and verbal reassurances that thunderstorms are harmless will do nothing to alleviate the fear of a child who has the example of a frightened mother to follow. Similarly, a child seeking sexual information may learn more from the inappropriate embarrassment of a parent than from verbal reassurance that sexual behavior is normal, natural, or even "nice."

An interesting experimental demonstration of the nonverbal communication of affect in monkeys was reported by Mirsky and his associates. Two monkeys were trained to press a lever in order to avoid receiving an electric shock several seconds after being shown a visual stimulus. Then, only one of the animals was shown the visual warning signal, while only the other animal was able to press a lever to prevent them both from receiving an electric shock. In order to eliminate communication by sound or odor, the monkeys were placed in different experimental rooms at a distance from each other, and closed circuit television was used to enable the monkey with the lever to observe the facial expressions of the monkey that was shown the warning signal. The latter monkey was restrained to avoid violent movements, and the monkey with the lever was able to discriminate minute changes in facial expression that were not recognizable to the human experimenter, even when only parts of the transmitting monkey's face (such as the eyes or mouth) were shown on the television screen.

The *communication of role-expectation* regarding appropriate behavior may be based upon the perception of emotions in others, but may also occur in the absence of such conscious awareness. If a cat is frightened by a dog and runs away, the dog will usually oblige by pursuing it, though he may show no aggressive behavior if he should happen to catch up. The female of many species will retreat from the male in order to invite pursuit.

A former mental hospital superintendent used to tell the story of an occasion when he was being visited by a member of the Board of Trustees, and the latter asked to talk with one of the patients. The psychiatrist selected a male patient who was convalescing from a manic episode, was quite cheerful and genial, and hence was not likely to complain about conditions of life in the hospital. The patient carried on an intelligent and entertaining conversation with the Board member until the latter rose to terminate the interview and turned to leave. Suddenly the patient leaped on him from behind, wrestled

him to the floor, and put his hands around the man's throat — but was easily restrained by a male attendant. After the hurried departure of the Board member, the psychiatrist remarked to the patient that the latter had been overactive but not aggressive on admission, and that now he appeared in better control of his behavior than previously, so that the psychiatrist wondered what had prompted the patient to assault the Board member. "Well," replied the patient cheerfully, "he so obviously *expected* something like that to happen, and I didn't want to disappoint him."

It has long been recognized that to give a dog a bad name is to hang him. It is comparatively recently, however, that investigators have documented the many subtle ways in which parents may communicate their expectation and approval of antisocial behavior to their delinquent children. Johnson and Szurek postulated that unconscious permissive sanctioning by parents is a major and specific cause for children to live out antisocial impulses. Litin, Griffin, and Johnson also called attention to the role of parental influences in determining unusual sexual behavior in children. Johnson subsequently elaborated her thesis that antisocial acting out in a child is unconsciously fostered and sanctioned by the parents, who vicariously achieve gratification of their own poorly integrated forbidden impulses through the child's acting out.

Our society contains many examples of *conflicting communications* regarding role-expectation. A variety of behaviors are forbidden verbally or even by law, but are permitted or encouraged by failure to enforce such regulations, and the example of other members of society. Words are one thing and actions another, as the Russians have pointed out in diplomatic negotiations. It is not infrequent to find "no smoking" signs in the same rooms as ashtrays, so the expectation is clear that some people will ignore the signs. In military service, officers may be required to harangue enlisted men going on leave against the moral or health dangers of sexual indulgence—but the same enlisted men may each be given a prophylactic (condom) at the same time they draw pay before going on leave. The communication of conflicting role-expectations within the family has also been postulated as a significant factor in the etiology of schizophrenia (e.g., Bateson et al.), and the double bind in which the patient is then placed will be discussed in a later chapter on the schizophrenias.

SELECTED REFERENCES

Abraham, K. 1927. *Selected Papers.* London, Hogarth Press.

Alexander, F. 1948. *Fundamentals of Psychoanalysis.* New York, W. W. Norton & Co., Inc.

Alexander, F. 1952. Development of the fundamental concepts of psychoanalysis. In *Dynamic Psychiatry*. ed. F. Alexander and H. Ross. Chicago, University of Chicago Press.

American Psychiatric Association. 1952. *Psychiatry and Medical Education.* Washington, D.C., American Psychiatric Association.

American Psychiatric Association. 1964. *A Psychiatric Glossary,* 2nd edition. Washington, D. C., American Psychiatric Association.

Bateson, G., Jackson, D. D., Haley, J., and Weakland, J. 1956. Toward a theory of schizophrenia. Behavioral Science *1,* 251-264.

Benedek, T. 1952. Personality development. In *Dynamic Psychiatry,* ed. F. Alexander and H. Ross. Chicago, University of Chicago Press.

Benedek, T. 1946. *Insight and Personality Adjustment.* New York, The Ronald Press Co.

Breuer, J., and Freud, S. 1936. *Studies in Hysteria.* New York, Nervous and Mental Disease Publishing Company.

Burton, R. V., and Whiting, J. W. M. 1961. Merrill-Palmer Quarterly on Berhavior Development 7, 85-95.

Cleckley, H. M., and Thigpen, C. H. 1955. The dynamics of illusion. American Journal of Psychiatry *112,* 334-341.

Engel, G. E. 1962. *Psychological Development in Health and Disease.* Philadelphia, W. B. Saunders Co.

Fenichel, O. 1945. *The Psychoanalytic Theory of Neurosis.* New York, W. W. Norton & Co., Inc.

Freud, A. 1937. *The Ego and the Mechanisms of Defence.* London, Hogarth Press.

Freud, S. 1920. *A General Introduction to Psychoanalysis.* New York, Boni & Liveright.

Freud, S. 1924-1950. *Collected Papers,* Vol. 1-5. London, Hogarth Press.

Freud, S. 1927. *The Ego and the Id.* London, Hogarth Press.

Freud, S. 1950. *An Outline of Psychoanalysis.* New York, W. W. Norton & Co., Inc.

Frings, H. 1962. Animal communication. American Journal of Psychiatry *118,* 872-880.

Hall, C. S., and Lindzey, G. 1957. *Theories of Personality.* New York, John Wiley & Sons, Inc.

Hoch, P. H., and Zubin, J., editors. 1958. *Psychopathology of Communication,* New York, Grune & Stratton, Inc.

Johnson, A. M. 1959. Juvenile delinquency. In *American Handbook of Psychiatry*, ed. S. Arieti. New York, Basic Books, Inc. Vol. I, ch. 42.

Johnson, A. M., and Szurek, S. A. 1952. The genesis of anti-social acting out in children and adults. Psychoanalytic Quarterly *21,* 323.

Josselyn, I. M. 1948. *Psychosocial Development of Children.* New York, Family Service Association of America.

Levine, M. 1952. Principles of psychiatric treatment. In *Dynamic Psychiatry*, ed. F. Alexander and H. Ross. Chicago, University of Chicago Press, ch. II.

Litin, E. M., Griffin, M. E., and Johnson, A. M. 1956. Parental influence in unusual sexual behavior in children. Psychoanalytic Quarterly 25, 37-55.

Masserman, J. H. 1961. *Principles of Dynamic Psychiatry,* 2nd edition. Philadelphia, W. B. Saunders Co.

Mirsky, I. A., Miller, R. E., Banks, J. H., and Ogawa, N. 1961. *The Communication of Affects,* Proceedings of the Third World Congress of Psychiatry, Montreal, June, 1961. Montreal, McGill University Press, Vol. 1, pp. 88-91.

Munroe, R. L. 1955. *Schools of Psychoanalytic Thought.* New York, The Dryden Press.

Nemiah, J. C. 1961. *Foundations of Psychopathology.* New York. Oxford University Press, Inc.

Ruesch, J., and Bateson, G. 1951. *Communication, The Social Matrix of Psychiatry,* New York, W. W. Norton & Co., Inc.

Ruesch, J., and Kees, W. 1961. *Non-verbal Communication.* Berkeley. University of California Press.

Sullivan, H. S. 1953. *The Interpersonal Theory of Psychiatry.* New York, W. W. Norton & Co., Inc.

CHAPTER 4

Etiology: The Analysis of Causation

LOGICAL POSSIBILITIES IN CAUSATION

In the process of expanding his scientific knowledge, it is usually necessary for man to ask such questions as Who? What? When? and Where? before he can attempt to answer the more difficult questions of How? and Why? In the study of psychopathology, it is logical first to define and describe the nature of abnormality (Chapter 2) and next to study the dynamic intrapsychic forces underlying the external manifestations of abnormality, before searching for further causative factors involved in the development of this behavior (Chapter 3). As previously indicated, the term development implies a gradual unfolding and fuller working out of the details concerning growth. Hence the study of development involves both observation and inferences about causation. The term genetic pertains to origin, and may either be restricted to causation by heredity or alternatively applied to various other processes involved in development.

Etiology is the science or philosophy of causation. The analysis of causation sometimes involves the application of experimental methods of investigation, but the field of experimental psychopathology is not restricted to the study of etiology. On the contrary, experiments of relevance to psychiatry may relate to either causation or treatment, and may involve "normal" persons, persons with known psychopathology, or experimental animals.

The analysis of causation has long been of interest to philosophy and mathematics. Aristotle proposed that each event is the result of four causes: firstly, the material cause or matter (for example, the stone on which the sculptor works); secondly, the formal cause or form (the law according to which the thing develops); thirdly, the efficient cause or agent whose initial impulse started the process; and fourthly, the final cause, the purpose, goal, or end that the whole process is seeking to reach. It has since been argued that only two basic types of causation are involved: (1) mechanism, according to which every event is and must be determined by an immediately preceding event; and (2) teleological causation (derived from the Greek word meaning end or goal) according to which events are determined by what lies ahead and not by what went before. The latter type of causation is compatible with concepts of free will and of philosophical idealism. Scientific determinism and philosophical materialism, however, rejected teleological interpretations of events in favor of hypotheses that may be tested for conformity with mechanistic concepts of causation.

Another fundamental concern of philosophy and mathematics has been the analysis of logic, involving the laws and processes of correct reasoning. The elements of formal logic were laid down by Aristotle, but many of his doctrines have been rejected by modern mathematical logicians—for example, the doctrine that every proposition ascribes a predicate to a subject, his classification of the types of propositions, and his reduction of every deductive process to the form of the syllogism (a statement of two premises, leading to a conclusion). An example of the syllogism is the following: All men are mortal; and all farmers are men. Therefore, all farmers are mortal.

One of the most important contributions that mathematics can make to the solution of a scientific problem is to provide an exhaustive analysis of the

logical possibilities for the problem. (See for example Kemeny, Snell, and Thompson.) The role of science is then to discover facts that will eliminate all but one possibility. Another important function of mathematical logic involves *checking the validity of arguments and proofs,* a proof being an argument which shows that a conditional statement is logically true. In the remainder of the present section, we shall examine a variety of logical possibilities in enumerating categories of causation.

The simplest notion of causation is that of a single determinant ("cause," antecedent, or independent variable) leading inevitably to a single result ("effect," consequence, or dependent variable). It is however generally recognized that a *single cause may lead to multiple different consequences.* In some instances, these consequences constitute a chain, each being followed in sequence by another result, as illustrated in the nursery rhyme quoted at the beginning of this chapter, in which the loss of the horseshoe nail led through various intermediate events to the loss of a kingdom. In other instances, a single cause may lead concurrently to multiple different end results. The variety of physiological consequences that may result from a single defect in metabolism (which may be controlled by a single pair of genes) is illustrated in Figure 4-1.

It is also widely recognized that *the same apparent end result may be reached through different mutually exclusive pathways,* and that such pathways may each involve single or multiple determinants. In the latter event, multiple antecedent events may lead from one to another in the form of a chain, or interact together simultaneously to constitute a pattern of causation. The genetically controlled chemical reactions taking place in the individual body cell are not a series of straight-line reactions, but a complex web of interrelated reactions. At the next level of structural and functional integration, that of the organ

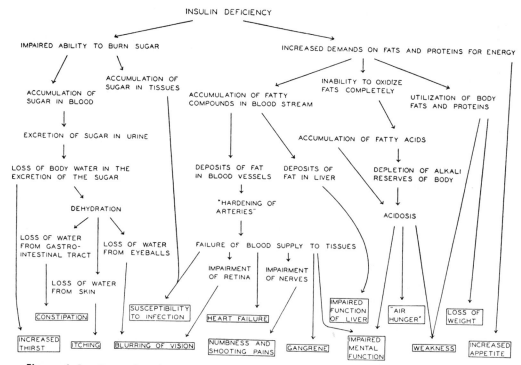

Figure 4–1. Some physiological consequences of the relative deficiency of insulin which occurs in diabetes mellitus. (From Neel, J. V., and Schull, W. J., *Human Heredity.* Reprinted by permission of The University of Chicago Press. Copyright © 1954, The University of Chicago.)

rather than the cell, what appears to be a single disease may result from several different types of inheritance. Neel and Schull pointed out that the diseases of the eye known as choroidoretinal degeneration may be transmitted through five different genetic mechanisms: simple autosomal recessive, autosomal dominant, sex-linked recessive, partially sex-linked dominant, and partially sex-linked recessive.

A further problem is that of circular causation in which a given situation may be both cause and effect, resulting in perpetuation of a given interaction. A simple clinical example is that of hostile interaction between husband and wife, which tends to be perpetuated in a vicious cycle, and also to generalize and derive further feedback from involvement of their children. A further example is the "self-fulfilling prophecy" of the paranoid individual who mistrusts others, and therefore invites and receives some measure of rejection, which makes him more alienated and mistrustful. Berelson and Steiner have referred to such interactions as "the spiral finding," as follows:

Deprived children tend to become poor parents, whose own children then tend to be deprived; the unpopular child, feeling rejected, withdraws, becomes more ingrown and, as a result, more unpopular; a deteriorating area of the city attracts social delinquency, as a result of which it deteriorates further; the official leadership of a formal organization, when opposed by the informal channels of personal relations within it, will tend to tighten up bureaucratic controls, and as a result the informal channels become more cohesive still; a deprived group such as Negroes in the United States are restricted in such social opportunities as education, as a result of which they are thought to be less educable and hence deprived further.

It is convenient to conceptualize the

interaction of multiple causes by means of Venn diagrams, in which each cause (independent variable) is represented by the area contained within a circle, and the consequence (dependent variable) by the shaded areas within overlapping circles. In diagrams of this nature, a single cause acting by itself is represented by the area within a circle that is *not* also contained in any other circle, whereas interaction between causes is depicted by any area falling within two or more intersecting circles. The simplest form of interaction involves only *two* causes, which may be represented by two intersecting circles

A and B. Figure 4-2 represents an exhaustive (i.e., complete) enumeration of all possible combinations of these two independent variables, which may either (1) be *sufficient* to produce a given end result (shaded area) when acting alone; (2) be *necessary* to produce *all* instances of the required end result; or (3) *suppress* the required end result (shaded area) and prevent it from appearing in situations in which an otherwise sufficient cause is operating.

The next simplest example of interaction involves three independent variables represented by the circles A, B, and C, which may act to produce a

AN EXHAUSTIVE ENUMERATION OF ALL POSSIBLE RELATIONSHIPS BETWEEN TWO CAUSES (OR INDEPENDENT VARIABLES, DEPICTED BY CIRCLES A AND B) AND A SINGLE EFFECT (OR DEPENDENT VARIABLE, DEPICTED BY SHADED AREA IN EACH DIAGRAM)

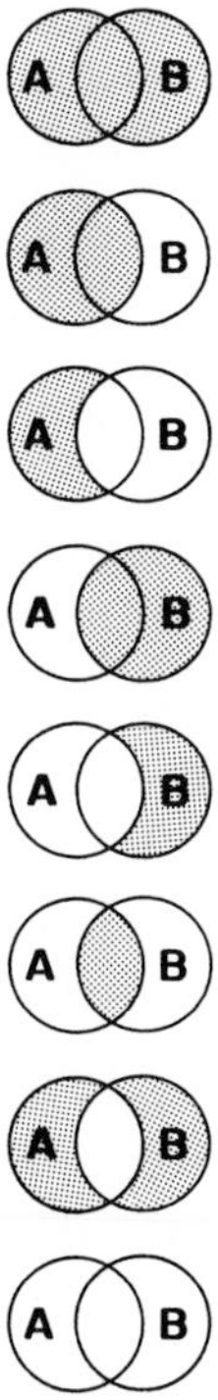

		SUFFICIENT CAUSES	NECESSARY CAUSES	NEGATIVE CAUSES OR SUPPRESSORS
1.	(A B)	A or B	—	—
2.	(A B)	A	A	—
3.	(A B)	A	A	B
4.	(A B)	B	B	—
5.	(A B)	B	B	A
6.	(A B)	—	A and B	—
7.	(A B)	A or B	—	A and B (interacting)
8.	(A B)	—	—	—

Figure 4-2

dependent variable represented by the shaded areas in the diagrams of Figure 4-3. An exhaustive (complete) enumeration of all possible combinations of three independent variables would require a total of 128 diagrams, and only a few of these situations have therefore been selected for reproduction in Figure 4-3. It should be noted, however, that there is now a fourth category of causation (in addition to those previously defined as sufficient, necessary, or suppressor) which may be described as *contributory* — i.e., sufficient or necessary to produce the required end result, but only when acting in combination with one or more other independent variables.

There is a simple mathematical relationship between (a) the number of independent variables *plus* possible interactions, and (b) the number of logically possible combinations associated with a single outcome or dependent variable. In Figure 4-2, the number of separate areas enclosed by the *two* intersecting circles is three, and the total number of possible combinations is 2^3 (i.e., 8). In Figure 4-3, the total number of areas enclosed within the *three* intersecting circles is seven, and the maximum possible number of

A PARTIAL ENUMERATION OF POSSIBLE RELATIONSHIPS BETWEEN THREE CAUSES (OR INDEPENDENT VARIABLES, DEPICTED BY CIRCLES A, B AND C) AND A SINGLE EFFECT (OR DEPENDENT VARIABLE, DEPICTED BY SHADED AREA)

	SUFFICIENT CAUSES	NECESSARY CAUSES	CONTRIBUTORY CAUSES	NEGATIVE CAUSES OR SUPPRESSORS
 I.	A, B or C	—	—	—
2.	 —	A, B and C	—	—
3.	—	—	 A, B or C	—
4.	 —	A	B or C	—
5.	 —	A and B	—	C
6.	 A	—	B and C	—
7.	 A	A	—	B and C
8.	 A	A	—	B or C

Figure 4-3

combinations is 2^7 (i.e., 128). If we try now to conceptualize interactions between *four* independent variables (which might be represented by intersecting spheres rather than circles) the total number of separate areas involved would be 13, and the maximum theoretical number of combinations would be 2^{13} (i.e., 32,768). Many of these outcomes are disjoint and inherently unlikely, while many others represent duplications of combinations observed with only two or three independent variables. It should be emphasized, however, that the preceding logically possible combinations of causal variables involve only a single result or outcome, and the situation becomes much more complex if we recognize that interactions between causal factors may involve qualitatively or quantitatively different outcomes. It is not surprising therefore that widely used models in the analysis of etiology concern themselves only with interactions between two or three separate groups of independent variables.

RELATIVITY IN ETIOLOGICAL MODELS

It has long been recognized that the tubercle bacillus is a necessary but *not* sufficient cause for the development of clinical tuberculosis. Other etiological factors may be conveniently divided into those that affect the susceptibility or vulnerability (immunity or resistance) of the individual, and those environmental factors governing the magnitude, frequency, and nature of his exposure to infection. The study of epidemiology, the basic science of preventive medicine and public health, led to the formulation of an etiological model involving these three groups of causative factors: the *agent of disease* (for example, virus, bacterium, parasitic worm, or toxic chemical); the *host vulnerability* (a combination of hereditary and environmental factors affecting predisposition); and the *environmental situation* (physical, biological, and social) favoring the development and spread of the agent.

In general medicine, one of the traditional models in analyzing etiology involves the distinction between *predisposing, precipitating,* and *perpetuating* factors. In psychiatry and psychology a widely used model involves distinctions between (1) *biological* factors, including both heredity and environmental factors operating primarily on the body or biological organism; (2) *psychological* factors mediated through learning and environmental experiences, particularly those involving interpersonal relationships; and (3) *sociocultural* factors, shared by other members of similar groups within the society and culture in which the individual lives, and generally (though not universally) regarded as mediated through psychological rather than biological mechanisms. In the next four chapters, evidence concerning the etiology of psychiatric disorder will be presented within the later conceptual framework.

There is, however, a further problem to which attention should be drawn in this preliminary discussion, namely the relativity of both the external stress (whether biological, psychological, or sociocultural) that may lead to psychopathology, and of the individual's ability to adapt or react in an abnormal manner (likewise the result of the interaction between biological, psychological, and sociocultural variables). A number of attempts have been made to relate this concept of varying response to varying stress with clinical observations concerning the generally recognized psychiatric syndromes. One such attempt is shown in Figure 4-4, adapted from Marmor and Pumpian-Mindlin. This diagram does *not* consider *qualitative* variations in types of environmental stress or personal vulnerability, but proposes that each is distributed *quantitatively* along a continuum. Minor stress is sufficient to precipitate severe emotional disorder in unstable individuals, which conforms with clinical

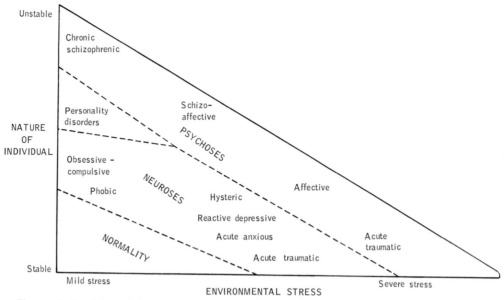

Figure 4–4. Adapted from Marmor, J., and Pumpian-Mindlin, E., 1950. Toward an integrative conception of mental disorder. Journal of Nervous and Mental Diseases 3, 19.

experience. However it should be emphasized that the locations of clinical diagnoses in this diagram are hypothetical.

While not concerned with specificity in clinical diagnosis, Langner and Michael presented an interesting analysis of lifelong adaptation based on analogy with the physical concepts of stress and strain, defining *stress* in terms of adverse environmental influences and *strain* as manifested by psychiatric impairment or disorder. Their illustrative diagram is reproduced in Figure 4-5, in which the letters SES refer to socioeconomic status. It is significant that these authors include in their diagram the concept of positive factors, favoring healthy adaptation, corresponding with the suppressor variables in our earlier diagrams, Figures 4-2 and 4-3. However, it may also be noted that they represented the magnitude of these positive factors as diminishing throughout life, whereas the magnitude

of adverse environmental stress was depicted as progressively increasing.

In the light of the preceding concepts regarding etiology and relativity, it may now be appropriate to return to the model of "abnormal behavior" that was used at the beginning of Chapter 2. At that point, *the wearing of sunglasses under conditions of low light intensity* (i.e., minimal stress) was used to illustrate relativity in terms of defining abnormality, rather than analyzing its causes. Let us now consider several alternative hypotheses about causal factors that might lead an individual to act in this manner. First, there is a possibility of hereditary susceptibility or sensitivity to relatively low intensities of light. This might be determined by a single pair of major genes as in albinism (a rare recessive characteristic), or by the interaction of more than one pair of genes as in the lack of pigmentation occurring in blue-eyed individuals. Other biological factors that might result in this be-

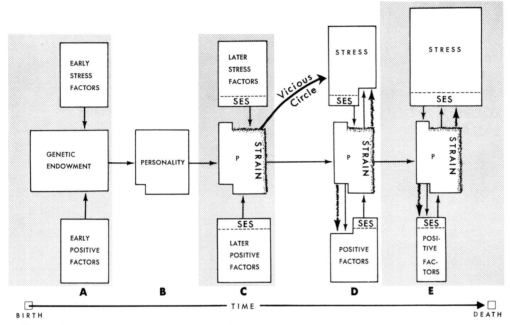

Figure 4–5. Interaction of environmental factors, endowment, and personality. (Reprinted with permission of The Macmillan Company from *Life Stress and Mental Health*, by T. S. Langner and S. T. Michael. Copyright © The Free Press of Glencoe, Inc., a division of The Macmillan Company, 1963, page 11.)

havior include intoxication (e.g., the morning after alcoholic overindulgence, when "even the kittens are stamping"), localized infection (e.g., conjunctivitis), or part of a more generalized infectious process (e.g., the photophobia of measles).

From a psychological point of view, the wearing of sunglasses may sometimes represent a defensive denial and withdrawal from painful reality. The eyes may be sensitive indicators of emotions or motivation, which the individual would prefer to conceal behind the dark lenses that he interposes between himself and others. On several occasions, the author has observed relatives of psychiatric patients wearing sunglasses in a relatively dimly lighted office during interviews that mobilized feelings of guilt, depression, anger, or fear. This particular form of learned defensive behavior would be most likely to be adopted by those who perceive others as potentially critical or hostile: the insecure neurotic, or the isolated and mistrustful schizoid or paranoid individual.

Emotional insecurity may also lead to the wearing of sunglasses because it is considered fashionable in the sociocultural group (or "in-group") with whom the individual identifies, and whose opinions and role-expectations are vitally important to him Certain groups in our society frequently wear sunglasses indoors, and in a number of other countries the wearing of sunglasses may be regarded as a behavior characteristic of foreigners or of their own upper socioeconomic class. Technology and socioeconomic status influence a great many behaviors, as well as the extent to which these behaviors are considered normal or abnormal. From the preceding illustrations it can also be seen how a *single be-havior may at one time be determined pre-dominantly by one category of causation, and at another time by a quite different determinant or combination of determinants.*

LOGICAL ARGUMENT AND FALLACY

It was pointed out earlier that one of the important tasks of mathematical logic involves checking the validity of arguments. An argument consists of an assertion that a certain statement (the conclusion) follows logically from certain other statements (the premises). The truth or falsity of the premises and conclusion are entirely irrelevant to the question of logical validity of the argument. Thus, a false conclusion may be derived by valid argument from false premises. On the other hand, if all the premises were false, a true conclusion might still result from a valid argument. An example of a valid argument is the syllogism stated earlier, which may be restated in the following form:

$$p \to q \qquad \text{All farmers are men.}$$
$$q \to r \qquad \text{All men are mortal.}$$
$$\therefore q \to r \qquad \text{Therefore, all farmers are mortal.}$$

An argument that is *not valid* is called a *fallacy*, one example of which is the following:

$$p \to q \qquad \text{All farmers are men.}$$
$$q \to r \qquad \text{All men are mortal.}$$
$$\therefore r \to p \qquad \text{Therefore, all mortals are farmers.}$$

A common type of fallacy involves drawing conclusions about causation from association or correlation. Thus, Eysenck pointed to the arguments on which three different types of theory may be developed to account for associations between the behaviors of *parents* and *their children* (Figure 4-6). In this figure P refers to the parental generation, F to the filial generation, x to a certain parental practice (in this example, early weaning), and y to a certain filial practice (in this case, aggressive behavior on the part of the children). Now x (early weaning) is found to be consistently and reliably correlated with y (aggressive behavior). One form of environmental theory (A) is shown, according to which the child's aggressive behavior is the direct result of the early weaning. An equally plausible but also invalid argument (B) is that certain temperamental characteristics (such as "aggression") are inherited, and manifest themselves independently in parent and child. A third type of argument (C) suggests that aggressive behavior on the part of the child modifies the parental behavior and hence leads to early weaning (reaction theory).

This common type of fallacy is sometimes known as post hoc reasoning (from the Latin *Post hoc, ergo propter hoc,* meaning "After this, therefore because of this"). In an amusing chapter entitled "Post Hoc Rides Again" Huff gave some pertinent illustrations of this fallacy,

---

$$(A) \quad P \to x \qquad \text{ENVIRONMENTAL}$$
$$ \quad F \to y \qquad \text{THEORY}$$
$$ \quad \therefore x \to \to y$$

$$(B) \quad P \to x \qquad \text{HEREDITARY}$$
$$ \quad F \to y \qquad \text{THEORY}$$
$$ \quad \therefore P \to \to F \to \to y$$

$$(C) \quad P \to x \qquad \text{REACTION}$$
$$ \quad F \to y \qquad \text{THEORY}$$
$$ \quad \therefore F \to \to P \to \to x$$

Figure 4–6. Three different types of theory to account for behavior resemblances between parents and children. (Reproduced by permission from Eysenck, H. J., ed. 1960. *Handbook of Abnormal Psychology*. London, Pitman Medical Publishing Company, Ltd.)

and his introductory paragraphs are reproduced herewith:*

Somebody once went to a good deal of trouble to find out if cigarette smokers make lower college grades than nonsmokers. It turned out that they did. This pleased a good many people and they have been making much of it ever since. The road to good grades, it would appear, lies in giving up smoking; and, to carry the conclusion one reasonable step further, smoking makes dull minds.

This particular study was, I believe, properly done: sample big enough and honestly and carefully chosen, correlation having a high significance and so on.

The fallacy is an ancient one which, however, has a powerful tendency to crop up in statistical material, where it is disguised by a welter of impressive figures. It is the one that says that if B follows A, then A has caused B. An unwarranted assumption is being made that since smoking and low grades go together, smoking causes low grades. Couldn't it just as well be the other way around? Perhaps low marks drive students not to drink but to tobacco. When it comes right down to it, this conclusion is about as likely as the other and just as well supported by the evidence. But it is not nearly so satisfactory to propagandists.

It seems a good deal more probable, however, that neither of these things has produced the other, but both are the product of some third factor. Can it be that the sociable sort of fellow who takes his books less than seriously is also likely to smoke more? Or is there a clue in the fact that somebody once established a correlation between extroversion and low grades—a closer relationship apparently than the one between grades and intelligence? Maybe extroverts smoke more than introverts. The point is that when there are many reasonable explanations you are hardly entitled to pick one that suits your taste and insist on it. But many people do.

To avoid falling for the *post hoc* fallacy and thus wind up believing many things that are not so, you need to put any statement of relationship through a sharp inspection.

*Reprinted from *How to Lie With Statistics*, by Darrell Huff. Pictures by Irving Geis. By permission of W. W. Norton & Company, Inc. Copyright 1954 by Darrell Huff and Irving Geis.

The correlation, that convincingly precise figure that seems to prove that something is because of something, can actually be any of several types.

One is the correlation produced by chance. You may be able to get together a set of figures to prove some unlikely thing in this way, but if you try again, your next set may not prove it at all. As with the manufacturer of the tooth paste that appeared to reduce decay, you simply throw away the results you don't want and publish widely those you do. Given a small sample, you are likely to find some substantial correlation between any pair of characteristics or events that you can think of.

A common kind of co-variation is one in which the relationship is real but it is not possible to be sure which of the variables is the cause and which the effect. In some of these instances cause and effect may change places from time to time or indeed both may be cause and effect at the same time. A correlation between income and ownership of stocks might be of that kind. The more money you make, the more stock you buy, and the more stock you buy, the more income you get; it is not accurate to say simply that one has produced the other.

Perhaps the trickiest of them all is the very common instance in which neither of the variables has any effect at all on the other, yet there is a real correlation. A good deal of dirty work has been done with this one. The poor grades among cigarette smokers is in this category, as are all too many medical statistics that are quoted without qualification that although the relationship has been shown to be real, the cause-and-effect nature of it is only a matter of speculation. As an instance of the nonsense or spurious correlation that is a real statistical fact, someone has gleefully pointed to this: There is a close relationship between the salaries of Presbyterian ministers in Massachusetts and the price of rum in Havana.

Which is the cause and which is the effect? In other words, are the ministers benefiting from the rum trade or supporting it? All right. That's so farfetched that it is ridiculous at a glance. But watch out for other applications of *post hoc* logic that differ from this one only in being more subtle. In the case of the ministers and the rum it is easy to see that both figures are growing because of the influence of a third factor: the historic and world-wide rise in the price level of practically everything.

STATISTICAL INFERENCE AND SCIENTIFIC PROOF

Statistics may be defined as that branch of science governing the collection, analysis, and interpretation of data. It enables the control or elimination of any of the conceivable sources of error or distortion of knowledge. Two sources of error or bias are commonly distinguished: (1) random or chance, and (2) systematic. Much of the formal content of statistics is concerned with the study and hence elimination of error due to random or chance variation. The term *descriptive statistics* has been applied to the estimation of certain characteristics of the population from which a sample is drawn (for example, measures of central tendency and dispersion). The term *inferential statistics* refers to the use of these procedures in reaching decisions regarding the probable truth or falsity of a given hypothesis.

The process of using a sample to test whether a hypothesis concerning a given population is true or false is called a statistical proof of the truth or falsity of the hypothesis. In reaching a decision regarding its probable truth or falsity, there are *two types of random error* that may be made. The mistake of rejecting a true hypothesis is termed a Type 1 or alpha error, whereas the mistake of accepting a false hypothesis is termed a Type 2 or beta error. In practice the probability of making a Type 1 or alpha error can usually be specified accurately and is termed the "level of significance" of a test, whereas the probability of making a Type 2 error is known as the power of the test and cannot usually be determined so precisely. It is therefore usually a much stronger statement to reject a statistical hypothesis (with a specified small probability of making a Type 1 error), than to conclude that one's data conform with the hypothesis (with a much larger and usually uncertain probability of making a Type 2 error). The establishment of a statistical

hypothesis therefore involves disproof of various alternative hypotheses.

Sources of systematic error or bias that should be recognized and avoided include the following: (1) shifting definitions of what is being studied, (2) inaccurate measurement or classification, (3) selection of samples that are not representative of the population from which they were drawn or of the group about which inferences are being made, (4) a number of types of inappropriate comparisons, (5) differential composition of groups, (6) misinterpretation of association or correlation, which does not necessarily imply causation (see preceding section), (7) disregard of dispersion, (8) technical errors such as miscomputation, (9) misleading statements, charts, and graphs.

Wittkower remarked that successive steps in rigorous research design consist of problem formation, review of knowledge, preliminary observation, theory construction, verification by empirical tests, controlled experiments, repetition of observations by independent investigators, and prediction of behavior on repetition. While predictability and manipulation of the experimental situation are scientific desiderata, they are not however essential prerequisites of a research design. In astronomy, for example, the principles of replication and prediction can be applied, but manipulation is obviously impossible.

Kline wrote that, in the development of a scientific "proof," the following factors are contributory, but none sufficient of itself: explanation, regularity, replication, control and prediction. The most useful single procedure to establish the validity of a theory is its ability to provide a correct disjunctive prediction. He elaborated on these statements as follows:*

---

*Excerpted by permission from Kline, N. S. 1961. On the relationship between neurophysiology, psychophysiology, psychopharmacology, and other disciplines. Annals of the New York Academy of Science *92*, 1009-1011.

...In point of fact, we are never able to "prove" anything; we can only accumulate more and more evidence that our hypothesis is not *incorrect*. There are a number of ways of doing this; although some of the methods are contributory they are not of themselves sufficient.

Explanation Is Not Sufficient

To explain, post hoc, what psychodynamics were involved or how a molecule broke down to produce a particular effect, can be done in dozens or hundreds of different ways. If mere explanation were sufficient, all of these ways would be "true." The fanciful manner in which chemical formulas are sometimes drawn to show a presumed relationship to other chemical formulas is as imaginative as anything in psychoanalytic theory. Embellishment, "interpretation," or extension of a theory to meet the nonconforming case is usually a reason for suspicion and closer examination.

Regularity Is Not Sufficient

Because a certain event in, let us say, the psychological area regularly follows or occurs simultaneously with a neurophysiological event is not proof that the two are directly—or even indirectly—related. Such a correlation certainly constitutes an invitation to investigate if there is a common causal nexus, but a theory relating the two is suitable only as a working hypothesis. All too often we have been told that this or that chemical (or sociological factor or electrophysiological event) is the *cause* of some mental state or feeling tone, simply because the two were associated. Even the existence of such pairing has usually been shown to be false when more extensively and intensively investigated.

Replication Is Not Sufficient

One of Koch's postulates is widely misunderstood and abused. It is not sufficient to be able to induce or replicate part of a disease; the entire natural history of the disorder must be reproduced. For instance, to stimulate the globus pallidus and produce symptoms of parkinsonism does *not* prove that a disorder of the globus pallidus is the cause of the disease. This nucleus may be involved only as an intermediate step, or may not be involved in the causal chain at all,

and the fact that stimulation reproduced certain symptoms may be artifactual. Similarly, the chemical structure of drugs that are known to produce psychoticlike behavior is no demonstration that a similar type of chemical structure occurs in the human patient and produces mental disorder. The fact that electrical activity of the reticular activating system is markedly different during sleep, wakefulness, and under a variety of specified conditions does not itself prove it is the alertness center of the brain. It, too, may only be part of the causal chain, or it may be coincidentally involved. All of these findings are, however, invitations to further investigation, since they constitute preliminary but insufficient "proof."

Control Is Not Sufficient

A patient is treated by a psychiatrist who believes in Pavlovian theory (or Freudian theory or Jungian theory) and who uses techniques compatible with his theory. The fact that the patient recovers does not constitute a "proof" of the psychiatrist's beliefs. The same holds true in the more "exact" disciplines. Many chemical reactions were well controlled on the basis of alchemy, with its astrological theories, and the phlogiston theory was the basis for much practical work. An ability to control predicated on a particular hypothesis, although it is not sufficient in itself, does, however, tend to lend support to a theory.

Even Prediction Is Not Sufficient

At the core of the scientific method is the ability to predict, and if this is done with two special qualifications observed it is the strongest evidence that we can educe for correctness. The first qualification is that the prediction must be in respect to an irregularly occurring, rare, or new event. The other qualification is that the prediction should be disjunctive, that is, that various incompatible alternative possibilities are enumerated, and the ones that will *not* occur, as well as the one that will occur, are specified.

Hence it is not sufficient to say that if a patient has a severe psychic trauma his condition will change. Specifically, what he *will* do and what he *will not* do must be described. Similarly it is not sufficient to say that "the addition of copper and other trace metals will change the effect of the phenothiazines," nor does the statement "stimulation of the septum pellucidum will change the electroencephalogram" mean nearly as much as it would if the disjunctive possibilities were enumerated and the correct one predicted.

It should be emphasized that while the last-named approach is the most desirable, there are many occasions in which theory is not adequately developed nor techniques available for proceeding in this manner. Under these circumstances it is perfectly legitimate to base our working hypothesis and our practice on such evidence as is available. We should, however, strive to develop theory and technique to the point at which new and disjunctive events are predicted and their occurrence empirically verified.

MULTIPLE CAUSATION OF PSYCHIATRIC DISORDERS

Attempts to establish the significant determinants of personality and psychiatric disorders require an open-minded skepticism, an exact specification of the problems to be studied, and a constant awareness of both systematic and random sources of error. It may now be appropriate to summarize some of the main problems involved in etiological studies of psychopathology:

(1) The analysis of causation must recognize the possibilities of multiple consequences from single agencies, single outcomes from multiple causal events, and different consequences from the interaction of two or more causes than from either operating independently. It is also necessary to bear in mind the possibility of circular causal relationships, and the existence of suppressor or inhibitory factors as well as unfavorable etiologic agents or experiences. The analysis of psychopathology involves a search for hereditary and other biological determinants, psychological and sociocultural influences, each of which may require competence in different techniques of investigation.

(2) Consistent association or correlation (as between a given psychiatric disorder and some metabolic anomaly or alternatively, membership in some sociocultural group) *may* indicate a direct cause-and-effect relationship: the psychiatric disorder being either the cause or the effect, or both cause and effect. On the other hand, any causal relationship between the associated variables may be only an indirect one, mediated through one or more other associated variables.

(3) Retrospective information concerning antecedent factors presumed to be significant in the development of a disorder may be extremely difficult to obtain and is subject to falsification — particularly when a long time has elapsed since the presumed causal situation, as the patient may have been a young child at the time and other informants may also distort information because of their emotional involvement.

(4) Prospective or anterospective information based upon longterm observations may also be extremely difficult to obtain, due to the excessive time and expense involved in making extensive observations upon large numbers of individuals — all of whom must be followed in spite of various changes in residence, although only a small proportion may be expected to develop the abnormality that is being studied.

(5) Evidence in support of a hypothesis ordinarily involves elimination or rejection of all alternative hypotheses, since the rejection of the hypothesis is usually a much stronger statement than its acceptance. The statistical significance of a test is the probability of rejecting a true hypothesis (making a type 1 or alpha error), which can be accurately specified, whereas the probability of accepting a false hypothesis (type 2 or beta error) can frequently not be specified accurately.

(6) The strongest positive evidence in support of a hypothesis, in contrast with the negative evidence resulting from the elimination of alternative hypotheses, is the ability to predict correctly. This is

particularly so when the two qualifications stipulated by Kline are both met—namely that the event should be irregular and rare or new, and that the prediction should be disjunctive.

(7) Experimental replication of naturally occurring psychiatric disorder, or of various hypothetical causal situations, is not usually possible. Attempts at reproducing "functional" psychiatric syndromes such as schizophrenia by means of a number of toxic agents ("psychotomimetic drugs") or biological deprivation (for example, of oxygen, vitamins, or sleep) result in incomplete replication of naturally occurring syndromes, and constitute one form of argument by analogy.

(8) Success or failure with a variety of treatment procedures (whether these are psychosocial or organic therapies) has frequently been used to support a bias in favor of some particular hypothesis of causation, but this represents another form of argument by analogy that is fallacious. A treatment may be effective in the absence of etiological knowledge, as in the surgical excision of some neoplasms. On the other hand, effective treatment may *not* be possible in spite of accurate etiological knowledge—as in chronic brain syndromes resulting from a variety of agencies, including deprivations (e.g., anoxia, hypothyroidism, or thiamine deficiency). Limited effectiveness of current psychosocial therapies in treating certain disorders does *not* necessarily indicate that learning or other psychological factors were unimportant in the etiology of these disorders.

In spite of the preceding difficulties in analyzing causation, such knowledge does lead to more rational and effective techniques of both treatment and prevention. The analysis of complex etiological factors requires skepticism but not nihilism. Research into the causation of psychiatric disorders has already yielded considerable relevant information, which will be reviewed in the next four chapters (5 through 8). We shall then turn to established techniques of evaluation and treatment (Chapters 9 through 12).

SELECTED REFERENCES

Bachrach, A. J. 1962. *Experimental Foundations of Clinical Psychology.* New York, Basic Books, Inc.

Berelson, B. and Steiner, G. A., 1964, *Human Behavior: An Inventory of Scientific Findings,* New York, Harcourt, Brace & World, Inc.

Bliss, E. L., ed. 1962. *Roots of Behavior.* New York, Hoeber Medical Division, Harper & Row, Publishers, Inc.

Dixon, W. J., and Massey, F. J., Jr. 1957. *Introduction to Statistical Analysis,* 2nd edition. New York, McGraw-Hill Book Co., Inc., ch. 7.

Eysenck, H. J. 1960. *Handbook of Abnormal Psychology.* London, Pittman Medical Publishing Company, Ltd., ch. 1.

Fessel, W. J. 1964. Interaction of multiple determinants of schizophrenia, AMA Archives of General Psychiatry *11*, 1-18.

Finch, J. R. 1966. Scientific models and their application in psychiatric models. AMA Archives of General Psychiatry. *15*, 1-6.

Galdston, I., ed. 1964. *Beyond the Germ Theory.* New York, New York Academy of Medicine, Health Education Council.

Group for the Advancement of Psychiatry. 1954. *Collaborative Research in Psychopathology.* New York, G.A.P. Report No. 25.

Group for the Advancement of Psychiatry. 1959. *Some Observations on Controls in Psychiatric Research.* New York, G.A.P. Report No. 42.

Hebb, D. O. 1958. *A Textbook of Psychology.* Philadelphia, W.B. Saunders Co., ch.6.

Hoch, P. H., and Zubin, J., eds. 1957. *Experimental Psychopatholgy.* New York, Grune & Stratton, Inc.

Huff, D. 1954. *How to Lie With Statistics.* New York. W. W. Norton & Co., Inc.

Joad, C. E. M. 1946. *Guide to Philosophy,* 14th edition. London, Gollancz, ch. 5, 7, 8, and 18.

Johnstone, H. W., Jr. 1954. *Elementary Deductive Logic.* New York, Thomas Y. Crowell Co.

Kemeny, J. G., Snell, J. L., and Thompson, G. L. 1956. *Introduction to Finite Mathematics.* Englewood Cliffs, New Jersey, Prentice-Hall, Inc., ch. 1 and 2.

Kline, N. S. 1961. On the relationship between neurophysiology, psychophysiology, psychopharmacology, and other disciplines. In *Pavlovian Conference on Higher Nervous Activity.* Annals of the New York Academy of Sciences *92*, 1009.

Kluckhohn, C., Murray, H. A., and Schneider, D. M., eds. 1953. *Personality in Nature, Society, and Culture,* 2nd edition. New York, Alfred A. Knopf, Inc., ch. 2.

Langner, T. S., and Michael, S. T. 1963. *Life Stress and Mental Health.* New York. The Free Press of Glencoe. (The Macmillan Co.) ch. 1.

MacIver, R. M. 1942. *Social Causation.* Boston. Ginn & Co.

Marmor, J., and Pumpian-Mindlin E. 1950. Toward an integrative conception of mental disorder. Journal of Nervous and Mental Disease *111*, 19-29.

Mednick, M. T., and Mednick, S. A., eds. 1963. *Research in Personality.* New York, Holt, Rinehart & Winston, Inc.

Michotte, A. 1963. *The Perception of Causality.* New York, Basic Books, Inc.

Milbank Memorial Fund. 1950. *Epidemiology of Mental Disorder.* New York, Milbank Memorial Fund.

Milbank Memorial Fund. 1953. *Interrelations between the Social Environment and Psychiatric Disorders.* New York, Milbank Memorial Fund.

Neel, J. V., and Schull, W. J. 1954. *Human Heredity.* Chicago, University of Chicago Press, ch. 12 and 17.

Reid, D. D. 1960. *Epidemiological Methods in the Study of Mental Disorders.* Geneva, World Health Organization, Public Health Paper No. 2.

Rosenblith, J. F., and Allinsmith, W., eds. 1967. *The Causes of Behavior,* 2nd edition. Boston, Allyn and Bacon, Inc.

Sarbin, T. R., ed. 1961. *Studies in Behavior Pathology.* New York, Holt, Rinehart & Winston, Inc.

Scott, J. P. 1958. *Animal Behavior,* University of Chicago Press. ch. 4-7.

Standen, A. 1950. *Science Is a Sacred Cow.* New York, E.P. Dutton & Co., Inc., Paperback No. D16.

Wardwell, W. I., and Bahnson, C. B. 1964. Problems encountered in behavioral science research in epidemiological studies. American Journal of Public Health *54*, 972-98.

Wittkower, E. D. 1955. Psychoanalysis as science — A psychophysiological approach. Canadian Psychiatric Association Journal *2*, 125.

CHAPTER 5

The proper time to influence the character of a child is about 100 years before he is born.

William Ralph Inge

Cruelty and compassion come with the chromosomes; all men are merciful and all are murderers.

From "Ape and Essence" by Aldous Huxley

Hereditary Factors in Etiology

PRINCIPLES OF HEREDITY

If the dichotomy between nature and nurture, between heredity and environment, between innate and acquired characteristics, were carried to its ultimate conclusion, it would become necessary to define hereditary characteristics (including behavior) as those that appear in the absence of environment, and environmental characteristics (or behavior) as those that require no organism. It is therefore a truism to say that every characteristic of a living organism depends upon interaction between hereditary predisposition and environmental influence. In practice, however, differences between individuals or groups of individuals may be determined predominantly by differences in their hereditary predisposition, or in their environmental experiences, or by varying degrees of interaction between them.

A trait is called hereditary if most of the variation within a population is related to differences in genetic endowment, as in the determination of blood groups or of predisposition to Huntington's chorea, mongolism, or phenylketonuria (PKU). A trait may be termed environmental or acquired if it

has little or no genetically determined variance, as in the case of social customs and language. A large group of traits, however, is significantly affected by both genetic and environmental factors; this group includes many characteristics that vary quantitatively over a wide range such as body height and weight, skin color, intelligence, temperament, and behavior. Fraser Roberts (1959) distinguished between five different degrees of hereditary and environmental determination as follows:

A characteristic may be exhibited:

— In persons of a certain genetic constitution only, always occurring in those persons and in those persons only. This is complete hereditary determination as with the blood groups or hemophilia.

— In persons of a certain genetic constitution only, but not in all such persons, the cooperation of environmental influences being necessary for the exhibition of the trait.

— In persons of several different genetic constitutions, but with different frequencies in persons of the various genetic constitutions, that is, in different proportions of persons of the several genetic groups.

— In persons of any genetic constitution, but with different frequencies in persons of different genetic constitution.

—In persons of any genetic constitution and with the same frequency in any genetic constitution. This is complete environmental determination.

The term *constitution* is used repeatedly in the preceding statement and requires clarification. Constitutional characteristics are associated with bodily structure and function, including immunity or predisposition to disease, and hence with certain forms of psychopathology. It is sometimes erroneously assumed that such characteristics imply hereditary causation, or alternatively that all such characteristics are congenital, i.e., present at birth. There is widespread recognition, however, that constitution represents the momentary product of original endowment and of all the physical and psychological processes of the past, so that it is therefore constantly changing as the individual passes through life.

The term *congenital* is also sometimes erroneously considered as synonymous with heredity, but is more correctly applied to those characteristics present at the time of birth. The latter may be either inherited or the result of environmental influences acting during intrauterine life: for example, bodily deformity or mental retardation due to prenatal infections such as rubella or syphilis. While hereditary determination implies that the potentiality for a given characteristic is present at conception, and also implies a constitutional predisposition, the characteristic itself may not be manifested until many years later as in the case of Huntington's chorea, which usually has its clinical onset during adult life.

Characteristics or disorders that are transmitted by heredity appear more frequently in other members of an affected individual's family than in the general population. It is important to recognize, however, that *familial* traits or disorders do not necessarily indicate a specific hereditary transmission. An increased frequency of a characteristic among family members may in fact result from three different varieties of causation: (1) similar hereditary predispositions; (2) direct environmental transmission from one affected individual to other members of the family (of pathogenic agents or experiences); (3) the sharing of similar environmental experiences, or exposure to the same pathogenic agent. In a number of instances, an increased familial concentration appears to involve all three of these mechanisms, as in the case of clinical tuberculosis.

It is assumed that the reader already has some basic knowledge of genetics, but there have been rapid advances in this field with some revision in basic concepts, which will now be reviewed briefly.

The units of biological inheritance are the *genes*, which are submicroscopic particles arranged in linear sequence along the length of the *chromosomes*. The latter are small bodies of various shapes and sizes, located in the cell nucleus, which stain darkly with certain dyes. The number of chromosomes contained in the cells of animals varies greatly from species to species, but it has now been established that most of the cells in the human body contain 23 pairs of chromosomes, one member of each pair being derived from the father and the other member from the mother. Twenty-two pairs of chromosomes are homologous (always match each other) and the remaining two chromosomes determine the sex of the individual. In females the sex chromosomes are also homologous and are known as the X chromosomes, whereas in males they consist of one X and one smaller Y chromosome. Studies of abnormal individuals with varying numbers of sex chromosomes indicate that the human Y chromosome strongly promotes the development of male bodily characteristics.

In the ovaries or testes the process of reduction division (meiosis) results in only 23 chromosomes (one sex chromosome and 22 autosomes) being contained in each of the ova or spermatozoa. Since none of the cells in the female body contain Y chromosomes, the ovum invariably contains an X chromosome. Cells in the male body, on the other hand, contain both X and Y chromosomes; and after reduction division, approximately half of the spermatozoa contain an X, and half a Y chromosome. Which of these two types of spermatozoa unites with the ovum determines the sex of the offspring. Since there are numerous submicroscopic genes on each chromosome, the exact number of genes in a human cell is not known, but has been estimated as somewhere between 40,000 and 80,000, approximately half of this number derived from the mother and half from the father (although males will have slightly fewer genes than females on account of their smaller Y chromosome). Characteristics or abnormalities transmitted by genes located in the sex chromosomes are known as *sex-linked,* whereas characteristics or abnormalities due to genes carried in any of the remaining chromosomes are said to result from *autosomal* inheritance.

The alternative forms of a gene that may occur at some particular point on a chromosome (i.e., "genetic locus") are termed allelomorphs or simply alleles. A given gene *A* is described as *dominant* to an allele *a* when it is impossible by any known test to distinguish between *AA* and *Aa* individuals. A gene *a* is described as *recessive* to an allele *A* when there is no detectable effect of *a* in *Aa* individuals. The terms dominant and recessive are therefore *not* attributes of the *genotype* (associated with specific, fixed, and immutable properties of the genes), but characteristic of the *phenotype* (which is externally recognizable to the geneticist in the light of knowledge at a given time.)

The criteria of inheritance by a single completely dominant gene, and by a single pair of completely recessive genes, depend on the frequency of the alleles (alternative forms of the gene) in the general population, as well as on whether they are located on autosomes or sex chromosomes (and in the latter instance also on which particular sex chromosome). The frequency of the alleles in the general population determines which of the six varieties of mating (between *AA, Aa,* and *aa* individuals) is most likely to contribute to the appearance of each of the three types of individual in the population. This situation is *least* complicated when we are dealing with a characteristic transmitted by a *rare* dominant gene, or a single pair of rare recessive genes, having a frequency of less than one in 1000 of the general population. The criteria of inheritance due to rare autosomal dominant and rare autosomal recessive genes are given below (modified after Neel and Schull):

Inheritance due to a single completely dominant rare autosomal gene (e.g., Huntington's chorea). Affected individuals will nearly all be heterozygous *Aa* individuals, and result from a mating of one heterozygous *Aa* (similarly affected) individual with one homozygous *aa* (unaffected) individual. The criteria of this form of inheritance are therefore as follows: (1) the trait is transmitted directly from affected parent to affected child without skipping of generations; (2) the two sexes are affected in equal numbers; (3) approximately half the children of an affected individual, and half the siblings of an affected individual, also show the trait.

Inheritance due to a single pair of completely recessive rare autosomal genes (e.g., phenylketonuria or PKU). In this situation affected individuals are homozygous *aa* individuals, and will usually be the offspring of two heterozygous *Aa* (unaffected) individuals. The criteria for this type of inheritance are therefore (1) father, mother, and more remote ancestors of an affected individual are usually normal; (2) approximately one quarter of the siblings of affected individuals will be similarly affected; (3) the two sexes are affected in equal numbers; (4) there tends to be a higher frequency of consanguinity among the parents of affected individuals than among the general population (including marriages between first cousins).

Differences between individuals that are attributable to the presence or absence of a single major gene at a given genetic locus, as in the preceding examples, may be described as caused by *simple Mendelian inheritance,* or sometimes monogenic inheritance. It is also possible however that differences between individuals may be attributable to the cumulative effects of multiple minor genes, which may be described as multifactorial or *polygenic inheritance.* It has previously been pointed out that a number of characteristics such as height, weight, intelligence, and blood pressure are distributed continuously throughout a given range of values. and the frequency of specified measurements within a given population tend to correspond approximately with the normal or Gaussian curve. Such continuous distributions of graded characteristics may be determined by a combination of hereditary and environmental factors. The genetic component of such quantitative variation is believed to depend mainly on the cumulative effects of minor genes distributed at multiple loci through various chromosomes. It has hitherto been impossible to define sharply the genetic and nongenetic components of variation in particular cases, but *the following criteria are considered suggestive of* polygenic or multiple gene inheritance: (1) continuous quantitative variation or gradation of measurements; (2) suggestion of a strong hereditary component resulting from foster child and twin studies, which will be outlined in the next section; (3) correlations between values for different classes of relatives, proportionate to the degree of their blood rela-

tionship — i.e., correlations decreasing in the following sequence: between uniovular twins, between midparental values (the average for *both* parents) and their children, between binovular twins or other full siblings (brothers and sisters), between *one* of the parents and his or her children, between grandparents and grandchildren, between uncles (or aunts) and nephews (or nieces), and between first cousins.

A polygenic hypothesis of inheritance does *not* imply an exact correspondence between measured values of a characteristic among parents and their offspring. In the event of complete hereditary determination by multiple minor genes, the expected correlation between *one* of the parents and his or her children would be +0.5. It would also be expected that the average value among children (e.g., for intelligence or the sex-adjusted value for height) would lie half way between that obtained for the parent and the average value for the general population. Similarly, it would be expected that the average value for each parent would lie half way between that observed among his or her children and the average for the general population. This tendency is sometimes described as *regression toward the mean* (for the general population).

The situation is a little more complicated when we compare midparental values (consisting of the average value for *both* parents) with those of their children. In the event that we start with a sample of *parents,* we should expect the average value for their offspring to correspond exactly with the midparental value. In the event that we start with a sample of *children,* however, we should expect their midparental values to lie halfway between those of the children and the mean for the general population. Combining both of these expectations into a correlation coefficient between midparental measurements and measurements for children, the expected correlation would be +0.71

(which is the geometric mean of 1.0 and 0.5).

The expected correlation between full siblings (including binovular twins) depends upon the extent of resemblance between their parents. In the event that there is *random mating,* and the parents resemble each other no more than any other two members of the population, the expected correlation between full siblings would be +0.5. With some characteristics, however, there is a strong tendency for like to marry like, which is known as *assortative mating.* Correlation coefficients between husband and wife with respect to physical traits such as eye color, height, and physique have been reported in the order of +0.2 to 0.33, and correlations between husband and wife for intelligence have been estimated in the order of +0.5. It has also been shown that the frequency of severe psychopathology in *both* husband and wife greatly exceeds that to be expected on a random basis, and it is probable that there is a strong tendency to assortative mating with respect to a variety of psychological characteristics. This would mean that full siblings would be expected to resemble each other, with respect to the same characteristics, to greater degree than that implied by a correlation of +0.5 but the magnitude of this effect is difficult to estimate and it may be cumulative from generation to generation.

Hitherto we have been concerned with the implications of hereditary transmission through single major genes, and the cumulative effects of multiple minor genes. It is also possible for genetic effects to manifest themselves through the *absence of an entire chromosome,* the *presence of one or more supernumerary chromosomes,* or *the translocation of part of one chromosome to another.* Advances in cytogenetics have permitted the microscopic analysis of chromosomal structure, and this has proved of relevance to psychiatry in two particular areas. One of these involves the psychiatric implications of intersexuality, sometimes determined by the presence of an abnormal number of sex chromosomes. The other major area is that of mental retardation, in which mongolism or Down's syndrome is now a classic example of etiology related to an abnormal complement of chromosomes. Further aspects of these chromosomal anomalies will be discussed in later chapters on sexual deviation and on mental retardation.

SELECTED METHODS OF GENETIC INVESTIGATION

It has been remarked that the main differences between man and other animals are that man drinks without being thirsty and mates all the year around. Unfortunately for the human geneticist, there are a number of other differences that make man a difficult subject for genetic study: for example the length of time elapsing between generations, the small number of offspring derived from mating two individuals, inability to control matings or environmental experiences, and man's relatively large number of chromosomes and genes. It is for these reasons that the study of human genetics has required the development of sophisticated statistical techniques that have not been necessary for the genetic study of other organisms.

It may still be possible, however, to learn much about heredity in man from the experimental study of inherited traits in lower organisms. In their excellent book on behavior genetics, Fuller and Thompson pointed out that there was some advantage in studying *Drosophila* (the fruit fly), other insects, fish, and to some extent birds, since the relationship between the gene and the behavior-trait is more direct than is typically true in mammals. On the other hand, difficulties in generalizing findings regarding the behavior of lower organisms to the kinds of behavior characteristic of man apply somewhat less in the case of other mammals, such as the mouse and the dog, the latter being particularly suitable because of its highly developed social behavior.

Since the mechanisms of gene transmission and the primary physiological action of genes are broadly similar in a wide variety of species, *cross-species comparisons* may reveal general principles that would not be evident in more limited studies (e.g., Ford and Beach). Valid conclusions regarding the hereditary basis of differences between naturally occurring species, however, require careful control of environmental experiences that might also determine such differences. The same is true for the two main types of animal experiments regarding the inheritance of behavior, namely, *the method of selective breeding* and *the method of pure strains*. The former involves the separation of two strains that score high and low on a certain behavioral continuum by mating high scorers and low scorers with animals of similar type throughout a number of generations. The latter method involves selected matings between pure strains obtained by a series of many consecutive brother-sister matings.

In a review of *methodology in human genetics,* Steinberg pointed out that detailed analysis of hereditary patterns in man had hitherto been limited for technical reasons almost entirely to characters determined by single gene differences. In general, the sequence of questions concerning the genetics of such simple Mendelian characteristics is the following: (1) Is the characteristic hereditary? (2) If so, what is the genetic mechanism? (3) How frequent is the gene in the population? (4) What is its mutation rate? (5) What are its linkage relations? He went on to quote a question asked by David and Snyder, "What are the necessary and sufficient criteria for establishing that genetic consitution is significant in the etiology of a disease?" and their answer to this question "An incidence of cases among the relatives of propositi significantly in excess of the incidence in the general population can be taken as substantial evidence that genetic factors are etiologically involved, *but only if it is shown that environmental factors cannot account for the increased incidence.*"

Pedigree Studies. Human genetics is therefore concerned with the analysis of family data. Such family resemblances have long been recognized in such statements as "like father, like son," but the scientific *study of human pedigrees* only began in the latter part of the nineteenth century. Sir Francis Galton's study of eminent men indicated that the chances of their having eminent relatives were fairly high, but unfortunately the pedigree method could provide no evidence as to whether this reflected similarities in genetic endowment, environmental opportunity, or both. In fact, the greatest contribution of the pedigree method in human genetics has been in suggesting hypotheses of inheritance by single genes, particularly rare dominant and sex-linked characteristics, for subsequent testing by more refined methods.

In the case of *discrete* characteristics, which are either present or absent, the latter involves statistical comparison of observed *frequencies* of the characteristic in various classes of relatives, with the frequencies expected under the hypothesis of a specified mechanism of inheritance. In the case of a characteristic having a continuous (graded) distribution, it involves comparison of observed *correlations* for the characteristic between various classes of relatives, with correlations expected on the basis of inheritance by multiple minor genes.

Foster Child Studies. Two further approaches have found considerable application in studying the role of heredity and determining human behavior: namely, foster child and twin studies. *Foster child studies* involve comparison of (a) similarities between the characteristics of foster children and their foster parents with (b) similarities between characteristics of children and their true biological parents. Osborne summarized the requirements to be met by adequate foster child studies as follows: (1) foster children must be placed in the adoptive homes sufficiently early to be relatively uninfluenced by the environment of the original home, (2) there must be little or no selective placement of the children, (3) an adequate sample of adoptive homes and various social levels must be included in the survey, and (4) the foster children should be of one race and nationality to eliminate racial sources of variation.

Twin Studies. *Twin studies* have been used extensively in attempts to establish the importance of heredity in determining human physique, intelligence, temperamental characteristics, and psychiatric disorders. Theoretically, twins might arise from at least five different types of biological situations, but in practice only two of these origins are distinguished in man: (1) separate fertilization of two different ova which proliferate independently, and (2) the fertilization of only one ovum, which subsequently divides into two separate individuals at some early stage in development. Binovular twins, arising from two fertilized eggs, may be alike or unlike in sex and are known as dizygous, dizygotic, DZ, or "fraternal" twins. Uniovular twins, arising from a single fertilized egg, are always of the same sex, and are known as monozygous, monozygotic, MZ, or "identical" twins. Among twin births in the United States, approximately one-third are monozygotic, one-third dizygotic twins of the same sex, and one-third dizygotic twins of different sexes.

Theoretically, the comparison of pairs of monozygotic twins with pairs of dizygotic twins (preferably of the same sex) should provide an indication of the relative importance of heredity and environment in determining a given characteristic, since MZ twins have identical genotypes (genetic constitution) and any difference in phenotypic (externally manifested) characteristics must be due to environmental influences—in contrast with DZ twins, in whom differences may be due to either hereditary or environmental influences. In practice, however, there are serious methodological difficulties, such as uncontrolled factors in the prenatal or postnatal environment, and misdiagnosis of zygosity, or of the characteristics to be studied. These problems have been regarded by some geneticists as sufficiently serious to invalidate conclusions based on the studies of twins, and will be considered briefly toward the end of this section. Nevertheless, it is desirable to review certain information that may be obtained from *three different types of twin studies* that may be undertaken. These are (1) comparisons between monozygotic twins, (2) comparisons between monozygotic twins reared apart and monozygotic twins reared together, (3) comparisons between monozygotic twins who are dissimilar or discordant for a given characteristic.

A rough index of the proportion of phenotype variance attributable to heredity may be obtained by *comparison of MZ with DZ twins* and the application of a simple formula that depends on the nature of the characteristic under comparison. If this characteristic is discrete (i.e., present or absent, as in the case of a clearly defined abnormality), the members of a given twin pair may be described as either concordant (if they both develop the characteristic) or discordant (if only one of them develops it). The contribution of heredity in determining the development of this characteristic in the population may then be estimated by the statistic

$$H = \frac{CMZ - CDZ}{100 - CDZ},$$

where H represents heritability, while CMZ and CDZ are the percentages of concordant MZ and like-sexed DZ twins respectively. If, on the other hand, the characteristic that is being compared (in MZ and DZ twins) is distributed along a continuous range of values (such as measures of height, weight, intelligence, or blood pressure), the contribution of heredity may be estimated by means of the statistic

$$H = \frac{r_{MZ} - r_{DZ}}{1 - r_{DZ}}$$

where r_{MZ} is the correlation coefficient between MZ twins and r_{DZ} is the correlation coefficient for like-sexed DZ twins.

There are several aspects of the preceding estimate of "heritability" that require clarification. Firstly, this is an estimated value for the population from which the sample was drawn, and makes no sense when applied to a single individual member of that population (since both heredity and environment are essential to the survival of the individual). Secondly, the estimate is subject to random error, and the statistical significance of differences between variance for MZ twins and variance for DZ twins should be tested by means of the F-ratio. Thirdly, the index of heritability for a given characteristic will be expected to vary from one population to another: i.e., according to time, place, and the subgroup of the population studied. It is particularly important to note that changes in the heritability for a given characteristic may be brought about by modifying the environmental situation. The more uniformly favorable the environmental situation, the greater is the likelihood that the individual will attain his maximal hereditary potential, and the greater the extent to which variability within the population will then depend upon heredity.

A specified contribution by heredity to the population variance for a given characteristic might theoretically result from a *uniform* contribution by heredity to the determination of the characteristic among *different* groups of the population. If there were a 50 per cent heritability for a characteristic, the figure might mean that heredity was the predominant (or theoretically the exclusive) determinant in about half the population, whereas environmental factors were the predominant (or theoretically the exclusive) determinants for the remaining 50 per cent of the population. In practice, however, it is highly probable that identifiable subgroups of the population (according to intelligence, socioeconomic status, or psychiatric diagnosis) will differ from one another in the relative contribution of heredity and also in the genetic mechanisms through which the characteristic is transmitted.

To return to the second type of twin study, a rough index of the proportion of phenotype variance attributable to "environment" may be obtained by *comparison of identical twins reared together with identical twins reared apart.* The total number of identical twins reared apart, however, is relatively small, and hence no comparisons have been made between rates of concordance and discordance for relatively uncommon discrete characteristics or abnormalities, although there is no reason why a statistic estimating environmental influences should not be derived from concordance rates in MZ twins reared together and MZ twins reared apart. Such comparisons have hitherto been restricted to continuous (graded) distributions of characteristics, and the following statistic has been used to estimate the percentage of phenotype variation attributable to environment (i.e., to the effect of differing environments on the same genotype):

$$E = \frac{r_{MZT} - r_{MZA}}{1 - r_{MZA}}$$

where E represents environmental influence, r_{MZT} is the correlation coefficient for MZ twins reared together, and r_{MZA} is the correlation coefficient for twins reared apart.

The third type of twin study involves

comparisons between MZ twins who are discordant for a given characteristic: for example, only one of whom develops schizophrenia or manifests overt homosexual behavior. Since such twins are identical in genetic endowment, the observed differences in phenotype must result from differing environmental influences, for which an exhaustive search is made in this type of study. It will, therefore, be noted that both of the latter types of twin study (involving MZ twins alone, without comparison with DZ twins) are concerned primarily with environmental influences and provide no evidence concerning the possible contribution of heredity. It may further be noted that the first type of twin study, involving comparisons between MZ and DZ twins, permits estimates of the *magnitude* of contribution of hereditary factors, but provides no indications of the *type* of genetic mechanism involved.

Limitations of the Twin Method. In view of the extent to which genetic studies of human behavior and psychiatric disorders have relied upon twin data, it is necessary to point out that many geneticists regard the validity of such studies as dubious. Neel and Schull pointed out that the inferences drawn from twin data are subject to reservations of both a statistical and biological nature. In addition to the statistical and biological biases outlined by these authors, however, there are a number of specific criticisms that apply to all but a few studies of twins with psychiatric disorders:

(1) Incorrect determination of zygosity based on the use of techniques other than modern serological tests, which permit accurate calculation of the probability of a given pair being MZ or DZ from an analysis of the various blood group systems. Gottesman compared the accuracy of various methods of zygosity determination, and found errors in about 20 or 30 percent of cases when older methods such as fingerprinting and photographs were used. Almost all of the studies of twins with psychiatric disorders undertaken prior to 1960 employed only these older and less accurate methods of zygosity determination, and sometimes merely hearsay evidence.

(2) Variable criteria for the clinical diagnosis of psychiatric disorders—a discrepancy of about 30 percent being found for major diagnostic categories in studies involving the admission of the same patient to different hospitals within close geographic proximity of each other (see Chapter 2).

(3) Unconscious bias of the investigator may influence psychiatric diagnosis of cotwins, when this diagnosis is made with full knowledge of the psychiatric diagnosis of the twin index case (or propositus) and the probable zygosity of the twins.

(4) Further statistical problems involving the estimation of concordance rates among cotwins may result from the following: (a) counting twin pairs twice whenever a pair contains two propositi, which is only appropriate when the abnormal individuals have been detected independently of one another; (b) attempts to estimate the lifetime concordance rates for cotwins who have not passed through the period of risk during which they may develop the abnormality.

In view of such difficulties, it is not surprising that Neel and Schull should conclude that "in its present context the twin method has not vindicated the time spent in the collection of such data," or that Penrose should remark, "The study of twins, from being regarded as one of the easiest and most reliable kinds of researches in human genetics must now be considered as one of the most treacherous."

In spite of the preceding cautions, it should be mentioned that a genetic basis for mongolism or Down's syndrome was strongly suspected on the basis of twin studies, long before the chromosomal aberrations were discovered. In a study reported in 1951, mongolism was found to occur in 16 cotwins out of 18 pairs (89 percent) considered as monozygotic, in comparison with only four cotwins out of 60 pairs (i.e., seven percent) who were considered dizygotic. It may be noted that the latter figures result in a heritability index for mongolism of approximately 88 percent. This degree of correspondence with the evidence provided by more recent cytogenetic studies, strengthens the credibility of other results obtained by twin methods, although the latter should certainly employ modern serological techniques of zygosity determination, objective criteria for the characteristic under study, and independent determination of these two sets of variables.

In the remainder of this chapter, we shall apply the background information that has been presented to various genetic studies concerning perception, intelligence, emotion, and behavior.

SENSORY AND PERCEPTUAL PROCESSES

It has been said that no two animals or people live in exactly the same world, because no two have precisely identical capabilities for sensory perception. Gross defects such as blindness and deafness have important psychological consequences, and certain forms of both are known to be due to simple Mendelian inheritance. In addition, however, there are a variety of major or minor anomalies of vision, hearing, and other senses that are related to genetic endowment.

A well known example of inherited variation in human perception is red-green color blindness, which has frequently been cited as an example of sex-linked inheritance. However, this is an oversimplification, since red-green color blindness is not a unitary characteristic, and it has been possible to distinguish between at least four (phenotypic) subgroups, suggesting the operation of genes at two or more genetic loci.

Another form of visual anomaly is night blindness, in which the rods in the retina take much longer than usual to become adapted to darkness. This defect exists in a number of forms that may appear as an isolated trait or in association with other forms of genetically determined eye disease. In some instances it appears to be transmitted as a simple dominant autosomal characteristic, and in other instances as a sex-linked characteristic (Figure 5-1).

Many forms of deafness in man and other animals are inherited as simple Mendelian characteristics. There have also been a number of attempts to establish a genetic basis for auditory discriminations of pitch, intensity, time, or interval. A more complex form of auditory discrimination that may have some genetic basis is known as tone deafness or "tune deafness" (inability to sing in tune or recognize errors made by others).

There is also some evidence for genetic basis for another defect on a higher level of perception, known as dyslexia. This consists of an inability to read and spell that is very persistent in spite of high overall intelligence.

Apart from vision and hearing, there may be widespread differences in sensitivity to other types of perception, such as smell, taste, touch, pain, or temperature. There is every reason to believe that such differences may well be partly genetically determined, but in most instances definite evidence is lacking. Some years ago, however, the accidental discovery was made that phenylthiocarbamide (PTC) tasted very bitter to some people, but was tasteless to others. Initially it was postulated that the inability to taste PTC was inherited as a simple recessive characteristic, but it was later found that the taste threshold in the two groups of people differed quantitatively rather than absolutely. Nevertheless, the distribution of taste sensitivity to PTC is definitely bimodal, and it appears that one major cause of the individual differences in taste sensi-

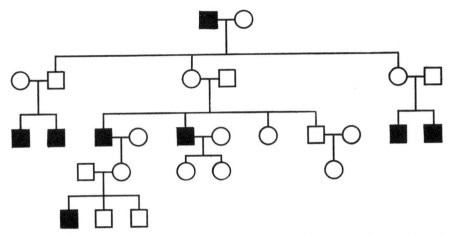

Figure 5-1. Pedigree of one kind of night blindness shows that males *(squares)* and females *(circles)* can transmit defect but that only males *(shaded squares)* are affected by it. (From Kalmus, H. Inherited sense defects. Scientific American 186:66 [May]. Copyright © 1952, Scientific American, Inc. All rights reserved.)

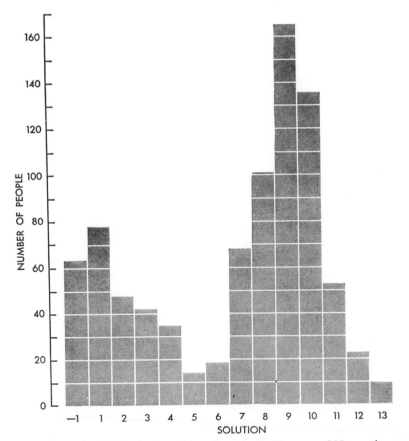

Figure 5-2. Taste threshold of phenylthiocarbamide (PTC) among 855 people was oddly distributed in two peaks. Solution 1 was 1.3 grams of PTC per liter; each number indicates a solution half as strong as the one preceding it. (From Kalmus, H. Inherited sense defects. Scientific American 186:68 [May]. Copyright © 1952, Scientific American, Inc. All rights reserved.)

tivity is a single recessive gene (Fig. 5-2). Among other factors known to influence the taste threshold for PTC (and a number of related compounds) are age, sex, and racial origin.

Fuller and Thompson concluded that "sensory and perceptual processes are generally more alike in related individuals. Heritability is not limited to anatomical defects (blindness, deafness) or to chemical defects (color blindness), but is found less clearly in more complex perceptual processes. Few studies, however, have been carried out with adequate controls for environmental effects."

INTELLIGENCE, EMOTION, AND MOTOR RESPONSES

Both the definition of intelligence and its measurement have been a subject of controversy, but of recent years there has been considerable acceptance of the pragmatic definition that intelligence is that which is measured by an intelligence test. From the viewpoint of the human geneticist, the most pertinent data regarding the relative importance of heredity and environment in determining intelligence test scores consist of certain foster child studies undertaken a generation ago. The requirements to be met by satisfactory foster child studies were summarized in the section on methodology, and the studies by Burks and Leahy appear most nearly to satisfy these requirements. The data from these two studies are reproduced in Table 5-1; it may be noted that in each instance the correlation between the intelligence scores of children and their true parents is consistently higher than the correlation between the intelligence scores of foster parents. These findings appear to indicate that heredity is of considerable importance in determining parent-child similarities in intelligence, a conclusion that is supported by a

TABLE 5-1. Correlations of Intelligence between Parent and Own Children and Parent with Foster Children*

	FOSTER GROUP: CHILDREN AND FOSTER PARENTS		CONTROL GROUP: CHILDREN AND TRUE PARENTS	
	r	N	r	N
(a) Data of Burks (1928)				
Father's MA	.07	178	.45	100
Mother's MA	.19	204	.46	105
(b) Data of Leahy (1935)				
Father's Otis score	.15	178	.51	175
Mother's Otis score	.20	186	.51	191

*Reprinted from Neel, J. V. and Schull, W. J. *Human Heredity.* By permission of the University of Chicago Press. Copyright 1954 by the University of Chicago, p. 113.

number of twin studies that have been undertaken.

Most of these twin studies have been restricted to comparisons between test correlations for monozygotic and dizygotic twins (e.g., Table 5-2) from which a numerical estimate of heritability may be derived. It should again be noted that heritability is an estimate that applies to the degree of hereditary determination within a given population and *not* a given individual. In the five twin studies of intelligence summarized in this table, the estimated heritable component of population variance varies between 0.57 and 0.77 (i.e., between 57 percent and 77 percent of the overall variation).

In one of these five studies (Newman, Freeman, and Holzinger) certain comparisons were also possible between monozygotic twins reared together and 19 pairs of monozygotic twins reared apart from early childhood. Correlations for height, weight, and intelligence between MZ twins reared apart, MZ twins reared together, and DZ twins are shown in Table 5-3 together with resultant estimates of the heritable and environmental determinants of variation in this sample. The estimates of H are derived from comparison of MZ

TABLE 5–2. Correlation Coefficients between Monozygotic and Dizygotic Twins for Intelligence and Other Psychological Tests*

TEST AND INVESTIGATOR	r_{MZ}	r_{DZ}	$H = \dfrac{r_{MZ} - r_{DZ}}{1 - r_{DZ}}$
Intelligence tests			
Wingfield (National Intelligence Test and McCall's Multimental Scale)	0.90	0.57	0.77
Herrman and Hogben (Otis)	0.84	0.48	0.69
Newman, Freeman and Holzinger (Binet)	0.88	0.63	0.68
Blewett (factor score)	0.76	0.44	0.57
Eysenck (data of Blewett and McLeod) (factor score)	0.82	0.38	0.71
Other psychological tests			
Mechanical aptitude (Brody)	0.69	0.28	0.57
Motor skills (McNemar)	0.79	0.43	0.63
Bernreuter's neurotic inventory (Carter)	0.63	0.32	0.46
Woodworth-Matthews' neurotic tendencies (Holzinger)	0.56	0.37	0.30
Strong's vocational interests (Carter)	0.50	0.28	0.31
Autonomic factor (Eysenck, data of Blewett and McLeod)	0.93	0.72	0.75
Neuroticism factor (Eysenck and Prell)	0.85	0.22	0.81
Extraversion factor (McLeod)	0.77	0.03	0.76
Extraversion factor (Eysenck, data of Blewett and McLeod)	0.50	−0.33	0.62

*Adapted from Shields, J., and Slater, E. 1960. Heredity and psychological abnormality. In Eysenck, H. J., ed. *Handbook of Abnormal Psychology*. London, Pitman Medical Publishing Company, Ltd., p. 333.

with DZ twins, and the estimates of E are derived from comparison of MZA with MZT twins (as already described in the section on methodology). It should be noted in passing that none of these estimates of heritability or environmental influence should have a negative value, and also that for any given characteristic E + H should add up to exactly one (i.e., 100 percent of the total variability is determined by the sum total of heredity and environment). It may be seen from the table that this is far from true, which brings home the point that these figures are rough estimates, with errors depending partly upon the size of the example examined. In this instance, the numbers of twin pairs involved in estimating H were considerably larger than the number involved in estimating E, so that the estimates of H can be regarded as somewhat more reliable than those of E.

While foster child studies and twin studies may give some indication of a significant hereditary component in determining intelligence (or other

Table 5–3. Degree of Similarity between Monozygotic Twins, Reared Apart or Together, and Dizygotic Twins*

CHARAC-TERISTIC	CORRELATION			E	H
	MZA	MZT	DZ		
Height	.969	.932	.645	− 0.544	0.808
Weight	.886	.917	.631	+ 0.272	0.775
I.Q.	.670	.881	.631	+ 0.639	0.678

*Data of Newman, Freeman, and Holzinger. 1937. Reprinted from Neel, J. V., and Schull, W. T., *Human Heredity*. By permission of The University of Chicago Press. Copyright 1954 by The University of Chicago, p. 276.

characteristics), by their nature these studies are unable to provide any information concerning the probable mechanism of inheritance. The latter must be evaluated by comparison of the observed findings for various classes of relatives with those expected on the basis of a specified type of inheritance. In the case of intelligence, test scores are distributed throughout the general population in very close approximation with the normal or Gaussian curve, and correlations between various classes of relatives roughly correspond with those expected if the genetic component of intelligence were multifactorial or polygenic (Table 5-4).

Comparisons between MZ and DZ twins have been made for a wide variety of psychological tests other than those designed to measure intelligence. In many of these tests a strong heritable component is suggested, and it is generally conceded that the most probable mechanism of inheritance involved is polygenic.

While it is uncertain to what extent their findings have relevance to the study of human intelligence and temperament, a number of interesting *animal* experiments have been carried out concerning the inheritance of learning ability, problem-solving ability, emotionality, and various forms of behavior. Tryon bred rats selectively for their performance on a series of trials in a specialized automatic maze (mating

the brightest with the brightest, and the dullest with the dullest through a series of generations). The results up to the eighth filial generation (F_8) are outlined in Figure 5-3. There is no doubt from the results that the maze performance of these rats was genetically determined, but there is considerable doubt as to whether maze performance indicated intelligent behavior or something else. In fact the "dull" rats were found either equal to or better than the "bright" rats on three out of five other maze tests, and the two groups differed in a number of ways other than their maze performance.

Thompson described an experiment in selective breeding of rats for intelligence that was designed to minimize the deficiencies involved in these and other early studies. The influence of motivational and emotional differences was reduced by selective breeding on the basis of rat "intelligence" as measured by the Hebb-Williams maze, and the results of selective breeding over six filial generations are shown in Figure 5-4. Among the many other characteristics for which animals have been selectively bred are their preference for a high or low cage temperature, the amount of voluntary activity they display, their speed of reaction, wildness or tameness, aggressiveness, emotionality, and susceptibility to audiogenic seizures (precipitated by auditory stimuli). In the majority of instances, the heritable determinant of such behavioral characteristics has been considered polygenic in nature.

A major contribution of animal studies is the experimental confirmation that a *single type of behavior* (for example, fighting or drug addiction) *may be determined predominantly by heredity under one set of circumstances and predominantly by learning under another set of circumstances.* Scott has reported that fighting between fox-terriers of the same litter is so strongly inherited that a litter of more than three animals cannot be reared together without one of the

TABLE 5-4. Correlations for Stature and Intelligence, According to Degree of Relationship*

DEGREE OF RELATIONSHIP	CORRELATION FOR STATURE	CORRELATION FOR INTELLIGENCE
Siblings	.54	.51
Parents and children	.51	.49
Grandparents and grandchildren	.32	.34
Uncles (or aunts) and nephews (or nieces)	.29	.35
First cousins	.24	.29

*Data from Burt, C., and Howard, M. 1956. The multifactorial theory of inheritance and its application to intelligence. British Journal of Statistical Psychology 9:59.

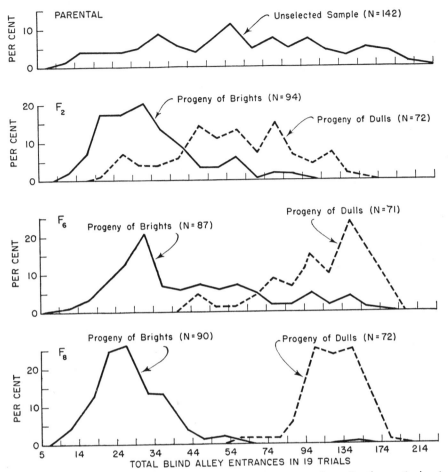

Figure 5–3. Error scores made by animals of successive generations. On the vertical axis is indicated the percent of the total group of rats of any one generation making the number of errors indicated on the horizontal axis. (Adapted from Tryon, R. C. Individual differences. In Moss, F. A., ed. 1942. *Comparative Psychology*. New York, Prentice-Hall, Inc.)

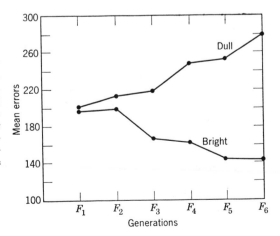

Figure 5–4. Mean error scores of "bright" and "dull" rats selectively bred for performance on the Hebb-Williams maze. (From Thompson, W. R. 1954. In Hooker, D., and Hare, C. C., eds. *Genetics and the Inheritance of Integrated Neurological and Psychiatric Patterns*. Research Publication of the Association for Research in Nervous and Mental Diseases, Vol. 33. Baltimore, The Williams & Wilkins Co.)

animals being killed by another. A mouse on the other hand can be trained to fight and aggressively attack any other mouse placed in its cage, by insuring success in a number of experimentally provoked encounters with another animal. Williams and others have bred strains of rats in which a preference for alcohol consumption is based on genetic differences. Masserman and Yum, on the other hand, demonstrated the learning of addiction to alcohol in cats who were subjected to motivational conflict.

Two further general principles may be mentioned at this point. Firstly, that certain *critical periods in development* have been established, during which a certain kind of behavior (for example, social interaction) may be learned very much more readily than at any subsequent age, and that such critical periods appear to be genetically determined (Chapter 7). Secondly, that the *behavior of primates in general,* and man's behavior even more than that of other primates, is *relatively more strongly determined by learning from environmental experience than that of lower animals.* Thus, sexual behavior in the lower animals may be instinctive, appearing without any previous opportunity for learning, in response to genetically controlled levels in hormone balance. In primates, on the other hand, developmental interaction with other animals of the same species may be essential for the learning of mature sexual behavior manifested by adults, and the varieties of sexual behavior manifested by man appear to be strongly dependent upon his early learning experiences. With the latter considerations in mind let us now turn to an overview of the possible contributions of heredity to the determination of psychiatric disorders.

PSYCHIATRIC DISORDERS

A large number of "behavior mutants" have been described in mammals and birds, usually involving circling or choreic behavior and sometimes convulsive seizures. The inheritance of these conditions has always proved to be of a simple Mendelian (single gene) type, and in those cases that have been fully investigated, lesions of the nervous system have been found associated with the behavioral anomaly (Fuller and Thompson).

In man there are also known to be a large number of hereditary degenerations of the central nervous system (hereditary ataxias) and of the peripheral neuromuscular apparatus ("muscular dystrophies" and "neural atrophies"), determined by a variety of single genes, dominant or recessive, autosomal or sex-linked. When the onset is during early childhood, degenerations involving the brain may be associated with mental retardation (intellectual subnormality); when the onset is later in life degenerations involving the brain may result in chronic organic brain syndromes (or dementia). In these disorders, however, abnormalities of sensation, coordination, and motor function are usually much more obvious than pathological changes in intellectual function, emotion, and behavior. Hence they tend to remain of much greater concern to the neurologist than to the psychiatrist or psychologist, as is also true of epilepsy, another type of brain disorder not usually associated with obvious psychiatric symptoms.

Convulsive seizures may occur in the presence or absence of observable brain pathology, and twin studies appear to discriminate between these *two categories* of epilepsy: (1) *idiopathic* epilepsy, occurring in the absence of obvious brain damage appears to have a major heritable component: (2) *symptomatic* epilepsy, occurring in association with various forms of brain disease, however, seems to have a relatively small heritable component. Family studies of the first variety (idiopathic) indicate considerably higher frequencies of epilepsy among close relatives of epileptics than the general population, but these frequencies are still much smaller than those required by hypotheses of transmission by single dominant or recessive genes, and it is probable that the heritable component is polygenic in nature. The concept of a low seizure threshold, determined partly by the cumulative action of multiple minor genes, is supported by animal experiments in selective breeding for vulnerability to seizures, the latter being found to increase progressively over several generations as expected with polygenic determination of a quantitative characteristic.

Genetic studies also appear to discriminate between *two categories of mental retardation or intellectual subnormality:* (1) *mild subnormality* (with an IQ of approximately 50 to 70) occurring in the absence of observable brain pathology, corresponding with the lower end of the normal distribution of intelligence in the population, and determined to a similar extent by genetic factors; (2) *severe subnormality* (with an IQ of less than 50), associated with a wide variety of organic brain lesions, usually environmental in origin but occasionally attributable to rare varieties of simple Mendelian inheritance. In recent years, cytogenetic studies (involving microscopic examination of cell nuclei) have also revealed the consistent occurrence of abnormal numbers of chromosomes in certain patients with mental retardation (e.g., mongolism).

Among the many *organic brain syndromes* resulting in psychiatric symptoms that usually develop for the first time in adult life, several forms are believed to have a strong heritable component. Huntington's chorea is unique, however, in having the mechanism of inheritance established beyond reasonable doubt, namely a single autosomal dominant gene with a high rate of manifestation. The same mechanism has been postulated for Pick's presenile psychosis, whereas polygenic transmission has been considered more

probable for the genetic component of Alzheimer's presenile psychosis, and for the organic psychoses of senility.

Among the large group of *"psychophysiologic" disorders,* in which somatic pathology appears related to emotional stresses, the significance of hereditary factors remains largely undetermined. Single major genes are believed to contribute to the etiology of hyperthyroidism and peptic ulceration (at least in certain families). However, persons of blood group O are about 40 per cent more susceptible to peptic ulceration than persons with other blood groups, thus suggesting multifactorial inheritance. Arterial blood pressure (and hence essential hypertension) is also thought to have a considerable heritable component, involving the cumulative effects of multiple minor genes.

There has been considerable controversy concerning the function of hereditary predisposition in determining the vulnerability of certain individuals to the common *"functional" psychiatric disorders,* having no consistently demonstrated organic bodily pathology. It should of course be recognized that to whatever extent vulnerability to these disorders is determined by specific hereditary predisposition, it must also involve specific organic bodily structure and function, regardless of whether or not the latter is currently recognized. However, at the present time, neither the relative importance of heredity and environment, nor specific mechanisms of inheritance, can be regarded as conclusively established with respect to these common "functional" psychoses, neuroses, and disorders of personality, character, and behavior.

The most extensive twin studies for psychiatric disorders have been carried out with respect to schizophrenia. Until comparatively recently there was considerable consistency in their results (a heritable component estimated as somewhere between 63 and 84 per cent) but more recent studies suggest a much lower contribution by heredity. The methodological difficulties of twin studies have been emphasized earlier, and the increased frequencies of schizophrenia in various classes of relatives do *not* conform with a hypothesis of transmission by a single dominant or recessive gene. The results of both twin and family studies for manic depressive psychosis and other "functional" psychiatric disorders have been based on smaller numbers than in the case of schizophrenia and have been even less consistent. With most of these disorders it appears conclusively established that close relatives are much more vulnerable than members of the general population to develop psychiatric disorders similar to those of the patient, but the relative significance of hereditary and environmental determination, and possible mechanism of inheritance involved, remain uncertain.

Human geneticists consider it extremely unlikely that any of the common psychiatric disorders known as the schizophrenias, manic depressive reactions, neuroses, or sociopathic personality disorders is determined by a single dominant gene or a single pair of recessive genes. To whatever extent they are determined by specific hereditary predisposition, this predisposition is much more likely to result from transmission by several different major genes, or the cumulative effects of multiple minor genes. As Fraser Roberts (1959) remarked, "Almost without exception simply inherited diseases due to single fully expressed genes are rare or very rare. . . . In our own community the commonest is probably fibrocystic disease of the pancreas, with a frequency of the order of 1 in 2000." In the vast majority of the more common diseases to which heredity contributes appreciably, the probabilities are in favor of multifactorial inheritance.

In conclusion, therefore, it may be stated that single gene substitutions have been established or are strongly suspect as determinants of a wide variety of rare structural disorders of the brain and nervous system (associated with neurological symptoms, organic brain syndromes, or mental retardation) and possibly certain psychophysiologic disorders. On the basis of present evidence, however, it is probable that most common "functional" psychiatric syndromes (defined by clinical diagnosis) will each prove to consist of several different syndromes with varying degrees of hereditary predisposition. These syndromes may include some discrete abnormalities transmitted by single major genes (probably rare), but are at least as likely to involve continuous variables resulting from the cumulative effects of multiple minor genes, and of environmental influences.

SELECTED REFERENCES

Anderson, V. E. 1964. Genetics in mental retardation. In *Mental Retardation*, ed. H. A. Stevens and R. Heber. Chicago, University of Chicago Press, pp. 348-394.

Bliss, E. L., ed. 1962. *Roots of Behavior*, New York, Hoeber Medical Division. Harper & Row, Publishers, Inc. ch. 1-6.

Burks, B. S. 1928. The relative influence of nature and nurture upon mental development. XXVII Yearbook, National Social Studies in Education, part I, pp. 219-318.

Burt, C. 1966. The genetic determination of differences in intelligence: a study of monozygotic twins reared together and apart. British Journal of Psychology 57, 137-153.

Burt, C., and Howard, M. 1956. The multifactorial theory of inheritance and its application to intelligence. British Journal of Statistical Psychology 9, 95-131.

Cowie, V. and Slater, E. 1959. Psychiatric genetics. In *Recent Progress in Psychiatry*, ed. G.W.T.H. Fleming and A. Walk. New York, Grove Press, Inc. Vol. III, pp. 1-53.

David, P. R., and Snyder, L. S. 1954. Genetics and disease. In *Proceedings of the Second National Cancer Conference*. New York, American Cancer Society.

Erlenmeyer-Kimling, L., and Jarvik, L. F. 1963. Genetics and intelligence: a review. Science 142, 1477-1479.

Ford, C. S., and Beach, F. A. 1951. *Patterns of Sexual Behavior*. New York, Hoeber Medical Division, Harper & Row, Publishers, Inc.

Fuller, J. L., and Thompson, W. R. 1960. *Behavior Genetics*. New York, John Wiley & Sons, Inc.

Gedda, L. 1951. *Studio Dei Gemelli.* Rome, Rome Edizioni Orizzonte Medico.

Gottesman, I. I. 1961. The efficiency of several combinations of discrete and continuous variables for the diagnosis of zygosity. Proceedings of the Second International Conference of Human Genetics, Rome, 1961. Acta Genetica.

Gottesman, I. I., and Shields, J. 1966. Schizophrenia in twins: 16 years' consecutive admissions to a psychiatric clinic. British Journal of Psychiatry *112*, 809-818.

Gregory, I. 1959. Husbands and wives admitted to mental hospitals. Journal of Mental Science *105*, 457-462.

Gregory, I. 1960. Genetic factors in schizophrenia. American Journal of Psychiatry *116*, 961-972.

Heston, L. L. 1966. Psychiatric disorders in foster-home-reared children of schizophrenic mothers. British Journal of Psychiatry. *112*, 819-825.

Hooker, D., and Hare C., eds. 1954. *Genetics and the Inheritance of Integrated Neurological and Psychiatric Patterns.* Research Publication of the Association for Research in Nervous and Mental Disease, Vol. 33. Baltimore. The Williams & Wilkins Co.

Kallmann, F. J. 1953. *Heredity in Health and Mental Disorder.* New York, W. W. Norton & Co., Inc.

Kallmann, F. J., ed. 1962. *Expanding Goals of Genetics in Psychiatry* New York, Grune & Stratton, Inc.

Leahy, A. M. 1935. Nature-nurture and intelligence. Genetic Psychology Monographs *4*, 236-308.

Lewis, A. J. 1957. The offspring of parents both mentally ill. Acta Genetica *7*, 349-365.

Lindzey, G., Lykken, D. T., and Winston, H. D. 1960. Infantile trauma, genetic factors, and adult temperament. Journal of Abnormal and Social Psychology *61*, 7-14.

Lindzey, G., Lykken, S. T., and Winston, H. D. 1961. Confusion, conviction, and control groups. Journal of Abnormal and Social Psychology *63*, 221-222.

Lindzey, G., Lykken, D. T., and Winston, H. D. 1961. Trauma, emotionality and scientific sin. Psychological Reports *9*, 199-206.

Neel, J. V., and Schull, W. J. 1954. *Human Heredity.* Chicago, University of Chicago Press.

Newman, H. H., Freeman, S. N., and Holzinger, K. 1937. *Twins: A Study of Heredity and Environment.* Chicago, University of Chicago Press.

Osborne, F. 1951. *Preface to Eugenics*, Revised ed. New York, Harper & Row, Publishers, Inc.

Penrose, L. S. 1959. *Outline of Human Genetics.* New York, John Wiley & Sons, Inc.

Penrose, L. S. 1962. *The Biology of Mental Defect.* 2nd edition. New York, Grune & Stratton, Inc.

Roberts, J. A. F. 1950. The genetics of oligophrenia. In *Congress International de Psychiatrie, Paris, 1950.* VI. *Psychiatrie Sociale. Genetique et Eugenique.* Paris, Hermann et Cie., pp. 55-113.

Roberts, J. A. F. 1959. *An Introduction to Medical Genetics,* 2nd edition. New York, Oxford University Press, Inc.

Rosenthal, D. 1962. Problems of sampling and diagnosis in the major twin studies of schizophrenia. Journal of Psychiatric Research *1*, 116-134.

Rosenthal, D., ed. 1963. *The Genain Quadruplets: A Case Study and Theoretical Analysis of Heredity and Environment in Schizophrenia.* New York, Robert Brunner.

Rosenthal, D. 1966. The offspring of schizophrenic couples. Journal of Psychiatric Research *4*, 169-188.

Scott, J. P. 1958. *Aggression.* Chicago, University of Chicago Press.

Scott, J. P. 1962. Critical periods in behavioral development. Science *138*, 949-958.

Scott, J. P., and Fuller, J. L. 1965. *Genetics and the Social Behavior of the Dog.* Chicago, University of Chicago Press.

Shields, J. 1962. *Monozygotic Twins Brought Up Apart and Brought Up Together.* New York, Oxford University Press, Inc.

Shields, J. and Slater, E. 1960. Heredity and psychological abnormality, *In Handbook of Abnormal Psychology,* ed. H. J. Eysenck. London. Pitman Medical Publishing Company, Ltd.

Steinberg, A. G. 1959. Methodology in human genetics. Journal of Medical Education *34*, 315-334.

Stern, C. 1960. *Principles of Human Genetics.* 2nd edition. San Francisco, W. H. Freeman & Co.

Thompson, W. R. 1954. The inheritance and development of intelligence. In *Genetics and the Inheritance of Integrated Neurological and Pscyhiatric Patterns,* ed. D. Hooker and C. C. Hare. Research Publication, Association for Research in Nervous and Mental Disease, Vol. 33, Baltimore, The Williams & Wilkins Co.

Tryon, R. C. 1942. Individual differences. In *Comparative Psychology,* ed. F. A. Moss. Englewood Cliffs, New Jersey. Prentice-Hall, Inc.

Vandenberg, S. G. 1962. The hereditary abilities study: hereditary components in a psychological test battery. American Journal of Human Genetics *14*, 220-237.

Vandenberg, S. G. 1965. Multivariate analysis of twin differences. In *Methods and Goals in Human Behavior Genetics,* ed. S. G. Vandenberg. New York, Academic Press, Inc.

Vandenberg, S. G. 1966. Contributions of twin research to psychology. Psychological Bulletin *66*, 327-352.

Vandenberg, S. G., Clark, P. J., and Samuels, I. 1965. Psychophysiological reactions of twins: hereditary factors in galvanic skin resistance, heart beat, and breathing rates. Eugenics Quarterly *12*, 7-10.

Woodworth, R. S. 1941. *Heredity and Environment.* New York, Social Science Research Council, Bulletin 47.

CHAPTER 6

Let me have men about me that are fat;
Sleek-headed men, and such as sleep o' nights.
Yond Cassius has a lean and hungry look;
He thinks too much; such men are dangerous.

From "Julius Caesar" by William Shakespeare

Other Biological Factors in Etiology

SOMATIC CAUSATION, ASSOCIATION, AND ANALOGY

During the past century, intensive efforts have been made to correlate symptoms of disease observed during life with pathological changes in bodily structure found after death. The postmortem study of patients who, during their lives, had manifested various forms of insanity was sometimes rewarded by findings of gross or microscopic pathology in the brain or other parts of the body. In some instances these pathological changes in the brain or elsewhere in the body were found to be associated with the presence of pathogenic microorganisms. In other cases degenerative changes were found, following previous exposure to other agents of disease such as chemical poisons or physical trauma.

In still further instances, degenerative changes were found to occur in the absence of prior exposure to any known damaging agent, and were eventually found to result from *deficiency* of some substance essential to the continued life of the cells involved. Such degenerative changes were sometimes attributable to a defective blood supply, and sometimes to the lack of a specific metabolic requirement carried in the blood, such as oxygen, vitamins, or thyroid hormone. Some degenerative changes occur, however, in the absence of any known noxious agent or deficit of essential substances. The latter changes may be described as "idiopathic," and are sometimes found with increased frequency among other members of the families of affected individuals. This familial distribution may conform with that expected on the basis of an inherited characteristic, and in these cases it is assumed that the inherited defect involves some metabolic malfunction, whether the latter is currently recognized or not.

Some naturally occurring organic brain syndromes and the resulting abnormalities in behavior are associated not with any recognizable changes in brain structure ("morphological lesion"), but with disturbances in metabolic function ("biochemical lesion") that are widespread throughout the body and involve the brain sufficiently to cause psychopathology.

The age of the individual at the time of onset of such changes (biochemical and morphological) is of crucial importance in determining the outcome of the pathological process and also the behavioral manifestations. While a significant degree of brain damage occurring in adult life may result in a chronic irreversible brain syndrome (with accompanying impairment of intellectual functions and social behavior), the same process occurring during the course of intrauterine life may result in lifelong mental retardation or intellectual subnormality. Even during intrauterine life, the time of onset of the process is important in determining the outcome, and damage occurring soon after conception may have more severe consequences (including gross bodily deformity and death of the fetus) than damage resulting from the same process occurring shortly before the birth of the infant.

The tremendous variety of pathological processes known to result in acute or chronic brain syndromes and in certain varieties of mental retardation will be outlined in later chapters concerning these disorders. At this time, however, it should be emphasized that there is no one-to-one relationship between (1) the nature, location, and duration of brain damage, and (2) the exact intellectual, emotional, and behavioral manifestations of consequent psychopathology. These latter manifestations depend in part upon the personality characteristics of the individual in whom the brain damage develops, and hence are dependent on all those factors that contribute to his personality development.

In view of the variety of disorders in brain structure or function that are known to precipitate or aggravate psychopathology, as well as the variety of abnormal psychological manifestations precipitated by such brain disorders, it is not surprising that a tremendous amount of research effort has been devoted to searching for bodily correlates or causes of "functional" psychoses, neuroses, and personality disorders. A number of experimental attempts have also been made to replicate the symptoms of various naturally occurring disorders (for example, the schizophrenias or neuroses) by means of toxic drugs or various forms of deprivation (for example, of oxygen, vitamins, or sleep).

The reader is reminded, however, of several considerations that were discussed in the latter part of Chapter 4. Association or correlation of somatic findings (or sociocultural variables) with psychopathology does not necessarily indicate causation. Nor does success or failure to modify psychopathology by somatic or psychosocial therapies necessarily indicate the role of such variables in etiology. Psychopathology that has been induced experimentally by drugs or biological deprivation may be similar to, but not identical with, the manifestations of naturally occurring "functional" psychopathology.

In the remainder of this chapter we shall consider first some immediate, proximate, or precipitating somatic causes of psychopathology, and then some more remote antecedent or predisposing somatic causes. It should be borne in mind, however, that the experimentally induced psychopathology illustrated in the next section is generally regarded as more similar to that found in naturally occurring acute brain syndromes than spontaneous manifestations of "functional" disorders such as the schizophrenias, depression or neuroses—although the latter symptoms may also be accentuated or produced in vulnerable individuals.

PRECIPITATING SOMATIC FACTORS—AGENTS, DEPRIVATION, AND STRESS

NOXIOUS AGENTS

Exogenous noxious agents (originating outside the body) that cause somatic damage and disease include *physical* injury (trauma) and radiation (e.g., x-rays), a wide variety of harmful *chemical* substances, and numerous living organisms or *biological* agents (bacteria, viruses, protozoal or metazoal parasites, and fungi). The recognition of the latter agents, the increasing availability of drugs to destroy them within the human body, the development of methods to prevent their spread through the environment, and methods of increasing human resistance or immunity to specific agents have all contributed to the spectacular diminution in morbidity and mortality from these diseases during the present century. However, a large number of these noxious agents may still on occasion affect the brain and mind, leading to acute or chronic brain syndromes or to lifelong mental retardation. Such noxious agents are frequently regarded as necessary and sufficient causes of the specific types of organic brain syndrome or mental retardation that they produce, but vulnerability to specific agents or groups of such agents varies considerably from one individual to another, so that several predisposing factors may contribute to the determination of this vulnerability.

In addition to organic brain syndromes and mental retardation in which noxious agents are a necessary (if not always sufficient) cause, these agents may also sometimes act as precipitating causes of "functional" psychoses and neuroses, for the development of which they are neither necessary nor sufficient. In the latter instances, predisposition appears to be relatively more important, so that vulnerable individuals may develop symptoms of schizophrenia, depression, or neuroses following an exposure to some noxious agent such as the organisms causing influenza or infectious hepatitis.

In attempts to replicate experimentally the manifestations of various "functional" psychiatric disorders, particularly schizophrenia, a number of toxic drugs have been administered to human subjects — both normal individuals who have no overt signs of psychopathology, and patients already suffering from some form of emotional disorder. Although a wide variety of drugs are known to produce toxic psychoses, these acute brain syndromes are usually characterized by delirium, with visual illusions and hallucinations, impairment of memory and other intellectual functions, and disorientation for time and place. A few *hallucinogens* or *psychotomimetic drugs*, however, tend to produce more subtle alterations in consciousness than most chemical agents, and their manifestations sometimes have

a closer resemblance to certain forms of schizophrenia. Hoch pointed out that what is particularly schizophrenia-like in these experimental psychoses is the ability to be aware of happenings in the outside world and at the same time aware of happenings in the inside world, i.e., a double registration of consciousness.

The manifestations of these experimentally induced *model psychoses* depend upon interaction between (1) the dose and effects of the drug administered, (2) the personality of the subject, and (3) the experimental setting in which the drug is administered. Not only may the effects of the same dose of the drug vary from one subject to another, but also within the same subject from one time to another. The experimental setting can of course be manipulated, and it may be noted that there are several different purposes for which these drugs have been used:

Self-administration has been known for centuries, and is related to the stimulant or "exaltatory" properties of certain of these drugs. In some cultural settings, the alterations in consciousness and behavior have been accompanied by Dionysian revelry, and in others by mystical or religious contemplation.

As an *experimental model of mental illness*, the administration of moderately large doses of such drugs has been considered relevant in studying the etiology of naturally occurring psychopathology.

Basic research on perception generally involves the administration of smaller doses without gross psychotomimetic effects, in order to evaluate changes such as those in visual acuity and ability to judge the passage of time (e.g., Fischer).

As adjuncts to psychotherapy, various drugs of this nature have been used in attempts to treat patients with functional psychoses, neuroses, or addiction to alcohol or other drugs.

In an article on mushrooms, folklore, and experimental psychoses, Rome cited a number of historical references to the hallucinogenic and intoxicant properties of mushrooms. One of the earlier authors cited was Bernardino de Sahagun, who lived and worked among the Indians in Mexico from 1529 to 1590 and wrote as follows:

The mushrooms they ate with honey, and when they began to get heated from them, they began to dance and some sang and some wept, for now they were drunk from the mushrooms. And some cared not to sing but to sit down in their rooms and stay there pensive-like and some saw in a vision that some wild beast was eating them, others saw in a vision that they were taken captives in war, others saw in a vision that they were to be rich, others saw in a vision that they were to own many slaves, others saw in a vision that they were to commit adultery and that their heads were to be bashed in therefore, others saw in a vision that they were to steal something—all the disastrous happenings that are wont to happen, these they saw in visions—then when the drunkenness of the mushrooms passed, they spoke with one another about the visions they had seen.

Two centuries later Georg Wilhelm Steller, a German scientist and traveler in the service of Peter the Great, explored the Russian Pacific coast together with the Dane Vitus Bering, and reported that mushrooms were in common use for their intoxicating properties. In the present century, several species of mushroom food in Mexico have been established as having hallucinogenic properties, and an active principle isolated from certain of them has been marketed under the name of *psilocybin*. The effects of this drug have been found very similar to those of several other hallucinogens, notably *mescaline, LSD-25,* and *bufotenin*.

The first hallucinogen that was studied at all intensively was *mescaline*, one of the alkaloids isolated by Lewin (1888) from a cactus, the sliced-off tops of which (mescal buttons or peyote) have been used by the Aztecs and subsequently other residents of Northern Mexico and southwestern United States to produce intoxication. Weir Mitchell and Havelock Ellis were among the first to describe their experiences after taking mescaline, and during the first half of this century numerous investigators reported their subjective experiences after taking the drugs. The outward behavior of the subject usually appears relatively normal, but he experiences distorted and hallucinatory sensory perceptions (particularly visual ones), in combination with varying degrees of clouded consciousness, intellectual impairment and confusion, paranoid thinking, and emotional lability. Osmond and Smythies drew attention to similarities between (1) the chemical structures of mescaline and epinephrine (adrenaline) and (2) the clinical manifestations of mescaline intoxication and *acute* schizophrenia. This stimulated a search for breakdown products of epinephrine, or other chemically related substances, capable of reproducing the clinical manifestations of schizophrenia. While several such toxic substances have been reported, none has received widespread confirmation as a universal correlate of schizophrenia.

Another hallucinogenic substance which has been widely investigated in recent years is a semisynthetic derivative of ergot known as *lysergic acid diethylamide* or *LSD-25*. The bibliography of the effects of this drug is already very extensive. The following account of his experiences under LSD was narrated by a Canadian journalist.*

On the morning of Thursday, June 18, 1953, I swallowed a drug which, for twelve unforgettable hours, turned me into a madman. For twelve hours I inhabited a nightmare world in which I experienced the torments of hell and the ecstasies of heaven.

I will never be able to describe fully what happened to me during my excursion into madness. There are no words in the English language designed to convey the sensations I felt or the visions, illusions, hallucinations, colors, patterns and dimensions which my disordered mind revealed.

I saw the faces of familiar friends turn into fleshless skulls and the heads of menac-

---

*Reprinted by permission from Katz, S. 1953. "My 12 Hours as a Madman." Toronto, Maclean's Magazine.

ing witches, pigs and weasels. The gaily patterned carpet at my feet was transformed into a fabulous heaving mass of living matter, part vegetable, part animal. An ordinary sketch of a woman's head and shoulders suddenly sprang to life. She moved her head from side to side, eyeing me critically, changing back and forth from woman into man. Her hair and her neck-piece became the nest of a thousand famished serpents who leaped out to devour me. The texture of my skin changed several times. After handling a painted card I could feel my body suffocating for want of air because my skin had turned to enamel. As I patted a black dog, my arm grew heavy and sprouted a thick coat of glossy black fur.

I was repeatedly held in the grip of a terrifying hallucination in which I could feel and see my body convulse and shrink until all that remained was a hard sickly stone located in the left side of my abdomen, sur-rounded by a greenish-yellow vapor which poured across the floor of the room.

Time lost all meaning. Hours were tele-scoped into minutes; seconds stretched into hours. The room I was in changed with every breath I drew. Mysterious flashes of multicolored light came and went. The dimensions of the room, elasticlike, stretch-ed and shrank. Pictures, chairs, curtains and lamps flew endlessly about like planets in their orbits. My senses of feeling, smelling and hearing ran amuck. It was as though someone had rooted out the nerve nets in my brain which control the senses then joined them together again without thought of their proper placings.

But my hours of madness were not all filled with horror and frenzy. At times I beheld visions of dazzling beauty, visions so rapturous, so unearthly that no artist will ever paint them. I lived in a paradise where the sky was a mass of jewels set in a back-ground of shimmering aquamarine blue; where the clouds were apricot colored; where the air was filled with liquid golden arrows, glittering fountains of iridescent bubbles, filigree lace of pearl and silver, sheathes of rainbow light all constantly changing in color, design, texture and dimension so that each scene was more lovely than the one which preceded it.

In addition to various perceptual disturbances (of vision, hearing, and tactile sensations), this subject reported marked fluctuations in mood during the course of the day, ranging from fatigue and depression to excitement and elation, from anger and suspicion to fear and apprehension. The diminished span of memory and intellectual im-pairment were illustrated in excerpts from a tape recording made at the time, as in the following passage:

Q. A bird in the hand is worth two in the bush. What does that mean?
A. A bird?
Q. A bird in the hand is worth two in the bush.
A. A bird in the hand . . . let's see . . . now it's becoming more difficult to figure these things out.
Q. Try it again. A bird in the hand is worth two in the bush.
A. A bird in the hand . . . well, I gotta make a running stab at it or I can't get it.
Q. Try again. A bird in the hand is worth two in the bush.
A. If you get a job, the first job you get . . . you see, now I put my hand up and I get preoccupied with my hand because there are all sorts of engrossing dis-tortions . . . .

I never did give the correct answer. My mind would click from one subject to an-other, like the lens of a camera, making concentration impossible. At other times, I saw visions which made me oblivious to everything else in the room. By blurting out the answers quickly, I was able to define concrete objects like *hat, bicycle* and *knife*. I couldn't handle abstract definitions like *bad* and *brave*. The word *join* made no sense to me whatsoever.

The unsuccessful effort to think both fatigued and depressed me . . . . How could I explain that I was perched on the edge of an abyss of horror, and that every second I feared being toppled into it, doomed to an eternal life of indescribable pain and wretchedness.

The effects of the drug, however, dis-appeared within 12 hours and the subject later wrote the following:

I awoke next morning at nine o'clock from a deep dreamless sleep. The events of the preceding day came rushing back to me. I looked cautiously about the room. My clothes were neatly laid out on the chair, my wallet, keys, pen and cigarettes were on the bureau. Outside the sky was blue and the sun was shining. I was happy and relieved to find that everything was nice and normal. The only visible effect of the LSD experiment on me was a hangover but it was no more painful than the morning-after-the-night-before variety.

In 1959 two reports appeared on the effects of a new psychotomimetic drug named *Sernyl*. After receiving this drug, the subject experiences distortions of perception and body image, feelings of unreality and depersonalization, inability to maintain directed thinking, and other manifestations similar to those that have been observed in experiments on sensory isolation (which will be discussed in the next chapter). The following year Cohen et al. reported that the effects of Sernyl were greatly reduced when persons receiving the drug were simultaneously subjected to environmental sensory deprivation. Pollard et al. compared the effects of Sernyl, psilocybin, and LSD-25 in individuals subjected to diminished sensory input.

These results suggest that drugs such as psilocybin, LSD, and mescaline act by *increasing* neural firing in the sensory pathways independently of inputs, whereas Sernyl *decreases* sensory activity with effects similar to those of sensory isolation (or alternatively has no effects on sensation). In either case, the psychotomimetic effects are also related to the structuring of the experiment and the personalities of the subjects.

BIOLOGICAL DEPRIVATION

During the latter part of the nineteenth century, Pasteur's discovery of the bacteria responsible for fermentation attracted numerous workers to the new science of bacteriology. Between 1880 and 1890 more than 20 specific microorganisms were shown to be responsible for human diseases. After the discovery of these and other pathogenic organisms, it is not surprising that many members of the medical profession

should have resisted the idea that diseases such as scurvy, beriberi, and pellagra could be due to a *deficiency* of some essential substances in the diet (rather than an exogenous infection or intoxication). However, the notion of dietary causation of disease was by no means new, as evidenced by the routine administration of citrus fruits (particularly limes) to British sailors following the publication of James Lind's classic book *A Treatise on Scurvy* in 1752. A century later, the dietary deficiency notion was held by only a minority, although Hirsch (1883) was able to cite extensive evidence in support of his contention that scurvy was "most of all associated with want of fresh vegetables in the diet."

The deficiency disease pellagra was attributed to a poor diet as long ago as the eighteenth century, and beriberi was replicated experimentally shortly before the end of the nineteenth century in fowl receiving a diet of polished rice. It was subsequently shown that both the disease occurring in fowl and beriberi in man could be cured by the addition to the diet of rice polishings or an extract prepared from them. However, it was not until 1911 that Funk obtained from rice polishings a crystalline substance, small quantities of which were capable of preventing or curing beriberi, and which he named "vitamine" (in view of its evident importance to life and in the erroneous belief that it had the chemical structure of an amine). Other essential vitamins were subsequently discovered and isolated in chemically pure form. A variety of other substances are now known to be needed in the diet for the maintenance of health, and minimal requirements have been established for protein and for certain minerals such as calcium and iron.

Deficiency of certain vitamins — particularly members of the B complex such as thiamine, niacin, and vitamin B_{12} — may result in organic brain syndromes (with gross impairment of intellectual functions) or release latent symptoms of functional *psychosis or neurosis.* An interesting account of the experimental induction of neuroses by starvation was given by Keys, who studied 36 "normal" young men during three months of control on a good diet, six months of semistarvation on a diet of the European famine type, and subsequent months of nutritional rehabilitation. In the semistarvation period the men lost about one-fourth of their previous body weight and developed all the classical signs of severe semistarvation. Self-ratings of these subjects during the prestarvation and semistarvation periods are shown in Table 6-1. Further evaluation of their emotional status during the course of the experiment was obtained through their responses to the Minnesota Multiphasic Personality Inventory, and Figure 6-1 shows their mean profiles during the prestarvation control period (C), after 24 weeks of semistarvation (S 24), and after 32 weeks of rehabilitation (R 32). The most noticeable elevations during the period of semistarvation involved the three neurotic scales commonly associated with hypochondriacal bodily complaints, depression of mood, and hysteria (Hs, D, and Hy respectively).

There are other substances that are equally necessary for the continuation of life and proper function of the brain and mind. These include oxygen, glucose (from which about 90 percent of

Table 6–1. Self Ratings of the Subjects in the Minnesota Experiment. Mean Values for 32 Men for the Pre-starvation Control (C), for 12 and for 24 Weeks of Semi-starvation (S12 and S24)*

SYMPTOM	C	s12	s24
Depression	0	.69	1.38
Moodiness	0	.84	1.50
Irritability	0	1.31	1.81
Apprehension	−.03	.34	.41
Apathy	0	1.09	1.81
Sensitivity to noise	0	1.31	1.81
Ambition	0	−1.19	−1.75
Self-discipline	0	−.56	−1.72
Mental alertness	0	−.84	−1.53
Concentration	0	−.91	−1.66
Comprehension	0	−.44	−1.03

Ratings: Normal 0, and deviations from normal: More 1, some more 2, much more 3, very much more 4, extremely much more 5.
Less −1, some less −2, much less −3, very much less −4, extremely much less −5.

*Reprinted by permission from Keys, A. 1952. Experimental induction of psychoneuroses by starvation. In *The Biology of Mental Health and Disease.* New York, Hoeber Medical Division, Harper & Row, Publishers, p. 520.

the energy used by brain cells is derived), and thyroid hormone. Severe deficiency of glucose brought about by injections of insulin (used for many years in the insulin coma treatment of schizophrenia) results in the temporary production of an organic brain syndrome, with clouding of consciousness, impairment of intellectual functions, and the release or accentuation of be-

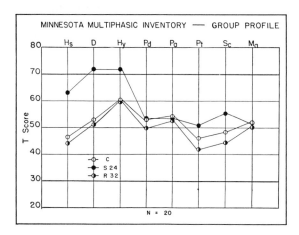

Figure 6–1. Mean profiles on the MMPI during experimental induction of neuroses by starvation. (Reprinted by permission from Keys, A. 1952. Experimental induction of psychoneuroses by starvation. In *The Biology of Mental Health and Disease.* New York, Hoeber Medical Division, Harper & Row, Publishers, Inc.)

havior abnormalities already present. Deficiencies of oxygen and hormones may occur for a variety of reasons and result in a diversity of abnormal behavior. In addition the concept of biological deprivation may also be applied to the consequences of prolonged loss of sleep and diminished sensory input. Sensory isolation will be considered in the next chapter, but some of the effects of oxygen lack and sleep deprivation will now be reviewed.

Windle reviewed the *effects of anoxia on the structure of the brain and the behavior of experimental animals.* It has been established that structural changes in the adult brain follow anoxia induced by breathing atmospheres lacking in oxygen, by profound nitrous oxide anesthesia, or by stopping the circulation of the blood to the brain. Neurons are very sensitive to oxygen lack, and complete anoxia need only be of brief duration in order to cause profound and permanent damage. Somewhat milder degrees of oxygen deficiency acting over a longer period of time may also result in permanent brain damage in adult animals. While the fetus and the newborn are more resistant to oxygen deficiency than the adult, severe degrees of oxygen deficiency around the time of birth may result either in death, in structural damage to the brain with consequent neurological symptoms (as in congenital cerebral palsy), or in defective intellectual function, which may persist throughout life (mental deficiency). The maze-learning ability of experimental animals subjected to anoxia at birth was found consistently lower than that of litter mates who were not subjected to anoxia. In passing it may also be mentioned that vitamin deficiencies during early embryonic development have also been shown to result in death or congenital deformities, certain of which may affect the brain (for example, see Woollam and Millen).

McFarland undertook a comprehensive survey of *the effects of anoxia on the physiology and biochemistry of the brain and on behavior.* In a series of studies he demonstrated relationships between quantitative alterations in a sensory function (light sensitivity) and the amount of oxygen in the arterial blood (also, diminished blood sugar following administration of insulin and the reduced oxygen combining power of the blood produced by carbon monoxide poisoning). He went on to evaluate the effects of anoxia on complex mental functions such as memory, judgment, and insight, as demonstrated through experiments at high altitudes in the Andes as well as in low-oxygen chambers at sea level. Figure 6-2 shows the impairment of immediate memory resulting from increasing altitude. Figure 6-3 shows the deterioration of handwriting during the course of one hour in which the oxygen content of the atmosphere was lowered from that found at sea level to that found at a simulated altitude of 28,000 feet. The latter experiment is particularly interesting in showing the subject's loss of insight into his intellectual impairment. He is reported to have remained cheerful throughout the test and felt quite all right except for occasional temporary blanks. At 23,000 feet (8.5 per cent oxygen) he began to omit letters from common words and his writing became quite illegible. He complained of his feet feeling a long way off and of his inability to orient other parts of his body. At 26,000 feet (7.4 per cent oxygen) he was greatly incapacitated and yet he appeared cheerful and was well satisfied with his performance. He was quite annoyed when he was removed from the apparatus and insisted that he could go much higher.

In another experiment, ten subjects spent six months in the Andes studying the effects of diminished oxygen pressure on the blood circulation, respiration, metabolism, brain, and sense organs. A series of psychological tests involving complex mental functions was administered, and the mean performances on these tests diminished with increasing altitude. Each subject

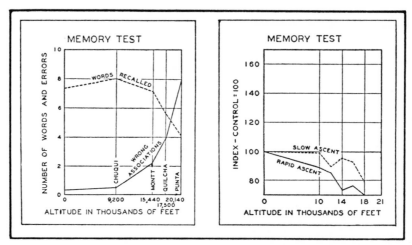

Figure 6–2. Immediate memory is affected by altitude. Acclimatized subjects on an Andean high altitude expedition *(left)* show a marked impairment in words recalled and an increase in wrong associations. During simulated flights *(right)* at altitudes of about 10,000 feet and over, there is a significant decrement in objective tests for immediate memory. (From McFarland, R. A. 1937. Journal of Comparative Psychology 24; and McFarland, R. A. 1941. C. A. A. Technical Development Report 11. Government Printing Office, Washington, D.C.)

was also asked to check a list of physiological and psychological complaints frequently associated with the effects of high altitude. The ten most commonly observed physiological changes in order of frequency were: shortness of breath on exertion or fatigability, breathing irregularities, cold extremities, dry skin, disturbed sleep, gas in the stomach or intestines, headache, sore throat, irregular pulse, and lassitude. The ten most common psychological alterations in behavior in order of frequency were as follows: greater effort to carry out tasks, more critical attitude toward other people, mental laziness, heightened sensory irritability, touchiness on various subjects, dislike of being told how to do things, difficulty in concentrating, slowness in reasoning, frequently recurring ideas, and difficulty in remembering.

Let us turn now to *sleep deprivation,* which has interested a number of investigators during recent years. Sleep deprivation was used in the Spanish Inquisition no less effectively than by modern inquisitors who have employed it in their efforts to impair personality

function for political reasons, as in the false confessions of "germ warfare" extorted from American fliers during the Korean War. Until recently, however, there was relatively little serious study of the physiological and behavior effects of prolonged wakefulness. Patrick and Gilbert (1896) kept three students awake for 90 hours and found decreases in sensory acuity, reaction time, motor speed, and memorizing ability; they reported hallucinations in one of the subjects. Kleitman (1939) kept 35 subjects awake for 60 to 68 hours, and reported greater sensitivity to pain, irritability, occasional hallucinations, and peculiar verbal responses and behavior. In a series of studies, Tyler and his associates reported on the effects of sleep deprivation up to 112 hours in large numbers of subjects. Tyler grouped the abnormal psychological reactions observed into psychoneurotic reactions, schizophrenic-like reactions, and paranoid reactions. Some of the subjects received stimulant drugs (amphetamines) which are known to precipitate psychotic reactions in certain individuals, but psychotic episodes were

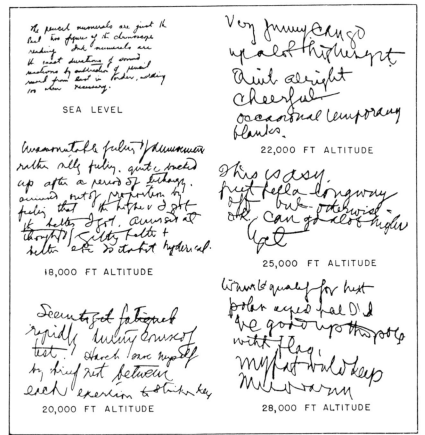

Figure 6–3. The handwriting of a subject gradually deteriorated at progressively higher altitudes (simulated). In comparison with the normal handwriting, that at higher altitudes shows an increase in size, muscular incoordination, and omission of letters. (From McFarland, R. A., 1932. The physiological effects of oxygen deprivation (anoxemia) on human behavior. Archives of Psychology 145.)

also observed in persons who had received an inactive placebo or no drug at all.

Brauchi and West published the following interesting case report on the effects of sleep deprivation:*

... a patient has been studied who was continuously wakeful while under constant observation for more than seven days and nights in June, 1957. The setting was a radio marathon contest in which both the

challenger (the patient) and the previously self-acclaimed champion were competing for the "title" and a $500 prize. Both men remained awake for 168 hours and 33 minutes, at which time the contest was declared a tie and terminated by the attending physician.

During the marathon the contestants had fairly comfortable quarters. Guards (firemen and policemen) were present at all times to observe whether either contestant fell asleep (in which case his opponent would be the victor). A doctor examined each contestant twice a day. The participants took 30-minute shifts at the microphone. From the fourth day on they received 5 mg. of dextroamphetamine twice a day. Both drank a great deal of coffee and, when not broadcasting, stayed awake by walking around,

*Reprinted by permission from Brauchi, J. T., and West, L. J. Sleep deprivation. Journal of the American Medical Association, Sept. 5, 1959, Vol. 171, pages 11–14. Copyright 1959 by the American Medical Association.

smoking, and conversing with friends. Abnormal symptoms were noted in both contestants from the fourth day onward. Only those of the patient . . . will be reported in detail; however, the other contestant was described by the guards and by the attending physician as having shown many similar symptoms.

During the fourth day and subsequently the patient thought that various parts of the equipment were in different cities. He began to experience "memory lapses." These occurred at frequent intervals and for increasing periods until the contest was stopped. His broadcasting performance during these memory lapses was not impaired, however. Although he was inside a building the patient could not understand why there were no cars going up and down the aisle. At one point the patient saw a manikin standing by a refrigerator at a nearby exhibit in the same building and thought that it was a woman waiting to get into her car. He actually opened the refrigerator door to assist the "woman" in out of the rain. He developed the feeling that he was being punished by being made to stay awake. He accused his girl friend of kissing one of the guards, although she was in the broadcasting booth with him alone at the time. He felt that he and his competitor belonged to a secret club of nonsleepers.

During the last two days both contestants became increasingly disorganized and were often delusional. Nevertheless, they continued to force themselves to remain awake and to broadcast every 30 minutes, although much of the broadcast material was confused, disorganized, and rambling. Transient auditory and visual hallucinations apparently occurred increasingly in both subjects at various times after the fourth day. Increased suggestibility was noted to the extent that on one occasion a brief period of *folie à deux* took place, in which the delusions and hallucinations of one contestant were accepted by the other.

Because of progressively psychotic behavior, tremors, and ankle edema in both contestants, the attending physician finally insisted that the contest be brought to an end. The two contestants were taken to a local hospital. The patient was resistive and irritable. He ran out the door and was found four hours later wandering around town, an episode of which he has no memory. He was returned to the hospital, sedated, and put to bed. The following morning he

signed a release and left for a week's vacation at a resort. However, he merely drove around the countryside during that week. When he returned to work he continued to have memory lapses similar to those which had been present during the contest, the last three days of which he recalled very little. His close friends observed a marked change in his personality after the marathon. He told conflicting stories about his past and seemed overwhelmed when confronted by the discrepancies. His thinking developed a bizarre flavor. He developed the delusion that he was responsible for the Egyptian-Israeli conflict and that a female secret agent in Florida was trying to get him to return to the Suez Canal zone. He used poor judgment in the management of personal and financial affairs. He was irritable, restless, began to drink heavily, became tardy and irresponsible in his work, and often failed to show up at all. He was troubled by insomnia at night and lapses of attention and memory during the day.

Finally the patient's affairs became so confused that he sought hospitalization . . . in September 1957, at which time positive findings were limited to the psychiatric sphere, except for electrocardiographic changes compatible with a right bundle-branch block which had been noted for many years. There was also roentgenologic evidence of previously noted interstitial fibrosis of the lungs. The patient was oriented in all spheres. Memory for the previous two or three days was hazy and circumscribed, with areas of amnesia. Attention and concentration were somewhat impaired. However, there was no disturbance of reasoning, judgment, abstract thinking, symbolization, or intelligence. No hallucinations or delusions were present at the time of the examination, although the patient gave a history of these occurring during the marathon. He was markedly anxious and apprehensive, and his speech was hesitant, halting, and vague. He feared that recently experienced feelings of depersonalization, estrangement, derealization, and *déjà vu* might recur. He was afraid of what he might do during one of his brief periods of amnesia, which had been taking place about once a week. His electroencephalogram was normal.

The patient's history revealed that he had been discharged from the Army in 1945 for physical reasons; however, anxiety state and emotional instability had been diagnosed at that time. His personal and professional life during the subsequent decade reflected a certain amount of instability, with three hospitalizations for nervous disorders. In November, 1956 (during a period of prolonged sleep deprivation related to nighttime working conditions), he first began to experience some dissociative symptoms which were relatively mild and infrequent. In March, 1957, three months prior to the big contest, he undertook a radio marathon alone under very difficult conditions, including social isolation in a small cramped booth. This lasted 89 hours, during which dissociative symptoms became increasingly prominent and the patient's mental state became progressively confused. On receiving sedation and a night's sleep the patient recovered from the acute symptoms, but he had "memory lapses" lasting 20 to 30 minutes several times during the three-month interval preceding the record-breaking marathon previously described.

In the hospital the patient was assigned to occupational, recreational, and group therapy and was in addition seen twice a week in psychotherapy. He responded rapidly and showed marked improvement. During his hospitalization of four months he had only one dissociative reaction, a short fugue in which he wandered off the ward with subsequent amnesia. After his discharge from the hospital in January, 1958, he returned to work and has remained in reasonably good health since that time.

Luby and his associates remarked that sleep deprivation provides a unique model for correlative studies of energy transfer systems, behavior, psychological functioning, and psychophysiology. In a careful multidisciplinary study, they found progressive depletion of the biochemical energy transfer systems, corresponding with similar findings reported by their group in patients with schizophrenia, which will be referred to in a later chapter.

BIOLOGICAL STRESS

The great French physiologist Claude Bernard (1878) pointed out that "in animals with complex organization the living parts exist in the fluids bathing them, such as blood and lymph, which constitute the internal environment," and went on to state that "it is the fixity of the internal environment which is the condition of free and independent life." He also wrote that "all the vital mechanisms, however varied they may be, have only one object—that of preserving constant the conditions of life in the internal environment." These concepts were elaborated by Walter Cannon (1926), who described the internal environment as being a fluid matrix, and gave the name of *homeostasis* to the constancy that was maintained by continually active physiological processes of regulation. He also applied the term *stresses* to those external and internal conditions affecting the regulators of homeostasis, and thereby tending to disturb the constant state of the fluid matrix. Among these stresses he included cold, oxygen deficiency, loss of blood, and low blood sugar.

The responses of the organism to stress have been studied over several decades by Hans Selye and his associates. Their observations on various species of animals indicated that the organism responded in a stereotyped manner to a variety of very different agents, including infections, intoxications, trauma, nervous strain, heat, cold, muscular fatigue, and x-rays. Each of these agents had specific effects different from the others, and their only common feature was in placing the body in a state of stress. They therefore concluded that the stereotyped response (which was superimposed on the various specific effects) represented a reaction to stress per se.

The first manifestations of this stress response to be noticed were enlargement of the cortex of the adrenal gland (with microscopic evidence of hyperactivity), involution of the thymus and lymph gland system (with accompanying changes in the blood count), and ulcers of the stomach and intestines, often accompanied by other signs of damage or "shock." In view of the involutional or degenerative changes of most organs of the body, it was quite

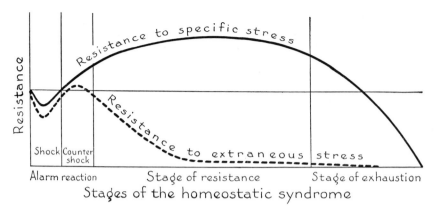

Figure 6–4. Changes in resistance to specific and extraneous stresses during the general adaptation syndrome. During shock, the organism is less resistant to the specific and extraneous stresses. During countershock, the organism builds up a resistance to all stresses. During the period of resistance, there is an increase in the resistance to the specific stress. At the same time the resistance to other (extraneous) stresses decreases, so that the organism may easily succumb to them. (After Selye, H. 1946. General adaptation syndrome and diseases of adaptation. Journal of Clinical Endocrinology 6, 177.)

striking that the cortex of the adrenal gland should *increase* in size and activity. It was suspected that this adrenal response played an important part in a nonspecific defense mechanism, which was therefore termed the "alarm reaction."

Subsequent investigations showed that the alarm reaction was merely the first stage of a much more prolonged *general adaptation syndrome,* evolving in three distinct stages: (1) the *alarm reaction* (with an initial phase of *shock,* followed by a phase of *countershock*); (2) the stage of *resistance* (involving successful adaptation to the specific stressor agent); and (3) the stage of *exhaustion,* following prolonged exposure to the stressor (to which resistance had developed but could no longer be maintained.) The stages of the general adaptation syndrome are illustrated in Figure 6-4, which also shows that the resistance of the organism to all *other* (extraneous) stressor agents is diminished, even during the stage of resistance to the specific stressor involved.

Nonspecific changes in bodily function and structure may occur in any of the three stages, evidence of tissue degeneration (e.g., ulcers of the stomach and intestines) being most marked in the initial phase of the alarm reaction and again in the final stage of exhaustion. It has been established that these changes in bodily function and structure may follow prolonged emotional stress, as will be illustrated in the next chapter, and it appears that Selye's general adaptation syndrome is of great relevance to the development of certain psychophysiologic disorders in man. At the present time, however, its significance in the development of other forms of psychiatric disorder is not at all clear.

In concluding this section on biological stress, we may summarize the three major groups of immediate, proximate, or precipitating biological causes of psychiatric disorders as follows: (1) too much (noxious agents), (2) too little (deprivation of biological essentials), (3) too fast (exposure of the individual to sudden and marked changes which subject him to stress in excess of his adaptive capacity or tolerance). We may also add that it is a general principle of biology that *noxious agents, deprivation, and stress all tend to produce the most severe and lasting damage when they affect young, immature, and rapidly developing tissues or individuals.*

Similarly, it appears that adverse interpersonal relationships and life experiences exert their maximal harmful effects when they are severe and prolonged and involve the infant or child (see next chapter).

REMOTE ANTECEDENT OR PREDISPOSING CAUSES

DIFFERENCES IN CONSTITUTIONAL PREDISPOSITION

The preceding section was concerned with the immediate responses of the organism to noxious agents, deprivation, and stress. Little emphasis was placed on differences in responses observed between different individuals, but such responses do vary considerably from one person to another. Thus, McFarland demonstrated differences in the response of psychoneurotic patients and normal control subjects to the same degrees of anoxia (Figure 6-5). Similarly, in the case report of sleep

deprivation by Brauchi and West, both the subjects who kept awake for the same period of seven days and seven nights showed some similar disorders of mental function and behavior, but in one instance they cleared up quickly whereas in the other they persisted and led to hospitalization and treatment. The history revealed that the latter subject had already been hospitalized for "nervous disorders" on three previous occasions. In another study of sleep deprivation, Koranyi and Lehmann deprived six chronic schizophrenic patients of sleep for 100 hours and observed the reappearance in these patients of acute symptoms of schizophrenia that had not been present for several years. On the other hand, Gulevich, Dement, and Johnson reported no gross psychotic symptoms in a healthy 17-year-old male subjected to 264 hours of continuous wakefulness.

In a comprehensive survey of constitutional factors and abnormal behavior, Rees remarked that the term *constitution* is variously used, and most frequently in the limited sense of sus-

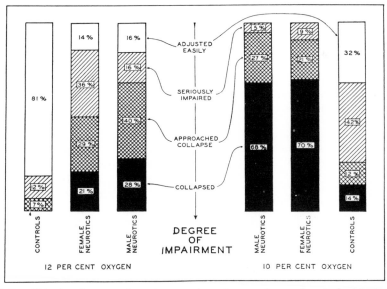

Figure 6–5. Altitude tolerance of psychoneurotic patients and normal control subjects at simulated altitudes of 14,500 feet (12 percent oxygen) and 19,000 feet (10 percent oxygen). A larger percentage of both male and female neurotic patients collapsed or approached collapse than of the normal controls. (From McFarland, R. A., and Barach, A. L. 1937. The response of psychoneurotics to variations in oxygen tension. American Journal of Psychiatry 93, 1315.)

ceptibility to disease — and hence vulnerability or predisposition to abnormal behavior. Two paragraphs later he expressed the view that "the concept of human constitution connotes predominant genetic determination and the relative constancy of constitutional attributes within the individual." Constitution, however, is far from being static and is *not* determined at the time of conception, nor by the time of birth (that is to say, it is neither hereditary nor congenital). As indicated in the preceding chapter, it is far more appropriate to regard constitution as the momentary product of original endowment and of all the physical and psychological processes of the past, and one which therefore is constantly changing as the individual passes through life.

Various aspects of human constitution may be recognized, and Rees classified these as follows:

1. *Morphological.* Among various morphological characteristics studied in human constitutional research are general bodily configuration (physical type, bodily *habitus,* somatotype); body size; the distribution and relative development of tissue components, e.g., muscle, fat, skeletal and connective tissue; relative development of various physical attributes, e.g., disharmonious growth (dysplasia); the relative development of masculine and feminine characteristics (androgyny, gynandromorphy), etc.

2. *Physiological.* Particularly relevant in constitutional studies are the functional characteristics of the autonomic, central and peripheral nervous systems; cardiovascular and other visceral functions; anabolic-catabolic processes; biochemical characteristics; endocrine balance, etc.

3. *Psychological.* Aspects of human constitution include personality in its manifold aspects, temperament, character, intelligence, perceptive characteristics, psychomotor functions, etc.

4. *Immunological.* This classification includes relationships between various constitutional attributes and disease susceptibility, including physical illnesses, psychiatric and psychosomatic disorders.

In view of the diversity of characteristics included under this broad concept of constitution, it should be evident that certain of them are likely to be relatively much more constant than others, and certain of them are likely to be determined by hereditary predisposition to a far greater degree than others. Furthermore, limitations in current knowledge prevent accurate specification of the relative contributions of various interacting causes of these constitutional characteristics. Nevertheless, interesting associations have been reported between various aspects of constitution and abnormal behavior, some of which will now be reviewed briefly. For convenience we shall distinguish only two aspects of constitution: (a) somatic structure or physique, and (b) somatic functions (physiological, metabolic, and immunological).

SOMATIC STRUCTURE OR PHYSIQUE

Notions of some correspondence between behavior and bodily configuration have at least the respectability of antiquity. According to Rees, the ancient Hindus classified men into types designated the hare, the bull, and the horse, and women into types referred to as the mare, the elephant, and the deer. Physicians of ancient Greece and Rome postulated connections between body build and the susceptibility to certain diseases. In the second century A.D. Galen gave detailed descriptions of nine temperamental types, which he considered to be determined by various mixtures of the four humors (blood, lymph, and black and yellow bile), and attempted thereby to relate body structure with both behavioral characteristics and susceptibility to specific diseases. Galen's teaching dominated medical thought and practice for many centuries, and as recently as the eighteenth century Laycock at Edinburgh proposed a fourfold classification of temperaments into the sanguine, phlegmatic, choleric, and melancholic types. Little objective evidence was provided, however, until Beneke (1878) published data on variations in size of internal organs in relation to age, disease, and body type. At approximately the same time diGiovanni (1880) attempted to relate susceptibility to diseases with external bodily measurements.

Modern studies on possible relationships existing between bodily constitution, temperament or personality, and psychiatric disorders was stimulated by the publication of Kretschmer's book, *Korperbau und charakter*, the first English translation of which appeared in 1925. The four main types of physique described by Kretschmer were (1) *the asthenic or leptosomatic type* (slender individuals with long bones and poor muscular development), which he considered almost invariably associated with schizoid personality and vulnerability to overt schizophrenia; (2) *the athletic type* (sturdy and strong with wide shoulders and well developed muscles); (3) *the pyknic or pyknosomatic type* (stocky, plump, rounded persons), which he considered almost invariably associated with cyclothymic personality and vulnerability to manic depressive psychosis; and (4) *the dysplastic type* showing endocrine disturbances and disproportionate development as in persons with

disorders of the pituitary gland. (See Figure 6-6 for illustrations of the first three of these types.)

Many classifications of body types have appeared during the present century, and it is interesting that a number of different authors have described closely similar types—apparently in many cases without knowledge of each other's work. Generally, two extremes of body build have been described (corresponding with Kretschmer's asthenic and pyknic types), together with a third type (corresponding with Kretschmer's athletic type) in many classifications (Table 6-2).

In more recent years, however, it has been increasingly recognized that these typologies imply discontinuity or concentrations in measurements that are essentially continuous distributions, with the majority of observations intermediate rather than at the extremes. Frequently these continuous distributions correspond closely with those expected theoretically according to the normal or bell-shaped curve. Recent studies of physique have therefore tended to permit a number of different observations to be made on each of several scales of measurement.

Sheldon and his associates rated each

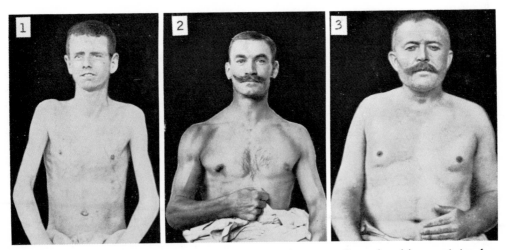

Figure 6-6. 1. Asthenic type. 2. Athletic type. 3. Pyknic type. (Reproduced by permission from Kretschmer, E. *Korperbau und Charakter*, 23rd and 24th editions. Berlin-Gottingen-Heidelberg: Springer 1961.)

TABLE 6–2. Comparison of Classification of Physical Types*

	1	2	3
Hippocrates (460-400 **B.C.**)	*H. apoplecticus*	—	*H. pthisicus*
Rostan (1828)	Digestive	Muscular	Respiratory-cerebral
Beneke (1876)	Rachitic	Carcinomatous	Scrofulous-phthisical
di Giovanni (1880)	3rd Comb.	2nd Comb.	1st Comb.
Manouvrier (1902)	Brachyskeletal	Mesoskeletal	Macroskeletal
Virenius (1904)	Connective	Muscular	Epithelial
Stiller (1907)	—	Hypertonic	Atonic
Sigaud (1908)	Digestive	Muscular	Respiratory-cerebral
Bean (1912)	Hypo-entomorph	Meso-entomorph	Hyper-entomorph
Bryant (1915)	Herbivorous	Normal	Carnivorous
Mills (1917)	Hypersthenic	Sthenic	Asthenic
Viola (1919)	Macrosplanchnic	Normosplanchnic	Microsplanchnic
Kretschmer (1921)	Pyknic	Athletic	Leptosomatic
Bauer (1924)	Hypersthenic	Sthenic	Asthenic
Aschner (1924)	Broad	Normal	Slender
Bounak (1924)	Euryplastic	—	Stenoplastic
McAuliffe (1925)	Round	—	Flat
Stockard (1925)	Lateral	Intermediate	Linear
Draper (1925)	Gall bladder	—	Ulcer
Weidendreich (1926)	Eurysome	—	Leptosome
Pearl (1926)	Pyknic	Intermediate	Asthenic
Pende (1927)	Macrosplanchnic	Normosplanchnic	Microsplanchnic
Von Rohden (1928)	Endodermic	Mesodermic	Ectodermic
Boldrini	Brachytype	—	Longitype
Wiersma (1933)	Eurysomic	—	Leptosomic
Sheldon (1940)	Endomorph	Mesomorph	Ectomorph
Conrad (1941)	Pyknomorphy	Metromorphy	Leptomorphy
Burt (1947)	Pachysome	—	Leptosome
Martigny (1948)	Entoblastique	Mesoblastique	Ectoblastique
Hammond (1953)	Pachymorph	—	Leptomorph
Hammond (1957)	Eurysome	Mesosome	Leptosome
Rees and Eysenck (1945) and Rees (1950)	Eurymorph	Mesomorph	Leptomorph
Lindegard (1953)	Fat factor high	Muscle and sturdiness factors high	Length factor high
Parnell (1957)	Fat factor (F) dominant	Muscle factor (M) dominant	Linear factor (L) dominant

*Reproduced by permission from Eysenck, H. J., ed. 1960. *Handbook of Abnormal Psychology.* London, Pitman Medical Publishing Co., p. 348.

individual on a seven-point scale in each of three dimensions of physique (the relative visceral, muscular, and skeletal development) as shown by standardized photographs taken from three directions (Figure 6-7), and on each of three corresponding groups of temperamental characteristics. They reported high correlations (of the order of +0.8) between physique and temperamental characteristics: (1) predominantly *endomorphic* body build tending to be associated with *viscerotonic* characteristics (such as relaxation, love of physical comfort, and sociability); (2) predominantly *mesomorphic* body build with

somatotonic characteristics (assertiveness, energy, and competitiveness); and (3) predominantly *ectomorphic* body build tending to be found with *cerebrotonic* personality characteristics (restraint, love of privacy, and sensitivity). The main temperamental characteristics associated with Sheldon's three main somatotypes are listed in Table 6-3 and summarized in the following anonymous verses, which appeared some years ago.

Oh, I'm a little endomorph asittin' in the sun.
I dote on beer and skittles; and I like my bit of fun.
I'm just a trifle lardy, just a trifle fat,
I may be somewhat tardy, but I like to be like that.

Table 6–3. Sheldon's Scale for Temperament*

I VISCEROTONIA	II SOMATOTONIA	III CEREBROTONIA
1. Relaxation in posture and movement	1. Assertiveness of posture and movement	1. Restraint in posture and movement tightness
2. Love of physical comfort	2. Love of physical adventure	2. Physiological over-response
3. Slow reaction	3. The energetic characteristic	3. Overly fast reactions
4. Love of eating	4. Need and enjoyment of exercise	4. Love of privacy
5. Socialization of eating	5. Love of dominating, lust for power	5. Mental overintensity, hyperattentionality, apprehensiveness
6. Pleasure in digestion	6. Love of risk and chance	6. Secretiveness of feeling, emotional restraint
7. Love of polite ceremony	7. Bold directness of manner	7. Self-conscious motility of the eyes and face
8. Sociophilia	8. Physical courage for combat	8. Sociophobia
9. Indiscriminate amiability	9. Competitive aggressiveness	9. Inhibited social address
10. Greed for affection and approval	10. Psychological callousness	10. Resistance to habit and poor routinizing
11. Orientation to people	11. Claustrophobia	11. Agoraphobia
12. Evenness of emotional flow	12. Ruthlessness, freedom from squeamishness	12. Unpredictability of attitude
13. Tolerance	13. The unrestrained voice	13. Vocal restraint and general restraint of noise
14. Complacency	14. Spartan indifference to pain	14. Hypersensitivity to pain
15. Deep sleep	15. General noisiness	15. Poor sleep habits, chronic fatigue
16. The untempered characteristic	16. Overmaturity of appearance	16. Youthful intentness of manner and appearance
17. Smooth, easy communication of feeling, extraversion of viscerotonia	17. Horizontal mental cleavage, extraversion of somatotonia	17. Vertical mental cleavage, introversion
18. Relaxation and sociophilia under alcohol	18. Assertiveness and aggression under alcohol	18. Resistance to alcohol and to other depressant drugs
19. Need of people when troubled	19. Need of action when troubled	19. Need of solitude when troubled
20. Orientation toward childhood and family relationships	20. Orientation toward goals and activities of youth	20. Orientation toward later periods of life

*From Sheldon, W. H. Constitutional factors in personality. In *Personality and the Behavior Disorders,* Vol. 1, ed. by J. McV. Hunt. Copyright 1944. The Ronald Press Company, New York.

Oh, I'm a busy *mesomorph* encased in gorgeous muscle,
My thinking is a trifle short, I'm long on vim and hustle.
I'm a certified go-getter; I'm the boy who will succeed
(Minus reason even better) perspiration is my creed.

Oh, I'm a spectral *ectomorph*, full of ratiocination.
The mind's my happy hunting ground and I loathe participation.
Lonelier than any cloud, I'm always quite superior
To the mouthings of the motley crowd and grunts of the inferior.

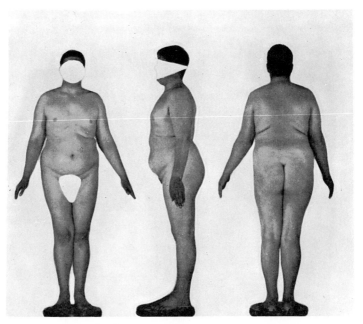

Predominant endomorphy (7-1-1).

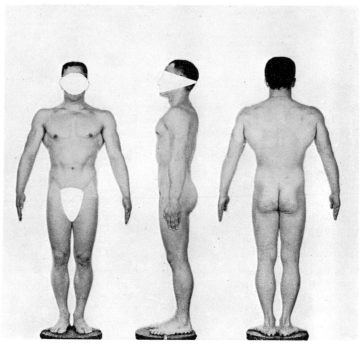

Predominant mesomorphy (1-7-1).

Figure 6–7. Reprinted by permission from Sheldon, W. H. 1954. ***Atlas of Men.*** Copyright 1954, Harper & Row, Publishers, Inc.

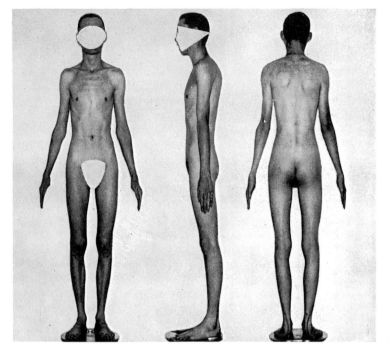

Predominant ectomorphy (1-1-7).

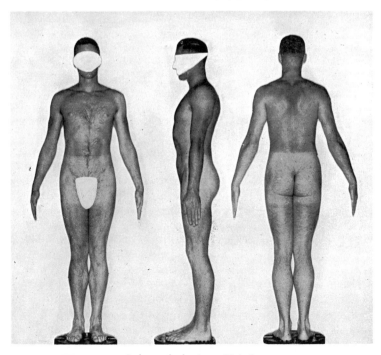

Balanced physique (4-4-4).

Figure 6–7. See legend on opposite page.

Some workers such as Parnell have deplored the subjective elements of Sheldon's photographic technique, and have relied more heavily on direct bodily measurements (physical anthropometry), either alone or in conjunction with photography. They have also made extensive use of factorial analysis of the bodily measurements so obtained. Regardless of the precise techniques adopted, nevertheless, three reported associations between body build and psychopathology show a considerable degree of consistency. The results of several studies appear to indicate statistical (*not* individual) associations between (1) predominant endomorphy and manic depressive psychosis: (2) predominant mesomorphy and delinquency; and (3) predominant ectomorphy and schizophrenia. In most studies, however, variables such as age have not been adequately controlled. Thus, samples of patients with manic depressive psychosis might show a relatively higher association with endomorphy than samples of patients with schizophrenia, because they are also apt to contain a higher proportion of older persons.

Lombroso (1911) studied morphological anomalies in criminals and postulated the presence of various physical stigmata as evidence of a degenerative constitutional basis for criminality. His data were not corroborated, but more recent studies suggested a statistical relationship between somatotype and delinquency. In an extensive study of 500 persistently delinquent boys and a group of 500 nondelinquents (matched by age, intelligence, racial origin, and residence in underprivileged neighborhoods), Glueck and Glueck found their delinquent group considerably more mesomorphic and less ectomorphic than their controls.

Even provided that the preceding associations are valid, the nature of ultimate causation still remains in doubt since (1) physique may influence behavior—either directly, or indirectly by modifying the experiences to which an individual is subjected; (2) behavior may influence physique—either directly, or indirectly by modifying some factor which acts directly on physique; or (3) both physique and behavior may be independently determined by some other determinant, such as hereditary endowment or experiences connected with membership in a certain family or socioeconomic group. Certain of these possible variations in relationship between physique and behavior have been elaborated by Anastasi.

In his book, *Hereditary Genius: An Inquiry into Its Laws and Consequences*, Francis Galton (1870) laid the foundations for the psychological study of individual differences in human abilities and behavior. Following his observations that men of genius tend to be above the average in height and weight, numerous other studies were reported, which sometimes asserted and sometimes denied the existence of a close correlation between bodily characteristics on the one hand and intelligence on the other. A large part of the evidence regarding a relationship between intelligence and physique was reviewed by Paterson, who concluded by quoting Pearson's comment on his own negative results in studying one aspect of this problem: "Much of science is the verification or refutation of impressions and opinions, and the mainly negative conclusions of this paper place at any rate on a sounder quantitative basis the view that even for the mass, and therefore much more for the individual, little can be judged as to intelligence from the more obvious anthropometric measurements."

Nevertheless, Pearson (1920) did demonstrate a weak but positive and significant relationship between intelligence and measurements of the size of the head (correlation coefficients varying between +0.097 and +0.139). In a subsequent investigation of mentally defective patients, Ashby and Stewart (1933, 1934) found a correlation between brain weight and mental age of +0.15, However, they pointed out that overall body weight was significantly correlated with mental age (r = +0.24) and was closely correlated with brain size, so that the association between brain weight and mental age might be attributed to mentally defective patients being generally smaller than members of the general population. Penrose added that all of the mean (bodily) measurements diminish slightly with IQ until the imbecile level is passed, below which there is a sharp fall. He also pointed out that mentally defective patients are much more susceptible to various forms of physical disability (both congenital and acquired after birth) than members of the general population, but that the reason for this finding remains in doubt. Reported relationships between intelligence, education, socioeconomic status, bodily illness, and psychopathology will be discussed further in subsequent chapters.

In the continuing search for correlations between bodily structure and psychopathology, Coppen studied a group of 41 male homosexuals whom he compared with 22 heterosexual neurotics and 53 control subjects selected by attendance at a clinic for mass radiography. The discriminate androgyny score, an index of relative "maleness" or "femaleness" of bodily development, was found to be significantly lower (more "female") in the homosexual group than in the control subjects. However, a similar deviation (in the "female" direction) was found for the group of heterosexual neurotics, and the homosexual group did not differ appreciably from the group of neurotic patients.

Doust studied a variety of morphological characteristics in a large sample of healthy adults and mixed psychiatric patients. He reported an excess among the patients of characteristics that he considered indicative of "morphological immaturity," and that relatively distinct patterns could be distinguished for each group of the psychiatric patients. He concluded that delayed or deviant biological maturation probably made a considerable contribution to the causation of "functional" mental disorders. Other evidence for this view was provided by a number of workers who studied the structure of the peripheral blood capillaries in patients displaying "functional" mental disorders, particularly schizophrenia. Numerous deviations from the normal numbers and structure of capillaries were reported, and cited as evidence of constitutional developmental defect, but Cobb and others pointed out that structural changes of this nature may well be determined by environmental situations or intercurrent disease.

SOMATIC FUNCTIONS (PHYSIOLOGY, METABOLISM, AND IMMUNOLOGY)

In the section concerned with biological stress, the concept of homeostasis was introduced, and it was pointed out that both life and normal brain function depend upon a considerable stability in the chemical constituents which go to make up the internal environment of the organism. It was also shown that relatively small or rapid changes in this internal environment may rapidly produce gross disturbances in intellectual functions and behavior. It is also reasonable to suppose, therefore, that minor deviations in the chemical function of various cells may be associated with differences in vulnerability or predisposition to the various forms of psychopathology. Indeed, in the absence of structural pathology, any hereditary determinants of behavior must be assumed to act through their effects upon biochemical equilibrium (whether or not such effects are currently being recognized). However, such changes in biochemical function might equally well result from a variety of environmental influences, prenatal or postnatal.

Roger Williams presented many examples of anatomical and biochemical variations between individuals, which

included differences in their requirements for various nutritional essentials.
He succeeded in breeding strains of
rats differing from each other in their
tendency to drink large amounts of
alcohol, and also reported differences
in the metabolism of human alcoholics
and nonalcoholic controls. On the basis
of these findings, he postulated that
"the uncontrolled craving for alcohol
in certain individuals is a nutritional
deficiency disease." However, it is by
no means certain that metabolic anomalies in established alcoholics have
in fact existed before the onset of their
alcoholism, or that any such anomalies
predispose to the development of alcoholism. While Williams and his associates drew attention to an interesting
line of investigation, they did not
demonstrate the significance of biochemical anomalies in the etiology of
alcoholism or any other "functional"
psychiatric disorder in humans.

Other workers have reported a wide
variety of deviations from normal metabolic function in various "functional"
psychiatric disorders, particularly the
schizophrenias. However, the extensive
investigations that have been carried out
along these lines have generally encountered serious difficulties such as the following: (1) Abnormal findings have not
been repeated consistently in similar
groups of patients (either by different
investigators or sometimes by the same
investigators at different times). (2) The
average (mean) observations on schizophrenic patients have tended to be very
similar to those of control groups, in
contrast to the variability or dispersion
(standard deviation), which tends to be
considerably wider. This applies to such
observations as blood circulation rate,
body temperature, basal metabolic
rate, blood chemistry, thyroid activity,
and excretion rate of adrenocortical
steroids. (3) Even consistent metabolic
findings do not necessarily indicate the
causation, since they may be genetically
controlled or due to various forms of
environmental biogenesis or psychogenesis.

It has been remarked that trying to
differentiate between psychiatric patients and normal persons by means of
various biochemical tests is comparable
to trying to distinguish between different makes or models of automobiles
by measuring gasoline consumption,
engine revolutions per minute, or speed
at a given moment of time. Many of the
positive metabolic findings reported in
"functional" psychiatric disorders have
been found to be due to idiosyncrasies
involving the nutritional intake, secondary to the behavior disturbance and
presence in a mental hospital.

In his introductory chapter to a
symposium of papers on *psychoendocrinology,* Reiss has remarked that "the
efforts of all the biochemists and en-
docrinologists who wanted to find a
cause for a psychopathological phenomenon are best likened to the
labors of the Danaids or of Sisyphus.
Labors and efforts, including the evaluation of the sometimes 'statistically significant' results, could have been saved
had all these workers not been the
victims of some serious misconceptions." He emphasized that no one-to-
one relationship has been established
between any form of psychiatric disturbance and some simple form of endocrine dysfunction. However, he went
on to state, "There is no doubt that the
ductless glands are the main regulators
of the biochemical equilibrium of the
organism, and the more we learn about
their physiology, the more we can see
how even the simplest metabolic functions are finally dependent on the
function of the endocrines, and how the
body equilibrium, which can ultimately
be defined as a tendency to maintain a
constancy in the chemical patterns of
blood and tissue, is dependent on the
cooperative effort of various ductless
glands. It is obvious that a decrease or
increase in the functions of a ductless
gland will have its repercussions on the
width and stability of the biochemical
equilibrium."

Reiss pointed out that Cannon's
theory concerning the body's regulation

toward emergency function (preparation for "fight or flight") involved only the regulation that was afforded by the adrenal medulla and the sympathetic nervous system. Selye's general adaptation syndrome, on the other hand, emphasizes the role of the interaction between the anterior lobe of the pituitary gland and the adrenal cortex. In fact, however, a large number of mechanisms could be described governing endocrine and biochemical adaptation to everyday life and its demands. Reiss concluded that it is more economical to investigate possible endocrine disturbances before studying special biochemical disturbances, the occurrence of which may be secondary to a primary disturbance in the total hormone equilibrium. He added, "At present, it does not appear very probable that special biochemical substances will ever be isolated which can, in spite of the existence of preformed personality patterns, produce specific disturbances of mentation and elucidate the pathogenesis of psychiatric disease entities."

In an extensive survey of interrelationships between endocrine secretions and patterns of overt behavioral response, Beach remarked, "It is impossible to overemphasize the importance of the fact that the effects of a given hormone upon behavior are not determined solely by its chemical constitution but may depend upon a variety of other factors ranging from the species, sex, and age of the animal, to the time of year the hormone is administered." Among the varieties of behavior most strongly influenced by hormones are tendencies toward dominance or submission (in relation to other animals of the same or different species), and the frequency and variety of sexual behavior. However, in a comprehensive study of sexual behavior of human beings and animals, Ford and Beach present considerable evidence that "in the course of evolution the extent to which gonadal hormones control sexual behavior has been progressively

relaxed, with the result that human behavior is relatively independent of this source of control." This question of physiological factors versus learned patterns of sexual behavior will be explored further in a later chapter concerning sexual deviation.

The function of the *autonomic nervous system* is of relevance to questions concerning both hormonal control and nervous system control of behavior. Extensive observations have been made on the neurophysiology of emotion and motivation (e.g., Ruch) and on somatic reactivity (e.g., Martin) that are beyond the scope of the present brief survey.

However, mention may be made of one index of central autonomic reactivity known as the Funkenstein test. This consists of the response in systolic blood pressure following intramuscular injection of 10 mg. of Mecholyl (acetylcholine). This response was recorded in a wide variety of psychiatric patients and normal individuals subjected to stress. On the whole, responses following injection of Mecholyl showed less convincing association with various diagnostic categories than with the clinical responses of patients to empirical treatment. More significant than either, however, appeared to be the associations between response to Mecholyl on the one hand and predominant moods of fear and anger on the other. Autonomic nervous system reactivity may be of particular relevance in the etiology of certain neuroses and sociopathic personality disorders.

A number of studies have indicated statistical associations between vulnerability to behavior disorders and *vulnerability to bodily illness or death*. Findings reported include the following: (1) unusually high frequencies of physical illness or death among patients with recognized behavior disorders; (2) diminished capacity of patients with certain forms of behavior disorder to develop the usual quantity of specific antibodies that confer immunity against reinfection; (3) an unusually high frequency of psychopathology among patients seeking treatment for bodily illnesses; (4) high frequencies of both bodily illness and psychopathology among certain groups of the population, for example, those of limited intelligence and socioeconomic status. To a number of authors it has appeared that the association existing between vulnerability to certain forms of psychopathology and inadequate resistance or immunity to bodily disease (noxious agents, deprivation, or stress) indicated a common constitutional predisposition. Once again, however, it may be pointed out that the reported associations may result from various causes.

Other associations that may be of relevance to the concept of constitutional predisposition include the relatively high frequency of *electroencephalographic abnormalities* in persons with certain forms of psychopathology (for example, excessive compulsive neuroses or antisocial behavior disorders); the increased frequencies of certain forms of psychopathology among individuals of limited *intelligence*; and associations between psychopathology and either *age or sex* of the patient—for example, a high frequency of neuroses and certain psychophysiologic disorders in the female, as contrasted with a high frequency of antisocial personality, alcoholism, and sexual deviation in the male. Such associations, however, may be variously interpreted, and we shall now turn to the evaluation of learning and other psychological factors in the etiology of psychiatric disorder.

SELECTED REFERENCES

Anastasi, A. 1958. *Differential Psychology.* 3rd edition. New York, The Macmillan Co., ch. 5 and 6.

Bakker, C. B., and Amini, F. B. 1961. Observations on the psychotomimetic effects of Sernyl. Comprehensive Psychiatry 2, 269-280.

Beach, F. A. 1948. *Hormones and Behavior.* New York, Hoeber Medical Division, Harper & Row, Publishers, Inc. Reprinted, 1961, by Cooper Square Publishers, Inc.

Berger, R. J., and Oswald, I. 1962. Effects of sleep deprivation on behaviour, subsequent sleep, and dreaming. Journal of Mental Science *108,* 457-465.

Bliss, E. L., ed. 1962. *Roots of Behavior.* New York, Hoeber Medical Division, Harper & Row, Publishers, Inc., ch. 7-15.

Brauchi, J. P., and West, J. J. 1959. Sleep deprivation. Journal of the American Medical Association *171,* 11-14.

Cohen, B. D., Luby, E. D., Rosenbaum, G., and Gottlieb, J. S. 1960. Combined Sernyl and sensory deprivation. Comprehensive Psychiatry *1,* 345-348.

Cohen, S. 1965. *The Beyond Within: The LSD Story.* New York, Atheneum Press.

Coppen, A. J. 1959. Body-build of male homosexuals. British Medical Journal *2,* 1443-1445.

Doust, J. W. L. 1952. Psychiatric aspects of somatic immunity. British Journal of Social Medicine *6,* 39-67.

Doust, J. W. L., 1952. Dysplastic growth differentials in patients with psychiatric disorders. British Journal of Social Medicine *6,* 169-177.

Fischer, R. 1954. Factors involved in drug-produced model psychoses. Experientia *10,* 435-436.

Fischer, R. 1966. Time contraction and psychomotor performance produced by psilocybin. Nature *209,* 433-434.

Fischer, R. 1966. The realities of hallucinogenic drugs: a compendium. Criminologica *4,* 2-15.

Ford, C. S., and Beach, F. A. 1951. *Patterns of Sexual Behavior.* New York, Hoeber Medical Division, Harper & Row, Publishers, Inc.

Fowlie, H. C. 1962. The physique of female psychiatric patients. Journal of Mental Science *108,* 594-603.

Galdston, I., ed. 1954. *Beyond the Germ Theory,* New York Academy of Medicine, Health Education Council.

Gellhorn, E., and Loofbourrow, G. N. 1963. *Emotions and Emotional Disorders: A Neurophysiological Study.* New York, Hoeber Medical Division, Harper & Row, Publishers, Inc.

Glueck, S., and Glueck, E. 1956. *Physique and Delinquency.* New York, Harper & Bros.

Gregory, I. 1955. The role of nicotinic acid (niacin) in mental health and disease. Journal of Mental Science *101,* 85-109.

Gulevich, G., Dement, W., and Johnson, L. 1966. Psychiatric and EEG observations on a case of prolonged (264 hours) wakefulness. Archives of General Psychiatry *15,* 29-35.

Harlow, H. F., and Woolsey, C. N., eds. 1958. *Biological and Biochemical Bases of Behavior.* Madison, University of Wisconsin Press.

Hoch, P. H. 1957. The problem of schizophrenia in the light of experimental psychiatry. In *Experimental Psychopathology,* ed. P. H. Hoch and J. Zubin. New York, Grune & Stratton, Inc., p. 206.

Hollister, L. E., and Sjoberg, B. M. 1964. Clinical

syndromes and biochemical alterations following mescaline, lysergic acid diethylamide, psilocybin and a combination of the three psychotomimetic drugs. Comprehensive Psychiatry 5, 170-178.

Katz, S. 1953. My twelve hours as a madman. Macleans Magazine, October 1, p. 9.

Keys, A. 1952. Experimental induction of psychoneuroses by starvation. In *The Biology of Mental Health and Disease*. New York, Hoeber Medical Division, Harper & Row, Publishers, Inc., ch. 30.

Kleitmann, N. 1939. *Sleep and Wakefulness as Alternating Phases in the Cycle of Existence*. Chicago, University of Chicago Press.

Koranyi, E. K., and Lehmann, H. E. 1960. On experimental sleep deprivation in psychotic patients. Archives of General Psychiatry 2, 534-544.

Kretschmer, E. 1925. *Physique and Character* (tr. W. J. H. Sprott from *Korperbau und Charakter*, 2nd edition). New York, Harcourt, Brace & World, Inc.

Luby, E. D., Grissell, J. L., Frohman, C. E., Lees, H. Cohen, B. D., and Gottlieb, J. S. 1962. Biochemical, psychological and behavioral responses to sleep deprivation. Annals of the New York Academy of Sciences 96, 71-78.

McFarland, R. A. 1952. Anoxia: its effects on the physiology and biochemistry of the brain and on behavior. In *The Biology of Mental Health and Disease*. New York, Hoeber Medical Division, Harper & Row, Publishers, Inc., ch. 22.

Martin, I. 1960. Somatic reactivity. In *Handbook of Abnormal Psychology*, ed. H. J. Eysenck. New York, Basic Books, Inc., ch. 11.

Osmond, H., and Smythies, J. 1952. Schizophrenia: a new approach. Journal of Mental Science 98, 309-315.

Oswald, I. 1962. *Sleeping and Waking: Physiology and Psychology*. Amsterdam, Elsevier Publishing Company.

Parnell, R. W. 1958. *Behaviour and Physique*. London, Edward Arnold and Co.

Paterson, D. G. 1930. Intelligence and physique, reprinted in *Studies in Individual Differences*, ed. J. J. Jenkins and D. G. Paterson. 1961. New York, Appleton-Century-Crofts, Inc., pp. 291-318.

Penrose, L. S. 1962. *The Biology of Mental Defect*, 2nd edition. New York, Grune & Stratton, Inc., pp. 35-40.

Pollard, J. C., Bakker, C., Uhr, L., and Feuerfiele, D. F. 1960. Controlled sensory in-put: a note on the technic of drug evaluation with a preliminary report on a comparative study of Sernyl, psilocybin and LSD-25. Comprehensive Psychiatry 1, 377-380.

Rees, L. 1960. Constitutional factors and abnormal behaviour. In *Handbook of Abnormal Psychology*, ed. H. J. Eysenck. New York, Basic Books, Inc., ch. 9.

Reiss, M., ed. 1958, *Psychoendocrinology*. New York, Grune & Stratton, Inc., ch. 1.

Rinkel, M., and Denber, H. C. B., eds. 1958. *Chemical Concepts of Psychosis*. New York, McDowell, Obolensky.

Roessler, R., and Greenfield, N. S., ed. 1962. *Physiological Correlates of Psychological Disorder*. Madison, University of Wisconsin Press.

Rome, H. 1959. Mushrooms, folklore, and experimental psychoses. In *Scientific Papers and Discussions*, ed. J. S. Gottlieb and G. Tourney. Washington, D. C., American Psychiatric Association, District Branches Publication No. 1, pp. 188-201.

Ruch, T. C. 1961. Neurophysiology of emotion and motivation. In *Medical Physiology and Biophysics*, 18th edition. Ed. T. C. Ruch and J. F. Fulton. Philadelphia, W. B. Saunders Co., ch. 22.

Selye, H. 1946. General adaptation syndrome and diseases of adaptation. Journal of Clinical Endocrinology 6, 117-230.

Selye, H. 1956. *The Stress of Life*. New York, McGraw-Hill Book Co., Inc.

Sheldon, W. H. 1954. *Atlas of Men*. New York, Harper & Row, Publishers, Inc.

Sourkes, T. L. 1963. *Biochemistry of Mental Disease*. New York, Hoeber Medical Division, Harper & Row, Publishers, Inc.

Trouton, D., and Eysenck, H. J. 1960. The effects of drugs on behaviour. In *Handbook of Abnormal Psychology*, ed. H. J. Eysenck. New York, Basic Books, Inc., ch. 17.

Tyler, P. B. 1955. Psychological changes during experimental sleep deprivation. Diseases of the Nervous System 16, 293-299.

Unger, S. M. 1963. Mescaline, LSD, psilocybin and personality change: a review. Psychiatry 26, 111-125.

West, L. J., and Greenblatt, M., eds. 1960. *Explorations in the Physiology of Emotions*. Washington, D.C. American Psychiatric Research Report No. 12.

West, L. J., Janszen, H. H., Lester, B. K., and Cornelison, F. S., Jr. 1962. The psychosis of sleep deprivation. Annals of the New York Academy of Sciences 96, 66-70.

Williams, R. J. 1953. *Free and Unequal*. Austin, University of Texas Press.

Williams, R. J. 1956. *Biochemical Individuality*. New York, John Wiley & Sons, Inc.

Windle, W. F. 1952. Anoxia; its effect on structure of the brain. In *The Biology of Mental Health and Disease*. New York, Hoeber Medical Division, Harper & Row, Publishers, Inc., ch. 23.

Woollam, D. H. M., and Millen, J. W. 1956. Role of vitamins in embryonic development. British Medical Journal 1, 1262-1265.

Wortis, J., ed. 1960. *Recent Advances in Biological Psychiatry*. New York, Grune & Stratton, Inc.

CHAPTER 7

Psychological Factors in Etiology

PRINCIPLES OF LEARNING

In Chapter 2 we considered psychiatric symptoms within the framework of topics relevant to psychology, and pointed to some relationships which exist between perception, cognition, emotion, motivation, and behavior. Preliminary mention was made of situations that generally lead to the appearance of dysphoric emotions, particularly danger, loss, and frustration. In Chapter 3, we focused on unconscious dynamic forces and mechanisms of adaptation, psychoanalytic concepts of personality development, and the interpersonal communication of affect and role-expectation.

The extent to which all of these processes are influenced by learning may differ from one individual to another. Most psychiatrists and psychologists, however, are of the opinion that maladaptive learning is crucial in determining predisposition, precipitation, and perpetuation of many forms of psychopathology—particularly neuroses, psychophysiological disorders, delinquency and sociopathic personality, sexual deviations, and addictions; but probably also the major affective and schizophrenic psychoses, and many of the behavioral manifestations that accompany mental retardation and organic brain syndromes.

Learning is of critical importance not

only in respect to the development of psychopathology, but also in determining the nature and extent of behavioral modification occurring as a result of the psychosocial therapies that will be discussed in Chapter 11. Failure to respond to psychotherapy, however, does *not* prove that learning was unimportant in the etiology of the disorder, since we know that certain forms of learning result in relatively fixed and permanent patterns of behavior. An analogy may also be drawn with the somatic pathology resulting from severe avitaminosis, which may fail to improve in spite of administration of large doses of the vitamin whose deficiency caused the lesion to develop.

Man's behavior is more dependent upon learning than is the behavior of lower animals, and there are aspects of learning and forgetting that can be studied only in the human organism. However, the types of learning most significant in the development of personality and psychopathology may also be studied experimentally in animals, and this chapter will therefore include a number of illustrations based on such animal studies. Before proceeding to outline the main processes involved in learning, however, it is necessary to clarify what is meant by this term.

Learning may be defined as any relatively permanent change in behavior that results from past experience. Not all learning involves improvement in behavior, and in fact some learning may be undesirable in its consequences. Moreover, some changes in behavior that take place with repetition are not the result of learning but of growth, fatigue, or physical damage. Hilgard therefore offered the following more comprehensive definition: "Learning is the process by which an activity originates or is changed through reacting to an encountered situation, provided that the characteristics of the change in activity cannot be explained on the basis of native response tendency, maturation, or temporary states of the organism (e.g., fatigue, drugs, etc.)."

One factor common to many situations in which learning takes place is *association*, which involves some connection in time and place between two events. The fact of association became the basis of a school of British philosophy in the seventeenth century, by virtue of being regarded as the sole mental operation except for sensation. The associationists continued to hold this view until the latter part of the nineteenth century, and attempted to formulate laws regarding the conditions under which ideas were learned by association. While association is a basic process in learning, however, *motivation* is often an important prerequisite for learning to take place or for the practical application of previous learning to the solution of new problems.

In the present section, we shall outline several of the major varieties of learning, including classical conditioning, instrumental learning, escape and avoidance learning, perceptual learning, and imitation. In succeeding sections, we shall consider frustration and conflict, and other forms of precipitating and predisposing psychological stress and deprivation.

CLASSICAL OR RESPONDENT CONDITIONING

Classical conditioning refers to the type of learning studied in the classical experiments of the Russian physiologist Ivan P. Pavlov (1849-1936). The process is sometimes known as respondent conditioning, because it involves a simple reflex or response to specific stimulus, which is paired with a hitherto neutral stimulus during the process of conditioning. Pavlov worked with dogs and measured their salivary secretion in response to various stimuli, but subsequent workers have used other species including man, and other forms of response to stimulation.

If a hungry animal is presented with food it will salivate. In this situation, food represents an *unconditioned stimulus* (UCS) and salivary secretion represents the corresponding *unconditioned response* (UCR). If now the presentation of food is accompanied by the presentation of some hitherto neutral stimulus (for example the sound of a tuning fork), the latter becomes a *conditioned stimulus* (CS) capable of eliciting a *conditioned response* (CR, in this case salivation) when presented in the absence of the unconditioned stimulus, i.e., without the concurrent presentation of food. (See Figure 7-1.)

The appearance of a conditioned response takes place through *reinforcement* of the conditioned stimulus, by pairing it with the unconditioned stimulus or reward (i.e., food). When the conditioned stimulus is presented alone, without the unconditioned stimulus or reward, the conditioned response is *nonreinforced*. When there is repeated presentation of the conditioned stimulus with nonreinforcement, the conditioned response will then tend to diminish in strength or to disappear completely through the process of *extinction*. Complete extinction does not mean that a

response has been permanently eliminated or unlearned, however. If the animal is subsequently returned to the laboratory after a period of rest, without any further reinforcement, the conditioned response is usually found to have reappeared (with diminished strength) through *spontaneous recovery*. Moreover, it will tend once more to attain maximal strength with less reinforcement of the conditioned stimulus than was necessary in the original process of conditioning.

Classical conditioning is a process of *stimulus substitution*, in which a previously neutral stimulus acquires the power to evoke a response originally evoked only by some other specific stimulus. At first, however, there is a strong inclination to *stimulus-generalization*, so that a dog conditioned to salivate at the sound of a tuning fork may also salivate at the sound of a buzzer or bell, or almost any other noise that is made in the laboratory. The more similar the new stimulus is to the conditioned stimulus, the greater the tendency for the conditioned response

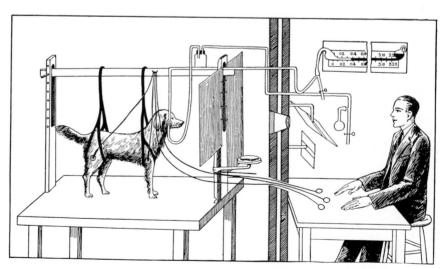

Figure 7–1. Studying the conditioned reflexes of salivation. The dog and experimenter are in separate rooms. In front of the experimenter's hands are the controls for the conditioned stimulus (CS) which is tactile (note the attachments on the dog's shoulder and thigh) and the unconditioned stimulus (UCS), the food (the food dish swings around within the dog's reach). A tube attached to the dog's cheek by cement leads to the manometer *(upper right),* by which the amount of salivary secretion is measured. (From Pavlov, I. P. 1928. *Lectures on Conditioned Reflexes,* tr. W. H. Gantt. New York, International Publishers, p. 270.)

to occur in the absence of reinforcement. If, however, all stimuli with the exception of the specific conditioned stimulus go unreinforced, the animal will learn perceptual *discrimination*, and the conditioned response will be elicited only by the appropriate conditioned stimulus, such as the sound of a tuning fork with a specific frequency or tone.

Each of the situations previously outlined involves *primary reinforcement* of the conditioned stimulus with the specific unconditioned stimulus (i.e., food). Pavlov also found, however, that a conditioned stimulus (i.e., the signal alone, without food) would serve effectively as a form of *secondary reinforcement* for another different conditioned stimulus to produce the desired response. The strength of the latter response tends to be less than that of the original conditioned response, since secondary reinforcement is accompanied by gradual extinction of the response (which is no longer paired with the primary reinforcer). Pavlov was able to carry this higher-order conditioning one step further, and obtained weak responses to a third-order stimulus, but this was the limit of the process, because of extinction of the lower-order stimuli.

In much of the literature on classical conditioning, both the unconditioned and conditioned stimuli have been presented through the *exteroceptive* organs of sensation such as the eyes and ears. Nevertheless, a considerable body of Russian literature has accumulated concerning experiments on *interoceptive conditioning*, involving internal bodily perceptions and responses in both animal and human subjects. Razran reviewed a number of these experiments and pointed out that interoceptive conditioning is readily attainable, and is by its very nature largely unconscious in character. It is somewhat slower in formation than is exteroceptive conditioning, but is more fixed and irreversible, i.e., less readily extinguished. It appears probable that early conditioning of this nature has considerable

significance as regards the etiology of psychophysiologic disorders in humans. Without denying or minimizing the role of perceptual and adjustive factors in higher and more complex levels of learning, Razran has suggested that simple unconscious interoceptive learning should be accorded the status of a prime model of all learning, with subsidiary principles being sought in the case of more complex forms of learning only when this basic model had proved inadequate.

INSTRUMENTAL OR OPERANT LEARNING

In classical conditioning, reinforcement is paired with a stimulus that is capable of producing an automatic response. In instrumental conditioning on the other hand *reinforcement follows, and is contingent upon, a given behavioral response being made*, often by trial and error on the part of the subject. One of the first attempts to study the changes in behavior brought about by its consequences was reported by Edward Lee Thorndike in 1898. He placed a hungry cat in a box from which it could escape by unlatching the door, and thereby get access to food outside the box. At first the animal exhibited various kinds of agitated behavior, and considerable time elapsed before it opened the door by accident. However, on being placed in the box repeatedly, the behavior leading to its escape tended to occur at increasingly short intervals, until eventually it could leave the cage immediately. Thorndike used the term "*The Law of Effect*" to describe this learning of behavioral responses from their consequences. It subsequently became known as instrumental learning, inasmuch as the behavior is instrumental in generating reinforcing consequences or alternatively as operant learning, since the behavior operates on the environment to attain a desirable result.

In order to measure the strength or quantitative aspects of operant learning, B. F. Skinner designated a darkened, sound-resistant box in which hungry rats are able to obtain a pellet of food by pressing a lever. The lever is connected with a recording system that produces a graphic tracing of the number of lever pressings, plotted against the length of time that the rat is in the box. The strength of learning under various conditions may then be shown by the rate of response (lever pressing) during reinforcement, and by both the rate of response and total number of responses occurring during nonreinforcement and extinction.

These experiments with rats have been supplemented by many further studies of pigeons and other organisms trained to perform a variety of behavioral responses. These instrumental learning situations differ from classical conditioning in two general ways: (1) that the conditioned response (e.g., lever pressing) is different from the unconditioned response (e.g., eating), and (2) that reinforcement is controlled by the behaving organism rather than by the experimenter. Instrumental learning appears more relevant to the study of human behavior than does classical conditioning, but there are many similarities between the two processes, including the general laws of reinforcement, extinction, spontaneous recovery, generalization, and discrimination that have already been outlined.

The principle of reinforcement is conveyed in the statement that reinforcement is necessary for the formation or maintenance of a conditioned response. Without reinforcement, the desired response either is not formed or is extinguished. It is appropriate however to distinguish between *positive reinforcement* through the *presentation* of desirable factors (for example, food, water, or sexual contact); and *negative reinforcement* resulting from the *removal* of unpleasant factors (such as loud noise, a very bright light, extreme cold or heat, or painful electric shock). The latter unpleasant factors are termed negative reinforcers, because their withdrawal does in fact strengthen the probability of the desired response.

This negative reinforcement should consequently be distinguished from *punishment*, which consists of either the *presentation of a negative reinforcer*, or the *removal of a positive*, and will be considered in the following section concerning escape and avoidance learning.

Extinction requires that responses be made in the absence of reinforcement, and is generally a more effective way of reducing or eliminating such responses than either punishment or forgetting. In *forgetting*, the effect of conditioning wears off gradually as time passes, but no nonreinforced responses are elicited during this time. Extinction of a response may occur quite rapidly, whereas forgetting is apt to be a slow process, and Skinner reported sizeable extinction curves in pigeons, as long as six years (about half the life span of the pigeon) after the response had been reinforced. The effectiveness of extinction in eliminating a response may be further increased by *reinforcement of an incompatible response*, resulting in competitive or reciprocal *inhibition* of the response it is desired to eliminate.

As in the case of classical conditioning, the satisfaction of any primary physiological drive (e.g., for food, water, or sexual contact) for purposes of learning may be termed *primary reinforcement*, while the satisfaction of drives toward learned goals may be termed *secondary reinforcement*. Any stimulus or situation that can motivate the learning of association through being paired with a primary reinforcer may become a secondary reinforcer. A secondary reinforcement is positive when the reinforcement with which it is correlated is positive, and negative when the reinforcement is negative. A secondary or conditioned reinforcer may also provide *generalized reinforcement* (positive or negative), when it has been paired with more than one primary reinforcer. Skinner noted that several important generalized reinforcers arise when behavior is reinforced by other people. Thus, behavior is reinforced when it secures the *attention* of others, is reinforced more strongly when it obtains their *approval* and more strongly still when it results in manifestations of *affection*. Another example of the learned or secondary reinforcement that is generalized is the rewarding of behavior by *money*.

In instrumental learning, new behavior may be acquired through *differential reinforcement* by the method of *successive approximations*. This procedure involves the reinforcement of those elements of available responses that resemble the final form of the behavior it is desired to produce, while component responses having little or no similarity to this behavior are left unrewarded and hence extinguished. By gradually raising the requirements for reinforcement in the direction of the final form the behavior is to take, available responses can be *shaped* into patterns that did not previously exist in the repertory of the given organism. Throughout the time we are awake, we act upon the environment constantly, and many of the consequences of our actions are reinforcing. Skinner pointed out, however, that operant reinforcement does more than build a behavioral repertoire, in that it improves the efficiency of behavior and maintains behavior in strength long after acquisiton or efficiency has ceased to be of interest.

Partial or intermittent reinforcement consists of reinforcing a response some of the time, but not every time it occurs. This may be accomplished in a *fixed-ratio* schedule by reinforcement after a given number of responses have occurred, or in a *fixed-interval* schedule by reinforcement after a given period of time has elapsed, if a response has occurred in this time. Partial reinforcement is therefore a mixture of a conditioning process and an extinction process. Inasmuch as there is intermittent reinforcement, however, the subject continues to respond, and in fact there is greater resistance to extinction than if reinforcement has been given following each appropriate response.

Even greater resistance to extinction is likely to result from the *variable-ratio* and *variable-interval* schedules of reinforcement, in which either the number of unreinforced responses or the time interval between reinforced responses is permitted to vary around some average value. In everyday life, most social reinforcers are dispensed on *variable combined schedules*, in which both the number of unreinforced responses *and* the time intervals between the presentation of reinforcers are allowed to vary. Furthermore, such social reinforcement is likely to depend upon the frequency as well as the nature and magnitude of the response. If variable reinforcement is administered only when the subject is responding at a high rate, the outcome is likely to be a stable *high* rate of response; whereas variable reinforcement administered only when the subject is responding at a low rate results in stable *low* rates of response. Variable schedules of reinforcement therefore result in behavior sustained at the frequency at which it is maximally reinforced, and it is suspected that much maladaptive behavior is developed and perpetuated by the unwitting reinforcement of undesirable responses of high magnitude and frequency. Such behavior is therefore persistent, difficult to extinguish, and baffling for the agent (e.g., parents) who have been responsible for its origin and maintenance.

ESCAPE AND AVOIDANCE LEARNING, AND PUNISHMENT

As indicated previously, reinforcement involves pleasurable consequences that may be of two different varieties. Hitherto, we have considered classical conditioning and instrumental learning resulting from *positive* reinforcement, involving the addition of pleasant consequences such as food, water, or an opportunity for sexual contact. Learning may also result from the administration of *negative* reinforcers or aversive stimuli that are unpleasant, such as excessive noise, light, cold, heat, or electric shock. In the latter situation, reinforcement results from withdrawal of the negative reinforcer.

Escape learning involves learning how to get away from or to eliminate an unpleasant situation once the organism is in it. *Avoidance learning* involves learning to avoid or prevent the unpleasant situation before it occurs. Both these latter forms of learning appear to involve elements of classical conditioning and instrumental learning, and the learning of avoidance behavior is generally preceded by learning how to escape from the situation once it has arisen. The following is an experimental illustration of avoidance learning reported by Solomon and Wynne:

A dog was placed in a compartment that was divided in two by a low fence that the dog could easily jump over. Each side of the floor of the compartment consisted of an electric grid through which shock could be administered to the dog. In each training trial, a buzzer was turned on, and ten seconds later the side of the compartment the dog was in was electrified. If the dog jumped over the fence to the other side of the compartment within the warning ten second period, the buzzer was turned off and no shock was administered. If he failed to jump over the fence he received a shock that was continued until he did so. Since the jumping response was instrumental in terminating shock, this escape behavior was reinforced. The dog in this experiment went for a number of trials without getting any reinforcement from escape or avoidance. Relatively suddenly he began to learn escape behavior, and within a few more trials he was consistently avoiding any shock by jumping within the ten second warning period.

In analyzing the preceding learning experiment, it appears that there are three recognizable stages. The first involves the classical conditioning of a fear response to the buzzer, which is associated with unpleasant shock. Instrumental learning then involves rein-

forcement due to escape from the negative reinforcer, and finally avoidance of any further negative reinforcement.

Once such avoidance learning has taken place it is extremely resistant to extinction. In some experiments, dogs have been known to jump at the sound of the buzzer for thousands of trials after the shock was completely turned off. One reason for this may be that avoidance learning involves partial reinforcement through relief from fear. Moreover, the avoidance response keeps the subject away from the primary reinforcement so that there is no opportunity for the fear response to be extinguished. From a therapeutic point of view, however, the avoidance response *may* be extinguished by presenting the conditioned stimulus, in the absence of the negative reinforcer, while preventing escape or avoidance behavior from taking place. In the experimental situation just described, this would involve keeping the dog on the *same* side of the compartment while sounding the buzzer, but *not* administering electric shock.

Punishment may involve either the addition of a negative reinforcer or the removal of a positive one. While punishment may result in escape or avoidance learning and may produce *suppression* of an existing learned response, it does *not* lead to extinction of the latter (which results only from the absence of reinforcement). In general, punishment reduces or eliminates learned responses only temporarily, and does *not* diminish the total number of responses obtained during a subsequent program of extinction. When a response is strongly motivated and there is not an alternative response available, punishment is relatively ineffective in eliminating that response. In the case of child training, frequent or severe punishment by the parents has the added disadvantage that it tends to drive the child away from the potential sources of most positive reinforcement for socially acceptable and desired behavior.

What made punishment effective in the avoidance learning situation outlined previously may be summarized as follows: failure to make a response was punished, not some already established habit. The motivation to make any response at all was low, but a response for avoidance of the punishment was readily available. There was a definite cue, in this case the stimulus buzzer, that warned of an impending punishment; this punishment was consistently administered for failure to make the correct response. Finally, the punishment was a strong one.

It has been established that mild punishment may sometimes serve as a secondary *positive* reinforcer in the learning of new responses, and in maintaining them once they have been learned. Eroseyeva (1916) noticed that if a hungry dog were fed only after a mild electric shock to its leg, it would soon learn to welcome the experience as a preliminary to feeding. Slutskaya (1928) showed that human infants would manifest pleasurable interpretation of a previously resented needle-prick if it were followed repeatedly by feeding. Masserman demonstrated a similar association of pain with pleasure in cats, and gave a number of examples of this type of learning in humans, including that of the sexual masochist who first attains orgasm under circumstances of discomfort or pain, and subsequently continues to obtain sexual gratification by submitting himself to whipping or other painful experiences. Skinner pointed out that punishment may act as a generalized reinforcer since this type of attention may be preferable to being completely ignored. Such findings are of considerable relevance to Freud's hypothesis of the repetition-compulsion, whereby an individual repeatedly reenacts certain life situations, regardless of unpleasant emotions and consequences. It has also been postulated that some forms of accident-proneness involve the same type of learning.

Perceptual Learning. In both classical conditioning and instrumental learning (and hence also avoidance learning) what is learned initially is an association of a response with a stimulus. In each instance we have been concerned mainly with the acquisition, reinforcement, and extinction of the behavioral responses that are involved. However, a number of studies have also focused on perceptual learning, involving the ability to discriminate between different stimuli.

The process of classical conditioning is readily adapted to the study of perception in animals and their ability to discriminate between various stimuli of increasing similarity. At first there is a tendency to *stimulus-generalization*, so that a dog conditioned to salivate at the sound of a tuning fork may also salivate at the sound of a bell or almost any noise that is made in the room. If he is reinforced only at the sound of the buzzer, however, the conditioned response soon becomes specific to this stimulus, and he may also learn to *discriminate* between this conditioned stimulus and other tuning forks of slightly higher or lower pitch. If the task of discrimination is made too difficult, however, there may be a major and persistent change in emotionality and behavior that has been termed an experimental neurosis, an example of which will be given later in this chapter.

Instrumental learning, as well as classical conditioning, affords opportunities for study of the acquisition of perceptual discriminations. The reinforcement of operant behavior, such as pressing a lever to obtain a food reward, may be made contingent upon stimuli that are associated with one lever but not another. Discriminations may additionally be acquired spontaneously through curiosity, and only subsequently applied through selective reinforcement that involves the ability to make such discriminations. Learning may also be accomplished by reasoning and insight, but the basic processes here outlined appear to be of greater significance in the development of personality and maladaptive patterns of behavior. There are, however, certain aspects of learning through imitating others that we should consider briefly before turning to studies on psychological stress and deprivation.

Imitation. Dollard and Miller conceptualized imitation as a special case of instrumental learning in which the social cues serve as the discriminative stimuli, and the learner's responses are differentially rewarded or not rewarded according to whether they match or fail to match those made by the model. According to this view, novel responses would never suddenly emerge, but would always be the consequence of a relatively prolonged process of instrumental learning. Bandura and Walters, however, considered it doubtful that many of the responses exhibited by almost all members of our society would ever be acquired, if social training proceeded solely by the method of successive approximations. They presented considerable evidence that learning may occur through observation of the behavior of others, even when the observer does *not* reproduce the model's responses during acquisition and therefore receives no *direct* reinforcement. Since elicitation and maintenance of imitative behavior are highly dependent on the response consequences *to the model,* an adequate social-learning theory should also take account of the role of *vicarious reinforcement,* by which the behavior of an observer is modified on account of the reinforcement administered to the model.

The same authors pointed out that effective social learning requires both adequate generalization and sharp discriminations. Thus mild physical aggression expressed toward peers is frequently rewarded as a "sign of masculinity" in boys, but more intense responses of this kind are usually punished. Physical aggression toward parents or siblings, even when mild, is considered to be undesirable, and consequently goes unrewarded or may be punished. On the other hand, specific forms of physical aggression may be permitted, encouraged, and rewarded in certain social contexts. Highly aggressive boys have been found to have parents who strongly disapprove of aggression *in the home,* and who reprimand and punish them for it, but encourage and reward aggression *outside the home.* Similarly, prejudices toward minority groups, and the "scapegoating" of outgroup members, may also be looked upon as the outcome of discrimination learning in which hostile-aggressive attitudes and behavior toward members of these groups have long been observed and rewarded.

Social training is viewed largely as teaching a child to express aggressiveness, dependency, and other social responses only in certain ways. Social-learning concepts of personality development consequently *emphasize the continuity of behavioral responses within the individual,* and *differences between individuals* (which may result from biological, psychological, or sociocultural determinants). In this respect, these concepts differ from stage theories of personality development that emphasize variations within the individual over periods of time, and similarities among individuals at specified age periods. Psychoanalytic concepts of personality development have already been presented in Chapter 3. It should be noted, however, that analysts differ in respect to the emphasis they place upon universal stages in psychosexual development, or alternatively upon the differences between individuals at a particular stage, and the multiple determinants of these differences. It may further be noted that Freud was relatively more impressed with the role of biological factors in determining the universal stages of development, whereas neo-Freudian analysts have tended to emphasize individual differences attributable to social learning, psychological stress, and deprivation.

PRECIPITATING TRAUMA, STRESS, OR DEPRIVATION

The changes in behavior that are known as learning generally require some repetition of the reinforcing experiences. Similarly, maladaptive behavior of any duration is unlikely to follow a single isolated traumatic or stressful event, but rather arises from a traumatic situation that has adverse effects on the organism over a period of time, regardless of any attempts the organism may make to change the situation.

A number of authors have attempted to conceptualize the nature of psychological stress. Hinkle remarked that any change in the environment (internal or external) which requires that the organism make an adaptation in order to maintain its homeostasis creates a stress. It is evident that stress involves a change that is relative and may vary in nature, intensity, duration, and timing. Stress situations may be nonspecific (tending to produce similar difficulties in most of the individuals so exposed), or highly specific to the individual concerned. Among the many nonspecific situations that tend to provoke psychological stress, Hinkle cited the following: situations involving a choice of courses of action, none of them wholly satisfactory; situations of uncertainty, in which past experience does not suggest the next logical move; situations of prolonged frustration; situations of deprivation and losses concerned with cultural or social positions or values; and situations which produce excessive demands upon the individual.

Among the factors determining specificity of stress are the preexisting situation of the individual and the direction of change. A sudden moderate change for the worse in a previously good situation may be viewed as disastrous, as illustrated by the suicide of a wealthy man who undergoes sudden financial losses but still remains financially secure. On the other hand, a slight improvement in a very poor situation may be greeted with great optimism. It has often been remarked that one man's meat is another man's poison, and such situations as promotion at work or the arrival of a new baby may bring joy in one household and misery in another. Such observations, however, reflect individual differences or idiosyncrasies in vulnerability or predisposition, and we shall return to these in a later section of the present chapter.

In the present section, we are concerned more with the common denominators of psychological stress and deprivation that may result in dysphoric emotions and maladaptive behavior among many individuals. We shall first consider certain aspects of frustration and conflict, next review some animal studies on experimental neuroses, and then take up some human studies on sensory isolation and interpersonal deprivation.

FRUSTRATION AND CONFLICT

Three general categories of *frustration* have been distinguished as follows: (1) *environmental* obstacles that prevent the individual from attaining his goals, such as the obstacles that are generally imposed by parents during childhood; (2) *personal* frustration of motives toward learned goals that are unattainable because they are out of reach of the individual's abilities, as is frequently the case with respect to educational and occupational strivings during later childhood and adolescence; (3) *conflict* between motives, one of which cannot be satisfied without frustrating another.

The nature of motivational conflict

has been studied in experimental animals and humans, and three major types have been distinguished. (1) In *approach-approach* conflict, there are two positive goals both of which the individual finds attractive. When possible, the individual tends to solve this conflict by approaching first the one and then the other goal (unlike the donkey that is reputed to have starved to death between two bales of hay). Nevertheless, the approach-approach conflict may be much more difficult to solve when the two alternative choices are mutually exclusive, and may then result in indecisive or maladaptive behavior. (2) In the *avoidance-avoidance* conflict, the individual is caught between the devil and the deep blue sea, and tends to vacillate or if possible to withdraw from the situation. It has been hypothesized that the characteristic interpersonal aversiveness of the schizoid or preschizophrenic individual is a consequence of avoidance learning in just such a conflictual situation, particularly where the individual is forced into choosing one of the unpleasant alternatives ("the double-bind hypothesis"). (3) In the *approach-avoidance* conflict, the individual is simultaneously attracted and repelled by the same goal, since the latter involves both reward and punishment. When the reward is highly desired, and the punishment strongly feared, this type of conflict becomes extremely difficult to resolve and may lead to various manifestations of fear and neurotic behavior. Examples of *approach-avoidance* conflict include those between (a) the desire for social approval, and (b) the desire to express anger, or the desire for sexual gratification, or the desire for self-preservation in military combat.

The *consequences of frustration and conflict* may be described as emotional and behavioral. The main emotional response manifested in many of the experimental situations to be described is *fear*, related to anxiety or apprehension over future discomfort or punishment. The main behavioral responses corresponding with this emotion are vigilance, avoidance, and escape. In many human situations of frustration and conflict, however, the predominant emotional response is one of *anger* or hostility, and the associated behavior involves retaliation, aggression, fighting, or destruction. Attack is one of the most primitive and effective forms of defense but there are many situations in which aggressive behavior would be dangerous or inappropriate: dangerous because of social disapproval or retaliation, or inappropriate because the desired goal is irretrievably lost (as in the death of a loved person). In the latter situation, the most frequent emotion perceived is *sorrow* or depression, and the corresponding behavior involves inhibition and immobility. In defending himself against the pain of grief and guilt, however, the individual may occasionally show a paradoxical reaction of denial associated with inappropriate *joy* or euphoria with overactivity, as in the case of mania following loss of health or the death of a loved person.

In addition to the preceding emotional and behavioral responses, there are a number of other possible consequences of frustration and conflict. In the first place, the latter may serve as motivation for *learning* new techniques of adaptation, and a variety of behavioral responses may be tried until an effective technique is found by trail and error. Any response that is effective in diminishing frustration will be reinforced, and may readily become a habitual pattern of behavior, even in situations quite different from the one in which it first proved effective. A severely frustrated person or animal may show a *fixation* of response, associated with inability to learn further patterns of adaptation and hence an inappropriate rigidity of behavior. Maier demonstrated fixation of this nature in rats that were trained to discriminate between light and dark cards, and to jump through a hole behind which the dark card was displayed in order to obtain a food reward. The experimenter then began randomly rewarding jumps to either card 50 per cent of the time and after repeated frustration the animals developed a stereotyped habit of jumping to the same card all the time. In a number of the rats, their fixation became so rigid that they continued to jump to this same card even when the other side of the apparatus was removed altogether, and food was placed there in full sight of the animal. (See Fig. 7-2.)

Other characteristic responses of the individual to frustration and conflict include *regression* to primitive or earlier patterns of behavior, and the use of a number of intrapsychic defense mechanisms that have already been

Figure 7–2. Fixation caused by conflict. The rat was given an insoluble, conflict-producing problem. In this conflict, the rat developed the habit of jumping to the window on the right. Below, it jumps compulsively to that window, which is locked, while food in the left window is readily visible. (Reprinted from Maier, N. R. F., 1949. *Frustration.* By permission of The University of Michigan Press. New York, McGraw-Hill Book Co., Inc.)

outlined in Chapter 3. It should be emphasized, however, that some degree of frustration and conflict, psychological stress, or deprivation, is universal as well as necessary for the development of a normal tolerance for frustration and stress that is characteristic of the mature individual. Maladaptive emotional responses and behavior are likely to occur and persist under the following circumstances: (1) when frustration or stress is excessive; (2) when frustration and stress are perceived as excessive, only because they have not previously been experienced (i.e., in the presence of previous overgratification); and (3) when any maladaptive response is reinforced and hence perpetuated.

EXPERIMENTAL NEUROSES IN ANIMALS

One of Pavlov's students, Shenger-Krestovnikova, discovered in 1914 that serious and persistent aberrations of behavior can be induced in dogs by subjecting them to adaptational stresses beyond their integrative capacities. The experimenter was testing the ability of the dog to discriminate between increasingly small differences in shape between a circle and an ellipse. The dog was trained to salivate in expectation of a food reward each time it was shown a card marked with a circle, and was trained *not* to salivate when shown a card with an ellipse. No punishment was given if the dog failed to discriminate correctly between the circle and the ellipse. Gradually the axes of the ellipse were made increasingly similar so that it more closely resembled a circle. When the axes of the ellipse approached the ratio of 8:9, the dog could apparently no longer discriminate between this stimulus and the circle, and its whole behavior suddenly changed. Instead of standing quietly in the experimental apparatus waiting for the next signal to appear, it struggled and howled, salivated irregularly, and ceased feeding. Instead of coming readily to the experimental room, it now struggled to avoid the ordeal, and its performance on simpler tests (of which it had previously been capable) was now grossly impaired and disorganized. Even after a period of prolonged rest away from the experimental situation, the disturbance never completely disappeared, and the dog was restless and agitated when reintroduced to the experimental harness.

In the United States, considerable work on the experimental production of abnormal behavior in dogs was subsequently reported by Gantt and his associates, and a variety of other laboratory animals have been used in the study of conditioning and responses to experimental stress. Liddell and his associates selected sheep and goats, on the assumption that their behavior pattern was so simple that their responses would permit generalization to all mammals. In 1927, they were studying the effects of removing the thyroid gland on conditioned reflexes in sheep, and suddenly doubled the duration of their daily laboratory tests and the number of conditioned responses elicited. The control sheep that had *not* undergone thyroidectomy developed a state of chronic agitation that made it useless for further testing. There were continuous movements of head, limbs, and body, the breathing became rapid and irregular, the heart rate was high and variable, and there was frequent urination and defecation. The disturbed behavior persisted in the barn at night, and the animal vigorously resisted being led back to the laboratory. When approached in the pasture it would dash away from the rest of the flock, and its disturbed behavior remained unchanged after three years away from the laboratory.

If a sheep or a goat were given a warning signal followed immediately by a mild electric shock to the forelimb, it soon began to flex this leg on receiving the warning signal in anticipation of the shock to come. There was also a stimulus-generalization to the entire experimental situation. *In the absence of any kind of warning signal,* the animal remained in a state of alert vigilance, and its apprehension may be illustrated by its increase in respiration from about 40 per minute to as high as 135 per minute during a period of an hour. Prolonged *anticipation* of danger or unpleasant experiences may be much more stressful than the experiences themselves. The worst bridges may well be those we never cross. Similarly, the threat of punishment may be a much stronger deterrent to future behavior than punishment itself.

The emotional stress resulting from standing and waiting, however, may be greatly increased by giving the animal a *series of signals* that *are not reinforced* by the painful stimulus. *Uncertainty* regarding the future may be more stressful than an unpleasant experience that is certain, and inconsistent punishment may be more productive of fear and anxiety than consistent punishment.

Further stressful effects, resulting from *prolonged vigilance combined with the possibility of avoiding unpleasant stimulation by appropriate action,* are illustrated by some experiments that have been carried out on monkeys. Brady placed an experimental monkey and a control subject side by side in specially designed chairs that permitted considerable freedom of movement and access to food and water. During alternating periods of six hours they rested or were subjected to an experimental regimen. During the latter periods both monkeys received a mild electric shock on the foot every 20 seconds, unless the experimental monkey pressed a nearby switch at least once within each 20 second interval. The first time that this procedure was carried out, the experimental monkey died suddenly after 23 days with what appeared to be a stomach ulcer, which is known to be one of the consequences of various forms of stress (as described in the preceding chapter). In subsequent experiments, several of the other experimental monkeys died or were found at autopsy to have developed ulcers, whereas none of the control monkeys did so. Since the behavior of the experimental monkeys was characterized by vigilance, decision making, and avoidance action, these interesting findings were reported under the title "Ulcers in 'Executive' Monkeys" (Figure 7–3).

Masserman undertook an extensive program of experiments with cats, designed to produce a variety of neurotic symptoms associated with fear, such as vacillation and disorganized or maladaptive behavior (including addiction to alcohol). The role of *motivational conflict* in the production of an experimental neurosis was demon-

strated as follows. A cat was first trained by a flash of light or the sound of a bell to open a box and obtain a pellet of food; then it was trained to depress a switch to operate the feeding signals at will and obtain access to the food. If on several occasions the animal was now subjected to an unexpected air blast or electric shock at the moment it operated the switch, a conflict arose between the animal's desire for food and fear of experiencing an unpleasant stimulus. Under these circumstances the animal crouched, trembled, and breathed rapidly, had a rapid pulse and an elevated blood pressure, and showed all the manifestations that ordinarily follow an injection of epinephrine or a generalized stimulation

Figure 7–3. Reprinted by permission from Brady, J. V., et al. 1958. Avoidance behavior and the development of gastroduodenal ulcers. Journal of Experimental Analysis of Behavior 1, 70.

of the sympathetic nervous system. These manifestations increased if food signals were given, if the animal were forced toward the food box by a movable barrier, or if it were offered food pellets similar to those previously obtained from the food box. These aversions readily became even more generalized, and the animal tried to escape from the experimental cage and subsequently resisted returning to it. Its emotional and behavioral disturbance persisted even in comfortable and familiar surroundings.

Masserman drew an analogy between the motivational conflict and behavior that were observed in such experimental neuroses, and those often found in man in the so-called "acute war neuroses" ("shell shock" of World War I, or "combat fatigue" of World War II). In the latter situation it is certainly possible to recognize the conflict between fear of death and fear of social disapproval, but a number of other etiological factors may also be recognized, such as prolonged deprivation of sleep, excessive sensory stimulation or perceptual isolation (information overload or underload), and sometimes the loss of a love object. Furthermore, the manifestations of neuroses or psychoses precipitated in combat are not always those of acute fear or anxiety, nor of readily recognized defenses against such emotions, but may be more related to predisposing personality characteristics and experiences.

As a result of his extensive studies, Masserman formulated four major "biodynamic" principles of behavior:

1. Behavior is actuated by the physiological needs of the organism and is directed toward the satisfaction of those needs.

2. Behavior is contingent upon, and adapted to, the organism's interpretations of its total milieu based on its inherent developmental capacities and experiences.

3. Behavior patterns tend to become deviated or fragmented under stress, and when further impeded, to assume substitutive and symbolic forms.

4. When, in a given milieu, two or more motivations come into conflict in a sense that their accustomed consummatory patterns are partially or wholly incompatible, kinetic tension (anxiety) mounts and behavior becomes hesitant, vacillating, erratic, and seemingly maladaptive (i.e., neurotic), or excessively substitutive or symbolic (i.e., psychotic).

DEPRIVATION INVOLVING SENSORY ISOLATION

There are many substances and experiences that an organism needs to maintain life and health and to develop normally in body, intellectual function, emotional response, and social behavior. If any one of these needs remains unsatisfied for long, a state of *deprivation* develops that may motivate the animal to various forms of adaptive or maladaptive behavior. The deprivation of certain biological essentials such as vitamins, oxygen, and sleep has already been considered in the preceding chapter. The motivation for some of the experiments described in the present chapter was provided by deprivation of food, and deprivation of water or opportunity for sexual contact has also been used to provide motivation for experiments on learning. Of recent years, however, there has also been increasing interest in the study of other forms of deprivation—notably (1) the absence of normal perceptual stimuli, (2) the absence of opportunity for normal social interaction, and (3) the absence of intimate relationships characterized by affection.

During past centuries there were many situations in which human beings were voluntarily or compulsorily isolated from contact with any other human being for prolonged periods of time, and in some instances these isolation experiences were accompanied by overall reduction or extreme monotony in sensory input through the exteroceptive organs of sensation. Although such isolation is sometimes the result of preexisting psychopathology (as occurs in the schizoid individual who seeks prolonged solitude), it is important to recognize that normal individuals as well may develop psychopathology under conditions of isolation, and to distinguish between the effects of reduction in human contact and those of reduction in overall sensory stimulation.

Solitary confinement in a prison cell has been a frequent expression of man's inhumanity to man, and many have recognized its harmful effects upon personality and behavior. Early in this experience, the individual may attempt to compensate for the loss of human relationships by imagining that he has companions with whom he converses, plays, or fights. As time goes on he may become increasingly withdrawn into his inner world of fantasy, and may have great difficulty in reestablishing his contact with reality when he is removed from isolation. When placed with fellow prisoners after 18 months in solitary confinement, Christopher Burney was afraid to speak for fear that he would show himself to be insane. After several days of listening to others, however, he recaptured the usual criteria of sanity and could then permit himself to speak.

Living alone in the polar night, isolated in a small hut for weeks or months on end, is another experience that involves both absence of human contact and monotony in sensory stimulation. There are several detailed accounts of such experiences, among which those of Byrd and Ritter are outstanding. In his book *Alone*, Admiral Richard Byrd gave excerpts from his diary and analyzed his thoughts and behavior during four and one-half months of isolation in the Antarctic at latitude 80°, during the southern winter of 1934. His situation was complicated by the fact that after two months of isolation he was stricken by what was probably severe carbon monoxide poisoning which led to delirium, malnutrition, exhaustion, and despair of surviving the ordeal. However, his account of the first two months appears to illustrate first the consequences of the lack

of human relationships, and second the effects of reduced sensory input. After three weeks of isolation (April twenty-first), he wrote:*

The morning is the hardest time. It is hard enough any where for a man to begin the day's work in darkness; where I am it is doubly difficult. One may be a long time realizing it, but cold and darkness deplete the body gradually; the mind turns sluggish; and the nervous system slows up in its responses. This morning I had to admit to myself that I was *lonely*. Try as I may, I find I can't take my loneliness casually; it is too big. But I must not dwell on it. Otherwise I am undone.

The following day he wrote:

. . . I find that I crave light as a thirsting man craves water; and just the fact of having this lantern alive in the night hours makes an immense difference. I feel like a rich man.

During April he took walks during which his fantasy life would become more active.

. . . Yet, I could, with a little imagination, make every walk *seem* different. One day I would imagine that my path was the Esplanade, on the water side of Beacon Hill in Boston, where, in my mind's eye, I often walked with my wife. I would meet people I knew along the bank, and drink in the perfection of a Boston spring. There was no need for the path's ever becoming a rut. Like a rubber band, it could be stretched to suit my mood; and I could move it forward and backward in time and space, as when, in the midst of reading Yule's *Travels of Marco Polo*, I divided the path into stages of that miraculous journey, and in six days and eighteen miles wandered from Venice to China, seeing everything that Marco Polo saw. And on occasion the path led back down the eons, while I watched the slow pulsations of the Ice Age, which today grips the once semi-tropical Antarctic Continent even as it once gripped North America.

While he found such fantasy enjoyable it was also dangerous, in that he was so preoccupied on one occasion

*Reprinted by permission of G. P. Putnam's Sons from *Alone* by Richard E. Byrd. Copyright 1938 by Richard E. Byrd.

that he temporarily lost his way back to the hut. In May he developed an increasing awareness of reduced sensory stimulation.

The senses were isolated in soundless dark; so, for that matter, was the mind; but one was stayed, while the other possessed the flight of a falcon; and the free choice and opportunity of the one everlasting by emphasized the poverty of the other. . . .I find, too, that absence of conversation makes it harder for me to think in words. Sometimes, while walking, I talk to myself and listen to the words, but they sound hollow and unfamiliar. . . .I've been trying to analyze the effect of isolation on a man. As I said, it is difficult for me to put this into words. I can only feel the absence of certain things, the exaggeration of others. . . .The silence of this place is as real and solid as sound. . . .It seems to merge in and become part of the indescribable *evenness*, as do the cold and the dark and the relentless ticking of the clocks. . . .I'm getting absent-minded. Last night I put sugar in the soup, and tonight I plunked a spoonful of cornmeal mush on the table where the plate should have been. . . .Well, this is the one continent where no woman has ever set foot; I can't say that it is any better on that account. In fact, the stampede to the altar that took place after the return of my previous expedition would seem to offer strong corroboration of that. Of the forty-one men with me at Little America, thirty were bachelors. Several married the first girls they met in New Zealand; most of the rest got married immediately upon their return to the United States.

On the last day of May, disaster struck in the form of inhaled gases from a gasoline engine, and Byrd's heroic struggle for survival against these overwhelming odds during the next two and one-half months of Antarctic winter makes inspiring reading. Part of his strong motivation for survival may be found in the following brief passage.

At the end only two things really matter to a man, regardless of who he is; and they are the affection and understanding of his family. Anything and everything else he creates are insubstantial; they are ships given over to the mercy of the winds and tides of prejudice. But the family is an everlasting anchorage, a quiet harbor where a man's ships can be left to swing to the moorings of pride and loyalty.

Christiane Ritter was isolated in the Arctic for periods up to 16 days at a time and described a variety of perceptual and cognitive disturbances. She saw a monster, hallucinated her past as if in bright sunshine, became "at one" with the moon, and developed a compulsion to go out over the snow, but was saved by another person. There are also numerous accounts of abnormal perception, cognition, affect, and behavior among persons who have endured long periods of relative isolation at sea. From examining these records it appears that those individuals who survive in groups, even as small as two or three, are less apt to have signs of severe psychopathology, whereas those who survive singly almost invariably show evidence of psychosis. Unfortunately, however, the effects of isolation in such instances are usually compounded by serious physiological stresses, such as dehydration and sleep deprivation, so that it is impossible to distinguish between the effects of each.

From such examples as the preceding, Lilly concluded as follows:

(1) Published autobiographies are of necessity incomplete. Social taboos, discretion to one's self, suppression and repression of painful uncomfortable material, secondary elaboration, and rationalization severely limit the scope of the material available. (Interviews with two men, each of whom lived alone in the polar night, confirm this impression.)

(2) Despite these limitations, we find that persons in isolation experience many, if not all, of the symptoms of the mentally ill.

(3) In those who survive, the symptoms can be reversible. How easily reversible, we do not know. Most survivors report, after several weeks exposure to isolation, a new inner security and a new integration of themselves on a deep and basic level.

(4) The underlying mechanisms are obscure. It is obvious that inner factors in the mind tend to be projected outward, that some of the mind's activity which is usually reality-bound now becomes free to turn to

phantasy and ultimately to hallucination and delusion. It is as if the laws of thought are projected into the realm of the laws of inanimate matter and of the universe. The primary process tends to absorb more and more of the time and energy usually taken by the secondary process. Such experiences either lead to improved mental functioning or to destruction. Why one person takes the healthy path and another person the sick one is not yet clear.

Scientific interest in the consequences of isolation was awakened during the Korean War, in an attempt to find reasons for the success of communist techniques of indoctrination, "brain washing," and extorting false confessions. Lifton stated that whatever its setting, thought-reform consists of two basic elements: *confession*, the exposure and renunciation of past and present "evil"; and *reeducation*, the remaking of a man in the communist image. The techniques employed to achieve these ends, however, may be varied and complex as indicated in an analysis of the process by Farber et al.

These authors pointed to the production of debility, dependency, and dread by the combined effects of such factors as physical pain and injury, malnutrition, disease, sleep deprivation, isolation, and actual or implied threats as of death, of pain, of nonrepatriation, of deformity or permanent disability, of harm to loved ones at home, and of absolute inability to satisfy the demands of interrogators. Studies on the effects of sleep deprivation have been described in the preceding chapter, and during recent years there have also been a number of studies of sensory deprivation.

Heron, Bexton, and Hebb presented a preliminary report on the cognitive effects of a decreased variation in the sensory environment. In their experiments, college students were paid $20 a day to do nothing but remain lying down on a comfortable bed with their eyes, ears, and hands shielded to minimize the perception of their environment. (See Figure 7-4.) These conditions were relaxed only to permit the

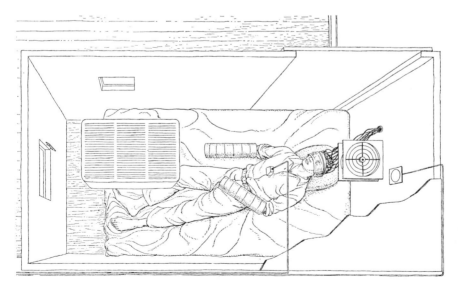

Figure 7–4. The subject in the isolation experiment (seen from above, with the ceiling cut away). Cuffs prevented somesthetic perception by the hands; the plastic shield over the eyes admitted light but prevented pattern vision. A foam-rubber U-shaped cushion covered the subject's ears; here it has been removed so that EEG tracings can be undertaken. The air conditioner is on the ceiling *(upper left)*, and just above the subject's chest is the microphone by which he could report his experiences. (From Heron, W. 1957. The pathology of boredom. Scientific American 196, 52 [Jan.]. Copyright 1957, Scientific American, Inc. All rights reserved.)

subject to eat or go to the toilet, but most subjects could endure them for only two or three days (the upper limit being six days), and then sought other jobs with less financial incentive. Subjects experienced marked boredom, and some did not remain long enough to permit the detection of cognitive changes. Others developed a significant decrease in their ability to solve problems, together with persistent and vivid visual imagery or hallucinations. In a subsequent report on changes in perceptual function after isolation, Doane et al. provided quantitative data concerning both visual and somesthetic sensory and perceptual processes. The findings following such sensory isolation included hallucinations of extreme vividness, impairment of thought processes, sensory and perceptual changes, together with changes in the electroencephalogram.

These findings were substantiated by other investigators who used different techniques for the reduction of sensory stimuli, and a number of such studies were presented in a book edited by Solomon et al. In this book, Lindsley compared common factors to be found under conditions of sensory deprivation, sensory overload, or sensory distortion (which may be accomplished by delayed auditory feedback).

PREDISPOSING PSYCHOLOGICAL STRESS AND DEPRIVATION

It is firmly established that the age of an organism and its degree of biological differentiation profoundly influence its response to various experiences of equivalent intensity. In general, the younger an organism when confronted with adaptational stress or deprivation, the more profound and generalized are the adverse consequences. Teratogenic agents applied during embryonic life produce severer effects in terms of death or gross generalized deformities

the sooner after conception the embryo is exposed to their adverse influence. Similarly, the homeostatic mechanisms of the young child are less well developed than those of the adult, so that infections and various stresses may produce much more severe consequences—for example, high fever, epileptiform seizures, or lifelong mental retardation.

Early postnatal behavioral experience is presumed to be of special importance for two general reasons. First, it appears that some consequences of such experience are particularly fixed or irreversible, regardless of subsequent experiences to which the organism is exposed. Second, the consequences of early experience appear to be more generalized and less specific than those of the same experience at a later age. The adult rat that receives electric shock while eating from a white dish learns to avoid white dishes but is otherwise much the same as before. The younger rat shocked in a roughly similar manner shows excessive emotionality in many situations.

In the present section, we shall first consider some animal studies concerning critical developmental periods for certain forms of learning, then review some of the possible consequences of childhood parental deprivation in humans, and finally examine some further aspects of childrearing practices and family influences on personality development.

CRITICAL DEVELOPMENTAL PERIODS FOR EARLY LEARNING

At the beginning of the present century, Craig noted that certain animals exhibited sexual fixations upon objects that were not appropriate species members. In order to be able to cross two species of wild pigeons, he found that the young of one species had to be reared with foster parents of the other species. Upon reaching adulthood, the birds that had been reared in this manner were found to prefer mates of the same species as their foster parents. Heinroth subsequently observed other interspecies sexual and social fixations. He reared several species of European birds by hand and found that filial and social responses became directed toward the human keeper rather than to members of the same species. Konrad Lorenz extended these experiments using geese, and applied the term *imprinting* to this process, since there appeared to be a rapid and lasting stamping in of the impression of the mother object on the young animal, resulting in the observed fixation. He noted that there seemed to be a *critical period* early in the life of the animal during which the experience must occur in order to develop such an attachment. In a series of extensive laboratory investigations, Eckhard Hess found that the critical period for imprinting in chicks and ducklings was in the first 32 hours after hatching, with maximum effectiveness lying between the thirteenth and sixteenth hours after hatching.

Evidence concerning the existence of critical periods for the formation of social bonds has also been provided for a variety of other species including fish, insects, and mammals. John Paul Scott undertook a detailed analysis of critical learning periods in the puppy, and found that a period of great change and sensitivity with regard to social relationships commenced at approximately three weeks of age. The puppy's experiences at this time were found to determine which animals and human beings would become his closest social relatives. Scott and Fuller therefore *defined a critical period as a special time in life when a small amount of experience will produce a great effect on later behavior.* They drew the analogy of pulling the trigger on a high power rifle, whereby a small amount of effort causes the bullet to travel at high speed and produce a smashing impact at a great distance. However, they also recognized that the *critical period is a relative*

rather than an absolute concept. "The difference between the amount of effort needed to produce the same effect at different periods determines just how critical the period is. In the case of the puppy, it looks as if a small amount of contact shortly after three weeks of age will produce a strong social relation, which can be duplicated only by hours or weeks of patient effort at later periods in life—if, indeed, it can be duplicated at all."

This development of social bonds does not appear to be dependent upon feeding or contact comfort. Whether rewarded, punished, or treated indifferently, the young animal of the proper age proceeds to form an emotional attachment to whatever is present in the environment at that time. Furthermore, it appears that organization *inhibits reorganization*, so that organization of function or behavior can be most strongly modified only when active processes of organization are proceeding.

Immature organisms of a variety of species have been exposed to a number of adverse experiences such as those involving unpleasant stimulation by electric shock or understimulation through isolation. Chimpanzees reared in darkness and in situations of restricted somesthetic perception provide evidence that normal adult perception is a function of early experience, and hence that any higher behavior depending upon perception is also dependent on the learning process of infancy.

Liddell found that the withdrawal of maternal care during a daily period of stressful training greatly affected the behavior of lambs and kids, and apparently increased their mortality (a finding previously reported in human infants). In his experiments, twin lambs and kids were subjected to 20 darkness signals of ten seconds each, followed by shock to the foreleg, and spaced two minutes apart. One lamb or kid was tested in a room with its mother present, and its twin was simultaneously tested alone in an adjoining room. At the end of the test, the lone lamb or kid rejoined its mother and twin. In each instance, the twin tested in the presence of the mother freely explored the room in the intervals between signals, and although the twin developed the usual anticipatory flexion of the forelimb prior to shock, it showed no adverse effects from the training procedure. The lone twin, on the other hand, showed progressive inhibition of movement and soon remained motionless, either standing or lying on the floor without even moving the head slightly when the lights were dimmed, and only rolling slightly at the shock. After training for a thousand signals, 20 each day, the animals were returned to the pasture. Both the lamb and kid trained in isolation died within a few months, whereas their twins given similar training in the presence of their mothers remained living and healthy two years later.

The preceding study indicates some potential hazards of repeated severe stress in the absence of the mother during early development. By contrast, Levine showed that both painful shocks and gentle handling may enhance the development of the normal stress responses in infant rats, whereas the absence of such treatment may lead to disordered physiology and behavior when the animal matures. The original experiment was repeated many times, subjecting infant rats to a variety of stresses and degrees of handling. Invariably, however, it was the non-manipulated "controls" that exhibited deviations of behavior in physiology when they were tested as adults. When adult rats were placed in unfamiliar surroundings, the nonmanipulated animals tended to cower in a corner or to creep cautiously about, frequently urinating or defecating, whereas animals that had been handled and subjected to stress in infancy explored their surroundings freely and showed no evidence of undue emotionality. The

impaired behavioral response of non-manipulated animals in strange situations corresponded with a diminished output of steroid hormones by the adrenal cortex (see Figure 7-5). It is not surprising, however, that subsequent experiments showed that both behavioral and physiological responses to stress are influenced by heredity, as well as by infantile experience.

In a series of fascinating experiments on monkeys, Harlow and his associates provided considerable evidence concerning relationships between early experiences and subsequent behavior. The early experiences of different groups of laboratory-reared monkeys were different from each other in several important respects, as follows.

Some infant monkeys were raised and nursed by their mothers, whereas others were separated from their mothers six to twelve hours after birth and suckled on tiny nursing bottles. Among the latter group, some were raised in isolation in a wire cage, whereas others were permitted to

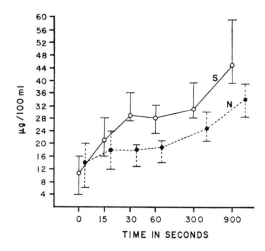

Figure 7–5. Circulating corticosteroids following electric shock in stimulated and non-stimulated rats. The zero time is the control value without shock. The circles represent the means of the groups; the bars indicate the range. (From Levine, S. 1962. Psychophysiological effects of infantile stimulation. In *Roots of Behavior*, ed. E. L. Bliss. New York, Hoeber Medical Division, Harper & Row, Publishers, p. 249.)

establish physical contact with and emotional dependence upon a cloth-covered substitute or "mother-surrogate." In all instances, the surrogate was preferred to a similar plain wire frame without the cloth covering. In an early report, Harlow and Zimmermann pointed out that the inanimate cloth mother surrogate could readily become an object loved with intensity and for a long period of time. They concluded that satisfactory body contact is an extremely strong affectional variable, and may well prove to be the most important affectional variable for primates. (See Figure 7-6.)

In an attempt to establish experimental neuroses in infant monkeys, various mother surrogates were constructed that subjected the monkey to unpleasant stimuli or experiences, but these were apparently ineffective in destroying the security and satisfaction obtained from clinging to the surrogate or in producing evidence of subsequent abnormal behavior.

Monkeys living with their own mothers and some of the monkeys reared with cloth surrogates were permitted interaction, in a controlled playpen or playroom situation, with other young monkeys of the same and of the opposite sex. An outstanding finding in both the playroom and playpen was that male and female infants showed differences in sex behavior from the second month of life onward, together with early differences in other forms of behavior. Young males demonstrated a much higher frequency of threatening behavior towards animals of both sexes, whereas young females demonstrated a much higher frequency of withdrawal and immobility. Young males initiated play contact with other animals much more frequently than did young females, while "rough-and-tumble" play was

Figure 7–6. Infant monkey clinging to cloth-covered mother surrogate. (Courtesy of Professor Harry F. Harlow.)

largely restricted to pairs of young males.

On reaching adult life, male and female monkeys reared in isolation, and also those reared on cloth surrogates *without* opportunity to interact with other infant monkeys, were totally unable to participate in normal sexual union with other mature monkeys. They also showed other behavioral abnormalities which included an absence of grooming responses with other monkeys, exaggerated aggression, and an absence of affectional interaction as measured by cooperation. With prolonged, patient education by sexually sophisticated male monkeys, some of the isolated females became sexually receptive, but none of the isolated males ever succeeded in mating with sexually sophisticated females. In spite of the fact that a number of isolated females were impregnated, however, they tended to make most unsatisfactory mothers (as illustrated in Figure 7-7). As Harlow remarked, "Month after month female monkeys that never knew a real mother themselves become mothers—helpless, hopeless, heartless mothers devoid, or almost devoid, of any maternal feeling."

The absence of opportunity for close interaction with other young monkeys appears to have profound implications for subsequent sexual, maternal, and social behavior. It is tempting to generalize from these findings to the etiology of similar behavior disorders in humans, particularly certain patients diagnosed as schizophrenic. An interesting biochemical study by Beckett et al. has suggested some further similarities between certain of Harlow's monkeys and human patients with schizophrenia. Biochemical tests were conducted blind on a total of 31 monkeys, which had been divided for purposes of analysis into four groups: 11 control animals reared in the wild, 10 surrogate animals that were reared in the laboratory with inanimate cloth-covered mother surrogates, four cage-shock animals reared in isolation but

Figure 7-7. Typical behavior of unmothered mother toward her infant. Mother is looking upward while crushing her baby against the cage floor. (Reproduced by permission from Harlow, H. F. 1962. The heterosexual affectional system in monkeys. American Psychologist *17*, 1–9.)

also experiencing electric shock conditioning in infancy, and six cage-non-shock animals reared in isolation in a bare cage. Both of the latter groups showed severe behavioral disturbances of the type described earlier, but the results of the experiment indicated that only the final group, reared in the environment with the least stimulation and the most tactile monotony, showed evidence of the same blood plasma factor that had been reported by this group in human schizophrenic patients. They recognized that these findings were extremely tentative, but they appear to offer further corroboration of the relationship between infantile experience and adult behavior and physiological function.

Fuller and Waller summarized *the unique features of early experience* in a three-component model, reproduced in

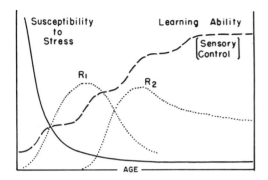

Figure 7-8. A diagram of a three-component model illustrating unique features of early experience. Susceptibility to stress is high in young animals and decreases sharply to a relatively constant level. The probability of eliciting response R_1 is high in young animals but low in older animals, which are more likely to give response R_2. As animals age, the probability of all responses (when no prior training has occurred) decreases gradually. Learning ability is represented as increasing progressively in stepwise fashion — and eventually reaching a constant level. (From Fuller, J. L., and Waller, M. B. 1962. Is early experience different? In *Roots of Behavior*, ed. E. L. Bliss. New York, Hoeber Medical Division, Harper & Row, Publishers, p. 243.)

Figure 7-8. The first factor involved is that the cells of young organisms are very sensitive to direct physical and chemical changes, and that they may be exposed to wide fluctuations in body chemistry because of imperfect functioning of homeostatic mechanisms. Second, there appears to be a gradual shift with age in the probability that any specified response will occur when an animal is confronted with a novel stimulus. The period of maximum response is the stage of playfulness in mammals. The third aspect of this model involves progressive changes in the possible complexity of stimulus control of behavior with advancing age. These authors remarked that the failure of experience-deprived animals to profit from delayed training is more likely to be caused by the fixation of incompatible responses than by an upper age limit for the development of learning.

PARENTAL DEPRIVATION IN HUMANS

In adults with psychopathology, Freud considered that we are often confronted with a chronic scar rather than with an acute bleeding wound. Throughout the present century, there have been extensive and intensive searches for the original traumata or the childhood roots of adult psychopathology. As mentioned previously, it is generally conceded that traumatic situations operative over long periods of time are more likely to have lasting adverse consequences than are isolated traumatic events. The problem still remains of identifying and measuring both the traumatic situations of childhood and their presumed consequences in adult life.

It has seemed to many investigators that permanent loss of a parent during childhood represents an objective event or situation that should be related to subsequent psychopathology, or at least to increased vulnerability to certain forms of psychopathology. Although he recognized that death of a patient is not a single isolated variable, Pollock still wrote the following: "The death of a parent in childhood is always a traumatic event affecting the development of the survivor's personality. The trauma is not only mediated through the separation, loss, and absence of the deceased parent, but also through contact with the surviving parent and family members who may themselves have mourning reactions that may alter their contact with the child."

Along similar lines, Brown et al. stated: "Our hypothesis is that a child can be sensitized by situations of loss of love and emotional deprivation, so that he breaks down in various ways in later life when faced with subsequent situations of loss and rejection." The alternative possibility that hardship and deprivation, including orphanhood, may lead to *increased* adaptability and creativity, with *diminished* vulnerability to adult psychopathology, has rarely been considered, although Goertzel and Goertzel provided some narrative evidence along these lines derived from studying the biographies of eminent men and women. Some tentative statistical support for the latter assumption was provided by a couple of studies of college students who had previously lost a parent, one of these studies being by the present author.

In this connection, it may be appropriate to relate an anecdote told by Hirsh about a psychiatrist and a behavioral scientist who were members of a wartime assessment panel. At one meeting, the psychiatrist presented an evaluation of a man who had lost both parents at an early age and who had been subjected to all the adversities that could be visited on a developing youngster. The psychiatrist's evaluation was that through hardship this man had developed excellent emotional stability, independence, and other such characteristics, and could surely be depended upon in a crisis. Several hours later the same psychiatrist reported on another man who had experienced practically the identical developmental history. He had lost both parents at an early age. He had been subjected to all the insecurities, buffetings, and adversities that could be visited by modern society on a developing youngster. Therefore, concluded the psychiatrist, this man is now very dependent, insecure, and emotionally unstable, so that he most certainly would *not* be dependable in a crisis. At this point, the behavioral scientist reminded the psychiatrist of the earlier case that had led to opposite conclusions, on the basis of identical background information. Patiently, and in an unruffled manner, the psychiatrist turned to the behavioral scientist and said, "Don't you know, young man, that the same fire that hardens steel melts butter?"

While Hirsh used the preceding illustration to emphasize the possible role of heredity in determining personality and behavior, it would be equally valid to maintain that *differences in previous social learning experiences* might result in different responses to parental loss as well as other forms of deprivation. Furthermore, the latter responses *may be greatly modified by subsequent social learning experiences* provided by the remaining parent and other members of society, one or more of whom may provide an effective substitute for the parent who has been lost.

In the light of these considerations, let us examine some of the data that have been provided regarding the possible significance of parental loss in early childhood upon subsequent behavior and upon manifestations of psychopathology. Many of these studies involve the *direct* impact of separation from parents upon the physical health and behavior of young children, from which inferences are then made about presumed psychopathology in adult life. Another large group of studies deals with *retrospective* reports on childhood parental loss among adolescents or older persons who have already demonstrated various forms of psychopathology. Very few studies involve longterm *anterospective* comparisons with respect to subsequent behavior among groups of individuals who have or have not been subjected to various forms of earlier parental deprivation.

The human infant is so dependent upon adults for his physical care that it is doubtful he can survive in total isolation from other human beings. There are a number of accounts of wolf-children and feral man, involving children who have been found living alone in the wild or in the company of wild animals whom they resemble in their behavior (e.g., see Singh and Zingg). When found by human beings, such children have been unable to speak, might still be walking on all fours, and have behaved like other animals. After prolonged and patient efforts at socialization, they have sometimes acquired language and other social skills, but their intellectual development has invariably remained retarded in comparison with other children of the same age. Among questions that have been raised about these feral children are (1) how long had they been living in the wild or with animals prior to being found by humans; (2) whether they may have been intellectually subnormal (mentally retarded) from conception or birth, and hence whether their retarded social development may have been largely attributable to biological factors including heredity.

Since a definitive answer to these questions is impossible, the study of feral children has contributed relatively little to our knowledge of normal and deviant socialization. Studies by Spitz and others, however, suggest that young children removed from the care of their parents, and exposed to the impersonal surroundings of some orphanages and other institutions, may have a much higher mortality than other children of the same age. Confounding factors in the latter studies include prior exposure to parents or siblings with communicable infectious disease, and also low socioeconomic status, since it is known that the latter is associated with high mortality at all ages but particularly during early childhood.

Direct studies of children separated from their parents, however, do indicate a high probability of a severe grief reaction, with social withdrawal and impaired appetite, that might well be expected to result in cachexia and increased vulnerability to intercurrent disease. Over a period of time, children who survive in such institutional settings have also manifested a high frequency of delinquent behavior and other personality characteristics similar to those of the adult sociopathic individual. It has *not* been conclusively established to what extent the grief reaction of childhood may sensitize the individual toward developing severe depression under provocation during adult life.

A number of early *retrospective studies* of delinquent adolescents indicated that a high proportion of these youngsters came from homes that were broken by death of a parent or by permanent separation. One of the best controlled studies in this area was reported by Glueck and Glueck, who compared 500 persistently delinquent boys with 500 nondelinquent boys, matched for age, intelligence, ethnic background, as well as residence in underprivileged neighborhoods. They found that the delinquents had experienced all varieties of parental loss during early childhood much more frequently than had the nondelinquent control group. However, one aspect of this study that has not received adequate recognition is that the permanent loss of *father* was much more frequent than the permanent loss of mother among these delinquent boys. Evidence from three other types of study suggest that it is the boy's relationship with his father that is most important in preventing delinquency, and one of these studies (by the present author) suggested that the same is true for the girl's relationship with her mother.

In his well-known monograph on maternal care and mental health John Bowlby undertook an extensive review of evidence concerning the effects of parental deprivation during childhood, but chose to emphasize the significance of the early relationship with the *mother* as follows:*

Evidence that the deprivation of mother-love in early childhood can have a far-reaching effect on the mental and personality development of human beings comes from many sources. It falls into three main classes:

(a) Studies, by direct observation, of the mental health and development of children in institutions, hospitals and foster-homes — direct studies.

(b) Studies which investigate the early histories of adolescents or adults who have

---

*Reprinted by permission from Bowlby, J. 1951. *Maternal Care and Mental Health.* World Health Organization Monograph Series No. 2, p. 15.

developed psychological illnesses—retrospective studies.

(c) Studies which follow up groups of children who have suffered deprivation in their early years with a view to determining their state of mental health—follow-up studies.

The extent to which these studies, undertaken by people of many nations, varied training and, as often as not, ignorant of each other's conclusions, confirm and support each other is impressive. What each individual piece of work lacks in thoroughness, scientific reliability or precision is largely made good by the concordance of the whole. Nothing in scientific method carries more weight than this. Divergent voices are few. Indeed, only three have come to light, all follow-up studies, but of a quality which bears no comparison with that of the research the conclusions of which they challenge.

The direct studies are the most numerous. They make it plain that when deprived of maternal care, the child's development is almost always retarded—physically, intellectually, and socially—and that symptoms of physical and mental illness may appear. Such evidence is disquieting, but skeptics may question whether the retardation is permanent and whether the symptoms of illness may not easily be overcome. The retrospective and follow-up studies make it clear that such optimism is not always justified and that some children are gravely damaged for life. This is a somber conclusion which must now be regarded as established.

Gardner discussed the consequences of prolonged or permanent parental separation, particularly absence of the *father*, upon (1) the child's developing *concept of self*—his sense of separateness, integrity, worth, and security as an individual; and (2) the child's *concept of human beings* that comprise his outer-world. The child may feel that he and his mother were abandoned because they were worthless, or alternatively, that mother abandoned father and hence may also abandon the child himself at a later date. He may also feel that human beings as a whole are not trustworthy, and that love relationships with other human beings are too hazardous because they may eventually lead to hatred and abandonment. Further problems may arise in the changed relationship with mother after the father has left the home. The child may come to be regarded as an economic burden (necessitating her going out to work), as a reminder of her deficiencies (her failure to retain her husband and home), and may be identified with all the bad and undesirable characteristics of the father. On the other hand, the mother may seek from the child the emotional satisfaction she could not obtain from her husband, overprotecting the child and smothering him with possessive demonstrations of affection which he is unable to reciprocate. Gardner remarked however that "despite repeated attempts at reassurance on the part of the parent who is to remain with him, he is rarely convinced that that parent alone has the power to supply all his needs—and, of course, this intuitive feeling of the child is essentially a correct one and is so proved in time." This is not to say that parental deprivation inevitably leads to psychiatric disorder, since adequate relationships may exist or be developed with other human beings important to the child. Such factors as broken homes, quarrels between parents, poverty, neglect, and malnutrition are significant only in their effects on the child's capacity to form relationships that influence his emotions and behavior.

In the event that a child loses one parent by death or divorce and the remaining parent remarries, the child may experience considerable insecurity and hostility toward the step-parent, who is a rival for the affection of the true parent. When children are born to this new union, the child of the former marriage is apt to feel increasingly alienated from both the true parent and the step-parent, and to develop hostility toward them as well as the new half-siblings. This feeling of alienation may be accentuated in the situation where the young child has lost his father, the mother has changed her name by remarriage, but the child has retained his former surname and grows up in a family whose members have a different name from his own. Even more severe difficulties confront the illegitimate child who grows up with his mother's maiden name, in spite of the fact that mother may subsequently marry and have children of another name. The latter situation, however, serves only to illustrate the lifelong rejection of this unwanted child, by the step-father who has failed to adopt him, and usually also by the mother to whom he is a continual reminder of her past mistakes, and hence to emphasize that it is these relationships themselves that are of significance.

The present author has published half a dozen studies, some retrospective and some anterospective, in the area of parental deprivation. From reviewing the extensive literature on this subject, the discrepancies in results reported appear to reflect difficulties in making controlled comparisons, particularly with respect to socioeconomic status and year of birth of the subjects. During the present century, mortality rates for both sexes (and hence for both parents) have been declining progressively, whereas the rates for parental divorce or permanent separation have been progressively increasing. Throughout this period of time, however, the highest rates of parental death and separation have been found among those having a low socio-economic status.

When controlled comparisons are made, it appears that the *separation* of parents is associated with a high frequency of *delinquency* among their offspring, and that *death* of a parent is also followed by a somewhat higher frequency of delinquency among the *offspring of the same sex as that parent*, although not as high as in the case of permanent parental separation. The role of the father in preventing delinquency among his sons is also substantiated by comparisons on quality of relationships existing in intact families

(Andry), and by transcultural studies (Bacon, Child, and Barry).

A number of reports have suggested an unduly high frequency of parental death (particularly of mother) during the childhood of adults who demonstrate schizophrenic reactions, but this finding appears to be confounded by low socioeconomic status, since the latter is associated with both high frequencies of mortality and high frequencies of schizophrenia leading to admission to state hospitals.

A number of authors have reported an association between death of a parent during childhood and vulnerability to *depression* during adult life, which the present author has been unable to confirm. However, Beck et al. reported increased frequencies of childhood bereavement among adult patients displaying various psychiatric disorders, who scored high on an inventory that was designed to measure depression. These findings were not only independent of clinical diagnosis, but probably also independent of age of the patients (as indicated by an analysis of variance).

In an interesting longterm follow-up study, Paffenbarger and Asnes examined the college case-taking records relative to 40,000 former students of the University of Pennsylvania and Harvard University for characteristics precursive of eventual suicide. Two hundred and twenty-five *male suicides* were identified, and for each of these two control subjects known still to be alive were randomly chosen from the same school and case-taking year. Early loss or absence of the *father* was the dominant distinguishing characteristic of the college records of these males who subsequently committed suicide. However, the suicides also had *fathers* who tended to be of higher educational and occupational status than the non-suicidal control group. Other studies also suggest that successful suicide, unlike most forms of psychopathology, is statistically associated with a high rather than a low socioeconomic status, and hence with tendencies to postpone immediate impulse gratification in favor of anticipated longterm future reward.

In the next and final section of this chapter we shall review some further aspects of childhood relationships, particularly with parents and siblings, and in the following chapter turn to some of the evidence relating psychopathology to membership in various sociocultural groups.

CHILDHOOD RELATIONSHIPS WITH PARENTS, SIBLINGS, AND PEERS

In Chapter 3, some psychoanalytic concepts of personality development were presented, which tended to emphasize the common denominators of relationships between children and their parents at given ages or stages of psychosexual development. Earlier in the present chapter, it was pointed out that social learning theory tends rather to emphasize continuities in these relationships over a period of time, and individual differences existing at any given point in time.

It is, nevertheless, exceedingly difficult to establish causal relationships between qualitative differences in childhood human relationships and vulnerability to development of specific forms of psychopathology many years later. Hitherto, most of the evidence provided has been retrospective, and based on the subjective recall by patients of events that are presumed to have occurred in the remote past. Not only is such information subject to distortion on the basis of current and previous emotional states, but also the greater our search for evidence of childhood trauma, the greater the probability that we shall find it even in the historical background of normal individuals who have made an effective adaptation throughout their lifetime. In spite of the difficulties that arise in proving the etiological significance of early relationships of childhood, however, clinical experience continues to

dictate that they be accorded a major role in the determination of adult psychopathology. This statement is true regardless of the degree of success or failure that may be derived from psychotherapy oriented toward giving the patient insight into the maladaptive learning that has resulted from ineffectual or traumatic childhood relationships.

According to principles of learning, there are *four major ways in which parental behavior may influence childhood personality development:* first through the nature and frequency of rewards or reinforcement, second through the circumstances and frequency under which behavior is ignored and extinguished, third through the direct or indirect punishment of new or well established behaviors, and fourth through the child's imitation of the attitudes and behavior of parents, older siblings, and other models. Actions speak louder than words, and children are sensitive to the nonverbal communications of affect and role expectation that may belie the accompanying words. Parents and peers may reinforce inappropriate affect and maladaptive behavior in a variety of subtle ways, as already indicated in the final section of Chapter 3.

For normal social development, it appears that children require close and enduring relationships with a parent or parent substitute of each sex, and with peers of both sexes outside of the family (which normal parents ordinarily encourage during the preschool years). It has been remarked that discipline without love is revenge, whereas love without discipline is anarchy. The parent who is emotionally secure is able to accept the emotional lability and periodic anger of the young child, enforce firm but compassionate controls on the child's behavior, and encourage gradual appropriate emancipation and independence. Discipline is not based upon the inconsistent angry feelings of the parent, as is frequently found in the histories of delinquent or sociopathic patients. Rather, disapproval or punishment is directed toward the prevention of socially unacceptable behavior, rather than the provocation of guilt within the child as is found in neurotic and depressed patients.

Various workers have noted that the form of discipline employed may serve as a sensitive indicator of the parents' feelings toward the child. Greenfield presented interesting retrospective data concerning the *form of childhood discipline* recalled by 58 outpatients of a university student psychiatric clinic and 58 matched control subjects. Four forms of "direct" physical or unambiguous means of discipline expression were distinguished from several forms of "indirect" or psychological techniques of discipline that would tend to arouse guilt feelings in the child, and express disappointment or denial of love by the parents. The direct forms of discipline consisted of being scolded or reasoned with, being spanked, being sent away from the group, or being denied some pleasure. The indirect forms of discipline consisted of being made to feel less good than a brother, a sister, or other children, being made to feel that he had hurt the mother or father, being made to feel that he had fallen short of what was expected of him, being denied any demonstration of affection by mother or father, or being told by mother or father that they cannot love him when he is bad. In this study, the students with psychopathology reported significantly higher frequencies of exposure to indirect forms of childhood discipline, while the control group reported higher frequencies of exposure to direct discipline. It should be pointed out, however, that the diagnosis of the students with psychopathology ranged from relatively mild adjustment reactions to long-standing schizophrenic reactions, and that different findings might be anticipated in the case of patients with antisocial behavior disorders than in the case of such patients who display neurosis or schizophrenia. Nevertheless, consistent associations have been found between various forms of parental behavior and various forms of psychopathology in their children, as illustrated in Table 7-1 from Kanner.

The nature and consistency of the complicated system of rewards and

TABLE 7-1. Principal Types of Parental Attitudes

Attitude	Characteristic verbalization	Handling of the child	Reaction of the child
Acceptance and affection	"It's the child that makes the home interesting."	Fondling; play; patience	Security; normal personality development
Overt rejection	"I hate him." "I won't bother with him."	Neglect; harshness; avoidance of contact; severe punishment	Aggressiveness; delinquency; shallowness of affect
Perfectionism	"I do not want him as he is; I must make him over."	Disapproval; fault-finding; coercion	Frustration; lack of self-confidence; obsessiveness
Overprotection	"Of course, I like him; see how I sacrifice myself for him."	Spoiling; nagging; overindulgence or hovering domination	Delay in maturation and emancipation; protracted dependence on mother; "spoiled child" behavior

From Kanner, L. 1957. *Child Psychiatry*, 3rd edition. 1957. Courtesy of Charles C Thomas, Publisher, Springfield, Illinois.

punishment that obtains during childhood, together with the quality of significant personalities available for identification and emulation, are important determinants of personality and psychopathology. The harsh internal control system of the typical neurotic patient tends to be associated with a history of excessive demands for conformity during childhood (reinforced by rewards and punishment), and identification with individuals having high ideals and standards of behavior. The defective internal control system of the patient showing consistent antisocial behavior, on the other hand, tends to be associated with a history of parental absence or indifference, inconsistent rewards and punishment, and identification with individuals having inadequate ideals and controls.

Of critical significance in the development of adult attitudes and patterns of behavior is the prevailing affect or emotional tone throughout childhood. Those reared in an atmosphere of acceptance, reasonable indulgence, and consistent firm limit-setting tend to develop confidence, trust, and affection; whereas those reared in an atmosphere of danger (e.g., inconsistent harsh punishment), indifference (e.g., absence of adequate rewards), rejection, and humiliation are likely to develop prevailing emotions of fear and hostility. These learned emotional responses tend to be generalized from the original person or situation onto other similar persons or situations. There may, however, be specificity as well as generalization in the *displacement* of emotion from its original source onto other specific individuals — as from a hostile punitive parent onto other representatives of authority, or onto other persons of the same sex as that parent, including the ultimate spouse of the subject. Many wives appear to suffer for the earlier sins of their husbands' mothers, and many husbands are punished for the earlier behavior of their wives' fathers.

The basic responsibilities of the parents include protection of the child from physical and social dangers, and the provision of regular gratification for physiological needs, of affection and emotional security, of accurate information about reality, of consistent firm but reasonable controls, and the opportunity to learn from independent decisions and behavior. The relative predominance of each of these parental functions varies during the normal course of a child's development from infancy through adolescence, toward complete independence and the mature acceptance of full responsibility for the consequences of his decisions. The division of labor within the family is ordinarily such that mother has the greatest responsibility for the care and training of the infant and preschool child, whereas the father's role in the setting of limits and as an example of identification becomes relatively more important during the school years, and particularly in boys; but father may also have a profound influence on the preschool child, both directly and indirectly through his relationship with mother.

There is a tendency for persons to marry other persons of equivalent emotional maturity, and either or both parents may reinforce maladaptive behavior, or may arouse in the child excessive fears or hostilities by transmitting their own anxieties, fears, or hostilities; by their direct behavior towards the child (verbal or nonverbal); and by transmitting inaccurate information about reality (e.g., regarding physical dangers or the trustworthiness of other people).

The human family is unique in frequently containing two or more dependent offspring of different ages. The different children in a family do not all grow up in an identical environment, but may have somewhat different relationships with one or both parents, as well as with their brothers and sisters. *Sibling rivalry* involves feelings of competition and jealousy between siblings, primarily for the affection, attention, and approval of the parents — particularly between siblings that are close together in age and of the same sex. Evidence of sibling rivalry is often particularly noticeable immediately after the birth of a new baby, in the form of aggressive or regressive behavior in the child who was previously the youngest member of the family. Such behavior is apt to be most severe and persistent when excessive attention is showered on the baby (for example a first-born son occurring after the birth of several girls), or when the displaced child is ignored, punished, or invited to display rivalry (by the parents' expectation that there would inevitably be difficulties). It is a clinical impression that manifestations of sibling rivalry may be more marked in the eldest (who has never previously competed with other children for his parents' attention) than in the case of subsequent additions to the family. It is also not uncommon for the displaced father to regress, and to manifest hostility toward his eldest child or first-born son (or the wife who has provided him with this child). The precise significance of this type of rivalry in personality development, however, is not established, and many psychological studies of birth order and ordinal position have failed to reveal consistent associations in respect to adult personality characteristics or psychopathology.

There does, however, appear to be an interesting association between birth order and scholastic aptitude. Not only do the eldest born children exceed youngest born on the campuses of the most academically selective colleges by a factor that may be as high as two to one, but Altus also reported that the eldest born have higher scholastic aptitude test scores in the verbal rather than the mathematical subtest. The latter fact would suggest that the economic factors influencing college attendance of the eldest child are less significant than his selection by the college on the basis of demonstrated academic ability. Since this ability is unlikely to reflect inherent hereditary differences, it has been interpreted as due to different child rearing attitudes and practices on the part of the parents. Sears et al. provided evidence that the father plays a greater role in the upbringing of the eldest child than of subsequent children, and it appears probable that parents are more demanding and communicate higher academic expectations to the eldest.

Other objective family data that have been studied include family size and parental age, and it may be mentioned in passing that there is a consistent association between mongolism (Down's syndrome) and advanced maternal age. It should also be mentioned that the only child represents a size of family rather than an ordinal position, as has frequently been assumed. It is unfortunate that such seemingly objective factors are also associated with a number of other interrelated variables that have hitherto proved impossible to disentangle: for example, socioeconomic status, intelligence, mortality (among both parents and children), frequencies of separation and divorce, and child-rearing practices. In searching for the childhood roots of adult psychopathology, it appears that the child-rearing practices involved are the more basic and critical variables to evaluate.

The relationships between siblings are determined to a considerable extent by the relationships of each of the siblings with the parents. Similarly, the relationships of the child with other children his own age outside the family are initially determined to an important degree by his parents. The development of communication and cooperative behavior with others his own age may be increased by encouraging the child to play with other children in the neighborhood and to bring them into his own home if he wishes, and by enrolling him in a nursery school—or they may be greatly impaired by restrictions placed upon his socialization. Excessive attention showered upon his young playmates by the parents of an insecure child may lead him to regard them as rivals rather than companions for cooperative enterprises. However, in the normal course of development the child will gradually establish increasing loyalties to his peer group and will tend to identify himself with their goals and values, which may or may not be socially acceptable. In the next chapter, we shall consider other sociocultural factors that may be related to the development of psychopathology.

SELECTED REFERENCES

Altus, W. D. 1965. Birth order and scholastic aptitude. Journal of Consulting Psychology *29*, 202-205.

Altus, W. D. 1966. Birth order and its sequelae. Science *151*, 44-49.

Andry, R. G. 1960. *Delinquency and Parental Pathology.* London, Methuen and Co.

Bacon, M. K., Child, I., and Barry, H. 1963. A cross-cultural study of correlates of crime. Journal of Abnormal and Social Psychology *66*, 291-300.

Bandura, A., and Walters, R. H. 1963. *Social Learning and Personality Development.* New York, Holt, Rinehart & Winston, Inc.

Beck, A. T., Sethi, B. B., and Tuthill, R. W. 1963. Childhood bereavement and adult depression. Archives of General Psychiatry *9*, 295-302.

Beckett, P. G. S., Frohman, C. E., Gottlieb, J. S., Mowbray, J. B., and Wolf, R. C. 1962. Schizophrenic-like mechanisms in monkeys. Paper presented at annual meeting of The American Psychiatric Association, May, 1962.

Bexton, W. H., Heron, W., and Scott, T. H. 1954. Effects of decreased variation in the sensory environment. Canadian Journal of Psychology *8*, 70-76.

Bliss, E. L., ed. *Roots of Behavior.* New York, Hoeber Medical Division, Harper & Row, Publishers, Inc., ch. 16-19.

Bowlby, J. 1951. *Maternal Care and Mental Health.* Geneva, World Health Organization, Monograph series No. 2.

Brady J. V. 1958. Ulcers in "executive" monkeys. Scientific American *199*, 95-100.

Brill, N. Q., and Liston, E. H., Jr. 1966. Parental loss in adults with emotional disorders. Archives of General Psychiatry *14*, 307-314.

Brown, F., Epps, P., and McGlashan, A. 1961. The remote and immediate effects of orphanhood. Proceedings of the Third World Congress of Psychiatry. Montreal, McGill University Press, Vol. 2, pp. 1316-1319.

Burney, C. 1952. *Solitary Confinement.* New York, Coward-McCann, Inc.

Byrd, R. E. 1964. *Alone.* New York, G. P. Putnam's Sons.

Doane, B. K., Mahatoo, W., Heron, W., and Scott, T. H. 1959. Changes in perceptual function after isolation. Canadian Journal of Psychology *33*, 210-219.

Dollard, J., and Miller, N. E. 1950. *Personality and Psychotherapy.* New York, McGraw-Hill Book Co., Inc.

Engel, G. E. 1962. *Psychological Development in Health and Disease.* Philadelphia, W. B. Saunders Co.

Farber, I. E., Harlow, H. F., and West, L. J. 1957. Brainwashing, conditioning, and D. D. D. (debility, dependency, and dread). Sociometry *20*, 271-285.

Franks, C. 1960. Conditioning and abnormal behavior. In *Handbook of Abnormal Psychology,* ed. H. J. Eysenck. London, Pitman Medical Publishing Co.

Fuller, J. L., and Waller, M. B. 1962. Is early experience different? In *Roots of Behavior,* ed. E. L. Bliss. Hoeber Medical Division, Harper & Row Publishers, Inc., ch. 16.

Gardner, G. E. 1956. Separation of the parents and the emotional life of the child. Mental Hygiene *14*, 53-57.

Glueck, S., and Glueck, E. 1950. *Unraveling Juvenile Delinquency.* Cambridge, Massachusetts, Harvard University Press, pp. 88-91, and 122-125.

Goertzel, V., and Goertzel, M. G. 1962. *Cradles of Eminence.* Boston, Little, Brown & Co. Inc., pp. 149-152, 214-216, and 272.

Greenfield, N. S. 1959. The relationship between recalled forms of childhood discipline and psychopathology. Journal of Consulting Psychology *23*, 139-142.

Gregory, I. 1958. Studies of parental deprivation in psychiatric patients. American Journal of Psychiatry *115*, 432-441.

Gregory, I. 1965. Anterospective data concerning childhood loss of a parent.
I. Delinquency and high school drop-out. Archives of General Psychiatry *13*, 99-109.
II. Pathology, performance, and potential among college students. Archives of General Psychiatry *13*, 110-120.

Gregory, I. 1966. Retrospective data concerning childhood loss of a parent.
I. Actuarial estimates versus recorded frequencies of orphanhood. Archives of General Psychiatry *15*, 354-361.
II. Category of parental loss by decade of birth, diagnosis, and MMPI. Archives of General Psychiatry *15*, 362-367.

Harlow, H. F. 1962. The heterosexual affectional system in monkeys. American Psychologist *17*, 1-9.

Harlow, H. F., and Harlow, M. K. 1965. The Affectional Systems. In *Behavior of Nonhuman Primates,* ed. A. M. Schrier, H. F. Harlow, and F. Stollnitz. New York, Academic Press Inc., Vol. 2, 287-334.

Harlow, H. F., and Harlow, M. 1966. Learning to love. American Scientist *54*, 244-272.

Harlow, H. F., and Zimmermann, R. R. 1958. The development of affectional responses in infant monkeys. Proceedings of The American Philosophical Society *102*, 501-509.

Heron, W., Bexton, W. H., and Hebb, D. O. 1953. Cognitive effects of a decreased variation in the sensory environment. American Psychologist *8*, 366.

Hess, E. H. 1962. Imprinting and the "critical period" concept. In *Roots of Behavior*, ed. E. L. Bliss. New York, Hoeber Medical Division, Harper & Row, Publishers, Inc., ch. 18.

Hilgard, E. R. 1956. *Theories of Learning*, 2nd edition. New York, Appleton-Century-Crofts, Inc.

Hinkle, L. E. 1954. Normal stress in normal experience. In *Beyond The Germ Theory*, ed. I. Galdston. New York Academy of Medicine, Health Education Council, ch. 7.

Hirsch, J. 1962. Discussion of a paper by J. P. Scott. American Journal of Orthopsychiatry *32*, 891-893.

Hoch, P. H. and Zubin, J., eds. 1957. *Experimental Psychopathology*. New York, Grune & Stratton, Inc.

Kanner, L. 1957. *Child Psychiatry*, 3rd edition. Springfield, Illinois, Charles C Thomas, Publisher, p. 131.

Levine, S. 1960. Infantile stimulation. Scientific American *202*, 81-86.

Levine, S. 1962. The effects of infantile experience on adult behavior. In *Experimental Foundations of Clinical Psychology*, ed. A. J. Bachrach. New York, Basic Books, Inc., ch. 5.

Levine, S. 1962. Psychophysiological effects of infantile stimulation. In *Roots of Behavior*, ed. E. L. Bliss. New York, Hoeber Medical Division Harper & Row, Publishers, Inc., ch. 17.

Liddell, H. S. 1952. Experimental induction of psychoneuroses by conditioned reflex with stress. In *The Biology of Mental Health and Disease*. New York Medical Division, Harper & Row, Publishers, Inc., ch. 29.

Liddell, H. S. 1954. Sheep and goats: the psychological effects of laboratory experiences of deprivation and stress upon certain experimental animals. In *Beyond The Germ Theory*, ed. I. Galdston. New York Academy of Medicine, Health Education Council, ch. 7.

Liddell, H. S. 1960. Experimental neuroses in animals. In *Stress and Psychiatric Disorders*, ed. J. M. Tanner. Oxford, Blackwell Scientific Publications.

Lifton, R. J. 1961. *Thought Reform and The Psychology of Totalism*. New York, W. W. Norton & Co., Inc.

Lilly, J. 1956. Mental effects of reduction of ordinary levels of physical stimuli on intact, healthy persons. Washington, D.C., American Psychiatric Association, Psychiatric Research Reports No. 5, pp. 1-9.

Lindsley, D. B. 1961. Common factors in sensory deprivation, sensory distortion, and sensory overload. In *Sensory Deprivation*, ed. P. Solomon et al. Cambridge, Massachusetts, Harvard University Press, ch. 12.

Maier, N. R. S. 1949. *Frustration*. New York, McGraw-Hill Book Co., Inc.

Masserman, J. H. 1961. *Principles of Dynamic Psychiatry*, 2nd edition. Philadelphia, W. B. Saunders Co.

Masserman, J. H., Aarons, L., and Wechkin, S. 1963. The effect of positive-choice conflicts on normal and neurotic monkeys. The American Journal of Psychiatry *120*, 481-484.

Mednick, M. T., and Mednick, S. A., eds. 1963. *Research In Personality*. New York, Holt, Rinehart & Winston, Inc.

Miller, N. E., and Dollard, J. 1941. *Social Learning and Imitation*. New Haven, Yale University Press.

Moore, A. U. 1958. Conditioning and stress in the newborn lamb. In *Physiological Bases of Psychiatry*, ed. W. H. Gantt. Springfield, Illinois, Charles C Thomas, Publisher.

Morgan, C. T. 1961. *Introduction To Psychology*, 2nd edition. New York, McGraw-Hill Book Co., Inc., ch. 5 and 7.

Paffenbarger, R. S., and Asnes, D. P. 1966. Chronic disease in former college students III. Precursors of suicide in early and middle life. American Journal of Public Health *56*, 1026-1036.

Pavlov, I. P. 1928. *Lectures On Conditioned Reflexes*. New York, International Publishers, Inc.

Razran, G. 1960. The observable unconscious in current Soviet psychophysiology: Survey and interpretation of experiments in interoceptive conditioning. In *Progress in Clinical Psychology*, vol. 4. New York, Grune & Stratton, Inc.

Ritter, C. 1954. *A Woman In The Polar Night*. New York, E. P. Dutton & Co.

Sarbin, T. R., ed. 1961. *Studies In Behavior Pathology*. New York, Holt, Rinehart & Winston, Inc.

Scott, J. P. 1962. Critical periods in behavioral development. Science *138*, 949-958.

Scott. J. P., and Fuller, J. L. 1965. *Genetics And The Social Behavior Of The Dog*. Chicago, The University of Chicago Press, ch. 5.

Sears, R. R., Maccoby, E. E., and Levin, H. 1957. *Patterns of Child Rearing*. Evanston, Illinois, Row, Peterson & Co.

Simon, N. M., and Senturia, A. G. 1966. Adoption and psychiatric illness. American Journal of Psychiatry *122*, 858-868.

Singh, J. A. L. and Zingg, R. M. 1942. *Wolf-children and Feral Man* (Denver: University contribution No. 4). New York, Harper & Row, Publishers, Inc.

Skinner, B. F. 1953. *Science and Human Behavior*. New York, The Macmillan Co.

Solomon, P., Kuzmansky, P. E., Leiderman, P. H., Mendelson, J. H., Trumbull, R., and

Wexler, D., eds. 1961. *Sensory Deprivation.* Cambridge. Massachusetts. Harvard University Press.

Solomon, R. L. and Wynne, L. C. 1953. Traumatic avoidance learning: Acquisition in normal dogs. Psychological monographs *67,* No. 4 (whole No. 354).

Spitz, R. 1954. Unhappy and fatal outcomes of emotional deprivation and stress in infancy, In *Beyond The Germ Theory,* ed. I. Galdston. New York Academy of Sciences, Health Education Council, ch. 8.

Thorndike, E. L. 1932. *The Fundamentals of Learning.* New York, Teacher's College.

Toman, W. 1961. *Family Constellation.* New York, Springer Publishing Co., Inc.

Weybrew, B. D. and Parker, J. W. 1960. *Bibliography of Sensory Deprivation, Isolation, and Confinement.* New London, Connecticut, U.S. Naval Medical Research Laboratory, Memorandum report No. 60-1.

Some are born great, some achieve greatness, and some have greatness thrust upon them.

From "Twelfth Night" by William Shakespeare

In Boston they ask, "How much does he know?" In New York, "How much is he worth?" In Philadelphia, "Who were his parents?"

Mark Twain

Habit is thus the enormous fly-wheel of society, its most precious conservative agent. It alone is what keeps us all within the bounds of ordinance, and saves the children of fortune from the envious uprisings of the poor.

From "Principles of Psychology" by William James

CHAPTER 8

Sociocultural Factors in Etiology

SOCIAL ORGANIZATION AND STRATIFICATION

Aristotle remarked that man is a political animal, but he is far from being the only organism to have developed a complex social organization. Biological and social scientists have frequently compared human society with groups of other organisms and have attempted to define the basic requirements and characteristics of all such groups. Very simple organisms may form groups without showing any differentiation of behavior and hence without organization. Simple aggregations of this kind, however, may still confer biological advantages on the individual members—as in obtaining shelter or mutual protection—and are a necessary preliminary to various forms of social organization.

The individual organism involves a complex system of relationships between the various cells composing it, and in a similar fashion any society involves a complex system of relations between the various organisms com-posing it. The three basic needs for the perpetuation of each are nutrition, reproduction, and protection. A society gives the strength of numbers and of specialization to its members; this strength enables them to meet their needs more efficiently together than as separate individuals.

There are three general ways in which biological factors lead to the differentiation of behavior. The first involves hereditary differentiation into two sexes, and sometimes also into nonsexual forms. Another determinant of differentiation is based on the type of nutrition of the young, and a third variety is based on the maturation or growth and development of the young. All three types of biological determinants can be found in an ant colony, while termites may be further differentiated into several classes of sexual individuals and specialized worker-classes of soldiers and nest-builders.

Such differentiation of behavior is based on differences in structure determined largely by heredity, and societies organized on this basis may be

161

known as *biosocial systems.* The differentiation of behavior between individual members however may also result predominantly from learning and habit formation, in which event the system may be spoken of as *sociocultural.* Biologically speaking, man may be divided into three or possibly four groups: the mature male and female, the dependent young, and possibly the aged. The complex differentiation occurring within these groups has been attributed largely to learning and habit formation, and mankind is the only species generally recognized as having a sociocultural system of organization.

Scott pointed out that two things are necessary for the differentiation of behavior into a social relationship. One of these is the ability of an organism to discriminate between different individuals, and the other is some kind of behavior that can be differentiated either by biological or by psychological factors. A crucial example of this is the *establishment of dominance* over another individual of the same species. Thus, in establishing a pecking-order, hens must be able to distinguish between the various other hens, and must be capable of either fighting or escape behavior. Any group of organisms that is capable of fighting can set up a dominance order, which may involve both male and female, the very young and the very old. Such dominance orders have a wide variety of functions but *all result in the division of something that is relatively limited in supply* such as mates, territory, or food. In groups of animals that have relatively prolonged sexual as well as social relationships, *dominance may be conferred* by one animal onto others that would otherwise be far less dominant. The females and their young may thus become dominant over mature males that are physically larger and stronger.

History was defined by Ambrose Bierce as an account mostly false, of events mostly unimportant, which are brought out by rulers mostly knaves, and soldiers mostly fools. Be this as it may, man has always been a fighter, whether he has used his hands or brains, his weapons or words. The account of his progress to the concrete jungle of the modern city is an account of *conflict:* conflict between groups and within groups. The problem for society has been one of minimizing dangerous conflicts between individuals and groups, and of channeling man's aggressive energies into the service of the community. In order to accomplish these things it has been necessary to establish certain common goals, while still permitting certain satisfactions to individual members of the group. Unfortunately, this plan has frequently been accomplished through encouraging discrimination and conflict with another social group. In a series of interesting experiments in group conflict involving boys attending summer camps, Sherif demonstrated that when two groups had conflicting aims—i.e., when one group could achieve its ends only at the expense of the other—their members became increasingly hostile toward each other, whereas working for common goals that neither could achieve without the other promoted the development of harmony.

Unbridled conflict and competition among the individual members of society would result in the hypothetical state of life described by Hobbes as "solitary, poor, nasty, brutish and short." Society must therefore demand some degree of cooperation and conformity with certain ideals or *social norms,* expressed informally in its folkways and mores, and finding formal expression in its laws. The institutions of society, such as marriage, consist of various combinations of folkways and mores and laws built around one or more functions. Conformity with these social norms is accomplished by means of a complex system of rewards (such as property, prestige, or esteem) and punishment (which may involve mild censure or disapproval, restrictions of opportunity, or the loss of property, personal freedom, or life). Asch provided impressive evidence of the effects of relatively mild social pressure in changing the opinions expressed by individuals who disagreed with a majority of group members confronted with a simple task of perceptual discrimination. In effect, a considerable proportion of individuals were prepared to report that black was white if all other members of the group said so.

Rettig and his associates undertook a series of experimental studies designed to test the "ethical risk" hypothesis, which postulates that unethical behavior varies as a function of perceived risk. Ethical propositions are considered to be among the most fundamental determinants of human behavior, and it was established that the severity of anticipated social censure was the most important source of variation in predictive judgments of unethical behavior. The expectancy of censure, although a separate and significant source of variation in predicting unethical behavior, proved to be no more crucial than either the expectancy or the reinforcement value of the anticipated gain from such unethical behavior. The concept of "ethical risk" in predicting unethical behavior should therefore be interpreted more in terms of the risk of public exposure and censure, than in terms of the risk of "getting caught." Interpreted in the latter manner, the concept of ethical risk appeared to be the single most important antecedent condition for engagement in unethical behavior.

Davis remarked that the essence of any situation lies in the mutual expectations of the participants, and that these expectations rest to a great extent on the norms applicable in the situation. Each actor therefore has some idea of what he expects of other persons in a given situation, and believes he has an idea of what they expect of him, and of what they expect that he expects them to expect. Certain rights and obligations are inherent in an individual s *position or status* within the social structure. In contrast with these rights and obligations, the manner in which an individual actually performs in a given position is termed his *role*. Selective social approval and disapproval may be determined by either status or role, the rewards for high status being termed *prestige*, while the rewards for satisfactory role performance may be termed *esteem*. The *power* of an individual is the extent to which his wishes determine the behavior of others, and is partly related to both prestige and esteem.

In a complex society, each individual may fill a number of different statuses at a given time, and even more during the course of his life time. Sometimes status is *ascribed* independently of individual qualities, and sometimes it is *achieved* according to individual accomplishment, as recognized in the quotation from Shakespeare found at the beginning of this chapter. In his well known passage on the seven ages of man, Shakespeare also described some common changes in the status of an individual during his life time:

All the world's a stage,
And all the men and women merely
    players.
They have their exits and their
    entrances;
And one man in his time plays many
    parts,
His acts being seven ages. At first the
    infant,
And then the whining schoolboy, with
    his satchel
And shining morning face, creeping
    like snail
Unwillingly to school. And then the
    lover
Sighing like a furnace, with a woful
    ballad
Made to his mistress' eyebrow. Then a
    soldier
Full of strange oaths, and bearded like
    the pard;
Jealous in honour, sudden and quick in
    quarrel,
Seeking the bubble reputation

Even in the cannon's mouth. And then
the justice,
In fair round belly with good capon
lined,
With eyes severe and beard of formal
cut,
Full of wise saws and modern instances;
And so he plays his part. The sixth age
shifts
Into the lean and slipper'd pantaloon,
With spectacles on nose and pouch on
side;
His youthful hose, well saved, a world
too wide
For his shrunk shank; and his big
manly voice,
Turning again toward childish treble,
pipes
And whistles in his sound. Last scene of
all
That ends this strange eventful history,
Is second childishness, and mere
oblivion,
Sans teeth, sans eyes, sans taste, sans
everything.
As You Like It, Act II, Scene VII

Status is most likely to be *ascribed* on the basis of sex, age, and kinship, and it is most likely to be *achieved* on the basis of success in an occupation valued by the society, or of marriage to an individual of high status. In every culture, status is determined partially by ascription and partially by achievement, but there are marked differences between cultures in the opportunities for achieving status by upward social mobility. In a *closed society*, as exemplified by the Indian caste system or medieval European feudal system, the opportunities for achieving status are relatively small; whereas in a more *open society* such as the United States, the opportunities for achieving status are relatively greater. Both systems have their advantages and disadvantages for society as well as for the individual. Thus ascribed status conveys a sense of personal security, and the closed society obtains stability at the expense of inefficiency and the frustration of many gifted individuals. Achieved status on

the other hand, permits gifted individuals to make their maximum contributions and stimulates competition, but at a cost of insecurity and instability. Unlimited individual competition may lead to disorganization, and failure to achieve may be accompanied by serious feelings of personal inadequacy. This is particularly true when the society professes that all men are born equal, thus denying the facts of inherent differences in ability and existing inequalities in opportunity.

The usual situation is that broad outlines of status are laid down by ascription, while many specific statuses are open to achievement. There are, of course, many yardsticks by which status may be measured, as illustrated in Mark Twain's words, quoted at the beginning of this chapter. When a number of yardsticks are used, a pattern of *social stratification* emerges, in which individuals can be grouped according to membership in one of several different *social classes*, and it has become customary to make a distinction between five or six such classes. The criteria usually employed by sociologists for this purpose include occupation, education, source of income (e.g., inherited wealth, salary, welfare), type of house, and residential area.

In his grim prediction about life in 1984, George Orwell remarked that throughout recorded time there have been three kinds of people in the world, the High, the Middle, and the Low, the aims of whom are entirely irreconcilable. "The aim of the High is to remain where they are. The aim of the Middle is to change places with the High. The aim of the Low, when they have an aim ... is to abolish all distinctions and create a society in which all men shall be equal ... but no advance in wealth, no softening of manners and no reform or revolution has brought human equality a millimeter nearer. From the point of view of the Low, no historic change has ever meant much more than a change in the name of their masters."

In a popular documentation of social class differences in modern America, Packard cited evidence of marked differences in the *time-orientation* of these three major groups. For upper class private-school boys the important time dimension was the *past*, whereas for middle class public school boys the significant time dimension was the *future*. By contrast, people in the lower classes were predominantly orientated to the *present*. Evidence to be presented later suggests that the predominant time-orientation of the major social classes is related to the form and frequency of psychopathology manifested by their members. Upper class orientation toward the past involves preservation of the status quo, and may be accompanied by dissatisfaction with the present, and the sense of failure that accompanies *depression and suicide* (the highest frequencies of which may be found at this level). Middle class orientation towards future achievement involves postponement of impulse-gratification, frequently accompanied by anxiety and *neurotic* conflict. Orientation to the present among members of the lowest social class is accompanied by tendencies to hedonistic impulse-gratification, with sexual and aggressive behavior that may be regarded as antisocial, dyssocial, or *sociopathic*.

It has been noted earlier that one of the two prerequisites for the differentiation of behavior into social relationships is the ability to discriminate between different individuals. The members of all social classes are able to make such discriminations with respect to members of their own and other social classes on the basis of such characteristics as appearance, behavior and conversation. As Professor Higgins commented on Eliza Doolittle in *My Fair Lady* (the musical version of Shaw's play *Pygmalion*), "It's 'Ow' and 'Garn' that keep her in her place—not her wretched clothes or dirty face." Stereotyped characterizations of members of different classes vary, however, relative to the individual's own social status, as

may be seen from examination of Table 8-1.

Discrimination does not stop with ability to recognize differences, but is also reflected in different forms of behavior towards the individual. There is a widespread tendency for human beings to identify with powerful individuals and with the majority or "*in-group*," while stigmatizing and rejecting members of various minorities or "*out-groups*." The lowest social class is viewed and treated in such a manner by members of all other classes, but such behavior may also be directed toward members of out-groups identified by characteristics such as age, sex, race, religion, and national origin. Any differences in appearance, behavior, or belief tend to be regarded as undesirable, bad, or incomprehensible, and to arouse corresponding feelings of mistrust and hostility, with varying degrees of criticism, ridicule, deprivation, isolation, or aggression. The process is illustrated in Table 8-2, which shows the percentages among 1725 native born Americans who stated many years ago that they would "willingly admit" members of four minority groups to each of five degrees of relationship listed. However, this particular study may be considered applicable only to this specific sample at that time and place.

The study of social and cultural factors in determining psychopathology is exceedingly complex, and must take into account differences between various groups in their definition of what constitutes abnormality and their behavior toward individuals showing such abnormality, as well as differences in the form and frequency of various forms of abnormal behavior according to time, place, and group membership. In the remainder of this chapter, we shall first review certain historical trends in attitudes toward social disorganization and stress, then discuss the measurement of various forms of abnormal behavior and interpretation of reported differences, and finally review

TABLE 8-1. The Social Perspectives of the Social Classes*

UPPER-UPPER CLASS		LOWER-UPPER CLASS
"Old aristocracy"	UU	"Old aristocracy"
"Aristocracy," but not "old"	LU	**"Aristocracy," but not "old"**
"Nice, respectable people"	UM	"Nice, respectable people"
"Good people, but 'nobody'"	LM	"Good people, but 'nobody'"
	UL	
"Po' whites"	LL	"Po' whites"

UPPER-MIDDLE CLASS		LOWER-MIDDLE CLASS	
"Society" { "Old families"	UU	"Old aristocracy" (older)	"Broken-down aristocracy" (younger)
"Society" but not "old families"	LU		
"People who should be upper class"	UM	"People who think they are somebody"	
"People who don't have much money"	LM	**"We poor folk"**	
	UL	"People poorer than us"	
"No 'count lot"	LL	"No 'count lot"	

UPPER-LOWER CLASS		LOWER-LOWER CLASS
	UU	
	LU	
"Society" or the "folks with money"	UM	"Society" or the "folks with money"
"People who are up because they have a little money"	LM	"Way-high-ups," but not "Society"
"Poor but honest folk"	UL	"Snobs trying to push up"
"Shiftless people"	LL	**"People just as good as anybody"**

*Reprinted from Davis, A., Gardner, B., and Gardner, M. *Deep South.* By permission of The University of Chicago Press. Copyright The University of Chicago Press, 1941. p. 65.

TABLE 8-2.   Responses (in Percentages) of Native-Born Americans
on the Bogardus Social Distance Scale*

SCALE ITEM	ENGLISHMEN	GERMANS	JEWS	NEGROES
1. To close kinship by marriage	94	54	8	1
2. To my club as personal chums	97	67	22	9
3. To my street as neighbors	97	79	26	12
4. To employment in my occupation	95	83	40	39
5. To citizenship in my country	96	87	54	57

*Adapted from Bogardus, E. S. 1928. *Immigration and Race Attitudes.* Boston, D. C. Heath & Co.

data regarding group differences in abnormal behavior within Western society and between different cultures.

SOCIAL DISORGANIZATION AND STRESS

The many ways in which society influences the adaptation of its individual members may be summarized as follows: (1) It *defines* certain obligations in terms of norms and role expectations; (2) it *demands* acceptance of status and role, and conformity with the overall goals of the community; (3) it *discriminates* between individual members in accordance with their potential and actual contributions; (4) it *disciplines* through a variety of rewards and punishments; (5) it *develops* over a period of time in terms of technology, complexity of organization, and the changing expectations of its individual members. It is readily apparent that there are numerous ways in which society may impose on certain of its members pathogenic influences involving situations of uncertainty, frustration, conflict, stress or deprivation. For example, the obligations of the individual may be poorly defined and ambiguous, the demands of society may exceed the individual's capacity for conforming with them, discrimination may be arbitrary and unsympathetic, discipline may be harsh or inconsistent,

and development may result in changes to which the individual is unwilling or unable to adapt.

The potentially harmful effects of social stress on individual personality integration have been recognized since at least the eighteenth century and have been reflected in the writings of many physicians and social scientists, which were extensively reviewed by George Rosen. In Rosen's article he quoted some interesting observations by Benjamin Rush, "the father of American psychiatry," on the comparative health and adjustment of the patriots and loyalists at the time of the American Revolution. In general the revolutionists enjoyed good health. "An uncommon cheerfulness prevailed everywhere among the friends of the Revolution. Defeats and even the loss of relations and property were soon forgotten in the great objects of the war." Marriages were more fruitful than in former years, and many sick persons were restored to perfect health, including a number of women with hysterical symptoms. In sharp contrast with this, there was a high frequency of mental and physical breakdown among those Americans who remained loyal to England. The latter frequently suffered from a form of hypochondriasis (bodily complaints without apparent organic basis), which Rush termed *Revolutiana* and which was popularly known as "protection fever" because it appeared to arise from the excessive concern of the loyalists for the protection of their persons and their possessions. Other factors apparently involved were the loss of power and influence, the suspension of the established church, changes in manners and diet as a result of inflation, and the legal and extralegal oppression to which the loyalists were subjected. Following the successful conclusion of the war, Rush also observed abnormally unrestrained behavior among the American people, concerning which he wrote in part "...The extensive influence which these opinions had upon the understandings, passions and morals of many of the citizens of the United States constituted a species of insanity, which I shall take the liberty of distinguishing by the name of *Anarchia.*"

A generation later two British authors expressed profound concern over the supposed adverse effects of civilization upon mental stability. Rosen quoted Sir Andrew Halliday as follows: "The finer the organs of the mind have become by their greater development, or their better cultivation, if health is not made a part of the process, the more easily are they disordered. We seldom meet with insanity among the savage tribes of men; not one of our African travelers remark their having seen a single madman. Among the slaves of the West Indies it very rarely occurs; and, as we have elsewhere shown from actual returns, the contented peasantry of the Welsh Mountains, the Western Hebrides, and the wilds of Ireland are almost free from this complaint." Rosen went on to quote George Burrows, writing at about the same time, as follows: "Many of the causes inducing intellectual derangement, and which are called moral, have their origin not in individual passions or feelings, but in the state of society at large; and the more artificial, i.e., civilized, society is, the more do these causes multiply and extensively operate. The vices of civi-

lization, of course, most conduce to their increase; but even the moral virtues, religion, politics, nay philosophy itself, and all the best feelings of our nature, if too enthusiastically incited, class among the causes producing intellectual disorders. The circumstances influencing their occurrence are to be sought in all the various relations of life, in constitutional propensities, and, above all, perhaps in education."

A few years later W. A. F. Browne, superintendent of a Scottish asylum, cited figures suggesting a much higher frequency of insanity in the United States than in Europe and offered the following interpretation. "This disparity probably depends on the rapid acquisition of wealth, and the luxurious social habits to which the good fortune of our transatlantic brethren has exposed them. With luxury, indeed, insanity appears to keep equal pace. ... With civilization... come sudden and agitating changes and vicissitudes of fortune; vicious effeminacy of manners; complicated transactions; misdirected views of the objects of life; ambition, and hope, and fears, which man in his primitive state does not and cannot know. But these neither constitute nor are they necessarily connected with civilization." Browne went on to discuss the relative frequency of insanity according to social class and occupation, but did not accept the figures uncritically and raised pertinent questions regarding their validity.

The view of insanity as related to the complexities of civilization, however, persisted on both sides of the Atlantic, and Woodward wrote in 1855 as follows:

"Here (in Massachusetts) the mind, and body, too, are often worked to an extreme point of endurance. Here wealth and station are the results of well-directed efforts; as the general diffusion of intelligence among the whole people stimulates a vast many of them to complete successfully for these prizes. But in the contest, where so many strive, not a few break down. The results on their minds may not, perhaps, be any less disastrous, whether wealth and station are obtained or not. The true balance of the mind is disturbed by prosperity as well as adversity."

Although lacking objective verification, this view has persisted into modern times, and the additional opinion has frequently been expressed that individual breakdowns are merely indices of a sick society. Lawrence K. Frank wrote as follows: "There is a growing realization among thoughtful persons that our culture is sick, mentally disordered and in need of treatment . . . The disintegration of our traditional culture, with the decay of those ideas, concepts, and beliefs upon which our social and individual lives were organized, brings us face to face with the problem of treating society, since individual ˙ therapy or punishment no longer has any value beyond mere alleviation of our symptoms."

In her book *The Neurotic Personality of Our Time*, Karen Horney described three contradictions in our culture that underlie the typical neurotic conflicts, these contradictions being between (1) competition and success on one hand, and brotherly love and humility on the other; (2) stimulation of our needs, and our factual frustrations in satisfying them; (3) the alleged freedom of the individual, and all his factual limitations. She went on to say, "These contradictions embedded in our culture are precisely the conflicts which the neurotic struggles to reconcile: his tendencies toward aggressiveness and his tendencies toward yielding; his excessive demands and his fears of never getting anything; his striving toward self-aggrandizement and his feelings of personal helplessness. The difference from the normal is merely quantitative."

In a book entitled *Psychosocial Medicine: A Study of the Sick Society*, James Halliday presented statistics suggesting progressive increases in the frequency of certain psychosomatic or psychophysiological disorders. Various other authors have pointed to rising mental

hospital admission rates as evidence of increasing social pressure and disorganization. However, these figures may represent increased awareness of abnormality, increased demand for and availability of treatment, and changing fashions in medical diagnosis, rather than any true increase in frequency of specific abnormalities.

The most satisfactory analysis of *hospital admission rates over a prolonged period of time* is that of Goldhamer and Marshall, who carefully examined all available data for Massachusetts for the 100 year period from 1840 to 1940. They found that there had been a very marked increase in hospital admission rates for the older age groups, but that when appropriate comparisons were made (equating the class of patients received and conditions affecting hospitalization) admission rates for patients under the age of 50 were just as high during the last half of the nineteenth century as at the termination of the period studied. While the nineteenth century admissions to hospital contained a larger proportion of psychotic and severely deranged patients, there was no longterm increase during the˙ century in the frequency of the psychoses of early and middle life.

Whether or not psychoses or other manifestations of emotional and social pathology have been increasing or fluctuating in frequency over a period of time, the widespread conviction remains that various forms of abnormal behavior are intimately and causally related to the complexities of social existence. In his book *The Sane Society*, Erich Fromm concerned himself not with individual pathology, but with the pathology of normalcy, particularly with the pathology of contemporary western society. In his introductory chapter he cited Victor Cherbulliez as estimating that from 1500 B.C. to 1860 A.D. no fewer than approximately 8000 peace treaties were signed, each one supposed to secure permanent peace, and each one lasting an average of two years. He also presented interesting tabulations concerning the frequency of suicide, homicide, and alcoholism reported to the World Health Organization by countries sufficiently developed to make reasonably accurate estimates of these figures.

Calhoun reported interesting experimental evidence of social disorganization among populations of domesticated albino rats which were permitted to develop in rooms that were subdivided into four interconnecting pens. The manner in which these pens were connected with each other and the elevation of burrows on the wall led to a theoretical biasing residence ratio of 3:4:3:2 along the series of four pens, which corresponded with the observed residence ratio of rats in these pens. Although each pen contained a large food hopper, the rats developed a new definition of the feeding situation to include the presence of another rat, and eventually 60 to 80 percent of all food consumption took place in only one of the four pens. The manifestation of this atypical aggregation or "pathological togetherness" was accompanied by many abnormal behaviors and disturbances in reproduction. Male rats developed a pansexuality in which they would mount other rats, regardless of their age, sex, or receptivity. They also inflicted wounds during mounting and bit the tails of other rats. Nest-building behavior was completely disrupted, and female rats developed a mortality rate three and a half times that for males. Transport of young by lactating rats was so disorganized that the young became scattered and were no longer nursed. The several conditions and processes involved in this situation were described by Calhoun as a "behavioral sink."

While such studies *may* have relevance for the high frequencies of sociopathic and psychotic behavior in the central disorganized slum areas of our large cities, the direct study of human psychopathology requires controlled comparisons between members of various groups found in human society.

Unfortunately, it may be exceedingly difficult to interpret correctly the recorded frequencies of psychiatric disorder in human society, and it has been remarked that such statistics are frequently used as a drunken man may use a lamp post—more for support than illumination. Nevertheless, they are of great potential significance and we shall now consider problems in measurement and interpretation.

MEASURING THE FREQUENCY AND DISTRIBUTION OF PSYCHOPATHOLOGY

There are three main approaches to the study of disease or abnormality: intensive clinical investigation of the individual patient, laboratory experiment under controlled conditions, and extensive analysis of disability in whole populations. The last approach led to repeated advances in knowledge concerning epidemic infectious diseases, and became the traditional method of medical epidemiology. The major goals of such epidemiological studies have consisted of defining the nature and extent of health problems, searching for causative factors and consequent principles of control, and evaluating results of control measures.

Epidemiology has been described as the diagnostic discipline of mass disease, or the basic science of public health. Elkind wrote on the epidemiology of mental disorder as long ago as 1927, and by 1950 Gruenberg was able to collect an extensive bibliography of relevant material including many articles by social scientists interested in ecology, thus lending support to Gordon's concept of epidemiology as "medical ecology." Gordon and co-workers elaborated on their interpretation of these terms as follows: "Ecology is a biologic and social discipline concerned with the general phenomena of mutual relationships between living organisms and their reaction to animate and inanimate surroundings. That part of human ecology relating to health and disease is medical ecology and medical ecology as it concerns communities of people is epidemiology."

During the past generation, measurement of the frequency and distribution of abnormal behavior has been of increasing concern to the converging disciplines of medical epidemiology, psychiatry, and the social sciences, including representatives of anthropology, of sociology, and of social psychology. As a result of this convergence of interest, there has been considerable interdisciplinary communication and cooperation in the emerging field of social psychiatry. Differences in backgrounds and interests, however, still lead to conflicting interpretations of reported observations, as we shall see in the next section.

Apart from difficulties that exist in interpretation, there are also problems in defining each form of abnormality to be studied, and in objectively measuring its frequency in the various segments of the population. The difinition of abnormality or of "what constitutes a case" is frequently relative rather than absolute, since abnormal behavior is not distinguished from normal as black from white, but is a matter of degree comparable with discriminating between various shades of gray. Thus, the degree of abnormality likely to be diagnosed as some form of "functional" psychosis may involve some three percent of the population during their lifetime (in a given community); the degree of abnormality likely to result in admission to mental hospital sometime during their lifetime may involve 15 or 20 percent of the population (in the same community); whereas a degree of abnormality that is defined as "significant psychopathology" by a research worker may involve 80 percent of the population (as in the study of mental health in Midtown Manhattan reported by Srole et al.).

Prior to counting noses, therefore, it is necessary to define precisely which noses are to be counted, and to specify the total sample of the population from which their owners shall be drawn. There are three general sources from which statistics on abnormal behavior have usually been derived, namely (1) patients in hospitals or other institutions at a given point in time, or admitted within a specified period of time; (2) census investigations of all persons in the community receiving psychiatric treatment, or recognizably abnormal, at a given time; (3) unselected samples of the general population, the members of which have been evaluated as a part of the investigation. The extensive literature concerning those studies carried out prior to the year 1950 was reviewed in some detail by Stromgren. A number of more recent North American studies on the epidemiology of mental disorder were reported in a volume edited by Pasamanick.

There are four general measures of frequency that may be used to compare the distribution of various abnormalities in the population or in selected groups of the population. (1) *Proportionate or percentage frequency* may be used to outline the relative proportions of selected diagnoses among specified groups of patients, and the age and sex distribution of selected diagnostic groups, for example. (2) *Prevalence rates* consist of the *total* number of cases (all or selected diagnostic groups) at a given point in time, divided by the comparable general population at the same point in time. (3) *Incidence rates* consist of the total number of *new* cases (of all or specific diagnostic groups) becoming sick within a specified period of time (usually one year), divided by the comparable general population at the midpoint of this period of time. (4) *Expectancy rates* may be regarded as the lifetime incidence (of all or specific diagnostic groups)—or as the probability of developing abnormality during a life time, provided that the individual lives long enough to pass through the "period of risk" during which he may manifest the abnormality that is under consideration.

Since prevalence and incidence may vary for each sex and for different age groups, they are frequently expressed as *age-sex-specific rates*, each consisting of the number of cases (of all or selected diagnostic groups) of a given age group, divided by the comparable general population in the same age group and sex. Sometimes a single statistic known as an *age-sex-standardized* or *age-sex-adjusted rate* of prevalence or incidence may be calculated from all the different age-sex-specific rates (by applying these to a standard population) in order to enable overall comparisons between segments of the population having dissimilar age distributions. Lifetime expectancy is already a single figure expressing the risk at all ages, and expectancy rates are therefore not described as being age-specific or age-standardized, but may be computed separately for the two sexes (as in the case of prevalence and incidence rates).

All these measures of frequency vary somewhat from one time to another, from one place to another, and among various social groups in the population—for example, according to education or marital status. We shall now consider each of them in somewhat more detail.

Proportionate or Percentage Frequency. The clinician is usually aware that "the commonest disorders occur most often" and that he sees or at least recognizes and diagnoses certain types of abnormality more frequently than he does others. Just which disorders the psychiatrist sees and diagnoses depends largely on selective factors related to his theoretical orientation, the type of treatment he prefers to apply, and the setting in which he has therefore chosen to practice. In a study of Connecticut psychiatrists, MacIver and Redlich reported that the most commonly used diagnosis for patients seen by Analytic-Psychological practitioners was character neurosis; that among Directive-Organic private practitioners the most common diagnosis was anxiety state and depression; whereas among patients seen by state hospital psychiatrists the most common diagnosis was schizophrenia.

Table 8-3 shows the percentage distribution of various diagnoses among (a) patients admitted for the first time during the year, and (b) total patients resident at the end of the year, for state and county mental hospitals in the United States for the year 1964. It may be seen that patients with a diagnosis of schizophrenia constitute about 20 percent of all first admissions to such institutions, but that, because of a rela-

TABLE 8–3. Percentage Frequency of Selected Diagnoses Among First Admissions and Resident Patients in U.S. State and County Mental Hospitals, 1964*

DIAGNOSIS	FIRST ADMISSIONS	RESIDENT PATIENTS
Acute brain syndromes	3.4%	0.8%
Chronic brain syndromes	24.4	25.0
Schizophrenic reactions	19.0	50.2
Other psychotic disorders	7.3	8.6
Psychoneurotic reactions	11.3	1.6
Personality disorders	23.2	3.5
Other diagnoses	11.4	10.3
All diagnoses—percent	100.0	100.0
—numbers of patients	122,453	430,636

*Adapted from *Patients in Mental Institutions 1964*, Public Health Service Publication No. 1452, Part II. Washington, D.C., U.S. Department of Health, Education and Welfare, 1966.

tively lower overall rate of separation (resulting from the combined effects of death and discharge) they constitute about one-half of all the patients resident in such institutions. On the other hand, relatively higher discharge rates among patients with acute brain syndromes, psychoneurotic reactions, and personality disorders, result in lower proportions of these disorders among chronic resident patients than among first admissions to state hospitals.

During the past several decades the proportions of various diagnostic categories among admissions to state hospitals have changed, smaller percentages of such patients having psychoses due to syphilis, but larger percentages of patients being admitted with organic psychoses attributable to senility, with psychoneuroses, and with personality disorders including alcoholism. By comparison with state hospitals, other institutions have tended to restrict the admission of certain categories of patients, particularly those with aggressive or antisocial behavior, those with established chronic disorders, and those with limited economic resources. General hospital psychiatric wards have tended to accept few patients with organic brain syndromes or established addiction to alcohol or drugs. Private psychiatric hospitals have tended to admit relatively fewer schizophrenics, and relatively more patients with affective disorders or neuroses (due to economic factors), and these patients have also constituted a high proportion of patients seen in the offices of private practitioners.

Another aspect of relative frequency distribution with which most clinicians are familiar involves the association of age and sex with diagnosis. Thus, among patients admitted to state institutions for the first time, about three-quarters of those with mental retardation (without psychosis) are under the age of 20 years; about two-thirds of those with schizophrenia and with antisocial personality are between the ages of 20 and 40 years; about two-thirds of those displaying paranoid reactions, involutional psychoses, alcoholism, and syphilis of the central nervous system are between the ages of 40 and 70 years; and a similar proportion of those with the organic psychoses of senility are over the age of 70 years. The two groups of disorders spread most uniformly throughout the adult age range are manic depressive reactions and various forms of neurosis. A predominance of female patients is most marked among the affective disorders and neuroses, whereas a predominance of male patients is found in antisocial personality, alcoholism, and syphilis of the central nervous system. On the whole, nevertheless, these relative frequency distributions are less informative than the absolute rates of prevalence, incidence, and expectancy, all of which are based on the general population at risk.

Prevalence at a Point in Time. Incomplete or partial estimates of prevalence may be obtained by examining the rate per 100,000 general population of patients resident in various forms of institution at a given point in time. Such rates for patients (of all ages combined) who were resident in state hospitals approximately doubled during the first half of the present century. This increase is *not* related to the growth in overall population during the same period (since the rates are based on a fixed unit of population) but does reflect the increasing age of the population (since elderly persons have higher rates of admission), an increasing tendency to hospitalize persons with relatively mild forms of abnormality, and the provision by governments of facilities for their care.

The total patients resident in such hospitals at a given time, however, obviously represents a very incomplete picture of the total prevalence of that abnormality in the community, since some patients are treated in general hospitals, others are cared for as outpatients, and still others go unrecognized or untreated. Numerous attempts have been made to estimate overall prevalence in various communities by means of census investigations and surveys of general population samples. Crosscultural comparisons of frequency have been concerned mainly with prevalence, and some of these studies will be mentioned in the final section of this chapter. Two extensive studies of social class differences undertaken in nearby cities in the United States will also be reviewed in a later section. Both the last studies showed a differential prevalence of psychiatric patients among the various social classes, and one of them also analyzed the distribution of untreated psychopathology according to socioeconomic status and other demographic variables.

Incidence of New Cases during a Given Time. Incomplete or partial estimates have traditionally been based on the annual rates of first admissions to hospitals accepting psychiatric patients, frequently simply the public state hospitals. Many investigators have presented such data, among the most extensive data being those of Dayton for the state of Massachusetts, of Malzberg for the state of New York, and of Odegaard for Norway. Some of these investigators expressed a high degree of confidence that their data represented an accurate estimate of true incidence, particularly for the major functional psychoses, since they considered that in their particular area all such patients must sooner or later be admitted to mental hospitals. However, it is generally recognized that a high proportion of persons committing suicide have shown previous symptoms of abnormality without receiving any treatment, and that other persons with functional psychoses also remain untreated in the community and may undergo spontaneous remission. In a

TABLE 8–4. Age and Sex Specific First Admission Rates per 100,000 Population, for Selected Diagnoses, U.S. State and County Mental Hospitals, 1964*

DIAGNOSIS	SEX	UNDER 15 YEARS	15–24 YEARS	25–34 YEARS	35–44 YEARS	45–54 YEARS	55–64 YEARS	65–74 YEARS	75 YEARS AND OVER
Brain diseases of the senium	Male						2†	72	250
	Female						1†	58	187
Alcoholic brain syndromes and alcohol addiction	Male		1‡	27	47	51	35	10§	
	Female		–‡	5	10	10	5	1§	
Schizophrenic reactions	Male	2	28	34	24	14	8	2§	
	Female	1	19	34	30	18	9	2§	
All diagnoses	Male	8	109	132	124	114	106	175§	
	Female	4	66	96	87	74	66	131§	

*Adapted from statistics for admissions with no prior psychiatric inpatient experience, prepared by the Office of Biometry, National Institute of Mental Health, U.S. Public Health Service, 1966.
†All ages under 65 years
‡All ages under 25 years
§All ages 65 years and over

Swedish investigation, Larsson and Sjogren reported that the number of patients in mental hospitals with manic depressive psychoses was only about one-seventh of the total persons with this disorder.

The age and sex distribution of first admission rates to mental hospitals with various diagnoses may be of some interest (see Table 8-4). but does not represent an accurate picture of all new cases. Factors other than incidence that influence admission figures include the following: social judgment as to what constitutes abnormality, social demand for mental hospital care, availability of psychiatric hospital accommodation, availability of alternative facilities for psychiatric treatment, and variations in diagnostic criteria.

A few attempts have been made to estimate the total incidence of new cases more completely by including data from other treatment facilities. Hollingshead and Redlich reported figures for new cases of neurosis and psychosis in relation to social class. The incidence of psychosis was higher in the lower classes than the upper (the difference being relatively less marked than in the case of total prevalence), whereas the incidence of neurosis was noticeably more evenly distributed throughout the various social classes (although the prevalence of neuroses in treatment was higher among members of the upper classes). These data will be reviewed later.

Lifetime Expectancy. Lifetime expectancy, lifetime incidence, or the probability of developing abnormality during a life time is obviously going to be more difficult to estimate than any measurement of frequency hitherto described. Estimates of lifetime expectancy in the general population are essential, however, for any meaningful comparisons with recorded lifetime frequencies of various abnormalities in the relatives of persons manifesting abnormality. Various methods of estimating lifetime frequency were discussed by Norris, and two such estimates will now be presented briefly.

A partial or incomplete lifetime expectation of mental disorder may be obtained by calculating the probability of being admitted to a mental hospital (with or without a specific clinical diagnosis). This may be done by applying age-sex-specific first admission rates to a life-table population, showing the proportion of individuals remaining alive at successive ages. Norris calculated the expectation of being admitted at least once to a mental hospital in London, England (on the basis of rates for the years 1947-1949), and compared these with similar figures previously calculated for New York state (on the basis of rates for the years 1940-1941). These probabilities of being admitted to mental hospital during a life time and receiving certain diagnoses are shown in Table 8-5.

More thoroughgoing attempts at enumeration of the lifetime expectation of various abnormalities involve the longterm follow-up of large samples of the general population. The most satisfactory study of this nature to date is probably that of Fremming who succeeded in tracing more than 92 percent of 5500 persons born in the Danish Island of Bornholm during the years 1883-1887, up to the time of death or of his inquiry conducted in 1947. By the start of their eleventh year 4130 remained available, and 2710 were still living in Bornholm at the time of their death or of Fremming's retrospective inquiry. The figures he computed for the expectation of mental disorders in this particular sample are shown in Table 8-6, and it should be noted that they apply only to the age range 10 to 54 years. The relatively high expectation of abnormality first recognized or treated after the age of 55 years is not included in this table, and some of the figures probably represent underestimates (particularly those involving relatively minor degrees of abnormality).

TABLE 8–5. Expectation of Being Admitted at Least Once to a Mental Hospital in London and in New York State*

| DIAGNOSIS | EXPECTED NUMBER OF FIRST ADMISSIONS PER 1,000 BIRTHS | | | |
| | London 1947/49 | | N.Y.S. 1940/41 | |
	Male	Female	Male	Female
Schizophrenia	8.4	10.6	15.8	16.1
Manic-depressive and involutional psychoses	8.0	14.4	6.3	14.2
Psychoses of old age	20.6	27.6	31.5	38.2
Psychoneuroses	2.9	2.4		
Organic psychoses (excluding cerebrovascular psychosis)	1.9	2.2	31.4	17.5
Puerperal psychosis	—	0.8		
Other disorders	3.2	3.2		
All disorders	45.0	61.2	85.0	86.0

*From Norris, V. 1959. *Mental Illness in London*. Maudsley Monograph No. 6. London, Oxford University Press.

The latter figures correspond closely with those obtained in an earlier census investigation of Bornholm conducted by Stromgren, and with a number of other studies carried out in Europe. However, it should be borne in mind that these findings refer to a predominantly rural population born in Europe before the beginning of the present century and subjected to diagnostic criteria acceptable in their country of origin. Some of the figures may therefore be expected to differ greatly from those found in a sample population born in an American city within the past few decades, and subjected to diagnostic criteria in this part of the world.

INTERPRETING GROUP DIFFERENCES IN PSYCHOPATHOLOGY

It is generally recognized that both the nature and frequency of different forms of psychopathology vary greatly among different groups of individuals, who may be distinguished from each other by the time or place in which they live, by their age or sex, or by their membership in groups having different sociocultural background and characteristics. The study of such qualitative and quantitative differences has attracted representatives of numerous disciplines, but the interpretation of findings has often been restricted by the investigator's background, knowledge, interest, or by his individual bias. It is not surprising that biological scientists (including some psychiatrists and psychologists) should interpret such differences on the basis of differential hereditary predisposition or various other forms of *biogenesis*, whereas most psychologists and social scientists (who have constituted the majority of investigators in this country) should prefer to implicate *psychogenesis* (involving differences in learning, frustration, and

TABLE 8-6. Expectation of Mental Disorders during Ages 10 to 54 Years, among Fremming's Sample of Danish Population*‡

TYPE OF MENTAL DISORDER	EXPECTATION PER CENT
Schizophrenia	0.88
Manic-depressive psychosis	1.64
Epilepsy	0.35
Dementia paralytica	0.27
Reactive psychosis	0.93
Other psychoses	0.50
Mental defect	1.33
Dull (underestimate)	1.67
Psychopathy (minimal figures)	2.95
Alcoholism	1.74
Psychoneurosis	2.22
Minor affective disorders	0.26
Total	14.74 †

*5500 persons born in the island of Bornholm 1883–1887, of whom 4130 remained available by start of eleventh year and 2710 were still domiciled in Bornholm at time of death or Fremming's inquiry (1947).

†Over-all expectation allowing for multiple disorders in the same person—11.9 per cent.

‡From Fremming, K. H. 1951. *The Expectation of Mental Infirmity in a Sample of the Danish Population.* Occasional Papers on Eugenics No. 7. The Eugenics Society and Cassell & Co., p. 10.

experiences of stress and deprivation) or *sociogenesis* (emphasizing the impact of society and culture).

Frequently a given investigator has assumed that the data demonstrate one type of causation for certain forms of abnormal behavior, and a different type of causation for other abnormalities. Thus, Linton considered that the presence of the major psychoses in all societies was indicative of "some general pattern of damage to the nervous system," whereas the variability of neurotic manifestations indicated different psychogenetic influences among the societies involved. In fact, however, the interpretations of observed sociocultural correlates remains hypothetical since (1) the nature and frequency of abnormal behavior in different sociocultural groups may not have been accurately established and (2) true differences between groups may involve certain interactions between various biological, psychological, or sociocultural determinants—i.e., predisposing, precipitating, and perpetuating (Chapter 4). In the interpretation of such findings as have been reported and are reviewed in the remainder of this chapter, the following considerations should therefore be borne in mind.

1. *The definition of what constitutes abnormality* is sociocultural in nature and is unrelated to causation. Abnormal thinking or behavior is that which is deviant from that of the social group of which the affected individual is a member, and which is recognized by the individual or the group as being unusual or unsatisfactory. Whether the wearing of sunglasses is regarded as normal or abnormal depends upon the opinion of society as well as on the external situation (intensity of light) and the multiple individual determinants considered in Chapter 4. History indicates that western societies have long distinguished between the defective (intellectually subnormal from birth), the delinquent (characterized by his criminal or antisocial behavior), and the "distraught" (or insane). Such social judgment of what constitutes abnormality involves majority opinion, which is not determined by single individuals or even groups of individuals (such as psychiatrists) although it may be influenced by them. Such judgment may also be modified or changed with the passage of time, as illustrated by an increasing tendency to transfer sexual deviation and alcoholism from the category of "delinquency" to that of "sickness" or abnormal behavior.

2. *Action toward individuals judged abnormal* has been related to society's interpretation of their condition, and consequently to prevailing community beliefs, attitudes, understanding, and resources. Abnormal individuals have sometimes been regarded as possessed

by a god or alternatively by demons or witches. Sometimes it has been thought that their souls were absent from their bodies, or more recently that their bodies, minds, or souls were sick. Such beliefs are related to the treatment that the abnormal individual has received, which has included death (from neglect or deliberate action), exorcism or torture, worship, kindly tolerance (or sometimes ignoring the abnormality), custodial care in home, jail, or hospital (either for punishment or protection), and medical treatment in hospital or community. It should be evident that the recognition of abnormality and the type of community action anticipated will have an enormous influence upon the reported frequencies of various forms of abnormality in different social and cultural groups.

3. *Stresses that may precipitate abnormality* in a vulnerable individual may be biological (e.g., a toxic or infective agent), psychological (e.g., frustration or loss of a loved one), or social (e.g., economic distress, unemployment, or war). However, such social stresses (1) have a differential impact on various segments of the population, and (2) precipitate abnormality only in certain members of the group on which they have their maximum impact. Variations in the frequency of suicide and other abnormalities during the twentieth

century appear to reflect mainly the impact of such precipitating stresses. Rates of suicide have tended to *increase in times of economic distress and unemployment* and to *decrease in times of war* when most persons are employed and united against the common enemy (see Figure 8-1). In countries that have been defeated in war, however, and occupied by the enemy, there have been marked increases in rates of suicide among vulnerable segments of the population. Moreover, during wartime, rates of admission to civilian mental hospitals have tended to decrease, whereas high frequencies of mental breakdown have been reported among the vulnerable combatant military personnel. The more remote predisposing effects of war and its aftermaths (mediated through such situations as illegitimacy, widowhood, orphanhood, and difficulties in vocational readjustment), are impossible to separate from the precipitating stresses reflected in the statistics of later years.

4. *Predisposition or vulnerability to stress* may be attributable to heredity, other biological factors, psychogenesis, or circumstances related to membership in a certain sociocultural group. However, there is still tremendous variability in the susceptibility of individuals within such vulnerable sociocultural groups; this variability may be related to indi-

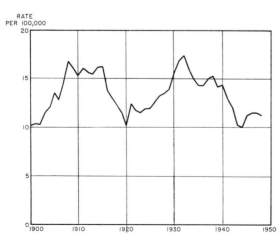

Figure 8-1. Suicide rates per 100,000 population, United States, 1900–1948. (From Vital Statistics of the United States, 1948, National Office of Vital Statistics, Federal Security Agency, U. S. Public Health Service.)

vidual differences in genetic endowment, or biological or psychosocial experiences.

The *contribution of heredity* to the differential sociocultural distribution of abnormal behavior is frequently ignored, but is strongly suggested in the case of those disorders related to intelligence, occupation, and social class. In Chapter 5 it was pointed out that the distribution of intelligence among the general population approximates the normal or bell-shaped curve, and that part of this variation in intelligence (usually estimated as one-half to three-quarters of the total variability) is attributable to genetic factors, probably the cumulative effects of multiple minor genes. It has also been established that childhood intelligence is related on the one hand to *parental* occupational status (Table 8-7), and on the other hand to the *child's* subsequent educational attainment, adult occupational and socio-economic status, mortality experience, and susceptibility to various forms of psychiatric disorder (Terman and Oden). It cannot be assumed that the same genetic factors which partially determine intelligence also partially determine sociocultural status, mor-

tality, and susceptibility to certain forms of psychopathology, but it is a reasonable hypothesis that has not been disproved.

The *contributions of other biological factors* have sometimes been apparent in comparisons between economically advanced and underdeveloped countries. The organic psychoses of senility have become increasingly frequent in countries where many persons survive to old age, but are still infrequent in the underdeveloped countries. On the other hand, underdeveloped countries still have relatively high rates of psychiatric disorder associated with such conditions as malaria, trypanosomiasis (sleeping sickness), massive infestation with intestinal parasites, and nutritional deficiencies such as pellagra (niacin deficiency) and kwashiorkor (protein deficiency). Organic psychoses due to exogenous toxins also show marked geographical and cultural variation, those due to alcohol and certain industrial chemicals being frequent in western countries, whereas a number of primitive tribes may develop intoxications with a variety of exotic drugs.

The *contribution of different child-rearing practices* to sociocultural patterns

TABLE 8-7. I.Q. in Relation to Occupational Status*

OCCUPATIONAL LEVEL	CHILDREN		ADULTS	
	U. S.	ENGLAND	U. S.	ENGLAND
Professional	116	115	120	132
Semi-professional and managerial	112	113	113	117
Clerical, skilled trades, retail business	107	106	108	109
Rural owners, farmers	95	97	94	(No data)
Semiskilled, minor clerical, minor business	105	102	104	105
Slightly skilled	98	97	96	84
Day laborers, rural and urban	96	95	95	96

*From Johnson, D. M. 1948. Application of the standard-score I.Q. to social statistics. Journal of Social Psychology 27, 217.

of behavior and maladaptation is extremely difficult to evaluate, partly because there is much individual variation within families of different social and cultural groups. However, anthropologists such as Benedict and Mead have provided considerable narrative evidence with respect to relationships between prevailing child-rearing practices (involving the majority of children in the primitive groups concerned) and prevailing attitudes and behavior in the adult members of the same societies (including sexual role differentiation and paranoid distortions of reality). Behavioral scientists such as Sears, Maccoby, and Levin have also documented extensive differences in patterns of child-rearing according to the socioeconomic status of the parents, and there is a widespread conviction that such differences are of vital significance in determining the form and frequency of normal and abnormal behaviors in adolescent and adult members of the various social classes.

The *contributions of various social and cultural determinants* in predisposing to the development of abnormal behavior are even more difficult to isolate and evaluate. It is reasonable to suppose that predisposition to abnormal behavior may be partly determined by such social factors as the ambiguous definition of obligations, conflicting or excessive demands on the individual, invidious discrimination, unreasonable discipline, and developmental changes in the goals and behavior of the majority. It would appear necessary for the mental health of its members that a society provide them with opportunities for satisfying basic needs (e.g., for food and shelter); of finding acceptable outlets for sexual and aggressive impulses; of establishing satisfying human relationships (tolerance, friendship, and support in times of stress); of acquiring an education, property, and prestige; and of avoiding situations involving severe stress, anxiety, deprivation, and frustration. It must be concluded, however, that the precise

significance of such social and cultural factors in determining individual abnormality remains undetermined, and must continue to be the subject of sophisticated but open-minded research.

COMPARISONS WITHIN WESTERN SOCIETY

The distribution of various forms of abnormality within western society has been studied extensively according to *time, place* and numerous *demographic characteristics* such as age, sex, marital status, race, country of birth, religion, education, occupation, economic status, and residence. Limitations in the information available regarding changing trends in frequency over a period of time have already been discussed, and certain geographical differences in frequency will be outlined in the present and final sections of this chapter.

The major differences in frequency of various diagnoses according to age and sex have already been reviewed. The distribution of abnormality is also closely related to *marital status*, the rate for most diagnoses being consistently lowest among the married, next among the widowed, then the single, and highest among the divorced. In one typical study of this variable, the present author found that age-sex-standardized (age-sex-adjusted) first admission rates to mental hospitals were as follows: married, 56; widowed, 89; single, 115; and divorced, 286 (annual first admissions per 100,000 standard population). It has long been recognized that such variations in frequency might be attributable either to *protection* against precipitating stresses (for members of those groups having low frequencies), or *selection* on the basis of predisposition to abnormality. Thus, the higher rates in the single than the married may be largely attributable to selection by marriage, particularly against mentally retarded and preschizophrenic males, but also against members of both sexes with other predispositions or existing pathology. The higher rates in the widowed than the married may reflect partly the stress of widowhood, but also selection against remarriage of vulnerable individuals. Similarly the high rates of breakdown in the divorced may reflect either the precipitation of divorce by psychiatric disorder, the precipitation of psychopathology by divorce, or selection against remarriage of certain divorced persons.

Frequencies of abnormalities in relation to race, country of birth, and religion are related to membership in minority groups, and also associated with economic handicaps. When corrections are made for the age and sex composition of such groups, psychiatric hospital admission rates in North America remain relatively higher among Negroes, the foreign born, and members of certain minority religious groups. Such findings may partly reflect a differential tendency to hospitalize members of various social groups with the same degree of abnormality. Population surveys, however, have tended to confirm the existence of higher prevalence rates for certain disorders among such groups, and explanations have again been sought on the basis of either protection against precipitating stress (for the majority), or selection by predisposition. Thus, Odegaard postulated a vulnerability to schizophrenia among those choosing to migrate, whereas subsequently Srole et al. distinguished between the vulnerability of former immigrants of low socioeconomic status and the lower frequency of psychopathology among better endowed immigrants of later years.

Geographical comparisons made between states, or between different parts of individual states, have tended to reflect a strong association between first admission rates (for most "functional" psychiatric disorders) and the urbanization, industrialization, and population density of the area. The latter may, of course, reflect greater social demand for hospital care and provision of such facilities in the more highly industrialized areas. In the case of organic psychoses of senility, for example, it has been shown that admission rates are inversely related to the distance of the patient's residence from the mental hospital.

Marked differences in both hospital admission rates and community prevalence of psychopathology have been found to exist within different areas of the same city, and have been found highly correlated with various indices of the overall socioeconomic status. The surveys of the British sociologist Charles Booth, conducted during the years 1886 to 1901, originated the idea of a "submerged tenth" of the population, particularly evident in the large cities that had developed following the industrial revolution. In Lidbetter's subsequent studies he emphasized the frequency of social dependency among certain families, and many other workers became interested in the "social problem group" of the population, this term being introduced in 1929 by the Mental Deficiency (Wood) Committee. The latter analyzed the findings of six comprehensive and well planned inquiries, including a large proportion of respondents with mild mental retardation, and reported in part as follows.

Let us assume that we could segregate as a separate community all families in this country containing mental defectives of the primary amentia type. We should find that we had collected among them a most interesting social group. It would include, as everyone who has extensive practical experience of social service would readily admit, a much larger proportion of insane persons, epileptics, paupers, criminals (especially recidivists), unemployables, habitual slum dwellers, prostitutes, inebriated and other social inefficients than would a group of families not containing mental defectives. The overwhelming majority of the families thus collected will belong to that section of the community, which we propose to term the "social problem" or "subnormal" group. This group comprises approximately the lowest ten percent in the social scale of most communities. Though a large majority of its members are not so low grade mentally that they can be actually certified as mentally defective, it is possible that a not inconsiderable number of them might prove, if examined by expert and experienced medical practitioners, to be certifiable and subject to be placed under care and control.

Blacker reviewed the results of several other British studies and concluded that the problem family commonly presents five features: a subnormal intelligence in one or both parents, an instability of character distinguishable from subnormal intelligence, intractable ineducability, a squalid home, and the presence of neglected and often numerous children. While there is considerable difficulty in distinguishing between cause and effect (among the preceding and many other associated characteristics of these families), it appears that the most essential features are intellectual subnormality and antisocial behavior (sociopathic personality characteristics) in one, or more commonly, both parents.

It has long been recognized that the frequency of many physical illnesses and the overall rates of mortality are highest among those of lowest socioeconomic status, and particularly within certain families of the lowest socioeconomic group. More recent studies have also documented the higher frequencies in the same families of mental abnormality, delinquency, or other social problems. Buell reported as follows:

Although about 23 percent of St. Paul's families were being served by one or more of the 90-odd agencies and services in the fields of economic dependency, health and maladjustment, we found that a group amounting to 6 percent of the community's families suffered from such compounding of these human ills that they were absorbing more than 50 per cent of the services. Though some such ideas long have been accepted by most of our experienced practitioners, this was the first time it had been documented in precise fashion. For our research purposes we have since referred to this small group as the 'multiproblem' families. . . . In St. Paul the multiproblem group accounted for 77 percent of the relief load, 51 percent of the drain on health services, 56 percent of the load carried by adjustment services in the mental health, casework and corrections fields.

Sociologists in the United States have tended to ignore the associations between social class and intelligence, mental retardation, and bodily illness (together with the possible significance of heredity and other biological factors in causation). They have, however, provided considerable evidence of relationships between locality of urban residence, socioeconomic status, and the frequency of psychoses, neuroses, and behavior disorders.

Between 1929 and 1942, Shaw and McKay stimulated a number of sociologists to undertake ecological studies of high delinquency areas in various cities in the United States. Shaw and McKay themselves found high correlations in Chicago between rates of male juvenile delinquency and zones or areas of the city; these correlations remained the same despite differences in the demographic composition of the populations residing in these areas over a period of time. In Baltimore, Lander observed high positive correlations between juvenile delinquency, overcrowding, and substandard housing conditions; with high negative correlations between delinquency, median rentals, and median years of schooling. However, he hypothesized that these were only surface relationships and that high delinquency rates were best interpreted in terms of *anomie*, according to which the group norms of behavior are no longer binding or valid in an area or for a population subgroup. Morris further drew attention to the finding that within *high* delinquency areas, there were certain streets and families with *low* rates of delinquency, and that family membership was more crucial than residence in underprivileged neighborhoods.

Faris and Dunham analyzed the distribution of mental hospital admission rates for various diagnoses from different areas within the city of Chicago. They found that overall admission rates per 100,000 population increased progressively from the periphery of the city (residential zone of single family dwellings) to the central areas of social disorganization and slum dwellings. The distribution of admissions with schizophrenia, alcoholism, drug addiction, and general paresis (central nervous system syphilis) all corresponded to the overall distribution of admissions, in contrast with manic depressive psychosis, which was randomly distributed throughout the city. Different patterns of distribution were found for different subtypes of schizophrenia, high rates of paranoid and hebephrenic types being recorded for communities in which the populations were highly mobile, whereas high rates of catatonic types were related principally to foreign born slum areas.

These authors considered the possiblity that the central concentration of admission rates, particularly for schizophrenia, might be due to *downward drift* of mentally abnormal individuals who had failed in economic competition. However, they pointed out that many of the patients with schizophrenia had been born in and had always lived in deteriorated areas, and they suggested that *social isolation* and other conditions of life in these areas combined to produce mental abnormality. While a similar distribution of mental disorders, particularly schizophrenia, has been found by a number of other workers in the United States and elsewhere, their interpretation has remained a matter of dispute. There are some authors who have continued to postulate that social and geographical drift may be at least as important as social isolation or stress in determining this distribution.

In their important study of social class and mental illness, Hollingshead and Redlich undertook a sophisticated and extensive analysis based on a census of all psychiatric patients from the city of New Haven, Connecticut, at a given point in time, and all new patients admitted to treatment during a period of six months (in the year 1950). Their enumeration included patients receiving treatment outside the city of New Haven, such as those currently residing in state or private psychiatric hospitals, and those commuting to New York for psychoanalysis. Their data permitted estimates of prevalence at a point in time, and incidence of new cases, for both psychoses and neuroses, each according to social class membership, as shown in Table 8-8. It may be seen that the incidence of *new* cases of neurosis was fairly evenly distributed, whereas the *total* prevalence of neurotics *receiving treatment* was highest in members of the upper classes. The incidence of *new* cases of psychosis was highest among the lowest social class, but the *total* prevalence of patients with psychoses *receiving treatment or custodial care* was relatively even higher in the lowest class, reflecting a tendency to chronicity. The authors related this chronicity to the inadequate treatment received by members of the lowest class, and documented social class differences in the prevailing patterns of

TABLE 8-8. Incidence and Prevalence Rates per 100,000 for Neuroses and Psychoses (New Haven, Conn., Receiving Treatment, 1950)*

CLASS	SIX-MONTH INCIDENCE	PREVALENCE
Neuroses		
I-II	69	349
III	78	250
IV	52	114
V	66	97
Psychoses		
I-II	28	188
III	36	291
IV	37	518
V	73	1505

*Adapted from Hollingshead, A. B., and Redlich, F. C. *Social Class and Mental Illness.* Copyright 1958 by John Wiley & Sons, Inc., p. 235.

treatment—but the tendency toward chronicity might be independent of treatment. Patterns of psychiatric treatment have also changed since the time of this study.

In a subsequent study of family and class dynamics in mental illness, Myers and Roberts undertook an intensive analysis of the data available on 50 patients identified in the course of the preceding study. Twenty-six of the 50 were members of Class III and 24 were members of Class V (the lowest class); approximately half of each group were neurotic and the remainder schizophrenic. Among the Class III patients, the highly regarded values of respectability and success figured prominently in the patients' socialization, and were considered to result in three types of stress: (1) conflict between instinctive drives and moral values; (2) frustration from inability to achieve respectability and success; (3) tension arising from upward mobility striving. By contrast, the Class V patients were exposed to adverse economic conditions and to isolation from community institutions, which were associated with five distinct patterns of stress: (1) most patients were reared in an environment containing little love, affection, protection, and stability; (2) most of them were constantly on the defensive in their relationships with their parents; (3) they felt neglected or rejected all their lives, first by their parents, brothers, and sisters, and later by the institutional representatives of society and higher status persons in general; (4) most experienced lifelong economic insecurity; (5) their more direct expression of their instinctual impulses resulted in stresses based on the reciprocal behavior of others. In this particular study, Class III patients were more upwardly mobile in society than their brothers and sisters and a comparable group of nonpatients, whereas Class V patients had achieved no more success than their siblings or the nonpatients.

An investigation of comparable magnitude and significance was undertaken by a group of Cornell University scientists, who undertook both a census of psychiatric patients and a home survey among the population of Midtown

TABLE 8-9. *Home Survey Sample (Age 20-59), Distributions of Respondents on Mental Health Classification by Parental-SES Strata†*

Mental health categories	PARENTAL-SES STRATA					
	A (highest)	B	C	D	E	F (lowest)
Well	24.4%	23.3%	19.9%	18.8%	13.6%	9.7%
Mild symptom formation	36.0	38.3	36.6	36.6	36.6	32.7
Moderate symptom formation	22.1	22.0	22.6	20.1	20.4	24.9
Impaired*	17.5	16.4	20.9	24.5	29.4	32.7
Marked symptom formation	11.8	8.6	11.8	13.3	16.2	18.0
Severe symptom formation	3.8	4.5	8.1	8.3	10.2	10.1
Incapacitated	1.9	3.3	1.0	2.9	3.0	4.6
N = 100%	(262)	(245)	(287)	(384)	(265)	(217)

*x^2=28.81, 5df, $p < .001$.
†From Srole, L., Langner, T. S., Michael, S. C., Opler, M. K., and Rennie, P. A. C. *Mental Health in the Metropolis.* Copyright 1962, McGraw-Hill Book Company. Used by permission of McGraw-Hill Book Company.

Manhattan, thus enabling estimates of the prevalence of both treated and untreated psychopathology. In the first volume analyzing their findings, Srole et al. presented detailed information dealing with the distribution of psychopathology according to age, sex, marital status, original and current socioeconomic status, generation in the United States and rural-urban origins, and national and religious origins. Of particular interest to the present discussion is the mental health category of the individual in relation to *parental socioeconomic status* (Table 8-9) and also the mental health category of the individual according to his own mobility in occupational status (Table 8-10). These would appear to provide clearcut evidence that good mental health is most frequent in those with parents of superior socioeconomic status (SES), and also tends to be associated with occupational stability or upward mobility; whereas psychiatric impairment is most frequent in those with parents of low socioeconomic status (SES) and also is most likely to be seen in association with downward occupational mobility. Further data showed that among men originating in or ascending into the top occupational class, their "sick-well ratio" was approximately 15 for non-mobile men, 30 for upward-mobile

men, and 300 for downward-mobile men (as compared with an overall sick-well ratio of 127).

In the final chapter of this volume, Srole attached paramount importance to the findings that respondents' SES-origin and age showed a separate but mutually reinforcing input relationship to frequencies of both mental morbidity and wellness among Midtown's sample adults. Srole went on to postulate that (1) handicaps in personality resources, social skills, and cohesions of parents, (2) the complex of effects directly generated by poverty, and (3) the community's stigmatize-rejection process, mutually reinforcing each other, may go far toward explaining the finding that offspring of low SES-origin families at all adult age levels reflect maximum vulnerability to mental morbidity and minimum fulfillment of wellness. He suggested that SES-origin pinpoints locations of differential "sowing" of latent pathology, whereas the age factor highlights clustering points in the "reaping" of overt morbidity. The third variable significantly related to mental health was immigration, and this factor was subjected to intricate analysis. Srole's conclusion was that each of these three demographic variables (SES-origin, age, and immigration) involve varying com-

TABLE 8-10. Home Survey Sample (Age 20-59), Distributions on Mental Health Classification of Age 20-29 Respondents by Occupational Mobility Types

Mental health categories	Mobility types		
	Up	Stable	Down
Well..........................	21.0%	22.6%	12.7%
Mild symptom formation...........	41.6	37.0	33.8
Moderate symptom formation......	23.8	16.8	23.4
Impaired*......................	13.6	23.6	30.1
N = 100%.....................	(315)	(297)	(299)
Sick-Well ratio...................	65	104	235

*$x^2=24.57$, $2df$, $p < .001$.

†From Srole, L., Langner, T. S., Michael, S. C., Opler, M. K., and Rennie, P. A. C. *Mental Health in the Metropolis.* Copyright 1962, McGraw-Hill Book Company. Used by permission of McGraw-Hill Book Company.

binations of three potentially malignant socially linked phenomena, namely (1) the poverty complex, (2) the role-discontinuity predicament, and (3) the stigmatize-rejection mechanism.

Further results of the Midtown, Manhattan, study were presented by Langner and Michael in a volume entitled *Life Stress and Mental Health.* These authors attempted to analyze the lifelong cumulative impact of differential social stresses and their consequences for individuals and groups, in terms of strain or manifestations of psychopathology as illustrated in their model which was presented briefly in Chapter 4. At the end of their final chapter, they contrasted the experience and behavior of lower and higher socioeconomic status groups, in a six-page table of findings and hypotheses that is strongly recommended for reference by any serious student of relationships between social status and psychopathology.

TRANSCULTURAL COMPARISONS

Regional differences in attitudes within the United States may be illustrated in a number of ways, one of which is a report attributed to Amy Vanderbilt on the word preferred by photographers in order to produce an animated expression in their subjects. In Hollywood, this word was reputed to be "sex"; in the Midwest, it was "cheese"; in the South, it was "honey" or "really"; and in Manhattan, it was "money."

Others have related similar differences between members of various nations. For example, it has been remarked that in Germany what is forbidden is not allowed; in France, what is not forbidden is allowed; and in the United States, what is forbidden is allowed. Someone suggested that national characteristics were exemplified in the naming of rockets. Americans named theirs Titan, Thor, Jupiter, Atlas, and Saturn; the English called theirs Black Knight, Bloodhound, and Thunderbird; whereas the French named their rockets Veronica and Monica.

An accumulation of such impressions may be integrated into national or *cultural stereotypes*, but it is good to emphasize that such judgments of national characteristics are frequently based on the *impressions created by a visible minority of its members.* American concepts of the "Latin temperament" may be colored by either the volatile emotional displays or the sedentary habits of a small proportion of the population. European concepts of the American character in turn may be determined largely by movies originating in Hollywood, or impressions derived from personal contact with a few travelers from the United States.

Clinical impressions of psychiatrists have suggested that certain forms of psychopathology may be more frequent among some cultures than others. For example, it was stated many years ago that male homosexuality was relatively frequent in Germany, female homosexuality and oral sexuality in France, and sado-masochistic practices in England. In recent years, increasing reliance has been placed on statistical comparisons between the frequency of specific forms of psychopathology in different countries. Many of these comparisons are of questionable validity, but differences in the frequency of alcoholism, based on deaths from hepatic cirrhosis, may reflect true differences in prevalence, and show some interesting differences in the ratio between sexes. In the United Kingdom the latter ratio is approximately two males to one female, in North America approximately five males to one female, and in Scandinavian countries approximately 20 males to one female alcoholic. Apparently such differences reflect different degrees of cultural tolerance or prohibition directed towards drinking behavior in females. Similar differences probably exist with respect to a variety of other behaviors which include child-rearing practices, although similarities in widely separated cultures may be as impressive as observed differences.

Wittkower and Fried reported on correspondence involving psychiatrists and social scientists in over 30 countries, and remarked on four questions that had been raised repeatedly: (1) Are there any significant differences in the prevalence and incidence of mental disorders in different cultures? (2) Are there any mental disorders common in some cultures but nonexistent in others? (3) Are there any nosological differences in the manifestations of mental disease in comparisons of different cultures? (4) Are there any psychiatric syndromes specific to certain geographical areas or cultural confines?

The reader may recall similarities between these questions and those that have been raised regarding variations in abnormality in our own civilization over the course of the past two centuries. Both types of question are related to the more basic issues of whether culture may cause or modify abnormal behavior in its individual members, and how it may accomplish this. Crosscultural comparisons have hitherto provided no more categorical answers to the latter questions than the analysis of time trends within our own society. However, problems of methodology have been increasingly recognized, techniques of measurement have become more refined, and the extensive literature of the past few decades suggests several preliminary generalizations such as the following: (1) that concepts of normality vary greatly from one culture to another, (2) that socially sanctioned behavior towards different forms of individual deviation also varies widely, (3) that all forms of psychiatric disorder known to western society may also be observed in more primitive societies, (4) that the frequency of these disorders may vary greatly from one primitive society to another, but that accurate estimates of such frequency are still lacking, (5) that the manifestations of a given disorder (for example, schizophrenia) may vary greatly from one culture to another, (6) that a number of syndromes reported in various primitive societies have not been observed in economically advanced countries.

In discussing the concept of normality, Arieti and Meth pointed out that in the west, suicide has long been considered to be a sign of emotional disorder, whereas in Japan it may have been normal in certain circumstances. They went on to state that "among the islanders of Dobu (Melanesia), no sane woman leaves her cooking pot unguarded for fear of being poisoned. To us, this behavior would indicate paranoia. Among some Eskimo tribes the mother accepts the killer of her son in her son's stead. Among the Papuans it is traditional for an uncle and nephew (mother's brother and son) to practice homosexuality. In Tibet a group of brothers inherit their father's second wife when he gets old. A Navajo male may marry a widow with a daughter, then later discard the mother and marry the daughter. It is not unusual for an Arapesh to marry simultaneously a mother and her daughter. These are a few behavior patterns which we consider abnormal but which are entirely normal in other civilizations." They also remarked that "one could easily yield to the weight of the factor of cultural variability and conclude that culture is by far the most important element in the etiology of mental conditions," but they continued as follows: "Actually, there is a great uniformity in the psychiatric nosology of people whose cultural norms vary widely. . . .The majority of psychiatric cases of all times and all places are similar to ours."

Malinowski compared three primitive societies and concluded that the type of culture determines the amount and kind of neurosis. Faris found few or no psychoses among natives in the Congo and attributed this to their having a simple and integrated social organization. Carothers reported mental hospital admission rates in Kenya were only a fraction of the comparable rates for England and North America. It has been maintained that the frequency of depression and suicide is particularly low among the African Negroes and that various forms of neuroses and psychophysiologic disorders are much less common in primitive than civilized societies. Such findings, however, have been treated with increasing skepticism in recent years. Linton has correctly pointed to such other considerations as the lack of facilities for the care of the insane or deviant, the concealment of insanity by families who view it as a disgrace, and the fact that troublesome psychotics may be allowed to die (if they cannot take care of themselves) or may be killed (if they become violent). It has also been pointed out that it is even more difficult to make an estimate of the frequency of milder abnormality such as neurosis or psychophysiologic disorders in primitive societies than in more highly developed countries.

Eaton and Weil undertook a detailed analysis of psychopathology in a relatively isolated cultural group living within North America. They measured the prevalence and estimated the lifetime expectancy of various disorders among members of the Hutterite sect, and compared the expectancy of psychoses in this group with estimates derived from previous studies of nine other population groups. The Hutterites had a higher enumerated rate of psychoses than seven of these populations, but the authors were rightly skeptical regarding the validity of this finding, and placed much greater emphasis on the *relatively high frequency of depression among the Hutterites associated with relatively low frequencies of schizophrenia and antisocial behavior.* They related this to the extreme emphasis of the Hutterites on communal cohesiveness and remarked, "There is much stress on religion, duty to God and society, and there is a tendency in their entire thinking to orient members to internalize their aggressive drives.

Children and adults alike are taught to look for guilt within themselves rather than in others." While this hypothesis is plausible, the crosscultural comparisons of frequency remain unconvincing.

It has been established, however, that certain organic brain syndromes (infections or intoxications) occur more frequently in certain countries than in others, and that the symptoms of "functional" psychiatric disorders may be modified considerably by the culture in which the individual resides. It has been reported that hospitalized schizophrenic patients are less aggressive and violent in India and Japan than in western mental hospitals. The content of schizophrenic delusions is also related to the cultural milieu. Schizophrenics from primitive tribes tend to complain of feeling bewitched or poisoned, whereas those from more highly developed countries are more apt to blame radio, television, and various other electrical devices.

Among many interesting syndromes that have been reported from various other cultures, mention may be made of *latah* (characterized by echolalia, echopraxia, and coprolalia), *amok* (a sudden homicidal mania, tending to result in social retribution leading to the death of the affected individual), *coro* (a phobia that the penis will disappear into the abdomen and result in death), *witigo* (whitico or windigo, involving cannibalism attributed to supernatural possession), and *voodoo death* (thanatomania or death resulting from transgression of a taboo or a delusion of having been bewitched). These disorders have been discussed by Linton and by Arieti and Meth.

Among the extensive crosscultural comparisons of recent years may be mentioned books on patterns of sexual behavior (Ford and Beach), personality (edited by Kaplan), and mental health (one edited by Opler, and another by Soddy). One of the largest programs of crosscultural studies on the prevalence of psychiatric disorders has been coordinated by Leighton. This includes the Stirling County study in Eastern Canada, and studies of an Eskimo village, two Mexican communities, and the Yoruba people of Nigeria. Books describing these studies have already appeared. The overall program was reviewed in an article by Murphy, in which she related the prevalence of psychiatric disorders to concepts of social integration and disintegration. In defining the latter she wrote, "To our way of thinking, a disintegrated environment is characterized by proportions and combinations of a number of conditions such as rapid sociocultural change (either in terms of the environment changing or of individuals migrating from one setting to another), poor economic conditions, secularization or ideological conflict, fractured social relationships especially in the basic living units of home or lineage, ill health or diseaster, and residence in groups which lack adequate leadership, education, recreation, association, communication, and control of crime and delinquency." The search for specific sociocultural correlates and determinants of psychopathology still continues.

SELECTED REFERENCES

Anastasi, A. 1958. *Differential Psychology*, 3rd edition. New York, The Macmillan Co., ch. 15-18.

Arieti, S., and Meth, J. M. 1959. In *American Handbook of Psychiatry*, ed. S. Arieti. New York, Basic Books, Inc., ch. 7.

Asch, S. E. 1955. Opinions and social pressure. Scientific American, November issue.

Benedict, R. 1934. *Patterns of Culture*. Boston, Houghton Mifflin Co. Reprinted, 1936, New York, Mentor Book No. 89.

Blacker, C. P. 1952. *Problem Families: Five Inquiries* London, Eugenics Society.

Bliss, E. L., ed. 1962. *Roots of Behavior*. New York, Hoeber Medical Division, Harper & Row, Publishers, Inc., ch. 20-23.

Bogardus, E. S. 1928. *Immigration and Race Attitudes*. Boston, D. C. Heath and Co.

Buell, B. 1955. Preventing and controlling disordered behavior. Mental Hygiene *39*, 365-375.

Calhoun, J. B. 1962. A "behavioral sink." In *Roots of Behavior*, ed. E. L. Bliss. New York, Hoeber Medical Division, Harper & Row, Publishers, Inc., ch. 22.

Carothers, J. C. 1959. *The African Mind in Health and Disease*. Geneva, World Health Organization, Monograph Series No. 17.

Clausen, J. A. 1959. The sociology of mental illness. In *Sociology Today*. New York, Basic Books, Inc., ch. 22.

Davis, A., Gardner, B., and Gardner, M. 1941. *Deep South*. Chicago, University of Chicago Press, p. 65.

Davis, K. 1948. *Human Society*. New York, The Macmillan Co., ch. 2, 3, 4, 10, and 14.

Dayton, N. A. 1940. *New Facts on Mental Disorders.* Springfield, Illinois, Charles C Thomas, Publisher.

Eaton, J. W., and Weil, R. J. 1955. *Culture and Mental Disorders*. Glencoe, Illinois, The Free Press, division of The Macmillan Co.

Engel, G. L. 1962. *Psychological Development in Health and Disease*. Philadelphia, W. B. Saunders Co. ch. 26-28.

Faris, R. E. L., and Dunham, H. W. 1939. *Mental Disorders in Urban Areas.* Reprinted, 1960, New York, Hafner Publishing Co., Inc.

Ford, C. S., and Beach, F. A. 1951. *Patterns of Sexual Behavior*. New York, Hoeber Medical Division, Harper & Row, Publishers, Inc.

Frank, L. K. 1936. Society as the patient. American Journal of Sociology *42*, 335-344.

Fremming, K. H. 1951. *The Expectaion of Mental Infirmity in a Sample of the Danish Population*. London, Eugenics Society and Cassell and Company, Occasional Papers on Eugenics No. 7.

Freud, S. 1930. *Civilization and Its Discontents*. New York, Cape and Smith.

Fromm, E. 1955. *The Sane Society*. New York, Holt, Rinehart & Winston, Inc.

Goldhamer, H., and Marshall, A. W. 1949. *Psychosis and Civilization*. Glencoe, Illinois, The Free Press, division of The Macmillan Co.

Gordon, J. E., O'Rourke, E., Richardson, S. L. W., and Lindemann, E. 1952. Preventive medicine and epidemiology—the biological and social sciences in an epidemiology of mental disorder. American Journal of the Medical Sciences *223*, 316-343.

Gregory, I. 1956. Factors influencing first admission rates to Canadian mental hospitals. I. An analysis of trends, 1932, 1953. Canadian Psychiatric Association Journal *1*, 115-143.

Gregory, I. 1959. Factors influencing first admission rates to Canadian mental hospitals. II. An analysis of provincial differences, 1950-1952. Canadian Psychiatric Association Journal *4*, 51-60.

Gregory, I. 1959. Factors influencing first admission rates to Canadian mental hospitals. III. An analysis by education, marital status, country of birth, religion, rural-urban residents, 1950-52. Canadian Psychiatric Association Journal *4*, 133-151.

Group for the Advancement of Psychiatry. 1961. *Problems of Estimating Changes in Frequency of Mental Disorder*. New York, GAP Report No. 50.

Halliday, J. L. 1948. *Psychosocial Medicine: A Study of the Sick Society.* New York, W. W. Norton & Co., Inc.

Hollingshead, A. B., and Redlich, F. C. 1958. *Social Class and Mental Illness.* New York, John Wiley & Sons, Inc.

Horney, K. 1947. *The Neurotic Personality of Our Time.* New York, W. W. Norton & Co., Inc.

Johnson, D. M. 1948. Application of the standard-score I.Q. to social statistics. Journal of Social Psychology 27, 217-27.

Kaplan, B., ed. 1961. *Studying Personality Cross-Culturally.* Evanston, Illinois, Row, Peterson & Co.

Kardiner, A. 1954. Social stress and deprivation. In *Beyond the Germ Theory*, ed. I. Galdston. New York, Academy of Medicine, Health and Education Council, ch. 10 and 11.

Kinsey, A. C., Pomeroy, W. B., Martin, C. E., and Gebhard, P. H. 1953. *Sexual Behavior in the Human Female.* Philadelphia, W. B. Saunders Co., pp. 685-687.

Kluckhohn, C., Murray, H. A., and Schneider, D. M., eds. 1953. *Personality in Nature, Society and Culture*, 2nd edition. New York, Alfred A. Knopf, Inc.

Kramer, M., Goldstein, H., Israel, R. H., and Johnson, N. A. 1955. *A Historical Study of the Disposition of First Admissions to a State Mental Hospital.* Washington, D. C., U.S. Department of Health, Education, and Welfare, Public Health Monograph No. 32.

Lander, B. 1954. *Towards an Understanding of Juvenile Delinquency.* New York, Columbia University Press, pp. 77-90.

Langner, T. S., and Michael, S. T. 1963. *Life Stress and Mental Health.* New York, The Free Press of Glencoe (The Macmillan Co.)

Larsson, T., and Sjogren, T. 1954. *A methodological, psychiatric and statistical study of a large Swedish rural population.* Acta Psychiatria Supplementum 89.

Leighton, A. H., Clausen, J. A., and Wilson, R. N., eds. 1957. *Explorations in Social Psychiatry.* New York, Basic Books, Inc.

Lindesmith, A. R., and Strauss, A. L. 1956. *Social Psychology*, revised edition. New York, Holt, Rinehart & Winston, Inc.

Linton, R. 1956. *Culture and Mental Disorders.* Springfield, Illinois, Charles C Thomas, Publisher.

Malinowski, B. 1927. *Sex and Repression in Savage Society.* New York, Harcourt, Brace & World, Inc.

Malzberg, B. 1940. *Social and Biological Aspects of Mental Disease.* Utica, New York, State Hospitals Press.

Mead, M. 1935. *Sex and Temperament.* Reprinted 1950, New York, Mentor No. M.D. 133.

Mead, M. 1949. *Male and Female.* Reprinted 1955, New York, Mentor No. M.D. 150.

Milbank Memorial Fund. 1950. *Epidemiology of Mental Disorders.* New York, Milbank Memorial Fund.

Milbank Memorial Fund. 1953. *Interrelations Between the Social Environment and Psychiatric Disorders.* New York, Milbank Memorial Fund.

Milbank Memorial Fund. 1957. *The Nature and Transmission of the Genetic and Cultural Characteristics of Human Populations.* New York, Milbank Memorial Fund.

Milbank Memorial Fund. 1961. *Causes of Mental Disorders: A Review of Epidemiological Knowledge.* New York, Milbank Memorial Fund.

Morris, T. 1958. *The Criminal Area.* London, Routledge and Kegan Paul, pp. 92-105.

Murphy, J. M. 1962. Cross-cultural studies of the prevalence of psychiatric disorders. World Mental Health 14, 53-65.

Myers, J. K., and Roberts, B. H. 1959. *Family and Class Dynamics in Mental Illness.* New York, John Wiley & Sons, Inc.

Norris, V. 1959. *Mental Illness in London.* London, Oxford University Press, Maudsley Monograph No. 6.

Opler, M. K., ed. 1959. *Culture and Mental Health.* New York, The Macmillan Co.

Packard, V. 1959. *The Status Seekers.* Reprinted by Pocketbooks, Inc., New York, Cardinal Edition, G.C. 601.

Pasamanick, B., ed. 1959. *Epidemiology of Mental Disorder.* Washington, D.C., American Association for the Advancement of Science, Publication No. 60.

Pasamanick, B., and Knapp, P. H., eds. 1958. *Social Aspects of Psychiatry.* Washington, D.C., American Psychiatric Association, Psychiatric Research Reports, No. 10.

Plunkett, R. J., and Gordon, J. E. 1960. *Epidemiology and Mental Illness.* New York, Basic Books, Inc., Joint Commission on Mental Illness and Health, Monograph Series No. 6.

Rainwater, L. 1960. *And the Poor Get Children.* Chicago, Quadrangle Books, Inc.

Reid, E. D. 1960. *Epidemiological Methods in the Study of Mental Disorders.* Geneva, World Health Organization, Public Health Papers No. 2.

Rettig, S. 1966. Ethical risk taking in group and individual conditions. Journal of Personality and Social Psychology, in press.

Rettig, S., and Pasamanick, B. 1964. Differential judgment of ethical risk by cheaters and noncheaters. Journal of Abnormal and Social Psychology 69, 109-113.

Rettig, S., and Rawson, H. E. 1963. The risk hypothesis in predictive judgments of unethical behavior. Journal of Abnormal and Social Psychology 66, 243-248.

Rose, A. M., ed. 1955. *Mental Health and Mental Disorder.* New York, W. W. Norton & Co., Inc.

Rosen, G. 1959. Social stress and mental disease from the eighteenth century to the present: some origins of social psychiatry. Milbank Memorial Quarterly 37, 5-32.

Scott, J. P. 1958. *Animal Behavior.* Chicago, University of Chicago Press, chapter 8.

Sears, R. R., Maccoby, E. E., and Levin, H. 1957. *Patterns of Child Rearing.* Evanston, Illinois, Row Peterson, & Co., ch. 12.

Shaw, C. R., and McKay, H. D. 1942. *Juvenile*

Delinquency and Urban Areas. Chicago, University of Chicago Press, pp. 60-68.

Sherif, M. 1956. Experiments in group conflict. Scientific American, November issue.

Soddy, K., ed. 1961. *Cross-cultural Studies in Mental Health.* London, Tavistock Publications.

Srole, L., Langner, T. S., Michael, S. C., Opler, M. K., and Rennie, P. A. C. 1962. *Mental Health in the Metropolis: The Midtown Manhattan Study,* Vol. 1. New York, McGraw-Hill Book Co., Inc.

Stromgren, E. 1950. Statistical and genetical population studies within psychiatry, methods and principal results. In *Congres Internationale de Psychiatrie, Paris, 1950. VI. Psychiatrie Sociale. Genetique et Eugenique.* Paris, Hermann and Cie.

Terman, L. M., and Oden, M. H. 1959. *The Gifted Group at Mid-Life.* Stanford, California, Stanford University Press.

Tyler, L. E. 1956. *The Psychology of Human Differences,* 2nd edition. New York, Appleton-Crofts, Inc., ch. 10-14.

Wanklin, J. M., Buck, C. W., and Hobbs, G. E. 1956. The distribution of mental disease. Mental Hygiene *40,* 275-282.

Whiting, J. W. M., and Child, I. L. 1953. *Child Training and Personality: A Cross-Cultural Study.* New Haven, Connecticut, Yale University Press.

Wittkower, E. D., and Fried, J. 1959. A cross-cultural approach to mental health problems. American Journal of Psychiatry. *116,* 423-428.

Wolfgang, M. E., Savitz, L., and Johnston, N., eds. 1962. *The Sociology of Crime and Delinquency.* New York, John Wiley & Sons, Inc.

My mother says that he is my father, but myself I do not know,
for no man can know who was his father.

Homer

You start a question and it's like starting a stone from on top of a hill;
Away the stone goes, starting others.

Robert Louis Stevenson

A friend is a person with whom I may be sincere.
Before him, I may think aloud.

Ralph Waldo Emerson

Psychiatric Interviewing and Evaluation

THE INITIAL PSYCHIATRIC INTERVIEW

During the present century, there has been increasingly widespread recognition of the high frequency of psychiatric disorders and of emotional factors related to bodily illness. Psychiatric treatment has also become more widely available, and there has been increasing public demand for such treatment, together with dramatic increases in medical school curriculum time for clinical psychiatry and relevant basic behavioral sciences.

Concurrently, there has been a worldwide trend toward recognition of the dignity of the individual member of society, and psychiatrists have advocated customs and laws that promote reasonable self-determination and responsibility on the part of psychiatric patients, provided that these are compatible with the safety of the patient and other members of society. Many hospitals accepting a high proportion of psychotic patients now do so on the patient's own voluntary application

instead of following legal commitment procedures, and within such hospitals there has been an increasing trend toward open-door policies, with an accompanying reduction in maximum security precautions.

Such factors have combined to make it increasingly likely that the psychiatric patient will recognize at least some aspects of his emotional disorder, and voluntarily consult a physician or other member of society perceived as having special competence in helping persons with similar problems. Nevertheless, the patient's expectations may be unrealistic, and may still be contaminated by prejudices that he has learned from others. His ambivalence toward psychiatry may be reflected in the ambiguous concept that "anyone who consults a psychiatrist should have his head examined." He may also have a cultural stereotype of the psychiatrist as a man who "administers the talking cure," or as one who dispenses some medical magic in the form of pills or electroshock.

The physician or psychiatrist in his turn responds to the role-expectations placed upon him by his training, his peers, the general public, and the specific individual who consults him as a patient. Sometimes these role-expectations conflict with one another, and it should be recalled that "the man who pays the piper calls the tune," so that a physician engaged in private practice may respond somewhat differently from one who is a full-time salaried employee of an institution or social agency.

Such considerations have resulted in varying attitudes toward what should be accomplished in an initial psychiatric interview. In some situations, the emphasis has been upon standardized questioning and recording of mental examination and psychiatric history for purposes of diagnostic evaluation. In other situations, *the first psychiatric interview is correctly viewed as the first therapeutic interview*, which attitude requires a much greater degree of flexibility on the part of the interviewer. The latter approach is most consistent with the perceived needs of the patient, and is increasingly widely favored by those responsible for teaching psychiatric evaluation. We shall therefore emphasize certain aspects of the interpersonal relationship before proceeding to the standardized recording of information that may be obtained. In passing it should be noted that the previous chapters of this book most relevant to the present chapter are those on definition and description (Chapter 2), dynamics and development (Chapter 3), and psychological determinants of psychopathology: learning, psychological stress, and deprivation (Chapter 7).

It has been remarked that "the beginning is the most important part of anything," and the relationship developed with the patient during the first interview may foster or impair the behavioral changes that may be anticipated from subsequent interviews. It has also been said that "it is not the words but the music" that is significant in effecting therapeutic change. The physician must be particularly aware of the nonverbal communications (of affect and role-expectation) by himself toward the patient, as well as by the patient toward the physician.

The patient may approach this new situation with attitudes of fear or mistrust, and with expectations that he will be criticized, ignored, deceived, or rejected. It is up to the physician to convey to the patient an attitude of respect and warm acceptance, upon which a relationship or trust may be developed. This may be done more easily if the physician recognizes that such negative feelings as the patient may have toward him are largely the result of *displacement* resulting from the patient's previous experiences and relationships with parents and others in authority, for example. The patient may also view the physician as someone who is in league with hostile relatives or other members of society who have lowered his self-esteem by suggesting or arranging the interview. The patient's first impression of the physician may either confirm his fears or lead to their modification and eventual abandonment. The physician must therefore show interest in, understanding of, and acceptance of the patient and his feelings — though not necessarily approval of his behavior. The patient should be interviewed alone, in quiet and comfortable surroundings. The interview should be for an adequate period of time (usually 45 or 50 minutes) and should be uninterrupted, as for example by telephone calls or by the physician's referring to his watch.

Effective interviewing involves catalyzing and maximizing the patient's ability to communicate both verbally and nonverbally. Complete lack of structure in the interview situation, and uncertainty about what is required of him, may provoke excessive anxiety in the patient, and long periods of silence should be avoided. On the other hand, the physician may effectively block the patient's communications about significant problems by means of frequent questions that turn the interview into an interrogation.

Initially, the physician should encourage the patient to tell his own story as freely as possible and should listen without interruption. At the outset it may be desirable to stimulate the patient by such questions as "What led to your coming to see me?" or "Whose idea was it that you should come and see me?" and "Why do you think they felt it would be a good idea?" When the patient stops spontaneously, he can often be encouraged to proceed or elaborate by the physician's nodding, changing position (e.g., sitting forward in his chair), or by minimal verbal cues such as "yes," "and then. . . ," "go on. . . ," or a repetition of the last few words in the patient's narrative. When the time comes for the physician to ask questions, they should be of as general a nature as possible—for example "How did you feel about that?" or "How do you feel most of the time?" rather than specific questions that may be answered briefly—for example "Do you feel happy or sad?" Questions that can simply be answered "yes" or "no" should be avoided initially, as should all leading questions suggesting a definite answer—for example "Do you feel unhappy?"

Similarly, in inquiring about the patient's childhood relationships with his parents, it is preferable to start with a very general question such as "Tell me something about your mother (father)," before proceeding to more specific questions based on the patient's earlier statements. The latter may include such questions as "What did you like the most about your mother (father)?" "What didn't you like about him (her)?"; "Were there times when he (she) became very angry with you—and what did he (she) do at such times?"; and "Were there times when he (she) made you feel very angry (frightened, unloved), and what did you do when you felt that way?"

To some extent, patients will tend to say what they think the physician wants to hear. Physicians in turn may hear what they want to hear, and encourage patients to say what the physician wants to hear. The latter process may be either deliberate or unconscious, and the patient's verbalizations may be highly colored by the selective attention or inattention of the physician. Increased attention on the part of the physician may lead the patient to elaborate on his dreams or fantasy life, on his sexual behavior or early childhood experiences. It is in such ways that therapists of varying persuasions seduce or direct the content of therapy along the lines that they consider most significant. It is particularly important, however, to avoid overlooking aspects of his communications that the patient considers important, because the physician happens to have some preconceived notions that some other area is much more significant.

During the process of evaluation, certain information may be required that would be threatening to the patient if it was sought by direct questioning early in the interview. It is necessary for the physician to establish whether there is any danger of suicidal or homicidal behavior, to form some estimate of the patient's intelligence and any evidence of organic brain disease, the presence of hallucinations or delusional beliefs, and the patient's sexual behavior and relationships with various members of his family, among other things. It is frequently possible to obtain some of this information without direct questioning by encouraging the patient to elaborate on some of his spontaneous statements.

It may be appropriate to ask direct questions about factual information (such as his age at the time his father died) but there are certain techniques that may be more helpful when dealing with more sensitive information: (1) *narrowing* involves asking a sequence of questions that proceeds from general areas to specific issues; (2) *progression* involves arranging a sequence of questions to progress from less intimate to more intimate matters; (3) *embedding* involves concealing a question that is significant in the middle of a sequence of questions that appear routine and affectively neutral; (4) *leading questions* are based on an assumption that has not been previously admitted — for example "What do you usually do when you get angry with your wife?" (5) *hold-over* questions involve ignoring emotionally charged material about which a patient blocks early in an interview, and asking about it later in another context; (6) *projective questions* involve general attitudes or values — for example "If you could rub a magic lamp, and have three wishes all come true, what would they be."

The *recording of information* during interviews presents certain problems, and it is easy to agree with Menninger that a great deal of nonsense has been written and spoken about taking notes. Some written notes may be desired by the physician for a number of reasons: in order that he may refresh his memory about what transpired before he next sees the patient; in order that he may review his basis for evaluation and therapeutic formulations; or in order that he may prepare systematic records of the psychiatric history and mental examination for administrative, legal, educational, or possible research purposes. With such goals in mind, it may be desirable to record a number of the patient's statements (and even the physician's comments) verbatim. Most patients will in fact accept the physician's need to make some written notes, and their acceptance will be enhanced by the physician's confidence in assuming that some note-taking is reasonable.

On the other hand, the more detailed and accurate the recording of notes, the more obtrusive this will become in the interview situation, and the more it will interfere with spontaneous communication by both the patient and the physician. Following some fixed sequence of questions on a printed (or memorized) questionnaire will suppress the patient's spontaneity further, and significant information will be overlooked in the interest of stereotypy. While it is impossible therefore to preserve flexibility in interviewing and simultaneously to record the information obtained on some standardized mental examination or history outline, it is still desirable to make sufficient notes during the interview to permit adequate subsequent recall and recording, if the latter is required. In order to eliminate the need to take written notes, and to analyze the interaction between patient and physician in more detail subsequently, increasing use has been made of tape recordings, but these should not be obtained without the knowledge and consent of the patient. It should also be borne in mind that interviews carried out in the presence of a tape recorder, one-way observation window, or television or movie camera may lead to quite different interactions between patient and physician from those which occur when they communicate with each other in complete privacy.

Redlich and Freedman directed attention to three successive phases of the initial interview. The *opening phase* includes the ordinary rituals and greetings of a first meeting, the expert and unobtrusive observation of the patient, and the introduction of the theme for the meeting by certain initial statements. The *middle phase* is a free-wheeling and unhurried inquiry to which most of the interview is devoted, and is a time for conscious clarification rather than for interpretation of unconscious dynamic processes. The *end phase* of the first interview involves a casual inventory of what has been communicated, and the making of proper arrangements for the next step, whether or not this is a second interview with the patient. Before the end of the initial interview, the physician should have reached an opinion whether there is any likelihood of the patient's harming himself or others, what further information about him is necessary or desirable, and whether further evaluation or treatment should be carried out in the community or in the hospital. If the patient is in good contact with reality, such future plans should be discussed with him fully. An effort should also be made to be explicit about the cost of further evaluation and treatment, and the basic obligations of the patient and therapist.

The initial psychiatric interview may sometimes also be the last, and it is always possible to use a single interview as the basis for recording a *psychiatric examination*, which may also be known as a mental status or psychological examination. On the basis of a single interview, it is sometimes necessary to express a summary opinion regarding the patient—for example that he is mentally retarded or suffering from an organic brain syndrome; that he shows psychotic reality distortion or requires involuntary admission to a hospital; that he is or is not competent to handle his financial affairs, to make a will, to stand trial, or to care for his children.

More frequently, however, such opinions or plans for treatment are *not* formulated on the basis of a single cross-sectional view of the patient, but on a longitudinal developmental account of his life history and patterns of adaptation, which may be given primarily by the patient or supplemented extensively by interviews with other persons. The comprehensive evaluation of the patient also involves physical examination and indicated laboratory investigations, as well as clinical psychological tests that will be described in the following chapter. In the remainder of the present chapter, we shall consider the kind of organization of data frequently adopted in recording the patient's psychiatric history and examination.

RECORDING THE PSYCHIATRIC HISTORY

Menninger pointed out that the psychiatric case history differs from the medical case history in a number of ways. One difference concerns the multiplicity of sources from which psychi-

atric information may be obtained. Some of this information may be available before the patient is interviewed, and its nature will depend upon the source of referral and the reasons for psychiatric evaluation. Patients referred by general physicians have usually had recent extensive somatic investigations; those referred by social agencies may be accompanied by extensive information about their family and interpersonal relationships; those referred by courts of law may have considerable documentation of circumstances leading up to the referral; those who have already been committed to mental hospitals will have had written statements made about the reasons for their admission.

Once the physician himself has access to the patient, however, it is preferable to interview the patient prior to interviewing any relatives, friends, or other informants who may be accompanying the patient. In many instances, it will also be desirable to interview significant relatives and even involve them in therapy, but this should always be done with the full knowledge and consent of the patient, except when he is grossly irrational or a young child. Psychoanalysts and other therapists engaged in longterm intensive psychotherapy generally interview relatives only in the presence of the patient, and will not communicate with other persons about the patient without the latter's consent and complete knowledge of the content of such communications.

Structuring the therapeutic situation in the latter manner serves to emphasize to the patient that the physician's primary concern is with the patient's own problems rather than those of his family, but there has been a movement toward involving other significant family members in the primary interaction with the therapist. An alternative that is still preferred in a number of situations is that of having a psychiatric social worker interview the relatives for purposes of information and therapy. The social worker generally tends to prefer a therapeutic role, but in a number of clinic or hospital settings may still be a major contributor to the psychiatric history—sometimes by conducting the initial intake interview with the patient. The latter situation is most frequent, however, in psychiatric clinics for children where the parents provide the initial information in an intake interview with the social worker.

Information obtained from other persons than the patient is likely to be greatest when the patient is a young child, has been mentally retarded from birth, has an organic brain syndrome or functional psychosis, or has a personality disorder characterized by antisocial behavior. Some therapists prefer to record all historical information obtained from other persons separately from that obtained from the patient. This is not the usual practice, however, and it is customary for the psychiatric history to be a composite record obtained from various sources, with specific mention of the informants' names and opinions when their accounts conflict with one another. In general the history begins with identifying data about the patient, a summary of the presenting problem and a history of the present illness, followed by family history, the developmental life history of the patient, and his adult patterns of adjustment.

Identifying Data and Presenting Problem. Identifying data include the patient's name, clinic or hospital file number, date of initial interview or admission, address, telephone number, sex, age last birthday, date of birth, place of birth, race, religion, education completed, occupation, marital status, and next of kin.

The presenting problem may be perceived differently by the patient, by his family, by his referring physician or other source of referral, and by the physician undertaking the psychiatric evaluation. These varied perceptions of the situation should all be recorded, with inclusion of a verbatim statement by the patient if possible.

In this connection, it is frequently helpful to record the date and time of the initial referral, the referring source (patient, relatives, friends, physician, social agency, police, court), the nature of the initial contact (verbal, telephone, written), reasons given for the referral, the attitude of the referring source towards the patient and any other information obtained at the time of referral.

It is also desirable to summarize information about informants other than the patient, such as their names, relationships, and attitudes towards the patient, the dates of interviews, and nature of other information received.

Present Illness. This should consist of a chronological and well-organized account of the duration and development of the present difficulties, of all changes noted in the patient's behavior and conversation, and of all changes in his physical health or environmental situation that may have precipitated his present difficulties or contributed to them.

Have there been any recent changes in intellectual performance or memory, in mood or activity level, in sleeping habits, in eating or weight, in elimination, menstruation, or sexual behavior? Has there been any evidence of hallucinations or delusions, of suicidal or homicidal preoccupation? Do the patient's symptoms vary from one time to another, and are such changes regular (e.g., according to the time of day) or related to contact with certain other persons? What changes have taken place in the patient's relationships with other members of his family, with his employer, fellow employees, or friends? In what way has his usual performance at work and interest in other activities been affected?

In addition to information about possible *precipitating factors*, or perpetuating factors such as secondary gains from his illness, there should be a statement regarding *any treatment* the patient has recently received for psychiatric disorder. This should include the name of the physician, the type of treatment, and the amounts of any medications being taken. If the patient has been undergoing psychotherapy or has been hospitalized on a psychiatric service, the dates, diagnostic formulations, and nature of the treatment should be described.

Family History. Detailed knowledge of the patient's family of origin (close blood relatives) and family of orientation (with whom he lived most of his childhood) may provide information about his hereditary endowment, the interpersonal relationships during his childhood, and the sociocultural milieu in which he developed. From all these points of view, it is much more important to have data concerning close relatives — whether biological parents and siblings or step-parents, adoptive or foster parents, and siblings — than concerning more remote ancestors such as grandparents, aunts, uncles, and cousins (although gross abnormalities in the latter may also be significant).

The most important objective data to obtain on parents and siblings — biological or social — are their sex and ages in relation to the patient, their educational and occupational status, their history of bodily illness, and any evidence of psychopathology: mental retardation, organic brain syndromes, suicide, psychosis, neurosis, delinquency, and alcoholism, for example. It may also be desirable to record miscarriages and stillbirths, and any consanguinity in the parents (the exact relationship being specified). The exact age and causes of death of any of these close relatives should also be recorded, together with the age of the patient at the time and the apparent impact of this event in the patient's life. Details concerning separation and divorce of the parents are also significant, and again the age of the patient and reaction to such parental loss should be recorded. The details of the patient's relationships with parents and siblings may be elaborated here or in succeeding sections.

Developmental History. This is frequently recorded in chronological sequence under such headings as birth, infancy, early childhood, school and later childhood, the adolescent period, and adult adjustment patterns. This approach emphasizes age-appropriate and-inappropriate behaviors, but sometimes results in fragments of related information being widely separated in the format of the history. Some clinicians and teachers, therefore, prefer to organize data along several developmental sequences, each of which proceeds from early childhood into adult life — for example, intellectual maturation, school and occupational history, religion and relationships with authority, social interaction with peers, and sexual and marital history. The latter approach, however, also tends to result in some fragmentation of information that is related in time. It therefore appears desirable to encourage flexibility in recording developmental data, as well as in securing such information from the patient or others.

Details of the mother's health during pregnancy are relevant to the patient's intrauterine development, and any history of toxicity or difficult delivery should be noted. Although there is often considerable retrospective falsification, it may be significant to inquire whether the patient's pregnancy was wanted and planned, the nature of breast or bottle feeding, the presence of colic or early feeding difficulties, bowel and bladder training, and the ages at which the patient sat up, crawled, walked, and talked. The history of convulsions and other physical illnesses should be noted, and the age and duration of any early admission to hospital or other institutions. Details of any early problem behavior such as temper tantrums, excessive masturbation, enuresis, night terrors, or stuttering should be explored.

Retardation in intellectual or social development may become evident during the preschool years, and opportunities for social interaction with peers may be provided or prevented by parents. It may be significant whether the patient brought friends to his own home or visited other children in their homes, whether he had birthday parties or was invited to other children's birthday parties, whether he was deprived in comparison with siblings or other children in the neighborhood, whether he had friends to stay in his home overnight or was invited and permitted to stay in their homes overnight, whether there were more prolonged periods of separation from his parents (such as sickness, vacations, summer camp, boarding school), and at what ages such separations occurred. Were the parents of the same religion, and was religious observance important to them? How did the patient come to feel about religious observance, and how is this reflected in his adult behavior?

Early interactions with the patient's parents may be mirrored in subsequent relationships with teachers, employers, the police, and military authorities. The adjustment of the patient during his school years should include information on the numbers and locations of different schools, with reasons for transfer, irregularity of attendance (including absences due to physical illness, emotional problems, or truancy), academic progress (advancing through grades, repeating grades, and class standing), extracurricular activities (athletic and social), and interpersonal relationships with teachers and other students. The subsequent occupational history should include information about the nature of employment, the nature and location of jobs, approximate income and reasons for changing employment, relationships with employers and fellow workers. Details of military service should include reasons for enlistment or rejection, duties performed, rank and nature of discharge, and particulars of any periods in hospital or conflict with military authorities. Appearances in juvenile court, contacts with social agencies and the police, and reformatory or jail sentences should also be noted.

Information should progressively become available from the patient concerning the nature and sources of sexual information, his recollection of childhood fantasies and explorations, the reaction of parents and others toward his sexual curiosity and experimentation, preparation for and reaction to the onset of ejaculation or menstruation, any formal sexual instruction received, sexual feelings aroused by persons of either sex or other sources of gratification, and overt sexual behavior including masturbation and homosexual and heterosexual activities. There should be some attempt to evaluate the main characteristics of sexual partners and the nature, extent, and variety of premarital, marital, and extramarital or postmarital relationships. Information may include conscious reasons for marriage, probable unconscious factors influencing the selection of a mate, the personality characteristics of the mate, significant aspects of marital interaction, communication and compatibility, decisions about family planning and contraceptive measures employed, the ages and characteristics of the patient's children, his attitudes toward them, family problems and conflicts, and reasons for any separation or divorce.

The *medical history* should include a chronological record of all illnesses, accidents, and operations, noting their severity, duration of disability, and any lasting sequelae. Under certain circumstances it may be necessary to make special inquiries about a history of convulsions, encephalitis, head injury, and venereal disease. Other significant information may include the patient's use of alcohol and tobacco, barbiturates and other sedatives, and narcotics or patent medicines, and his exposure to various occupational toxins such as lead, arsenic, and mercury.

Adult personality and psychopathology may have become evident in summarizing the present illness or some of the longitudinal trends in the developmental history, but will usually require further elaboration. What have been the patient's predominant mood, activity level, interests, degree of social participation, and his greatest sources of satisfaction and dissatisfaction? What have been his main personality characteristics, intrapsychic dynamics and defenses, and his significant adult interpersonal relationships? What have been his main attitudes toward himself, attitudes toward others, and aspirations for the future? What evidence is there of previous maladaptation—intellectual, emotional, or behavioral? Is there any history of previous psychiatric evaluation, treatment, or hospitalization that has not already been reviewed under the history of the present illness? If so it will frequently be desirable to obtain further information from those who were responsible for the patient's treatment at any such time, and the patient's signed consent to obtain this information should be requested.

RECORD OF PSYCHIATRIC EXAMINATION (MENTAL OR PSYCHOLOGICAL STATUS)

The topics and questions itemized in the preceding section do *not* constitute an exhaustive list of all relevant factors in personality development, and need *not* be asked or answered for each separate patient—particularly not in any rigidly prescribed sequence. Similarly, the current trend is toward flexibility in recording data relevant to the psychiatric examination. While the latter may always be written on the basis of a single interview, observations made during several interviews with the patient are often combined into a portrait of his current adaptation over a period of several days or even weeks.

Information relevant to the psychiatric examination has already been presented in parts of Chapters 2 and 3, and it may be organized and presented in a similar manner in the record of the mental status examination: for example, under perception, intellectual function, affect, motivation, behavior, conversation, dreams, fantasy life, and dynamics (intrapsychic and interpersonal). More frequently, however, clinical interaction with the patient results in information's being obtained in a different sequence from the preceding, and it is often recorded in the sequence in which it is obtained, which proceeds from relatively objective observational data to more subjective interpretations based on inference.

A simple summary of findings on psychiatric examination may be arranged *in alphabetical sequence*: Appearance, Behavior, Conversation, Delusions and hallucinations, Emotional tone and reaction, Fantasy and dreams, Intellectual functions including memory and orientation, Judgment including conscience and insight, and the like. This sequence is somewhat arbitrary and forced, however, and many psychiatrists prefer to organize the relevant data in a different sequence, one example of which follows.

Appearance and Behavior. This may include a general statement of such characteristics as the patient's age, sex, height, weight, posture, clothing and facial expression. Does the patient appear to be well-groomed and neatly dressed, or is he careless of his appearance and disheveled or inappropriately dressed? Does he appear composed, relaxed and at ease, or tense, uncomfortable, apprehensive, fearful, restless, or agitated? Is he alert and responsive, or somnolent, withdrawn, disinterested, or dejected? Is there increased or decreased motor activity, or does he show any unusual involuntary movements, peculiar mannerisms, bizarre gestures, or repetitive and stereotyped movements? Is there any aggressive, violent, or destructive behavior? Is the facial expression mobile or unchanging, bland or miserable, angry or fearful? Does the patient make and maintain eye-contact with the examiner, or avoid looking at him directly, particularly at certain times in the interview? Does the patient laugh, smile, weep, or blush?

Conversation or Verbal Behavior. The stream of conversation often corresponds with the level of motor activity, and may be either increased or decreased. Speech may be clear and animated, or the voice may be quiet and monotonous. The patient may converse spontaneously, or only in response to questions, or not at all. Questions may be answered readily or reluctantly, promptly or after considerable delay, relevantly, circumstantially, or irrelevantly. The predominating thought content may be revealed by spontaneous productions or digressions in response to questions, and may indicate preoccupation with a wide variety of interpersonal or intrapsychic problems. It may reveal disorders of mood (e.g., euphoria or depression), perception (e.g., illusions or hallucinations), and ideation (e.g., delusions). Disordered thought processes may also be indicated by poverty of ideas, flight of ideas, loose associations, concrete (literal) or overinclusive thinking, or neologisms (new words).

Samples of conversation may be recorded verbatim in the patient's own words. Such samples may include his initial statements or other spontaneous remarks, evidence of predominant thought content, evidence of unusual ideation and significant responses to questions, including any time lag before such questions are answered.

Emotional Tone and Reaction. The predominant affect, mood, or *emotional tone* should be noted—for example anxiety, fear, anger, euphoria, depression, or apathy. These should be distinguished from the *emotional response or reaction*, which may be characterized by overall variability (either lability or shallowness) and by its appropriateness to the situation and thought content (see Chapter 2).

Disorders of Perception and Ideation. It should be recalled that illusions and hallucinations may affect any of the five senses. Such disturbances of perception may sometimes be inferred from the patient's behavior: for example, if he appears to be picking imaginary objects out of the air, or holding a one-sided conversation when he is in a room by himself. Alternatively, distortions of perception may be reported in response to a general question such as, "Have you had any unusual or strange experiences lately?" but it may be necessary to make more specific inquiries regarding unusual smells, a strange taste in the food, unusual sensations in certain parts of the body, hearing voices when there is no one in the immediate vicinity, or seeing things that other people do not seem able to recognize. The nature of any such experiences should be explored, and also the patient's interpretations of what is causing them. It may be helpful to ask if he thinks many people have such experiences, and why they should happen to him or why he was chosen to have such experiences.

Delusions may be intimately related to disorders of perception, as when auditory hallucinations are interpreted as messages from God, or the voices of imagined persecutors. Frequently, however, delusions occur in the absence of hallucinations or illusions, and appear more related to the prevailing emotional tone. Various types of delusion were described in Chapter 2, and may or may not be evident in an initial interview. Unrealistic ideas of grandeur (wealth, power, or prestige) or of self-accusation, worthlessness, and hopelessness, are more likely to be apparent than delusions of reference, active or passive influence, or persecution—which may be deliberately concealed because the patient recognizes that other persons disbelieve his own convictions. Sometimes the latter may be revealed by asking general questions such as, "Have any other people been showing an unusual interest in you?" or alternatively, "Has anyone been interfering in your life, or deliberately making life difficult for you?" It may also be necessary to ask more specific questions whether other people appear to have access to private information about the patient, whether they watch him, talk about him, spread information about him, try to control his thoughts or actions, exploit him, hold him back, or discriminate against him in other ways. The evidence on which he bases any such beliefs should be explored, and also the reasons why he thinks he is being subjected to such experiences.

Fantasy, Dreams, and Dynamics. The patient's behavior may be likened to Salome's dance of the seven veils. With casual acquaintances she may shed one or two of these veils. Perhaps she will tantalize more intimate friends or confidants by shedding a third or fourth. She may, however, be so ashamed of her own nakedness that she is unwilling to shed the final coverings in private, let alone in the presence of a relative stranger.

The same key will not open the locks of every door, and the physician must accumulate a variety of "skeleton keys," each of which may be helpful in gaining access to the patient's trust and innermost feelings and fantasies. Some patients will reveal considerable inner fantasy in response to simple questions about the nature and frequency of their daydreams. Others unwittingly reveal a great deal more, albeit in symbolic and distorted form, in their reports of the nighttime dreams that they recall after awakening. The analysis and interpretation of such dreams constitutes one of the tasks of analytically oriented psychotherapy, but unconscious dynamic defense mechanisms may be evident to the physician in a variety of behaviors that the patient demonstrates in his daily living and interaction with others. Such mechanisms of adaptation should be recorded in the mental examination, as well as summarized in connection with subsequent diagnostic formulations and plans for treatment.

Intellectual Capacity and Function. The maximum *intellectual capacity* or potential and the current *intellectual function* on performance may both be estimated by means of psychological tests that will be outlined in the following chapter. Nevertheless, the physician should be alert for clues re-

garding the patient's current level of intellectual function in comparison (1) with other persons of the same age, and (2) with the maximum level at which the patient has ever functioned. In children and adolescents up to the age of 16 years, the Intelligence Quotient may be expressed as a percentage of the Mental Age (in comparison with the average member of the general population) divided by the Chronological Age of the patient. A 12-year-old child functioning at the intellectual level of the average nine-year-old child would have an IQ of approximately 75. Any adult patient functioning at the intellectual level of the average eight-year-old child would have an IQ of approximately 50 (i.e., eight divided by 16).

It should be recognized, however, that questions intended to measure intellectual function may be considered insulting by the patient when they are asked in a clinical interview situation. It is, therefore, generally preferable to estimate intellectual capacity (or maximum potential) based upon the patient's previous education, current vocabulary, comprehension, and general information. Under special circumstances, it may be appropriate to ask a few general questions such as the population of the United States, and the state or town or city in which he lives, the distance from his current location to certain well-known cities, or other information about well-known places or persons. Persons of similar intelligence may vary in their knowledge of such general information, and accurate answers may not be as significant as the nature of the response and incompatibility between responses—for example, that the population of the United States is "about 20 billion," while the population of one of its constituent states is given as "about 24 billion." Such questions as well as simple arithmetical calculations can be presented within the context of what the patient remembers from the time he was in school. However, it should again be emphasized that in most patients such questions will be unnecessary, and may be perceived as insulting and damaging to the relationship with the physician.

Memory and Orientation. Impairment of intellectual functions generally includes some degree of memory impairment and disorientation. Remote memory concerning such events as date and place of birth, schools attended, employment, marriage, and children is usually better preserved than memory for recent events. The latter may be tested by asking the patient to count to 42 and then stop, to recall three objects after several minutes, to recall the name of the physician or other person on the ward, and to recall such things as when he was admitted or what he ate at recent meals. Similarly, orientation as to person and place is usually better preserved than orientation as to time, day of the week, date of the month, and even month or year. Here again, some questions can be introduced much more readily than others, as by the physician remarking, "Let's see now, what's the date today?" (without waiting a lengthy period for a reply), or asking the patient's date of birth, date of marriage, or date of admission to the hospital. Indirect evidence of memory and orientation, however, is generally preferable in the clinical interview situation to direct questioning that assumes the form of a frontal assult.

Conscience, Judgment, and Insight. Superego functions, conscience, aspirations, and internal controls are *not* static, but may vary with mood and other factors, such as the ingestion of alcohol or other drugs. In this connection, it should be recalled that actions speak louder than words, and a reliable history of past behavior provides the best information concerning former ethical standards and motivation. However, some estimate of present superego functions may be revealed by the patient's currently verbalized attitudes towards past behavior (e.g., regrets, guilt, and remorse), and his ideals and plans for the future. An evaluation should also be made of other aspects of the patient's judgment, and of his insight into the nature of his current problems. Insight may vary from a partial recognition by the patient that he has some psychiatric problem—which may be present in some psychotic patients along with other "milder" disorders—to a much more thorough understanding of the origin, nature, and dynamics of his personality and psychopathology. If he has such detailed knowledge but is unable to modify maladaptive behavior, he is sometimes described as having "intellectual insight," whereas such knowledge associated with modification or abandonment of maladaptive behavior may be described as "emotional insight." In the past, analytically oriented psychotherapy was focused on interpretation of unconscious dynamics leading to intellectual insight, but has become increasingly concerned with the "corrective emotional experiences" that may lead to emotional insight and abandonment of maladaptive behavior.

FURTHER EVALUATION, DIAGNOSIS, TREATMENT PLANNING, AND OUTCOME

In this chapter, we have so far considered three aspects of the patient's evaluation—the initial psychiatric interview or consultation, the subsequent elaboration and recording of a more comprehensive psychiatric history, and the main areas of concern in recording a mental status or psychiatric examination. There are three further broad categories of information that may be sought by the physician before he formulates his diagnosis and plans for treatment. The extent to which the physician utilizes these additional techniques of evaluation may vary greatly, however, according to the problems presented by the individual patient, as well as the training of the physician, and the type of situation in which he is practicing. Before considering diagnosis and treatment, we shall therefore review the types of information that may be obtained through the use of hypnosis or drugs, the administration of standardized psychological tests, and the somatic investigations in which every physician has been trained.

Psychiatric Examination under Hypnosis or Drugs. Sometimes pertinent information remains inaccessible during psychiatric interview because the patient is mute, shows marked emotional blocking, or has amnesia for a certain period of time. Under such circumstances, he may become much more accessible and productive through hypnosis or administration of any one of a variety of sedative, tranquilizing, or stimulant drugs. Some psychiatrists have long employed such techniques as adjuncts to therapy, particularly in overcoming amnesia and promoting emotional catharsis or abreaction involving the release of pent-up emotion associated with consciously intolerable thoughts or events. The therapeutic benefits of such procedures, however, are often questionable or very short-lived, although the widespread use of tranquilizing drugs is often regarded as increasing the accessibility of patients to psychotherapy.

Since the time of the ancient Romans it has been known that alcohol tends to decrease inhibition and increase conversation about emotionally charged subjects, as reflected in the dictum "in vino veritas." During World War II, intravenous barbiturates such as sodium Amytal or Pentothal were widely used in the treatment of "combat fatigue," and were subsequently popularly misrepresented as "truth sera." There is in fact no guarantee that a patient will tell all or even a significant part of the truth when under the influence of such drugs. However, intravenous narcosis with these agents may greatly facilitate conversation, and sometimes the increased verbalization will be dramatic. On the other hand, a marked increase in speech

and emotional response may also occur after the intravenous injection of a stimulant such as dimethyl amphetamine (Desoxyn), or after inhalation of such drugs as nitrous oxide, carbon dioxide, or ether. Less dramatic but quite effective increases in communication may be accomplished by the oral administration of sedative or tranquilizing drugs, without the undesirable side effects of overstimulation such as prolonged agitation, insomnia, or fragmentation of thinking.

The use of hypnosis and drugs in psychiatric evaluation has diminished progressively since the years immediately following World War II. In the event that any such adjuncts are used in psychiatric evaluation, however, the dates and details of such diagnostic interviews should be recorded separately, and it should also be borne in mind that the mental state of the patient is *not* the same when he is under their influence as it is at other times.

The Administration of Standardized Psychological Tests. The extent to which standardized psychological tests are employed in psychiatric evaluation and treatment-planning depends upon a number of factors. These include the training and theoretical orientation of the physician, as well as the availability of competent clinical psychologists and the training and orientation of the latter toward diagnosis or therapy. Psychological tests employed routinely or on specific referral and request include measurement of intelligence and intellectual impairment, objective behavioral or subjective personality (self-report) inventories, projective techniques (such as sentence completions, the Rorschach ink blots, the Thematic Apperception Tests, and the House-Tree-Person drawings), and tests of vocational interests, preferences, or aptitudes.

In a number of clinic and hospital settings, it has been customary to administer routine batteries of several psychological tests to be supplemented by additional tests in specific areas when indicated. One basic battery of tests employed in a number of centers consists of the Wechsler Adult Intelligence Scale (or other test of intellectual function) and the Rorschach and Thematic Apperception Tests. Another battery that is much more economical of time in screening large numbers of patients consists of the Shipley-Hartford (or other brief instrument for estimating intelligence), the Minnesota Multiphasic Personality Inventory (self-report based on 566 standardized questions), and one of the numerous Sentence Completion Tests that have been devised.

The training of a psychiatrist usually includes some formal instruction and considerable clinical familiarization with the practical applications of selected psychological tests, although the sample of such instruments with which he becomes familiar will be selected according to the setting in which he obtains his training. With increasing curriculum time in medical schools for instruction in clinical psychiatry and basic behavioral sciences, many other physicians also receive some basic instruction and experience in the application of psychological tests prior to graduation. Increasing numbers of physicians in general or specialist practice now make use of such knowledge after graduation, and request psychological tests for their patients without necessarily referring the patient for psychiatric evaluation. The next chapter contains summary information on a number of psychological tests in widespread use.

Somatic Investigations. Physical examination, including a brief or detailed neurological examination as indicated, should be performed and recorded as soon after the initial psychiatric interview or admission to the hospital as possible. This is considered desirable for two general reasons: (1) a variety of psychopathology may be precipitated or perpetuated by neurological or other somatic illness, and (2) the psychiatric patient with somatic complaints may need this evidence that the latter have been investigated thor-

oughly, before he is ready to accept the fact that his bodily complaints may have a psychological etiology and may respond to psychiatric treatment. There are, however, certain problems and exceptions to be considered in making the preceding generalizations.

Due to their training and interest in conducting longterm intensive individual psychotherapy, many psychiatrists prefer *not* to perform physical examinations on their patients, and over a period of time may lose their original competence to do so. Such psychiatrists prefer to be regarded as "talking" rather than "touching" doctors, and this preference may be reflected in their rejection of the physician's white coat, stethoscope, and other armamentaria. Since patients referred to psychiatrists by other physicians have generally had recent (and sometimes extensive) somatic investigations, it may indeed be unnecessary or undesirable to repeat the latter after the patient's referral. If, on the other hand, the patient has had no such somatic investigations prior to referral, the psychiatrist may prefer to refer the patient to a general physician or neurologist for the necessary physical examination and laboratory investigations.

Repeated somatic investigations with equivocal or negative results concerning which the patient is not informed may strongly reinforce the patient's belief in a somatic etiology. Even more reinforcing of such a conviction is the patient's being subjected to a number of medical treatments or surgical procedures prior to his referral for psychiatric evaluation. On the other hand, there is a need for prompt investigation (whether by the therapist or another physician) of somatic complaints appearing for the first time during psychotherapy. This is particularly likely to be a problem when the patient has previously cried "wolf, wolf" on a number of occasions through numerous bodily complaints for which no organic basis was found. It is necessary to bear in mind, however, that a hypochondriacal or hysterical patient may develop organic pathology, and the latter should be evaluated by a physician.

In addition to a general examination and a reasonably comprehensive neurological examination, a number of routine laboratory investigations may be included in the initial evaluation, such as hemoglobin determination, complete blood count, serological test for syphilis, urinalysis, and chest x-ray. Some psychiatrists have recommended routine tests of thyroid function or electroencephalography. Other studies of patients with suspected neurological lesions include lumbar puncture, brain scan, skull x-rays, pneumoencephalography or angiography. Positive findings on physical examination or laboratory investigations may or may not be causally related to the patient's presenting psychopathology, but should always be summarized in the overall diagnostic evaluation.

Diagnostic Formulation and Treatment Planning. *Psychiatric diagnosis* is generally summarized under several headings, the first of which may be termed the *descriptive (or clinical) diagnosis*, based on the standard nomenclature of psychiatric syndromes, which was summarized in Chapter 2. A second general heading is the *dynamic diagnosis,* which includes predominant intrapsychic defense mechanisms, significant current interpersonal relationships, precipitating and perpetuating stress, and deprivation. A third heading consists of the *developmental (or genetic) diagnosis,* which constitutes a summary of adverse factors perceived as significant in personality development and in determining predisposition to psychopathology. A fourth heading consists of the *somatic diagnosis* and its probable relationship to the presenting psychiatric problems.

Comprehensive *plans for psychiatric treatment* may also be summarized under several headings, and should include the nature and frequency of proposed psychotherapy: individual, family, or group; the proposed social and milieu

therapy in a hospital setting; social casework to be undertaken with relatives or other key persons in the patient's environment; pharmacological agents to be administered; any proposal for electroshock or other somatic treatment of psychopathology; and any somatic treatment indicated for organic bodily illness.

A variety of forms of psychiatric treatment will be outlined in Chapters 11 and 12. In recording the psychiatric evaluation, however, it may also be desirable to *predict the outcome* of whatever treatments are recommended, taking into account the nature of the patient's problems, his age, intelligence and personality resources (or ego-strength), as well as his family and socioeconomic circumstances (external reality situation).

Progress Notes and Final Summaries. The frequency and content of *progress notes* will depend upon the nature of evaluation and treatment, and the setting in which it is undertaken. Many psychotherapists make some written notes of communications by their patients and themselves (verbal or nonverbal) during the course of each interview, and neither elaborate upon nor summarize these notes until the time of termination. Others interview the patient without taking any notes, and after each interview write a summary statement which may consist of one sentence or a brief paragraph. A number of institutions require progress notes at specified intervals—for example, daily during the first week or month after the patient's admission, or at intervals of one week, one month, or even one year in some state hospitals. In the opinion of many psychiatrists, there should be flexibility in both the frequency and content of such progress notes, but a written note is recommended each time the patient is seen, no matter how brief the note may be.

Final summaries are also required in many settings, and may vary from half a page to many pages in length. The content usually includes identifying data, presenting problems, a summary of the initial interview and evaluation, history of present illness and personality development, a summary of the psychiatric examination and psychological tests, positive findings in the physical examination and laboratory investigations, the psychosocial and somatic treatment procedures, progress of the patient during therapy, and evaluation of the patient's reality situation and adaptational resources at the time of termination. This type of summary, written while the information is still fresh in mind, may prove most valuable to the therapist in the event that the patient returns for further consultation or therapy after a lapse of time, and it can always be supplemented by making brief progress notes in the event of any such further interviews or written communications.

SELECTED REFERENCES

Alexander, F., and French, T. M. 1946. *Psychoanalytic Therapy.* New York, The Ronald Press Co.

Appel, K. E., and Strecker, E. A. 1936. *Practical Examination of Personality and Behavior Disorders.* New York, The Macmillan Co.

Aring, C. D. 1958. Sympathy and empathy. Journal of The American Medical Association *167,* 448.

Bartemeier, L. H. 1951. The attitude of the physician. Journal of The American Medical Association *145,* 1122-1125.

Bird, B. 1955. *Talking with Patients.* Philadelphia, J. B. Lippincott Co.

Carter, G. H. 1955. History-taking and interviewing technique. Journal of Medical Education *30,* 315-326.

Deutsch, F., and Murphy, W. F. 1955. *The Clinical Interview.* New York, International Universities Press, Inc.

Dewan, J. G., and Spaulding, W. D. 1958. *The Organic Psychoses.* Toronto, University of Toronto Press, ch. 10.

Finesinger, J. E. 1948. Psychiatric interviewing. 1. Some principles and procedures in insight therapy. American Journal of Psychiatry *105,* 187.

Frank, J. D. 1961. *Persuasion and Healing.* Baltimore, The Johns Hopkins Press.

Garrett, A. 1942. *Interviewing: The Principles and Methods.* New York, Family Welfare Association of America.

Gill, M. M., Newman, R., and Redlich, F. C. 1954.

The Initial Interview in Psychiatric Practice. New York, International Universities Press, Inc.

Group for the Advancement of Psychiatry. 1961. *Reports in Psychotherapy: Initial Interviews.* New York, Group for the Advancement of Psychiatry, Report No. 49.

Hall, B. H., and Wheeler, W. 1957. The patient and his relatives: Initial joint interview. Social Work *2,* 75-80.

Hendrickson, W. J., Coffer, R. H., and Cross, T. N. 1954. The initial interview. Archives of Neurology and Psychiatry *71,* 24.

Kahn, R. L., and Cannell, C. F. 1963. *Dynamics of Interviewing.* New York, Basic Books, Inc.

Menninger, K. A. 1962. *A Manual for Psychiatric Case Study,* 2nd edition. New York, Grune & Stratton, Inc., The Menninger Clinic Monograph Series No. 8.

Meyer, A. 1957. *Psychobiology: A Science of Man.* Springfield, Illinois, Charles C Thomas.

Pittenger, R. E., et al. 1960. *The First Five Minutes: A Sample of Microscopic Interview Analysis.* Ithaca, New York, Martineau.

Preu, P. W. 1943. *Outline of Psychiatric Case Study,* 2nd edition. New York, Hoeber Medical Division, Harper & Row, Publishers, Inc.

Redlich, F. C., and Freedman, D. X. 1966. *The Theory and Practice of Psychiatry.* New York, Basic Books, Inc., ch. 7.

Redlich, F. C., Dollard, J., and Newman, R. 1950. High fidelity recording of psychotherapeutic interviews. American Journal of Psychiatry *107,* 42.

Reider, N. 1939. The reaction of psychiatric patients to physical and neurological examinations. Bulletin of the Menninger Clinic *3,* 73-81.

Reik, T. 1948. *Listening with the Third Ear.* New York, Farrar, Straus & Giroux.

Reisman, D. 1959. Some observations on interviewing in a state mental hospital. Bulletin of the Menninger Clinic *23,* 7.

Rogers, C. R. 1951. *Client-Centered Therapy.* Boston, Houghton Mifflin Co.

Ruesch, J., and Bateson, G. 1951. *Communication, The Social Matrix of Psychiatry.* New York, W. W. Norton & Co., Inc.

Stevenson, I. 1960. *Medical History-taking.* New York, Hoeber Division, Harper & Row, Publishers, Inc.

Stevenson, I., and Sheppe, W. M., Jr. 1959. The psychiatric interview, and the psychiatric examination. In *The American Handbook of Psychiatry,* ed. S. Arieti. New York, Basic Books, Inc., vol. 1, ch. 9 and 10.

Stevenson, I., and Matthews, R. A. 1950. The art of interviewing. General Practitioner *2,* 59-69.

Sullivan, H. S. 1954. *The Psychiatric Interview.* New York, W. W. Norton & Co., Inc.

Wallen, R. W. 1956. *Clinical Psychology.* New York, McGraw-Hill Book Co., Inc., ch. 4-6.

Whitehorn, J. C. 1944. Guide to interviewing and clinical personality study. Archives of Neurology and Psychiatry *52,* 197-216.

CHAPTER 10

Psychological Tests

by Philip A. Marks and John O. Kangas

INTRODUCTION

Psychological testing is a method of securing a sample of a person's behavior under standardized conditions and employing explicit techniques of evaluation. The clinical value of psychological tests depends upon the ability to make useful inferences about behavioral and psychological characteristics outside of the testing situation.

We all act as psychological testers at least some of the time. We perceive the behavior of ourselves and others, we more or less explicitly describe and classify (score) that behavior, we make implicit or explicit comparisons of that behavior and the occurrence of similar behavior among other people we know, and we infer from our observations what people might be thinking and feeling and how they might behave at other times in other places.

The difference between such informal assessment procedures and a formal psychological test is a difference of degree, not of kind. Since its birth as a scientific discipline, psychology has studied man as a judge of the psychological characteristics of his fellow man. The accumulated research has exposed some of man's foibles, including expertman's foibles, as such a judge. Formal psychological tests use scientific principles of measurement to improve upon man's informal, more or less intuitive methods of assessment. Use of these

principles has led to specifying what to observe and count in naturally occurring behavior, to structuring interviews and standardizing test questions and materials, to adopting formal scoring procedures, and to establishing norms and studying the relationships between test scores and the behaviors or psychological characteristics of interest.

It may be instructive to draw an analogy between a psychological test and a physiological laboratory test. Their similarity is striking if one substitutes for the kind of specimen or behavior being sampled. Both represent methods of producing useful information about man which is not as readily or as accurately available without the use of the test or laboratory procedure. Both employ standardized ways of collecting the sample for study and of evaluating or scoring the sample collected. Both emphasize reduction of the scoring process to numbers. This ideal is not always reached in either, and the result is sometimes graphic or semiquantitative. For both kinds of tests, score values are collected for various populations. Finally, in both instances, it is recognized that sound clinical decisions rest on a much broader information base than the laboratory test findings alone.

The total number of psychological tests available in the United States is very large, well over 2000 (Buros, 1961). They measure a wide variety of psycho-

208

logical and behavioral characteristics: aptitudes, skills, achievement levels, sensory and perceptual acuities, motor abilities, emotions, motives, attitudes, interests, values, moral and ethical qualities, and personality functioning. For virtually every psychological dimension, there is a test designed to measure it.

Psychological tests differ considerably in the nature of the test materials employed, and in the methods of administration, scoring, and interpretation. Thus, some tests are called *paper-and-pencil* tests, whereas others requiring more elaborate materials or instrumentation are referred to as *apparatus* tests. Tests which employ spoken, written, or printed words to ask or answer questions are commonly called *verbal* tests; tests where words do not play such an obvious role are known as *performance* tests. In performance tests, the subject is required to draw, sort, point, construct something, or to manipulate the test materials in some way.

Some printed verbal tests, especially those measuring attitudes, interests, and personality are called *questionnaires* or *inventories*. Such tests are often also described as *structured*, because of the relative lack of ambiguity in the meaning of the test questions and because of the restrictions that are placed on the form the answer must take. Many inventories, for example, require that the person taking the test answer the question either True or False, Yes or No.

The term *unstructured* is used in describing those tests in which either the test materials (stimuli) or the task is relatively ambiguous, such as telling what a particular inkblot looks like, or telling a story about a picture; or in which there are few constraints on the form the answer must take. Some unstructured personality tests are labeled *projective techniques* on the assumption that the process by which the subject ascribes meaning and organization to the relatively ambiguous stimulus materials involves a projection of his inner psychological needs, motives, conflicts, and the like.

The nature of many psychological tests requires that the test be *individually administered* by a skilled examiner. Such tests often involve timing of individual responses or further questioning depending upon the character of the subject's initial response. *Group tests*, in contrast, can be given to many subjects simultaneously and do not require close subject-examiner interaction during test administration. Some group tests are called *self-administered* tests because the role of the examiner or proctor seems to involve little more than asking the subject to read the instructions on the test booklet and to proceed at his own pace. The term self-administered is somewhat misleading, however, since the examiner may play a crucial role in eliciting an appropriate test-taking attitude on the part of the subject and in correcting misunderstandings.

The scoring of some psychological tests gives primary attention to the final *product* of the subject's efforts. Did he say True or False to the question? Did he pronounce the word correctly? What did he see in the inkblot? Other tests emphasize the *process* by which the subject reaches his final answer. What chain of reasoning led him to say True to the question? To what extent did he use phonic skills in trying to pronounce the word? What aspects of the inkblot did he emphasize in ascribing meaning to it? Whether scoring pertains to process or product, the test is considered *objective* to the degree that all persons who follow the scoring rules arrive at the same summary test scores.

The testing method variations reviewed in the preceding paragraphs represent efforts by test-makers to construct better, more sensitive tests of whatever psychological characteristic is being measured. Whichever testing materials and procedures are employed, all psychological tests need to be judged for their worth on the basis of certain common standards. These standards are discussed and summarized in the following paragraphs.

Reliability. Reliability is a generic

term referring to the stability and consistency of tests. A highly reliable (stable) psychological test will yield similar results when administered on different occasions. The degree of test reliability varies considerably according to the characteristics of the test and of the psychological or behavioral variable being measured. Some aspects of vocational interests, for example, and some features of intellectual functioning seem to be relatively stable over long periods of time. Our reliability expectations for tests in these areas are much more stringent than they are for tests which measure moods or emotions which may undergo rather marked changes in relatively short periods of time.

The reliability issue is in point of fact a rather complex one, and the reader who wishes to pursue inquiry into it is referred to Tryon (1957), Cronbach (1960), or Horst (1966). It is sufficient here to conceptualize reliability as the degree of reproducibility of scores by the same tests over an interval of time.

Validity. Validity of a psychological test has to do with whether the test does in fact measure whatever it is the test purports to measure, namely, the criterion. Most samples of behavior which are collected by means of psychological tests are not particularly important and useful in and of themselves. What difference does it make clinically if a person does or does not see something that looks like a bird on a particular inkblot, or knows the capital of Turkey, or answers True to the statement, "I drink a lot of water every day"? A psychological test assumes potential importance when, from such responses, one can infer clinically important extratest behaviors or psychological characteristics. The question of validity is the question of the veracity of such inferences. Because it may be possible to draw many different inferences from a particular psychological test, the validity of a test cannot be described by some single statement or index number. Rather, a test has as many validities as there are inferences which one may draw from its scores.

As with biological tests, some psychological tests possess reasonable levels of reliability and validity for the variables being measured and the inferences drawn from them. Others are hardly worth the paper they are printed on. Some "tests," such as those appearing in Sunday newspaper supplements, rest their case for reliability and validity on their appearance of being related to some psychological variable. The standards of reliability and validity for a well-constructed psychological test are of course much more stringent, and demand empirical documentation through research. The reader is referred to *Standards for Educational and Psychological Tests and Manuals*, published by the American Psychological Association (1966), for a detailed account of the characteristics that a well-constructed psychological test should possess.

Utility. The usefulness of a psychological test in a clinical context cannot be evaluated by resolution of reliability and validity questions alone. A number of issues often considered under the label "utility" must be raised.

RELEVANCE. Inferences drawn from a test must be relevant to a clinical question or decision. A psychological test of acoustic pitch discrimination may be very reliable and valid, but is not of any obvious utility in designing treatment procedures for a seriously depressed person; whereas a test which predicts response to electroshock therapy might have considerable utility for that purpose.

BASE RATES. The relative incidence (i.e., base rate) of some criterion behavior in a target population has bearing on the usefulness of a psychlogical test. If, for example, the incidence of suicide among psychiatric outpatients is three per 1000 per year, and a psychological test were able to predict who would and who would not commit suicide better than chance, such a test would still be of dubious value clinically. Assume that this test has a 75 percent accuracy in separating suicidal from nonsuicidal patients. Out of the 1000 patients in our example it would correctly identify two, possibly all three, of the potential suicides. But since it would also misclassify 25 percent, it would incorrectly identify 249 of the 997 nonsuicidal patients as potential suicides. If the test scores are taken seriously two or three suicides have been identified and possibly prevented, but at the price of mislabeling and mismanaging 249 other patients as suicidal risks. In this instance, a valid psychological test might create more problems than it would solve. An article by Meehl and Rosen (1955) offers a sophisticated discussion of the base rate issue and its import for the utility of psychological tests. In general, psychological tests are likely to be clinically useful when the target population is fairly evenly divided on whatever characteristic the test is purporting to measure.

Cost Factors. Frequently there is more than one source of available information from which a clinically important inference can be made. Since psychological tests as a source of such information require time, effort, and expense, it is appropriate to consider whether there might not be a more economical information source. If one needs only approximate knowledge of a college coed's intellectual functioning level, it may be much more economical to inquire about her school achievement, past and present, than to administer an hour-long intelligence test. Similarly, there is no need to administer a lengthy personality test to determine if a patient has psychotic mentation when existing nursing notes document wild accusations of sexual intent on the part of the entire male staff toward the patient. And it may not be worth requesting psychological testing if the information could be secured during the next scheduled interview, assuming there was no need for it earlier. Referral for psychological testing should imply that testing is the most economical means available of obtaining the necessary information.

The Band-Width Fidelity Dilemma. For the sake of decision making, we sometimes need very precise information on some point. This usually implies the expenditure of considerable time in measurement to achieve the necessary degree of precision. Sometimes though we can tolerate a larger margin of error, especially when the time saved can be used to collect other needed information. Psychological tests usually present us with choices of this sort. Those tests which are most reliable and valid in measuring some particular behavior or psychological characteristic are often the most costly and time-consuming to use. Other tests may be only moderately valid or reliable, but may at the same time provide information about many other characteristics of importance to a clinical problem. Given limited testing time, the choice of tests depends upon both accuracy and coverage considerations.

SUMMARY

The chapter so far has defined psychological tests and has reviewed variations in the characteristics of such tests.

It has also emphasized that the usefulness of a test depends not only upon its intuitive appeal and apparent relevance, but more importantly upon its known reliability and validities, and further upon features of the clinical context in which it will be used. The next section will review selected psychological tests. The final section will discuss current testing practices.

CATALOGUE OF TESTS COMMON IN USE

Choice of a limited number of psychological tests for individual description is difficult and necessarily somewhat arbitrary. In making this selection, the authors have been guided in part by survey reports of test usage (e.g., Sundberg, 1962), and also by their judgment of test relevance to the clinical problems encountered in general medical and psychiatric settings. Tests of *ability* are reviewed first, followed by *personality* tests further classified as inventories and projective techniques. Finally an assortment of less frequently used tests is described. Most of the tests in this latter group were included either because they represent new techniques which show promise of wider future use, or because they represent different testing techniques or methods.

As a guide to the reader, each test description is accompanied by one or more references to facilitate further study of that instrument. For tests not included here, the reader is directed to the *Mental Measurement Yearbook* series edited by Buros (1941, 1949, 1953, 1959, 1965). Here he will find descriptive information about published tests, one or more critical reviews of each, and a list of references. A number of single-volume texts of psychological testing are also available, which provide more comprehensive and detailed coverage of psychological tests than is possible in this chapter. (See, for example, Cronbach, 1960; Anastasi, 1961; and Kleinmuntz, 1967.)

GENERAL ABILITY TESTS: ADULT

Wechsler Intelligence Scales (W-B I, II, and WAIS). The most popular individual intelligence test for adults was developed by David Wechsler at Bellevue Hospital in 1939. Prior to this, the most widely used intelligence test for adults, the Stanford-Binet, had been developed and standaridized for use with children. The widespread use during World War II of the W-B Form I led to the development of Form II which was published in 1946. Today the Wechsler Adult Intelligence Scale (WAIS) has largely superceded both earlier forms, and as early as 1955 became the most widely used individual test for measuring adult intelligence (ages 16 and over).

The WAIS consists of 11 subtests, six of the subtests constituting a *Verbal Scale*

and five a *Performance Scale*. For each subtest, with the exception of Digit Symbol of the Performance Scale, the items are arranged in order of ascending difficulty. The Verbal subtests are *Information, Comprehension, Digit Span, Similarities, Arithmetic,* and *Vocabulary*; the Performance subtests are *Picture Completion, Picture Arrangement, Object Assembly, Block Design,* and *Digit Symbol.*

Information. This 29-item subtest samples the subject's fund of general information. Included are items such as, "How many make a pair?" "Where is France?" "What is the freezing point of water?"

Comprehension. The 14 items in this subtest require the subject to solve practical problems, explain social and physical laws, and interpret proverbs. For example, "What should you do if you witnessed an automobile accident?" "What does this saying mean: It is an ill wind that blows no good'?" "Why do automobiles have wheels?"

Arithmetic. A series of 14 problems is presented orally which the subject must solve without the use of paper and pencil within a given period of time. Example: "How much is two dollars and three dollars?" "How many inches are there in two feet?" "Six men can build a boat in five days. How many men will be needed to build the boat in a half day?" Both time and accuracy are scored.

Similarities. The subject is asked to state the way in which two words are alike or similar. There are 13 word pairs arranged in order of increasing difficulty. Example: "In what way are 'apple and peach,'. . . 'arm and leg,'. . . 'bird and flower' alike?"

Digit Span. The items in the first half of this subtest consist of three to nine digits read by the examiner at a prescribed rate. The subject must reproduce the digits in correct order. In the second half the subject must reproduce a series of two to eight digits, but in reverse order.

Vocabulary. The subject is required to define up to 40 words arranged in order of increasing difficulty. Example: "What does 'summer,'. . . 'haven,'. . . 'sanctimonious' mean?"

Digit Symbol. This is the first test of the performance scale. The subject is shown nine digits paired with nine simple geometric designs. The test presents a random series of 90 digits without their corresponding symbols. The task requires filling in the correct symbol for each digit within a specified time.

Picture Completion. Each of the 21 pictures in this series has a part missing. The pictures are shown to the subject one at a time and he is asked to identify the most essential detail missing.

Block Design. In this test the subject must reproduce up to ten designs of increasing complexity using either four or nine multicolored blocks. Both time and accuracy are scored.

Picture Arrangement. Each of the eight items consist of cartoon-like picture cards. These cards are presented out of order and the subject is instructed to rearrange them so that they tell a sensible story. Both time and accuracy are scored.

Object Assembly. This test consists of four jigsaw puzzles of varying difficulty. The subject is instructed to complete each as quickly as he can. Both time and accuracy are scored.

The WAIS, like the other Wechsler scales, requires about 60 to 90 minutes to administer by a skilled examiner. In scoring the WAIS, the raw score on each subtest is converted into a standard score (derived from the standardization sample) with a mean of ten and standard deviation of three. All subtests scores are thus expressed in comparable units. The sum of the standard scores on the six verbal subtests represents the total score for the Verbal Scale. Similarly, the sum of the subtest scores on the five nonverbal tests represents the total score on the Performance Scale. The Full Scale score is obtained by adding these two sums.

The scoring of the WAIS provides tables for transforming each total score into a deviation IQ, comparing a sub-

ject's scores with those of the standardization subjects of his age group. For each age level the mean IQ has been fixed at 100 with a standard deviation of 15. It is common practice to report three separate IQ estimates: Verbal IQ, Performance IQ, and Full Scale IQ.

Guertin, W. H., Ladd, C. E., Frank, G. H., Rabin, A. I., and Hiester, D. S. 1966. Research with the Wechsler Intelligence scale for adults: 1960-1965. *Psychological Bulletin 66*, 385-409.

Wechsler, D. 1958. *The Measurement and Appraisal of Adult Intelligence.* Baltimore, The Williams & Wilkins Co.

Shipley Institute of Living Scale. The Shipley Institute of Living Scale (S-H), formerly the Shipley-Hartford Retreat Scale, is a paper-and-pencil test developed in 1939 as a measure of intellectual impairment.

The S-H consists of two parts, each of which has a ten minute time limit. The first part is a *vocabulary* test of 40 multiple choice items (e.g., SHIP animal flower spoon boat; INANE obese timely silly damp); the second part is an *abstraction* test consisting of 20 completion items (e.g., PALET PALE PAL____; bib bib part trap 479____). The items for each part are arranged in order of increasing level of difficulty. The test yields four scores: vocabulary, abstraction, conceptual quotient (CQ), and intellectual quotient (IQ). The CQ is derived from the difference in performance on the two tests. A CQ below 100 would indicate that the subject's performance was poorer on the abstraction part than on the vocabulary part. Such a result is regarded as an indicator of intellectual impairment which may be due either to brain damage or some functional disorder. According to the manual, CQ scores above 90 are "normal" and those below 70 are "probably pathological." Values between 70 and 90 are considered "slightly suspicious," "moderately suspicious," and so on.

One earlier limitation of the S-H was that age norms were not provided and therefore no correction could be made for the normal decline in mental ability with age. Recently, however, a number of studies have reported age-based norms which permit the conversion of total raw vocabulary and abstraction score to a Full Scale Wechsler IQ estimate (e.g., Sines, 1958).

Monroe, K. L. 1966. Note on the estimation of the WAIS FULL Scale IQ. *Journal of Clinical Psychology 22*, 79-81.

Prado, W. M., and Taub, D. V. 1966. Accurate prediction of individual intellectual functioning by the Shipley-Hartford. *Journal of Clinical Psychology 22*, 294-296.

Shipley, W. C. 1940. *Shipley-Hartford Retreat Scale: Manual of Directions and Scoring Key.* Hartford, Connecticut, Institute of Living.

Sines, L. K. 1958. Intelligence test correlates of Shipley-Hartford performance. *Journal of Clinical Psychology 14*, 399-404.

GENERAL ABILITY TESTS: Child and Infant

The Stanford Binet Scales (Forms L, M, and L-M). The first practical intelligence test was developed by Alfred Binet in Paris and published in 1905. A widely accepted American revision was prepared by Lewis Terman at Stanford University in 1916 and became known as the Stanford-Binet. This revision was replaced in 1937 when Terman and Merrill introduced Forms L and M of the Standford-Binet. The latest revision (1960) combines the best subtests of the 1937 revision into a single Form L-M. In clinical practice the Binet Scales are by far the most widely used individual tests for measuring children's intelligence (ages two to 18 years).

Test items for the younger child require observing, manipulating, and identifying common objects. For example, at an early preschool level the child is asked to identify parts of the body on a large paper doll. At a slightly later age he is asked to build a bridge with blocks. Beginning with the middle age levels increasing use is made of such verbal material as vocabulary, completion of analogies, memory for sentences, and inductive and deductive reasoning. The items are grouped and arranged in age levels, with approximately six items of equal difficulty appearing at each level. Months of mental age credit

are earned for successes beyond the age level at which all items have been passed. This yields a total score expressed in years and months of mental age. In earlier revisions of the Binet the IQ score was a ratio between such a mental age and the subject's chronological age, multiplied by 100. The present Binet L-M like the WAIS employs deviation IQ scores with a mean of 100 and a standard deviation of 16. Testing involves about 30 to 40 minutes for the younger child and approximately 90 minutes at the later ages.

Terman, L. M., and Merrill, M. A. 1937. *Measuring Intelligence.* Boston, Houghton Mifflin Co.

Terman, L. M., and Merrill, M. A. 1960. *Stanford-Binet Intelligence Scale: Manual for Third Revision, Form L-M.* Boston, Houghton Mifflin Co.

Himmelstein, P. 1966. Research with the Stanford-Binet, Form L-M: The first five years. *Psychological Bulletin 65*, 156-164.

Wechsler Intelligence Scale for Children. First published in 1949, the Wechsler Intelligence Scale for Children (WISC) is second only to the Stanford-Binet in frequency of use as an intelligence measure for children (ages five through 15 years).

The WISC is quite similar in design to Wechsler's adult scales with most of the items in the WISC coming from Form II of the Wechsler-Bellevue Adult Scale. The WISC consists of 12 subtests, six of which comprise a Verbal Scale and six a Performance Scale. The one additional performance subtest which does not appear on the WAIS consists of a series of paper-and-pencil mazes. Typically only ten subtests are included in the administration of the scale. The WISC also resembles the WAIS in yielding Verbal and Performance IQs as well as a Full Scale IQ based on total test performance.

IQ scores from the WISC and Stanford-Binet are highly correlated, but there are important differences between the two scales in the IQ values obtained especially at extreme levels. Because of this, WISC IQ's and Stanford-Binet IQ's are not identical nor necessarily interchangeable.

Weider, Noller, and Schramm have reported equivalent WISC and Stanford-Binet Full Scale IQ's throughout the range of 40 to 140, showing that whereas a Binet IQ of 40 is equivalent to a WISC IQ of 45, a Binet IQ of 140 is equal to a WISC IQ of 130.

In general, the WISC is an easily administered test for children who are not at the extreme ranges of intellectual ability. The Stanford-Binet is probably better suited for the younger or severely retarded child. For the older child or early adolescent the WISC is often preferred. An authorized Spanish-American translation of the WISC is also available.

Wechsler, D. 1949. *Wechsler Intelligence Scale for Children, Manual.* New York, The Psychological Corporation.
Weider, A., Noller, P. A., and Schramm, A. 1951. The Wechsler Intelligence Scale for Children and the revised Stanford-Binet. *Journal of Consulting Psychology* 15, 330-333.
Littell, W. M. 1960. The Wechsler Intelligence Scale for Children. Review of a decade of research. *Psychological Bulletin* 57, 132-156.

Wechsler Preschool and Primary Scale of Intelligence. Recently published, the Wechsler Preschool and Primary Scale of Intelligence (WPPSI) follows the theoretical and methodological approach of the WISC in providing a series of ability tests for measuring the intelligence of younger children (ages four to six and one-half years).

The WPPSI consists of 11 subtests, six comprising a Verbal Scale (information, vocabulary, similarities, comprehension, arithmetic, and sentences as an alternate) and five comprising a Performance Scale (animal house, picture completion, mazes, geometric design, and block design). Eight of the 11 subtests provide the same measures as the WISC, and are continuous with the WISC. As is characteristic of the other Wechsler scales, the WPPSI is an individually administered test which yields three separate IQ estimates (Verbal IQ, Performance IQ, and Full Scale IQ) and requires about one hour of testing time. As a lower extension of the WISC, it is

also suitable for testing the disadvantaged or mentally retarded child for whom the WISC tests are often too difficult.

Wechsler, D. 1967. *The Wechsler Preschool and Primary Scale of Intelligence, Manual.* New York, The Psychological Corporation.

Draw-a-Man. Perhaps the most "culture free" measure of children's intelligence is the Draw-a-Man (DAM), which was first introduced by Florence Goodenough in 1926. This relatively simple test provides the subject with a blank sheet of paper, and instructions to "draw a picture of a man" as best he can. This test is not timed and the subject is encouraged to work slowly and carefully. As a test of mental ability, the DAM has been used primarily with children (ages four to ten).

A new revision prepared by Harris (1963) is now available. Scoring emphasizes presence or absence of body and clothing detail rather than artistic skill. Thus, the subject is credited for correct point of attachment of arms to trunk; presence of eyes, nose, mouth, and the like. Raw scores are converted to mental age and IQ equivalents. In general, the DAM for children like the Shipley test for adults is a good screening measure of general intelligence.

Goodenough, F. L. 1926. *Measurement of Intelligence by Drawings.* New York, Harcourt, Brace & World, Inc.
Harris, D. B. 1963. *Children's Drawings as Measures of Intellectual Maturity: A Revision and Extension of the Goodenough Draw-a-Man Test.* New York, Harcourt, Brace & World, Inc.

Cattell Infant Intelligence Scale. The Cattell Infant Intelligence Scale (CIIS) represents an attempt to extend intelligence testing down to the infancy level. The scale was developed as a downward extension of the 1937 Stanford-Binet, with items grouped at 19 levels ranging from two to 30 months of age.

The CIIS utilizes considerable material from the Gessell Developmental Schedules and from various other infant tests. Typical items at the earliest infancy level include attending to objects and following movements. Items at the second half-year of life include playing with blocks, imitating motor behavior (e.g., ringing a bell), and making sounds and using words. Items earn mental age credit. An IQ is obtained from the ratio of total mental age credit to chronological age. The CIIS for most infants requires from 20 to 30 minutes for completion. Like other infant intelligence scales, the CIIS yields a reasonably reliable estimate of current psychomotor functioning. Such estimates, however, have not proven to be useful predictors of later intelligence as measured by the Stanford-Binet or WISC.

Cattell, P. 1947. *The Measurement of Intelligence of Infants and Young Children.* New York, The Psychological Corporation. (Third Printing, 1950, Revised 1960.)

SPECIAL ABILITY TESTS

Bender Visual-Motor Gestalt. One of the best known and most frequently used tests for evaluating perceptual-motor coordination is the Bender-Gestalt (B-G) developed by Lauretta Bender in 1938. Although commonly employed as a projective device for assessing personality dynamics, the B-G was originally designed as a test of organic brain impairment (ages ten and over). It is also used at earlier ages as a measure of neurological maturation.

The test consists of nine simple geometric designs presented individually on cards. The subject is provided with blank sheets of white paper and instructed to make free-hand copies of the designs. In clinical practice many examiners will then ask the subject to reproduce the designs from memory.

The subject's performance may be analyzed and interpreted qualitatively, or may be treated statistically following one of several formal scoring procedures (e.g., Koppitz, 1964). An interesting recent modification of the B-G, using two of the original designs in three different positions and providing both quantitative scoring and normative

data, is the Minnesota Percepto-Diagnostic Test (MPD) described by Fuller and Laird (1963).

Hutt, M. L., and Briskin, G. J. 1960 *The Clinical Use of the Revised Bender Gestalt Test* New York, Grune & Stratton, Inc.

Fuller, G. B., and Laird, J. T. 1963. The Minnesota Percepto-Diagnostic Test. Journal of Clinical Psychology *19*, 3-34.

Koppitz, E. 1964. *The Bender-Gestalt Test for Young Children.* New York, Grune & Stratton, Inc.

Wechsler Memory Scale (Forms 1 and 2). The Wechsler Memory Scale (WMS), introduced by David Wechsler in 1945, is one of few published measures of memory function. It was designed for adults (ages 25 to 50) and is available in two forms.

Form 1 of the WMS consists of seven subtests: *personal and current information* (e.g., "How old are you?" "Who is President of the United States?"), *orientation* (e.g., "What year is this?" "What day of the month is it?"), *mental control* (counting backward from 20 to one, repeating the alphabet, and counting by threes), *logical memory* (recall of paragraphs), *memory span* (recall of digits forward and backward), *visual reproduction* (drawing three geometric figures from memory), and *associate learning* (ten word pairs which the subject is required to learn in three trials).

Administration of the WMS takes an average of 15 minutes. The total raw score is corrected for age and converted into a memory quotient (MQ), which in turn can be compared with the Wechsler-Bellevue IQ. The equivalence of Form 2 to Form 1 has not yet been adequately established.

Wechsler, D. 1945. A standardized memory scale for clinical use. Journal of Psychology, *19*, 87-95.

Hall, J. 1957. Reliability (internal consistency) of the Wechsler Memory Scale and correlation with Wechsler-Bellevue intelligence scale. Journal of Consulting Psychology *21*, 131-135.

Porteus Maze Test. The Porteus Maze Test, first developed by Stanley Porteus in 1914, was published as a separate scale in 1924. It purports to assess judgment, planning, and self-control. Research to date indicates its sensitivity to organic brain impairment. It has been used with a variety of subjects including delinquents, criminals, lobotomized patients, mentally defectives, illiterates, normal children, patients with organic brain damage, and many different ethnic and cultural groups (ages three years and over).

The test consists of a series of printed line mazes, graded in difficulty. The subject is instructed to draw the shortest path from the entrance to the exit of the maze without lifting the pencil from the paper once he begins. Additional trials are provided following errors. There is no time limit. Typically testing begins at the five- or seven-year level and continues until the subject has failed two successive age levels. In addition to providing a quantitative measure of mental ability (TQ score), the scoring also permits a qualitative measure of temperament and emotional control (Q score).

Porteus, S. D. 1959. *The Maze Test and Clinical Psychology.* Palo Alto, California, Pacific Books.
Porteus, S. D. 1965. *Porteus Maze Test: Fifty Years Application.* Palo Alto, California, Pacific Books.

Vineland Social Maturity Scale.

The Vineland Social Maturity Scale, developed by Edgar Doll in 1935 and revised in 1953, is a developmental schedule which evaluates the subject's social competence and self-sufficiency. Although covering a range from birth to over 25 years, the scale is most commonly used with the younger child and the mentally defective. The scale consists of 117 items grouped into 17 age levels. Unlike the usual testing procedures, the information required for each item is obtained by interview with an informant intimately familiar with the subject (such as a parent or nurse) or with the subject himself.

The Vineland items cover eight areas of functioning: *general self-help, eating, dressing, self-direction, communication, occupation, locomotion,* and *social relations.* A score is computed from the total number of items successfully performed, with allowance given in scoring

for lack of opportunity and emerging skills. Both a social age (SA) and a social quotient (SQ) can be derived from the subject's performance. The Vineland is often used for differentiating between socially inadequate mental defectives and intellectually subnormal subjects who are nevertheless quite competent in managing their personal and social lives.

Doll, E. A. 1947. *The Vineland Social Maturity Scale: Manual of Directions.* Minneapolis, Educational Test Bureau.
Doll, E. A. 1953. *The Measurement of Social Competence.* Minneapolis, Educational Test Bureau.

PERSONALITY TESTS: INVENTORIES

The Minnesota Multiphasic Personality Inventory (Individual, Group, R and Tape Forms).

The Minnesota Multiphasic Personality Inventory (MMPI) is the most widely used objective personality test in existence today. Its popularity is attested to by the fact that over 2000 books and articles have been written about it, it has been translated into 14 different languages, and over 220 scales have been constructed using the original item pool. The MMPI is used routinely in many settings including psychiatric and medical facilities.

Developed at the University of Minnesota Hospitals by Hathaway and McKinley in 1940, the test consists of 550 questions which the subject is asked to answer True or False. The questions cover a wide range of subject matter: for example, general physical health, habits, social attitudes, and mood and morale.

There are four validity scales, *cannot say* (?), *Lie* (L), *Frequency* (F), *Correction* (K); and ten clinical scales, *Hypochondriasis* (1), *Depression* (2), *Hysteria* (3), *Psychopathic deviate* (4), *Masculinity-femininity* (5), *Paranoia* (6), *Psychasthenia* (7), *Schizophrenia* (8), *Hypomania* (9), *Social introversion - extroversion* (0) which make up the basic MMPI personality profile.

The MMPI is a prime example of an empirically developed personality test. Neither the scoring nor the interpretation of the MMPI involve any assumption regarding the theoretical or apparent meaning of the questions. Instead the items which comprise each of the scales were selected and grouped on the basis of differentiating patients classified into common descriptive psychiatric syndromes from general population "normal" adults. The items of each scale are keyed so that the higher the score the more deviant the subject is with respect to the traits empirically associated with that scale, the more dissimilar the subject is to the "normal" group, and the more similar he is to the criterion group used in the scale's construction. The interpretive assumption underlying this approach is that persons who are similar in their responses to a set of questions about themselves are likely to be similar in other aspects of their behavior as well.

The MMPI is provided in booklet, audio tape, and card-sorting forms. The test can be used with subjects as young as 12 years of age with a reading level at sixth grade or higher. Testing time ranges from 45 to 90 minutes for most subjects.

Directions for administering, scoring, and interpreting the MMPI appear in a number of sources. The *MMPI Manual* revised in 1951 is outdated and will soon be replaced by a new revision. Dahlstrom and Welsh's *Handbook* (1960) is the basic MMPI text, and provides comprehensive information on the use of the test in clinical practice and research. A good introductory source for medical students and physicians is the *Physician's Guide* of Good and Brantner (1961). Two sources of particular value in working with psychiatric patients provide not only basic test information, but also extensive material on the clinical and actuarial interpretation of MMPI profiles. The work of Gilberstadt and Duker (1965) is especially appropriate for use in Veteran's Administration medical and psychiatric settings. The Marks and Seeman Atlas (1963) was developed in a university hospital and is better suited for use

in working with psychiatric patients seen in such settings.

Dahlstrom, W. G., and Welsh, G. S. 1960. *An MMPI Handbook: A Guide for Use in Clinical Practice and Research*. Minneapolis, University of Minnesota Press.

Gilberstadt, H., and Duker, J. 1965. *A Handbook for Clinical and Actuarial MMPI Interpretation*. Philadelphia, 1961. W. B. Saunders Co.

Good, P. K-E., and Brantner, J. P. 1961. *The Physician's Guide to the MMPI*. Minneapolis, University of Minnesota Press.

Hathaway, S. R., and McKinley, J. C. 1951. *The Minnesota Multiphasic Personality Inventory Manual (Revised)*. New York, The Psychological Corporation (in revision).

Marks, P. A., and Seeman, S. 1963. *The Actuarial Description of Abnormal Personality: An Atlas for Use with the MMPI*. Baltimore, The Williams & Wilkins Co.

Tellegen, A. 1964. The Minnesota Multiphasic Personality Inventory. In *Progress in Clinical Psychology, Vol. VI.*, ed. L. E. Abt and B. F. Reiss. New York, Grune & Stratton, Inc., pp. 30-48.

California Psychological Inventory. The California Psychological Inventory (CPI), published in 1957 by Harrison Gough, is a 480 item true-false questionnaire which is similar to the MMPI in its empirical construction. However, unlike the MMPI, the CPI was derived using high school and college students selected by peer nomination techniques rather than psychiatric criterion groups. Moreover, high scores on CPI scales represent normal values of the variables. The CPI is intended primarily for use with "normal" subjects (ages 13 and over). It is published in English, Italian, French, and German editions.

At present the CPI consists of 18 scales: *dominance* (Do), *capacity for status* (Ca), *sociability* (Sy), *social presence* (Sp), *self-acceptance* (Sa), *sense of well-being* (Wb), *responsibility* (Re), *socialization* (So), *self-control* (Sc), *tolerance* (To), *good impression* (Gi), *communality* (Cm), *achievement via conformance* (Ac), *achievement via independence* (Ai), *intellectual efficiency* (Ie), *psychological mindedness* (Py), *flexibility* (Fx), and *femininity* (Fc).

The administration, scoring, and profiling of the subject's answers are similar to those of the MMPI. Both hand scoring stencils and machine scoring services are available. The CPI is a relatively new instrument which has not as yet achieved widespread use in clinical settings. Research suggests that it has special utility with delinquents and asocial groups.

Gough, H. G. 1957. *California Psychological Inventory Manual.* Palo Alto, California, Consulting Psychologists Press.

California Test of Personality (Grades Kgn.–3, 4–8, 7–10, 9–16, and Adult Forms). Originally published by Thorpe, Clark, and Tiegs in 1939, and revised in 1953, the California Test of Personality (CTP) is one of the few inventory personality tests with forms for young children.

Each form of the CTP provides two major scoring categories, personal adjustment and social adjustment. Within each category, scores may be obtained on six personality variables. Included under *personal adjustment* are self-reliance, sense of personal worth, sense of freedom, feeling of belonging, withdrawal tendencies, and nervous symptoms. Variables measured within *social adjustment* are social standards, social skills, antisocial tendencies, family relations, school or occupational relations, and community relations. Raw scores may be converted to percentile ranks and expressed on a profile for interpretation. Provision is also made for computing a summary index of "total adjustment," as well as summed category scores for "personal and social adjustment."

Thorpe, L. P., Clark, W. W., and Tiegs, E. W. 1953. *California Test of Personality Manual.* Los Angeles, California Testing Bureau.

Strong Vocational Interest Blank (Forms Men and Women). One of the most widely used interest tests is the Strong Vocational Interest Blank (SVIB), first published in 1927 by E. K. Strong, and revised in 1946 and again in 1966. Following a strictly empirical approach, the SVIB scales were developed by comparing the responses of persons successfully engaged in each occupation with a composite of these men and women. Scores on this test are more closely related to vocational choice and persistence rather than vocational satisfaction or success.

Both (Men and Women) forms of the SVIB contain some 400 items grouped into eight sections. The first five sections deal with occupational titles, school subjects, amusements, occupational activities, and the preferences for types of people. The subject records his answer by expressing "liking," "dislike," or "indifference." The remaining three parts request the subject to rank activities in order of preference, compare his interests in pairs of items, and rate his present abilities and other characteristics. The Men's form currently provides scales for 54 occupations (e.g., physician, psychiatrist, physicist, pharmacist) in 11 groups, and for five special variables (Occupational Introversion-Extroversion, Academic Achievement, Occupational Level, Specialization Level, and Masculinity-Feminity). The Women's form provides scales for 32 occupations (e.g., dietitian, occupational therapist, physical therapist, nurse, physician), and two nonoccupational scales (Feminity-Masculinity and Academic Achievement). The test is untimed, requiring about 30 to 45 minutes to complete (ages 16 and over).

Because of the SVIB's complicated item weighting procedures, hand scoring keys, although available, are impractical to use. Answer sheets are usually scored by a commercial test scoring center.

Layton, W. L. (ed.) 1960. *The Strong Vocational Interests Blank: Research and Uses.* Minneapolis, University of Minnesota Press.

Strong, E. K., Jr., and Campbell, D. P. 1966. *Strong Vocational Interest Blanks Manual.* Stanford, California, Stanford University Press.

PERSONALITY TESTS: PROJECTIVE TECHNIQUES

Rorschach. Sundberg's survey of psychological testing in the United

States (1962) reports that in 1959 the Rorschach was the most widely used clinical assessment procedure. Moreover, Buros' *Sixth Mental Measurements Yearbook* lists 3030 articles and books which have been written about this instrument alone. On the basis of Sundberg's survey, it can be estimated that the Rorschach is administered to about a million persons a year in the United States alone; that use of the instrument consumes on the average no less than 5,000,000 man-hours per year at a total cost to the clients of some $50,000,000.

Developed by the Swiss psychiatrist, Herman Rorschach, the technique was first described in 1921. In its original form, the Rorschach consists of ten cards, on each of which is printed a bilaterally symmetrical inkblot. Five are colored and five achromatic (shades of grey and black). In the typical examining procedure the subject is shown the cards one at a time and is asked what he sees—what the inkblot looks like to him. The responses during this *free association* period are recorded verbatim. Time of the response is also recorded as well as the position in which the cards are held, and any spontaneous remarks the subject may make. Following the presentation of all ten cards, the cards are again presented one at a time in the *inquiry* phase. Now the subject is asked to indicate what part of the blot is associated with each response (location) and what it was about the blot that influenced the response (determinants, e.g., form, movement, shading, color). A final stage of Rorschach administration, *testing limits*, often follows. Here an attempt is made to elicit by suggestion or direct questioning common location, determinant, and content responses which the subject may not have perceived during free association or inquiry proper.

There are numerous Rorschach scoring systems. The most popular in the United States are those of Klopfer, of Beck, and of Hertz. In addition to scoring location, determinants, and content, each system also evaluates responses in terms of popularity, originality, and accuracy of "fit" to the stimulus properties of the cards. Personality structure and dynamics are inferred from the subject's individual scores and their configural relationships, and also from detailed analysis of his individual responses. Most Rorschach interpretation is admittedly impressionistic or subjective in the sense that the interpreter relies heavily on skill gained from his clinical experience.

Although many variations of the original Rorschach have appeared, perhaps the most significant to date is the Holtzman Inkblot Technique (Forms A and B). Responses are scored in 22 categories (e.g., form definiteness, use of shading, anatomy content, hostility, popularity, rejection). The subject is instructed to give one response to each blot. Administration takes about 45 to 90 minutes. Normative information on these 22 variables is provided for eight groups, including normals (ages five through adult), schizophrenics, mental retardates, and others.

Beck, S. J., Beck, A. G., Levitt, E. E., and Molish, H. B. 1961. *Rorschach's Test*. 3rd edition. New York, Grune and Stratton, Inc.

Holtzman, W. H., Thorpe, J. S., Swartz, J. D., and Herron, E. W. 1961. *Inkblot Perception in Personality: Holtzman Inkblot Technique*. Austin, Texas, University of Texas Press.

Klopfer, B., and Davidson, H. H. 1962. *The Rorschach Technique: An Introductory Manual*. New York, Harcourt, Brace & World, Inc.

Rickers-Ovsiankina, M. A., (ed.) 1960. *Rorschach Psychology*. New York, John Wiley & Sons.

Thematic Apperception Tests. The Thematic Apperception Test (TAT) was developed by Henry Murray and his co-workers in the Harvard Psychological Clinic in 1935. Today it ranks second to the Rorschach in use among projective techniques. The purpose of the TAT is exploring dominant drives, emotions, sentiments, complexes, and conflicts of a subject's personality.

The test consists of 31 cards (30 pictures and one blank card) which are presented one at a time. The subject is asked to tell a story about each card— to tell what is happening, what led up to the picture, and what will be the outcome. Of the 31 card set, ten pictures plus the blank card are designed for all subjects, seven are designed for girls and older females, seven are designed for boys and older males, and the remainder for males and females of various ages. TAT administration practices differ widely and there is no standard number of cards used for all subjects. Typically an hour is required for a ten-card series.

Interpretation of the TAT, like that of other projective techniques, is largely subjective or impressionistic. A number of formal TAT scoring systems have been proposed but none has become widely used in clinical practice.

A number of adaptations of the TAT have been developed for special purposes. One such revision (Thompson, 1949) was prepared for use with Negroes after it was found that Negro subjects were often unable to identify with the characters portrayed on the original cards.

Although the TAT is designed for use with children as young as seven years, the Children's Apperception Test (CAT) developed by Bellak in 1948 is perhaps more interesting and better suited for the younger child. The CAT consists of 20 pictures of animals rather than humans and is designed for ages three to ten. The purpose of the CAT is to elicit information on feeding problems, sibling rivalry, and other childhood conflicts.

Bellak, L. 1954. *The Thematic Apperception Test and The Children's Apperception Test in Clinical Use.* New York, Grune & Stratton, Inc.
Murray, H. A. 1943. *Thematic Apperception Tests: Manual.* Cambridge, Massachusetts, Harvard University Press.
Thompson, C. E. 1949. *The Thematic Apperception Test: Thompson Modification.* Cambridge, Massachusetts, Harvard University Press.

House-Tree-Person. The House-Tree-Person (H-T-P) technique described by Buck in 1948 is a projective device designed for use in personality assessment with both children and adults.

The H-T-P derives its name from the requirement that the subject make a free hand drawing of a *house,* a *tree,* and a *person.* The subject is given paper, pencil with eraser, and crayons. Each drawing is made on a separate piece of paper. An inquiry phase follows in which the subject is asked to describe and explain his drawings.

Both quantitative and qualitative scoring methods are employed. Interpretation is based upon characteristics of drawing performance, drawing details, and the subject's verbalizations. A related projective technique is the Draw-A-Person in which only human figures are drawn. Notwithstanding the popularity of figure drawing techniques, the empirical evidence supporting their use is less adequate than one would desire (see Swenson, 1957).

Buck, J. N. 1948. The H-T-P technique, a qualitative and quantitative scoring manual. Journal of Clinical Psychology Monograph. No. 5.
Machover, K. 1948. *Personality Projection in the Drawing of the Human Figure.* Springfield, Illinois, Charles C Thomas, Publisher.
Swenson, C. H. 1957. Empirical Evaluation of Human Figure Drawings. Psychological Bulletin *54,* 431-466.

Word Association Methods. Originally known as the "free association test," the word association procedures antedated the present projective movement and were described by Francis Galton as early as 1879. The procedure involves the presentation of a stimulus word to a subject who is told simply to respond by giving the first word that comes to mind. Although there are many word association lists available, perhaps the most commonly used is the Kent-Rosanoff form originally developed in 1910. This form consists of 100 common, neutral words which were selected because they evoked the same association from people in general. For example, to the word "table" a majority of subjects respond "chair." Typical words of the Kent-Rosanoff list are table, black, woman, anger, justice, stove, doctor, and afraid.

Word association responses can be analyzed in a variety of ways. A response can be compared with normative data in order to establish whether it is common or idiosyncratic. Such frequency of response tables are available for various populations and diagnostic groups (e.g., see Kent and Rosanoff, 1910; Palermo and Jenkins, 1964; Rapaport, Gill, and Schafer, 1946).

Kent, G. H., and Rosanoff, A. 1910. *Free Association Tests.* Chicago, C. H. Stoelting.
Palermo, D. S., and Jenkins, J. J. 1964. *Word Association Norms: Grade School Through College.* Minneapolis, University of Minnesota Press.
Rapaport, D., Gill, M., and Schafer, R. 1946. *Diagnostic Psychological Testing, Vol. II.* Chicago, Yearbook Publishers, Inc.

Sentence Completion Techniques.

The sentence-completion or incomplete sentence method is one of the simplest and most popular procedures for obtaining information regarding a subject's attitude toward self and others, family relations, aspirations, sexual adjustment, and the like.

The method typically entails the use of a number of incomplete sentences which the subject is to complete with whatever thoughts come to his mind. In the form developed by Rotter (1950), *The Incomplete Sentences Blank,* there are 40 "stems" which are completed by the subject. The subject is asked simply to express his real feelings and make a complete sentence. Typical of the Rotter stems are the following: I like . . ., I regret . . ., When I was a child . . ., Marriage . . ., My father . . ., My greatest worry is . . . .

Although Rotter provides formal scoring procedures, such scoring is rarely used in daily clinical work. More often than not the examiner analyzes each response in a subjective way based on his clinical experience. The Rotter Blank is designed for use with adolescents and adults. It is untimed and requires between 20 and 40 minutes.

Rotter, J. B., and Rafferty, J. E. 1952. *The Rotter Incomplete Sentences Blank: Manual.* New York, The Psychological Corporation.
Rotter, J. B. 1952. The Sentence Completion Method. In *Projective Techniques,* ed. H. Anderson and G. Anderson. New York, Prentice-Hall, Inc.

MISCELLANEOUS TESTS AND RESEARCH TECHNIQUES

Adjective Check List. The Adjective Check List (ACL), first introduced in 1949 and reported by Gough and Heilbrun in 1964, is designed for use in personality assessment and research. The ACL consists of 300 adjectives (e.g., active, evasive, logical, tense) commonly used to describe individual attributes. The subject is required to check each adjective he would consider to be self-descriptive. Designed for adolescents and adults, the ACL can currently be scored on 24 variables (e.g., defensiveness, self-confidence, self-control, achievement, dominance, aggression, counseling readiness). Hand scoring of the 24 scales is extremely laborious, and special answer sheets are available for mechanical scoring.

Gough, H. G., and Heilbrun, A. B. 1964. *Manual for the Adjective Check List.* Palo Alto, California, Consulting Psychologists Press.

Minnesota Briggs History Questionnaire (FI, M, and W Forms). The Minnesota-Briggs History Questionnaire (M-B), formerly the M-B History Record, is a standardized objective case-history questionnaire with a form for use with family informants (FI), as well as self-administered forms for men (M) and women (W).

The FI form contains 175 items sampling all major areas of a standard psychiatric interview (e.g., identifying data, family background, educational history, occupational history, social patterns, dating and sexual history, trouble with law, health, personal characteristics, and marriage). A major advantage of the M-B is that it provides uniform coverage and a permanent record suitable for case-history research.

Briggs, P. F. 1961. *Manual for use with the M-B History Questionnaire.* Minneapolis, University of Minnesota. Author.

Missouri Children's Picture Series. The Missouri Children's Picture Series (MCPS), recently introduced by Sines et al. (1964), is an empirically derived nonverbal personality test for children (ages five to 16).

The MCPS consists of 238 pictures, each printed on a 3 × 5 card. The pictures show a child sometimes alone, sometimes with others, either apart from or participating in a wide range of typical activities for children. The child is presented the cards one at a time and instructed to "look at each picture. If it looks like fun, put it here (in a pile to his right). If it does not look like fun, put it here (in a pile to his left). Let me know when you are finished." Testing time is approximately 15 to 20 minutes individually and 30 to 45 minutes in groups. Scoring is objective and employs a hand scoring template for each scale. Raw scores are translated into standard scores based on age norms provided for each sex.

There are currently three cross-validated scales available: *conformity, masculinity-femininity,* and *maturity.* Three additional scales are in process of cross-validation: *aggression, inhibition,* and *hyperactivity.* Scales for at least four more personality variables are planned: *somatization, sleep disturbance, sociability,* and *socioeconomic status.* At its present state of development the MCPS is a promising device but is not yet ready for routine clinical use.

Sines, J. O., Pauker, J. D., and Sines, L. K. 1964. *The Missouri Children's Picture Series.* Columbia, University of Missouri.

Myers-Briggs Type Indicator (Forms F and Fs). The Myers-Briggs Type Indicator (MBTI), developed in 1943 and revised in 1962, is based upon a modification of Jungian theory of personality types (grades nine to 16 and adults).

The MBTI is a forced choice, self-report inventory consisting of 166 items which can be answered within 50 to 55 minutes. The test provides four dimension scores: Extroversion-Introversion, E-I (interests in the outer world of people and things, or in the inner world of concepts and ideas);

Sensation-Intuition, S-I (perceiving directly through the senses, or indirectly by intuitive processes); Thinking-Feeling, T-F (arriving at decision by impersonal logic, or by subjective processes); and Judging-Perceiving, J-P (arriving at a conclusion about something, or an awareness of something).

While the MBTI is not among the more popular tests in clinical use today, nonetheless it has considerable potential utility in that the type scores empirically relate to a wide range of personality, ability, interest, value, aptitude, academic, and behavioral variables.

Myers, I. T. 1962. *Manual (1962), The Myers-Briggs Type Indicator.* Princeton, N. J., Educational Testing Service.
Stricker, L. J., and Ross, J. 1962. *A Description and Evaluation of the Myers-Briggs Type Indicator.* Princeton, N. J., Educational Testing Service.

Psychotic Reaction Profile. The Psychotic Reaction Profile (PRP), developed by Lorr, O'Connor, and Stafford in 1961, is one of the most recent of published scales for rating the behavior of psychotic patients. The scale consists of 85 items which are marked either True or Not true by a psychiatric aide or nurse who has observed the patient over a three-day period. The PRP provides scores on four dimensions: *withdrawal, thinking disorganization, paranoid belligerence,* and *agitated depression.* Total rating time is about 15 minutes.

Lorr, M., O'Connor, J. P., and Stafford, J. W. 1960. The Psychotic Reaction Profile. Journal of Clinical Psychology *16,* 241-245.
Lorr, M., O'Connor, J. P., and Stafford, J. W. 1967. *Manual, Psychotic Reaction Profile.* Beverly Hills, California, Western Psychological Services.

Q Sort. The Q Sort, originally described by Stephenson in 1935, is a rating procedure whereby a judge may evaluate a subject in a form suitable for quantitative comparison and analysis. It permits computation of average ratings over several judges and estimates of degree of agreement between judges.

In the usual Q sort procedure, the sorter is presented with a standard set of sentences, phrases, or words and asked to distribute the statements into categories along a continuum ranging from *least* to *most* descriptive of the subject being judged. The number of categories as well as the number of statements placed in each category may vary depending upon the Q set used.

One example, the California Q set, reported by Block in 1961, consists of 100 statements designed to provide "a comprehensive description, in contemporary psychodynamic terms, of an individual's personality." Each statement appears on a separate card for convenience of sorting. Some statements describe phenotypic or observable characteristics of the subject (e.g., "Is cheerful," "Is verbally fluent," "Can express ideas well"); others are genotypic statements requiring varying degrees of inference from what can be observed (e.g., "Is self-indulgent," "Handles anxiety and conflicts by refusing to recognize their presence," "Has repressive or disassociative tendencies"). The California Q set requires about 30 minutes of working time.

Another example is the Marks set of 108 items, developed in 1959 and reported in 1961. In content the Marks Q set also includes both phenotypic (e.g., "Is tense, high-strung, and jumpy," "Is irritable") and genotypic statements ("Has a need to achieve; to strive to do something as well as possible," "Has a need to affiliate with others"). These statements were selected for their representative coverage of the personality domain from a pool of over 2000 items. In construction the items were empirically screened for applicability to children and adults of both sexes, for clinical pertinence, for ratability and for interpatient variability. Unlike the California Q set which requires most of the statements to be placed in the middle sorting categories, the Marks Q set distributes the statements evenly into all sorting categories.

Block, J. 1961. *The Q-Sort Method in Personality Assessment and Psychiatric Research.* Springfield Illinois, Charles C Thomas, Publisher.

Marks, P. A., and Seeman, W. 1962. The heterogeneity of some common psychiatric stereotypes. Journal of Clinical Psychology *3*, 266-270.

Semantic Differential. The Semantic Differential, developed in 1957 by Osgood, Suci, and Tannenbaum, offers a novel approach to personality assessment by focusing on the connotative meaning of key concepts to the subject. This is accomplished by having the subject rate each such key concept (e.g., mother, father, God, myself, husband) on a series of "simpler" bipolar dimensions such as good-bad, strong-weak, light-heavy, hard-soft. The fact that each concept is rated on the same dimensions permits scoring which plots the relative similarity of the key concepts to each other.

Thus the subject's ratings furnish a perspective on how he is viewing himself, significant others, and the world about him—a perspective on his individual meaning system.

The technique is appropriate in virtually any situation where assessment of, and changes in, meanings of concepts is desired. It may be used to compare a subject's self-ratings with the way he is rated by others; reratings permit evaluation of change in the meaning of concepts over time, for example. The Semantic Differential may be administered in group or individual form.

Osgood, C. E., Suci, C. J., and Tannenbaum, B. H. 1957. *The Measurement of Meaning.* Urbana, University of Illinois Press.

Sixteen Personality Factor Questionnaire (Forms A, B, and C). The Sixteen Personality Factor Questionnaire (16 PF) was devised by Raymond Cattell in 1949 and reported by Cattell and Eber in 1964. Cast in the format of an objective questionnaire, for ages 15 and over, it purports to measure all the main dimensions of personality. While not a popular personality assessment device, the 16 PF was developed by factor analysis and represents a fundamentally different approach to inventory construction from the MMPI.

The aim of factor analysis is to identify the basic dimensions of human personality following a particular statistical methodology. The assumptions underlying this approach are essentially twofold: that psychological variables have properties of continuity, and that the values of these variables are linear and at least nearly orthogonal. Such assumptions involve the belief that psychological variables correspond to most mathematical and physical models, a belief that is not endorsed by many applied psychologists.

The 16 PF provides three alternative responses to each question—e.g., yes, uncertain, or no). Three forms are available with 187, 187, and 106 items respectively; they may be used in combination to increase measurement reliability. Testing time varies with the form or forms used, and ranges from 20 minutes to approximately three hours, depending on the reading speed of the subjects. The various forms are self-administered in group or individual testing sessions. Both hand scoring keys and commerical machine scoring answer sheets are available.

Scoring of the 16 PF yields values on 16 dimensions: *Cyclothymia* vs. *Schizothymia, General Intelligence* vs. *Mental Defect, Emotional Stability* vs. *Dissatisfied Emotionality, Dominance* vs. *Submission, Surgency* vs. *Desurgency, Character Strength* vs. *Lack of Character Strength, Adventurousness* vs. *Shyness, Sensitivity* vs. *Tough Maturity, Paranoid Tendency* vs. *Relaxed Security, Bohemian Introversion* vs. *Practical Concernedness, Shrewdness* vs. *Naivete, Guilt Proneness* vs. *Confident Adequacy, Radicalism* vs. *Conservatism, Self-Sufficiency* vs. *Group Dependency, High Self-Sentiment* vs. *Low Self-Sentiment,* and *High Ergic Tension* vs. *Low Ergic Tension.*

In summary, while factor analysis provides a means of grouping items into internally consistent, relatively homogeneous, and independent clusters, there is still a need to demonstrate the relationships of such scales to external empirical criteria. It is for reasons such as these that the 16 PF, like other factorally derived tests, is still at an experimental stage and is not recommended for clinical use.

Cattell, R. B., and Eber, H. W. 1957. *Handbook for the Sixteen Personality Factor Questionnaire.* Champaign, Illinois, Institute for Personality and Ability Testing (With 1964 Supplementation).

CURRENT TESTING PRACTICES

A job analysis of psychological testing might divide the total task into the subtasks of (1) decision to use a test, (2) test selection, (3) administration, (4) scoring, (5) interpretation, and (6) applying interpretation to the solution of clinical problems. It is convenient to consider these subfunctions separately in reviewing contemporary testing practices in medical and psychiatric settings.

Deciding to Test. Use of a psychological test in a clinical setting implies that psychosocial information is relevant to optimal patient care and treatment, and that formal testing is the best way to get such information. Sensitivity to the need for such information typically rests with the clinician responsible for the patient. Choice of a test as a means of securing the necessary information usually implies a desire for corroboration of clinical impressions, or a recognition that some particular datum can be assessed with reasonable accuracy only through use of formal psychological evaluation procedures.

Widespread use is made of psychological tests in most modern psychiatric settings today. Test usage in general medical settings varies greatly, and is dependent upon the nature of the patient's presenting problems, the interest and attention given by the attending staff to the psychological aspects of their patient's problems, and, perhaps most important, upon the availability of psychological testing facilities.

Most frequently the decision to test is made on a patient-by-patient basis. Sometimes, either because of the character of the patient population or because of a conviction regarding the value of having certain kinds of psychological information available on all patients, a decision is made to administer a test or a battery of tests to all patients in that setting. Thus, all new psychiatry in- and out-patients at The Ohio State University Hospitals are now given a brief intelligence test (Shipley-Hartford), a personality inventory (MMPI), and a sentence completion blank; and all admissions to medical sections at The Mayo Clinic are given a personality inventory (MMPI). In such routine screening usage, these tests serve the additional function of alerting attending staff to psychological factors which may deserve further inquiry.

Selecting Tests. Optimal test selection requires adequate knowledge of the patient and of characteristics of available tests. Intelligence tests, for example, vary in their literacy requirements and in their dependence upon vision, hearing, speech, and hand-eye cordination. Some are designed for children, some for adults. Some are particularly appropriate for exceptional subjects such as the mentally retarded or the very gifted. Valid assessment of intellectual function presumes that an appropriate test has been chosen. Some physicians are competent in test selection by virtue of past training and experience; however, physicians rely typically upon a psychologist for selecting tests, much as they would rely upon a physiologist for selecting the appropriate test procedure to measure a physiological variable, when they themselves are not thoroughly conversant with the available techniques.

Administering Tests. Psychological tests are administered by a variety of people in a variety of professional settings. Many physicians, especially psychiatrists, do some psychological test administration themselves. In some instances they may use their office nurse or receptionist to assist them in much the same way she would assist with biological laboratory procedures done directly by the physician. As with any laboratory test procedure, adequate training and quality control are essential. Some medical schools now offer such training. There are a number of psychological tests which require considerable specialized skill in examiner-patient interaction. Such skills are not esoteric and can be learned; but this requires a major commitment of time both for learning these skills and for maintaining them. These factors place the valid administration of some tests beyond the interest and competence of most physicians. Thus, physicians turn to psychologists who as the primary developers of psychological assessment procedures have also remained active in giving and using tests in independent practice and in institutional settings. An increasing number of clinical psychologists are now questioning from the viewpoint of cost and efficient utilization of limited professional manpower whether time-consuming test administration is an appropriate function of Ph.D.-trained personnel. It is perhaps for such reasons that a new subprofession is emerging, that of the psychometrist, trained at the B.A. or M.A. level, a specialist in administering and scoring psychological tests. Today, psychometrists are likely to be found in settings where testing activity has been centralized. These units may bear names such as Student Testing Center in colleges and universities, or Psychometric Laboratory in hospitals and clinics.

At least brief mention should be made of the newest innovation in test administration practices — the "testing machine." Electronic equipment is now available which can display a wide variety of visual and auditory stimuli, which permits the subject's answers to be recorded in a number of different ways, and which responds to the subject's answers by altering the question or stimulus material presented next. Such devices are in common use in psychological research settings today and their future use in applied settings can be anticipated.

Scoring Tests. Variations in test scoring practices are dependent upon the character of the test. The scoring of most objective tests can be reduced to an explicit clerical procedure, which may be as simple as summing true and false answers to particular test items, and converting total raw scores to standardized values by means of a prepared transformation table. With such tests, careful attention to codified details of scoring procedure and clerical accuracy are the prime ingredients of scoring skill. Most objective tests are still hand-scored by the test administrator, but increased use is being made of computers and related test-scoring electronic hardware. Several commercial test-scoring services are now providing computer scoring on a mail-in basis. Other tests, especially unstructured tests, presently do not lend themselves to clerical, mechanical, or electronic scoring procedures. Scoring of the Rorschach, for example, still requires the skill and experience of a trained person.

The physician's competence in psychological test scoring raises issues comparable to those discussed under test administration. The physician can learn to score many objective tests with a modicum of training, and can in turn train his receptionist or nurse to assist him, or he can elect to bypass such learning and utilize a computer scoring service. In the case of tests involving a more subjective, less explicit, less codified scoring procedure, most physicians will continue to rely on the psychologist and the psychometrist.

Test Interpretation. Test "reading" or interpretation is the process of translating test scores into significant information about the patient's psychological functioning. Traditionally, the interpretive process has relied heavily upon the skilled clinician, his professional experience in the use of tests, and his knowledge of scientific literature regarding tests and what different scores and patterns of scores signify. At least for some tests and for some interpretations and predictions, the clinician-interpreter faces a challenge from actuarial (or statistical) methods (see Sawyer, 1966; also Sines, 1966). For example, research findings indicate that undergraduate academic performance can be predicted by using test scores in a mathematical equation as well as or better than by college counselors utilizing the same test score information. In the same actuarial tradition, Marks and Seeman (1963) have provided an interpretive "cookbook" listing personality characteristics empirically associated with each of 16 MMPI profile patterns. In earlier research with a prototype of an MMPI cookbook, Halbower (Meehl, 1956) found that skilled clinicians reading MMPI profiles could not surpass the accuracy attained by the use of his cookbook.

Computers can be and are being used to interpret as well as score psychological tests. The development of the first such computer program was described in the Proceedings of the Mayo Clinic in 1962. Automated or semiautomated programs for the MMPI were subsequently developed by Dr. Joseph Finney at the University of Kentucky, Dr. Raymond Fowler at the University of Alabama, Dr. Bernard Glueck at the Institute of Living, Dr. Philip Marks at the University of Kansas, and Dr. Alex Caldwell at U.C.L.A., among others. MMPI scoring and interpretation using The Mayo Clinic Program are now commercially available through the Psychological Corporation, 304 East 45th Street, New York, New York 10017. The Roche Psychiatric Service Institute, sponsored by Roche Laboratories of Nutley, New Jersey, also provides

MMPI scoring and interpretation to psychiatrists and psychologists utilizing the Fowler program.

Because of the necessary background of specialized experience and knowledge, clinical test interpretation has largely remained the province of the psychologist. There are notable exceptions especially among psychiatrists, pediatricians, and neurologists, some of whom have attained high levels of interpretive expertise with tests relevant to their clinical area. Actuarial and computer interpretive procedures make psychological test interpretations more readily available to the practicing physician without the arduous accrual of personal clinical interpretive skill.

TYPICAL MODELS OF TEST USAGE

The variations in contemporary psychological testing practices in medical and psychiatric settings today, described in the preceeding sections, can be summarized by three models of test usage. Each model has its advantages and disadvantages; together they probably represent current testing practice. As will be seen, they differ primarily in terms of the functions performed by the physician, the psychologist, the psychometrist, and the computer. They may be called (1) the laboratory model, (2) the interpreter model, and (3) the consultant model.

The Laboratory Model. This model assumes that the physician wishes summarized numerical data from some particular psychological test instrument, much as he might wish to know the specific gravity from a standard urinalysis. Of the three, this model places greatest responsibility upon the physician for appropriate test use. It implies that he knows which test to select for the information he is seeking. It requires either test administration and scoring skills on his part, or an available Psychometric Laboratory (psychometrist with or without a computer). Further-

more, it requires skill in interpreting test scores and in using this information. As behavioral science teaching increases in medical school curricula and as the services of psychometrists and computers become more widely available, it seems likely that this model will find wider acceptance.

The Interpreter Model. This is the traditional psychological testing model in medical settings. Here the physician asks the psychologist for test-based information regarding certain psychological characteristics of his patient. The psychologist assumes responsibility for selecting the most appropriate test(s), for administering and scoring them, and for interpreting the results. He may or may not use laboratory resources in performing these activities. This model implies that the physician has asked the right questions of the psychologist and his tests, and that the resultant information will be appropriately integrated with other findings by the physician in formulating a solution to a clinical problem. Within the framework of this model, the functioning of the psychologist is similar to that of the radiologist or the pathologist.

The Consultant Model. In this model the physician requests the psychologist's opinion and recommendations regarding certain aspects of the care and treatment of his patient much as he would request the advice of a neurologist, internist, or other specialist. Rather than focusing on test-based information, this model asks the consultant to formulate a solution to the psychosocial aspects of the patient's problem. Psychological tests and the use of laboratory resources may or may not play an important role as an information base in formulating the consultative opinion and recommendations. This model makes available not only the psychologist's knowledge of psychological tests but additionally his overall expertise concerning human psychological functioning.

SUMMARY

In conclusion, viable psychological tests like viable professions have grown out of social needs. Today there is ample evidence of the utility of these tests in many applied settings, including the hospital and the clinic. More sophisticated procedures and models for securing, condensing, and utilizing salient psychosocial information will undoubtedly develop in the service of comprehensive patient care.

REFERENCES

American Psychological Association. 1966. *Standards for educational and psychological tests and manuals*. Washington, D.C., American Psychological Association.

Anastasi, A. 1961. *Psychological testing*. New York, The Macmillan Co.

Buros, O. K., ed. *Mental measurements yearbook*. Highland Park, New Jersey, The Gryphon Press, 1941, 1949, 1953, 1959, 1965.

Buros, O. K., ed. 1961. *Tests in print*. Highland Park, New Jersey, The Gryphon Press.

Cronbach, L. J. 1960. *Essentials of psychological testing*, 2nd edition. New York, Harper & Row, Publishers, Inc.

Horst, P. 1966. *Psychological measurements and prediction*. Belmont, California, Wadsworth Publishing Co.

Kleinmuntz, B. 1967. *Personality measurement: An introduction*. Homewood, Illinois, Dorsey Press.

Marks, P. A., and Seeman, W. 1963. *The actuarial description of abnormal personality: An atlas for use with the MMPI*. Baltimore, The Williams & Wilkins Co.

Meehl, P. E. 1956. Wanted—A good cookbook. The American Psychologist *11*, 263-272.

Meehl, P. E., and Rosen, A. 1955. Antecedent probability and the efficiency of psychometric signs, patterns, or cutting scores. Psychological Bulletin *52*, 194-216.

Sawyer, J. 1966. Measurement and prediction, clinical and statistical. Psychological Bulletin *66*, 178-200.

Sines, J. O. 1966. Actuarial methods in personality assessment. In *Progress in experimental personality research*, ed. B. A. Maher. New York, Academic Press Inc., pp. 133-193.

Sundberg, N. D., and Tyler, L. E. 1962. *Clinical psychology: An introduction to research and practice*. New York, Appleton-Century-Crofts, Inc.

Tryon, R. C. 1957. Reliability and behavior domain validity: Reformulation and historical critique. Psychological Bulletin *54*, 229-249.

Oh, wad some power the giftie gie us
To see oursels as others see us.
It wad frae monie a blunder free us,
An' foolish notion.
>　　　　*Robert Burns*

He that complies against his will
Is of his own opinion still.
>　　　　*Samuel Butler*

If you will believe well of your fellow man,
You may create the good you believe in.
>　　　　*William James*

Children begin by loving their parents; as they grow
older they judge them;
Sometimes they forgive them.
>　　　　*Oscar Wilde*

What every psychiatric patient needs is a friend.
>　　　　*Clifford Beers*

The enemies of our enemies are our friends.
>　　　　*Anonymous*

One of the principal functions of a friend is to suffer
(in a milder and symbolic form) the punishments that
we should like, but are unable, to inflict upon our
enemies.
>　　*"Brave New World" by Aldous Huxley*

CHAPTER 11

The Psychosocial Therapies

LEARNING, COMMUNICATION, AND THERAPEUTIC INTERACTION

All forms of psychotherapy involve efforts to bring about changes in the patient's ideation, personality, or behavior, and fall within definitions of learning given at the beginning of Chapter 7. Before the learning of more effective adaptation can take place, however, it is generally necessary for the patient to unlearn well-established patterns of maladaptive behavior. The means by which such changes are brought about involve communication between patient and therapist, a preliminary consideration of which was undertaken in the final section of Chapter 3, and some further aspects of which were discussed in the opening section of Chapter 9 concerning the initial psychiatric interview. Before proceeding further with the present chapter therefore the reader may wish to remind himself of the content of the relevant sections in these preceding chapters (3, 7, and 9).

In attempting to extinguish *existing* maladaptive behavior, it should be recalled that this involves nonreinforcement, rather than criticism or punishment. The latter may be more effective in discouraging the adoption of *new* patterns of maladaptive behavior, but it should be borne in mind that negative reinforcement will tend to drive the patient away from the therapist, who would otherwise be a potent source of positive reinforcement through rewards. In addition to learning more effective behavior through positive reinforcement, the patient may also learn through imitation and identification with the perceived attitudes and behavior of the therapist, whether or not the therapist recognizes or fosters such identification.

Such principles of learning are involved in various different approaches to psychotherapy, and are being increasingly recognized by therapists of varying persuasions, whether or not this leads to any modification of therapeutic goals or techniques for accomplishing them. At the present time, a considerable number of psychologists and a smaller proportion of psychiatrists base their therapeutic efforts directly upon learning principles intended to modify behavior, rather than to change the patient's personality or help him obtain insight into hitherto unconscious dynamic processes. This approach to behavior modification will be the second of five major approaches to psychotherapy discussed in the present chapter. Each of these approaches is widely used in therapy with individual patients, with families or with groups of patients. Some of the special aspects of family and group therapy as well as social and milieu therapy will be outlined later in the chapter, after discussion of the major approaches to therapy.

Broadly speaking, the *goals of psychotherapy* may either be limited to symptomatic relief, alleviation of situational stress, and support of the patient in coping with difficulties; or alternatively involve more ambitious efforts to improve adaptive capacity and decrease vulnerability through reeducation or personality reconstruction. In striving toward either type of goal, the therapist places varying emphasis and interpretations on two major dimensions of the therapeutic interaction: the *emotional relationship* between patient and therapist, and the *verbal content* of their transactions. Some therapists consider that the words are less important than the music of the therapeutic relationship, but few emphasize one to the exclusion of the other. There remain, however, important differences between the emphasis on relationship and the nature of the relationship offered by different therapists. Some approach their patients as representatives of authority and decision-makers. Others may assume the role of protector or parent substitute, friend or educator. Analysts tend to remain listeners rather than talkers, onto whom the patient will displace feelings, and to whom the patient will attribute attitudes originating in his own earlier relationships with other significant persons. Nondirective or client-centered therapists consider that a relationship of trust can be established only on the basis of unconditional positive regard by the therapist for the patient. On the other hand, the transactional therapist concerned with the nuances of nonverbal communication may insist that trust must be based on honesty in communication, including disapproval of the patient's attitudes or behavior where reasonable and appropriate.

Prestige-suggestion that a patient will lose a symptom or otherwise improve because of an authoritarian communication to this effect from the therapist is widely regarded as superficial and unlikely to provide lasting benefit, particularly by analytically oriented therapists who emphasize the acquisition of insight or the value of a corrective emotional experience. Frank, on the other hand, emphasized the role of *the patient's faith in the therapist* in all forms of psychotherapy. This faith can exist only when the therapist has faith in himself and in the effectiveness of his therapy based on personal experience or knowledge acquired from others. Unfortunately, the scientific evaluation of the effects of psychotherapy is extremely difficult, and authoritative opinions that vary from the skeptical to the frankly nihilistic have been expressed. Scientific investigation requires an open-mindedness toward the effectiveness of a therapy, but nihilism or doubt will certainly be communicated to the patient and will adversely affect the results of any therapy.

Granted the knowledge and experience that promote confidence, the therapeutic approach may still be one of ego-support, insight, or behavioral change. Therapy may be directive or nondirective, suppressive or expressive, and involve clarification of conscious motivation or interpretation of unconscious dynamics.

In the glossary published by the American Psychiatric Association, psychotherapy is defined as "the generic term for any type of treatment which is based primarily upon verbal or nonverbal communication with the patient in distinction to the use of drugs, surgery or physical measures such as electro- or insulin shock, hydrotherapy, and others. Most physicians regard intensive psychotherapy as a medical responsibility." The last sentence reflects the official position of the American Psychiatric Association but requires a little clarification. In the first place this general opinion held by "most physicians" may be applied to all psychotherapy rather than restricted to intensive psychotherapy. Secondly, although psychiatrists are physicians, they do not necessarily hold the same opinions as other physicians or even other psychiatrists. There are many psychiatrists who consider it quite appropriate to apply the term psychotherapy to activities carried out by members of other professional disciplines, such as counseling or behavior modification undertaken by psychologists and case

work carried out by social workers. In recent years psychologists have contributed a great deal of literature on certain approaches to psychotherapy, counseling, and behavior modification, some of which will be outlined below.

Harper presented comparative data on 36 systems of psychoanalysis and psychotherapy. The American Handbook of Psychiatry, edited by Arieti, included ten different approaches in the second volume, and several additional chapters in the third volume. Stein's book on contemporary psychotherapies included eight major approaches to individual therapy, plus papers on family and group therapy, presented by different authors.

Certain similarities or common denominators among these therapies, however, have led certain authors to emphasize only a few major differences. In his large volume on the technique of psychotherapy, Wolberg distinguished two main approaches: *supportive therapy* and insight therapy, further dividing the latter into *insight therapy with reeducative goals* (concerned mainly with conscious conflicts and deliberate efforts at readjustment) and *insight therapy with reconstructive goals* (psychoanalysis and analytically oriented therapy concerned mainly with unconscious conflicts and attempts to achieve more extensive changes in character structure). While there is some merit in this simplification, the present author considers that two further approaches should receive separate discussion — namely *behavior therapy* that is directed towards the relief of symptoms (and reeducation without any concern over insight), and *transactional approaches* to therapy that utilize some psychoanalytic theory and techniques but emphasize the corrective emotional experience within the framework of learning and communication theory.

In the next five sections of the present chapter we shall therefore review the following major approaches to psychotherapy;)1) directive, suppressive, and supportive therapies; (2) behavior modification based on principles of learning; (3) nondirective, relationship, and reeducative therapies; (4) psychoanalysis and dynamic psychotherapies; and (5) transactional approaches to psychotherapy.

DIRECTIVE, SUPPRESSIVE, AND SUPPORTIVE THERAPIES

These approaches originate within the traditional framework of the doctor-patient relationship and have the respectability of antiquity. In the past, they have frequently been adopted by physicians with little or no training in psychiatry, or by those who work with large numbers of patients, or for patients who appear relatively inaccessible to more intensive psychotherapy. In an age of increasing psychiatric sophistication, these approaches are frequently regarded as superficial and symptomatic, although they may still be preferred by physicians who also rely heavily on drugs or other somatic therapies, especially in working with certain types of psychiatric problems.

The term *directive* implies that the physician understands the patient's problems and needs better than the patient, and accepts responsibility for seeing that his recommendations are carried out — whether these involve environmental manipulation, involuntary or voluntary admission to hospital, administration of drugs or other somatic therapy, or deliberate efforts to change the patient's attitudes and behavior by conscious persuasion, prestige-suggestion, or example.

Such an approach tends to ignore the possible contributions of unconscious motivation and dynamics, and may deliberately suppress such material as well as maladaptive behavior. In the words of Levine, "Suppressive psychotherapy employs such techniques as authoritative firmness and commands, the ignoring of symptoms and complaints, placebos used with dogmatic assurance, suggestions under hypnosis to repress symptoms, comparable waking suggestion, exhortation, and persuasion. Essentially, in this approach, the therapist acts as a dictator, as an adjunct to the forces of repression, as an omniscient and omnipotent father who expects to be obeyed."

In prestige-suggestion, the therapist assures the patient directly or indirectly that unpleasant or disabling symptoms are being relieved. Suggestibility of the patient may be increased by means of hypnosis, narcosis, or administration of a placebo, and is greater when the patient has little psychiatric sophistication and the therapist is perceived as having high status, prestige, and power.

Advocates of suppressive therapy have sometimes drawn an analogy between neurotic symptoms and a suitcase containing too many articles to permit its being closed. Three possible solutions involve discarding some of its contents (superficial expressive therapy), removing and repacking its contents more neatly (longer term reconstructive therapy), and sitting on the case until it does close (suppressive therapy). Sometimes direct coercion has involved deliberate attempts to frighten patients out of their symptoms and habits. Redlich and Freedman reported that an eight-year-old boy with nocturnal enuresis was told by his family physician: "Your little wee-wee will be burnt off with electricity if you don't quit wetting the bed." The boy promptly stopped bed-wetting but developed nightmares and a marked general passivity and dependency that lasted for years. Not only may suppressive therapy be damaging, but it may also be ineffectual, since other symptoms and maladaptive behavior may replace those that are suppressed.

In contrast with the preceding approach, *supportive therapy* uses those techniques that will make the patient more secure, reassured, accepted, protected, encouraged, safe, less anxious, and less alone. The therapist assumes an authoritarian but relatively *nondirective* role and attempts to boost the patient's self-esteem. He is warm, friendly, and reassuring, and permits the patient considerable temporary dependence upon him. He attempts to remove external stresses by environmental manipulation or by hospitalization of the patient, and encourages externalization of the patient's interests on various lines such as occupational and recreational therapy. He may provide guidance, advice, and a variety of measures for the relief of symptoms, including medication and somatic therapies which will be considered in the next chapter. Superficial approaches to group therapy as well as some forms of social and milieu therapy are essentially supportive in nature.

The term *expressive therapy* is sometimes applied to those forms of psychotherapy emphasizing the verbal productions of the patient, and the analysis of these productions with the aid of the therapist. Not infrequently, however, supportive therapy fosters verbal expression by the patient rather than the therapist, and includes such techniques as verbalization or ventilation, clarification, emotional catharsis or abreaction, and desensitization. *Verbalization or ventilation* concerns such matters as conscious problems, worries, doubts, fears, impulses, conflicts, and sources of anxiety and guilt. It is an extension of talking things out, getting things off one's chest, or confession (with implied or actual absolution) that many people employ in every day life relationships with friends and counselors. The therapist may discuss these problems with the patient and assist in *clarification* of their nature, origin, and solution.

Verbalization of emotionally charged material with the accompanying experience of strong emotions (such as grief or hate) may result in at least temporary relief of pent-up tensions or *emotional catharsis*, and may sometimes be followed by densensitization of the patient to the source of these emotions. Sometimes the strong emotion is displaced onto the therapist or other persons not responsible for originating

this feeling tone. The therapist should be aware of this, and hence experience no reciprocal antagonism toward the patient that might otherwise lead to retaliation or argument. The term *abreaction* is sometimes used as synonymous with the process of emotional catharsis, and sometimes in a more restricted sense to indicate the emotional release or discharge resulting from recalling the awareness of a painful experience that had been forgotten (repressed) because it was consciously intolerable.

BEHAVIOR MODIFICATION BASED ON LEARNING PRINCIPLES

The principles of classical conditioning, instrumental learning, avoidance learning, and desensitization have been established on a scientific basis during the present century, and were reviewed in Chapter 7. In recent years, these principles have been applied by psychiatrists and psychologists in attempts to remove undesirable symptoms or behavior, and replace these by more socially acceptable adaptation. The exponents of these techniques have generally been unconcerned with the possible significance of unconscious motivation and with effecting major changes in personality, and have been unimpressed by the results of psychotherapies intended to accomplish the latter, whether through insight into conscious or unconscious factors.

Bandura and Walters remarked that the techniques and goals of psychotherapy tend to be preselected on the basis of the therapist's training, with little reference to the diverse forms of behavior deviations exhibited by different patients, so that it is probable that therapeutic procedures will frequently fail to match the problems presented by the patient. They pointed out that the therapist may attempt to produce behavioral changes in opposite directions (in different patients) by means of the same therapeutic relationship and procedures, and they specifically questioned the value of (1) a relationship of "unconditional positive regard," (2) the attainment of insight by the patient (which may be secondary rather than primary in patients who undergo improvement), and (3) the beneficial consequences of emotional catharsis or abreaction which appears to increase aggressive behavior in patients with aggressive tendencies.

Eysenck vigorously attacked the theoretical foundations and practical results of psychoanalysis and other insight-oriented psychotherapies and provided some statistical support for his contentions, which were in turn criticized by a number of other authors. It has already been pointed out that comparative studies of the effects of psychotherapy are extremely difficult to carry out due to relativity in criteria of initial psychopathology, and also in criteria of changes in personality adaptation and behavior. While behavior therapists have not succeeded in demonstrating the superiority of their techniques in treating various forms of psychopathology, however, they have demonstrated symptomatic relief and short-term behavioral change in a number of instances. The focus of behavior therapy is on producing just such changes, and Eysenck summarized some of the differences he perceived between this approach and analytically oriented psychotherapy (Table 11-1).

Historically, one of the best known of these behavior therapies is the conditioned aversion treatment of alcoholism, which was originally used in Russia and was popularized in this country by Voegtlin et al. Varied techniques were employed by different authors, but all involved the concurrent administration of alcohol with emetics (such as emetine and apomorphine) in doses sufficient to produce severe nausea and vomiting. In terms of learning principles, this involves applying punishment to a well-established behavior and inducing a motivational conflict between the desire for alcohol and fear of extremely unpleasant consequences. As might be expected, a course of such aversive therapy is likely to suppress the undesirable behavior temporarily, and to require repetition at subsequent intervals. It is also evident that the treatment is only applicable to certain alcoholic patients—particularly those with neurotic rather than sociopathic personality characteristics, a history of moderately successful social adaptation prior to the onset of alcoholism, and those in good physical health. It may further be suspected that those patients who persist with such unpleasant treatment are likely to have a strong masochistic component, involving guilt and need for punishment, and that even for such patients the therapist will be perceived as a punitive figure who will ultimately be avoided and is unlikely to retain a capacity for fostering more successful social adaptation through positive reinforcement.

More recently, aversive conditioning has also been applied to the treatment of other behavior disorders such as sexual deviation, with a combination of punishment for deviant attitudes and behavior, and reinforcement of socially acceptable hetorosexual attitudes and behavior. A further well-known approach to reconditioning therapy was introduced by Wolpe, who conceptualized his techniques in terms of *reciprocal inhibition and desensitization*. In Wolpe's words, ". . .Neurotic behavior consists of persistent habits of learned (conditioned) adaptive behavior acquired in anxiety-generating situations. . . .If a response incompatible with anxiety can be made to occur in the presence of anxiety-evoking stimuli so that it is accompanied by a complete or partial suppression of the anxiety-responses, the bond between these stimuli and the anxiety-responses will be weakened."

This approach differs from aversive conditioning in that deliberate attempts are made to extinguish fear and avoidance responses through desensitization to the perceived sources of fear.

TABLE 11-1. Differences between Psychotherapy and Behavior Therapy

PSYCHOTHERAPY	BEHAVIOR THERAPY
1. Based on inconsistent theory never properly formulated in postulate form.	Based on consistent, properly formulated theory leading to testable deductions.
2. Derived from clinical observations made without necessary control observations or experiments.	Derived from experimental studies specifically designed to test basic theory and deductions made therefrom.
3. Considers symptoms the visible upshot of unconscious causes ("complexes").	Considers symptoms as unadaptive conditioned responses.
4. Regards symptoms as evidence of repression.	Regards symptoms as evidence of faulty learning.
5. Believes that symptomatology is determined by defense mechanisms.	Believes that symptomatology is determined by individual differences in conditionability and autonomic lability, as well as accidental environmental circumstances.
6. All treatment of neurotic disorders must be historically based.	All treatment of neurotic disorders is concerned with habits existing at present; their historical development is largely irrelevant.
7. Cures are achieved by handling the underlying (unconscious) dynamics, not by treating the symptom itself.	Cures are achieved by treating the symptom itself, i.e., by extinguishing unadaptive C.R.s and establishing desirable C.R.s.
8. Interpretation of symptoms, dreams, acts, etc. is an important element of treatment.	Interpretation, even if not completely subjective and erroneous, is irrelevant.
9. Symptomatic treatment leads to the elaboration of new symptoms.	Symptomatic treatment leads to permanent recovery provided autonomic as well as skeletal surplus C.R.s are extinguished.
10. Transference relations are essential for cures of neurotic disorders.	Personal relations are not essential for cures of neurotic disorder, although they may be useful in certain circumstances.

*Reprinted with permission from Eysenck, H. J. 1960. *Behaviour Therapy and the Neuroses.* New York, Pergamon Press Inc., p. 11.

In an attempt to compare the effectiveness of insight therapy and desensitization in relieving anxiety, Paul selected 96 students who requested treatment for anxiety from among a class of 710 students enrolled in a public-speaking course. Following a screening interview, 74 subjects were assigned to one of four groups, equated for observable anxiety, to receive: (a) modified systematic desensitization, (b) insight-oriented psychotherapy, (c) attention placebo treatment, or (d) no treatment. The remaining 22 subjects constituted a no-contact control. Five experienced psychotherapists were involved in the project, and systematic desensitization was found consistently superior to other techniques. No differences were found between the effects of insight-oriented psychotherapy and the nonspecific effects of the attention-placebo treatment, although both groups showed greater anxiety reduction than the no-treatment controls. These results, however, should *not* be interpreted as indicating a superiority of desensitization in all situations, since (1) the subjects were students who had not presented spontaneously with complaints of psychopathology, (2) none received more than five hours of treatment over a six-week period, and (3) there was no long-term follow-up of reduction in anxiety or other improvements in adaptation.

It is precisely this emphasis on short-term symptom reduction and behavioral change that makes most psychiatrists skeptical about the value of the behavior therapies in meeting the needs of many psychiatric patients. Nevertheless, there have been many further reports on the application of instrumental learning principles to produce behavioral change in a variety of patients with much more severe psychopathology, including those with clinical diagnoses of schizophrenia. Such techniques have used various types of reward and reinforcement schedules to foster socially desired behavioral responses, through the methods of successive approximation and shaping of behavior that were outlined in Chapter 7. Autistic, withdrawn, and mute patients have learned to speak and engage in approach behavior, which makes them accessible to other forms of psychotherapy emphasizing the interpersonal relationships or verbal content of interviews. For the interested student, many such studies of behavior modification have been reported in books edited by Eysenck, and by Ullmann and Krasner.

NONDIRECTIVE, RELATIONSHIP, AND REEDUCATIONAL THERAPIES

Adolf Meyer regarded psychotherapy as a matter of negotiation over viewpoints and attitudes. The patient presents one view of his difficulties, whereas the physician has another view. Therapy was viewed as a joint effort to bring about an approximation of those views that would be the most effective and the most satisfying in the situation. This interpretation of psychotherapy is of considerable interest in relation to Schelling's formulations regarding the strategy of conflict. According to the latter author, the essential feature of *all* strategy is the art of generating "bargaining power" which consists in the "power to bind one's self." One will win, that is, *impose* a choice upon the other by divesting *oneself* of the freedom to choose, while leaving the *other's* freedom unimpaired.

The term *directiveness* in psychotherapy is usually applied to deliberate efforts by the therapist to influence the patient's conscious behavior, and nondirectiveness implies permissiveness in fostering self-determination by the patient. Relationship and reeducative therapies, as well as psychoanalysis, usually offer the patient considerable apparent freedom of choice in decisions about conscious behavior. However, deliberately or unconsciously, the therapist tends to determine the relevant content of therapy and direct it along certain lines. Freud made this explicit in the following statement from the first lecture in his general introduction to psychoanalysis: "The physician listens, attempts to *direct* the patient's thought processes, reminds him, forces his attention in certain directions, gives him explanations and observes the reactions of understanding or denial thus evoked." Similarly, Bandura and Walters remarked that mild approval and disapproval, silence and nonresponsiveness, avoidance reactions, restatement of client's expressions, instigation, and topic transition, are used by almost every therapist to channel client's responses. In nondirective therapies, therefore, the direction provided by the therapist involves a relatively subtle process of seduction, rather than a crude frontal assult requiring the immediate change of overt behavior.

The approach to psychotherapy conceived by Adolf Meyer was termed "Distributive analysis and synthesis." It involved beginning with analysis of the patient's symptoms or complaints, and led first to an analysis of motives involved in symptom development, then to a study of habitual attitudes, motives, and long-term personality assets and liabilities. The goal of psychotherapy was a changing of habitual attitudes, which involved understanding their origins, attempting new activities based on new attitudes, and gradual maturation and emancipation of the patient from his dependency on the therapist. The whole approach is reeducative, and may be regarded as *genetic-dynamic* in that it involves a detailed analysis of the patient's personality development and patterns of adaptation. Unlike psychoanalysis, however, this approach concerns only *conscious* processes. It is still in use by a number of therapists, who consider that this type of therapy is more suitable than psychoanalysis in the treatment of many psychotic patients, and may also be helpful in patients with other psychiatric disorders that are milder in degree.

Relationship therapy is a term that has been applied to various approaches that permit the patient (a) the experience of being accepted as of value, or potentially so, and of not being condemned or rejected because of defensive distortions; (b) the growth of an identification with some of the more successful techniques and adjustments of the therapist as they may fit the individual needs of the patient; and (c) spontaneous corrective emotional experiences based on the fact that the therapist does not respond in the manner expected by the patient. The attitude and behavior of the therapist toward the patient resemble that of the ideal parent, and may involve a considerable measure of emotional support, but relationship therapy differs from more superficial supportive therapies previously described

in having a goal of reeducation (modification of adaptative patterns) — and hence is apt to be of much longer duration, to involve discussion of the remote past as well as the more recent past and present, and to encourage maturation and independence. The therapist avoids being too supportive but sets limits on unacceptable behavior, may point out mistakes, may be firm without hostility, and remains consistent and realistic.

Client-centered therapy was introduced by Carl Rogers, and found widespread acceptance among clinical psychologists but not psychiatrists. It is a form of nondirective relationship therapy based on a belief in the patient's right to self-determination and capacity for emotional growth. The therapist is expected to act as a catalyst of growth and not to impose his own opinions or decisions on the patient. The therapist remains permissive, tolerant, and nonjudgmental, but encourages the patient to verbalize his problems and emotions. The therapist may then rephrase the patient's words, and reflect to the patient the feelings he originally expressed. Clarification of the patient's problems and emotions are believed to lead the patient to an increased self-understanding and capacity for adaptive behavior.

In a restatement of his position, Rogers wrote that the client-centered point of view has a number of distinguishing characteristics:*

These include the developing hypothesis that certain attitudes in the therapist constitute the necessary and sufficient conditions of therapeutic effectiveness; the developing concept of the therapist's function as being immediately present to his client, relying on his moment-to-moment felt experience in the relationship; the continuing focus on the phenomenal world of the client; a developing theory that the therapeutic

---

*From Rogers, C. R. 1966. Client-centered therapy. In *American Handbook of Psychiatry*, ed. S. Arieti. New York, Basic Books, Inc., Vol. III, ch. 13.

process is marked by a change in the client's manner of experiencing and an ability to live more fully in the immediate moment; a continuing stress on the self-actualizing quality of the human organism as the motivating force in therapy; a concern with the process of personality change, rather than with the structure of personality; a stress on the necessity of research to discover the essential truths of psychotherapy; the hypothesis that the same principles of psychotherapy apply to the competently functioning business executive, the maladjusted and neurotic person who comes to a clinic, and the hospitalized psychotic on the back ward; a view of psychotherapy as one specialized example of all constructive interpersonal relationships, with the consequent generalized applicability of all our knowledge from the field of therapy; and finally, a concern with the philosophical and value issues that grow out of the practice of therapy.

Rogers wrote that it is the presence of certain *attitudes* in the therapist, which are communicated to, and perceived by, his client, which effect success in psychotherapy. He hypothesized that, if the therapist can provide three definable conditions in his relationship with the client and if the client can perceive to some degree the presence of these conditions, then therapeutic movement will ensue. These three conditions are the therapist's congruence or genuineness; unconditional positive regard, a complete acceptance; and a sensitively accurate empathic understanding.

While client-centered therapists have become somewhat more active in the interview situation than formerly, most psychiatrists would agree with Bettelheim that "love is not enough," and consider that one type of therapeutic relationship is unlikely to have universal therapeutic effectiveness. Unconditional positive regard may be undesirable in relation to maladaptive aspects of the patient's behavior. The therapist's congruence or genuineness may require the honest expression of negative feelings about such behavior, rather than about the patient as an individual. The patient should learn that there is a difference between antisocial impulses

or fantasies and antisocial behavior, and the therapist should provide an identification model that is compatible with the reality of the society in which both patient and therapist live. The relationship as well as the verbal content of therapy may need to be different for a neurotic patient and one who is sociopathic or psychotic. It is for reasons such as these that many psychiatrists prefer analytically-oriented and transactional therapies that will be outlined in the next two sections of this chapter.

PSYCHOANALYSIS AND DYNAMIC PSYCHOTHERAPIES

Psychoanalysis has been defined as the science of the unconscious functions of the mind and personality, developed by Freud and his students. It is frequently pointed out that psychoanalysis has three distinctly different connotations: (1) a psychological theory of human development and behavior, (2) a method of research, and (3) a system of psychotherapy. Freud was at least as interested in the investigative and theoretical aspects of psychoanalysis as in its therapeutic application, and he believed that the future will attribute far greater importance to psychoanalysis as the science of the unconscious than as a therapeutic procedure. During his career he tried a number of therapeutic techniques, and was at times dissatisfied with the results of therapy. Nevertheless, he continued to regard psychoanalysis as the most effective form of psychotherapy, likening his own techniques to pure gold and various modifications or other forms of psychotherapy to impure alloys.

In their early publications on hysteria, Breuer and Freud described their technique of "cathartic hypnosis" in order to recover a patient's early memories and feelings regarding some traumatic event. Such unconscious memories and feelings were believed to result in the development of the hysterical symptoms, which would be removed by catharsis or abreaction of the repressed feelings associated with the forgotten traumatic event. Freud soon found that the results of hypnosis were not lasting, and for a short period he employed a "concentration" technique whereby the conscious patient was encouraged to remember previous events related to his symptoms. This in turn was soon abandoned and replaced by the method of "free association," which consists of the patient's saying everything that comes to his mind without any conscious reservation. This technique has become known as the fundamental rule of psychoanalytic treatment, leading to knowledge of hitherto unconscious feelings, impulses, fantasies, and ideas.

In order to facilitate this process, the patient reclined on a couch during the interview, with the analyst seated a little behind and to one side of him. Interviews lasted from 45 minutes to one hour and were held four to six days a week for a period of one to five years. *The analysis of dreams* through free-association became an important means of access to unconscious motivation, and Freud regarded the dream as the royal road to the unconscious.

In spite of the patient's conscious attempts to free-associate, it was observed that there were obstructions to the associative process, and to the uncovering of unconsciousness motivation and repressed memories. These obstructions to the acquisition of insight became known as *resistances*, and an important part of the analyst's efforts became the recognition of resistances and the utilization of *interpretation* to improve the patient's insight. Interpretation may involve inferences about the patient's emotions or motives, the pointing out of similarities in certain life situations, increasing awareness of cause-and-effect relationships in the patient's life, or revealing hidden or symbolic meanings. The goal of interpretation is not to persuade the patient to believe something about himself, but to enable him to perceive something about himself.

In part, the process of interpretation has been likened to holding a mirror up to the individual so that he may see his own unconscious motives more clearly. In part it has also been likened to providing him with a pair of glasses that will enable him to perceive external reality and the motivations of others more accurately. In either event, it has been remarked that the patient may need his blindness, and may be disquieted by his improved vision. Premature interpretation may arouse dysphoric affect (e.g., anxiety or depression) and result in regression or other unconscious defenses. Resistance to the development of insight may also be manifested by such reactions as silence, denial, blocking, forgetting, evasion, embarrassment, or strong emotions including anger toward the analyst. Skilled therapists therefore undertake interpretation cautiously and tentatively, when they perceive the patient ready to accept and tolerate additional insight.

The major distinguishing feature of psychoanalytic therapy involves emphasis on the development, analysis, and resolution of the *transference relationship or neurosis*. Transference has been defined as a special form of displacement, involving the unconscious attachment to the analyst of emotions and attitudes that were originally associated with significant persons in the patient's early life (such as parents and siblings). The patient then reacts toward the therapist as if the latter were the person responsible for the original development of these positive, negative, or ambivalent feelings, and expects that the therapist will behave toward him in the same manner as the significant figure did in earlier relationships.

Fenichel described transference as follows: "The patient misunderstands the present in terms of the past; and then, instead of remembering the past, he strives, without recognizing the nature of his action, to relive the past and to relive it more satisfactorily than he did in childhood. He 'transfers' past attitudes to the present." The analyst in turn attempts to facilitate the development and eventual resolution of the "transference neurosis," as outlined in the following passage from Gitelson:

When the psychoanalytic technique is correctly applied, the events observed are relatively free from artifacts introduced by the activity of the observer. In this setting the phenomenon known as the transference neurosis develops. This is not created by the analyst. It appears under the pressure of the tendency of past attitudes and impulses to repeat themselves. It is permitted to establish itself and to evolve in its own terms and toward its own particular denouement. In the relationship to the analyst, there thus recur the significant emotional events of infancy and early childhood. These events do not present themselves as discrete transference episodes, but as part of a continuous process of recapitulation in the present of the continuous past, in the form of affects, fantasies, dreams, impulses, and somatic sets and tensions. It is this restoration of the past and the present that constitutes the microscopic field of psychoanalysis.

The aim of psychoanalysis is to replace unconscious acts by conscious acts, or in the words of Freud: "Where there was id, ego shall be." Loewald wrote that the patient who comes to analysis for help is led to self-understanding by the understanding he finds in the analyst. Redlich and Freedman added that the basic aim is to produce in the patient a profound insight into the relationship of his infantile neurosis to his present way of life, and particularly to its faulty aspects. In accomplishing this aim, the analyst recognizes that his own attitudes and behavior toward the patient may sometimes reflect displacement of his own unconscious motives through *counter-transference*, so that an important part of psychoanalytic training involves a personal analysis for the therapist, and close supervision and control of his early analytic work with patients by a training analyst. Such training and supervision is so close and prolonged that it is sometimes perceived as resulting in indoctrination of the trainee, with consequent perpetuation

of unproven dogma. The psychoanalytic trainee is indeed dependent upon his training analyst for graduation and accreditation as an analyst, which may imply acceptance and conformity with the values and attitudes of the training analyst. Nevertheless, the multiplicity and diversity of modifications in psychoanalytic technique and deviations from orthodoxy testify to the ability of many trained analysts to attain mature independence and make significant contributions in both theory and therapy.

Fenichel classified neuroses according to their accessibility to analysis in the following sequence: hysteria; compulsion neurosis and pregenital conversion neuroses; "neurotic" depressions; character disturbances; perversions, addictions, and impulse neuroses; psychoses, severe manic-depressive cases, and schizophrenias. In addition to diagnosis, certain other criteria are recognized as influencing the outcome of psychoanalysis or other forms of psychotherapy. These include the age of the patient (preferably 15 to 40); his intelligence, education, socioeconomic background, and ability to communicate in the same language as the therapist; the duration of symptoms, and presence or absence of marked secondary gain from them; and the reality situation of the patient, particularly his current relationships with other members of his family and of society.

Among the criticisms of psychoanalysis that have been raised are those involving the relationship between theory and technique, the results with classical methods as compared with other techniques, and the high cost and social inaccessibility of psychoanalytic therapy. Some analysts and other therapists oppose the fostering of regression within the transference neurosis, generally accompanied by an initial period of worsening symptoms and maladaptive behavior. They also maintain that analytic techniques foster undue dependency on the therapist, morbid introspection and narcissism, fixation

"I think I was better off when my hostility was latent."

THE SATURDAY EVENING POST

Figure 11-1. (Reprinted with permission from The Saturday Evening Post. Copyright © 1959, The Curtis Publishing Company.)

on past events to the exclusion of present and future adaptation, or a tendency toward *acting out* of sexual and aggressive impulses. (Figure 11-1). Frequently such criticisms are based on limited personal knowledge and misunderstanding of psychoanalytic techniques, whose ultimate goal is to improve current and future adaptation to reality. There is a world of difference between the acting out of unconscious conflicts and the process of working through, which involves active exploration of a problem by patient and therapist until a satisfactory solution has been found or until a symptom has been traced to its unconscious sources.

Many modifications of classical psychoanalysis have been introduced during the present century, some of which now have little more than historical interest. One of the major developments in this country, however, was the formulation of new concepts and techniques by the neo-Freudian analysts, particularly Karen Horney, Erich Fromm, and Harry Stack Sullivan. The neo-Freudians emphasize the interpersonal and sociocultural context within which personality and maladaptive behavior develop. They analyze the patient-therapist relationship, the patient's adaptation to his environment, and the development of his maladaptive social patterns. They also tend to rely on the interpretation of dreams and transference, but are more active in the therapeutic role and tend to employ less frequent therapeutic interviews, in a face-to-face interview situation. Psychoanalytically oriented psychotherapy (or "dynamic psychotherapy") is in even more widespread use, and tends to involve less frequent visits (once to three times per week), for a shorter overall duration, in a face-to-face interview situation, with even greater activity on the part of the therapist. Some of these technical similarities and differences between five psychotherapeutic approaches were summarized by Wolberg and are reproduced in Table 11-2.

Alexander pointed out that variations from the standard psychoanalytic technique have emphasized one or another of the following three therapeutic factors: (1) emotional abreaction, (2) intellectual insight, and (3) recovery of repressed infantile memories. He himself stressed the therapeutic significance of differences between the old family conflicts and the actual doctor-patient relationship. He considered that this difference is what allows a "corrective emotional experience" to occur, which he regarded as the central therapeutic factor both in psychoanalysis proper and also in analytically oriented psychotherapy. The new settlement of an old unresolved conflict in the transference situation became possible not only because the intensity of the transference conflict was less than that of the original conflict, but also because the therapist's actual response to the patient's emotional expressions was quite different from the original treatment of the child by the parents.

In order to increase the effectiveness of the corrective emotional experiences, he believed that the therapist should attempt to create an interpersonal climate suited to highlight the discrepancy between the patient's transference attitude and the actual situation as if he exists between patient and therapist. A number of authors criticized the latter type of "role-playing" by the therapist, on the basis that these consciously and purposefully adopted attitudes are artificial and will be recognized as such by the patient. Alexander maintained, however, that the therapist's objective, emotionally nonparticipating attitude is itself artificial, in as much as it does not exist between human beings in real life. Other modifications introduced by Alexander involved changing the number of interviews in appropriate phases of

the treatment in order to make the patient more vividly conscious of his dependency needs by frustrating them, and experimental temporary interruptions of treatment based on his assumption that there is a general trend toward "over-treatment," and that undue regression and dependency should not be fostered by the therapist.

Before proceeding to review the transactional approach to psychotherapy, it may be appropriate to conclude this section by reproducing Alexander's summary of the *areas of agreement among psychoanalysts of different theoretical persuasion*:*

1. During treatment, unconscious (repressed) material becomes conscious. This increases the action radius of the conscious ego: the ego becomes cognizant of unconscious impulses and thus is able to coordinate (integrate) the latter with the rest of conscious content.

2. The mobilization of unconscious material is achieved mainly by two basic therapeutic factors: interpretation of material emerging during free association and the patient's emotional interpersonal experiences in the therapeutic situation (transference). The therapist's relatively objective, non-evaluative, impersonal attitude is the principal factor in mobilizing unconscious material.

3. The patient shows resistance against recognizing unconscious content. Overcoming this resistance is one of the primary technical problems of the treatment.

4. It is only natural that the neurotic patient will sooner or later direct his typical neurotic attitude toward his therapist. He develops a transference which is the repetition of interpersonal attitudes, mostly the feelings of the child to his parents. This process is favored by the therapist's encouraging the patient to be himself as much as he can during the interviews. The therapist's objective non-evaluative attitude is the main factor, not only in mobilizing unconscious material during the process of free association, but also in facilitating the mani-

---

*Reprinted by permission from Alexander, F. 1963. The dynamics of psychotherapy in the light of learning theory. American Journal of Psychiatry *120*, 440;448.

Table 11-2. Technical Psychotherapeutic Similarities and Differences

	SUPPORTIVE THERAPY	INSIGHT THERAPY WITH REEDUCATIVE GOALS	INSIGHT THERAPY WITH RECONSTRUCTIVE GOALS		
			Freudian Psychoanalysis	Non-Freudian Psychoanalysis	Psychoanalytically Oriented Psychotherapy
Duration of Therapy	One to several hundred sessions	Several sessions to several hundred sessions	2-5 years	2-5 years	Several sessions to several hundred sessions
Frequency of Visits	1-3 times weekly	1-2 times weekly	4-5 times weekly	2-4 times weekly	1-3 times weekly
Detailed History-Taking	Usually	Often	Rarely	Occasionally	Occasionally
Psychologic Examinations	Intelligence testing, vocational battery	Intelligence testing, vocational battery, projective testing	Projective testing often employed	Projective testing often employed	Projective testing often employed
Patient's Communications	Interviews focused on symptoms and environmental disturbances	Interviews focused on daily events and interpersonal relationships	Unguided free associations	Interviews focused on current situations, interpersonal relationships, and other conflictual sources. Free associations sometimes used	Interviews focused on current situations, interpersonal relationships and other conflictual sources
General Activity of Therapist	Toward strengthening of existing defenses	Challenging of existing defenses. Activity—directiveness to non-directiveness	Challenging of existing defenses. Passivity, anonymity, non-directiveness. Constant analysis of transference and resistance	Challenging of existing defenses. Activity—moderate directiveness to non-directiveness. Constant analysis of transference and resistance	Challenging of existing defenses. Greater activity—directiveness to non-directiveness. Constant analysis of transference and resistance

	Often	Occasionally	Never	Rarely	Rarely
Advice-giving to Patient					
Transference	Positive transference encouraged and utilized to promote improvement	Positive transference controlled and, if possible, utilized to promote improvement. Negative transference analyzed as it develops in terms of the reality situation	Transference encouraged to point of development of a transference neurosis. Transference analyzed in terms of genetic origins	Transference encouraged to point of awareness of repressed attitudes and feelings. Transference neurosis avoided by some analysts. Transference analyzed in terms of character structure or genetic origins	Transference encouraged to point of awareness of repressed attitudes and feelings. Transference neurosis avoided as a rule. Transference analyzed in terms of character structure, and, occasionally, genetic origins
General Relationship of Patient to Therapist	Positive relationship fostered and utilized	Positive relationship fostered and utilized	Relationship permitted to develop spontaneously	Relationship permitted to develop spontaneously	Relationship permitted to develop spontaneously. Positive relationship occasionally fostered and utilized
Physical Position of Patient during Therapy	Sitting up, face-to-face	Sitting up, face-to-face	Recumbent on couch	Sitting up, face-to-face, or Recumbent on couch	Sitting up, face-to-face. Occasionally recumbent on couch
Dream Material	Not utilized	Not utilized	Constantly utilized	Constantly utilized	Constantly utilized
Adjuncts Utilized during Therapy	Bibliotherapy, art therapy, group therapy, physical therapy, drug therapy, hypnotherapy, occupational therapy	Group therapy, and bibliotherapy occasionally used	None	Few or none	Analytic group therapy, hypnoanalysis, narcotherapy, play therapy, and art therapy occasionally employed

*Reprinted by permission from Wolberg, L. R. 1954. *The Technique of Psychotherapy.* New York, Grune & Stratton, Inc., pp. 90–91.

festation of transference. The original neurosis of the patient, which is based on his childhood experiences, is thus transformed in an artificial "transference neurosis" which is a less intensive repetition of the patient's "infantile neurosis." The resolution of these revived feelings and behavior patterns—the resolution of the transference neurosis—becomes the aim of the treatment.

THE TRANSACTIONAL APPROACH TO PSYCHOTHERAPY

In the same article as the summary that ended the preceding section, Alexander also wrote as follows:

. . .the traditional descriptions of the therapeutic process do not adequately reflect the immensely complex interaction between therapist and patient. The patient's reactions cannot be described fully as transference reactions. The patient reacts to the therapist as to a concrete person and not only as representative of parental figures. The therapist's reactions also far exceed what is usually called countertransference. They include in addition to this, interventions based on conscious deliberations and also his spontaneous idiosyncratic attitudes. Moreover, his own values are conveyed to the patient even if he consistently tries to protect his incognito. The patient reacts to the therapist's overt but also to his nonverbal hidden intentions and the therapist reacts to the patient's reaction to him. It is a truly transactional process.

In studying this transactional material I came to the conviction that the therapeutic process can be best understood in terms of learning theory Particularly the principle of reward and punishment and also the influence of repetitive experiences can be clearly recognized. . .

Alexander did not spell out the details of the communication processes and learning principles that he considered so vitally important for effective psychotherapy. Other analysts and dynamically oriented therapists have increasingly incorporated such principles into their conceptual framework and therapeutic procedures. In discussing Alexander's article, however, Knobloch pointed to a fundamental difference between this position and the viewpoint of behavior therapists who deliberately utilize learning principles. Knobloch wrote as follows:

When contemplating psychotherapy in terms of a learning theory, the view of behavior therapists like Wolpe and Eysenck cannot be left out. Apart from differences, reflected in heated polemics, there is a basic similarity between the dynamically oriented psychotherapists and the behavior therapist. Both regard neurosis as a product of learning. Most adherents of both groups allow for an innate predisposition or vulnerability to become neurotic, called neuroticism or otherwise. Both conceive psychotherapy as an unlearning or relearning. But whereas the habits to be relearned are according to the behavior therapists, relatively simple and identical with "symptoms," according to the dynamically oriented psychotherapists they are very complex personality structures which create symptoms as secondary habits..

In a comparative study of psychotherapeutic attitudes and techniques, Strupp found that the therapist's initial attitude toward his patient cut across all theoretical orientations and was the most important determinant of the prognosis, treatment plans, and diagnosis. More experienced therapists tended to assume a more active role in therapy, to take more initiative, make more interpretations, and to behave more as individuals. With the confidence borne of experience, trained therapists were not afraid to be themselves or to use their particular style of communication with their patients. He felt that those who had been analyzed were sounder in their interpretations, that their interventions were more inferential, and that they tended to exhibit greater warmth, but there were many common elements in all approaches to psychotherapy as well as considerable differences between therapists of the same theoretical persuasion.

The transactional approach to psychotherapy has attracted therapists with varied background and training, including analysts, psychiatrists, and psychologists. Techniques of therapy and the relative activity of the therapist have tended to vary, but there is a consistent focus upon the two-way communications between therapist and patient, and the effects of these transactions on the unlearning of maladaptive patterns and the learning of more effective adaptation. Grinker remarked that the therapeutic field consists of the mutual understanding of transactions in which role processes, their antecedents, and patterned identifications are communicated and changed. He maintained that respect for the patient involves honesty on the part of the therapist in admitting his own positive and negative feelings as they develop within the therapeutic situation. While the therapist's attitude may therefore be judgmental, he also emphasized permissiveness on the part of the therapist, which is not incompatible with the therapist's admission of his own feelings to the patient. While permissiveness in expression is desirable, it is not necessary or desirable to include permission for acting-out for antisocial behavior. The therapist may therefore indicate to the patient his disapproval of the latter s behavior before it occurs, warn the patient that it may occur, and indicate disapproval after it does occur. This in effect confronts the patient with the reality of social relationships which the patient needs to learn.

In order to present more clearly some ways in which this transactional approach to psychotherapy differs from other approaches outlined in preceding sections, the following paragraphs by Grinker are reproduced herewith:*

Therapy is a learning process and its operations are concerned with facilitating that process. To do that, there has to be a certain attitude of permissiveness, and receptivity on the part of the therapist in relation to another human being who is sick, the therapist taking the role of the helper.

*Reprinted with permission of The Macmillan Company from Grinker, R. R. 1961. A transactional model for psychotherapy. In *Contemporary Psychotherapies*, ed. M. Stein. Copyright The Free Press of Glencoe, Inc., pp. 190-213.

Within that explicit framework, which is the structure of the therapeutic situation, communications will expose the implicit roles that the patient would like the therapist to take in complementarity with him. These roles, the therapist declines to assume, but instead interprets to the patient and points out to the patient that through the facade of the explicit role relationship, the patient really wishes another kind of relationship; and in that sense, the intelligent patient will generalize from that statement to other situations in which similar behaviors were used, and will learn. This will complete that particular therapeutic focus and the process begins again on another focus. The patient learns; this is the process of treatment. . .

In our procedures, we are considerably more active than those individuals who model their therapy after the psychoanalytic pattern. Strupp (1957) has shown that the most experienced therapists are much more active, whereas the younger, less experienced ones are passive, as if they await the patient's insight and his communication to the therapist of what should be interpreted. We are active in that we choose the focus; we communicate adequately with the patient; we avoid long silences and the impassivity of a nonparticipant. These silences in psychotherapy are deadly, deadly to the patient and deadly to the therapist, and are great stimulants to sleep. Not only do we choose the focus for the subject of communication, but we decide when a transaction should be dropped and a new one adopted. . .

We do not invite dreams, nor when they are recounted, do we interpret them. . .

Although we do not invite, and we certainly avoid, the development of a transference neurosis whenever possible, we are obviously still dealing with transference phenomena, which is another way of saying that we are dealing with back-and-forth implicit communications between therapist and patient in which the present is colored by the past. We don't induce a transference neurosis, which is facilitated by the frequent sessions, by the steady appearance of the same room or the patient lying on the couch, by a regression which evokes a patterned response of early infantile conflicts in which the therapist plays the central role. We do not induce these transference neuroses. . .

In the therapeutic process, we start out with the here and now—that is, the current real life which involves the communications between patient and therapist about their relationship. Although the time element is not restricted to the immediate relationship but will always bring in memories and communications about the recent or distant past, we do not emphasize the so-called genetic processes or the past experience of childhood; nor do we attempt to evoke early memories or feel particularly successful when we have been able to recapture childhood feelings. The patient himself will bring into communication as much of the past that is significant for the particular focus under discussion. Granted a modicum of intelligence, he will see, when he understands the implicit nature of the current transaction, that other experiences in different periods of his life conform and correspond to a category. We are content to work with what the psychoanalysts call derivative conflicts and we are not especially interested in his uncovering the so-called primary conflicts. Also in relation to the real life of the patient, we encourage him to experiment in relationships outside of the therapeutic situation, accepting whatever failures or successes may be reported as part of the learning process. . .

In summary, what I have proposed is a method of psychotherapy based on the operations derived from field, role and communication theories rather than on a theory of personality. This facilitates a vivid current understanding of the patient without recourse to reified variables of unconscious, transference, counter-transference, resistance, topological foci, processes involving energy, or any part functions of the human being in behavior. Here, I will make a very dogmatic statement: The more we understand theoretical psychodynamics and the less we are influenced by it operationally, the better we may understand our patients and ourselves.

GROUP AND FAMILY THERAPIES

Group therapy consists of psychotherapy undertaken by a single therapist (often accompanied by a non-participating professional observer) with groups of psychiatric patients or their relatives, or both. Groups have been conducted by a tremendous variety of professional personnel, differing widely in their training and theoretical orientations. Among such group leaders are included psychiatrists, analysts, psychologists, social workers, ministers, nurses, aides, and occupational or recreational therapists. Almost every system of individual psychotherapy has been applied to groups of individuals, and the latter have shown a corresponding diversity in size, as well as with respect to such variables as age, sex, and diagnosis. Group approaches have been employed widely both in hospitals and outpatient clinics, and in the treatment of patients with neuroses, psychoses, and behavior disorders.

This widespread development of group therapy arose out of three major considerations: (1) the desire to bring psychotherapy to larger numbers of patients than could be reached on an individual basis, (2) greater benefit that might be attained through group interaction than from individual therapies, and (3) increasing recognition of the sociodynamic nature of human maladjustment. The relative shortage of professional personnel in relation to the large numbers of patient's relatives requiring assistance is probably the least satisfactory reason for recommending group therapy. It is generally considered that group therapy is not a substitute for individual therapy, and a number of patients are concurrently involved in both individual and group therapies, often with different therapists. It is also believed that there are some patients for whom group therapy may be more effective than individual therapy — among these being patients with limited intelligence, those who have lacked adequate sibling or other social relationships, those with antisocial behavior disorders, those who find an individual therapeutic relationship too threatening, and those in whom there appears to be special danger of homosexual attachment to an individual therapist.

Frank suggested that all varieties of psychotherapies share three aims: the first being to strengthen the patient's self-respect, the second being to help the patient maintain a level of tension or distress sufficient to keep him working toward better solutions (but not so great as to force him back into his maladaptive patterns), and the third being to supply some guides or models to the patient as he struggles to modify his attitudes. The various approaches to psychotherapy offer the patient a different kind of emotional relationship, and present him with some sort of task. The main advantages of group therapy appear to lie in the opportunity for relationships with a variety of persons other than the group leader (with each of whom identification may occur, and onto each of whom there may be unconscious displacement of emotions and expectations related to earlier relationships), and in the increased opportunity for reality testing in an atmosphere that encourages the patient to experiment.

Groups may be described as open or closed, according to whether their membership is continually changing (due to some patients leaving and new members being added) or remains restricted to the original members of the group throughout the duration of the therapy. Sessions usually last for an hour or more, and their frequency may vary from once to five or six times a week. Groups that are oriented towards the attainment of insight (with reeducative or reconstructive goals) tend to be closed, to be restricted in numbers (from four to 12 members), to be relatively homogeneous in composition (e.g., in age, sex, diagnosis, and socioeconomic status), and to meet relatively frequently over a prolonged period of time. In such groups three phases of development are commonly recognized: a phase of *unification*, with development of group identity and cohesiveness; a phase of *interaction*, with observation and analysis of dynamic interrelationships; and a phase of understanding and *resolution*, with the development of insights and increasingly adaptive behavior.

As in the case of individual psychotherapy, some groups may have limited or more superficial goals, including direction and suppression of symptoms, emotional support, or verbal and emotional expression. Such groups are frequently *open-ended*, with changing membership and relatively infrequent sessions, and the techniques adopted include didactic lecturing and discussion, educational and directive counseling, and confessional and inspirational approaches. Group therapies intended to promote the development of insight include the reeducative approach of Moreno known as *psychodrama* (involving role-play, discussion, and interpretation), and modified psychoanalytic techniques developed by Slavson et al.

Of recent years there has been a tendency to regard *the family rather than the individual* as the unit in which psychiatric problems develop, and the unit toward which psychiatric treatment should be directed. This concept has long been held in the field of child and adolescent psychiatry, where individual therapy with the child has generally been supplemented by concurrent social case work, counseling or psychotherapy with one or both parents. In adult psychiatry, individual therapy with the hospitalized patient has frequently been accompanied by social case work with relatives, and recommendations have often been made that a parent or spouse receive more intensive individual therapy with a different therapist.

For some years, however, there have been psychotherapists who consistently involve more than one member of the primary family group in all or most of their therapeutic interviews. Such family therapy groups may consist of husband and wife, or parents and children. The techniques employed in such therapy correspond with the training and goals of the therapist, and may therefore be supportive, reeducative, or psychoanalytic. Among the approaches to family therapy are those elaborated by Ackerman and by Jackson.

Handlon and Parloff considered it

unfortunate that there is a tendency to equate family therapy with other forms of group therapy. They suggested that each family is a kind of subculture with its own valued role-structure and its own unique family mythology. In particularly pathological families, one of the important functions of this family mythology appears to be in supporting the denial of any interindividual conflict. They therefore explored certain similarities and differences between conventional and family group therapy, through postulating four conditions that appear to provide important sources of therapeutic leverage in the conventional group: (1) that the group provides support and acceptance of the patient through the development of a permissive atmosphere, (2) that the group provides an opportunity for the stimulation of typical interaction patterns which permit of their examination and analysis, (3) that the group provides an opportunity for reality testing in a relatively unthreatening atmosphere, and (4) that the group provides an opportunity for its members to display transference distortions which can be therapeutically useful.

In each instance, these authors pointed to ways in which family interactions operate in such a manner as to negate the preceding assumptions that appear to apply in conventional group therapy situations with nonfamily members. They concluded that seeing a family operate together as a group is an extremely useful way of learning about the family pathology that may have contributed to the patient's disorder. They also felt fairly sure that under some circumstances seeing the family in a group can have therapeutic results. However they felt much less sure that they could predict when such family therapy would work effectively, and that further research was necessary in order to specify the critical ingredients that must be present in family therapy. Such research is of course necessary in determining the critical ingredients of all forms of psychotherapy, but requires an open-minded attitude on the part of the investigator, rather than an unduly skeptical or nihilistic approach.

HOSPITALIZATION AND MILIEU THERAPY

The historical development of institutions for the care of psychiatric patients was outlined in Chapter 1, and it was pointed out that formerly society made no separate provisions for the confinement of the defective, the delinquent, and the distraught. If their behavior was troublesome, and their families either unable or unwilling to care for them, all persons viewed as socially incompetent were apt to be secluded in jails or workhouses, or to be forced to work on farms to contribute to their upkeep. The humane reforms of the nineteenth century, however, were accompanied by segregation of the mentally ill and later the mentally retarded in separate institutions for custodial care. Such institutions were often planned and constructed primarily to *protect society from the patient,* as reflected in their distance from centers of population, their prison-like buildings and routines, and commitment laws that specified that the patient should be "furious and violent and dangerous" rather than simply insane. The secondary role of such institutions in *protecting the patient from society* was implied in their becoming widely known as asylums of rest or refuge. As the latter role became more prominent, emphasis was placed on trying to make the surroundings more pleasant for the patients.

This goal persisted into the present century, and has only gradually be replaced by the goal of *making the patient's experiences in hospital therapeutic.* There has been a growing realization that all patients do not respond equally well to a single type of hospital routine, but that the nature of their therapeutic experiences should be individualized. One patient may require considerable responsibility for self-determination that would only increase anxiety and regression in another patient or in the same patient at a different time. Pleasant surroundings may sometimes be detrimental to therapy by fostering dependency and rewarding secondary gains from psychiatric disability.

In this connection, Kral and others documented their observations that certain psychiatric patients — particularly those with neuroses and psychophysiologic disorders — frequently lost their symptoms in the structured, though stressful, environment of a concentration camp, and did not always have a recurrence following their release. It has also been observed that some patients who failed to respond to prolonged intensive psychotherapy in an outpatient or inpatient setting (with continuing responsibility for socially acceptable behavior and decision-making), improved rapidly following brief periods in state hospitals where they received no specific psychotherapy, drugs, or other somatic therapy but were temporarily subjected to an organized routine with no responsbility for decision making. Sullivan interpreted such beneficial effects of custodial care as follows: ". . .the severity of any mental disorder is to an important degree a result of insecurity about one's status. . . . This part of the problem would be solved by removing the patient to a society in which vertical mobility is not possible. Just this, in effect, is achieved by his admission to the custodial institution."

The psychiatric patient in a hospital may be participating in individual psychotherapy (occasionally up to six hours a week) and receiving drugs or other somatic treatment, but in every case he is spending the majority of his time in an environment that may be either therapeutic or destructive. While certain patients tend to respond best to certain types of hospital environment, the latter should be modified as necessary to meet the needs of the individual patient. The effective modification of the hospital environment to meet the needs of patients involves awareness of communication and interaction between all patients and every staff member with whom they come into daily contact.

Gradual or rapid changes in the institutional care of psychiatric patients have often occurred during the past two centuries, but the modern systematic study of personality function as a part of institutional treatment appears to have been initiated by Sullivan, who organized an admission ward for young male patients with acute schizophrenia. At about the same time, Aichhorn reported on successful innovations in the institutional care of delinquent teenagers. Rowland subsequently reported on interaction processes in the state mental hospital, while Anna Freud and Burlingham were successful in establishing "artificial families" among young children and the staff of a nursery. Main wrote on the hospital as a therapeutic institution, and Bettelheim and Sylvester discussed the concept of a therapeutic milieu. Jones reported on the therapeutic community as an approach to treatment in psychiatry, and other authors such as Stanton and Schwartz, and Caudill, contributed more detailed information on the interpersonal relationships within psychiatric hospitals. The latter authors emphasized the significance of informal and unofficial transactions, the difficulties and importance of communication and honest decision-making, the emotional needs of staff as well as patients, and the therapeutic functions of patients as well as staff.

Powles examined the concept of milieu therapy and concluded that three dimensions are involved: (1) a *personalistic* dimension — the idea that a "therapeutic milieu" can be distinguished from an "institutional" one by its emphasis on considering the staff and patients as real people; (2) an *organismic* dimension — the idea that the hospital is a society or a community, with staff and patients playing integrated roles; (3) a *communal* dimension — the idea that traditional staff and patient roles are not helpful in psychiatric treatment, and that more active sharing of responsibility and more active communication and interaction between staff and patients will more effectively combat the regression of psychiatric patients.

During the time he is in the hospital, the patient may interact with other patients, with various members of the hospital staff, and with members of his family, friends, or other persons outside the hospital. Members of the hospital staff may interact with a given patient directly through their relationships with other patients, with other staff members, and with the patient's family, friends, or other members of the community. It therefore becomes imperative that all staff members have considerable understanding and constant awareness of interpersonal relationships and of the nature of psychotherapy. It is considered important that all staff members be completely honest and truthful with patients, capable of providing accurate information and correcting misinformation, and showing a genuine interest in the welfare of the individual patient that should sometimes be verbalized as well as demonstrated nonverbally. What has already been said about approaches to psychotherapy also applies to the relationships and communications between patients and staff members other than the psychiatrist. While the goals of milieu therapy have traditionally been supportive in nature, there has been an increasing tendency for staff members other than the psychiatrist to adopt therapeutic techniques intended to promote new learning and improve overall adaptation.

An effective way of improving communication and reality-testing among patients and staff at all levels is the establishment of a variety of organized groups for discussion or therapy. Patients learn to communicate with other patients and staff members in ward councils, and in activity or verbal psychotherapy groups, which are conducted by personnel with varying training: psychiatrists, psychologists, social workers, nurses, or occupational therapists. Such formal patient groups may focus their attention on problems in a variety of areas such as orientation of the patient following admission to hospital, treatment, ward management, recreational activities, problems anticipated following discharge, or factors influencing personality development and adaptation in society. Staff members may also use group techniques effectively in working with patient's families, and there should be regular staff conferences for discussion of patient management and problems of interpersonal relationships at all levels.

Since the end of the second world war there has been a radical change in the operation of state mental hospitals in many countries, which has been facilitated (though not initiated) by the advent of phenothiazines and other drugs. Snow reported on extensive changes in one 2200 bed state hospital during a period of four years, associated with the introduction of *tranquilizing drugs* and of an *open door policy*. Within a few months after the introduction of chlorpromazine, the number of patients in this hospital requiring physical restraint had been reduced from about 35 or 40 patients per day to about six or eight patients a day. Many patients became more amenable, could be engaged in conversation, and became interested in occupational therapy recreation. However, by the end of a year, the restraint rate had again risen to a average of 14 patients a day, in spite of the continued use of drugs and the increased ancillary program. During the following year, many wards were opened for eight hours a day and the patients were allowed to go outside without interference or being questioned. Escapes, accidents, assaults, and pregnancies did *not* occur, and it was observed that there was a general diminution in tension among patients, between patients and staff, and among the staff themselves. The restraint rate diminished to practically zero, and regressive behavior became far less evident. At first patients used their new-found freedom to explore, but soon there was a marked increase in their voluntary attendance at occupational therapy and church, and increased utilization of various recreational facilities. Concurrently there was a liberalization in the regulations concerning visiting by relatives and friends.

Improvements in patients' behavior may frequently be related to nonverbal communications by staff or role-expectations regarding appropriate behavior on the part of patients. Such changes are accompanied by improvement in relationships between the hospital (patients and staff) and members of the nearby community. Volunteers from the community are apt to develop recreational programs and facilities (within and outside the hospital), and to assist in the rehabiliation of patients by offering them homes and jobs. Changing community attitudes are likely to lead to a much higher proportion of voluntary admission, with decreased reliance on commitment procedure for involuntary admission.

It is increasingly recognized that there should be *continuity of psychiatric care* before, during, and after any period of hospitalization. It is therefore desirable that every psychiatric inpatient facility have an active outpatient clinic or department to which patients may be referred before they require admission, or following a period of treatment in the hospital, and that there be continuity in the staff involved in such treatment. Another logical extension of treatment facilities involves the establishment of a *day-hospital* unit in which patients may remain for treatment all day, but return to their homes at night. Still another development particularly suitable for those patients who are now well enough to work in the community involves the establishment of a *night-hospital* unit, to which patients return following their day's work, to participate in treatment during the evening and remain over-

night. In addition to such units geared to daytime or evening treatment, there are also *halfway houses*, where patients who have recently left hospital may live until they have again become established in the community. There are also programs of *foster home placement* for selected patients requiring continuing care of this nature.

With decreasing emphasis on custodial care and increasing efforts to provide a therapeutic milieu more closely integrated with the community, many changes in architecture and organizational structure of psychiatric hospitals have been recommended. It has been proposed that no such hospital should contain more than 1000 beds, and many would prefer to see a number of much smaller units established within the community from which they draw patients, as part of a local general hospital or at least in close proximity to one. Federal legislation concerning grants for the construction of *comprehensive community mental health centers* stipulate that such centers should provide for part-time hospitalization and 24 hour emergency psychiatric consultation, as well as full-time inpatient care and adequate outpatient clinic facilities.

FUNCTIONS OF PSYCHIATRIC HOSPITAL PERSONNEL

In the preceding section, general concepts and developments in milieu therapy were reveiwed. Such developments come about through the cooperative efforts of members of various professional disciplines involved in specific aspects of patient care. Some of these professional disciplines are engaged in outpatient evaluation and treatment, particularly psychiatry, clinical psychology, and social work. Others are engaged primarily or exclusively in the care of psychiatric inpatients, e.g., nursing or occupational therapy. The roles of various members of the psychiatric team, and relationships between them, may vary considerably between different clinic or hospital settings. In some, the clinical psychologist is involved primarily in administering and interpreting psychological tests, while in others he may be engaged largely in therapy, teaching, or research. In some settings the psychiatric social worker is responsible for intake interviews or obtaining information about the developmental history of the patient, whereas in others she is predominantly involved in therapeutic case work with relatives or rehabilitation and placement of hospital patients. In the present section, it is proposed to elaborate further on some specific aspects of the roles of certain personnel having specific functions in the treatment of hospitalized psychiatric patients.

PSYCHIATRIC NURSING

During the earlier part of his stay in the hospital, the patient usually spends the greater part of his time on a ward in close personal contact with nurses, nursing aides, and orderlies. It is of vital importance that they contribute to the evaluation of the patient and establish the foundations of therapeutic relationships that will continue during the latter part of the patient's stay in hospital, during which he will be spending an increasing proportion of his waking hours elsewhere in recreational, occupational, or industrial activities.

Immediately after the patient's admission, the nurse should receive from the physician as much information about the patient as is currently available, together with written orders regarding his evaluation and initial goals of management. Such information should include the circumstances leading up to the patient's admission, the manner of admission (voluntary, or type of involuntary admission), special precautions that may be required (in relation to factors such as aggressive behavior, suicide, escape tendencies, seizures, accidental injury, or physical illness), activities to be permitted or encouraged, the degree of supervision

indicated, and any special instructions regarding visitors, incoming or outgoing mail, and telephone calls. The nurse will arrange for investigative procedures to be carried out, will keep accurate and comprehensive written records on the patient's behavior and conversation, and will discuss with the physician any special information or problems that may arise.

In her initial contact with the patient she should attempt to provide accurate information about the ward and hospital, explain any procedures that he does not understand or resents, and answer any questions of special concern to the best of her ability. Sometimes it will be necessary to consult the physician, or to ask the patient to consult his physician, for the answers to certain questions; and sometimes the patient's concern over family or financial matters may require prompt consultation with a social worker. In any event, the nurse should be as informative and helpful as possible, and should grant as many of the patient's requests as are permissible within the specific limits and restrictions set by the physician and the ward environment to which the patient has been admitted.

In her relationship with the patient, the nurse has been viewed as having at least half a dozen roles: as parent-substitute, technician, manager, teacher, socializing agent, and counselor or psychotherapist. In discussing the role of the nurse in therapy, the Group for the Advancement of Psychiatry made the following statement:*

A chief responsibility of the psychiatric nurse is to create a therapeutic ward atmosphere. More specifically, she should be able to influence favorably the group interaction in social, recreational and occupational activities on the ward. It should be emphasized that the nurse s role in this regard should enable her to make a unique contribution in

*Reprinted by permission from Group for the Advancement of Psychiatry. 1952. *The Psychiatric Nurse in the Mental Hospital.* G.A.P. Report No. 22, p. 2.

the ward care of hospitalized mental patients. Through her continued presence on the ward, the nurse has many opportunities for daily direct contacts with individual patients as well as with the total patient group. In these manifest day-by-day situations occurring in the ward's society, the nurse needs to know the significance of both the patient's behavior and his relationships with personnel and with other patients. A dynamic understanding of the patient's behavior in its manifestations will enable the nurse to respond appropriately to the behavior. This is the essence of the nurse's therapeutic activity. The psychiatric nurse must also be competent in her ability to assist the psychiatrist with the special therapies used in present-day psychiatric practice.

The treatment of the patient can and should be enhanced by the nurse's participation in frequent staff meetings wherein she has an opportunity to discuss with the psychiatrist his therapeutic plans for each patient. Discussion seminars provide an effective means to aid the nurse's own professional development—not only do they increase the nurse's fund of psychiatric knowledge, but also they provide an opportunity for critical appraisal of herself in her relationship with patients and personnel.

In a number of psychiatric inpatient facilities, specific management devices and forms of attitude therapy are prescribed by the psychiatrist for individual patients, to guide all staff members interacting with the patient. The main *management devices* include encouraging the sublimation of aggression, encouraging direct verbal expression of conscious hostility, encouraging suppression of conscious hostility, encouraging relief from a conscious or unconscious sense of guilt, giving "love" unsolicited or encouraging the patient to "earn love," offering substitutions for inappropriate sexual identifications, and encouraging socially acceptable narcissistic gratification or compulsive defenses. Such management devices and various forms of *attitude therapy* have been defined in detail (with rationale and examples) in a mimeographed guide to the order sheet published by the Menninger Foundation. Similar techniques designed to meet the needs of individual patients have been adopted in a number of centers emphasizing the contribution of a therapeutic milieu to the overall treatment program.

RECREATIONAL, OCCUPATIONAL, AND INDUSTRIAL THERAPY

It has long been considered that the devil finds work for idle hands, and that those who can be interested in some form of activity tend to appear more contented that those who remain inactive. Activity programs within custodial institutions originated for various reasons including attempts to have patients contribute to their own upkeep, to diminish problem behavior on the part of patients, and to make their life situations more pleasant for patients who must remain in the hospital for prolonged periods of time. Of recent years increasing emphasis has been placed on the therapeutic role of various activities for patients who will probably be remaining in the hospital even for relatively short periods of time.

During the patient's stay in the hospital there will usually be increasing opportunity and responsibility for recreational and occupational activities, under the supervision of staff members other than the nurses and attendant on the ward where he resides. Much of what has already been said about the therapeutic relationship provided by nurses also applies to the relationships that should be provided by these other staff members. In individualizing the management of each patient, it is important that there be consistency and continuity in management techniques adopted by various members of the staff. The latter requires that information regarding management devices and attitude therapy be transmitted to the occupational therapist not only at the time of the patient's initial referral, but also in ongoing team meetings between members of the staff involved in the patient's care.

In prescribing recreational and occupational therapy, there should be consideration of the nature of specific activities to be encouraged, the person or agency for whom projects should be undertaken (the patient, his relatives or friends, other patients, or the hospital, and whether there should be any financial reward for work undertaken. A number of hospitals are reluctant to accept former patients on their staff, but others have found the arrangement quite satisfactory, and convalescent patients may be enabled to commence paid employment in the nearby community prior to their discharge from hospital. A social worker may be able to help the patient find suitable employment, but a number of patients experience considerable uncertainty over vocational goals and should have the opportunity for appropriate vocational counseling and rehabilitation training where appropriate.

PSYCHIATRIC SOCIAL WORK

Whereas other members of the hospital staff work primarily with the patient, the social worker is more concerned with the patient's relationships with other members of the family and community outside the hospital. Apart from interviews with the patient, therefore, the social worker is involved in interviews and other contacts with relatives, friends, employers, and community agencies. The knowledge and skills of the social worker may be valuable at any time during or after the patient's stay in the hospital.

It has previously been mentioned that the roles of social workers vary greatly in different hospital or clinic settings. They may be involved to a varying degree in securing information about a patient immediately following his admission, in finding jobs and financial assistance for patients ready to leave hospital, or in counseling patients and their families following discharge. There has been an increasing tendency, however, for social workers to participate in evaluation and treatment throughout the patient's stay in hospital,

to meet regularly with other members of the therapeutic team, and to work with the patient's relatives and significant community resources.

In private practice and in most training centers, the physician or student supplements information obtained from the patient by interviewing close relatives. Even when this is current practice, however, it may be helpful for the patient's relatives to be interviewed by a social worker at the time the patient first comes to the clinic or hospital. Such interviews may not only provide additional information about the patient, but also provide the relatives with more accurate information about such matters as the nature of the patient's problems, the nature of psychiatric treatment, and visiting hours. This initial interview with the social worker may also be concerned with financial problems and the care of the patient's home and children, and may initiate the establishment of a therapeutic relationship with relatives on which continuing casework will be based.

Casework with the patient's relatives may be expected to increase their understanding and sympathy with the patient's difficulties in interpersonal relationships, and to modify their destructive attitudes and behavior toward the patient in the interest of their own future happiness as well as that of the patient. Sometimes a social worker will be involved in individual casework or group therapy with hospitalized patients, but these functions are frequently assumed by other personnel. The social worker, however, has an important role to fill in the rehabilitation of the convalescent patient, which may involve helping him to find a job, a place to live, and temporary financial assistance. Continuing casework after discharge from hospital may enable the patient and his family to make satisfactory adjustments and reinforce more effective adaptation than hitherto.

PSYCHIATRIC ADMINISTRATION

In hospitals oriented toward custodial care, it has been traditional for all patients on a given ward to be assigned to a single physician, and for any patient transferred to another ward to become the responsibility of the physician in charge of that ward. In psychiatric inpatient settings focusing on active treatment and rehabilitation, however, it is customary for each patient to remain under the care of a single psychiatrist for as long after his admission as there remains hope for his return to the community. The physician undertaking individual psychotherapy with the patient will also be responsible for arranging any other treatment procedures that may be indicated, although the latter may sometimes be carried out by another physician (as for example group therapy or electroshock treatment).

The psychiatrists should arrange regular team meetings with all other personnel directly involved in the therapy of the patient and casework with relatives, in order to communicate information about the patient's progress and reach a common understanding and agreement on the goals of future treatment. The psychiatrist carries the ultimate medical responsibility for the patient and functions as the leader of the group. He should learn to know the potentialities of each member of the team, should establish a regular procedure for the team meetings, should share his own thinking with other members of the group, and should react verbally to the contributions made by other members. He should be able to clarify the ideas expressed by others and keep the discussion focused on relevant issues. It may be necessary to impose time limits on the discussion of a certain issue, and he should attempt to summarize what has been said in a form that may be recorded for future reference.

The basic administrative duties of the psychiatrist are to coordinate the efforts of members of the interdisciplinary team in the care and treatment of the individual patient. In a hospital setting, however, senior psychiatrists are also required to coordinate and administer all clinical services, teaching and research activities, and sometimes other aspects of hospital operation. The latter functions are beyond the scope of the present chapter, but the personal qualifications must include an ability to bring about the resolution of conflict through communication and compromise. In the words of the Chinese philosopher, Laotzu:

Of the best leaders
the people only know that they exist;
the next best they love and praise;
the next they fear;
and the next they revile.
When they do not command the people s faith,
some will lose faith in them,
and then they resort to recriminations.
But of the best, when their task is accomplished,
their work done,
the people remark
"we have done it ourselves. '

SELECTED REFERENCES

Ackerman, N. W. 1958. *The Psychodynamics of Family Life.* New York, Basic Books, Inc.

Ackerman, N. W. 1966. Family therapy. In *The American Handbook of Psychiatry,* ed. S. Arieti. Vol. 3, ch. 14.

Aichorn, A. 1935. *Wayward Youth.* New York, The Viking Press, Inc.

Alexander, F. 1956. *Psychoanalysis and Psychotherapy.* New York, W. W. Norton & Co., Inc.

Alexander, F. 1963. The dynamics of psychotherapy in the light of learning theory. American Journal of Psychiatry *129,* 440-448; reprinted 1965, International Journal of Psychiatry *1,* 189-197.

Alexander, F., and French, T. M. 1946. *Psychoanalytic Therapy. Principles and Application.* New York, The Ronald Press Co.

Alexander, F., and Ross, H., eds. 1952. *Dynamic Psychiatry.* Chicago, The University of Chicago Press.

American Psychiatric Association. 1964. *A Psychiatric Glossary,* 2nd edition. Washington, D.C., American Psychiatric Association.

Arieti, S., ed. 1959. *The American Handbook of Psychiatry.* New York, Basic Books, Inc., Vol. 2, ch. 64-73.

Arieti, S., ed. 1966. *The American Handbook of Psychiatry.* New York, Basic Books, Inc., Vol. 3, ch. 13-19.

Bachrach, A. J., ed. 1962. *Experimental Foundations of Clinical Psychology.* New York, Basic Books, Inc., ch. 14-18.

Bandura, A. and Walters, R. H. 1963. *Social Learning and Personality Development.* New York, Holt, Rinehart & Winston, Inc., ch. 5.

Bettelheim, B. 1950. *Love Is Not Enough.* Glencoe, Illinois, The Free Press, division of The Macmillan Co.

Betz, B. J., and Whitehorn, J. C. 1956. The relationship of the therapist to the outcome of therapy in schizophrenia. In *Psychiatric Research Reports* No. 5, ed. N. S. Kline. Washington, D.C., American Psychiatric Association.

Bierer, J. 1951. *The Day Hospital.* London, Lewis.

Brenman, M., and Gill, M. M. 1947. *Hypnotherapy.* New York, International Universities Press, Inc.

Breuer, J., and Freud, S. 1936. *Studies in Hysteria.* New York and Washington, Illness and Mental Disease Publications.

Bryan, W. A. 1958. *Administrative Psychiatry,* New York, Pageant Book Company.

Burton, A., ed. 1965. *Psychotherapy of the Psychoses.* New York, Basic Books, Inc.

Caudill, W. A. 1958. *The Psychiatric Hospital as a Small Society.* Cambridge, Massachusetts, Harvard University Press.

Colby, K. M. 1951. *A Primer for Psychotherapists.* New York, The Ronald Press Co.

Diethelm, O. 1951. *Treatment in Psychiatry.* New York, The Macmillan Co.

Dollard, J., and Miller, N. E. 1950. *Personality and Psychotherapy.* New York, McGraw-Hill Book Co., Inc.

Dollard, J, Auld, F., and White, A. M. 1953. *Steps in Psychotherapy.* New York, The Macmillan Co.

Eisenstein, V. W., ed. 1956. *Neurotic Interaction in Marriage,* New York, Basic Books, Inc.

Eysenck, H. J. 1965. The effects of psychotherapy. International Journal of Psychiatry *1,* 97.

Eysenck, H. J., ed. 1960. *Behaviour Therapy and the Neuroses.* New York, Pergamon Press, Inc.

Eysenck, H. J., ed. 1964. *Experiments in Behaviour Therapy.* New York, Pergamon Press, Inc., and The Macmillan Co.

Fenichel, O. 1945. *The Psychoanalytic Theory of Neurosis.* New York, W. W. Norton & Co.

Frank, J. D. 1955. *Group Therapy in the Mental Hospital.* Washington, D.C., American Psychiatric Association, Mental Hospital Service, Monograph Series No. 1.

Frank, J. D. 1961. *Persuasion and Healing.* Baltimore, The Johns Hopkins Press.

Freud, A. 1931. *Introduction to the Technic of Child Analysis.* London, George Allen and Unwin.

Freud, S. 1917. *Introductory Lectures on Psychoanalysis.* London, George Allen and Unwin.

Freud, S. 1933. *New Introductory Lectures on Psychoanalysis.* New York, W. W. Norton & Co.

Fromm, E. 1955. *The Sane Society.* New York, Rinehart.

Fromm-Reichmann, F. 1950. *Principles of Intensive Psychotherapy.* Chicago, The University of Chicago Press.

Gill, M. M., and Brenman, M. 1960. *Hypnosis and Related States.* New York, International Universities Press, Inc.

Gitelson, M. 1951. Psychoanalysis and dynamic psychiatry, AMA Archives of Neurology and Psychiatry *66,* 280-288.

Goldston, S. E., ed. 1965. *Concepts of Community Psychiatry.* Washington, D.C. U.S. Department of Health, Education, and Welfare, Public Health Service Publication No. 1319.

Grinker, R. R. 1961. *Psychiatry and Social Work; A Transactional Case Book.* New York, Basic Books, Inc.

Grinker, R. R. 1961. A transactional model for psychotherapy. In *Contemporary Psychotherapies,* ed. M. I. Stein. New York, The Free Press of Glencoe, division of The Macmillan Co., pp. 190-213.

Group for the Advancement of Psychiatry. 1952. *The Psychiatric Nurse in the Mental Hospital.* New York, G.A.P. Report No. 22.

Group for the Advancement of Psychiatry. 1960. *Administration of the Public Psychiatric Hospital.* New York, G.A.P. Report No. 46.

Handlon, J. H., and Parloff, M. B. 1962. The treatment of patient and family as a group: is it group psychotherapy? International Journal of Group Psychotherapy *12,* 132-141.

Harper, R. A. 1959. *Psychoanalysis and Psychotherapy: 36 Systems.* Englewood Cliffs, New Jersey, Prentice-Hall, Inc.

Hendrick, I. 1958. *Facts and Theories of Psychoanalysis,* 3rd edition, New York, Alfred A. Knopf, Inc.

Hinsie, L. E. 1937. *Concepts and Problems of Psychotherapy.* New York, Columbia University Press.

Horney, K. 1939. *New Ways in Psychoanalysis.* New York, W. W. Norton & Co.

Ingham, H. V., and Love, L. R. 1954. *The Process of Psychotherapy.* New York, McGraw-Hill Book Co., Inc.

Jones, M. 1953. *The Therapeutic Community—A New Treatment Method in Psychiatry.* New York, Basic Books, Inc.

Klein, M. 1961. *New Directions in Psychoanalysis.* New York, Basic Books, Inc.

Knobloch, F. 1965. Discussion of paper by Franz Alexander. International Journal of Psychiatry *1,* 199-203.

Koegler, R. R., and Brill, N. Q. 1966. *Treatment of Psychiatric Outpatients.* New York, Appleton-Century-Crofts, Inc.

Kral, V. A. 1951. Psychiatric observations under severe chronic stresses. American Journal of Psychiatry *108,* 185.

Kubie, L. S. 1936. *Practical Aspects of Psychoanalysis.* New York, W. W. Norton & Co.

Levine, M. 1952. Principles of psychiatric treatment. In *Dynamic Psychiatry,* ed. F. Alexander and H. Ross. Chicago, The University of Chicago Press, ch. 11.

Loewald, H. W. 1960. On the therapeutic action of psychoanalysis. International Journal of Psychoanalysis *41,* 16.

Lorand, S. 1946. *Technique of Psychoanalytic Therapy.* New York, International Universities Press, Inc.

Main, T. F. 1946. The Hospital as a therapeutic institution. Bulletin of the Meninger Clinic *10,* 66.

Masserman, J. H., and Moreno, J. L., eds. 1957. *Progress in Psychotherapy*, Volume 2. New York, Grune & Stratton, Inc.

Menninger, K. 1958. *Theory of Psychoanalytic Technique*. New York, Basic Books, Inc.

Monroe, R. L. 1955. *Schools of Psychoanalytic Thought*. New York, The Dryden Press.

Moreno, J. L. 1946. *Psychodrama*. New York, The Beacon Press.

Mowrer, O. H. 1953. *Psychotherapy: Theory and Research*. New York, The Ronald Press Co.

Paul, G. L. 1966. *Insight vs. Desensitization in Psychotherapy*. Stanford, California, Stanford University Press.

Powdermaker, F. B., and Frank, J. D. 1953. *Group Psychotherapy*. Cambridge, Massachusetts, Harvard University Press.

Powles, W. E. 1960. An examination of the concepts of milieu therapy. Canadian Psychiatric Association Journal 5, 203.

Rado, S. 1956. *Psychoanalysis of Behavior; Collected Papers*. New York, Grune & Stratton, Inc.

Rangell, L. 1954. Similarities and differences between psychoanalysis and dynamic psychotherapy. Journal of the American Psychoanalytic Association 2, 734-744.

Redlich, F. C., and Freedman, D. X. 1966. *The Theory and Practice of Psychiatry*. New York, Basic Books, Inc., ch. 10.

Reznikoff, M., and Toomey, L. C. 1959. *Evaluation of Changes Associated with Psychiatric Treatment*. Springfield, Illinois, Charles C Thomas, Publisher.

Rogers, C. R. 1942. *Counselling and Psychotherapy*. New York, Houghton Mifflin Co.

Rogers, C. R. 1966. Client-centered therapy. In *The American Handbook of Psychiatry*, ed. S. Arieti. New York, Basic Books, Inc., Vol. 3, ch. 13.

Rosen, J. N. 1947. The treatment of schizophrenic psychoses by direct analytic therapy. Psychiatric Quarterly 21, 3.

Sager, C. J. 1966. The treatment of married couples. In *American Handbook of Psychiatry*, ed. S. Arieti. New York, Basic Books, Inc., Vol. 3 ch. 15.

Schilder, P. 1951. *Psychotherapy*. New York, W. W. Norton & Co.

Schofield, W. 1964. *Psychotherapy: The Purchase of Friendship*. Englewood Cliffs, New Jersey, Prentice-Hall, Inc.

Slavson, S. R. 1948. *The Practice of Group Therapy*. New York, International Universities Press, Inc.

Snow, H. B. 1958. The open door hospital. Canadian Journal of Public Health 49, 363.

Stanton, A. H., and Schwartz, M. H. 1954. *The Mental Hospital*. New York, Basic Books, Inc.

Stein, M. I., ed. 1961. *Contemporary Psychotherapies*. New York, The Free Press of Glencoe, division of The Macmillan Co.

Strupp, H. H. A multidimensional analysis of technique in brief psychotherapy. Psychiatry 20, 387-397.

Strupp, H. H. 1958. The psychotherapist's contribution to the treatment process. Behavioral Science 3, 34-67.

Strupp, H. H., and Luborsky, L., eds. 1962. *Research in Psychotherapy, Volume 2*, Washington, D.C., American Psychological Association, Inc.

Sullivan, H. S. 1953. *The Interpersonal Theory of Psychiatry*. New York, W. W. Norton & Co.

Thorne, F. C. 1957. Critique of recent developments in personality counselling theory. Journal of Clinical Psychology 13, 234.

Ullmann, L. P., and Krasner, L., eds. 1965. *Case Studies in Behavior Modification*. New York, Holt, Rinehart & Winston, Inc.

Voegtlin, W. L. 1940. The treatment of alcoholism by establishing a conditioned reflex. American Journal of Medical Sciences 199, 802.

Voegtlin, W. L., Lemere, F., and Broz, W. R. 1940. Conditioned reflex therapy of alcohol addiction. Quarterly Journal of Studies in Alcohol 1, 501.

Wolberg, L. R. 1945. *Hypnoanalysis*. New York, Grune & Stratton, Inc.

Wolberg, L. R. 1954. *The Technique of Psychotherapy*. New York, Grune & Stratton, Inc.

Wolpe, J. 1958. *Psychotherapy by reciprocal Inhibition*. Stanford, California, Stanford University Press.

World Health Organization. 1959. *Social Psychiatry and Community Attitudes*. Geneva, W.H.O. Technical Reports Series No. 177.

CHAPTER 12

Somatic Treatments in Psychiatry

by B. C. Schiele

INTRODUCTION

The present chapter is concerned with certain procedures and chemicals having their primary effects upon the body, which have found empirical application in the treatment of the "functional' psychiatric disorders (in which no consistent somatic pathology has been established). A large number of drugs and physical agents have been introduced in the hope of ameliorating these "functional" disorders (affective disorders, the schizophrenias, paranoid states, psychoneuroses, personality and behavioral disorders), and the rationale underlying their introduction has frequently been an expressed belief in the ultimate discovery of some form of underlying brain pathology (e.g., Sargant and Slater, 1964). However, there is little connection between the development of the individual empirical somatic treatments, and the one point they all have in common is that they are based on the belief that psychiatric conditions, especially the psychoses, can be influenced therapeutically by nonpsychological methods (Kalinowsky and Hoch, 1961).

The nonpsychological therapy most commonly used in treatment of the psychiatric disorders is drug therapy. Since time immemorial, mankind has used a variety of drugs having depressant or stimulant effects on the central nervous system. Such drugs include alcohol, opium, hashish, caffeine (in tea or coffee), and cocaine (in coca leaves). Alcohol has found application in a particularly wide variety of circumstances including the reduction of anxiety and fear in situations of physical danger (e.g., before battle), the reduction of tension to permit freer social interaction or emotional release, and the relief of bodily pain, mental anguish, or insomnia.

It is necessary to distinguish between the pharmacological actions of such drugs on the central nervous system and their effects upon mood or behavior. Drugs which are truly depressant in their action on nerve cells (e.g., alcohol) may appear to be stimulant in their external effects on the whole organism, since small doses first remove cortical inhibition and may thereby elevate mood and facilitate speech and motor activity. On the other hand, small doses of drugs which stimulate nerve cell

260

function may increase cortical inhibition and anxiety, and lead to further blocking of speech and motor activity. With larger doses of either depressant or stimulant drugs, the external effects on motor activity show increasing conformity with the direct effects on the central nervous system.

Such drugs have long been prescribed for psychiatric patients, either in an attempt to relieve the patient's distress (e.g., insomnia, anxiety, or depression) or to control behavior that was disturbing to others (e.g., aggressive, destructive, or hyperactive behavior). During the past century, most of the drugs available for these purposes have been central nervous system depressants, but of recent years increasing use has been made of drugs with a stimulant action on the central nervous system and drugs designed to improve a mood of depression (regardless of their central effects).

Since 1953 the extensive use of major tranquilizing drugs, particularly the phenothiazines, has resulted in diminished reliance on other somatic therapies, and many psychotic patients are now treated predominantly by such drugs or by a combination of drugs and psychotherapy. A large number of psychiatrists regard this as the most important therapeutic development of recent years, but for different reasons. Those with an analytic-psychological orientation tend to view the importance of this development as being the extension of psychotherapy to hitherto inaccessible patients. Those with a directive-organic orientation are more apt to regard drug therapy as effective in its own right, and to look forward to the discovery of specific metabolic anomalies which may be controlled by specific drug therapy (rather than by current empirical symptomatic treatment). Regardless of these differences in theoretical orientation, however, the advent of these drugs has led to considerable rapprochement in the methods of treatment adopted by different psychiatrists. There are still some psychiatrists who feel that the use of tranquilizers removes anxiety which is a necessary incentive to psychotherapy (particularly in neurotic patients), but increasing numbers of analytically trained psychiatrists are using drugs as an adjuvant to psychotherapy and many directive-organic psychiatrists are placing increasing reliance on psychotherapy in management. It should be borne in mind, however, that success or failure with any of the empirical treatments used in psychiatry (psychotherapy, drugs, or other somatic treatments) does not necessarily bear any relationship to the causation of the disorders involved.

The groups of drugs affecting the central nervous system which will be discussed in the present chapter include: (1) anticonvulsants, sedatives, hypnotics, and narcotics, (2) major tranquilizers, ataractics, or neuroleptics, and (3) stimulants and antidepressants. Somatic treatments discussed will include: (1) electroconvulsive therapy, (2) insulin coma therapy, (3) psychosurgery, and (4) other physical therapies.

DIFFERENTIAL USE OF DRUGS IN PSYCHIATRY

It frequently is difficult to decide from which pharmacological category the drug for a specific patient should be chosen. Unfortunately, formal differential diagnosis, even when made by the most capable and experienced psychiatrist, often does not lead to differential therapy. This is due, at least in part, to the fact that complex and various behavioral phenomena are not easily compressed into simple categories. Therefore, although the physician will still use the diagnosis as a partial guide in the choice of treatment, he must depend heavily on what may be termed target symptoms. For example, an excited, hyperactive, or agitated patient logically would be given a sedative or suppressant rather than a stimulant, no matter what the basic diagnosis is. By becoming thoroughly familiar with one or two drugs of each pharmacological type, the physician will develop a base of reference. In most instances, he will be able to rely on the compounds he knows best. Other drugs within specific groups, whose action varies only slightly from that of the "standard" drug, will be needed only for special indications.

The classification under which the newer psychopharmacological agents will be discussed is a modification of one based on both clinical considerations and pharmacological characteristics. In this brief review, only general indications for the use of the various types of compounds and the most common or serious associated hazards can be discussed.

ANTICONVULSANTS, SEDATIVES, HYPNOTICS, AND NARCOTICS

Bromides were introduced in 1857 for the control of epilepsy, in which it was found that they would reduce the frequency and severity of seizures. Their action, however, is not confined to the motor cortex, and they have a general depressant action on the central nervous system, so that they gradually found extremely wide application in the management of hyperactivity, anxiety, and tension. They are long-acting and cumulative, and prolonged administration is frequently accompanied by the development of depression (of mood), intellectual impairment, gross mental confusion (toxic "delirium") and an acneiform skin rash. The blood level at which symptoms of toxicity develop varies in different individuals, but unpleasant symptoms are usually associated with a blood level of over 250 mg per 100 ml, and death may result if the level reaches 350 to 500 mg per cent. Treatment consists of discontinuing bromides and administering sodium chloride and fluids.

Phenobarbital was first used as an anticonvulsant in 1912 and still finds application in the control of grand mal epileptiform seizures. It is usually prescribed by mouth in doses of 50 to 150 mg three times a day, but larger doses may be given, by injection if necessary. It is slowly absorbed, long acting and may be cumulative. Like the bromides, it produces a generalized depression of the central nervous system and, prior to the advent of the newer tranquilizing drugs, it was widely used for the symptomatic control of neurotic anxiety and tension. However, it may also produce a depression of mood and impairment of intellectual functions, which may be quite severe if administration is prolonged. The bromides and phenobarbital were the only drugs used in the control of epilepsy up to 1938, when diphenylhydantoin (Dilantin) was introduced for the control of grand mal seizures. Soon afterward, trimethadione (Tridione) was found to be helpful in the management of petit mal attacks, and a large number of other synthetic drugs have since been developed for use in epilepsy.

Apart from drugs designed to control epileptic seizures or relieve anxiety, three other groups of central nervous system drugs were in widespread psychiatric use during the first half of the present century: long-acting drugs for the control of prolonged excitement and overactivity, shorter-acting drugs for the relief of insomnia, and drugs which could be given by injection for the prompt control of sudden acute disturbances.

The *sulfonals* are long-acting sedatives which enjoyed considerable popularity in the management of prolonged states of excitement (manic and schizophrenic), and it was found that their toxic effects could be minimized by avoiding constipation. A number of psychiatrists, however, preferred *barbital* (in doses of five to ten grains several times a day), but the effects of these drugs on motor activity was apt to be accompanied by considerable intellectual impairment and ataxia.

Among the shorter-acting drugs which enjoyed a long period of popularity are *chloral hydrate* and *paraldehyde*, but these have been partially displaced by the relatively short-acting barbiturates such as *amobarbital* (Amytal), *pentobarbital* (Nembutal), and *secobarbital* (Seconal). These drugs may be useful for the symptomatic relief of insomnia (even in patients who are also receiving tranquilizing or antidepressant medication), and the student should become familiar with their dosage and duration of action.

Two drugs which were often given by injection (frequently in combination with one another) for the control of disturbed behavior were *hyoscine* and *morphine*. Although they were prompt, predictable, and effective, the danger of addiction (and sometimes consequent perpetuation of episodes of disturbed behavior) resulted in the gradual replacement of these drugs by injectable preparations of barbiturates, and more recently the latter have been largely superseded by injectable tranquilizing drugs such as those described in the next section.

MAJOR TRANQUILIZERS, ATARACTICS, OR NEUROLEPTICS

Some of the disadvantages of barbiturates and other sedatives in controlling excited patients have already been outlined. Such drugs tend to increase intellectual impairment and confusion and to leave the patient ataxic but still antagonistic, so that he may injure himself or others. A number of drugs have been discovered, however, that diminish activity, anxiety, and aggression without marked impairment of intelligence or consciousness; and these drugs have been described as ataractic (from ataraxy, meaning freedom from confusion). These drugs were also found to diminish the intensity and duration of other psychotic symptoms such as hallucinations and delusions, and they became generally known as the major tranquilizers. Because these agents produce sustained relief of symptoms in many mentally ill people without causing marked sedation, they have added a new dimension to psychiatric therapy that did not exist when only the sedative drugs were available.

The amelioration of psychotic symptoms associated with the major tranquilizers is often referred to as their "antipsychotic" action. A better term would be psychotostatic, as no cure is effected. The observed reduction in psychotic symptoms is somewhat analogous to the reduction of convulsive seizures in epilepsy. An antiepileptic drug will not cure the patient, but it will enable him to lead a much more successful life and to have fewer and less severe seizures.

If one looks at this "antipsychotic" effect closely, it is obvious that the reduction in emotional turmoil effected by the drug allows the patient to become interested in his family and community affairs and to participate more effectively in environmental and interpersonal therapies. A gross measure of the impact of the major tranquilizers in mental hospitals can be seen in the marked reduction of violent behavior and the consequent reduction in the need for restraint and seclusion.

Some patients do not respond at all to the major tranquilizers. On the other hand, the majority of both acute and chronic schizophrenic and other psychotic patients do benefit from these drugs. One of the most striking benefits of the widespread use of these drugs in this country is the dramatically decreased bed occupancy rate in mental hospitals.

MECHANISMS OF ACTION OF THE MAJOR TRANQUILIZERS

Whereas the mechanisms of action of the tranquilizers remain in doubt, a good deal of information is available about their central effects. This is particularly true in the case of the major or true tranquilizers. Although both the phenothiazine and rauwolfia groups have essentially the same marked effect against psychomotor excitation, their pharmacological action in achieving this effect is quite different. Compounds of both groups are capable of reducing sympathetic excitation at the central level, yet each does this in a different manner. To better understand these actions from a physiological basis, the reader is referred to the publications of Magoun and associates.

The most widely studied of the phenothiazines and a drug known to have marked adrenergic blocking activity is chlorpromazine (Thorazine), which raises the threshold for sympathetic excitation at the hypothalamic level, where the sympathetic nervous system has its headquarters. This suggests a blocking action against the sympathetic neurohumoral transmitter substance. Although Hess in 1948 first suggested the possible existence of a distinct central sympathetic transmitter substance, it remained for Vogt in 1954 and Brodie and Shore in 1957 to demonstrate the presence of norepinephrine in the hypothalamus. Norepinephrine, a precursor of epinephrine, is blocked by chlorpromazine.

If norepinephrine is established as the true transmitter substance necessary for excitation of the sympathetic center in the posterior hypothalamus, it may be reasonably assumed that chlorpromazine achieves its effect by preventing norepinephrine from exciting those nerve cells that generate widespread sympathetic effects. In 1953, Courvoisier and coworkers confirmed this postulate by demonstrating widespread reduction of sympathetic tone in the body when chlorpromazine was administered. There is vasodilation and hypotension with compensatory tachycardia, relaxation of smooth muscle, and an alteration in pupillary size and salivary and gastric secretions. Most peripherally active adrenergic blocking agents fail to block the adrenergic influence on the heart.

Reserpine (Serpasil*), a member of the rauwolfia group, acts in a somewhat different manner. It has the unusual property of causing a depletion in central stores of norepinephrine and serotonin. Reserpine has been demonstrated to enter and leave the cells of the brain readily, but to exert a more lasting effect by interfering with the binding of norepinephrine in the cells. As quickly as norepinephrine is formed, it is dissipated. It fails to enter into preformed stores—a step presumably necessary for the subsequent excitation of the sympathetic effector cells. Thus, as with chlorpromazine, the result is a failure to transmit the intended neurohumoral message to the effector cells of the central sympathetics. In both instances, the tone of the sympathetic division of the autonomics is diminished. Again, evidence for this is the marked hypotension that results. Simultaneously, according to evidence furnished by Bein and coworkers, the balance of autonomic activity is shifted in favor of the parasympathetic system, which results in the increase in gastrointestinal activity and gastric secretion, bradycardia, pupillary constriction, and salivation.

Thus, although the mechanisms of action are different for the rauwolfia and phenothiazine groups, their overall effect is to decrease sympathetic, adrenergic activity (and ergotropic responses) and to favor parasympathetic, nonadrenergic (or trophotropic) activity. In either case, psychomotor agitation is lessened. This concept may not be correct, since other modes of action (now under investigation) may in reality be occurring. However, the currently favored hypothesis is that the threshold of excitability of the sympathetics is raised while simultaneously the

---

*One of several brand names.

threshold of excitability of the parasympathetics is lowered.

The major tranquilizers are able to suppress central sympathetic activation without significantly depressing the reticular activating system. This favors the control of psychomotor agitation without loss of cortical activity or consciousness. This effect is in marked contrast to the action of the barbiturates, which control hyperactivity of the hypothalamus but also are prominently active in suppressing the reticular activating system. As a consequence of this latter action, sleep ensues and control of the overactive emotional state occurs at the expense of loss in intellectual function.

Drugs which have the antipsychotic or neuroleptic action described above are known as the major tranquilizers and comprise the following four categories:

(1) The rauwolfia alkaloids
(2) The phenothiazine compounds
(3) The thioxanthene compounds
(4) The butyrophenones

THE RAUWOLFIA DRUGS

Medications derived from the snake root plant (*Rauwolfia serpentina*) have been used for centuries in India to treat insanity and other disorders. Modern evaluations of their efficacy in the treatment of mental disorders began in 1954. Although they share many of the antipsychotic and tranquilizing effects of the phenothiazine derivatives, the rauwolfia compounds are administered in lower doses and are much slower acting. Differences in the mechanisms of action of the two classes suggest that the rauwolfia drugs might benefit some psychiatric patients who are not helped

Rauwolfia Group

STRUCTURE	GENERIC NAME	TRADE NAME
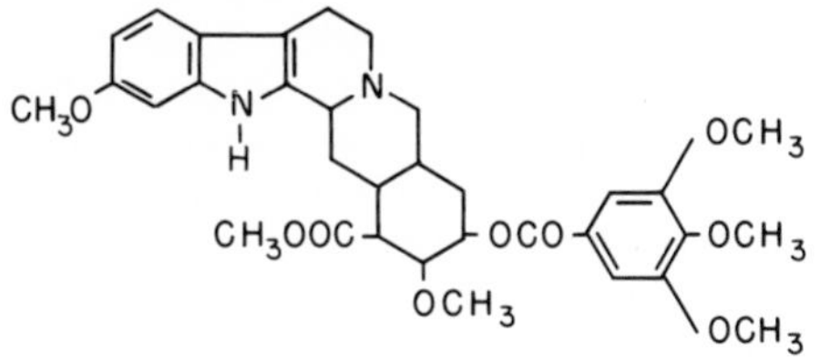	*Reserpine*	Serpasil
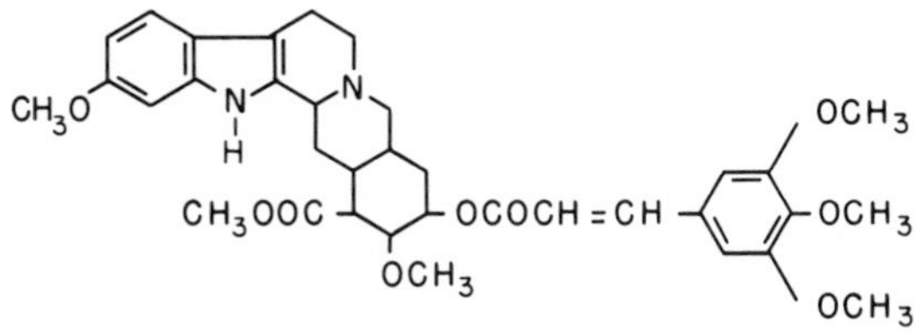	*Rescinnamine*	Moderil
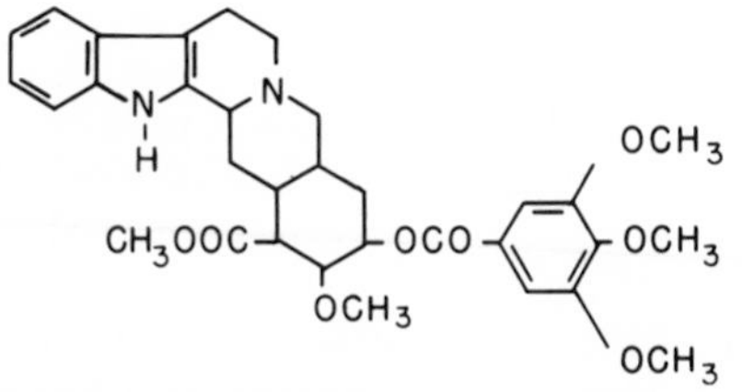	*Deserpidine* *(Recanescine)*	Harmonyl

Figure 12–1. (From Benson, W. M., and Schiele, B. C. 1962. Tranquilizing and Antidepressive Drugs. Courtesy of Charles C Thomas, Publisher, Springfield, Illinois, p. 24.)

by the phenothiazine derivatives. However, the rauwolfia compounds have not been as well accepted in psychiatric therapy as the phenothiazine drugs, and a number of comparative studies have indicated that they are not as effective. The use of these drugs for psychiatric effect is decreasing, and they are reserved chiefly for patients who do not benefit from other procedures.

The rauwolfia compounds appear under many brand names and in combination with many other drugs. Of the many alkaloids which have been extracted from this plant, three are available for clinical use: reserpine, deserpidine (Harmonyl), and rescinnamine (Moderil) (see Figure 12-1). Other pharmaceutical preparations contain the whole root (Raudixin) or the alseroxylon fraction (Rauwiloid). These drugs are widely prescribed for the reduction of hypertension. When rauwolfia derivatives are administered, either alone or in combination with other drugs, it must be borne in mind that serious mental depressions may occur.

These compounds are capable of producing extrapyramidal phenomena somewhat similar to those induced by phenothiazine derivatives (to be described). Seizures also may occur. Untoward effects on the autonomic nervous system include bradycardia, cutaneous flushing, salivation, vomiting, diarrhea, and nasal congestion. Hypotension with syncope may be troublesome, particularly in aged or hypertensive patients. Activation of peptic ulcer with gastric hemorrhage and melena may be also occur.

Because of the danger of vascular collapse, patients about to undergo surgery or electroshock should not be given rauwolfia compounds. These drugs may also aggravate allergic disorders such as asthma or urticaria. Patients may experience unwanted weight gain or edema of the extremities. Impotence and loss of libido have been noted. Although the use of rauwolfia compounds has not resulted in leukopenia, there have been reports of nonthrombocytopenic and thrombocytopenic purpura.

THE PHENOTHIAZINE COMPOUNDS

Members of the phenothiazine class are generally useful in relieving emotional tension, agitation, and excitement, with subsequent lessening of delusions and hallucinations. Although some compounds tend to be more effective than others and some patients respond better to one compound than to another, the antipsychotic and tranquilizing action of all these agents is essentially similar. Therefore, the choice of an individual drug often depends on the patient's susceptibility to various side effects.

The phenothiazines are commonly divided into three groups: the dimethyl, the piperidyl, and the piperazine. These designations refer to the characteristic configuration of the long side chain for compounds within each group (Figure 12-2).

Although the individual compounds have their own profiles of action, there is an overall similarity of pattern for each group. For example, drugs of the piperazine subgroup are distinguished by greater potency on a milligram basis than the other compounds. They also have less sedative effect.

Compared to the piperazine group, the dimethyl and piperidyl compounds have greater sedative action and a lower milligram potency (Table 12-1). Therefore, for convenience and simplicity, they can be grouped together.

Individual Compounds. Only a few representative compounds will be mentioned. *Chlorpromazine*, a member of the dimethyl subgroup, was the first phenothiazine compound introduced and therefore serves as a standard for comparison. Because of this drug's extensive use throughout the world since 1953, comparatively more is known about its side effect pattern than about those of the other phenothiazines. Despite the frequency of side effects with this drug, chlorpromazine remains an effective

CHEMICAL STRUCTURE OF PHENOTHIAZINE COMPOUNDS

Basic Phenothiazine Nucleus

Dimethyl Subgroup	POSITION R_{10}	POSITION R_2	Piperazine Subgroup	POSITION R_{10}	POSITION R_2
Triflupromazine	$-CH_2-CH_2-CH_2-N\begin{smallmatrix}CH_3\\CH_3\end{smallmatrix}$	CF_3	Fluphenazine	$-CH_2-CH_2-CH_2-N\bigcirc N-CH_2-CH_2-OH$	CF_3
Chlorpromazine	$-CH_2-CH_2-CH_2-N\begin{smallmatrix}CH_3\\CH_3\end{smallmatrix}$	Cl	Trifluoperazine	$-CH_2-CH_2-CH_2-N\bigcirc N-CH_3$	CF_3
Methoxypromazine	$-CH_2-CH_2-CH_2-N\begin{smallmatrix}CH_3\\CH_3\end{smallmatrix}$	OCH_3	Perphenazine	$-CH_2-CH_2-CH_2-N\bigcirc N-CH_2-CH_2-OH_2$	Cl
Promazine	$-CH_2-CH_2-CH_2-N\begin{smallmatrix}CH_3\\CH_3\end{smallmatrix}$	—	Prochlorperazine	$-CH_2-CH_2-CH_2-N\bigcirc N-CH_3$	Cl
Piperidyl Subgroup			Thiopropazate	$-CH_2-CH_2-CH_2-N\bigcirc N-CH_2-CH_2-O-CH_3$	Cl
Thioridazine	$-CH_2-CH_2-\bigcirc$	SCH_3	Acetophenazine	$-CH_2-CH_2-CH_2-N\bigcirc N-CH_2-CH_2-OH$	$COCH_3$
Mepazine	$-CH_2-\bigcirc N-CH_3$	—	Carphenazine	$-CH_2-CH_2-CH_2-N\bigcirc N-CH_2-CH_2-OH$	COC_2H_5

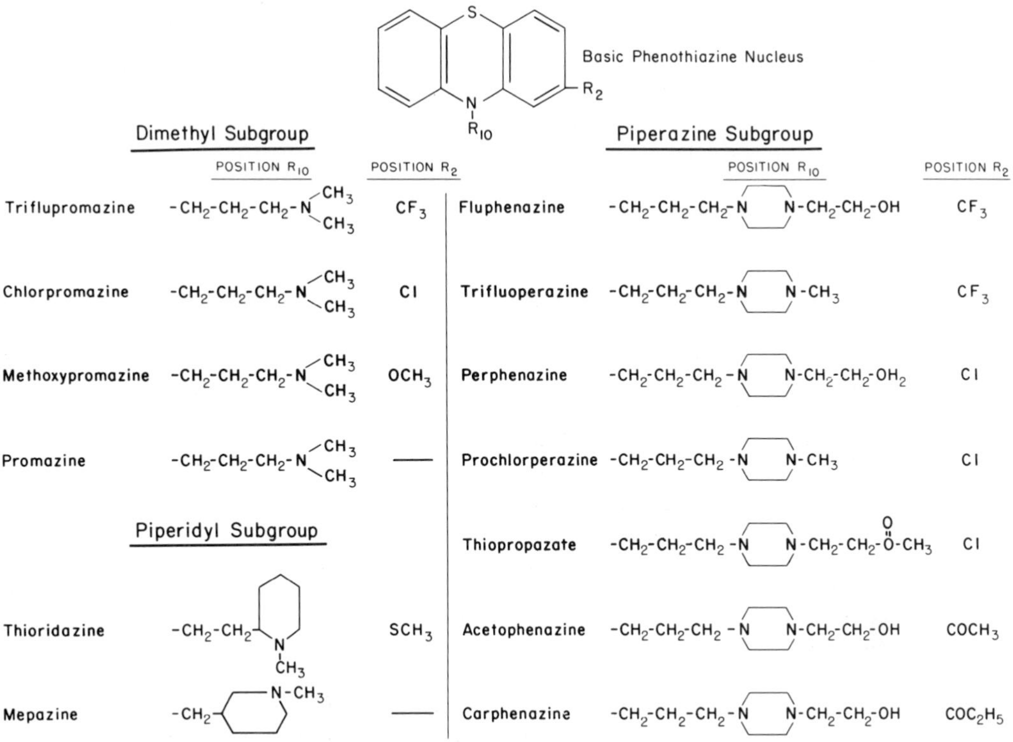

Figure 12-2. (From Schiele, B. C. 1962. Newer drugs for mental illness. Journal of the American Medical Association *181*, 126.)

TABLE 12–1. Phenothiazine Compounds in Order of Milligram Potency as Compared to Chlorpromazine†

MORE SEDATIVE			LESS SEDATIVE		
Dimethyl Subgroup		APPROX. ORDER OF	*Piperazine Subgroup*		APPROX. ORDER OF
GENERIC NAME	TRADE NAME	POTENCY	GENERIC NAME	TRADE NAME	POTENCY
Triflupromazine	Vesprin	2	Fluphenazine	Prolixin	20
Chlorpromazine	Thorazine	1		Permitil	
Methoxypromazine	Tentone*	¾	Trifluoperazine	Stelazine	10
Promazine	Sparine	½	Perphenazine	Trilafon	6
			Prochlorperazine	Compazine	4
Piperidyl Subgroup			Thiopropazate	Dartal	4
			Acetophenazine	Tindal	4
Thioridazine	Mellaril	1	Carphenazine	Proketazine	3
Mepazine	Pacatal	½			

*Removed from the market.
†Modified from Schiele, B. C. 1962. Newer drugs for mental illness. Journal of the American Medical Society *181*, 126.

and useful agent with a broad spectrum of action.

Thioridazine (Mellaril), a member of the piperidyl subgroup, is a nearly unique compound; it is the only effective neuroleptic which has almost no extrapyramidal side effects. It has a potency comparable to that of chlorpromazine with a much lower incidence of adverse effects. When given in excessive dosages, however, thioridazine sometimes produces toxic retinitis (largely reversible). For this reason, it is unwise to prescribe over 800 mg. per day of thioridazine. Patients with refractory conditions who require a large dosage of a phenothiazine compound should be given another drug. Occasionally, male patients have experienced inhibition of ejaculation while on thioridazine therapy, but this disappears when the drug is discontinued.

Trifluoperazine (Stelazine) and *perphenazine* (Trilafon), both piperazine compounds, are, like the other members of this subgroup, effective and useful agents. The piperazine agents are characterized by greater milligram potency and milder sedative action than drugs in the other two subgroups. The piperazine drugs occasionally have the effect of activating or alerting some withdrawn and depressed patients, but it is not uncommon for these compounds to produce sedation, particularly when first administered. Both trifluoperazine and perphenazine are potent compounds with a rapid onset of action and wide usefulness. The chief limiting factor for all piperazine compounds is their tendency to produce neurological side effects in susceptible individuals.

Side Effects and Toxicity. The term "side effect" is commonly used to denote any consistent action of a drug that is not a desired therapeutic action. Most side effects are nuisances rather than threats to the efficacy of treatment. However, there is a marked individual variation, and some patients do not tolerate even low doses of certain types of drugs. As a general rule, side effects are readily reversible by reduction of dosage or discontinuation of medication.

Toxic reactions may be defined as abnormal or idiosyncratic responses to a drug that are not part of its usual effects. Toxic reactions may be very serious, but, fortunately, they are quite rare. Here again, individual susceptibility is an important factor. Therefore, a patient who has had a serious toxic reaction to an agent would be wise to avoid similar agents because of the risk of cross sensitivity.

None of the phenothiazine compounds produces sedation of the degree occurring when barbiturates and other sedative agents are used. Chlorpromazine and thioridazine are the most sedative of the phenothiazine compounds now available. However, some untoward effects are common to all drugs of this class. The action of the phenothiazines, which includes effects on the autonomic nervous system, may cause dryness of the mouth, tachycardia, pallor, constipation, blurred vision, unwanted weight gain, edema, and vivid dreams. With high dosage, seizures may ensue; this is especially likely to occur in patients with brain damage or epilepsy. These reactions tend to be dose related, although they develop in some patients more readily than in others.

Although any phenothiazine compound can produce extrapyramidal phenomena in susceptible patients, these reactions are much more readily elicited by the piperazine compounds. These extrapyramidal phenomena may appear as motor restlessness, parkinsonian syndrome, or some type of dyskinesia. The latter may take one of several forms, including opisthotonos, perioral dyskinesia, dystonic movements, torsion spasms, or oculogyric crisis. The dystonia and dyskinesia may be confused with hysteria, acute encephalitis, or other neurological disorders.

Although these extrapyramidal disturbances can be annoying or even alarming to the patient and physician, they are seldom serious. Control is usually easily achieved by using one or a combination of the following methods: (1) lowering the dosage or discontinuing the precipitating drug, (2) adding an antiparkinsonian agent to the regimen, or (3) changing the compound administered to one that rarely produces extrapyramidal disturbances.

Although the neurological side effects which develop early in phenothiazine therapy are readily controlled, there is a type of neurological involvement known as tardive dyskinesia that usually occurs in patients over 55 years of age who have been on neuroleptic drugs for many months. Such patients may develop abnormal movements of the tongue and mouth, usually accompanied by abnormal movements of the trunk and extremities. These do not disappear upon discontinuation of drug therapy, and administration of antiparkinson agents is also without benefit. The etiology of these conditions is not clear, but normal persons and mental patients in comparable age groups who have not received neuroleptic drugs rarely exhibit this type of neurological disorder. Thus, it seems likely that these disorders are related to drug therapy. The physician should therefore regard with caution the appearance of neurological side effects in older patients.

In this connection, it might be well to mention the hazards associated with the use of antiparkinson drugs. Since such agents can dramatically ameliorate acute phenothiazine-induced neurological disturbances, there is a tendency for these drugs to be used too liberally. Whenever possible, it is preferable to control neurological side effects by lowering dosage. This is particularly important when a patient is on long-term therapy, as giving an antiparkinson agent will increase the likelihood of his developing atropine-like side effects (blurred vision, dry mouth, and so on, and even toxic psychosis).

The ability of drugs to induce extrapyramidal symptoms roughly parallels milligram potency (Table 12-1). The single exception to this is thioridazine, an effective and moderately potent compound which rarely produces extrapyramidal side effects. The milligram potency also gives a rough indication of the antiemetic properties of a compound. As a rule, the more potent drugs have much stronger antiemetic properties than do the less potent compounds; thioridazine, however, has no antiemetic activity. Piperazine compounds also have strong antinauseant activity. Among the dimethyl compounds, chlorpromazine and triflupromazine also have this property.

The incidence of postural hypotension (palpitation, dizziness, fainting) and skin disorders (including solar erythema) is higher with use of dimethyl and piperidyl compounds than with use of the piperazine drugs. The same relationship is probable for jaundice and possible for blood dyscrasias.

Blood dyscrasias are the most serious complications that may be associated with the administration of phenothiazine derivatives. Those most commonly occurring are leukopenia and eosinophilia; thrombocytopenic and nonthrombocytopenic purpura and hemolytic and hypoplastic anemia also have been reported. Although none of these disorders occur frequently, the physician must be aware of the possibility that blood dyscrasia will develop after the administration of any phenothiazine compound. However, experience to date indicates that this side reaction is less likely to occur with use of the piperazine compounds.

Jaundice of the obstructive type is an uncommon but well known complication of therapy with chlorpromazine. It has also been reported occasionally with the use of promazine, mepazine, and triflupromazine, but not with thioridazine. A lower incidence of this type of complication appears to be one of the advantages of the piperazine group. Such jaundice has occasionally been reported with prochlorperazine (Compazine), but rarely if at all with other piperazine compounds.

If phenothiazine medication is discontinued at the first sign of jaundice, the condition will clear up within two to four weeks in most patients; however, it may persist for several months in a few patients. Fatalities have occurred, but only rarely.

Serial needle biopsy and liver function studies done on patients who have recovered from phenothiazine-induced jaundice would indicate that the disease is more prolonged histopathologically than it is clinically. Therefore, although many patients have successfully been given phenothiazine compounds after recovery from an attack of jaundice, such a practice may be hazardous. Recurrence of a severe attack of jaundice or permanent liver damage might ensue.

The jaundice that occurs with the use of phenothiazine derivatives should not be confused with that due to the antidepressant hydrazine monoamine oxidase inhibitors. The latter is necrotic in nature and frequently fatal.

The described disparities in patterns of adverse effects explain why a patient may continue to receive phenothiazine therapy and yet may be relieved of certain distressing symptoms by changing from one subgroup of compounds to another. This is often true of patients in whom extrapyramidal symptoms, skin disorders, or hypotension develop. Thus, a patient in whom extrapyramidal reactions develop while he is taking one of the piperazine compounds, such as perphenazine, would not be likely to have these reactions with the piperidyl compound, thioridazine. If this same patient were given another drug of the piperazine group, however, he would probably continue to have such symptoms. Similarly, a patient with a skin reaction or postural hypotension resulting from therapy with one of the dimethyl or piperidyl compounds would probably not have this complication if a drug from the piperazine group were used.

In a patient in whom a blood dyscrasia has developed during treatment with a phenothiazine compound, use of another drug in this class would be hazardous, as cross sensitivity may occur. Danger also exists when patients have a history of phenothiazine-induced jaundice. However, if psychiatric indications warrant desperate measures, one of the more potent piperazine compounds may be tried under close medical supervision.

Most skin disorders occurring with phenothiazine therapy are not serious and usually subside promptly when use of the precipitating drug is discontinued. Often medication with the same compound can be resumed later without recurrence of the reaction. However, since severe solar erythema may develop rapidly, caution is indicated. Patients receiving drugs of the more sedative dimethyl and piperidyl groups may have to wear protective clothing much of the time until they develop a tan.

Although most skin disorders are not serious, physicians should beware of the development of the melanosis syndrome in patients who have been on long-term chlorpromazine therapy. Ever since the phenothiazine drugs became widely used in long-term maintenance therapy, there has been concern that unforeseen chronic toxicities could develop, and it is not surprising that chlorpromazine, the phenothiazine with the longest history of use, should be implicated in such an adverse reaction.

The melanosis syndrome is characterized by a brownish or purplish discoloration of the skin over the exposed areas of the body, principally the cheekbones, nose, forehead, and chin. Fine granular deposits of pigment have also been found in the conjunctiva, the lens, and the cornea of the eye (visible to slit-lamp examination). These deposits tend to form in a stellate pattern which may be seen as a lens opacity in severe cases. Vision is surprisingly unaffected unless the opacity is far advanced. Some patients have been observed to have only skin pigmentation, some to have only eye pigmentation, and others to have both. A few patients affected with this syndrome have been known to die suddenly, apparently from acute heart failure. Upon autopsy, extensive similar pigmentation has been found in the parenchymal organs. The condition develops very slowly, and there have been reports that it may be reversible, receding very gradually over a period of months after drug therapy has been discontinued.

Although a thorough and satisfying explanation of the etiology of the melanosis syndrome is not available, it is clear that the pigmentation is associated with long-term, high-dosage chlorpromazine therapy. Exposure to light may also be a factor. However, the most important variable seems to be individual susceptibility, as many patients who have been treated with high dosages of chlorpromazine over long periods of time have not been affected.

While it is apparent that chlorpromazine is the drug involved in this adverse reaction, there is no assurance that other phenothiazines may not be capable of producing similar changes. In patients who develop skin or eye changes, chlorpromazine should be discontinued at once, and, ideally, no other phenothiazine should be given. However, it seems logical that if phenothiazine therapy is a necessity, those phenothiazines which do not characteristically induce skin reactions and light sensitivity might be tolerated. These belong to the piperazine subgroup and include compounds such as prochlorperazine, trifluoperazine, perphenazine, and fluphenazine (Prolixin, Permitil). It would not seem logical to use the more sedative phenothiazines such as thioridazine, triflupromazine, and promazine, which might not be as safe. It might also be well to have affected patients avoid excessive exposure to sunlight, particularly for the first few weeks after chlorpromazine has been discontinued.

Special Precautions. Precautions are indicated for some patients. The older patient generally can tolerate only low doses of the major tranquilizers, for toxic, confusional states readily develop when high or ordinary doses are given. Postural hypotension may occur in any susceptible person, but it is more likely to result in injury from falling with the aged patient. Hypotension is also a potential danger in patients with acute coronary disease. In persons with epilepsy or brain damage, seizures may develop or increase in frequency. Major tranquilizers may potentiate analgesia in patients under heavy sedation or in a coma from alcohol or other drugs. Patients with kidney impairment should be closely supervised and, in those with liver disorders, the risk of jaundice is believed to be increased.

In most patients, no noticeable withdrawal symptoms occur after use of the major tranquilizers is discontinued. However, double-blind studies do indicate that some persons will be restless and complain of mild abdominal discomfort for a few days when administration of large doses of a phenothiazine drug is stopped abruptly. Addiction or drug dependency has not been noted as a result of the use of major tranquilizers.

Deaths attributable to these compounds are quite rare. Most deaths have occurred in association with blood dyscrasia and a few with jaundice. Asphyxiation during a convulsive seizure has been reported, as has death from vascular collapse. In a few instances, mostly in mental hospitals, toxic encephalopathy with hyperpyrexia has resulted in fatalities. Occasionally, patients who appeared to be physically healthy have unexpectedly been found dead, and in many cases routine autopsy has not provided an explanation. Most of these patients have been on long-term, high-dosage therapy. Although these deaths are largely unexplained, some investigators have reported histopathologic changes in the cardiac muscle which may have resulted in cardiac failure.

In spite of the facts that there are hazards to the administration of major tranquilizers and that deaths have occurred, the overall death rate in psychiatric hospitals does not appear to have increased since the widespread use of these drugs began. It may even have declined, since there is less need for other physiological therapies with their attendant risks.

Efficacy. Davis, who reviewed numerous controlled studies comparing various phenothiazines and phenobarbital to placebo, concluded that the majority of the phenothiazine compounds are clearly more effective than placebo in the treatment of schizophrenia (see Table 12-2). Unexpectedly, one-fourth

of the studies surveyed failed to show a difference between chlorpromazine and placebo therapy, but the negative chlorpromazine studies suffered from various design defects (low dosage, small sample, short treatment period) that reduced the likelihood of finding significant differences when such differences existed. For example, the majority of the negative studies used fixed dosages in the range of 75 to 400 mg chlorpromazine daily. In contrast, studies that allowed for a flexible dosage schedule, with some patients receiving a dosage as high as 800 to 1600 mg chlorpromazine daily, all showed

TABLE 12–2. Double-Blind Placebo-Controlled Studies of the Efficacy of the Tranquilizing Drugs on Hospitalized Psychotic Patients, Comparing the Number of Studies in Which the Drug Was More Effective than Placebo Versus the Number of Studies Finding the Drug Equal to Placebo in Effectiveness*

DRUG		NO. OF STUDIES IN WHICH	
GENERIC NAME	TRADE NAME	DRUG MORE EFFECTIVE THAN PLACEBO	DRUG EQUAL TO PLACEBO
Chlorpromazine	Thorazine Largactil	36	11
Triflupromazine	Vesprin Vespral	5	1
Perphenazine	Trilafon Fentazine	4	0
Prochlorperazine	Compazine Stemetil	3	1
Trifluoperazine	Stelazine	10	1
Fluphenazine	Prolixin Permitil	5	0
Thioridazine	Mellaril	6	0
Mepazine	Pacatal Pecazine	0	4
Promazine	Sparine	2	3
Phenobarbital	—	0	3

*From Davis, J. M. 1965. Efficacy of tranquilizing and antidepressant drugs. Archives of General Psychiatry *13*, 552.

chlorpromazine to be superior to placebo.

Davis also surveyed the literature on controlled studies that compared various phenothiazine compounds and phenobarbital to chlorpromazine (see Table 12-3). These studies suggest that triflupromazine, perphenazine, prochlorperazine, trifluoperazine, thioridazine, and fluphenazine are comparable in efficacy to chlorpromazine and that promazine and mepazine are considerably less effective than chlorpromazine. A survey of studies comparing reserpine to chlorpromazine showed chlorpromazine to be clearly superior, although reserpine was more effective than placebo.

Since most of the above studies indicating the efficacy of the phenothiazine drugs were done on chronically ill schizophrenic patients, the question remained as to their efficacy in acute cases. That they also can bring about rapid symptom remission in acute cases was shown in a well designed study involving more than 400 patients and conducted cooperatively by nine public and private hospitals under the sponsorship of the Psychopharmacology Service Center of the National Institute of Mental Health (Cole, 1964). The population was notable in that it was composed exclusively of newly admitted, acute schizophrenics who were selected by very rigid criteria. The study was double blind and was conducted for six weeks; the patients were randomly assigned to one of four treatment groups: chlorpromazine, thioridazine, fluphenazine, or placebo. This group of investigators found that the effect of the active drugs was superior to that of placebo and that, among themselves, the drugs differed principally in the pattern of side effects produced. There were only one to three treatment failures in each drug group, but in the placebo group, there were 36 treatment failures. Ninety-five per cent of the drug-treated patients showed some degree of improvement within six

TABLE 12-3. Comparative Effectiveness of Phenothiazine Drugs Compared to Chlorpromazine as a Standard Using Controlled Studies, Indicating Number of Studies in Which a Drug Was Found More Effective, Equally Effective, or Less Effective Than Chlorpromazine[†]

DRUG GENERIC NAME	TRADE NAME	NUMBER OF STUDIES IN WHICH:		
		DRUG MORE EFFECTIVE THAN CHLORPROMAZINE	DRUG EQUAL TO CHLORPROMAZINE	CHLORPROMAZINE MORE EFFECTIVE
Mepazine	Pacatal	0	1*	3
Promazine	Sparine	0	1*	4
Triflupromazine	Vesprin	0	9	0
Perphenazine	Trilafon	0	5	0
Prochlorperazine	Compazine	0	7	0
Trifluoperazine	Stelazine	0	6	0
Thioridazine	Mellaril	0	7	0
Fluphenazine	Prolixin	0	5	0
Phenobarbital		0	0	6

*These studies were just short of reaching statistical significance which would show chlorpromazine more effective than the drug in question.

[†]Adapted from Davis, J. M. 1965. Efficacy of tranquilizing and antidepressant drugs. Archives of General Psychiatry *13*, 552.

weeks, 75 per cent showed either marked or moderate improvement, and 46 per cent were so much improved that they were rated as having no symptoms or only borderline illness. In contrast, only 23 per cent of the placebo group showed marked or moderate improvement, although over half of these patients showed some degree of betterment. Not only were these phenothiazines generally effective over a large population, but a variety of symptoms and behaviors were affected (for example, thought disturbance, paranoid symptoms, social withdrawal, delusions, agitation, anxiety, careless appearance). Thus, the phenothiazines seem to be effective in achieving rapid symptom remission in acute schizophrenia as well as being efficacious in the management of more chronic cases.

Maintenance Therapy. There is considerable evidence that long-term maintenance therapy with major tranquilizers can assist patients to live with reasonable success outside the hospital, even though they may not be completely well. In other words, continued treatment with a major neuroleptic compound is necessary to prevent relapse in many individuals. Among the many studies which support this contention is one by Schiele and coworkers (Figure 12-3). In a double-blind study comparing the then-new compounds thioridazine and trifluoperazine to chlorpromazine and placebo, these investigators found that patients receiving placebo deteriorated rapidly. All placebo patients were chronic hospitalized schizophrenics who had improved and been maintained for a year or more on chlorpromazine or another phenothiazine. Engelhardt and coworkers, who followed a large series of patients discharged from mental hospitals, also found that continued treatment with an effective phenothiazine like chlorpromazine was far more valuable in preventing relapse than treatment with a placebo or with a less effective drug like promazine.

Maintenance therapy with the pheno-

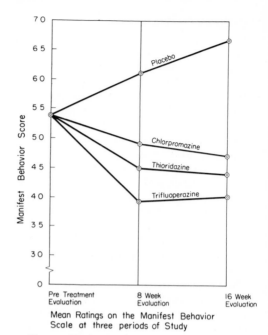

Mean Ratings on the Manifest Behavior Scale at three periods of Study

Figure 12-3. Mean ratings on the Manifest Behavior Scale at three periods of study. (Higher rating = clinical worsening.) (From Schiele, B. C., Vestre, N. D., and Stein, K. E. 1961. A comparison of thioridazine, trifluoperazine, chlorpromazine, and placebo: a double-blind controlled study on the treatment of chronic, hospitalized, schizophrenic patients. Quarterly Review of Clinical and Experimental Psychopathology and Quarterly Review of Psychiatry and Neurology 22, 151.)

thiazines does present some problems, however, the most important being the tendency of patients placed on maintenance therapy to discontinue their medication. For this reason, the physician should prescribe the drug which the patient tolerates best and adjust the dosage as finely as possible to reduce annoying side effects. This should be done before the patient is discharged from the hospital.

Although some patients may require treatment with a neuroleptic drug indefinitely, others are able to discontinue these drugs without relapse. For this reason, and because long-continued maintenance therapy involves some risk, as indicated in the section on side effects, it is desirable to discontinue medication whenever it is not needed. Unfortunately, the physician has very poor guidelines in this situation. The problem is further complicated by what is known as the "lag effect.' Most patients who relapse following discontinuation of phenothiazine therapy do not experience a return of symptoms until several weeks or months have elapsed. Keeping this in mind, the physician may proceed somewhat as follows: if the patient has maintained improvement over a period of several months, a cautious trial without the drug may be undertaken. The medication should be reduced gradually over a period of one to two months. During this time, and for the next few months, the patient should be seen periodically; the physician and the patient's family should be alert for the possibility of delayed relapse and medication should be resumed at full dosage if symptoms begin to reappear. The role of the family is important because, unfortunately, most individuals who have had a serious psychosis do not clearly recognize the return of their symptoms, or at least they do not seem to be able to ask for help. Once again, it should be emphasized that the physician's main problem is to persuade patients to remain on the medication. Even though the nonpsychiatric physician may not actively treat psychotic individuals, he is likely to have a significant number of regular patients who have had some kind of psychiatric disorder and for whom maintenance therapy may be indicated.

THE THIOXANTHENES

This class of neuroleptic compounds has some similarity to the phenothiazines in spite of pharmacological and structural differences. The thioxanthene nucleus contains a carbon atom instead of the nitrogen atom found in the central ring of the phenothiazine nucleus. Two thioxanthenes will be discussed: chlorprothixene (Taractan) and thiothixene (Navane). (See Figure 12-4.)

Chlorprothixene has been available since 1960. This drug has significant sedative properties and is viewed by many as a moderately effective major neuroleptic which also has some antidepressant activity. The latter claim is not surprising in view of the fact that, structurally, it is also somewhat similar to amitriptyline (Elavil), one of the tricyclic antidepressant agents.

A variety of other thioxanthene compounds are receiving clinical evaluation and at least one, Navane, has been introduced commercially. It is an effective neuroleptic with moderately high milligram potency (comparable to that of the mid-range of the piperazine phenothiazines) useful in the treatment of acute or chronic schizophrenia. Its side effect profile appears to be favorable. Extrapyramidal symptoms occur with moderate intensity, as is usually the case with compounds which have a pipera-

STRUCTURE	GENERIC NAME	TRADE NAME
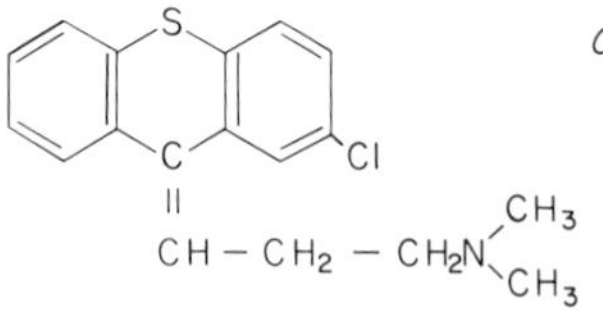	*Clorprothixene*	Taractan
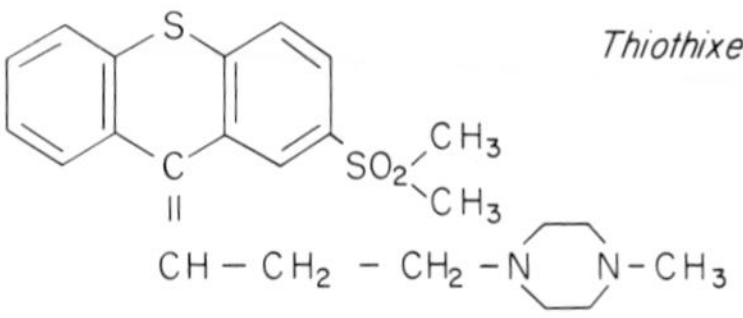	*Thiothixene*	Navane

Figure 12–4. The thioxanthene neuroleptics.

zine side chain. However, this drug produces very little drowsiness, and, in some patients it has been reported to have an alerting or activating effect. Again, similar action has occasionally been reported in other compounds with piperazine side chains.

THE BUTYROPHENONES

These drugs are major neuroleptic agents which are chemically distinct from the phenothiazine class (see Figure 12-5). One of the butyrophenones, haloperidol (Haldol), has been used in medical practice for some years in Europe. Clinical opinion and controlled studies, including a few done in the United States, show it to be an effective compound. It became commercially available in the United States in the spring of 1967. This drug has a higher milligram potency than any of the phenothiazine drugs, and it has very little tendency to produce sedation, skin disturbances, or hypotension, side effects which are commonly associated with the low-potency sedative phenothiazines. In common with other compounds which have a high milligram potency, its use is associated with a high incidence of neurological side effects. How it will compare in overall efficacy with the various phenothiazine agents remains to be seen. In any event, it does appear to be of value in treatment-resistant schizophrenics and other patients who have failed to benefit from phenothiazine therapy.

ANTIANXIETY AGENTS (MINOR TRANQUILIZERS)

Whereas the major tranquilizers produce a type of emotional calmness with relatively little sedation, the antianxiety agents have a mild sedative effect. The major tranquilizers are efficacious in the treatment of disturbed psychotic patients, while the effectiveness of the minor tranquilizers is generally limited to psychoneurotic conditions and common nervous tension. The major tranquilizers are capable of producing a reversible extrapyramidal syndrome characterized by rigidity, tremors, and drooling, while the antianxiety agents are free of such side effects. The incidence of side reactions is relatively high in major tranquilizer therapy, and dangerous toxicities have been reported; in therapy with the antianxiety agents, the incidence of side reactions is low and dangerous reactions very rare. Habituation is virtually unknown with the major tranquilizers, but it can be a problem with the minor tranquilizers. Some of the antianxiety agents have muscle-relaxing properties which may contribute to their effectiveness, and others have a mild antihistaminic effect. Aside from these effects, and in contrast to promotional claims, most show little evidence of any specific action. Indeed, the chief advantage claimed for the antianxiety agents over the older sedatives like phenobarbital is that the newer drugs produce less sedation than the older agents.

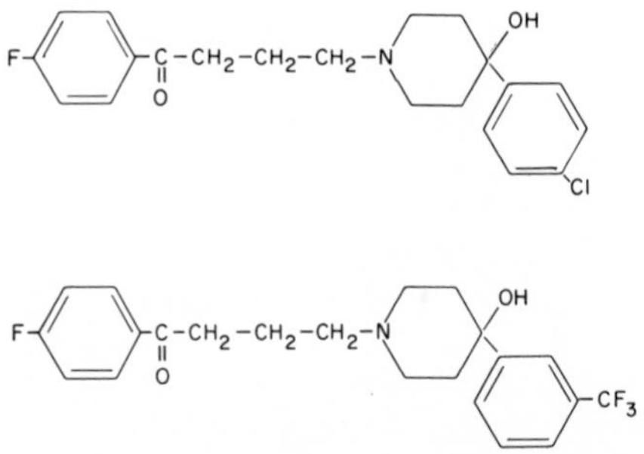

Figure 12–5. The butyrophenone neuroleptics.

Any compound that will relieve anxiety may be useful in the symptomatic treatment of neuroses and anxiety states or as an adjunctive therapy. These compounds may be particularly useful in mild depressions and in psychosomatic disturbances. Many such illnesses are of a self-limiting nature, and it is usually not necessary for the patient to continue the use of antianxiety agents over any extended period of time. Many patients find them especially helpful during periods of stress. Because of their relative safety, many physicians prefer to try them first in any ambulatory case or when in doubt. Since the use of these agents generally presents no problem, and since most patients have no adverse reaction to them, there is a tendency on the part of both patient and physician to overuse these compounds.

In spite of the wide use and great popularity of the antianxiety agents, less is known about their efficacy and specific indications than is known about the major tranquilizers. It is much more difficult to conduct and evaluate controlled studies in an ambulatory population of psychoneurotic or anxious patients than it is in a population of hospitalized, seriously ill patients. In addition, changes brought about by the antianxiety agents are less marked and therefore more difficult to measure than are changes wrought by the more potent major tranquilizers. In spite of the dearth of objective and scientific evidence, however, the great popularity of the minor tranquilizers supports the contention that they are of value in the relief of many nervous symptoms.

MECHANISM OF ACTION

Claims have been made for a true tranquilizing action of the diol-carbamates, but little evidence has been obtained for the kind and degree of action exhibited by the major tranquilizers. Meprobamate (Miltown, Equanil) and chlordiazepoxide (Librium) exhibit striking activity on polysynaptic reflexes of the spinal cord which suggests that their main mode of action is that of reducing skeletal muscle tension. Reduction of muscle tension decreases the number of afferent proprioceptive impulses that tend to aggravate existing tension and anxiety. This concept is confirmed by the fact that meprobamate is useful in treating tension headaches. Meprobamate has little effect in migraine headache and has little if any effect in the treatment of psychomotor agitation. In very high dosages, it simultaneously impairs motor and intellectual function, as do the barbiturates.

The mechanism of action of the diphenylmethanes is even more difficult to resolve. However, some evidence is available that use of benactyzine (Suavitil), for example, results in a significant block of conditioned responses. The compound has strong anticholinergic activity, but such activity, including the role of the autonomics in conditioned behavior, still needs to be elucidated.

INDIVIDUAL COMPOUNDS

The antianxiety agents are listed in Figures 12-6, 12-7, and 12-8. Those in common use are meprobamate, chlordiazepoxide, and its two analogues, diazepam (Valium) and oxazepam (Serax).

Meprobamate, the first minor tranquilizer to be introduced, has received extremely wide acceptance. Although the overall toxicity of the drug is low, it may induce the following: skin rash, chills and fever, gastrointestinal disturbances, paradoxical excitement, and acute nonthrombocytopenic purpura. Aplastic anemia has been reported. Skin eruptions may be maculopapular, erythematous, urticarial, or any combination of these. Less commonly, they may be vesicular or petechial.

Overdosage can result in marked drowsiness or even coma, slurred speech, and ataxia in susceptible persons. Other persons can take excessive doses without developing any of these reactions. Drug dependency and

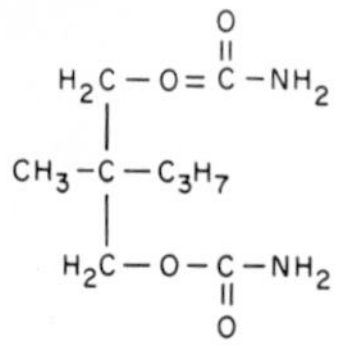

Meprobamate — Miltown / Equanil

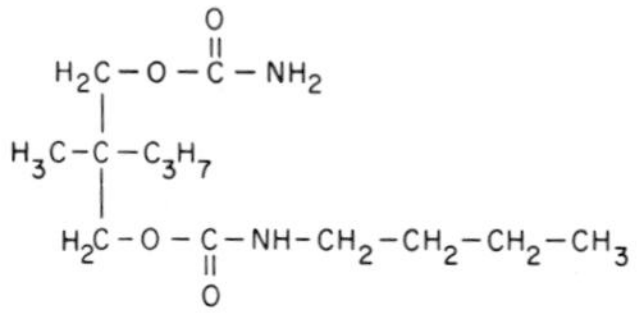

Tybamate — Solacen

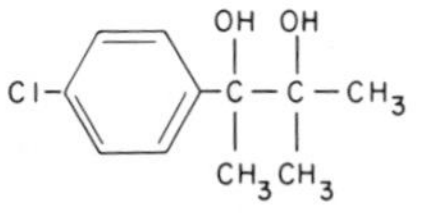

Phenaglycodol — Ultran

Figure 12-6. Antianxiety agents, I.

addiction are possible. Withdrawal symptoms including convulsions have been observed. Suicidal death is possible, but this occurs only with massive overdosage.

Chlordiazepoxide is a much more potent compound than meprobamate and it is also a muscle relaxant. It has wide patient acceptance and has become the most popular single psychotropic agent, replacing meprobamate which once held this position.

In susceptible persons, overdosage may result in drowsiness, ataxia, or con-

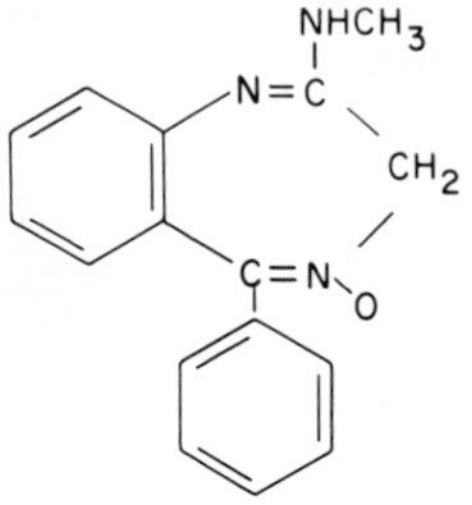

Chlordiazepoxide — Librium

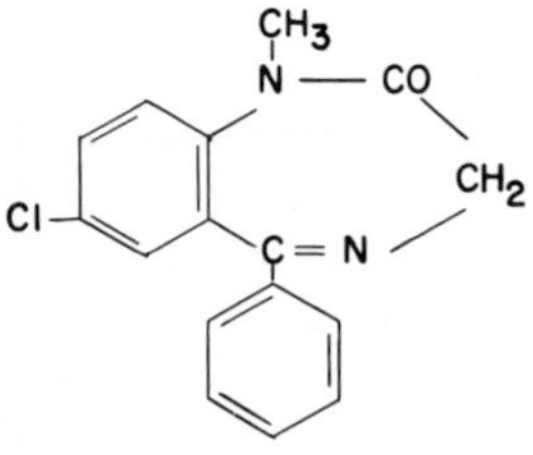

Diazepam — Valium

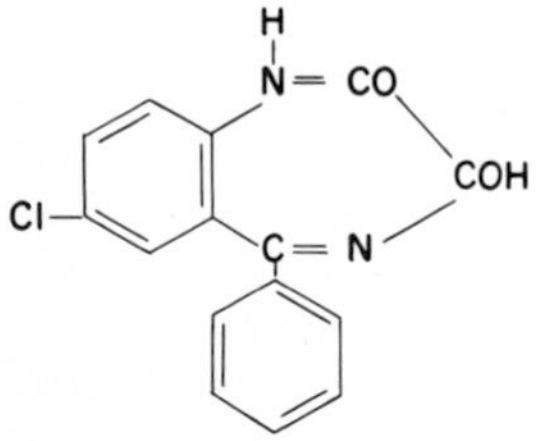

Oxazepam — Serax

Figure 12-7. Antianxiety agents, II.

Diphenylmethane Group

STRUCTURE	GENERIC NAME	TRADE NAME

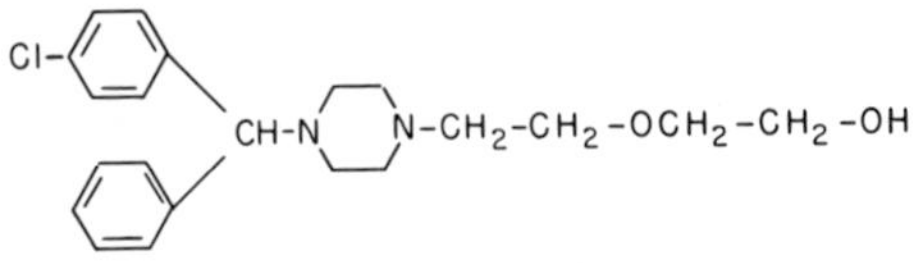

Hydroxyzine — Atarax, Vistaril

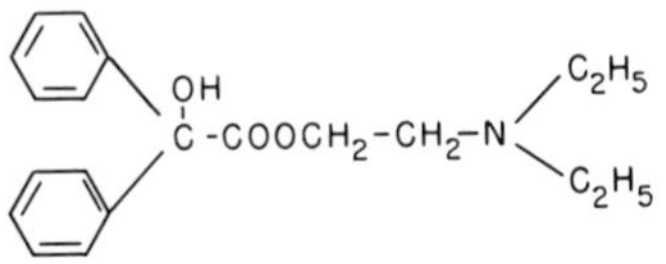

Benactyzine — Suavitil

Figure 12–8. Antianxiety Agents, III. (Adapted from Benson, W. M., and Schiele, B. C. 1962. Tranquilizing and Antidepressive Drugs. Courtesy of Charles C Thomas, Publisher, Springfield, Illinois.)

fusion. Patients occasionally suffer from syncope, paradoxical excitement or rage, skin eruptions, nausea, constipation, menstrual irregularity, or altered libido. On rare occasions, blood dyscrasia or jaundice has been associated with the use of chlordiazepoxide. Withdrawal reactions may occur if large doses are given.

Diazepam and oxazepam are recently introduced analogues of chlordiazepoxide (see Figure 12-7). These agents have the same general pattern of indications and contraindications as chlordiazepoxide. Diazepam is somewhat more sedative than its parent compound.

Benactyzine (see Figure 12-8), when given alone, has not been very effective in the treatment of anxiety. It is capable of producing atropine-like effects including dryness of the mouth, metallic taste, blurred vision, inhibition of accommodation, dizziness, giddiness, ataxia, nervousness, palpitation, nausea, diarrhea, general apathy, and indifference. Probably the chief use of benactyzine today is in combination with meprobamate as Deprol. This medication is being promoted as an antidepressant. In addition to producing the side effects of meprobamate, Deprol is also potentially capable of producing some of the just-mentioned atropine-

like effects. These are not very likely, however, since the amount of benactyzine in the combination tablet is small.

Hydroxyzine (Atarax) (see Figure 12-8) has both sedative and antispasmodic action, which makes it useful as a calming agent. It is advocated for treatment of cardiac arrhythmias, but its efficacy for this use needs further evaluation. The toxicity and incidence of side reactions with this drug are low. Apparently it has little or no tendency to cause habituation and, therefore, is of value when this effect becomes a potential problem.

Other minor tranquilizers include phenaglycodol (Ultran), chlormezanone (Trancopal), promoxolane (Dimethylane), emylcamate (Striatran), mephenoxalone (Trepidone), buclizine (Softran), and hydroxyphenamate (Listica).

STIMULANTS, ENERGIZERS, AND ANTIDEPRESSANTS*

A number of drugs are known to have a direct stimulant effect on central

---

*Part of this material on antidepressants was presented at the American Psychiatric Association meeting, May 11, 1967. It is reproduced with permission.

nervous system activity, some of these acting most intensely on the cortex, others on the medullary centers, and others mainly on the spinal cord. In large doses they produce convulsions, the nature of which is determined by the predominant site of action of the drug. Members of this group of drugs are used to counteract the inhibition or depression of the central nervous system that results from overdosage with anesthetic, hypnotic, or other sedative drugs. Direct stimulants of this nature are often termed analeptics, and they have also been used therapeutically to induce epileptiform convulsions and in attempts to relieve psychiatric depression (of mood) or "nervous exhaustion." None of these direct stimulants, however, has proved really effective in relieving psychiatric depression, and they tend to aggravate the insomnia, anxiety, tension, and motor agitation that frequently accompany the depression of mood. However, there are two distinct classes of drugs which have significant antidepressant action and which are useful in the treatment of severe depression. These are the tricyclic antidepressants and the monoamine oxidase inhibitors.

THE TRICYCLIC ANTIDEPRESSANTS

The tricyclic or imipramine-like antidepressants are so designated because of their central structure, which has three rings. In this way these drugs are structurally similar to the phenothiazines (compare Figure 12-1 with Figures 12-9 and 12-10). Four tricyclic antidepressants, namely, imipramine (Tofranil), desipramine (Pertofrane, Norpramin), amitriptyline (Elavil), and nortriptyline (Aventyl), are available in clinical practice in the United States. Imipramine, an iminodibenzyl compound which was once thought to be a potential antihistaminic agent, is the best known. In the early 1950's, when the usefulness of the phenothiazines became known, imipramine was studied as a possible antipsychotic agent because of its structural similarity to the phenothiazines. A Swiss clinical investigator, R. Kuhn, must be credited with recognizing the antidepressant nature of imipramine. He observed that this drug was not nearly as effective as chlorpromazine in the treatment of schizophrenia, but that patients with depressive symptoms showed elevation of mood and general improvement. This clinical action was not predictable from the available pharmacology and animal data, and, as is frequently the case, this significant clinical advance was made possible by the observations of an astute clinician.

Imipramine. Imipramine is generally considered to be reasonably safe and reasonably effective in a wide

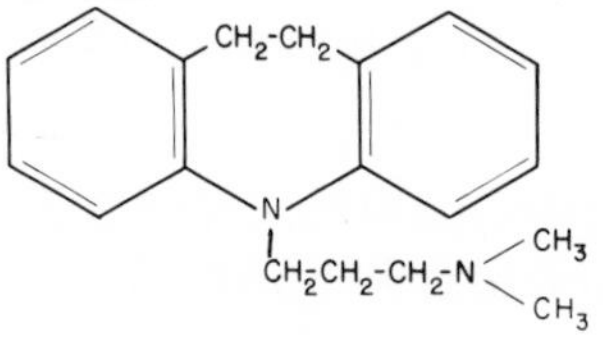

Imipramine   Tofranil

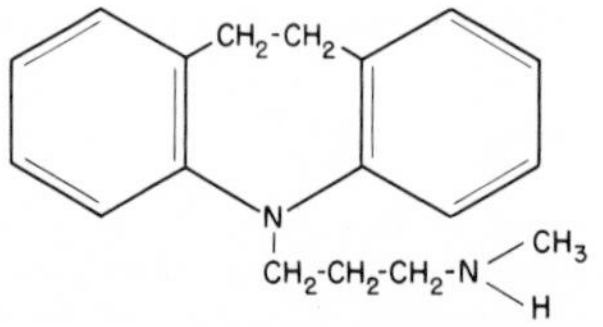

Desipramine   Norpramin

Pertofrane

Figure 12–9. Tricyclic antidepressants, I. Imipramine and its demethylated derivative.

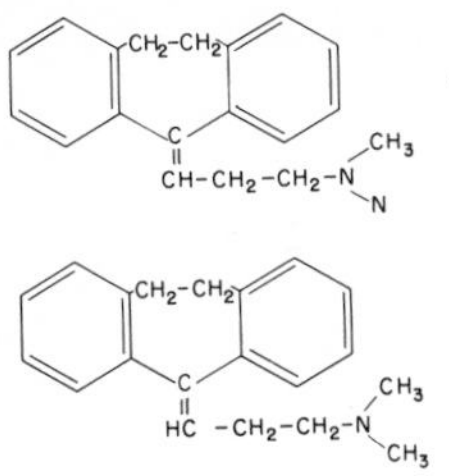

Figure 12–10. Tricyclic antidepressants, II. Amitriptyline and its demethylated derivative.

variety of clinical depressions, including some which are severe. It is widely used in clinical practice, and, since it was the first of the tricyclic antidepressant compounds to be discovered, it has been more extensively studied than the others. In controlled studies of imipramine versus placebo (see Table 12-4), patients have demonstrably benefited from imipramine therapy, although in some studies a superiority to placebo has not been evident. Some patients do not respond to imipramine at all, even after extensive treatment with high dosages, and other patients respond with an observable but not marked degree of improvement. As Klerman and Cole have stated, some improved patients were not sufficiently improved to satisfy either the patient or the phy-

sician. Some patients respond to imipramine therapy rapidly by showing improvement within few days, and others, while responding well, do not show improvement for several weeks. For this reason, it is generally conceded that the patient should be given a minimum of three weeks' therapy, assuming the drug is reasonably well tolerated. If a patient fails to improve on adequate dosage after three and one-half to four weeks, the physician can be fairly certain that the patient will not benefit from this regimen. It should be noted, however, that early response to imipramine therapy is generally a good prognostic sign.

Adequate dosage is important, and the manufacturer's suggested dosage is usually a good guide with drugs of this type. A dosage of 250 to 300 mg daily is indicated for the average patient. In order to evaluate the patient's individual sensitivity and lessen the possibility of unusual side effects, it is wise to begin administration of the drug at a lower dosage, perhaps 150 mg daily, for the first few days. This precaution is a wise one to take with all the tricyclic antidepressant compounds.

If a patient responds favorably to imipramine, he should stay on a maintenance dosage for about two months

TABLE 12–4. Effectiveness of Antidepressants Over Placebo in Depressive Patients*

| | | NUMBER OF STUDIES IN WHICH: | |
| | DRUG | DRUG MORE EFFECTIVE THAN PLACEBO | PLACEBO EQUALLY EFFECTIVE |
GENERIC NAME	TRADE NAME		
Amitriptyline	Elavil	4	1
Imipramine	Tofranil	17	6
Iproniazid	Marsilid	2	1
Isocarboxazid	Marplan	3	2
Phenelzine	Nardil	3	2
Nialamide	Niamid	1	1
Tranylcypromine	Parnate	2	0
Amphetamine		0	2

*From Davis, J. M. 1965. Efficacy of tranquilizing and antidepressant drugs. Archives of General Psychiatry *13*, 552.

TABLE 12–5. Treatments of Depression Compared
With Imipramine as a Standard*

	NO. STUDIES WHERE:		
TREATMENT	TREATMENT INFERIOR TO IMIPRAMINE	TREATMENT EQUAL TO IMIPRAMINE	TREATMENT BETTER THAN IMIPRAMINE
ECT	0	0	3
Phenelzine (Nardil)	2	3	0
Isocarboxazid (Marplan)	2	1	0
Tranylcypromine (Parnate)	0	2	0
Amitriptyline (Elavil)	0	2	3
Thioridazine (Mellaril)	0	1	0
Chlorpromazine (Thorazine)	0	1	0

*From Davis, J. M. 1965. Efficacy of tranquilizing and antidepressant drugs. Archives of General Psychiatry 13, 552.

after clinical symptoms have subsided. Dosage should then be reduced gradually, and the physician should be alert for possible signs of relapse for an additional two months.

Amitriptyline. Amitriptyline is similar to imipramine in its general mode of action, its indications, and its dosage range. It has slightly greater sedative effects than imipramine, and controlled studies comparing it to imipramine have indicated that it produces somewhat more favorable results (see Table 12-5). However, both drugs are viewed with favor by medical practitioners.

Desipramine and Nortriptyline. Desipramine and nortriptyline are demethylated analogues of imipramine and amitriptyline, respectively (see Figures 12-9 and 12-10). Demethylation is believed to be one of the first metabolic changes undergone by imipramine and amitriptyline; hence, it would appear that their demethylated analogues should have a more rapid onset of action, offsetting one of the chief disadvantages of the parent substances. A slow onset of action coupled with the uncertainty of success is a bad combination in the treatment of patients who are miserable, severely depressed, and potentially suicidal. Animal studies provide some evidence that desipramine and nortriptyline do possess a more rapid onset of action, but clinical studies have not given these drugs any clear advantage, although, because of their recent introduction, this point is not entirely certain. The few controlled studies comparing desipramine and nortriptyline to placebo or to imipramine also show no clear evidence of a more rapid onset of action or of any greater efficacy.

In general, the indications, side effect pattern, and administration of desipramine and nortriptyline are similar to those of imipramine. However, desipramine is considered to be slightly more potent than imipramine, and nortriptyline appreciably more potent than amitriptyline, so that the dosage of the demethylated analogues are correspondingly smaller than the dosages of the parent compounds.

Side Effects and Toxicity. Since the tricyclic antidepressants are structurally similar to the phenothiazines, it is not surprising that the pattern of side effects and toxicity associated with them is also similar. Atropine-like side effects (dryness of the mouth, constipation, tachycardia, and, less commonly, blurring of vision) are among the less serious reactions associated with these drugs. Very rarely, paralytic ileus and urinary retention or aggravation of glaucoma occurs. A mild parkinsonian syndrome is a possible neurological side effect, but patients are more likely to have tremors, dysarthria, ataxia, unsteady gait, and mental confusion. The antiparkinson drugs may add to these atropine-like effects and these should be used cautiously if at all with the tricyclic compounds. Dizziness, nausea, and paradoxical excitement may also ensue. Insomnia has been reported, but drowsiness is more common; skin reactions have occasionally been seen. In many patients, increased perspiration is a prominent side effect with the tricyclic antidepressants.

As with the phenothiazine compounds, the incidence of annoying side reactions is high, but serious toxic reactions are rare. Among such toxic reactions is blood dyscrasia, or jaundice. The jaundice which occurs with these drugs, however, is of the cholestatic type, similar to the jaundice that occurs with the phenothiazines, and it should not be confused with the more serious liver disorders associated with the monoamine oxidase inhibitors. If any of these reactions should appear, therapy must be discontinued at once.

Postural hypotension is another and commoner problem associated with the tricyclic antidepressants, but it is usually not serious, although it can be a limiting factor in the use of these compounds in patients with cardiac disorders and in geriatric patients. The possibility of a fall is much more hazardous in aged than in young patients. In spite of potential annoying side effects and the more dangerous toxic reactions, however, these drugs are well tolerated by the average patient, and, as most of these reactions are dose related, they usually are not severe enough to interfere significantly with treatment.

THE MONOAMINE OXIDASE INHIBITORS

The monoamine oxidase (MAO) inhibitors act by stimulating the central nervous system. They do not have the direct excitative effect on neural cells which characterizes direct central nervous system stimulants like the amphetamines. Rather, the MAO inhibitors have a predominantly indirect stimulating action and are mediated through changes in the availability of neurohumor substances. One mechanism of action postulated for drugs belonging to this class is the inhibition of the enzyme monoamine oxidase, which would result in increased brain levels of various biogenic amines such as the catecholamines. Other mechanisms of action are also possible, however, even though the compounds belonging to this group have become widely known by the term MAO inhibitors.

The MAO inhibitors fall into two classes, the hydrazines and the nonhydrazines. Drugs belonging to the latter class combine direct and indirect actions and therefore can be designated as bimodal stimulants (see Figures 12-11 and 12-12).

Hydrazine MAO Inhibitors. Iproniazid (Marsilid), which was first introduced in 1951 for the treatment of tuberculosis, caused hyperactivity and euphoria and occasional short-lived psychotic episodes in the patients to whom it was given. Several years later, this drug was tried in the treatment of psychiatric depressions with favorable results. It was at one time commercially available in the United States, but its toxic effect on the liver caused it to be withdrawn in this country, although it is still available in many other countries, including Canada, where it is considered to be one of the most efficacious drugs of its type.

The fact that iproniazid was known to be an inhibitor of MAO and that it was also effective in the treatment of serious depression led to increased research activity concerning the physiological and chemical changes associated with the depressive state and the possible benefits of antidepressant drugs. It seemed likely that this mechanism of action could be used to explore the pathologi-

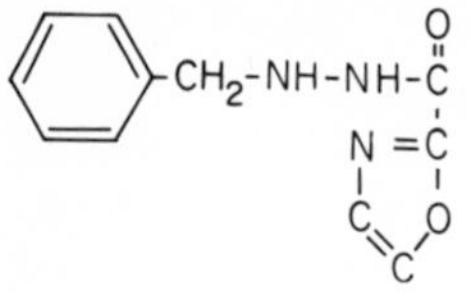

Isocarboxazid — Marplan

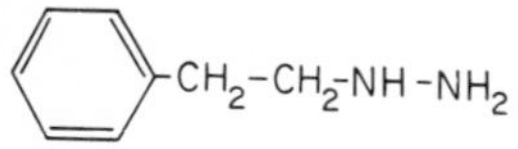

Phenelzine — Nardil

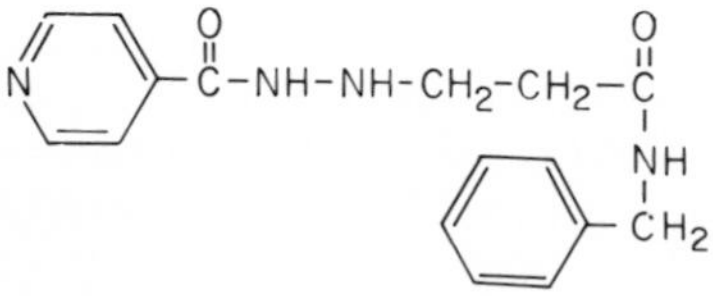

Nialamide — Niamid

Figure 12–11. The hydrazine monoamine oxidase inhibitors. (From Benson, W. M., and Schiele, B. C. 1962. *Tranquilizing and Antidepressive Drugs.* Courtesy of Charles C Thomas, Publisher, Springfield, Illinois. p. 52.)

cal physiology associated with depression and to shed light on the action of other antidepressant agents. The flurry of research which followed led to the development of many compounds which inhibited MAO. A number of such drugs were subsequently made available in the United States. Among them were four hydrazine compounds: pheniprazine (Catron), phenelzine (Nardil), isocarboxazid (Marplan), and nialamide (Niamid). Pheniprazine was withdrawn from the market because it has a toxicity similar to that of iproniazid, but the other three drugs remain available (see Figure 12-11).

The disadvantages of the hydrazine MAO inhibitors include their slow action, which frequently requires two to three weeks before clinical improvement becomes apparent, and the difficulty with which dosage is regulated because of their cumulative effect.

Of the three hydrazine compounds, phenelzine appears to be the most effective (see Table 12-5). This compound is the most similar chemically to tranylcypromine and the amphetamines (see Figure 12-12). Isocarboxazid is probably the next most effective, and nialamide the least.

The Nonhydrazine MAO Inhibitors. Tranylcypromine (Parnate) is the only antidepressant agent which has both a reasonable potency in the relief of serious depression and a rapid onset of action. It also seems probable that there is a small but significant number of pa-

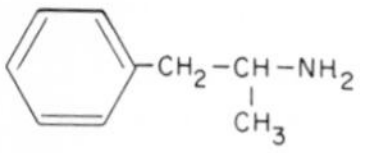

Amphetamine — Benzedrine

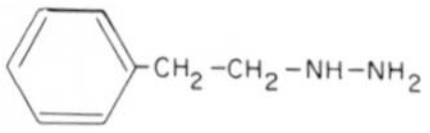

Phenelzine — Nardil

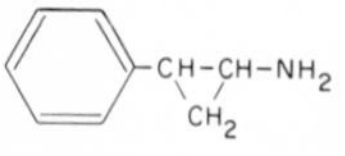

Tranylcypromine — Parnate

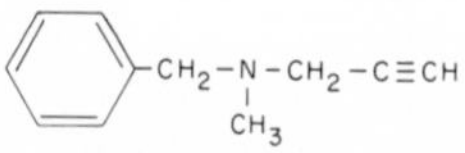

Pargyline — Eutonyl

Figure 12–12. The structural similarity between amphetamine (a direct central nervous system stimulant), phenelzine (a hydrazine monoamine oxidase inhibitor), and the two nonhydrazine MAO inhibitors.

tients who respond to MAO inhibitors and not to other antidepressant treatments such as electroconvulsive therapy, and, for these patients, tranylcypromine is frequently the most useful drug. Most patients who respond to tranylcypromine do so within two or three days, and a clinical trial of one week is considered adequate with this drug even though there are occasional patients who appear to benefit from tranylcypromine therapy only after several weeks treatment. Unfortunately, not many controlled studies of tranylcypromine have been done, but the few that have been published tend to support this statement. In addition, no controlled comparison of tranylcypromine and the other MAO inhibitors has ever been made. The general utility of tranylcypromine is hindered by the fact that it is blamed for the highest incidence of paradoxical headache reaction of any of the MAO inhibitors (see following section).

Pargyline (Eutonyl), another nonhydrazine MAO inhibitor, is considered an antihypertensive agent, although it does have mild antidepressive properties. A third nonhydrazine MAO inhibitor, etryptamine (Monase), was available for a short time but was withdrawn because of toxicity.

Side Effects and Toxicity. The hydrazine MAO inhibitors have been associated with toxic effects on the liver. In the case of iproniazid (which is still used in other countries), a significant incidence of jaundice and death (as high as 25 percent mortality for those affected) led to its removal from the American market. However, for unknown reasons, the incidence of jaundice is now markedly lower than when the drug was first introduced (Pare reports one case of jaundice for every 5000 patients and one death for every 20,000 patients). The three hydrazine MAO inhibitors still available in this country (isocarboxazid, phenelzine, and nialamide) have also been associated with hepatotoxicity, although this reaction is very rare with these drugs.

The hydrazine MAO inhibitors may also cause a number of autonomic side effects such as dry mouth, orthostatic hypotension, constipation, delayed micturition, and delayed ejaculation. They may also be associated with excessive perspiration, tremulousness, insomnia, weight gain, and overstimulation, and they may precipitate short-lived psychotic episodes in unstable persons.

A serious but rare complication which occurs occasionally in patients taking MAO inhibitors is the paradoxical hypertensive headache syndrome. It may be found on rare occasions with any of the MAO-inhibitor type drugs, but it is more likely to occur with tranylcypromine. The reaction is characterized by a sudden rise in blood pressure and a pounding, throbbing headache of violent proportions, but it may also be accompanied by neck stiffness or soreness, nausea and vomiting, sweating, photophobia, dilated pupils, or tachycardia or bradycardia associated with chest pain. This reaction will subside spontaneously in an hour or two and usually has no unfavorable sequelae. However, occasional patients may suffer subarachnoid hemorrhage, hemiplegia, or even death. Such reactions are believed to be triggered by some exogenous factor. Blackwell observed that a significantly high percentage of patients who devloped this "Parnate headache" did so after eating well ripened cheese such as Camembert or cheddar. These cheeses contain large amounts of tyramine, an amino acid with pressor effects. Apparently the pressor effects of tyramine are potentiated because it is protected from destruction by MAO inhibition. Attacks of this type are also precipitated by certain alcoholic beverages, certain other food substances such as broad beans, and drugs like amphetamine and ephedrine. The physician should periodically review precautions contained in the manufacturer's labeling, particularly when prescribing an inhibitor, as the labeling is constantly being revised as new information becomes available. (The manufacturer's labeling may be found in the package insert which comes with the drug or in the *Physicians' Desk Reference*.)

The occurrence of hypertensive headache crisis caused tranylcypromine to be removed from the American market for a time in 1964. Many physicians protested the removal of this drug, however, claiming that some of their patients responded better to tranylcypromine than to any other treatment. The drug was therefore returned to commercial use with the restriction that it not be given to patients more than 60 years old, to anyone who had previously had a hypertensive headache crisis, or to anyone with serious hypertension or cardiovascular disease. The occurrence of this paradoxical reaction is one of the chief reasons why the MAO inhibitors, particularly tranylcypromine, are used less frequently than formerly.

Tranylcypromine does not appear to cause jaundice or liver toxicity, but it does share two of the side effects commonly found with the hydrazine MAO inhibitors, namely, overstimulation and postural hypotension. Other untoward effects are uncommon with this drug. Postural hypotension may manifest itself as dizziness, light-headedness, palpitation, and, occasionally, syncope. As a rule, these symptoms are easily managed by lowering the dosage for a few days; the dosage may then be increased gradually as tolerance develops. Because the overstimulation associated with tranylcypromine may cause onset or increase of insomnia, some patients do not tolerate this drug.

Precautions. In our present state of knowledge, it appears unwise to give any MAO inhibitor in conjunction with a tricyclic antidepressant drug. This precaution should be applied particularly to tranylcypromine, the most potent of the MAO inhibitors and the one with the most rapid onset of action. Frequently, the administration of such combinations will cause no difficulties, but severe atropine-like reactions with tremor, hyperpyrexia, convulsions, and occasionally death have been reported with the combination of one of the MAO inhibitors and a tricyclic antidepressant agent. This reaction is more likely if the tricyclic agent is added after the MAO inhibitor has been in use for some time. If the physician wishes to discontinue the use of one type of antidepressant drug and prescribe the other type, he should allow at least a one-week interval, or longer if possible, before administering the second compound. During the intervening period, a phenothiazine compound or an antianxiety agent could be given without unusual hazard. The dosage of the second antidepressant compound should be increased gradually, and during the first two weeks of its administration the patient should be closely supervised. Hospitalization or close supervision of patients taking any antidepressant drug is also called for if there is any reason to believe suicidal tendencies are present.

DIRECT CENTRAL NERVOUS SYSTEM STIMULANTS

Direct central nervous system stimulants are also known as psychomotor stimulants. Included in this group of drugs are the amphetamines, which have been available for many years, and methylphenidate (Ritalin) and pipradrol (Meratran), both introduced in the mid-1950's. As a group, these drugs are characterized by a rapid onset of action (within one hour) and a short duration of action (several hours). They are stimulating compounds which have value in combating drug-induced drowsiness and in reducing fatigue on a short-term basis. They are also useful in the treatment of narcolepsy and some types of hyperkinetic disturbances in children. Although they may benefit an occasional mildly depressed patient, they cannot be considered antidepressant drugs in the true sense of the word. They rarely help seriously depressed patients, and in controlled studies on the treatment of depression they frequently do little better than placebo.

Habituation is possible with this group of drugs, particularly with the amphetamines, and sympathomimetic effects that may cause anxiety and palpitation also occur. Anorexia is produced by these drugs, and this effect is often utilized in chemotherapy for weight reduction. The two newer compounds have less sympathomimetic activity than the older amphetamines. Partly for this reason and partly because of its low order of toxicity, many physicians prefer methylphenidate for its mild cortical stimulating action in the treatment of psychiatric conditions.

MECHANISMS OF ACTION OF THE ANTIDEPRESSANT DRUGS

The exact mechanisms by which the antidepressant drugs achieve their effects has not yet been worked out. Much research has been done to show that stimulating compounds such as the MAO inhibitors and central nervous system depressants such as imipramine may have similar antidepressant effects although they achieve these effects through different actions. One of the most appealing theories is the catecholamine hypothesis described by Schildkraut (see Table 12-6):*

The "catecholamine hypothesis of affective disorders" proposes that some, if not all, depressions are associated with an absolute or relative decrease in catecholamines, particularly norepinephrine, available at central adrenergic receptor sites. Elation, conversely, may be associated with an excess of such amines. . . .

Data from pharmacological studies, mainly in animals, suggest that the actions of both major classes of antidepressant drugs are mediated through the catecholamines. The monoamine oxidase inhibitors increase brain concentrations of norepinephrine while imipramine-like agents potentiate the physiological effects of nor-

epinephrine. Reserpine, a drug which can cause clinical depression, depletes catecholamines, but other amines may also be involved in its mechanism of action. A rigorous extrapolation from pharmacological studies to pathophysiology clearly cannot be made. Clinical studies relevant to the catecholamine hypothesis are limited and the findings are inconclusive.

It is not possible, therefore, to confirm definitively or to reject the catecholamine hypothesis on the basis of data currently available. It must be stressed, moreover, that this hypothesis is undoubtedly, at best, a reductionistic oversimplification of a very complex biological state and that the simultaneous effects of the indoleamines, other biogenic amines, hormones and ionic changes will ultimately have to be included in any comprehensive formulation of this biochemistry of the affective disorders. In our present state of knowledge, however, the catecholamine hypothesis is of considerable heuristic value, providing the investigator and the clinician with a frame of reference integrating much of our experience with those pharmacological agents which produce alterations in human affective states.

The tricyclic antidepressants resemble the phenothiazines chemically and pharmacologically, but they are not effective antipsychotic agents. The crucial difference between the two is that the phenothiazines block central adrenergic synapsis, while the tricyclic antidepressants increase their sensitivity.

Dosage and Administration of Antidepressant Drugs. The manufacturer's recommendations constitute a good guide to dosage and administration, although these recommendations tend to be conservative. As the physician becomes familiar with a compound, he may have occasion to deviate from the manufacturer's suggested dosage schedule. Dosage is started low in order to test the patient's sensitivity and is built up over a period of several days, depending on the patient's response and the severity of his symtoms.

While high dosages may produce needless side effects without concomitant therapeutic gain, it is important

---

*Modified by permission from Schildkraut, J. J. 1965. The catecholamine hypothesis of affective disorders. American Journal of Psychiatry *122*, 509-522.

TABLE 12-6. Summary of the Pharmacological Observations
Consistent with the "Catecholamine Hypothesis
of Affective Disorders"†

DRUG	EFFECTS ON MOOD IN HUMANS	EFFECTS ON BEHAVIOR IN ANIMALS	EFFECTS ON CATECHOLAMINES IN BRAIN
Reserpine	Sedation Depression (in some patients)	Sedation	Depletion (intracellular deamination and inactivation)
Tetrabenazine	Sedation Depression (in some patients)	Sedation	Depletion (intracellular deamination and inactivation)
Amphetamine	Stimulant	Stimulation Excitement	Releases NE* (? onto receptors) Inhibits cellular uptake (and inactivation) of NE*
Monoamine oxidase (MAO) inhibitors	Antidepressant	Excitement Prevents and reverses reserpine-induced sedation	Increase
Imipramine	Antidepressant	Prevents reserpine-induced sedation Potentiation of amphetamine effects	Inhibits cellular uptake (and inactivation) of NE* ? Potentiates action of NE* (as in periphery)
Dihydroxyphenylalanine (DOPA)	? Reverses reserpine effects	Excitement Reverses reserpine effects	Increase

*NE=Norepinephrine.
†From Schildkraut, J. J. 1965. The catecholamine hypothesis of affective disorders: a review of supporting evidence. American Journal of Psychiatry *122*,509.

to give sufficient medication to control the patient's symptoms or at least to establish that a particular patient will not respond to the agent in question. Some individuals will respond to a very small dosage while others require a large quantity of drug for the same level of symptom reduction. Also, tolerance to side effects varies widely, so that dosage must be individualized. Controlled studies show most of the antidepressant drugs to be more efficacious than placebo, and most of the studies that do not give the advantage to the drugs have used fixed low-level dosages.

Usually there is a latent period between the beginning of drug administration and the appearance of definite signs of improvement, and this period is frequently as long as two weeks. Therefore, a three- to four-week trial is necessary to determine whether or not an antidepressant drug will be effective in a given situation. The earlier the benefit from the drug and the smaller the dosage required, however, the better the prognosis.

The antidepressant drugs are almost always given by the oral route and there is little advantage to parenteral administration.

Indications for Use. There are many varieties of depressive disorders, and many of these are self-limiting, especially when they are associated with situational difficulties like the death of a loved one or a business failure. Depression is commonly associated with anxiety, and it is widely recognized that persons who live with a pattern of personal strain or persistent anxiety are vulnerable to depression. Most common depressions are of this neurotic, anxiety-related type and occur in people who have a history of pathological anxiety.

However, not all depressions develop in chronically anxious persons, nor do all depressions display manifest anxiety symptoms. It has long been considered that there are at least two distinct types of depression: the neurotic depression with anxiety features and the endogenous depression. Unfortunately, depressions occur in such a variety of forms that no satisfactory classification has been developed that would enable the physician to pinpoint diagnosis and treatment or to predict results. Part of the problem is that the human mind has great difficulty in correlating complex masses of data. By the use of modern statistical techniques and electronic computers, however, correlations are now possible and there are a number of studies which provide evidence to support the traditional dichotomous diagnosis of depressive states. For example, Kiloh and Garside (1963) have used techniques like factor analysis and discriminate function on historical and symptomatic data from large numbers of depressed patients. They found two computer-derived symptom clusters which appear to distinguish two kinds of depression. Among the most important items associated with neurotic depression were the following: self-pity, variability of symptoms, immature personality, insomnia (difficulty in falling asleep), hypochondriacal concern, and obsessional tendencies. Among the items associated with endogenous depressions were the following: insomnia (early awakening), depression worse in the morning, retardation rather than agitation, patient is usually 40 years old or older at onset of illness, severe depression of mood, inability to concentrate, weight loss of seven pounds or more, and history of previous attack.

Although they are not all of equal validity or importance, there are a large number of other studies supporting the concept of two essentially distinct varieties of depression. However, it is still very often impossible to differentiate these two kinds of depression because of the frequency of overlapping symptoms. When we *are* able to make a diagnosis, however, we find it a valuable guide in treatment.

Many physicians feel that the antidepressant drugs act against the endogenous elements in a depressive illness, and that the greater the neurotic or reactive factor, the less effective the antidepressant drugs. Pare says, however:

> This is not to say that antidepressants should be reserved for typically endogenous illnesses. Efforts to improve or strengthen a patient's personality in a predominantly reactive or neurotic depression may be unavailing, yet the small improvement brought about by antidepressant therapy may enable the patient, with help, to overcome or adjust the circumstances which previously were insurmountable.

The Choice of Drug. The chief problem in choosing an antidepressant drug is the decision whether to use a drug of the MAO inhibitor type or one of the tricyclic antidepressants. We are unable to define clear-cut, differential indications, but a trend does exist. It is widely held that the tricyclic antidepressants are more effective in endogenous disorders, and it is generally conceded that these are the drugs to try first if one is to use an antidepressant agent. Since the MAO inhibitors are associated with troublesome side effects and dangers, many physicians shy away from them and reserve these drugs for patients who have failed with other treatments. Though it is not possible to describe the type of patient with certainty, there are individuals who respond better to the MAO inhibitors than to the tricyclic antidepressants. These patients are usually found to have atypical depressions with obsessional features and phobias.

Efficacy. In the current controversy over the antidepressant drugs, all shades of opinion have appeared in print, backed up by clinical evidence, and in some cases by controlled studies. The most enthusiastic supporters of these agents claim that the antidepressants represent a major breakthrough, both in the treatment of depression and in our understanding of related psychophysiological mechanisms. The detractors claim that the antidepressants are of little practical value and that the symptomatic improvement ascribed to their use really results from the spontaneous remissions that most depressions are liable to. Other detractors concede that the antidepressants may afford some mild symptomatic relief, but go on to say that their onset of action is slow, their benefits uncertain, the risk of toxicity and side effects too great, and knowledge of indications for specific drugs largely lacking. Observers in the middle ground have pointed out, however, that although all patients do not benefit equally from these drugs, some patients benefit a great deal; while others, who have proved resistant to electroconvulsive and other therapies, respond only to certain antidepressant compounds.

It is the author's opinion that the antidepressant drugs leave much to be desired, that their antidepressant action is not powerful enough to greatly benefit the seriously depressed patient, that some individuals are not helped at all, but that many patients do obtain a certain amount of clinical benefit which is sufficient to speed their recovery and to enhance natural healing processes and other kinds of therapy.

Drug Combinations. Polypharmacy is sometimes held in disrepute because it is easily abused. An over-enthusiastic physician eager to relieve his patient of multiple miseries may prescribe, for example, an antidepressant drug to combat depressive symptomatology, a phenothiazine for schizoid tendencies, an antiparkinson agent for resultant neurological side effects, a barbiturate for insomnia, a minor tranquilizer for anxiety, a psychomotor stimulant for drug-induced hypersomnolence, and medications designed to lessen postural hypotension, constipation, and so on.

Although giving so many drugs is obviously poor practice, there are times when combination drug therapy is indicated. A single compound cannot be expected to provide all the therapeutic action needed in a complex clinical picture. The following are examples of justifiable drug combinations commonly employed in clinical practice.

(1) A phenothiazine plus an antidepressant is commonly used in schizophrenia with depressive features, as the antipsychotic effect of the phenothiazine drug is needed. The same combination is also widely used in the treatment of agitated depression, in which the greater sedative properties of a phenothiazine agent are desired. A common combination is thioridazine (Mellaril) plus imipramine, or perphenazine (Trilafon) plus amitriptyline. The latter combination is commercially available in a single tablet marketed under the trade name Etrafon or Triavil.

There are few well conducted controlled studies of combination phenothiazine-antidepressant drug therapy. The few studies that do exist provide little evidence that such combinations are very valuable. Overall and Hollister compared thioridazine to imipramine in a population of depressed patients and schizophrenic patients and found thioridazine superior. Further analysis, however, showed that if the patient sample were subdivided, the anxious and hostile depressed patients responded best to thioridazine, whereas the patients with retarded depressions responded best to imipramine. These findings seem to indicate that if we had better diagnostic criteria and more specific indications for various therapeutic agents, hit-or-miss combination therapy might prove less beneficial than treatment with a single drug.

(2) A second widely used drug combination consists of an antianxiety agent like chlordiazepoxide (Librium) or dia-

zepam (Valium) plus an antidepressant agent like phenelzine or tranylcypromine.

Here again, although such combinations have wide acceptance, it is possible that the antianxiety agents alone might be just as effective in the milder depressions associated with anxiety. In case of doubt, it might be well to begin treatment with an antianxiety agent alone, as this type of medication is easier to regulate and is better tolerated than the antidepressant drugs. The latter could then be added to the therapeutic regimen at a later time if necessary.

Drug versus Electroconvulsive Therapy in Depression. As yet, no published study has demonstrated the superiority of antidepressant drug therapy over electroconvulsive therapy in the treatment of depression (see Table 12-5). However, drug therapy is usually given a trial before electroconvulsive therapy is considered because of its numerous conveniences if successful. Also, as a large percentage of patients with affective disorders have recurrent attacks, it is worthwhile to find out whether drug therapy will benefit such patients. (See also discussion of electroconvulsive therapy.)

The advantages of electroconvulsive therapy, on the other hand, are impressive. Electroconvulsive therapy brings rapid relief to the majority of depressed patients and is still probably the most potent and certain antidepressant treatment available. The principal disadvantage of electroshock is patient resistance, particularly if more than one treatment series is required or if maintenance therapy is indicated. In addition, the memory deficit induced by electroconvulsive therapy is a serious problem for some persons. If he benefits from the treatment, a patient whose normal personality is characterized by ongoing, aggressive activity and confidence will be able to endure a period of memory loss without great difficulty, but the individual whose usual personality is characterized by compulsiveness and uncertainty will be

distressed by the same level of memory deficit. Other disadvantages of electroconvulsive therapy are the necessity of hospitalization, entailing loss of time at work, and the failure of some patients to respond adequately or at all to this treatment. Physical injury and death can occur, but with modern techniques the risk is very low, particularly in view of the seriousness of the condition being treated and of the high incidence of suicide in untreated depressions.

To recapitulate, drug therapy in depression is less certain and less potent than electroconvulsive therapy and is therefore not the best choice in very severely depressed patients or in patients with acute suicidal drives. It is also usually less rapid in its onset of action, but it does have the advantages of high patient acceptance, of producing no memory deficit, and of enabling the patient to continue to work while undergoing treatment. There is also some slight evidence that antidepressant drugs may offer some preventive action in patients who are subject to recurrent episodes of depression.

REST, SLEEP, AND FEVER TREATMENTS

Organic treatments of psychiatric patients carried out under medical auspices that may be of historical interest include bloodletting, emetics, purgatives and, more recently, attempts to eradicate supposed infection. Toward the end of the last century, however, a therapeutic program was introduced by Weir Mitchell (1885) which received widespread acceptance and persisted in modified form up until recent years. This program was applied mainly to neurotic patients (particularly young women with "nervous exhaustion") and consisted of removal from environmental stress ("the cause of breakdown"), enforced rest, moral exhortation or suggestion, and restoration of normal physique by dietary supplementation (together with massage for at least an hour a day and electrical stimulation of the muscles). Mitchell remarked,

If I succeed in first altering the moral atmosphere which has been to the patient like the very breathing of evil, and if I can add largely to the weight and fill the vessels with red blood, I am sure of giving relief to a host of aches and pains and varied disabilities. If I fail, it is because I fail in these very points or else because I have overlooked or undervalued some serious organic tissue change.

In patients who were already obese, he tried to replace "unhealthy fat" with "healthy fat" by first placing them on a reducing diet before building them up again by his standard methods (a technique reported from Russia in more recent years). While the latter technique has not found favor in Western countries, extensive use has been made of insulin during the last few decades, both for the promotion of appetite and weight gain, and also for its sedative action in relieving neurotic anxiety. For these purposes, insulin may be administered in doses of about ten units three times a day, half an hour before meals, or alternatively in a single dose of from ten to 100 units to the conscious but recumbent patient. The latter treatment results in moderate hypoglycemia (without loss of consciousness) of several hours' duration and has been termed *modified, sub-coma, or somnolent insulin therapy* to distinguish it from the much more severe hypoglycemia of full insulin coma therapy used in schizophrenia (which will be described later).

Continuous narcosis or prolonged sleep treatment involves the administration of hypnotic drugs in sufficient dosage to keep the patient asleep for 18 to 20 hours out of the 24, for a period of about two weeks. It apparently originated in Sweden around the beginning of the present century, but it was not until 1922 that Klaesi of Switzerland introduced barbiturates for this purpose, and the method found extensive application in the treatment of psychiatric patients. It has been regarded as the most important predecessor of the

"shock treatments" and was used in a variety of patients including those with excessive psychomotor activity (manic or catatonic excitement), severe anxiety and depression, and various forms of schizophrenia. A number of workers advocated the supplementary administration of insulin (ten to 20 units) and glucose, and of recent years some workers have used massive doses of phenothiazines to produce the same result. However, many psychiatrists consider that the risks of such treatment greatly outweigh its advantages. In the early days, mortality sometimes reached as high a figure as five per cent, the main dangers being collapse and pneumonia (hypostatic, or from aspiration). To prevent such complications patients require skilled nursing supervision 24 hours a day with hourly recording of pulse, respiration, temperature and blood pressure, and adequate measurement of fluid intake and output. The patient should be turned frequently to prevent pressure sores and hypostatic pneumonia, and suction apparatus should be available continuously for the removal of excessive secretions. The prophylactic administration of atropine and penicillin may be advisable in all cases, and any organic disease or debility must be regarded as a contraindication.

Various forms of *fever therapy* were introduced as a result of the observation that certain psychiatric patients improved during intercurrent infections. In 1907 Lundvall attempted to produce fever and leukocytosis by means of sodium nucleinate, and in 1917 Wagner-Jauregg of Vienna introduced malaria in the treatment of general paresis (central nervous system syphilis). Six of his first nine patients improved and three of them were able to return to work and remained symptom-free several years later. Until the introduction of penicillin, malaria remained the standard treatment of general paresis, social remission being achieved in about one-third of cases and arrest of the disease process in another third.

Tertian malaria was used for this purpose and the patient was usually allowed to have eight to 12 bouts of fever prior to termination by means of quinine. A variety of other pyrexial agents were introduced—biological (e.g., typhoid vaccine, and killed *E. coli* suspension), chemical (e.g., sulfur in oil), and physical (e.g., thermostatically controlled fever cabinets or simply hot baths and packs). These agents were applied in turn in attempts to treat patients with "functional" psychoses such as schizophrenia, but the results were inconsistent and proved less satisfactory than those obtained by means of insulin coma therapy, convulsive therapy, and brain surgery.

The latter treatments will be outlined in the next three sections of the present chapter, and certain other forms of somatic treatment will be reviewed briefly in the final section.

INSULIN COMA THERAPY

Not long after the introduction of insulin for the control of diabetes, it was found that small doses of this drug were effective in promoting appetite and weight gain and in exerting a sedative effect in hyperactive patients. Steck (1932) reported on the use of insulin in patients with delirium tremens, and Manfred Sakel of Vienna found somewhat larger doses effective in controlling the withdrawal symptoms in patients addicted to morphine. Hypoglycemia had hitherto been considered dangerous, but Sakel found it was readily controlled by the administration of sugar and used increasing doses of insulin for the purpose of producing coma in schizophrenic patients. Repeated comas were followed by marked improvement in a certain proportion of patients with schizophrenia, and within a few years this method of treatment had found widespread application and acceptance. By the time of the 1950 International Congress of Psychiatry in Paris, insulin coma therapy was re-

garded by many psychiatrists as the most effective treatment available for patients with schizophrenia, particularly during the first year of illness. Since the introduction of the major tranquilizing drugs, insulin coma therapy has been discontinued in many centers where it was formerly used extensively, but a few psychiatrists maintain that it still has a place in the treatment of schizophrenia, particularly in cases that have failed to respond to phenothiazine therapy.

Procedure. Injections of regular insulin are administered about 6:30 to 7:00 A.M. to patients who have been fasting since the previous evening. After receiving the injection, they remain in bed until the termination of hypoglycemia, about three and one-half hours after the initial injection. Termination is brought about by the administration of glucose (by mouth, by stomach tube, or intravenously), followed by a meal. The dose of insulin is increased until coma results two or three hours after the injection and may then be maintained or reduced, according to the depth and duration of coma desired. Insulin is usually administered five or six mornings a week (preferably the latter) until the patient has had about 50 comas, which usually requires about 60 treatments (from ten to 12 weeks of continuous treatment).

Since the patient may have a recurrence of hypoglycemia, which may proceed to coma at any time during the 24 hours following a treatment, he requires constant skilled nursing supervision and should not be allowed out of hospital for visits during this time. He should also be under constant medical observation throughout the period of controlled hypoglycemia each morning, and it is customary for patients receiving this form of treatment to live together in groups on the same ward. Each unit of 12 patients requires one physician and three or four nurses, all familiar with the treatment procedures and its common complications. If there are fewer than 12 patients of either sex receiving treatment at the same time, there is no reason why subunits of each sex should not be treated in close proximity under the supervision of a single physician. Since some of the beneficial effects of insulin coma therapy are attributed to group psychotherapy, activities, and interaction during the time that patients are partly or fully conscious, there are some therapists who consider that insulin units should contain patients of both sexes whenever possible.

The stages and symptoms of hypogly- cemia are shown in Table 12-7. Coma is usually considered to be reached with the onset of State II, when the patient is no longer consciously aware of his environment and cannot respond purposively to painful stimuli (although reflex and nonpurposive responses are still possible). It is generally considered desirable that the duration of coma should be about one hour, but there are some therapists who prefer to consider the onset of therapeutic coma as being at a much deeper level (e.g., State V,

TABLE 12-7. Hypoglycemic Symptoms*

STAGE	PSYCHOLOGICAL	MOTOR	SENSORY	AUTONOMIC

I
Depression of cerebral and cerebellar functions
	1. Gradually increasing clouding of consciousness with defects in:
	  a. orientation
	  b. attention
	  c. understanding
	  d. perception
	2. Wild excitement, with or without psychotic syndromes
	3. Sleep
		1. Muscular relaxation (hypotonia)
		2. Tremors
		  Imperfect voluntary acts (apraxia)
		4. Imperfect (incoherent) speech
			1. Visual disturbances	1. Parasympathetic overactivity
				  a. Watery sweat
				  b. Watery saliva
				  c. Bradycardia
				  d. Constricted pupil or
				2. Sympathetic overactivity
				  a. Viscid sweat
				  b. Viscid saliva
				  c. Tachycardia
				  d. Dilated pupil
				3. Vital signs vary within normal limits—temperature dropping

II
Release of sub- corticodien- cephalon
	1. Loss of environmental contact, i.e., coma	1. Stereotyped (primitive) movements
		  a. Involuntary grasping
		  b. Involuntary sucking
		  c. Protrusion of tongue
		  d. Kissing
		  e. Snarling
		  f. Grimacing
		2. Motor restlessness
		3. Choreiform, athetoid, and hemiballistic movements
		4. Fine myoclonic twitchings
		——→clonic spasms——→
		convulsions (release of subcortical motor nuclei)
			1. Increased sensitivity to external stimuli (release of the sensory thalamus)	1. Sympathetic overactivity in waves
				  a. Tachycardia
				  b. Dilated pupils (react to light)
				  c. Exophthalmos
				  d. Flushing
				  e. Viscid perspiration
				  f. Viscid salivation
				  g. Increased blood pressure and perspiration (release of hypothalamus)

III
Release of the midbrain
	1. Deep coma	1. Loss of primitive movements
		2. Increasing hypertonus
		3. Spasm
		  a. Tonic (flexion of upper extremities with extension of rest of body)
		  b. Torsion
		4. Dissociated eye movements
		5. Pathological pyramidal reflexes most easily elicited
			1. Decreased sensitivity to external stimuli	1. Parasympathetic signs, which are overcome periodically by sympathetic signs with each spasm (dilated pupils do not react to light)
				2. Paradoxical pupillary dilation and hippus
				3. Vital signs variable

IV Release of upper medulla	1. Deep coma	1. Recurrent extensor spasm in all extremities 2. Magnus and de Kleijn reflex	1. Loss of sensitivity	1. Sympathetic signs with each spasm (pupils dilate but do not react)

V
Release of lower medulla
	1. Deep coma	1. Muscular flaccidity
		2. Depressed reflexes
			1. Loss of all sensitivity
			2. Loss of corneal reflex
				1. Parasympathetic signs
				  a. Pallor
				  b. Pinpoint pupils (do not react)
				  c. Slow heart rate
				  d. Depressed respiration

*Table modified from Himwich. From Noyes, A. P., and Kolb, L. C. 1963. *Modern Clinical Psychiatry*, 6th edition. Philadelphia, W. B. Saunders Co., p. 545.

with loss of corneal reflexes), in which case the maximum duration permitted is usually about 15 minutes.

Dosage. The dose of insulin required to produce a given level of coma varies enormously in different patients, the average coma dose being somewhere in the neighborhood of 200 to 400 units. Some patients may become comatose with less than 50 units and others may prove resistant with doses up to 4000 units. Two techniques have commonly been adopted for increasing the dosage up to the required level, the more conservative method being that of starting with ten units and increasing by ten to 20 units daily until coma results. A faster method which achieved widespread popularity involves starting with a dose of ten units and doubling a dose each day until a dose of 320 units is achieved, then increasing it by 100 to 200 units a day until coma is reached. The latter method obviates the technique of "zig-zagging" (high and low doses being given on alternative days), which was sometimes effective in initiating coma after relatively high doses had been reached by the conservative method without producing coma.

Hyaluronidase, in doses of 75 to 150 units, may be added to the insulin to promote absorption of the latter and produce coma with lower doses than would otherwise be possible. Atropine should be given routinely at the same time as the insulin, or within an hour afterward, and a further injection of atropine may be administered later in the event that electroconvulsive therapy is given to a patient who has already received insulin. Barbiturates and anticonvulsant medications such as Dilantin may be given to prevent undue motor excitement or spontaneous seizures occurring during insulin therapy. Vitamins B and C are given routinely to prevent deficiencies resulting from the intake of large quantities of carbohydrates. Airways, suction, and oxygen should always be available in the event of respiratory embarrassment. In case of delayed response to intravenous administration of glucose, brain metabolism may be stimulated by means of oxygen, injections of vitamin B complex, and direct central nervous system stimulants.

Complications. The most frequent complications of treatment are delayed or secondary hypoglycemic reactions occurring later in the day (or the night) following treatment, but they usually respond readily to administrations of glucose. Excitement and spontaneous seizures occurring during the course of treatment can usually be readily controlled by appropriate medication. The most serious complication of insulin therapy is the prolonged or irreversible coma which may vary in duration from a few hours to several weeks. Following a brief prolonged coma, the patient usually shows symptoms of an acute reversible organic brain syndrome, but following a more severe episode there may be considerable irreversible intellectual impairment. Occasionally, an irreversible coma will terminate in death, but the mortality of insulin coma therapy in skilled hands is only about 0.5 percent of all patients treated.

Nevertheless, it should be recognized that insulin coma therapy involves several hours of daily stress on the cardiovascular and central nervous systems. This stress is very much more severe than in the case of convulsive therapy (or, for that matter, psychosurgery), and insulin coma therapy has therefore been reserved for young physically healthy adults (usually between the ages of 15 and 45 years). Among the many contraindications may be mentioned diabetes, hypertension, any form of cardiac or chronic respiratory disease, hyperthyroidism, and pregnancy. Treatment should also be suspended during any acute intercurrent infection or fever.

ELECTROCONVULSIVE THERAPY

Weickhardt is said to have recommended the administration of camphor to produce convulsions as long ago as 1798, and his example was apparently followed by a number of other physicians. Convulsive therapy was again introduced in 1933 by Meduna of Budapest, who recommended intramuscular injection of 25 percent solution of camphor in oil to schizophrenic patients, on the assumption of an infrequent association (and therefore "biological antagonism") between epilepsy and schizophrenia (which was subsequently discredited). Camphor was found to be unpredictable in its effects and was therefore soon replaced by other analeptic drugs, particularly pentamethylenetrazol (Metrazol or Cardiazol). It was found empirically that convulsive therapy was relatively more effective in depressed patients than in those with schizophrenia, but the production of seizures by intravenous medication had several serious disadvantages: difficulty in determining the minimum adequate dosage to produce a single seizure, extremely unpleasant subjective sensations between the time of injection and onset of seizure, and a high proportion of violent convulsions with accompanying musculoskeletal damage.

In 1937 Bini of Italy first suggested the possible use of an electric current as a convulsive stimulus and the following year, after extensive animal experiments, Cerletti and Bini advocated electroconvulsive therapy in psychiatric patients. A number of different machines have since been developed that may be plugged into the standard electrical outlet (usually 110 volt, 60 cycle, alternating current), the simplest consisting of a variable transformer, a voltmeter, and an automatic timer. The convulsive threshold varies (increasing with age and following the administration of sedative drugs), but a seizure is usually produced by a voltage of 70 to 150 volts continued for 0.1 to 0.5 second. The electric current is ordinarily applied to bitemporal electrodes (skin resistance being reduced by a jelly containing electrolytes). The appropriate dose is the minimum current required to produce a typical grand mal epileptiform convulsion with instantaneous loss of consciousness, immediate onset of the tonic phase (which lasts about ten seconds), followed by the clonic phase (which lasts about half a minute) and then the period of postconvulsive coma, from which the person awakes with signs of an acute reversible organic brain syndrome (impairment of intelligence, memory, and orientation of variable duration). While a moderate subconvulsive electric shock produces immediate loss of consciousness (petit mal) and mental confusion without a sensation of pain, the experience may be unpleasant for the patient and result in increased apprehension before subsequent treatments, so that an unintentional subconvulsive shock should always be followed immediately by a higher dose sufficient to produce a grand mal seizure. Very low voltages of electricity may be administered continuously without producing loss of consciousness but are painful and should never be administered without anesthetic (and in any event their therapeutic value is questioned by most psychiatrists).

Complications. The frequency and various technical modifications of electroconvulsive therapy have been designed to minimize the risk of complications, the most frequent of which are the following: (1) impairment of memory and other intellectual functions (closely related to the frequency of treatments); (2) biting the tongue and breaking teeth with danger of aspiration (controlled by removal of dentures and use of a semicircular rubber mouth gag, preferably with airway incorporated); (3) musculoskeletal damage, such as fractures (particularly compression fractures of the bodies of the dorsal vertebrae, usually asymptomatic), dislocation (particularly of the jaw, which may be readily reduced immediately following treatment), and, more rarely, ruptured muscles or tendons; (4) vomiting with danger of aspiration (avoided by giving treatment after the patient has fasted); and (5) cardiovascular complications such as fibrillation, coronary infarction, or stroke. Cardiovascular complications may be minimized by the routine administration of atropine prior to treatment. Death from electroconvulsive treatment is extremely rare and has been estimated as around one in 5000 treatments, even when patients treated include so-called "calculated risks" (such as the very aged and those with hypertension, cardiac pathology, or other somatic disease). Deaths in such cases have usually been attributed to cardiac failure (sometimes related to unrecognized hypothyroidism) or to overdosage with one of the less reliable muscle relaxants such as curare.

Indications. Classical involutional melancholia is the most clear-cut indication for electroconvulsive therapy. The vast majority of such patients are permanently relieved of their symptoms and may be considered recovered within a period of 30 to 50 days after the beginning of treatment. Prior to the advent of such therapy, these patients were doomed to suffer for months or years, with only about half of them recovering at the end of two years. Other forms of depression also may respond favorable to electroconvulsive therapy, but the benefits of such treatments are often short-lived, particularly in those patients who are prone to relapse, as electroconvulsive therapy does nothing to prevent the recurrence of future attacks. Patients with manic excitement or excited schizophrenic states also frequently respond favorably to electroshock. Here again, the treatment is not very satisfactory for the patient who is prone to have frequent episodes.

Although electroconvulsive therapy is effective in reducing depression, agitation, and excitement, it probably ought to be considered a symptomatic treatment, as it may relieve a severe depression associated with a neurosis but leave the neurosis itself untouched. Such treatment is usually ineffectual in the behavioral disorders and is contraindicated in organic brain syndromes, although a few judicious treatments may relieve associated symptoms of depression or excitement.

Frequency. The usual regimen recommended is to give electroconvulsive treatments three times a week. Most depressed patients receive a total of from eight to 12 treatments, but patients with manic excitement usually require more than this, and schizophrenic or paranoid patients usually need 20 or more treatments.

Intensive electroshock treatment, also known as regressive, depatterning, or annihilation treatment, involves the administration of about 50 treatments over a period of two to four weeks and has been recommended for a variety of patients (with psychotic, neurotic, or behavioral disorders), sometimes in preference to insulin coma therapy or lobotomy. In spite of the fact that intensive electroshock treatments produce recognizable brain damage (e.g., diffuse punctate hemorrhages) in experimental animals, and that patients show some permanent residual amnesia (which is maximal for the period of several months immediately preceding and during the treatment), some advocates of this method claim that there is little or no permanent impairment of intellectual function. Cameron (1960) reported that there is considerably greater amnesia for schizophrenic behavior than for concurrent normal behavior in the period prior to treatment and suggested that there is an important degree of correlation between the persistence of this differential amnesia and the stability of the patient's recovery. Sargant and Slater (1964), however, have stated that it is a mistake to regard electroconvulsive therapy as a substitute for leukotomy, and that the organic changes produced by a heavy dosage of convulsive therapy and those produced as a planned procedure by the surgeon are different in nature, in site, and in result.

The degree of memory and intellectual impairment produced by electroconvulsive therapy varies considerably from one individual to another, and tends to increase with advancing age. Thus, an old person with arteriosclerosis may become quite confused after only three treatments, whereas a young adult may show little or no impairment after 20 treatments given over a period of about six weeks. The degree of impairment is related more closely to the frequency than to the total number of treatments. Before the introduction of the tranquilizing drugs, a number of chronic state hospital patients received weekly maintenance treatments over a period of years for the symptomatic control of disturbed behavior. Maintenance treatments (inappropriately termed "prophylactic electroshock"), varying in frequency from once a week to once a month, were also found helpful in preventing recurrence of manic-depressive episodes in patients subject to frequent and prolonged attacks, but few patients were prepared to continue treatment indefinitely, and the ultimate results were probably less favorable than those following lobotomy.

Prevention of Musculoskeletal Complications. Several modifications of electroshock treatment have been designed to minimize the likelihood of musculoskeletal complications, which are particularly apt to occur at the beginning of the first treatment in males with well developed musculature. One involves the incorporation into the machine of a glissando, whereby the voltage is gradually increased from zero to its peak level over a period of one or two seconds instead of instantaneously. Another involves giving the patient a subconvulsive stimulus (petit mal) to produce muscular relaxation, followed immediately by a stimulus sufficient to produce a grand mal seizure. The most effective modification, however, is the intravenous administration of a drug which relaxes or paralyzes the muscles. Curare was formerly used for this purpose, but its action is slow and prolonged, and there was danger of subsequent death from respiratory paralysis

(even when Prostigmin was administered routinely as an antidote). Many therapists now routinely administer a quick and brief-acting depolarizing agent such as succinylcholine chloride (Anectine) in doses of about 20 mg per 100 pounds of body weight. This substance is ordinarily destroyed quickly in the tissues and should be injected rapidly and followed by a convulsive stimulus when muscular relaxation has occurred (after about 45 seconds). If the patient is awake during this time, he may experience pain from muscular fasciculation and a sense of suffocation from respiratory paralysis. The latter may be prevented by previous inhalation of oxygen, and there may also be a total amnesia for this period following the treatment, but not infrequently there is some recollection and consequent apprehension of further treatments. Many therapists, therefore, routinely employ intravenous Pentothal prior to the administration of Anectine through the same needle. Some therapists, however, prefer to avoid the increased risk of Pentothal administration by using a subconvulsive electric shock to produce the required amnesia.

Drugs or Electroconvulsive Therapy? Since the advent of the psychotropic drugs, electroconvulsive therapy has not been as widely used as it once was, but it does still have a prominent place in psychiatric practice. The major tranquilizing drugs are most effective in the treatment of schizophrenia, where electroconvulsive treatment was always of limited value, but even here, electroconvulsive therapy can be of occasional help, particularly in certain drug-resistant patients.

Electroconvulsive treatment has its most clear-cut indication today in the treatment of severely depressed patients who may be suicidal or in extremely agitated patients. Here electroconvulsive therapy is more certain, more rapid, and more potent than drug therapy.

Whenever it is feasible, it is wise to give the patient an adequate therapeutic trial with antidepressant drugs prior to the initiation of electroshock treatment. Since many patients can expect to have other episodes of depression later in life, it is worthwhile to discover whether drug therapy will be of value in individual cases. When drugs do provide symptom relief for the patient, treatment will be much more satisfactory than with electroconvulsive therapy, as the patient often will be able to continue to work and will not be burdened with memory deficit. Drug therapy also interferes less with psychosocial therapies, which are often concurrently administered, and it engenders none of the fear and resistance sometimes encountered by electroshock in patients who have had more than one course of treatment.

Electroconvulsive therapy is often given while patients are receiving tranquilizers alone or together with antidepressant drugs. Electroshock should not be given when a patient is receiving a rauwolfia compound because of the danger of cardiovascular collapse. There is no indication, however, that it is dangerous to give electroconvulsive treatments to patients receiving the phenothiazines, antianxiety agents, or antidepressant agents. On the other hand, there is not much evidence of any real advantage, and it would seem better in most cases to discontinue these psychotropic agents when electroshock is given. In the case of patients who are prone to relapse or who are otherwise treatment-resistant, it might be prudent to start an appropriate psychotropic agent immediately at the termination of electroconvulsive therapy.

PSYCHOSURGERY

It has been reported that in medieval Rome it was observed that insanity sometimes improved following a sword wound that broke the skull, and some attempts were apparently made to let out the evil humors by boring into the skull (with occasional beneficial results).

The method fell into disuse, and it was not until 1888 that the Swiss psychiatrist Burkhardt undertook his first operation on the anatomically intact brain of a psychotic patient. In his report he remarked,

Doctors are different by nature. One stands fast on the old principle "*primum non nocere*"; the other states: "*melius anceps remedium quam nullum.*" I belong, naturally, to the second category. . . .

His first patient was an extremely disturbed woman who had been in his asylum for 15 years and was continually hallucinated. He believed that her mental condition was due to these hallucinations and that the latter were caused by localized disease of the cerebral cortex. He therefore performed four successive operations at intervals of several weeks, at each of which he removed several grams of tissue from the left side of the cortex, following which there was considerable improvement. He subsequently operated on five further patients, but the results were not spectacular.

It remained for Egas Moniz of Lisbon to recommend the treatment of psychotic patients by surgical interruption of the frontal association pathways, and the first such operation was carried out under his direction by Almeida Lima in 1935. Moniz believed that these patients had fixed arrangements of cellular connections (related to their persistent delusions), particularly in the frontal lobes, and that these connections must be destroyed by means of an alcohol injection or a cut (made through a trephine opening over the prefrontal region).

In 1936 Moniz reported on the results of surgery on his first 20 patients, one-third of whom he considered recovered, one-third improved, and one-third unimproved. Similar reports have since been reported by a number of different workers using fairly extensive, bilateral, destructive procedures on patients consisting mainly of chronic distrubed schizophrenics who had failed to respond to all other methods of treatment available. Results are least favorable among those who have been sick the longest and among those who are inactive and apathetic. They are much better among schizophrenics who remain tense (though not necessarily aggressive), and who are treated within a year of their admission to hospital (during which they have failed to respond to other forms of treatment). Results may also be improved by some of the less destructive surgical techniques involving cuts that are bilateral, but quite far forward, and confined to the medical quadrants (particularly the inferomedial quadrant) of the frontal lobe. Regardless of duration, the best results in the latter type of operation are seen in patients who have been crippled by extreme anxiety and recurrent depression (rather than schizophrenia). As Sargant and Slater (1964) have pointed out, the better preserved the personality and the more reluctant the physician to recommend this form of treatment, the better the end result is likely to be. Lobotomy is contraindicated in patients with organic brain syndromes and sociopathic personality or behavior disorders.

Types of Operation. Freeman and Watts introduced lobotomy in the United States in 1936 and recommended a bilateral closed operation (through burr holes) from the side. This "standard" operation was widely adopted but involved extensive cuts being made rather posteriorly and was apt to be followed by considerable organic intellectual and emotional impairment (accentuated by the selection of chronically withdrawn schizophrenic patients for operation). A variety of other procedures have been developed, which differ in the direction from which the brain is approached (from above, from the side, from the front, or through the superior conjunctival sac and orbit); in whether the skull remains closed (except for a burr hole) or is opened (by means of a bone flap to enable direct vision); in whether the operation is unilateral or bilateral (results appear to be consistently better with the latter); and in the nature of the procedure undertaken (cutting of the thalamofrontal radiation, undercutting certain areas of the cortex, removal of parts of the cortex, or electrocoagulation of the inferior medial quadrant or of the thalamic nucleus). Various procedures still have their advocates, but there is considerable agreement on the desirability of minimal anterior inferomedial cuts bilaterally in severe neuroses and affective disorders; and on slightly more posterior and extensive cuts in schizophrenia. While the use of lobotomy has diminished greatly since the advent of the tranquilizing drugs, and has been abandoned altogether in a number of centers, it still remains an effective empirical treatment if both the patient and operative techniques are carefully selected.

Results. Following suitable operative procedures in appropriate patients, there is little or no recognizable impairment of intellectual function, emotional reaction, or social behavior, and the patient may have much more satisfactory interpersonal relationships and occupational adjustments than formerly. In many cases, however, there is some degree of residual impairment which may be related to either the patient's psychiatric disorder or the surgical procedure. The main complications of operation are due to extensive cutting or bleeding, resulting in intellectual and emotional deterioration, hemiplegia, or, occasionally, death (three percent in some series, but less than one percent in other large series of patients). Epileptiform seizures have been reported to develop in about five percent of patients who have undergone lobotomy (and may also develop as a somewhat rarer complication following insulin coma therapy), but are usually readily controlled by anticonvulsant medications.

Although lobotomy will be reserved

for patients who have failed to respond to other forms of treatment, it should never be performed with the idea that no further treatment is necessary, desirable, or possible. Patients who have undergone lobotomy and continue to receive psychotherapy, active social and milieu therapy, and visits from interested relatives tend to make a much more satisfactory adjustment than those who are neglected following the operation. Morever, every form of psychiatric treatment is still available to the patient following lobotomy and may prove much more effective than the same treatment prior to operation (with the exception of insulin coma therapy). In the event that symptoms of anxiety, tension, and depression are incompletely relieved by lobotomy and other forms of treatment subsequently, it may be desirable to consider a second bilateral lobotomy (still inferomedial, but slightly more posterior and extensive than the first). However, this should not be undertaken too hastily since there is often continued improvement over a period of many months after the operation and the maximum benefit may not be observed until after a year has elapsed.

OTHER SOMATIC TREATMENTS

Insulin coma therapy, electroconvulsive therapy, and modern techniques of frontal lobe surgery were developed independently within a few years of one another and have been widely accepted forms of somatic treatment for functional psychiatric disorders. However, a large number of other somatic treatments have been introduced for the same purpose, some of which originated before the three methods just described, and others of which were proposed subsequently as being more effective or less drastic (often based on theoretical assumptions regarding the probable mode of action of the treatment they were designed to replace).

A number of workers have regarded the common denominator of insulin coma and convulsive therapies as being diminished cerebral metabolism with anoxemia. Loevenhart (1926) had used carbon dioxide, and Zedor (1928) had administered nitrous oxide to psychotic patients. After the introduction of insulin and convulsive therapy, there was renewed interest in the therapeutic production of anoxia by means of nitrous oxide and pure nitrogen, but the results of systematic comparisons with patients receiving insulin and Metrazol were entirely unsatisfactory. Some years later Meduna (1947) reported on the beneficial effects of carbon dioxide inhalations in psychoneurotic patients, and his technique enjoyed a few years of popularity prior to the introduction of the tranquilizing drugs. Following the administration of carbon dioxide there is often considerable excitation and abreaction, effects which may also be achieved by a variety of other agents including nitrous oxide, ether, trichlorethylene, and injections of methamphetamine (Desoxyn, Methedrine or Pervitin).

Fiamberti (1937) considered the only common factor in insulin and convulsive therapy to be the production of violent vascular changes and advocated the intravenous injection of acetylcholine for this purpose. The latter drug produces cardiac arrest and loss of consciousness, but results are not generally considered comparable with those of other shock therapies. Marshall and Tarwater (1938) recommended histamine injections, on the theory that psychoses might be allergic responses to which the patient could be desensitized, and a number of other workers pursued this treatment on the basis of the marked vascular responses noted in this and other forms of shock treatment, but the results have been generally discredited. Cameron (1945) attempted to desensitize the sympathetic nervous system in patients with anxiety states by repeated injections of epinephrine, and other workers have used adrenergic blocking agents to relieve anxiety associated with excessive sympathetic activity.

Among the many other drug therapies which have been tried in psychiatric patients, three deserve special attention, namely lithium ion and nicotinic acid therapy and the therapeutic administration of psychotomimetic agents, especially lysergic acid diethylamide (LSD-25). The latter two therapies, however, are included in this discussion principally because of popular interest displayed by both physicians and the laity rather than because of any proven scientific merit.

LITHIUM THERAPY

The lithium salts have been used occasionally as sedative agents since the early 1900's. The lithium ion is capable of producing severe toxic disturbances, including incoordination, somnolence, vascular collapse, and death, and it is contraindicated in serious renal and cardiovascular disorders. In 1949, the indiscriminate use of lithium chloride as a salt substitute caused a number of deaths.

Studies of the therapeutic properties of lithium were retarded not only by the above-mentioned toxicity but also by the advent of the psychotropic drugs, which absorbed the interest of the majority of investigators. Nonetheless, European and Australian workers and, more recently, American investigators continued to explore the therapeutic potentialities of the lithium ion, eventually evolving techniques which now allow the drug to be administered with much less risk. Lithium can be given with reasonable safety if the following precautions are taken: (1) The patient should be kept under clinical observation, preferably in the hospital, particularly during the first three weeks of therapy, in order to determine correct dosage and tolerance of the lithium ion. The drug should be temporarily discon-

tinued if early toxic signs such as nausea, vomiting, diarrhea, or incoordination appear. (2) While clinical observation constitutes the most important precaution, it is also wise to monitor serum lithium levels, particularly during the first three weeks of therapy and approximately once a month thereafter. The best therapeutic results without side effects are usually obtained if the serum lithium level is held between 1.0 and 2.0 milliequivalents per liter of plasma.

The best results for lithium therapy are claimed in the control of manic excitements, although motor overactivity in schizophrenia and other types of disorders may also respond to lithium. In particular, lithium therapy is indicated for those patients who do not respond to treatment with the phenothiazines. Lithium therapy does not appear to be effective in the treatment of depression, although there is some preliminary evidence that it may of be value in the prevention of relapse in either manic-depressive or relapsing depressive disorders. Baastrup and Schou (1967) reported a six and one-half year follow-up study of 88 patients suffering from recurrent depressive disorders or from repeated manic-depressive episodes. They found that during lithium treatment, relapses occurred on the average only every 60 to 85 months but that without lithium treatment, relapses occurred on the average every eight months. Without lithium therapy, patients spent an average of 13 weeks a year in a psychotic state, but with lithium treatment, this mean was reduced to two weeks a year. If these claims are substantiated by other researchers, lithium will be the first drug ever demonstrated to give prophylaxis against one of the major psychoses.

The few other controlled studies which have appeared, plus the universally favorable reports found in uncontrolled studies, suggest that this treatment may become an established therapy in certain psychiatric disorders.

However, the final status of lithium therapy is still to be determined. Many centers are now investigating this agent, but since no pharmaceutical company currently sponsors lithium (as it cannot be patented), each investigator has to file his own investigational new-drug application with the Food and Drug Administration before he can legally use this agent to treat his patients.

LSD-25 AND OTHER HALLUCINOGENS

There are a large number of toxic substances capable of producing an altered mental state in man. Cohen (1964) cited the use of such various toxic plants in religious rites in different parts of the world over a period of many centuries. Among the hallucinogenic substances that have been used in the North American continent are mescaline extracted from Mexican peyote cactus, and psylocybin extracted from the Mexican mushroom. Lysergic acid diethylamide (LSD-25) was first synthesized in 1938 by the Swiss chemist Albert Hoffman, who also discovered its hallucinogenic properties. LSD immediately created a great deal of interest and has since been reviewed as a promising research tool. One of its fascinating qualities is the fact that an infinitesimal amount (100 to 200 micrograms) produces an intense mental state that lasts as long as eight to ten hours. The chemical structures of LSD, mescaline, and psylocybin are similar to endogenous neurohumoral substances such as norepinephrine and serotonin.

Although the altered mental state produced by LSD has often been called a model psychosis, it is actually a form of short-lived toxic psychosis which can be prevented or reversed by the administration of a phenothiazine.

LSD produces a few minor physical symptoms which appear within the first half hour after administration. These are most commonly enlargement of the pupils, a sensation of chilliness, and mild nausea. The psychological response of the subject is extremely variable. Some subjects suffer fear, depression, and anxiety, and find the whole experience so unpleasant that they refuse to take the drug again. More often, however, anxiety sensations are short-lived and are replaced by a variety of interesting subjective changes during which the subject may have a vivid awareness of things about him and experience vivid visual hallucinations and illusory distortions.

Dangers of Use. In some sections of the country there is much illicit use of LSD and other hallucinogenic agents. LSD obtained on the black market is of uncertain composition and the dosage is also uncertain. There have been a number of reports of prolonged personality disturbances, including psychotic episodes, and a few suicides among such illicit users of the drug. In most of these cases it seems likely that the role played by medication may have been to accentuate a dormant psychotic potential. However, in the hands of a responsible and experienced investigator, LSD is quite safe. Although it is possible for unstable subjects to be precipitated into a transient paranoid episode or a period of depersonalization, the usual outcome of such an incident is recovery from the episode, often with improvement over the pretreatment status.

There have been claims that LSD is valuable as an adjunct to psychotherapy in the treatment of alcoholics, drug addicts, and treatment-resistant psychoneurotics. For example, some patients appear to gain new insights and to acquire an improved attitude toward their problems after an LSD experience. To what extent these claims are true, however, awaits further investigation. At present, LSD is an investigational drug and is not available commercially.

NICOTINIC ACID

For some years, Hoffer and Osmond have claimed that nicotinic acid (niacin) given in massive doses over a long period will benefit many persons suffering from schizophrenia, alcoholism, and certain types of organic brain disorders. They use a total daily dose of 3000 mg (50 mg daily is an adequate dosage in the treatment of nicotinic-acid deficiency). Hoffer and Osmond also claim that patients treated with nicotinic acid are more likely to maintain improvement than are patients treated with other modalities, and that other forms of therapy are enhanced, particularly psychotropic medications, which have greater milligram potency when used concurrently with nicotinic-acid therapy.

Many physicians have scoffed at this treatment, but the claims made for it have created considerable public interest. For this reason, carefully-designed controlled studies are currently being conducted, and it is hoped that they will help determine the actual value of this therapy.

SELECTED REFERENCES

American Medical Association Council on Drugs. 1967. Antidepressants. In *New Drugs*. Chicago, AMA.

Arieti, S., ed. 1955. American Handbook of Psychiatry, Vol. II. New York, Basic Books, Inc., ch. 74, 75, 76, and 78.

Arieti, S., ed. 1966. American Handbook of Psychiatry, Vol. III. New York, Basic Books, Inc., ch. 28, 29, and 30.

Ayd, F. J., Jr. 1961. A survey of drug-induced extrapyramidal reactions. Journal of the American Medical Association *175*, 1054.

Baastrup, P. C., and Schou, M. 1967. Lithium as a prophylactic agent. Archives of General Psychiatry *16*, 162-172.

Benson, W. M., and Schiele, B. C. 1962. *Tranquilizing and Antidepressive Drugs*. Springfield, Charles C Thomas, Publisher.

Blackwell, B., Marley, E., Price, J., and Twylor, D. 1967. Hypertensive interactions between monoamine oxidase inhibitors and foodstuffs. British Journal of Psychiatry *113*, 349-365.

Caffey, E. M., Jr., et al. 1964. Discontinuation or reduction of chemotherapy in chronic schizophrenics. Journal of Chronic Disorders *17*, 347-358.

Caffey, E. M., Hollister, L. E., Kaim, S. C., and Pokorny, A. D. 1966. Antipsychotic, antianxiety and antidepressant drugs. Medical Bulletin *11*, 1-27.

Cameron, D. E. 1960. Production of differential amnesia as a factor in the treatment of schizophrenia. Comprehensive Psychiatry *1*, 26.

Cohen, S. 1965. *The Beyond Within—The LSD Story*. New York, Atheneum.

Cole, J. E., and Wittenborn, J. R. 1966. *Pharmacotherapy of Depression*. Springfield, Charles C Thomas, Publisher.

Cole, J. O. 1964. Therapeutic efficacy of antidepressant drugs. Journal of the American Medical Association *190*, 448.

Cole, J. O., et al. 1964. Phenothiazine treatment in acute schizophrenia: effectiveness. Archives of General Psychiatry *10*, 246.

Davis, J. M. 1965. Efficacy of tranquilizing and antidepressant drugs. Archives of General Psychiatry *13*, 552-572.

Englehardt, D. M., et al. 1964. Phenothiazines in prevention of psychiatric hospitalization. Archives of General Psychiatry *11*, 162-169.

Freeman, W., and Watts, J. W. 1942. *Psychosurgery*. Springfield, Charles C Thomas, Publisher.

Garattini, S., and Dukes, M. N. G. 1967. *Anti-Depressant Drugs*. New York, Excerpta Medica Foundation.

Gershon, S., and Yuwiler, A. 1960. Lithium ion: a specific psychopharmacological approach to the treatment of mania. Journal of Neuropsychiatry *1*, 229-239.

Glueck, B. C., Jr., et al. 1957. Regressive electric shock therapy. Psychiatric Quarterly *31*, 117.

Gordon, H. L. 1948. Fifty shock therapy theories. Military Surgeon, 103, 397.

Greenblatt, M., Arnot, R., and Solomon, H. C., eds. 1950. *Studies in Lobotomy*. New York, Grune & Stratton, Inc.

Greenblatt, M. K., Grosser, G. H., and Wechsler, H. 1964. Differential response of hospitalized depressed patients to somatic therapy. American Journal of Psychiatry *120*, 935.

Greenblatt, M., et al. 1965. *Drug and Social Therapy in Chronic Schizophrenia*. Springfield, Charles C Thomas, Publisher.

Hordern, A. 1965. *Depressive States*. Springfield, Charles C Thomas, Publisher.

Kalinowsky, L., and Hoch, P. 1961. *Somatic Treatments in Psychiatry*. New York & London, Grune & Stratton, Inc.

Kiloh, L. G., and Garside, R. F. 1963. The independence of neurotic depression and endogenous depression. British Journal of Psychiatry *109*, 451-463.

Klerman, G. L., and Cole, J. O. 1965. Clinical pharmacology of imipramine and related antidepressant compounds. Pharmacological Reviews *17*, 101-141.

Medical Bulletin. 1966. Antipsychotic, antianxiety and antidepressant drugs. MB No. 11. Washington, D.C., Veterans Administration.

Medical Research Council. 1965. Clinical trials of the treatment of depressive illness. British Medical Journal *1*, 881-886.

Mitchell, S. W. 1885. *Fat and Blood*, 4th edition. Philadelphia, J. B. Lippincott Co.

Pare, C. M. B. 1965. Some clinical aspects of antidepressant drugs. In *The Scientific Basis of Drug Therapy in Psychiatry*, ed. J. Marks and C. M. B. Pare. New York, Pergamon Press, Inc.

Richardson, H. L., Graupner, K. I., and Richardson, M. E. 1966. Intramyocardial lesions in patients dying suddenly and unexpectedly. Journal of the American Medical Association *195*, 254-260.

Rosenthal, S. H., and Gudeman, J. E. 1967. The endogenous depressive pattern. Archives of General Psychiatry *16*, 241-249.

Sargant, W., and Slater, E. 1964. *Physical Methods of Treatment in Psychiatry*, 4th edition. Baltimore, The Williams & Wilkins Co.

Schiele, B. C. 1962. Newer drugs for mental illness. Journal of the American Medical Association *181*, 126-133.

Schildkraut, J. J. 1965. The catecholamine hypothesis of affective disorders: a review of supporting evidence. American Journal of Psychiatry *122*, 509-522.

Solomon, P. 1966. *Psychiatric Drugs*. New York & London, Grune & Stratton, Inc.

Uhr, L. M., and Miller, J. G. 1960. *Drugs and Behavior*. New York, John Wiley & Sons, Inc.

Wittenborn, J. R. 1966. *The Clinical Psychopharmacology of Anxiety*. Springfield, Charles C Thomas, Publisher.

Wittenborn, J. R., and May, P. R. A. 1966. *Prediction of Response to Pharmacotherapy*. Springfield, Charles C Thomas, Publisher.

CHAPTER 13

All prevention of disease prevents mental disease; all treatment of disease has as one aim the prevention of psychiatric complication of disease.

Paul Lemkau[8]*

Preventive Psychiatry†

by Charles A. Roberts

During many discussions the terms "mental health," mental illness," and "psychiatry" are used almost interchangeably. Psychiatry is the medical specialty concerned with diseases of the mind; psychiatrists are medical specialists concerned with diseases of the mind. As the main objective of all medicine is the elimination of illness, psychiatrists are also concerned with the prevention of psychiatric illnesses. Mental health should appropriately be seen as a broad field which concerns itself with the whole range of psychosocial problems and the promotion of more effective living. While many may not agree, it would appear that there are many disciplines qualified to participate in and direct mental health programs, not exclusively the field of psychiatry, nor are psychiatrists necessarily the best qualified to direct such programs. On the other hand, a sick person is morally and legally a medical responsibility and thus patients with psychiatric illness should be examined and treated by physicians, although many other disciplines will participate in their treatment.

In a recent paper, Lemkau says

. . . The term "mental illness" is a misnomer −. . . the term could hide some important issues in thinking about the prevention of mental illnesses. In my estimation, it has done so. It leads one to think of a prevention and treatment programme that would prevent and treat all kinds of mental illnesses. It seeks to apply a panacea rather than to deal with the multiple, specific and treatment needs. . . .

In other fields of medicine, there seems to be much less confusion between prevention and treatment: the cardiologist deals with treatment comprehensively and when preventive measures (e.g., the use of penicillin in rheumatic illnesses) of wide or universal application become available he assists public health personnel, health educators, and other community services to apply these preventive measures to the population at risk. Those to whom psychiatrists act as consultants and even psychiatrists themselves might be less confused if the areas of prevention and treatment were clearly defined for mental problems. There are present in our society many endemic mental illnesses for which we do not at this time have primary preventive measures available. Primary, secondary, and tertiary activities in prevention may be recognized, although many professional colleagues and most people in our communities think only of primary activities as being preventive.

Primary prevention, in its strictest sense, covers those measures and activities which will reduce the number of cases of a disorder or illness in the community. Or in other words, "Prevention

---

*For numbered references, see list at end of the chapter.

†A more detailed discussion of this subject may be found in *Primary Prevention of Psychiatric Disorders.* Toronto Press, 1968.

may be accomplished in the pathogenesis period by measures designed to promote general optimum health or by specific protection of a man against disease agents or the establishment of barriers against agents in the environment."[10]

Secondary prevention aims at lowering the frequency of sick persons in the community through the successful treatment of established cases, particularly by the early treatment of such disorders, so that the total number of cases is reduced and the acute and chronic phases of the illness are prevented from developing.

The concept of *tertiary prevention* includes all of those measures , other than or in addition to the treatment of the disease itself, which are designed to reduce the frequency and severity of disability associated with mental illness. That much of the disability seen in the mentally ill is not necessarily inherent to the disease process is a basic assumption. Social crippling is often a by-product of the social experiences and deprivations to which the mentally ill are commonly subjected.[13]

Efforts to define mental health have been notoriously unsuccessful. Efforts to obtain an understanding or appreciation of mental health might be more fruitful if they were directed toward the reality in which we live and not toward abstract conceptual models of that which constitutes mental health.

DAILY ROUTINE AND COMMUNITY ORIENTATION

While it may appear naive to review certain aspects of our way of life which are well known to all of us but which few of us seldom think about, it would seem desirable to do so at this time in order to set the stage for the discussion which follows. The average community has developed a set of mores on the basis of which the individual is expected to follow a certain pattern of behavior. If he follows this pattern, he is acceptable to the community, but on the other hand if he varies too far from these mores he will be rejected by the community in which he lives. Western communities have two ways of expressing severe rejection. Either one is admitted to a hospital if he is considered to be ill; or alternatively one comes under the judicial, penal, or reform system if he is considered to be unwilling, even though able, to conform to the mores of our society.

The average resident in our Western communities is first of all expected during each 24-hour period to involve himself in constructive and productive work averaging about eight hours per day; second, to participate in recreational or similar pursuits for about the same period of time; and third, to have a period of rest which for the average person is also about eight hours. In the further development of this theme, we must ask ourselves why people follow this pattern. It is easy but too superficial to suggest that they do it just because they grew up in this particular culture. Certainly most people have never given this matter any thought and follow the routine mechanically even though they frequently have a terrific resentment against the demands made upon them.

The average person rests six, seven, or eight hours per night because by the late teens or early 20's he has learned from experience the routine he must follow in order to function reasonably well. Everyone knows, that he can go a few nights without having his regular amount of rest, but he knows equally well that to do more than this is to endanger his health and to render him inefficient for a short period of time until he regains his equilibrium.

Insofar as work is concerned, it appears that three main factors are involved: satisfaction for oneself from his own activities, recognition of the value of one's activities by society, and the need to obtain a living.

Insofar as recreation is concerned, it appears to represent a change of activity and an opportunity to do something one would like to do without being dependent on it for income. There is good reason to believe that there is only one real difference of motivation insofar as work and recreation are concerned: namely, that one works in order to gain a living, whereas in recreation one does what he likes to do—something which gives him personal satisfaction; which has sufficient recognition from his own family, friends, and social contacts; but which does not require concern about its value in terms of dollars and cents.

The acceptance of this routine, and positive identification of the individual with one or more of the people with whom he has continuing contact or who are responsible for his therapy, are perhaps the most important factors in the treatment and prevention of all forms of disability.

People in our society appear to be ever more confused about their personal lives and seem to be increasingly involved in a search for satisfying activities as the status of and respect for work in our society changes. The attitudes of therapists and other gate-keepers in our communities with regard to work may be of great social significance. People work in order to gain personal satisfaction, and many of our present social and professional difficulties may be due to overemphasis on making a living with the shortest possible work week, with too little emphasis on personal satisfaction and on social recognition of the part individuals play in our society.

Traditionally, our communities have placed a high value on work and participation; the well-to-do who do not work are frequently referred to as playboys and spendthrifts. Historically, the only people excused from work are the sick or dependent, and all others who do not work are described as lazy or in some way undesirable. The group of dependent people includes the very young and the very old, who, either because of lack of development or because of progressive aging, are unable to participate in work. The introduction of various

welfare programs and more particularly unemployment compensation has further complicated this matter. A guarantee of income is quite different from a guarantee of employment. Socially, it would be much more appropriate to ensure that work would be available for everyone than to be concerned with income maintenance, as the guarantee of work would ensure income maintenance, whereas the guarantee of income alone may well interfere with the normal motivations of our society. What does all of this mean to the average person in our community and to the psychiatric patient? What does it mean to professionals? It is important to maintain a reasonable perspective with regard to these matters. There is no doubt that it was formerly necessary to work long hours because we did not have the means of production that are now available to us. As our means of production have improved, it has become possible to shorten work hours since we can meet the needs of our communities with much less work than was formerly necessary. It should be noted here that reference is made to production and not to personal care services. While technology has made surplus production possible, it has not had the same effect on the service industries. In education, health, welfare, and related personal care services, the shortened work week and changes in attitude toward work have only increased our problem: we are probably further away from meeting the needs of our population and the situation seems to be deteriorating. Increased emphasis on formal education, longer holidays, shorter hours, and so on seem to increase our basic shortage of personnel faster than we can increase the number available and one wonders if we can ever meet the needs of our population if the present trends continue.

The shortened hours of work have accentuated the importance of recreation. Furthermore, it is quite obvious that most workers engaged in mass production are unable to meet the needs of personal satisfaction and social recognition in their jobs, and their dissatisfaction is continuously expressed by demands for more and more income with less and less work. People do not talk about the lack of personal satisfaction or low status of the service which they perform, as this requires the admission of a personal problem or leads to a criticism, explicit or implicit, of one's superiors or of the organization where one is employed. Facing a problem in this way is unacceptable to most people.

It is in this area that professional people appear to be most confused. Professionals, being part of the communities in which they live, want a shortened work week, higher salaries, and other fringe benefits obtained by labor. At the same time they wish to obtain personal satisfaction and social recognition for the services they perform. It is quite possible that these two objectives are incompatible, at least for them.

NECESSITIES FOR MENTAL HEALTH

At the present time, we do not know the specific cause of many mental disorders. We do, however, have some useful assumptions regarding factors which encourage or discourage the development of mental health.

In the field of nutrition, for example, we are familiar with the importance of supplying the body with the right food, including vitamins, calories, and the like, to meet changing physical needs and to protect and enhance normal growth and development. In mental health, there are psychic, social, and physical needs which must be satisfied if mental health is to be protected and promoted.

Knowledge of these psychological "vitamins' is increasing. As in other fields of health, the child is of primary importance in preventive activities — we have known for generations that love, tenderness, and affection are essential for the healthy emotional growth of an infant and child. Adults, including the aged, have emotional needs which must be met if good mental health is to be maintained and psychiatric illness avoided. Parents, teachers, the clergy, recreational workers, and others associated with developing children must be similarly concerned about psychological development and must be informed about the emotional, social, psychological, and physical needs of the young. They must know how to provide adequate opportunities for healthy emotional development and must anticipate the critical reactions which can occur when too much stress is combined with inadequate satisfaction of emotional needs.

"Community psychiatry," "social psychiatry," and other names have been applied to programs concerned with a community organization approach to mental health programs designed to improve the total opportunities of people in our communities and to facilitate the utilization of all available resources when people need help.

While we know that psychiatric illnesses and symptoms are extremely common, the true extent of morbidity in this field is difficult to establish and is very largely dependent on the definitions used in any particular study. It is variously estimated that one in ten of the noninstitutionalized population has some recognizable psychiatric illness or defect, but some studies report that nearly half the population shows some sign of psychiatric disorder or precursor symptoms. According to Kraft,[4]

The recently issued volumes of the Joint Commission on Mental Illness and Health present us with a wealth of documentation establishing the proliferating roots of mental ill health and its connection with a multitude of related social problems, such as delinquency, poverty and alcoholism. A recent study of mental health in Manhattan concludes that as many as one out of four adults has levels of mental ill health requiring treatment.

It is more than possible that no other illnesses afflict our population to such an extent regardless of how we estimate the incidence of psychiatric illnesses. It is considered, though, that some common types of psychiatric illnesses may be as much diseases of our society as they are diseases of individuals in our society.

While a number of psychiatric illnesses are recognized as due to brain damage, infections, poisoning, injury, dietary deficiencies, and physical illness, these illnesses whose cause is known account for only a small part of the psychiatric illness seen in our society. Some illnesses, especially in the field of mental deficiency, seem to be family-related and may be either acquired or inherited or both. It is clear, however, that most psychiatric illnesses are not simply due to physical causes or inherited according to specific genetic patterns and, in fact, their specific causes are not known at this time.

Programs for Prevention of Mental Illness. Prevention must be attempted, as it is increasingly obvious that treatment alone can never deal with such widespread illnesses. The trained personnel are not available for all patients with psychiatric symptoms and illnesses to receive adequate treatment. These preventive programs must be developed even in the face of our ignorance of specific causes and of the natural course of many psychiatric conditions.

We must also face the fact that many of the services provided in our society to deal with social breakdown and psychiatric illness may, in fact, worsen or prolong these conditions rather than lead to improvement or prevention. Not only our penitentiaries and jails, not only welfare institutions, but also our hospitals, both general and special, are housing many individuals suffering from psychiatric illness and social breakdown and may indeed be contributing to the social disabilities from which these individuals suffer.

The increasing public interest in the size and nature of this problem is encouraging. Governments have historically been involved in mental health programs; most governments are now investing heavily in treatment programs, in the training of personnel, and in the facilitation of research. Historically great killers, cholera among others, were often reduced and controlled by sanitary measures *before* their specific causes were known. Some of our great pioneers in public health promoted sanitary organization to control infectious diseases although they lived before Pasteur began the science of bacteriology.

As we are acting so much on faith and on limited evidence in a complicated situation, we must ensure ongoing research to assess our efforts and to evaluate their impact. This is really epidemiological research supported by work in such fields as sociology, psychology, psychiatry, and others.

According to Rumke, "the phase in which we are now working may fairly be called 'pre-scientific'—a necessary precursor of more objectively scientific ways of working."[12]

PRIMARY PREVENTION

To develop primary prevention activities on a sound basis, many more studies will be necessary. For example, we must know more specifically the symptoms and signs of social or individual breakdown as they occur in any given community. Much will have to be done in the area of "case-finding"—both the public at large and workers in all fields of individual service will require more specific in-depth education regarding psychiatric signs and symptoms. It would also be helpful to develop ways and means of identifying those people in our communities who are vulnerable under conditions of stress and social change, and to understand the mode of action of the "noxious agents" to which they are susceptible.

We begin, in medicine, by symptomatic treatment. We hope to find a specific cause and apply specific treatment; if the cause is one which can be removed by environmental measures or by strengthening the host's resistance, we can carry out primary prevention.

In 1962, the American Public Health Association published *Mental Disorders — A Guide to Control Method.*[10] This publication follows the accepted ideas of "control" and deals with prevention at three levels, primary, secondary, and tertiary. Under the heading of primary prevention there are chapters entitled:

Chapter 2. Mental Disorders of Known Etiology.
Chapter 4. Conditions of Unknown Etiology
Chapter 5. Some General Measures for Prevention of Mental Disorders.
Chapter 6. Implications for Training of Administrators and other Specialists.

Insofar as mental disorders of known etiology are concerned, it is quite clear that primary prevention is not within the sphere of activity of the psychiatrist. Once the cause of mental illness is known, it becomes a matter of poison control, prenatal care, control of infectious diseases, genetic counseling, dietary advice, and so on. According to Lemkau.[7]

It appears to be the fate of psychiatrists that each time an illness once freely admitted as belonging in their bailiwicks yields up the secrets of its etiology, or even becomes subject to arrest by specific treatment, that disease is no longer considered psychiatric....

These causes fall in traditional areas of public health concern. Public health personnel and practicing physicians are prepared professionally for treating them; psychiatrists, in general, are not. Thus, practicing physicians and public health physicians or nurses should not feel uncomfortable in this area of primary prevention of mental disorders.

In all of these efforts it is necessary to recognize the importance of public health education. Some of our professional education programs include this as a study area. On the whole, however, practical efforts in public health education have been spotty and limited. It surely is an important area of concern but not one from which we can anticipate immediate results in direct response to our efforts. Health education programs can be frustrating for those involved in them, and particularly so when these programs are not well supported by other health workers. There can be no doubt of the changes in public attitudes toward mental illness during recent decades. Families, individuals, community agencies, employers, and others are now much more aware of mental illness. More and more they are demanding not only treatment services but efforts to bring these illnesses under control.

"Conditions of unknown etiology" are not yet in the area of primary control. They are, however, subject to control at the secondary and tertiary levels. Thus case-finding and follow-up are of great concern in the control of mental illnesses.

Under "Some general measures for prevention of mental disorders" we must consider the following: support in times of stress, prevention of maternal deprivation, improvement of child rearing practices, prenatal care, reduction of radiological exposure, and genetic counseling. The development of adequate services in these areas should not be seen as a responsibility of mental health services alone. Such programs are concerned with total health and welfare of which psychiatric illness is just one aspect. The role of the mental health professional in these areas is as a program consultant or advisor.

The social breakdown syndrome as postulated in the *Guide to Control Methods* is based on the concept that a capacity for development may be lost if social isolation is permitted during particular developmental periods. Social isolation

(Text continued on p. 315.)

TABLE 13–1. Some Poisons Producing Mental Disorders*

	SOURCE									TYPES OF EFFECT			
	Drugs	Animals	Food and Plants	Industrial	Malevolent Poisoning	Agricultural Chemicals	Addictive	In Consumers Goods and HH	Specific Antidote or Antagonist	Acute Symptoms	Toxic Psychoses	Perm. Brain Damage	Fatal
Abrin			FP		M					S			
Acetone				I				HH		S			
Acetylsalicylic Acid	D									S	P	BD	F
Aconitine			FP							S		BD	F
Alkyl Mercury				I		Ag				S			F
Aminophyllin	D									S			
Amphetamine	D								Barbiturates	S	P	BD	
Aniline				I						S	P	BD	F
Arsenic	D			I	M	Ag		HH	BAL	S	P	BD	F
BAL Dimercaprol	D									S			
Banthine	D									S		?	F
Barbiturates	D									S	P		
Benadryl	D								Stimulants	S	P	BD	F
Benzol				I						S	P		
Black Widow Spider		An							d-tubocurarine	S	P	?	
Bromides	D								i.v. NH_4Cl	S	P		F
Butazolidin	D								Antihistamines	S	P		F
Cadmium				I						S	P		
Caffeine	D		FP				A?		Sedatives	S	P		
Camphor	D		FP	I						S	P		
Cannabinol			FP							S	P		
Carbon Disulphide				I				HH		S	P	BD	F
Carbon Monoxide				I				HH		S	P	BD	F
Carbon Tetrachloride				I		Ag		HH		S	P	BD	F
Cholinesterase Inhibitors	D			I		Ag			Ca. gluconate; Atropine	S	P	BD	
Chlorothene	D			I						S			
Chlorothiazide	D									S			
Chlorpromazine	D								Methylphenidate	S	P		
Cocaine	D						Ad			S	P	BD	F
Colchicine	D								Atropine	S	P		F

Substance	D	FP	I	Ag	Ad	HH	Antidote	S	P	BD	F
Coniine								S			
Copper Salts	D	FP	I	Ag							
Cyanides			I	Ag			Sodium Nitrite and Sodium Thiosulfate		P		F
Daphnin		FP				HH	Barbiturates	S	P		
DDT							Barbiturates	S	P		F
Digitalis	D	FP					Potassium Cl.	S	P		F
Dilantin								S	P		
Ergot	D	FP			Ad						F
Ethanol	D						Caffeine	S	P		
Ethylene Glycol Acetate			I				Barbiturates	S	P	BD	F
							Na. acetate	S	P	BD	F
Germisol	D		I				Barbiturates	S			
Henbane	D						Paraldehyde	S			
Imipramine (Tofranil)	D		I				Barbiturates	S			
Iodine	D							S			
Iproniazid	D							S			
Iron			I					S			
Kerosene	D		I			HH	Analeptics	S	P		F
Lead	D		I			HH		S	P	BD	F
Lobeline		FP					Barbiturates	S	P		
Lysergic Acid Diethylamide								S			
Mercury	D						Dimercaprol	S	P	?	F
Mescaline	D		I				Barbiturates	S	P		F
Metaldehyde		FP		Ag				S			
Methanol	D		I		Ad	HH	NaHCO3	S	P	BD	F
Morphine	D				Ad		Nalorphine	S	P		F
Muscarine		FP					Atropine	S	P		F
Naphthalene			I			HH		S			F
Parathion				Ag			O2; atropine	S			F
Phenacetin (Acetophenetidin)	D							S	P		

*Reprinted by permission from Mental Disorders: A Guide to Control Methods. Copyright 1962 by the American Public Health Association, Inc., pp. 36-38.

TABLE 13–1. Some Poisons Producing Mental Disorders (Continued)

	SOURCE									TYPES OF EFFECT			
	DRUGS	ANIMALS	FOOD AND PLANTS	INDUSTRIAL	MALEVOLENT POISONING	AGRICULTURAL CHEMICALS	ADDICTIVE	IN CONSUMERS GOODS AND HH	SPECIFIC ANTIDOTE OR ANTAGONIST	ACUTE SYMPTOMS	TOXIC PSYCHOSES	PERM. BRAIN DAMAGE	FATAL
Phenergan	D								Paraldehyde	S	P		F
Phenmetrazine	D									S	P		
Phenol	D			I				HH		S	P		
Phenylbutazone	D							HH	Antihistamines	S	P		
Phosphorus (yellow)				I				HH		S	P		F
Pyrethrum				I		Ag		HH		S	P		
Quinacrine (Atabrine)	D									S	P		
Rauwolfia	D		FP							S	P		
Ricin	D		FP	I					Atropine	S	P		F
Saccharine				I				HH		S	P		
Scorpions		An							Serum; Barbiturates Noradrenalin	S	P		
Snake Venoms		An							antivenins	S	P		
Sodium Hypochlorite	D			I				HH		S	P		F
Solanin			FP					HH		S	P	Potatoes eaten by children	F
Squill	D	An							Barbiturates	S	P		
Strammonium	D		FP							S	P		
Strychnine	D				M				O₂; barbiturates	S	P		
Sympathomimetic Amines	D						A			S	P		
Thallium	D					Ag		HH	BAL	S	P		F
Thiocyanates	D							HH		S	P	BD	
Toluene				I						S	P		
Tricresylphosphate				I				HH		S	P		
Turpentine				I						S	P		F
Vanadium					M					S			

or alienation is a breakdown in communication. If we can keep people communicating (e.g., verbally, socially, and emotionally) and if we help them through crisis situations, we should prevent many psychiatric conditions. Alienation or social isolation is a progressive and vicious circle; if we can impinge on the circle and break through the isolation, much good will result.

Many approaches are being developed to deal with the problems of social isolation. These efforts include the establishment of counseling and guidance services, using both group and individual methods: related support in times of stress; anticipation of significant life experiences; special social groupings; and so on. Goldfarb[3] states:

What shines through is that older persons bring practical problems to the leader, that they focus their attention upon him and that they benefit from the opportunity to bring things to him and from his attitude toward them. . . . Because it favors the development of a relationship which the older person may otherwise be disinclined to accept or may be unable to find, the group may prove to be a practical . . . as well as less expensive . . . way of providing what many aged persons need if they are to learn, relearn, or release their capacities for adjustment to a community which tends to pose them difficult problems as their ability decreases.

Further examples of this type of activity are provided by "The Well-Being Clinics,"[9] developed by Dr. Allister Macleod and Mrs. Phyllis Poland in conjunction with the Y.W.C.A. in Montreal, and the group discussion methods used in the Crestwood Heights project in Toronto.[11]

The chapter "Implications for the Training of Administrators and Other Specialists"[10] is well worth reading. It is apparent that all of us in our different specialties require more knowledge of each other's roles and of how our activities can augment or minimize each other's efforts. While recent developments have been encouraging, it is also true that some of the major changes that

appear to be desirable, particularly in respect to preventive activities and the provision of patient care, are being impeded and delayed by many existing attitudes toward mental illness and the mentally ill. There is reason to believe that the public at large and many community groups are ahead of the professions and governmental authorities in their attitude toward mental illness and in their desire to see improvements in the services provided. Ways must be found to mobilize this general public support to bring about necessary changes.

THE IMPORTANCE OF COMMUNITY STRUCTURE

The work of Dr. Alexander Leighton[2, 5, 6] and his associates seems destined to make major contributions to our understanding of communities and the development of mental illness therein. While biology, heredity, current circumstances, life experiences, and so on may all play a part in the etiology of psychiatric and psychological disorders in an individual, Leighton appears to accept that psychoneurotic patterns are primarily derived from life experiences with varying degrees of hereditary and physiological predisposition; that personality disorders are conceived of as being basically "constitutional" (i.e., whatever the cause, the condition arises early, pervades the personality, and remains relatively fixed throughout life); and that heredity is a major factor in both schizophrenia and the affective psychoses. Thereafter, the sociocultural environment can influence the development of disorders or the prevention of them. These sociocultural conditions may well have selective influences on the appearance and persistence of malfunctioning which may lead to psychiatric disorders. Social disintegration — not just a moving away from functional effectiveness but also a relative lack of patterning in the system — may be incited by a high frequency of broken homes, few and weak associa-

TABLE 13-2. Infections Producing Mental Disorders

	AGENT	RESERVOIR	VECTOR	PERSONAL CONTACT	EFFECTIVE IMMUNIZATION ACTIVE/PASSIVE	EFFECTIVE RX TO PREVENT BRAIN DAMAGE	OCCURRENCE	ACUTE SYMPTOMS	PERMANENT BRAIN DAMAGE FETAL	CHILDHOOD	ADULT	NOTES
Meningococcus meningitis	B	Man		PC	None	Sulfas and antibiotics	Sporadic and Epidemic	Ac		Ch	Ad	Especially dangerous in infants. Mental deficiency.
Mononucleosis	Unkn.	Man?		PC?	None	None	Common	1% children		Ch		
Mumps	V	Man		PC	Active; lasts two years	None	Universal	Ac	?	Ch?	?	
Pneumococcal pneumonia	B	Man		PC	None	Sulfas and antibiotics	Common	Ac				
Rheumatic fever	?	Man		PC	None	None	Frequent	Ac	?	Ch?	?	Is a complication of streptococcal disease
Rubella	V	Man		PC	Passive-gamma globulin	None	Universal		F			About 10% of fetal infections in first trimester result in anomalies
Syphilis	Sp.	Man		PC	None	Penicillin	Frequent		F	Ch	Ad	
Toxoplasmosis	Prot.	Many mammals		Congenital	None	Sulfonamides?	Scattered		F?			
Tuberculosis	B	Man		PC	Active	Isoniazid	Scattered			Ch	Ad	

V=virus, B=Bacterium or Bacillus, Sp=Spirochete, Prot.=Protozoon, ?=suspected, Blanks=Not known, F=fetal.

*Reprinted by permission from *Mental Disorders: A Guide to Control Methods.* Copyright 1962 by the American Public Health Association, Inc., pp. 40 – 41.

TABLE 13-2. Infections Producing Mental Disorders (Continued)

	AGENT	RESERVOIR	VECTOR	PERSONAL CONTACT	EFFECTIVE IMMUNIZATION ACTIVE/PASSIVE	EFFECTIVE RX TO PREVENT BRAIN DAMAGE	OCCURRENCE	ACUTE SYMPTOMS	PERMANENT BRAIN DAMAGE FETAL	CHILDHOOD	ADULT	NOTES
Aseptic meningitis Group B Coxsackie	V	Man		PC	No	No	Common	Ac				
Chicken pox	V	Man		PC	No	No	Universal	Ac		Ch		
Smallpox	V	Man		PC	Yes		Not in USA	Ac				
Encephalitides	V	Birds?	mosquitoes	No	No See Text	No		Ac		Ch	Ad	
Eastern encephalitis	V	Wild birds	mosquitoes	No	No	No	Sporadic or Epidemic	Ac		Ch		
Western encephalitis	V	Wild birds	"	No	No	No	Sporadic or Epidemic	Ac		Ch		
St. Louis encephalitis	V	Wild birds	"	No	No	No	Sporadic or Epidemic	Ac		Ch	Ad	
Pertussis	B	Man		PC	Active	No	Common	Ac		Ch		
Encephalitis lethargica					No	No	Epidemic	Ac		Ch	Ad	Apparently has disappeared from the world.
Influenza	V	Man		PC	Active	No	Epidemic	Ac	No	Ch	Ad	
Measles	V	Man		PC	Passive-gamma globulin	No	Universal	Ac		Ch	Ad	0.02%

TABLE 13–3. Some Genetic Diseases Which May Produce Mental Disorders*

	Mendelian R=recessive D=dominant	Age of Manifestation	Treatment	Carrier Identification	Approx. Frequency	Lab. Diagnoses	Proportion of Cases Due to Mutations
Cerebral lipidoses	R	Various	None	Some types	1:25,000	No	Negligible
Galactosemia	R	Infant	Dietary	Yes	Unknown	Yes	Negligible
Phenylketonuria	R	Infant	Dietary	Yes	1:20,000	Yes	Negligible
Gargoylism	R	Infant	None	No	<1:25,000	Yes	Negligible
Gargoylism (sex-linked)	R	Child	None	No	<1:50,000	Yes	Approx. ⅓
Acrocephalosyndactyly	D	Congenital	None	Yes	Unknown	No	Most
Ocular hypertelorism	D	Congenital	None	Yes	Unknown	No	Unknown
Huntington's chorea	D	Late adult	None	No	1:25,000	No	Approx. ⅕
Tuberous sclerosis	D	Variable	None	Yes	1:30,000	No	Approx. ¼

*Reprinted by permission from *Mental Disorders: A Guide to Control Methods.* Copyright 1962 by The American Public Health Association, Inc., p. 43.

tions, few and weak leaders, few patterns of recreation, a high frequency of hostility, a high frequency of crime and delinquency, and weak and fragmented communication.

Communities, according to Leighton, are apt to become disintegrated under the following circumstances: recent disasters, widespread ill-health, extensive poverty, cultural confusion, widespread secularization, extensive migration, and rapid, widespread social change. Community social disintegration results in psychological stress, lack of resources for dealing with stress, and thereafter psychiatric disorders. Leighton and his coworkers pose a number of hypotheses which are then examined in the light of the data gathered in their community studies.

1. *Sociocultural disintegration leads to physical insecurity and then to psychiatric disorder.* Their findings indicate that individuals living in depressed areas have a high risk of psychiatric disorder regardless of their own position of economic advantage, and conclude that psychiatric illness is not the result of physical insecurity.

2. *Sociocultural disintegration fosters mental health by the degree to which it permits freedom of sexual expression.* They found that the highest prevalence of psychosomatic symptoms were present in those with the least sexual restraint. They do not refute this hypothesis but raise doubts as to its validity.

3. *Sociocultural disintegration fosters mental health by the degree to which it permits freedom of hostile and aggressive expression.* Their evidence indicates that groups in which aggression and hostility are freely expressed have the greatest prevalence of symptoms.

4. *Sociocultural disorder fosters psychiatric disorder due to the limitations put on the giving and receiving of love.* Their evidence supports this: great numbers of broken homes, separation of parents, membership in few associations, overt hostility, and poor communication characterize disturbed groups.

TABLE 13–4. Nutritional Diseases Which Produce Mental Disorders

Name	Deficiency Foods	Acute Brain Syndrome	Chronic Brain Syndrome	Mental Retardation	Notes
Beriberi	Thiamine	S			
Kwashiorkor	Multiple, especially protein	S	Chr	MR	Anorexia in weaning infants
Pellagra	Niacin	S	Chr	?	
Wernicke's encephalopathy	Thiamine	S	Chr		Especially in chronic alcoholics
Anoxemia	Oxygen	S	Chr	MR	

S=Acute brain syndrome.
Chr=Chronic brain syndrome.
MR=Mental retardation as a residual.
*Reprinted by permission from *Mental Disorders: A Guide to Control Methods.* Copyright 1962 by The American Public Health Association, Inc., p. 44.

5. *Social disintegration fosters psychiatric disorders by interfering with the achievement of socially valued ends by legitimate means.* Their evidence supports this hypothesis.

6. *Sociocultural disintegration fosters psychiatric disorders by interfering with spontaneity.* The evidence suggests that while people can get away with more things in a disintegrated area, the choice of things one might like to do is very limited. The integrated communities appear to offer a wider range of opportunities.

7. *Social disintegration fosters psychiatric disorders by interfering with a person's orientation regarding his place in society and sense of membership in human groups.* This is supported by the evidence that people in depressed areas feel mentally and morally inferior.

8. *Social disintegration fosters psychiatric disorder by interfering with the individual's sense of membership in a moral order.* Their evidence suggests that cultural confusion, secularization, lack of membership in associations, lack of leaders, and poor communication all contribute to high incidence of psychiatric disorders; and conversely that the moral order of a community has a regulative power in terms of mental health.

Paul Lemkau at a recent meeting of the World Federation for Mental Health reviewed the activities of public health and mental health workers, and demonstrated how they are coming together around our common concern about morbidity and disablement. He indicated his belief that psychiatrists may not be fully aware of how much prevention has taken place, and that programs appear to be moving on to firmer ground with respect to certain disorders at least. While recognizing the multifactorial nature of certain mental disorders such as senility and arteriosclerosis, he stressed knowledge of the social breakdown syndrome and of social deprivation of children and their potential importance in primary prevention.

While specific preventive measures are not yet available for certain illnesses such as schizophrenia, it would seem that a recognition of the contributions of Crestwood Heights[11] and Stirling County.[2, 5, 6] the concept of the social breakdown syndrome and social depri-

TABLE 13–5. Mental Diseases Caused by General Systemic Diseases*

		Brain Syndromes		Prevention	Corr. Rx	Effective Maintenance Rx
		Acute	Chronic			
Addison's disease	Adrenocortical deficiency	Ac	Chr	No	No	Corticosteroids
Pernicious anemia	Inability to absorb Vitamin B12 due to absence of "intrinsic" gastric enzyme	Ac		No	No	Liver
Cushing's syndrome	Hypercortisone	Ac			Operate if due to basophilic adenoma	
Erythroblastosis fetalis	Maternal antibodies destroy fetal blood cells		Chr	Rh typing	Exchange transfusion	No
Hyperbilirubinemia	Liver defect		Chr		" "	
Hyperthyroidism		Ac		No	Operative	Yes
Cretinism	Hypothyroidism	Ac	Chr	Iodine in salt?	No	Yes
Diabetes	Hyperinsulinism	Ac	Chr	No	No	Insulin
Intracranial masses		Ac	Chr	No	Surgery or antibiotics	No
Arteriosclerosis		Ac	Chr	No	No	No
Senile deterioration		Ac	Chr	No	No	No
Mongolism			Chr	No	No	No

*Reprinted by permission from *Mental Disorders: a Guide to Control Methods.* Copyright 1962 by The American Public Health Association, Inc., p. 46.

vation in childhood could provide reasonably firm ground on which to base a social program for the improvement of mental health and the prevention of at least some psychiatric illnesses.

THE ROLE OF SOCIETY AND GOVERNMENT

At this time it is necessary to consider in the broadest terms the importance of social action in the promotion of mental health and the prevention of mental ill health. On the basis of research findings, it would seem reasonable to suggest that such social action should have the following objectives:

1. Sociocultural disintegration should be avoided.
2. The maintenance of group standards of behavior should be emphasized.
3. Personal, racial, religious, cultural, and other differences should not be exploited for economic, political, and other reasons, as there is an indication that groups in which hostility and aggression are freely expressed have the highest prevalence of symptoms.
4. Social programs should promote the integrity of the family, group activities, and other community developments which will support the individual and his family.
5. Socially valuable objectives should be established as goals for our society, and individuals should receive recognition of their contribution toward the achievement of these goals.
6. Programs should clarify and ensure the place of the individual in our society.
7. The environment of children in all socioeconomic-educational groups should be enriched to permit the maximum development of their individual potential.

When existing social and psychiatric problems are viewed against these principles, there may well be reason for concern. It would not appear unreasonable to suggest that Western society is becoming increasingly hedonistic: the individual must have immediate gratification or satisfaction of needs regardless of the social cost, or in the long run, the cost to the individual concerned. Too commonly, we hear expression of concern about one's place in society, of disillusionment regarding one's contribution to society, and of isolation and loneliness. This hedonistic standard is now affecting all of our social structures. Social structures and sanctions on behavior have always existed for the good of society as a whole even though it has been recognized that individuals might well suffer personally in order to preserve society as a whole. While it is true that Freud postulated the psychological theme which demonstrates the difficulties which repression and other psychological defense mechanisms cause for the individual, he always recognized that these were socially necessary and that sublimation of the individuals drives or instincts through socially acceptable activites might well be essential in the development and maintenance of a reasonable society. It would appear that all social groups need acceptable group objectivies, with which the individual can identify and from which he can gain personal satisfaction and a sense of social value, which justify to him his continuing contributions to society and the deferment of gratification of some of his intense innate needs.

All individuals have basic needs for which they seek gratification. If gratification is not forthcoming, then anger and aggression develop followed by feelings of guilt. This guilt is dealt with either by depression which is directed inward or by paranoia which is directed outward. These reactions are accompanied or followed by efforts at reparation. However, it is important to realize that immediate and selfish satisfaction of these basic drives can lead to the same processes. Gratification must, therefore, be obtained through constructive social activities (a euphemism for work) which will lead to acceptable satisfaction of these basic drives or wishes. While there may be immediate and temporary relief following the expression of aggression or the satisfaction of sexual drives, it is clear that the individual will not make a satisfactory long-term adjustment unless there is a concurrent satisfactory level of personal and social acceptance. Demonstration of such ways of dealing with the individual's instinctual drives is perhaps the most critical task of a parent or parent substitute, and it would appear that adults who as children did not assimilate this way of behavior may well have mental health problems.

There are many interesting contradictions in the mental health field. In psychoanalysis and in psychotherapy, there is frequent reference to the maintenance of a level of frustration, and gratification of many of the patient's demands is avoided. Many, by no means all, therapists insist that patients will not make progress unless they themselves pay for their therapy. In this scheme of things, the patient's ego should be consistently strengthened so as to provide an acceptable state of balance between the internal drives, the internal restrictions on behavior, and the real world in which the patient lives. The patient must pay or must give up something (i.e., make a choice regarding the time when a particular drive is to be satisfied and which drive it is to be), in order to feel justified in taking "treatment" from the therapist. It is interesting, by contrast, to observe the number of people in the area of social action who advocate gratification of impulses without requiring effective social participation; this appears to be so in the field of industrial relations, education, family life, and so on. As Leighton observed in his comments on freedom of sexual expression, these ideas are usually more popular with social scientists than with mental health professionals, although they would appear to be gaining an increasing number of adherents in the mental health field as well. It is quite

possible that the efforts of those working in the field of pathology to extend into areas of prevention are based on the experience of what happens to "sick" individuals rather than to those members of our society who maintain an acceptable level of social function, and it is clear that much more information is needed about total populations rather than abnormal populations on which to base specific programs in these fields.

As an example of this we have a recent study of college students in the United States. In this study college students were asked to select their most mentally healthy classmates. This group of mentally healthy students was found to have a significantly higher proportion of serious conflicts with parents (in many cases, the student had left home because of this) than had occurred in a random sample of other students. If the choice had been "sick students" instead of "the most healthy," we could probably have attributed their illness to "conflict with authority."

All experiences to date would, however, indicate that our society must provide opportunities for individual development, for individual satisfaction, for a sense of individual worth, and for social recognition and participation if we are to look forward to better mental health in the future.

It would be easy to avoid mention of political systems and national policies when discussing primary prevention in the mental health field. It would, however, be unrealistic to do so. For too many years we have concerned ourselves with individual action in the mental health field. As indicated earlier, we must now of necessity enter the arena of social action.

Transcultural psychiatry has not yet clarified the effects of different cultures on mental health. From the evidence available it seems reasonable to assume that the incidence and nature of serious psychotic illnesses may not vary much from culture to culture, although ways of handling them certainly affect the apparent need for hospital and other health services for such patients. These psychotic illnesses can, however, be relatively effectively controlled through treatment, hospital care, supportive services, and so on. Some day many of these may be preventable. For the moment, however, effective treatment and rehabilitation may be the best primary prevention, and it should minimize the effects of these illnesses on other people and on the community at large. Of much greater concern are the psychosomatic and neurotic illnesses, character and personality disorders, and antisocial behavior in general.

The western world prides itself on its physical accomplishments, individual freedom, and social welfare programs. There is, however, a qualification for all of these. Are they developed as part of a social action program or are they political expedients? Older citizens, less privileged families with young children, widows, and other dependent members of our society must feel that they have a recognized place in our communities. Adequate services must be provided for young children, adolescents, and the handicapped; services are too grudgingly given, often on a gratuitous basis rather than as a right of a free citizen in a free society which is proud of its accomplishments and of its recognition of the individual's essential dignity. There is reason for hope. We have had John Kennedy's vision to help us: The Peace Corps, The Messages on Mental Health and Retardation, and sweeping changes in social welfare philosophy in the United States followed by President Johnson's Great Society; in Canada, C.U.S.O., the Company of Young Canadians, A.R.D.A., and the Canada Assistance Act. If only these can be mobilized to give every individual a feeling of participation in a valued and valuable program—an attachment to ideals which would make each one feel worthy and participant in a great system—perhaps many of the problems faced by each of us and our society as a whole would be reduced.

The rationalization of federal, state (provincial), and municipal systems is essential if every family, every expectant mother, every child, every immigrant, every adolescent, and every handicapped person, is to have housing, educational, counseling, recreational, social welfare, and health programs which are essential to a truly preventive program in the primary sense. No one must be denied the essential opportunity of personal and social fulfillment because of some argument over jurisdiction. In times of war these difficulties can be overcome; surely they can be overcome in times of peace. Nor should services necessary for personal and social fulfillment be denied on the basis of cost: society can afford that which is necessary; and it must be accepted that automobiles—now the greatest killers and maimers in the western world—are only as good as their users, great physical monuments, subways, airports, and so on are often useful as symbols of the aims, objectives, and value systems of a society. They are often essential to physical comfort, but they may remain as monuments to our social failures unless concurrently necessary opportunities are provided for the individual members of our society to find a satisfying and accepted place.

Many, no doubt, will feel that all of this has nothing to do with the prevention of mental illness, but it is suggested that programs such as "Head Start" may in a few years contribute more to the mental helath of our citizens than will all of our health services. In the health field, morbidity has been reduced and life expectancy has increased markedly; society must now provide opportunities for effective satisfying "living" for those whose physical health has been improved and whose lives have been lengthened.

CAUSES AND PREVENTION OF PSYCHOSOCIAL CONDITIONS

There are a number of conditions which may be collectively referred to as psychosocial: alcoholism, drug addiction, suicide, behavior disorders and delinquency, and much of the symptomatology seen in geriatric psychoses. The more these conditions are studied, the more it appears that they result from the failure of present social patterns to adequately meet the needs of many individuals. Thus, to ask the question "Can we prevent alcoholism or drug addiction?" is to ask whether it is possible to prevent the many psychosocial ills which confront us today.

Failure of social patterns to provide for the individual needs of people is the basis of many of today's psychosocial ills. The child who becomes delinquent is seeking an outlet for himself which will make him stand out in his group, which will give him a feeling of importance and through this an inner satisfaction. The aging person who becomes a problem usually feels abandoned, and in fact often is. To him, life no longer seems to have meaning and he feels himself to be a burden to his relatives rather than a contributing member of his family or social group. The drug addict is similarly seeking escape from unpleasant realities which are often based on the feeling of not being wanted or of not belonging to a group. He frequently seeks escape through association with other individuals in an environment which accepts him without question, and it is here that his addiction is usually developed.

It is difficult to understand and to work with the delinquent, the drug addict, and the aged because most of us have not experienced feelings similar to theirs. Only as we appreciate the environment as it appears to them, only as we appreciate their feelings, will we be able to understand them and to provide the support they need.

The prevention of psychosocial illness, of which drug addiction is an example, presents one of the major problems of our day. There is no evidence that the increased availability of alcohol, LSD, marijuana and other drugs, or the recognition of addictions as being illnesses, has contributed to a reduction in the extent and nature of these problems. There is evidence in Great Britain that the restriction of alcohol during the Second World War may have reduced alcoholism, and to quote Professor Carstairs,[1] "the reduction in severe alcoholism in this country (i.e., Great Britain) can confidently be ascribed to taxation which has made it too expensive to drink really heavily. Similarly, legal sanctions have cut down the amount of drug addiction." It would seem reasonable to assume that the incidence of these conditions is increasing as the addicting agents become more widely available and as the social sanctions against such conditions are reduced. The philosophy of increased availability, maintenance of addiction, and the lowering of social sanctions may well be nihilistic, as these tend to support pathology rather than health. The prevention of these conditions is a challenge which can be met if our communities are prepared to make the necessary efforts.

In doing this, the first essential is that the homes in which our children are brought up should provide for their full needs. Naturally this includes the necessities of life such as proper diet, proper clothing, warmth, and comfort; but more important it also means love and security—the infant must feel wanted. One wonders how such a climate can be provided in the overcrowded slums of our cities; in homes where there is discord between parents; in homes torn by alcoholism, separation, or divorce; or when other such factors are present to mar the environment of the growing child.

The second need is for a reëvaluation of moral and ethical standards. To develop normally, a child must grow in a proper atmosphere of right and wrong, of good and bad. From the first he must learn that certain actions on his part are to his advantage while others bring undesired results; that his behavior in a group is necessarily related to that of others in the group and, if he wants to get along, he has to give as well as to receive benefits. As adults, we must realize our responsibility to older people and recognize the contribution they have already made to our society and to us individually. Today, too many older people are living in very small rooms, too many are in municipal homes, and far too many are entering mental hospitals. No one would ever advocate that a mentally disturbed old person should be elsewhere than in a mental hospital, but too many older people are deteriorating mentally because they are made to feel unwanted and that they have no further useful part to play.

In meeting the challenge of all of the psychosocial conditions, the clergy has a vital role. No other group in our society has the same access to the individual, and through this relationship the clergy has a responsibility to prescribe many of the social and moral standards of our communities and of the people who make up these communities.

Similarly, the school plays a leading part in the provision of better psychosocial conditions. The role of the school is to teach, and this includes teaching for future living. The school and, perhaps in a more personal and meaningful way the teachers, have a terrific impact on the growing child. The attitudes, behavior, and moral values of the teacher often set the behavior pattern for our children — this is particularly true of children coming from discordant homes.

In addition to these general effects, the school has a more specific contribution. During the early school years children are likely to show their first difficulties in adjusting to social situations. These may be seen in a variety of patterns, but in all cases of deviant behavior the child needs adequate assessment, guidance, and help so that he may learn proper methods of adjustment.

The community, through such organizations as church groups, youth centers, Boy Scouts and Girl Scouts, has an essential role in helping teenagers and young adults through this rather difficult period of growing up. Community programs must aim to meet the needs of the growing child through the development of healthful and health-giving activites. The basic need at this period is a desire for individual satisfaction as a useful member of the group. Children want to conform and yet they want the freedom of adults even before they have sufficiently matured to handle perplexing social situations. These programs must allow scope for individual initiative and group activity and, through proper guidance and organization, must help the very young and the teenagers to adjust and handle these situations. Recreation and group activities for teenagers and young adults ought not to be based on the negative idea of keeping them off the streets and away from undesirable hangouts, even though these may be worthy objectives, or should outside activities be intended to replace family activities or to make life easier for the parents. Rather, recreation should be provided to meet the needs of the teenager and young adult, so that they will develop through wholesome activities to healthy, satisfied, and useful members of our adult society.

What positive steps can be advocated to achieve proper development from infancy to maturity? When the home is broken, a child should be placed in a foster home or in other circumstances where parent substitutes and the love and kindness so necessary for him can, as far as possible, be provided. It is not suggested that our schools should replace the home in providing the essential background for the growing child, but rather that in receiving pliable children schools may beneficially influence the further development of their personalities. Home and school must work together to develop children who can become happy and useful members of our free society. Attitudes toward civic affairs, toward drugs and other depressing influences, are subtle. They are seldom successfully taught in an intellectual way; rather, the young child absorbs attitudes from his total environment. Early help is essential if he is to achieve adequate adjustment in the future. Within a few years, patterns of behavior are established which will be very difficult to overcome even by individual therapy. Most of our social deviates, delinquents, addicts, and neurotics, have a background of poor adjustment during this period, and we know too well how difficult it is to alter these behavior patterns in later life.

When social and moral standards are threatened, should not the churches and other community organizations assume the initiative in exercising an increasing influence in all our communities which are underprivileged — whether physically, morally, or socially — to organize these areas so that their residents can gain motivations which will enable them to go forward together toward self-improvement and improvement of the community around them? And when age has met and succumbed to the overwhelming pressure of frustration and abandonment, our prosperous society should provide adequate, useful, and individually satisfying activities for these older people.

In addition to adequate preparation of our youth for future life, we must remove the slums and undesirable hangouts from our communities and provide proper accommodation, healthy environments and, more important, individually satisfying activities for those who live in these areas. In community planning, let us ever be conscious of the inner needs of our people — conscious that these are in many ways more important than their physical needs which today we are striving to fulfil. The sum total of these activities would represent the basis for the community effort.

CONCLUSION

This chapter has concentrated on general measures in the area of social action rather than on those specific items covered in Chapter II of the

American Public Health Association Manual, as, on the basis of our present knowledge, it appears that general social measures which can be achieved could do much more for the mental health of a population than can the limited number of specific preventive actions now available, even though each of these must be individually applied as they become available to us.

The question "Who is to prevent mental illness?" is frequently asked. Obviously, all have a responsibility in this area: the physician (regardless of his specialty or area of work) with respect to medical action; all of the helping professions with respect to social and psychological opportunities for development; and the total community, particularly its leaders, with respect to social action. In this connection, the institutionalization of responsibility gives cause for concern. As our communities become larger, as family relationships change, and as tax-supported programs replace individual responsbility, there may be a continuing shift of total responsibility to impersonal institutions. This is surely the antithesis of a good situation for mental health, which requires that the individual feel accepted, worthwhile, and contributing, and that he be able to gain satisfaction from his meaningful, responsible activities as an individual, as a member of a family, and as one of the individuals in the larger social groups which make up our communities.

Lemkau summarises the present position as follows:[7]

First; every model of pathological process produces disease that have psychiatric symptoms. Preventive psychiatry is an inevitable component of all disease prevention and every physician has a role as preventor of psychiatric illnesses. Regardless of how narrow his concept of his specialty, he cannot avoid this role. Second: Social deprivation, emotional conflict and environmental stress are included as models of processes which produce pathological behaviour. The first of these, because of successful research in the last two decades, has begun to have increased specificity while the other two remain too much for anyone's satisfaction as influences of a general type leading to various types of ill health. Each of the three offers opportunities for direct prevention action; however, because of their non-specific character and probably because of time relationships, the evaluation of preventive effect is extremely difficult. Nevertheless, it can be said that the concept of preventive psychiatry is a little less vague and tenuous than it was a decade ago. The theory is tighter and the opportunity for action is more inviting.

REFERENCES

1. Carstairs, G. M. 1958. Preventive psychiatry: Is there such a thing? Journal of Mental Science *104*, 63–71.
2. Hughes, C. C., Tremblay, M. A., Rapoport, R. N., and Leighton, A. 1960. *People of Cove and Woodlot*. New York, Basic Books, Inc.
3. Klein, W., et al. 1965. *Promoting Mental Health of Older People Through Group Methods — A Practical Guide*. New York, Mental Health Materials Center.
4. Kraft, I. 1964. Preventing mental ill-health in early childhood. Mental Hygiene *14*, 413–423.
5. Leighton, A. 1959. *My Name is Legion*. New York, Basic Books, Inc.
6. Leighton, D., Harding, J. A., Macklin, D. R., Leighton, A., and Macmillan, A. M. 1963. *The Character of Psychiatric Symptoms in Selected Communities*. New York, Basic Books, Inc.
7. Lemkau, P. V. 1965. Prevention in psychiatry. American Journal of Public Health *55*, 554–560.
8. Lemkau, P. V. 1966. Prospects for the prevention of mental illness. Mental Hygiene *50*, 172–179.
9. Macleod, A., and Poland, P. 1961. The well-being clinic. Social Work, January, 1961.
10. Program Area Committee on Mental Health. 1962. *Mental Disorders: A Guide to Control Methods*. New York, American Public Health Association.
11. Seeley, J. R., Sim, R. A., and Loosley, E. 1956. *Crestwood Heights*. Toronto, University of Toronto Press.
12. Soddy, K., and Ahrenfeldt, R. H., eds. 1965. *Mental Health in a Changing World*. Philadelphia, J. B. Lippincott Co.
13. United States Department of Health, Education, and Welfare. 1962. *The Prevention of Disability in Mental Disorders*. Mental Health Monograph No. 1. Public Health Service Publication, No. 924, Washington, Government Printing Office.

CHAPTER 14

Psychiatry and the Law

LEGAL ASPECTS OF THE PHYSICIAN-PATIENT RELATIONSHIP

A preliminary consideration of interpersonal relationships, involving the communication of affect and role-expectation, was undertaken in the final section of Chapter 3. Further aspects of the physician-patient relationship were developed in connection with the initial psychiatric interview (Chapter 9), and the psychosocial therapies in which the therapeutic relationship is a major factor in determining outcome (Chapter 11). The physician-patient relationship, however, also constitutes a legal contract, involving a promise or set of promises by the physician, the performance of which the law considers to be a duty, and for breach of which the law gives remedy to the patient.

The physician should therefore recognize his obligations to the patient, and the rights of the patient to confidentiality and privacy, to self-determination, to competent evaluation and treatment, and to information regarding the probable outcome of treatment, including any known potential hazards. The physician should distinguish between the therapeutic communication of realistic optimism and unwarranted promises of "cure" that may lead to subsequent disillusionment and hostility on the part of the patient, and may result in litigation. On the other hand, the physician should avoid undue defensiveness, which will be communicated verbally or nonverbally to the patient, and may well provoke a hostile patient to bring the legal action that he recognizes the physician fears.

The physician should recall that verbal transactions are subject to retrospective falsification, and should therefore keep adequate written records, as well as routinely obtaining the written consent of the patient to release confidential information, to seek admission to the hospital, or undertake special treatment procedures. Apart from such safeguards, however, the physician's professional security rests in the integrity of his relationship with the patient—his genuine interest in the welfare of the patient, his competence and self-confidence, and his honesty in communicating with the patient.

A *contract* between two persons may be either expressed or implied, de-

328

pending on whether the parties have specifically set forth (either orally or in writing) the terms of their agreement, or whether the conditions are to be inferred or deduced from the conduct of the parties rather than from any definite language. The contract between doctor and patient is usually implied by the patient's visit to the doctor's office, or the doctor's response to a call from the patient. There is no obligation for a physician to accept a request that he attend a patient, even though no other physician is available. The mere rendering of such services as may be necessary in an emergency does not automatically result in a contract for subsequent services, although the physician is required to use due skill and care in administering emergency treatment. By special agreement with the patient, the physician may limit his contract to treating the patient in one particular time or place, or by means of one particular procedure. Once the physician has accepted responsibility for the patient's evaluation and treatment, however, his obligation continues for the duration of the patient's illness and until the physician's services are no longer necessary unless the physician is relieved of this obligation by the patient, or unless he gives the patient reasonable notice of his intention to withdraw, giving the patient an adequate opportunity to secure the services of another physician.

In addition to complying with the law that he possess a valid license to practice medicine, the physician is obligated to possess the same degree of skill and learning possessed by other members of his profession at the time and place he renders services (not simply at the time of his graduation); he should exercise ordinary and reasonable care and diligence in applying this knowledge and skill, should employ such available remedies as experience has shown to be most beneficial, and in case of doubt he should recommend consultation with a colleague who has special skill and knowledge of patients with similar problems or disorders. A psychiatrist or other specialist must possess that degree of additional skill and knowledge possessed by physicians who devote special study and attention to his particular field of specialization.

The omission or failure to perform his duties to the patient constitutes *negligence*, and the physician may be considered guilty of *malpractice* if injury or damage to the patient results directly therefrom. Malpractice has been defined as the treatment of a case by a surgeon or physician in a manner contrary to accepted rules and with injurious results to the patient; hence, any professional misconduct or any unreasonable lack of skill or fidelity in the performance of professional or fiduciary duties. The elements constituting a cause of action based on negligence are as follows: (1) a legal duty or obligation requiring the individual to conform to a reasonable standard of care in order to protect others from unreasonable risk, (2) a failure on the part of the individual to adhere to the standard required, (3) actual loss or damage resulting to the person or property of another, and (4) a reasonably close causal connection between the substandard conduct involved and the resulting injury. It should also be noted that the physician may be liable for the negligence of his partner, assistants, agents, or employees, even though the latter were not acting under his immediate supervision or control, and even though the agent exceeded his authority or undertook actions directly contrary to the physician's express instructions. In the case of nurses not employed by the physician, he may still be held responsbile while they are acting on his behalf and under his direction.

A physician requires the *consent* of an individual or of his legal guardian in order to undertake either examination or treatment. Failure to obtain such consent may constitute assault, which is punishable even though no actual harm has been done. If asked to examine an individual by a third party (e.g., employer, police officer, or judge), the physician should tell the individual concerned that he has the right to refuse, and that if he consents the results of the examination will be conveyed to the third party. In such instances, the patient's signed consent to examination and release of information should be obtained immediately before the latter is carried out. It is also necessary to obtain the patient's signed consent for special treatment procedures, such as those involving injections or loss of consciousness, including electroshock treatments. In order to be legally valid, the signed consent for a given procedure must be an intelligent or informed consent, with full understanding of what is to be done and of any risks involved. Informed consent for treatment should *not* be incorporated into a routine application form for admission to hospital, but should consist of a separate form, to be signed only when the treatment has been recommended and planned in the immediate future. Informed consent forms should include a description of the nature of the procedure and of possible complications or risks. Such informed consent forms should be signed by all human subjects involved in research investigations (whether patients or volunteers). However, the signing of these forms will not absolve the physician from carrying out appropriate investigations beforehand, or from exercising reasonable skill and care during and after the treatment procedure.

The physician is required to give the patient and others responsible for his care (e.g., his guardian or nursing attendants) such *information and instructions* as will enable him to comply with recommended treatment or act intelligently on behalf of the patient. Frequently, information concerning diagnosis and prognosis has been withheld from patients with incurable disease, but a number of patients may seek such information directly. Under some circumstances it has been held that the physician has an obligation to volunteer such information to the patient (in

order that he may make a valid will, for example) and in other circumstances that the responsible next-of-kin must be informed. However, the law has distinguished between passive concealment (mere silence) and active concealment (the deliberate suppression of fact, or deceit). Some courts have held that the physician is not required to volunteer such information, but has a duty to disclose it if asked. In view of many misconceptions about psychiatric diagnosis and prognosis, it has sometimes been questioned whether this should ever be discussed with patients, but here again the patient or responsible next-of-kin has a right to a truthful interpretation of such information as is within their comprehension.

It is a general principle that information obtained from the patient is to be kept *secret and confidential*. This obligation has its roots in antiquity and was included in the Hippocratic Oath: "Whatsoever in my capacity as physician or even when not so acting, I see or hear that ought never to be published abroad, I will not divulge, but consider such things to be holy secrets." The same principle is recognized in the more recent Geneva Oath: "I will respect the secrets that are confided in me." In the event that the physician passes on any such information and thus does hurt to the patient, he is liable to be sued in an action for damages. However, disclosure is permissible with the express signed consent of the patient (or guardian), and in certain instances the consent to divulge information to a third party may be required by law, or may be considered necessary to prevent the patient from committing suicide or homicide. In some instances, a privileged communication *by the physician* may be regarded as one that would have been defamatory and actionable, but is prevented from being so by reason of circumstances rebutting the existence of malice—as where the physician has a legal, moral, or social duty to perform in making this communication to another person, such other person having a corresponding interest or duty toward the patient. This principle is taken for granted by many physicians in communicating information about a patient to others responsible for his care and treatment. However, it should be mentioned that those conducting individual psychotherapy frequently keep separate records to which other staff members do not have access.

In the preceding paragraph, reference was made to privileged communications by the physician, but there is more widespread emphasis on *privileged communication as a legal right belonging to the patient and not the doctor.* The Group for the Advancement of Psychiatry defined medical privileged communication as a right existing only by statute, whereby a patient may bar his doctor from testifying about his medical treatment and the disclosures which are an integral part of it. In 1828, the state of New York enacted a statute protecting such communications by patients to their physicians, and a majority of the United States have statutory provisions protecting the confidentiality of the patient's communications to his physician. In 1959 the state of Georgia specifically granted this privilege to patients under psychiatric treatment, and in several states a similar privilege has been extended to patients consulting psychologists. The Group for the Advancement of Psychiatry recommended the following model statute for privilege of the psychiatrist-patient relationship: "The confidential relationship and communication between the psychiatrist and patient shall be placed on the same basis as regards privilege as provided by law between attorney and client." There remain some jurisdictions, however, in which the confidentiality of the patient's communications to his physician may conflict with the legal expectation that he will divulge such information when required to do so in court.

In concluding this section concerning legal aspects of the physician-patient relationship, reference may be made to a booklet containing 47 *medicolegal forms*

with legal analysis, prepared and published by the American Medical Association. These form letters and authorizations, consents, or refusals cover the more common situations in which written communication between physician and patient may be desirable or necessary. Such forms require modification to conform with prevailing local conditions, and many are irrelevant for psychiatric practice, but those concerning the topics we have discussed are based on a sound body of legal opinion.

In the following sections of the present chapter we shall consider legal aspects of psychiatric hospitalization; incompetency and guardianship; marriage, adoption, and sterilization; criminal responsibility; and psychiatric testimony.

HOSPITAL ADMISSION, TREATMENT, AND DISCHARGE

Early laws relating to the insane or mentally defective individual were concerned more with the preservation of his property in the interest of his heirs than with the custody of his person, which was generally assumed to be the responsibility of his family. In the event that he had no immediate family, however, or became so violently disturbed that he could not be managed by them, he then became a charge on the community, and provisions were established for his detention in a jail or later an asylum. A New York statute enacted in 1788 noted that "There are sometimes persons, who by lunacy or otherwise are furiously madd, or are so far disordered in their senses that they may be dangerous to be permitted to go abroad," and authorized two or more justices to direct constables by warrant to apprehend and keep safely locked up the "furiously madd" and dangerous. This statute specified, however, that it should not be interpreted as restraining or preventing any friend or relation of such a lunatic from taking him under their own care and protection.

Often the procedures under which the mentally disordered were taken into custody were quite informal, and some were detained for prolonged periods of time on a brief written order by the person in charge of the custodial institution, based on verbal allegations by members of the community. During the nineteenth century, public concern was aroused over the legality of detaining persons against their will when they might not be severely mentally disordered, and states enacted a wide variety of commitment laws, which still tend to constitute the basis for involuntary detention of the mentally disordered. Since the term commitment also applies to the legal detention of criminals, it has been increasingly replaced by the less offensive term "hospitalization" in statutes relating to the confinement of noncriminal mentally disabled persons.

There are at least five general matters that may be covered, with varying degrees of adequacy, by legislation relating to the voluntary and involuntary hospitalization of the mentally disordered: (1) *Who may be admitted*—the mentally ill (formerly described as insane), with or without dangerous propensities to themselves or others; the mentally retarded or subnormal; epileptics, with or without mental illness or retardation; alcoholics and drug addicts; sexual psychopaths or criminals with mental illness. (2) *Where they may be admitted*—to jail, state hospitals, or other state institutions such as training schools for the retarded; to private psychiatric hospitals; to university-affiliated psychiatric hospitals or units; to psychiatric units in general hospitals; and so on. (3) *How long they may be detained*—indefinitely, until the hospital authorities or court considers that discharge is appropriate and desirable; or alternatively for a temporary period specified at the time of admission, for example 30 or 90 days, sometimes also specified as a period of observation and evaluation rather than treatment. (4) *How the patient shall be admitted and discharged*—on his own voluntary application; involun-

tarily on the application of any responsible member of the community, or some specific class of persons such as a police officer; involuntarily, on the basis of medical opinion from one or more independent physicians or a board of physicians; involuntarily by judicial order, with or without court hearing, sometimes entailing trial by jury. (5) *What rights the patient has after admission to hospital*—these include the rights to accept or refuse recommended treatment, to retain control over property and enter into legal contracts, to communicate with family or attorney, to initiate proceedings for release from hospital, and so on. The latter rights may differ in the case of a voluntary or involuntary patient, may be specified clearly or remain somewhat nebulous, and are related to whether hospitalization automatically involves the patient's being considered mentally incompetent, which will be considered further in the following section of this chapter.

Within a single state, separate admission forms and procedures (as well as differential preservation of civil rights and the right to determine treatment or discharge) may apply, not only in the case of voluntary or various forms of involuntary admission, but also according to the type of institution to which the patient is admitted, and according to the nature of the mental disorder that leads to his admission. For example, separate laws may apply to patients admitted to a state hospital and those admitted to other psychiatric facilities. Similarly, separate laws may apply to voluntary or involuntary admission of patients with mental illness, and of those with mental retardation, or of those with alcoholism or drug addiction.

In the present section we shall focus mainly on laws concerning voluntary and involuntary admission of *the mentally ill*. Such laws were enacted to permit the detention of psychiatric patients in locked wards in public or private institutions, while protecting the rights of such persons to a fair and impartial judgment of the necessity of depriving them of their liberty. At the time such laws were first enacted, the mere existence of insanity was not generally considered sufficient grounds for restraining a person in hospital, but the patient also had to be dangerous either to himself or to others, or alternatively incapable of taking care of himself. Since commitment was frequently limited to the dangerously insane, the resulting laws tended to perpetuate the stigma of criminality in mental illness. In many states, involuntary admission to mental hospitals involved arrest and detention in jail, pending a trial in court before a judge (and sometimes a jury), followed by transportation to mental hospital by police or other legal authorities.

Such procedures have been defended by some lawyers and members of the general public concerned with civil rights, as the only way to prevent "railroading" and unjust detention of the patient in hospital. Many psychiatrists and a number of lawyers, however, have been concerned that such procedures tend to dehumanize the patients, cause them to be regarded as criminals and to regard hospitals with fear, and may interfere with the right of the patient to receive appropriate treatment. In his presidential address to the American Psychiatric Association, Bowman included the following illustrative remarks:

Following the regular procedure, the wife swore out a warrant, the sheriff arrested the patient and he was taken to the jail to await a hearing. He hanged himself in the jail. To those sticklers for the defense of the legal rights of the patient, I would point out that his legal rights were well preserved . . . he was not sent to a hospital without due process and a chance to appear before the judge. Perhaps if he had he might be alive today. . . . The public is so obsessed with the alleged infallibility of legal procedure that they insist on protecting . . . the legal rights of the patient without thinking of what his medical rights are.

After examining existing commitment procedures, the Group for the Advancement of Psychiatry proposed four essentials of a satisfactory commitment law: a minimum of legal formalism, devices which aim to get maximum patient participation and treatment which includes intramural detention, minimal psychic traumatization in admission procedures, and removal of stigmata resulting from archaic legal phraseology. The committee recommended a uniform law embodying the following general features: certification by two qualified physicians (not necessarily psychiatrists), safeguard of the patient's rights to petition for release by "hearing," emergency admission, and voluntary admissions.

Despite the desirability of voluntary hospitalization from a medical point of view, statistics cited by the World Health Organization indicated that only ten percent of admissions to State mental hospitals in the United States were voluntary during the year 1949. By way of contrast, in the year 1952, nearly 70 percent of the admissions in England and Wales, 67 percent of those in Scotland, and 31 percent of those in France were voluntary. Unfortunately, the existence of a legal procedure permitting voluntary admission to state hospitals does not necessarily ensure that this procedure will be widely used, since acceptance of the voluntary application for admission may be at the discretion of the state hospital staff. Furthermore the voluntary patient may still be deprived of civil rights, may be detained in the hospital for a period of time after he requests release, and may then become subject to proceedings for compulsory indeterminate hospitalization.

Nevertheless, increasing reliance on voluntary admission of the mentally ill is recognized as desirable by physicians, patients, and legislators. In this country, a number of states have based more recent legislation on the Draft Act prepared and published by the United States Public Health Service (1951). This model act consisted of four parts: (1) definitions of terms used in the act;

(2) admission and discharge provisions concerning voluntary hospitalization; (3) admission, post admission, and discharge provisions concerning involuntary hospitalization; (4) provisions applicable to patients generally.

In order to promote and extend the practice of *voluntary hospitalization*, the act stipulated that a voluntary patient who requests his release, or whose release is requested in writing by his legal guardian, parent, spouse, or adult next-of-kin, shall be released *forthwith*, except under three general circumstances: (1) if the patient was admitted on his own application and the request for release was made by another person, a release should be contingent upon the agreement of the patient; (2) if the patient was admitted on the application of another person by reason of his age, his release prior to the age of sixteen years should be contingent upon the consent of his parent or guardian; (3) if, within 48 hours of receiving the request for discharge, the head of the hospital filed with the probate court or judge a certification that in his opinion the release of the patient would be unsafe for the patient or others, release should be postponed pending the commencement of proceedings for judicial hospitalization, but in no event for more than five days.

Four general procedures were recommended for *involuntary hospitalization*, initiated by someone other than the patient. The first of these was hospitalization on *medical certification; standard nonjudicial procedure*, involving written application to the hospital by a friend, relative, spouse, guardian, or specified official, and certification by two designated medical examiners. The second procedure involved hospitalization on *medical certification; emergency procedure*, involving written application to the hospital by any health or police officer or any other person, and certification by at least one licensed physician regarding the nature of the emergency. The third method of involuntary admission involved hospitalization *without endorsement or medical certification; emergency procedure*, initiated by any health or police officer believing that the individual was mentally ill and likely to injure himself or others. The fourth method involved hospitalization upon *court order; judicial procedure*, following the filing of a written application together with a medical certificate, supplemented by the reports of two further designated medical examiners before examination in court (with the stipulation that the patient shall not be required to submit to an examination against his will). The Draft Act specified the due process of law to be followed in such circumstances, and indicated that the order of hospitalization shall state whether the individual should be detained for an indeterminate, or for a specified temporary, period of time.

In the event that involuntary hospitalization is based on *medical certification*, it is essential the latter be completed only after careful and comprehensive examination; that the medical certificate should include written evidence of the patient's disorder (appearance, behavior, verbatim conversation, and statements made by persons other than the patient). It may be stipulated that two physicians should examine the patient separately, and that they should not be related to each other, to the patient, or to the head of the hospital, either by blood, by marriage, or by any business affiliation. The physician's shield against subsequent litigation by the patient is that he has acted in good faith and with reasonable care. He should charge his usual fee for the time involved, and should keep a record of his examination and a copy of his medical certificate.

A distinction is sometimes made between compulsory hospitalization and *nonprotested involuntary hospitalization*. Lindman and McIntyre pointed out, however, that the nonprotested admission may represent either (1) procedures identical or similar to those classified as involuntary hospitalization by *medical certification* (with the patient having ability to prevent hospitalization on this basis), or alternatively (2) those *judicial hospitalization* procedures involving a waiver of the right to a court hearing (either explicit, or implied because neither the patient nor someone acting on his behalf requests a hearing). The model act recommended that the patient should always have a right to a court hearing, which should be arranged as soon as possible after the initiation of commitment proceedings. It is also considered preferable that the patient be detained in a hospital rather than a jail, and that the hearing itself be conducted in a hospital rather than in open court.

As indicated previously, various states have adopted separate laws and procedures for the voluntary or involuntary hospitalization of different types of mentally disordered individuals: those with mental illness, mental retardation, epilepsy, or addiction to alcohol or other drugs. There may also be different laws and procedures for the admission of the same type of patient to a public hospital, a private hospital, or a university-affiliated facility. A number of states have legal provisions whereby a person charged with a criminal offense, or convicted and awaiting sentence, may be hospitalized involuntarily for a limited period of observation and evaluation during which no form of treatment may be permitted. There may be separate legal provisions governing the involuntary hospitalization and treatment of convicted and sentenced prisoners who develop signs of mental illness during the period of their confinement. In view of the diversity of laws governing the hospital treatment of psychiatric patients, every physician entering practice in a new state should familiarize himself with the laws and procedures of that state, and should find out what types of medical certificate he will be permitted and expected to complete. Sometimes the completion of such medical certificates requires certain qualifications other than medical licensure, such as citizenship, and a certain duration of residence or of medical practice in that state.

Following involuntary admission to hospital, by any of the three methods other than court order, the Draft Act recommended that any patient (or his legal guardian, spouse or adult next of kin) have a right to make *written application for judicial determination*, and that the patient should be released within 48 hours after receipt of this request, except if the head of the hospital certified to the court that such release would be unsafe for the patient or for others, in which event release would be postponed for a period not to exceed five days pending the commencement of proceedings for a judicial determination. It was also specified that any individual detained in a hospital should be entitled to a *writ of habeas corpus* upon proper petition by himself or a friend to any court empowered to issue such writ in the county in which he was detained. This has long been accepted practice, but some jurisdictions place restrictions on the frequency with which an individual may apply for a writ of habeas corpus.

The Draft Act contained other provisions applicable to patients generally, including the right to humane care and treatment, safeguards concerning the use of mechanical restraints, the right to communication and visitation and to exercise all civil rights, including the right to dispose of property, make purchases or enter contractual relationships, and to vote—*unless the patient has been adjudicated incompetent and has not been restored to legal capacity*. It was also recommended that all information about the patient be kept confidential, and not be diclosed except with the consent of the patient or his legal guardian, or as necessary to carry out any of the provisions of the Act, or on direction of the court that failure to make such disclosure would be contrary to the public interest.

INCOMPETENCY, GUARDIANSHIP, AND RESTORATION

Between puberty and the age of 21 years, society recognizes the increasing responsibility of the adolescent, and his or her increasing capacity to make independent decisions, which may be contrary to the wishes of his parents or guardians. At the age of 14 an alien child is required to sign his own annual registration or change of address card, and at the age of 16 he may make independent application for citizenship. The adolescent is permitted to drive an automobile, and by the age of 18 years he has attained many of the privileges and obligations of the adult. In addition to military service, and trial for offenses in adult rather than juvenile courts, he may now be able to leave home or enter a hospital against the wishes of his parents. This is frequently the age at which females may consent to sexual relations, and no longer involve the male in charges of statutory rape. It may also be the age at which the female may marry without parental consent, although her husband may be regarded as her legal guardian until she reaches the age of 21 years. The latter is generally regarded as the age of full emancipation and responsibility, including the right to vote, and the right for males to marry without parental consent.

It has long been recognized that some persons may need hospital care, and yet be capable of handling their affairs. Others may be incapable of managing their property, but may be quite capable of living in society, with varying degrees of supervision by others. Historically, laws concerning the property of the mentally incompetent individual long preceded laws concerning the care of his person. In the Twelve Tables of Rome (449 B.C.) it was provided that: "If a person is a fool, let his person and goods be under the protection of his family or his paternal relatives, if he is not under the care of anyone." In thirteenth-century England, the law distinguished between the idiot (having no understanding from his nativity) and the lunatic (who had lost the use of his reason), and the king was granted custody of his lands throughout the

lifetime of the idiot (retaining the profits after providing for his maintenance), but only temporarily in the case of the lunatic (returning the profits to him after his recovery).

The Group for the Advancement of Psychiatry (1948) considered the common acceptance of involuntary hospitalization as equivalent to legal incompetence to be one of the worst features of contemporary commitment laws. In a number of states these two issues are regarded as independent, although a judgment of mental incompetence may be given at the judicial hearing leading to involuntary admission. However, hearings to determine incompetency for some specific responsibility (usually financial management) may be held on patients who are not being admitted to the hospital. In this event, it is not sufficient to demonstrate symptoms of mental illness (for example, disorientation, hallucinations or delusions), but it must be shown that the patient has a disorder of thinking that causes impaired judgment and results in squandering, hoarding, or self-injurious gullibility.

When the patient has been declared incompetent, it becomes necessary for the court to appoint a guardian, trustee, curator, or committee to manage his estate and protect his interests. In some jurisdictions this may be an autonomous public body specifically established for this purpose, which remains responsible for the patient's affairs as long as the latter is considered incompetent. In those states where incompetence is implicit in involuntary hospitalization, legal competency is usually automatically restored on complete discharge from the hospital—but *not* when he is absent from the hospital on leave, parole, probation, or trial visit (which may sometimes be prolonged for an undesirably long period of time, and include loss of other rights than control over property). When incompetency has been established separately from involuntary hospitalization, however, another court hearing will usually be necessary to restore the patient's competence and discharge his guardian.

Although there is considerable variation in legislation, Lindman and McIntyre appropriately summarized the main differences between incompetency and hospitalization as follows:

	INCOMPETENCY	HOSPITALIZATION
TEST	Unable to care properly for one's property or person due to one of the following conditions:	Dangerous to self or others, or in need of treatment due to one of the following conditions:
APPLICABLE TO CASES OF	Mental illness Mental deficiency Drug addiction Alcoholism Senility Physical disability Spendthrifts	Mental illness Mental deficiency Drug addiction Alcoholism Epilepsy
PURPOSES	Protect estate from dissipation and provide protection for persons who are unable to care for themselves	Removal from society for protection of the individual or of society and/or for treatment of the illness
PRIMARY RIGHT AFFECTED	Civil rights	Freedom to be at large
COMPARABLE TO	Legal status of a minor	Person removed from society for a contagious disease

*From *The Mentally Disabled and The Law*, ed. F. T. Lindman and D. M. McIntyre, Jr., Chicago, The University of Chicago Press. Copyright 1961 by the American Bar Foundation.

As indicated in the preceding table, the legal status of the incompetent individual is comparable with that of a minor, and he usually loses other rights than the power to dispose of his property, as for example the right to drive an automobile or to enter into a contract. Most courts distinguish between the contracts of an incompetent individual made prior to the adjudication of his condition and those executed after such an adjudication. A majority of courts hold that contracts made prior to an adjudication of incompetency are voidable, and under certain conditions may be disaffirmed by the incompetent, but that they remain in full force until disaffirmed. Legal transactions made by an incompetent individual after a guardian has been appointed are usually considered void, except that in some jurisdictions they may be enforced for the benefit of the incompetent.

Testamentary capacity is the statutory right to make a will, and is usually dependent upon "sound mind and memory." Lindman and McIntyre stated that the person making a will must be able to do the following:

1. Know, without prompting, the nature and extent of the property of which he is about to dispose;
2. Know the nature of the act he is about to perform;
3. Know the names and identity of the persons who are to be the objects of his bounty;
4. Know his relation toward them;
5. Have sufficient mind and memory to understand all of these facts;
6. Appreciate the relations of these factors to one another;
7. Recollect the decision which he has formed.

Davidson summarized these requirements of the testator as being (1) that he must know the executed document is a will, (2) that he must consciously sign the instrument, (3) that he must know the nature and extent of the property he possesses, and (4) that he must know the natural objects of his bounty. A will may be declared invalid if mental disorder interferes with any one of these criteria. However, the mentally retarded may make valid wills if they understand what they mean and what they are distributing; and psychotic patients with delusions may make valid wills provided the delusions do not materially affect the disposition of property. In upholding any will made during or shortly after a period of known mental disorder, it will be necessary to prove the patient had testamentary capacity at the time the will was made. This is best accomplished by having the patient examined separately by two competent psychiatrists on the same day that the patient signs his will, and preferably within the same hour.

MARRIAGE, ADOPTION, AND STERILIZATION

Prohibitions against a marriage of mentally disabled persons appear in the common law, and arose from two separate sources of concern: (1) the prevention or voiding of a marital contract, when one of the partners is incapable of understanding the nature of the relationship; and (2) to prevent reproduction by persons whose offspring might become a public charge. The first of these two policies is older and has figured more prominently in legislation. It is generally held that a person cannot contract a valid marriage if at the time he was so insane, retarded, or drunk that he did not understand the nature of the marriage relationship, or its implications and obligations. In some states a petition for *annulment* of such a marriage, however, may be made only by the incompetent spouse, although in other states the competent spouse may petition for annulment provided that he left the incompetent partner as soon as the incompetence was discovered. In some states insanity prevents any action for *divorce*, whereas in other states divorce may be granted on grounds of prolonged or incurable insanity.

The legal rights of the mentally disabled are more fully protected by divorce statutes than by statutes governing the *adoption* of their children. A majority of states allow children of the mentally ill to be adopted without their parents' consent, and only a minority demand that parental disability be hopeless or incurable. It is evident here that society is concerned with the rights of the child as well as those of the parent, as reflected in the following recommendations by the World Health Organization:*

1. Every child needs a family and a home.
2. Adoption should have as its main object the well-being of the child.
3. Appropriate practical advice should be available to the natural mother so that she may decide freely whether to keep her child or whether to have him adopted.
4. If adoption is decided upon, it should be effected expeditiously so that the child may be safeguarded from the difficulties involved in undue delay. When immediate placement is not possible, for example, for older children, abrupt changes in care should be avoided.
5. Adoptions of brothers and sisters should not be arranged in such a way that their ties with one another are severed.
6. The adopted child should be given the same status, opportunities, and rights as those of a child established in its own family.
7. Adopting parents should be prepared to accept the normal risks which come the way of natural parents.
8. A mere material assessment of the prospective home should be replaced by an evaluation of the whole situation.
9. It is no amateur matter to decide which parents and home will fit each child, and no child should be placed haphazardly with adoptive parents.
10. Normality of family life is furthered when the age of the adopting parents is within the age-range of usual parenthood. Parents who must build their families through adoption can best do so by aiming at natural age intervals between the children.
11. The child should be aware from a young age that he is adopted.
12. Adequate training facilities are necessary to develop the special skills required by social workers dealing with adoption.
13. Among the matters needing further research are the improvement of methods of prediction and other methods of diminishing risks; the study of differences of development as between adopted and other children; and the skills involved in carrying out adoption procedures.

Voluntary or involuntary sterilization, and sometimes abortion, have been recommended for psychiatric patients, but objective evidence of the consequences is hard to come by. Ekblad published

---

*Reprinted by permission from *Mental Health Aspects of Adoption*. 1953. World Health Organization Technical Report Series No. 70, p. 18.

two monographs containing considerable follow-up information on fairly large samples of Swedish women subjected to each of these procedures. Lindman and McIntyre distinguished among four fundamental reasons advanced for the use of sterilization: (1) for therapeutic purposes, involving the treatment of disease and preservation of health in women: (2) socioeconomic reasons prompting a number of people to undergo such operations purely for birth control; (3) punitive measures existing in some states, which authorize the sterilization of "hereditary criminals" or sexual offenders and (4) eugenic purposes.

Proponents of statutes providing for the sterilization of criminals or of the mentally disabled usually argue for such laws on *eugenic grounds,* on the questionable assumption that such disorders are transmitted primarily by heredity. There are two general approaches to eugenics which have received the unfortunate terms of (a) "positive eugenics," which consists of an attempt (usually nebulous) to encourage reproduction among those whom society would consider useful and valuable citizens; and (b) "negative eugenics" (which actually has a more definite or "positive" program to offer), consisting of efforts to discourage by various means the reproduction of physically, mentally, or socially handicapped individuals whose handicap is attributable to heredity. Neel and Schull remarked:

The eugenic movement has had a lurid and disquieting history. In Nazi Germany the positive aspect was perverted to the doctrine of a race of supermen whose illustrious racial heritage conferred special rights, while the negative aspects were interpreted as permitting the wholesale extermination of elements whom the supermen had judged undesirable. During that same period there was in the United States a great deal of loose thinking, based primarily upon failure to develop a critical attitude both toward the nature-nurture problem and the precise mathematical consequences of either positive or negative selection. These developments combined to bring discredit upon the entire eugenic movement, an opprobrium from which a sounder eugenics movement is only now emerging.

The exact mathematical consequences of negative selection (as by sterilization) on the frequency of a trait determined by a single major gene, may be computed over a number of generations (each of which represents a period of about 25 to 30 years in the human). In Figures 14-1 and 14-2, the effects of 100 percent negative selection (as by sterilization during childhood of *all* affected individuals) is compared with the effects of negative selection that is only 50 percent effective (which would be an unduly high figure in the case of disorders manifesting themselves for the first time during the reproductive life of the individual). *Figure 14-1* shows the effects of such selection over a period of five generations, in the case of a trait determined by a single dominant gene, whereas *Figure 14-2* shows the effects of such selection over a period of 20 generations in the effect of a trait determined by homozygosity for a single pair of recessive genes. It may be seen that selection against a simple recessive characteristic is likely to be considerably less successful than against a simple dominant characteristic.

It was pointed out in Chapter 5 that single gene inheritance of this nature is responsible for the development of a number of *rare* forms of *severe* mental retardation and chronic brain disease in adults (and the severely retarded do not ordinarily reproduce themselves). The genetic component of *mild* mental retardation, however, appears to be transmitted by multiple minor genes, and any hereditary contributions to the various common forms of functional psychopathology probably involves (a) genetic heterogeneity (two or more different major genes), and/or (b) polygenic inheritance (multiple minor genes). The results of negative selection against such heterogeneous and genetically poorly defined material does *not* permit a precise mathematical pre-

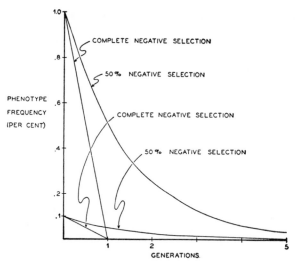

Figure 14-1. The results of complete and 50 per cent selection for five generations against a trait determined by a single dominant gene. In the one case the initial frequency of the trait is placed at 1 percent and in the second case at 0.1 percent. (Modified by permission of Dr. Nils von Hofsten and Hereditas. From Neel, J. V., and Schull, W. J. 1954. *Human Heredity.* By permission of the University of Chicago Press. Copyright © 1954, the University of Chicago.)

diction, and hence *competent geneticists have rightly concluded that it is difficult to justify sterilization of the mentally ill or retarded on genetic grounds.* Nevertheless, it is on such genetic grounds that a number of states and countries have adopted eugenic laws permitting voluntary or involuntary sterilization and sometimes abortion. In a review of "genetic-hygienic experiences in Denmark in recent years," Kemp stated that "genetic-hygiene corresponds in the main to negative qualitative eugenics" and reported that just over two-thirds of the individuals submitting to sterilization (on a "voluntary" basis) were mental defectives, of whom about two-thirds were females.

While geneticists have tended to emphasize our ignorance concerning the precise significance of heredity and of negative selection against the common psychiatric disorders, they have also tended to ignore the *euthenic or sociological argument that certain parents have a high proportion of children with psychiatric disorders because of the postnatal experiences to which they inevitably expose these children.*

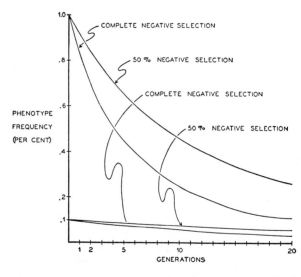

Figure 14-2. The results of complete and 50 percent selection for 20 generations against a trait determined by homozygosity for a single recessive gene. In the one case the initial frequency of the trait is put at 1 percent and in the second case at 0.1 percent. (Modified by permission of Dr. Nils von Hofsten and Hereditas. From Neel, J. V., and Schull, W. J. 1954. *Human Heredity.* By permission of the University of Chicago Press. Copyright © 1954, the University of Chicago.)

Many persons consider the latter a much stronger argument in favor of various forms of family planning than the genetic argument considered hitherto. Regardless of which is the more important, however, the empirical fact remains that parents in certain families and social groups have an unduly high proportion of children with psychopathology.

Those who have recognized the implications of such findings have often been reluctant to recommend state support for family planning programs, particularly in areas where birth control is a subject of heated religious or political controversy. Nevertheless, deliberate efforts to promote voluntary family planning or compulsory sterilization have been reflected in the laws or practices of various states. Penrose summarized the main methods for controlling the reproduction of the mentally retarded as being (1) segregation during a major part of the reproduction period (the commonest device in general use), (2) voluntary or compulsory sterilization, (3) contraception, (4) abortion, (5) euthanasia (the last named being the only method that has not been considered acceptable in any democratic country).

In support of *involuntary sterilization* the following statement was made in the Supreme Court of the United States by Justice Oliver Wendell Holmes (1927):

We have seen more than once that the public welfare may call upon its best citizens for their lives. It would be strange if it could not call upon those who already sap the strength of the State for these lesser sacrifices, often not felt to be such by those concerned, in order to prevent our being swamped with incompetence. It is better for all the world, if instead of waiting to execute degenerate offspring for crime or to let them starve for their imbecility, society can prevent those who are manifestly unfit from continuing their kind. The principle that sustains compulsory vaccination is broad enough to cover the fallopian tubes.

In support of a more moderate program, involving *voluntary rather than compulsory birth control measures*, Kanner wrote the following:

More harm comes to children from parental instability than from low I.Q.'s of their parents. Sterilization laws, desirable though they are, can – and should – reach only a small group of people who combine feeblemindedness with the inability to rear children properly. This inability is not restricted to those of low intelligence. It is found among highly educated, sophisticated people as well; among them are persons who have sense enough to know their emotional shortcomings and their lack of readiness for parenthood. Much unhappiness of parents and children (and many illegitimate abortions) could be prevented if expert contraceptive advice could be dispensed among them. The Planned Parenthood Association is doing pioneer work in this direction; it needs the support of an enlightened population. Those who see in their daily work the pathetic results of unplanned and unwanted parenthood can readily appreciate the prophylactic value of such efforts.

In concluding this section, reference is made to the report of the American Bar Foundation on the rights of the mentally ill, edited by Lindman and McIntyre. In this report it was noted that regulation of marriage of the mentally disabled is inadequate under present statutes; that the majority of statutes allowing divorce for postnuptial "insanity" do not adequately protect the mentally ill; and that the adoption statutes fail to protect the rights of the mentally disabled, although the present author and others would also emphasize the rights of the offspring. This report also recommended a reëvaluation of the basis for statutes providing for the compulsory sterilization of the mentally disabled, with every reasonable procedural protection being afforded to the individual concerned.

CRIMINAL RESPONSIBILITY

The Group for the Advancement of Psychiatry (1954) remarked that in the Middle Ages responsibility, identified with individual salvation, was attributable to everyone and also to animals, corpses, and inanimate objects. Today, however, responsibility is generally disavowed in the small child and in certain psychotic patients, and should be diminished in a larger intermediate group (the mentally retarded and neurotic) who cannot be fitted into conventional legal categories of either the sane or the insane.

Insanity apparently first became a defense to a criminal charge in England in the fourteenth century, but the degree of insanity required to absolve the individual was extreme, and in 1724 Judge Tracey instructed a jury that for an accused to escape punishment he must "not know what he is doing, no more than . . . a wild beast." Later in the same century, Hawkins wrote "those who are under a natural disability of distinguishing between good and evil as infants under the age of discretion, idiots and lunatics, are not punishable by any criminal prosecution whatever."

The test of criminal responsibility that has been widely accepted in American courts during the past century is based on the opinions of fifteen English judges following the M'Naghten trial of 1843, in which the accused was acquitted of murder on grounds of insanity. The House of Lords subsequently posed five questions to the judges of England, whose relevant answers can be reduced to two rules for determining the responsibility of a person who pleads insanity as a defense to a crime:

1. To establish a defense on the ground of insanity it must be clearly proved that, at the time of committing the act, the party accused was laboring under such a defective reasoning, from disease of the mind, as not to know the nature and quality of the act he was doing, or if he did know it, that he did not know he was doing what was wrong.

2. Where a person labors under partial delusions only and is not in other respects insane (and commits an offense in consequence thereof) he must be considered in the same situation as to responsibility as if the facts with respect to which the delusion exists were real.

The essence of these M'Naghten rules is that the defendant is *not* held responsible provided that he did not know (1) the nature of his act, (2) the quality (harmfulness) of his act, or (3) that the act was generally considered wrong; and also provided that any such lack of knowledge was the result of a mental disorder. Unfortunately these answers, which were given with respect to a specific system of paranoid delusions, were subsequently accepted as a declaration of comprehensive law on criminal responsibility, applicable in any case involving a defense of mental illness. Although these rules were adopted by the majority of American courts, in 1869 the Supreme Court of New Hampshire recognized that *an accused person is not criminally responsible if his unlawful act was the result of mental disease or mental defect.*

In some states, *irresistible impulse* may be accepted as a valid defense, provided that the temporary mental disturbance destroyed the patient's free agency at the time or prevented him from refraining from the crime. A defense of irresistible impulse may involve impulsive acts in a psychotic patient, compulsive neurotic behavior, or rage reactions in otherwise normal people, but this defense may not be considered valid in most states. Similarly the traditional view has been that *voluntary drunkenness* is not a valid defense against prosecution for a crime committed while drunk, although intoxication may affect the degree of intent, premeditation, deliberation, or willfulness. More recent decisions have tended to recognize alcoholism as evidence of mental disorder, with correspondingly diminished responsibility for criminal behavior.

In 1954 the District of Columbia Court of Appeals ordered a retrial on a former psychiatric patient named Durham, who had been convicted of housebreaking. The opinion regarding criminal responsibility expressed in the *Durham decision* attracted widespread attention, and included the following statements:

We find that as an exclusive criterion the right-wrong test is inadequate in that (a) it does not take sufficient account of psychic realities and scientific knowledge, and (b) it is based upon one symptom and so cannot readily be applied to all circumstances. We find that the "irresistible impulse" test is also inadequate in that it gives no recognition to mental illness characterized by bruting and refection and so relegates facts caused by such illness to the application of the inadequate right-wrong test. We conclude that a broader test should be adopted. . . .

The rule we now hold must be applied on the retrial of this case and in future cases is not unlike that followed by the New Hampshire Court since 1870. It is simply that an accused is not criminally responsible if his unlawful act was the product of mental disease or mental defect.

The same year the Committee on Psychiatry and Law of the Group for the Advancement of Psychiatry recommended the following bill.

SECTION I DEFINITION OF MENTAL ILLNESS:

"Mental illness" shall mean an illness which so lessens the capacity of a person to use (maintain) his judgment, discretion, and control in the conduct of his affairs and social relations as to warrant his commitment to a mental institution.

SECTION II WHEN MENTAL ILLNESS IS A DEFENSE:

No person may be convicted of any criminal charge when at the time he committed the act with which he is charged he was suffering with mental illness as defined by this Act, and in consequence thereof, he committed the act.

SECTION III

When the defendant is acquitted on the defense of mental illness, such a finding shall be recorded as part of the verdict.

SECTION IV

When such a verdict is recorded, the court shall immediately permit the defendant to a public institution for the custody, care and treatment of cases of the class to which the defendant belongs, and the defendant shall not be discharged therefrom unless and until the court has adjudicated that he has regained his capacity for judgment, discretion and control of his affairs and social relations.

Since this time there has been continuing controversy regarding the formulation of adequate tests of criminal responsibility, and the procedural implementation of such tests, as well as the concept of *partial responsibility*, according to which the mental condition reduces the degree of crime for which the accused is held responsible. After comprehensive review of these problems, the report of the American Bar Foundation edited by Lindman and McIntyre contained the following conclusions and recommendations:*

1. It is desirable to broaden the class of the mentally disabled who are held criminally irresponsible without removing the issue from the jury. . . .

2. Statutes should require that notice of intent to defend on the ground of mental irresponsibility be served on the prosecuting agency and the court a reasonable time before trial. . . .

3. Any accused raising the defense of irresponsibility should undergo a thorough mental examination by a panel of impartial experts. . . .

4. Further study should be initiated to determine whether the policies of the law are better furthered by allocating the burden of persuasion on the issue of responsibility to the prosecution or by placing it on the accused. . . .

5. A mandatory period of hospitalization for the purposes of observation should be imposed upon any defendant found not guilty by reason of insanity. . . .

6. The defense of partial responsibility should be available to defendants but the reduced prison confinement should be followed by a period of indeterminate hospitalization when necessary for the public safety. . . .

7. The present mental condition of all persons charged with serious crimes should

---

*Reprinted by permission from Lindman, F. T., and McIntyre, D. M., eds. 1961. *The Mentally Disabled and The Law*. Chicago, the University of Chicago Press, pp. 366-368. Copyright 1961 by the American Bar Foundation.

be carefully investigated by experts prior to trial and those found to lack the capacity to be proceeded against should be hospitalized in a mental institution until sufficiently recovered to stand trial. . . .

8. Frequent periodic mental examinations should be made of defendants hospitalized as incompetent and those found presently competent should be returned promptly for further proceedings. . . .

9. Statutes should take cognizance of the civil rights and property interests of persons hospitalized in connection with criminal proceedings. . . .

10. The courts of all states should be empowered to stay the execution of a condemned prisoner found incompetent and should be authorized to conduct the hearing on that issue in the court's discretion whenever reasonable doubt of competency is created in the mind of the court. . . .

11. Where inadequate post-conviction procedures now exist, others should be adopted which will enable defendants who were effectively prevented from raising the issue of incompetency or irresponsibility during the proceedings against them to attack their convictions collaterally. . . .

PSYCHIATRIC TESTIMONY

From the variety of topics discussed in preceding sections of the present chapter, it is evident that there are many psychiatric problems concerning which a physician may be asked or required to give courtroom testimony. He may either be called to give evidence as a witness to facts (which may be medical or nonmedical), or as an expert witness on matters of opinion. As a *witness to facts* perceived through his own senses, he can be subpoenaed and compelled to answer questions involving facts observed by himself, but may refuse to answer questions calling for conclusions, opinions, and diagnosis, prognosis, or estimates of incapacity. As an *expert witness*, on the other hand, he must qualify as having special competence in the relevant field of knowledge, and is expected to answer questions calling for conclusions and opinions as

to diagnosis, prognosis, and so on, although he can still be compelled to answer only questions of fact. As a witness to fact he is entitled only to the subpoena fee, but as an expert witness he is entitled to be paid for his time on his regular hourly basis.

The adversary system of law sometimes leads to reluctance on the part of the physician to testify, and has been a matter of some dispute between the legal and medical professions. "He that is not for me is against me," and many psychiatrists would prefer to present impartial testimony *to the court*, rather than limited evidence perceived as in the interests of one side or the other. Frequently, however, the attorney for the defense or for the prosecution will arrange with the physician for his testimony as an expert witness. The opposition will therefore attempt to discredit his evidence through cross examination, and by calling its own expert witnesses to express a contrary opinion. The group for the Advancement of Psychiatry (1954) recommended that, whenever prior to the verdict the issue of mental illness of a defendant is raised, the court may call disinterested, qualified experts to testify *in limine* or at the trial and, if the judge does so, he shall notify counsel of the witnesses so designated, giving their names and addresses. Several states have statutes providing that the trial judge may appoint disinterested witnesses to testify in a case where insanity is set up as a defense, and this was one of the recommendations of the American Bar Foundation listed at the end of the preceding section.

In preparing evidence, the physician should recall that he will be allowed to refresh his memory in court by referring to notes made at or shortly after the time of examination, but that such records may be subject to seizure by the court as an exhibit, particularly if he reads from his records verbatim. In any event, his records should be accurate and comprehensive, show the source of referral, dates of all visits, dates of treatment and payment, and contain copies of all letters and reports sent out. The witness should have the subject matter clear in his own mind, and should have a pretrial *conference* with the attorney by whom he has been called. At this time it may be desirable to frame a hypothetical question to be asked by the attorney on the basis of facts known to the physician, in the light of the patient's history and complaints—which are themselves only hearsay for the physician, and cannot therefore ordinarily be included in his testimony. The pretrial conference should also consider possible lines of cross-examination for which the physician should be prepared.

In court the physician should be careful of his appearance, behavior, and speech. He should address the judge by his appropriate title, should speak distinctly and audibly, use simple nontechnical language, give direct and relevant answers, avoid exaggeration, put aside all bias, and avoid arguing with counsel or any display of anger. In cross-examination the physician should be prepared for questions regarding his qualifications, the number of similar cases he has seen, the thoroughness of his examination, and the conformity of his opinion with those of recognized authority. If a book is cited to discredit the physician's testimony, he should ask the date of publication to see if it is obsolete; he may also deny that the author is an authority (about this patient, this particular problem, or any problem); and he should also be prepared to cite other authorities in support of his testimony. After completing his testimony, the physician should ordinarily leave the courtroom without delay, to indicate his impartiality in the outcome of the trial.

SELECTED REFERENCES

American Bar Association Special Committee on the Rights of the Mentally Ill. 1947. American Bar Association Reports No. 72, 295.

American Medical Association. 1961. *Medicolegal Forms with Legal Analysis.* Chicago, Illinois, American Medical Association.

Biggs, J. 1955. *The Guilty Mind.* New York, Harcourt, Brace & World, Inc.

Birnbaum, M. 1960. The right to treatment. American Bar Association Journal *46*, 499.

Bowman, K. 1946. Presidential Address. American Journal of Psychiatry *103*, July issue.

Davidson, H. A. 1952. *Forensic Psychiatry.* New York, The Ronald Press Co.

Davidson, H. A. 1959. The commitment procedures and their legal implications. In *American Handbook of Psychiatry,* ed. S. Arieti. New York, Basic Books, Inc. Vol. 2, ch. 96.

Deutsch, A. 1949. *The Mentally Ill in America,* 2nd edition. New York, Columbia University Press.

Ekblad, M. 1955. *Induced Abortion on Psychiatric Grounds.* Acta Psychiatrica et Neurologica Scandinavica, Supplementum 99.

Ekblad, M. 1961. *The Prognosis after Sterilization on Social-Psychiatric Grounds.* Acta Psychiatrica Scandinavica, Supplementum 161.

Gray, K. G. 1955. *Law and the Practice of Medicine,* 2nd edition. Toronto, Ryerson Press.

Group for the Advancement of Psychiatry. 1948. *Commitment Procedures.* Topeka, Kansas, G.A.P. Report No. 4.

Group for the Advancement of Psychiatry. 1950. *Psychiatrically Deviated Sex Offenders.* New York. G.A.P. Report No. 9.

Group for the Advancement of Psychiatry. 1954. *Criminal Responsibility and Psychiatric Expert Testimony.* New York, G.A.P. Report No. 26.

Group for the Advancement of Psychiatry. 1960. *Confidentiality and Privileged Communication in the Practice of Psychiatry.* New York, G.A.P. Report No. 45.

Guttmacher, M., and Weihofen, H. 1952. *Psychiatry and the Law.* New York, W. W. Norton & Co., Inc.

Hoch, P. H., and Zubin, J., eds. 1955. *Psychiatry and the Law.* New York, Grune & Stratton, Inc.

Holdsworth, W. 1956. *A History of English Law,* 7th edition. London, Methuen and Company, Vol. 1.

Kanner, L. 1957. *Child Psychiatry,* 3rd edition. Springfield, Illinois, Charles C Thomas, Publisher, ch. 21.

Kemp, T. 1957. Genetic-hygienic experiences in Denmark in recent years. Eugenics Review *49,* 11-18.

Lindman, F. T., and McIntyre, D. M., eds. 1961. *The Mentally Disabled and the Law.* Chicago, University of Chicago Press.

Litin, E. M. 1960. Should the cancer patient be told? Post-graduate Medicine *28,* 470.

Neel, J. V., and Schull, W. J. 1954. *Human Heredity.* Chicago, University of Chicago Press, ch. 18 and 20.

Overholser, W. 1953. *The Psychiatrist and The Law.* New York, Harcourt, Brace & World, Inc.

Overholser, W. 1959. Major principles of forensic psychiatry. In *The American Handbook of Psychiatry,* ed. S. Arieti. New York, Basic Books, Inc., Vol. 2, ch. 95.

Penrose, L. S. 1954. *The Biology of Mental Defect.* London, Sidgwick and Jackson, ch. 12.

Perry, R. L., and Cooper, J. C. 1959. *Sources of Our Liberties.* Chicago, American Bar Foundation.

Ray, I. 1871. *A Treatise on The Medical Jurisprudence of Insanity,* 5th edition. Boston, Little, Brown & Co., Inc.

Szasz, T. S. 1956. Some observations on the relationship between psychiatry and the law. Archieves of Neurology and Psychiatry *75,* 297.

Szasz, T. S. 1957. Commitment of the mentally ill; "Treatment" or social restraint? Journal of Nervous and Mental Disease *125,* 293.

Szasz, T. S. 1957. The concept of testamentary capacity. Journal of Nervous and Mental Disease *125,* 474.

Szasz, T. S. 1958. Psychiatry, ethics and the criminal law. Columbia Law Review *58,* 183.

U. S. Public Health Service. 1951. *A Draft Act Governing Hospitalization of the Mentally Ill.* Washington, D.C., Government Printing Office, USPHS Publication No. 51.

World Health Organization. 1953. *Mental Health Aspects of Adoption.* Geneva, WHO Technical Report Series No. 70, p. 18.

World Health Organization. 1955. *Legislation Affecting Psychiatric Treatment.* Geneva, WHO Technical Report Series No. 98.

Zilboorg, G. 1944. Legal aspects of psychiatry. In *One Hundred Years of American Psychiatry,* ed. G. Zilboorg and J. K. Hall. New York, Columbia University Press.

CHAPTER 15

Neurotic Disorders

The Scottish physician William Cullen (1710-1790) introduced the term neurosis, and regarded neuroses as one of four major varieties of pathology confronting physicians. During the following century, distinctions were made between psychosis (major reality-distortion or insanity), psychoneurosis, and neurosis. These distinctions were related to then current notions of etiology, according to whether the disorder was regarded as originating primarily in the brain or in the peripheral nervous system. It is now recognized that multiple etiological factors may contribute to the development of all these disorders. While the distinction between psychosis and neurosis has been preserved, the term psychoneurosis has long been used interchangeably with neurosis, and applied to a variety of syndromes and maladaptive personality disorders.

Neurotic disorders may be manifested primarily by excessive anxiety, fear, or depression, disturbances of consciousness or disordered bodily functions, repetitive thoughts and behavior, or difficulties in interpersonal relationships. They are generally considered as less severe *in degree* than psychoses, since neurotic patients do *not* show gross distortions or misinterpretation of external reality (such as hallucinations or delusions) and do *not* undergo gross disorganization of personality. However, longitudinal or lifelong studies of neurotic individuals usually show evidence of periodic or constant maladjustment from early childhood which may sometimes be severely incapacitating. Superimposed frustration, conflict, stress, or deprivation may then precipitate the more acute symptoms or manifestations of neurosis.

Neurotic disorders are generally regarded as attempts at resolution of unconscious emotional conflicts in a manner that handicaps the patient's effectiveness in living. According to the anxiety theory of neurosis proposed by Freud, the common denominator of all neuroses is anxiety, which may either be directly felt and expressed, or may be unconsciously and automatically controlled by the utilization of various ego defense mechanisms that were described in Chapter 3. Neurotic symptoms such as dissociation, conversion, phobias, obsessions, or depression are then viewed as maladaptive defenses against the overwhelming conscious anxiety that would be aroused by recognition of unacceptable unconscious impulses—particularly repressed sexual and hostile wishes.

In many ways, neurotic individuals may be regarded by others as socially desirable and useful citizens. They tend to have a rigid superego, conscience, or internal control system, and to be moral, reliable, responsible, truthful, civilized, and conforming. Their thoughts and behavior are overly inhibited and they have difficulty in recognizing or tolerating sexual and hostile impulses in themselves as well as in others. Neurotic women tend to be frigid and to obtain no satisfaction from sexual relations, while neurotic men frequently show some degree of impotence or premature ejaculation. Neurotic patients of both sexes try not to express anger or hostility directly, but frequently hurt or frustrate others unconsciously as a consequence of their behavior. They want to love and feel loved, but are emotionally insecure and sensitive to the opinions and criticisms of others. They may have high ideals and ambitions, but feel inferior, inadequate, and dissatisfied with themselves. They are frequently anxious, tense, and worried, and devote much energy to plans, doubts, and fears of the future.

Since their suffering is largely internal and they do not usually appear grossly abnormal to others, they tend to seek help voluntarily themselves rather than being forced into accepting treatment by others. Because of the variety of manifestations, however, they may seek help from any of a number of sources such as a family physician, religious advisor, marriage counselor, or social agency. They are sometimes reluctant to accept that there is any emotional basis for their symptoms, but most neurotics have sufficient insight to accept referral to a psychologist or a psychiatrist, although they do not have insight into the significance of unconscious psychodynamic and interpersonal relationships. Psychotherapy can frequently be carried out on an outpatient basis, although at times their symptoms may be so acute that a short period of treatment in hospital may be recommended.

Initial appraisal of the patient may show no gross deviation from normal in appearance, attitude, or behavior, but a number of suggestive signs may be evident to an alert observer. Occasionally there are obvious manifestations of disability, as in the hysterical patient who is paralyzed or moving his limbs

uncontrollably, but frequently the signs consist of minor suggestions of inner difficulties. However, in spite of the enormous variation in neurotic symptoms and in the intelligence and socio-economic status of individual patients, there are still some generalizations that may be made.

The clothing of neurotic patients is usually neat, tidy, and somewhat conservative. They tend to be cooperative, communicative, and reasonably sociable but inhibited, cautious and lacking self-confidence. In hospital they tend to conform with what is expected in the way of ward activities, but may have difficulties in sleeping. There may be outward signs of anxiety, tension, or fearfulness such as a tremor of the hands or voice, or a marked startle reaction to unexpected sounds. Compulsive patients are prone to be fastidious in appearance, meticulous, and repetitive in their habits. Depressed patients may be careless concerning their clothing and appearance and show evidence of fatigue, or indifference to their surroundings, or have crying spells.

Conversation is spontaneous, and attention can be gained, maintained, and directed. There is no undue pressure or retardation of speech, and responses to questions are relevant and appropriate. Thought content frequently shows preoccupation with the neurotic symptoms or problems that have led them to seek help. In hysterical patients, however, there is frequent use of the defense mechanism of denial of consciously intolerable thoughts, wishes, or needs or of external reality. Apart from hysterical dissociative states, the patient is in good contact with reality and is able to supply detailed information concerning his personal history, which will tend to correspond with that obtained from any other reliable sources.

Intelligence may be of any level, and there will be no impairment of intellectual function, memory, or orientation (except in some hysterical dissociative states). The hysterical patient may be quite calm, and appear indifferent to the consequences of his severe disability. Other patients will tend to be anxious, tense, fearful, or depressed but the emotional reaction remains appropriate and usually quite adequate.

Neurotic patients frequently give a history of previous treatment for a variety of bodily complaints due to real or imagined illnesses, and a higher frequency of surgical operations (of all types) than any other group of psychiatric patients of the same age and sex. At the time they are referred for psychological or psychiatric evaluation, however, medical examinations and tests are likely to be negative.

Psychological tests may be helpful in evaluation, and show marked individual differences in intelligence, personality, and unconscious psychodynamics. On the Minnesota Multiphasic Personality Inventory the first scale (Hs) consists mainly of a set of physical complaint items characteristic of neurotic patients with hypochondriasis, the second scale (D) indicates symptoms of depression, the third scale (Hy) was derived chiefly from patients with symptoms of conversion hysteria, and the seventh scale (Pt) is sensitive to "psychasthenic" traits and was derived from obsessive-compulsive persons. Patients with neurotic symptoms tend to show elevations of various combinations of these scales, sometimes together with other scales. Patients with code types 12 and 21 have been characterized by somatic pain and concern, and have usually been diagnosed as neurotic (mainly hypochondriacal or hysteric). Code types 23 or 32 have been predominantly female and depressed (either psychotic or neurotic). Code types 27 and 72 indicate depression, and have more often been diagnosed as psychotic than neurotic. Code types 31 and 13 have been described as "the conversion V" or "hysteroid valley" and have been regarded as typical of conversion hysteria with complaints of pain. Code types 78 and 87 have been divided fairly evenly between neurosis and psychosis, the neurotics being mainly depressed, psychasthenic, or mixed.

In the Rorschach test, obsessive-compulsive patients sometimes give a very large number of responses, many of them small or rare detail, which tend to be of good form level and well elaborated. Some depressed or grossly disturbed hysterical patients may give a very small number of responses, but the majority of neurotic patients give an average number of responses, of form level appropriate to their intelligence. With the exception of obsessive-compulsives, who are inclined to give rare detail responses, the distribution of responses according to location is usually within normal limits. There tend to be several popular responses, with no very unusual or bizarre content, and few outright rejections of cards, although there may be considerable variation in reaction time from one card to another, which may be related to "shading shock" or "color shock." There is often an unusually high proportion of straight form responses (indicating constriction) and some preponderance of introtensive movement responses over extratensive color responses. Animal movement responses frequently exceed human movement and CF may exceed FC, both suggesting immaturity and impulsivity.

Responses to both the Rorschach and Thematic Apperception Test may give the therapist considerable insight into the patient's unconscious dynamics and characteristic ways of responding to emotional stimuli. Similarly, various Sentence Completion tests may also provide valuable insights into the patient's problems and patterns of adaption. Here are some characteristic responses given by a young hysterical woman, who had been married a few months previously, but was currently living apart from her husband so that they could both continue their education independently. These responses indicate a denial of unacceptable motives in both herself and others.

Marriage... has brought to me more happiness than I ever dreamed possible.
Most women... should strive to remember to

be feminine, though capable and not overly feminine.

My body. . .satisfies me the way it is. I won't let it be defiled. I know I must not be ashamed of it.

Most bosses. . .aren't nearly as nice as mine. He is the best in the world, I'm sure.

A husband. . .must be prepared to stand by and understand through thick and thin — as mine is doing now. His love for his wife must take second place only to his love for God.

I like. . .to like people and to be liked by them. Perhaps love would be a better word. I like to be in the wild free outdoors and to run uninhibitedly.

My mother. . .is one of the dearest, most precious persons in the whole world. I'd do almost anything to make her happy.

If I were in charge. . .of the world, I'd arrange things so that everyone loved everyone else all of the time.

My father. . .has always and still does refuse to let me grow up. At least he won't admit to himself that I have.

Most men. . .are wonderful, fascinating creatures who never forget that women are female.

This place. . .is wonderful. It is more like a hotel than a hospital and does everything possible to prevent us from thinking we're really very, very sick.

My job. . .is perfect. Though the work gets boring, the people are wonderful beyond words.

It is easy for me to. . .love many people and animals and friends all at the same time.

My health. . .is good and bothers me only when I think something is psychosomatically wrong again.

Nothing cheers me up as much as. . .my husband or a good talk with God.

I am the sort of person who. . .is so full of love it just bursts out and sometimes in the wrong ways.

I am ashamed when I think of. . .my past relations with a man named X — also hurt and regretful.

Things look hopeless when. . .I'm all depressed, excited, angry and don't know why. Really, I don't think things have ever looked really hopeless!

I need. . .help to understand myself and loads of love.

Most of the time, I am. . .a very pleasant, likeable (I think and hope) person.

If I saw a firetruck. . .I'd like to follow it and always hope no one was hurt and that it wasn't too bad.

Everywhere. . .around me I find people who love me and want to help me now when it's so important.

If I were the boss, I. . .would arrange for everyone to love everyone else.

I really think my place in life. . .is and will be wonderful and satisfying.

Some people don't like me because. . .I don't know of anyone who dislikes me.

In psychoanalytic usage, the term neurosis has often been used to refer to any form of abnormal behavior other than mental retardation and organic brain syndromes. Psychophysiologic disorders have been referred to as organ neuroses, sociopathic personality disorders have been referred to as impulse neuroses, and schizophrenic reactions as narcissistic neuroses. In general psychological and psychiatric usage, however, the term neurosis (or psychoneurosis) has been restricted to a limited number of syndromes classified according to the predominant symptoms, which may be either anxiety, hysterical dissociation or conversion, phobias, obsessions and compulsions, or various manifestations of depression. Each of these neurotic syndromes will now be described and illustrated, and we shall then review certain other neurotic syndromes, particularly traumatic and character neuroses.

ANXIETY REACTION

Anxiety is a state of apprehension, tension, uneasiness, uncertainty, or helplessness associated with the anticipation of danger, the source of which is largely unknown or unrecognized. Anxiety is therefore often spoken of as "vague," "object-less," or "free floating" in contrast to *fear*, which is the emotional response to a consciously recognized, specific, and usually external threat or danger. Karl Abraham (1911) noted that anxiety and depression are related to each other in the same way as are fear and grief. Anxiety and fear, however, are frequently accompanied by similar bodily changes which involve overactivity of the sympathetic nervous system and may be regarded as a preparation for "fight or flight."

Anxiety may be regarded as pathological when it is present to such an extent as to interfere with effectiveness in living, the achievement of desired realistic goals or satisfactions, or reasonable emotional comfort. Neurotic anxiety is distinguished from normal anxiety in that (1) it is disproportionate to the objective threat; (2) it involves repression, dissociation, or other defenses against unconscious conflict; (3) it is handled by various forms of retrenchment of activity and awareness, inhibitions, and the development of other neurotic symptoms; (4) it is not relieved by amelioration of the objective situation. Anxiety neurosis is therefore characterized primarily by the direct conscious experience of anxiety, which may be of acute or gradual onset, with subjective uneasiness or apprehension out of proportion to any apparent external cause. The conscious anxiety remains uncontrolled, and there is only a minor degree of utilization of various specific defense mechanisms common in other neuroses.

A 20-year-old boy was referred for psychiatric evaluation at the beginning of his final year in a highly competitive college where he was carrying a B-plus average, and hoping to improve on this so that he might graduate magna cum laude. Since the beginning of the fall quarter, he had been feeling acutely apprehensive and jittery, with moist sweaty palms, and had temporarily become discouraged to the point of wanting to withdraw from school and return home. However, he dated the onset of his anxiety to almost one year previously, during the fall quarter of his junior year, when he was in hospital for a month with a virus infection diagnosed first as infectious mononucleosis and then as hepatitis. At that time he had become very worried that he might be going to die, and for a couple of weeks he had received minor tranquilizing medication. He was also worried about losing a year before graduation, but he had previously accumulated credits in summer school sufficient to offset those he lost due to sickness. His situation was complicated, however, by an intense emotional relationship with a girl he had been dating for eighteen months, and with whom he had been exchanging letters daily. Up to that time there had been no sexual relationship, and they were making plans to become engaged after his graduation from college, with the anticipation of getting married when he was in graduate school and having children after he had completed the latter.

During the winter quarter of his junior year he worried excessively whether they had made the right decision, and also studied extremely hard in order to get A's in all his courses. During the spring quarter he had several minor infections and became even more apprehensive about his health, about examinations, about wasps getting into his room, and about other matters. He became very sensitive to trivial noises, and lay awake for an hour or two before he was able to get to sleep. The night before an examination he couldn't sleep at all, and became very discouraged but got an A in the course anyway. During the summer he felt obliged to undertake a research fellowship which he didn't enjoy. He was apprehensive that the chemicals he used at work might harm him, and worried that he might catch tetanus. He worried about noise being made by bats, and thought he might be bitten and get rabies. He developed a tight feeling in his throat and became very irritable and frightened, worried about dying, and not being able to see the people that he loved again. He was again given a minor tranquilizer for a couple of weeks.

When he returned home he wanted his girl friend with him constantly, and the increased intensity of their emotional relationship led to intercourse, but they did not use contraceptives since he "didn't want it to become a habit," and instead relied on the "safe period" and coitus interruptus. He felt obliged to make a commitment to her that they would become engaged during the Christmas vacation of his senior year, and would get married immediately after he graduated. He was frightened of losing her, and still frightened of dying, but also felt increasingly trapped by their impending plans for engagement and marriage.

This patient was the second child and only son of Jewish parents who had high expectations that he would achieve success for the entire family. He viewed his father as permissive but distant, constantly preoccupied with business concerns over which he worried excessively. He felt closer to his mother, and had always tended to confide in her more, or sooner, than in his father. Both parents, however, were anxiously overprotective, and extremely concerned about any somatic complaints. He recalled that when he was about ten years old he had been sent away to summer camp but hadn't liked it, and had gone to the infirmary with a stomach ache, following which his parents came and took him home from camp.

At first he denied that there had been any sibling rivalry between him and his elder sister, but he soon reported that she had felt discriminated against, and treated unfairly in comparison with himself. During the past few months before he was referred for psychotherapy, his sister had been seeing a psychiatrist twice a week and there had been many violent scenes at home in which she verbally abused their parents. At one point he rationalized his own plans for engagement to his girl friend on the basis that it would give his parents a little happiness. During the course of therapy it also became apparent that he had been emotionally insecure throughout his adolescence, and had experienced considerable guilt over masturbation and over earlier heterosexual fantasies involving his sister. Sporadic sexual relationships with other girls had not involved conscious guilt, and had been unaccompanied by any strong emotional attachment. However, he had at times adopted compulsive defenses and rituals such as counting to five, tapping his wrist, saying a prayer, and repeating over to himself the things that he wanted the most, such as to graduate magna cum laude and Phi Beta Kappa.

He remained in therapy for one academic quarter and attained considerable insight into hitherto unconscious psychodynamics. At first he received small doses of supplementary tranquilizing medication but this became less necessary as time went on, and he reached an agreement with his girl friend to postpone their engagement until the time they had originally planned. During the same period of time he also learned of his acceptance in the graduate school of his choice, but this partial relief from academic pressure appeared less significant in alleviating symptoms than his diminished sense of obligation to his girl friend. Although improved adaptive capacity might have followed more prolonged psychotherapy, the removal of situational stress also removed his motivation for further personality change at that time.

DISSOCIATIVE REACTION

Dissociation is an automatic and unconscious defensive mechanism by which emotional significance and affect are separated and detached from an idea, situation, or object. Dissociative reactions include a wide variety of symptoms, some of which involve gross personality disorganization and may superficially resemble schizophrenic psychoses. However, the onset is usually abrupt, in response to obvious emotional stress or conflict, and an early remission of the symptoms of a given attack may be expected, although they are prone to recur from time to time. The most common type of dissociative reaction consists of an attack of *amnesia* (loss of memory) that is sudden in onset and remission, and usually involves quite circumscribed periods of time — unlike the amnesia associated with organic brain syndromes, which tends to be diffuse, maximum for events in the recent past, and gradual in onset and recovery.

When amnesia is associated with physical flight, the syndrome is known as a hysterical *fugue*, as in the case history presented below. Dissociative reactions also include *sleepwalking* and *multiple personality*, in which the same individual may behave at different times in ways that are as incongruous as those depicted in Stevenson's novel "Dr. Jekyll and Mr. Hyde."

Brief dissociative reactions may occur in patients who have also shown symptoms of conversion hysteria (to be described later), or in the absence of other obvious neurotic symptoms. They are relatively uncommon in comparison with other forms of neurosis, but their dramatic nature has resulted in their attracting considerable public as well as scientific attention. Reports of amnesic episodes and fugues have not infrequently appeared in the lay press, and a fascinating account of one such individual was narrated by Berton Roueché. Multiple personality is much rarer and even more dramatic, and classic accounts of such patients were written by Morton Prince (1906) and by Thigpen and Cleckley (1957).

A middle-aged woman was found one night in an empty parking lot by police who were on routine patrol. She was untidy in appearance and had no possessions with her other than the clothes she wore. She offered no spontaneous conversation, but followed simple instructions and made some attempt to answer questions. However, she had no idea who or where she was, and the police took her to the emergency department of a nearby hospital. Her shoes were worn and her feet were blistered and swollen, but otherwise the preliminary physical examination was negative, except for a small elevation in temperature that returned to normal a few hours after she had been given plenty of fluids to drink. In the absence of any identification or obvious bodily illness, she was admitted to a psychiatric ward as "Jane Doe." Further medical and neurological examinations and tests were carried out, but no organic basis was found for her mental condition. During the first couple of days she was on the psychiatric ward, she dressed neatly, ate and slept well, and socialized with the other patients. At interview she appeared somewhat anxious and unhappy, complained of a lump in her throat (globus hystericus), and that she felt as though she was looking through a wet windshield. However, she answered questions relevantly to the best of her ability, was soon correctly oriented, and was able to remember most of the events that had happened *since* the time she had been found by the police. Prior to this time she recalled vaguely having been walking through the woods, but she was unable to remember any details of her previous life. She pictured her mother as a very young girl, but could not picture her father and stated angrily, "I don't want to know about him." She had a pervading feeling of personal loss, but had no idea what she might have lost.

Three days after her admission to the psychiatric ward she was hypnotized, and under hypnosis she recalled vividly the details of her previous life. It turned out that she was 43 years old and had been an only child who had never known her father. Her mother had worked as a domestic in private homes and in hotels, and when possible the patient had lived with the mother, but this was only for a few months at a time. The remainder of her childhood she had lived with an uncle and aunt, who were a middle-aged couple without any chil-

dren of their own. Until the age of ten she had assumed that her father was dead, but at this time her mother told her that he had deserted before she was born, and this information came as a shock to her. When the patient was aged 14, her mother committed suicide and the patient recalled having felt so unhappy that she wished her mother had taken her with her. She had previously had a number of friends her own age, but during the next couple of years she became quite socially withdrawn and she left school at the age of 16 after completing grade ten in order to help her uncle in his business. He had promised that he would subsequently put her through nightschool, but the business folded within a couple of years and he was unable to do so.

At the age of 18 she married a man three years older than herself who lived next door and was currently working in a factory. Their sexual relationship was unsatisfactory from the start. In retrospect, she attributed this to both her own lack of information and experience, and her husband's lack of consideration for her. There were other sources of conflict between them and her husband began to drink heavily and to go out with other women, so that after several years they were separated. World War II came along and her husband enrolled in military service, following which they were reconciled and she spent several happy years with him (as he was never stationed overseas). Three children were born in quick succession but the youngest died at the age of a few months. After the war was over, however, her husband returned to his former pattern of excessive drinking and going out with other women, and when she was 30 he finally left her with two preschool children to look after. She made arrangements with her husband's parents to look after the children and went out to work as her mother had done in a variety of unskilled jobs, in factories, laundries, as a waitress, and in domestic service. She never obtained a divorce from her husband but led everyone to believe that she had.

In her late 30s she was working in a large city and met a man to whom she became very attached. He was married but his wife was a chronic patient in a mental hospital and he was unable to obtain a divorce. The patient went to live with him as his wife, but experienced a great deal of guilt over this and wished that they were free to marry each other. Twice she left him and returned to live with her mother-in-law but there was conflict between them and she felt unwanted. On the second such occasion she had a brief episode of amnesia and was found by the police walking down the highway, but this episode only lasted three days, following which she again returned to live with her boy friend. Once again the conflict was too much for her and she left him to work in another city. While there she received word from him that he had finally obtained a divorce and that he now wished to marry her. She felt unable to tell him that she was not free to do so, and was ambivalent about returning to live with him as before. She was trapped in her own lies and conflicts.

In this situation, she packed all her belongings in a suitcase, checked this in a locker at the railroad station, put the key in her purse which also contained all her money (which she would have needed to buy a railroad ticket) and then lost the purse. This occurred several weeks before her admission to hospital, and she had only vague recollections of what had transpired during these weeks. It was summertime and she slept outside and in abandoned houses. She was afraid of people and came out mainly after dark, when she would frequently walk aimlessly for hours. She was unable to recall eating but would drink water wherever she could find it. The night that she was found by the police was her forty-third birthday and she was very close to a house where she had lived with her husband.

Once the events of her previous life had been recalled, she had no recurrence of her former amnesia, and was able to participate in psychotherapy. When asked what three wishes she would make if she could have anything she wanted, she replied only, "a home and my children." However, she was able to accept the reality of her situation, and her feelings of depression gradually diminished with emotional support and supplementary medication. She gained considerable insight into the sources of emotional conflict and after a couple of months in hospital she felt in a better position to establish herself independently than she had done for many years. Supportive outpatient therapy was continued for some months following her discharge, and she appeared to be making an effective adaptation at the time the latter was terminated.

CONVERSION REACTION

In patients with conversion symptoms, conscious anxiety is avoided by the conversion of unacceptable impulses into disordered functions of parts of the body, usually parts that are mainly under voluntary control, in contrast with the disturbance of autonomic and visceral functions that occur in psychophysiologic or "psychosomatic" disorders. The three main types of disordered bodily function observed in conversion reactions are:

(1) Altered sensation, which may consist of anesthesia (total loss of sensation), hypoesthesia (reduced sensitivity), hyperesthesia (excessive sensitivity), or paresthesia (unusual sensations such as tingling). Partial or complete hysterical blindness or deafness are special types of anesthesia or hypoesthesia.

(2) Paralysis, or loss of ability to perform voluntary movements, usually affecting specific parts of the body. The total inability to use both lower limbs is known as paraplegia, while a total inability to use the arm and leg on one side of the body is known as hemiplegia. Total inability to speak is known as aphonia, and may also result from functional hysterical paralysis.

(3) Involuntary movements or dyskinesias include a wide variety of forms that may superficially resemble every known type of involuntary movement that occurs in physical diseases of the nervous system. The most common varieties of hysterical involuntary movements are tics, tremors, and seizures that may closely resemble those observed in epilepsy.

In conversion reactions, the changes in bodily functions are often thought at first to be caused by some physical illness, and the patient or his relatives are apt to consult a general physician. The physician often suspects some organic disease of the nervous system and refers the patient to a neurologist rather than a psychiatrist or psychologist. However, careful neurological examinations and tests usually show obvious discrepancies between the patient's symptoms and the known anatomical distribution of motor and sensory nerves, such as "glove" or "stocking" anesthesias, and inconsistent losses of motor function. The patient frequently shows no anxiety or concern over grossly impaired function ("la belle indifférence" of Charcot), and the symptoms are often symbolic of underlying mental conflict. The onset is usually sudden, in response to recognizable emotional stress, and the symptoms enable the patient to escape temporarily from an unpleasant situation and obtain "secondary gains" in the form of attention and consideration from relatives and others.

A 27-year-old married woman was referred to a neurologist by her family physician for evaluation of headaches, nausea, vomiting, blurred vision, and seizures characterized by uncontrollable generalized bodily movements. Frequent complaints of headache had been present for eight or nine years, but these had become worse during the preceding three months, during which time she had also developed all the other symptoms. The muscular movements occurring during her seizures superficially resembled those of epilepsy (a period of rigidity followed by rhythmical violent jerking movements), but she did not lose consciousness at these times and could still be involved in conversation. There was no period of time that she was unable to remember subsequently, she had never fallen to the floor, turned blue, frothed at the mouth, bitten her tongue, or injured herself accidentally, nor had she lost control of her bowels or bladder. Clinical examination and neurological tests were negative, and she was referred for psychiatric evaluation.

She was the eldest of four girls and led an unhappy childhood. Her father drank excessively and her parents quarreled continually. Her father molested her sexually when she was three or four years old and she apparently developed gonorrhea, which led to her being removed from the home by the Welfare Board for treatment, and subsequent placement for three or four years in a foster home with two elderly women. There were no other children in this home and she was restricted from playing with other children in the neighborhood, frequently being kept alone in a fenced yard. She did not start school until the age of six, at which time her next younger sister was also enrolled, and at about this time she returned to live with her mother. Her father had deserted the family shortly after her removal to the foster home, but her mother would repeatedly tell her that she was just like her father. When the patient was aged nine or ten the mother remarried, but this marriage was no more successful than the first and soon ended in another divorce.

The patient was happy neither at home nor at school, where she found the work difficult although she made average grades. She was always a shy, quiet child with few friends. At the age of 16 she had some abdominal pain and her appendix was removed. She was in grade ten at the time but did not subsequently return to school and took several brief jobs as a salesgirl. She started dating a boy five years older than herself who lived next door, and soon she became pregnant. When she told her mother, the latter remarked, "You made your bed, now lie in it." Her pregnancy led to a forced marriage and during the next 11 years the patient gave birth to a total of eight living children. At the time of her referral for psychiatric evaluation, she was asked if she had any problems and she replied, "Eight of them," referring to her eight children. Soon afterwards, however, she found it necessary to deny that she had any problems except her physical health. It is probably significant that her headaches began when her second child was about five months old and she found herself pregnant for the third time. She and her husband were Catholic but had used contraceptives at times and this had been a source of emotional conflict for both of them. However, she maintained that her husband was a good provider and was considerate of her, and denied any other problems than the desire to avoid further pregnancies.

At first she found it difficult to accept that her bodily complaints could have an emotional basis, and to accept psychiatric treatment. However, she came regularly for weekly interviews and other problems soon became evident. She admitted an extramarital affair several years previously, which she believed had led to one of her pregnancies, and she had subsequently experienced much guilt over this. Her relationship with her husband was not as perfect as she had originally maintained, and he was also involved in therapy, in an attempt to modify his attitudes and behavior toward her. Over a period of time she gained considerable insight into her previously unconscious hostility towards her husband, its various manifestations, and its origins in her childhood relationships with her father and stepfather. At one time there was an increase in the severity of her symptoms which necessitated a brief period in the hospital, but over the course of several years she was able to establish a more mature adjustment, without undue reliance on bodily symptoms.

PHOBIC REACTION

A phobia has been defined as an obsessive, persistent, unrealistic fear of an external object or situation such as heights, open spaces, dirt, and animals. The fear is believed to arise through a process of displacing an internal unconscious conflict onto an external object symbolically related to the conflict. Excessive, unrealistic fears of death or disability from bodily disease (germs, cancer, and so on) frequently reach phobic intensity and usually appear attributable to repressed sexual and hostile impulses. A number of phobic reactions were formerly described and classified as "anxiety hysteria," but some phobias gain an obsessive quality by their intensity and repetitiveness so that there has been an increasing tendency to group phobic reactions with obsessive-compulsive reactions which will be described next.

A 35-year-old unmarried kindergarten teacher sought psychiatric help with a history of long-standing dissatisfaction with herself, and fears that were manifested in several specific situations. She was terrified of crowds and of riding in an automobile, which made it difficult for her to get to work, significantly impaired her social relationships, and increased the intensity of her ambivalent dependency upon her parents with whom she lived. She had always felt nervous and insecure in her relationships with other people, felt inferior to others, and had long been dissatisfied with her life at home with her parents, her inability to enjoy her work, and her failure to attract a man whom she would find acceptable for marriage. For several months she had had difficulty in sleeping and had been increasingly tired. It had become more and more of an effort to force herself to go to work, and she was more than usually threatened by her daily contact with other teachers, and with the parents of the children she was teaching. She was also more than usually irritated by those whom she thought she loved the most, mainly her parents and her current boyfriend. She felt miserable most of the time and had often wondered if life was worth living, although she had never seriously considered suicide.

She had one sister a few years older than herself who was subject to attacks of asthma, but the patient did not recognize that these might have any relationship to emotional problems. She considered her sister, who was married with several young children, as being much more aggressive, secure, and capable than herself. There were no other siblings, and the two girls had grown up in a middle class family with anxious, conforming, and overly protective parents. Their father was a conscientious hard-working manager of a small business, who worried excessively about small details and was only able to assert himself in the security of his own home, where he was frequently irritable, and would shout at the children with little provocation. He was, however, provoked to anger by his wife who continually worried and nagged him and the children. Several times during her life, the patient's mother had suffered brief "nervous breakdowns," at which times she was unable to look after her home and family adequately, but on only two of these occasions had she seen a psychiatrist, and the latter had been unable to modify her lifelong neurotic personality.

When first asked about her early life at home, the patient hastily replied that it was "nice," and then went on as follows: "I was quite happy I think. I can't think of anything specific. Mother was very, very fussy about the house. The housework was the most important thing in the world — whether everything was picked up. She couldn't give the love a child needed. Nothing satisfied her. She's inadequate and critical of what everyone does. The main thing was keeping the house in order. She was always nagging my father."

When asked about parental discipline during her childhood, she replied: "Mother would say 'you'll have to do this or your father will take care of you.' He's kind but has a very bad temper. He'd scream and yell, and I was afraid of him. I was the good one. Everyone would say how sweet and quiet and good I was. My sister was the problem—she'd have temper tantrums. Father always worried about money. He loved us and thought the world of his family." Later, when asked if she ever got angry, the patient replied "It's hard for me to get angry at anybody. Sometimes at my mother but not outwardly. It's usually better not to say anything. If I get angry with her, I feel bad afterwards. She always makes me feel wrong. I still feel she is my mother and I owe her respect. Everything I do, I'm trying to please her, but then I can't. I can't feel like an adult in that household." Both her parents were overconcerned about her physical health, and repeatedly cautioned her to be careful in order to avoid any possiblity of accidents. They never provided her with any useful information about sexual relationships, pregnancy, or childbirth. "I always had a lot of dates. I always wanted to get married badly, but when I get close to it I can't. I was always naive and overprotected about sex. I'm sure this must have a lot to do with it. Sex was never discussed at home. I never knew how a baby was born till I went to college. I never thought much about it. I was so innocent I'd flirt, and not know what it was all about. I like to be loved or feel there is someone around. I liked to be kissed at the time, but afterwards I get upset, like it

was wrong or bad. My present boy friend has emotional problems, and doesn't earn enough to support us if we got married unless I also worked. We're both Catholic and we couldn't afford to have any children. When I see him I want to be close to him but I think it's wrong. I think we should stop seeing each other, but then I miss him terribly."

At one time, a physician had recommended that the patient live away from home, but she was so dependent upon her parents that she had soon become more anxious and unhappy when she was away from them. However, her ambivalent feelings of love and hostility towards them, and towards her boy friend, remained unresolved. Her hostile and sexual feelings were the source of much fear, guilt, and need for punishment in the form of self-blame and depression. Analytically oriented psychotherapy enabled her to achieve insight into previously unconscious dynamics, but her unacceptable motivation was a source of continuing fear and depression that was not relieved by antidepressive medication. There was a marked improvement in mood following a short course of electroshock treatments (Figure 15-1), and she was subsequently able to participate more effectively

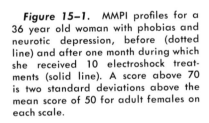

Figure 15-1. MMPI profiles for a 36 year old woman with phobias and neurotic depression, before (dotted line) and after one month during which she received 10 electroshock treatments (solid line). A score above 70 is two standard deviations above the mean score of 50 for adult females on each scale.

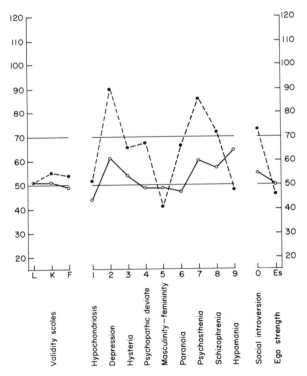

in psychotherapy. Reduction of excessive fear was accomplished by small doses of a minor tranquilizer, and she was able to involve herself more readily in relationships with other adults. She began teaching grade one instead of kindergarten, and was able to relate more effectively to the parents of the children and to the other teachers. Although she still remained uncomfortable in new social situations, she lost her irrational fear of crowds and was able to drive an automobile. She was still unable to emancipate herself from her parents, but her increased mobility and social relationships outside her home diminished the intensity of her former ambivalent dependency upon them.

OBESSIVE COMPULSIVE REACTION

An *obsession* is defined as a persistent, unwanted idea or impulse which cannot be eliminated by usual logic or reasoning. A *compulsion* is an insistent, repetitive, intrusive, and unwanted urge to perform an act that is contrary to the individual's ordinary conscious wishes or standards. Obsessional thoughts and fears (as of contamination by dirt, excreta, or germs) are often accompanied by compulsions to repetitive actions and rituals such as hand-washing, touching or counting objects, or repeatedly checking doors and windows, taps, ashtrays, or clocks.

A 37-year-old unmarried woman, born in Austria, was the second of four children. Both her sisters were described as nervous, excitable, high strung, and hysterical, but both had married and remained in Austria. Her only brother was the youngest member of the family and was described as clever and studious, but had been taken prisoner by the Russians and had not been heard of since. Her father was a wealthy man who had worked for the government until the age of 32, retired with a pension, lived in a large house with servants and married at the age of 40. He had acquired syphilis prior to his marriage, and for several years before his death he had increasingly frequent heart attacks. The infection also involved his nervous system and for many years he was forgetful, apathetic, and emotionally unstable. He took no interest in the children and sometimes they wouldn't see him for

weeks on end. He finally died at the age of 59, several days after having a stroke. The patient's mother had developed severe tuberculosis at the age of 18 and had had part of a lung removed surgically before her marriage at the age of about 35. Her tuberculosis persisted, and she frequently coughed up blood. Every time a child was born she had to go to a sanitarium for several months. She was described as intelligent, studious, nervous, high strung, and quarrelsome, having no friends. She was subject to frequent migraine headaches, was strict, and not interested in her children. She rejected the patient as being "stupid and ugly." Some of her actions were quite strange—she didn't wash at all and she invariably used a washbasin as a toilet.

The patient was told that her mother didn't want her and attempted to produce an abortion prior to her birth. She was always weak and sickly as a child, had dysentery during her first year of life, was hospitalized for some months and was not expected to live. She developed rickets (vitamin D deficiency) and didn't walk until four years old. From the ages of two to four her mother left her with foster parents and she was always deprived of security and affection. After returning to live with her family, her mother frequently told her she was weak, stupid, and ugly. The patient was a quiet and fearful child, rarely doing anything wrong, but mother frequently beat her so that she and one of her sisters used to think that she wasn't their real mother, but their stepmother. From the age of about nine she consciously hated her mother and used to pray every night that she would die. She was an intelligent child, but was only allowed to attend school until the age of 15 and for the following year she had two menial jobs near home. At the age of 16 her mother sent her away to an agricultural school as a punishment, but the patient enjoyed this year very much. During the next five years she did domestic service and was promoted to being a governess for the children. She studied hard in her spare time and obtained a job in the post office for six years, followed by seven years of office work for the American Occupation Forces. At the age of 36 she immigrated and then worked as a saleswoman.

Her awareness of sex dated back to the age of nine when she was sent away to a boarding house where she had to share a single bedroom with the landlady and three other boarders. The landlady frequently entertained different men at night and the patient became very frightened and ran away to a friend. She was placed in another boarding house where she shared a room with an older girl who lied and stole money, tried to teach the patient to do likewise and also introduced her to mutual masturbation. After returning home the patient always stayed awake until after her parents went to bed, and if either parent went to the room of the other, she would scream and cry, which would make her mother shout at her or beat her. At the age of 13 she started to masturbate and at the age of 16 she told her mother about this. Mother told her that this was terrible, that it would drive her crazy, that she would never be clean again, and that she was just like her father. Mother also told the patient's sisters and other relatives about it publicly, and the patient said for years afterward she was unable to laugh or smile anymore. She was afraid to go to sleep at night because she sometimes had an erotic dream, and she constantly felt dirty so that she began to wash her hands "hundreds of times a day."

She went out with a boy friend for the first time when she was 26 years old and felt that he was the first human being that was ever interested in her. They went out together every day for a year but there were no sexual relations until the last night before he went away, and she did not like the experience. She subsequently went with another man for about 18 months, "the first man I really loved," and had frequent intercourse which she enjoyed. After this she had a number of protracted sexual relationships with men for whom she was usually working, and who were already married. She said that she just wanted someone to talk to and didn't want a sexual relationship, but it always finished up that way. Sometimes they promised her marriage and she was engaged five times, four times to men who were already married, and promised to obtain a divorce. During these years she became pregnant on three occasions, on the first of which her legs became completely paralyzed and lost all feeling (apparently a conversion reaction) and she obtained an abortion at four months. The two subsequent pregnancies terminated in spontaneous abortion.

For as long as she could remember she had had many fears, and had had difficulty in sleeping at night. She gradually overcame the intense shyness of her childhood, but she remained lonely, anxious to please others, and meticulously clean and tidy. "Migraine" headaches started at the age of about 13 and severe compulsive washing of her hands and genitals developed at the age of 16 (after telling her mother about masturbation). On one occasion at the age of about 30 she lost her voice for several days following an emotional shock (probably another conversion reaction). Six weeks after immigration she had severe pain in the stomach and the presence of a peptic ulcer was confirmed by x-rays, but this cleared up following three months of medical treatment.

She first sought psychiatric help at the age of 33, at which time she commenced a partial psychoanalysis which lasted six hours a week for two years. At the end of this time she had considerable intellectual insight and there had been some symptomatic improvement, but she remained dependent on medication at times for the relief of anxiety, fear, and insomnia. Following her immigration there was an increase in her neurotic symptoms, in addition to the development of peptic ulcer. She developed kleptomania and compulsively appropriated many items of little value, such as pencils, pens, small amounts of money, and even pins. This type of behavior had previously been present in childhood, and she describe it as an attempt to obtain pleasure by deceiving her mother, but she always felt very guilty afterwards.

She had a phobia of electric light sockets and had to frequently check and recheck whether various lights and electrical appliances had been turned off. She had to check that all doors were shut, and again washed her hands and genitals very frequently. Whenever one obsessive thought, phobia, or compulsive action ceased, another one commenced, and she had a compulsion to do anything that she was explicitly forbidden to do. On one occasion she felt that her compulsive behavior was under the control of some external source, but this transient delusion of influence persisted only briefly, and there was no other evidence of reality distortion or psychosis. Sometimes she experienced feelings of depression but this was of neurotic intensity and was not accompanied by thoughts of suicide. Usually these episodes of depression were of brief duration, but on one occasion her depression lasted longer than usual and she received a short course of electroshock treatments. This resulted in rapid improvement in mood, but had no effect on her fears, obsessions, and compulsive behavior. The latter did not usually incapacitate her from working, however, and with supportive psychotherapy she was able to abandon her former dependency on medication.

DEPRESSIVE REACTION

Normal grief or sadness is an appropriate emotional response to an external and consciously recognized loss. When neurotic depression results from loss, it exceeds normal grief in degree and/or duration, in proportion to the loss sustained. Symptoms of depression frequently develop, however, in individuals with a history of previous neurotic symptoms or personality characteristics, in response to frustration and conflict rather than loss. These are typically situations that the normal individual would avoid, or to which he would react with anger rather than grief, but the neurotic individual is usually unable to express anger directly, and his depression frequently appears to represent retroflexed rage (anger turned backward upon himself).

Whatever the source of the neurotic's depression, it is more severe than normal grief, but less severe and incapacitating than psychotic depressions, which will be considered in Chapter 17. While the neurotic person may think of committing suicide, or be afraid of harming himself or others, the patient with a psychotic depression is very much more likely to succeed in doing so. Thus, the diagnostic manual of the American Psychiatric Association suggests that neurotic depression be differentiated from psychotic depression on the following grounds:

(1) Life history of patient, with special reference to mood swings (suggestive of psychotic reaction) to the personality structure (neurotic or cyclothymic) and to precipitating environmental factors, and

(2) Absence of malignant symptoms (hypochondriacal preoccupation, agitation, delusions, particularly somatic, hallucinations, severe guilt feelings, intractable insomnia, suicidal ruminations, severe psychomotor retardation, profound retardation of thought, stupor).

A 20-year-old male sought psychiatric assistance during the winter quarter of his third year in a highly competitive college. He was of superior intelligence and during the preceding two years had worked hard enough to bring his cumulative grade point average from C-minus to a solid B average. However, he had not found much satisfaction in his work and was currently expressing uncertainty regarding his vocational goals. He was quite introverted, had not participated in many athletic or social activities, and tended to become deeply involved in relationships with a few other students of both sexes and to become disappointed when they failed to reciprocate or live up to his expectations.

The depression that led to his seeking psychotherapy had been precipitated by the loss of his current girl friend, but he did not report this immediately. His presenting complaints were as follows. "I've been depressed—just different things bothered me. My relation to my parents. I can't be free of them, and my ideas are very different from theirs. And I have a strong fear of social gatherings, and inability to make friends. And my home life was very unhappy. My parents have not been happy. It's been more like a battleground than a home. The depression comes and goes. Sometimes I feel I don't want to do anything. Sometimes I go for months thinking that the world doesn't make sense. If my feelings didn't change I would't want to go on living. In high school I remember feeling miserable because my parents nagged me. In the seventh grade I wished I could put aside the next ten years and live my own life."

When asked about his father he replied that the latter came from a farm, married the daughter of a college president, and lived miserably ever after. He had spent 20 years as a minister, and had then turned to teaching high school, apparently due to economic pressures following the birth of the patient's younger brother. When asked about his mother, the patient reported that her father had died when she was nine years old, and that she seemed very frustrated with her existence. She had been working full time as a teacher since shortly after the birth of the patient's younger brother, and she had always pushed both of them very hard to achieve in school. She nagged her husband and her two sons. There had been frequent arguments between the two parents, and they had stopped sleeping together many years previously.

When the patient was a child, the family had moved frequently and tended to live in the country, where he felt relatively isolated from other children his own age. At one time he was in a class in school that was taught by his mother, and he felt she demanded more of him both in and out of school than of other children. He had a feeling of rejection and frequent abandonment by his parents, who placed religion and obligations to others above personal satisfaction. He generalized these feelings about his parents to include all teachers, and remarked "all that's ever important to teachers is achievement and duty and work. They are always breaking up boys and girls. I hate them. Everyone recognizes that teachers are puritans." He was subjected to constant criticism and disapproval, and developed a harsh and punitive superego, with low self-esteem.

He verbalized considerable conflict between his religious convictions and sexual and aggressive feelings. "The two parts of religion that bothered me most were 'don't lust after other people's women, and don't get angry.' When I was a teenager I could only go four or five days without masturbating. It was awful—demoralizing. I tried to ignore the sexual attraction that girls had for me and regard them as people, and I couldn't and it bothered me." After leaving home and entering college he had consciously rejected religion, and become quite bitter, cynical, and disillusioned. However, his relationships with others remained ambivalent, with strong repressed hostility that he could not express directly, but that nevertheless alienated him from those on whom he was emotionally dependent.

His recent deep attachment to a girl friend involved unrealistic expectations on his part, and when she continued to go out with other boys he felt abandoned and rejected, as he had in his lifelong relationships with his mother. During the course of analytically oriented psychotherapy he vacillated between unrealistic positive evaluation (idealization) of others, and unrealistic negative distortion (cynicism) regarding all human motivation and behavior. The same applied to his evaluation of the therapist in the transference relationship, but eventually he was able to make more rational intermediate discriminations, and to involve himself in more realistic interpersonal relationships than hitherto. He was also able to recognize and modify slightly his exceptionally high goals for achievement that had led to much internal frustration, and during the following year there was far less tendency to episodes of intense depression than hitherto. His age and intelligence were in his favor in making a more mature and effective lifelong adaptation. The fact that he had already left home enabled him to learn to view his relationships with his parents more objectively, and he was still young enough for considerable modification of emotional attitudes and behavior.

TRAUMATIC NEUROSES

This term has frequently been applied to neurotic syndromes that develop immediately following some severe precipitating situational stress or trauma. The symptoms may be any of those described already, but most frequently consist of anxiety, dissociation, conversion, or depression. What these symptoms *primarily* accomplish for the patient is to provide him with an acceptable means of escape from an intolerable situation in which he was trapped. Frequently, however, symptoms are perpetuated by considerable *secondary gains*, which may include (1) release from other obligations (e.g., employment, housework, care of husband or children, sexual relationships with spouse); (2) changed behavior on the part of other family members (e.g., "my husband used to drink and run around, but has behaved much better since I've been sick"); (3) greatly increased attention from physicians, attorneys, insurance claims adjusters, and others); (4) direct financial remuneration so long as sickness continues (e.g., disability insurance, workman's compensation, Veterans Administration pensions, or Social Security).

The term traumatic neurosis has generally been taken to include combat fatigue, and occupational and compensation neuroses. However, the causative factors involved in the precipitation and perpetuation of symptoms may be different in these different conditions. Three case histories will serve to illustrate some of the differences in etiologic factors, manifestations, and prognosis.

COMBAT FATIGUE

In the American Psychiatric Association diagnostic manual, one of the *transient situational personality disorders* described is the *gross stress reaction,* occurring either (1) in combat, or (2) in civilian catastrophe (such as fire, earthquake, explosion). These are reactions occurring in more or less "normal" persons who have experienced intolerable stress, and frequently represent reactions to overwhelming fear. However, it should be recognized that in combat, sleep deprivation and other biological factors are often superimposed upon the conflict between fear of death and conformity to social expectations. The amount of stress required to provoke decompensation varies enormously from one individual to another. Some individuals, particularly those with a history of previous neurotic symptoms, will show severe and persistent symptoms following exposure to minimal degrees of stress. The extremely persistent nature of some *war neuroses* has been documented by long-term follow-up studies such as those of Brill and Beebe, and of Archibald, et al. By definition, however, the *gross stress reaction* is only a temporary diagnosis, and symptoms should resolve rapidly following prompt and effective treatment, as in this illustrative case history reported by Grinker and Spiegel.*

A 20-year-old platoon sergeant in the infantry had had no anxiety in civilian life, and none in the six major engagements prior to the Battle of Mateur, where he developed acute anxiety in a very confused military situation. His platoon had orders to take a hill and had been told that they would meet with no opposition. The reverse proved to be the case, and most of the men were wiped out by enemy machine gun fire. The patient and a friend wandered about trying to get back to their own lines, when they were caught in

*From *War Neuroses* by Grinker, R. R., and Spiegel, J. P. Copyright, the Blakiston Company. Used by permission of McGraw-Hill Book Company.

the fire of their own artillery. They finally made their way to a foxhole, where they found a dead German and a dead American soldier, the latter having been a member of their company. The patient's friend threw the bodies out, and got into the foxhole. Shells were falling all about them and there was no room in the foxhole for the patient. He then developed intense anxiety and did not know what to do; finally he lay prone on the ground and flung the dead bodies of the two soldiers over his own for protection. He lay there for a long time, trembling and terror-stricken, until finally an artillery shell exploded very close by and blew the two bodies off the patient, ripping off his shirt at the same time. The two dead soldiers had actually saved his life. His mind at that point went blank. He wandered about, and was picked up by some men from his company, who brought him back to the bivouac area, from where he was returned to the rear. When he entered one of the forward hospitals he had acute anxiety, persistent tremor, great restlessness, loss of appetite, and insomnia with battle dreams. After a few days of rest these symptoms improved considerably. The acute anxiety and tremor disappeared, and he was sent back to our hospital. On admission he complained of restlessness, lack of appetite, and a "shaky" feeling in his body. He had only very fine tremors of the hands. There were terrible dreams, in which he re-lived his battle experience, and also nightmares, in which he saw himself being attacked by gorillas. After Pentothal therapy all anxiety disappeared, as did the battle dreams, and he was shortly sent back to noncombatant duty.

OCCUPATIONAL AND COMPENSATION NEUROSES

Occupational neuroses involve escape from an unpleasant work situation, and compensation neuroses involve the continuation or anticipation of financial rewards for disability that has developed suddenly following an accidental injury, often sustained during the routine performance of the patient's occupation. In each of the two following patients it may be possible to recognize the interaction of multiple predisposing, precipitating, and perpetuating factors leading to the development and continuation of their neurotic symptoms, for which both of them refused therapy.

A 61-year-old married man was referred to a neurosurgical service for evaluation of severe pain in the back and the neck that had persisted for nearly a year following an accident occurring during the course of his employment. Lately he had also complained of headache and of feeling dizzy, tired, and completely lacking in energy. His wife had found him much more irritable than usual, and incapable of completing simple tasks around the home such as mowing the lawn. Careful medical and neurological examinations and tests failed to reveal an adequate organic basis for his complaints, and he was referred for psychiatric and psychological evaluation.

At interview he reported that he had worked regularly for the same company for 15 years prior to his accident and had taken very little time off for sickness. His accident occurred when he was standing on a ledge some ten or 12 feet above the floor, and involved his having been hit in the back by a beam that was being moved by another workman. He was knocked off the ledge and barely escaped falling to the floor by grabbing some pipes and pulling himself back up again. It soon developed that he believed he had narrowly escaped death or much more severe and permanent disability. After the accident he took two or three days off work and consulted an osteopath who told him he had a severe injury to the spine. At first the patient's feet did not seem able to hold him, but the osteopath gave him several treatments and recommended he wear a brace following which he returned to work. His symptoms persisted and he consulted an orthopedic surgeon who arranged for a special brace to be made for him, which was very heavy and uncomfortable. Being a conscientious man, the patient forced himself to go to work every day but he found the brace almost unbearable and was tired and sore all over when he got home at night. Six months after the accident he was admitted to the hospital for a couple of weeks for intensive investigations and unpleasant physical manipulations but there was little change in his symptoms and he began to feel increasingly tired and depressed. When he was in hospital or remained home from work, he received workman's compensation payments but most of the time he tried conscientiously to return to work, which he found increasingly difficult.

On reviewing his history it was learned that he was the youngest of three children and grew up in a lower middle class home with strict standards of behavior to which the children were expected to conform. His parents both lived to a ripe old age, and neither they nor his brother nor sister had shown any obvious signs of psychopathology. His grades in school were average or somewhat below, and he left after completing grade 11 to go to work. He became an electrician and was employed regularly all his life up until the time of his accident. He married at the age of 21 and had four daughters, all of whom had married some years previously. Both he and his wife regarded their marriage as successful, but his wife had undergone treatment for stomach ulcers, and sexual relations had been infrequent for some years. They rarely expressed anger or argued with each other, but the patient had been more irritable than usual since his accident.

The patient was asked to enter hospital for psychiatric evaluation, but when he arrived he insisted that he had expected to be admitted to a surgical service for operation. However, he agreed to come into hospital and was placed on an open ward with neurotic patients, none of whom were acutely disturbed. However, he resisted the idea that his symptoms could have an emotional basis and said that it was against his pride to be on a psychiatric ward. He resented the MMPI test because it contained some questions about sex, and his replies showed considerable defensiveness (with marked elevations on both the F and K Scales). None of the clinical scales showed marked elevations, but the two highest were scales one and two (hypochondriasis and depression). His resentment about being admitted to the psychiatric ward increased rapidly and he left hospital the day after admission. It was recommended that he receive antidepressive medication and return for outpatient psychotherapy, but he remained convinced that his symptoms required surgical treatment. This conviction had already been reinforced by the extensive somatic investigation and treatment extending over almost a year prior to his referral for psychiatric evaluation, and by the financial compensation he received on the basis of his somatic complaints. Secondary gains from continued disability also include escape from an unpleasant or frightening situation (employment, marital responsibilities, and so on), and may be perpetuated by lawyers who insist that the patient recover completely before instituting litigation to secure final financial settlement.

A 33-year-old married woman was referred by her family physician to a neurosurgical service for evaluation of severe pain in the back and legs which had persisted since a minor accident some months previously, and which incapacitated her from looking after her home and family. Careful neurological examinations and tests failed to reveal an adequate organic basis for her symptoms, and she was referred for psychiatric and psychological evaluation.

At interview she related without emotion that she had been sick ever since an evening some months previously when she and her husband had been out to a party. After the party, she was standing outside waiting for her husband to bring the car, when a man who had been drinking heavily came up to her and gave her a shove, so that she sat down sharply and felt pains going down both her legs. The man who had pushed her apparently phoned her a couple of days later and told her not to worry about the cost of medical expenses, saying that he would have an adjustor come over to see her, and she put the whole matter in the hands of her lawyer. She consulted her physician who had x-rays taken which were negative, but she continued to feel stiff and sore and her symptoms interfered with her ability to do the housework, prepare meals for her husband and daughter, or have sexual relations with her husband. She continued to consult her physician frequently and was admitted to hospital briefly for further studies. She felt that all medical and hospital expenses incurred since the time of the accident should be paid by the man who had pushed her, but her lawyer advised her against accepting any final settlement of her claim until she was completely well again.

On reviewing her earlier development it was learned that she was the third of four children, having two older sisters and a younger brother who received a great deal of attention when he arrived and throughout their childhood. She grew up in a lower middle class family which emphasized conformity, did not permit expression of anger, and provided the girls with little sexual information. She completed high school, trained for a further year as a teacher, taught school for a year, and then married for the first time. One child was born the following year, but she described her husband as irresponsible and he left her soon after the birth of the child, following which she obtained a divorce and lived with her parents until her second marriage at the age of 22. One further child was born the following year and she maintained that her second marriage was satisfactory in every respect. Her husband was a good provider and considerate of her, and she denied any source of conflict between them. She claimed that their sexual relationship had been quite satisfactory up until the time of her accident, but this was not substantiated by interview with her husband. Her MMPI was quite defensive (with minor elevations on both the L and K scales), but in spite of this she also showed an elevation on Scale 3 (hysteria) and a minor elevation on Scale 1 (hypochondriasis).

It was recommended that she accept final settlement of her claim for compensation, and that she receive outpatient psychotherapy at a nearby mental health clinic, but she refused to accept the possibility of any emotional basis for her symptoms.

OTHER NEUROTIC DISORDERS

Hypochrondriasis refers to the presence of various bodily complaints without demonstrable organic pathology, and may be found in patients with other neurotic symptoms (particularily conversion or depressive reactions), or sometimes associated with psychotic distortion of reality (in depressive or schizophrenic reactions).

Neurasthenia is an obsolescent term introduced by Janet to describe symptoms attributed to weakness or exaustion of the nervous system. Such patients tended to complain of fatigue, feelings of inadequacy, and poor concentration, and the symptoms are nowadays more likely to be diagnosed as depressive in nature.

Psychasthenia is another term that was introduced by Janet, which was formerly used to describe obsessive compulsive reactions with impairment of initiative and energy. This term has also become largely obsolete, and the associated symptoms are generally attributed to depression.

CHARACTER NEUROSES

One of the unsatisfactory aspects of symptomatic diagnosis in neurotic disorders is that the same patient may manifest symptoms of more than one of the reactions hitherto reviewed. Another problem is that patients with none of the typical symptomatic manifestations may still encounter serious difficulties through personality characteristics that in other patients are associated with neurotic symptoms. Hendrick remarked that neurosis is a diagnosis based on evidence of a fundamental need to suffer beyond what environmental accident or physical illness justifies, in a person with a well developed interest in other people, and a potential capacity for erotic, tender, friendly, or sublimated love. Evidence for such a need to suffer (resulting from unconscious guilt) may be overt, disguised, or apparent only in extensive inhibitions.

According to this view, neuroses may be of two kinds: those in which symptoms predominate, and those in which neurotic character traits predominate. The various syndromes described previously may be regarded as *"symptomatic neuroses"* and may be contrasted with *character neuroses*, whose most conspicuous feature is the compulsive repetition of characteristic behavior leading to excessive suffering or failure. Some authors, however, perfer to contrast character neurosis with *situation neuroses*, which are reaction of a person whose personality was otherwise intact and undisturbed by an external situation filled with conflict.

Of recent years, *the term character neurosis has been used in at least three different ways*: (1) to describe persons with many typical neurotic personality characteristics, having their main difficulties in the area of interpersonal relationships rather than any of the symptoms previously described; (2) as synonymous with character disorder, referring to "unhealthy patterns of behavior and emotional response which are to varying degrees socially unacceptable or disap-

proved, accompanied by minimal outward evidence of anxiety or symptoms as ordinarily seen in the neuroses." This concept is closely related to the psychoanalytic definition of impulse neurosis and the general psychiatric diagnoses of sociopathic personality, sexual deviation, and drug addiction (which will be reviewed in Chapters 20 through 23); (3) as a residual category to describe "patients who do not belong in one of the specific reaction types. . . (but) exhibit mixed symptoms as well as relative mild character and, to a lesser extent, some behavior disturbances" (Hollingshead and Redlich, 1959).

DYNAMICS, DEVELOPMENT, AND ETIOLOGY

In psychoanalytic theory, neuroses may be classified according to the nature of defenses that the ego employs, or according to the nature of the repressed impulses. Freud postulated a connection between characteristic defenses employed and particular forms of neuroses. Thus in hysteria the main defenses used are repression and denial; in phobic reactions there is displacement of fear from its original source; and compulsive rituals represent reaction formation against aggressive and sadistic impulses, with symbolic atonement or undoing to alleviate guilt. Anna Freud suggested that repression may be used against sexual impulses, whereas other defenses may be employed against agressive impulses. In any event, the chronic failure of ego functions and maladaptive defenses are considered to originate in disturbed interpersonal relationships during childhood.

Retrospective information on early childhood relationships appears to implicate parental domination or deprivation (rejection, death, or separation) with repression of aggressive and sexual impulses. Internalization of parental instruction and prohibitions, and identification with the high ideals and aspirations of rigid parents are accompanied by the development of a harsh and dominant superego, with displacement of hostility which continues to be expressed indirectly during adult life.

Unfortunately, such retrospective information may result partly from distortion by the informant. Even when the facts can be established beyond reasonable doubt, the consistent association of adult neurosis with disturbed interpersonal relationships during childhood may still not indicate direct cause and effect, but indirect or mutual causation through other factors such as inherent personality characteristics of the child producing inevitable patterns of response from the parents. Long-term follow-up studies of children separated from their parents at birth and adopted through agencies shortly afterwards would offer some hope of eventually clarifying this issue. In the absence of such studies, however, the majority of psychiatrists and psychologists are convinced that most neurotic disorders are due to maladaptive learning, frustration and conflict, psychological stress, and deprivation. This belief is supported both by a paucity of positive findings in biological studies of neurotic patients, and by the frequent response of neurotic patients to predominantly psychosocial therapies.

HEREDITARY FACTORS

There have been few attempts to estimate the frequency of specific neurotic syndromes among the parents and siblings of patients with similar disorders, but some suggestive findings were reported by Brown (1942) and are summarized in Table 15-1. According to the diagnostic criteria employed in this study, there appeared to be a strong tendency toward familial specificity in neurotic disorders: anxiety reactions were the most common form of neurosis among the relatives of patients with anxiety reactions, hysteria the most common form of neurosis among the relatives of patients with hysteria, and obsessional symptoms the predominant form of neurosis among the relatives of patients with obsessional symptoms. Although these findings are compatible with a hypothesis of specific genetic predisposition, they may equally well be explained by postnatal transmission of predisposition to specific neurotic disorders through the childhood learning of maladaptive behavior.

In an extensive study of twins with neurotic and psychotic disorders, Slater (1953) provided data concerning 52 pairs of twins, one of whom was diagnosed as "psychopathic or neurotic." In this relatively small and heterogeneous group, he recorded an age-corrected frequency of similar abnormality among 26 percent of their siblings and 32 percent of their parents. The concordance rates for their cotwins were only two out of eight pairs diagnosed as monozygotic, and eight out of 43 pairs diagnosed as dizygotic. If we apply Holzinger's index of heritability to the latter

TABLE 15-1. Expectancy Rates for Various Kinds of Neurotic Disorders in Parents and Sibs of Index Cases*

TYPES OF INDEX CASES	PER CENT OF AFFECTED RELATIVES					
	Anxiety Neurotics		Hysterics		Obsessives	
	Parents	Sibs	Parents	Sibs	Parents	Sibs
Anxiety neurotics	21.4	12.3	1.6	2.2	0	0.9
Hysterics	9.5	4.6	19.0	6.2	0	0
Obsessives	0	5.4	0	0	7.5	7.1

*Modified after Brown. 1942. *In* Fuller, J. L., and Thompson, W. R. 1960. *Behavior Genetics.* New York, John Wiley & Sons, Inc.

data, it appears that the overall contribution of heredity is only somewhere in
the neighborhood of ten percent of the
variance. Even if this group had consisted solely of patients with neurotic
disorders, however, the small numbers
involved would make us even more
skeptical about these results than those
of the much larger series of twins with
manic depressive and schizophrenic
reactions.

Eysenck and Prell (1951) attempted to
study the inheritance of neuroticism by
administering psychological tests to 25
monozygotic (MZ) and 25 same-sexed
dizygotic (DZ) pairs of normal school
children, and a group of 21 neurotic
children for purposes of comparison.
The tests were intercorrelated for the
twin populations studied, and factorial
analysis was undertaken. Correlations
with respect to a "neuroticism factor"
were + 0.85 for MZ twins and + 0.22
for DZ twins. On the basis of these
data, Holzinger's approximate index of
heritability is given by the formula

$$H = \frac{r_{MZ} - r_{DZ}}{1 - r_{DZ}} = \frac{0.85 - 0.22}{1 - 0.22} = 0.81.$$

This result would suggest that about 81
percent of the variance or susceptibility
toward neuroticism could be attributed
to heredity. However, the serious difficulties and objections inherent in twin
studies were outlined in Chapter 5 and
cannot be emphasized too strongly. In
addition to the general defects of the
method, it is extremely questionable
what relationship may exist between
presumed neurotic traits in these normal twin children and overt manifestation of neurosis in adults.

The latter objections apply less to a
study undertaken by Gottesman (1962),
who administered the Minnesota Multiphasic Personality Inventory to 34
pairs of monozygotic and 34 pairs of
same-sexed dizygotic adolescent twins.
The determination of zygosity was
based on modern serological techniques
(involving nine blood groups), and the

MMPI scales were derived from psychiatric patients and standardized against a
large sample of the general population.
Six of the ten standard MMPI scales
have been found to occur with high
frequency in the configurations associated with various neurotic disorders, and four of these six scales had
appreciable indices of heritability in this
study: social introversion (scale 0) 60
percent, depression (scale 2) 44 percent,
psychasthenia (scale 7) 33 percent, and
schizoid (scale 8) 29 percent. The first
two of these indices of heritability (for
social introversion and depression) attained probable statistical significance
(as tested by the F ratio), so that a
genetic contribution to these factors
appears quite likely.

It should be noted, however, that
such findings *do not* suggest a specific
Mendelian mechanism as a determinant
of neurosis. Whatever hereditary predisposition may exist (and this is by no
means established) would be expected
to exert its effects through the cumulative actions of multiple minor genes
(polygenic transmission), such as those
which might contribute to the determination of physique, intelligence, endocrine and autonomic functions,
immune or allergic reactions, and other
responses to stress or deprivation.

SOMATIC FACTORS

The investigation of Sheldon and his
coworkers into physique suggested correlations between body structure and
personality traits of the order of + 0.8.
Endomorphic body build was correlated
with viscerotonic characteristics of relaxation, love of comfort, and sociability; mesomorphic structure with somatotonic characteristics of vigor and assertiveness; and ectomorphic structure with
cerebrotonic characteristics of restraint
and inhibition. Rees and Eysenck (1945)
compared 100 normal soldiers with 200
successive admissions to a neurosis
center and found that the neurotic
showed greater variability in body build
than the normals. Hysterics tended to

be concentrated toward the eury-morphic (or endomorphic) end of the scale, while neurotics with anxiety, depression, or obsessions tended to be concentrated at the opposite (leptmorphic or ectomorphic) end of the scale.

No consistent changes in brain structure have been observed although some authors have postulated a diffuse cortical atrophy in severe obsessive-compulsive reaction (a clinical diagnosis made at the time of lobotomy). Obsessive-compulsives have also been said to show a high frequency of EEG abnormalities, but many such changes found in neuroses and functional psychoses have appeared to be related to age rather than diagnosis. The only consistent physiological findings in neurosis consist of overall increased nervous activity, particularly of the autonomic nervous system, both sympathetic and parasympathetic (Gellhorn, 1943). Adrenosympathetic hyperactivity is indicated by such manifestations as increased heart rate, blood pressure, and respiration; dilatation of blood vessels in skeletal musculature and constriction of blood vessels in skin and intestines; pallor, cold sweats, erection of hair, dilatation of the pupils, and inhibition of peristalsis and salivation (with dry mouth). Variable and frequently localized increased parasympathetic activity is indicated by contrary findings to the preceding.

Funkenstein and his coworkers (1951) found that in a state of anger the hypotensive action of Mecholyl is slight and noradrenaline is secreted, whereas in a state of fear the hypotensive action of Mecholyl is marked and adrenaline is secreted. Gellhorn has concluded that the hypotensive action of Mecholyl is determined by the sympathetic excitability of the posterior hypothalamus. The Mecholyl test, vascular reactions, and urinary excretion in a state of anger suggest increased excitability of the hypothalamus and a dominant secretion of noradrenaline, as contrasted with diminished hypothalamic excitability and a dominant secretion of adrenaline in a state of fear. Gellhorn postulated that the predisposition of certain individuals to react to situations of stress with anger, whereas others react with fear, is explained on the basis of the individual variations in hypothalamic sympathetic excitability, but he recognized that this may be due to either hereditary or environmental factors or both.

PSYCHOLOGICAL FACTORS

The most common unconscious ego defense mechanisms utilized by neurotic individuals are implicit in the modern classification of these disorders and have already been mentioned. In their conformity to social ideals and expectations, most neurotics make excessive use of the mechanisms of repression, sublimation, and displacement of affect. In a patient with an anxiety reaction, such defenses have proved inadequate, and unconscious conflict is associated with conscious anxiety. Hysterical patients also rely heavily on the mechanism of denial, and conscious anxiety is largely prevented by the maladaptive defenses of dissociation and conversion. The development of phobias is interpreted as evidence of unconscious displacement of affect, resulting from fear of punishment for intolerable sexual and hostile impulses. Compulsive behavior is interpreted as symbolic undoing or atonement for unconscious guilt over unacceptable wishes, and depression is associated with loss of a love object, retroflexed rage, and need for punishment resulting from unconscious guilt.

There are many individual differences in the developmental dynamics and adult personality characteristics of patients with various forms of neurosis, but we may expect to find a history of interpersonal relationships favoring reliance on the characteristic intrapsychic defenses. The reader will have noticed some similarities in the case histories of patients manifesting different symptoms of neurosis, and may have recognized certain common denominators in their early experiences. They have become conforming, inhibited and anxious to please others because this type of behavior has been expected and demanded of them. Parents and other significant adults have strongly emphasized and reinforced "good" behavior, while attempting to extinguish or actively punishing all signs of "bad" impulses and behavior.

The superego, conscience, or internal control system is developed partly through the internalization and automatization of the repeated instructions and prohibitions of childhood, and partly through identification with the ideals and example of those in authority. Typically, the parents of the neurotic patient have fostered the development of an unusually harsh and rigid superego, so that the neurotic tends to feel as guilty over unacceptable impulses as normal persons would do if they had acted upon such impulses. Since antisocial impulses are universal, the neurotic attempts to avoid guilt by repressing them from consciousness and adopting various other defenses.

One or both parents of the neurotic individual are apt to be overprotective. Not only are they overconcerned with good behavior and moral development, but also with attempting to protect the child against physical illnesses and cautioning them repeatedly against common physical dangers. It may soon appear to the child that the physical environment and interpersonal relationships are dangerous and should therefore be feared. In some instances the parent may give verbal reassurance regarding the absence of danger (for example, in thunderstorms or the dark), but words are readily nullified by the example of an apprehensive parent who is forever expressing concern over trivialities. Overprotection also implies overcontrol and possessive domination of the child. If he is never given the responsibility for making decisions and learning from his own mistakes, the child then becomes overdependent on the parent, and in adult life is apt to remain tied to his mother's apron strings.

Along with the parents' concern that the child be a credit to them goes emphasis on achievement, and often attempts to elicit behavior that is normally expected at a later stage of development, as in the premature attempts at toilet training that have often been reported in patients with obsessive-compulsive neurosis. Such parents are usually also intolerant of noise and disorder, and establish in childhood the characteristic obsessional patterns of cleanliness, meticulous attention to detail, and perfectionistic strivings.

The parents are frequently undemonstrative of affection toward each other or toward the children. They also tend to inhibit all expression of anger by the child, either through harsh retribution or guilt-provoking moralization. Some parents, however, indulge themselves in violent temper outbursts, against which the frightened child can offer no retaliations. In general, however, Greenfield (1959) reported that patients with neurotic and schizophrenic reactions had suffered less *direct* discipline (such as scolding, spanking and isolation) than *indirect* discipline such as being made to feel that he is not as good as other children, being made to feel that he had hurt his parents, being made to feel that he had fallen short of expectations, and being denied any demonstration of affection. These techniques of indirect discipline, combined with frequent criticism or nagging give the neurotic individual a lasting sense of guilt and inadequacy.

It has been remarked that the worst bridges are those we never cross, and experimental evidence suggests that uncertainty is more anxiety-provoking than unpleasant experiences that cannot be avoided. During his childhood, the neurotic individual has frequently been warned of dangers that remain vague and undefined, and this is particularly apt to apply in the area of sexual behavior. The child's simple questions about where babies come from or how they start to develop may be met with embarrassment and evasion, or alternatively, with detailed explanation far beyond the child's current interest or ability to comprehend. There is no easy communication of simple sexual information, and the subject usually remains shrouded in mystery and danger of disgust. A sexual story told by a child across the street may be brought home to the parents for interpretation and result only in criticism or forbidding further play with the neighbor child. If masturbation is discovered, the child may be threatened with dire consequences to physical or mental health. There may be no preparation for menstruation in girls, or the onset of nocturnal emissions in boys. When dating begins, there may be vague admonitions toward good behavior, without specific advice on what should be avoided. It is not surprising that neurotics frequently reach adult life without adequate sexual information, and that their relationships with adults of the opposite sex should be marred by conflict and frigidity or impotence. It was the latter observation that led to Freud's dictum that in a normal sex life no neurosis was possible. Some of the other factors involved, however, may be equally significant.

There has been considerable speculation as to whether the early relationship with mother or that with father is the more significant in the development of neurosis. Since mother is the primary agent of socialization during the preschool years, it has generally been assumed that her personality and behavior are the most likely to have both positive and negative effects on the development of the child. However, there is a strong tendency for people to marry others of equivalent emotional maturity, and for psychopathology in the mother to be accompanied by various forms of psychopathology in the father. Moreover, in recent years, there has been an increasing tendency to recognize the direct effects of father's behavior on the child from an early age,

and also the indirect effects on the child of father's behavior toward mother.

Objective evidence of psychopathology in the parents of neurotic patients is relatively scarce. In one study (Gregory, 1959) involving 142 neurotics (103 female and 39 male) admitted to mental hospitals at a median age of 35 years (age range 18 to 50 years) only one had apparently lost his father by suicide, but 3.5 percent had a father who had been admitted to mental hospital. Nine percent of the fathers were reported to have consumed excessive amounts of alcohol. A further eight percent of fathers and 18 percent of mothers were recorded as having other significant personality abnormalities. By the time of their admission to hospital, 2.3 percent of these patients' siblings had also been admitted to mental hospital and 5.8 percent of the siblings were reported as showing other significant abnormalities.

A slightly higher proportion of these neurotic patients had lost their fathers by death before the age of ten years than would be expected on the basis of figures for the comparable general population. A similar excess of paternal deaths during the first ten years of life was recorded by Norton (1952) and did not appear to be related to increased age of the father at the time the patient was born. Very few neurotic patients had been permanently separated from mother during childhood except by death of the mother, but a considerable further number had lost their fathers during childhood due to parental discord and separation. Altogether by the age of ten years, 13 percent had permanently lost their fathers and six percent their mothers. Further investigations into the nature and pattern of parental deprivation during the childhood of neurotics appears to be indicated, but the *qualitative* nature of existing relationships would seem to be more generally significant.

SOCIOCULTURAL FACTORS

The frequency and form of neurotic

symptoms vary considerably in different cultures, social classes, and over a period of time. The variations noted in different social and cultural groups have sometimes been attributed to heredity and sometimes to environmental factors (particularly differences in child rearing practices), according to the persuasion of the investigator concerned. However, rapid and marked changes in frequency and form during a relatively short period of time would argue strongly against hereditary predisposition for certain of the symptoms under consideration, particularly conversion hysteria. Gross manifestations of conversion hysteria appear to have been very much more frequent in civilized countries during the latter part of the nineteenth century than in these well-developed areas of recent years. A number of authors have attributed this diminution in frequency and severity to diminished sexual repression resulting from more liberal sexual mores and patterns of child rearing. However, it is noteworthy that gross motor hysteria has frequently been observed during the past few decades as an acute stress reaction among soldiers from underdeveloped countries. The conflict here would appear to be related to self-preservation rather than sexual motives, and a number of psychiatrists have regarded the frequency of hysterical symptoms as an index of psychiatric sophistication in the society or culture concerned.

Hollingshead and Redlich found hysterical reactions virtually absent in class I, II, and III, but present in limited numbers in classes IV and V of the New Haven Population. The prevalence of obsessive-compulsive reactions, neurotic depressive reactions, and "character neuroses" (receiving treatment) were all positively correlated with socioeconomic status. They simplified their observations to the following statement: "The class V neurotic behaves badly, the class IV neurotic aches physically, the class III patient defends fearfully, and the class I-II patient is dissatisfied with himself." It is important to realize,

however, that these generalizations may be bound both to local ethnic or cultural factors and to prevailing vagaries of psychiatric diagnosis.

In most primitive tribes there is remarkable freedom from obsessive-compulsive neurotic symptoms, but there are a few tribes where obsessive ritual constitutes a major component of the culture. Such findings have usually been attributed to observed differences in child rearing practices, but biological scientists also point to the different genetic endowment of these widely separated groups.

TREATMENT

Every variety of psychosocial and organic psychiatric treatment has at some time been applied in the treatment of patients with neurotic disorders. However, both the etiological evidence regarding the importance of psychological factors and the pragmatic results of psychosocial therapies have combined to render the latter the predominant current approach to the treatment of neurotic patients. No other group of psychiatric disorders appears to respond as favorably to long-term intensive individual psychotherapy. Patients are often motivated to continue in such therapy for long periods of time through their rigid superego and personal discomfort in the form of anxiety or depression. However, there are many neurotic patients who are not so motivated, or for whom such therapy is not available or is not considered to be indicated. The factors likely to contribute to such a decision are the age and intelligence of the patient, as well as his socioeconomic status and the reality situation confronting him.

The various current approaches to psychosocial and organic psychiatric therapies have been reviewed in some detail in Chapters 11 and 12. They will therefore *not* be discussed in detail in the present chapter or in any of the following chapters concerning the various clinical syndromes. It may be noted, however, that Fenichel classified various forms of psychopathology in the following sequence, according to their accessibility to psychoanalysis: (1) hysteria, with early cases of anxiety hysteria (or phobic reactions) having the best outlook; (2) compulsion neuroses and pregenital conversion neuroses, cases showing anxiety being more favorable than "cases in a relatively stable and hardened equilibrium"; (3) neurotic depressions; (4) character disturbances, which are regarded as always more difficult to treat than symptomatic neuroses; (5) perversions, addictions, and impulse neuroses; (6) functional psychoses.

A wide variety of other treatments has been employed with varying degrees of success, according to the nature and severity of the neurosis and the theoretical orientation of the therapist. Those therapists with a directive-organic orientation have long favored management by means of environmental manipulation and short-termed directive therapy, including the use of such techniques as hypnosis, narcosis, and drug-induced abreaction. Numerous medications have been prescribed for the symptomatic relief of autonomic hyperactivity, and of subjective feelings of anxiety, fear, or depression. The most popular of these drugs at the present time are minor tranquilizers such as meprobamate and chlordiazepoxide, and antidepressive agents such as imipramine and amitriptyline. These drugs appear to be relatively more effective in relieving neurotic anxiety and depression than either the major phenothiazine tranquilizing drugs (used largely in schizophrenia) or stimulant antidepressive agents (e.g., tranylcypromine) that may intensify anxiety and insomnia.

Electroshock therapy may produce at least temporary relief of neurotic depression, but the depression is apt to recur when it represents a definite reaction to loss or frustration that remains unchanged. Moreover, electroshock therapy is likely to accentuate symptoms of anxiety and apprehension,

and lasting relief from neurotic depression generally requires more intensive efforts directed toward other manifestations of the neurosis and their underlying dynamics. In patients with very severe neuroses, who have been chronically incapacitated by extreme anxiety or obsessive-compulsive symptoms and have failed to respond to all other methods of treatment, lobotomy has occasionally led to dramatic and lasting relief for which patients and relatives alike have been grateful. However, the primary approach to treatment in most patients with neurotic disorders consists of various combinations of individual, family, and group psychotherapy together with environmental manipulation.

SELECTED REFERENCES

Abse, D. W. 1959. Hysteria. In *American Handbook of Psychiatry*, ed. S. Arieti, New York, Basic Books, Inc., vol. 1, ch. 14.

Ackerman, N. W. 1958. *The Psychodynamics of Family Life*. New York, Basic Books, Inc.

Alexander, F., and Ross, H., Editors. 1952. *Dynamic Psychiatry*. Chicago, University of Chicago Press, ch. 5 and 6.

Archibald, H. C., and Tuddenham, R. D. 1965. Persistent stress reaction after combat. AMA Archives of General Psychiatry *12*, 475-481.

Archibald, H. C., Long, D. M., Miller, C., and Tuddenham, R. D. 1962. Gross stress reaction in combat—a 15 year follow-up. American Journal of Psychiatry *119*, 317-322.

Brill, N. Q., and Beebe, G. W. 1955. *A Follow-up Study of War Neuroses*. Washington, D.C., V.A. Medical Monograph.

Brown, F. W. 1942. Heredity in psychoneuroses. Proceedings of the Royal Society of Medicine *35*, 785-790.

Buck, C. W., and Ladd, K. L. 1965. Psychoneurosis in marital partners. British Journal of Psychiatry *111*, 587-590.

Buck, C. W., and Laughton, K. B. 1959. Family patterns of illness: the effect of psychoneurosis in the parent upon illness in the child. Acta Psychiatrica Et Neurologica Scandinavica *34*, 165-175.

Chrzanowski, G. 1959. Neurasthenia and hypochondriasis. In *American Handbook of Psychiatry*, ed. S. Arieti. New York, Basic Books, Inc., vol. 1, ch. 13.

Cullen, W. 1781. *First Lines of The Practice of The Physic*, 3rd edition. Edinburgh, William Creech.

Eisenstein, V. W. 1956. *Neurotic Interaction in Marriage*. New York, Basic Books, Inc.

Errera, P., and Coleman, J. V. 1963. A long-term follow-up study of neurotic phobic patients in a psychiatric clinic. Journal of Nervous and Mental Disease *136*, 267.

Eysenck, H. J., and Prell, D. B. 1951. The inheritance of neuroticism. Journal of Mental Science *97*, 441-465.

Fenichel, O. 1945. *The Psychoanalytic Theory of Neurosis.* New York, W. W. Norton & Co., Inc.

Friedman, P. 1959. The phobias. In *The American Handbook of Psychiatry*, ed. S. Arieti. New York, Basic Books, Inc., vol. 1, ch. 15.

Freud, A. 1946. *The Ego and the Mechanisms of Defence.* New York, International Universities Press.

Freud, S. 1920. *A General Introduction to Psychoanalysis.* Reprinted 1953, Perma Books No. M-5001.

Freud, S. 1923. The ego and the id. Reprinted 1961 in *Standard Edition.* London, Hogarth Press.

Freud, S. 1926. Inhibitions, symptoms and anxiety. Reprinted 1959 in *Standard Edition.* London, Hogarth Press.

Funkenstein, D. H., Greenblatt, M., and Solomon, H. C. 1951. Autonomic changes paralleling psychologic changes in mentally ill patients. Journal of Nervous and Mental Disease *114*, 1.

Gellhorn, E. 1943. *Autonomic Regulations.* New York, Interscience Publishers, Inc.

Gellhorn, E. 1960. Recent contributions to the physiology of the emotions. In *Explorations in The Psychology of Emotions*, ed. L. J. West and M. Greenblatt. Washington, D.C., American Psychiatric Association, Psychiatric Research Reports No. 12, pp. 209-223.

Gottesman, I. I. 1962. Differential inheritance of the psychoneuroses. Eugenics Quarterly *9*, 223-227.

Greenfield, N. S. 1959. The relationship between recalled forms of childhood discipline and psychopathology. Journal of Consulting Psychology *23*, 139-142.

Gregory, I. 1959. An analysis of family data on 1000 patients admitted to a Canadian mental hospital. Acta Genetica *9*, 54-96.

Grinker, R. R., and Spiegel, J. P. 1945. *War Neuroses.* Philadelphia, The Blakiston Company, pp. 18-19.

Grinker, R. R., and Spiegel, J. P. 1945. *Men Under Stress.* New York, McGraw-Hill Book Co., Inc.

Gutheil, E. A. 1959. Reactive Depressions. In *American Handbook of Psychiatry*, ed. S. Arieti. New York, Basic Books, Inc., vol. 1, ch. 18.

Hendrick, I. 1958. *Facts and Theories of Psychoanalysis*, 3rd edition. New York, Alfred A. Knopf, Inc.

Hollender, M. H. 1965. Perfectionism. Comprehensive Psychiatry *6*, 94-103.

Hollingshead, A. B., and Redlich, F. C. 1958. *Social Class and Mental Illness.* New York, John Wiley & Sons, Inc.

Horney, K. 1937. *The Neurotic Personality of Our Time.* New York, W. W. Norton & Co., Inc.

Kardiner, A. 1941. *The Traumatic Neurosis of War.* Menasha, Wisconsin, G. Bonta Publishing Company.

Kardiner, A. 1959. Traumatic neuroses of war. In *American Handbook of Psychiatry*, ed. S. Arieti. New York, Basic Books, Inc., Vol. 1, ch. 12.

Leveton, A. F. 1962. Reproach: The art of shamesmanship. British Journal of Medical Psychology *35*, 101-111.

May, R. 1950. *The Meaning of Anxiety.* New York, The Ronald Press Co.

Michaels, J. J. 1959. Character structure and character disorders. In *American Handbook of Psychiatry*, ed. S. Arieti. New York, Basic Books, Inc., Vol. 1, ch. 19.

Naumberg, M. 1953. *Psychoneurotic Art: Its Function in Psychotherapy.* New York, Grune & Stratton, Inc.

Nemiah, J. 1961. *Foundations of Psychopathology.* New York, Oxford University Press.

Nemiah, J. 1966. Neurotic aggression. In *American Handbook of Psychiatry*, ed. S. Arieti. New York, Basic Books, Inc., Vol. 3, ch. 7.

Norton, A. 1952. Incidence of neurosis related to maternal age and birth order. British Journal of Social Medicine *6*, 256.

Portnoy, I. 1959. The anxiety states. In *American Handbook of Psychiatry*, ed. S. Arieti. New York, Basic Books, Inc., Vol. 1, ch. 16.

Prince, M. 1906. *The Dissociation of Personality.* New York, Longmans, Green & Co., Inc. (reprinted 1920, Meridian).

Rado, S. 1942. Pathodynamics and treatment of traumatic war neurosis. Psychosomatic Medicine *4*, 362.

Rado, S. 1959. Obsessive behavior. In *American Handbook of Psychiatry*, ed. S. Arieti. New York, Basic Books, Inc., Vol. 1, ch. 17.

Rees, L., and Eysenck, H. J. 1945. A factorial study of some morphological and psychological aspects of human constitution. Journal of Mental Science *91*, 8.

Ross, W. D. 1966. Neuroses following trauma and their relation to compensation. In *American Handbook of Psychiatry*, ed. S. Arieti. New York, Basic Books, Inc., Vol. 3, ch. 9.

Roueché, B. 1954. Lost. In *The Incurable Wound.* New York, Berkley Pub. Corp., No. G-188, pp. 7-32.

Saul, L. J. 1956. *The Hostile Mind.* New York, Random House, Inc.

Slater, E. 1953. *Psychotic and Neurotic Illnesses in Twins.* London, Her Majesty's Stationery Office, Medical Research Council, Special Reports Series No. 278.

Stern, R. L. 1947. Diary of a war neurosis. Journal of Nervous and Mental Disease *106*, 583-586.

Sullivan, H. S. 1953. *The Interpersonal Theory of Psychiatry.* New York, W. W. Norton & Co., Inc.

Thigpen, C. H., and Cleckley, H. M. 1957. *The Three Faces of Eve*, reprinted 1961. New York, Popular Library No. SP117.

CHAPTER 16

So neither ought you attempt to cure the body without the soul; and this is the reason why the cure of many diseases is unknown to the physicians of Hellas, because they are ignorant of the whole, which ought to be studied also. For this is the great error of our day in the treatment of the human body, that physicians separate the soul from the body.

Plato

The sorrow which has no vent in tears may make other organs weep.

Henry Maudsley

Psychophysiologic Disorders

From time to time we have drawn attention to the essential unity of the individual, involving a two-way interaction between mind and body. In Chapters 5 and 6 we considered how disturbances in bodily functions may determine psychopathology, and we shall return to this problem again in later chapters concerning mental retardation and organic brain disorders. In the present chapter, however, we are concerned with disturbances of bodily function and structure that may result in part from the same kind of psychological and social determinants as were considered in Chapters 7 and 8. These psychosomatic or psychophysiological disorders involve real changes in physiological function and anatomical structure of the body, in contrast with certain bodily symptoms of neurosis (conversion hysteria and hypochondriasis) that were considered in the preceding chapter.

Psychoanalysts have often employed the term *organ neuroses* to distinguish these physiological and anatomical disorders (frequently considered to be associated with neurotic conflict and personality conflicts) from the symbolic disturbances in function occurring in conversion hysteria. However, some analysts greatly expanded the concept of organ neurosis, and Fenichel included the following in his definition: "(1) affect equivalents; (2) results of changes in chemistry of the unsatisfied and dammed-up person (expressions of 'unconscious affects'); (3) physical results of unconscious attitudes or unconsciously determined behavior patterns; (4) all kinds of combinations of these three possibilities." By including the category "physical results of unconscious attitudes" he extended this category beyond the range of disorders that we shall be describing in this chapter, since the indirect bodily consequences of personality and emotional conflict may include such pathology as suicide, homicide, proneness to "accidental" injury, the manifestations of venereal diseases, and the bodily complications of cigarette smoking, alcoholism, or addiction to other drugs.

A number of psychiatrists have used the term *somatization reaction* to describe the same group of bodily disorders that we are referring to as psychosomatic or psychophysiologic. According to this view, all somatization reactions are considered to be varieties of psychoneurosis, whereas the American Medical

Association and American Psychiatric Association agreed to give psychophysiologic disorders a separate grouping between psychotic and psychoneurotic reactions "to allow more accurate accumulation of data concerning their etiology, course and relation to other mental disorders."

The term *psychosomatic disorders* was formerly used to refer to the same group of conditions that are now known as psychophysiologic disorders, and was used with exactly the same implications regarding the probable or frequent role of emotional factors in causation. As the term psychosomatic was popularized, however, it became applied to describe a holistic orientation toward the discipline of medicine as a whole. From this point of view, any disorder, although it may predominantly affect either body or mind, may be regarded as affecting the organism as a whole and hence psychosomatic.

In an attempt to define this group of conditions more accurately, therefore, the term *psychophysiologic autonomic and visceral disorders* was introduced to describe the following conditions: "These reactions represent the visceral expression of affect which may be thereby largely prevented from being conscious. The symptoms are due to a chronic and exaggerated state of a normal physiological expression of emotions, with the feeling or subjective part repressed. Such long continued visceral states may eventually lead to structural changes." A distinction between the bodily manifestations of psychophysiologic disorders and those of neurotic anxiety reactions is made on the basis of "predominant, persistent, involvement of a single organ system." The bodily manifestations of psychophysiologic disorders are distinguished from those of conversion hysteria by "(1) involvement of organs and viscera innervated by the autonomic nervous system, hence not under full voluntary control or perception; (2) failure to alleviate anxiety; (3) physiological rather than symbolic origin of symptoms; (4) frequent pro-

duction of structural changes which may threaten life."

A person with a psychophysiologic disorder first becomes aware that something is the matter with him when he experiences some form of bodily discomfort such as pain, vomiting, diarrhea, or difficulty in breathing. If symptoms such as these persist or inconvenience him sufficiently, the source of help to whom he most frequently turns is his family physician. Even if he is sensitive to the presence of psychopathology in his patients, however, the physician is unlikely to find any gross abnormality in appearance, behavior, or conversation. A patient with a psychophysiologic disorder is able to tell his story spontaneously, answer questions readily and relevantly, and give a detailed family and developmental history that usually corresponds closely with information obtained from other sources. Sometimes there is a strong preoccupation with bodily functions and frequently a denial of emotional problems, with reluctance to accept the possibility that any such problems have existed or might cause his bodily symptoms. It may be much easier for another person such as the physician to perceive associations between the onset of symptoms and periods in the person's life when he has been experiencing unusual emotional stress. Unfortunately, some physicians may be so preoccupied with bodily functions and laboratory investigations that they fail to recognize the person's concurrent emotional problems and fail to help him deal with them effectively.

Ordinarily the person with a psychophysiologic disorder is neither psychotic nor suffering from an organic brain syndrome, and hence there is no impairment of intellectual function or memory and no evidence of illusions, hallucinations, or delusions. The mood is usually within normal limits, although there may be some evidence of anxiety, depression, or hostility. The person usually has a strongly developed superego, conscience, or internal control system, and it has become part of the popular stereotype that people with ulcers or high blood pressure, for example, are ambitious and hard-driving. Like other stereotypes, however, this is an oversimplified view of the situation, and to which there are many exceptions.

In the Minnesota Multiphasic Personality Inventory the first clinical scale (Hs) was almost wholly made up of a set of physical complaint items that were considered characteristic of patients with a diagnosis of neurotic hypochondriasis. An elevation of this scale is also likely to be found in hypochondriasis associated with psychotic depression or schizophrenia. Patients with known organic diseases of the body may obtain somewhat higher Hs scores than average, on the basis of the psychological complaints attributable to their pathology, but elevation of the Hs score above 65 has been regarded as strong evidence of a psychological component even in patients who are physically very ill. In addition to elevation of this first scale, persons with psychophysiologic disorders are also more apt to show elevations of other scales commonly associated with depression or neurosis (i.e., scales 2, 3, and 7) than they are to show elevations of scales commonly associated with psychosis (scales 6, 8, and 9).

Projective psychological tests are also more likely to be suggestive of neurotic constriction and inhibition than of affective disorder or psychotic reality distortion. On the Rorschach test, the total number of responses is likely to be within normal limits and to contain several popular but relatively few original responses. They tend to be consistently elaborated to a degree compatible with the individual's intelligence, but there may be some fluctuations in form level and reaction time following the presentation of cards with shading or color (shading or color shock). An unduly high proportion of the responses may be determined predominantly by form (F) and there may be a predominance of introtensive

movement over extrotensive color responses. There may also be a suggestion of immaturity and impulsiveness associated with a high proportion of animal responses, an excess of animal movement (FM) over human movement (M), and an excess of relatively uncontrolled color responses (FC or even occasionally C) over responses involving the controlled use of color (FC). Dynamic interpretations from either the Rorschach or other projective tests such as the Thematic Apperception Test may be informative in individual patients, but do not show consistent patterns for groups of patients.

The term *psychophysiologic autonomic and visceral disorders* implies that this group of conditions has its main impact on the internal organs or viscera, and also that the effects of certain emotions or psychological stresses are transmitted from the brain to these viscera via the autonomic nervous system. Stimulation of the sympathetic nervous system has effects similar to injection of epinephrine into the blood stream, and results in preparation of the organism for emergency action such as fighting or running away. These effects include increases in the heart rate, blood pressure, rate of breathing, and blood flow to the muscles of the limbs, accompanied by decreases in the activity of the digestive system and blood flow to the intestines and skin. Stimulation of parasympathetic nerve supply, on the other hand, has opposite effects on various organs, and tends to occur when it is safe for the organism to relax, digest its food, and sleep. Ordinarily, the antagonistic effects of sympathetic and parasympathetic systems are controlled by centers in the hypothalamus and the effects of each remain approximately balanced. However, the predominance of either sympathetic or parasympathetic activity may vary in the same individual from one organ system to another, and from one time to another.

A wide variety of disorders have been described as psychophysiologic and in some of these disorders the mediating role of the autonomic nervous system is not clearly established. A number of widely accepted psychophysiologic disorders are given in the list below, from the American Psychiatric Association Diagnostic Manual. It should be emphasized that emotional factors are *not* usually regarded as the only significant causative factors, and that they may be more important in some individual cases than in others.

Skin reaction—such as neurodermatitis or some varieties of eczema.

Musculoskeletal reaction—as in some types of backache or tension headache.

Respiratory reaction—as in some kinds of asthma.

Cardiovascular reaction—as in some cases of tachycardia, high blood pressure, or migraine headache.

Hemic or lymphatic reaction—involving changes in blood or lymphatic systems.

Gastrointestinal reaction—as in some cases of peptic ulcer, ulcerative colitis, constipation, vomiting, and anorexia nervosa.

Genitourinary reaction—as in some types of impotence, frigidity, dyspareunia, menstrual disturbances, unusual frequency of urination, and dysuria.

Endocrine reaction—as in some cases of hyperthyroidism.

Nervous system reaction—as in some cases of fatigue or "neurasthenia."

Reactions of organs of special sense—such as the eye or ear.

We shall now present a series of case histories illustrating some of the most frequent types of psychophysiological disorder, and shall then consider the dynamics, development, etiology, and treatment.

NEURODERMATITIS

This woman's husband sought psychiatric help when they were both 31 years old, regarding a whole complex of problems involving his wife and himself and also affecting their children. He had recently completed graduate studies and accepted an appointment that involved moving to a new locality. Both he and his wife were currently undergoing an exacerbation of preexisting depression, and this was accompanied by regression and problem behavior on the part of their children, particularly the eldest boy who was shy but rebellious, wet his bed at night, and chewed his clothing.

The husband at first related the onset of all their emotional difficulties to seven years previously, when his wife was pregnant with their first child and developed a very severe neurodermatitis that had since fluctuated in intensity but persisted throughout the intervening years. At that time the husband was a student and they were living in a poor neighborhood, with no prospect of improvement in their financial situation for some years to come. The wife had nevertheless sought psychiatric help, which took the form of individual analytically oriented psychotherapy for a period of about six months. During this time she became increasingly depressed and was given Tofranil but there was no improvement in her symptoms or their reality situation by the time that therapy was terminated. Both of them were quite pessimistic about the outcome of therapy when they again sought psychiatric help seven years later.

At this time the wife spoke as follows: "The outlook for myself is dim. If we consider me as depressed, then I have been chronically since the age of 12. I probably wouldn't waste your time coming in, if it wasn't for the sake of my husband and children. I'm a miserable excuse for a human being, and it's not fair to him my being this way—smouldering. He can see from the way I am, that things are not the way he would want them to be. I don't know if I'm lazy or just don't have the drive or push to do things. I'm easily discouraged. Sometimes I just can't tolerate the children and I'm terribly impatient with them. My husband is easy to get along with—except he is a bit too much like a mother. I think he reminds me of my stepmother, and it makes me aggravated and want to do the opposite. He makes a list and wants things done. He has a tendency to take over and I think he'll do it better. The other day I asked him not to wash the clothes and he did, and it aggravated me. How do you think it makes me feel? Useless. I feel so ambivalent. I have a poor relationship with my stepmother and have ambivalent feelings about my father and our oldest child and about my husband."

It developed that she was an only child and that her mother had died when she was only 11 years old. Prior to this her mother had been sick for many years and there had been no entertaining in their home. The patient used to visit the homes of other children, but felt shy, inferior, and ashamed of being unable to bring them to her own home, both before and after her mother died. For several years after this, her grandmother lived with the patient and her father, but died soon after the latter had remarried. Father worked extremely hard, never had time to talk to the child, emphasized duty and obligation to others, and was very critical of failure to live up to his high standards of behavior. Her stepmother was also very efficient "like an army sergeant," and was very intolerant of other people's inadequacies, constantly criticizing and nagging the patient. The latter never received any sexual information or instruction from her own family and was very ashamed when menstruation started. She dated a number of boys, but never permitted petting and there was no premarital intercourse with her husband.

She married a man who had also suffered an emotionally deprived childhood. He was also an only child, and his mother committed suicide when he was eight years old. Although he thought of his life as normal up to that time, he had hated school and missed weeks each year on account of sickness prior to his mother's death. After this, he and his father went to live with his maternal grandmother, in spite of the fact the latter denounced his father and claimed that the latter had in effect killed the patient's mother. A year or so later his father remarried and the patient got along well with his stepmother. In school he moved within a year from the bottom of the class to the top, but the father's second marriage soon terminated in divorce. The boy remained with his father, who worked extremely hard and demanded the same of his son. The only rewards in his life were for working hard at school and outside of school, for helping his father. The work always had to be done before he could play with other children, and by the time he could join them their baseball game or other activities were over. As time went by he became increasingly introverted, ambitious to achieve, perfectionistic and compulsively neat and orderly, since he was also responsible for much of the housework. However he dated a little, and had some sporadic premarital sexual experience.

He and his wife were married when they were both 21, and at first she was quite frigid and uninterested in sexual relations. She was working full time and was their only source of income when she became pregnant. After the birth of the child she had to continue working full time and leave her husband babysitting and studying at home. She felt trapped and was in emotional turmoil. She recalled feeling so angry that she wanted to break everything in sight, and she couldn't sleep at night. It was in this setting of impotent rage that she developed neurodermatitis and severe depression. It was also about this time that there was a dramatic change in their sexual relationship. She had now learned to enjoy intercourse, but her husband became increasingly preoccupied with his work, fatigued, and uninterested in sex. She became aware, however, that he did not find all girls equally unattractive, and he became involved in a platonic relationship with another girl. While the latter relationship did not involve sexual consummation, he told his wife that he loved this other girl, and didn't want to be married to her anymore. She perceived this as the most crushing thing that had ever happened to her. She just wanted to be dead, but couldn't because of the children. She punished him for this in many ways, including constant nagging to the point of almost driving him away. He wanted to leave home, but she begged him to stay and he agreed to do so for the sake of the children. However, there was no resumption of their previous sexual relationship. For a while intercourse took place about three or four times a year, but the husband tended to be impotent and resented any initiative taken by his wife. Although they still slept in the same bed, he would consistently fall asleep in the living room, reading or watching television, and would only join her some hours after she had gone to bed and was already asleep. There had been no sexual relations for about a year before they again came for psychiatric treatment.

At this time both husband and wife were depressed and involved in a mutually hostile interaction that was having repercussions on their children. They were therefore both involved in conjoint family therapy, with goals of insight and reeducation. Both had hitherto been frustrated and defeated by their perfectionistic strivings and displaced hostilities. They were, however, motivated to continue working together toward improving communication and resolution of conflict. There had, moreover, been an improvement in their reality situation, and reasonable anticipation of further improvement in the years to come. Insight and conscious efforts to compromise led to more mature and effective interaction than hitherto. After 15 hours of therapy there was a resumption of sexual relations that became more mutually satisfying than at any time previously. There was also gradual diminution in the wife's neurodermatitis, and in her tendency to use this and neurotic techniques to manipulate her husband's behavior. As he became more comfortable in his new employment situation, he found it less necessary to rely on compulsive defenses, and accepted a division of labor according to which his wife assumed a major responsibility for their home, while they collaborated in child rearing and no longer undercut each other. Increased consistency and security for the children also led to diminished problem behavior, and therapy was terminated after six months.

MUSCULOSKELETAL PAIN LEADING TO POLYSURGERY

A 22-year-old woman had enjoyed remarkably good health until several years after her marriage when she became pregnant for the first time. During the last three months of her pregnancy she complained of considerable pain in the lower part of her back and her right side. The pain disappeared after the birth of the child, but three months later it returned and she had several severe attacks during which her physician found tenderness and rigidity of the muscle wall in the lower right quadrant of her abdomen. She had no fever or other signs of infection, but it was concluded that she had a chronic appendicitis and the offending organ was removed surgically. It did not show obvious evidence of pathology and no other organs were found abnormal at operation, but the patient's pain disappeared and she returned home. Within a few months she was again complaining of severe attacks of pain in the right side, and at this time it appeared to be worse in the region of the right kidney. The surgeon found that she had a "floating kidney" which descended so far in the abdominal cavity that pain might result from temporary obstruction of the urinary outflow and stretching of the nerve supply in its supporting structures. A second operation was undertaken to secure the kidney firmly in its proper place. Again the patient was free of pain for several months after her return

home, but it then became even more severe and extensive than previously. Not only did she have pain in the whole of her right side, but it radiated down the back of her leg in the same manner as pain caused by a ruptured intervertebral disc. A myelogram showed a small protrusion on the left side which was thought to be due to a degenerating disc. Although pain was all on the right side, this disc was held responsible for her symptoms and attempts were made to relieve the supposed pressure on her nerve roots by means of a back brace and sleeping on a fracture board. Her pain grew worse and she was completely unable to do her housework so that a third operation was undertaken in order to remove the spinal disc. At operation no protruding disc was found and therefore none was removed. Exploration of the area was entirely negative, but following the operation the patient again completely lost her symptoms and was able to move freely without pain. Three weeks after leaving hospital the pain returned and was more extensive than on the last occasion, involving the whole of her right side from the knee up to the shoulder. At last the surgeons were convinced that her symptoms must be emotional in origin and referred her for psychiatric evaluation.

The patient was the youngest of five children and one of her sisters had been born with epilepsy, which was only partly controlled during childhood and adolescence and led to her death during a convulsion at the age of 22. Her other two sisters were married and her brother was an unskilled laborer. Their father had never learned to read or write and had worked all his life as a hired man on a farm. The family had been raised in mariginal circumstances, but the parents had enjoyed good health, had made their children feel loved and wanted, and had raised them to be conscientious citizens. As the youngest member of the family the patient had been somewhat overprotected throughout childhood. She started school at the of six and attended regularly until the age of 12 but she was backward and repeated two grades. During her last year in school she was in grade four but was not promoted to grade five and left school rather than repeat a grade for the third time. During the next five years she did domestic work for several neighbors. At the age of 17 she married a farmer for whom she had been working. This man was a widower 40 years older than herself who had a son older than the patient. At interview the patient remarked, "Quite a difference, isn't it, 40 years? I wish it were four years. We get along pretty well but he doesn't like me to go out at all. He wants me to stay home all the time. He takes me to see my father and mother but he won't take me to see my brother or sisters or anyone else. I've only been to a show twice since the baby was born and I've not been to a dance since we were married. I'm just an old woman at home. I just sit home and knit. Well, I haven't felt like going out much."

The patient was unable to give the year of her birth and her general information was very limited. She was obviously mentally retarded and formal testing revealed a full scale IQ of 46. She showed no evidence of psychotic reality distortion or of severe depression and it was concluded that her bodily symptoms represented a means of escape from the intolerable aspect of her marriage. In hospital she improved rapidly with physiotherapy and strong prestige-suggestion. She was soon walking freely and there were neither pain nor physical signs in her shoulder, back, or leg. On leaving hospital she returned to live with her parents and resumed caring for her two-and-a-half-year-old child.

STUTTERING

A 20-year-old male presented himself for psychiatric evaluation of emotional problems associated with very severe stuttering that was accompanied by a number of tics, including blinking of the eyes and grinding of the teeth. With great difficulty, he related that he had had a problem with stuttering as long as he could remember but that he could often converse freely with friends his own age. His speech was very much worse when he was anxious and frightened, and his stuttering was more severe when he was talking with his father than with his mother. At the first interview he was extremely tense, the palms of his hands were sweating profusely, and he sat rigidly upright on the edge of the chair.

Although he was introverted and anxious in new social situations, much of his fear was focused on his father. He described his father as a hot tempered man who had sworn a great deal for as long as the patient could remember. His father had been explosive, verbally critical of him (more than of his younger brother), and frequently physically punitive. By contrast, he viewed his mother as kindly, permissive, and understanding, always willing to listen to him no matter how long it took him to communicate with her.

During school, his athletic and social participation had been limited, and he had concentrated on getting better grades in school than might have been anticipated from his bright normal intelligence. He had always been inhibited and conforming, and it was not until he entered college that anyone suggested he have speech therapy. At the outset of speech therapy he also received small doses of a minor tranquilizer, but this was discontinued after a few months. He remained in speech therapy for more than a year, with gradual but marked improvement in his ability to communicate, and total abandonment of the related tics that had been so apparent at the time of his initial referral.

ASTHMA, ASSOCIATED WITH NEUROTIC DEPRESSION

A 34-year-old married woman was admitted to a psychiatric hospital with a history of asthmatic attacks which had been increasing in frequency and severity during the preceding twelve years, together with feelings of fatigue, insomnia, and depression which had been increasing progressively over the preceding three months. She reported that her maternal grandmother and one maternal aunt had suffered from severe asthma, and she claimed that she was allergic to several fruits and vegetables. However, she had had extensive medical investigations and sensitivity tests but no program of desensitization had ever been recommended by the physicians caring for her, and her asthmatic attacks tended to be precipitated and aggravated by emotional stress.

The patient was the eldest of eight children and her mother was pregnant with her at the time of her marriage. This probably led to unconscious resentment and partial rejection of the patient by her mother who appeared to discriminate against the patient and favor some of the younger children. The patient perceived no such discrimination or favoritism on the part of her father who was a conscientious man, regularly employed, and well liked by everyone. In this home, however, he was rather passive and ineffectual, whereas the mother was dominant and aggressive. The patient described her mother as being moody and "a martyr type" who was critical and demanded high standards of behavior from all members of the family. During her childhood the patient was given a great deal of responsibility in caring for her younger siblings and during adolescence she was frequently deprived of social activities with her friends in order to help at home. The patient was never able to express anger as a child and at the age of 34 she still felt that the opinion of her parents was as important as when she was a child.

The patient obtained little sexual information from her mother but started dating about the age of 15 and had a number of boy friends. During her junior year in high school she started going steady with a boy slightly older than herself and within six months she began a pregnancy which led to a forced marriage. Her parents disapproved of her husband, who was not a Catholic, but after marriage he changed his religion and their children were raised in this faith. During the first 12 years of her marriage the patient was pregnant 11 times. Six of these pregnancies terminated in spontaneous abortions and one child died a few days after birth, so that she was left with four living children. Pregnancy was always stressful for her and her first attack of asthma occurred shortly after the birth of her second child. The attacks became more frequent and severe during subsequent pregnancies, and after 12 years of marriage she submitted to a sterilization operation which freed her from this particular source of stress. However, a couple of years prior to this she became aware that her husband was going out with another woman. This made her feel nervous and angry inside, but she never confronted him with the fact or expressed her anger directly. Instead she punished him by denying him sexual relations, which she had in fact feared from the time of her first spontaneous abortion. Her husband's interest in the other woman was of very brief duration, but she continued to deny him sexual relations until about two years after her sterilization operation at which time he was involved in an automobile accident and sustained a whiplash injury to his neck. He felt unable to work and began drawing regular unemployment insurance which probably prolonged his disability (see previous chapter regarding compensation neuroses). In addition, the patient became more solicitous of him and went out to work to supplement the family income. When the husband's insurance payments ran out, he looked for work sporadically but remained unemployed. He visited various employment offices and was offered several jobs, but turned them down for various reasons such as poor wages, no chance for getting ahead, or simply because he did not feel he would like the work.

In this situation the patient was unable to express resentment directly to the husband, but felt obliged to continue providing for the family and became increasingly worried about their financial situation. She became tired, had difficulty in sleeping, lost interest in her usual recreations, lost her appetite and some weight, and felt miserable. On admission to hospital her MMPI was technically invalid (21 F and only seven K responses), and it was considered that she was admitting to psychopathology that she did not in fact have. At interview she was in good contact with reality, and projective tests indicated neurotic constriction of personality with some hysterical denial and evidence of depression. She maintained that her husband and children were wonderful and initially she denied the marital conflict already outlined. During several weeks of psychotherapy, however, she was able to verbalize freely her sources of frustration and conflict and to gain considerable insight into previously unconscious psychodynamics. She also received antidepressive medication (Parnate) and gained about ten pounds in weight. Her husband was seen on several occasions, and eventually found employment. The patient left hospital much improved and was felt to be somewhat less vulnerable to developing overt psychopathology than formerly.

MIGRAINE HEADACHES, WITH NEUROTIC DEPRESSION

A 46-year-old married woman was admitted to a psychiatric ward with a history of migraine headaches for the preceding 40 years, increasing in frequency and severity during the preceding ten years. During the past few months they had become so incapacitating that she had quit her job and remained home, unable to do her housework or to sleep at night, and feeling so acutely miserable that she had spoken of suicide. She had consulted numerous physicians over the years and had received a tremendous variety of drugs, only one of which (a combination of caffeine and ergotamine) had appreciably reduced the intensity of her headaches, and even this had been completely ineffective recently. She had had intensive medical and neurological examinations and laboratory investigations without any evidence being found of bodily disease, but at the time of her admission to the psychiatric ward she denied having any emotional problems whatever and maintained that she was the happiest, sanest wife there ever was, except that she had these headaches. During her first interview she repeated about ten times, "I have a wonderful husband and children. I have no problems," and the psychiatrist was moved to comment in the chart, "Methinks the lady doth protest too much."

The patient was the third of nine children, and she believed that she was the favorite of her father, whom she described as a wonderful man who was much like herself in that he was quiet and never liked to argue much. She also described her mother as wonderful but not so easygoing as her father. Throughout childhood she recalled her mother's having been subject to migraine headaches, which had apparently developed shortly after her marriage and which ceased around the time of her menopause. Throughout the intervening years mother would have a headache about once a month, and at these times, "Father would do anything for her. I would care for her also because I had a taste of what it was like."

At the age of about five or six the patient started having severe headaches which usually developed in the frontal region, behind one of the eyes, and spread backwards until she experienced a severe throbbing throughout one side of her head. These headaches would incapacitate her about one day each month, and she would have to stay home from school and go to bed in a dark room. However, she apparently enjoyed school and studied hard, graduating from high school the third in her class. Her family had no money to send her to college so she went to work as a bookkeeper. She claimed she got along well with others her own age, but her parents did not approve of many of her friends and had little faith in her judgment of them. They provided her with little or no sexual information but greatly restricted her relationships with boys and she was not allowed to go out on dates until after she graduated from high school.

At first she reported having been married only once and then that she had been married previously but that her first husband had died in an automobile accident.

Eventually she admitted that at the age of 20 she had met and married a man with little education, who was currently employed in highway construction. She had become pregnant immediately after marriage, but within three months her husband had been convicted of holding up a gas station and sent to a reformatory. She returned to live with her parents and after the birth of her child she went out to work. Her first husband never returned to her and she apparently obtained a divorce.

At the age of 27 she met a man 16 years older than herself who claimed to be a minister. She could think of nothing better than being married to a minister and after a brief courtship, they were married against the advice of her parents who did not like her husband. Not long after their marriage the patient learned that her husband was not a minister, and had never even attended high school. Moreover, he was extremely jealous and possessive of her and he soon sold their home so that he could buy a farm where he could keep her away from other men. She was crushed by his deceit and irrational jealousy, but could not bring herself to admit she had made another mistake and return to her family. Her husband knew nothing about farming and soon lost enough money that he sold the farm and they returned to town, but he remained jealous of her and they had little social life. When she was sick, he sometimes refused to call a doctor as he did not want any other men around her. The child by her first marriage came to live with them and became known by the same surname, but her husband never formally adopted this child which led to difficulties later in connection with the name to be used on the child's high school diploma and marriage license.

The patient never enjoyed sexual relations with her husband, but there were a total of eight pregnancies through the years, terminating in five spontaneous abortions and the birth of three living children who were aged 18, 15, and 12 at the time of her admission to the psychiatric ward. She had an early menopause shortly after the age of 40 and was discouraged to find that her headaches did not diminish as her mother's had done, but rather increased in frequency and intensity. Her husband had previously dominated her completely, but at about this time he had a surgical operation for stomach ulcers and after this she found he was much more considerate at times that she complained of severe headache. He even permitted her to go out to work as a nurse's aide, although he still objected to the fact that this might throw her into contact with other men.

Several years after their marriage the patient had learned that her husband had also been married previously, but he had told her that he had divorced his first wife because of the latter's infidelity. The patient was now told by her husband's sister that this was quite untrue, and that the first wife had divorced him because of his paranoid jealousy and unreasonable behavior. Her hostility towards him increased, but she was trapped in a marriage from which she saw no acceptable escape. Her headaches increased and she was rewarded by his becoming more solicitous and attentive to her every whim. She could not feel angry with such a kind man and her internalized hostility was transformed into guilt and depression. In hospital she received intensive psychotherapy, learned to verbalize her feelings freely, and gained considerable insight into previously unconscious dynamics. She received antidepressive medication with some temporary improvement, but again became more depressed and was therefore given a course of 14 electroshock treatments. There was marked improvement in mood and she gained about 15 pounds in weight. Following this she received further supportive individual and group psychotherapy and her husband was seen on several occasions to discuss how he could contribute to a lasting improvement in her condition. Her family physician was advised to prescribe only the single medication that had proved most effective and to avoid rewarding the secondary gains of her sickness. After leaving hospital she was able to return to work and her headaches remained less frequent and severe than for many years previously.

PEPTIC ULCERS, ASSOCIATED WITH DEPRESSION AND EXCESSIVE DRINKING

A 46-year-old married man was admitted to a psychiatric hospital immediately after having been discharged from a senior executive position in a large company because of excessive drinking and unreliability in keeping appointments. Apart from a few years in military service he had been with this company for the preceding 25 years, had worked extremely hard, and felt personally responsible for much of the company's growth and expansion during the preceding 15 years. He had spent much time away from home traveling on company business and had worked evenings and weekends, and had not taken a vacation with his family for some years. However, he had come to feel that his talents and dedication were not appreciated or adequately rewarded. During the preceding five years he had perceived his future as bleak, with little or no opportunity for further advancement financially or in terms of prestige. Every morning he would feel sick over the dismal prospect of another day's exhausting demands. He would not express his feelings of frustration and resentment directly at work, but became increasingly irritable at home with his family. He started to drink excessively to relieve his tension and he developed peptic ulcers which were treated medically. He was given some sedative medication, but remained dependent on alcohol and became increasingly depressed, although he never reached the point of considering suicide.

He was born the fourth child in a family of five boys, and his father was an unsuccessful farmer whom he never respected and disliked from an early age. He felt much closer to his mother, who was nervous and physically frail, with numerous chronic bodily complaints that the family regarded as 90 percent emotional. This hypochondriacal mother, however, dominated her husband, criticized him, and nagged her sons into striving for the success that their father had never achieved.

Poverty and small physical stature contributed to making the patient feel inferior to other children in the neighborhood, but he overcompensated for this by striving for academic distinction. In spite of having to work in a store during noon hours, after school, and on Saturdays, he remained at the top of his class in school and graduated as valedictorian. He left home soon afterward, worked in an office during the daytime, and attended night school, where he claimed to have completed four years of college work, including two years of law school, although he never obtained a degree. At the age of 24 he married, and subsequently had three children, who he hoped would all go to college. It was a bitter blow to him when his eldest daughter got married shortly after leaving high school. Although his work always came ahead of his family, there was little conflict between him and his wife until the last few years during which he had been resentful, depressed, irritable, and drinking excessively.

At the time he was admitted to hospital after losing his job he was angry, tense, tremulous, and unhappy, but he showed no evidence of organic intellectual impairment, was in good contact with reality, and his depression appeared to be of neurotic intensity. The MMPI was valid and none of the clinical scales were elevated with the exception of scale 2 (depression). For several years he had been dissatisfied with his way of life, and the loss of his job freed him from its obligations and confronted him with the necessity of reevaluating his patterns of behavior and goals in life. He participated actively in individual and group psychotherapy, and rapidly acquired considerable insight into developmental psychodynamics. His tension and depression diminished, his excessive smoking decreased, and he gained about seven pounds in weight. He was given a mild tranquilizing drug and after six weeks he left hospital much improved. There was no recurrence of his former symptoms during the next two years.

ULCERATIVE COLITIS, ASSOCIATED WITH ANXIETY AND DEPRESSION

A 19-year-old married girl was admitted to hospital two months after the delivery of her first-born child, with a history of persistent diarrhea throughout most of the preceding two years. During her recent pregnancy the diarrhea had increased in intensity until she was having ten to 15 watery bowel movements each day. At times she was also passing a little blood, and she had lost almost 20 pounds in weight during the preceding year. She appeared undernourished and felt weak, tired, and depressed. Direct examination showed evidence of ulcers of the large bowel (ulcerative colitis). She was admitted to hospital for both medical and psychiatric treatment, but she accepted the former and rejected the latter.

She was the third of four children and was six years younger than either of her elder siblings. She remained the youngest in the family until the age of 12 and even after this she still remained extremely dependent on her parents. Her father was conscientious, hard-working and a respected member of the community. He had received treatment for both asthma and peptic ulcers and the patient remarked, "He looks grouchy but he isn't that way." The only really negative

remark about him that she would permit herself was that he had plenty of money but he was stingy. Her mother was one year older than her father and appeared to have been somewhat anxious, tense, and overprotective. The patient never spent any time away from her parents prior to marriage, and since this time she had frequently wished she were back home living with them. In hospital she stated that she missed her parents more than she missed her husband and baby.

During her junior year of high school she started going steady with a boy she was very fond of, and toward the end of the school year she permitted some petting which stopped short of intercourse. When school ended, she went on a vacation with her parents and her menstrual period was delayed. She had received no sexual instruction from her parents and could not ask them now, but was frightened that she must be pregnant. She felt a little nauseated and had a funny feeling in her stomach which confirmed her fears. When she returned home her boy friend was out of town and it was at this time that her diarrhea started. After his return they dated a few weeks and then he terminated their relationship. She denied any conscious anger but experienced grief and her diarrhea persisted. A few months later the same boy got another girl pregnant and married her. This other girl happened to be one that the patient did not like and she could not understand how her former boy friend could prefer this girl to herself. Again she denied hostility toward him and grieved that she had not been the girl who became pregnant. Her diarrhea persisted.

In the middle of her senior year in high school she started going steady again, and by the time she graduated she again believed she was pregnant, but the baby did not arrive until ten months later and then weighed less than five pounds. In any event she was married in the late fall at which time she thought she was five months pregnant and she and her husband rented a small apartment. Her husband was two years older than herself, had previously attended college for one semester, had spent six months in the army and had "goofed around" in various unskilled jobs. By the time of their marriage he had started operating a small restaurant of his own but found he had to work very long hours to make ends meet. He was away from home about 15 hours a day, seven days a week, and the patient spent most of her time alone or visiting her family. Her diarrhea became worse and by the time the baby was delivered the young couple owed $1000 for medical and hospital expenses. Her husband continued to work long hours and the patient found it extremely difficult to meet the demands of her newborn infant. She was afraid of further pregnancy but her religion did not permit her to use contraceptives, and she complained of severe pain on intercourse which prevented sexual relations. At the time of her admission to hospital two months after the birth of the child, however, she was still adamantly denying the existence of emotional problems. Her MMPI at this time was defensive (with a K score of 68), but still showed T scores over 70 on scales 2 and 3 (depression and hysteria) with minor elevations on scales 7 and 8 (psychasthenic and schizoid). When asked what three wishes she would make if she could have anything she wanted, she replied that she wished her husband would become Catholic, that he would get along better with her parents, and that he would spend more time with her. Intensive medical treatment, including considerable sedative medication, brought her diarrhea largely under control and within the following month she gained about six pounds in weight. Although she resisted dynamically oriented psychotherapy, a repeat MMPI obtained at this time showed a reduction in all four clinical scales that had previously been elevated, with no change whatever in the K score. At the time she left hospital, therefore, she had undergone considerable symptomatic improvement, but there had been no apparent change in her reality situation or vulnerability to stress.

VOMITING, WITH ANOREXIA NERVOSA

An 18-year-old girl was referred for psychiatric evaluation because of repeated attacks of vomiting with loss of appetite and loss of weight. She had been admitted to a general hospital during these attacks several times during the preceding year, and had had numerous medical examinations and laboratory investigations but no evidence of organic disease had been discovered.

The girl was the youngest of five children, and was an unwanted child, born to middle-aged Catholic parents. When the mother discovered she was pregnant with the patient, she seriously considered seeking an abortion but did not actually attempt to do so.

Instead, mother apparently utilized the defense mechanism of reaction formation against her hostility toward the child, and after the birth of the patient the mother behaved toward her in an overprotective manner. Among other things she was overly concerned that the child should have enough to eat, and this concern led to the patient's being regarded as a feeding problem. However, the mother was persistent and controlling and the patient became a conforming, conscientious child.

Her parents were undemonstrative of affection toward each other or the children, and her mother remarked to one doctor that she thought kissing was foolish and added, "I would rather that my husband pick up a heavy load of laundry than give me a peck on the cheek." Not only was affection inhibited, but also any demonstration of other emotions such as anger or sorrow. The patient never felt free to cry or express anger toward anyone, and in turn she was very threatened by any disapproval shown her by others. She constantly sought approval by good behavior, acts of consideration for others, and achievement in school. On one occasion that she was awarded a medal for scholastic achievement, mother ridiculed this several times and justified her behavior by saying, "I don't want my daughter to become overconfident." The patient ceased confiding either her achievements or her problems in her parents, but sought satisfaction in her school work and extracurricular activities.

She was of superior intelligence and was usually second or third in her class, but in her senior year in high school she studied extremely hard and eventually succeeded in graduating as valedictorian. During this year, however, she had experienced other sources of stress and conflict. She had been prepared for the onset of menstruation but had little access to any other sexual information, and sexual functions were shrouded in mystery, fear, shame, and disgust. Her menstrual periods were often accompanied by nausea, and any physical contact with boys was apt to produce anxiety and vomiting. During the preceding year, however, she had been dating a boy regularly, had been contemplating marriage, and had permitted some petting, which she found distasteful and which tended to be followed by episodes of vomiting. During this time she had also established with a priest a relationship which she thought of as entirely platonic; but she became extremely dependent on him, and unconscious sexual feelings toward him apparently contributed to her anxiety and physiological disturbances. On one occasion she had a brief episode of hysterical dissociation which involved sleep walking, and she was found walking around the rectory at three o'clock in the morning. When she was awakened by the priest, she wondered what on earth she was doing there.

Her vomiting spells became worse and started to last several days at a time. She had little appetite, frequently felt disgusted by food, and lost weight until at one time she was 20 pounds below her previous maximum. Occasionally her appetite would return and she would gorge herself compulsively to the point of acute discomfort that was then relieved by further vomiting. She would seek medical help only when she was weak and exhausted, and she consistently denied any emotional basis for her symptoms. Her MMPI was very defensive (low F and high K) and all the clinical scales were within normal limits, the only minor elevation being on scale 3 (hysteria). The sentence completion test and the Rorschach also showed marked defensiveness, denial of sexuality and hostility, and neurotic constriction of personality. She refused psychiatric help, but each time she was in hospital she underwent rapid symptomatic improvement, which was apparently maintained after her enrollment in college away from her home town and the conflicts that had overwhelmed her.

PREMATURE EJACULATION AND IMPOTENCE

A 30-year-old college instructor sought psychiatric assistance with complaints of consistent premature ejaculation and periodic total impotence. He related that many years previously he had suffered a great deal from neurotic anxiety, and had benefited greatly from two years of analytically oriented psychotherapy (three hours a week), but that he had remained inhibited and had not engaged in heterosexual relationships until a couple of years previously. He had no homosexual fantasies or relationships and his sexual activities had previously been confined to masturbation, which his father had long since told him would cause insanity, and concerning which he had experienced a great deal of conscious guilt.

It developed that his father was a dynamic and aggressive man who had grown up in the slums of a large city but had worked his way through college and became a dentist. He worked hard and was critical and demanding of his children, and the patient was afraid of him throughout much of his childhood. By contrast, his mother was passive and was perceived as warm but possessive and overprotective. She was physically frail, anxious, and tense, worried a lot, and got her own way by crying and making other members of her family feel guilty.

The patient was the eldest child of a Jewish family and said that his grandfather had prophetic dreams that the patient was going to be a college professor. The expectations of high achievement were clearly reinforced throughout his childhood, and while he was in elementary school he started stuttering, which led to his being placed in a special high school. He also developed generalized anxiety, tremors, tics, and insomnia, but these symptoms were all relieved after he went away to college and had his first period of psychiatric treatment. He had since been moderately effective as a teacher, but still tended to intellectualize his personal problems. He recognized his profound ambivalence towards others, including the girls with whom he had started to have sexual relationships. He overcompensated for his feelings of inadequacy, and attempted to impress other men with tales of his sexual conquests. He said that he derived conscious sadistic satisfaction from making women love him and then rejecting them. He interpreted this as a Don Juan complex based on his edipal relationship with his mother. He reported that his mother had been seductive toward him and that he had consciously wanted to hurt her ever since the age of five or six.

During the course of further analytically oriented psychotherapy it became evident that he was ready to assimilate and work through the conflicts into which he had only intellectual insight. Apart from neurotic discussions of his sexual problems with various girl friends, he had not in fact communicated about the sources of his emotional problems with anyone else since he had previously been in therapy. During the course of several months there was considerable resolution of his ambivalent sexual and aggressive feelings, together with an emotional commitment to a single partner with whom there was mutual satisfaction and eventually marriage. Toward the end of therapy he reported an interesting dream that involved the death of his mother many years previously. In the dream, the corpse was no longer able to control the behavior of others, and he felt that he was now emancipated from her possessive domination. In any event, his overt behavior demonstrated mature independence, responsibility for the consequences of his own behavior, and greater consideration for the feelings of others than hitherto.

FRIGIDITY WITH DYSPAREUNIA

A 28-year-old married woman was admitted to a general hospital psychiatric unit with a history that for three years she had been growing increasingly fearful that she had some form of serious physical illness. She had never had much somatic illness, but had first become frightened that her circulation might close off and her hand might turn blue, then that she might have a brain tumor, and then that she might have some form of cancer. When admitted to hospital she was pregnant for the first time, and was very frightened that she might have cancer of the uterus.

The patient was the younger of two girls and described her parents as perfectionistic. Her father was a traveling salesman who was apparently happier when he was away from home. When things went wrong, he would bring his troubles home and vent his hostility on his wife and children. The parents were undemonstrative of affection toward each other or the children, and the mother would threaten the girls with the homecoming of their father. If they had misbehaved during his absence, they would then be spanked when he arrived. They attended church regularly, and at home the parents reinforced that the girls should never do anything morally wrong, frequently without giving them explicit instructions. They were given no specific information about sexual relations, pregnancy, and childbirth, but learned simply that sex was something dirty. They were expected to do well at school, and subsequently completed college. The patient had many friends and was happier with them than at home. She dated a number of boys but never permitted petting, and would never date a boy again if he "got fresh." She denied masturbation or any thoughts of sex before marriage.

While in college she met a man who was currently a salesman but soon afterwards entered the ministry. They were married when she was 22 years old, and throughout the six years of their marriage she had never experienced orgasm. Intercourse was never enjoyable for her and was simply a duty to her husband. She succeeded in depriving him of pleasure through her persistent frigidity, complaints of dyspareunia, and insistence on contraception as she did not yet feel ready to look after a child. Shortly after the development of her hypochondriacal somatic concerns, her husband had been assigned to a small rural parish where she no longer had access to the friends and entertainment she had previously enjoyed in the city where she had always lived.

She denied conscious hostility toward her husband or anyone else, but found indirect expression in her frigidity and other neurotic manifestations. She showed no evidence of psychotic thinking or behavior, and her intelligence was in the high average range. Her MMPI showed elevations on scales 3, 2, and 7 (hysteria, depression, and "psychasphenia"). During the time she was in the hospital she became involved in analytically oriented psychotherapy, and gained partial insight into her hostile interaction with her husband and its relationship to the repressed hostility of her childhood. An unsuccessful attempt was made to involve her passive ineffectual husband in therapy, but following her discharge from hospital she remained in therapy for some months, and there was evidence of further emotional maturation. She was able to meet the dependency needs of her child, and experienced some pleasure in her sexual relationship with her husband as well as losing her former symptoms of anxiety and hypochondriasis.

DYNAMICS, DEVELOPMENT AND ETIOLOGY

According to the anxiety theory of neurosis, the disordered bodily functions and structure occurring in psychophysiological disorders arise through the mechanism of *somatization*, which represents a maladaptive defense against the experience of intolerable conscious anxiety, provoked by unconscious conflict involving unacceptable sexual and aggressive impulses. Thus Weiss and English remarked that "The psychopathology of psychosomatic disorders does not differ essentially from that of the neuroses. Freud's theory of the libido and his concept of anxiety prove just as useful in this as in the latter field."

There is considerable direct evidence to support the hypothesis that anxiety plays a decisive role in the occurrence and maintenance of psychophysiological disorders, and also some indirect evidence such as that from a study of 67 psychotic patients who were subjected to lobotomy (Franks, et al). In this study there was little change in symptoms of psychophysiologic disorders during the prepsychotic and psychotic periods; but a great change—a notable loss of symptoms—from the psychotic to the postlobotomy period. These results are in keeping with observations that other nonspecific methods of relieving anxiety and tension, such as the administration of tranquilizing drugs, frequently result in symptomatic relief of psychophysiologic disorders. They offer no explanation, however, for the origins of the anxiety nor for the specific nature of the autonomic imbalance associated with the development of somatic pathology.

Freud provided evidence that the bodily symptoms of conversion hysteria were symbolic of the unconscious conflict leading to their development. Before long, analysts began offering similar interpretations regarding the origin of organ neuroses or psychophysiologic disorders. According to this view, the bodily symptoms of psychophysiologic disorders may be interpreted through a kind of "organ language," some of which has found its way into common usage. For example, difficulty in swallowing food that is not caused by organic disease may be interpreted as evidence of something unpalatable in the person's life situation. Nausea and vomiting in the absence of physical disease may be interpreted on the basis of disgust, inability to "stomach" something unpleasant, and its symbolic rejection in the act of vomiting. Difficulty in breathing in the absence of organic disease may suggest

that the patient has a "load on his chest." Pain in the shoulder or arm may suggest that the subject would like to use this arm to strike someone but is unconsciously restrained from doing so. Pain or itching in other parts of the body may also be interpreted as resulting from unconscious hostility, as illustrated in statements such as "He gives me a pain in the neck," or alternatively, "He sure gets under my skin." Some of the symbolic interpretations concerning origins of bodily symptoms, however, have been extremely fanciful and improbable. Of recent years, analysts have tended increasingly to search for other factors that may be more consistently associated with the development of specific psychophysiologic disorders.

The *problem of specificity* is central to understanding the causation of these or any other group of disorders. Do the disorders represent nonspecific responses of bodily organs to a variety of nonspecific stresses, or can we find some specificity in either the stress or the bodily reponse, or both? The last possibility is inherently more likely, and considerable evidence has been accumulated during recent years, usually designed to relate the development of a specific type of psychophysiologic disorder to one of the following specific factors:

1. The nature of the precipitating stress or conflict (including unconscious symbolism outlined above).
2. The predominant type of emotion experienced.
3. The personality characteristics of the patient.
4. Early life experiences (particularly the interpersonal relationships of infancy and early childhood) thought to result in the development of this type of personality.
5. Hereditary factors thought responsible for the development of this type of personality.
6. A hereditary vulnerability of all, or of the affected part, of the autonomic nervous system.

The term *target-organ* is frequently applied to the organ or organ system that is regarded as having a specific vulnerability to either specific or nonspecific stress. An attempt to investigate the question of specificity of target organ (regardless of what might be responsible for determining this) was undertaken by Buck and Hobbs, who examined the insurance records of 87 individuals (who constituted a 5 percent sample of subscribers to a prepaid plan for medical care) over a 5 year period. Four groups of psychophysiologic disorders were studied (allergic disorders, and psychosomatic disorders of the cardiovascular, gastrointestinal, and musculoskeletal systems) as well as a fifth category consisting of behavioral and character disorders and nonsomatic neuroses. Calculations were made of the expected number of persons with illness in two of the five categories, if the illnesses occurred absolutely independently. It was found that there was a significant excess of individuals having disorders in two categories, for six of the ten possible combinations. The authors concluded that their data indicated *no evidence of organ or system specificity*, but rather of a tendency for psychosomatic illness to be diffuse in its manifestations within the individual. While this may be true of a number of bodily symptoms or syndromes commonly regarded as psychophysiologic, it remains questionable whether this holds true for certain forms of major illness commonly considered to have a partial emotional basis (for example, asthma, peptic ulcer, ulcerative colitis, high blood pressure, and coronary heart disease). We shall now discuss what is known about heredity, other biological factors, and psychological and sociocultural factors in the causation of psychophysiologic disorders.

HEREDITARY FACTORS

In one large scale study of the families of patients with ulcers of the stomach or duodenum, 11.5 percent of the patients' brothers also had ulcers, in contrast with five and a half percent of the comparable general population. There have also been reports of increased frequencies among close relatives of patients with other presumed psychophysiologic disorders including asthma, high blood pressure, migraine headaches, and hyperthyroidism. These increased frequencies appear to be specific for the single type of disorder being considered, and there is no indication whether there may also be an increase in nonspecific vulnerability to other forms of psychophysiologic disorder among the relatives of persons so affected. We have pointed out earlier that an increased family frequency of various forms of psychopathology may be due to the postnatal transmission of learned patterns of maladaptation, but this familial tendency for certain specific psychophysiologic disorders is suggestive of hereditary transmission.

While the extent of hereditary vulnerability (either general vulnerability to autonomic imbalance, or specific vulnerability of a given organ or organ system) still remains to be determined, it should be recognized that competent and conservative human geneticists regard some form of hereditary predisposition as probable in at least certain of these disorders. Fraser Roberts remarked that in general the probabilities are in favor of multifactorial inheritance (due to the cumulative effects of multiple minor genes), which is considered responsible for the genetic component of high blood pressure or of any other continuously graded characteristic such as height, weight, or intelligence. Figure 16-1 shows the distribution of blood pressures among a sample of the general population and among the relatives of persons with high blood pressure, in whom there is evidence of a familial tendency.

Roberts also points out that major genes may well contribute to multifactorial systems. In addition to the increased frequency of duodenal ulcers among the relatives of persons with this

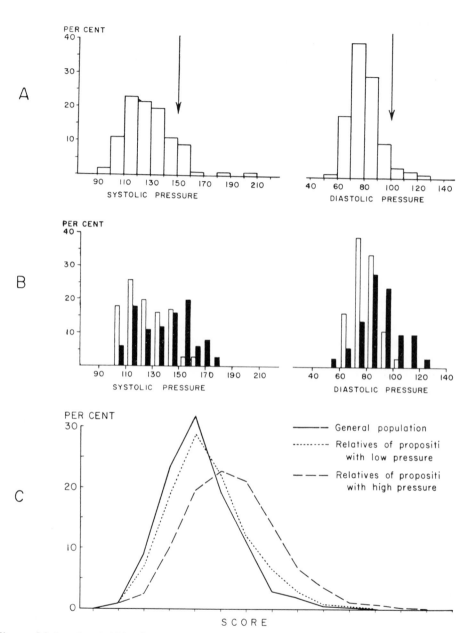

Figure 16–1. Arterial blood pressures. **A,** Sample of 227 women, 30 to 39 years of age. The arrows point to the systolic and diastolic pressures that are often chosen to separate groups with normal and high blood pressure. **B,** Forty-six female relatives of propositi with low pressures (light columns represent controls), as compared with 41 female relatives of propositi with high pressures (dark columns represent hypertensives); 30 to 39 years of age. **C,** Frequency distributions of diastolic pressures for 867 persons from the general population, 371 relatives of controls, and 1062 relatives of hypertensives; males and females, 10 to 79 years of age. The curves are adjusted for age and sex, because different age groups as well as both sexes have different mean pressures. (After Hamilton, Pickering, Roberts, and Sowry. 1954. *Clinical Science* 13:273–304.)

condition, it has been found that persons with blood group O are about 40 percent more likely to suffer from such ulcers as those belonging to the other ABO blood groups, and that nonsecretors are almost twice as likely to suffer from this disease as secretors. The associations are, however, far too small to account for the observed frequency of duodenal ulcers in siblings. It therefore appears that both major genes and multiple minor genes may contribute toward the genetic component in peptic ulcers. In the case of hyperthyroidism, however, the proportion of affected sisters is so much higher than that of affected mothers that an underlying recessive gene or genes have been considered plausible.

As yet there have been few twins studies in this area, but Pilot reported on seven pairs of monozygotic twins, one member of which had developed a psychophysiologic disorder. Vandenberg reported on differences in the psychophysiologic reactions of healthy pairs of monozygotic and dizygotic twins. His preliminary results suggested a significant hereditary component in the reaction of the heart beat frequency and breathing rate to a startling event such as an unexpected light flash or the falling of a hammer-like device near the subject's arm. No hereditary component was found for the galvanic skin resistance. It is evident, therefore, that hereditary predisposition *may* be significant in determining the development of these and other psychophysiologic manifestations at any period throughout life, but that it is also vitally important to consider other biological, psychological, and sociocultural determinants.

SOMATIC FACTORS

It is only a few decades since Walter Cannon investigated the physiological concomitants of fear, hunger, pain, and rage. In another series of well-known studies, H. G. Wolff and his associates observed changes in the stomach lining and secretion during various emotional states. When their subject became angry, his stomach lining was red and there was an increase in its rhythmic contractions and in the secretion of hydrochloric acid. When the same man was depressed or frightened, his stomach was pale and there was a decrease in its movements and acid secretion.

Funkenstein and his associates studied the blood pressure responses of psychotic patients following an injection of mecholyl, and their work was subsequently extended by Gellhorn, Ax, and others. Gellhorn agreed with Funkenstein that the pattern of *increased* central sympathetic reactivity was generally found in persons or patients expressing anger toward others, whereas the pattern of *decreased* central sympathetic reactivity was associated with fear or depression (the latter being interpreted as retroflexed anger, turned inward upon the self).

Ax examined a series of psychological responses in situations associated with either anger or fear, and found statistically significant differences in a number of these physiological responses, as shown in Figure 16-2. A number of biochemical studies have suggested that the response to fear resembles that following an injection of epinephrine, and that the response to anger resembles a combined response to epinephrine and norepinephrine. Other workers have been concerned with localizing centers in the hypothalamus of the brain that exert neural controls over the physiological concomitants of anger and fear. Such studies are still in progress, but for the purposes of the present chapter the important thing is to recognize that specific emotional states may be associated with specific physiological responses.

Nonspecific stress or deprivation may also produce a series of bodily changes, among which are included peptic ulcers of the stomach and intestines. In Chapter 6 we outlined the three stages of Selye's general adaptation syndrome,

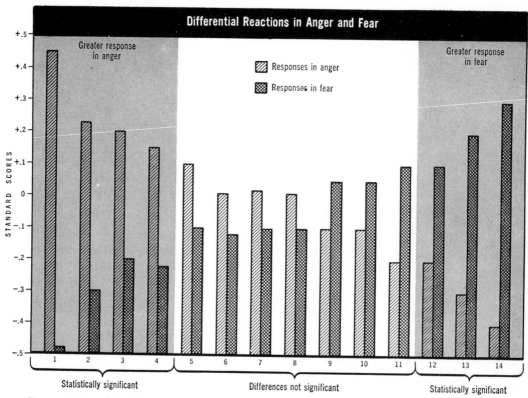

Figure 16-2. Physiological responses in anger and fear. The chart plots changes from the normal (zero) level for 14 indicators all simultaneously recorded. The indicators are numbered to correspond to the numbers at the base of the chart. 1, Galvanic skin responses (increases in number); 2, heart rate decreases; 3, muscle tension increases; 4, diastolic blood pressure rises; 5, face temperature decreases; 6, heart stroke volume decreases; 7, heart stroke volume increases; 8, hand temperature decreases; 9, systolic blood pressure increases; 10, face temperature increases; 11, heart rate increases; 12, muscle tension peaks; 13, skin conductance increases; 14, respiration rate increases. (From Hilgard, E. R. 1957. Introduction to Psychology. 2nd Ed. Harcourt, Brace and Company.)

and mentioned that degeneration such as ulcers of the stomach and intestines is most prominent in the initial phase of the alarm reaction and again in the final stage of exhaustion. Under experimental conditions, exposure to nonspecific noxious agents has also produced such disorders as high blood pressure and degenerative changes in the heart, kidneys, and joints, which Selye has attributed to excessive amounts of pituitary and adrenal cortical hormones.

PSYCHOLOGICAL FACTORS

It is still being investigated whether any of the psychophysiologic disorders develop on the basis of a specific type of interpersonal relationship (particularly with mother) during infancy or early childhood, or whether they are invariably associated with a specific group of personality characteristics in the adult. In patients with any of these disorders, a history is frequently obtained of experiences during early childhood that indicate persistent or recurrent stress or deprivation (involving inter-personal relationships or bodily dysfunctions).

Psychophysiologic disorders may be found in either sex, at any age or socio-economic status, and may be associated with a wide variety of personality characteristics or psychiatric disorders, including neuroses, "functional" psychoses, sociopathic personality, or alcoholism. However, they are more commonly associated with neurotic personality characteristics (and sometimes neurotic symptoms), and the developmental history is more apt to resemble that of patients with neuroses than of those with other forms of psychiatric disorder. It is therefore common to obtain a history of excessive parental anxiety and concern, over-protection, restriction of activities, domination, and demands for conformity, together with deprivation of overt demonstration of affection and other rewards. It is an impression of many authors that the dominant parent, and the one with whom there is the most pathological relationship, is apt to be mother, whereas father is more apt to contribute to faulty patterns of adaptation by his absence (e.g., from death, divorce, or excessive involvement in activities outside his home) or ineffectuality when present, than by harsh and rigid domination when present (although this pattern is also found).

There is also an empirical impression that children later developing these disorders have less opportunity for interaction with other children of both sexes than usual—for example, that they may more often be only children, have no siblings of about the same age, or have only siblings of the same sex, and have restrictions imposed upon their relationships with peers outside the home (by overprotective or dominating parents). Such impressions, however, hitherto lack statistical validation in large groups of patients with specific psychophysiologic diagnoses.

The history of school adjustment is usually one of conformity and competitiveness, with the exception that athletic and social participation has sometimes been restricted by medical and/or parental decree. If symptoms of psychophysiologic disorder do not appear until later life, however, the pattern of conformity and striving for success frequently leads to a high degree of occupational achievement and upward mobility in socioeconomic status. In the past, some of these disorders have been more frequently recognized and diagnosed in persons of the upper socioeconomic classes and have been regarded as the price to be paid for the inevitable tensions and pressures experienced by the successful executive. More recently, however, it has become increasingly apparent that untreated or at least undiagnosed cases are at least as common or may be relatively more frequent among those of limited education and socioeconomic status, whose life situation (marital, occupational, and so on) has been one of chronic frustration.

In view of the wide age range, as well as the variety of psychophysiologic disorders and associated personality characteristics under consideration, the history may reveal various patterns of psychosexual development and marital adjustment. In keeping with the common association with neurotic personality characteristics, however, the prevailing pattern among patients with psychophysiologic disorders is one involving inhibition of aggressive and sexual impulses. A somewhat higher frequency of these disorders may therefore be expected among the single, widowed, or divorced than among the married population of equivalent ages. There is also apt to be a history of limited (and guilt-ridden) premarital sexual experience, together with some persistent sexual inhibition after marriage that may amount to frigidity or impotence. There is a tendency for like to marry like, and disinclination, distaste, or disgust with sexual relations on the part of either the patient or spouse may contribute toward marital discord and accentuate the patient's emotional conflict and psychophysiologic symptoms. Persistent marital discord may also contribute to a perpetuation of similar problems among the children.

It has already been pointed out that peptic ulcers and other bodily disorders may result from acute or chronic biological stress. At this point we may remind the reader of an experiment described in Chapter 7, in which Brady produced ulcers in "executive" monkeys by prolonged psychological stress involving vigilance combined with the possibility of avoiding unpleasant stimulation by appropriate action. Corson suggested that it is *chronic* exposure to *unavoidable* stressful stimuli or their symbols that may lead to cerebrovisceral pathology. His studies on dogs demonstrated that visceral and neuroendocrine response patterns to chronic exposure to conditioned and unconditioned noxious stimuli may be quite different from those exhibited by the same animals during the early presentation of these stimuli. He concluded that failure to differentiate between the effects of acute and chronic stress, and between avoidable and unavoidable stressful situations, is very likely responsible for a good deal of confusion in the attempts to relate psychological stress to somatovisceral and behavioral disturbances.

A study involving human subjects would appear to indicate that *neither predisposition nor precipitating stress alone are ordinarily sufficient to produce duodenal ulcers*, but that a combination of both appear to be necessary. Weiner, et al. obtained measurements of serum pepsinogen (an index of secretory activity of the stomach) for each of 2073 Army inductees. From this total sample, they selected 63 men with values in the upper 15 percent and 57 men with values in the lower nine percent of the blood pepsinogen distribution. Each of these subjects was given a battery of psychological tests and a radiological examination of the upper gastrointestinal tract before being sent to basic training. One hundred and seven subjects were reexamined between the eighth and sixteenth week of basic training, and nine subjects were found with either healed or active duodenal ulcers. All of these men were in the upper 15 percent of the blood pepsinogen distribution, and independent evaluation of the psychological data revealed that these men showed evidence of major unresolved and persistent conflicts about dependency and oral gratification. The authors concluded that neither a high rate of gastric secretion nor a specific psychodynamic constellation is independently responsible for the development of peptic ulcer, but that both constitute the essential determinants in the precipitation of ulcers, on exposure to social situations noxious to the specific individual. Similar findings may be anticipated in intensive studies of persons with other forms of psychophysiologic disorder.

SOCIOCULTURAL FACTORS

In his book on psychosocial medicine, Halliday remarked,

Psychosomatic affections comprise many of the chronic and recurring forms of sickness. They are disorders which incapacitate rather than kill. In only a few does psychophysiological dysfunction lead to organic change which as an end result may ultimately prove lethal, as sometimes occurs in exophthalmic goiter, peptic ulcer, diabetes, and the hypertensive cardiovascular disorders. Statistics of sickness or morbidity should therefore provide the primary source of information. Unfortunately, these are rare and those which do exist are often imperfect. However, while accurate figures are not available, there is general agreement that these disorders are responsible for considerable disability in the general population.

Halliday drew attention to a disproportion in the sex ratio for many of these disorders, in some cases males being in excess (e.g., for childhood asthma and duodenal ulcer) and in other cases females (e.g., for hyperthyroidism). He also noted a reversal in the age and sex ratio for perforated peptic ulcer in England between 1900 and 1930 (at the turn of the century the condition was most frequent in young adult females, and to a lesser extent in older males; but by 1930 it was very much more frequent in young adult males and to a lesser extent in older females.) A number of these disorders appear to show some relationship to rural or urban residence and to occupational and socioeconomic status.

Statistics from the United States Army showed interesting changes in the annual frequency of peptic ulcers diagnosed during World War I and World War II. Ulcers of the stomach appeared to *decrease* slightly in frequency from 0.43 to 0.25 per 1000 men, whereas ulcers of the duodenum *increased* considerably from 0.28 to 2.50 per 1000 men. These figures probably reflect other findings indicating that ulcers of the stomach and duodenum represent two completely different disease-entities, emotional factors having very little relation to the onset of the former but being much more significant in the causation of the latter. It cannot be emphasized too strongly, however, that methods of medical investigation and fashions in medical diagnosis may well be responsible for apparent differences in frequency occurring over a period of time. Similarly, radical differences in the nature of medical care available may be responsible for reported differences in frequency between members of different social classes or of different cultures.

Paffenbarger and his associates undertook a large scale epidemiological study, in which they searched for precursors of mortality from coronary heart disease. This study involved over 45,000 former students of the University of Pennsylvania and of Harvard University, and undertook to relate physical, social, and psychological data recorded during college years (1921-1950) with later health status as measured through self-administered questionnaires, physical examinations, and death certificates. Observations on coronary heart disease were limited to the first 590 *male* former students known to have died from this cause, who were contrasted with 1,180 randomly chosen classmates of equivalent age who were known to be still alive. Analyses of college case-taking and other records of these subjects identified nine precursors of fatal coronary heart disease: heavy cigarette smoking, higher levels of blood pressure, increased body weight, shortness of body height, early parental death, absence of siblings, nonparticipation in varsity athletics, higher emotional index, and scarlet fever in childhood. Some precursors correlated only with early death from coronary disease, and some with death throughout the range of ages studied. The outcome of this research is of particular interest since it involves extensive anterospective data, and implicates multiple etiological factors in a single psychophysiologic disorder. Future research may be expected to indicate the relative significance and relationships between various etiological factors and each of the many psychophysiologic disorders.

TREATMENT

Accurate knowledge of etiology leads to more logical and effective methods of prevention and therapy, but much of the treatment of psychophysiologic disorders is somatic rather than psychological. Severe bodily pathology will require medical and sometimes surgical treatment. Hemorrhage from peptic ulcers may necessitate transfusion, and perforation may require prompt surgical repair. Ulcers that cannot be controlled by an adequate period of medical and psychosocial treatment may lead to severe complications, the prevention of which may also involve surgical intervention. Symptomatic medical treatment of other psychophysiologic disorders may involve a variety of therapeutic efforts such as the use of specific pharmacological agents, diets, or topical applications.

Psychosocial therapies have been widely employed in conjunction with medical treatment, or in attempts to diminish vulnerability during quiescent phases of the disorder. Frequently, however, physicians and surgeons have been reluctant to recognize the significance of psychological factors in etiology, and have referred patients for psychiatric treatment only as a last resort, when the somatic pathology has been firmly established for many years and has proved resistant to symptomatic treatment. Even in a much shorter period of time, extensive somatic investigations and treatment may convince the patient of the importance of organic factors, and render him extremely reluctant to consider emotional factors in etiology or psychological techniques of therapy. Some psychiatrists have unwisely made optimistic pronouncements about the outcome of therapy, when they were becoming involved in psychiatric treatment efforts that were doomed to failure.

In appropriate circumstances, a great deal may be accomplished through supportive psychotherapies and environmental manipulation, and sometimes through more ambitious efforts at personality reconstruction. It should be recognized, however, that the latter may be accompanied by temporary increases in anxiety or depression, with regression and exacerbation of somatic pathology. When indicated, this may be at least partly controlled by administration of tranquilizing or antidepressive medication. Occasionally, depression may be so severe as to suggest electroshock treatment. It has also been mentioned previously that a marked reduction in psychophysiologic disorders has been observed following lobotomy, although brain surgery has rarely been performed specifically in order to relieve such conditions. The psychosocial therapies more generally employed in the treatment of psychophysiologic disorders have al-

ready been elaborated in Chapter 11, and the organic psychiatric therapies in Chapter 12. The special problems of intensive psychotherapy in the patient with a psychophysiologic disorder are well expressed in the following paragraph by Alexander and Szasz:*

Although every physician must be able to make at least a rough psychological diagnosis, decisions concerning psychotherapy—as in the case of other specialized treatments—must rest with the psychiatric specialist. It is important to emphasize that whenever the psychological approach consists of more than providing emotional support, that is to say, whenever it attempts to penetrate behind the ego's defenses and uncover etiological factors, it is likely to activate emotional tension and cause an exacerbation of somatic symptoms. Indeed, we are only now beginning to understand the functional value of somatic illness for the total personality. Also in patients with organic disease, psychological treatment may have to be supplemented by, or intelligently coordinated with, somatic measures whenever the latter type of treatment is indicated. Finally, it should be noted that attempts to treat patients with certain organic diseases through psychoanalysis are of relatively recent origin, and that the analysis of such patients often presents special problems not unlike the problems encountered in the analysis of psychotic patients.

SELECTED REFERENCES

Alexander, F. 1950. *Psychosomatic Medicine: Its Principles and Application.* New York, W. W. Norton & Co., Inc.

Alexander, F., and Szasz, T. S., 1952. The psychosomatic approach in medicine. In *Dynamic Psychiatry,* ed. F. Alexander and H. Ross. Chicago, University of Chicago Press, ch. 12.

Anokhin, P. K. 1967. *The Conditioned Reflex and Internal Inhibition,* tr. and ed. S. A. Corson. London, Pergamon Press, Ltd.

American Psychiatric Association. 1952. *Diagnostic and Statistical Manual.* Washington, D.C., American Psychiatric Association.

---

*Reprinted from *Dynamic Psychiatry,* ed. F. Alexander and H. Ross, by permission of the University of Chicago Press. Copyright 1952 by the University of Chicago.

Asratian, E. A. 1965. *Compensatory Adaptations, Reflex Activity, and the Brain*, tr. and ed. S. A. Corson. London, Pergamon Press, Ltd.

Association for Research in Nervous and Mental Disease. 1950. *Life Stress and Bodily Disease*. Baltimore, The Williams & Wilkins Co., Research Publications of the Association for Research in Nervous and Mental Disease, Vol. 29.

Ax, A. F. 1953. Physiological differentiation between fear and anger in humans. Psychosomatic Medicine *15*, 432-442.

Ax, A. F. 1960. Psychophysiology of fear and anger. American Psychiatric Association, Psychiatric Research Reports No. 12, pp. 167-175.

Bachrach, A. J., ed. 1962. *Experimental Foundation of Clinical Psychology*. New York, Basic Books, Inc., ch. 10-14.

Barbara, D. A. 1959. Stuttering. In *American Handbook of Psychiatry*, ed. S. Arieti. New York, Basic Books, Inc., Vol. 1, ch. 47.

Benedek, T. F. 1959. Sexual functions in women and their disturbance. In *American Handbook of Psychiatry*, ed. S. Arieti. New York, Basic Books, Inc., Vol. 1, ch. 37.

Bliss, E. L., and Branch, C. H. 1960. *Anorexia Nervosa*. New York, Hoeber Medical Division, Harper & Row, Publishers, Inc.

Block, J., Jennings, H., Harvey, E., and Simpson, E. 1964. Interaction between allergic potential and psychopathology in childhood asthma. Psychosomatic Medicine *26*, 307.

Brady, J. V. 1958. Ulcers in "executive" monkeys. Scientific American *199*, 95-100.

Buck, C., and Hobbs, G. E. 1959. The problem of specificity in psychosomatic illness. Journal of Psychosomatic Research *3*, 227-233.

Bykov, K. M., and Kurtsin, I. T. 1966. *The Corticovisceral Theory of the Pathogenesis of Peptic Ulcer*, tr. and ed. S. A. Corson. London, Pergamon Press, Ltd.

Cannon, W. B. 1929. *Bodily Changes in Pain, Hunger, Fear and Rage*, 2nd edition. New York, Appleton-Century-Crofts, Inc.

Cleghorn, R. A., and Brown, W. T. 1964. Psychogenesis of emesis. Canadian Psychiatric Association Journal *9*, 299-311.

Corson, S. A. 1966. Conditioning of water and electrolyte excretion. In *Endocrines and the Central Nervous System*. Baltimore, The Williams & Wilkins Co., Association for Research in Nervous and Mental Disease Publications, Vol. 33, ch. 7.

Corson, S. A. 1966. Neuroendocrine and behavioral response patterns to psychologic stress and the problem of the target tissue in cerebrovisceral pathology. Annals of the New York Academy of Sciences *125*, 890-918.

Corson, S. A., and Corson, E. O. 1966. Neuroendocrine and behavioral correlates of constitutional differences. Proceedings of the Fourth World Congress of Psychiatry, Madrid, September 1966.

Dunbar, F. 1954. *Emotions and Bodily Changes*, 4th edition. New York, Columbia University Press.

Engel, G. L. 1962. *Psychological Development in Health and Disease*. Philadelphia, W. B. Saunders Co., ch. 33.

Fenichel, O. 1945. *The Psychoanalytic Theory of Neurosis*. New York, W. W. Norton & Co., Inc., ch. 13.

Franks, J., et al. 1959. Role of anxiety in psychophysiological reactions. AMA Archives of Neurology and Psychiatry *81*, 227-232.

Funkenstein, D. H., Greenblatt, M., and Solomon, H. C. 1951. Journal of Nervous and Mental Disease *114*, 1.

Gellhorn, E. 1960. Recent contributions to the physiology of the emotions. In *Explorations in the Physiology of the Emotions*, ed. L. J. West and M. Greenblatt. Washington, D. C., American Psychiatric Association, Psychiatric Research Reports No. 12 pp. 209-223.

Gottlieb, J. S., et al. 1956. *Research in psychosomatic medicine*. Washington, D.C., American Psychiatric Association, Psychiatric Research Reports No. 3.

Gutheil, E. A. 1959. Sexual dysfunctions in men. In *American Handbook of Psychiatry*, ed. S. Arieti. New York, Basic Books, Inc., Vol. 1, ch. 36.

Halliday, J. L. 1948. *Psychosocial Medicine*. New York, W. W. Norton & Co., Inc.

Hamilton, M., Pickering, G. W., Roberts, J. A. F., and Sowry, G. S. C. 1954. The aetiology of essential hypertension. 4: The role of inheritance. Clinical Science *13*, 273-304.

Hanley, W. B. 1964. Hereditary aspects of duodenal ulceration: serum-pepsinogen level in relation to ABO Blood Groups and salivary ABH secretor status. British Medical Journal *1*, 936-940.

Jost, H., and Sontag, L. W. 1944. The genetic factor in autonomic nervous system function. Psychosomatic Medicine *6*, 308-310.

Kimball, R. W. 1961. Studies on the pathogenesis of migraine. In *Recent Advances in Biological Psychiatry*, ed. J. Wortis. New York, Grune & Stratton, Inc., Vol. 3, p. 200.

Knapp, P. H., ed. 1963. *Expression of the Emotions in Man*, New York, International Universities Press, Inc.

Lidz, T. 1959. General concepts of psychosomatic medicine. In *American Handbook of Psychiatry*, ed. S. Arieti. New York, Basic Books, Inc., Vol. 1, ch. 32.

Lidz, T., and Rubenstein, R. 1959. Psychology of gastrointestinal disorders. In *American Handbook of Psychiatry*, ed. S. Arieti. New York, Basic Books, Inc., Vol. 1, ch. 35.

Mahl, G. F. 1949. Effect of chronic fear on the gastric secretion of HCl in dogs. Psychosomatic Medicine *11*, 30.

Mendelson, M. 1966. Psychological aspects of obesity. International Journal of Psychiatry *2*, 599-612.

Mirsky, I. A. 1958. Physiologic, psychologic, and social determinants in the etiology of duodenal ulcer. American Journal of Digestive Diseases *3*, 285.

Paffenbarger, R. S., Wolf, P. A., Notkin, J., and Thorne, M. C. 1966. Chronic disease in former college students. I. Early precursors of fatal coronary heart disease. American Journal of Epidemiology *83*, 314-328.

Paffenbarger, R. S., Notkin, J., Kreuger, D. E., Wolf, P. A., Thorne, M. C., LeBauer, E. J., and Williams, J. L. 1966. Chronic disease in former college students. II. Methods of study and observations on mortality from coronary heart disease. American Journal of Public Health *56*, 962-971.

Pearl, J. M., Ritchie, W. P., Gilsdorf, R. B., Delaney, J.P., and Leonard, A.S. 1966. Hypothalamic stimulation and feline gastric mucosal cellular populations. Journal of the American Medical Association *195*, 281-284.

Pilot, M. L. 1961. Psychosomatic disorders in monozygous twin pairs. Proceedings of the Third World Congress of Psychiatry, Montreal, 1961. McGill University Press, Vol. 1, pp. 534-538.

Razran, G. 1960. The observable unconscious in current Soviet psychophysiology: survey and interpretation of experiments in interoceptive conditioning. In *Progress in Clinical Psychology*. New York, Grune & Stratton, Inc., Vol. 4, pp. 1-31.

Reiser, M. F., and Bakst, H. 1959. Psychology of cardiovascular disorders. In *American Handbook of Psychiatry*, ed. S. Arieti. New York, Basic Books, Inc., Vol. 1, ch. 33.

Rennie, T. A. C., and Srole, L. 1956. Social class prevalence and distribution of psychosomatic conditions in an urban population. Psychosomatic Medicine *18*, 449-456.

Richter, C. P. 1957. On the phenomenon of sudden death in animals and man. Psychosomatic Medicine *19*, 191-198.

Roberts, J. A. F. 1959. *An Introduction to Medical Genetics*, 2nd edition, New York, Oxford University Press.

Roessler, R., and Greenfield, N. S., eds. 1962. *Physiological Correlates of Psychological Disorder*, Madison, Wisconsin, University of Wisconsin Press.

Russek, H. I. 1960. Emotional stress and coronary heart disease in American physicians. American Journal of the Medical Sciences *240*, 711-721.

Selye, H. 1956. *The Stress of Life*. New York, The McGraw-Hill Book Co., Inc.

Sontag, L. W. 1950. The genetics of differences in psychosomatic patterns in childhood. American Journal of Orthopsychiatry *20*, 479-489.

Stevenson, I. P., and Wolff, H. G. 1949. Life situations, emotions and the bronchial mucus. Psychosomatic Medicine *11*, 223.

Stunkard, A. 1959. Obesity and the denial of hunger. Psychosomatic Medicine *21*, 281.

Vandenberg, S. G., Clark, P. J., and Samuels, I. 1965. Psychophysiological reactions of twins: hereditary factors in Galvanic skin resistance, heartbeat, and breathing rates. Eugenics Quarterly *12*, 7-10.

Wahl, C. W. 1966. Commonly neglected psychosomatic syndromes. In *American Handbook of Psychiatry*, ed. S. Arieti. New York, Basic Books, Inc., Vol. 3, ch. 11.

Wahl, C. W., and Golden, J. S. 1966. The psychodynamics of the polysurgical patient: report of sixteen patients. Psychosomatics *7*, 65-72.

Wardwell, W. I., Bahnson, C. B., and Caron, H. S. 1963. Social and psychological factors in coronary heart disease. Journal of Health and Human Behavior *4*, 154-165.

Weiner, H., Thaler, M., Reiser, M. G., and Mirsky, I.A. 1957. Etiology of duodenal ulcer. I. Relation of specific psychological characteristics to rate of gastric secretion (serum pepsinogen). Psychosomatic Medicine *19*, 1-10.

Weiss, E., and English, O.S. 1957. Psychosomatic Medicine, 3rd edition. Philadelphia, W. B. Saunders Co.

West, L. J., and Greenblatt, M., eds. 1960. *Explorations in the Physiology of Emotions*. Washington, D. C., American Psychiatric Association, Psychiatric Research Reports No. 12.

Wittkower, E. D., and Cleghorn, R. A., eds. 1954. *Recent Developments in Psychosomatic Medicine*. Philadelphia, J. B. Lippincott Co.

Wittkower, E. D., and Russell, B. 1953. *Emotional Factors in Skin Disease*. New York, Hoeber Medical Division, Harper & Row, Publishers, Inc.

Wittkower, E. D., and White, K. L. 1959. Psychophysiologic aspects of respiratory disorders. In *American Handbook of Psychiatry*, ed. S. Arieti, New York, Basic Books, Inc., Vol. 1, ch. 35.

Wolf, S., and Wolff, H. G. 1942. Evidence on the genesis of peptic ulcer in man. Journal of the American Medical Association *120*, 670-675.

Wolf, S., and Wolff, H. G. 1947. *Human Gastric Function: An Experimental Study of a Man and His Stomach*. New York, Oxford University Press.

Wolf, S., and Wolff, H. G. 1953. *Headaches: Their Nature and Treatment*. Boston, Little, Brown & Co., Inc.

Wolf, S., Cardon, P. V., Shephard, E. M., and Wolff, H. G. 1955. *Life Stress and Essential Hypertension*. Baltimore, The Williams & Wilkins Co.

O! that this too too solid flesh would melt,
Thaw and resolve itself into a dew;
Or that the Everlasting had not fix'd
His canon 'gainst self-slaughter.
O God! O God!
How weary, stale, flat, and unprofitable
Seem to me all the uses of this world.

From "Hamlet," by William Shakespeare

I'll change my state with any wretch,
Thou canst from gaol or dunghill fetch;
My pain's past cure, another hell,
I may not in this torment dwell
Now desperate I hate my life,
Lend me a halter or a knife;
All my griefs to this are jolly,
Naught so damn'd as melancholy

From the "Anatomy of Melancholy," by Robert Burton

And if I laugh at any mortal thing,
Tis that I may not weep.

George Noel Gordon, Lord Byron

CHAPTER 17

Psychotic Depressive and Manic Disorders

Psychotic affective disorders are characterized by severe deviations from the normal affect, mood, or emotional feeling tone. The predominant mood may be either abnormally low (depression) or abnormally high (euphoria). Associated with severe depression or euphoria, there may also be marked disturbances of perception, thinking, or behavior, including hallucinations, delusions, and suicidal or homicidal tendencies. However, any such secondary disturbances in thinking or behavior are appropriate to the prevailing mood, and disappear when the pathological mood returns to normal.

Depression is associated with an attitude of extreme and unrealistic pessimism, whereas euphoria involves extreme and unjustified optimism. The term optimism was formerly applied by philosophers to Leibnitz's doctrine that this world is the best of all possible worlds—since God, being all-wise, must know all possible worlds; being all-powerful must be able to create whatever he might choose; and being all-good must choose the best. Satirical refutations of this position are contained in some of the writings of Voltaire and in the later writings of Mark Twain, published posthumously in his "*Letters from the Earth.*" During a period of pessimism, the individual is apt to perceive the world and himself as evil, and to anticipate the worst outcome of any event. By contrast, an optimistic individual places the most favorable interpretation on events, minimizing their adverse aspects and anticipating the best possible outcome.

399

In a debate on optimism and pessimism, one of the speakers told how two men were out walking, when one of them was struck by droppings from a bird flying overhead. Turning to his companion he remarked, "How fortunate it is that cows cannot fly." Obviously, said the speaker, the man was an optimist. This contention, however was immediately challenged by another speaker who maintained that the man was a pessimist because he had anticipated the worst. In extreme form, either position involves denial and distortion of reality, and it has long been recognized that unrealistic optimism may represent a defense against overwhelming feelings of misery. Aristotle remarked that melancholy men may be the most witty, and the same concept is evident in the quotation from Byron at the beginning of this chapter.

In most religions, men have been promised that good behavior would be rewarded by joy and bliss in the life hereafter. The heaven of Norse mythology is interesting in being devoid of any such hope of the future. It was instead a solemn place, over which hung the threat of inevitable doom. The gods knew that someday they would be defeated and destroyed by their enemies. Men and women must be even more helpless against evil. Although a hero's death would entitle a man to a seat in Valhalla, yet in the last battle between good and evil, he would die together with the gods. In more recent times, a similar philosophy has been expressed in the statement, "You can't win, but you don't have to lose right away." We shall turn now to consider some of the contrasting clinical manifestations of syndromes characterized by depression or euphoria.

DEPRESSION AND SUICIDE

If a person is severely depressed, it may be possible to recognize this from his appearance, attitude, and behavior even before any attempt is made to converse with him. He may be retarded and motionless, sitting or standing for long periods of time in an attitude of dejection, completely preoccupied with his inner misery and indifferent to his appearance and surroundings. Alternatively he may be agitated and restless, pacing the floor or wandering aimlessly, wringing his hands, or even occasionally tearing his hair or clothing. These extreme behavioral manifestations of depression are seen relatively infrequently nowadays, because of earlier recognition and more effective treatment than formerly. However, severely depressed persons still require close supervision to prevent suicide.

The facial expression is apt to be immobile and unsmiling. The features may look haggard and drawn, with accentuation of angular creases in the upper eyelid, and a tendency to frequent weeping. Persons who are severely depressed may be completely uncommunicative, and unresponsive to questioning. More commonly, depressed individuals make little or no spontaneous conversation, but answer questions briefly and in a quiet monotonous voice. Their replies are relevant and appropriate to the question asked, but tend to reflect a uniformly gloomy and morbid outlook. They complain of feeling tired, listless, weary, fatigued, and lacking in pep or energy. They feel "run down," or "dragged out," have no ambition or initiative, and are no longer interested in activities they have previously enjoyed.

There is difficulty in sleeping, which may consist of an inability to go to sleep or to remain asleep for any length of time. The mornings often seem to be the worst time of day. There is usually loss of appetite and weight, and often associated constipation. Diminished sexual desire is usual, and in severe depression there may be complete frigidity or impotence. In women it is not uncommon for menstruation to cease temporarily during an episode of depression and to resume spontaneously after recovery. A depressed person is also apt to be unduly sensitive to disturbed bodily functions or minor degrees of pain, and hence to have numerous hypochondriacal complaints for which no organic basis can be found. If his depression is not recognized, however, his complaints may lead to unnecessarily prolonged and expensive medical investigations, or even surgical operation, in addition to a dangerous delay in initiating psychiatric treatment.

Intellectual capacity is distributed throughout the normal range and in mild cases of depression there may be little or no evident impairment of intellectual function, whereas in severe depression the impairment of intellectual function is profound. Similarly, in mild depression, there is no impairment of memory or orientation (except when there is also an organic brain syndrome), but these functions may appear to be disturbed in the severely depressed patient.

Illusions and hallucinations are not characteristic of simple depressive syndromes, but were formerly described in about 30 percent of persons with manic-depressive psychoses. Of recent years there has been an increasing tendency to include such persons among the schizo-affective disorders, which will be considered in the next chapter. Delusional distortion of reality, however, is consistently found in psychotic depressions, the characteristic delusions being those of self-accusation, worthlessness, hopelessness, and nihilism (the last being a belief that the self or part of the self is non-existent).

The emotional reaction shows little or no variation from the prevailing mood or affect of depression. This all-pervasive feeling tone may be described by a variety of words among which are the following: discontented, displeased, dissatisfied, disconsolate, discouraged, despondent, dejected, defeated, desolate, destitute, and desperate. Mixed in with feelings of depression, however, may be emotions of fear or outwardly directed anger. The latter appears to have considerable dynamic significance in certain forms of depression, which have been interpreted as representing retroflexed rage: i.e., impotent rage that cannot be expressed against the source of frustration, or the love-object that has been lost, and hence is turned backward upon oneself. Under the surface, the depressed person may have a great deal of repressed resentment and hostility that may be recognized and expressed during the course of successful therapy.

Just as a depressed person is more sensitive to physical pain, so also is he more sensitive to psychic pain resulting from harsh judgment by his conscience, superego, or internal control system. He may be preoccupied with regrets for past mistakes, and experience severe guilt and remorse over quite trivial misdemeanors. Since depressed persons tend to blame themselves and to inflict suffering primarily on themselves (although secondarily also on others), they are sometimes described as *intrapunitive*. In the bitterness of their defeat their rationalizations may approximate the following: "I have failed, I shall fail again, and in fact I am a failure." The second part of this statement implies that the future is hopeless, and the third that the individual is worthless. In the depths of despair, the individual may conclude that life is no longer worth living, that the world would be a better place without him, and that he should commit suicide.

Studies of mortality among diagnosed psychiatric patients (e.g., see Norris) indicate the highest frequencies of *suicide* among patients with diagnoses of manic-depressive psychoses. Retrospective psychiatric evaluations of successful suicides indicate a high frequency of psychotic depression (whether manic-depressive, schizoaffective, or involutional), in contrast with psychiatric evaluations of living persons who have made unsuccessful suicidal attempts (who are relatively more likely to have neurotic or sociopathic personality disorders). In this society it is generally assumed that those who commit suicide or make serious attempts are depressed to a psychotic degree, whether or not they have shown previous symptoms. Hirsh remarked "whether precipitate or calculatedly deliberate, there is an overwhelming body of evidence to suggest that the suicide is rarely a rational being eliminating himself for thoroughly valid reasons. More often than not, he is emotionally and often physically ill."

In a study of 134 successful suicides, Robins et al. diagnosed 60 as having manic-depressive depression, 31 as being chronic alcoholic, five with chronic brain syndromes, three with schizophrenia, and two with drug addiction. Twenty-five were undiagnosed but considered definitely psychiatrically ill, five were suffering from terminal medical illnesses, and only three were apparently clinically well. It is a popular misconception that people who speak of committing suicide do not carry out their threats. In this study, Robins et al. found that 68 percent had communicated suicidal ideas, and 38 percent specifically stated that they intended to kill themselves. The extent to which persons with suicidal ideas or other signs of abnormality are recognized and brought to psychiatric attention, however, will depend upon such factors as the psychiatric sophistication of the community and the availability of adequate treatment resources.

Although it is widely recognized that severe depression carries the potential danger of suicide, it is less commonly realized that the lives of other persons may also be in danger. It is not uncommon for depressed persons to take the lives of other members of their family preparatory to their own suicide. Sometimes the consent of the other person is obtained, as in a suicide pact between two lovers, but on other occasions the distorted judgment of the depressed person includes the conviction that life is as hopeless for other family members as for himself and he may kill his wife and children prior to taking his own life.

EUPHORIA

Euphoria consists of a mood of elation or exaltation, together with acceleration of thought and speech and motor excitement. It is found in manic and hypomanic phases of manic-depressive psy-choses, and also in some toxic or organic brain syndromes. In many respects, euphoria represents the opposite side of the coin from depression. In extreme euphoria, appearance, attitude, and behavior may be so unusual that the condition may be recognized without any attempt at interview. The person tends to be careless or decorative in appearance, gay and animated, energetic and overactive, impulsive, and reckless of consequences. The hypomanic individual is usually outgoing, sociable, and friendly, genial, and good-natured. However, with increasing psychomotor activity, the manic patient is apt to become sarcastic, irritable, vulgar, aggressive, and even assaultive or violent.

There is an increased stream of thought and spontaneous speech, which may continue uninterrupted until the patient becomes hoarse or loses his voice. He is continually stimulated, both by new thoughts arising internally and by the external environment. It is usually possible to get his attention long enough to answer brief questions appropriately, or at least start to do so. However, there is frequently a flight of ideas to other subjects that are only related tangentially, although associations of ideas are not so disconnected that speech is completely fragmented as it may be in schizophrenia. The content of speech tends to reflect a prevailing mood of unjustified optimism, and the individual is inclined to be relaxed, jovial, humorous, and witty. With increasing pressure of ideation, there is a tendency to make puns, to associate by rhyming, and in extreme cases to show evidences of clang associations (associations being made simply to sounds rather than ideas).

Intellectual capacity is distributed throughout the normal range and there is little or no impairment of intellectual function with mild hypomania. However, increasing carelessness results in numerous errors and impairment of measured intellectual function which can be extreme in severe mania. Similarly, memory and orientation are unimpaired except in advanced cases of manic delirium. Illusions and hallucinations are not characteristic, but were formerly reported in 30 percent of manic-depressive psychoses and are frequently found in severe mania.

While the prevailing emotional tone is one of euphoria, there is usually considerable lability or fluctuation in the emotional reaction, and in some individuals there may be repeated episodes of tears or other evidence of depression. The euphoria is characteristically associated with delusions of grandeur involving unrealistic ideas of power, wealth, strength, beauty, intelligence, and so on. Any frustration of the individual's impulses may lead to considerable outwardly directed hostility, which may be associated with sarcasm, delusions of persecution, or assaultive behavior.

It has been pointed out that the depressed person is hypersensitive to pain and victimized by conscience. The euphoric individual, by contrast, is "feeling no pain," either bodily or intrapsychic. He is insensitive to pain, inconsiderate of the feelings of others, and indifferent to the consequences of his impulsive behavior. The author has seen a hypomanic patient walk around the ward singing happily with a temperature over 104 degrees due to an acute appendicitis, which was found at operation to have perforated. The impaired superego or internal control system permits promiscuity, financial irresponsibility, and other antisocial behavior. There is also a danger that the individual's impulsive behavior will lead to accidental self-injury (or even death), or that externally directed aggression will result in assault and injury to others.

DIAGNOSTIC CATEGORIES OF AFFECTIVE DISORDER

The obvious differences between melancholia (depression) and mania (excitement) have been recognized since antiquity, and Aretaeus noted attacks of depression and excitement in the same individual. Falret (1854) described an alternating form of mood disorder as "la folie circulaire" or "folie à double forme," and Kraepelin (1899) proposed the term manic-depressive psychosis. A few years later Adolf Meyer proposed abandoning the term melancholia in favor of depression, and by 1907 Kraepelin had become convinced that involutional melancholia was not an independent entity. However, it is still considered as such in the standard nomenclature of the American Psychiatric Association.

Many psychiatrists have considered that a basic distinction should be made between *exogenous* reactions, which follow some obvious precipitating stress, and *endogenous* reactions, in which no such external stress is apparent. This view is still widespread in Europe, and was expressed as follows by Hoff:

Three forms of depression must be carefully distinguished. The first, reactive or exogenous depression, is caused and maintained by unfavorable external conditions of life. It is obvious that someone who experiences a major tragedy in the family or a business setback will be affected by it, but this is a perfectly normal reaction and not a disease. The second form of depression, neurotic depression, occurs during the course of a neurosis and is due to the secondary reaction of the personality after failing to deal with the primary neurotic symptoms. The patient is aware of the impoverishment of his personality arising out of the struggle with the irrational unconscious conflict and of the subsequent regression and reacts to this with a depression. The third form of depression, endogenous depression or melancholia, is the expression of a genuine, possibly organic disease belonging to the group of manic-depressive psychoses. . . .

Roth pointed out that the presence or absence of a precipitant for the illness is of dubious value as a basis for the classification of depressive states. In fact, either the manic or the depressive phase of a manic-depressive psychosis (which has traditionally been considered endogenous) may develop immediately following an obvious precipitating stress (either biological or psychological) and may therefore appear to be exogenous. Nevertheless, a majority of psychiatric opinion has favored the preservation of various diagnostic distinctions. Moreover, these relatively crude distinctions, based on clinical symptoms and history, appear to have some empirical validity in that they may enable more accurate prediction concerning the probable outcome of the disorder, with or without specific forms of treatment.

In the A.P.A. diagnostic manual the term *"affective reactions"* is reserved for "psychotic reactions . . . characterized by a primary, severe disorder of mood," and only two such disorders are listed, namely manic-depressive reactions and psychotic depressive reactions. However, the category of involutional psychotic reaction (which includes the former diagnosis "involutional melancholia") is usually primarily affective. Similarly, although neurotic depressive reaction and normal grief reaction are not psychotic in quality or intensity, they are often regarded as falling into the broad group of affective disorders or reactions and are therefore mentioned here. Affective symptoms may also be prominent features of certain schizophrenic (schizoaffective) reactions and of organic brain syndromes. It should be noted that a mood of depression may occur in any of the affective disorders, but that a mood of euphoria is only found in manic-depressive reactions or in association with schizophrenia or organic brain syndromes. We shall now summarize the main characteristics of the affective disorders, with some illustrative case histories.

MANIC-DEPRESSIVE REACTIONS

These disorders are characterized by severe mood swings, with a tendency to remission and subsequent recurrence. Various accessory symptoms such as illusions, hallucinations, and delusions may be added to the basic mood disorder; but in recent years there has been an increasing tendency to diagnose such patients as having "schizoaffective psychoses" which are classified with schizophrenias (see next chapter).

In manic episodes there is euphoria, emotional lability, overtalkativeness, flight of ideas, and increased motor activity. Symptoms vary in degree or intensity (from hypomania through acute mania to delirious mania). In depressive episodes there may be either uneasiness, apprehension, perplexity and agitation, or mental and motor retardation and inhibition which may reach the point of stupor.

A given individual may show any combination of manic and depressive episodes: e.g., a single episode of either depression or mania, repeated attacks of depression alone (or mania alone), a periodic alternation of manic and depressive episodes (either of which may follow the other closely or be separated in time), or a completely irregular sequence of manic and depressive episodes. In 70 to 80 percent of all cases, the first attack is depressive.

The strong tendency toward recurrence is illustrated by Rennie's series of 208 cases followed up for over 30 years. Only 21 percent of these patients had a single attack, 79 percent had a second, 63 percent third attacks, and 45 percent had fourth attacks.

Attacks may appear to be "endogenous" (unrelated to any evident environmental stress or deprivation), in which event there may be a regular periodicity (consistent intervals between attacks), or irregularity in time and nature of attacks. On the other hand, such attacks frequently appear to be "exogenous," either manic or depressive episodes following closely some biological or emotional stress or deprivation (e.g., physical illness or the loss of a loved one). Attacks may remain of brief duration and be unaccompanied by chronic personality deterioration. However, there appears to be a tendency toward increased frequency and duration of attacks with advancing age, and chronic mania may be associated with personality deterioration.

MANIC-DEPRESSIVE DEPRESSION LEADING TO SUICIDE

A 20-year-old male college student was referred for psychiatric treatment early in the winter quarter of his junior year, after he had made a serious suicidal attempt by cutting one wrist and then his neck quite deeply with a razor. He appeared dejected and retarded, but was still able to communicate verbally and presented his problems as follows: "It's something that's been gnawing at me all my life, particularly last quarter. Why I did that (attempted suicide) I don't know — I'm running away I guess. There's a political club I got to be president of. I didn't ask to be, and I'm not qualified for it — along with many other things I go into. I'm not really qualified for anything — not qualified to live — not qualified to die either. I can't think anymore. I'm a robot. Nobody else seems to think there's anything wrong. I don't know if that's because I'm a good actor. I can't think. Nothing is satisfying. There are plenty of things that should be but aren't. I've been a listener all my life."

When asked how long he had been feeling depressed he replied, "Intensely, like this, for the past quarter. Maybe before that all my life. In high school a lot of nice things started to happen to me. I got into a good college. I was no student before. I still can't spell. All the time I am ill at ease. I can't

laugh. I don't think I have had a real deep laugh more than four or five times all my life. I was thinking of killing myself constantly for the past three weeks. I have never felt quite this bad before. I feel I want to hide from things. I don't like or dislike people. Everybody's fine. I don't have opinions of my own."

He had profound feelings of worthlessness and hopelessness. During the preceding quarter he had increasing difficulty in sleeping, had lost appetite and weight, and had experienced increasing lack of energy, but had continued to drive himself in multiple activities. He was taking seventeen credits and maintaining a B average in a competitive college. He was playing first string football and had been elected cocaptain of the team for the next year. He had been elected president of the letter club and president of the political club. He was waiting on tables in the dining room and had a morning and evening paper route. He was also expecting to be a proctor during his senior year.

The patient was an only child and his father had committed suicide by carbon monoxide when the boy was ten years old. His mother had told him that his father's death

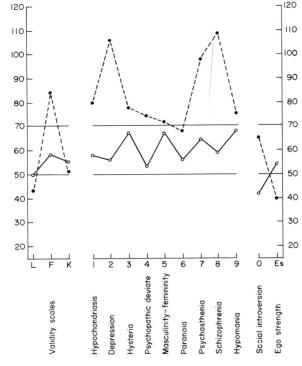

Figure 17–1. MMPI profiles for a 20 year old male, with psychotic depression (dotted line), and after one month of daily psychotherapy and imipramine (solid line). A score of 70 is two standard deviations above the mean score of 50 for adult males on each scale.

was due to a heart attack, and chose the day after the boy's own suicidal attempt to tell him that his father's death had in fact been suicide. At interview, the mother appeared to be distant and unemotional. Following her husband's death she had been left in comfortable financial circumstances and did her best to raise her son to be socially responsible, but she seemed surprised by his need to achieve, and his inability to decline any responsibility that was placed on him. She remarked that whenever he was chosen he must always do a good job, that he wanted approval, wanted to do the right thing, and had never been a problem to her. She had apparently never gone out of her way to encourage and foster relationships with other children his own age, and she appeared surprised that he was insecure in such relationships, and in conflict over his vocational goals.

Following his unsuccessful suicidal attempt there was some spontaneous improvement in mood, which is not uncommon, and has been interpreted as due to partial atonement and reduction in guilt. He also received imipramine and intensive psychotherapy, and returned to college a month later, with the understanding that he would be continuing in long-term psychotherapy. (See Figure 17-1.) As his mood improved, however, he denied the reality of his problems, and was no longer motivated to work on their solution. At this point he sought vocational guidance but rejected further therapy. However, the fall quarter of the following year he again became overwhelmed by the magnitude of his self-imposed schedule, and on this occasion he sought psychiatric treatment himself. Supportive psychotherapy and medication were completely ineffectual and he became more deeply depressed so that he was admitted to hospital for a course of electroshock treatments. After half a dozen treatments, there was a dramatic change in his mood and he became mildly hypomanic.

When his mood stabilized he again left hospital and returned to college but once more rejected further involvement in long-term psychotherapy. It was later learned that there was a recurrence of mild hypomanic behavior during which he became exuberant, talkative, told vulgar jokes, had too much to drink, and made embarrassing propositions to girls he scarcely knew. The episode was of brief duration, and he graduated from college uneventfully and went on to graduate school. A few years later it was learned that he had had another episode of psychotic depression and had succeeded in committing suicide.

MANIC-DEPRESSIVE DEPRESSION, ASSOCIATED WITH HOMICIDE

A married woman was admitted to state hospital at the age of 45 years, for psychiatric evaluation after having killed her two adopted children by strangulation and subsequently having attempted suicide by the same method.

She was the ninth of 11 children of Catholic parents and was brought up on her parents' farm in rather poor socioeconomic circumstances. Her father committed suicide by drowning when she was ten years old, and three of her older brothers also committed suicide by shooting themselves. One of her younger brothers had repeated admissions to mental hospital over a period of about six years, and finally had a lobotomy (brain surgery) which was followed by marked improvement. Two of her sisters had died from infections, and the other two sisters remained unmarried (one of them was a nun).

The patient left school at the age of 13 after completing grade eight, and remained home working on the farm for the next five years. At the age of 18 she started working for the telephone company for six months, then entered a convent for 14 months, and subsequently returned to the telephone company, where she continued to work until after her marriage. At the age of 32 she married a man four years younger than herself and at the time of her admission to hospital he reported that the first two or three years of their marriage were extremely difficult — that his wife frequently flew off the handle and bawled him out, and that on several occasions he had become so angry he was afraid he would kill her so that he left their home for a couple of days at a time. He believed that she had never enjoyed intercourse but had regarded this as a duty to her husband which she had felt guilty if she failed to fulfill. She didn't confide much in him and it wasn t until seven years after their marriage that he learned about her father's suicide. At first she didn't want any children and they used the rhythm method of birth control for a couple of years. She said that she was afraid of having children because of her age and physical health, but she was also worried that the insanity in her family might be hereditary. They finally adopted the elder child when she was aged 35 and the younger child when she was aged 38. The elder was described as high strung and was out of school a year following tonsillectomy. Of the younger child the patient's husband said, "She was always delicate, never wanted to eat, and we always had to pound hell out of her to get her to eat."

The patient started complaining of pain in her right side at the age of about 17. At the age of 23 she had an appendectomy and at the age of 30 she had one ovary removed, but the pain persisted. She also reported having diarrhea (diagnosed as colitis) five or six times a day from the ages of 27 to 43. During the two years immediately preceding her admission she was under treatment for "stomach trouble" (diagnosed as gastritis).

She had episodes of severe depression for at least 20 years prior to her admission. She worried a great deal over the suicides of her father and brothers, and her husband stated that from the early days of their marriage he had expected to come home some time and find her on the floor. She saw a psychiatrist briefly at the age of 36 and received a few electroshock treatments. These apparently helped her but she disliked the treatment and never wished to return. Depressive episodes subsequently returned several times a year, lasting for several weeks at a time, and at these times she spoke of being a burden to her husband, and also said that if she should die before her husband then the children would be a burden to him.

The episode of depression immediately preceding her admission to hospital had lasted about a month before she killed her children and attempted suicide. On arrival she was tense, tremulous, and tearful. She offered little spontaneous conversation, but answered questions briefly in a quiet monotonous voice. When asked why she had killed the children, she replied, "Because I am depressed a lot of the time and I just don't feel good. I've often wanted to take my own life before, and I didn't want to leave them to be neglected. That was why I wanted to take them." In spite of her constant depression, she was able to complete extensive psychological testing and she obtained a full scale IQ of 108.

Since no other treatment was known that might diminish or abolish her long standing tendency to recurrent episodes of severe depression (which might now be accentuated by guilt over having caused the deaths of her children), she underwent lobotomy (brain surgery), following which there was marked and lasting improvement in mood, and also in the bodily symptoms of which she had complained for many years. Several years after the operation she was discharged from hospital and returned to live with her husband.

MANIC REACTION, FOLLOWED BY DEPRESSION AND SUICIDE

A 38-year-old widow was admitted to state hospital exactly two weeks following the death of her husband in a railroad crossing accident. She had previously been considered outgoing, gay, and talkative, but had never shown evidence of psychopathology. She had genuinely loved her husband and felt partly responsible for his death. In this situation the usual response would be grief or depression, but the patient reacted by becoming overtalkative, loud, boisterous, and overactive. She went on a spending spree, calling herself "the merry widow," and her admission to hospital was arranged by puzzled relatives.

The patient was the eldest of four children, all girls, and two of them were married with children of their own. Their parents were still living together and there was no history of psychopathology or of disturbed interpersonal relationships within the family.

The patient was raised on her parents' farm in average economic circumstances and was apparently a happy, sociable youngster. She left school at the age of 17 after completing grade 11 and one year of business school. She enjoyed school and had a good work record in a single job for five years prior to her marriage at the age of 23. Her husband was a farmer nine years older than herself, and was described as a calm, stable person who had a steadying influence on the patient. The couple had three children, who were aged nine through 13 at the time of the patient's admission to hospital. The patient was highly regarded by her family and friends and was described as being talkative and carefree. At times she seemed to be overly excitable and sometimes lost her temper with the children, but her husband could always calm her down, and she had never shown evidence of either pathological euphoria or depression.

On the day of her husband's death, she and her husband were driving with four other people to attend a plowing contest near their home. The patient was riding in the back seat of the car and complained of feeling carsick. Her husband, who was driving, suggested that she trade places with him, and she took over the driving. On approaching a railroad crossing, the warning signal indicated a train was approaching and she stopped short of the track. Another car that was coming behind them, however, failed to see the warning signal or the train, and ran into her car from behind with some force, pushing it onto the tracks. The car stalled and she was unable to start it in time and at the last minute she yelled for everyone to jump out. However, the patient's husband and his sister were unable to get out in time and were still in the car when it was hit by the train. The patient's sister-in-law subsequently recovered, but her husband was killed in the crash.

For a day or two after the accident the patient seemed to be numb and in a state of shock, but by the time of the funeral she appeared to have recovered her spontaneity. Within a day or two after the funeral, there was an abrupt change in her usual personality and she became quite euphoric, saying that her husband was far happier with the angels than he would have been with her. She immediately bought a new car to replace the car that had been wrecked in the accident, and she drove this so recklessly that her friends and neighbors became concerned. At the time of her admission to the hospital, one of her friends described her behavior as follows, "She is clear in her mind and thinks this is her normal thinking. She is fanatic in her ideas and crude in her jokes. The doctor told me this morning that he listened to more stories about her yesterday in his office than ills of his patients." Besides the new car, the patient bought a new big tractor and truck and implements for the tractor. She bought a new coat and hat and an electric blanket and insisted that her mother buy a new coat also. She bought bunk beds not only for her own family but also for a neighbor, and ordered a freezer for her sister. She asked for a private line on her telephone and arranged for a new oil burning furnace and insulation for her house. When asked how she could pay for all this, she said that she was going to get $100,000 from the driver of the car that had pushed her and her husband onto the railroad tracks.

She was overtalkative and laughed and made fun of things, which ordinarily she would not do. She had a feeling of importance and thought nothing of telling everybody off. She phoned people constantly and at odd times such as five o'clock in the morning, to tell them to come over to visit her or that she was coming over to visit them. She phoned one neighbor and told her to do her ironing and cleaning. She phoned another neighbor to say that the family were coming over there for supper. She lost her temper easily with the children, and the night before her admission to hospital she threw a butcher knife across the room at them. On another occasion she struck her three-year-old nephew and when the child did not cry, she was so pleased that she promised to take out a large life insurance policy on him. She was too busy to eat properly and she was too active to sleep at night. Her disturbed and potentially dangerous behavior finally led to her commitment to the hospital.

On arrival she was very angry about being taken to the hospital and began writing two lists of names, one group of which she was going to sue and the other group she was going to reward with sums of $1000 each. Part of her conversation to her physician was as follows, "If you send me out of here, I'll give you $1000. You understand I can sue you for anything. I'm not mental and I won t stay here. My children need me. My mother will be frantic. You will have to drive me home. People don t know why I am so happy after my husband died. They can't understand that I have got religion to help me now whereas others have not. I have to get out so I can plant bulbs on my husband's grave. I don't want anyone else to do it for me. You're a doctor. I can tell you the real reasons for all this. I want to get married again and I wanted to get everything straightened up before I do. Once you've been married you need the security of marriage. I've gotten well rested now and I'll be able to carry on at home." She also wrote a number of letters: to one woman whom she called stupid and asked never to visit her again; to a bachelor whom she decided to marry; to the son of another patient in the hospital, telling him that his mother was not being looked after properly; and others.

Chlorpromazine was given soon after admission, with partial control of her hypomanic symptoms, and she then received a short course of electroshock treatments, with complete remission of the remaining symptoms. She left hospital within three months of her admission, but on her return home she immediately began to feel depressed and to blame herself for the silly things she had done just after her husband's death. She began to feel that she would never be able to live down the fact that she had appeared happy after her husband's death and even talked about remarriage. Less than two weeks after leaving the hospital she was sufficiently depressed to take half a dozen sleeping pills in a suicidal attempt, and she was readmitted to hospital.

She received a further brief course of electroshock treatments and temporarily lost her symptoms of depression, but for several months afterward her mood continued to change rapidly from euphoria to depression. Six months after her second admission to hospital, however, her mood had been stabilized for several weeks and she was allowed to leave the hospital again. Litigation concerning the accident was still pending, and the patient's farm was put up for sale. Thirteen months after the death of her husband, and four months after leaving hospital for the second time, the patient drove her car onto a railroad crossing early one morning and parked it in the path of a fast train she knew would be coming. On this occasion her suicidal attempt was successful, and shortly afterward her three children were awarded a total of $24,000 in damages to compensate them for the loss of both their parents.

PSYCHOTIC DEPRESSIVE REACTION

This reaction is described as differing from the manic-depressive reaction, depressed phase, principally in (1) absence of history of repeated depressions or of marked cyclothymic mood swings, and (2) frequent presence of environmental precipitating factors. It is suggested that this diagnostic category be used when a "reactive depression' is of such quality (severity) as to place it in the group of psychoses. However, it should be emphasized that the first (or subsequent) manic or depressive episode of a typical manic-depressive psychosis may appear as a "reaction' to exogenous environmental stress or deprivation. A number of authors therefore question the validity of this diagnostic category. The following case history illustrates a single episode of *postpartum psychotic depressive reaction*:

A 31-year-old married woman was admitted to state hospital about three months after the birth of her fifth child, with symptoms of severe depression. Soon after the birth of the youngest child she became increasingly tired, had been unable to sleep, had lost her appetite and any interest she had previously had in sexual relations, had been increasingly apprehensive of further pregnancy, had been worrying unduly about her

family's financial situation and had gradually become unable to look after her home and family. She felt completely hopeless and thought of suicide, although her strong religious convictions prevented her from making any attempt on her life. She felt she had been driven by the devil to do wrong and became preoccupied with guilt feelings over masturbation as a child. Her inactivity and depression finally led to her admission to hospital.

The patient grew up on her parents' farm in average economic circumstances and left school at the age of 14 after completing grade eight. She helped her mother at home for a couple of years and then did housework for neighbors. At the age of 22 she left home to work in the kitchen of a nearby hospital and the following year she married a man four years older than herself who was regularly employed as a cabinetmaker.

She obtained no information about sex from her parents or peers but discovered masturbation on her own and experienced considerable guilt over this over the years. She had no premarital sexual relations and following her marriage she was initially quite frigid and was afraid of becoming pregnant. Her religious beliefs, however, limited attempts at contraception to the rhythm method which was quite ineffectual. During her nine years of marriage, she had been pregnant seven times and had five living children, one spontaneous abortion, and one tubal pregnancy which had been removed surgically. Her only source of discord with her husband involved various debts which had been incurred from time to time which he regarded as the inevitable result of raising a large family, but which the patient regarded as unnecessary. She had had minor brief episodes of depression following the birth of her second and fourth children, but had never previously shown any symptoms of psychotic intensity.

On arrival in hospital she said that her trouble had started a couple of months before the birth of her youngest child. "The main thing was that I couldn't sleep and things got on my nerves, like if the radio was turned on loud and if the children didn't behave. After the baby was born my appetite wasn't good and I felt very tired so I couldn't do the housework." She said that her main worry was that her children had come too close together and that her husband had got into debt. She expressed guilt over former masturbation and admitted having felt so hopeless that she had considered suicide.

Her mood of depression was rapidly relieved following a course of electroshock treatment, and while she was in hospital a physical disorder of the uterus was discovered which led to its surgical removal. This in effect solved her main problem, since she could no longer become pregnant. She left hospital two months after her admission, returned home to look after her family and had no recurrence of psychopathology during the following five years.

INVOLUTIONAL PSYCHOTIC REACTION, DEPRESSED TYPE

This is described in the American Psychiatric Association manual as

Characterized most commonly by depression occurring in the involutional period, without previous history of manic-depressive reaction, and usually in individuals of compulsive personality type. The reaction tends to have a prolonged course and may be manifested by worry, intractable insomnia, guilt, anxiety, agitation, delusional ideas, and somatic concerns. Some cases are characterized chiefly by depression and others chiefly by paranoid ideas. Often there are somatic preoccupations to a delusional degree.

It is emphasized that it may be extremely difficult to differentiate between these and other psychoses (e.g., manic-depressive or paranoid) having their onset during the involutional period, and that the diagnosis should not be made simply on the basis of age of onset. However, some authors have continued to regard involutional melancholia as merely the first clinical depressive episode of a manic-depressive psychosis, which happens to have its onset during the involutional period. Others point to the frequent occurrence of schizophrenia (and *not* manic-depressive psychosis) in the blood relatives of patients having a clinical diagnosis of involutional psychosis (and Kallmann speculated that this familial association may have a genetic basis).

A 53-year-old married women was admitted to a state hospital with a history that for several weeks she had been worrying more than usual, particularly about imagined financial difficulties, and that she was unable to eat or sleep. She became convinced that something terrible had happened, and it was impossible to convince her to the contrary. She became increasingly agitated and during the week preceding her admission she paced restlessly day and night, and scarcely ate or drank anything at all.

She was born the fourth in a family of six children, having four sisters and one brother who was two years younger than herself. Both parents lived to an old age and there was no family history of severe psychopathology, although her father had a tendency toward episodes of mild depression and her mother had some mild impairment of memory shortly before her death. The patient was brought up on her parents' farm in marginal economic circumstances, and left school at the age of 14 after failing to complete the examinations at the end of grade eight. She then helped at home and worked out for awhile in domestic service prior to her marriage at the age of 19. Her husband was ten years older than herself and had sustained a leg wound during World War I (prior to their marriage) which periodically led to his receiving treatment in hospital. However, he worked as a farmer for most of their married life. When the patient was 39, her husband developed pulmonary tuberculosis which progressed gradually over the next ten years, and for three years prior to her admission to state hospital her husband had been in a TB sanitarium constantly. She had remained with her two sons who were working the farm.

Her elder son described his mother as overly conscientious, a meticulous housekeeper who hated dirt and disorder, whose chief interests were her home and her church. She attended the latter regularly but lacked other recreations. She was fairly good-natured but nervous and always found something to worry about. For as long as he could remember she had episodes when she felt low in spirits for a few days at a time, but had never previously had any major episode of depression. He felt she had always worked too hard and on the morning of her admission to hospital she was up at 6:00 o'clock to cook breakfast for her sons.

On her arrival at the hospital her lips were dry and cracked and it was evident that she had been taking insufficient fluids so that she was given some intravenously. During the next few days she remained completely careless of her appearance. Her hair and clothing were always untidy and she used no cosmetics. At times she would pace about restlessly, but much of the time she sat motionless in an attitude of dejection. Her facial expression was one of constant misery and she would periodically moan out loud. From time to time she would wring her hands, pull her fingers, examine her nails, and pick and scratch at her clothing. At first she made no spontaneous remarks, and frequently failed to respond to questions. When asked for information about herself and her family, she repeatedly stated, "I don't know." At the time of her admission she appeared to be disoriented as to time, place, and person, and to have gross impairment of memory for recent and remote events. When unable to answer some of these questions, she remarked, "Something went wrong with my head. I don't seem to remember at all. I can't tell you that. There is something wrong with my head. I don't remember." However, within a few days her state of confusion disappeared and she answered questions relevantly and appropriately. Her sole preoccupation at this time remained the welfare of her two sons, and her desire to get her brother to help them since she believed they were in financial difficulty on the farm. At this time she stated, "I just realized what I have done. I have done something I shouldn't have done. I have caused the boys to lose the place on account of my worrying. I guess it's too late to do anything about it now." She felt that disaster had occurred and that she was the sole cause of this. She expressed ideas of self-accusation and worthlessness, and felt that the future was completely bleak and hopeless, although she denied any thoughts of committing suicide.

A week after her admission she started a course of electroshock treatments, and there was marked improvement in mood and activity level but she relapsed soon after the treatments were discontinued, and received a further course of treatment. On this occasion her response was more lasting. Three months after her admission she returned home to live with her family and follow-up interviews during the next two years indicated a more satisfactory adjustment than hitherto.

AFFECTIVE DISORDERS ASSOCIATED WITH OTHER SYNDROMES

Neurotic depressive reactions were discussed and illustrated in Chapter 15, but they are often considered as forms of affective disorder. They usually occur in individuals with a history of previous neurotic symptoms or personality characteristics, are precipitated by emotional stress or deprivation, and are intermediate in severity between normal grief reactions and psychotic depressive reactions. The A.P.A. diagnostic manual suggests that differentiation from psychotic depressive reactions be based on the following:

(1) life history of patient, with special reference to mood swings (suggestive of psychotic reactions), to the personality structure (neurotic or cyclothymic) and to precipitating environmental factors; and (2) absence of malignant symptoms (hypochondriacal preoccupation, agitation, delusions, particularly somatic, hallucinations, severe guilt feelings, intractable insomnia, suicidal ruminations, severe psychomotor retardation, profound retardation of thought, stupor).

It has been pointed out that psychiatric diagnoses are not mutually exclusive, and that the same person may develop signs of two or more diagnostic syndromes, either consecutively or concurrently. Moderate deviations in mood (particularly depression) are quite frequent, and may be associated with paranoid or schizophrenic reactions, sociopathic personality, alcoholism, or any of the other syndromes that we shall be considering in subsequent chapters. Organic brain syndromes lead to both primary symptoms of intellectual impairment, and secondary "functional" symptoms due to the release of hitherto latent personality characteristics. Among the latter are tendencies to affective disorders, so that either depression or excitement may occur as a prominent manifestation of an organic brain syndrome.

DYNAMICS, DEVELOPMENT, AND ETIOLOGY

Karl Abraham regarded *ambivalence* as the basic characteristic of the depressed patient, and remarked that the patient is as ambivalent toward himself as he is toward external objects (other persons). He also pointed to a pregenital origin of this ambivalence, associated with enormously increased oral eroticism. In his classic paper on mourning and melancholia, Freud analyzed the self-reproaches of depressed patients, and found them to have meaning if the name of an ambivalently regarded object (i.e., loved and hated person) was substituted for the person's own name. The depressed person may say, "I am bad because I am a liar," when he has reason to say "X is bad because he is a liar," or, more specifically, "I am angry with X because he has lied to me." This *introjection* of the ambivalently loved object has been considered the opposite of the defense mechanism of projection, and the most characteristic mechanism observed in depression. However, depression also involves subjugation of the ego by a dominant and punitive (sadistic) superego. The difference between a neurotic and a psychotic depression has been regarded as reflecting the depth of narcissistic regression, involving the withdrawal of libido from relationships with external objects.

Rado interpreted the self-reproaches of the depressed person as an ambivalent ingratiation of the external love-object and of the individual's own superego. He also explained the periodic alternation of manic and depressive episodes as a special case of the general periodicity of transgression and expiation, which he viewed as ultimately related to the fundamental biological periodicity of hunger and satiety in the infant. In subsequent papers he developed an adaptational theory of depression which he summarized as follows:

The depressive spell is a mood-cyclic disorder. We interpret it as a particular form of emergency dyscontrol. The patient has suffered a severe loss or, in any case, behaves as if he has suffered one. His emotional reaction to this actual or presumed emergency is overwhelming and threatens to destroy his capacity for adaptive control. At first he is torn between coercive rage and guilty fear, which drive him in opposite directions. Then his mounting guilty fear gains the upper hand. It splits his defeated coercive rage into two unequal parts that undergo different vicissitudes. The smaller part—the stubborn core—is forced underground. There it remains what it was, coercive rage directed against the environment. The larger part of defeated rage escapes repression because its flexibility permits its assimilation to the now prevailing pattern of guilty fear. This portion of defeated rage is turned against the patient himself and is vented in remorseful bouts of self-reproach. Though such self-punishment from retroflexed rage is excruciatingly painful, the patient's remorse is but a facade. Beneath this facade he has utmost contempt for himself because of his inability to live up to his expectations. Bitter with wounded pride, he thus punishes himself—not in contrition—but for his failure to gain his coercive ends. This deeply hidden meaning of self-punishment from retroflexed rage makes mockery of the patient's remorse and reveals the real root of his sense of unworthiness.

Lewin and other analysts have interpreted manic excitement as a defense against depression through the denial of loss and frustration and the use of reality as distraction in the constant pursuit of fleeting object-relationships. Similarly, Rado remarked "Elation is for the organism a calamitous way of cutting short the agony of depression. We attribute it to an automatic process of miscarried repair work." Such dynamic interpretations are, however, descriptive of repair mechanisms rather than etiologic, and we shall now review some of the findings regarding the role of heredity, other biological factors, psychological experience, and sociocultural determinants in the development of affective disorders.

HEREDITARY FACTORS

Several series of *twins with manic-depressive psychoses* have been studied and the results are summarized in Table 17-1. It may be seen that estimates of concordance rates among monozygotic cotwins

TABLE 17–1. Estimated Concordance Rates in Monozygotic and Dizygotic Cotwins of Manic-depressive Twins†

INVESTIGATOR	APPARENT ZYGOSITY OF TWINS	NUMBER OF PAIRS	ESTIMATED CONCORDANCE RATE (PER CENT)	HERITABILITY $H = \dfrac{CMZ - CDZ}{100 - CDZ}$
Rosanoff et al., 1935	MZ	23	70	0.64
	DZ	67	16	
Luxenburger, 1942 (cited by Gedda, 1951)	MZ	56	84	0.81
	DZ	83	15	
Kallmann, 1953	MZ	27	100°	1.00
	DZ	58	26°	
Slater, 1953	MZ	8	57°	0.39
	DZ	30	29°	
Da Fonseca, 1959	MZ	21	75	0.60
	DZ	39	38	

*Corrected for age.

†Modified after Shields, J., and Slater, E. 1960. Heredity and psychological abnormality. In *Handbook of Abnormal Psychology*, ed. H. J. Eysenck. London, Pitman Medical Publishing Company, Ltd., p. 326.

has varied between 57 and 100 percent while estimates of concordance rates among dizygotic cotwins has varied between 15 and 31 percent. When Holzinger's index of "heritability" is computed from these figures (as shown in the extreme right hand column of the table) the significance of heredity in determining predisposition to manic-depressive psychoses is estimated as somewhere between 39 percent (Slater's data) and 100 percent (Kallmann's data). Apart from the enormous variation in these results, which may be related in part to the relatively small numbers of twins involved, there are important methodological reasons to doubt the validity of such twin studies as have been conducted hitherto (as previously discussed in Chapter 5).

Twin studies can give no information concerning possible mechanisms of hereditary transmission, but the latter may be inferred from the observed frequency of manic-depressive psychoses among different classes of relatives of patients with this diagnosis. A number of such estimates are shown in Table 17-2, and

here again a marked variation should be noted. In spite of this, some workers have confidently hypothesized that predisposition to manic-depressive psychosis is transmitted from parent to child by a single dominant gene with irregular frequencies of manifestation (associated with a relatively low penetrance and/or expressivity). It may be recalled that rare disorders due to a single dominant gene (with 100 percent frequency of manifestation) would result in frequencies of 50

TABLE 17–2. Expectancy (Percent) of Manic-Depressive Disorders Among Relatives of Manic-Depressive Probands†

INVESTIGATOR	PARENTS	SIBS	CHILDREN
Banse, 1929	10.8	18.1	
Röll and Entres, 1936	13.0		10.7
Slater, 1938	15.5		15.2
Strömgren, 1938	7.5	10.7	
Sjögren, 1948	7.0	3.6	
Kallmann, 1950	23.4	23.0	
		26.3°	
Stenstedt, 1952	7.4	12.3	9.4

°Dizygotic twins.

†Modified after Shields, J., and Slater, E. 1960. Heredity and psychological abnormality. In *Handbook of Abnormal Psychology*, ed. H. J. Eysenck. London, Pitman Medical Publishing Company, Ltd., p. 306.

percent among siblings, parents, and children. Moreover, even with reduced rates of manifestation, the frequency of the disorder should at least be the same in siblings, parents, and children if it is in any way attributable to a single dominant gene.

Burch reëxamined mental hospital first-admission rates for manic-depressive psychoses, and found certain features resembling comparable statistical data for diseases that are widely believed to have an autoimmune etiology. From these data he postulated that predisposition to manic-depressive psychosis is confined to individuals of a subpopulation characterized by a particular genotype, for which he suggested the following specific genetic requirements: one dominant allele at an X-linked locus, and one dominant allele at an autosomal locus. He maintained that phenotypic initiation of the disease then depends upon the accumulation in a carrier of three specific random events.

This and other similar hypothetical constructs must be regarded as extremely speculative. Most competent and conservative geneticists consider that whatever genetic predisposition is required for the development of manic-depressive psychoses is likely to consist of several different major genes ("genetic heterogeneity") or the cumulative effects of multiple minor genes ("polygenic transmission"). The relatively higher frequency of affective disorders in females than in males, and the associations of manic-depressive reactions with endomorphic (pyknic) body build, and with a tendency toward high blood pressure and heart disease, are all consistent with the latter type of genetic hypothesis.

There is little direct evidence of genetic predisposition to other forms of affective disorder except for Kallmann's data on *involutional psychoses*. He studied 29 pairs of monozygotic twins and 67 pairs of dizygotic twins, at least one of whom was suffering from an involutional psychotic reaction. He reported a concordance rate among monozygotic cotwins of 61 percent and among dizygotic cotwins of six percent, from which Holzinger's index suggests a heritable component of about 59 percent. He also reported that about six percent of the parents and six percent of the siblings of affected individuals suffered from involutional psychoses. Less than one percent of their parents and siblings, however, suffered from manic-depressive psychoses whereas over four percent of parents and siblings suffered from schizophrenia. He therefore concluded that involutional psychoses were genetically related to schizophrenia and in fact their sufferers represented some of the heterozygous carriers of the recessive gene that he considered responsible for schizophrenia. In our present state of knowledge, however, this must be regarded as speculation, as must the more complex genetic hypothesis proposed by Burch for the etiology of involutional psychoses.

In spite of the difficulties in establishing any specific genetic mechanism, the twin and family data constitute strong evidence of some form of hereditary predisposition in affective disorders. In some of these studies, the concordance rates in cotwins and the observed frequencies in siblings and parents are higher than the corresponding frequencies for similar twin and family studies of schizophrenia. These findings have frequently been interpreted as indicating that the evidence for hereditary predisposition to manic-depressive reactions is stronger than the evidence for hereditary predisposition toward schizophrenia or any other "functional" psychosis, neurosis, or personality disorder. However, the numbers of manic-depressive twins and other index cases involved in these investigations are smaller, and the ascertainment of similar disorders in various classes of relatives probably less complete than in the case of similar studies of schizophrenia. Clinical diagnostic criteria are also uncertain, and there is greater variability in the recorded frequencies of manic-depressive psychosis among the various classes of relatives than in the case of similar investigations of schizophrenia.

SOMATIC FACTORS

A great variety of bodily dysfunctions may act as *precipitating stresses* leading to the development of an affective disorder. The expression "seeing things through jaundiced eyes" implies that jaundice is usually accompanied by depression. However, while jaundice involves some degree of intoxication throughout the whole body, many localized conditions may also lead to affective disturbances. A study of suicide was mentioned earlier in which five out of 134 persons were found to have been suffering from terminal medical illnesses unaccompanied by any known psychiatric disorders. However, instead of depression and suicide, bodily illness may also result in a paradoxical reaction of euphoria, and the onset of manic attacks may occur shortly after the sudden onset of blindness or discovery of cancer.

The mechanism by which such bodily dysfunctions precipitate affective disorders may be either primarily biological or primarily psychological. Theoretically at least, the affective disorder may result directly from either the disturbed body physiology or alternatively from the emotional impact of loss of health and earning power or anticipated death and separation from loved ones. In practice, it appears that psychological stress is nearly always the more significant factor, and the only primarily biological precipitating events that have been definitely incriminated appear to be the administration of excessive doses of certain hormones (cortisone and adrenocorticotrophic hormone [or ACTH] from the pituitary gland), and possibly certain sedative and tranquilizing drugs. A fascinating account of a manic episode precipitated by cortisone was written by Berton Roueché under the title "Ten Feet Tall." However, none of these agents invariably produces an affective disorder, so that probably individual vulnerability or predisposition is of greater significance in etiology.

Attempts to establish the existence of some form of constitutional predisposition to affective disorder date back more than 2000 years. Burton's *Anatomy of Melancholy* contained a reference to Hippocrates finding Democritus dissecting various animals in the hope of finding evidence of the bile that he assumed responsible for his own melancholy temperament. However, it appears that no consistent bodily correlates were established until Kretschmer found an association between manic-depressive psychoses and pyknic (endomorphic) body build. The strength of this association dwindled with subsequent work that was controlled for the greater average age of manic-depressive than of schizophrenic patients. Nevertheless, there does appear to be a somewhat greater vulnerability to affective disorders among those of endomorphic physique, and among females than among males. The causal significance of these associations, however, is not at all clear.

The dearth of consistent biochemical findings in affective disorders is evident in the volumes edited by Bellak, and by Hoch and Zubin, as well as in the subsequent literature. It has been remarked that the biological work on manic-depressive psychosis is comparable with that on schizophrenia, in that the range of whatever somatic function one examines is considerably wider than that found in normal control groups.

A variety of physiological correlates of affective disorder has been reported. Thus, Funkenstein claimed that depression was associated with excessive secretion of epinephrine, in contrast with an association between externally directed anger and the secretion of norepinephrine. Shagass reported changes in the electroencephalogram of depressed persons following intermittent photic (light) stimulation, and also following the administration of an intravenous sedative drug. Kaplan presented evidence that the normal regulation of vision by means of the autonomic nervous system was impaired in patients with depression. However, the consistency and significance of these and similar findings remains to be clarified.

PSYCHOLOGICAL FACTORS

Bellak cited Abraham as postulating five factors basic to melancholy: (1) a constitutional tendency to oral eroticism, (2) a fixation of libido at the oral-aggressive level, (3) successive disappointments in love objects (that is, repeated narcissistic trauma), (4) severe disappointment in the mother before the resolution of the Oedipus complex, (5) a repetition of this disappointment later in life, leading to the immediate onset of melancholy. There has since been considerable theoretical speculation and empirical investigation concerning the roles of psychological precipitating factors and predisposition.

Travis studied 70 patients with manic-depressive psychoses and found that the precipitating factors fell into seven main categories: (1) marital maladjustment, (2) death in the family, (3) childbirth, (4) physical condition, (5) economic stress, (6) antagonism toward parents, (7) sickness in the family. In a more recent study, Bruhn compared the histories of 91 persons attempting suicide with those of 91 nonsuicidal psychiatric outpatients. Even when comparisons were restricted to persons in both groups who had lost one or both parents prior to the age of 15 years, the following precipitating factors were found to be more prevalent among those who had attempted suicide than among the psychiatric outpatients: (1) absence or death of a family member in the preceding year, (2) unemployment of the breadwinner in the family, (3) greater residential mobility, and (4) a greater degree of marital disharmony.

In an important paper on childhood mourning and its implications for psychiatry, Bowlby pointed out that a number of workers have sought to relate together psychiatric illness, loss of a loved object, pathological mourning, and childhood experience. He cited Abraham as concluding that "in the last resort melancholic depression is derived from disagreeable experiences in the childhood of the patient." Bowlby emphasized the adverse effects of loss of mother during the period between about six months and six years of age. However, retrospective statistical studies of the frequency of parental loss during the childhood of persons developing various psychiatric disorders invariably show a high *absolute* frequency of loss of father (by death or separation) than of mother, as is the case in the comparable general population. The present author found that loss of the parent of the same sex during childhood is followed by an increased frequency of delinquency but not necessarily by an increased vulnerability to depression or other forms of psychopathology.

In a paper on depression and childhood bereavement, Brown presented statistical evidence that loss by death, both of father and of mother, was much more frequent during the childhood of a large series of depressed patients than of either of two control populations (a census population, and a group of patients attending nearby general medical practitioners). Forty-one percent of depressive patients had lost either parent before the age of 15 as compared with 16.6 percent of the census population and 19.6 percent of patients attending general medical practitioners. The increased loss of mothers occurred fairly evenly throughout each five year period of childhood, whereas the increased frequency of loss of fathers was particularly noticeable during later childhood.

Brown recognized that childhood bereavement is not always followed by depressive illness, and that depressive illness may also occur in the absence of bereavement. However, in a subsequent paper, Brown et al. stated, "Our hypothesis is that a child can be sensitized by situations of loss of love and emotional deprivation so that he breaks down in various ways in later life when faced with subsequent situations of loss and rejection. It can be compared with an anaphylactic reaction or a kind of delayed conditioned reflex of the emotions."

The comparative historical data concerning persons attempting suicide and nonsuicidal psychiatric outpatients presented by Bruhn provides some confirmation, both of an increased frequency of parental deprivation during the childhood of those attempting suicide, and also of increased vulnerability of these deprived persons to subsequent loss. Thus, 42 percent of those attempting suicide had lost one or both parents prior to the age of 15 years, as compared with 25 percent of nonsuicidal psychiatric outpatients (p < 0.02). The precipitating factor of prolonged absence or death in the family during the preceding year was found among 66 percent of the attempted suicides from broken homes, as contrasted with 22 percent of nonsuicidal psychiatric outpatients from broken homes (p < 0.001), or as contrasted with 42 percent of those attempted suicides who had not come from broken homes (p < 0.05). These data are suggestive that the repetition of a traumatic experience similar to that experienced in earlier childhood may have contributed to the suicide attempt.

Beck and his associates administered an inventory designed to measure depression to a group of 297 psychiatric patients, and found a significantly higher frequency of orphanhood among the 100 patients scoring highest on the depression inventory than among the 100 patients scoring lowest. Although this finding was partly related to age, analysis of variance indicated that orphanhood was probably a more significant determinant.

Further evidence of relationships between childhood death of parents and adult depression comes from a controlled study by Dennehy. In a series of 1020 consecutive psychiatric admissions (under the age of 60) to three hospitals serving areas of London, there were 111 males and 250 females with depressive diagnoses. Among the latter, she found

an excess of *male* depressives who had lost their *mother* and an excess of *female* depressives who had lost their *father* prior to the age of 15 years. While some excess of parental loss was observed prior to the age of ten years, it was most marked and statistically significant for depressive patients of both sexes between the ages of ten and 15 years.

In the preceding chapter, reference was made to a large scale epidemiological study by Paffenbarger et al. involving a search for precursors of mortality from coronary heart disease. These authors had access to extensive data concerning more than 40,000 former students of the University of Pennsylvania and of Harvard University, relating physical, social, and psychological information recorded during college years (1921–1950) to later health status. As part of the study, Paffenbarger and Asnes identified the records of 225 *male* subjects who subsequently committed suicide, and matched each of these with two controlled subjects known to be still alive, and randomly chosen from the same school and case-taking year. Several contrasting features of their family background at the time of college case-taking are of interest, and are shown in Table 17-3.

Among the suicides, a higher proportion of both mother and father had attended college, and father's occupation was more frequently professional than among the controls. More of these male suicides had lost their father by death during childhood, and their parents had more frequently separated than had those of the controls. Among the data *not* presented in this table may be mentioned findings that the suicides had more often attended secondary boarding schools; that they had more frequently reported insomnia, social isolation, anxiety, and depression; and that they had more frequently failed to graduate from college than had the control population. Apart from the high frequency of paternal death and parental separation, therefore, the suicides appeared to come from families of higher

TABLE 17-3. Family Background at Time of College Case-Taking†

Item	Suicides		Controls		P
	Ratio*	%	Ratio*	%	
Parental education					
Father, college	124/166	74.7	192/325	59.1	<0.01
Mother, college	52/123	42.3	75/245	30.6	0.03
Father's occupation					
Professional	93/164	56.7	130/325	40.0 ⎫	
Managerial	38/164	23.2	93/325	28.6 ⎬	<0.01
Other	33/164	20.1	102/325	31.4 ⎭	
Parents separated	24/141	17.0	31/297	10.4	0.05
Parental morbidity					
Father, poor health	19/181	10.5	24/382	6.3	0.08
Mother, poor health	24/176	13.6	39/387	10.1	0.21
Parental mortality					
Father dead	32/224	14.3	30/447	6.7	<0.01
Mother dead	16/222	7.2	32/442	7.2	0.99
Parents separated or father ill or dead	55/160	34.4	69/316	21.8	<0.01

*Numerator equals number with item; denominator equals number at risk.
†From Paffenbarger, R. S., Jr., and Asnes, D. P. 1966. Chronic disease in former college students. III. Precursors of suicide in early and middle life. American Journal of Public Health 56, 1026–1036.

socioeconomic status which placed a higher premium on achievement, which they themselves, however, failed to attain.

An increased frequency of parental deprivation during childhood is not specific to the affective disorders, but has also been reported in a number of other forms of psychopathology. Moreover, among persons developing affective disorders, situations involving loss are not the only type of predisposing or precipitating factors found. Thus, affective disorders may also be precipitated by situations involving the threat of future danger of disaster (which ordinarily provokes the primary affective response of fear) and by situations involving frustration (which ordinarily provokes the primary response of anger). Among the other nonspecific factors predisposing to the development of affective disorders may be included anything leading to the development of an unduly strict and dominant superego, such as religious doctrine and parental discipline de-signed to produce excessive guilt. Thus, Greenfield's findings regarding an increased frequency of indirect or psychological forms of childhood discipline may be expected to apply to patients with affective disorders as well as with other psychiatric syndromes. The same applies to Hollender's formulations on perfectionism and Leveton's analysis of reproach (the art of shamesmanship).

Fromm-Reichmann and her associates searched for specific factors in the family background and early life experience of manic-depressive patients, and their findings were elaborated by Gibson. It was postulated that families of manic-depressive patients were set apart in some way from their environment and that they attempted to counteract this situation in two major ways. First, the families had placed a high premium on conforming to the expectations of the community. Second, they had made a prodigious effort to raise the economic level of the family. This led to a situation in which the status of the family was of primary importance, while each member was important only in terms of the contribution he could make to the family. Children in these families were used as instruments for achieving prestige. This need for winning prestige was frequently inculcated by the mother, who was usually the dominant parent and was regarded as strong and reliable. By contrast the fathers were thought of as weak but lovable. The patient often occupied a special position in the family which subjected him to the envy of other siblings and of the parents, but neither the patient nor the parents were usually aware of this envy. Gibson attempted to compare such developmental factors for two series of manic-depressives and one series of schizophrenic patients, but there is a strong element of selective bias in his findings which may be illustrated by the fact that only 27 out of 120 manic-depressive patients in one series were found acceptable for intensive study. Further investigations will need to compare findings for specific patient populations with those for control groups of normal individuals, and to attempt to avoid systematic bias in the selection of all samples. Meanwhile, our empirical impressions of development, which still require validation, include the following.

The interpersonal relationships of early childhood (particularly with parents and siblings) *do not appear to be disturbed in any consistent fashion*, but may be characterized by various patterns of parental deprivation or domination. In some instances there may have been a warm and satisfactory relationship with both parents that was interrupted and changed by death (less commonly desertion) of a parent, usually the father. In other cases the father might be absent from the home much of the time on account of involvement in heavy business responsibilities or commitments. In others, the father might be home much of the time but ineffectual and distant (although this appears much less frequently than in the background of schizophrenic patients), or alternatively be periodically incapacitated and inaccessible owing to episodes of depression. There are many cases in which relationships with either or both parents show marked fluctuation from time to time, in association with marked mood swings of one or the other parent (sometimes associated with one or more admissions to a mental hospital). On the whole, however, the relationships with mother appear to be fairly continuous and characterized by domination, excessive protection, demands, and control. Conformity on the part of the child may be insured by a variety of means, particularly threats, pleas, punishment, and withdrawal of affection.

Patients developing different types of affective disorders may give very different histories regarding their degree of social participation (or introversion versus extroversion) during childhood. Typically, the manic-depressive patient is reported to have been active and outgoing or extroverted; the patient with involutional melancholia is said to have been shy, withdrawn, and introverted; the patient with a neurotic depressive reaction is characterized as having been anxious, tense, and inhibited. These portraits, however, are not consistent; and it is interesting to note that Kohn and Clausen found as high a proportion of manic-depressives as of schizophrenics had been socially isolated or partially isolated at age 13 to 14 years. In both these diagnostic groups the proportion of isolates exceeded those of a normal control group, but amounted to only one-third of all the patients studied.

Within wide limits of activity level and social participation, then, the adjustment of these children at school (both academic and athletic) may usually be described as conscientious, conforming, and competitive. Their inherent intellectual ability varies considerably, however, and so does their achievement level in school and in their subsequent occupational, residential, and economic status. The activity and fortunes of the manic-depressive patient may vary greatly from time to time according to his mood, whereas the status and achievements of patients with other affective disorders remain more constant. Patients are often able to maintain a good relationship with a single employer over a long period of time, except where severe or prolonged symptoms of affective disorder disrupt this relationship. Similarly, most of these patients are able to maintain or even gradually improve their social and economic status over the years. They are often active in religious and other social organizations. They do not usually have records with police or other social agencies, except sometimes in connection with symptoms of their affective disorder.

Individuals prone to develop manic-depressive psychosis are often able to establish fairly mature relationships with adult members of the opposite sex, and may present no overt problems in their sexual adjustment prior to the onset of clinical symptoms. However, sexual interests and activity are closely related to mood; and during episodes of depression the patient will show disinclination for sexual relations, whereas the euphoric patient will tend to show increased sexual drive with lack of inhibition and sometimes promiscuity. After remission of the hypomanic episode, the patient may experience considerable guilt and remorse for sexual behavior during the period of euphoria. During hypomanic episodes, however, impulsive decisions may be made regarding marriage or divorce, or alternatively the spouse may initiate divorce proceedings on account of the patient's extramarital relationships or other hypomanic behavior. It therefore follows that there is some increase of marital instability among patients subject to hypomanic episodes, but not infrequently the family learns to recognize and accept the temporary episodes of abnormality without conscious deliberate retaliation. Nevertheless, in a number of these latter cases latent hostilities receive indirect expression, and marital discord may contribute toward a perpetuation of the manic-depressive symptomatology. Individuals who develop involutional or neurotic depressive reactions are more likely to have a history of stable but restricted and inhibited sexual relationships, and there appears to be some selection against marriage of these persons.

The characteristic prepsychotic personality of the manic-depressive patient is described as being "cyclothymic." The A.P.A. diagnostic manual states that "such individuals are characterized by an extrotensive and outgoing adjustment to life situations, an apparent personal warmth, friendliness and superficial generosity, an emotional reaching out to the environment, and a ready enthusiasm for competition. Characteristic are frequently alternating moods of elation and sadness, stimulated apparently by internal factors rather than by external events." While this generally is regarded as the typical picture, it has been mentioned earlier that patients with a diagnosis of manic-depressive psychosis have also been found to give a history of social isolation during adolescence more often than a control group of normal subjects. Patients with a diagnosis of involutional melancholia are commonly characterized as having compulsive personalities with excessive or obsessive concern over adherence to standards of conscience, conformity, and cleanliness. Patients with a diagnosis of neurotic depressive reaction are usually described as having been overinhibited, overconscientious, and prone to episodes of anxiety or other overt neurotic symptoms.

SOCIOCULTURAL FACTORS

It is generally agreed that suicide is less frequent among primitive tribes than among civilized communities. However, there are no reliable statistics among the former, and it should also be recognized that the self-induced death of a person may result indirectly from behavior that would not ordinarily be considered suicidal. A native who runs amok and starts attacking or killing other members of his tribe is in effect committing suicide since he knows that the inevitable consequence of such behavior is death at the hands of the majority. Nevertheless, outwardly turned aggression is the direct manifestation of his behavior and inwardly turned aggression only the indirect consequence.

In our own society, suicide rates have shown a great deal of consistency over the past half century, although there have been temporary increases in times of economic distress with high unemployment, and temporary decreases during war time with high employment and approval of externally directed aggression against the enemy. An inverse relationship between suicide and homicide may be observed, not only with respect to war time versus peace time, but also as between male versus female, the old versus young, white versus nonwhite, and those of superior versus those of inferior socioeconomic status. The frequency of suicide in the United States during a given year, according to age, sex, and race, is show in Table 17-4. The figures indicate higher frequencies in male than female, in the old than in the young, and in the white than in the nonwhite population. The rates of successful suicides in males increase progressively throughout the life, whereas in females they reach a peak during the involutional period (ages 45 to 65) and subsequently decline. The act of homicide (*not* death from homicide) is *relatively* even more characteristic of the male, the young adult, and those of lower socioeconomic status.

In an open society, there is a strong positive correlation between intelligence and socioeconomic status, and the frequency of suicide also appears to be higher among those of superior intelligence. In their 35 years' follow-up study of intellectually superior California school children, Terman and Oden found that by a median age of 44 years suicide among the gifted women had already passed the corresponding expectation of suicide in the general population, whereas the suicide rate among the gifted men had reached two-thirds of the lifetime expectation of suicide

TABLE 17–4. Age-Sex-Race-Specific Rates of Death by Suicide, United States, 1963*

AGE IN YEARS	WHITE MALE	WHITE FEMALE	NONWHITE MALE	NONWHITE FEMALE
Under 5 years	—	—	—	—
5–9	0.0	—	0.1	—
10–14	1.0	0.2	0.6	0.3
15–19	6.4	1.9	3.7	2.0
20–24	12.9	4.6	12.5	3.2
25–29	16.1	6.6	14.2	4.4
30–34	17.7	8.4	17.6	5.5
35–39	22.2	10.9	16.6	4.5
40–44	25.0	10.9	13.1	3.4
45–49	29.4	12.3	11.7	2.5
50–54	37.0	13.6	15.8	3.0
55–59	41.4	12.3	13.8	2.5
60–64	38.7	10.9	11.3	2.1
65–69	37.8	10.0	16.6	5.2
70–74	43.4	8.9	20.0	4.8
75–79	50.9	8.3	21.6	1.6
80–84	56.0	6.8	14.3	1.4
85 years and over	59.5	5.1	12.1	4.4

*Death rates per 100,000 living general population.

Data from U.S. Department of Health, Education, and Welfare. Vital Statistics of the United States, 1963, Volume II – Mortality.

among the corresponding general population (with the years of the highest suicide rates still ahead of them).

Frequencies of diagnosed affective disorders among different groups of the population are less readily determined and probably much less reliable than differences between rates of suicide. However, Faris and Dunham found certain characteristic patterns of first admission rates of public mental hospitals from the city of Chicago. The frequencies of admission for manic-depressive psychoses were randomly distributed throughout the city, in contrast with those for schizophrenia which showed an increasing gradient from the residential suburbs to the central areas of disorganized dwellings. Subsequent studies suggested that the frequency of manic-depressive psychoses was positively correlated with socioeconomic status, in direct contrast with the frequency of schizophrenia. However, Hollingshead and Redlich reported a higher frequency of affective *psychoses* among classes IV and V than among the upper three classes, in contrast with depressive *neuroses*, which were more common in the upper three classes than in classes IV and V. In fact, they typified the class I-II neurotic as being dissatisfied with himself, and it has been noted that feelings of depression almost invariably accompany lowered self-esteem.

Crosscultural comparisons of frequency are likely to be even less reliable than those made between different groups in a highly developed society, but one such study is of great potential interest to the causation of affective disorders. Eaton and Weil reported that the Hutterites had a higher frequency of manic-depressive psychoses than nine other cultural groups with whom they were compared. If this did in fact represent a true difference in frequency, it might of course be attributable in differences in hereditary predisposition, but the authors pointed to the Hutterites' extreme emphasis on communal cohesiveness. "There is much stress on religion, duty to God and society, and there is a tendency in their entire thinking to orient members to internalize their aggressive drives. Children and adults alike are taught to look for guilt within themselves rather than in others."

TREATMENT

As in treating other forms of psychopathology, it is appropriate to distinguish between (1) reparative or symptomatic therapy, involving efforts to effect remission of the psychotic episode; and (2) reconstructive therapy, involving more prolonged efforts to improve adaptive capacity and prevent future recurrences. The incapacitating and dangerous nature of severe affective disorder frequently leads to an initial period of treatment in hospital, followed by more prolonged outpatient psychotherapy whenever the latter can be accomplished.

Unfortunately, the patient who is euphoric tends to lack insight and motivation for therapy, and the individual who has been severely depressed may no longer be motivated for therapy once his acute misery has been alleviated. There are other problems in undertaking intensive psychotherapy with patients who are known to be susceptible to psychotic affective disorders. Increased insight or awareness of hitherto unconscious motivation, or of the external reality situation, may of themselves mobilize increased depression. It has been remarked that the psychiatric patient may need his blindness, and may be sufficiently disturbed to undergo marked regression when there is an improvement in his vision and perception of himself and others. Prolonged reconstructive psychotherapy is therefore much more likely to be both practicable and effective in neurotic depressive reactions than in a patient with psychotic affective disorders.

When the amphetamines were first introduced, it was hoped that these stimulants might prove effective in the treatment of depressive syndromes.

Among their unpleasant side effects, however, is a marked tendency to accentuate symptoms of anxiety, anorexia, insomnia, difficulty in concentration, and psychomotor agitation. Even when they produce a temporary elevation of mood, this is frequently followed by a rebound phenomenon involving increased fatigue and depression, during which there may be mobilization of suicidal impulses.

Attempts were made to overcome such unpleasant side effects by combining amphetamines with sedatives, particularly barbiturates, but most psychiatrists have regarded such combinations as almost equally ineffectual and potentially dangerous. Short-acting sedatives alone, (particularly barbiturates) have been found helpful in relieving insomnia and associated symptoms of sleep deprivation. It should be borne in mind, however, that such sedatives have frequently been used by depressed patients in suicidal attempts, and that a number of anxious patients have become addicted through using them for daytime relief of tension.

The major phenothiazine tranquilizing drugs were found most effective in the treatment of manic and schizophrenic reactions, but frequently intensify symptoms of depression (except in schizoaffective reactions). Minor tranquilizers such as meprobamate (Equanil or Miltown) and chlordiazepoxide (Librium) tend to provide symptomatic relief of neurotic anxiety and depression, but are of limited value in psychotic affective disorders, and also carry the same potential hazards as barbiturates (addiction and use for suicidal attempts). The most effective drugs in the symptomatic treatment of psychotic affective disorders are several members of the diverse group of antidepressive agents, which include imipramine (Tofranil), amitriptyline (Elavil) and tranylcypromine (Parnate). The latter agents have been reviewed in Chapter 12, but none of them is consistently effective in relieving psychotic depressive reactions.

Convulsive therapy by means of injected Metrazol was originally introduced in the hope of modifying schizophrenic reactions, but was soon found more effective in the treatment of psychotic depression, particularly involutional melancholia and manic-depressive depression. Within a few years, Metrazol injections were replaced by electroconvulsive therapy, various modifications of which have persisted to the present time. Electroshock is still considered by many psychiatrists to be the most consistently effective single treatment for producing remission in psychotic depression. Although it is now used much less frequently than formerly, electroconvulsive treatment is frequently effective in severe or drug-resistant depressive syndromes, the usual number of treatments being somewhere between six and 12 during a period of two to four weeks. Attempts to prevent or greatly diminish the intensity of recurrent suicidal depression have included long-term medication, maintenance electroshock treatment (once a week to once a month), and psychosurgery. When a patient has been repeatedly and severely incapacitated by symptoms of depression, lobotomy may reduce the intensity of the symptoms, and hence the danger of suicide or need for repeated hospitalization. In recent years, however, lobotomy has rarely been recommended, and antidepressive medication has greatly diminished the widespread use of electroshock treatment.

Symptoms of manic excitement tend to respond less favorably than psychotic depression to electroshock treatments, in that the patient is apt to require a longer course of treatment and to relapse more frequently after its termination. However, the major phenothiazine tranquilizing drugs provided a significant advance in the control and management of increased psychomotor activity, and persistent manic symptoms are now infrequent. Since 1949 there have been a number of reports on the use of lithium to control manic episodes. While recognizing its potential hazards, Wharton and Fieve suggested that lithium may be the treatment of choice for phenothiazine-refractory or phenothiazine-allergic manic patients treated in a research setting.

Both manic and psychotic depression may respond to medication currently available, and it may be anticipated that more effective pharmacological agents will become available 'in the future. Whenever feasible, however, symptomatic therapy should be supplemented by psychosocial therapy directed toward diminishing environmental stress and the patient's vulnerability to react to such stress in a pathological manner.

SELECTED REFERENCES

Abraham, K. 1911. Notes on the psychoanalytic investigation and treatment of manic depressive insanity and allied conditions. In *Selected Papers on Psychoanalysis*, 1949. London, Hogarth Press, pp. 137-156.

American Psychiatric Association. 1952. *Diagnostic and Statistical Manual.* Washington, D.C., American Psychiatric Association.

Arieti, S., ed. 1959. Manic depressive psychosis. In *American Handbook of Psychiatry.* New York, Basic Books, Inc., Vol. 1, ch. 22.

Beck, A.T. 1963. Thinking and depression: I. Idiosyncratic content and cognitive distortions. AMA Archives of General Psychiatry 9, 324-333.

Beck, A. T. 1964. Thinking and depression: II. Theory and therapy. AMA Archives of General Psychiatry 10, 561-571.

Beck, A. T., Sethi, B. B., and Tuthill, R. W. 1963. Childhood bereavement and adult depression. AMA Archives of General Psychiatry 9, 295-302.

Bellak, L. 1952. *Manic-Depressive Psychosis and Allied Conditions.* New York, Grune & Stratton, Inc.

Bigelow, N., 1959, The involutional psychoses. In *American Handbook of Psychiatry*, ed. S. Arieti. New York, Basic Books, Inc., Vol. 1, ch. 26.

Bowlby, J. 1961. Childhood mourning and its implications for psychiatry. American Journal of Psychiatry 118, 481-496.

Brown, F. 1961. Depression and childhood bereavement. Journal of Mental Science 107, 754-777.

Brown, F., Epps, P., and McGlashan, A. 1961. The remote and immediate effects of orphanhood. Proceedings of the Third World Congress of Psychiatry, Montreal, Canada, McGill University Press, Vol. 2, pp. 1316-1319.

Bruhn, J. G. 1962. Broken homes among attempted suicides and psychiatric out-patients: a comparative study. Journal of Mental Science 108, 772-779.

Burch, P. R. J. 1964. Manic depressive psychosis: some new aetiological considerations. British Journal of Psychiatry 110, 808-817.

Burch, P. R. J. 1964. Involutional psychosis: some new aetiological considerations. British Journal of Psychiatry 110, 825-829.

Campbell, J. D. 1953. *Manic-Depressive Disease.* Philadelphia, J. B. Lippincott Co.

Cohen, M. B., Baker, G., Cohen, R. A., Fromm-Reichmann, F., and Weigert, E. V. 1954. An intensive study of twelve cases of manic-depressive psychosis. Psychiatry 17, 103-137.

Dennehy, C. M. 1966. Childhood bereavement and psychiatric illness. British Journal of Psychiatry 112, 1049-1069.

Dublin, L. I. 1963. *Suicide: a Sociological and Statistical Study.* New York, The Ronald Press Co.

Durkheim, E. 1930. *Suicide*, tr. J. A. Spaulding and G. Simpson, 1951. Glencoe, Illinois, The Free Press.

Eaton, J. W., and Weil, R. J. 1955. *Culture and Mental Disorders.* Glencoe, Illinois, The Free Press.

Engel, G. L. 1961. Is grief a disease? Psychosomatic Medicine 23, 18.

Faris, R. E. L., and Dunham, H. W. 1939. *Mental Disorders in Urban Areas*, reprinted 1960. New York, Hafner Publishing Co., Inc.

Fenichel, O. 1945. *The Psychoanalytic Theory of Neurosis.* New York, W. W. Norton & Co., Inc., ch. 17.

Freud, S. 1917. Mourning and melancholia. In *Standard Edition*, 1935. London, Hogarth Press, p. 14.

Funkenstein, D. W. 1954. Psycholophysiologic studies of depression: some experimental work. In *Depression*, ed. P. H. Hoch and J. Zubin. New York, Grune & Stratton, Inc., pp. 183-189.

Gibson, R. W. 1958. The family background and early life experience of the manic-depressive patient. Psychiatry 21, 71-90.

Greenacre, P. 1953. *Affective Disorder.* New York, International Universities Press, Inc.

Greenfield, N. S. 1959. The relationship between recalled forms of childhood discipline and psychopathology. Journal of Consulting Psychology 23, 139-142.

Gregory, I. 1958. Studies of parental deprivation in psychiatric patients. American Journal of Psychiatry 115, 432-442.

Gregory, I., 1966. Retrospective data concerning childhood loss of a parent. I. Actuarial estimates vs. recorded frequencies of orphanhood. AMA Archives of General Psychiatry 15, 354-361.

Gregory, I. 1966. Retrospective data concerning childhood loss of a parent. II. Category of parental loss by decade of birth, diagnosis and MMPI. AMA Archives of General Psychiatry 15, 362-367.

Grinker, R. R., Miller, J., Sabshin, M., Nunn, R., and Nunnally, J. C. 1961. *The Phenomena of Depressions.* New York, Hoeber Medical Division, Harper & Row, Publishers, Inc.

Gutheil, E. 1959. Reactive depressions. In *American Handbook of Psychiatry*, ed. S. Arieti. New York, Basic Books, Inc., Vol. 1. ch. 18.

Hirsh, J. 1959-1960. Suicide (parts 1-4). Mental

Hygiene *43*, 516-524; *44*, 3-10; *44*, 274-280; *44*, 382-388.

Hoch, P. H., and Zubin, J., eds. 1954. *Depression.* New York, Grune & Stratton, Inc.

Hoff, H. 1959. Indications for electro-shock, Tofranil and psychotherapy in the treatment of depressions. Canadian Psychiatric Association Journal *4*, special supplement, pp. S55-S64.

Hollender, M. H. 1965. Perfectionism. Comprehensive Psychiatry *6*, 94-103.

Hollingshead, A. B., and Redlich, F. C. 1958. *Social Class and Mental Illness.* John Wiley & Sons, Inc., pp. 230-240.

Hopkinson, G. 1964. A genetic study of affective illness in patients over 50. British Journal of Psychiatry *110*, 244-254.

Kallmann, F. J. 1950. The genetics of psychoses. In *Congrès International de Psychiatrie*, Paris, 1950. VI. *Psychiatrie Sociale.* Paris, Hermann and Cie, pp. 1-30.

Kaplan, S. D. 1960. Autonomic visual regulation. Part II, differential spectral centralization to autonomic drugs in depression. In *Explorations in the Physiology of Emotions*, ed. L. J. West and M. Greenblatt. Washington, D.C., American Psychiatric Association, Psychiatric Research Report No. 12, pp. 115-118.

Kline, N.S., et al., eds. 1957. *Research in Affects.* Washington, D.C., American Psychiatric Association, Psychiatric Research Report No. 8.

Kohn, M. S., and Clausen, J. A. 1955. Social isolation and schizophrenia. American Sociological Review *20*, 265-273.

Leveton, A. F. 1962. Reproach: the art of shamesmanship. British Journal of Medical Psychology *35*, 101-111.

Lewin, B. D. 1950. *The Psychoanalysis of Elation.* New York, W. W. Norton & Co., Inc.

Macdonald, J. M. 1964. Suicide and homicide by automobile. American Journal of Psychiatry *121*, 366-370.

McGill University Conference on Depression and Allied States. 1959. Canadian Psychiatric Association Journal *4*, special supplement.

McGill University Research Conference on the Depressive Group of Illnesses. 1966. Canadian Psychiatric Association Journal *11*, special supplement.

Meerloo, J. A. M. 1962. *Suicide and Mass Suicide.* New York, Grune & Stratton, Inc.

Menninger, K. A. 1938. *Man Against Himself.* New York, Harcourt, Brace & World, Inc.

Norris, V. 1959. *Mental Illness in London.* London, Chapman and Hall, Maudsley Monograph No. 6, ch. 10.

Paffenbarger, R. S., and Asnes, D. P. 1966. Chronic disease in former college students. III. Precursors of suicide in early and middle life. American Journal of Public Health *56*, 1026-1036.

Rado, S. 1954. Hedonic control, action-self and the depressive spell. In *Depression*, ed. P. H. Hoch and J. Zubin. New York, Grune & Stratton, Inc., 153-182.

Rado, S. 1961. The automatic motivating system of depressive behavior. Comprehensive Psychiatry *2*, 248-260.

Rennie, T. A. C. 1942. Prognosis in manic-depressive psychoses. American Journal of Psychiatry *98*, 801.

Robins, E., Murphy, G. E., Wilkinson, R. H., Gassner, S., and Kayes, J. 1959. Some clinical considerations in the prevention of suicide based on a study of 134 successful suicides. American Journal of Public Health *49*, 888-899.

Roth, M. 1959. The phenomenology of depressive states. Canadian Psychiatric Association Journal *4*, special supplement, pp. S32-S54.

Roueché, B. 1954. Ten feet tall, reprinted 1958. In *The Incurable Wound.* New York, Berkley Books, G-188, pp. 114-143.

Schneidman, E.S., and Farberow, N.L., eds. 1957. *Clues to Suicide.* New York. McGraw-Hill Book Co., Inc.

Shagass, C. 1957. Neurophysiological studies of anxiety and depression. In *Research in Affects*, ed. N. S. Kline, et al. Washington, D.C., American Psychiatric Association, Psychiatric Research Report No. 8, pp. 100-117.

Shields, J., and Slater, E. 1961. Heredity and psychological abnormality. In *Handbook of Abnormal Psychology*, ed. H. J. Eysenck. New York, Basic Books, Inc., pp. 326 and 328.

Terman, L. M., and Oden, M. H. 1959. *The Gifted Group at Mid-Life.* Stanford, California, Stanford University Press, pp. 30-32.

Travis, J. H. 1933. Precipitating factors in manic depressive psychoses. Psychiatric Quarterly *7*, 411-418.

Weiss, J. M. A. 1966. The suicidal patient. In *The American Handbook of Psychiatry*, ed. S. Arieti. New York, Basic Books, Inc., Vol. 3, ch. 8.

Wharton, R. N., and Fieve, R. R. 1966. The use of lithium in the affective psychoses. American Journal of psychiatry *123*, 706-712.

CHAPTER 18

Schizophrenic Disorders

The term *démence precoce* was introduced in 1860 by the Belgian psychiatrist Morel to describe a severe mental illness occurring in a fourteen-year-old boy, who had previously been a good student but rapidly underwent a deterioration of intellect and personality progressing to dementia. A few years later, Kahlbaum (1863) defined *paranoia* as a well-systematized delusional state without gross disorganization of intellectual processes or behavior, whereas patients showing both prominent delusions and gross disorganization were considered as having *dementia paranoides*. Hecker (1871) applied the term *hebephrenia* to malignant mental illnesses having their onset around the time of puberty, and followed by rapid and lasting personality disorganization (as in the boy reported by Morel). Another form of mental illness in which the patient remained mute and motionless was described by

Kahlbaum (1874) as *catatonia* or "tension insanity."

Emil Kraépelin (1896) used the term *dementia praecox* to include Hecker's hebephrenia, Kahlbaum's catatonia, and the group of dementia paranoides, later also including a fourth category termed *dementia praecox simplex*, that had been proposed by Diem (1903). For Kraepelin, the common denominators of these syndromes were an early onset, and a progression to permanent and irrecoverable dementia. However, the Swiss psychiatrist Eugen Bléuler (1911) pointed out that many such syndromes did *not* involve either early onset or irrecoverable dementia, and he redefined them as *the group of schizophrenias*. The term schizophrenia means literally "splitting of the mind," and it is a popular misconception that this is synonymous with having a "split or multiple personality," whereas the latter is a rare manifestation of hysterical dissociation that has already been reviewed in Chapter 15. In schizophrenia, on the other hand, the "split" or incongruity is between various functions of the mind such as thinking, emotion, and behavior.

Kraepelin distinguished between paranoid dementia praecox and other paranoid psychoses (paranoia and paraphrenia) in which the personality of the individual remained relatively well-integrated, and which did not therefore justify the term dementia. Long-term follow-up studies of his own patients, however, showed that most patients with these other forms of paranoid psychosis did eventually develop symptoms considered characteristic of schizophrenia. Many psychiatrists therefore prefer to regard such paranoid states or conditions as forms of schizophrenia, but the standard nomenclature has still retained the distinction made by Kraepelin. While paranoid schizophrenia will be discussed and illustrated in the present chapter, therefore, certain other aspects of paranoid disorders will also be reviewed in the next chapter.

In the American Psychiatric Association glossary, schizophrenia has been defined as a severe emotional disorder of psychotic depth, characteristically marked by a retreat from reality with delusion formation, hallucinations, emotional disharmony, and regressive behavior. During the present century, different authorities have regarded one particular aspect of the symptomatology as being the most characteristic feature of schizophrenia—either the thought disorder, the shallow or inappropriate emotional response, the impaired capacity for experiencing pleasure ("anhedonia"), the withdrawal from social contact and reality, the regressive behavior, or the frequently poor prognosis.

Jung (1903) remarked that "if a man could walk and talk in his dreams, his total behavior would be in no way different from that of a patient with schizophrenia." The inability to perceive logical relationships, to distinguish between fantasy and reality, or to

separate thought from action has generally been viewed as central to all the varied manifestations of schizophrenia. Eugen Bleuler distinguished between certain symptoms of schizophrenia that he regarded as primary or essential characteristics of the process, and those that he regarded as secondary elaborations present only in certain individuals. His *primary* symptoms consisted of the alterations in thinking and associations, autism (introversive preoccupation with self), and ambivalence. His *secondary* symptoms consisted of the frequently observed delusions, hallucinations, catatonic and hebephrenic features, and regressive phenomena.

Storch (1924) regarded the thinking and behavior of schizophrenic patients as being archaic, and having much in common with that of primitive man, both being apt to think in terms of *concrete* images rather than abstract ideas, and both tending to act directly on the basis of emotion. The same may also be true of normal children, and other authors such as White (1926) interpreted schizophrenic thinking in terms of regression from the abstract reasoning of the adult to the concrete level of the child.

Vigotsky (1934) emphasized the disturbance in logical reasoning that is observed in schizophrenia. In normal logical thinking, a conclusion is true only if the major premise implicitly contains the minor. Given the premises (1) All men are mortal, and (2) Socrates is a man, the logical conclusion follows that (3) Socrates is mortal. In the *paralogical thinking* of schizophrenia, by contrast, false conclusions may be reached from inadequate bases. Thus, given the premises (1) Certain Indians are swift, and (2) Stags are swift, the paralogical conclusion might be that (3) Certain Indians are stags. Vigotsky therefore observed that "The logician accepts identity on the basis of identical subjects (that about which something is said), the paralogician on the basis of identical predicates (that which expresses what is said about the subject)."

Cameron (1938) analyzed the language and thought of disorganized schizophrenics, and characterized their communications as follows: (1) asyndetic—lacking essential connectives, (2) metonymic—lacking precise definitive terms for which approximate but related terms or phrases are substituted, (3) interpretative—having parts of one theme appearing as intrusive fragments, (4) overinclusive—including material only remotely related, (5) noncorresponding—lacking a relationship between what is done and what is said, (6) requiring transformation in the rules of procedure to justify failures, (7) shifting verbal generalizations concerning solutions that were inadequate.

Arieti (1959) interpreted schizophrenia as a form of progressive teleologic (i.e., purposeful) regression in which there is a resurgence of lower levels of mental integration, such as (a) concretization of the abstract, (b) paleologic thinking, and (c) desymbolization. He recognized that there may be a reproduction of all the stages of symbolization and socialization, and that all of these stages may overlap or appear in various proportions which may account for the tremendous diversity in clinical symptoms. We shall now review the major manifestations of abnormality that may be observed.

APPEARANCE AND BEHAVIOR

The appearance and behavior of schizophrenic patients may vary greatly according to the type, phase, or stage of the illness. In early or well-integrated cases there may be very minor deviations in appearance and behavior, but more regressed patients are apt to be described as incongruous, peculiar, bizarre, strange, or unusual. They may be quiet, withdrawn, isolated, and uncommunicative, or, on the other hand, quite active, argumentative, aggressive, or even violent. The *simple* form is often described in such terms as careless, indifferent, disinterested, lacking initiative, apathetic, inactive, shy, quiet, with-

drawn, preoccupied, and socially isolated. The *hebephrenic* form is also apt to involve preoccupation with internal fantasy, but the patient is more active, and appearance and behavior are frequently bizarre. There may be grimacing, mannerisms, strange gestures, silly laughter and giggling, or quick impulsive actions, all without any relation to external stimuli.

In *catatonic stupor* there is marked withdrawal and inactivity that may amount to complete immobility, being associated with either rigid or flexible posturing (in the latter instance known as flexibilitas cerea or waxy flexibility). There may be automatism or stereotyped movements such as rocking the body backward and forward for hours on end. There is commonly negativism, which may include refusal of food and fluids, and impulsive behavior in response to either external or internal stimuli. The pupils of the eyes may show hippus (irregular contraction and dilation) or the eyelids may be tightly closed (frequently fluttering). Although unresponsive to external stimuli, such patients may be acutely aware of what is going on around them, and may be able to report events or conversations some months later. There may be an abrupt change from catatonic stupor into *catatonic excitement* or the latter may commence without any preceding phase of stupor. In the excited phase there is extreme psychomotor hyperactivity and agitation, which is often accompanied by assaultive behavior to others or impulsive self-destructive attempts. Patients in this phase remain negativistic and usually refuse food and fluids. Their behavior is commonly very bizarre and regressed, involving destruction of clothing and bedding, or smearing of excreta, and the like.

Paranoid schizophrenics are less overtly disturbed in appearance and behavior. Because of their delusions, they are often serious, unsmiling, intense, and may have a hostile glaring expression. If engaged in conversation, they may be talkative, argumentative, or aggressive and assaultive. With progressive personality deterioration, however, they often become quiet, withdrawn, apathetic, and indifferent, careless of their appearance and regressive in behavior, and for example may hoard valueless objects or engage in repetitious stereotyped rituals.

Other forms of schizophrenia involve combinations of the preceding varieties, or association of schizophrenic symptomatology with affective, neurotic, or sociopathic symptoms.

SPEECH AND THINKING

Conversation may be completely absent in catatonic stupor, or continually present in catatonic excitement. Other patients who have regressed will carry on spontaneous but unintelligible conversations in response to internal stimuli, and will fail to respond to questions or other external stimuli. Others will fail to initiate conversation, but will respond to questions, while a number of patients will also converse spontaneously. Speech, however, reveals some degree of the characteristic thought disorders present in schizophrenia, which have received some preliminary consideration and will now be elaborated further.

1. *Prelogical, paralogical, paleological, autistic, dereistic, magical, or primary process thinking* is a primitive or regressive type of reasoning that constitutes a basis for other disorders of ideation and speech observed in schizophrenia, such as overinclusive thinking, loose association and fragmentation, condensation and neologism, and delusional formation. Primary process thinking has been defined as the type of mental activity and thought process that is characteristic of unconscious mental life at all times, and which in infancy often characterizes conscious mental life as well. It is marked by the free discharge of psychic energy and excitation without regard to the demands of the environment, reality, or logic. It includes the type of paralogical thinking that has been already defined, and may be illustrated by reference to a patient who was admitted to hospital expressing the delusion that he was God. On exploring the basis for his belief, it turned out that he had been dating the same girl for many years but had never made any sexual advances to her. She had eventually gone out with another man, became pregnant by him, and told the patient. The latter knew that he was not responsible for the pregnancy, and concluded that this must have been an immaculate conception, that his girl was the Virgin Mary and that he was God.

2. *Overinclusive thinking* was defined by Cameron as the inability to preserve conceptual boundaries, as a result of which distantly associated and even irrelevant ideas become regarded as essential parts of a concept. This necessarily makes thought more abstract and less precise, and may lead to the overlapping of mutually exclusive concepts that share some elements in common. Payne reviewed the literature, and provided additional evidence that schizophrenics are significantly more overinclusive than normal adults, neurotics, or depressives. Comparisons with normal children, and patients with organic brain syndromes or mental retardation, however, appear to be lacking.

3. The *loose associations* of schizophrenics make for *irrelevant replies* to questions and *flight of ideas* from one subject to another, in which no logical connection is apparent (in contrast with the flight of ideas found in hypomanic patients). The patient attempts to express vague concepts in stilted language, and loose associations contribute to make conversation *fragmented*, disconnected, and unintelligible. Forms of speech disorder characteristic of advanced schizophrenia include *echolalia,* the automatic repetition of phrases or words; *verbigeration,* stereotyped and seemingly meaningless verbal responses without relevance to the attempt of another person to converse; and *word salad,* a mixture of words or phrases which lack comprehensive meaning or logical coherence. The following is an example given by Cameron (1947) of a

schizophrenic patient's response to the question, *"Why are you in the hospital?":*

I'm a cut donator, donated by double sacrifice. I get two days for every one. That's known as double sacrifice; in other words, standard cut donator. You know, we considered it. He couldn't have anything for the cut, or for these patients. All of them are double sacrifice because it's unlawful for it to be donated any more. (*Well, what do you do here?*) I do what is known as the double criminal treatment. Something that he badly wanted, he gets that, and seven days' criminal protection. That's all he gets, and the rest I do for my friend. (*Who is the other person that gets all this?*) That's the way the asylum cut is donated. (*But who is the other person?*) He's a criminal. He gets so much. He gets twenty years, criminal treatment, would make forty years; and he gets seven days' criminal protection and that makes fourteen days. That's all he gets. (*And what are you?*) What is known as cut donator Christ. None of them couldn't be able to have anything; so it has to be true works or prove true to have anything, too. He gets two days, and that twenty years makes forty years. He loses by causing. He's what is known as a murder. He causes that. He's murder by cause because he causes that. He can't get anything else. A double sacrifice is what is known as where murder turns, turns the friend into a cut donator and that's what makes a daughter-son. (*A daughter-son?*) Effeminate. A turned Christ. The criminal is a birth murder because he makes him a double. He gets two days' work for every day's work. . . .(*What is "a birth murder"?*) A birth murder is a murder that turns a cut donator Christ into a double daughter-son. He's turned effeminate and weak. He makes him a double by making him weak. He gets two days' work for every one day's work because after he's made a double, he gets twice as much as it is. He's considered worth twice that much more. He has to be sacrificed to be a double.*

4. The patient tends to coin *neologisms or new words*, which may be condensed combinations of two or more words, used to expressed personalized meanings not readily understood by others. Some examples of neologisms are contained in the verse from Lewis Carroll's poem "Jabberwocky" cited at the beginning of this chapter.

Carroll's definition of these words (interpreted in the book by Humpty Dumpty) was as follows: *"Brillig"* means four o'clock in the afternoon—the time when you begin broiling things for dinner. *"Slithy"* means lithe and slimy. *"Toves"* are something like badgers, something like lizards and something like corkscrews. *"Gyre"* is to go round and round like a gyroscope. *"Gimble"* is to make holes like a gimlet. *"The wabe"* is the grass plot around a sun-dial, because it goes a long way before it and a long way behind it. *"Mimsy"* is flimsy and miserable. *"Borogrove"* is a thin shabby looking bird with feathers sticking out all around, something like a live mop. *"Rath"* is a sort of green pig. *"Mome"* is short for from home, and *"outgrabing"* is something between bellowing and whistling with a kind of sneeze in the middle.

5. In *concrete or literal thinking* there is inability to make a normal abstract interpretation of commonly understood concepts, as may be illustrated by a very literal interpretation of well known proverbs. This type of thinking is *not* specific to schizophrenia, but may also be found in organic brain syndromes and mental retardation, as well as in normal children. However, the responses of schizophrenics when asked to interpret proverbs may be either concrete, autistic, or overinclusive. The following are a number of responses given by schizophrenic patients to the proverbs indicated:

Q. A stitch in time saves nine.
   A. If you had a tear in your clothing and sewed it up right away, you'd be saving time.
   A. If I would take one stitch ahead of time, I would know nine times better how to do another stitch.
   A. I could do something and it would help everyone else.
Q. A rolling stone gathers no moss.
   A. It won't grow any grass.

---

*Reprinted by permission from Cameron, N. 1947. *The Psychology of Behavior Disorders*. Boston, Houghton Mifflin Co., pp. 466-467.

A. A person could answer that better if they were a stone.

A. The stone keeps rolling endlessly.

Q. *People in glass houses shouldn't throw stones.*

A. Because they'd break the glass.

A. You shouldn't throw stones at people.

A. You shouldn't throw stones through windows—that's what I've been trying to avoid doing.

Q. *When the cat's away, the mice will play.*

A. There's nobody to watch the kittens—I mean the mice.

A. If the father is away, things get harmed, too.

Q. *Still waters run deep.*

A. How deep is the ocean.

Q. *A new broom sweeps clean.*

A. No it doesn't because the bristles are stiff.

Q. *A golden hammer breaks an iron door.*

A. If we'd love the Russians, they'd probably love us back.

Q. *A bird in the hand is worth two in the bush.*

A. If you've got something, hang onto it rather than look for something else.

Q. *Don't count your chickens before they're hatched.*

A. If it looks like something is going to happen to benefit you, don't count on it.

Q. *You catch more flies with honey than vinegar.*

A. Flies are drawn to something sweet; something sour drives them away.

Q. *The tongue is the enemy of the neck.*

A. Just like Patrick Henry said, "Give me liberty or give me death."

Q. *Where there's a will, there's a way.*

A. Faith in God, believing that he lives.

Q. *Rome was not built in a day.*

A. It takes a lot of people, a long time to build a city or a country.

Q. *Barking dogs seldom bite.*

A. It depends on what they are barking for. When they are loose it is all right, but when they are tied up they get mean and will bite.

Q. *A stream cannot rise higher than its source.*

A. As far as your faith in God is, that is as far as you can go.

Q. *Don't swap (trade) horses when crossing a stream.*

A. Don't give up your faith and your ways for people who don't believe, keep going on your own faith.

Q. *The used key is always bright.*

A. But you have no right to it yourself, everybody keeps you locked up.

Q. *Gold goes in at any gate except heaven's.*

A. Gold is really *in* heaven, it's heaven's glories.

Q. *One swallow (bird) doesn't make a summer.*

A. Not one, it's *many* things that make it beautiful, birds and bees, everything. Nothing can be out of order.

Q. *The wife is the key to the house.*

A. She has to see that everything has a place and is in order. And sometimes she has to get mad and blow up, otherwise the husband would keep beating her and beating her and they never would find the ways to heaven's glories.

Q. *Riches serve a wise man but command a fool.*

A. The poor people are the fools, but they are the ones that know the way to heaven's glories; for the King, not for themselves.

Q. *Don't cast pearls before swine (pigs).*

A. Everybody that is greedy you shouldn't trust.

SENSORIUM AND EMOTION

Schizophrenia may occur in persons of either subnormal or superior intelligence, but there is some indication of an increased frequency among those of limited intellectual capacity and socioeconomic status. Regardless of this, it is well established that schizophrenia is frequently accompanied by either sudden or gradual impairment of intellectual function that may be very severe in regressed patients. This "cognitive slippage" is associated with the same impoverished ideation and stereotyped repetition of a few concepts that may also be observed in organic brain syndromes. In many patients with symptoms of schizophrenia, however, intellectual function remains within the average range. Similarly, orientation and memory show no evidence of gross impairment except in patients showing considerable regression.

Hallucinations and illusions are common, and may involve any type of sensation. Most frequently they consist of auditory hallucinations, such as the voices of real or imaginary persons talking to or about the patient, but they may also involve any of the other senses. The patient may see visions, perceive an unusual taste in his food (frequently associated with a belief that someone is trying to poison him), perceive an unusual smell that he may attribute to his own body odor (frequently with sexual significance), or perceive various unusual bodily sensations that may be attributed to electricity or involve the genitals (and be associated with delusions of magical communication or sexual assault).

Delusions are associated with autistic thinking and may be based on hallucinatory experiences. They are characteristic of paranoid schizophrenia but may also be found in other forms, and involve gross distortion of reality. The delusions most commonly found are those of reference, active or passive influence, and persecution or grandeur, but hypochondriacal or somatic delusions are also quite frequent, and delusions of self-accusation, worthlessness, or hopelessness may be found when there is an associated affect of depression.

In regressed patients the emotional tone is bland or neutral and the emotional reaction is either shallow, flat, and inadequate (leading to an overall picture of indifference and apathy) or else frankly inappropriate to the patient's thought content or external reality (such as the giggling or sudden tears of a hebephrenic patient). In paranoid schizophrenia there may be marked chronic hostility associated with the patient's delusions, and in the schizoaffective reactions there may be no evident change from a constant mood of depression.

The incipient or well-integrated schizophrenic frequently has high standards of conscience and morality, although there may sometimes be a history of promiscuous or impulsive acting-out behavior, particularly in catatonic patients. Judgment and insight may also be fairly well preserved in early or mild cases but are grossly impaired in regressed patients or those with marked thought disorder, hallucinations, and delusions.

The four syndromes that Kraepelin included in his unifying concept of dementia praecox have been retained in the American Psychiatric Association classification of schizophrenic reactions. However, the diagnosis of simple and hebephrenic types of schizophrenia has gradually become infrequent, and it is generally considered that these represent advanced chronic forms that may be at least partly prevented by means of early intensive therapy. Catatonic and paranoid forms of schizophrenia are still observed quite frequently, and several additional categories have been diagnosed with increasing frequency — namely acute and chronic undifferentiated schizophrenia, schizoaffective disorders, and childhood and residual varieties.

SIMPLE SCHIZOPHRENIA

Simple schizophrenia is characterized chiefly by reduction in external attachments and interests, and by impoverishment of human relationships. There is a lack of initiative, inactivity, indifference, apathy, and withdrawal from social relationships. It is not usually associated with either hallucinations or delusions. The onset tends to be early and insidious, and the course chronic. In time the patient shows increasing evidence of schizophrenic thinking and impairment of intellectual functions.

An unmarried woman was first admitted to the state hospital at the age of 28 and was accompanied by her mother and sister, who reported that during the previous five years she had gradually become increasingly inactive and withdrawn from social contact. She would do some housework, reading, sewing, and listening to the radio, but she would not do anything the family asked her to do. When they went out, she would usually remain home and would frequently just lie on her bed. During the preceding two years she had become more careless of her appearance and at times wouldn't bother answering questions that were asked her. Sometimes she would appear tense, get red in the face, and bite her arm. At other times the family noticed her talking to herself, both during the daytime and at night.

The patient was the third of four children, having an older brother and sister and brother two years younger than herself. None of the patient's siblings had married by the time of her admission to the hospital. Her father was 44 and her mother 38 at the time she was born. At interview her mother appeared quiet, inactive, and overcontrolled. Her father had worked as a farmer up to five or six years prior to the patient's admission, since when he had been increasingly incapacitated by Parkinson's disease.

Her mother stated that the patient was never strong as a child, did not walk until 17 months, appeared white and pale, and vomited a great deal. She attended school until the age of 16, completing grade ten and subsequently two years of a commercial course. She stayed at home with her mother until the age of 21, went to a nearby town and worked as a stenographer for about 16 months, and then returned home where she remained up to the time of her admission. She was always very quiet, but during her adolescence she was fairly active in girls' club work and was treasurer of the Sunday School. She never had any boy friends and was apparently never asked out on dates.

On arrival in hospital she said, "I really don't know why they sent me here. I know I have a bad heart, but otherwise I don't know." When asked how her heart bothered her, she replied, "Just weakness. I just haven't as much life in me as most people have." She didn't admit to any hallucinations, and when asked to whom she talked when she was alone, she replied, "I guess it's to myself." When asked what sort of things made her angry, she replied, "I guess mother and I don't get along as well as we might. She tells people everything she knows. She can't seem to sit down. She is on the go all the time." While she was in hospital, however, the patient remained completely apathetic and showed no evidence of any strong emotions. There was no impairment of memory or orientation, and her full scale IQ was 110.

She gave only ten responses to the Rorschach test, which suggested strong feelings of insignificance and inferiority. There was little or no change in her condition following phenothiazine medication, electroshock treatments, and insulin coma therapy, but she was able to return home to live with her family upon whom she remained completely dependent.

HEBEPHRENIC SCHIZOPHRENIA

Hebephrenic schizophrenia is characterized by a shallow and inappropriate emotional response, with frequent giggling, hallucinations and transient delusions, bizarre and impulsive behavior. The onset tends to occur during adolescence, and to be followed by rapid and lasting regression.

An 18-year-old girl was admitted to the state hospital with the history that during the preceding year there had been a gradual disintegration of her personality leading to failure in school, disorganization of her thinking and behavior, inappropriate laughing and giggling, and bizarre conversation and behavior.

She was the eldest of four children, having a brother one year younger than herself, a sister three years younger, and a sister 13 years younger than herself. Her mother was already pregnant with the patient at the time of her marriage, but the patient was apparently accepted, and nothing unusual was learned about interpersonal relationships within the family during her early childhood. The patient apparently felt loved and wanted by her parents and was regarded as her father's favorite. When the second World War was declared, her father was called into military service and the family moved to another town. The patient experienced some difficulties in her new school and had to repeat grade two, but following this she had no academic difficulties and obtained good grades up to her final year in high school, when she became sick. In addition to studying hard, she enjoyed social activities and had many friends in school.

When she was 13 years old, however, her father returned from military service, and from this time on he was drinking excessively. One year prior to the patient's admission to hospital, her father attempted to rape the sister who was three years younger than the patient. The attempt was interrupted by the youngest sister and reported by the patient to her mother, who called the police. Father was placed in jail for three weeks and was not allowed to return to live with his family. He went to work in another town, sent money for a few months, but then stopped, so that mother was obliged to go to work as a waitress.

Following the patient's admission to the hospital, her mother reported that her illness had started soon after her father's departure from the household. "She started to worry about a year ago. My husband left, and she began to think about him all the time. She used to talk funny—funny things like she would hear an airplane and stand on the kitchen table looking at the ceiling. She would look out of the kitchen window at children who were playing at school about a mile away and ask if the other children could see her. She would stay away from school and wouldn't help with the housework, but stood outside staring at nothing. At the end of the school year she failed all of her examinations. About a month after this she started throwing clothes about her room and slept with her nightgown up above her head. She would say, 'I don't know whether I am a boy or a girl. Do you think I will ever get married and have a baby?' and she would say to me, 'You are staying young and I am growing old.'" She went to see her father in another town but when she arrived there, he had gone. She started complaining of a cramp in her stomach and began to cry and laugh alternatively. She would fall to the bathroom floor for no apparent reason. She stopped eating and had to be fed with a spoon. When her mother visited her in hospital, she said, "Go on home. You make me worse," and threw things on the floor. She called her mother and aunt obscene names and laughed and cried alternatively.

On arrival in hospital she said, "Things don't work right in my mind the way they should, and I know it definitely. It seems to be lately that whenever I read or write, well that is the whole question, it affects my whole mind. I sort of. . .I don't know what you call it, but when I think of one thing, I don't take it the way I should take it at the time. My mind seems to wander at the time—I don't hit the right target at the right time. I am all someplace else. I feel as if it is crossing and then coming down. . ." and then she waved her finger over her head several times. She failed to respond to any of the treatments that were currently available, and as time went by her contact with reality diminished further, her intellectual functions deteriorated, her emotional response remained inappropriate, and her behavior was impulsive, manneristic, and bizarre.

CATATONIC SCHIZOPHRENIA

Catatonic schizophrenia is characterized by marked disturbances in motor activity which may take the form of either generalized inhibition (retardation, mutism, or stupor) or excessive activity (excitement). Although the disturbances of thinking and affect are typically schizophrenic, the disordered psychomotor activity shows considerable similarity with that observed in manic depressive reactions. Thus, a single catatonic patient may have repeated episodes of stupor without excitement, repeated episodes of excitement without stupor, or may dramatically and unpredictably swing from one extreme of motor activity to the other. In the absence of treatment there may be spontaneous remission, either partial or apparently complete, but catatonic stupor frequently used to be prolonged indefinitely and catatonic excitement used to terminate in death from exhaustion. Tranquilizing drugs and electroshock treatments, however, have played a major part in rendering the prognosis of individual attacks relatively favorable.

Catatonic Stupor. A 19-year-old college student suddenly became acutely confused, delusional, and mute toward the end of the fall quarter of his third year in a highly competitive college situation. He was extremely intelligent, had completed senior high school in only two years, and had obtained a National Merit Scholarship. He was currently attempting to complete the requirements for his bachelor's degree in three years, carrying a heavy load of courses and maintaining an A-minus average. His first episode of acute regression and catatonic stupor developed in the middle of a graduate school entrance examination, which he was unable to complete. The college authorities called his parents who took him home the same day and arranged for his immediate admission to the psychiatric unit of a general hospital in their community.

At first he was completely mute, withdrawn, preoccupied, and showed gross psychomotor retardation, paying no attention to his surroundings and refusing food. He was started immediately on phenothiazine medication, but his behavior persisted throughout the first week after his admission to hospital, and his few responses to questions were irrelevant and largely unintelligible. He was then started on electroshock treatments and received a total of seven treatments during the next two weeks, accompanied by marked improvement in reality contact and activity level. As he became accessible to psychotherapy, he verbalized diffuse delusions of persecution and passive influence, believing that his thoughts and behavior were under the control of other persons. With continuing phenothiazine medication and psychotherapy, however, he rapidly reintegrated, and was able to leave hospital and return to college at the beginning of the winter quarter. Medication was continued in reduced dosage and he remained in psychotherapy throughout the balance of the academic year.

He was the eldest child and only son of a college professor whose name was the same as his own. Father had been absent in military service for the first two and a half years after the patient was born. The boy and his mother had lived with his maternal grandparents, who were overindulgent and undercut the discipline that his mother tried to impose. Long after they had left the home of the grandparents, the patient had been very resentful of the discipline imposed by mother, and had made her feel guilty by saying how much he loved his grandmother and disliked her. Following his return from military service, his father had entered graduate school, and had remained distant and aloof throughout the boy's childhood. As expressed by the patient, "I never did adjust when he came back from overseas. He seems cold and has high standards of behavior. I've never been able to live up to them and satisfy him. He just tells me how he thinks I should act, and expresses disappointment that I'm falling short. He expresses his own beliefs and doesn't tolerate my own ideas." When asked what he liked the most about his father he answered, "The fact that he seems to know what he is doing, and has a good life worked out for himself." When asked what he liked

the least he replied, "The fact that I don't feel very close to him. He seems always to want to be in control and to have his ideas accepted." When asked about his mother, he said that she had always seemed very impatient and was forever bawling him out. He was unable to state anything that he particularly liked about her. In spite of the fact that he had not lived with his grandparents since the age of three, he still regarded them as his "emotional parents," and he always enjoyed visiting them.

His parents had provided little opportunity for social interaction with other children his own age, and he had never participated in athletic activities. After entering college he had started dating, but a few months prior to his breakdown he had become confused by communication he had received from his girl friend's mother, which he had interpreted as license for them to go ahead and have sexual relations. He had never attempted to do so, however, and wondered if this had something to do with the girl friend's breaking up their relationship immediately after their return to college in the fall.

He continued to demonstrate a general inhibition of emotional expression and retained his motivation to achieve academically, but modified his plans to permit graduation after four years of college instead of three. He carried a somewhat reduced course load throughout most of the following year, and had no difficulty in getting A's in most of these courses. During his senior year he had a brief episode of emotional blocking with difficulty in concentration and verbalization, but this responded rapidly to further phenothiazine medication. He graduated magna cum laude, was accepted in an outstanding graduate school, and was confident of his future ability to withstand stress and seek further psychiatric help if necessary. It was felt, however, that only limited gains had been made in fostering emotional maturation and social interaction.

Catatonic Excitement (Postpartum). A 23-year-old married woman was admitted to the state hospital two weeks after the birth of her first child, in a state of constant agitation and excitement which it had been impossible to control in a general hospital psychiatric unit in spite of large doses of chlorpromazine (Thorazine).

The patient was the only child of parents who were in their early 20s at the time she was born and who were still living together at the time of her admission to the hospital. Her father was a farmer and she was raised in adequate socioeconomic circumstances. Both parents claimed that there were no problems in interpersonal relationships during the patient's childhood, but after the patient had reintegrated somewhat, she reported frequent battles with her mother for as long as she could remember. Her socialization may also have been hindered by several changes in residence during her adolescence. She left school at the age of 15 after completing grade ten, following which she worked in a grocery store and lunchroom that her parents were operating at that time. At the age of 21 she married a man six months younger than herself who earned a living driving a dump-truck. The patient experienced some guilt over premarital sexual relations with her husband, but their marital adjustment was described as satisfactory and she showed no evidence of psychopathology until after the birth of their eldest child two years after their marriage. She was described as outgoing, and always made friends easily. She worried readily about other peoples' troubles and would often cry in movies. She never attended church regularly but enjoyed reading, knitting and getting together with friends.

Nothing unusual was noticed until five days after the baby was born when she seemed to be over-exuberant, grabbed her aunt and swung her around, and asked her to dance with her. At this time she said she was happy because she was leaving the hospital where the baby had been born, but the day after leaving the hospital she cried frequently and that night she scarcely slept at all. She became increasingly agitated and tearful and was readmitted to the psychiatric ward of the hospital where she was found to be hallucinating and delusional, and her behavior was agitated, excited, and assaultive. Following her transfer to the state hospital, she remained acutely disturbed, impulsive, and assaultive and she refused all food and fluids. Her replies to questions were frequently irrelevant, and her conversation showed flight of ideas and evidence of autistic thinking. When asked how she had come to the hospital, she replied, "Came in a boat. Came to get better. I didn't know it was rugged like this. My husband just did it for me. Did we save any from having the boat? They are trying to make me better. I was insane but I am not any more. Can we rent skates here?" At first she misidentified the physician as her husband and then asked him, "Are you the baby?" Shortly after admission she wrote a note to her mother-in-law saying, "Dear Mrs. X.: We were really married, but if you want us to do it again, we will. I love my husband, and I haven't lost a dime—teach me tonight—me or baby." At times she thought she heard the voices of her husband or mother talking to her and at times she expressed the delusion that her child had been born dead. Sometimes she was correctly oriented and her memory was accurate, but at other times she was confused, disoriented, and appeared to have marked impairment of memory. After she had reintegrated, she was found to have a full scale IQ of 100.

Her state of excitement and disturbed ideation failed to respond completely to Thorazine or to a long course of electroshock treatments. However, she appeared to have a complete and lasting remission following a full course of insulin coma therapy. She was discharged from hospital within six months after admission and apparently had no recurrence of acute psychopathology during the next few years.

PARANOID SCHIZOPHRENIA

Paranoid schizophrenia is characterized by autistic or paralogical thinking with delusions of reference, influence, persecution, or grandeur. The delusions are poorly systematized and accompanied by hallucinations, particularly auditory. The average age of onset is slightly higher than with the preceding forms of schizophrenia, and decompensation may be either abrupt or insidious. When the onset of symptoms is acute, there are often obvious precipitating stresses and the response to treatment tends to be relatively favorable. On the other hand, when there is a gradual development of paranoid schizophrenia in an isolated and hypersensitive individual, with no evidence of precipitating stresses, the psychosis is much more likely to become a permanent way of life.

A 30-year-old unmarried man who was an instructor in a small college was admitted to a psychiatric hospital because he had begun freely expressing the delusion that he was a pope and demanding that he be treated accordingly. On admission to hospital his main complaint was, "I've been made a pope and left to shift for myself." It was soon learned, however, that he had been delusional for almost two years previously. At this time he had been a teaching assistant in another small college, trying desperately to complete the requirements for a Ph.D. degree (which he failed to obtain). He had been living a life of social isolation and studying very hard, when one day he experienced "a delicious cold feeling inside" followed by a feeling that everything inside him was aflame, as if his heart had "opened up." This ecstatic feeling lasted about six hours and he regarded it as the most wonderful spiritual experience of his life. There was apparently no voices or visions but he interpreted this as a religious calling and for several months afterward he seriously considered entering a seminary. During this time, however, he became aware that he was being singled out for some additional special attentions.

The day after his religious experience, a low flying airplane passed near his apartment several times and he felt that he was being buzzed. Other ideas of reference appeared, probably associated with auditory illusions or hallucinations. He thought he heard strangers on the street making remarks about him such as "There goes the big shot" and "There goes number one." Letters that he wrote went unanswered, and a number of job applications resulted in his acceptance at only two small colleges that he regarded as inferior. He came to feel that his correspondence was being censored and that he was being discriminated against unjustly.

In spite of his paranoid ideation, his intellectual performance was unimpaired and his behavior was not recognized as abnormal, so that he was able to teach effectively in the small college for a year and a half. During this time he lived with an older couple and had very little social contact with anyone his own age. However, one day he recognized a nun in a teaching order as being someone that he had known a few years previously and had regarded as very attractive — "too beautiful to have her talents covered by the robes of her order of nuns." He perceived her as being like himself, a victim of circumstances, condemned to "teach in the sticks." He never spoke to her, but began to ponder how he might have her released from her vows so that he could marry her. He felt that she was watched and guarded very closely to prevent him from doing so. He felt that many people recognized him as the lay pope and that he could thereby grant the nun a dispensation from her vows so that she could marry him.

During the last few weeks before he was admitted to hospital, however, his delusions of grandeur would change rapidly and assume some other form. On one occasion he telephoned the President of the United States, giving the name of a fictitious ambassador. On another occasion he wrote the following letter to a general in Washington, signing it with the name of a fictitious general:

This morning the secretary very rudely handed me some routine University matters as if to say, tend to your knitting or we'll get rid of you. Also, she has consistently refused to handle my typing, causing me to handle the entire burden myself. I can no longer bear the brunt of this despicable treatment. I think the secretary ought to be fired.

General, I have been subject to the most unspeakable treatment in a community I have been earnestly trying to defend. I have appealed to Admiral X (his father's name) but he has left me entirely to my own resources, causing much hardship and crippling the operation of the entire. . . Strategic Command.

What are the services coming to, if her own officers are muzzled and fear to speak out in defense of each other?

Sincerely yours,

General XXX, Commandant
. . .Strategic Command.

He also wrote a letter to his father, saying as follows:

I cannot welcome back to this community a person who will not defend his own flesh and blood as an individual upon whose shoulders has been laid the highest title in Christiandom. You had definite knowledge of this whole matter last summer and you did nothing. How foolish can a person be! I refuse to accept your correspondence of phone calls unless you address me by my proper title.

He had no insight into the fact that he was in any way sick, but when admitted to hospital he was pleasant and cooperative. When asked what three wishes he would make if he could have anything that he wanted, he replied as follows:

1. To get married to a girl who is a nun.

2. People are calling me pope, and I'd rather have training to be that than remain a college instructor.
3. I'm not so awfully hard to please—so long as I have a responsible position and am supported in this. One of the things that galls me is that I haven't got a Doctorate—I've got more than enough credits piled up but I've not been permitted to register.

The patient was the eldest of five children, was given the same name as his father, and was expected to follow in his father's footsteps, or even to achieve what his father had been unable to do. He was born soon after his father's appointment to the faculty of a well-known university, where he was to remain for the next 30 years building an international reputation for himself and a large research establishment for the university. At the time of the patient's admission to hospital, his father submitted a wealth of documentary information including a two page history written at the time the boy was 12, a supplementary two page history on subsequent events, a two page curriculum vitae on the patient and a four page curriculum vitae on himself (the father). This may suggest a certain degree of narcissism and it is interesting to note that the father had never earned a Ph.D. degree, in spite of his own research accomplishments and his pressure on the patient to obtain the degree. By comparison with the boy's father, his mother appears to have been quite inconspicuous, and the only information submitted by her was signed with her husband's name rather than her own.

The patient described his father as engrossed in his work and neglecting his family and religion. When asked what he liked the most about his father, he replied that it was the latter's ability to establish contacts the world over and his professional ability. When asked what he disliked about his father, he replied that the latter always kept his world to himself and never drew others into it. He always liked his mother and said that he cheerfully performed many tasks that his father should have done himself. His only criticism of his mother was that she took part in no community activities.

During the first three months of his life the patient had feeding difficulties which were attributed to a faulty metabolism of carbohydrates and led to frequent measurements of his blood sugar throughout his childhood. From the age of six months to about 16 months, he was subject to "nervous spells" that occurred about every six weeks. These "nervous spells" consisted of waking from sound sleep, between 9 and 10 o'clock at night, screaming violently and remaining terrified for about 30 minutes. His parents claimed that he started to speak about the seventh month and walked at nine months and that he learned to read in his third year. However, he was always nervous and "high-strung." At the age of five he had an attack of vomiting which lasted for three days, following which he developed twitching around the mouth and eyes and tremors in the hands, which was diagnosed as chorea (a brain infection, usually associated with psychological abnormalities). His muscular coordination remained below average and he was nine years old before he could tie his shoelaces. He also stuttered, lacked energy, and failed to establish any satisfactory relationships with other children his own age. His parents regarded him as an exceptionally well-behaved boy, and encouraged him in intellectual pursuits, so that by the age of 12 he was playing an excellent game of chess and reading widely in newspapers, magazines, and journals such as the National Geographic and Science. At school, however, his nervousness and apparently uncontrollable movements frequently got him into trouble with his teachers. He was scolded and punished for his restlessness and was punished again for attempting to control this by sitting on his hands. In response to such treatment his parents stated that he developed a persecution complex and on occasions came home from school completely shaken and exhausted. At the age of 12 he had an attack of sleepwalking. Medical and neurological examinations carried out at this time were essentially negative, but the boy and his parents did not get the psychiatric help they needed. Father was apparently convinced that all the boy's problems were due to low blood sugar, and for a period of several years he had an extensive series of blood sugar tests undertaken, and attempts were made to ward off attacks of nervousness by controlling the boy's diet.

During his adolescence he was a choir boy and developed deep religious convictions which subsequently led him to consider entering a seminary. He was serious and studious, a shy, reserved, overconforming intellectual who wanted desperately to achieve distinction, but didn't know how to get along with members of his own or the opposite sex.

After he finished high school his father

could not afford to send him away to school so he remained at home and attended the same university where his father was teaching. One summer his father sent him to stay with friends in a Spanish American country to learn Spanish, and another summer to acquaintances in a French-speaking community so that he could learn French. He obtained his bachelor's degree in four years, cum laude, and then enrolled in an outstanding graduate school on a scholarship. He again received little or no financial support from his father and had to live with his grandfather a considerable distance from the university, and he neglected his diet. He studied extremely hard and obtained an A average during his first semester, but then broke down with an apparent acute schizophrenic reaction. He was admitted to hospital, had a short course of electroshock treatments, and reintegrated rapidly. After this he obtained work as a clerk and machine operator for nearly a year, until he was drafted into the Army (at the age of 24). After basic training he was assigned to duties as a clerk typist, but it is suspected that he had a further brief psychotic episode and in any event he was discharged from the Army in less than two years. Following this he returned immediately to the task of trying to obtain his Doctor of Philosphy degree. During the next two years he accumulated academic credits at two small colleges, while also working part time to support himself and it was at the end of this period that he experienced the religious revelation which ultimately led to his readmission to hospital.

For the first few months after his admission he was treated by means of phenothiazine tranquilizing drugs and fairly intensive psychotherapy, but his delusional convictions remained unchanged, and it was therefore decided that he should have a long course of electroshock treatment. During the next few months he received about 20 treatments, but rapidly relapsed and expressed various delusions of grandeur—that he was God, the devil, a brigadier general, and once again, the pope. He now received an intensive course of about 30 further electroshock treatments in less than two weeks. At the end of this time he was profoundly confused, but the treatments accomplished their purpose and there was no recurrence of his former delusions. He subsequently received further phenothiazine drugs and supportive psychotherapy, was able to recognize his former beliefs as unrealistic and left hospital with the idea that he would abandon his long struggle for the Ph.D. degree. His measured intellectual performances was still in the very superior range, however, and he had no interest in seeking a teaching position at the high school level. After a few months at home with his parents, he planned once more to return to college teaching.

Another example of paranoid schizophrenia follows:

A married woman was first admitted to state hospital at the age of 42. She had separated from her husband six months previously, immediately after their only son had married and left home. Following this the patient had been living alone in a single room, and a few days prior to admission she confided in her sister that she thought her food and cigarettes were being poisoned. She was admitted to the psychiatric ward of a general hospital and told the psychiatrist that she could hear the voices of men and women engaged in intercourse, and also that she was being doped by her food so that she could be used sexually. Her hallucinations and delusions were extremely disturbing to her, and she was anxious, miserable, and agitated. She remained only briefly in the general hospital and then left and registered in a hotel where she locked herself in her room and refused to let anyone in. The police were called, and eventually broke the door down and took her to the state hospital.

The patient was born in Roumania and was the second of three children, having a brother two years older and a sister only 16 months younger than herself. Her father died from meningitis when she was nine years old, and her mother remarried two years later, but the patient never got along with her stepfather and claimed that he treated her unkindly. When she was 13 years old the whole family immigrated and she apparently had very little schooling after this, ending at the age of 14 with grade seven education. Following this she worked in factories until her marriage at the age of 18 to a man 14 years older than herself. Their only child was born the year after their marriage, and three years after his birth she returned to factory work. There was severe discord between her and her husband for many years and she claimed that this arose from financial problems, in that her husband was irresponsible, frequently changed jobs, and did not pay their bills so that she had to work. However, she also admitted that their sexual relationship was never satisfying to her and that she never wished to have intercourse with him or with anyone else. The sexual content of her delusions is significant.

On arrival in the hospital she was tense, anxious, restless, and agitated. She would frequently pace the floor, at times talking to herself or weeping uncontrollably. At interview her manner was pleasant and cooperative but her response to questions was frequently irrelevant and she sometimes continued talking to herself under her breath. She spoke in a quiet, monotonous voice with her eyes averted, and at times spoke inaudibly or unintelligibly. When interviewed soon after admission she did not know where she was and when asked if she had inquired this from anyone, "I don't know whether they would tell me the truth or not. I locked the doors at my mother's and left the light on all night because I thought they were going to poison me and rob me when I was locked in that room. They asked me how I could talk, different ones, and I don't know how they could see me because the blinds were drawn. They were going to burn me to prove that I am what they say I am. You know what they are saying about me. I guess everybody does. They are saying that I am a prostitute and a bitch." She said she had been unhappy for a long time because she had been alone and added, "If you are not with the one you love, you are unhappy." When asked who she loved, she replied, "Ray." When asked how this name was spelled, she replied, "W-r-a-y, I think. There is x-ray, too. I don't know. They are forcing me to holler so that they can say I am crazy." There was no impairment of memory or other intellectual functions and she obtained a full scale IQ of 81. On the MMPI, the only T-score over 70 was on scale 6 (paranoid).

She was admitted to the hospital before phenothiazine tranquilizing drugs were in general use, and she showed only temporary responses to long courses of electroshock treatment and insulin coma therapy. A year after her admission to the hospital, lobotomy (brain operation) was performed, and a month later she returned home to live with her husband. All went well for a couple of months but then there was a recurrence of her hallucinations and delusions, together with some disturbed behavior. She was readmitted to hospital and on this occasion received chlorpromazine (Thorazine) medication. Although she continued to have auditory hallucinations while on medication, she no longer reacted to them and again went home to live with her husband three months

after her second admission to hospital. She and her husband were advised that medication should be continued indefinitely. Her improvement was maintained for about a year when she again became increasingly seclusive, delusional, and hostile. She developed the delusions that she was divorced from her husband, that she was married to a king whose first name was Raymond, that she herself was a princess, that her father was Jesus and that she had given life to quintuplets during her last admission to hospital. Three years after her first admission to hospital she was again admitted for long-term care and subsequently continued to express numerous delusions of grandeur.

ACUTE AND CHRONIC UNDIFFERENTIATED SCHIZOPHRENIA

Acute and chronic undifferentiated schizophrenia show no consistent predominance of any of the four preceding groups of symptoms. However, the acute variety frequently presents marked catatonic or paranoid features, and the chronic undifferentiated variety often used to be diagnosed as simple schizophrenia.

A 21-year-old college student began showing symptoms of abnormality at the beginning of his senior year. He had been out of town all summer working for a man who was at first extremely kind to him and praised his work. However, the man eventually made homosexual advances to the patient, which the latter refused, following which the admired employer became very angry and critical and told him he had no ability. Shortly after this he went to visit a former girl friend in another city, but she had not expected him and told him that she was too busy to see him. He drove home alone, did not take as much time as he should to sleep on the trip, and arrived exhausted. He started back to college right away, but had difficulty in concentrating and was confused, disorganized and inactive. He was preoccupied with sex and religion, and asked both his mother and father intimate questions that they found embarrassing. He also spoke of certain strange experiences which involved people trying to deceive him for some obscure purpose. He appeared apathetic and there were long delays in his replies to questions. When he did reply, his answers showed evidence of concrete thinking and tended to be irrelevant.

It was learned that he was the youngest child and only boy born to a middle class Jewish family. He was born with deformities involving both hands and one foot, which required a number of surgical operations during childhood. His father was passive and ineffectual, and the patient stated, "He is quiet, lazy, never made use of opportunities, and I never was able to talk to him." His mother was also socially incompetent, but talkative and dominant within the home. She expected her son to achieve, and told him repeatedly that he could do not only as well, but better than other people without physical handicaps. He was driven to compete successfully both in athletics and academically. His three elder sisters all completed college and it was expected that he would not only obtain his bachelor's degree but go on into a professional school. He did not feel able to take money from his parents, and therefore had to achieve all this entirely on his own. He entered college with a scholarship, but this was discontinued when he failed to obtain the necessary grades.

In hospital this patient received phenothiazine tranquilizing medication and fairly intensive psychotherapy, and reintegrated rapidly. At this time he was found to have a full scale IQ of 112 (bright normal). He also underwent a program of vocational testing which helped him to set more realistic and satisfying goals than in the past. He left hospital after a couple of months but continued to receive medication and supportive psychotherapy for several more months, and made further improvement in interpersonal relationships.

SCHIZOAFFECTIVE DISORDERS

Schizoaffective disorders are characterized by a combination of schizophrenic thinking and behavior with prominent symptoms of affective disorder (euphoria or depression). The usual form of schizoaffective reaction represents a combination of paranoid schizophrenia with severe depression as illustrated in the following case histories. Over a period of time the affective disorder usually varies in intensity, whereas the schizophrenic symptoms are apt to become more prominent unless regression is arrested or reversed by treatment.

A twenty-year-old girl sought psychiatric help toward the end of her second year in a highly competitive college where she was carrying an A-minus average. She reported severe depression and persistent ideas of suicide, which had been intensified by a recent visit from her mother and sister whom she feared and hated. Her mistrust of others was generalized, however, and there was a lifelong history of interpersonal aversiveness and social isolation. Recently she had also developed delusions of reference and persecution, believing that she was being followed by unknown hostile persons in automobiles, from whom she fled in terror. It appeared that the precipitating factors for her psychotic episode included the imminent prospect of spending the summer months in close contact with the members of her family whom she mistrusted the most.

She was admitted to a general hospital psychiatric unit, and attempts were made to administer both phenothiazine and antidepressive medication, but she tolerated all drugs poorly, complaining of many side effects on small doses, and it was evident that she would not continue to take them as an outpatient. On the other hand, she readily became involved in intensive analytically oriented psychotherapy, which was the primary treatment undertaken throughout the next two and a half years. It was recognized from the outset however that dramatic personality change was unlikely, in view of her lifelong social inadequacy and tendency to project hostility as well as to become severely depressed.

The patient was the older of two girls, born to parents who were both socially withdrawn and advanced in age. Her father was a college professor who had been married previously and had no children by his first marriage. A few years after the death of his first wife he married the patient's mother who was then over forty and had never previously been married. The father was sixty when the patient was born and retired before she entered school, following which the family traveled, and the children had no opportunity for enduring social relationships with others their own age or with teachers. Within a few months after the patient started grade one she had already attended three different schools, and there was no satisfaction from interpersonal relationships that must always be terminated and followed by grief.

Before her birth, the patient's father had hoped she would be a boy and had selected a boy's name for her, that he frequently used as a nickname during her early childhood. When her younger sister was born the latter displaced the patient completely from the affections of her mother, who also allowed the demands of the younger sister to reduce her own contact with the patient's father. A symbiotic bond became firmly established between the mother and the younger sister, and the patient attempted to relate increasingly to her father but the latter frequently preferred to pursue isolated activites by himself. The patient had no one in whom she could really confide. Mother had never prepared her for the onset of menstruation, and for many years she was terrified each time she had a period. Her few childhood inquiries about sex were answered by evasion or embarrassed suppression. Around the age of puberty she recalled having asked her mother about sexual activity involving their family cat and another cat, and being met only with the reply that she should never speak to anybody else about this again. She had not in fact done so until after ten hours of therapy.

When the patient was nearly 15 years old her father died, and she reacted with grief and psychotic denial of reality. During the months that followed she sometimes thought she saw him walking on the street and that she heard his voice talking to her. She became more preoccupied with inner fantasy, and sometimes had difficulty distinguishing between this fantasy and external reality. There was temporary impairment of her school work but she gradually reintegrated spontaneously, graduated near the top of her high school class, and maintained good grades in college. She found the time that she had to spend with her mother and sister increasingly intolerable, but did seek some solace in relationships with others her own age. It is not surprising that she should have experienced some confusion in psychosexual identification, since she partially rejected her own femininity. On occasion she thought of cutting off her own breasts and had made a number of superficial cuts with a razor blade. She had also experienced some conscious homosexual fantasy, but she preferred the company of males her own age and also had some heterosexual fantasy. However she had strong religious convictions and inhibited all sexual expression except for masturbation, which made her guilty and which she had

abandoned a few years before she entered therapy.

In the few intimate human relationships she had been able to establish, she had unrealistically high expectations, which led to disillusionment, followed by projection of her own hostile impulses in the form of paranoid distortion of reality. The two boys with whom she had become most friendly in college were both emotionally disturbed and currently in psychiatric treatment. One was severely depressed and withdrew from college, which had led to withdrawal of a major source of temporary emotional support and reactivation of feelings of abandonment similar to those she had experienced following her father's death.

In therapy, she again repeated the same pattern through an initial unrealistic positive transference followed by a strong negative transference, and she demonstrated guilt and masochistic behavior for her expressed hostility. She became increasingly preoccupied with suicide and cut her wrists as well as her breasts. She was readmitted to hospital and on this occasion cooperated more readily in taking phenothiazine and antidepressive medication. Following a visit home however she returned to hospital with a supply of sedative medication that had been prescribed for her mother and took an overdose in an apparent suicidal attempt. However, she took the medication at midday, and the following note that she wrote shows both her narcissistic preoccupation and ambivalence toward others:

Ye shall again behold me, and your heart shall be joyful, and joy no man taketh from you.

This is to free Dr. X from all guilt in connection with this act against myself. He has been good to me beyond belief, and I love him dearly for it, but this kind of love he does not understand. I feel it is best to remove myself from his presence forever.

I sincerely hope that Y (a male orderly) will be able to forget me very shortly. He has tried to be a friend to me, but I in my weakness have not been able to accept friendship. Forgive me.

I want Z (a boy friend outside the hospital) to have all my music and books.

I wish to be buried in my white dacron dress.

I have always wanted to be buried without a coffin.

I do not really want to die, but in the end

I think it will be better for all concerned if I no longer burden with my personal difficulties which I ought to have the strength to overcome anyway.

An impasse in therapy occurred after 120 hours, and she manifested psychotic depression with severe regressive behavior. At this point she therefore received a course of electroshock treatments which was followed by marked improvement in mood and activity level. She again became accessible to psychotherapy, returned to college, and continued in outpatient therapy throughout the following 18 months. Throughout the following year she continued to get A's in most of her courses, but her lack of capacity for pleasure (anhedonia) led her to withdraw from college prior to graduation, and she subsequently worked part time in two churches. When faced with the prospect of therapeutic termination she underwent temporary regression, and was readmitted to hospital a week for reevaluation, but received no further medication or electroshock treatments and was soon ready to return to her own apartment.

At the age of 21 she had become financially independent through a trust established by her father, and she had subsequently avoided all contact with her mother and sister. She also continued to view other interpersonal relationships as potentially dangerous, and to live in relative social isolation, rarely making emotional investments in more than two or three other human beings at the same time. The process of therapeutic termination was prolonged and painful, because of the intensity of the dependency through which she had previously attempted to relate to the therapist. However, she showed no further regression nor psychotic behavior, and became sufficiently emancipated to lead an independent existence. She remained emotionally fragile, but less vulnerable to minor stress and deprivation than prior to therapy.

Another example of a schizoaffective disorder follows:

This married woman was first admitted to a state mental hospital at the age of 28, with a history that during the previous three years she had felt other people were watching her and talking about her. She became increasingly withdrawn from social contact, and spent a great deal of time in a room by herself. She was also extremely unhappy,

wept a great deal, and expressed concern over various bodily complaints for which her physician could find no organic basis. She was afraid of going to bed and was unable to sleep. Occasionally she became angry for no apparent reason, but for the most part she was frightened and miserable and it was for the latter symptoms that her husband finally sought help for her.

She was the second child in a family of six and was the only girl. Her older brother was mentally defective and was admitted to a state institution as a child. As the eldest child remaining in the family and the only girl, the patient was expected to help a great deal around the home and with the care of the younger brothers. Her father was a laborer who was employed irregularly, and she was raised in marginal economic circumstances. Father had a violent temper and when he became angry he would break furniture. Mother would cry a great deal and would accuse the father of unfaithfulness, apparently with some justification. Mother was also domineering and overprotective toward the patient and would never allow her to go out on dates for fear she would become pregnant. At the age of 12, the patient was forced to discontinue school while she was in grade seven, as her mother was pregnant at the time and wanted the patient to help at home. At the age of 17 she started to work in factories, and at the age of 21 she married a man seven years older than herself. Her own parents separated soon after this and each established a common law marriage with other partners.

The patient was always shy and sensitive, never had any close friends, and felt uncomfortable in even small social groups, preferring to spend her spare time alone reading. She had acquired little sexual information prior to meeting her husband and their premarital relations frightened her. They had one child who was born two years after their marriage, and the patient subsequently stated that she did not want any more children until she was well mentally. Their child slept in the same room as the patient and her husband, and this probably added to inhibition in their sexual relationship.

After the birth of her child the patient returned to factory work but quit this about three years prior to her admission to hospital when she felt that the other girls at the factory were watching her and talking about her. She thought she heard someone say, "I wish I could make faces at her." She also heard a man say, "She looks like an Indian and won't talk to anyone." On the bus she overheard a remark, "There must be something wrong with that woman. She acts as if she is doped." In a movie she heard six girls laughing and heard one of them say, "If there is nothing wrong with that woman, why does she act like that?" Apart from these ideas of reference she also expressed delusions of both active and passive influence. She felt that by watching people with her eyes she could bring harm to them. She also felt that other people were able to influence her by staring into her eyes. She felt she was being hypnotized, but didn't know why other people should be picking on her. Her feelings of depression, self-blame, and hopelessness were related to her paranoid delusions. However, she was currently oriented and showed no gross impairment of intellectual functions, obtaining an IQ of 84.

In spite of the long-standing psychopathology, she reintegrated rapidly following a short course of electroshock treatments, and left hospital a couple of months following admission. After returning home she apparently remained well for three months but then became increasingly tired, inactive, disinterested, and depressed, and developed the same type of delusions as previously. She was readmitted to hospital a year after her first admission at which time she had auditory hallucinations, together with delusions of reference, influence, persecution, and hopelessness regarding the future. On this occasion she received a full course of insulin coma therapy, together with supplementary electroshock treatments for the symptomatic control of depression. There was considerable improvement during this program of treatment but she subsequently relapsed again and a lobotomy was performed (involving limited anterior bimedial cuts). She left hospital a month after the operation and had no difficulty in looking after her family. A year later she returned to factory work and there had been no further recurrence of schizophrenic ideation or of depression by the time of the last follow-up interview three years after the operation. (See Figure 18-1.)

CHILDHOOD SCHIZOPHRENIA

Childhood schizophrenia has its onset at any time prior to the age of 15 years and may assume any of the forms that have already been outlined above. Since schizophrenia may involve mutism and

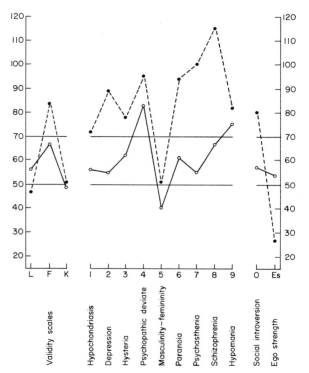

Figure 18–1. MMPI profiles for a 28-year-old woman with severe schizo-affective psychosis, before (dotted line) and one year after a bimedial lobotomy (solid line). A score of 70 is two standard deviations above the mean score of 50 for adult females on each scale.

intellectual impairment, however, a young child with this condition may fail to develop speech and show other evidence of intellectual subnormality, which may result in the mistaken diagnosis of mental retardation. Alternatively, the schizophrenic child may be brought for psychological or psychiatric evaluation because of either neurotic symptoms or delinquent behavior. Such schizophrenic children may therefore be described as pseudodefective, pseudoneurotic or pseudopsychopathic. Childhood schizophrenia will be referred to again in a later chapter on the disorders of childhood and adolescence.

The term *pseudoneurotic schizophrenia* has become increasingly popular since Hoch and Polatin (1949) pointed out that many patients presenting initially with neurotic symptoms were subsequently found to have clear-cut evidence of schizophrenic thought-disorder. The most frequent form of pseudoneurotic symptoms consisted of excessive, diffuse, or free-floating anxiety ("pananxiety").

The term *pseudopsychopathic schizophrenia* was introduced by Dunaif and Hoch (1955) to describe a group of patients in whom the schizophrenic symptoms were initially masked by delinquent, antisocial, or "acting-out" behavior. The latter behavior usually involved sexual deviation and offenses, based on what has frequently been referred to as the schizophrenic's chaotic sexuality, but the concept has generally been expanded to include any form of schizophrenia associated with prominent manifestations of impulsive, antisocial, or sociopathic behavior.

The term *nuclear* has sometimes been applied to those forms of schizophrenia with the most obviously disturbed behavior (e.g., hebephrenic or catatonic types), as contrasted with *peripheral* forms in which there might be less obvious behavioral abnormality (e.g., simple and paranoid types.) More commonly, however, the concept of *nuclear* schizophrenia has been applied to those forms having an early, gradual, insidious

onset and poor prognosis (particularly simple and hebephrenic types), as contrasted with *peripheral* schizophrenia characterized by a more adequate prepsychotic personality, having a later and more acute onset, with some tendency to spontaneous remission or favorable response to treatment (e.g., some catatonic and paranoid types).

This dichotomy on the basis of prepsychotic personality, rapidity of onset, and prognosis has been widely discussed in the psychological literature as a contrast between process and reactive forms of schizophrenia. *Process* schizophrenia, occurring in socially inadequate persons and having a gradual onset and poor prognosis, has also been viewed by a number of investigators as the "true" form of schizophrenia, having an endogenous biological basis. *Reactive* forms of schizophrenia, on the other hand, occurring in more adequate individuals in response to stress, with acute onset and favorable prognosis, have been viewed by these workers as schizophreniform psychoses, having an exogenous, experiential, or psychological etiology. In the present state of our knowledge, such generalizations are unjustifiable, as recognized in the following statements by Benjamin (1958), "That this assumption is premature in the present state of our knowledge of schizophrenia is clear. Perhaps it is true; perhaps not. But the demonstration of qualitative differences between the two types of illness and a reliable method of distinguishing between them, would surely obligate the investigators in this field to consider the possibility of differences in etiology and pathogenesis, and to conduct his researches accordingly, whether these be along psychological or neurophysiological lines."

Garmezy and Rodnick (1959) reviewed an interesting series of psychological studies carried out under their direction, indicating that poor prognosis was not only related to poor premorbid adjustment, but also to a greater sensitivity to censure and to a certain type of family organization, presumably correlating with different types of experience in early childhood. These findings will be discussed further in the following section on etiology.

Zigler and Phillips (1962) examined the case histories of 806 patients referred to the psychology department of the Worcester State Hospital for personality study. Two hundred and ninety-eight were diagnosed as schizophrenic, 74 as manic-depressive, 159 as psychoneurotic, and 275 as having various forms of character disorder. They attempted to test two hypotheses: (1) that within a schizophrenic population the symptom pattern of patients who have exhibited a relatively good level of premorbid social competence will be more characterized by a "turning against the self," whereas the symptom pattern of patients who have exhibited poor premorbid social competence will be more characterized by either an "avoidance of others" or "self-indulgence and turning against others"; and (2) that this relationship between premorbid social competence and symptomatology is not unique to schizophrenia but would also obtain in the nonschizophrenic portion of the pathological population. Both hypotheses were confirmed, and the authors concluded that the process-reactive distinction was reducible to the social maturity dimension which in turn was applicable to all of the psychopathology rather than to schizophrenia alone. Insofar as it is applicable to etiological research on schizophrenia, however, this distinction should be borne in mind in evaluating the results of various studies to be discussed in the next section of this chapter.

DYNAMICS, DEVELOPMENT, AND ETIOLOGY

In an early paper on the defense of neuropsychoses, Freud (1894) concerned himself with interpreting hallucinations, and he subsequently regarded the majority of schizophrenic symptoms as indicative of regression to the state of narcissism that is characteristic in normal infants. He interpreted the impairment of social relationships as withdrawal of libido from external objects, and the content of paranoid delusions as a projection onto others of the individual's own unacceptable, unconscious wishes. Paul Federn also made major contributions to the psychoanalytic interpretation and treatment of the schizophrenias and was the first to describe them as disorders of the ego.

Fenichel (1954) pointed out that the following psychoanalytic formulations mean one and the same thing, only varying in point of view: the schizophrenic has regressed to narcissism, the schizophrenic has lost his object, the schizophrenic has parted with reality, the schizophrenic's ego has broken down. Moreover, there is nothing implicit in any of these statements regarding a somatic or psychological origin of the regression. In different cases, the regression might have different causes and a different range, but it always reaches a greater depth and involves an earlier level of development than in the neuroses.

Harry Stack Sullivan and other neo-Freudian analysts became less preoccupied with intrapsychic dynamics and possible biological interpretations, and much more concerned with the interpersonal relationships of the schizophrenic patient, both in their current and developmental significance. Sullivan and Fromm-Reichmann both made considerable contributions to the modified psychoanalytic treatment of schizophrenia, and emphasized the probable role of disturbed interpersonal relationships in etiology.

While avoiding a reductionistic interpretation emphasizing only one type of etiology Arieti remarked as follows:

All cases which have been studied psychodynamically by various authors have demonstrated, without variation, severe and early psychological maladjustment, poor family relations, unhappy childhood, severe conflicts, and a paucity of adequate defenses.

Severe and badly compensated conflict seems a necessary antecedent to schizophrenia. However, schizophrenia is not a necessary *consequence* of severe or badly compensated conflict.

He also postulated that the potentiality of experiencing or manifesting schizophrenic symptoms exists in every member of the human race irrespective of the culture and society. However, there are many persons who disagree with his viewpoint, and insist that there must be a specific hereditary vulnerability in at least the majority of persons who develop schizophrenia.

Rado made the following dogmatic assertion: "Schizophrenia originates with the presence of certain mutated genes in the fertilized egg from which the patient developed. Although the nature of these mutated genes is not known, their existance is established." Borrowing a genetic term, he described such a person as a schizophrenic phenotype or more briefly, a schizotype, and he postulated that schizotypal organization involved two fundamental forms of damage of the integrative apparatus of the psychodynamic cerebral system:

1. The capacity for pleasure is diminished; pleasure's usually strong motivating action is enfeebled. This damage is designated as integrative pleasure deficiency. Its neurochemical basis is unknown.

2. The individual's awareness of his own body is, or tends to become, distorted. This clinical fact is interpreted as damage of the action-self, precipitated by what we provisionally call a *proprioceptive (kinesthetic) diathesis*. The physiological nature of this disturbance is still unexplored.

Meehl also concluded that schizophrenia, while its content is learned, is fundamentally a neurological disease of genetic origin, and developed his thesis as follows:

This neural integrative defect, which I shall christen *schizotaxia*, is all that can properly be spoken of as inherited. The imposition of a social learning history upon schizotaxic individuals results in a personality organization which I shall call, following Rado, the *schizotype*. The four core behavior traits are obviously not innate; but I postulate that they are universally learned by schizotaxic individuals, given any of the actually existing social reinforcement regimes, from the best to the worst. If the interpersonal regime is favorable, and the schizotaxic person also has the good fortune to inherit a low anxiety readiness, physical vigor, general resistance to stress and the like, he will remain a well-compensated, "normal" schizotype, never manifesting symptoms of mental disease. He will be like the gout-prone male whose genes determine him to have an elevated blood uric acid titer, but who never develops clinical gout.

We shall now review some of the extensive evidence regarding the relative significance of heredity, other biological factors, psychological, and sociocultural factors in the etiology of the schizophrenias.

HEREDITARY FACTORS

It has long been known that there is a much greater frequency of schizophrenia among the relatives of schizophrenic patients than among the general population. Such intrafamilial concentration, however, might be due to any combination of three different causal mechanisms: (1) inheritance of a similar predisposition or vulnerability, (2) direct nongenetic transmission of pathogenic agents or experiences from one affected individual to another, (3) common exposure of affected persons to similar pathogenic agents or experiences.

A variety of approaches have now been adopted to the study of genetic factors in schizophrenia, which include the following: (1) statistical estimates of lifetime frequency of schizophrenia in the relatives of patients with schizophrenia, (2) studies of the children of two schizophrenic parents, (3) comparisons of the frequency of schizophrenia in cotwins of monozygotic or dizygotic twins with schizophrenia, (4) analysis of the etiology of schizophrenia occurring in the Genain quadruplets (Rosenthal), (5) study of the children of schizophrenic mothers reared from infancy by foster parents, (6) chromosome studies of schizophrenic patients.

During the first half of the present century, a number of estimates were made of the frequency of schizophrenia in various classes of relatives of schizophrenic patients. Attempts were then made to force these data into conformity with a simple Mendelian hypothesis of transmission by a single pair of recessive genes (or a single dominant gene). The expected frequency of schizophrenia in various classes of relatives, under either of these simple Mendelian hypotheses, is dependent upon the estimated frequency of schizophrenia in the general population, which was for many years

accepted as approximately 0.8 percent. Based on the latter assumption, the theoretical frequencies of schizophrenia in various classes of relatives, according to these single gene hypotheses, are shown in Table 18-1, and compared with frequencies actually recorded by various investigators. The latter do *not* correspond with these simple Mendelian hypotheses, which led some investigators to invoke concepts of partial penetrance or expressivity, according to which clinical schizophrenia was only manifested in certain of the individuals assumed to have the genetic potentiality for the disorder.

On the basis of his extensive studies,

TABLE 18–1. Theoretical Expectancies of Schizophrenia, If Inherited Through Completely Dominant or Recessive Autosomal Genes, and Frequencies Recorded by Various Investigators‡

CATEGORY	THEORETICAL EXPECTANCY IF INHERITED THROUGH		FREQUENCIES RECORDED (CORRECTED FOR AGE) WITH STANDARD ERRORS
	COMPLETELY DOMINANT GENE	COMPLETELY RECESSIVE GENE	
General population	—	—	0.008 ± 0.0008 (Fremming, 1951)
Children of first cousins	0.008	0.013	0.011 (quoted by Slater, 1958)
Relatives of schizophrenics* Parents	0.503	0.089	{ 0.093 ± 0.008 (Kallmann, 1950) 0.041 ± 0.011 (Slater, 1953)
Children†	0.503	0.089	0.164 ± 0.013 (Kallmann, 1938)
Children of *two* schizophrenics	0.751	1.000	{ 0.634 ± 0.075 (Kallmann, 1938) 0.454 ± 0.063 (Schulz, 1940) 0.392 ± 0.130 (Elsässer, 1952)
Full siblings	0.503	0.297	{ 0.142 ± 0.008 (Kallmann, 1950) 0.054 ± 0.009 (Slater, 1953)
DZ cotwins	0.503	0.297	0.000 to 0.22 } See Table 18–2.
MZ cotwins	1.000	1.000	0.000 to 0.862 }
Half siblings	0.256	0.152	0.071 ± 0.029 (Kallmann, 1950)
Nephews and nieces	0.252	0.047	0.039 (quoted by Kallmann, 1946)
First cousins	0.133	0.028	0.026 (quoted by Kallmann, 1946)

*Ascertained through affected individuals.
†Children of either one or two schizophrenics.
‡Modified after Gregory, I. 1960. Genetic factors in schizophrenia. American Journal of Psychiatry *116*, 964.

Kallmann long maintained that predisposition to schizophrenia was transmitted as a simple autosomal recessive unit characteristic, with incomplete penetrance or expressivity, determined by a "genetically nonspecific constitutional defense mechanism" (probably polygenic in nature). Böök, on the other hand, considered that the type of schizophrenia prevalent in his north Swedish isolate was due primarily to a major, partially dominant autosomal gene. Slater examined some of the consequences of generalizing the latter theory of partial dominance. He concluded that certain recorded frequencies of schizophrenia in the relatives of schizophrenics were compatible with this theory, and would correspond with a manifestation rate in the heterozygote of about 0.26 and a gene frequency of about 0.015. Since only 3 percent of schizophrenics would be homozygous under these conditions, it follows that more than 70 percent of all persons having the genetic potentiality for schizophrenia would fail to manifest the disorder because of modifying genetic factors or environmental influences or both.

The present author examined the expected frequencies of schizophrenia in various classes of relatives under each of three genetic hypotheses involving incomplete penetrance or expressivity (in homozygote and/or heterozygote), and concluded that *no single gene hypothesis was compatible with all the data recorded.* This would leave three alternative hypotheses, that are *not* mutually exclusive: (a) genetic heterogeneity, (b) polygenic inheritance, and (c) predominantly environmental causation. On the basis of mental hospital first admission rates, Burch postulated that schizophrenia is restricted to a carrier population (about 2.7 percent cent at birth of the general male and female populations of New York state) that is homozygous for certain alleles at two nonlinked autosomal loci, and that its phenotypic initiation (in males and females) depends upon the accumulation of two specific random events that are probably auto-

somal somatic mutations. At the present time, however, this hypothesis must be regarded as speculative, and it is equally likely that other genetic mechanisms are involved in whatever hereditary predisposition exists to various forms of schizophrenia.

Studies of the offspring of schizophrenic couples, i.e., having *both parents diagnosed as schizophrenic,* are of particular interest in relation to a simple Mendelian hypothesis. If schizophrenia were due to a single pair of fully expressed recessive genes, then the frequency of schizophrenia in the offspring of two affected parents should be 100 percent (as also in monozygotic cotwins). If schizophrenia were due to a single fully expressed dominant gene, then the frequency among the offspring of two affected parents should be at least 75 percent. Rosenthal (1967) reviewed such studies and found a frequency of schizophrenia amounting to only 34.3 percent among the offspring of schizophrenic couples, suggesting considerable environmental influence in determining outcome, at least among these subjects.

While they provide no information regarding possible mechanisms of genetic transmission, a number of *twin studies* do suggest that such predisposition exists, at least in certain of the schizophrenias. The results of ten such studies of twins with schizophrenia are summarized in Table 18-2. The latter shows estimated concordance rates in monozygotic and dizygotic cotwins, together with Holzinger's index of heritability derived from these concordance rates. The consistency evident in the first six of these studies is impressive, but it should be noted that the first five did *not* involve serological determination of zygosity, and that they all involved hospital samples with a high proportion of chronic patients. The four most recent studies involve serological determination of zygosity, and sampling that included more acute forms of schizophrenia (which may also be partly related to more modern techniques of therapy available). Gottesman and

TABLE 18–2. Estimated Concordance Rates in Monozygotic and Dizygotic Cotwins of Schizophrenics

INVESTIGATOR, COUNTRY, AND YEAR	APPARENT ZYGOSITY OF TWINS	NUMBER OF PAIRS	ESTIMATED CONCORDANCE RATE PERCENT	HERITABILITY $H = \dfrac{CMZ - CDZ}{100 - CDZ}$
Luxenburger, Germany, 1928	MZ DZ	17 33	67 0	0.67
Rosanoff, United States, 1934	MZ DZ	41 101	67 10	0.63
Essen-Möller, Sweden, 1941	MZ DZ	7 24	71 17	0.65
Slater, England, 1953	MZ DZ	41 115	76 14	0.72
Kallmann, United States, 1953	MZ DZ	268 685	86 15	0.84
Inouye, Japan, 1961	MZ DZ	55 17	76 22	0.69
Tienari, Finland, 1963	MZ DZ	16 21	0 10	minus 0.11
Harvald and Hauge, Denmark, 1965	MZ DZ	7 59	29 5	0.25
Kringlen, Norway, 1966	MZ DZ	50 175	28 7	0.23
Gottesman and Shields, England, 1966	MZ DZ	24 33	42 9	. 0.36

Shields pointed out that concordance rates have tended to be higher in female than male pairs, in chronic rather than acute schizophrenias, and in countries other than Scandinavia and Finland. There is indeed no reason to expect that the hereditary contribution to the schizophrenias should be identical throughout all populations or countries studied. Within our own society, the extent of hereditary predisposition might well be related to intelligence, socioeconomic status, or other variables.

Several studies suggest that some forms of schizophrenia may be predominantly determined by heredity and some predominantly by environmental factors. Rosenthal (1959) examined the case histories of monozygotic twins with schizophrenia that had been previously published by Slater. He found an almost total absence of schizophrenia among the families of the discordant twin pairs (in which the cotwin did not develop schizophrenia), in contrast with a positive history of schizophrenia among about 60 percent of the families of the concordant twins (in which the cotwin also developed schizophrenia). Moreover, the discordant male twins (whose cotwin was unaffected) tended to have a later age of onset and more favorable prepsychotic personality and outcome than the concordant male twins (whose cotwin was also affected). The clinical diagnosis of the discordant tended to be paranoid, and of the concordant to be catatonic schizophrenia. Rosenthal concluded that, biologically speaking, at least two broad groups of schizophrenia were differentiated by this method of analysis: in one the genetic contribution was absent or minimal; in the other, the genetic contribution was probably considerable.

Another study suggesting a genetic distinction between process and reactive forms of schizophrenia was that conducted by Inouye, who divided his monozygotic schizophrenic twins into three groups, the two largest of which each contained 23 cases. Among those with chronic progressive schizophrenia, he found 17 cotwins (i.e., 74 percent) to be concordant, whereas among those with mild or transient schizophrenia, he found only nine cotwins (i.e., 39 percent) to be concordant. In a further detailed analysis of his material, he postulated that both dominant and recessive forms of Mendelian inheritance were recognizable, but such impressions gained from pedigree studies of individual families require statistical evaluation of extensive family data (independently of twin studies).

In relation to the proposition that the genetic component of schizophrenic disorders is polygenic in nature, attention may be drawn to associations between schizophrenia and several presumed polygenic systems such as those involving intelligence, resistance to bodily disease, and somatotype. Thirty-five year follow-up studies of intellectually superior California school children (Terman and Oden) indicated high adult socioeconomic status and a low frequency of schizophrenia in individuals who had then passed through the period of risk (eight recorded cases of schizophrenia among a total of 1468 subjects, indicating a frequency of schizophrenia among this sample of 0.545 ± 0.19 percent). It may be regarded as established that a considerable component of adult intelligence is genetically determined (Chapter 5), and a genetic connection between mental retardation and schizophrenia has been suggested. Since intelligence is also related to socioeconomic status, a postulated genetic connection between schizophrenia and intelligence would be quite compatible with those studies relating frequency of schizophrenia to lower social class. The increased mortality of mothers during the early childhood of schizophrenics may also be associated with the latter relationship to social status.

Two further relevant studies may be cited in this review of genetic factors in schizophrenia. Heston compared the psychosocial adjustment of 47 adults born to schizophrenic mothers with 50 control adults, where all subjects had been separated from their natural mothers from the first few days of life. A significant excess of both schizophrenic and sociopathic personality disorders were found among the offspring of schizophrenics, in comparison with the offspring of normal adults. The offspring of schizophrenic mothers included five with schizophrenia, four with mental deficiency, nine with sociopathic personality, and 13 with neurotic personality disorders. The offspring of the normal controls (also separated from their natural mothers) included none with schizophrenia or mental deficiency, two with sociopathic personality, and seven with neurotic personality disorders. The results are suggestive of both specific and nonspecific hereditary transmission, but require verification from further foster child studies.

Raphael and Shaw reported on chromosome studies in schizophrenia. Among 210 patients in their study, they found one with Klinefelter syndrome and one triple-X syndrome, suggesting that specific abnormalities of sex chromosomes may be more frequent among schizophrenics than in the general population. Of greater significance, however, is the finding that most of these schizophrenic patients had no chromosome abnormality. In most instances, therefore, it may be assumed that hereditary factors predisposing to schizophrenic disorders involve a few major gene substitutions or the cumulative effects of multiple minor genes.

SOMATIC FACTORS

On a morphological basis, Kretschmer classified individuals into four types. He considered that persons with asthenic or leptosome habitus were psychologically schizothymic and introverted with a potentiality for schizophrenic breakdown. It is nowadays generally considered preferable to abandon the concept of types in favor of bodily measurements or indices having means and standard deviations. More recently Sheldon and his coworkers measured physical development using three dimensions of variation (the relative visceral, muscular, and skeletal development) and postulated a correlation between predominantly ectomorphic body build and schizophrenia. The latter workers failed to consider variations in stature but Rees and Eysenck analyzed both size and body type (the latter in terms of length and breadth). A group of schizophrenics examined by Rees were found to be both smaller in stature than normal and also leptomorphic in body type.

Doust (1952) studied a number of morphological characteristics which he considered indicative of biological maturation and found among his psychiatric patients an undue persistence of characteristics of morphological immaturity together with dysplastic features. Among schizophrenics he reported "a scanty upper lip without discrete lobulation; a high interpupillary index, double jointedness, and persistent remnants of the epicanthic fold."

Lewis (1936) reported on 600 autopsies in which a hypoplastic heart and circulatory system were found consistently in catatonics and hebephrenics. Olkon (1939) considered that cutaneous capillaries of schizophrenics showed striking deviations from the normal, including a reduction in number, lack of uniformity in size, variety of bizarre

shapes, a rate of flow both faster and slower than normal, and more frequent occurrence of hemorrhages. Some workers have regarded such findings as evidence of constitutional developmental defects, but Cobb and others have pointed out that even such morphological changes may actually be determined by environmental situations or intercurrent disease.

In chronic cases of schizophrenia, Alzheimer and other workers reported a loss of brain tissue with nonspecific degenerative neuronal changes, particularly in the frontal area, but many of the subjects have been over the age of 60 at the time their brains have been examined and other degenerative processes may well be involved. Dunlap (1928) found similar nerve cell losses and degenerative changes in control brains as in schizophrenics. However, such authors as Winkelman (1952) have continued to report that gross findings of cortical atrophy plus a hypoplastic arterial system in the brain are frequently found in schizophrenia; and that the main microscopic findings include focal and general loss of nerve cells, especially in the anterior half of the brain. The presence of numerous nerve cells shows degenerative changes (such as shrinkage, vacuolization of cytoplasm, "ghost cells," loss of polarity, and fatty infiltration), a fairly uniform hyperplasia and hypertrophy of macroglia, and a diffuse mild subcortical demyelination.

Wolf and Cowen (1952), on the other hand, concluded as follows:

It would appear from a review of the histopathologic findings in patients with schizophrenia that one is not dealing with obvious or even unequivocal changes in the central nervous system. The abnormal findings in other organs are even more ambiguous and ill-defined. It seems reasonable to conclude that if there are microscopic variations from the norm, they are of such a subtle nature as either not to be detectable by ordinary methods of microscopic observation or to be masked by the effects of tissue death or those due to manipulation incidental to preparation of the material for histologic study. All the reported microscopic abnormalities have been challenged as nonspecific by a group of competent histologists and have been attributed to misjudgment of the limits of normal variation, misinterpretation of artifacts, or the uncritical attribution of special significance to casual, coincidental findings.

Among the infectious agents that have been considered responsible for schizophrenia, most frequently cited has been the tubercle bacillus. Loewenstein reported tuberculosis bacteremia as a cause of schizophrenia in 1931, and in 1944 reiterated his belief that the latter was due to tuberculous emboli lodged in the brain. Others such as Kallmann have viewed a frequent association of schizophrenia with tuberculosis as due to a shared hereditary susceptibility to the two disorders. In her study of mental illness in London, however, Norris (1959) failed to find an increased frequency of tuberculosis in schizophrenia, and other reports of increased frequency may well have been due to increased exposure. Other workers have maintained that the most important causative factor in schizophrenia is some area of focal sepsis, and several studies have implicated chronic rheumatic brain disease. Papez and Bateman used special stains to study the brain cells of schizophrenic patients, and maintained that there were constant changes consisting of inclusion bodies (suggestive of a virus infection) in the nucleus and cytoplasm, but their findings remain unconfirmed.

Doust (1952) found that the physical illness experience of a group of schizophrenic patients was significantly in excess of that of a control group of normals (and was also higher than that of neurotic or psychopathic patients). The schizophrenics appeared to carry an undue load of musculoskeletal and cardiovascular diseases. In discussing these findings the author referred to other studies in which schizophrenic subjects failed to develop normal antibody titers in response to injections of antigenic substances (in one instance pertussis and another instance TAB

vaccine.) He considered that a relationship between immunity and psychiatric factors was at least as important as any demonstrated relationship between immunity and nutritional status, but this proposition remains to be demonstrated.

Many deviations in thyroid and adrenal cortex function have been reported in psychiatric patients, but no specific endocrine disturbance has been found in schizophrenia or other functional mental disorders. However, long-term investigations of patients with periodic catatonia have shown changes in basal metabolic rate, nitrogen excretion or 17-ketosteroid excretion correlating with phasic changes in clinical condition, and benefiting from hormone therapy. It has also been reported (Doust, 1952) that constitutional, nuclear, or process schizophrenics (defined by him as simple, catatonic, and hebephrenic types) show a significant degree of chronic anoxemia, whereas paranoid schizophrenic patients show a low normal base line level of oxygen saturation, but readily tend to become anoxemic under the impact of various stresses. These findings have been criticized on the basis that spectroscopic oximetry of the ear lobe or nail bed may bear little relationship to oxygen levels in brain capillaries, and a number of other workers have reported a normal rate of cerebral circulation and oxygen consumption in schizophrenic patients. Still others have reported normal cerebral glucose consumption.

Kety (1959) reviewed various biochemical theories of schizophrenia and grouped them under the following five headings: (1) oxygen, carbohydrate, and energetics, (2) amino acids and amines, (3) the epinephrine hypothesis, (4) ceruloplasmin and taraxein, and (5) serotonin. Uncontrolled factors in early work suggested that a defect in carbohydrate metabolism was characteristic of the schizophrenic process. However, an abnormal glucose tolerance and other evidence of hepatic dysfunction do not completely exclude incidental hepatic disease of nutritional deficiencies. Similarly, there are numerous mechanisms whereby vitamin deficiencies may cause substantial changes in the complex patterns of the intermediary metabolism of amino acids. Again, a low level of ascorbic acid in the blood is an important and uncontrolled variable in the rapid in vitro oxidation of epinephrine by plasma from schizophrenic patients. A number of workers have failed to confirm the hallucinogenic properties initially reported to be possessed by adrenochrome (postulated as a product of the faulty metabolism of epinephrine). A reported increase in serum copper in schizophrenia, with the demonstration that practically all of the serum copper was in the form of ceruloplasmin, led to the development of a color reaction known as the Akerfeldt test, but it was not long before the high ceruloplasmin levels in schizophrenics was found to be due to low ascorbic acid levels due to dietary insufficiency.

Several groups of workers have applied modern biochemical techniques in attempts to isolate an active factor from the blood serum of schizophrenic patients. Heath and his associates (1958) reported having extracted from schizophrenic serum a substance, presumably a protein, that was capable of reproducing certain psychotic symptoms (difficulty in thinking and depersonalization) in volunteer control subjects. They termed this substance "taraxein" and also reported that it produced abnormal behavior and electroencephalogram changes when administered to monkeys. Other workers in this country were unable to reproduce their results, but Swedish and Russian workers reported experimental verification.

An extensive series of biochemical investigations in schizophrenia has been reported by Gottlieb, Frohman, Luby, Beckett, and their associates. Beckett et al. (1960) reported correlations between disturbances in the biochemical energy transfer systems of schizophrenic patients and their clinical manifestations. Intermediates of glucose metabolism were measured in 30 control and schizophrenic subjects before and after stress, which consisted of administering ten units of regular insulin intramuscularly. A failure of mobilization of biological energy to meet stress (as measured by a change in the specific activity of fructose-1, 6-diphosphate) was related to the presence of schizophrenia and to the degree of incapacity rather than to chronicity. A continual overproduction of biological energy (as measured by the prestress specific activity of adenosine triphosphate) was found in some schizophrenic patients and appeared to be related to clinical chronicity and to aggressive destructive outbursts. Frohman et al. (1962) reviewed additional evidence of disturbed intermediary carbohydrate metabolism in schizophrenic subjects, and of the presence of a slow-moving alpha globulin in the serum of these patients. Gottlieb (1962) remarked that, on the basis of these studies, one cannot say whether this is a substance normally present in the serum of all individuals but quantitatively elevated in patients with schizophrenia, or a qualitatively abnormal substance characteristic of schizophrenia itself. He has recognized, moreover, that all these biochemical findings may be attributable to (1) inborn errors of metabolism, (2) inborn errors that reveal their pathophysiology under specific environmental conditions, or (3) environmentally induced maladaptive biochemical mechanisms. However, if continuing research along these lines accomplishes nothing more than the objective identification of certain groups of schizophrenic and possibly preschizophrenic individuals, it would thereby open the door to more satisfactory research into both causation and treatment than has been possible hitherto.

The investigations of the preceding group were not confined to schizophrenia, but also involved the study of model psychoses produced by sleep deprivation, sensory isolation, and the administration of psychotomimetic drugs. Luby et al. (1962) reported that prolonged sleep deprivation resulted in disturbed carbohydrate metabolism and the appearance of a serum factor believed similar to that found in schizophrenia. While sleep deprivation has been found to accentuate the symptoms of schizophrenia, they found that sensory isolation was better tolerated by schizophrenic subjects than by normal controls, and they suggested that schizophrenic withdrawal may represent an attempt by the patient to reduce input overload (resulting in a form of learned self-imposed sensory isolation). In their experiments with various psychotomimetic drugs, they found that Sernyl reproduced the primary symptoms of schizophrenia in normal volunteers, in contrast with other psychotomimetic drugs that caused hallucinations and other secondary manifestations. They hypothesized that the effect of Sernyl was mediated through the reduction of proprioceptive feedback, or impairment of the central integration and interpretation of input from this sensory modality. When Sernyl was administered to schizophrenic subjects, they became profoundly disorganized and regressed. On the other hand, normal volunteers who received Sernyl underwent less disorganization when they were subjected to conditions of sensory isolation. They concluded that schizophrenia involves disturbed neural integration that might result either from the presence of an inhibitor substance or from a defect in energy production. However, the ultimate causation of any such disturbance in body function may well be found in the field of interpersonal relationships, and we shall now turn to a consideration of developmental experiences.

PSYCHOLOGICAL FACTORS

Social isolation has long been recognized as one of the characteristic manifestations and possible causal factors in the development of schizophrenia. As long ago as 1908, Eugen Bleuler remarked, "The overt symptomatology certainly represents the expression of a more or less successful attempt to find a way out of an intolerable situation."

Many subsequent authors have sought the source of this withdrawal within the schizophrenic individual himself, either in terms of biological abnormality or intrapsychic dynamics. Many others, however, have sought to find environmental circumstances from which withdrawal was inevitable. Sullivan and others concluded that the withdrawal represented an avoidance of painful interpersonal relationships characterized by criticism, threats, and inevitable failure. Schilder (1939) interpreted the failure of such patients to differentiate adequately among cues in the environment as follows: "It is as if the schizophrenic would say, 'This fully differentiated world of yours is much too difficult and dangerous and therefore I content myself with a more primitive world.'" Fromm-Reichmann (1950) attributed schizophrenic aloofness to the desire to avoid another rebuke in a long row of thwarting rebuffs which the schizophrenic has experienced in childhood and has been conditioned to expect in repetition.

The search for adverse childhood experiences led many investigators to examine the relationship presumed to have existed between schizophrenic patients and their parents, together with other characteristics of family organization. Kasanin, Knight and Sage (1934) examined 45 unselected case histories of schizophrenics and reported that maternal overprotection or rejection was present in 60 percent of the cases (overt rejection, however, was present in only two cases). Gerard and Siegel (1950) examined the family background of 71 male schizophrenics through histories obtained from their parents and relatives. They concluded that the parents were immature and had a poor marital relationship, and that the child was often exposed to markedly overprotective attitudes. Reichard and Tillman (1950) emphasized the dominating, egocentric, and manipulative role of the mother, whom they perceived as unable to form a proper respect for the individual's need to be himself and to be accepted in his own right.

Mark (1953) administered an attitude survey to 100 mothers of male schizophrenics and to a control group of 100 mothers of male nonschizophrenics. Out of 139 items in the survey, 67 differentiated between the two groups of mothers at the 0.05 level of significance or better. On analyzing the content of these items, it appeared that the mothers of schizophrenics were mainly restrictive in their control of the child. When it came to the warmth of the relationship, they exhibited attitudes of both excessive devotion and cool detachment.

In a subsequent study of the mother-child relationship in schizophrenia, McGhie (1961) concluded that overprotection was more typical of the early background of the neurotic than of the schizophrenic. However, he found that the mother of the schizophrenic patient shows a remarkable capacity for denial in her attitude to the patient's earlier difficulties. "Not only does she distort reality in projecting the cause of the patient's abnormal reactions outside of him, but she also accepts, approves and actively encourages the deviant features in his development. Her influence on the patient is almost specifically designed effectively to cripple the child's attempts to reach an independent and stable level of adjustment." In his interviews with these mothers, some interesting material emerged concerning their own previous life history. They tended to report an unhappy early home life which was often disrupted further by parental loss. As children they were unhappy, insecure, and unable to make good contact with others. They remained to some extent social isolates throughout their lives, their marriages predestined to failure by their rejection of their own femininity.

In addition to the mother-child relationship, several investigations have focused attention on the relationships between father and child, and between the mother and father of schizophrenic patients. In a preliminary study, Lidz and Lidz (1949) compared the clinical histories of 50 schizophrenic patients with 50 depressive psychotic patients, and concluded that fewer than ten percent of the schizophrenics had come from homes that were well integrated and contained two reasonably stable parents. Lidz and Fleck (1960) reviewed the results of subsequent intensive analyses of families containing a schizophrenic member. Among the characteristics of the mothers of schizophrenic patients they include an imperviousness to what the child seeks to convey, combined with an inordinate intrusiveness; a tendency to confuse the child's needs with her own needs projected on the child; and disparity between what is expressed verbally and emphatically. They found that the fathers were as frequently and as severely disturbed as the mothers, and that they were often insecure in their masculinity, and needed constant admiration and attention to bolster their self-esteem. The quality of imperviousness to the feelings and sensitivities of others that epitomized many of the mothers also applied to many of the fathers. They also pointed out that the fathers may exert an adverse influence on the child, either directly or indirectly through their relationship with the mother. Some of the relationships between mother and father were characterized by severe chronic disequilibrium and discord, which they termed marital schism. In other instances the rather serious psychopathology of one marital partner dominated the home, and they described this situation as marital skew. In a more recent publication, Fleck, Lidz, and Cornelison (1963) compared the parent-child relationships of male and female schizophrenic patients and reported that schizophrenic males often came from skewed families with passive, ineffectual fathers and disturbed, engulfing mothers; whereas schizophrenic girls typically grew up in schismatic families with narcissistic fathers who were often paranoid and, while seductive of the daughter, were disparaging of women, and with mothers who were unemphatic and emotionally distant.

Bowen and his associates (1959) reported on their intensive observations of a small number of families containing a schizophrenic child. They stated that

The family members, particularly the father and mother, function in reciprocal relation to each other. They are separated from each other by an emotional barrier which, in some ways, has characteristics of an "emotional divorce." Either father or mother can have a close relationship with the patient when the other parent permits. The patient's function is similar to that of an unsuccessful mediator of the emotional differences between the parents. The most frequent family pattern is an intense two-some between mother and patient which excludes the father and from which he permits himself to be excluded. The family pattern changes under varying individual family circumstances in the course of daily living.

Bateson et al. (1956) advanced the concept of a "double-bind" as a pattern of communication provoking behavior characteristic of schizophrenia. Weakland (1960) subsequently redefined the essential characteristics of the double-bind situation as follows. (1) In a double-bind situation a person is faced with a significant communication involving a pair of messages of different level or logical type which are related but incongruent with each other. (2) Leaving the field is blocked. (3) It is therefore important to respond adequately to the communication situation which includes responding to its duality and contradiction. (4) An adequate response is difficult to achieve because of the concealment, denial, and inhibition inherent in or added to the basic contradictory pair of messages.

As thus defined, it is difficult to find concrete examples of double-bind communication, although clinical experience with patients provides a number of examples of conflicting instructions by one or both parents, leading to situations where the individual is damned if he does and damned if he doesn't take a certain course of action. Thus, a mother may tell her daughter, "Have some cake. I baked it especially for you" (and implicitly, "You'll hurt my feelings if you don't"),

and immediately afterwards remark, "You're overweight" (and implicitly, "I don't approve of people who are overweight"). Another mother of a schizophrenic daughter asked what she was doing, and the patient told her she was finishing a letter to her fiancé so that it would catch the last mail that day. The mother repeatedly scolded the daughter into helping with the supper dishes and when she did so, remarked, "You don't really like him very much, do you?"

In another household, a 15-year-old girl became pregnant out of wedlock. Her parents ignored this until she was six months pregnant, at which time she spoke to her mother, who said that she must not tell her father because it would upset him. After the baby was born, both parents told her not to bring it home because it would make everyone sick. Because of the girl's age, however, the signature of the girl's parents was required before the baby could be placed for adoption, but the parents refused to sign the necessary papers. At the time this occurred, this patient was not schizophrenic, but was showing many signs of rebellion more characteristic of a developing sociopathic personality. For reasons such as this, it has been seriously questioned whether conflicting instructions or double-bind communication are any more likely to lead to schizophrenia than to other forms of psychopathology. Nevertheless, it is evident that schizophrenic patients frequently spend their entire childhood with parents who have a poor perception of reality, considerable uncontrolled hostility, and who use various defensive distortions such as denial and projection. Double-bind communication may then serve to generate additional anxiety and reality distortion.

The following verbatim letter to a hospitalized schizophrenic and its double-bind interpretation are quoted from Weakland and Fry.* (The patient's

---

*From Weakland, J. H., and Fry, W. F. 1962. Letters of mothers of schizophrenics. American Journal of Orthopsychiatry 32, 604-623. Copyright, The American Orthopsychiatric Association, Inc. Reproduced by permission.

mother and father were divorced. The father had remarried and the parents visited the patient separately. The "Clem" referred to in the letter was the patient's husband, reportedly sadistic to her. He did not visit her in the hospital.)

Dear Janet

Just a few lines again.

I talked to your Dad on the phone and he said you dident answer his letter. You better write to him.

I want to have you visit me one of these days & maybe you can visit him too.

And by the way you havent written to me. (You did call me.)

And you know Janet I dont like to even think of Clem it seems to remind me of trouble. Id rather just not think of him.

And dont you let the cigarette habit get stronger than you are.

Sometimes these habits have a way of doing that.

When I get a chance Ill get you a Carton.

But too much smoking is bad business.

I want so much too have you visit me as soon as possible, so be good and write to me.

Your Dad said you dident answer his letter so maybe you ought to, but dont tell him I told you.

Well I better close now. Hope I can visit you soon.

Lots & Lots of love.

Mother

Weakland and Fry comment as follows on the letter:

The letter begins with self-deprecation, "Just a few lines again," which also may 1) reflect deprecatively on the recipient as not worth more, and 2) make any strong impact it might have difficult to attribute to the communication. That is, since it is "just a few lines," if the patient should be upset on reading it one implication is that this outcome reflects something wrong with the patient rather than with the letter or its author.

Next, mother benevolently minds the patient's business in telling her to write her father, although the parents are divorced and avoid meeting. Similar influence is continued in the suggestion about possibly visiting father. Coupled to this is an ex-pression of a wish that Janet might visit her, the mother. This looks positive, but may be difficult for the patient. In the first place, the statements about visiting father and visiting mother are closely juxtaposed and similar in phrasing, but very different fundamentally: One is a controlling suggestion concerning another person, the other expresses a wish of the writer; moreover, the people involved in the similarity are at odds with each other. This combination of similarity and difference is confusing in itself. Second, the apparent invitation to visit mother is vague and casual, an indefinite "one of these days" statement. Seen in context, with the recipient a daughter confined in a mental hospital, this casualness must to some extent convey a raising of hopes but treating them lightly, brushing the patient off again. Even this feeble overture toward contact is immediately followed by an underplayed ("and by the way") reproach ("You haven't written me"), and then another reversal ("You did call me"), with this also underplayed by being put in parentheses. The mother next reminds the patient of her own estranged husband; this appears as a gratuitous recalling of this painful topic to the daughter's mind while saying, "I'd rather just not think of him."

After this brief but comprehensive handling of family relationships, the mother turns to the bad habit of smoking. She cautions her daughter, imputing a weakness or inability to take charge of her own smoking, though Janet is a grown married woman. Yet this as a personal accusation is obscured by the impersonal phrasing concretizing the "cigarette habit" and its influence. Then, having indirectly told Janet "Don't smoke so much," she promises to send a whole carton of cigarettes. And the gift offer, like the visit offer, is casual—"When I get the chance." Again, though, she disqualifies this offer by "too much smoking is bad business."

The letter then returns to the family themes. Again a completely indefinite hope about a visit home is held out, followed abruptly by an implied condition for such a visit—"so be good and write me." The more complete message here then appears to be "I want to see you if you behave as I like." Yet this is uncertain too; the original statement is so inexplicit that nothing is even testable. There is also a further development on controlling the relationship of Janet and her father ("You ought to answer his letter" again) plus suggested conspiracy to conceal the mother's influence ("don't tell him I told you"). The letter is then terminated by unspecific, indefinite positive — "Hope I can visit you soon," and "Lots and lots of love."

This detailed recital of incongruent alternations; yes-only-no, do-only-don't, come-yet-wait — which may not be visible to the patient because of the vagueness and generality in the letter, its "played-down" nature, and its over-all framing as benevolent — provides recurrent exemplification of messages fitting our double-bind concept.

Garmezy and his associates undertook an extensive series of experimental investigations into psychological factors discriminating between normal individuals and various groups of schizophrenic patients. On the assumption that the highly generalized withdrawal tendencies of schizophrenic patients represent an inability to differentiate among environmental stimuli, Garmezy (1952) hypothesized that such patients would have greater difficulty in responding differentially to stimuli along a given dimension than would normal subjects. Since social stress often accentuates withdrawal behavior by patients, he further hypothesized that the introduction of social punishment for incorrect responses would produce even more marked differences in the differentiating ability of schizophrenic and normal subjects. These hypotheses were confirmed, and learning curve data indicated that, under threat of punishment, avoidance responses to all stimuli came to dominate the behavior of the schizophrenic patients, overshadowing and negating previously effective rewards.

In a study of visual discrimination, Dunn (1954) presented schizophrenic and normal control subjects with stimulus scenes consisting of a series of silhouetted mother-boy figures depicting scolding, whipping, and feeding interactions, and a neutral series representing objects (house and tree). No differences were found between the groups for the whipping, feeding, and object scenes, but for scolding the schizophrenic patients showed a markedly flatter gradient and presumably poorer discrimination than the control group. When the Phillips Scale was later used to subdivide the schizophrenic sample into those with good and poor premorbid personality adjustment, the results indicated that the variance in the scolding scene was produced primarily by the poor premorbid schizophrenics.

Garmezy and Rodnick (1959) reviewed the results of subsequent studies relating the differential reaction sensitivities of good and poor premorbid schizophrenics to differences in the organization of their families. In one study, patients were asked to answer child rearing attitude scales as they believed their mothers and fathers would have answered these when they were "growing up." Poor premorbid patients assigned more deviant attitudes to both parents than good premorbid patients and normal controls. However, intra-family comparisons based on the same items indicated maternal dominance in the families of the poor premorbid group, as contrasted with paternal dominance in the families of the good premorbid group of patients. Normal controls indicated a shared pattern of parental authority with very little indication of conflict between parents. These results were substantiated by those of a study in which Farina (1960) used a structured situational test to examine directly the patterns of dominance and conflict in the parents of schizophrenic patients.

A series of studies on monkeys deprived of contact with their mothers and with other young monkeys were undertaken and reviewed by Harlow (1962). When fully grown these deprived monkeys show gross abnormalities of behavior, and may be described as both asocial and asexual. After long and patient education by a sexually sophisticated male monkey, some of the deprived female monkeys have been impregnated (although they tend to reject and abuse their infants severely), but none of the deprived male monkeys have been ever induced to mate successfully. It is of particular interest that these and other behavioral abnormalities appear more related to an early absence of play contact with other young monkeys than to early separation from their mothers. It is tempting to speculate that a similar deprivation of peer relationships in human children may be one of the most important factors in developing a predisposition to schizophrenia. Such a deprivation of satisfactory peer relationships may be, of course, largely accomplished through the intervention of parents who are themselves apt to be socially isolated and to perceive normal interpersonal relationships as dangerous or unrewarding. Clinical experience with schizophrenic patients does in fact suggest that they have frequently been subjected to partial social isolation during early childhood, but it is very difficult to provide objective verification.

It should be noted that the presence of pathological personality characteristics, attitudes, and behavior in the parents of schizophrenics does not indicate to what extent such psychopathology might be transmitted by heredity and to what extent by postnatal environmental influence. Those with a hereditary and constitutional viewpoint maintain either (a) that parent and child both manifest abnormal thought and behavior because of similar gene-determined pathology, or (b) that the abnormal parental attitudes and behavior are a normal reaction to the behavior of the child who manifests abnormality from birth or shortly afterward. Those with a psychogenic viewpoint maintain that every child is born with the potentiality to develop schizophrenia if exposed to sufficiently pathogenic influences during early childhood. It appears that the question will be resolved only after the development of more objective criteria for diagnosis and their application in careful and extensive genetic and developmental analyses.

SOCIOCULTURAL FACTORS

What is known of the distribution of schizophrenia among different social and cultural groups is no more capable of providing an answer to this question of ultimate etiology than are the metabolic studies detailed earlier. Thus it has long been recognized that the relatively lower frequency of schizophrenia among the married than the unmarried might be interpreted as due to either protection against stress, or determination of marital status by selection on the basis of mental and personal characteristics. Similar interpretations have been applied to other differential rates between sociocultural groups. Odegaard has remarked that "the problem of selection versus protection-stress is largely identical with the more general problem of nature and nurture, constitution and environment." This generalization appears unjustified, since any protection afforded by a certain status is only against precipitating (environmental) stress or deprivation, whereas selection is on the basis of predisposition or established abnormality determined by the complex interaction of hereditary endowment with biological and/or psychosocial stress or deprivation.

Relatively high rates for schizophrenia have also been found among the foreign-born (particularly recent immigrants); among Negroes; among those of low educational, socioeconomic, and occupational status; and in certain urban areas. Faris and Dunham (1939) studied the distribution of first admission rates in Chicago and found them highest in the central areas of social disorganization, decreasing progressively toward the periphery of the city. They concluded that the conditions of social life in certain areas are causal for psychosis, but it was not long before the alternative hypothesis was advanced that preschizophrenics tend to drift into the disorganized areas. Gerard and Houston (1953) analyzed the ecological distribution of schizophrenia in Worcester, Massachusetts, in relation to family setting and found that the overall pattern corresponded with the residential pattern of a minority of patients: single, separated, and divorced men alone. They attributed the central concentration of these male schizophrenics to drifting or residential instability. Their findings were supported by Hare (1956) on the basis of a similar study in Bristol, England. The latter author considered that the principal cause of the excess of schizophrenic cases in the central areas was that personality difficulties had led them to move there (attraction or drift hypothesis, related to selection), and that a lesser, but still probable, causative factor was the social isolation of individuals parted from their families by force of circumstances ("breeder' hypothesis, related to protection against stress).

Of revelance to the relationship between social isolation and schizophrenia is a careful retrospective study by Kohn and Clausen (1955) of the adolescent (prepsychotic) activities and interpersonal relationships of 45 schizophrenics and 13 manic-depressives in Hagerstown, Maryland, admitted to various hospitals in Maryland during the period 1940 to 1952. On the basis of comparisons with a control group matched by age, sex, and occupation (or father's occupation), they concluded that their data did not support the hypothesis that social isolation in adolescence was a predisposing factor in either schizophrenia or manic-depressive psychosis. An interpretation in harmony with the findings of this study was that, as a result of the inadequacies in their social relationships both within and outside the family, certain individuals came to feel that they did not really belong to their peer-groups — that is, they became alienated from their peers — and that under severe enough conditions, alienation might lead to a withdrawal from social interaction, i.e., to isolation.

In a subsequent paper Kohn and Clausen (1956) attempted to evaluate the significance of both parental authority behavior and the quality of affectional relations with parents in the development of schizophrenia. Since they made specific comparisons between schizophrenics and normal individuals, according to both sex and socioeconomic status, their findings are of particular interest. They found (a) that schizophrenic patients more frequently than normal persons of comparable background reported that their mothers played a very strong authority role and their fathers a very weak authority role; (b) that normal males reported different patterns of parental authority from those reported by normal females, but schizophrenic males reported much the same pattern as schizophrenic females; (c) normal respondents of differing socioeconomic background reported different patterns, but schizophrenics of differing socioeconomic background reported much the same patterns of parental authority relations; (d) female schizophrenics who reported strong maternal and weak paternal authority said they were closer to their fathers than to their mothers, while male schizophrenics who reported such authority relations said they were closer to their mothers.

In their extensive study of social class and mental illness, Hollingshead and Redlich (1958) found the overall prevalence of schizophrenia (receiving treatment or custodial care) inversely related to social class, the rates being 111 per 100,000 general population for Classes I and II combined, 168 in Class III, 300 in Class IV, and 895 in Class V. The incidence of newly diagnosed cases of schizophrenia showed a similar, though less marked, inverse relationship with socioeconomic status, increasing from 28 new cases per 100,000 general population during a six-month period in Classes I and II combined to 73 in Class V during the same period. These authors tentatively concluded that the excess of psychoses from the poorer classes was a product of the life conditions entailed in the lower socioeconomic strata of society, and also that the greater tendency to chronicity among members of the lower classes was related to the poorer quality of psychiatric treatment they received. Myers and Roberts (1959) provided detailed evidence concerning the different life experiences and family relationships of schizophrenic and neurotic patients in Classes III and V, but it remains questionable to what extent the development of schizophrenia is related to these different life experiences, and also to what extent the ultimate prognosis is related to the type of treatment that such patients receive.

In addition to the preceding studies with a sociological orientation, numerous crosscultural comparisons have been made concerning the manifestations and frequency of the schizophrenias in different ethnic groups. Unfortunately, most such studies have been essentially descriptive in nature and have then proceeded to unjustified inferences concerning causation. Some authors such as Linton have viewed the universal prevalence of schizophrenia as evidence of an organic disease process, whereas others such as Opler have viewed the same observations as indicative of universal compensatory and repressive psychic mechanisms or defenses, varying in frequency and intensity in different cultural contexts.

In an excellent review of mental illness in primitive societies, Benedict and Jacks (1954) pointed out that most of the schizophrenics observed in these settings appeared to be of "nuclear" type, whereas relatively "intact" forms were under-represented. They noted a high frequency of states of confused excitement, frequently accompanied by homicidal behavior, as contrasted with the low frequency of depressed and suicidal states among primitive peoples. The psychodynamic interpretation was offered that in these groups the hostility of the psychotic individual tends to be directed outward whereas in western societies this hostility is more often directed inward. They also suggested that western culture, as it abandons the supernaturalism of the past and drives almost compulsively toward goals of objectivity and rationality, is making it progressively more difficult for the psychotic individual to adjust, especially the schizophrenic. Primitive cultures, in contrast, may afford a maximum of buffering, magical devices whereby the defenses of a poorly adapted or disorganized ego-structure can be culturally reinforced. These authors correctly concluded that the evidence available did not answer the ultimate questions of constitutional (genetic) versus environmental or dynamic (cultural) factors in the etiology of schizophrenia.

In conclusion, we wish to emphasize again that reported associations between membership in a given sociocultural group and the nature of frequency of schizophrenia do not establish direct causal relationships, but that such findings may be attributable to such variables as heredity, intellectual endowment, biological stress, and various types of interpersonal relationships. It is evident that future studies should integrate genetic, metabolic, psychodynamic, and sociocultural concepts and techniques; and attempts should also be made to adopt longitudinal or long-term follow-up methods of investigation.

TREATMENT

During the present century, many attempts have been made to utilize modified psychoanalytic techniques or other forms of intensive individual psychotherapy as the primary approach to treatment in patients manifesting schizophrenic regression. Harry Stack Sullivan pioneered in the development of social and milieu therapy for young hospitalized schizophrenics, and many private psychiatric institutions in this country emphasized both the therapeutic milieu and the value of intensive psychotherapy in relatively long-term hospital treatment of schizophrenic patients able to afford and benefit from such therapy. Since schizophrenia is relatively more common, however, among those of low socioeconomic status, and these people are far more numerous in the general population, the great majority of schizophrenics have been treated in public mental hospitals that tended to emphasize organic therapies, sometimes to the exclusion of psychosocial techniques. This situation started to change following the end of World War II, when greatly increased numbers of physicians entered training in psychiatry. The introduction and widespread application of phenothiazine tranquilizing drugs also rendered many schizophrenic patients more accessible to psychosocial therapies, which have been increasingly emphasized during recent years. Historically, however, organic therapies have played a major role in the treatment of schizophrenia that will be summarized in the present section.

Insulin coma therapy was introduced by Manfred Sakel of Vienna in 1933, and at the 1938 International Congress there were reports of favorable results in schizophrenia from various countries. By the time of the 1950 International Congress of Psychiatry in Paris, many psychiatrists regarded this as the best available treatment for early schizophrenia. A New York state hospital commission in 1944 compared the outcome in 1128 patients who had received insulin coma therapy in the Brooklyn State Hospital with 897 matched control patients admitted during the same period to other state hospitals where insulin treatment was not given. Eighty percent of the treated patients had left hospital as compared with 59 percent of the untreated patients. The patients treated with insulin had an average length of stay in the hospital of four months less than the untreated group, and the quality of their remission was considered better in all subgroups. Follow-up studies by other workers, however, indicated relapse rates among discharged patients that were sometimes as high as 50 percent. Others reported that patients having a remission following insulin therapy were more likely to relapse than patients

having spontaneous remission without treatment.

In view of the difficulties and risks of insulin coma therapy, a number of psychiatrists preferred electroshock therapy, although they recognized that the latter was not as likely to produce remission in schizophrenia as in affective psychoses. However, Rees compared schizophrenic patients treated by insulin with others treated by electroshock and a control group receiving no treatment, and reported that only the insulin group showed much better results than the untreated patients. Sargant and Slater (1954) remarked that the principal fault of current hospital practice was in not giving insulin treatment early enough, and losing valuable time through trying electroshock treatment first. However, the latter is still employed by some psychiatrists, particularly in the symptomatic control of patients in catatonic stupor or excitement.

Following the introduction of lobotomy by Moniz in 1936, many schizophrenic patients were subjected to psychosurgery. This was usually reserved for those who failed to undergo improvement with all other forms of organic treatment currently available, and was frequently used in chronic regressed patients of many years duration. As might be expected, the results in such chronic schizophrenic patients were not as beneficial as those reported in other forms of psychiatric disorder. A further problem was that the standard lobotomy performed was more extensive and damaging than certain modified operations not in general use. In spite of the chronicity in patients selected for psychosurgery, and the nature of the operation itself, however, a number of reports indicated that about two-thirds of such chronic patients could return to the community after brain surgery, and that as many as one-third might again become self-supporting.

Following the advent of chlorpromazine in 1953 and the introduction of many other tranquilizing drugs, there was a dramatic change in both the therapy and the prognosis of patients with schizophrenia. Within a few years, insulin coma therapy and psychosurgery were discontinued completely in most centers, and the use of electroshock treatment was greatly reduced in frequency. While the tranquilizing drugs were initially found to be most helpful in the symptomatic control of excessive psychomotor activity and aggressive behavior, they were soon found to have a significant influence on ideation and emotional response, and to render many schizophrenic patients much more accessible to psychotherapy.

Certain of the phenothiazine drugs such as trifluoperazine (Stelazine) are relatively more effective than others in withdrawn and inactive or anergic schizophrenics. Efforts to develop energizing drugs to stimulate the apathetic patient, however, have hitherto met with less success than those that are useful in reducing excessive psychomotor activity and fragmentation of thinking. In most instances, stimulants such as amphetamines or tranylcypromine should be avoided in schizophrenia, since they tend to increase anxiety and fragmentation of thinking. It may be anticipated that other drugs will be introduced that are more effective in the symptomatic treatment of schizophrenia than any currently available. However, the problem also remains of finding more effective techniques of psychosocial therapy to enable such patients to adapt more effectively to their reality situations, and to diminish their vulnerability to future schizophrenic regression. All the psychosocial therapies reviewed in Chapter 11 have been applied in treating schizophrenia and will not be elaborated further in the present chapter. However, it is necessary to emphasize the application of such therapies, both in treating hospitalized patients, and in treating the increasingly large numbers of schizophrenic patients who can now adapt to long-term treatment in an outpatient setting.

SELECTED REFERENCES

Arieti, S. 1955. *Interpretation of Schizophrenia*. New York, Brunner.

Arieti, S., ed. 1959. Schizophrenia. In *American Handbook of Psychiatry*. New York, Basic Books, Inc., ch. 23 and 24.

Arieti, S. 1960. Etiological considerations of schizophrenia. In *The Out-Patient Treatment of Schizophrenia*, ed. S. C. Scher and H. R. Davis. New York, Grune & Stratton, Inc. ch. 2.

Arieti, S. 1962. Hallucinations, delusions, and ideas of reference treated with psychotherapy. American Journal of Psychotherapy 16, 52-60.

Bateson, G., Jackson, D. D., Haley, J., and Weakland, J. H. 1956. Toward a theory of schizophrenia. Behavioral Science 1, 256-264.

Beckett, P. G. S., Frohman, C. E., Gottlieb, J. S., Mowbray, J. B., and Wolf, R. C. 1963. Schizophrenic-like mechanisms in monkeys. American Journal of Psychiatry 119, 835-842.

Beckett, P. G. S., Frohman, C. E., Senf, R., Tourney, G., and Gottlieb, J. S. 1960. Energy transfer systems and the clinical manifestations of schizophrenia. In *Scientific Papers and Discussions*, ed. J. S. Gottlieb and G. Tourney. Washington, D.C., American Psychiatric Association, District Branches Publication No. 1, pp. 278-296.

Beckett, P. G. S., Senf, R., Frohman, C. E., and Gottlieb, J. S. 1963. Energy production and premorbid history in schizophrenia. AMA Archives of General Psychiatry 8, 155-162.

Bellak, L. 1938. *Dementia Praecox*. New York, Grune & Stratton, Inc.

Bellak, L. 1958. *Schizophrenia: A Review of The Syndrome*. New York, Logos Press.

Benedict, P. K., and Jacks, I. 1954. Mental illness in primitive societies. Psychiatry 17, 377-389.

Benjamin, J. D. 1958. Some considerations in biological research in schizophrenia. Psychosomatic medicine 20, 427-445.

Bleuler, E. 1911. *Dementia Praecox or The Group of Schizophrenias*, tr. J. Zinkin, 1950. New York, International Universities Press, Inc.

Böök, J. A. 1953. A genetic and neuropsychiatric investigation of a North Swedish population. Acta Genetica 4, 1-100.

Bowen, M. M. Dysinger, R. H., and Bassamania, B. 1959. The role of the father in families with a schizophrenic patient. American Journal of Psychiatry 115, 1017-1020.

Burch, P. R. J. 1964. Schizophrenia: Some new aetiological considerations. British Journal of Psychiatry 110, 818-824.

Cameron, N. 1938. Reasoning, regression and communication in schizophrenics. Psychological Monographs 50, 1.

Cameron, N. 1947. *The Psychology of Behavior Disorders*. Boston, Houghton Mifflin Co., ch. 15.

Doust, J. W. L. 1952. Psychiatric aspects of somatic immunity. British Journal of Social Medicine 6, 49-67.

Doust, J. W. L. 1952. Dysplastic growth differentials in patients with psychiatric disorders. British Journal of Social Medicine 6, 169-177.

Dunaif, S. L., and Hoch, P. 1955. Pseudopsychopathic schizophrenia. in *Psychiatry and The Law*, ed. P. H. Hoch and J. Zubin. New York, Grune & Stratton, Inc., pp. 169-195.

Dunn, W. L., Jr. 1954. Visual discrimination of schizophrenic subjects as a function of stimulus meaning. Journal of Personality *23*, 48-64.

Durell, J., and Schildkraut, J. J. 1966. Biochemical studies of the schizophrenic and affective disorders. In *The American Handbook of Psychiatry*, ed. S. Arieti. New York, Basic Books, Inc., Vol. 3, ch. 28.

Farina, A. 1960. Patterns of role dominance and conflict in parents of schizophrenic patients. Journal of Abnormal and Social Psychology *61*, 31-38.

Faris, R. E. L., and Dunham, H. W. 1939. *Mental Disorders in Urban Areas*, reprinted 1960. New York, Hafner Publishing Co., Inc.

Federn, P. 1952. *Ego Psychology and the Psychoses*. New York, Basic Books, Inc.

Fenichel, O. 1945. *The Psychoanalytic Theory of Neurosis*. New York, W. W. Norton & Co., Inc., ch. 18.

Fessel, W. J. 1962. Blood proteins in function psychoses. AMA Archives of General Psychiatry *6*, 132-148.

Fessel, W. J. 1964. Interaction of multiple determinants of schizophrenia. AMA Archives of General Psychiatry *11*, 1-18.

Fleck, S., Lidz, T., and Cornelison, A. 1963. Comparison of parent-child relationships of male and female schizophrenic patients. AMA Archives of General Psychiatry *8*, 1-7.

Frohman, C. E., Goodman, M., Beckett, P. G. S., Latham, L. K., Senf, R., and Gottlieb, J. S. 1962. The isolation of an active factor from serum of schizophrenic patients. Annals of the New York Academy of Sciences *96*, 438-447.

Fromm-Reichmann, F. 1950. *Principles of Intensive Psychotherapy*. Chicago, University of Chicago Press.

Garmezy, N. 1952. Stimulus differentiation by schizophrenic and normal subjects under conditions of reward and punishment. Journal of Personality *20*, 253-276.

Garmezy, N., and Rodnick, E. H. 1959. Premorbid adjustment and performance in schizophrenia: Implications for interpreting heterogeneity in schizophrenia. Journal of Nervous and Mental Diseases *129*, 450-466.

Gerard, D. L., and Houston, L. G. 1953. Family setting and the ecology of schizophrenia. Psychiatric Quarterly *27*, 90-101.

Gerard, D. L., and Siegel, J. 1950. The family background of schizophrenia. Psychiatric Quarterly *24*, 47-73.

Gottesman, I. I., and Shields, J. 1966. Schizophrenia in twins: 16 years' consecutive admissions to a psychiatric clinic. British Journal of Psychiatry *112*, 809-818.

Gottlieb, J. S. 1962. Biochemistry and schizophrenia: Implications for the future. In *The Future of Psychiatry* ed. P. Hoch and J. Zubin. New York, Grune & Stratton, Inc., pp. 103-115.

Gregory, I. 1960. Genetic factors in schizophrenia. American Journal of Psychiatry *116*, 961-972.

Hare, E. H. 1956. Family setting and the urban distribution of schizophrenia. Journal of Mental Science *102*, 753-760.

Harlow, H. F. 1962. The heterosexual affectional system in monkeys. American Psychologist *17*, 1-9.

Harvald, B., and Hauge, M. 1965. Hereditary factors elucidated by twin studies. In *Genetics and the Epidemiology of Chronic Diseases*, ed. J. V. Neel, M. W. Shaw, and W. J. Schull. Washington, D.C., U.S. Department of Health, Education, and Welfare, pp. 61-76.

Heath, R. G., Krupp, I. M., et al. 1967. Schizophrenia as an immunologic disorder. I.-III. A.M.A. Archives of General Psychiatry *16*, 1-33.

Heath, R. G., Martens, S., Leach, B. E., Cohen, M., and Angel, C. 1958. Effect on behavior in humans with the administration of taraxein. American Journal of Psychiatry *114*, 14-24.

Heston, L. L. 1966. Psychiatric disorders in foster home reared children of schizophrenic mothers. British Journal of Psychiatry *112*, 819-825.

Hobbs, G. E., Wanklin, J. M., Buck, C., and Egener, K. M. 1966. The prepsychotic characteristics of schizophrenic patients. Canadian Psychiatric Association Journal *11*, 140-145.

Hoch, P., and Polatin, P. 1949. Pseudoneurotic forms of schizophrenia. Psychiatric Quarterly *23*, 248-276.

Hoch, P. H., Cattell, J. P., Strahl, M. O., and Pennes, H. H. 1962. The course and outcome of pseudoneurotic schizophrenia. American Journal of Psychiatry *119*, 106-115.

Hollingshead, A. B., and Redlich, F. C. 1959. *Social Class and Mental Illness*. New York, John Wiley & Sons, Inc., ch. 8.

Horwitt, M. K. 1956. Fact and artifact in the biology of schizophrenia. Science *124*, 429-430.

Hoskins, R. G. 1946. *The Biology of Schizophrenia*. New York, W. W. Norton & Co., Inc.

Inouye, E. 1961. Similarity and dissimilarity of schizophrenia in twins. *World Congress of Psychiatry*, Montreal, Canada, McGill University Press, Vol. 1, pp. 524-530.

Jackson, D. D., ed. 1960. *The Etiology of Schizophrenia*. New York, Basic Books, Inc.

Jung, C. G. 1936. *The Psychology of Dementia Praecox*. New York, Nervous and Mental Disease Publishing Company, Monograph No. 3.

Kallmann, F. J. 1953. *Heredity in Health and Mental Disorder*. New York, W. W. Norton & Co., Inc., pp. 143-181.

Kasanin, J., Knight, E., and Sage, P. 1934. The parent-child relationship in schizophrenia. Journal of Nervous and Mental Disease *79*, 249-263.

Kety, S. S. 1959. Biochemical theories of schizophrenia. Science *129*, 1528-1532.

Kohn, M. L., and Clausen, J. A. 1955. Social isolation and schizophrenia. American Sociological Review *20*, 265-273.

Kohn, M. L., and Clausen, J. A. 1956. Parental authority behavior and schizophrenia. American Journal of Orthopsychiatry 26, 297-313.

Kringlen, E. 1964. Schizophrenia in male monozygotic twins. Acta Psychiatrica Scandinavica, Supplementum 178.

Kringlen, E. 1966. Schizophrenia in twins: An epidemiological-clinical study. Psychiatry 29, 172-184.

Lawes, T. G. G. 1963. Schizophrenia, Sernyl and sensory deprivation. British Journal of Psychiatry 109, 243-250.

Leveton, A. F. 1962. Reproach: The art of shamesmanship. British Journal of Medical Psychology 35, 101-111.

Lidz, R. W., and Lidz, T. 1949. The family environment of schizophrenic patients. American Journal of Psychiatry 106, 332-345.

Lidz, T., and Fleck, S. 1960. Schizophrenia, human integration and the role of the family. In The Etiology of Schizophrenia, ed. D. D. Jackson. New York, Basic Books, Inc., ch. 11.

Lidz, T., Parker, B., and Cornelison, A. 1956. The role of the father in the family environment of the schizophrenic patient. American Journal of Psychiatry 113, 126-132.

Lidz, T., Cornelison, A., Terry, D., and Fleck, S. 1958. Intrafamilial environment of the schizophrenic patient: VI. The transmission of irrationality. A.M.A. Archives of Neurology and Psychiatry 79, 305-316.

Luby, E. D., Gottlieb, J. S., Cohen, B. D., Rosenbaum, G., and Domino, E. F. 1962. Model psychoses and schizophrenia. American Journal of Psychiatry 119, 61-67.

Malis, G. Y. 1959. Research on the Etiology of Schizophrenia, tr. B. Haigh. New York, Consultanta Bureau, The International Behavioral Sciences Series, ed. J. Wortis.

Mark, J. C. 1953. The attitude of the mothers of male schizophrenics toward child behavior. Journal of Abnormal and Social Psychology 48, 185-189.

McGhie, A. 1961. A comparative study of the mother-child relationship in schizophrenia. British Journal of Medical Psychology 34, 195-221.

Meehl, P. E. 1962. Schizotaxia, schizotypy, schizophrenia. American Psychologist 17, 827-838.

Mishler, E. G., and Waxler, N. E. 1966. Family interaction and schizophrenia. A.M.A. Archives of General Psychiatry 15, 64-74.

Myers, J. K., and Roberts, B. H. 1959. Family and Class Dynamics in Mental Illness. New York, John Wiley & Sons, Inc.

Opler, M. K. 1956. Culture, Psychiatry and Human Values: The Methods and Values of a Social Psychiatrist. Springfield, Illinois, Charles C Thomas, Publisher.

Opler, M. K., and Singer, J. 1956. Ethnic differences in behavior and psychopathology: Italian and Irish. International Journal of Social Psychiatry 2, 11-23.

Payne, R. W. 1961. Cognitive abnormalities. In Handbook of Abnormal Psychology, ed. H. J. Eysenck. New York, Basic Books, Inc., ch. 6.

Payne, R. W., and Friedlander, D. 1962. A short battery of simple tests for measuring overinclusive thinking. Journal of Mental Science 108, 362-367.

Rado, S. 1960. Theory and therapy: The theory of schizotypal organization and its application to the treatment of decompensated schizotypal behavior. In The Out-Patient Treatment of Schizophrenia, ed. S. C. Scher and H. R. Davis. New York, Grune & Stratton, Inc., ch. 4.

Raphael, T., and Shaw, M. W. 1963. Chromosome studies in schizophrenia. Journal of the American Medical Association 183, 1022-1028.

Reichard, S., and Tillman, C. 1950. Patterns of parent-child relationships in schizophrenia. Psychiatry 13, 247-257.

Rennie, T. A. C. 1939. Follow-up study of 500 patients with schizophrenia admitted to the hospital from 1913-1923. A.M.A. Archives of Neurology and Psychiatry 42, 877.

Rosenthal, D. 1959. Some factors associated with concordance and discordance with respect to schizophrenia in monozygotic twins. Journal of Nervous and Mental Disease 129, 1-10.

Rosenthal, D. 1961. Sex distribution and the severity of illness among samples of schizophrenic twins. Journal of Psychiatric Research 1, 26-36.

Rosenthal, D. 1962, Problems of sampling and diagnosis in the major twin studies of schizophrenia. Journal of Psychiatric Research 1, 116-134.

Rosenthal, D., ed. 1963. The Genain Quadruplets: A Case Study and Theoretical Analysis of Heredity and Environment in Schizophrenia. New York, Basic Books, Inc.

Rosenthal, D. 1967. The offspring of schizophrenic couples. Journal of Psychiatric Research 4, 169-188.

Sanua, V. D. 1961. Sociocultural factors in families of schizophrenics. Psychiatry 24, 246-265.

Sargant, W., and Slater, E. 1954. An Introduction to Physical Methods of Treatment in Psychiatry 3rd edition. London, E. and S. Livingstone.

Schilder, P. 1939. The psychology of schizophrenia. Psychoanalytic Review 26, 380-398.

Simon, W., and Wirt, R. D. 1961. Prognostic factors in schizophrenia. American Journal of Psychiatry 117, 887-890.

Slater, E. 1953. Psychotic and Neurotic Illness in Twins. London, Her Majesty's Stationery Office, Medical Research Council Special Reports Series No. 278.

Smith, K., Tumphrey, M. W., and Hall, J. C. The "last straw": The decisive incident resulting in the request for hospitalization in 100 schizophrenic patients. American Journal of Psychiatry 120, 228-233.

Solomon, P., and Glueck, B. C., Jr., eds. 1964. Recent Research on Schizophrenia. Washington, D.C., American Psychiatric Association, Psychiatric Research Reports No. 19.

Storch, A. 1924. The Primitive Archaic Forms of

Inner Experiences and Thoughts in Schizophrenia. New York Nervous and Mental Diseases Publishing Company, Monograph Series No. 36.

Sullivan, T. M., Frohman, C. E., Beckett, P. G. S., and Gottlieb, J. S. 1966. Biochemical studies of families of schizophrenic patients. American Journal of Psychiatry *122,* 1040-1044.

Tienari, P. 1963. *Psychiatric Illnesses in Identical Twins.* Acta Psychiatrica Scandinavica, Supplementum 171.

Vaillant, G. E. 1966. The prediction of recovery in schizophrenia. International Journal of Psychiatry *2,* 617-627.

Vigotsky, L. S. 1934. Thought in schizophrenia. A.M.A. Archives of Neurology and Psychiatry *31,* 1063-1077.

Weakland, J. H. 1960. The "double-bind" hypothesis of schizophrenia and three-party interaction. In *The Etiology of Schizophrenia* ed. D. D. Jackson. New York, Basic Books, Inc., ch. 13.

Weakland, J. H., and Fry, W. F. 1962. Letters of mothers of schizophrenics. American Journal of Orthopsychiatry *32,* 604-623.

White, W. A. 1926. The language of schizophrenia. A.M.A. Archives of Neurology and Psychiatry *16,* 395-413.

Winkelman, W. W. 1952. Histopathology of mental disease. In *The Biology of Mental Health and Disease.* New York, Hoeber Medical Division, Harper & Row, Publishers, Inc., pp. 486-491.

Wolf, A., and Cowen, D. 1952. Histopathology of schizophrenia and other psychoses of unknown origin. In *The Biology of Mental Health and Disease.* New York, Hoeber Medical Division, Harper & Row, Publishers, Inc., ch. 28, pp. 469-486.

Zigler, E., and Phillips, L. 1962. Social competence and the process-reactive distinction in psychopathology. Journal of Abnormal and Social Psychology *65,* 215-222.

CHAPTER 19

The fault, dear Brutus, is not in our stars,
but in ourselves, that we are underlings.

From "Julius Caesar" by William Shakespeare

Trifles light as air
are to the jealous confirmations strong
as proofs of holy writ. . . .

From "Othello" by William Shakespeare

Paranoid Disorders

Paranoid disorders or reactions are psychoses characterized by persistent delusions, usually of reference, influence, persecution, or grandeur, frequently occurring in the absence of hallucinations. Paranoia and other paranoid reactions are distinguished from paranoid schizophrenia on the basis of age of onset; the logical development of well-systematized delusions; the preservation of intellectual function, appropriate emotional response, and social behavior; and a tendency for minimal personality deterioration over prolonged periods of time. However, many psychiatrists have long regarded paranoia and other paranoid reactions as being schizophrenic disorders that have a later onset than usual and are not accompanied by rapid personality disorganization.

Paranoia is derived from Greek roots meaning beside (or beyond or near) one's mind (or intellect or reason). The term was in use before the time of Hippocrates to describe any form of insanity, but virtually disappeared from medical literature around the second century A.D. It was reintroduced during the eighteenth century, and gradually came to be applied to those mental disorders characterized by delusional thinking. Kahlbaum (1863) defined paranoia as a well systematized delusional state of gradual development, little influenced by life experience, and without hallucinations or other disturbances in thinking. The term has sometimes been regarded as synonymous with *monomania*, in which an entire system of delu-

sions may follow logically upon a single false premise.

Kraepelin distinguished paranoia from the paranoid variety of dementia praecox or schizophrenia. However, Kolle (1931) reëvaluated 66 patients in whom the diagnosis of paranoia had been made earlier (including 19 cases described by Kraepelin) and in 62 of these he found evidence of primary delusions. Ninety percent of the patients became ill after the age of 35 years and a number of family histories were positive for schizophrenia. Most psychiatrists and psychologists have long regarded paranoia as extremely rare, and have seen at most a handful of cases in whom they were prepared to make this diagnosis. Many in fact regard the diagnosis of paranoia as of only historical interest, but consider the concept useful in providing a frame of reference in diagnosing and treating other paranoid reactions.

Paranoid states are psychoses characterized primarily by delusions, and are regarded as intermediate in form between the extremes of paranoid schizophrenia and the theoretical concept of true paranoia. The delusions occurring in paranoid states are fairly well systematized, although less logically than in true paranoia, and the patient does not show the gross thought disorder or regression that occurs in schizophrenic reactions. Kraepelin (1920) described these delusional states without personality deterioration under the term *paraphrenia* but one of his coworkers found that more than half the

78 patients Kraepelin diagnosed as paraphrenic had subsequently developed other signs of typical schizophrenia.

Paranoid personality characteristics involve being egocentric, narcissistic, and making excessive use of the mechanism of projection (whereby that which is emotionally unacceptable in the self is unconsciously rejected and attributed (projected) onto others). Such individuals tend to be extremely sensitive, unable to trust others, suspicious, jealous, and unreasonably ambitious. They are usually defensive, unable to admit mistakes or accept criticism, hostile, conscientious, and introverted.

Well-integrated patients with paranoid disorders may show little or nothing unusual in their appearance and social behavior. They may be dressed neatly and appropriately, eat and sleep satisfactorily, and be quite cooperative and communicative. On the other hand, their appearance, manner, and behavior may all reflect suspicion and intense hostility. They may be reserved and unsociable, superior or sarcastic in manner, or angry and aggressive to the point of being assaultive.

There may be some pressure of speech, and conversation may show continual preoccupation with the substance of the patient's delusions. Usually, however, the patient's attention can be gained, maintained, and directed, and he will answer questions relevantly. When there is no evidence of schizophrenic thought disorder, the paranoid individual's reasoning may appear intact, and his whole delusional system may seem to follow logically upon a single erroneous belief *(monomania)*. This situation may be likened to the claim attributed to Bertrand Russell that, given the basic assumption that zero equals one, anything can be proved mathematically. When asked to prove he was the Pope, he is said to have answered as follows: "If zero equals one, then one equals two (by adding one to each side of the equation). Now the Pope and I are two; therefore we are one."

Hallucinations may be present, but the typical feature of the paranoid psychosis is the presence of delusions of reference, active or passive influence, persecution, or grandeur. (See Figure 19-1.) Delusions of infidelity by the marital partner are not infrequent, and it may be difficult to establish beyond reasonable doubt that these are in fact delusional.

The intellectual capacity of the individual paranoid patient may be dull to normal or very superior, but there is some evidence that the average intellectual capacity and function of well-preserved paranoid patients is somewhat higher than that of paranoid schizophrenics, and may be slightly above average. Intellectual function remains unimpaired. Orientation is accurate, and there is no gross impairment of memory for recent or remote events.

The emotional tone may be within normal limits and the emotional reaction both adequate and appropriate. More frequently, associated with the delusional beliefs is a mood of anger and hostility from which there is little variation. True mirth is unusual, and humor is apt to be confined to sarcasm. However, it has been noted previously that paranoid ideation may be found associated with affective disorders, either mania or depression.

Conscience and judgment are well preserved except in so far as they are affected by the delusional system. Patients lack insight into the fact that their beliefs are delusional, but may gain such insight during the course of treatment, or they may become aware that other people regard their beliefs as delusional and hence cover up or no longer admit them.

It has already been pointed out that the main distinctions between paranoid schizophrenia, paranoia, and other paranoid states have been made on the basis of age of onset and degree of personality disorganization. However, within the group of paranoid disorders, distinctions have also been made on the basis of the predominant type of delu-

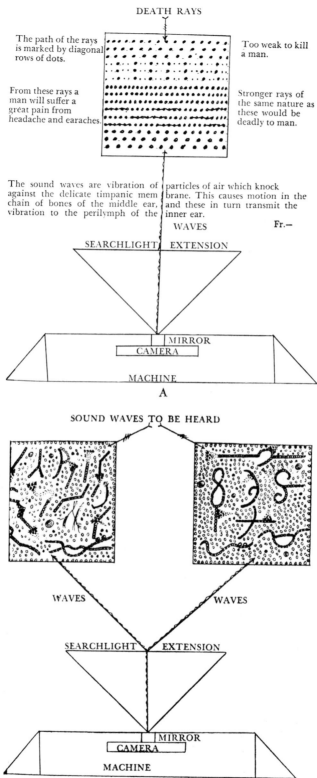

DEATH RAYS

The path of the rays is marked by diagonal rows of dots.

Too weak to kill a man.

From these rays a man will suffer a great pain from headache and earaches.

Stronger rays of the same nature as these would be deadly to man.

The sound waves are vibration of particles of air which knock against the delicate timpanic mem brane. This causes motion in the chain of bones of the middle ear, and these in turn transmit the vibration to the perilymph of the inner ear.

WAVES   Fr.—

SEARCHLIGHT EXTENSION

MIRROR

CAMERA

MACHINE

A

SOUND WAVES TO BE HEARD

WAVES   WAVES

SEARCHLIGHT   EXTENSION

MIRROR

CAMERA

MACHINE

These rays can be thrown almost in any color, such as red, dark red, blue and silver.

B

Figure 19-1. Legend on opposite page.

sions and the behavior to which these delusions may lead.

The most frequently observed syndrome involves delusions of reference, influence, and persecution, which are sometimes therefore described as "paranoid" delusions, although this is a tautology since the word paranoid itself means delusional. In any event, as such individuals search for and find increasing evidence of persecution by others, they frequently come to believe in the existence of what Cameron termed a "pseudocommunity." He defined the paranoid pseudocommunity as an imaginary organization, composed of real and imagined persons, whom the patient represents as united for the purpose of carrying out some action upon him. Once such beliefs have crystallized, a certain form of action may then appear logical and justifiable to the patient. One such possible course of action is attempted escape. An alternative form of action, however, involves retaliation, and this may result in litigation, assault, or homicide.

Other common forms of paranoid reaction involve delusional jealousy in which the patient has an unjustified conviction of the infidelity of the spouse; erotic delusions involving unjustified fears of imminent sexual assault by others; and paranoid grandiosity (or megalomania) in which the patient has an exaggerated view of his own importance, wealth, or power. Delusions of grandeur are apt to be very persistent, since they usually involve a greater degree of reality distortion than delusions of persecution.

We shall now present several further examples of typical paranoid behavior and one of folie a deux, which involves the sharing of paranoid ideas by two persons.

CONJUGAL PARANOID STATE

A 37-year-old married woman was referred for psychiatric evaluation because she had become convinced that other people were talking about her relationship with her husband, and that her husband was having an affair with another woman. The husband and other persons in the small town where they lived insisted that there was no basis for such beliefs, and the patient would be temporarily reassured, but she would soon become aware of further "evidence" in support of her doubts and fears, and the latter would once more attain the certainty of delusional conviction. At her first interview with the psychiatrist she reported as follows:

"I thought someone was talking about me and I let it become an obsession. It's never happened before—if someone has disapproved of me before, I've never let it bother me—a lot of illness in my husband's family— his father died last fall and his mother was taken to hospital right afterward with a recurrence of cancer. She was in hospital two months and was never the same again men-

---

Figure 19-1. " 'An influencing machine.' A forty-year-old paranoiac drew these diagrams of a mysterious 'machine' which, he claimed retrospectively, his 'enemies' had been using since his birth to read and control his thoughts and feelings, govern his actions through 'hip-not-ism' and 'electronic waves,' cause him to entertain evil sexual and other forbidden desires, and suffer trances, illnesses or, if they finally willed it, eventual death. The patient's persecutors were vaguely and variously identified as secret police, 'astrologers,' or supernatural cosmic agents possessed of an omnipotent influence called 'Sumna Loqui' (the 'highest word'?) but presumably jealous of his own great powers. These delusions evidently served a number of purposes: they replaced feelings of failure and deep inadequacy with fantasies of vicarious self-aggrandizement; they projected his erotic, homosexual and destructive impulses onto others and thus relieved him of responsibility for any counter-action he might take, and, less directly, they made it necessary for him to regress, in effect, to the custodial safety of a psychiatric hospital. The fixity of the patient's basic delusional formations is symbolized by the fact that, although the patient drew many diagrams of this machine, the ground plan of the construction was always the same and the object it influenced varied within narrow limits (compare A and B)." (Material courtesy of Adrian H. Vander Veer, M.D., from Masserman, J. H. 1961. *Principles of Dynamic Psychiatry.* 2nd edition. Philadelphia, W. B. Saunders Co.)

tally. We were remodeling the business and there were so many pressures — I was involved in so many civic affairs and practically never saw my husband. I felt very insecure — I felt I wasn't satisfying my husband although I was bending over backwards. He has never given me cause for jealousy but I got it in my mind that his secretary was talking about me — she was always laughing when I saw her. My husband and I went on a trip this spring and when we got back I got it in my head that he must be stepping out on me and he says he isn't but I just can't get it out of my mind. The more I sit at home, the more I think about it. I thought the secretary and others were talking about his stepping out on me. Then there were some other little incidents. When a certain woman's name came up, and there was a pause in conversation, people looked at me and I thought everything seemed to fit together. We went to a party one night and this woman was there and she gave me an odd look — my interpretation of the look was, 'Do you or don't you?' When my husband joined us she got up and walked away. I felt that something was the matter with our relationship. It just happened very innocently — the first time was after our return from the trip when this woman's name came up, she was supposed to be on a committee and the others stopped talking. I felt my husband was talking about her more than he ever had and was driving past her place more than he ever had. This last year we have had our problems and I felt I wasn't satisfying my husband — I wasn't doing anything as well as he wanted. I'd just draw into myself and let him make all the decisions. When I speak up and tell him what I want, he doesn't want to do it that way." When asked if there had been any change in their sexual relationship, she replied, "No, except I thought he was paying more attention to me — more than he needed to or wanted to. He was making love to me more often than he ever had, and I didn't feel it was spontaneous — as though he thought I expected him to do it that way."

The most crucial predisposing event of her childhood appeared to have been the divorce of her parents when she was only three years old. However, this traumatic event was only significant insofar as it was followed by years of adverse relationships and experiences. She was the youngest of six children, the next of whom was five years older than herself. She grew up in economic and emotional insecurity. Lacking any contact with her father, her main childhood relationship was with a hostile, demanding

mother. "Mother worked awfully hard bringing up us kids and she was rather bitter and I can remember her telling me many times how horrible men were. And she was very suspicious of me in high school. She was strict with me and suspicious of where I'd been and it used to bother me. She accused me of smoking and I'd never even tried it. She'd often accuse me of things I hadn't thought of doing. I always used to excuse her because she had a hard life, but it hurt me. Money bothered me — there just wasn't any extra — and I still have that feeling now. We had the necessities of food and clothes, but mother made my dresses too big — she was very practical — I had to go without toys and party dresses. I didn't blame her, but it always bothered me that I didn't have a father. In the sixth grade we copied a poem about father and made a booklet that we were supposed to take home to father. I took it home to my eldest brother and everyone in the family laughed at me — it hurt me and I ran to my room and cried. My four brothers teased me a lot and everybody told me what to do. I was never sure whether I would be able to do something — whether there would be enough money. The other girls were all so free and easy — I felt better when I started earning money babysitting in high school, but I remember saving money for material for a dress and my mother made it but all the same she complained about it — she did that lots of times with things that seemed important to me — she made me feel constantly guilty. I've been wondering why I'm so inhibited and don't speak up when I disagree. I don't remember being terribly unhappy as a child, but there were a lot of people who expected me to do things a certain way — I've always tried to be a good girl and I want people to like me." The mother was very strict and religious and would control the patient largely by indirect methods of discipline, particularly with withdrawal of love and approval.

After completing high school the patient got employment which also enabled her to obtain a college degree, and at the age of 24 she married a man several years older than herself who was from a well-to-do business family. They had one child who was born a couple of years later. Both she and her husband regarded their sexual relationship as mutually satisfactory although the patient said she didn't know anything about sex until she was a senior in high school. "I wondered if Mother was frigid. She wasn't demonstrative — she always kept her feelings to herself — she never touched the children —

she never told me anything about sex or menstruation."

The main difficulties in the patient's married life appear to have been related to her feelings of insecurity and alienation from other human beings. When she and her husband moved to a new town where he was a prominent member of the community, she and her son each at first found it difficult to make new friends. Having made this adjustment, however, she continued to remain reluctant to entertain as frequently as her husband wished. The most significant precipitating factor for her illness appeared to be a violent argument with her husband over her reluctance to entertain members of his family, during which he remarked to her, "Maybe we should get a divorce." The patient stated, "That really upset me. I think from that time on I was very very worried about our relationship — the mention of divorce. I've felt very insecure — worried that anything I might do might be the wrong thing." She felt so threatened by this that she was unable to mention it in any subsequent discussions with her husband.

She remained in hospital only three weeks, during which she was involved in daily psychotherapy, and also received phenothiazine medication which was continued for some months after her discharge. Her husband was also interviewed at the beginning and end of her brief stay in hospital, and there appeared to have been an improvement in their relationship, as well as abandonment of her paranoid ideation.

PARANOID STATE LEADING TO ATTEMPTED MURDER

A 75-year-old married man had been separated from his wife for approximately forty years, and had since been living by himself in a rundown shack, together with a number of chickens, dogs, cats, and other animals. He was always eccentric and suspicious, but was very interested in civic affairs, and for 20 years previously had been trying to get elected to the city council. One year he stood for election as mayor. He felt that the taxpayers were not getting a fair deal, and claimed that many of the members of the city council were crooked and dishonest. During the preceding ten years he had been brought to court on a total of 12 occasions, charged with a variety of offenses including gambling, leaving his animals at large, assault, and possession of an unregistered re-

volver. For several years prior to his admission to state hospital, he believed that the wife of his next door neighbor was a witch who caused small animals to come to him, and his admission to hospital was precipitated by his shooting her one day while she was hanging out the family washing.

This man was born in Italy and was one of four children. His parents were both illiterate and his father worked a small piece of land. He himself had little schooling and said that he attended irregularly due to frequent sickness as a child. One of his eyes was injured in a fight with another boy during his childhood and his vision from this eye was permanently reduced. He also lost the upper portion of one ear in a street fight as a boy. He remained at home until the age of 20, worked three years on a railroad in Germany, and then returned to Italy. At the age of 27 he married and a month later he emigrated. His wife joined him a year later and they apparently had four children, but after living together for four years he sent his wife and the children back to Italy. For the next ten years he lived with another woman, but became tired of her and ordered his wife to return to him. She did come back but after only two weeks he became upset by her nagging and left her and the children. He subsequently established residence in his shack and lived as an eccentric recluse up to the time of his admission to hospital.

On arrival in hospital he appeared to be having auditory hallucinations, and was observed talking to himself when there was no one nearby. He believed that as a child he and his mother were confronted by a witch who had been the cause of the deaths of two other children in the neighborhood. He claimed that his mother stood her ground and extracted from the witch a promise that no witch would harm her children for seven generations. The second time he came into contact with a witch was during his three years in Germany, when she criticized the way he was acting and annoyed him for about three weeks. The third witch he encountered was the wife of his next door neighbor, whom he claimed had been annoying him for four to five years prior to his admission to hospital. He believed that she frequently visited him in the form of wind, smoke, misty colors, and animals. He claimed that she and other witches tried to kill children on Wednesday and Friday nights. He described slashing with a knife at wind in his house when he was certain it was the witch, and he was pleased to see the neighbor's wife exhibiting a limp the following day. He also took a bottle of liquor which he believed to have been poisoned by the witch to various physicians and finally to the city council.

He was correctly oriented and showed no gross impairment of memory for recent or remote events, although he obtained a Memory Quotient of only 79 on the Wechsler Memory Scale. It was considered that this was not incompatible with a lifelong limitation of other intellectual functions, but he would not cooperate with formal intelligence testing. In view of his longstanding psychopathology and his danger to others, he remained in hospital for permanent custodial care.

LITIGINOUS BEHAVIOR IN A PARANOID INDIVIDUAL

The following abstract from a 1962 newspaper illustrates the seclusive and litiginous behavior of an unmarried woman who died suddenly of a heart attack at the age of 72 and left an estate of $106,000.

She was known as the eccentric victim of a persecution complex, and was popularly but erroneously supposed to have been a lawyer, or at least to have received formal training in the law.

A successful business woman before she succumbed to her obsession, she undertook her own study of legal matters when, in the 1920's, barristers refused to act in her behalf. She attempted to bring so many suits that in April, 1930, the Legislature passed the Vexatious Proceedings Act to control her passion for litigation. Under this act, she, or any person to whom it was applied, could only bring court actions with the permission of a Supreme Court judge. The act has since been applied to only two other persons.

Despite her familiarity with legal processes, Miss X left no will that can be found by the administrators of her estate. Her estate, when it has been probated, will be divided among her six surviving brothers and sisters.

As a younger woman, Miss X had run a prosperous fuel business. In her declining years she lived frugally in the isolation of her home, which had been barricaded against her imagined persecutors. Although she spent little on her own comfort, she dispatched a voluminous correspondence of letters and telegrams to public figures in Canada and the United States.

As a result of an action she brought against the postal authorities in 1939, there was no postal delivery to her home; she had complained that persons unknown were reading her mail; the post-office held her mail for her. A large bagful of letters and circulars was sorted in the process of winding up her estate.

Although she was frequently at odds with other people, Miss X had her own concept of integrity. After her death it was found that her debts amounted to less than $50, chiefly accounts owing large corporations which had not presented their bills.

FOLIE A DEUX

Baillarger (1860) reported the admission to hospital on the same day of two persons from the same family suffering from similar delusions. Lasegue and Falret (1877) introduced the terms folie à deux and folie communiquée. Marandon de Montyel (1891) divided folie à deux into three subgroups: folie simultanée (in which neither partner is dominant), folie communiquée (which was attributed to hereditary predisposition), and folie imposée (in which the delusions of one patient appeared completely dependent upon those of the other). Flournoy (1927) regarded the latter as a phenomenon of suggestion rather than a true psychosis, and stressed the affective relationship between the two persons involved. Gralnick (1942) also described folie à deux as "*the psychosis of association*" and emphasized its preponderance in persons who had been living together in intimate contact for a long time. Among 103 pairs recorded in the literature, he reported that 40 consisted of two sisters, 26 pairs of husband and wife, 24 of mother and child, 11 of two brothers, six of brother and sister, and 2 of father and child. The following is an example of folie imposée, in which the delusions of an only daughter were also adopted by her elderly mother.

The daughter was 28 years old and her mother 65 years old at the time of their admission to mental hospital, from the women's jail of a large city. Both they and the father were born in Poland and had immigrated to Canada over 20 years previously, but had still retained their Polish citizenship. They were of Jewish faith and poor financial status. The mother had received no education. The daughter had attended school to seventh grade and then left, due to financial difficulties. They had both lived with the father until six months before their admission to hospital, at which time he was admitted to an old people's home. However, mother and daughter had worked, eaten, and slept together for many years.

On arrival at the hospital, the daughter told the story that six years previously she had developed a nasal obstruction and had consulted a plastic surgeon in the United States who had performed an operation on her nose. After this, she was driving to the doctor's office when she was involved in an automobile accident and was thrown against the windshield of the car in which she was riding. She complained that ever since that time she had had excruciating pains all over her face and neck, and that her nose had also caused her a lot of trouble. She had attempted to sue the doctor for half a million dollars, but no lawyer would handle her case, so she and her mother had entered his house and had refused to leave until he had paid them this amount. They were arrested and taken to court, and after being detained for some time, they were deported to Canada.

On five occasions after this she and her mother entered the United States and attempted to sue the doctor. Finally the United States Immigration Officer in Canada refused to issue them a visa, and it became obvious to them that he was being paid by the doctor to keep them out of the country. Accordingly, they tried to collect the half million dollars from the immigration officer. She and her mother waited in his office every day for several weeks until they were arrested and taken to jail prior to their transfer to the mental hospital. In addition to her primary delusions, the daughter showed poorly integrated delusions of persecution by others, and reported that she and her mother had had a lot of trouble in their rooming house during the preceding few months due to the fact that other people were after their money.

The mother told exactly the same story as her daughter, felt that her daughter's claims were well founded, and also told of their persecution in various rooming houses. In addition, she said that the doctor had ruined her daughter's health and that the latter would be unable to marry until her nose was healed. The mother was very anxious for her daughter to get married, in which case she would, of course, live with her daughter and son-in-law. Both of them wished to be released from the hospital as soon as possible in order to return to the United States and collect from the doctor.

Shortly after their admission to the hospital, mother and daughter were separated for a period of about three months during which the daughter underwent an intensive program of electroshock treatments and insulin coma therapy. Initially there was a change in her delusional system, in that she felt the doctor wished to pay her the half million dollars, but was being prevented from doing so by her relatives. Thereafter she reverted to her former beliefs and these remained quite unshakable. During this period of separation the mother became at first severely depressed, and then appeared to lose her conviction in her daughter's delusional system. However, she could not accept the fact that her daughter was sick, and remained anxious for them both to leave the hospital at the earliest opportunity. When the daughter's program of treatment was terminated, and her delusional system was found to be unchanged from the time of her admission, she and her mother were reunited and thereafter remained inseparable companions in one of the chronic wards of the hospital.

DYNAMICS, DEVELOPMENT, AND CAUSATION

Cameron (1959) pointed out that from a dynamic standpoint the position of paranoid reactions is an anomalous one. On the one hand, the existence of delusions that tend to expand and their resistance to correction by reality contradiction indicate that these conditions are psychotic. On the other hand, the paranoid patient may be in much better contact with reality than other psychotic patients, both affective and schizophrenic, and may give the outward appearance of a normal or psychoneurotic adaptation. Freud (1896) recognized this situation in describing a paranoid reaction as both a defense neurosis and a defense psychosis. In his subsequent analysis of Schreber's autobiography, Freud (1911) made his classic interpretations of the paranoid mechanism of denial and projection. He drew attention to Schreber's transient conscious wish to be a woman during sexual intercourse, his subsequent denial and projection of this wish, and its return in the form of a conscious expectation of sexual assault. Freud therefore proposed as verbal approximations for the paranoid denial, the statement, "I do not love him. I hate him." and for the paranoid projection, "He hates (persecutes) me, which justifies my hating him."

A number of analysts postulated that all paranoid reactions in men and women involve denial and projection of latent homosexual impulses. Others emphasized that the paranoid patient may be denying and projecting hostility or heterosexuality rather than homosexuality. Thus, the following verbal approximations may be offered for delusions of infidelity occurring in paranoid women: "I do not hate my husband and reject him sexually; I love him, but he is unfaithful to me and rejects my love." Similarly, paranoid women with delusions of sexual assault may be saying in effect, "I do not want sexual relations with anyone other than my husband, but someone else is trying to seduce me."

Since paranoid reactions are widely regarded as late-onsetting forms of paranoid schizophrenia, it is generally assumed that the same causal factors are operative. The fact that paranoid reactions are also diagnosed far less frequently than schizophrenic reactions has also contributed to their attracting only a fraction of the research effort that has been devoted to the schizophrenias. We shall therefore mention only a few additional studies concerning paranoid disorders.

Miller (1941, 1942) reviewed the histories of 400 hospitalized psychotic patients with marked paranoid trends and found evidence of paranoid illness in the ancestors of only eight of these patients (i.e., two percent). Forty-four of these patients (11 percent) were direct descendants of persons known to have suffered from psychiatric disorders.

Kay and Roth (1961) undertook a clinical follow-up and genetic study of 99 patients aged 60 years and over, suffering from "late paraphrenia," who had been admitted to a Swedish and an English mental hospital. Both groups showed similar characteristics, which included a predominance of females over males (in a ratio of about seven to one) and an excess of unmarried patients among both sexes. In contrast with comparable patients having affective disorders, significantly more paraphrenics were living alone at the time they became ill, and among those living alone many more of the paranoid patients were socially isolated. The authors related this social isolation to deafness, personality abnormalities, and relatively few surviving relatives. They concluded that late paraphrenia was the mode of manifestation of schizophrenia in old age, and that social isolation was partly a consequence of self-segregation but partly also a contributing causal factor.

Lucas et al. (1962) attempted to relate the content of delusions in a series of hospitalized schizophrenics to the patient's age, sex, and some of his social and familial characteristics. They found that delusions with religious or supernatural content were more frequent in persons of higher social status, and also in the unmarried. Grandiose delusions were more frequent in persons of higher social status and in eldest as compared with youngest siblings. Delusions of inferiority tended to have the opposite distribution. Paranoid (persecutory) delusions increased in frequency with increasing age of onset, were more common in persons born in other parts of the country than those born in the locality of the hospital, and were more common in youngest as compared with eldest siblings. Sexual delusions occurred much more often in women than men, and tended to be more frequent in the married than the single.

Several authors described well-integrated paranoid reactions which they regarded as different from schizophrenia, among displaced persons from Eastern European countries who subsequently immigrated to North America or Australia. Such authors speak of "the persecutory delusions of lingually isolated persons" and "aliens' paranoid reactions," pointing out that such persons are displaced both horizontally (to a new country with a new language and new jobs) and vertically (to a lower economic and social level), and exposed to loneliness and adaptational stresses. Ruth Benedict described a paranoid personality as a universal feature of the Dobu tribe of New Guinea, and it seems probable that the frequency of paranoid personalities of psychoses varies considerably from one culture or subculture to another. However, the relative significance of biological, psychological, and sociocultural determinants remains as uncertain as in the schizophrenic reactions.

TREATMENT

The main differences between the treatment and prognosis for patients with paranoid states and those with paranoid schizophrenia are related to differences in the age of onset, duration of abnormality prior to treatment, and reality situation to which the patient must adapt. The more advanced age of most patients with paranoid states has both positive and negative aspects in comparison with the treatment of the patients with paranoid schizophrenia. The observation that "you can't teach an old dog new tricks" may be translated into the concept that older patients are less likely to undergo radical personality reconstruction with prolonged intensive individual psychotherapy. On the other hand, a later age of onset of psychotic reality distortion may imply more successful adaptation throughout earlier periods of stress or deprivation. It may therefore be relatively easier to bring

about reintegration to the prepsychotic level of personality function.

Of critical importance in this respect is the duration of paranoid systematology prior to the initiation of treatment. The former view that paranoid disorders were more consistently chronic than schizophrenic disorders may well have been related to a more prolonged duration of psychosis prior to treatment. During the period when insulin coma therapy was popular in the treatment of schizophrenia (approximately 1933 through 1953), the treatment of middle-aged or elderly paranoid patients may also have been relatively less effective, since this treatment was generally considered too dangerous for patients over the age of 40 to 45 years. In other respects, however, the treatment of patients with paranoid disorders has been very similar to that employed in the treatment of younger patients with schizophrenia. Of recent years, this has generally involved a combination of psychosocial therapies with phenothiazine medication. The latter approach has resulted in a greatly improved prognosis for patients with paranoid disorders, which may also be partly attributed to greater availability of community psychiatric resources and earlier acceptance and utilization of such services.

In symptomatic paranoid states associated with acute reversible organic brain syndromes, it may be anticipated that resolution of the organic brain syndrome will usually be accompanied by restoration of the prepsychotic personality. Similarly, paranoid ideation associated with depressive and manic disorders also tends to resolve when the affective disorder undergoes remission. In either instance, however, paranoid ideas and behavior may persist after the resolution of organic intellectual impairment or affective disorder, and require continuing psychotherapy and medication. Efforts toward resocialization also require the involvement of available family and community resources, and lasting remission may be anticipated following the removal of adverse precipitating and perpetuating psychosocial stress or deprivation.

SELECTED REFERENCES

American Psychiatric Association. 1952. *Diagnostic and Statistical Manual of Mental Disorders.* Washington, D.C., American Psychiatric Association.

Ascher, E. 1949. Folie à deux. AMA Archives of Neurology and Psychiatry *61,* 177-182.

Benedict, R. 1934. *Patterns of Culture.* Boston, Houghton Mifflin Co. Reprinted 1946, Mentor Book #M89.

Cameron, N. 1947. *The Psychology of Behavior Disorders.* Boston, Houghton Mifflin Co., Ch. 14.

Cameron, N. 1959. Paranoid conditions and paranoia. In *American Handbook of Psychiatry.* Ed. S. Arieti. New York, Basic Books, Inc., Vol. 1, Ch. 25.

Flournoy, H. 1927. Folie à deux. Schweiz. Arch. f. Neurol. u. Psych. *20,* 44.

Freud, S. 1896. Further remarks on the defense neuro-psychoses. In *Standard Edition.* London, Hogarth Press, 1955, Vol. 1.

Freud, S. 1911. Psychoanalytic notes upon an autobiographical account of a case of paranoia (dementia paranoides). In *Standard Edition.* London, Hogarth Press, 1955, Vol. 14.

Gralnick, A. 1942. Folie à deux: the psychosis of association. Psychiatric Quarterly *16,* 230-260.

Gregory, I. 1950. The therapeutic problem of folie à deux. McGill Medical Journal *19,* 64-67.

Kay, D. W. K., and Roth, M. 1961. Environmental and hereditary factors in the schizophrenias of old age ("late paraphrenia") and their bearing on the general problem of causation in schizophrenia. Journal of Mental Science *107,* 649-686.·

Kolle, K. 1931. *Primary Paranoia.* Leipzig, G. Thieme.

Listwan, I. A., 1956. Paranoid states: social and cultural aspects. Medical Journal of Australia, May 12, 1956. Reprinted in World Mental Health *11,* 171-177.

Lucas, C. J., Sainsbury, P., Collins, J. G. 1962. A social and clinical study of delusions in schizophrenia. Journal of Mental Science *108,* 747-758.

Miller, C. W. 1941. The paranoid syndrome. AMA Archives of Neurology and Psychiatry *45,* 953-963.

Miller, C. W. 1942. Factors affecting the prognosis of paranoid disorders. Journal of Nervous and Mental Disease *95,* 580-588.

Modlin, H. C. 1963. Psychodynamics and management of paranoid states in women. AMA Archives of General Psychiatry *8,* 263-268.

Moore, R. A., Selzer, M. L. 1963. Male homosexuality, paranoia and the schizophrenias. American Journal of Psychiatry *119,* 743-747.

Planansky, K., and Johnston, R. 1962. The incidence and relationship of homosexual and paranoid features in schizophrenia. Journal of Mental Science *108,* 604-615.

Tyhurst, J. S. 1958. Paranoid patterns. In *Explorations in Social Psychiatry.* ed. A. H. Leighton, J. A. Clausen, and R. N. Wilson. New York, Basic Books, Inc., Ch. 2.

CHAPTER 20

The only way to get rid of a temptation is to yield to it.

from "The Picture of Dorian Gray" by Oscar Wilde

Delinquency and Sociopathic Personality

Man is not born with a knowledge of right and wrong, and the child is dependent on others to communicate this information to him by their words and example. However, neither is he born with a conscience or internal control system that ensures he will always behave in accordance with such communicated knowledge. He is motivated primarily by self-interest, and will learn to conform with the demands of others when such demands are consistently reinforced by rewards and punishment, approval and disapproval. Initially, he will abandon unacceptable behavior through fear of inevitable detection and unpleasant external consequences. Later, with the development of conscience, he will reject unacceptable behavior from habit, and from the knowledge that it would be accompanied by unpleasant internal consequences in the form of guilt and remorse.

Different societies and individual families within these societies vary enormously in their definitions of unacceptable behavior, their efficiency in detecting such behavior, and their behavior toward the individual who has been discovered breaking any given one of their rules. The sum total of the individual's previous experience, together with the current responses of authority and peers to a specific behavior, then determines the probability with which

that behavior will be rejected or repeated in future.

A *crime* has been defined as any act or omission prohibited by public law for the protection of the public, and made punishable by the state in a judicial proceeding in its own name. It is a public wrong, as distinguished from a mere private wrong or civil injury to an individual. Since crime has no inherent universal property, it is unreasonable to expect that all criminals will share any single personality characteristic. As MacIver (1942) pointed out, the crime committer may be a maniac or a genius, a scoundrel or a patriot, a man without scruple or a man who puts his scruples above the law, a reckless exploiter or a man in desperate need.

Delinquency is a term traditionally applied to juvenile offenders against any law, whether civil or criminal. Bovet (1951) pointed out, however, that in many European countries a minor is legally considered a delinquent only if his breach of the penal code is an offense for the whole population. In the United States, on the other hand, the charges on which a minor appears before a court cover a wide range of behavior including truancy from school, consistent disobedience to parents, consumption of alcohol, and smoking in public. The most objective criterion of delinquency is simply an established

479

police or court record for apprehension and conviction. Within this group, however, the severity of the problem in individual cases may be reliably differentiated on the basis of frequency and severity of offense. Only a small proportion of delinquents manifest persistent criminal behavior in adult life, although a somewhat larger proportion of adult criminal offenders have a history of delinquent behavior during adolescence.

Prichard (1835) used the term *moral insanity* to describe certain criminals with an absence of feeling, absence of control, and absence of all ethical sense. The concept of moral insanity or moral imbecility remained influential throughout the remainder of the nineteenth century until Koch introduced the term *psychopathic inferiority* to describe patients with a severe type of impulsive antisocial behavior disorder. In the United States, the term *psychopathic personality* persisted throughout the first half of the present century, and was defined in the American Psychiatric Association glossary as "a person whose behavior is predominantly amoral or anti-social and characterized by impulsive, irresponsible actions satisfying only immediate and narcissistic interests, without concern for obvious and implicit social consequences, accompanied with minimal outward evidence of anxiety or guilt."

During the same period of time, such individuals were described by a number of psychoanalysts who applied terms such as *impulse neuroses, instinct-ridden characters*, or simply *character disorders*. There is some ambiguity in the latter term, however, since it has also been used to include a very different group of patients with neurotic personality characteristics, whose difficulties involve their relationships with other people but not antisocial behavior.

The behavior of the typical psychopath is directed toward immediate gratification of his own selfish impulses. He wants what he wants when he wants it, without any consideration for the wishes of others. It is therefore not he but the other members of society who suffer primarily, although he may well suffer the consequences of their retaliation. Since, however, it is primarily other members of society who suffer from his behavior, the term psychopathic personality has been increasingly replaced by the term *sociopathic personality disturbance*, which has been defined as follows: "Individuals to be placed in this category are ill primarily in terms of society and of conformity with the prevailing cultural milieu, and not only in terms of personal discomfort and relations with other individuals." This latter group of disorders includes antisocial and dyssocial reactions, sexual deviation, alcoholism, and drug addiction. However, sexual deviation, alcoholism, and addiction are very heterogeneous disorders that include many persons with neuroses or psychoses, and will therefore be considered separately in subsequent chapters. The remainder of the present chapter will be devoted to delinquency and sociopathic personality, the main characteristics of which are contrasted with those of the neurotic personality in Table 20-1.

Appearance, manner, and language may all be typical of certain groups of adolescents and young adults who are in rebellion and conflict with their parents and society at large. The details change from time to time, but frequently include a certain type of haircut, certain items of clothing (e.g., a black leather jacket or clothing tailored in a certain way), a truculent and hostile manner, and an extensive slang vocabulary. In many other cases, however, the sociopathic personality is not readily distinguishable from normal. These people may be of either sex, from any social class, good-looking and intelligent, and quite skillful in hiding their antisocial attitudes and history.

Motor activity is within normal limits; attention can be gained, maintained, and directed; speech is coherent and intelligible; and replies to questions are usually relevant and logical. Patients are

TABLE 20–1. Typical Neurotic and Sociopathic Personality Characteristics

NEUROTIC PERSONALITY	SOCIOPATHIC PERSONALITY
(Symptomatic, Situational or Character Neuroses)	*(Antisocial or Dyssocial Personality; Psychopathic Personality; Instinct-ridden Character; Character or Behavior Disorders)*
Predominantly female (approx. 3:2)	Predominantly male (approx. 3:1)
First psychiatric contact at any age.	First psychiatric contact prior to age of 40 years.
Equal distribution of new cases in all social classes, but concentration of treated cases in upper classes.	Concentration in lower socioeconomic classes and areas.
Rigid superego, conscience of internal control system.	Defective or absent superego, conscience and internal controls.
Frequent regrets, guilt, and depression over minor or imagined past mistakes or misdeeds.	Minimal or no regrets, guilt, or depression over serious past antisocial behavior.
Excessive inhibition of present impulses (particularly sexual or aggressive) in anticipation of long-range advantage. Conformity with standards of civilized society.	Uninhibited acting-out of hedonistic impulses, with inability to postpone immediate gratification for future reward. Reckless antisocial behavior.
Moral, reliable, responsible, but lack self-confidence and may be indecisive. Devout or conflicted over religion.	Amoral, unreliable, irresponsible. Pathological liar, cheat, swindler, thief. May be promiscuous, violent, or addicted to alcohol or drugs. Indifferent to religion.
Ambitious plans and striving for goals in remote future, and intangible ideals with much doubt, fear, anxiety, and apprehension.	Absence of long-range plans or efforts, and freedom from worry or anxiety; confident and carefree.
Strives to attain and retain affection of others. Insecure and sensitive to criticism. Frequent feelings of inadequacy and worthlessness.	Does not care what other people think of him, so long as this does not frustrate his immediate goals.
Capable of deep affection, but latent (unconscious) hostility often interferes with ability to maintain warm relationships.	Incapable of true affection for others, but uses superficial charm and plausibility to manipulate others.
Sexual impulses or behavior appear dangerous or disgusting, with resulting frigidity or impotence.	Transient enjoyment of uninhibited sexual behavior with wide variety of partners.
Aggressive impulses not permitted direct expression, but may be displaced onto others, or achieve indirect expression.	Hostility may be expressed directly and violently if this does not interfere with goals of the moment.
Autonomic lability and tendency to ectomorphic body build (except in hysteria).	Frequent electroencephalographic abnormalities and tendency to mesomorphic body build.
Frequent history of similar disorder in parents and siblings; parental deprivation, discord, domination and demands; restricted relationships with siblings and peers; high achievement in school and occupation with continued social conformity.	Frequent history of similar disorder in parents and siblings. parental deprivation, discord (often illegitimacy or desertion by parents) deceit, and lack of supervision, poor example or controls (occasionally overindulgence), association with delinquent peers or siblings; truancy, job instability, and nomadism; record of conflict with police or military authorities and often jail sentences.

quite capable of giving a detailed history of their background and development, but they are pathological liars and the history they give tends to conflict with that obtained from other sources. However, they will often admit to resentment and hostility toward their parents; rebellion leading to rupture with parents at adolescence; expulsion from, frequent changes of, or truancy from school; changes in job at intervals that average less than six months; repeated convictions for antisocial behavior; failure to respond to either appeals or punishment; and poorly defined or abandoned goals or plans for the future.

Intellectual capacity and function appear to be distributed in the same manner as in the general population, but the antisocial personality tends to have a higher intelligence than would be expected from his school achievement and occupation. There is no impairment of intellectual function, memory, or orientation; nor is there ordinarily evidence of illusions, hallucinations, or delusions. However, patients with sociopathic personality may sometimes develop psychoses (the most common being schizophreniform) or pseudopsychoses: e.g., Ganser's syndrome of approximate answers, usually developing in prisoners awaiting trial, on the basis of either malingering or of a dissociative reaction.

Mood and emotional reaction are frequently within normal limits, but there may be a prevailing attitude of hostility or mood of depression resulting from situational stress. The poor controls may permit the psychopath to react to these emotions impulsively by physical assault (even homicide), or suicidal attempts or gestures (often ineffectual and not repeated). Judgment and insight are both impaired, and careful evaluation of the patient's words and deeds will enable recognition of the defective conscience and internal control system.

The sociopath has a low tolerance of frustration and is oriented toward action without forethought. Frequently he comes to psychiatric attention because of *threats to harm himself or others*, as in the case of a middle-aged man who had recently been divorced by his second wife and was now threatening to kill her or himself unless she returned to him.

It developed that he had met her when he was in military service, and she was a prostitute. He was in the military police and would clear all the enlisted personnel off her premises, preparatory to returning and spending the night with her. After their marriage, they each continued a life of promiscuity, but he became increasingly jealous over her extramarital affairs and would sometimes beat her up. She divorced him for physical and mental cruelty but was terrified by his continued jealousy and threats to harm her. When she refused to return to him, he became genuinely depressed and threatened suicide, but even at this time he expressed no guilt nor remorse over considerable antisocial behavior including lying and cheating others besides his former wife. When she left the state, and it was evident that he could not get her back, his depression improved rapidly and he soon started living with another woman, to whom he promised marriage without any intention of keeping his word.

Sometimes the suicidal threat is at least temporarily successful in manipulating the behavior of the other person involved, and this is particularly true when the other person believes a genuine suicidal attempt has been made.

A girl who was rejected by her boy friend reported as follows:

"I decided he could not do this so I tried to talk him out of it, but it didn't work, so I thought I'd try to scare him more by trying to commit suicide. I didn't really want to die, I just wanted more or less to scare him, so I took a bunch of tranquilizers and sedatives and aspirin, and I meant to tell my roommate what I was doing (that I was committing suicide) but I got so sleepy I dropped off. My boy friend says he doesn't feel guilty but he does, and he thinks I did it for him, and that I really was trying to kill myself. The situation is now almost the same as it was before, except I've got more of a hold over him." The hold, however, didn't last, and the boy friend was glad to escape from the relationship a few months later.

The sociopath can resist anything but temptation, and the male will frequently use the words "I love you" simply as a key to unlock the door to intercourse, while the female will often picture herself as a girl who can't say no, as in the following lines from *Oklahoma* by Rodgers and Hammerstein.

It ain't so much a question of not knowing what to do.
I knew what's right and wrong since I've been ten.
I heared a lot of stories and I reckon they are true
About how girls are put upon by men.
I know I mustn't fall into the pit.
But when I'm with a feller I fergit.
I'm just a girl who cain't say no.
I'm in a terrible fix.
I always say "Come on let's go."
Just when I ought to say "Nix.". . .

The recklessness of some psychopaths is reflected in an undue susceptibility to accidental injury or "*accident-proneness*," one impulsive 20-year-old boy gave a history of a dozen accidents during adolescence, which included being thrown off horses he had been told not to ride and several injuries resulting from fighting with other boys his own age. On one of these occasions he and his brother had been fighting with knives, and on another they were "horsing around" with pitchforks. It is irresponsible behavior such as this that leads to a high frequency of accidental injury and death among adolescent and young males (Table 20-2). It is very probable that the higher rate of mortality among such individuals is one of the reasons for a lower frequency of sociopathic personality among the population surviving to older ages. Other reasons for the diminished frequency observed in middle age include gradual abandonment of sociopathic behavior, removal from circulation by prolonged prison sentences, and adop-

TABLE 20-2. Age-Sex-Race-Specific Rates of Death by Accidents, United States, 1963*

AGE IN YEARS	WHITE MALE	WHITE FEMALE	NONWHITE MALE	NONWHITE FEMALE
Under 1 year	80.3	63.3	165.6	156.0
1–4	32.2	22.8	57.8	46.7
5–9	22.3	11.3	34.5	24.8
10–14	24.8	8.8	38.1	12.1
15–19	81.0	23.1	82.2	18.9
20–24	108.6	21.8	121.4	22.9
25–29	76.4	15.5	119.8	27.5
30–34	65.1	14.9	108.6	28.8
35–39	63.6	17.3	111.8	26.6
40–44	63.2	19.7	120.0	29.0
45–49	71.0	22.5	118.8	31.1
50–54	80.5	25.4	132.5	39.7
55–59	87.9	28.8	130.4	37.6
60–64	92.7	36.3	148.9	59.3
65–69	105.5	47.0	165.5	72.2
70–74	138.0	76.7	172.8	91.9
75–79	197.2	137.6	173.9	127.8
80–84	321.5	272.2	236.5	164.4
85 years and over	657.8	669.0	339.4	357.8

*Death rates per 100,000 living general population.
Data from U.S. Department of Health, Education, and Welfare. Vital Statistics of the United States, 1963, Volume II — Mortality.

tion by some of a predominant pattern of chronic alcoholism.

Early attempts at *classification of psychopathic personality* resulted in profusion and confusion. Kraepelin described seven types of psychopath, Schneider ten types, and Kahn listed 16 types which included psychoneurotic reactions as well as a variety of eccentricities and frailties. Henderson's classification of psychopathic states, on the other hand, contained only three subgroups: (1) predominantly aggressive, showing impulsive violence toward themselves or others, which might be manifested by suicide, homicide, alcoholism and drug addiction, epilepsy, or sexual perversion; (2) predominantly inadequate or passive, which included both petty delinquents with thieving, lying, and swindling propensities, and those showing types of invalidism closely allied to psychoneurotic and psychotic states; (3) predominantly creative, or intellectually gifted individuals manifesting impulsive, egocentric, and socially unacceptable behavior.

In the United States, psychiatrists and psychologists have tended to divide persistent delinquents and sociopathic personalities into two broad groups distinguished from each other by their background and development instead of the nature of antisocial behavior manifested. Thus, Johnson (1959) distinguished between the unconsciously driven *individual delinquent* from the so-called "good or normal" family, and the gang or *sociologic group delinquent* operating at any economic level. The former group corresponds with what other authors have described as maladaptive delinquency or antisocial reaction, whereas the latter group corresponds with the concept of adaptive delinquency or dyssocial reaction. Examples of each will be given below.

The term *antisocial reaction* refers to chronically antisocial individuals who are always in trouble, profiting neither from experience nor punishment, and maintaining no real loyalties to any person, group, or code. They are frequently callous and hedonistic, showing marked emotional immaturity, with lack of sense of responsibility, lack of judgment, and an ability to rationalize their behavior so that it appears warranted, reasonable, and justified. Two such cases will now be reviewed.

A 20-year-old boy was admitted to a psychiatric hospital on a court order, at the request of his father, who hoped thereby to enable him to escape the legal consequences of his serious antisocial behavior, which included moving traffic violations, stealing parts from automobiles, and escaping from police custody. It developed that his father had previously sought the patient's admission to a psychiatric hospital because he was unemployed and uncontrollable at home, but he now wished to use the results of psychiatric evaluation to prevent the boy from being fined or admitted to jail. When asked about the circumstances of his admission to hospital, the boy replied as follows.

"My father put out a warrant for me to be put in hospital because I was sitting around the house doing nothing—so I got a job then, and was living with some friends in an apartment. I left home about four months ago, and then one day I went home and my folks weren't home—and I talked to a few of my friends and everyone was busy—so I sat watching TV and some friends came and we had a little party—and I was sitting out in this girl's car talking. I was behind the wheel (I don't have a license) and followed a friend home three blocks, and on the way the police stopped me. I had had my license suspended for speeding. After the police arrested me and handcuffed me, I ran away to a friend's house and took the handcuffs off—his father had a hacksaw and grinder—and then went out of town for a couple of months and worked in a gas station. Then the police came down and picked me up there and took me to jail for a night—but they found my father had a warrant out to take me to the hospital, so they had to take me there."

The patient was the oldest of three children, all boys, the next one being five years younger than himself. His father was a well-to-do business man, who had a part time job as a law enforcement officer, but thought nothing of driving considerably in excess of the speed limit because he could get away with it. Mother was quite anxious and concerned about the boy's behavior, and it may be significant that she belatedly paid the bill for his psychiatric evaluation, although this had been requested by father and the bill had been submitted to him. A joint interview with both parents revealed a very long history of rebellion and nonconformity on the part of the boy, which had been handled quite ineffectually by the parents, both of whom seemed quite amused by many incidents of antisocial behavior that they described. His father gave the following history.

"The problem started in the first grade of school. He was a nonconformist from the beginning. The teachers would say, 'Take out paper and pencil,' and he would if he felt like it. He skimmed through the first six grades not using his ability. We sent him to a private day school in the seventh grade and he continued the same pattern. He has always been skinny and sensitive about this. He wouldn't swim at the public beach—we'd have to go up aways. I could never work with him. *We were at each other's throats all the time.* He'd never cooperate. Whatever you did, he'd fight it every inch of the way. He was at the private school for three years and didn't participate in anything. They tried everything—marking him high, no pressure, then pressure, competition with other boys—nothing worked. They asked to have him withdrawn, so we put him back in public school and he got into lots of trouble. He just sat there and did nothing. They didn't want him back there any more. He had to repeat grade 11. He was only kept in high school to keep him off the street and he didn't graduate. He'd take the car without our permission. He stole hubcaps and there were traffic violations. He ran away from home for two-three days with the car. We had him see a psychiatrist and then took him to court. We tried voluntary probation but he did not keep his appointments. He was uncooperative at home, making life miserable for everybody. When he quit school, we told him he couldn't just sit home so he got a job. Our last dealings at home I couldn't talk to him at all. He lied to me brazenly. I couldn't believe anything he said. We sent him to summer camps but no one was ever able to change him. He worked for six months and then got into trouble. He won't take a bus. He'd walk several miles rather than ride a bus. When he has a job, it's all right as long as someone picks him up. On his own, he's late or sick and doesn't go.

"At the age of 17 he was in a psychiatric hospital for six weeks. He was incorrigible. He stole a car—I imagine a lot of boys his age do take a car now and then. He took this car and was speeding about 120 miles an hour to escape the police. He knocked one of the tires off the wheel by hitting the center island, but he still drove the car about half a mile trying to get away. They booked him for drunken driving, but didn't press charges on stealing the car. *I fixed that up with the owner and had it repaired.* Through all these escapades we finally talked to the judge about the question of whether he should go to the reformatory or was he mentally ill—so we put him in the hospital for six weeks. As far as the psychiatrist was concerned at that time, it was a character disorder, which could go one way or the other. After leaving hospital he fooled around in school for another year, then got a job for six months, then got into trouble with other boys stealing batteries or cars. He was in jail a couple of days and lost his job. His accident record was terrible—every time he took a car he'd be picked up. I talked his grandmother into giving him her car for half of what it was worth and he got risk insurance. He promised he wouldn't change the car but in a couple of weeks he did. He had his license taken away from him three times, but he continued driving anyway and he got picked up for having a loud muffler. You almost have the impression *he's trying to get punished.*

"Three things happened at the same time—stealing, driving after his license was suspended, and something else. He was locked up and the fine was $150. We wouldn't pay the fine but his friends pooled their cash and did. He promised the lawyer and judge to go into military service but he didn't. *He has never had to face consequences.* He just sat home and didn't go into service. It was impossible living with him. He'd do everything to aggravate us, so I gave him $100 to get out of the house and he rented a room. The landlord heard him pacing the floor all night and reported his friends were hoodlums. They had parties and made too much noise so he had to move. The landlord arranged with him to take a course at vocational school but he only went for a couple of days and then quit. At summer school he'd only go when he could drive the car. He sat home for three months doing nothing. We finally said he was going to go voluntarily for psychiatric help or we'd have him committed. His main job was aggravating his mother. We got the ambulance and he ran away and lived with friends in the neighborhood for six weeks. He came home to wash his clothes. The police had a warrant and told me to call the police, but I was afraid to. Then we went away for a weekend and he got into the house and had a party. He drove a girl home in her car and the police caught him. They handcuffed him and he ran away and went to a friend's house, got rid of the handcuffs and got the friend to take him out of town. He worked in a filling station until a couple of days before the police picked him up there and took him to jail."

He was of average intelligence and showed no evidence of organic intellectual impairment nor of psychotic reality distortion. There was no evidence of guilt or remorse over his antisocial attitudes or behavior, and the only elevation the MMPI showed was on the psychopathic deviate scale. When asked about his future plans, he replied, "I'd like to get married and have a few kids and get a good job. I don't know what. I'd like to build a car and sell it and get a job and go into service. That will help me decide." Since he was not committable as mentally defective or mentally ill, he was returned to stand trial and face the consequences of his antisocial behavior. It was considered that he would probably benefit more from compulsory group psychotherapy than from attempts at individual psychotherapy, but it is not known whether this recommendation was followed, or what type of subsequent adjustment he made.

The following is a history of another sociopathic personality:

Another patient was the second of three children, all boys, having a brother three years older and another two years younger than himself, both of whom apparently made a more adequate social adjustment than the patient. He said that his parents were both good to him, but his father soon began chasing around with other women and deserted the family when the patient was five years old. His mother divorced his father, who soon remarried a younger woman and continued living in the same community. The mother also remarried within a couple of years, and the stepfather was a police officer whom the patient described as kind but strict.

The patient was of average intelligence and learned easily in school but was an underachiever, and got into trouble because of his rebellious behavior. He started drinking at about the age of 12 and at the age of 14 he ran away from home for a couple of years and tried his hand at boxing. At the age of 16 he returned home and entered high school, but had to leave school half way through the year to marry his 21-year-old school teacher who was pregnant by him. The child was born the following year and the couple had no further children although the marriage survived for 19 years during which the patient was away from home most of the time. Throughout this period of his life he traveled extensively, and worked at a variety of occupations including boxing, wrestling, bronco-riding at rodeos, and training animals. At different times he claimed he had owned a meat market and was foreman in an aircraft factory. He had numerous brief extramarital affairs, spent his money freely, drank excessively, and on several occasions his drinking led to several days or weeks in psychiatric hospitals in different parts of the country. Toward the end of his first marriage, his wife began chasing around with other men and finally divorced him for doing the same thing, so that she could remarry.

Shortly after this he obtained a job working as an orderly in a state hospital, and married a psychiatric aide who was a divorcee with two sons by her previous marriage. The early years of their marriage were surprisingly stable and they had two further children. The patient quit drinking altogether for several years and remained employed in the same job where his work was highly regarded. His relationship with his wife then gradually deteriorated, and she started going out with other men while he resumed his former pattern of drinking excessively. On one occasion when he had been drinking he began to beat up his wife and pushed her down the basement stairs; when he continued to threaten her, one of her sons shot him in the leg, which had to be amputated.

He was now 48 years old, and his life entered on a new and discouraging phase. When he was ready to leave hospital, his wife and family no longer wanted him home, and he was unable to obtain any employment which he considered satisfactory. He was referred for vocational rehabilitation but would not accept the kind of help that they could give him, and was subsequently placed in boarding homes. He complained bitterly that he had no money to spend on his children, and talked of feeling so miserable that life was not worth living. Psychiatric evaluation, however, showed no clinical evidence of depression and the only elevation on the MMPI was the psychopathic deviate scale. His full scale IQ was 109, and there was no evidence of organic intellectual impairment nor psychotic reality distortion. He did, however, tend to deny responsibility for his own difficulties and to project the blame onto his wife and others. Because of persistent complaints of pain, depression, and difficulty in sleeping, he subsequently obtained supplies of analgesic, antidepressive, and hypnotic medications, each of which he tried taking in large doses to produce the same sort of effect he had previously obtained from alcohol. On one occasion he took an overdose of sleeping pills in a suicidal gesture, and was admitted to a psychiatric ward for a period of three weeks. On this occasion he was considered to be moderately depressed, but his mood improved rapidly following admission and he was taken off all medication. He was again referred to vocational rehabilitation, and many job opportunities were explored, but he was again found to be poorly motivated and returned to the same type of boarding house as previously.

The term *dyssocial reaction* applies to individuals who manifest disregard for the usual social codes and often come in conflict with them as the result of having lived all their lives in an abnormal moral environment. They may be capable of strong loyalties. These individuals typically do not show significant personality deviation other than those implied by adherence to the values or codes of their predatory, criminal, or other social group. Two illustrations of dyssocial reactions will now be given. The first is taken from a book by Shaw:*

When I started to play in the alleys around my home I first heard about a bunch of older boys called "Pirates." My

*Reprinted from Shaw, C. R. 1930. *The Jack-Roller.* By permission of the University of Chicago Press. Copyright 1930 by the University of Chicago.

oldest brother was in this gang and so I went around with them. There were about ten boys in this gang and the youngest one was eleven and the oldest one was about fifteen. . . .

Tony, Sollie, and my brother John were the big guys in the gang. Tony was fifteen and was short and heavy. He was a good fighter and the young guys were afraid of him because he hit them and beat them up. Sollie was a little guy about twelve years of age. He couldn't fight, but he was a smart guy and told stories and made plans for the gang. My brother was fifteen and was bigger than Tony and was a good fighter. He could beat up any guy in the gang by fighting, so he was a good leader and everybody looked up to him as a big guy and was proud to be his brother. . . .

When I started to hang out with the Pirates I first learned about robbin'. The guys would talk about robbin' and stealing and went out on "jobs" every night. When I was eight I started to go out robbin' with my brother's gang. We first robbed junk from a junk yard and sometimes from the peddlar. Sometimes we robbed stores. We would go to a store, and while one guy asked to buy something the other boys would rob anything like candy and cigarettes and then run. We did this every day. Sollie always made the plans and Tony and John would carry out the plans. . . .

The gang had a hangout in an alley and we would meet there every night and smoke and tell stories and plan for robbin'. I was little and so I only listened. The big guys talked about going robbin' and told stories about girls and sex things. The guys always thought about robbin' and bummin' from school and sometimes from home. . . .

Besides robbin', the gang went bummin' downtown and to ball parks and swimming. On these trips we always robbed everything we could get. . .

When I was ten the gang started to robbin' stores and homes. We would jimmy the door or window and rob the place. I always stayed outside and gave jiggers. The big guys went in and raided the place. They showed me how to pick locks, jimmy doors, cut glass and use skeleton keys, and everything to get into stores and houses. Every guy had to keep everything a secret and not tell anybody or he would be beat up and razzed. The police were enemies and not to be trusted. When we would get caught by the police we had to keep mum and not tell a word even in the third degree.

I looked up to my brother and the other big guys because of their courage and nerve and the way they could rob. They would tell me never to say a word to anybody about our robbin'. My mother didn't even know it. Some kids couldn't be in the gang because they would tell everything and some didn't have the nerve to go robbin'. The guys with a record were looked up to and admired by the young guys. A stool-pigeon was looked down on and razzed and could not stay in the gang. . . .

The guys stuck together and helped each other out of trouble. They were real good pals and would stick up for each other. They were always planning new crimes and new ways to get by without being caught. Everyone hated the police and looked upon them as enemies. Anybody who was friendly to the police was not trusted. The plans for stealing were always secret and anybody who talked about them to fellows outside of the gang or to the police was not trusted and became an enemy of the Pirates. . . .

Another example of dyssocial behavior follows:

An American Indian half-breed woman first came to psychiatric attention at the age of 24 when she presented herself in the emergency department of a large city hospital after slashing both her wrists superficially with a razor blade in an apparent suicidal gesture. She had previously had one child and claimed to have been married and divorced from the father of this child, but it was never established whether the relationship had been formalized. She was currently about two months pregnant out of wedlock by another man with whom she had been living, and she reported that he had been abusing her physically. Cutting her wrists was apparently an impulsive attempt at manipulating his behavior rather than a genuine attempt at killing herself. Nevertheless, she was admitted to the psychiatric ward of the hospital for observation and further evaluation.

Within the next few days she was found to be in good contact with reality and showed no clinical signs of depression. The psychopathic deviate scale was the only one that was elevated on her MMPI. Her boy friend was interviewed, admitted to paternity of the current pregnancy, and expressed the desire to marry her immediately following her discharge from hospital. She was discharged within a week and it was recommended that she return to the psychiatric outpatient department, but she never did so. However, she and her boy friend were married soon afterward, and during the next three years they had two further children. Her husband was irregularly employed in a variety of unskilled laboring jobs and they moved frequently from one neighborhood to another, in each of which they became well known to welfare agencies who provided financial assistance. The patient was considered to be a very poor housekeeper and mother, but did not neglect or abuse her children to such an extent that they were removed from her care. At the age of about 27, however, she began to go out drinking frequently with other men and there was a deterioration in her relationship with her husband, who threatened and sometimes beat her. On various occasions she presented herself at the emergency department of another general hospital with a number of minor bodily complaints. A few months later she began to complain of nervousness, said that her husband had beaten her senseless, and threatened to kill herself, which led to her being admitted to the psychiatric ward for evaluation.

The patient was one of 13 children born to an Indian woman living on a reservation. The father of all these children was apparently a white man who spent most of his time elsewhere, employed fairly regularly in construction work. He provided adequate financial support for the family, but the upbringing of the children was left to the mother and others living on the reservation. The children were allowed to run wild and lacked adequate adult supervision. Discipline was occasionally harsh, but inconsistent, and for the most part lacking. However, the patient attended school at home until the age of 13, when she was sent to a boarding school for Indian children in a nearby state, and she completed high school there. She subsequently moved to the city, held a number of unskilled jobs, and began a series of sexual relationships which led to pregnancy and marriage. She said that she lived with the father of her first child for 18 months, but that he was very jealous and wouldn't let her go out. Her current husband was apparently more like herself in being irresponsible and dominated by his impulses.

This husband arrived at the hospital a few days after his wife's admission and demanded her immediate release. When told that she did not wish to leave the hospital, he became extremely angry, threatened to bash her doctor's head in, told her he was going to divorce her, and left the hospital saying that he was going to get a "writ" to get her out immediately. A couple of weeks later he came back and talked to the social worker, at which time he was apologetic for his previous behavior and appeared serious and sincere. He complained of his wife's abusing their children and of her going out with other men, but he did not perceive her behavior as being particularly abnormal, and this was not considered surprising in view of his own sociopathic history. His mother had died when he was five years old, and his subsequent childhood had been emotionally deprived like that of the patient. He had been in trouble with the police on several occasions, and had served a brief sentence for driving without a license. He was financially irresponsible, impulsive, and inconsistent in his behavior. At times he would indulge his wife, saying that he didn't want to hurt her by denying her what she wanted, while at other times he became violently angry and assaultive. There were numerous inconsistencies in the stories told by the patient and her husband, and it was considered that both of them were pathological liars.

A program of psychological testing on the patient showed her to have a full scale IQ of 102, with no evidence of organic intellectual impairment nor of psychotic reality distortion. Her mood improved rapidly and she was discharged after three weeks, but she and her husband continued to remain a long-term problem for the welfare authorities.

DYNAMICS, DEVELOPMENT, AND CAUSATION

It is generally assumed that persistent delinquency and sociopathic personality involve a major defect in the development of the superego or internal control system. In discussing instinct-ridden characters, however, Fenichel wrote as follows:*

Analysis does not confirm the assumption that impulsive characters are happy "narcissistic psychopaths" who have no superego and can therefore gratify all their demands without any consideration for others. Assuredly a lack of lasting object relationships in early childhood or an oral fixation and traumatic experiences may make the complete and definite establishment of an effective superego impossible; for example, the parent figures may have changed in such rapid succession that there was objectively no time or opportunity to develop lasting relationships and identifications; however, persons of this kind also experience frustrations and develop reactions to them. Their superego is not lacking but incomplete and pathological, and the reactions of the ego to the pathological superego reflect the ambivalences and contradictions which these persons felt toward their first objects. Psychoanalysis of juvenile delinquents gives various examples of such distorted relations toward the superego. Cases of lesser severity are characterized by their chronic dissatisfaction; they are "hypersexual" and hyperinstinctual because of their state of being dammed up; cases of greater severity are governed by oral and cutaneous fixations, by extreme ambivalence toward all objects, by the identity of erotic and narcissistic needs, and by conflicts between rebellion and ingratiation.

Various authors have used the term *superego lacunae* (meaning holes or blind spots in the superego) to refer to specific defects in the internal control systems of individuals manifesting antisocial behavior. Johnson (1959) emphasized the subtle conscious and unconscious ways in which parental behavior directs the development of the child's superego, and pointed out that the child internalizes not only the positive, socially consistent attitudes of the parents, but also the frequently unexpressed,

*Reprinted from Fenichel, O. 1945. *The Psychoanalytic Theory of Neurosis.* By permission of W. W. Norton and Company, Inc. Copyright 1945 by W. W. Norton & Co., Inc.

ambivalent, antisocial feelings. She hypothesized that antisocial acting out in a child is unconsciously fostered and sanctioned by the parents, who *vicariously achieve gratification* of their own poorly integrated forbidden impulses through the child's acting out. In addition, one or both parents unconsciously experience gratification for their own hostile and destructive wishes toward the child, who is repeatedly destroyed by his behavior.

The term *"acting out"* was originally used by Freud to describe behavior observed during psychoanalytic therapy, in which the neurotic patient repeated in the transference, without insight, certain salient episodes of his earlier life. Persistent delinquents and sociopathic personalities unconsciously act out earlier experiences in their every day life, and in recent years the term acting out has come to be used mainly to refer to behavior against authority which is specifically forbidden by society. There are, however, various theories as to why the sociopathic personality develops a defective superego and impulsively acts out against society.

HEREDITARY FACTORS

Extreme difficulty in changing long-standing patterns of antisocial behavior by psychotherapy or any other means has been regarded by many psychiatrists as lending support to their belief in a hereditary or constitutional psychopathic inferiority. This argument is illogical, and is somewhat similar to postulating a hereditary basis for the structural changes resulting from severe vitamin deficiency on the grounds that these changes are not reversed by belated massive doses of the specific vitamin whose deficiency caused them in the first place. In fact, there is little objective evidence concerning the contribution of hereditary factors in the causation of sociopathic personality.

Several studies of adult twins manifesting criminal behavior were undertaken by Lange (1929), Rosanoff et al. (1934), Kranz (1936), Stumpfl (1936), and Borgstroem (1939). These were combined by Shields and Slater (1961), who gave the concordance rates among monozygotic twins as 68 percent and for same-sexed dizygotic twins as 35 percent. Holzinger's index of heritability computed from these rates is $\frac{68-35}{100-35} = 0.51$, suggesting that hereditary and environmental factors are about equally important in the causation of criminal behavior in adults. In twins manifesting juvenile delinquency, Rosanoff et al., found concordance rates of 85 percent in monozygotic pairs and 75 percent in same-sexed dizygotic pairs, so that the Holzinger index of heritability for this series is $\frac{85-75}{100-75} = 0.40$, which is reasonably consistent with that found for the larger series of adults. However, all these twin studies were conducted many years ago, and severe limitations due to methodological difficulties cannot be overemphasized.

The relative frequency of persistent delinquency or sociopathic personality among various classes of relatives has not been established. In comparison with other psychiatric patients, there is a low frequency of suicide or mental hospital admissions among the parents, but a high frequency of alcoholism or other behavioral abnormality. In one series of 95 psychopaths admitted to a mental hospital, Gregory (1959) found a history of excessive drinking among 15 percent of the fathers and five percent of their mothers. There was also a higher frequency of illegitimacy among the psychopaths than for any other type of psychiatric disorder, a higher frequency of desertion of either parent (but particularly father) during childhood, and a higher frequency of loss of *both* parents by the age of ten than for any other psychiatric disorder. In this particular study, ten and a half percent had lost both parents by the age of ten years, but in a number of studies such figures have been very much higher.

O'Neal et al. (1962) reported interesting data concerning parental deviance and the genesis of sociopathic personality. In a follow-up study of over 500 children seen in a child guidance clinic approximately 30 years earlier, they identified 84 males who were diagnosed sociopathic personality as adults, and compared the characteristics of their parents with those of 166 male cases with other psychiatric disorders and with 75 males showing no gross psychopathology. Only 13 percent of the sociopathic males had mothers with a probable diagnosis of sociopathic personality, as compared with nine percent of males with other psychiatric disorders and four percent of males without psychopathology. However, 51 percent of the sociopathic males had fathers with a probable diagnosis of sociopathic personality, as compared with 33 percent of the males with other psychiatric disorders, and 19 percent of the males without obvious psychopathology. Such figures, however, do not indicate whether sociopathic males inherit or learn their sociopathic behavior from their parents.

From the limited family data available, no specific hypotheses of Mendelian inheritance are justified, and in any event multifactorial inheritance would offer a much more reasonable explanation of the diverse manifestations of sociopathy. However, maladjusted parents and siblings also offer faulty models for identification, and subject the individual to adverse experiences throughout childhood, so that sociopathic personality has become widely regarded as a learned response to environmental circumstances rather than an inevitable manifestation of inherited inadequacy. Nevertheless, there is some evidence that other biological factors may predispose to at least certain forms of antisocial behavior.

SOMATIC FACTORS

There is a considerably higher frequency of sociopathic behavior among males than females, but it is not clear to what extent this reflects inherent biological differences as opposed to learned differences in socioculturally defined role-expectations. In a number of animal species, however, aggressive fighting behavior is mainly confined to the adult males and may be greatly reduced or disappear when the animal is castrated or otherwise sexually inactive. However, differences between the behavior of male and female animals may appear very early in life, as reported by Harlow (1962). He found that male and female infant monkeys showed marked differences in sex behavior from the second month of life onward, and that many other differences in behavior also appeared very early. Threat responses were characteristic of young males, whereas withdrawal was much more characteristic of the female. Play behavior was typically initiated by males, seldom by females. Contact play was much more frequent among the males and real "rough and tumble" was strictly for the boys. Grooming patterns and caressing, on the other hand, were characteristic of the female.

In the human animal, undue aggressiveness and recklessness tend to be maladaptive and frequently arouse social censure. On occasion, however, they may be not only adaptive but life-saving. Some time ago, a newspaper carried an account of a fire in which three girls, aged four to eleven years, perished because they were afraid to jump from the second floor of their burning home. Four brothers of comparable ages jumped to safety, although two of them were hospitalized with minor injuries. The a priori probability that the four boys would jump and the three girls remain behind is 1 in 128. Even assuming that four members of the family would jump and three will remain behind, the probability of this particular combination occurring is only 1 in 35. However, it is generally recognized that differences between the behavior of human males and females are determined largely by differences in social

TABLE 20-3. Incidence of Somatotype Component Dominance*

	496 DELINQUENTS (PER CENT)	482 NONDELINQUENTS (PER CENT)
Endomorphic dominance	11.8	15.0
Mesomorphic dominance	60.1	30.7
Ectomorphic dominance	14.4	39.6
Balanced types (No component dominance)	13.5	14.7

*Modified from Glueck, S., and Glueck, E. 1956. *Physique and Delinquency.* New York, Hoeber Medical Division, Harper & Row Publishers, Inc.

approval and disapproval of their actions rather than differences in their bodily structure and physiology.

Glueck and Glueck (1950) recorded extensive comparisons between 500 pairs of persistently delinquent and nondelinquent boys matched by age, intelligence, national origin, and residence in underprivileged neighborhoods. In a subsequent detailed analysis of physique and delinquency (1956), they reported a strong statistical association with mesomorphic or athletic body build (Table 20-3). In the latter study they stated the following conclusions:*

(1) The basic morphologic differentiation of the physique types is accompanied by differences in the incidence among them of certain traits, some of which are actually associated with delinquency, others potentially so.

(2) Differences in the physical and temperamental structure of body types bring about some variation in their response to environmental pressures.

(3) Differences in the incidence of certain traits among the physique types, as well as divergences in their reactions to the environment, are reflected in certain differences in the etiology of delinquency among the body types.

Thus, even if other researchers should confirm our finding that 60 percent of delinquents (at least in disorganized urban area) are of the mesomorphic body type, thereby suggesting a focus in prophylactic and therapeutic endeavors on the mesomorphs in the child population, the special characteristics of the other physique types

*From Glueck, S., and Glueck, E. 1956. *Physique and Delinquency.* By permission of Harper & Row, Publishers, Inc., pp. 249-250.

point to the need of some diversity of approach to the prevention and treatment of antisocial behavior in boys of different body structures. There is enough evidence of differences in clusters of traits and sociocultural factors that have a selective influence on the delinquency of the body types to warrant taking into account variations in bodily structure in the planning of general programs of prevention and control and in applying therapeutic measures for the individualized treatment of delinquents.

Doust postulated that psychopaths, in common with most other types of psychiatric patients, show evidence of morphologic immaturity when studied by the techniques of both physical anthropology and capillary microscopy. He also reported that aggressive psychopaths tended to show normal oxygen levels in peripheral capillaries, but that predominantly inadequate psychopaths tended to resemble neurotic patients in showing an impaired response to stress. However, these findings have been questioned, and no consistent changes in bodily structures or function have been established. In any event, such findings are compatible with either genetic or environmental hypotheses of causation.

In an interesting study of anxiety in the sociopathic personality, Lykken (1957) divided 49 diagnosed psychopaths into two groups according to Cleckley's criteria, and compared them with 15 control subjects on a battery of tests related to anxiety reactivity or anxiety condition-ability. In comparison with control subjects, the Cleckley or primary sociopaths showed significantly less anxiety on a questionnaire device, less Galvanic skin response reactivity to a conditioned stimulus associated with electroshock, and less avoidance of punished responses on a test of avoidance learning. The remaining or "neurotic" sociopaths scored significantly higher on the Taylor anxiety scale and on the Welsh anxiety index. It would appear from these results that certain groups of sociopaths differ from each other and from normal subjects in their perception of and responses to bodily and psychic pain or discomfort, but the exact nature and origin of these differences still require elucidation.

In an effort to evaluate the possible effects of war time experiences among British children on their subsequent behavior, Wilkins (1960) examined statistics on persons found guilty of indictable offenses during the years 1946 and 1957. The general theory that some birth years were associated with excessive criminality was sustained by his analysis, and involved both sexes and all adolescent age groups. From his data it appeared that disturbances of social or family life had the most marked effect on criminality if they occurred when the children concerned were passing through their fifth year. However, Stott (1962) subsequently reexamined the same data and reported that delinquency proneness in boys aged eight to 14 years was specific to those born during the early war years and closely resembled the war time peak for children dying from congenital malformation in the first four weeks of life. In a further comparison between delinquent and nondelinquent subjects, he found a close relationship between a number of bodily defects and behavior disorders. He considered but rejected the hypothesis that these correlations could be attributed to living conditions, compensation for feelings of inferiority or frustration, or an emotional origin for the bodily defects. He therefore argued that the only explanation that could account for the associations was that of congenital insult, which in some cases was seen both somatically and in

impairment of that part of the nervous system controlling behavior.

Other workers have suggested that sociopathic behavior is frequently or even invariably caused by some kind of organic disorder of the brain or nervous system. It is true that when the frontal lobes of the brain are damaged extensively by tumors, injury, or surgery, such persons become indifferent to social convention; and it is also true that certain forms of epilepsy are accompanied by aggressive antisocial behavior. Moreover, a relatively high frequency of electroencephalogram abnormalities have been found among persistent delinquents and sociopaths showing no clinical evidence of epilepsy. Correlations of this nature, however, do not indicate ultimate causation, and brain pathology has not been proven a significant factor in the majority of delinquents or sociopaths.

PSYCHOLOGICAL FACTORS

Levy (1951) pointed to two contrasting patterns in the development of delinquency: (1) parental rejection and other forms of deprivation, and (2) parental indulgence, permitting the child uncontrolled expression of his aggressions and desires. Sometimes the child is exposed to both of these apparently contradictory patterns, but it is not difficult to perceive overindulgence as either a manifestation of rejection (by a parent who does not care enough to control the child) or a reaction formation against feelings of guilt (that would arise if the parent consciously recognized his hostility and rejection). Moreover, the child may be exposed to inconsistent rewards and punishments, indulgence and rejection, whether he lives with both parents continually, whether one or both parents are absent from the home, or whether the child himself is moved from one home or institution to another.

Fenichel referred to one such patient who became extremely impulsive under the influence of a pathological and very inconsistent father who used to make generous presents one moment and take them back in the next, and to make promises that were not kept. Thus, the son learned to take immediately and quickly whatever he could get before it was taken away again, and to follow any impulse as soon as possible before any prohibition could be given.

Considerable evidence has accumulated indicating an unusually high frequency of both *parental death and separation* for various reasons during the childhood of individuals who subsequently become persistently delinquent or sociopathic. Among their extensive comparisons between 500 matched pairs of persistent delinquents and nondelinquent boys, Glueck and Glueck (1950) recorded some interesting data concerning parental deprivation which are shown in Table 20-4. It may be seen that 60 percent of the delinquents as compared with 34 percent of the nondelinquents came from homes that had been broken by separation, divorce, or death or prolonged absence of a parent by the time of the boy's inclusion in the research project at a mean age of approximately 14½ years. The first breach in family life had occurred before the age of five years in 170 delinquents, as compared with 80 nondelinquents. Statistically significantly greater numbers of delinquents than nondelinquents had been deprived of one or both parents for each of five categories

of deprivation described — namely, sporadic separation of parents, permanent separation or divorce, death, absence from the home for at least a year on account of criminalism or illness, and abandonment at birth.

Bowlby (1951) reviewed extensive evidence from a number of different countries concerning the high frequency of broken homes and admission to institutions during the childhood of individuals manifesting delinquency and other behavior disorders. He contended that loss of *mother* during early childhood was more damaging than loss of father, but statistically the loss of father is much more frequent than loss of mother. In the preceding study by Glueck and Glueck, 41.2 percent of their *male* delinquents (as compared with 24.8 percent of the nondelinquent controls) were no longer living with their own *father*, whereas only 15.6 percent of these delinquents (as compared with 7.2 percent of the nondelinquents) were no longer living with their own *mother*. In another retrospective study, the present author (1959) found that adult sociopaths of both sexes had lost *both parents* during childhood more frequently than patients with any other variety of psychiatric disorder, and about five times as frequently as expected on the basis of figures for the loss of one parent alone.

In a subsequent large scale anterospective study involving 11,329 Min-

TABLE 20-4. Nature of All Breaches in Family Life§

DESCRIPTION	DELINQUENTS		NON-DELINQUENTS		DIFFERENCE	P
	NUMBER	PER CENT	NUMBER	PER CENT	PER CENT	
Parents separated sporadically	136	27.2	46	9.2	18.0	<.01
Parents separated or divorced	111	22.2	64	12.8	9.4	<.01
One or both parents died°	100	20.0	68	13.6	6.4	<.01
One or both parents away from home for at least a year†	70	14.0	30	6.0	8.0	<.01
Parents abandoned boy at birth‡	24	4.8	5	1.0	3.8	<.01

Note: Percentages are based on totals of 500.
  *Four delinquents and two non-delinquents lost both parents.
  †Because of criminalism or illness.
  ‡Parents not married and did not live together after birth of boy either at all or for long.
  §From Glueck, S., and Glueck, E. 1950. *Unraveling Juvenile Delinquency.* Cambridge, Mass., Commonwealth Fund and Harvard University Press.

TABLE 20–5. Frequencies of Delinquency (Ratings 2, 3, and 4) among Statewide Sample of Minnesota Boys, According to Previous Family Status of Parents and Person with Whom Boy Was Living[†]

FAMILY STATUS OF PARENTS	PERSON WITH WHOM BOY WAS LIVING	NO. DELINQUENTS, RATINGS 2, 3, & 4	NO. NONDELINQUENTS, RATINGS 0 & 1	RATE OF DELINQUENCY (PERCENTAGE OF EACH CATEGORY)	χ^2
Parents living together	Both parents	1,073	3,609	22.9	3.41
	Neither parent	9	23	28.1	0.28
Father dead	Mother only	50	109	31.4	4.72*
	Neither parent	6	6	(50.0)	4.41*
	Step-parent	14	26	35.0	2.61
Mother dead	Father only	10	32	23.8	0.00
	Neither parent	6	9	(40.0)	2.08
	Step-parent	6	20	32.1	0.01
Both parents dead	Neither parent	1	3	(25.0)	0.00
Parents separated or divorced	Mother only	66	98	40.2	23.42‡
	Father only	9	27	25.0	0.01
	Neither parent	10	21	32.3	1.13
	Step-parent	13	36	26.5	0.16
Totals	—	1,273	4,019	24.1	42.24‡

*$P < 0.05$.
‡$P < 0.001$.
[†]From Gregory, I. 1965. Anterospective data following childhood loss of a parent. I. Delinquency and high school dropout. A.M.A. Archives of General Psychiatry *13*,99–109.

nesota school children, the present author (1965) examined frequencies of delinquency and high school dropout according to various categories of parental loss recorded several years earlier. Delinquency in boys was found to be much more frequent than average among those who had lost their father by parental separation or divorce, and somewhat more frequent than average among those who had lost their father by death, as well as among boys who had experienced other varieties of parental loss during childhood (Table 20-5). These findings were not restricted to any socioeconomic group. Delinquency in girls was most frequent among those whose parents had separated or divorced, those who had lost their mother by death, those who were living with their father only, and those who were living with neither parent. There were similar findings with respect to loss of

the parent of the same sex among nondelinquent boys and girls who dropped out of high school prior to graduation.

The preceding findings suggest that the identification model provided and the control normally exercised *by the parent of the same sex* are more crucial in preventing delinquency among boys and girls than any aspect of the relationship with the parent of the opposite sex. However, the majority of persistent delinquents and adults with sociopathic personality have grown up in homes where both parents were present throughout most of their childhood. Studies on the *quality of relationships* existing within these homes lend some support to the concept that the behavior of the parent of the same sex is particularly important. In his study of delinquent boys who did *not* come from broken homes, Andry found that they tended to perceive greater defects in their fathers' roles than in their mothers' roles, whereas nondelinquents tended to perceive the roles of both parents as being adequate. In a crosscultural study of 48 nonliterate societies, Bacon, Child, and Barry undertook separate correlations of the frequency of theft and personal crime with a number of variables that were suspected to be causal factors in the development of crime. Lack or limitation of opportunity for the young boy to form an identification with his father was associated with both types of crime.

The predominant pattern of early experiences appears to involve various combinations of parental absence, rejection, and indifference; inconsistent rewards and limits; conflict between the parents, and also with society at large; deceit; and the example or covert approval of antisocial behavior. Illustrations of these determinants are contained in the case histories of antisocial and dyssocial reactions that have already been presented, but are further illustrated in the background of a delinquent girl from a professional family.

She was the only child of an apparently intact family, but it developed that her parents had been in conflict throughout their marriage. Her mother had not wanted any children, but after some years she yielded to the demands of her husband. Very soon the child became the focus of conflict between the parents, with mother being overindulgent and protecting her from the supposedly unreasonable demands of the father. When the child developed temper tantrums, there were a few painful scenes when father spanked her while mother watched tearfully, wringing her hands. Father soon abandoned these attempts at controlling the child and resorted to dire threats of punishment or withdrawal of privileges which were never carried out. He pressed the mother to set simple tasks for the child around the home, such as tidying her room and helping with the dishes, but the mother preferred to wait on her hand and foot. When she began to associate with a family the father considered undesirable, he threatened her with expulsion from the family, but when she continued visiting them, he picked her up at their home without comment.

Father disapproved strongly of smoking but mother continued to do so. When the daughter started against his wishes he tried to bribe her financially to quit, but her mother rewarded her with private sessions when they would smoke and talk together. Meanwhile, the father, who verbalized a moralistic respect for the letter of the law, flagrantly disregarded traffic and other regulations that he did not find it convenient to observe. The stage was set for the girl to do likewise. When her misdemeanors came to the attention of her parents, mother was very concerned but indulgent, while father remained critical but unable to set limits to her behavior.

Frequently there are no incentives or rewards for good behavior at home or at school, and the values of the peer group tend to be accepted uncritically. Achievement in school therefore tends to be lower than native ability, although there may be considerable success in athletic and other extracurricular pursuits. In quite a high proportion of cases there is a history of temper tantrums in childhood, repeated difficulty with teachers, resentment of discipline, or open rebellion and truancy. Often such children are expelled or otherwise leave school prematurely and have to be satisfied with jobs below their native capability. There are frequent changes of occupation and residence, moves to another locality often resulting from situational difficulties of their own making. They tend to spend money freely when they have it, and they are usually in financial difficulties. Inquiry will usually reveal a long record of conflict with police or military authorities interspersed with jail sentences, followed by repeated offenses of the same nature, so that it appears that they are unable to learn from the unpleasant consequences of past mistakes.

SOCIOCULTURAL FACTORS

It has long been recognized that high rates of delinquency are found among boys resident in underprivileged areas of large cities. Shaw and McKay (1942) undertook an extensive ecological analysis of rates within the city of Chicago for the years 1900 to 1906, 1917 to 1923, and 1927 to 1933. For the first of these three series, the four areas with highest rates were all immediately adjacent to the Loop, and other high rate areas were in the Stock Yards district and in south Chicago. The areas with low rates, on the other hand, were located for the most part near the city's periphery. In comparison with subsequent series, the areas with very high rates were somewhat more closely concentrated around the central business district. The correlation coefficient for rates in the early and later series (in 113 geographical areas) was found to be + 0.70. This coefficient was greatly reduced by the fact that rates in six areas changed radically, but most of the areas of high rates in the early series also corresponded with those ranking highest in the two later series. Their principal conclusion was that sociologic delinquency was a subcultural tradition in the areas of the city inhabited by the lower socioeconomic classes. The rates of delinquency in these areas did not tend to change much in spite of marked changes in the ethnic origin of the persons living in these areas.

Many subsequent statistical studies tended to confirm the popular impression that gang delinquency is primarily a working class phenomenon. Thus, Lander (1954) reported that in Baltimore the zero order correlations between overcrowding, substandard housing conditions, and the juvenile delinquency rate were +0.73 and +0.69. On the basis of similar correlations, a number of persons have argued that bad housing has a direct causal effect on the delinquency rate, and that removal of slums would lead to removal of social ills, but Lander rejected this interpretation as insufficient. He found correlations between median years of schooling for the adult population, median rentals, and delinquency of −0.51 and −0.53, but regression analysis

and factor analysis indicated that these variables were not fundamentally related to the prediction or understanding of juvenile delinquency. In Baltimore he also found an inverse correlation of −0.16 between delinquency and the presence of foreign-born groups. He concluded that adequate explanations of the differential delinquency rates must involve consideration of the direct motivation of behavior, and invoked the concept of *Anomie*. "When the group norms are no longer binding or valid in an area or for a population sub-group insofar is individual behavior likely to lead to deviant behavior. Delinquency is a function of the stability and acceptance of the group norms with legal sanctions and the consequent effectiveness of the social controls in securing and forming juvenile behavior."

Cohen (1955) attempted to account for the delinquent subculture on the basis of the valid observation that birds of a feather flock together. Lower class children tend to be reared in surroundings that are quite different from the middle class standards of schools they must attend. Status frustration and loss of self-esteem leads such children to draw together in small groups or gangs. The delinquent subculture thus rewards those who attack or assault the middle class status system. However, not all boys from a high delinquency area rebel against the standards of the larger society and Scarpitti et al. (1960) have pointed to the long-term stability of "good" boys living in poor areas. They concluded that once a favorable self-image has been internalized by preadolescents with respect to friends, parents, schools, and the law, there is every reason to believe that it is as difficult to alter as a delinquent self-image.

Hathaway and Monachesi (1952) followed up a large sample of ninth-grade children to whom the Minnesota Multiphasic Personality Inventory had been administered and found that high points on certain scales were associated with an unusually low frequency of delinquency, whereas high points on certain other scales were associated with high rates of delinquency. The three suppressor scales associated with reduced rates of delinquency were 0, 2, and 5 (social introversion, depression, and femininity) whereas the three excitor scales were 4, 8, and 9 (psychopathic deviate, schizoid, and hypomanic). Wirt and Briggs (1959) undertook an extensive analysis of environmental factors related to delinquency and nondelinquency in each of the two groups characterized by unduly low or high overall frequencies of delinquency. Among both nondelinquent groups they found a high index of family sufficiency and family occupational-educational achievement, whereas both delinquent groups showed a low index of family sufficiency and occupational-educational achievement, together with low achievement by the child and a high frequency of conflict with parents.

In a British study of delinquency reviewed by Morris (1958) it appeared that there was no small degree of continuity between the antisocial attitudes and behavior of children and those of their elder brothers and sisters and parents. In this study, Carter and Jephcott (1952-1954) combined the techniques of the social survey with that of participant observation. Analysis of court records showed delinquency to be concentrated in five fairly small areas, and in each area a pair of streets were selected for study, one having a high frequency of delinquency and the other a lower frequency. These "black" and "white" streets appeared superficially similar, but *marked differences were found among individual families.* The majority of families in the "black" streets manifested domestic violence, street brawling, drunkenness, and sexual promiscuity. On the other hand, the majority of families in the "white" streets were houseproud and placed a premium on education as a means to social and economic advancement.

Hollingshead and Redlich (1958) not only found a higher frequency of antisocial behavior among members of the lowest social class, but also documented the very different ways in which misbehavior is apt to be viewed and handled among members of different social classes, as indicated in the following example:*

The case histories of two compulsively promiscuous adolescent females will be drawn upon to illustrate the differential impact of class status on the way in which lay persons and psychiatrists perceive and appraise similar behavior. Both girls came to the attention of the police at about the same time but under very different circumstances. One came from a core group class I family, the other from a class V family broken by the desertion of the father. The class I girl, after one of her frequent drinking and sexual escapades on a weekend away from an exclusive boarding school, became involved in an automobile accident while drunk. Her family immediately arranged for bail through the influence of a member of an outstanding law firm; a powerful friend telephoned a newspaper contact, and the report of the accident was not published. Within twenty-four hours, the girl was returned to school. In a few weeks the school authorities realized that the girl was pregnant and notified her parents. A psychiatrist was called in for consultation by the parents with the expectation, expressed frankly, that he was to recommend a therapeutic interruption of the pregnancy. He did not see fit to do this and, instead, recommended hospitalization in a psychiatric institution to initiate psychotherapy. The parents, though disappointed that the girl would not have a "therapeutic" abortion, finally consented to hospitalization. In due course, the girl delivered a healthy baby who was placed for adoption. Throughout her stay in the hospital she received intensive psychotherapy and after being discharged continued in treatment with a highly regarded psychoanalyst.

The class V girl was arrested by the police after she was observed having intercourse with four or five sailors from a

---

*Reprinted with permission from Hollingshead, A. B., and Redlich, F. C. 1958. *Social Class and Mental Illness.* New York, John Wiley & Sons, Inc.

nearby naval base. At the end of a brief and perfunctory trial, the girl was sentenced to a reform school. After two years there she was paroled as an unpaid domestic. While on parole, she became involved in promiscuous activity, was caught by the police, and sent to the state reformatory for women. She accepted her sentence as deserved "punishment" but created enough disturbance in the reformatory to attract the attention of a guidance officer. This official recommended that a psychiatrist be consulted. The psychiatrist who saw her was impressed by her crudeness and inability to communicate with him on most subjects. He was alienated by the fact that she thought masturbation was 'bad,' whereas intercourse with many men whom she hardly knew was "O.K." The psychiatrist's recommendation was to return the girl to her regular routine because she was not "able to profit from psychotherapy."

In a later follow-up of their large sample of school children, Hathaway and Monachesi (1963) reported that boys and girls from farms had the lowest delinquency rates. Professional families had a rate for boys (25 percent) that was more than twice the farmer rate and that was not much different from that for day-laborer families, where the highest rate occurred (30 percent). They found little correlation between delinquency and intelligence. The highest rate occurred with medium-low intelligence (26 percent), but the high intelligence group still had a rate of 20 percent. Boys who dropped out of school had a rate of 39 percent and those from broken families a rate of 37 percent. They went on to remark: "These figures seem to us to suggest that demographic data provide little encouragement for formulating any single urban or suburban community plan to decrease delinquency. These data warn us that delinquency is not now, if it every was, a low-income, low-intellect, subcultural outcome. It is a phenomenon almost as significant in suburbia as anywhere. Our fast-diminishing rural population is the only remaining low group."

TREATMENT

In their accessibility to psychoanalysis, Fenichel placed the sociopathic personality disturbances ("perversions, addictions, and impulse neuroses") after the symptomatic and character neuroses but before manic-depressive and schizophrenic psychoses. He remarked that they are "especially difficult, first because the symptom is either pleasurable or at least promises to be pleasurable, providing a new and severe form of resistance; and second, because the pregenital orientation, usually oral, is prominent." Hinsie (1938) reported on 23 cases accepted at the Berlin Psychoanalytic Institute of whom 18 discontinued treatment, four were unimproved and one was considered much improved.

Many psychiatrists have recorded failure to modify antisocial personality by means of other types of individual psychotherapy, and speak of their inability to establish an adequate emotional relationship or motivation. In view of the lack of internal controls, many consider that external controls are essential and that such individuals should receive training in special institutions (neither jails nor mental hospitals), with consistent nonpunitive discipline that would constantly deprive the psychopath of success in his antisocial behavior and would force him to face the consequences of his actions. Such authors tend to focus on *group rather than individual psychotherapy*, with gradual rehabilitation and a well-supervised parole system. An interesting experiment in socializing the antisocial individual was described by Maxwell Jones (1953), who established a *"therapeutic community"* in the 100-bed Social Rehabilitation Unit of the Belmont Hospital in England. Another interesting approach was the introduction of group therapy as a condition for probation of offenders (e.g., California).

Other attempts to modify antisocial behavior involve the use of drugs (e.g., amphetamine and stilbestrol), electroshock treatments, and even lobotomy. In a handful of criminal psychopaths with violent and destructive behavior, lobotomy was reported to have produced symptomatic benefit (but rarely social remission), but one would not expect such procedures to be indicated in persons with defective internal controls and anxiety perception. While psychosocial therapies represent the most logical and promising approach to treatment, however, they are relatively less effective than in patients with neurotic disorders.

SELECTED REFERENCES

Aichorn, A. 1935. *Wayward Youth.* New York, The Viking Press, Inc.

American Psychiatric Association. 1952. *Diagnostic and Statistical Manual for Mental Disorders.* Washington, D.C., American Psychiatric Association.

American Psychiatric Association. 1964. *A Psychiatric Glossary,* 2nd edition. Washington, D.C., American Psychiatric Association.

Andry, R. 1960. *Delinquency and Parental Pathology.* London, Methuen.

Bacon, M. K., Child, I. L. and Barry, H. 1963. A cross-cultural study of correlates of crime. Journal of Abnormal and Social Psychology *66,* 291-300.

Bovet, L. 1951. *Psychiatric Aspects of Juvenile Delinquency.* Geneva, World Health Organization, Monograph Series No. 1.

Bowlby, J. 1951. *Maternal Care and Mental Health.* Geneva, World Health Organization, Monograph Series No. 2.

Bromberg, W. 1961. *The Mold of Murder.* New York, Grune & Stratton, Inc.

Brown, F., and Epps, P. 1966. Childhood bereavement and subsequent crime. British Journal of Psychiatry *112,* 1043-1048.

Carter, M. P., and Jephcott, P. 1952-1954. *The Social Background of Delinquency.* Typescript available on loan from the University Librarian, Nottingham, England.

Cleckley, H. 1955. *The Mask of Sanity.* St. Louis, The C. V. Mosby Co.

Cleckley, H. 1959. Psychopathic states. In *American Handbook of Psychiatry,* ed. S. Arieti. New York, Basic Books, Inc., Vol. 1, ch. 28.

Cohen, A. K. 1955. *Delinquent Boys: The Culture of The Gang.* Glencoe, Illinois, The Free Press.

Doust, J. W. L. 1952. Dysplastic growth differentials in patients with psychiatric disorders. British Journal of Social Medicine *6,* 169-177.

Doust, J. W. L. 1952. Spectroscopic and photoelectric oximetry in schizophrenia and other psychiatric states. Journal of Mental Science *98,* 143-160.

Ernst, F. H., and Keating, W. C., Jr. 1964. Psychiatric treatment of the California felon. American Journal of Psychiatry *120,* 974-979.

Fenichel, O. 1945. *The Psychoanalytic Theory of Neurosis.* New York, W. W. Norton & Co., Inc., ch. 16.

Fotheringham, J. B. 1957. Psychopathic personality — a review. Canadian Psychiatric Association Journal *2,* 52-70.

Glueck, S., and Glueck, E. 1950. *Unraveling Juvenile Delinquency.* Cambridge, Massachusetts, Commonwealth Fund and Harvard University Press.

Glueck, S., and Glueck, E. 1956. *Physique and Delinquency.* New York, Harper and Row, Publishers, Inc.

Greenacre, P. 1945. Conscience in the psychopath. American Journal of Orthopsychiatry *15,* 495-509.

Gregory, I. 1959. An analysis of family data on 1000 patients admitted to a Canadian Mental Hospital. Acta Genetica *9,* 54-96.

Gregory, I. 1965. Anterospective data following childhood loss of a parent. I. Delinquency and high school dropout. AMA Archives of General Psychiatry *13,* 99-109.

Harlow, H. F. 1962. The heterosexual affectional system in monkeys. American Psychologist *17,* 1-9.

Hathaway, S. R., and Monachesi, E. D. 1952. The Minnesota Multiphasic Personality Inventory in the study of juvenile delinquents. American Sociological Review *17,* 704-710.

Hathaway, S. R., and Monachesi, E. D. 1963. *Adolescent Personality and Behavior: MMPI Patterns of Normal, Delinquent, Drop-Out and Other Outcomes.* Minneapolis, University of Minnesota Press.

Henderson, D. K. 1939. *Psychopathic States.* New York, W. W. Norton & Co., Inc.

Hollingshead, A. B., and Redlich, F. C. 1958. *Social Class and Mental Illness.* New York, John Wiley & Sons, Inc.

Johnson, A. M. 1959. Juvenile delinquency. In *American Handbook of Psychiatry,* ed. S. Arieti. New York, Basic Books, Inc., Vol. 1, ch. 42.

Johnson, A. M., and Szurek, S. A. 1952. The genesis of antisocial acting out in children and adults. Psychoanalytic Quarterly *21,* 323.

Johnston, N., Savitz, L., and Wolfgang, M. E., eds. 1962. *The Sociology of Punishment and Correction.* New York, John Wiley & Sons, Inc.

Kahn, E. 1931. *Psychopathic Personalities.* New Haven, Connecticut, Yale University Press.

Lander, B. 1954. *Towards An Understanding of Juvenile Delinquency.* New York, Columbia University Press, pp. 77-90.

Levy, D. M. 1951. Psychopathic behavior in infants and children: A critical survey of the existing concepts. American Journal of Orthopsychiatry *21,* 250-254.

Lichter, S. O., Rapien, E. B., Seibert, F. M., and

Sklansky, M. A. 1962. *The Drop-Outs.* New York, The Free Press of Glencoe (The Macmillan Co.).

Lykken, D. T. 1957. A study of anxiety in the sociopathic personality. Journal of Abnormal and Social Psychology *55*,6-10.

MacIver, R. 1942. *Social Causation.* Boston, Ginn & Co., pp. 88-95.

Morris, T. 1958. *The Criminal Area.* London, Rutledge and Kegan, Paul, pp. 92-105.

O'Neal, P., Robins, L. N., King, L. J., and Schaefer, J. 1962. Parental deviance and the genesis of sociopathic personality. American Journal of Psychiatry *118*, 1114-1123.

Prichard, J. C. 1835. *Treatise On Insanity.* London, Sherwood, Gilbert and Piper.

Quay, H. C. 1965. Psychopathic personality as pathological stimulation-seeking. American Journal of Psychiatry *122*, 180-183.

Reiner, B. S., and Kaufman, I. 1959. *Character Disorders In Parents of Delinquents.* New York, Family Service Association of America.

Robison, S. M. 1960. *Juvenile Delinquency, Its Nature and Control.* New York, Holt, Rinehart & Winston, Inc.

Scarpitti, F. R., Murray, E., Dinitz, S., and Reckless, W. C. 1960. The "good" boy in a high delinquency area: 4 years later. American Sociological Review *25*, 555-558.

Shaw, C. 1945. *The Jack-Roller.* Chicago, University of Chicago Press.

Shaw, C. R., and McKay, H. D. 1942. *Juvenile Delinquency and Urban Areas.* Chicago, University of Chicago Press, pp. 60-68.

Shields, J., and Slater, E. 1961. Heredity and psychological abnormality. In *Handbook of Abnormal Psychology,* ed. H. J. Eysenck. New York, Basic Books, Inc., pp. 298-343.

Stott, D. H. 1962. Evidence for a congenital factor in maladjustment and delinquency. American Journal of Psychiatry *118*, 781-794.

Thrasher, F. M. 1927. *The Gang.* Chicago, University of Chicago Press.

Whyte, W. F. 1943. *Street Corner Society.* Chicago, University of Chicago Press.

Wilkins, L. T. 1960. *Delinquent Generations* (Home Office Research Unit Report No. 3 in Studies in the Causes of Delinquency and the Treatment of Offenders). London, Her Majesty's Stationery Office, pp. 1-19.

Wirt, R. D., and Briggs, P. F. 1959. *Personality and Environmental Factors in The Development of Delinquency.* American Psychological Association, Psychological Monographs No. 485, Vol. 73, No. 15.

Wolfgang, M. E., Savitz, L., and Johnston, N., eds. 1962. *The Sociology of Crime and Delinquency.* New York, John Wiley & Sons, Inc.

CHAPTER 21

Sexual Deviation

A *sexual offense* is any form of sexual behavior that breaks a law. Any felony or misdemeanor that is sexually motivated may be considered a sexual offense. English and American legal codes forbid all premarital and extramarital intercourse; mouth-genital and anal contacts, whether in or out of marriage; all sexual contacts with children and animals; and the public exhibition of any kind of sexual activity. All such offenses are punishable by law, and culturally approved sexual behavior is therefore restricted to genital union between man and wife after marriage in private.

The term *sexual offender* might well be applied to a large proportion of the population, but it is usually reserved for persons who have been caught, charged with, and convicted of sexual offenses. Whether a person becomes a recognized sexual offender or not, therefore, fre-quently depends upon his current relationship with the sexual partner or "victim," the circumstances in which the offense was carried out, the moral feelings of the community in which he lives, and local practices of law enforcement. Glueck (1956) pointed out that about 25 percent of the Connecticut State prison population were sentences for sexual offenses, in contrast with about 10 percent of the New York State prison population, and that this difference appeared to reflect a much more severe set of penalties for various sexual offenses in Connecticut.

Sexual deviation or *paraphilia* may be defined as deviation of sexual aims and behavior from normal sexual activity. These terms are usually restricted to adults, and imply a persistent preference for any form of sexual behavior that does not terminate in genital union with an adult member of the opposite

502

sex, or that deviates from more or less culturally accepted sexual activity. All forms of sexual deviation are therefore also sexual offenses in our society, and the majority of convicted sexual offenders are sexual deviates. However, there are some sexual offenses such as prostitution which do not involve deviation, and the majority of sexual deviations do not result in prosecution and conviction. Moreover, there are enormous differences between the personality characteristics and behavior of persons convicted of different kinds of sexual offenses, and persons convicted of one type of offense may be most unlikely to commit another type of offense. The impotent old man, who becomes involved in sexual play with little children, presents a marked contrast with the sadistic young man who has raped or killed.

Abnormal sexual behavior may be described by a variety of other general terms such as *sexual perversion, aberration, and variation.* The term *sexual inversion,* on the other hand, refers to individuals in whom there is an inversion or reversal of gender role or psychological sex. That is to say, sexual inverts who are anatomically male tend to think and act as though they were female, whereas inverts who are anatomically female tend to think and act as though they were male. Sexual inversion is not absolute but relative, and is not synonymous with homosexuality. Many persons manifesting homosexual behavior are not psychosexually inverted, and many sexual inverts are not overtly homosexual but exclusively heterosexual, autoerotic, or asexual. Regardless of overt sexual behavior, a certain proportion of persons with sexual inversion manifest transvestitism, which consists of dressing in clothing appropriate to members of the opposite sex, or transsexualism, which involves requesting anatomical transformation into a member of the opposite sex.

Sexual psychopathy has been used both as a generic term, to refer loosely to all categories of sexual deviation or offen-

ses, and also with a more restricted meaning. The sexual deviate, however, does not necessarily have a sociopathic personality, but is frequently neurotic and occasionally psychotic. The term sexual psychopathy, therefore, should preferably be restricted to those deviates manifesting a persistent pattern of repeated sexual offenses that are potentially dangerous to others. The latter definition has been embodied in the sexual psychopath laws of a number of states. Thus, Illinois (1938) defined the criminal sexual psychopath as an individual who had been suffering from the condition at least one year, not insane or feeble-minded, with criminal propensities toward the commission of sex offenses. Such laws have frequently been enacted in order to permit indefinite detention of the persistent and aggressive sexual offender, but such individuals constitute only a small proportion of all persons committing sexual offenses, as we have mentioned already.

The tremendous diversity of sexual deviations and offenses is reflected in a corresponding diversity of the persons who commit them. The appearance, attitude and behavior of a few effeminate male homosexuals and a few masculine female homosexuals may strongly suggest this diagnosis, but there is nothing characteristic about the demeanor of most sexual deviates and offenders, even those who consistently prefer homosexual relationships. However, while some offenders may be active, energetic, outgoing, and aggressive, the majority of those apprehended show little obvious abnormality in appearance or behavior, but tend on the whole to be shy, reserved, timid, and uncomfortable in interpersonal relationships with other adults.

It is usually possible to gain, maintain, and direct the individual's attention. He may converse spontaneously, answer questions appropriately, and give a detailed history of his background and experiences that corresponds with that obtained from other sources. The more deviant his sexual behavior, however, the less communicative he is likely to be, and the more frequently his conversation shows evidence of reality distortion.

The distribution of intelligence tends to be much the same as in the general population, and there is no gross impairment of intellectual function, memory, or orientation among most homosexuals or those with relatively mild forms of deviation. Among those deviates showing psychotic disturbances of ideation, however, there may also be some impairment of intellectual function. Similarly, hallucinations, illusions, and delusions are absent except in the patient who is found to be grossly psychotic.

Emotional tone may be within normal limits and emotional reaction quite adequate and appropriate, but those with severe forms of sexual deviation may show marked signs of anxiety and depression, or alternatively of apathy and indifference. Conscience and judgment may be grossly impaired in the area of sexual behavior and associated interpersonal relationships, but well preserved in other areas, except in the case of the sociopath or psychotic individual.

Psychological testing, like clinical evaluation, reveals marked diversity in the personality characteristics and dynamics of individuals with sexual deviations. In the Minnesota Multiphasic Personality Inventory, the fifth scale (Mf) is a measure of masculinity and femininity of interests patterns. When they answer frankly, most if not all overt male homosexuals will obtain very high T-scores on this scale. However, one would never be justified in assuming the existence of an overt homosexual behavior on the basis of a high score on this scale. On the other hand, a strong elevation on Scale 4 (psychopathic deviate) together with an elevation in Scale 5 is considered suggestive of direct homosexual experiences.

Among male sex offenders, projective tests such as the Rorschach and Thematic Apperception Test tend to show a pervasive fear of sexual contact with adult females. In their study of over 200 sex offenders admitted to Sing Sing Prison, Hammer and Glueck (1955) remarked that this fear of sexual contact with adult females might best be illustrated by references to the responses to TAT card 13 Mf which depicts a seminude female lying in bed with her breasts and upper part of the body exposed and a man standing in the foreground. "The usual theme elicited by this card is one of sexual contact between the two figures, either in a marital or non-marital setting. In a random sampling of a hundred records from the sex-offender files, 93 percent of the subjects were unable to give such a theme; instead they offered stories of the female figure either being sick, dying or dead, thus exhibiting a rejection of heterosexuality and, at the same time, hostility toward the mature female sex object. These findings tend to support Rado's formulation of the inhibiting effect, on sexual performance, of fear of intimate sexual contact with the adult female." We shall return to psychodynamic interpretations concerning the rejection of adult heterosexuality after reviewing the main varieties of sexual deviation and offenses.

In the standard nomenclature, all forms of sexual deviation are classified as a subgroup of sociopathic personality disturbance. Many psychiatrists, however, consider that the majority of sexual deviates and offenders are more neurotic than sociopathic, and that an appreciable minority are suffering from psychoses, organic brain syndromes, or mental retardation.

There appear to be *three empirical ways in which one may classify sexual offenses and deviation,* namely: (1) according to the nature of the sexual act (e.g., masturbation, intercourse, mouth-genital or anal contacts, fetishism, or others), (2) according to the object of the sexual attentions (e.g., adult, adolescent or child of the opposite or same sex, animal, or inanimate object), and (3) according to the associated psychopathology in the deviate or offender (e.g., neurotic, psychotic, sociopathic personality, alcoholic, organic brain syndrome, or mental retardation). We shall now outline and illustrate the main categories of sexual deviation and offenses, according to each of these three methods of classification.

THE NATURE OF THE SEXUAL ACT

Masturbation is sexual pleasure obtained by manipulation of the genitals or other erogenous parts of the body. Individual masturbation is widely practiced by the higher animals and by all races of mankind, particularly by immature males who have not yet established an adult heterosexual relationship, and by adults of both sexes who have been deprived of a normal heterosexual outlet. The use of artificial genitalia resembling those of the opposite sex has been reported in literature since the time of Aristophanes' *Lysistrata,* and mutual masturbation may be practiced by males or females with members of the same or the opposite sex. During the middle ages, the Church condemned all forms of sexual indulgence other than genital intercourse between husband and wife with the express purpose of having children. Masturbation became regarded as evil and perverse, and was frequently referred to as "self-abuse." Even in the present century it was thought by many physicians and other educated people to lead to insanity or other tragic consequences, and masturbation in girls sometimes led to surgical removal of the clitoris. More recently it has become regarded as a normal part of sexual activity and the accumulative experience reported in the Kinsey studies amounted to 93 percent in males (decreasing from adolescence onwards) and 62 percent in females (increasing to middle age). It is therefore regarded as abnormal only if practiced in public, or to the exclusion by choice of heterosexual genital union, as frequently occurs following certain of the deviant acts to be considered later.

Mouth-genital contact is a form of sexual activity that was formerly regarded as even more perverse or deviant than masturbation. However, it has been reported since antiquity as a partial aim in heterosexual foreplay, particularly in French literature, and has become increasingly acceptable in English-speaking countries, being reported by about 50 to 60 percent of the younger generation in Kinsey's samples. Cunnilinctus is the term used for application of the mouth to the female genitalia, and fellatio for the application of the mouth to the penis. Either may be reciprocal, as in the practice of lambitus or "soixante-neuf" ("69"), and may occur with members of the same or opposite sex. Mouth-genital contact was the type of homosexual act preferred by each of the subgroups of male sexual offenders in Glueck's Sing Sing study.

Ano-genital activity is one of the most frequent homosexual practices, particularly between adult males (sodomy) but also between man and boy (pederasty). It has also been reported as not too uncommon between man and woman, but is very much less frequent than coitus a posteriore, a normal variation in which the male approaches the female from behind. Similarly, ano-genital intercourse with animals (zooerasty) is much less frequent than coitus between man and animal, which is the most common form of bestiality.

Voyeurism or scoptophilia consists of obtaining sexual gratification through looking at the genitalia or sexual behavior of others. The use of visual stimuli to increase sexual excitement is of course a normal partial aim, and the Kinsey surveys indicated that on the whole such visual stimulation was very much more important to the male than to the female. Society has long catered to his desire for visual and other sensual stimulation through a variety of art forms, including painting, sculpture, photographs, magazines, books, plays, movies, and impromptu or special performances in brothels. It has sometimes been considered acceptable (or sophisticated) for a man to take his wife or mistress to a brothel to watch the show, and even to have her engage in sexual activity with another partner so that he may be further stimulated to normal heterosexual gratification. In contrast with such culturally deplored, but at times widespread practices, the true voyeur obtains a maximum of sexual excitement from watching others, and orgasm occurs under these circumstances either spontaneously or through masturbation. The typical "peeping-Tom" is a socially isolated schizoid individual who prowls respectable neighborhoods after dark, looking through lighted windows for women who are in various stages of undress but are rarely engaged in sexual activities. A minority of voyeurs are primarily interested in watching deviant behavior, and in the past this frequently took the form of watching sadistic acts carried out on others. Thus, Hirschfeld (1944) quoted a 1792 account of the activities of a voyeur who liked to witness flagellations as follows:

There is a rich old banker in Broad Street who has arranged with the head mistresses of two girls' schools (one in Hackney, one in Stratford) to pay them a large weekly sum each for a most peculiar entertainment. At the time of his weekly visits at each school the children received their accumulated punishments. The old man stays in an adjacent room and watches through an aperture while the girls, one after the other, are brought in, bared behind, and chastised with the rod.

Exhibitionism may be defined as the exposure of the male genital in public and in sight of a female person as a final sexual aim. This final sexual aim distinguishes the act from exposure of the male genital for other motives which have been recorded since antiquity. Thus, Theophrastus (about 300 B.C.)

wrote that "the buffoon is one that will lift his shirt in the presence of free-born women," and Christoffel (1956) drew attention to genital exposure in primitive cultures as a form of aggression or defense (i.e., counterattack) against women. In our society, male genital exhibitionism constitutes one of the most frequent sexual deviations to be recognized, amounting to as high a proportion as one-third of all sexual offenses coming to court in some jurisdictions. Since the offender is likely to be placed on probation, exhibitionists constitute a small fraction of imprisoned sexual offenders but a relatively high proportion of those receiving psychiatric treatment on an outpatient basis. In an excellent study of exhibitionists attending an outpatient clinic, Mohr et al. (1962) stressed the need to distinguish between exhibitionists exposing themselves to girls as a final sexual aim, and pedophiles doing the same thing preparatory to further sexual activities with the child. They found that the girls and women to whom exhibitionists expose themselves were almost always strangers, and that the act itself might range from showing the penis without an erection or conscious sexual feelings, to masturbation with the use of obscene language in an intense sexual experience. Exhibitionism has frequently been regarded as closely related to voyeurism, and this group found that voyeurism was in fact the only other form of deviation that was at all common among exhibitionists. The age distribution of their sample of exhibitionists showed an interesting bimodal distribution, with the first peak culminating in adolescence and the other culminating in the 20s. The adolescent group were unmarried, but nearly all of the young adult group had married prior to the onset of exhibitionism. However, one-third of the latter group had been married less than a year, and the two outstanding factors related to exposing themselves seemed to have been impending or recent marriage and impending or recent birth of a child. Such data suggest that the urge to expose occurs at a time at which the patient is caught in a conflict with a female — the mother in adolescence and the wife or future spouse in the early 20s. It has also been remarked that the wife of the exhibitionist frequently appears to be a mother-substitute, and that the patient himself is usually self-effacing and not at all exhibitionistic or aggressive in most respects. The following case history illustrates some of these characteristics in one such persistent exhibitionist.

A 24-year-old married man was admitted to a psychiatric hospital for evaluation after his third court appearance for "indecent exposure."

The patient was the youngest of four children and was the only boy. His three older sisters were all married and none of them were known to have shown evidence of any psychopathology. His father, however, was an alcoholic who spent all his money on drinking parties and was a poor provider. He worked irregularly, changed jobs frequently, and never owned his own home until the patient had built him one (paying for the materials himself) a couple of years previously. The father was always inconsistent in discipline and was at times cruel to the patient and his sisters. The patient's mother, on the other hand, was described as good, kind, long-suffering, and easy to get along with. However, there was much open discord between the parents and the mother often said she would have left her husband if it hadn't been for the children.

The patient showed no retardation in development, and was well behaved and conforming. He left school at the age of 16, but obtained some further training to enable him to work as an electrical technician. He was always shy and immature, and did not participate in many athletic or social activities.

He obtained little or no sexual information from his parents or peers but at the age of about fourteen he started to expose his genitals to girls of the same age, and sometimes to masturbate in front of them. This behavior didn't get him into any serious difficulties until the age of 20, when he exposed himself in front of a 27-year-old woman, and was beaten up by her brother, taken to court, and fined $50. His pattern of periodic exhibitionism continued and at the age of 23 he exposed himself to a 16-year-old girl who took him to court, following which he spent a month in jail. Shortly after this he met his future wife, who was pregnant at the time, and two months later gave birth to an illegitimate child who was immediately adopted. During the next six months the patient established his first sexual relationship with a woman and they had intercourse on a number of occasions with mutual satisfaction. Six months prior to the patient's admission to hospital they were married, and for a while he continued to obtain satisfaction from intercourse, but he would often get hurt and resentful over trivial incidents and conflicts, and at these times he would refuse to have sexual relations with his wife even though she approached him. Two months prior to his admission to hospital his wife became pregnant and it was soon after learning this that the patient regressed to his former pattern of exhibitionism. He had never told his wife about this behavior, however, and it came as a complete surprise to her when he was again arrested and on this occasion was referred to hospital for evaluation.

On arrival he was neat and well behaved, but anxious and tense. There was no evidence of psychotic reality distortion nor of severe depression, and his intellectual function was bright normal (full scale IQ 118). He was introverted and expressed feelings of inadequacy, and on a sentence completion test, two of his responses were as follows: "*When I was a child* I always ran away or didn't fight back." And again "*My greatest mistake was* running away from everything." He also reported that during the preceding ten years he had had frequent attacks of a migraine type of headache, associated with blurring of vision, numbness on one side of the head and a buzzing in one ear, and frequently nausea or vomiting. He related the onset of these attacks to periods of emotional stress, anxiety, and tension. While he was in the hospital, a medication was found which aborted or relieved the headaches, and he appeared to gain considerable insight into the dynamics underlying his neurotic personality and exhibitionism, but it is not known whether the latter behavior subsequently recurred.

Fetishism is a form of erotic symbolism in which sexual stimulation and gratification are obtained only through some special part of the body or some inanimate object that has acquired special sexual significance. Such fetishes or sexual symbols are frequently exciting to the normal male, and may be objects of special significance in heterosexual foreplay. The parts of the body most frequently sexualized include the buttocks, thighs, legs, feet, breasts, and hair, while inanimate objects most apt to become fetishes include female underwear, stockings, shoes, silk garments, furs, and gloves. College administrators may encounter simple forms of mass fetishism in the form of panty-raids on girls' dormitories, and military censors have sometimes received large quantities of women's underwear and other fetish objects sent from home at the request of enlisted men serving overseas. In severe forms of fetishism, however, inanimate objects with no power to arouse most persons sexually become the only means through which the individual can obtain sufficient excitement to achieve orgasm. Such fetishists may be arrested by the police because of snipping hair or compulsively stealing fetish objects. The latter constitutes one form of kleptomania, although other kleptomaniacs steal compulsively without achieving any conscious sexual gratification. Similarly pyromania consists of compulsive fire-setting, which constitutes a form of fetishism when it is done to obtain sexual gratification, although here again some forms of pyromania do not involve conscious sexual motivation.

Transvestitism consists of dressing in clothing appropriate to the opposite sex, and has been recorded among both men and women since antiquity. As in other forms of sexual deviation, however, males have attracted most of the attention, and it is apparently to his data on males that Hirschfeld was referring when he stated that about 35 percent of transvestites are het-

erosexual, an equal percentage homosexual, about 15 percent bisexual, and the remaining 15 percent either restricted to autoerotic activities or completely asexual. This variety in sexual orientation of transvestites, however, is equally true of women who dress as men. Among both sexes there would appear to be three major categories of transvestitism: (1) a form of fetishism, in which the individual is predominantly heterosexual or autoerotic; (2) a predominant homosexual orientation in which transvestitism represents mainly a means to an end, namely attracting other members of the same sex; (3) associated with *transsexualism*, involving a conscious desire to change into a member of the opposite sex. Of recent years a number of males have in fact been transformed surgically into anatomical approximations of females, and a number of others have sought such operations. Such individuals have generally been both transvestites and homosexuals, but they represent only a small proportion of both groups. Randell reported a series of 50 transvestites, many of whom have been referred to psychiatry from an endocrine clinic where they had been seeking operations to change their sex. Among the 37 males in this selected series, 21 were seeking to change their sex, whereas among the 13 females, nine were expressing the wish to do so. Pauly presented evidence that transsexualism may involve a paranoid reaction, with denial of the physical reality of anatomical sexual identification. However, not all such patients should be regarded as psychotic. The following case history illustrates one patient with this syndrome who appeared to be in good contact with reality but reacted with depression when her hopes could not be fulfilled.

A 30-year-old patient presented in a medical outpatient clinic with the complaint, "My sexes are mixed up." The patient was using a man's name, dressed and acted like a man, and spoke in a hoarse voice. The history written by a medical student included the following interesting contradictions:

Patient raised as a male but always has been aware of his "female-like" sexual organs. He claims his "mind and desires" are those of a male and always have been, which is the reason he was raised as a male, even though his sex organs are those of a female. His sexual development has been female. No penis. Urinates like a girl. Pubic hair at age 13-15, axillary hair at about same time but later. Breasts developed by age 15. No voice change. Some fine facial hair growth. Shaves twice a week but probably more because of desire than need. General physique is male-like—broad shoulders, husky, well developed muscles in arms and legs. . . .

The same kind of confusion about the patient's sex is illustrated by the following excerpt from a letter written by her elder sister:

In school she was one of the guys, playing basketball, baseball, football, and even boxing against the fellows—and always beating them. X has always been very strong and muscular. . .as far as X's ability on the farm—he could hold a candle to any and all. Any kind of mechanical work as far as tractors, cars, farm machinery, carpentering, etc.—even to 'pulling' calves, castrating small pigs, milking cows, butchering etc.—are all part of his present and past. X has always had an unlimited amount of energy, never tiring from any amount of work or athletics. During corn picking season, he can work a week or two straight with only five or six hours sleep per night.

Menstruation had started about the age of 16 and was reported to be of brief duration, but occurred regularly once a month. Medical examination showed that anatomically the patient was a normal female, and further confirmation was obtained by examination of cells from a buccal smear which showed 28 percent sex chromosomes chromatin positive. (Normal value for males less than 5 percent, and for females about 35 percent). A 24-hour sample of urine showed 17-ketosteroids to be 5.6 mg (normal range for women 5 to 15, and for men 10 to 20 mg), thereby excluding the possibility of adrenocortical hyperplasia.

When scored as a female, her responses to the Minnesota Multiphasic Personality Inventory showed a marked elevation on Scale 5 (T-score 80) indicating masculinity of attitudes and interests, but all other scales were well within normal limits. In effect, she was psychologically a normal male. Furthermore, the patient wished to marry a girl three years younger. Neither of them was experienced sexually, but they had attemped sexual relations. The reason the patient had at last consulted a physician was that she wanted a surgical operation that would make her anatomically male.

Her family were all in favor of this and the patient herself wrote the following eloquent plea:

I am banking everything on this operation. I know there is going to be a lot of pain and it isn't going to solve all of my problems, but it is the biggest step that I have to take toward solving them. This is not a spur of the moment decision. I have thought about it ever since I knew it could be done and I am 31 years old and I decided it was now or never. The whole family has got their hearts set on it. They think (and so do I) it is the best thing that could happen to me. My dad isn't going to be here forever and when the time comes I am going to have to go out into this world on my own and I always hire out as a man, so I want to be one. It's the only kind of life I know and it's the only kind I want to know. I know how men talk and act when they are in a bunch, and anything they would say and do wouldn't shock me in the least. I don't see how this could affect me spiritually. I am not religious and besides that I don't think God judges you by your body but by your soul. My morals have always been very high and this operation won't change me any, except I will be a lot happier and I will feel as though I am as good as anyone else. Doctor, I would rather die on that operating table as not to have this done.

Sadism involves the attainment of sexual gratification through inflicting bodily or mental pain on others. The term is derived from the Marquis de Sade (1740-1814) who practiced or fantasied a wide variety of perversions which he recorded in his novel (*Justine and Juliette, or The Curse of Virtue and the*

Blessing of Vice). He was repeatedly taken into custody but released by virtue of his social position. Following one of his orgies at which two prostitutes died from an overdose of cantharides (an irritant, formerly used as an aphrodisiac to increase sexual stimulation), he was sentenced to death but soon afterwards was reprieved and set free.

It was not long before another woman was found unconscious after he had cut open her veins at several points and lacerated her skin all over her body. He was then taken to the Bastille, and later to a lunatic asylum where he eventually died. It is of some interest to note that extreme sadism was recognized as evidence of insanity as long ago as the beginning of the eighteenth century, although some societies have continued to tolerate or even institutionalize the sadistic treatment of minority groups up to the present time. Such sadism, of course, had its origin in antiquity, and has tended to be preserved most strongly in totalitarian, militaristic, and patriarchal cultures. Flogging or torture were frequently the lot of animals, captives, slaves, servants, children, and wife or concubine. Such treatment tended to become a male prerogative, and it is not surprising that in his sexual relationships the male should sometimes obtain additional pleasure from inflicting suffering on his partner. In civilized societies the infliction of pain before or during intercourse is generally minimal, and confined to such acts as will also intensify the pleasure of the partner, which may include biting, scratching, and squeezing. However, there are some deviant individuals for whom the infliction of severe pain, the sight of blood, or even death may constitute the only means by which they may attain the maximum of sexual pleasure. The greater the degree of sadism necessary to obtain sexual gratification, the greater the probability that the individual is psychotic. The following case history illustrates the development of sadism leading to murder and violation of the corpse (necrophilia).*

If you had seen Charles on the street in your city you would not have known him for a vicious killer. In prison, he still has a freshness of face which belongs in a choir stall. When I last saw him, he was scarcely twenty-one. . . .

Before Charles came to prison I had read about him in the newspapers. The case had made headlines for many days: it was composed of elements that were "naturals" for arousing public interest—a boy, a pretty girl—"Not so pretty," says Charles—an empty apartment, an ice pick.

The girl was a stranger who had come with samples of religious books and records and had asked to see the boy's mother. He waved her into the apartment, struck her on the head with a hammer, and stabbed her 69 times with an ice pick. Then he flung himself on the corpse and raped it.

He subsequently went for a leisurely walk and ate an ice cream cone, and then returned and nonchalantly reported his crime to the police. At psychiatric interview there was no definite evidence of psychosis, but he was emotionally flat and inappropriate and was suspected of having paranoid schizophrenia. He was then interviewed after an injection of pentothal and at this time he spoke of having heard a voice telling him to kill the girl. He subsequently claimed that he had told his mother about this, but that she didn't want him to plead insanity. "She didn't want the publicity. She's a buyer in one of the big department stores and she was afraid she'd lose her job. She wanted everything kept quiet. She was afraid to have her name connected with it. . .you see, she has a different name than mine so nobody connected her with me. . ."

Long before Charles was born the marriage between his parents was falling apart. They had not wanted each other nor the two children that followed. Under religious compulsion they maintained a semblance of harmony for over two years, but in the first month of their mar-

---

*From *The Fifty-Minute Hour* by Robert Lindner. Copyright 1954 by Robert Lindner. Reprinted by permission of Holt, Rinehart and Winston, Inc.

riage both had known it could not last. So Charles and his brother were marked before birth. In Charles' third (his brother's second) year, a religious dispensation permitted the parents to separate, and the figure of their father disappeared from their lives. For a few months their mother tried to maintain the home, but since she herself was a harassed, conflicted, easily disturbed person, she found the task too great. On the advice of her confessor the children were placed in an orphanage. For fifteen years thereafter the two boys were to live in homes and institutions. . . .

Charles' life in one institution and home after another was miserable and shocking to learn about. He lived in constant fear and terror. He was brutalized beyond description. In the first 'home,' a religious one, even at the age of four and thenceforward, he was beaten unmercifully for the smallest infractions and made to do extravagent penances for expressing the ordinary playfulness of a small boy. Supervisors, who by their faith alone should have been obliged to give him affection if not love, handled him — and all of their charges — as if he were not a child but a species of animal. In small sadisms these governors reflected their own frustrations, and it often seemed as if they acted under orders to grind out the lives committed to them. Existence was regimented under the pretense of piety. Before long Charles found himself regarding his person and his being with guilt; for under the warped codes and philosophies to which he was exposed he was forced to accept the idea that what was happening to him — his exile from normal life, his abandonment by his family — was somehow his own fault.

It was not long before Charles donned the only armor available to him. After a few years during which he had been the recipient of brutality, the target of assaults sexual and physical, the butt of sadisms that make a small boy's life a hell, he associated himself in spirit with his tormentors. The process of this identification began with a change in the fantasies he had so long employed for comfort when he nursed his wounds in the dormitory at night. In analysis, we learned that these first fantasies were heroic in stamp, epic with poetry and, though mean and pitiful

from such a distance, panoplied with the glory that life lets us know only once. But they did not help against the harsh realities of his environment. The heroes of his mind could not hold out against the inquisitors in his real life, nor could their gleaming swords avail against the sticks and blows of his masters and fellows. Into his reveries, then, there crept a new note. Richard Coeur de Lion was replaced by Genghis Khan, the Dragon Slayers by Bluebeards, and instead of dreams of chivalry he came to cherish fantasies of revenge. As the character of his inner life changed, so did Charles. Growing meanwhile, and acquiring physical strength, he was soon able to express the vengeful hate in him. Toward those smaller and weaker he behaved as he could not toward those larger and stronger. He passed on his hurts: he became an afflictor, delighting in giving pain. Also, he learned shrewdness and cunning; and soon he was accomplsihed at diverting hurt from himself to someone else. In sexual activities, where he was once the target he became the arrow, and on the vainly protesting forms of others he discharged the venom of his frustration. By the age of ten he had become perverted in every way to the roots of his being — already his soul had been twisted into that of a murderer.

During these years, when Charles was undergoing the changes described, he saw his mother only infrequently. Her occasional visits on his birthday or a holiday were always hurried. They left him with a feeling of something incomplete, undone and unsaid. Always laden with gifts, she made a small, excited flurry in his colorless life. He said to me, "She was like a fairy princess when she came. She smelled so good." But at the same time that he looked forward to her visits and dreamed of her after she had gone, part of him hated her, too, for having placed him in the purgatory of his daily life. It was this that made of her visits the incomplete episodes they were. He wanted to ask her to take him with her when she left, but he feared to ask, knowing her reply in advance. So an emptiness would seize him when she went away. At such times he would cast about for victims on whom to vent himself, and the record I have of his life shows that every visit was followed by a display of aggression. In it we read a tale of his acts and the punishment received; it is a story of small violences, swift retributions, long and hard penances.

On special occasions there were visits to his mother's home. Brief exposure to normal life, these were more confusing and destructive than solacing, for all they gave Charles was a taste of what he should have had, and they increased an appetite that, under the circumstances, could never be satisfied.

In the light of subsequent information it is evident that even the visits to his mother's home were far from being exposures to normal life. On one occasion at the age of nine he was removed from his mother's bed where he was sleeping by a strange man who then retired to the bedroom with his mother. Most of the time he was left alone in his mother's apartment while she went out. On one visit to his mother's at the age of 13, he discovered a trunk containing old letters, from which he learned that his father was not dead as his mother had told him but had remarried and was currently living in another city with a family by his second marriage. At the same time he found his mother's wedding ring which he used for some time afterwards as a fetish to achieve sexual orgasm. Later, when he first went with a prostitute, he was impotent until the woman had put on his mother's wedding ring. In the book Lindner presents further interesting evidence that in killing and raping the girl, Charles was symbolically destroying and possessing the mother. The whole story of his chaotic psychosexual development, with endurance of severe cruelty and development of extreme sadism, is typical of the small group of dangerous and probably psychotic sexual psychopaths.

Masochism consists of sexual gratification obtained through suffering bodily or mental pain, and is derived from the name of Leopold von Sacher-Masoch (1836-1895) who subjugated himself as a "slave" to women. His first great sexual experience was with Anna von Kottwitz, who was a dominating woman several years older than he, and was the model on whom he based two books, *Venus in Furs* and *The Divorced Woman or the Erotic Story of an Idealist*. A much more frequent and less deviant form of masochism involves the woman

in a primitive society or subculture of our own society who provokes her mate into abusing her so that he may then or later show her how much he loves her. The role of the victim in provoking physical abuse will be mentioned later at the beginning of the section on causation.

In the seventeenth and eighteenth centuries a number of English women became addicted to flagellation or whipping, which may well have been related to the treatment they had previously received at the hands of their parents and teachers. Hirschfeld quoted a contemporary description of a feminine flagellation club whose members were mostly married women who met once a week to whip each other. Similar homosexually oriented masochistic practices were widespread in monasteries, convents, and boarding schools. However, the origin of heterosexual masochism in males has frequently been attributed to a combination of punishment and sexual stimulation by sadistic females during their childhood. In their adult years, male masochists have been able to indulge their perversion in brothels equipped with a variety of ingenious machines on which they could be flagellated or tortured. Attempts to inflict pain on themselves have not infrequently led to genital mutilation, castration, or even death. Other forms of extreme masochism include the ingestion of excreta, and certain aspects of necrophilia. Once again it may be noted that the more extreme the deviant behavior, the greater the probability that the individual will show other evidence of psychosis.

THE OBJECT OF THE SEXUAL AIM

Heterosexual Activities between Consenting Adults. The extent of normal heterosexual activity occurring outside the sanction of marriage is well established. These offenses are frequently undiscovered or ignored, and probably represent the largest single group of sexual offenses. Promiscuity and less extensive premarital and extramarital coitus are relatively more frequent among those of limited socioeconomic status and also in sociopathic personalities than in any other group of psychiatric patients. At any given age and among any given social group, however, there are tremendous individual differences in the nature and frequency of normal heterosexual relationships between consenting adults, both within and outside of marriage. It should be emphasized that it is among such persons that we find most of the individuals characterized by unusually strong sexual drive or frequent sexual responses: *nymphomania* in the female, or *satyriasis* in the male. It is a popular misconception that most sexual deviates are characterized by a pathologically strong sex drive, and it is also an erroneous belief that persons with nymphomania or satyriasis are usually sexual deviants. While they may use a variety of techniques in foreplay, their goal is normal genital union as in the general population. Moreover, during the present century there has been increasingly widespread acceptance of uninhibited sexual behavior, including nudity, mouth-genital contact, and a variety of positions during coitus.

Homosexual Activity between Consenting Adults. Homosexuality is a broad term denoting any consistently preferred sexual activity between members of the same sex, including mutual masturbation, mouth-genital, and ano-genital contacts. Homosexual contacts have been observed in both males and females of a variety of infrahuman species of mammals, and in the case of males the mounting animal not infrequently reaches orgasm. Homosexual relationships between human males have at times been widely accepted and practiced in civilized cultures as well as primitive tribes. Homosexual behavior involving human females, also known as lesbianism or sapphism, has also been widely prac-

ticed at times, although it has generally been considered both less frequent than male homosexuality, and less likely to arouse social censure. At the present time there is considerable discrepancy between attitudes toward male homosexuality in different localities, and Glueck (1956) noted that New York State reduced a homosexual offense between two adult males from a felony to a misdemeanor at the same time as California was increasing the maximum penalty for the same offense from ten to 20 years. Nevertheless, the occurrence of mutual masturbation with members of the same sex is a widespread phenomenon during adolescence, and Kinsey et al. reported that, by the age of 45 years, approximately 37 percent of males and 13 percent of females admitted having had some homosexual experience to the point of orgasm. Among single persons in the age group 36 to 40 years, 40 percent of males and ten percent of females reported current involvement in active homosexual relationships. It is among members of the latter group that we should expect to find a high proportion of exclusively homosexual individuals with true psychosexual inversion. The majority of such persons have neither been convicted of homosexuality in court nor consulted a psychiatrist voluntarily. Those who do seek psychological or psychiatric assistance are more apt to do so on account of neurotic anxiety or depression than any great desire or expectation of changing their basic homosexual orientation. The following case history illustrates the neurotic manifestations of one such male homosexual.

This patient was the second of two children born to middle-aged parents of limited socioeconomic status. His father was an immigrant who was in his late 30s at the time of his marriage. He worked as a laborer and was a quiet man, although a satisfactory provider. The patient's mother was also somewhat withdrawn socially and was over 30 at the time of her marriage. Her first child was a boy, and six years went by before she became pregnant again. In the light of subsequent developments, it appears either that mother wanted a girl rather than a boy, or that she wanted no further children, and that her overprotection of her second son constituted a reaction formation against rejection.

In any event, the boy's mother is reported to have nearly died at the time of his birth, and from that time on she never again had sexual relations with her husband. Throughout childhood the child slept in his mother's bed, while the displaced father had to share a bed with the elder brother. The mother coddled and supported the patient throughout his childhood and they presented a united front against the father whom the patient came to consider as a surly, brutish man who would as soon slap him as look at him. In spite of a great deal of hostility toward his father, he was also expected to respect him, and the relationship was therefore one of marked ambivalence. In contrast with many negative feelings toward his father, his predominant feelings toward his mother were positive, and he identified with her, unconsciously patterning himself after her.

He was of average intelligence and made adequate progress in school but had few close relationships with children of either sex. At the age of 14 he was introduced to homosexuality by an older man who was living nearby. His extremely moralistic upbringing made it difficult for him to accept this behavior. He was shattered by an overwhelming sense of guilt, but was unable to tell anyone what was troubling him. He became anxious and depressed, withdrew from school (early in the eighth grade), and remained at home where he could be close to mother. When he grew older he worked in a variety of jobs, including janitor, desk clerk, gas station attendant, hair dresser, and cosmetologist.

At 18 he fell in love with an older man and went to another state with him for three months, but then returned home and consulted a psychiatrist because of feelings of guilt and depression. For the next 20 years he remained home most of the time. After his father died he continued to live with his aging mother, and with his brother who had a masculine identification but also failed to marry. At one time the patient dated a girl for awhile and had sexual relations with her, but found the relationship unsatisfactory

and broke it off. He did not associate regularly with any homosexual group, but had a few close friends over the years and felt acutely lonely most of the time. His speech and behavior were extremely effeminate and at times he dyed his hair, used makeup, and plucked his eyebrows. He had a strong interest in antiques, art, and religion.

At age 45 he was admitted to a psychiatric hospital briefly following several episodes of amnesia, involving his awakening in a strange hotel with no recollection of how he got there. When these episodes were reconstructed, it appeared probable that they represented a defense against conscious acknowledgement of intolerable homosexual impulses towards a younger man of whom he was sincerely fond. He was afraid to approach him sexually and afraid of losing him. He felt guilty and depressed. However, he responded rapidly to supportive psychotherapy and returned to his home and occasional homosexual relationships.

Rape or Sexual Assault of an Adult Female. In his study of male sexual offenders in Sing Sing Prison, Glueck found this group to have a more aggressive, outgoing, impulsive type of personality than any other group of sexual offenders. They were the youngest of the groups and contained the highest proportion of Negroes. The assault itself frequently occurred when control was diminished by alcohol or by a combination of sexual frustration and temptation. It is relevant in this connection that the sociopathic personality, even when sober, has a low tolerance of frustration, and can resist anything but temptation. It is also pertinent to note that the female victim may have deliberately or unconsciously provided a great deal of temptation to commit the offense of which she subsequently complained. We shall return to this role of the victim at the beginning of the section on causation.

Heterosexual Hebephilia. Hebe was the Greek goddess of youth, and hebephilia is a term used to describe sexual activity with adolescents, in contrast with pedophilia which involves sexual activity with children before puberty. Heterosexual hebephilia therefore includes any form of sexual activity with a female partner who is pubescent or adolescent through age 16. A sensitive fictional account of one such relationship is contained in the well-known novel *Lolita* by Nabokov. Truth in this instance presents a harsher picture than fiction. Glueck reported the men convicted of this offense were found to be close to the rapists and nonsexual offenders in their general adjustment, but showed marked disturbances in judgment which were considered related to a high proportion of "schizoadaptive patterns." Half of his cases of incest fell into this group.

Heterosexual Pedophilia. This includes those involved in any kind of sexual activity with a female partner who has not started to show any pubertal changes. In the Sing Sing study the men in this group tended to be somewhat older, to have a poor marital adjustment, and to have shown considerable disturbance in reality perception, particularly under the influence of alcohol. Among heterosexual pedophiles referred to an outpatient clinic, Mohr et al. found a distinct trimodal age distribution, with peaks occurring in adolescence, in the 30s, and in the 50s. Their adolescent group were characterized by retardation in psychosexual and social development. Their middle-aged group were more characterized by regression, with severe marital and social maladjustment, often compounded by alcoholism. Their older group were characterized by loneliness and actual impotence or concern about impotence. The last group is concerned with the type of pedophilia most commonly described in the literature, but the middle-aged group were more frequent in their sample, and the following case is illustrative of such individuals.

A 32-year-old man was referred for psychiatric evaluation by his family physician and presented himself with the statement that he was lacking in sexual control. It developed that he was married and had four children, but that his sexual relationship with his wife had never been entirely satisfactory to either of them, and that from the early years of his marriage he had periodically engaged in immature sexual relationships with young girls between the ages of six and ten years. One such relationship with a young sister-in-law had ceased five years previously when she was killed in an automobile accident. Following this the patient had continued to have immature sexual contacts with little girls, but had also started to have periodic extramarital relationships with adult females. During the previous three years two of these women had become pregnant but they had apparently been having intercourse with other men and the patient was not held responsible for these pregnancies. Nevertheless, his wife became aware of both his extramarital affairs and relationships with little girls. On a number of occasions she agreed to continue the marriage provided that her husband discontinued his infidelity and deviant behavior. He repeatedly promised to do so but after a while it would become evident to her that he had continued or resumed these activities. She finally decided to build a more satisfactory life for herself and her children, and applied for divorce. The patient succeeded in postponing the divorce proceedings by agreeing to legal separation, and it was a month after this that he came for psychiatric evaluation. It appeared to the psychiatrists who saw him that he was far less interested in changing his own behavior than in attempting to use involvement in psychotherapy as a means to persuade his wife that he was at last sincerely seeking help, and that she should therefore permit him to return to her and the children.

The patient was the eldest of eight children and was born soon after his parents' marriage when his father was 25 and his mother 18 years old. All of the remaining children were boys with the exception of the youngest, and his only sister was not born until the patient was 17 years old. The next child after the patient died at the age of one year, so that the patient was five years older than the next living sibling and was relatively isolated from him. His father was away from home a lot, supposedly buying and selling farm products, and when he was at home there was considerable conflict and argument between the two parents. The patient's mother was always tired and never wanted to go anywhere, and his father would accuse her unjustly of being a poor housekeeper.

From an early age the patient was given many responsibilities on the parents' farm, and had neither time nor opportunity for either studying or social activities with other children his own age. His father was very strict and frequently beat him with a belt, so that he was most unhappy at home and, between the ages of 14 and 17, he twice left home but returned at his mother's request. He left school altogether in grade nine, worked on his father's farm for another three years, spent four years in the Navy, returned to the farm for one year, and then moved to a city to work in a factory.

He always felt closer to his mother than to his father, but neither parent gave him any sexual information. During adolescence he discovered masturbation. At the age of 17 he started to date a 14 year old girl and they went steady together for the next four years, at the end of which time they were married. Neither of them had had any heterosexual experience prior to marriage, and the patient stated that he had never attempted premarital intercourse with his wife because he was scared and didn't know anything. After marriage the patient soon discovered that his wife was "very cool" sexually. She didn't refuse him intercourse but evidently considered it an obligation and remained totally unresponsive. Throughout their marriage he had felt that she had pushed him away sexually and then blamed him for seeking alternative outlets. It should be mentioned, however, that frigidity is accentuated by hostility and may sometimes develop for the first time after a woman has learned of her husband's infidelity or deviation.

In any event, at the time of his psychiatric evaluation the patient and his wife had four children, a boy aged ten and three girls aged seven, five, and four years. Apart from being a poor husband, the patient was also an extremely poor father, behaving in some ways just as his own father had done when the patient was a child. Thus, he was frequently away from home, and rationalized this on the basis of needing money from a second job. When at home he was strict with the children and sometimes beat them with his belt, and he would usually find a job around the house which would enable him to withdraw socially from his family. He felt hurt that all his children seemed to prefer their mother's company to his own, and that three of the four children actually seemed to reject him physically. He denied any conscious sexual feelings or approaches towards his own daughters, but his wife expressed concern over this possibility and gave this as one of her reasons for seeking divorce at this time.

At the time he presented himself for psychiatric evaluation, he claimed that during the previous 24 hours he had had several impulses to kill himself by cutting his wrists or by driving his car off the road. He was therefore admitted to a psychiatric ward for close observation. While there he was pleasant and cooperative in manner, but frequently ignored regulations that had previously been brought to his attention. When confronted with his failure to conform, he either maintained that he was not breaking the regulation but doing something else, or that he had not known it existed. He socialized quite readily but preferred to spend his time alone with one of several adolescent female patients, who were between the ages of 16 and 20 and were the youngest girls on the ward.

While in hospital he underwent extensive psychological testing. He obtained a full scale IQ of 88 and showed no evidence of organic intellectual impairment. On the Minnesota Multiphasic Personality Inventory he obtained marked elevation on scales 8 and 4 (schizoid and psychopathic deviate), together with borderline elevations on scales 9 and 6 (manic and paranoid), suggesting a personality characterized by very marked social alienation and withdrawal, together with a high probability of impulsive antisocial behavior. His stories on the Thematic Apperception Test suggested concern with inadequacy and poor masculine identification, together with suspiciousness. There were indications of a strict and domineering father, coupled with a weak, ineffectual, and nonsupportive mother. Some potential for poor impulse control and hostile acting out was also indicated. The Rorschach test suggested extreme anxiety and turmoil, together with an inability to perceive accurately. Extreme anxiety was indicated by many diffuse and poorly controlled shading responses, poor form level, inability to handle emotionality as expressed by color, and a rather eroded and malignant self-concept, all of which are considered more typical of schizophrenia than sociopathy.

Clinically he was also considered to be potentially schizophrenic, but no clear-cut evidence of schizophrenia was established and he was not found to be severely depressed as he had claimed at the time of his admission. In view of his anxiety and schizoid characteristics, he was given one of the phenothiazine drugs and an attempt was made to involve him in psychotherapy, but the patient terminated both forms of treatment within a few months after his short stay in hospital, when it became apparent to him that his wife was not going to change her mind about divorce.

Homosexual Hebephilia. This involves any form of sexual activity with a pubescent or adolescent male partner. In the Sing Sing study these men reported considerable traumatic sexual experience during childhood and showed evidence of marked impairment in their capacity for interpersonal relationships.

Homosexual Pedophilia. This involves any form of sexual activity with prepubertal boys. Glueck reported that these men showed the greatest amount of psychiatric disturbance among all the groups of offenders in the Sing Sing study, and a high proportion of them were diagnosed as frankly psychotic. They showed marked impairment of reasoning and judgment, and the only individuals with whom they could successfully relate were boys. In their study of offenders referred to an outpatient clinic, Mohr et al. found that the homosexual pedophiles showed the same trimodal age distribution as the heterosexual pedophiles, but that they showed a much greater tendency to seek orgasm during their sexual activities with the child. Thus, orgasm was sought in over 50 percent of the homosexual pedophile group as compared with only six percent of the heterosexual pedophile group. Furthermore, over half the offenses of heterosexual pedophiles occurred in the patient's or victim's own home, whereas the homosexual pedophiles had a greater tendency to seek out the victim and set up the situation for the offense.

Incest. Weinberg differentiated male incest into three main categories: (1) an indiscriminate promiscuity where the incest is part of a pattern of sexual psychopathology; (2) intense craving for young children or pedophilia, which also includes the daughter as a sexual object; and (3) the endogamic or intra-familial-oriented incest. In the Sing Sing study, the incest group was made up of offenders from several groups who also happened to commit incest with a primary relative, usually female. Half of this group involved heterosexual hebephilia, the most common form of which consisted of sexual relations between father and adolescent daughter. In their study of a group of incestuous daughters, Sloane and Karpinski found that there appeared to be more emotional damage when the incest occurred during adolescence than when it took place prior to puberty. The adolescent daughter participating in incest generally becomes involved in promiscuity and other maladaptive behavior. Barry and Johnson noted that incestuous daughters experienced little anxiety when they were young, and when the mother accepted the fact of incest. However, Cormier et al. pointed out that the daughter eventually rebels at the exclusive possessiveness of her father and seeks her freedom. She either runs away, makes another attachment, or she reveals the fact of incest. The following case history of father-daughter incest illustrates pathological relationships involving both parents, and rebellion on the part of the daughter, leading to promiscuity, escape from the home, punishment of the father by disclosure, and punishment of other men onto whom she had displaced some of her hostility.

A 15-year-old girl was admitted to a psychiatric hospital at her own request after she had charged five boys with giving her alcohol and forcing her to have intercourse with them. Following this she refused to return home and asked for psychiatric help.

She was the second of four children, and was the eldest girl. Her mother was described as being somewhat neurotic and the patient was afraid to ask her where babies came from or any other sexual information. However, she stated, "I started to menstruate when I was 11. At this time my father and I started to have intercourse about twice a week. I didn't know that it was wrong. My mother had never told me anything about sex. When I was 13 I went to babysit one night. A fellow about 18 came and gave me something to drink. I knew it wasn't ginger ale, but I didn't know what it was. I remember what happened, but it is all hazy. The fellow had intercourse with me and it was about 4:30 a.m. by the time I got home. My mom had phoned the police and they were at my home when I got there. They tried to find out if I had had intercourse with this fellow. I wouldn't tell them, but I told my mother that I and this fellow did what Dad and I did. Mom didn't understand until I said, 'You know, what you and Dad do.' Since this Mom has been very jealous of my father and me and our relationship. About a week ago my father wanted me to have intercourse. When I refused, he said he wanted me because my mother would only have intercourse with him about once a year."

She said that at one time she told her parents that she had a sexual urge after her menstrual period and her mother told her that at these times she could have intercourse with her father if she had her mother's permission. However, she also remarked, "My mother just doesn't trust me. She will not forget what I have done. She will not give me a second chance. She will not let me go out and when I do she picks me up in the car. She would kill me if she knew that I wanted to come in here." She felt unwanted at home where she was responsible for much of the housework, getting meals, and looking after the younger children. She was resentful of the frequent arguments between her parents and about their close supervision of her friends. She didn't feel free to bring any friends home and her mother broke up several relationships with "decent" boys by telling them in front of her that she was too young to go out. She rebelled and went by herself, and picked up boys and men with whom she satisfied her increasingly strong sexual urges. However, she felt guilty over her own behavior and resented that of the men with whom she went out. She had previously refused to lay a charge against her father, although she had

come to resent his advances greatly. In laying a charge against the five boys with whom she had spent one night, she was symbolically punishing her father and other men who had taken advantage of her. However, she continued to feel guilty and moderately depressed. In hospital she benefited from psychotherapy and was then placed in a residential home for girls with behavior problems, where her emotional and social maturation could continue.

Zoophilia or bestiality involves any form of sexual gratification obtained through contact with an animal. In the case of males, Kinsey et al. reported a cumulative frequency of eight percent, occurring mainly during adolescence and generally consisting of coitus with a female animal. In the case of females, Kinsey et al. reported a cumulative frequency of 3.6 percent, occurring mainly during adolescence and adult life, and consisting mainly of general body contact.

Voyeurism, exhibitionism, and the symbolic sexual offenses (fetishism, and so on) have already been outlined in the preceding section on classification according to the nature of the sexual act. In the following section we shall consider the types of sexual offenses and deviation most likely to be associated with the main syndromes of psychiatric disorder.

PSYCHOPATHOLOGY ASSOCIATED WITH SEXUAL OFFENSES

Neurotic Disorders. The sexual attitudes and behavior of the typical neurotic are inhibited, and these patients frequently manifest frigidity or impotence. Sometimes there may be attempts at compensation by means of guilt-ridden promiscuity, but direct sexual aggression is rare. However, neurotic personality characteristics and symptoms frequently accompany the fear of adult heterosexual relationships that is characteristic of many sexual deviates and offenders. Such neurotic manifestations are commonly found in persons with persistent preferences for homosexuality, voyeurism, exhibitionism, fetishism, and milder degrees of sado-masochism.

Sociopathic Personality. The sexual behavior of the typical sociopath involves promiscuity and uninhibited sexuality with a variety of partners of the opposite sex. Preferably such partners are obtained with their consent, but otherwise the sociopath may resort to force, fear, or fraud, and frequently becomes involved in charges of seduction or abduction. An otherwise willing female partner may complain that a sociopathic male abuses her excessively, or wants to tie her to the bed during prolonged periods of sexual indulgence. Sometimes the object of his attentions is an adolescent female, and somewhat less frequently he may participate in homosexual activity, usually with an adult and often for financial motives. More deviant forms of sexual behavior are less frequently associated with sociopathic personality, but Dunaif and Hoch drew attention to the frequency of sociopathic behavior among certain schizophrenic patients with severe forms of sexual deviation.

Functional Psychoses. The hypomanic patient tends to be sociopathic during his episode of euphoria, and frequently becomes involved in promiscuity, or more rarely in sadistic behavior or sexual assault of a female. In depression of psychotic intensity there is commonly profound inhibition of all sexual responses, with temporary frigidity or impotence. In some depressed patients, feelings of guilt and desire for punishment may lead to physical masochism, and it is probable that this was responsible for some of the medieval religious practices involved in "mortifying the sinful flesh." In schizophrenic and paranoid reactions, there is often a lifelong denial of direct heterosexual experience, which may range from impotence or frigidity to a total inability to establish a meaningful relationship with any other human being. Many schizophrenics rely exclusively on mastur-

bation for the relief of sexual tensions, while others turn to a variety of deviant sexual practices. A number of authors have viewed the chaotic sexuality of some schizophrenics as equivalent to the polymorphous perversity that Freud attributed to the infant. Dunaif and Hoch documented the severe sexual deviations and offenses of a group of patients whom they described as having "pseudo-psychopathic schizophrenia." In any event, it is widely agreed that the most bizarre forms of sexual offense and deviation, such as severe sadism or masochism, are carried out by individuals who are overtly schizophrenic.

Organic Brain Syndromes. No single form of sexual offense or deviation is characteristic of the patient with an organic brain syndrome, but a variety of abnormal sexual misbehavior may be precipitated by the onset of organic intellectual impairment, due to such disorders as prolonged alcoholism or the psychoses of senility. These offenses frequently involve older men and adolescent or prepubertal girls, a number of such relationships being incestuous in nature. However, the latter group of offenses are often attributable to impairment of sexual functions and marital relationships rather than to impairment of intellectual functions and superego controls.

Mental Retardation or Intellectual Subnormality is not found unduly frequently among sexual offenders charged and convicted in court. Severe or low-grade mental retardation is accompanied by sterility, and mild or high-grade mental retardation tends to be associated with irresponsibility and promiscuity, particularly among subnormal females. There is a selection against marriage of subnormal males and other sexual outlets may be blocked, which may be a factor in provoking occasional sexual assault and sometimes more primitive substitutive outlets, as with animals. On the whole, however, society recognizes their sexual behavior as an understandable manifestation of their intellectual subnormality and such individuals tend to be admitted to institutions for the mentally retarded rather than being brought to court for the offense itself.

DYNAMICS, DEVELOPMENT, AND CAUSATION

Before considering the psychodynamics of the sexual deviate and the significance of various biological, psychological, and sociocultural factors in predisposing to sexual deviation, it is appropriate to consider the role of the victim and other precipitating factors.

The Role of the Victim and Other Precipitating Factors

In the event that a sexual offense involves assaulting or molesting other people, ostensibly against their will, public opinion and the law have traditionally tended to regard the woman or child molested as an innocent victim of the offender. It has been observed, however, that many such victims deliberately or unconsciously invite, provoke, or seduce the offense of which they subsequently complain to the authorities.

Among a variety of infrahuman species the ritual of courtship and mating involves a display of desirable characteristics, aggressive behavior toward rivals, and the establishment of dominance over the mate. Often the role of the female is to stimulate the male by tantalizing him, to invite pursuit by running away, and to resist mildly before finally submitting. Many men have learned to recognize the discrepancy between the verbal protests and nonverbal cooperation of their partners, as typified in the line from *Don Juan* by Byron:

"And whispering, 'I will ne'er consent,' consented."

Many women, particularly in primitive societies or among the lower socioeconomic levels of our own society, may expect men to establish their worth as a sexual partner through a display of dominance that may involve physical force and even some bodily pain. That civilized women may experience a desire to be violated "innocently" is illustrated by a wartime story told by Hirschfeld:

The women and girls of many villages were instructed to keep out of sight during the passage of enemy troops through the locality. The ladies accordingly stayed indoors, but when the last of the enemy troops had left, they rushed out of their hiding places with the bitterly disappointed cry: "What about the violation?"

Willing submission to pain may result from a desire to intensify sexual excitement, or from more materialistic motives, as illustrated by the following brief excerpt from *A Harlem Tragedy* by O. Henry.

"I wouldn't have a man, "declared Mrs. Cassidy, "that didn't beat me up at least once a week. Shows he thinks something of you. Say! But that last dose Jack gave me wasn't no homeopathic one. I can see stars yet. But he'll be the sweetest man in town for the rest of the week to make up for it. This eye is good for theatre tickets and a silk shirtwaist at the very least.' A little later in the same short story, Mrs. Cassidy remarks, "What I want is a masterful man that slugs you when he's jagged and hugs you when he ain't jagged. Preserve me from the man that ain't got the sand to do neither!"

The invitation to sexual assault may be deliberate or unintentional. In the latter instance, the provocation may occur in one or two general ways. On the one hand a sadistic woman may knowingly arouse a man sexually with the conscious intention of frustrating him, only to find that he will not be denied what she had in effect promised him. On the other hand, through unconscious denial of sexuality, the hysterical or otherwise neurotic woman may unwittingly provide the temptation and provoke the sexual response that she consciously rejects. In either instance, however, the hostility of the woman who has provoked the assault may well lead to the man's being charged and convicted.

Similar conscious and unconscious motives may lead other victims to disclose and seek punishment for the offense that their behavior has precipitated. Bender and Blau pointed out that children were sometimes the initiators or seducers in their sexual relations with adults. Hirschfeld remarked that some children became remarkably astute at recognizing the male genital exhibitionist and encouraging him to commit an offense while one of their friends went to fetch a policeman. He also reported the following interesting case in which a middle-aged woman presented herself as a victim of a male exhibitionist, but was herself responsible for the circumstances about which she complained:*

In a small town in Württemberg a middle-aged business man was denounced for creating a public nuisance in that he exposed his erect member while lying in his bed. The complaint was made by a 40-year-old single woman, a school teacher, who lived in a garret flat in the house opposite. The accused admitted exposure, but denied the charge of having committed a public nuisance, because the teacher, in order to see him, had to climb on a rather high chest of drawers. He had lived opposite her for 11 years, and as she so far had not been shocked by his action he had come to think that he was doing her a favor in carrying it out. The investigation confirmed the argument that the man could not be seen except from the top of the chest of drawers, and the accused was acquitted. Apart from the latter discovery it also came out that the lady had not only stood on a chest of drawers, but had also used a pair of opera glasses. Why, after so many years, she suddenly turned moral and denounced the man, remained a mystery.

The significance of various *situational factors* in precipitating sexual offenses

---

*Reprinted by permission from Hirschfeld, M. 1944. *Sexual Anomalies and Perversions.* New York, Emerson Books, Inc., pp. 505-506.

has already been referred to on several occasions. Glueck remarked that sexual assault frequently occurred when control was diminished by alcohol or by a combination of sexual frustration and temptation. Mohr et al. noted that exhibitionism tended to occur when the individual was caught in a conflict situation with mother, fiancee, or wife — in the latter instance, either immediately before or after marriage or pregnancy. Cormier et al. cited a number of precipitating circumstances in cases of father-daughter incest, but concluded as follows:

. . .external reality such as the death or absence of the wife, disturbances in the marital relationship, the return of the father after a long absence, physical overcrowding, alcoholism, a relatively young father living close to an adolescent daughter, all these precipitating factors which are put forward are commonly found without leading to incest. In some predisposed fathers, however, they can reawaken concealed and suppressed incestuous temptation which is eventually acted out.

PSYCHODYNAMICS

In his *Three Contributions to the Theory of Sex*, Freud (1910) presented evidence of infantile sexuality, and postulated that the sexual aims of deviates or perverts are identical with those of children. He subsequently observed that occasional perverse acts or fantasies are universal, and in his *Introductory Lectures to Psychoanalysis* (1920) he remarked "If it is correct that the real obstacles to sexual satisfaction, or privation in regard to it, bring to the surface perverse tendencies in people who would otherwise have shown none, we must conclude that something in these people is ready to embrace these perversions; or, if you prefer it, that the tendencies must have been present in them in a latent form."

If sexual deviates or perverts are regarded as persons with infantile instead of adult sexuality, the latter may result from either fixation (i.e., arrested development) or from regression to earlier sexual aims. Freud concluded that persons who react to sexual frustrations with regression to infantile sexuality are perverts; whereas persons who react with other defenses, or employ other defenses after the regression are neurotics.

It soon became evident however that sexual deviates, like neurotics, have repressions, and certain of these came to be regarded as specific determinants in the development of their psychopathology. These consist of an unconscious Oedipus complex and an unconscious castration anxiety. However, since the anxiety and guilt feelings of the neurotic are perceived as directed against the Oedipus complex, castration anxiety is viewed as the decisive factor in the development of sexual deviation. Thus, Fenichel wrote as follows:

In perversions, adult sexuality is supplanted by infantile sexuality. Something must be repulsive in adult sexuality, and something especially attractive in infantile sexuality. While the latter factor is variable, the former is constant; it is always the castration complex that interferes with the capacity for enjoying full genital sexuality. Actually the differences in the male and the female castration complex directly corresponds to the differences between male and female perversions.

In elaborating this interpretation, Fenichel stated that the pervert is a person whose sexual pleasure is blocked by the idea of castration. Through the perversion he tries to prove that there is no castration; insofar as this proof is believed, sexual pleasure and orgasm become possible again.

In their study of psychodynamic patterns in the Sing Sing sex offenders, Hammer and Glueck presented considerable psychological test data indicating both (1) fear of sex contact with adult females, and (2) feelings of genital inadequacy. Projective tests administered and interpreted by three different psychologists were all considered to reveal unconscious castration fears, feelings of tremendous guilt in sexual areas, and anticipation of awful punishment. The castration factor also appeared as a feeling that they were damaged and that they were not a complete unit within themselves. The authors postulated that the sex offense represented an attempt on the part of the subject to employ substitute sex outlets for the mature female, due to the threatening sexual potential with which she was endowed by virtue of the offender's oedipal entanglement. This unresolved oedipal involvement appeared to be, in part at least, behind the guilt-dictated fear of genital damage in these men. In the various groups of offenders studied, there appeared to be a parallel increase between the intensity of castration feelings on the one hand, and the distance from the mature female as a potential sex object on the other.

Such formulations have not satisfied all psychoanalysts, and Balint attempted to look beyond the castration complex and its denial. He cited Ferenczi's view that we are all motivated by strong regressive longings for a return to early and more pleasureable conditions, typified ultimately by life within the mother's womb, and postulated that the male comes nearest to achieving this regression during coitus: with his semen in reality, with his penis symbolically, with his whole self in fantasy. This view is in accord with the epigram defining man as a creature who came out of woman and spends the rest of his life trying to get back in. Be this as it may, Balint contended that perversions are attempts to escape from the two main demands of mature genitality: (1) accepting as real the intense need in ourselves for periodic regressions in the form of heterosexual coitus, and (2) accepting the necessity of the work of conquest, i.e., changing an indifferent object into a cooperative genital partner. Such psychodynamic interpretations, however, are essentially descriptive, and we shall now turn to further studies of etiology.

HEREDITARY FACTORS

It has already been emphasized that sexual offenders and deviates represent a very heterogeneous group, and it is not surprising that their family histories should reveal a corresponding diversity of psychopathology. On theoretical grounds we should expect a relatively high frequency of neurotic personality characteristics and symptoms among the parents and siblings of those sexual deviates having prominent neurotic manifestations. Similarly, we should expect a high frequency of antisocial behavior and alcoholism in the families of sexual offenders with sociopathic personalities; and an unusually high frequency of psychosis and suicide among the parents and siblings of psychotic sexual offenders. Data hitherto recorded are compatible with these theoretical formulations, but positive family histories give no indication of the relative significance of heredity and maladaptive learning based on pathogenic postnatal experiences. None of the family data so far available support a hypothesis of simple Mendelian inheritance for any specific variety of sexual deviation.

Kallmann reported a series of 95 pairs of adult male twins, of whom at least one member (the index case) was predominantly or exclusively homosexual. Among 44 pairs of twins diagnosed as monozygotic, he recorded 100 percent concordance as to some overt homosexual behavior in cotwins, and a close correspondence in the quantitative rating of homosexual behavior after adolescence. Among 51 pairs of twins diagnosed as dizygotic, 40 percent were reported as concordant as to the presence of some form of overt homosexual behavior, and 11.5 percent of the cotwins received homosexuality ratings of five or six by Kinsey's criteria. The Holzinger index of heritability for overt homosexual behavior, computed from these data, is 100 percent, suggesting that consistently preferred adult male homosexuality is attributable to heredity alone. Kallmann concluded that, "The most plausible genetic explanation for these findings would seem to be a gene-controlled disarrangement in the balance between male and female maturation patterns, resulting in a shift toward an alternative minus variant in the integrative process of psychosexual maturation." However, the severe limitations of such twin studies must again be emphasized. Moreover, Kolb, Mesnikoff, et al. subsequently provided considerable data on five pairs of monozygotic twins (four male and one female) who were found to be discordant as to homosexual behavior, and in whom they related this discordance to differences in intrafamilial relationships during childhood.

In recent years *chromosomal* studies have revealed the existence of a number of individuals who survive to adult life in spite of the presence of only one sex chromosome or alternatively one or more extra sex chromosomes. A wide variety of such anomalies have been reported, the two most frequent of which result in the development of Turner's and Klinefelter's syndromes. It may be recalled that the normal female has two X chromosomes and the normal male has one X and one Y chromosome. In *Turner's syndrome* there is only a single X chromosome and these individuals are externally female but do not develop secondary sex characteristics, rarely menstruate, and are apparently always sterile. They frequently have malformations of the aorta, deafness, and mental retardation. Individuals with *Klinefelter's syndrome*, on the other hand, generally have three sex chromosomes, two X and one Y. They are externally male, but often somewhat feminine in build, usually sterile and often mentally retarded. The fact that such anomalies are apt to be associated with bodily malformations and intellectual subnormality, and *not* with any specific form of sexual deviation, is strong evidence against the existence of chromosomal abnormalities in those physically and intellectually normal individuals characterized by persistent preference for deviant sexual behavior.

During the first half of this century, the hypothesis was advanced that some male homosexuals are sex intergrades with male anatomical sex characteristics but a female chromosomal pattern. Several large scale studies indicated a relative excess of brothers among the siblings of male homosexuals, and one study revealed a substantial excess of sisters among the siblings of male exhibitionists. These studies were considered to provide indirect evidence in support of the hypothesis, but subsequently it became possible to provide direct evidence regarding the nuclear sex of male homosexuals. Pritchard reviewed this evidence, and examined the chromosomes in a small series of male homosexuals in all of whom he found the normal male complement of one X and one Y chromosome. The hypothesis of intersexuality as a basis for male homosexuality must therefore be rejected.

SOMATIC FACTORS

The search for a constitutional basis of homosexuality led some investigators to study the bodily physique of such persons. It is well known that normal men are relatively broader in the shoulders than the hips whereas the reverse is true of normal women. Accurate measurement of the underlying bony structure is relatively simple to carry out, and the two diameters may be compared in a single index termed the *discriminant androgyny score*, which is consistently higher in males than in females. Coppen compared the body build of 31 male homosexuals with that of 22 heterosexual neurotics and 53 control subjects selected by attendance at a clinic for mass radiography. He found the discriminant androgyny score to be significantly lower for the homosexuals than the control subjects, but

his group of heterosexual neurotics also showed a similar reduction in comparison with the control group. The author concluded that the homosexuals had a body build similar to that found in other psychiatric patients, and that it was not specifically related to their sexual abnormality.

It has long been postulated that normal and deviant sexual behavior must bear a close relationship to *endocrine function*. In the lower animals it has been found that sexual activity may be consistently decreased by castration, or increased and generalized to include homosexual as well as heterosexual activity by administration of *male* hormones to *male* animals. In the human, however, there tends to be a very poor correlation between blood hormone levels and overt sexual behavior. In females the marked changes in endocrine activity during puberty and menopause may be unaccompanied by any change in current sexual behavior. In males the sharp increase in hormone levels accompanying normal or precocious puberty are not necessarily accompanied by overt behavioral changes, and castration during adult life may have relatively slight effects on established patterns of sexual behavior. Following castration there is a tendency for sexual behavior to decrease in quantity, but for no change to occur in the direction of the sexual aim. Similarly, no consistent abnormalities of endocrine function have been observed in any group of sexual deviates or offenders.

Following an extensive *comparison of sexual behavior in many species of animals and 190 human societies*, Ford and Beach concluded that human beings are less dependent upon sex hormones than are subhuman primates, and that the latter in turn are somewhat freer of hormonal control than lower mammals. They therefore suggested that in the course of evolution the extent to which gonadal hormones control sexual behavior has been progressively relaxed, with the result that human behavior is relatively independent of this source of control. They continued as follows:

Review of the changes which have taken place in the structure of the brain during mammalian evolution showed that this structure has become increasingly complex and important as the primates and finally their own species developed. In particular, the cerebral cortex has assumed a greater and greater degree of direction over all behavior, including that of a sexual nature. It appears that the growing importance of cerebral influences accounts for the progressive relaxation of hormonal control over sexual responses. At the same time, increasing dominance of the cortex in affecting sexual manifestations has resulted in greater lability and modifiability of erotic practices. Human sexual behavior is more variable and more easily affected by learning and social conditioning than is that of any other species, and this is precisely because in our own species this type of behavior depends heavily upon the most recently evolved parts of the brain.

PSYCHOLOGICAL FACTORS

Harlow demonstrated that the learning of normal heterosexual behavior by adult monkeys is based on earlier opportunities for play activities and sexual experimentation with other young monkeys. Adult male monkeys that were denied such opportunities for early learning did *not* subsequently learn to mate successfully, and were observed masturbating even when alone with a sexually receptive female.

The diversity of deviant sexual behavior in humans suggests that many different types of experience are likely to contribute to its development. Following his study of the Sing Sing male sexual offenders Glueck remarked, "We could not demonstrate one specific traumatic episode in the sexual development of most of the men. There appeared to be a continuously traumatic, prohibiting and inhibiting attitude toward sexual behavior throughout the developmental years that was reflected in the serious distortions of the adult sexual patterns." Most of these sexual offenders showed a marked lack of knowledge about sexual activity and normal patterns of sexual behavior. Those with the greatest deviation in sexual aim correspondingly gave a history of the greatest modesty during childhood. Those showing most markedly deviant forms of sexual behavior similarly showed the greatest difficulty in approaching the adult female. The typical sexual offender is not aggressive but overly inhibited in his other sexual activities. Admittedly he fails to show consideration for the person with whom he commits the offense, but frequently he himself does not even obtain satisfaction from the deviant sexual activity.

Forty-four percent of Glueck's sample of sexual offenders remained unmarried at the time of the study (at a median age of 33.5 years) and tended to give such reasons as economic insecurity, sexual difficulties, and personality difficulties. Nearly half of those who were married stated that they were not usually satisfied by their marital sexual relationships. The disturbance in their ability to relate to other adults, illustrated in their relationships with their wives and other sexual partners, was further emphasized by their isolation in general areas of adult socialization. Those involved in the most deviant behavior tended to be the most shy and timid, and were also the most likely to show overt symptoms of schizophrenia or other psychosis. A considerable proportion used alcohol to excess, and this tended to intensify the pathological patterns of adaptation.

Hampson, Money, and their associates provided extensive evidence concerning the *relative significance of biological and psychosocial determinants* in the development of adult psychosexual orientation and behavior. Their findings were based on the intensive study of certain experiments of nature, consisting of individuals with a variety of endocrine and/or hermaphroditic disorders. True *hermaphroditism* involves the presence in one individual of both ovarian and testicular tissue, and is extremely rare. *Pseudohermaphroditism*, involving various types of genital malformation, is much more frequent, as also is *masculinization in females* resulting from excessive production of male hormones by an overactive adrenal cortex. In such individuals, it is possible to distinguish between seven variables relating to their sex, any one of which might be incongruent with some or all of the other variables. The latter are as follows: (1) chromosomal sex, (2) gonadal sex, (3) hormonal sex, (4) internal accessory organs, (5) external genital appearance, (6) assigned sex and rearing, (7) adult gender role or psychological sex. These workers found that the last variable of *adult gender role or psychological sex invariably corresponded with assigned sex and rearing*, regardless of existing contradictions with respect to any of the five preceding variables. Hampson concluded that gender role or psychologic sex is learned, and went on to state, "In place of a theory of innate constitutional psychologic bisexuality such as that proposed by Freud, we would substitute a concept of psychosexual neutrality in humans at birth. Such neutrality permits the development and perpetuation of diverse patterns of psychosexual orientation and functioning in accordance with the life experiences each individual may encounter and transact."

In the normal child there is a strong positive identification with the parent of the same sex, which leads to early and permanent adoption of the attributes and behavior that are culturally sanctioned in members of this sex. In individuals with psychosexual inversion, on the other hand, there is a decisive childhood identification with a parent or parent-surrogate (for example, an older brother or sister) of the opposite sex. The intensity of the latter identification, and the age of the child when it first develops, are significant determin-

ants of the degree of sexual inversion manifested in adult life. Among those individuals with extreme psychosexual inversion and an exclusive preference for homosexual relationships during adult life, identification with the parent or surrogate of the opposite sex has been evident since earliest childhood. The reasons for this identification with the opposite sex, however, have not been easy to establish retrospectively.

Kolb and Johnson emphasized the roles of both parents in fostering psychosexual inversion and homosexual behavior. Kolb, Mesnikoff, et al. studied the early parental attitudes and behavior of five pairs of twins who were discordant as to homosexual behavior in adult life. Four pairs of twins were male and in each case their mother was the dominant parent. The father was openly and actively derogated in three cases, and in the fourth assumed a passive role in the family. The male twin who became homosexual was most closely associated with the mother, whereas the male twin who became heterosexual was more closely associated with the father.

In a much more extensive comparison of 106 homosexual males and 100 heterosexual males undergoing psychoanalysis, Bieber et al. reported that the majority of homosexuals had overly close relationships with their mothers and mutually hostile relationships with their fathers. Almost half of the mothers of the homosexuals were dominant wives who minimized their husbands. Most of the mothers were explicitly seductive, and about two-thirds of the mothers openly preferred their homosexual sons to their husbands, and allied with the sons against the husbands. In about half the cases the patient was the mother's confidant. (Table 21-1.)

It is evident that well-adjusted parents will tend to reinforce normal psychosexual attitudes and behavior, and extinguish manifestations of deviant development in their children. Ab-

TABLE 21-1. Parental Relationships of 106 Homosexual and 100 Heterosexual Male Patients (All figures are percentages.)*

	HOMO-SEXUALS	HETERO-SEXUALS
Mother		
Demanded that she be prime center of patient's attention	61	36
Was seductive toward patient	57	34
Spent a great deal of time with patient	56	27
Tried to ally with patient against husband	62	40
Was more intimate with patient than with other male siblings	56	29
Encouraged masculine activities	17	47
Interfered with patient's heterosexual activity during and after adolescence	58	35
Father		
Patient was father's favorite	7	28
Patient spent little time with father	87	60
Patient hated and feared father	57	31
Patient admired father	16	47

*Data from Bieber, I., et al. 1962. *Homosexuality: A Psychoanalytic Study.* New York, Basic Books.

normal parents, on the other hand, may reinforce inappropriate identifications and deviant sexual behavior while extinguishing normal sexual curiosity and exploration. Various forms of sexual deviation may be expected to arise as substitutive phenomena when normal development towards heterosexuality meets with extreme frustration or actual punishment. In the case of masochism the punishment itself becomes associated with sexual gratification, as in the following illustration from Hirschfeld:*

The patient, at the age of 13 years, was on a visit at an estate, where there was also a boy of the same age and two girls aged 14 and 16 years respectively. The mother of the three children was an invalid and left the education of the three children in the hands of a governess. The governess in question was 28 years old, big and strong, with an energetic face and energetic gestures. One morning the attention of the visiting boy was attracted by the sound of weeping, shouting, and imploring words, and the crash of blows, all coming from the schoolroom. He looked through the keyhole and saw that Erna, the 14-year-old girl, was lying across a big

*Reprinted by permission from Hirschfeld, M. 1944. *Sexual Anomalies and Perversions.* New York, Emerson Books, Inc., pages 303-304.

table. The governess had raised her skirt and was beating her on her bare buttocks with a cane. At lunch Erna's eyes were red with weeping and she was restlessly fidgeting in her seat; she had difficulty in sitting—the chastisement must have been very severe. The boy then made friends with Erna, who confided to him that the governess took a great delight in beating her and Elsa, her 16-year-old sister, and that she beat them almost daily, either with a cane, or with a hazel switch, or with a birch rod. She used to lay Elsa too across the table and, raising her skirt, beat her on her bare buttocks. If the girls complained, the governess accused them of various misdeeds. On one occasion, after such a complaint, she beat one of the girls till she was black and blue. Elsa used to lie quietly; Erna always struggled a little. The visiting boy masturbated practically every evening with his school mate. One evening they were surprised in the act by the governess. She locked the door behind her and said: "You're now going to get a good hiding, and every evening for eight days, before bedtime, you're going to get the same." She fetched a stick, laid each of the boys across the arm of the sofa and raising his shirt—all that he was wearing—she laid on with the cane until his buttocks changed colour. Both boys submitted. "It burned my behind like fire, but at the same time it prickled so pleasantly, so delightfully. And it was the blows that did it; it had never been so nice when we masturbated, which we did again. And later I noticed that the governess's hands, during the now regular chastisements, frequently strayed between my legs and stayed there. So we were glad of the blows and when the happy days were over we longed for them."

SOCIOCULTURAL FACTORS

Characteristic of most sexual deviates is a profound lack of information concerning normal sexual activities, a diminished ability to achieve gratification from any form of sexual activity, and unsatisfactory interpersonal relationships with other adults. These characteristics appear to be related to continuously prohibiting and inhibiting attitudes toward sexual behavior throughout the developmental years. By and large, members of the upper and middle socioeconomic classes of our society are taught a greater degree of control over their sexual and aggressive impulses than members of the lower classes. These restrictive patterns of socialization during childhood and adolescence have been held responsible for the apparently higher frequency of deviant sexual behavior among the upper and middle classes, in contrast with a relatively higher frequency of sexual assault among members of the lower classes.

Differences in childhood experiences, however, are also related to adult differences in what is regarded as normal sexual behavior. Thus, members of lower classes may accept as normal a certain amount of promiscuity, so long as the sexual act consists simply of genital union, but may view as perverse the more varied sexual behavior of the upper and middle classes, which tends to include extensive premarital petting, prolonged kissing and foreplay, and a variety of positions in intercourse.

Ford and Beach undertook an extensive review of sexual behavior in primitive societies which vary from extreme permissiveness to severe restrictiveness. The latter is often combined with sadistic treatment of the adolescent during sexual initiation rites, and harsh punishment of offenders against the generally accepted sexual mores. The history of western civilization provides comparable examples of both extremes of sexual license and prohibition. Similarly, certain forms of deviant sexual practices have been recognized as widespread in certain societies and received some measure of social approval. Hirschfeld referred to the traditional forms of sexual deviation as being flagellation in England, mouth-genital contact and female homosexuality in France, and male homosexuality in Germany. Such practices, however, may be relatively widespread and culturally accepted at a given time and place, but tend to change gradually along with other characteristics of the society that has fostered them.

TREATMENT

Three attitudes are reflected in the behavior of society toward the offender, sexual or otherwise: namely (1) retaliation, involving harsh punitive measures; (2) restitution, insisting on the offender repairing the damage he has done; (3) rehabilitation, assisting the offender to avoid repetition of the offense. The reaction to the sexual offender has traditionally involved retaliation, and only more recently have attempts been made toward rehabilitation.

When a major sexual crime is committed in a given community, particularly if it should involve the murder and rape of a young girl, there is generally a public outcry for indiscriminate imprisonment of all sexual deviates and offenders, on the naive assumption that they are all equally likely to commit a similar offense. It would appear that the members of the community who are most vociferous in making such demands are also likely to be those who have the greatest conflicts over the control of their own sexual impulses. Hirschfeld quoted the case of a German judge who was unusually harsh in sentencing sexual offenders, but was eventually arrested for exhibiting his genitals to a young girl. A similar type of reaction-formation may be recognized in those persons who find it necessary to guard the public against obscene literature and various forms of art by having themselves appointed as censors — in which case they themselves are exposed to the sensual stimulation that they deny others. For some years past, however, there has been an increasing tendency towards objective evaluation of the sexual offender and attempts at rehabilitation.

Fenichel remarked that perversions,

addictions, and impulse neuroses are comparable to severe character disorders in their accessibility to psychoanalysis, but that they are always especially difficult (more so than either symptomatic or character neuroses), "First because the symptom is either pleasurable or at least promises to be pleasurable, providing a new and severe form of resistance; and second because the pregenital orientation, usually oral, is prominent."

Most authorities agree that psychotherapy is unlikely to change the direction of a long-established preference in sexual behavior, but that considerable modification may be achieved of (1) substitutive regression of recent onset, (2) deviant partial aims in a predominantly heterosexual individual, and (3) neurotic symptoms (such as anxiety states) frequently associated with deviant sexual behavior.

Tranquilizing or antidepressive drugs have frequently been used to provide symptomatic relief of neurotic symptoms accompanying sexual deviation. Somatic methods of treatment such as electroshock treatment (or even lobotomy) have been recommended for psychotic symptoms accompanying severe deviation, but such symptoms have usually been present for a long time, and the direction of the sexual aim itself is also unlikely to be changed.

Suppression of male sexual activity by means of female sex hormones or castration (either voluntarily or compulsorily) have been carried out in some areas. These procedures result in a diminution in sexual desire and behavior, but no change in the direction of residual sexual impulses. Psychosocial therapies already reviewed in Chapter 11 are therefore the main approach to treatment in patients with sexual deviation.

SELECTED REFERENCES

Allen, C. 1962. *A Textbook of Psychosexual Disorders.* London, Oxford University Press.

Balint, M. 1956. Perversions and genitality. *In Perversions: Psychodynamics and Therapy,* ed. S. Lorand and M. Balint. New York, Random House, Inc.

Barry, M. J., and Johnson, A. 1958. The incest barrier. Psychoanalytic Quarterly 27, 485-500.

Bender, L., and Blau, A. 1937. Reaction of children to sex relations with adults. American Journal of Orthopsychiatry 7, 500-518.

Bieber, I., et al. 1962. *Homosexuality.* New York, Basic Books, Inc.

Bieber, T. 1967. On treating male homosexuals. AMA Archives of General Psychiatry 16, 60-63.

Christoffel, H. 1956. Male genital exhibitionism. In *Perversions: Psychodynamics and Therapy,* ed. S. Lorand and M. Balint. New York, Random House, Inc.

Coppen, A. J. 1959. Body-build of male homosexuals. British Medical Journal 2, 1443-1445.

Cormier, B. M., Kennedy, M., and Sangowicz, J. 1962. Psychodynamics of father-daughter incest. Canadian Psychiatric Association Journal 7, 203-217.

Dunaif, S. L., and Hoch, P. H. 1955. Pseudopsychopathic schizophrenia. In *Psychiatry and the Law,* ed. P. H. Hoch and J. Zubin. New York, Grune & Stratton, Inc., pp. 169-195.

Ellis, A., and Abarbanel, A., eds. 1961. *The Encyclopedia of Sexual Behavior,* Vol. I and II. New York, Hawthorne Books.

Ellis, H. 1942. *Studies in The Psychology of Sex,* Vol. 1 and 2. New York, Random House, Inc.

Fenichel, O. 1945. *The Psychoanalytic Theory of Neurosis.* New York, W. W. Norton & Co., ch. 16.

Ford, C. S., and Beach, S. A. 1951. *Patterns of Sexual Behavior.* New York, Harper & Row, Publishers, Inc.

Freud, S. 1910. *Three Contributions to the Theory of Sex.* New York, Nervous and Mental Diseases Publishing Co.

Freud, S. 1920. *Introductory Lectures to Psychoanalysis.* Reprinted 1953, Perma Books, M-5001.

Friedman, P. 1959. Sexual deviations. In *American Handbook of Psychiatry,* ed. S. Arieti. New York, Basic Books, Inc., Vol. I, ch. 29.

Glueck, B. C., Jr. 1956. *Final Report, Research Project for the Study and Treatment of Persons Convicted of Crime Involving Sexual Aberrations.* New York, State Department of Mental Hygiene.

Gorman, G. F. 1964. Fetishism occurring in identical twins. British Journal of Psychiatry 110, 255-256.

Guttmacher, M. S. 1951. *Sex Offenses: The Problem, Causes and Prevention.* New York, A. A. Norton & Co. Hammer, E.F., and Glueck, B. C., Jr. 1955. Psychodynamic patterns in the sex offender. In *Psychiatry and the Law,* ed. P. H. Hoch and J. Zubin. New York, Grune & Stratton, Inc., pp. 157-168.

Hampson, J. L. 1963. Determinants of psychosexual orientation (gender role) in humans. Canadian Psychiatric Association Journal 8, 24-34.

Harlow, H. F. 1962. The heterosexual affectional system in monkeys. American Psychologist 17, 1-9.

Hirschfeld, M. 1944. *Sexual Anomalies and Perversions.* New York, Emerson Books, Inc.

Hoch, P. H., and Zubin, J., eds. 1949. *Psychosexual Development.* New York, Grune & Stratton, Inc.

Kallmann, F. J. 1953. *Heredity in Health and Mental Disorders.* New York, W. W. Norton & Co., pp. 116-119.

Karpman, B. 1954. *The Sexual Offender and His Offenses.* New York, Julian Press.

Kinsey, A. C. Pomeroy, W. B., and Martin, C. E. 1948. *Sexual Behavior in the Human Male* Philadelphia, W. B. Saunders Co.

Kinsey, A. C., Pomeroy, W. B., Martin, C. E., and Gebhart, P. H. 1953. *Sexual Behavior in the Human Female.* Philadelphia, W. B. Saunders Co.

Kolb, L. C., and Johnson, A. M. 1955. Etiology and therapy of overt homosexuality. Psychoanalytic Quarterly *24*, 506-515.

Kolb, L. C., Rainer, J. D., Mesnikoff, A., and Carr, A. 1961. Divergent sexual development in identical twins. Proceedings of the Third World Congress of Psychiatry, Montreal, Canada, McGill University Press, Vol. 1, pp. 530-534.

Krafft-Ebbing, R. 1906. *Psychopathia Sexualis, with Special Reference to The Antipathic Sexual Instincts, A Medico-forensic Study.* New York, Redman.

Lindner, R., 1955. *The Fifty-minute Hour.* Holt, Rinehart & Winston, Inc. Reprinted 1956, Bantam Books, H-2304, pp. 1-47.

Masters, R. E. L., ed. 1963. *Patterns of Incest.* New York, Basic Books, Inc.

Mesnikoff, A. M., Rainer, J. D., Kolb, L. C., and Carr, A. C. 1963. Intrafamilial determinants of divergent sexual behavior in twins. American Journal of Psychiatry *119*, 732-738.

Mohr, J. W., Turner, R. E., and Ball, R. B. 1962. *Exhibitionism and Pedophilia.* Corrective Psychiatry and Journal of Social Therapy, Volume 8, No. 4.

Mohr, J. W., Turner, R. E., and Jerry, M. B. 1964. *Pedophilia and Exhibitionism.* Toronto, University of Toronto Press.

Money, J. 1963. Cytogenetic and psychosexual incongruities with a note on space-form blindness. American Journal of Psychiatry, *119*, 820-827.

Nabokov, V. 1955. *Lolita.* Reprinted 1959, Crest Giant D-338.

Pauly, I. B. 1963. Female psychosexual inversion: trans-sexualism. Read before the American Psychiatric Association, St. Louis, May, 1963.

Pauly, I. B. 1965. Male psychosexual inversion: trans-sexualism. AMA Archives of General Psychiatry *13*, 172-181.

Pritchard, M. 1962. Homosexuality and genetic sex. Journal of Mental Science *108*, 616-623.

Rachman, S. 1961. Sexual disorders and behavior therapy. American Journal of Psychiatry *118*, 235-240.

Rado, S. 1949. An adaptational view of sexual behavior. *In Psychosexual Development,* ed. P. H. Hoch and J. Zubin. New York, Grune & Stratton, Inc., pp. 159-189.

Randell, J. B. 1959. Transvestitism and trans-sexualism. British Medical Journal *2*, 1448-1452.

Slater, E. 1962. Birth order and maternal age of homosexuals. The Lancet *1*, 69-71.

Sloane, P., and Karpinski, E. 1942. Effects of incest on the participants. American Journal of Orthopsychiatry *12*, 666-673.

Snell, J. E., Rosenwald, R. J., and Robey, A. 1964. The wife beater's wife. AMA Archives of General Psychiatry *11*, 107-112.

Weinberg, S. K. 1955. *Incest Behavior.* New York, The Citadel Press.

Wolfenden, J., et al. 1962. *Report of the Committee on Homosexual Offenses and Prostitution.* London, Her Majesty's Stationery Office.

CHAPTER 22

Alcoholism

The term *addiction* has a Latin origin and in Roman law constituted an assignment of property to another person, as by a debtor to a creditor. Over the years, addiction has come to mean the surrender of one's self to a constant and habitual practice. In this broad sense, the term may be applied to include any behavior that comes to dominate a person's motivation to an unusual degree, to the partial exclusion of various other normal forms of behavior. The concept of addiction has therefore sometimes been invoked with respect to such varied activities as excessive eating and drinking (including water or other innocuous beverages), excessive reading or working, excessive sexual activity or cigarette smoking, and the excessive use of various drugs including alcohol.

Addiction implies an intense desire or craving, which the individual must gratify regardless of adverse consequences. Psychoanalysts have frequently regarded such morbid craving as *impulsive* and *ego-syntonic* in nature, and assumed that it is irresistible only because the individual in question is intolerant of tensions. Psychiatrists have therefore tended to consider alcoholism and drug addiction as forms of character disorder or impulse neurosis, and in the standard nomenclature they have been classified as forms of socio-pathic personality disturbance. However, many addicted persons have intellectual recognition of the consequences of their behavior, which may be *compulsive* and *ego-alien* in nature. Indeed there are many pathways to the various forms of addiction, and affected individuals may be neurotic or even psychotic rather than socio-pathic.

Man seeks to attain pleasure or relief from pain. Over the course of the centuries, he has discovered various drugs that will temporarily enable him to achieve one of both of these goals. But there are wide differences in what various persons regard as pleasure, in what causes them pain or anguish, and in what they regard as acceptable means of attaining one and avoiding the other. When they take alcohol or other drugs, they may be seeking for frenzy or Nirvana, revelry or solitude, euphoria or apathy, exuberance or escape from misery, ecstasy or oblivion.

Certain drugs are more likely to produce one or another variety of emotional reaction, but there are marked differences in the responses of individuals to the same drug, and a single person may respond differently at one time than at another. For example, when mildly unhappy a person may find that alcohol helps him to drown his sorrows. When somewhat more de-

531

pressed, however, alcohol may only intensify his mood and lead to diminished self-control that may result in an impulsive attempt at suicide.

There are many similarities between certain patients with alcoholism and those addicted to other drugs. However, the use of alcohol is more widely socially acceptable than the use of other drugs. Alcoholism is more frequent and has been studied more intensively than other forms of drug addiction. In the present chapter we shall therefore consider alcoholism separately from other forms of drug addiction, which will be reviewed more briefly in the next chapter.

EFFECTS OF ACUTE AND PROLONGED ALCOHOL INTAKE

The various stages of alcoholic intoxication have been recognized since antiquity, and are aptly summarized in an ancient Hebrew myth. The story relates that Noah was plowing one day, and was approached by the Devil who asked what he was doing. Noah replied, "I'm planting a vineyard. When the fruit is ripe, the grapes are excellent to eat, either moist or dried, and when pressed the juices become wine which warms the body and the spirit." The Devil suggested that they become partners in the vineyard and Noah agreed, following which the Devil killed a sheep, a lion, a monkey, and a pig so that the blood of each animal flowed around the roots of the vines. This was interpreted as indicating that man is ordinarily like a sheep, mild and inoffensive. After he starts to drink, he feels like a lion, proud and confident of his strength. If he drinks deeper, he starts to chatter aimlessly, scamper about, and behave like a foolish monkey. If he drinks still more, he falls to the ground and wallows in food, drink, and filth.

It is widely recognized that alcohol causes (1) progressive dissolution of complex cerebral functions; (2) release of emotions and behavior normally inhibited by the cortex; and (3) relief from anxiety, fear, and sorrow related to maladaptive cortical function. In its direct action on brain cells, alcohol is never a stimulant, but invariably sedative. The stimulation of speech and motor behavior produced by small doses of alcohol result from sedative action on the cortical cells that ordinarily inhibit such behavior. It is this impairment of critical judgment and inhibition that has led to the statement that the superego is the part of the personality that is soluble in alcohol.

The old proverb, *in vino veritas*, is only a half-truth, since an intoxicated person may be more apt to tell lies as well as the truth, and its correct interpretation is that man's true nature is likely to be revealed under the influence of alcohol. He may become aggressive or amorous, and usually he is less considerate of others, but with small amounts of alcohol many persons become more sociable and considerate of others than usual. In the words of one female character in a play (*The Late Christopher Bean*) "A man is the same when he's drunk as when he's sober—only more so."

Scientists have attempted to quantify the behavioral changes following alcohol intake, and to relate these to the concentration of alcohol in the bloodstream, (e.g., see Miles, 1932). The degree of impairment of any given psychological function increases as the level of the blood alcohol concentration rises, but this relationship is logarithmic rather than rectilinear, and a small increase in the blood alcohol may result in a proportionately much larger increase in the degree of impairment. However, the same blood alcohol concentration does not bring about identical degrees of impaired function among all persons.

The alcohol concentration in the blood is determined by (1) the amount swallowed in a given time; (2) the rate of absorption, which is much greater on an empty stomach; (3) the weight of the individual, since alcohol spreads rapidly throughout the entire body; (4) the rate of metabolism by the liver, which is apt to be slower in small persons and those with liver disease, such as a number of chronic alcoholics. Individual tolerance to alcohol is often thought of mistakenly in terms of the effects of a given amount of alcohol consumed, rather than the behavioral effects of a given blood alcohol concentration. However, there is considerable variation in the true tolerance of different individuals to the same concentration of alcohol in the blood, and alcoholics generally acquire increased psychological or physiological tolerance to alcohol, which may disappear only following the onset of liver damage and various nutritional deficiencies.

A great deal of investigation has been undertaken on the relationship between automobile accidents and drinking on the part of their drivers. While recognizing that there are considerable individual differences in tolerance to alcohol, the widespread application of tests of blood alcohol concentration constitutes the most reasonable scientific approach to this problem. It has been found that a high proportion of persons killed in traffic accidents have blood alcohol levels of 0.10 percent and over. The probability of a driver's being involved in a motor vehicle accident increases as his blood alcohol concentration increases. There is evidence that an automobile driven by a person who has blood alcohol level of 0.10 percent or higher is a danger to others using the roads. However, since impairment of driving ability occurs in some drivers at a blood alcohol level of 0.05 percent, many authorities consider that this is the highest level that can be considered as consistent with highway safety.

There are many other forms of dangerous or antisocial behavior in which a person under the influence of alcohol may become involved. If he reaches a sufficient level of intoxication, he may not subsequently remember his behavior during this period, whether or not this included antisocial acts. "Blackouts" of this nature are most frequent among chronic alcoholics, but may occur following a single isolated episode of excessive drinking. Whether or not he subsequently remembers them, the law will still hold the individual responsible for antisocial acts committed while he was under the influence of alcohol, since it is considered that he voluntarily placed himself in this position and should have known the possible consequences.

Alcohol intoxication usually occurs during the evening, is frequently accompanied by an increased utilization of bodily energy, and followed by a deep sleep. The following morning, retribution awaits most persons in the form of a hang-over, with varying degrees of intellectual impairment, anxiety accompanying disturbed bodily physiology, and possible remorse over behavior of the preceding evening. It has been speculated that some persons become alcoholics because they can enjoy intoxication without suffering the usual consequences. Clinical experience, however, suggests that the reverse is more frequently the case, and that the alcoholic may start to drink in the morning to escape the increasingly intolerable burden of his misery, remorse, and deteriorating reality situation.

It has long been recognized that the habitual consumption of large amounts of alcohol may produce severe disturbances of a variety of bodily and mental functions. Among these may be mentioned cardiac decompensation, arterial hypertension, a hemorrhagic tendency, atrophic gastritis, cirrhosis of the liver, endocrine lesions (mainly of the thyroid and ovary), disturbances of the autonomic nervous system, peripheral neuritis, and a group of disorders of the central nervous system which include epileptic seizures, delirium tremens, Korsakow's syndrome, Wernicke's syndrome, and encephalopathy attributed to nicotinic acid deficiency.

There is considerable evidence that

the majority of these disorders may be attributed either to nutritional deficiencies accompanying the chronic alcoholism, or to sudden withdrawal of all alcohol from cells that have adapted to relatively high concentrations over prolonged periods of time. It is known, for example, that, independent of alcohol intake, deficiency of vitamin B-1 (thiamin) will cause cardiac decompensation, peripheral neuritis, and acute or chronic brain syndromes; that deficiency of nicotinic acid (niacin) will cause diarrhea, dermatitis, and acute or chronic brain syndromes; and that deficiencies of vitamins C or K will cause a hemorrhagic tendency. Moreover, the abrupt discontinuation of a variety of sedative drugs which have been administered over a prolonged period of time may provoke an acute brain syndrome resembling delirium tremens, with or without accompanying epileptic seizures (Kalinowsky, 1958). Regardless of their exact origin, however, the main psychiatric complications of chronic alcoholism consist of typical acute or chronic brain syndromes similar to a variety of other such disorders that will be discussed in Chapter 24.

Alcoholism has been variously regarded as moral depravity, antisocial behavior necessitating police action, and medical or psychiatric illness requiring treatment. Of recent years there has been an increasing recognition of its world-wide prevalence and staggering cost both to individuals and society, in terms of personal misery and economic underproductivity. In the United States alone it has been estimated that about five million persons may be classified as alcoholics.

During its first session, the World Health Organization Expert Committee on Mental Health (1949) recommended that a subcommittee be established to consider alcoholism separately from other mental health problems. This subcommittee helped considerably to clarify prevailing concepts of excessive drinking and alcoholism, and eventually agreed on the following definitions.

Excessive drinking consists of ". . . any form of drinking which in its extent goes beyond the conditional and customary 'dietary' use or the ordinary compliance with the social drinking customs of the whole community concerned irrespective of the etiological factors leading to such behavior and irrespective also of the extent to which such etiological factors are dependent upon hereditary, constitutional or required physio-pathological and metabolic influences."

Alcoholics are ". . . those excessive drinkers whose dependence upon alcohol has attained such a degree that it shows a noticeable mental disturbance or an interference with their bodily and mental health, their interpersonal relations, and their smooth social and economic functioning; or who show the predromal signs of such developments. They therefore require treatment."

The subcommittee concluded that all forms of excessive drinking begin with a symptomatic stage (symptomatic of psychological or physical pathology or of social conditions) and that sometimes this stage may be prolonged and not develop further. This initial phase of *irregular symptomatic excessive drinking* is apt, however, to proceed to such a dependence on alcohol as to satisfy the preceding definition of alcoholism. The early stages of alcoholism may be described as *habitual symptomatic excessive drinking*, which may consist of either daily drinking (particularly in wine-drinking and beer-drinking countries) or intermittent bouts of excessive drinking (particularly in countries or social groups where the pattern of drinking involves predominantly the use of distilled spirits). More advanced alcoholism is characterized by "inability to stop" drinking (wine or beer) or "loss of control" over alcohol intake (during bouts of drinking distilled spirits) in which case the alcoholic may be described as an *addictive drinker (alcoholic addict)*.

As a result of an analysis of more than 2000 drinking histories of male alcoholics, Jellinek (1951) described a number of symptoms commonly found in various phases of alcohol addiction. The *prealcoholic symptomatic phase* is said to last from several months to two years, and is characterized by occasional or constant drinking for the purpose of producing relief from excessive tension, and latterly by an increase in alcohol tolerance so that the drinker requires a larger amount of alcohol than formerly to reach the same stage of sedation. The beginning of the *prodromal phase* is characterized by the sudden onset of "blackouts" or amnesia for a recent period of drinking (also called alcoholic palimpsests). During this phase there is evidence of increasing dependency upon alcohol as a drug, some of the manifestations of this being surreptitious drinking, preoccupation with alcohol, gulping the first drink or two, guilt feelings about drinking, avoiding reference to alcohol in conversation, and an increasing frequency of alcoholic blackouts.

The crucial phase of addiction is initiated by loss of control over drinking behavior (or inability to stop), and at the same time the alcoholic begins to rationalize his drinking behavior by means of various "alibis." At about this time his drinking behavior becomes conspicuous and parents, wife, friends, and employer may begin to reprove and warn him. The alcoholic may respond with grandiosity, aggression, or persistent remorse and periods of total abstinence. He may change the pattern of his drinking, may begin to drop friends and lose jobs. There is a tendency toward increasing social isolation as his behavior becomes alcohol-centered. There may be a loss of outside interests, a reinterpretation of interpersonal relations, marked self-pity, and contemplated or actual geographic escape. At about this time there tends to be a change in family habits involving withdrawal from or increase in social activities on the part of wife and children. The alcoholic meanwhile develops unreasonable resentments toward them and others, be-

comes concerned with protecting his supply of alcohol, neglects a proper nutritional intake, and is frequently hospitalized for the first time. Metabolic changes often include a decrease of the sexual drive, and this may be associated with alcoholic jealousy concerning the wife, or even frankly paranoid delusions of infidelity. At about this time there is a beginning of regular morning drinking.

The *chronic phase of alcohol addiction* is initiated by prolonged intoxications or "benders" which often lead to marked ethical deterioration, impairment of thinking, and alcoholic psychoses (the latter in about ten percent of all alcoholics). The alcoholic now tends to drink with persons far below his social level, and may take recourse to "technical products" such as rubbing alcohol. A loss of alcohol tolerance is often noted at about this time, and may be related to decreased ability of the liver to accomplish oxidation. Other terminal symptoms described by Jellinek include indefinable fears, tremors, psychomotor inhibitions, obsessive drinking, the development of vague religious desires, and failure of the entire rationalization system. At this point the addict may admit defeat and become spontaneously accessible to treatment, although obsessive drinking continues as he does not see a way out.

Bacon (1958) described a similar sequence of increasingly deviant drinking behaviors in the American alcoholic, and concluded that somewhere in this progression the word drinking no longer applies to the man's use of alcohol. "He is no more a drinker than a kleptomaniac is a customer, or a pyromaniac is a camp fire girl. Alcoholics may consume alcohol. They do not drink."

Some years ago G. K. Chesterton remarked that the dipsomaniac and the abstainer both make the same mistake: they both regard wine as a drug and not as a drink. Alcohol is indeed a powerful drug that is readily available in a variety of palatable forms, and on which an individual may become both physiologically and psychologically dependent. Apparently, however, not all members of the population are equally vulnerable to alcoholism, and a number of workers have studied the personality characteristics of those persons who do become addicted. Most psychiatrists would agree with Armstrong (1958) that there is no such thing as one typical alcoholic personality, but that the histories of alcoholics show a wide variety of psychopathology. It is generally accepted that the most frequent forms of preexisting or associated psychopathology consist of sociopathic personality, neurosis, and depression. Among those male alcoholics referred for psychiatric evaluation and treatment, the proportion showing neurotic personality characteristics is probably much higher than among male alcoholics in general. The same may also be true of those female alcoholics who are referred for psychiatric evaluation and treatment, but it is widely believed that a higher proportion of the latter are basically sociopathic and poorer candidates for treatment than in the case of male alcoholics who have been referred. Two illustrative case histories follow.

At the time of his first admission to state hospital at the age of 24, this man was unemployed and unmarried, and had a long standing history of antisocial behavior, promiscuity, and addiction to alcohol and other drugs. From the age of 14 he had had numerous admissions to general hospitals and at least eight brief admissions to a private psychiatric hospital, on account of intoxication. He had also served at least eight jail sentences, six of them for intoxication and two longer terms for assault. On the first of these occasions he had assaulted his mother and was sentenced to a minimum of six months. On the second occasion he and another prisoner assaulted a guard, beat him up badly, and attempted to escape. On this occasion he was sentenced to a further two years in jail.

The patient was the elder of two children, having one sister six years younger than himself. They were born into a wealthy family in a small town who enjoyed a good deal of social prestige. The patient's father worked regularly in the family business as an insurance agent, had many friends, and was considered successful. However, he had used alcohol excessively from the time he was about 21, and alcoholism was one of the causes of his death at the age of 57. The patient's mother was 12 years younger than her husband, and also used alcohol excessively during her married life, particularly during the two years preceding her husband's death. Following this, however, she managed to abandon her dependency on alcohol and lived quietly with her adolescent daughter.

The patient and his sister was cared for by nursemaids during their early childhood and received minimal attention or discipline from their parents, and the parents exercised little control over the patient's behavior. From a very early age the patient's father would have him pour drinks for the guests and be present at the numerous alcoholic parties he held in the home. The patient stated that he used to drain the glasses at the age of five or six, and by the age of 12 he was drinking a 12-ounce bottle himself on weekends. By the age of 17 he was drinking from one to three fifths of liquor a day. His father provided him with plenty of money and rescued him from the consequences of any delinquent behavior.

The patient completed public elementary school and spent three months in the public high school but was expelled for striking a teacher. He was then sent to a private school until he reached grade 11 at which time he changed the date of his birth certificate and joined the army and became a paratrooper. The war ended soon afterwards and the following year he was discharged from military service, following which he remained at home unemployed for six months drinking heavily and having several brief admissions to a private sanitarium. A job was obtained for him but he quit it after a month. He returned home and soon afterwards was arrested for the third time for drunken driving and was placed in jail. Bail was set and paid by his father who then sent the patient out of town and told him that no more money would be forthcoming. When the patient ran out of money, he worked for six months in a gold mine. On hearing that his father had died, he returned home and soon afterward received a 14-day jail sentence for intoxication. After leaving the jail he had a few drinks and went home where he found his mother entertaining a male friend, and he gave her two black eyes. He was charged with assault and sentenced to jail, but was placed on probation after six months. He soon got drunk again and was returned to jail, and it was on this occasion that he seriously assaulted one of the guards in an attempt to escape. After his return home two years later, he soon began drinking again and began using a variety of stimulant, sedative, and narcotic drugs including amphetamines, barbiturates, and Demerol.

From an early age he was pleasant and plausible with his acquaintances until they frustrated or crossed him in any way, when he would become extremely angry and sometimes violent. In keeping with his general pattern of impulse-gratification, he had had a long series of heterosexual relationships, beginning at the age of 12 with older girls. At the age of 13 he established a regular sexual relationship with a girl twice his age, and during the next ten years he led a life of almost unbelievable promiscuity, never taking a girl out without having sexual relations with her and usually dropping her after one or two experiences in favor of some other girl of his acquaintance.

He was of muscular physique and bright normal intelligence (IQ about 115). On his first admission to the hospital, the female psychologist assigned to test him gave him a battery of psychological tests including the MMPI, in connection with which she reported "Only the psychopathic deviate scale is outside normal limits, indicating antisocial tendencies, inability to profit by experience, impulsive decisions and a lack of deep emotional responsiveness, and a rather shallow concern for other people and low frustration tolerance." At the end of a lengthy report she pointed out that his alcoholism was only one expression of his general psychopathic tendencies, but felt that treatment could be confined to a symptomatic attack on the drinking behavior itself. She undertook this treatment herself. The patient was discharged from hospital ten months after his admission and two weeks later the psychologist married him. During the next ten years the patient had seven further admissions to the same state hospital, and a number of other admissions to a nearby general hospital. However, he continued to live with his wife in the same locality, changing residence only three times during the ten years. Although he changed jobs on numerous occasions, he provided adequately for his family. His drinking became more episodic than constant, and he continued to supplement alcohol with stimulant drugs at times. On one of these occasions he became involved in a serious automobile accident and on another occasion he made a serious suicidal attempt by cutting his throat with a razor blade for which he required 42 sutures. On the last recorded admission to state hospital immediately following the suicidal attempt, he was quite amiable, pleasant and repentent, unlike his hostile manner on previous admissions.

The following is an example of alcoholism in a sociopathic female.

A married woman was first admitted to a state hospital at the age of 28, with a history of life long egocentric and impulsive behavior, with frequent temper tantrums, and manipulative behavior for the purpose of getting her own way. For several years she had become increasingly dependent on alcohol and excessive amounts of sedative drugs (barbiturates). Recently her behavior had become overactive and uncontrollable, and she had threatened suicide by throwing herself out of a moving car and then by cutting her wrists superficially.

She was the only child of parents who were both in their 40s at the time she was born. Her father was a professor who was preoccupied with research and other intellectual pursuits. Much of the time he was cold and distant, but when the patient started school he became critical of her academic performance, calling her "beautiful but dumb." He was disturbed by her temper tantrums and was unable to set consistent firm limits to her behavior. Behavior of which he didn't approve would sometimes bring stern lectures, but on subsequent occasions the same behavior would pass unnoticed. Little information was available regarding the patient's relationship with her mother, as she died of pneumonia when the patient was only eight years old. A couple of years later her father remarried, but the stepmother never established a satisfactory relationship with the patient and frequently left the home on account of dissention with the patient's father. The patient lived at home and attended public school until the age of ten, but was then placed in a series of private schools which she left either because she didn't like them or because her behavior was intolerable to the school authorities. She finally graduated from a technical high school in which she had been studying mainly art and a commercial course. She was a beautiful girl with considerable superficial charm and subsequently held a variety of positions as a model. She led a very active social life, although her father objected to the late hours she kept with some of her boy friends. Apparently, however, she had no premarital sexual relations except with her husband, whom she married at the age of 21. During the two years preceding her first admission to the hospital, she had been dissatisfied with her husband sexually, and also because she felt he hadn't advanced sufficiently rapidly in his career. For a year prior to her admission she had been considering divorce, and had started to have a number of extramarital sexual relations. At the patient's insistence she and her husband had lived in several major cities where she could get jobs modeling and have the kind of social life she felt she wanted. However, she had found no lasting satisfaction in this and for several years she had been drinking by herself to excess and had become dependent on large amounts of barbiturate sedatives which she took during the daytime as well as at night. She stated her reason for drinking and taking medication was boredom and an effort to forget her domestic and financial troubles. Anger with her husband led her to threaten suicide and make a superficial attempt by scratching her wrists which precipitated her admission to hospital. When asked about her temper tantrums and manipulative behavior, she replied, "I always do that. If they do me some good, I have them." She was incapable of genuine affection toward anyone else, and freely admitted that she used others only to gratify her immediate whims. On admission to hospital she obtained a full scale IQ of 107. Her MMPI showed abnormal elevations on scales 4 and 9 (psychopathic deviate and hypomanic).

On arrival in the hospital she threatened litigation for illegal detention, but her disturbed behavior was under conscious voluntary control and she became composed and cooperative as soon as she found that threats were not going to help her situation. She also entered psychotherapy when she found that this was expected of her, but interviews accomplished little beyond providing her with narcissistic gratification.

Her first admission to hospital lasted only three weeks, but during the following year there were several further brief hospitalizations, each precipitated by impulsive and manipulative behavior associated with continued addiction to alcohol and sedatives. One year after her first admission to hospital

she was out with another man and was involved in an automobile accident which resulted in a severe facial injury, thus destroying one of her most prized possessions. Plastic surgery was carried out and there was every reason to believe that there would be little or no facial disfigurement. However, she became quite depressed over the loss of her beauty and indulged in an orgy of self-pity and alcohol. She was readmitted to hospital, and shortly after this she received a letter from her husband stating that he intended to obtain a legal separation and that he might ultimately want a divorce (depending on her ability to control her behavior). A week after receiving this letter, she managed to obtain a large quantity of sedatives and swallowed them all immediately in what proved to be a successful attempt at suicide.

DYNAMICS, DEVELOPMENT, AND CAUSATION

In his earlier formulations on alcoholism, Freud (1912, 1917) emphasized the alteration of mood by alcohol as a form of defense, by means of which the individual is enabled to escape from reality and regress to the dependency and freedom from responsibility characteristic of early childhood, corresponding with the oral stage of psychosexual development. In later years, Freud (1930) revised his thinking, and equated alcoholism with the model of repressed homosexual traits he had used to describe the development of paranoid symptoms. He now maintained that disappointment in women (mothers, wives, and lovers) drove men to drink, and unconscious homosexual wishes led them to seek emotional satisfaction from the company of men which they could not obtain from their wives. When these latent homosexual feelings approached consciousness, they repressed them and returned to their wives. However, they also tended to project onto their wives their unacceptable feelings for the men they loved, and hence to develop paranoid delusions of infidelity by their wives. Other analysts have focused on various aspects of both earlier and later Freudian formulations.

The removal of cortical inhibition by small amounts of alcohol leads to increased sexual interest and stimulation. Abraham (1926) identified alcoholic intoxication with sexual gratification, and considered that drinking prowess was widely regarded as the equivalent of sexual prowess. A man who doesn't drink may be viewed by many with suspicion and distrust. An older man whose sexual potency is declining may grasp at alcohol as a substitute for sex, and Abraham likened this substitution to certain sexual perversions such as voyeurism and fetishism. The sexual development of the alcoholic was fixated at the oral level of development, and alcohol became the means of effortless gratification whereby the individual exchanged women for wine.

Abraham believed that the alcoholic was severely frustrated by his mother early in life, and hence forced to turn to his father, which resulted in over-identification with the father and development of homosexual tendencies. However, Chafetz and Demone remarked that latent homosexuality and confusion in sexual identity may play a significant role in the evolution of problems associated with alcoholism, but do *not* offer sufficient impetus for the development of so devastating a condition. "Much of the psychopathology of alcoholism may be tied to factors commonly seen in the patient with homosexual problems but these are not only insufficient to be the sole etiological agent for alcoholism; they are often misinterpreted. Since the fixation at the oral stage is so early in psychosexual development, the alcoholic has never achieved a genital level of differentiation and is so desirous of receiving love, he does not differentiate the sex of the provider."

Rado emphasized the euphoriant effect of alcohol which provided a unique source of satisfaction, elation, and achievement for many whose lives were otherwise ridden with boredom, frustration, and disappointment. In this manner, alcohol may permit fulfillment of the omnipotent and megalomaniac fantasies of the infant, uncurbed and undifferentiated, in which he perceives himself as the master of a disorganized world. According to Rado, a crisis arises when the pharmacothymic regime fails to provide elation, and this crisis may be resolved in one of three ways: (1) a free interval to rehabilitate the depreciated value of the drug, (2) suicide, and (3) psychosis.

Menninger emphasized the self-destructive drive of alcoholics and referred to alcoholism as a form of chronic suicide. He remarked that

Alcohol addiction . . . can be considered a form of self-destruction used to avert a greater self-destruction deriving from elements of aggressiveness excited by thwarting ungratified eroticism, and the feeling of a need for punishment from a sense of guilt related to aggressiveness. Its further quality is that in a practical sense self-destruction is accomplished in spite of, and at the same time by means of, the very device used by the sufferer to relieve his pain and avert his fear of destruction.

The significance of self-destructive urges in alcoholism was challenged by McCord et al. who undertook longitudinal studies of prealcoholics and did not find a higher frequency of suicidal trends among prealcoholics than nonalcoholics. On the other hand Robins et al. undertook a retrospective analysis of 134 successful suicides, and considered that 21 had been suffering from chronic alcoholism — the second most frequent psychiatric diagnosis in this series (after manic-depressive psychosis).

Fenichel stated that the identity of the decisive conflict explains the relation between drug addiction and the manic-depressive states, and remarked that in the final stages of their illness, addicts live in objectless alternating states of elation and "morning after" depression, which in the last analysis, correspond to the alternation of hunger and satiation in the mentally still undifferentiated infant. He also wrote as follows:

Patients who are ready to give up all object libido necessarily are persons who never estimated object relationships very highly. They are fixated to a passive-narcissistic aim and are interested solely in getting their gratification, never in satisfying their partners nor, for that matter, in the specific personalities of their partners. Objects are nothing else for them but deliverers of supplies. Erogenously, the leading zones are the oral zone and the skin; self-esteem, even existence, are dependent upon getting food and warmth.

Levy summarized a number of dynamic functions served through the use of alcohol as follows: (1) discharge function, permitting expression of otherwise unacceptable impulses; (2) narcotization, to exclude the world of reality; (3) symbolism, through which one achieves status; (4) infantomimetic functions involving oral gratification and the satisfaction of needs for love and dependency; (5) masochistic functions; (6) hostility; (7) homosexuality, latent or overt; (8) identification with a parental model. Armstrong commented that all of these patterns could be recognized in alcoholic patients, but that in each individual, alcohol may serve several purposes at the same time.

In an excellent review, Gibbins concluded that none of the psychoanalytic theories reveal any of the sufficient conditions for the genesis of alcohol addiction. "All the developmental elements which have been invoked as etiological may be found in behavior disorders of quite a different nature. Generally speaking, the analysts have only touched upon the necessary conditions of abnormal behavior." We shall now consider some of the further studies of etiology.

HEREDITARY FACTORS

There is evidence of unduly high frequencies of alcoholism, sociopathy, and criminality among the close relatives of alcoholics. In a study of 645 Swedish alcoholics, Amark found the frequency of alcoholism among their brothers and fathers to be about 25 percent. In an intensive study of 50 chronic alcoholics in New York City and 50 chronic alcoholics in Zurich, Switzerland, Bleuler found that for both groups schizophrenia, manic-depressive psychoses, epilepsy, and feeble-mindedness occurred with the same frequency among their relatives as among groups of the average population of the same social level. By contrast, alcoholism, neurotic, and psychopathic personality characteristics were found much more frequently among the relatives of alcoholics than in the general population. If his figures for the two groups of alcoholics are combined, we find that more than 28 percent of their fathers, five percent of their mothers, 15 percent of their brothers over the age of 40, and five percent of their sisters over the age of 40 were also alcoholic. Another 15 percent of their parents and nearly nine percent of all siblings were recorded as having neurotic or psychopathic personality disorders.

"Like father, like son" is an observation that does not imply any single reason for the resemblance. We have already emphasized that concentrations of general or specific forms of psychopathology within families may be related to heredity, imitative learning, or the sharing of similar adverse experiences. Even if the family concentration of alcoholism were attributed largely to heredity, there is still no simple genetic mechanism that would explain the observed differences in frequency between fathers, mothers, brothers, and sisters.

Kaij studied the drinking habits of 201 pairs of twins, which included 26 monozygotic pairs and 56 dizygotic pairs of the same sex. The concordance rates for drinking were 65 percent among MZ twins and 30 percent among same-sexed DZ twins, so that the Holzinger index of heritability for drinking behavior would be approximately 50 percent. Even if these findings were valid, and could be assumed relevant to alcoholism, the limitations of twin studies would prevent any inferences concerning possible mechanisms of genetic transmission.

SOMATIC FACTORS

Williams formulated a genetotrophic theory of alcoholism which constituted the basis for subsequent biochemical studies in postalcoholic and nonalcoholic humans, and experiments on alcohol consumption in animals. Now, it is generally accepted that individuals differ greatly in bodily structure, a variety of metabolic functions, and their needs for specific quantities of specific nutrients in their diet. It is also generally agreed that individual differences in structure, function, and dietary requirements result from the complex interaction of hereditary predisposition and lifelong environmental experience. According to Williams's theory, individuals develop alcoholism because of peculiarities in their nutritional requirements caused by inherited anomalies in their metabolism.

Williams and his associates subsequently reported differences in the alcohol consumption of genetically different strains of rats fed with identical vitamin-deficient diets. Mardones et al. also succeeded in demonstrating some degree of correlation (for a standardized body weight) between parent rats (bred selectively) and their offspring. Their combined results for generations three through seven are shown in Table 22-1.

These results strongly suggest that alcohol consumption *may* be determined partly by genetic factors in experimental animals, but give no indication of how important such factors *are* in predisposing to alcoholism in humans. Williams and his associates reported significant differences in biochemical determinations made on postalcoholic and nonalcoholic persons. Their findings were rightly criticized by Popham, both on statistical grounds and on the basis that biochemical anomalies in postalcoholics may well be the result of their drinking rather than the cause. Even if such biochemical anomalies were found consistently among prealcoholic individuals, they might still be the result of earlier experience rather than inherited defects. These same considerations apply equally to biochemical findings and to findings concerning hormonal or other somatic functions in alcoholics.

Some years ago it was postulated that established chronic alcoholics showed consistently diminished function of the adrenal cortex, which might be either primary (idiopathic or "constitutional"), or secondary to prolonged alcohol intake and inadequate nutrition. This

TABLE 22-1. Alcohol Intake of Offspring of Rats Selected with Respect to Alcohol Consumption*

PARENTS' CONSUMPTION†	PERCENTAGE OF OFFSPRING WHOSE ALCOHOL CONSUMPTION FALLS WITHIN INDICATED RANGE			
	.00-.19	.20-.39	.40-.59	.60+
.00-.19	61.4	29.6	5.8	3.2
.20-.39	29.6	42.4	22.5	5.6
.40-.59	27.6	31.9	26.1	14.5
.60+	25.0	19.5	22.3	33.3

*Data from Mardones, R. J., Segovia, N. M., and Hederra, A. D. 1953. Heredity of experimental alcohol preference in rats. II. Coefficient of heredity. Quarterly Journal of Studies on Alcohol *14*, 1–2.
†Consumption measured in cubic centimeters per day, per 100 grams of body weight.

finding was not established by subsequent research. However, Bleuler's intensive study of 50 American and 50 Swiss alcoholics revealed a wide variety of associated endocrine dysfunctions occurring in 28 percent of each of the samples. In some instances there appeared to be no causal relationship between the endocrine dysfunction and the alcoholism; in other instances the endocrine dysfunction was regarded as secondary to the alcoholism; but in a considerable proportion of this minority group, the endocrine dysfunction was thought to be causative of the personality disorder that preceded the onset of alcoholism.

In conclusion it should be emphasized that the establishment of a genetic basis for any bodily characteristic predisposing to alcoholism would require statistical comparisons of the frequency of this bodily characteristic among nonalcoholics, prealcoholics, and various classes of relatives of these prealcoholics.

PSYCHOLOGICAL FACTORS

In Bleuler's study, 22 percent of his American alcoholics and 28 percent of his Swiss alcoholics came from homes that were broken by death or separation of the parents before the patient reached the age of ten years. In a sample of Canadian alcoholics, the present author found that 23 percent had permanently lost one or both parents by ten years of age, and that 7.1 percent had in fact lost both parents by this age, the latter figure being more than five times as high as expected on the basis of the frequencies with which they lost a single parent. Both of these figures for permanent loss of one or both parents during early childhood were higher than the comparable figures for any other major diagnostic category with the exception of sociopathic personality. As for this category, they were also more frequently related to permanent parental separation, particularly desertion by father, than to the death of either parent.

More recently, Dennehy undertook a controlled study of childhood bereavement and adult psychiatric disorder. Both male and female alcoholics showed an excess of loss of mother when the total loss under 15 years of age was considered. Male alcoholics also showed an excess of loss of father between the ages of ten and 15 years. This pattern of parental death during childhood was somewhat similar to the pattern that she found for adult patients with depression.

Knight attributed the oral fixation of alcoholics to specific early family experiences, most frequently involving an indulgent mother and inconsistent father. According to this view, the child is overindulged by a permissive mother, fails to learn self-control, and reacts with intense rage to every frustration. This capacity for rage is fed by an inconsistent father who unpredictably gratifies at one time and denies at another. A pattern of dependence, rejection, and intense desire for indulgence is built into the personality, together with deep feelings of inferiority and guilt. During adolescence, drinking commences as a form of "manly" behavior, frequently in defiance of expressed parental wishes. This revolt would appear to be mainly against the prohibitions of the mother, since the father frequently presents a model of alcoholism and irresponsibility for the child to emulate.

Adler attributed addiction to a desire of the individual to remove powerful feelings of inferiority while escaping responsibilities. Schilder attributed alcoholism to a perpetual state of insecurity fostered by the parents in earliest childhood. According to this view, the child has been pushed deeper and deeper into an insecure abyss by ridicule, passivity, threat, corporal punishment, and degradation. Although the threats originally came from one or both parents, the child learns to expect them from all other human beings, so that all interpersonal relationships are viewed as dangerous. Strecker also regarded alcoholism as an escape from feelings of inadequacy related to excessive social introversion, but many alcoholics are predominantly extroverted before they commence drinking excessively, and the varied personality characteristics of alcoholics may be related to the diversity of their previous experiences.

In Bleuler's study, only 20 percent of the alcoholics in either the American or Swiss sample were recorded as spending their childhood with both parents in a favorable home environment, and only about 30 percent of each sample were recorded as spending their childhood in a favorable home environment regardless of whether they were living with their own parents or not. In view of the diverse pathways to alcoholism and drug addiction, however, it is not surprising that the adverse early relationships and experiences should be correspondingly diverse. It would therefore be expected that those alcoholics and addicts having neurotic personality characteristics and adjustment would also give a history of an overcontrolling, demanding, anxiety-provoking early environment; whereas those with lifelong antisocial personality characteristics would be more likely to give a history of deprived, rejecting, and indifferent early relationships. Among those alcoholics seeking psychiatric attention, and particularly among those persisting with long-term psychotherapy, neurotic characteristics and personality development are much more frequent than among the general population of alcoholics.

In an interesting series of experiments with cats, Masserman and Yum examined the influence of alcohol on "neurotic" behavior resulting from *motivational conflict.* They first trained cats to operate a switch that opened a box in order to obtain food, and then made the animals "neurotic" by subjecting them to air blasts or shocks whenever they opened the box. Under the latter regime, the cats became frightened, apprehensive, inhibited, indecisive, and immobile. When these animals which had learned to avoid the switch were given alcohol, they once more spontaneously operated the switch for the food reward in spite of continued air blasts or shocks. About half of these animals learned to take milk containing alcohol in preference to plain milk, and this preference persisted as long as their experimentally induced "neurotic" behavior.

Conger regarded the essence of the preceding experimental situation as a fairly simple *approach-avoidance conflict* in which the effect of alcohol was to reduce the drive of fear that kept the animals from the switch. Having determined that alcohol reduced a similar approach-avoidance conflict in albino rats, he created an approach tendency in one group of rats and an avoidance tendency in a second group. The strength of the tendencies to approach or avoid was measured by the animal's pull against a calibrated spring when it was temporarily restrained. Alcohol produced very little decrease in the pull of hungry animals toward food, but a marked decrease in the pull of frightened animals away from the place where they had been shocked in previous trials. Before alcohol, the avoidance was stronger than approach; after alcohol, the avoidance was weaker than approach.

These experiments demonstrate that alcohol may reduce fear and avoidance behavior in a conflict situation. They do not, however, provide evidence concerning the influence of alcohol on (1) anger and extrapunitive behavior, or (2) sorrow and intrapunitive behavior, in situations of frustration or loss, for example. Moreover, in the human animal, much learned behavior is related to superego development, and it is not clear why only some individuals with a generally strong superego should seek relief in alcoholism, or why only a proportion of persons with a generally weak superego should become addicted to the same drug. However, some important differences in alcohol usage appear to be related to the role-expectations and drinking customs of the culture, social groups, and individual families of which the individual is a member.

SOCIOCULTURAL FACTORS

Bacon remarked that what is unique about "drinking" is that it is of the order of phenomena called "a custom." It is a "way" that is characteristic of a given group of people, and that is learned by members of the group.

Different groups have different ways. One group ferments milk from horses, consumes it on certain days with particularly appropriate words, clothes, accompanying foods and so on; perhaps only males of a certain status activate this way. Another group utilizes fermented grapes, the resulting wine is mixed with three to five times the same amount of water and everybody uses the beverage three or four times a day, always with meals. A third group uses a millet beer; a fourth group a distilation from cereal or potatoes. Perhaps in one group the act is primarily a ritual of deep religious significance, in another the usage is always one whose purpose is that of getting everyone intoxicated.

In a cross-cultural study of drinking behavior in nonliterate societies, Horton concluded that the strength of the drinking response in a given society tends to vary directly with the level of anxiety in the society. "Anxiety is so universal and constant an experience of mankind that any means of alleviating this burden of pain must be valued." However, the estimation of overall anxiety levels among the different societies was largely speculative, and his views still lack objective validation.

Several studies have documented an unusually high frequency of alcoholism among Irish Americans, and an unusually low frequency of alcoholism among Jewish Americans—in spite of quite high frequencies of neurosis and other forms of drug addiction among the Jewish group. Bales postulated three general ways in which culture and social organization may influence such rates of alcohol addiction. The first is the degree to which the culture operates to bring about acute needs for adjustment or inner tensions in its members. The second is whether the attitude toward drinking positively suggests drinking to the individual as a means of relieving his inner tensions, or whether such a thought arouses a strong counteranxiety. The third is the degree to which the culture provides suitable substitute means of satisfaction.

He also distinguished four different attitudes toward drinking characteristics of various cultural groups, which appear to be related to the frequency of alcoholism among their members. The first is an attitude that calls for complete abstinence, as of the Moslems or the Mormons. The second is a ritual attitude toward drinking, generally associated with religious observances, as among orthodox Jews. The third is a convivial attitude in which drinking is regarded as a social rather than a religious ritual. The fourth attitude is termed utilitarian, since the effects of alcohol are intended to promote self-interest and personal satisfaction, as is typical among alcoholics.

The most reliable estimates of the frequency of alcoholism in a population are based on the application of Jellinek's formula to reported deaths from cirrhosis of the liver, a fairly constant proportion of which are attributable to alcoholism (51.5 percent for males, and 17.7 percent for females in the United States). Estimates of the prevalence of alcoholism in various countries have been obtained by this method, and are shown in Table 22-2. It may be seen at a glance that the highest and lowest frequencies recorded in this table refer to two wine-producing and wine-drinking

TABLE 22-2. Estimated Prevalence of Alcoholism in Various Countries*

	ALCOHOLICS PER 100,000 POPULATION (20 YEARS AND OLDER)	YEAR	SOURCE
France	5200	1954	Jellinek (1954)
United States	4360	1955	Keller & Efron (1957)
Chile	2960	1950	Popham (1956)
Sweden	2580	1946	WHO (1951)
Switzerland	2100	1953	Popham (1956)
Denmark	1950	1948	WHO (1951)
Canada	1890	1956	—
Norway	1560	1947	WHO (1951)
Finland	1430	1947	WHO (1951)
Australia	1340	1947	WHO (1951)
England and Wales	1100	1948	WHO (1951)
Italy	700	1954	Jellinek (1954)

*From Popham, R. E., and Schmidt, W. 1958. *Statistics of Alcohol Use and Alcoholism in Canada, 1871–1956.* University of Toronto Press, p. 120.

countries in close geographic proximity to each other. France is at the top of the list, with an estimated prevalence of alcoholism amounting to more than five percent of the adult population, while Italy is at the bottom of the list with a frequency of less than one percent of the population. The latter figure is particularly interesting in the light of a 1952 survey of drinking habits in Italy, according to which only one percent of the population consumed alcoholic beverages apart from meals. In France, by contrast, the dominant pattern of excessive drinking appears to consist of continual drinking throughout the day, without obvious signs of intoxication. Consequently, the diagnosis of alcoholism in France has tended to be reserved for those heavy drinkers who have developed an organic complication such as cirrhosis of the liver or one of the alcoholic psychoses. Alcoholism has therefore been regarded traditionally as a medical rather than a psychiatric problem, and the French literature even includes a treatment for alcoholism designed to permit the patient to continue daily drinking.

Clear-cut differences have been found in the frequency of alcoholism among males and females, and in the United States there are between five and six times as many male alcoholics as female. However, the sex ratio for alcoholism has also been found to vary considerably in different countries, from as low as two males to one female in England, to more than 20 males to one female in some Scandinavian countries. The most reasonable explanation of the latter differences is in terms of cultural approval of different drinking behaviors rather than inherent biological differences. Just as there is a double standard of sexual behavior for males and females, there is also a double standard of drinking behavior that varies from one cultural group to another, but consistently fosters more alcoholism among males than females.

In reviewing the various sociocultural backgrounds of alcoholism, Ullman concluded that in any group or society in which the drinking customs, values, and sanctions—together with the attitudes of all segments of the group or society—are well established, are known to and agreed upon by all, and are consistent with the rest of the culture, the rate of alcoholism will be low. Under conditions in which the individual drinker doesn't know what is expected, or when the expectation in one situation differs from that in another, it can be assumed that he will have ambivalent feelings about drinking. Ullman therefore regarded ambivalence as the psychological product of unintegrated drinking customs. To psychologists and psychiatrists, however, ambivalence is a highly individual phenomenon, having its roots in the intrafamilial relationships of early childhood, and involving drinking behavior only through displacement or generalization.

A theory which brings together the individual psychological approach and the group sociocultural approach to alcoholism is the *vulnerability-acceptance hypothesis* put forward by Jellinek and elaborated by Popham. According to this theory, various different populations contain individuals with similar degrees of vulnerability to psychopathology, but the populations differ in their overall acceptance of drinking. In countries or social groups with a low acceptance of drinking, one would expect to find a low frequency of alcoholism, and a high frequency of severe psychopathology among alcoholics. In those countries or social groups with a high acceptance of drinking, one would expect to find a higher frequency of alcoholism with severe medical complications, but a relatively low frequency of severe psychopathology among alcoholics. Unfortunately, the assumption that all countries and social groups contain a similar proportion of individuals with comparable psychopathology is unjustified. While *group* differences in vulnerability may be partly explained by sociocultural factors, the marked differences in *individual* vulnerability within such groups must be related to biological or psychological factors involved in personality development of the individual.

TREATMENT

Measures adopted in the treatment of established alcoholism or drug addiction may be separated into three main types: (1) disintoxication, (2) deterrents to continued use of the drug, (3) curative measures directed toward the removal of the causes of addiction.

A wide variety of drugs has been recommended in the process of *disintoxication*, which usually involves some combination of the following: (a) withdrawal or replacement of the drug concerned. Alcohol may be withdrawn abruptly with temporary substitution of tranquilizing drugs; (b) replacement of fluids (glucose in water or saline), and also Vitamin B complex and other nutrient substances; (c) a variety of supportive measures that may include insulin, ACTH, cortisone, and various stimulants.

Deterrent or suppressive measures are not in themselves likely to be curative. Their value is for insuring a period of freedom from the drug, during which it is hoped to apply other measures leading to more lasting remission. Such deterrents may be applied at the individual or at the social level of action and include punitive legislation (heavy fines or compulsory institutionalization); conditioned reflex treatment of alcoholism (to bring about nausea or vomiting on drinking alcohol); and the use of disulfiram (Antabuse) or citrated calcium carbamide (Temposil), both of which will react with alcohol to produce acetaldehyde, with resulting unpleasant toxic manifestations.

Administration of tranquilizing or antidepressive drugs or even electroshock treatment may be indicated in those cases where symptomatic alcoholism is associated with severe functional psychopathology (e.g., psychotic depressive or schizophrenic disorders). However, those responsible for the management of alcoholic patients usually stress that it is unsafe to rely on any medication to relieve tension, apart from small doses of sedatives or tranquilizers during the withdrawal period.

A certain proportion of alcoholics with a history of neurotic characteristics, considerable social conformity, and an interested family may be candidates for psychoanalysis or other intensive individual psychotherapy. Those alcoholics with strong antisocial personality characteristics, however, offer no better prospects of response to individual psychotherapy than other persons with sociopathic personalities (or "impulse neuroses"). However, a considerable measure of success has been reported by a number of workers using directive techniques of education as well as some attempts at insight therapy with *groups* of alcoholics and their relatives (particularly wives).

It is considered important at the outset that the alcoholic should recognize (1) that he can never revert to social drinking, (2) that it is unsafe to rely on any other medication to relieve tension, and (3) the nature of various compulsive and addictive phenomena.

The lay organization known as *Alcoholics Anonymous* has a group method of approach to the problems of alcoholism that may be described as both inspirational and spiritual, in addition to which they function as a social agency in bringing new members (and members who have relapsed) to treatment. They may also be able to help considerably in interpreting the nature of the problem to the individual's family and in enlisting their cooperation in treatment. In view of their considerable success in helping many alcoholics achieve and maintain sobriety, the "Twelve Steps" that they consider the basis of their program are listed below:

1. We admitted we were powerless over alcohol — that our lives had become unmanageable.

2. Came to believe that a power greater than ourselves could restore us to sanity.

3. Made a decision to turn our will and our lives over to the care of God as we understood Him.

4. Made a searching and fearless moral inventory of ourselves.

5. Admitted to God, to ourselves, and to the other human beings the exact nature of our wrongs.

6. Were entirely ready to have God remove all these defects of character.

7. Humbly asked Him to remove our shortcomings.

8. Made a list of all persons we had harmed, and became willing to make amends to them all.

9. Made direct amends to such people whenever possible, except when to do so would injure them or others.

10. Continued to take personal inventory and when we were wrong promptly admitted it.

11. Sought through prayer and meditation to improve our conscious contract with God as we understood Him, praying only for knowledge of His will for us and the power to carry that out.

12. Having had a spiritual experience as a result of these steps, we tried to carry this message to alcoholics and to practice these principles in all our affairs.

SELECTED REFERENCES

Abraham, K. 1926. The psychological relations between sexuality and alcoholism. International Journal of Psychoanalysis 7, 2-10.

Adler, A. 1941. The individual psychology of the alcoholic patient. Journal of Criminal Psychopathology 3, 74-77.

Amark, C. 1951. *A Study in Alcoholism*, clinical, social psychiatric and genetic investigations. Acta Psychiatrica Supplementum 70.

Armstrong, J. D. 1958. The search for the alcoholic personality. Annals of the American Academy of Political and Social Science 315, 40-47.

Armstrong, J. D. 1961. Psychiatric theories of alcoholism. Canadian Psychiatric Journal 6, 140-149.

Bacon, S. D. 1958. Alcoholics do not drink. Annals of the American Academy of Political and Social Science 315, 55-64.

Bales, R. F. 1946. Cultural differences in rates of alcoholism. Quarterly Journal of Studies on Alcohol 6, 480-499.

Bleuler, M. 1955. A comparative study of the constitutions of Swiss and American alcoholic patients. In *Etiology of Chronic Alcoholism*, ed. O. Diethelm. Springfield, Illinois, Charles C Thomas, Publisher, pp. 110-178.

Chafetz, M. E., and Demone, H. W. 1962. *Alcoholism and Society*. New York, Oxford University Press.

Conger, J. J. 1951. The effects of alcohol on conflict behavior in the albino rat. Quarterly Journal of Studies on Alcohol 12, 1-21.

Dennehy, C. M. 1966. Childhood bereavement and psychiatric illness. British Journal of Psychiatry 112, 1049-1069.

Fenichel, O. 1945. *The Psychoanalytic Theory of Neurosis*. New York, W. W. Norton & Co., Inc., pp. 375-382.

Fox, R. 1967. A multidisciplinary approach to the treatment of alcoholism. American Journal of Psychiatry 123, 769-778.

Freud, S. 1912. Contributions to the psychology of love: the most prevalent form of degradation in erotic life. In *Collected Papers*. London, Hogarth Press, Vol. 4, pp. 203-216.

Freud, S. 1917, Mourning and melancholia. In *Collected Papers*. London, Hogarth Press, Vol. 4, pp. 152-170.

Freud, S. 1930. *Three Contributions to the Theory of Sex*, 4th edition. Washington, D.C., Nervous and Mental Diseases Publishing Company.

Gibbins, R. J. 1953. *Chronic Alcoholism and Alcohol Addiction*. Toronto, Alcoholism Research Foundation and University of Toronto Press, Brookside Monograph No. 1.

Gregory, I. 1959. An analysis of family data on 1000 patients admitted to a Canadian mental hospital. Acta Genetica *9*, 54-96.

Himwich, H. E., ed. 1957. *Alcoholism, Basic Aspects and Treatment.* Washington, D.C., American Association for the Advancement of Science, Publication No. 47.

Horton, D. 1943. The functions of alcohol in primitive societies: a cross-cultural study. Quarterly Journal of Studies on Alcohol *4*, 199-320.

Jackson, C. R. 1944. *The Lost Week End.* New York, J. J. Little and Ives Company.

Jellinek, E. M. 1951, 1952. In World Health Organization Technical Report Series Nos. 42 and 48.

Kaij, L. 1957. Drinking habits in twins. Acta Genetica *7*, 437-441.

Kalinowsky, L. B. 1958. Withdrawal convulsions and withdrawal psychoses. In *Problems of Addictions and Habituation,* ed. P. H. Hoch and J. Zubin. New York, Grune & Stratton, Inc., pp. 49-56.

Knight, R. P. 1937. The psychodynamics of chronic alcoholism. Journal of Nervous and Mental Disease *86*, 538-548.

Mardones, R. J., Segovia, N. M., and Hederra, A. D. 1953. Heredity of experimental alcohol preference in rats. II. Coefficient of heredity. Quarterly Journal of Studies on Alcohol *14*, 1-2.

Masserman, J. H., and Yum, K. S. 1946. An analysis of the influence of alcohol on experimental neuroses in cats. Psychosomatic Medicine *8*, 36-52.

McCarthy, R. G. 1951. *Facts About Alcohol.* Chicago, Science Research Associates, Guidance Series Booklets No. 120.

McCord, W., McCord, J., and Gudeman, J. 1959. Some current theories of alcoholism: a longitudinal evaluation. Quarterly Journal of Studies on Alcohol *20*, 727-749.

Menninger, K. A. 1938. *Man Against Himself.* New York, Harcourt, Brace & World, Inc., ch. 3.

Miles, W. R. 1932. Psychological effects of alcohol in man. In *The Effect of Alcohol on Man in Health and Disease,* ed. H. Emerson. New York, The Macmillan Co.

Popham, R. E. 1953. A critique of the genetotrophic theory of the etiology of alcoholism. Quarterly Journal of Studies on Alcohol 15, 228-237.

Popham, R. E. 1959. Some social and cultural aspects of alcoholism. Canadian Psychiatric Association Journal *4*, 222-229.

Popham, R. E., and Schmidt, W. 1962. *A Decade of Alcoholism Research.* Toronto, University of Toronto Press, Brookside Monograph No. 3.

Rado, S. 1933. The psychoanalysis of pharmacothymia (drug addiction). Psychoanalytic Quarterly *2*, 1-23.

Robins, E., Murphy, G. E., Wilkinson, R. H., Gassner, S., and Kayes, J. 1959. Some clinical considerations in the prevention of suicide based on a study of 134 successful suicides. American Journal of Public Health *49*, 888-899.

Schilder, P. 1941. The psychogenesis of alcoholism. Quarterly Journal of Studies on Alcohol *2*, 277-292.

Strecker, E. A. 1941. Chronic alcoholism: a psychological survey. Quarterly Journal of Studies on Alcohol *3*, 12-17.

Williams, R. J. 1947. The etiology of alcoholism: a working hypothesis involving the interplay of heredity and environmental factors. Quarterly Journal of Studies on Alcohol *7*, 567-587.

Williams, R. J., et al. 1957. Identification of blood characteristics common to alcoholic males. Science 126, 1237.

World Health Organization. 1949, 1950, 1951. Geneva, W.H.O. Technical Report Series Nos. 19, 21, 42, and 48.

Zwerling, I., and Rosenbaum, M. 1959. Alcoholic addiction and personality. In *American Handbook of Psychiatry,* ed. S. Arieti. New York, Basic Books, Inc., Vol. 1, ch. 31.

CHAPTER 23

Habit is either the best of servants, or the worst of masters.

Nathaniel Emmons

Drug Addiction

In seeking relief from pain and boredom, man has learned to use a variety of drugs having one of three major pharmacological actions: sedation, stimulation, or the production of delirium. The sedative drugs include *hypnotics* used mainly to produce sleep and *narcotics* that relieve pain, produce numbness and insensibility, and eventually lead to stupor with arrested activity or unconsciousness. *Stimulant* drugs act predominantly on the brain and sympathetic nervous system, so that they increase alertness and motor activity, prevent fatigue and sleep, and usually increase neuromuscular irritability and anxiety. *Deliriant* drugs may be stimulant or sedative, but in moderate dosage they tend to produce an acute brain syndrome with confusion, illusions, and hallucinations, and at least temporarily increased psychomotor activity.

Table 23-1 shows the main drugs involved in habituation and addiction, according to their predominant pharmacological actions. It may be noted that cocaine is a stimulant, although it is considered by Federal Law as a narcotic on the basis of its strong tendency to produce addiction. While the acute effects of these drugs depend partly on their pharmacological actions, they also depend partly on the personality of the individual and his current mood. In certain vulnerable individuals a single large dose of a strong stimulant such as cocaine or amphetamine may release latent symptoms of psychosis that tend to disappear after the effects of the drug wear off. Similarly, the nature and duration of psychotic symp-

toms precipitated by the deliriant drugs depend to a considerable extent upon the personality of the individual and the circumstances under which the drug is administered.

The *prolonged use of narcotic drugs* such as morphine and heroin is accompanied by profound changes in bodily functions and personality. The body tends to adapt to the presence of the drug and to develop an increasing *tolerance* for the drug, which requires progressively increasing doses to produce the same physiological and emotional effects. Concurrently the individual develops an increasing emotional and physiological *dependence* on the effects of the drug so that he is acutely uncomfortable when a sufficient quantity of the drug is no longer present in his body. Other common side effects of prolonged use of narcotics include lack of appetite, constipation, and loss of weight, and lack of interest in sexual and social relationships. There is often accompanying moral deterioration, but superego development may well have been defective prior to the onset of the addiction. Since these drugs are profoundly sedative on a variety of bodily functions, their sudden discontinuation after prolonged use will result in a variety of withdrawal symptoms characterized by overactivity of various organ systems. Such manifestations of sudden withdrawal include psychomotor restlessness, nervousness, severe muscular cramps with pain, lacrimation, perspiration, shivering, nausea, vomiting, diarrhea, and rapid weight loss—as much as five to 15 pounds in

TABLE 23–1. Drugs Leading to Habituation and Addiction

I. SEDATIVE DRUGS

Narcotics
Opium and its products
Morphine, heroin, codeine, and others

Synthetic substitutes for morphine
Meperidine, Methadone, and others

Hypnotics
Barbiturates
Amobarbital, pentobarbital, secobarbital, and others

Nonbarbiturates
Bromides, paraldehyde, chloral hydrate, and others

Minor Tranquilizers
Meprobamate (Equanil, Miltown)

Benzodiazepines (e.g., chlordiazepoxide, diazepam)

II. STIMULANT DRUGS

Cocaine

Caffeine

Nicotine

Amphetamines and derivatives
Benzedrine, dexedrine, desoxyn, and others

III. DELIRIANT DRUGS (Hallucinogenic or psychotomimetic agents)

Marijuana (hashish, or Indian hemp)

Mescaline (from cactus or peyote)

Psilocybin (from mushrooms)

Bufotenin (from cohaba snuff)

Lysergic acid diethylamide (LSD–25)

---

24 hours. The intensity of withdrawal symptoms reaches its peak 72 hours after the last dose, and diminishes during the remainder of the first week, following which there is only some residual nervousness, insomnia, and weakness.

The *prolonged use of barbiturates and other sedatives* also results in increasing tolerance, psychological and physical dependence, and the occurrence of withdrawal symptoms following their abrupt discontinuation. Since these drugs act primarily on the brain and not so much throughout the rest of the body, the most common signs of prolonged use consist of impaired function of the cerebral cortex (poorer intelligence, memory, orientation, consciousness, and the like) and of the cerebellum (incoordination, ataxia, slurred speech, tremors, choreiform movements, nystagmus, and so on). Such effects are cumulative, even with short-acting barbiturates that are ordinarily eliminated from the body within a few hours.

Withdrawal symptoms following the abrupt discontinuation of such drugs may be even more dangerous than those following withdrawal of narcotics.

Two manifestations of withdrawal are particularly important (Kalinowsky, 1958) and these consist of typical *epileptic seizures*, and *acute brain syndromes* that appear identical with the delirium tremens observed in chronic alcoholism. Seizures and withdrawal psychoses have been observed following the abrupt discontinuation of all the major hypnotic drugs and also tranquilizers such as meprobamate. If not treated promptly by sedatives and anticonvulsants, seizures may terminate in death, and delirious episodes may last for several days. It is also possible that either of these manifestations may precipitate or aggravate more chronic brain syndromes characterized by impairment of various intellectual functions.

The *prolonged use of cocaine or other stimulants* may also lead to increasing tolerance and dependency, and the main complications of their use are the direct consequences of overstimulation. There is generally a loss of appetite and weight, accompanied by increased anxiety and irritability, sleep deprivation, and periodic delirious episodes that may be attributed either to the stimulation or to prolonged deprivation of normal sleep. Abrupt discontinuation of stimulant drugs is not followed by typical withdrawal symptoms, but what goes up must come down, and sudden withdrawal is apt to be followed by profound fatigue and exaggeration of preëxisting symptoms of depression.

The World Health Organization expert committee on drugs liable to produce addiction drafted the following *definition of drug addiction:**

---

*Reprinted by permission from *Expert Committee on Drugs Liable to Produce Addiction*. World Health Organization Technical Report Series No. 57, p. 9.

Drug addiction is a state of periodic or chronic intoxication, detrimental to the individual and to society, produced by the repeated consumption of a drug (natural or synthetic). Its characteristics include:

1. An overpowering desire or need (compulsion) to continue taking the drug and to obtain it by any means;
2. A tendency to increase the dose;
3. A psychic (psychological) and sometimes a physical dependence on the effects of the drug.

At the same time they distinguished between *habit-forming drugs* and those producing true addiction, and offered the following definition of the former:

A habit-forming drug is one which is or may be taken repeatedly without the production of all the characteristics outlined in the definition of addiction and which is not generally considered to be detrimental to the individual and to society. Because of continuing confusion between the term addiction and habituation, however, the committee decided to clarify the distinction between these two terms by the following statement.

The cycle of administration leading to addiction may begin in legitimate medical use, but becomes established as a serious problem through self administration beyond medical need. In the development of addiction there is an interplay between pharmacological action and the psychological make-up of the individual.

There are some drugs, notable morphine and pharmacologically morphine-like substances, whose specific pharmacological action under individual conditions of time and dose will always produce compulsive craving, dependence and addiction in any individual. Addiction will develop sooner in those individuals whose psychological make-up leads them to seek and find escape in the pharmacological action of drugs. Sooner or later there must come a time when the use of the drug cannot be interrupted without significant disturbance, always psychic (psychological) and sometimes physical. With these drugs pharmacological action is paramount; psychological makeup adjuvant. Such drugs cause individual and sociological damage and must be rigidly controlled.

There are other drugs which never produce compulsive craving, yet their pharmacological action is found desirable to some individuals to the point that they readily form a habit of administration, an habituation. Administration of such drugs can be interrupted without significant disturbances. With them psychological make-up is paramount; pharmacological action adjuvant. They cause no sociological change and do not need rigid control.

There are some drugs whose pharmacological action is intermediate in kind and degree between the two groups already delineated so that compulsive craving, dependence and addiction can develop in those individuals whose psychological make-up leads them to seek and find an escape in drugs. With these substances psychological make-up is the determining factor, but pharmacological action plays a significant role. In some instances individual and sociological damage may develop but since the incidence of the damage is not general, the type and degree of control of drugs of this group are better left at present to national consideration.

Coffee and tea contain caffeine, which is a mild stimulant that gives rise to greater mental and muscular efficiency and feelings of well-being. Continued use of caffeine leads to habituation and increased tolerance of its stimulating effects, but does not lead to addiction in the usual sense of the word. However, some individuals use such large doses of coffee or caffeine tablets that there may be a marked accentuation of neurotic symptoms (anxiety and depression), psychophysiologic disorders (high blood pressure and peptic ulcer), loss of appetite and weight, severe impairment of sleep, and impulsive outbursts of hostile aggression.

The inhalation of cigarette smoke results in the rapid absorption of nicotine, which produces mild stimulation of the sympathetic nervous system. Heavy cigarette smoking with inhalation results in chronic mild sympathetic stimulation, and controlled experimental reduction in the nicotine content of cigarettes smoked has been shown to result in slowing of the heart and lowering of blood pressure. Knapp et al. concluded that heavy cigarette smokers are true addicts, showing not only social habituation, but mild physiologic withdrawal effects. They also remarked as follows:

Clinically, smoking appears to represent a complex learned psychosomatic pattern. Primary pleasure from the habit occurs but appears to become subordinate to secondary use to ward off pain, especially anxiety or a sense of loss. Various aspects or layers contribute to the urge; (1) the symbolic and personal meaning of smoking to the smoker; (b) the numerous sensations accompanying smoking—gustatory, pulmonary, tactile, visual and kinesthetic; (c) the impulse to take in and eliminate, interwoven with but not identical with, alimentary urges, (d) the seeking in heavy smokers of a state of chronic low-grade arousal.

The drugs commonly associated with addiction and habituation have been grouped above according to their predominant pharmacological actions. We shall now consider some of the **common pathways to addiction.**

1. *Medical habituation* may occur among patients for whom drugs have been prescribed over a prolonged period of time, as in the case of morphine and synthetic narcotics administered for pain, hypnotics prescribed for insomnia, and meprobamate or various sedatives prescribed for the relief of neurotic anxiety. The term medical habituation may also apply to those doctors, nurses, and pharmacists who become addicted to various drugs, generally hypnotic but occasionally narcotic, partly because they have access to a relatively inexpensive source of supply.

2. *Sociocultural habituation* involves the widespread availability and use of certain drugs among large segments of a population. Examples include the widespread use of opium among certain Asiatic peoples, and of cocaine from chewing coca leaves in South America. Among various segments of our own

population, the term sociocultural habituation may be applied to the use of caffeine, nicotine, alcohol, barbiturates, marijuana, LSD, and heroin.

3. *Sociopathic personality* characteristics may predispose certain individuals to employ methods of obtaining gratification that do not conform with the prevailing cultural mores and may be expressly forbidden by law. In our own society this applies to the excessive use of alcohol and to any use of narcotic drugs.

4. *Neurotic personality* characteristics and symptoms may be temporarily relieved by tranquilizers and hypnotics obtained on medical prescriptions, or by alcohol which requires no such prescription. In either event, prolonged use tends to result in increasing tolerance and dependency, with increasing difficulty in withdrawal.

5. *Other forms of psychopathology* may well lead to excessive dependency and addiction. The hypomanic usually tends to seek the company of others, often in a drinking situation. Depressed, schizoid, and paranoid individuals may seek relief from a variety of drugs, either in the company of others or in solitude. While the major functional psychoses appear to be rare among confirmed adult drug addicts, a diagnosis of overt or latent schizophrenia has been relatively frequent among adolescent addicts.

In a summary of data on the first 1036 addicts treated at the Lexington (Kentucky) Hospital of the Public Health Service, Pescor (1943) gave the following percentages for various forms of psychopathology:

1. Psychopathic diathesis	54.5
2. Inebriate personality	21.9
3. Psychopathic personality	11.7
4. Psychoneurotic	6.3
5. Normal individual accidentally addicted	3.8
6. Psychosis associated with addiction	1.4
7. Addiction due to psychosis	.1
8. Not an addict (?)	.3

The average age of the preceding group of addicts at the time of their admission to the Lexington Hospital was 39.1 years, and the average age at which they had started to use drugs was 27.5 years. The majority had spent time in correctional institutions, and they are not therefore typical of all addicts, even those who have used narcotics rather than less socially unacceptable drugs. Thus, among 30 adolescent opiate addicts admitted to the same hospital, Gerard and Kornetsky (1954) considered that six showed evidence of overt schizophrenia, eight of incipient schizophrenia, 12 of delinquency-dominated character disorder, and four of inadequate personality.

Adolescent drug use appears to have increased rapidly since the second World War, and has led to both public concern and scientific investigation. Some convincing accounts of individual addicts are contained in the book *Monkey on My Back* by Brown, and an excellent review of the literature is contained in an article by Clausen.

From various sources, the general public has learned something of the addict's slang: his world of snorts (snuff) and shots (injections), of kicks and jolts (from the effects of drugs), and fixes to take the monkey off his back. It may have learned of pot or reefers or muggles (all names for marijuana), and of goof-balls (barbiturate capsules) which may also be known as yellow-jackets (Nembutal), red devils (Seconal), or blue angels (Amytal). It may have heard how a junkie (addict) has been hooked by progressing from Sneaky Pete (cheap wine) to Pot (marijuana) to Horse (heroin snuff) to Bang ("mainlining" the heroin by direct injection into the vein).

Familiarity, however, may breed contempt, and many persons still regard the addict as a "dope-fiend" to be feared and despised almost as much as the "sex-maniac." In part, this is related to the fact that the narcotics addict is regarded as a criminal in our society, and that the maintenance of his expensive habit requires him to engage in other criminal activities. There has been considerable argument as to which comes first, the chicken or the egg, the addiction or the criminal activities that sustain it. Clausen pointed out that if one relies on official records of arrest for delinquent activities as evidence of delinquency, it appears that many drug users did not become "delinquent" until after they had started using drugs. On the other hand, he noted a Chicago study suggesting that most young drug users had engaged in delinquent activities for some time prior to first arrest and prior to the beginning of drug use.*

With few exceptions known drug users engage in delinquency in more or less systematic form. Contrary to the widely held view that the delinquency of the young addict is a consequence principally of addiction, it was found that delinquency both preceded and followed addiction to heroin. . . .Three observations may be made about the effects of addiction upon the delinquent behavior of the person: (1) The pressure of need for money to support his addiction impels the user to commit violations with greater frequency and with less caution than formerly. (2) Delinquents, after becoming addicted to heroin, do not engage in types of delinquency in which they are not already skilled. The post-addict delinquent, in other words, does not generally engage in more serious crimes than those he committed prior to his addiction. (3) Delinquents who as pre-addicts tended to engage in riotous behavior such as street fighting and gang attacks tend after addiction to abandon this kind of activity. Three elements are probably responsible for the change: (a) the sedative effects of the opiate; (b) the desire to avoid attracting the attention of public and police; and (c) the tendency for adolescents to become quieter in their conduct as they approach maturity.

We shall now present case histories to illustrate the very different personalities and problems involved in the addictions of a young male sociopath and two other patients with severe neurotic and depressive disorders.

A 21-year-old man requested admission to the psychiatric ward of a general hospital and stated that he wanted help in terminating his dependency on several drugs which he had been using excessively during the past few years. He gave his occupation as a musician and accepted financial responsibility for his hospital bill, but he remained in hospital for one month and never made any payment on the bill. In retrospect, it appeared to his psychiatrist that he may have sought admission to hospital at this time in order to escape from one or more of four current difficulties in his reality situation: (1) his parents had recently threatened him with compulsory admission to a state hospital, (2) he may have known that he was currently under investigation by narcotics authorities; (3) his wife, from whom he was separated, had recently threatened him with divorce action; (4) another girl with whom he had had sexual relations had recently given birth to an illegitimate child, and had alleged that he was the father of the child.

The patient was the eldest of four children, all boys. During the time he was in the hospital, it was learned that his next younger brother had been involved in various delinquent activities including narcotic addiction for nearly as long as the patient, for which reason the brother was currently in a state hospital. The parents of these boys were still living together and were apparently conscientious and socially conforming individuals who had made the mistake of being overly lenient and permissive with their sons. The father had worked continuously in the same job for the previous 13 years, and the patient described him as steady and dependable. When asked what he liked most about his father, he gave no response, and when asked what he liked the least about him, he replied that his father was kind of strict. However, it turned out that the latter had never used corporal punishment and had only remonstrated with him when he stayed out late and became involved in various forms of serious antisocial behavior during adolescence. The patient described his mother as friendly, warm, religious, a nice person, and easy to get along with. There was nothing he didn't

---

*From "Social patterns, personality and adolescent drug use," by J. A. Clausen. Chapter VIII of *Explorations in Social Psychiatry*, edited by A. H. Leighton, J. A. Clausen, and R. N. Wilson. Basic Books, Inc., Publishers, New York, 1957.

like about her, and as in the case of his father, she appears to have been quite unable to set any consistent firm limits on the behavior of her son.

The patient was of at least average intelligence, and during elementary school he apparently made average grades. In high school, however, he barely obtained a "D" average and was expelled from school on three occasions, for playing hooky, for selling contraceptives to other students, and for horsing around and beating up a much smaller boy. This last offense led to his appearance in juvenile court, and on other occasions he was taken to court for driving without a license and for selling stolen goods, but he got by with being placed on probation.

Early in high school he started having sexual relations with a variety of different girls, and when he was 17 one of these girls became pregnant so that he was forced into marriage. He left school without completing grade ten, and for six months he and his wife lived with her parents before moving to an apartment of their own for the next two years. During this time he worked at several unskilled jobs including busboy and truck driving. He claimed that it was during this time that he started using drugs because he felt it would be exciting and that he could impress other people by doing something dangerous. He also started going out with other women, and his wife returned to live with her parents while he returned to his own parents' home.

At the time of his admission to the hospital he claimed that until six months previously his drug intake had been restricted to about 60 mg of Dexedrine (stimulant) and about four ounces of cough syrup containing codeine (narcotic) daily. He said that he had then increased his intake of Dexedrine to about 90 mg a day, usually taken in the evening together with 400 mg of Nembutal and 400 mg of Seconal (both hypnotics). This enabled him to be "high" all night, during the earlier part of which he would sometimes play in a dance orchestra, and he would then sleep during the daytime. He subsequently admitted, however, that he had also taken injections of Demerol and it was later learned that he had also been using heroin (both narcotics). When he could not steal these drugs, he would steal other articles and use the money obtained to buy the drugs he needed.

Immediately after his admission to hospital on a ward of 30 patients, he became friendly with the one other patient on the ward who was known to have had a previous history of drug addiction. The latter was a young male schizophrenic who had also used a variety of drugs and whose marriage had already ended in divorce. After the first few days, however, our patient spent most of his time socializing with young female patients. He was composed and cooperative with the staff, and did not develop severe withdrawal symptoms which may have been because of the therapeutic substitution of anticonvulsants and sedatives, or the possibility that he had succeeded in bringing into the hospital a sufficient supply of medication for his needs. In any event, all medication was apparently successfully withdrawn within a couple of weeks.

His Minnesota Multiphasic Personality Inventory showed a marked elevation on scale 4 (psychopathic deviate) and a lesser elevation on scale 2 (depression), suggesting the presence of mild depression in a bascially sociopathic individual. It gradually became apparent that his motivation in seeking admission to hospital was temporary escape from difficulties in his environmental situation. He was not motivated toward making any major changes in his antisocial personality characteristics, and at the end of a month he was discharged from hospital. Not long afterward he was charged with burglary in connection with the theft of gold, silver, and drugs from a dentist's office. He admitted this theft and also confessed to further theft of narcotics and other drugs from two drug stores. On this occasion he was admitted to the United States Public Health Service Hospital at Lexington, Kentucky, and placed on prolonged probation by the court.

Another example of drug addiction follows:

A 20-year-old boy was admitted to the psychiatric unit of a general hospital after an unsuccessful attempt at suicide by shooting himself with a 22-caliber pistol. He had completed high school the preceding year, graduating second in a class of about 350 students, with straight A's. He was currently a freshman in college studying premedical courses and obtaining average grades. On arrival in hospital, he related that he had had severe periods of depression throughout the preceding year, ever since he had been refused admission to the Air Force Academy on which he had set his heart for about four years previously. He had been told that this refusal was based on his reports of having experienced pain in the stomach for several years, which his family physician had diagnosed as due to a peptic ulcer, although this had not been demonstrated by means of x-rays. His response to this frustration was prolonged rage, which was largely retroflexed in the form of depression. The severity of this frustration for him was based on his intense ambition and desire to achieve, as illustrated by his response when asked what three things he would wish for most of all. His reply was, to be successful (1) in medicine, (2) in music, (3) in aviation.

Both of his parents were perfectionistic and demanding, and both had apparently suffered from peptic ulcers. His mother was the dominant member of the family and was a music teacher, described by the patient as '40 percent housewife and 60 percent piano teacher." His father was a high school mathematics teacher and also a part time professional musician, who had insisted that the boy study music with the best teacher available so that he could achieve the perfection for which the father strove unsuccessfully. Both parents were critical, strict, and quite religious. The patient was the eldest of their children, having an adopted sister aged 16, an adopted brother aged 14 who suffered from asthma, and a full sister nine years old. All of the younger children had emotional problems, and at one time a psychologist had attempted therapy with the whole family but had been unable to effect much change in the attitudes or behavior of the parents.

About a year prior to his admission to hospital, the patient had started having difficulty in sleeping, and had begun to take Doriden (a nonbarbiturate hypnotic) at bedtime. After he completed high school, he started to play regularly some evenings with a professional dance band to help put himself through college. The other musicians were all older than he, and a couple of them drank excessive amounts of alcohol. The patient felt he was more talented than they were, and also felt superior to the people for whom they played. He was cynical, bitter, and disillusioned and began to use Doriden during the evenings to numb the pain of his dissatisfaction. After awhile, he also began to use Dexamyl, a combination of Dexedrine (a stimulant) with amytal (a hypnotic), and he referred to these medications as "sky hooks" that enabled him to

lift himself above the petty strife and misery of this world. As time went by, he became more and more dependent on these drugs and used them during the daytime. He had increasing difficulty in sleeping, lost appetite and weight, and became more depressed. He was under the influence of drugs at the time he attempted suicide.

At the time of his arrival in hospital, he was found to be moderately anxious and depressed, which was reflected by approximately equal elevations on scales 2 and 7 of the Minnesota Multiphasic Personality Inventory. He received antidepressive medication (Parnate), and intensive analytically oriented psychotherapy with goals of partial personality reconstruction. After one month in hospital, his depression had improved sufficiently for him to be referred to Vocational Rehabilitation, and at this time he was found to have a full-scale Intelligence Quotient of 128. His interests and aptitudes were such that he was led to change his vocational goals and decided on a career in engineering. In psychotherapy, there were many resistances to be overcome and his gains were slow. During the first four months, however, progressive improvement in his mental condition was paralleled by a gain of 35 pounds in weight. When he finally left hospital six months after his admission, there had been tremendous gains in insight into hitherto unconscious psychodynamics, and his goals for the future were much more realistic than hitherto. He subsequently continued seeing an older female patient he had met in hospital who initiated him sexually, but the relationship did not last long, and he was able to concentrate on academic and social activities. He remained in psychotherapy throughout the following year and continued to make a much more satisfactory adjustment than hitherto.

A further example of drug addiction follows:

A 31-year-old woman was admitted to the psychiatric unit of a general hospital with a history of much previous psychiatric treatment and increasingly severe addiction to barbiturates, which no longer controlled her severe anxiety and depression, so that she had remained at home for several months and was increasingly preoccupied with thoughts of suicide. It was learned that she had first been referred to a psychiatrist at the age of 18, a few weeks after she had started attending college away from home, because of fatigue and loss of weight associated with depression. At that time she had been admitted to a general hospital psychiatric unit and had received a short course of electroshock treatments. Her mood and activity level had improved, but it had soon become evident that her depression was related to longstanding neurotic conflicts and anxiety that had been manifested from early childhood. During the following 12 years, efforts had been directed toward personality reconstruction through analytically oriented psychotherapy and symptomatic treatment through the administration of tranquilizing sedatives and antidepressive medication. She had had repeated readmissions to psychiatric units and several further courses of electroshock treatment, that had led to only temporary improvement in persistent depression.

At the age of 26 she had first been given a prescription for a proprietary medication containing several barbiturates that was intended to be used only for insomnia. However, the patient had discovered that if she used the medication during the daytime it controlled her previously overwhelming feelings of anxiety and fear, and tended to diminish the frequency and intensity of depression. The physician who prescribed the drug had failed to specify how many times each prescription could be refilled by the pharmacist, and the patient obtained supplies at different drug stores, gradually increasing her tolerance and also her dependency on the medication. For a period of five years, she had taken the drug continually and was able to continue working and avoid readmission to hospital. She then became engaged to a man of different religion, of whom her parents disapproved and toward whom she was ambivalent. In spite of continued medication, she had become severely depressed and unable to work. Electroshock treatment had again produced only temporary relief of depression and it was impossible to work through her longstanding conflicts.

In view of her chronic, incapacitating, and dangerous symptoms that had failed to respond to all other available forms of treatments, arrangements were made for her to have a lobotomy in the hope of producing more complete and lasting improvement. However, in order to avoid damaging her intelligence and positive personality attributes, a minimal anterior bimedial operation was performed. At first there was dramatic improvement, but this was only maintained for a few months before she again became anxious and depressed, resumed her former dependency on barbiturates and broke her engagement on the grounds that she would never make a satisfactory wife and mother. During the following year she continued taking medication and did not return to work, but remained at home in a hostile, dependent relationship with her parents. On the anniversary of her broken engagement, she was so depressed that she attempted suicide with an overdose of the pills on which she had been dependent for so long.

A second lobotomy was undertaken that still involved only a slight extension of the surgical cuts made previously. Following this second operation, however, there was marked and sustained improvement, with no recurrence of the former severe anxiety or depression, and no further dependency on any form of medication. Her hitherto severely abnormal Minnesota Multiphasic Personality Inventory Profile was now within normal limits, and she obtained a full scale IQ of 130 (prior to operation this had been 117). She was referred for vocational rehabilitation and found to have retained her skills as an exceptionally able stenographer. While she remained at home for nearly a year after the second operation, she then returned to work and to an apartment of her own with a more adequate social life than hitherto.

This patient was the younger of two children, both girls, and she repeatedly referred to her older sister as being more socially conforming and normal than herself. However, while this sister was able to remain regularly employed as a high school teacher, she also was unmarried and appeared to be insecure and overdependent on her parents. The parents were both children of ministers and were conscientious, overly conforming, insecure, and relatively socially isolated. Although father could express no hostility outside his home, with his family he was an authoritarian tyrant. The patient reported that he frequently had violent rages, but that no other member of the family was allowed to get angry, or indeed to express any strong emotion. As a child she had feared and hated her father more than any person she met then or subsequently. However, respect and obedience were demanded, and she was made to feel guilty for her hostility, so that she blamed her own behavior for his anger. As an adult, she was able to free him from responsibility by blaming his own childhood experiences as follows: "In defense of my father, he had a hellish childhood. Children were to be seen and not heard. They had to sit quietly at the table or be smacked on the face. He had to go to work and sell from door to door, and it kills him because he's so shy."

In retrospect, the patient believed that her parents had wanted a boy and were disappointed when she turned out to be a girl. She was a shy and frightened child, and automobile rides with her father would lead to attacks of vomiting. She got good grades in school, but following an appendectomy at the age of eleven she was frightened of returning to school. Neither her mother nor her older sister had prepared her for the onset of menstruation, and she thought that she must be sick. She received little or no sexual information from her family, had relatively few dates, and had no sexual experience until after the age of 30 when she was engaged. Apart from her fear of pregnancy, this aspect of her relationship with her fiance had been more satisfactory to her than most others, which were contaminated by displacement of her hostility towards her father.

She had been the first girl to be elected president of the senior class of her high school, and before dropping out of college she was one of three candidates for president of her freshman class there. After training as a stenographer she had held a responsible position as an executive secretary until she was finally incapacitated by her severe anxiety and depression. After her second lobotomy, she was again able to function effectively as a stenographer, although she did not return to a position with as much responsibility as she had previously held. However, she was much more comfortable in social relationships than at any time hitherto, and she retained the initiative and sense of responsibility that enabled her to live independently of her parents.

DYNAMICS, DEVELOPMENT, AND CAUSATION

Psychoanalytic interpretations of drug addiction have emphasized the same intrapsychic and interpersonal dynamics as previously discussed in the case of alcoholism. Similarly, the results of research into the causation of alcoholism have frequently been generalized to other forms of drug addiction for which less specific research has been undertaken. In the present section we shall therefore consider briefly a few additional formulations and findings concerning drug addiction.

Rado regarded the essential factor in the pathology of narcotic bondage as corruption of the organism's hedonic control by the superpleasure of narcotic drugs. By wiping out the adult's enlightened hedonic responses, the absolute priority of superpleasure reduces self-regulation to the precultural hedonic responses of the infant, aimed at immediate regard. He postulated a biological basis for the observed psychodynamics, and cited the discovery of "pleasure centers" in the brains of experimental animals as confirmation of his own hedonic theory. He remarked that electric stimulation of these centers gives the animals a unique pleasure reward strikingly similar to the superpleasure induced biochemically by narcotic drugs, and referred to the following quotation from Olds, who had implanted electrodes in the brains of experimental animals and provided them with levers for self-stimulation:

The animals seemed to experience the strongest reward or pleasure from stimulation of areas of the hypothalamus and certain mid-brain nuclei-regions which Hess and others had found to be centers of control of digestive, sexual, excretory and similar processes. Animals with electrodes in these areas would stimulate themselves from 500 to 5000 times per hour.

Electric stimulation in some of these regions actually appeared to be far more rewarding to these animals than an ordinary satisfier such as food. . . .Indeed a hungry animal often ignored available food in favor of the pleasure of stimulating itself electrically. Some rats with electrodes in these places stimulated their brains more than 2000 times per hour for 24 consecutive hours.

Lehmann commented that a model of addiction based on these observations would conceive of the addicting agent as being a suitable stimulator of the pleasure centers in the brain, and inducing a self-perpetuating cycle of behavior characterized by the continuous seeking of this special addicting agent. He added, however, that the presence of such centers in the human brain had not hitherto been demonstrated.

In an attempt to establish an inherited predisposition to cigarette smoking, Fisher cited a German study of smoking behavior in 51 pairs of monozygotic twins and 31 pairs of dizygotic twins. A major degree of concordance for smoking behavior was found among 76 percent of the monozygotic twins and 49 percent of the dizygotic twins, which would result in a Holzinger index of heritability amounting to 53 percent. The data could be rearranged in several ways according to the extent to which attention was given to minor variations in the smoking habit, but in all cases the monozygotic twins showed closer similarity and fewer divergencies than the dizygotic.

A number of studies have reported that groups of cigarette smokers have higher average levels of anxiety and neurotic traits than groups of non-smokers, but there is no direct evidence of a cause and effect relationship. In the present state of our knowledge, there is as much reason to suppose that cigarette smoking causes nervous tension as to believe that nervous tension causes cigarette smoking. Matarazzo and Saslow suggested that smoking behavior is determined by multiple factors, and that for any given individual, his smoking behavior may be socioculturally determined, age-sex linked, related to occupation, or associated with a variety of personality and other behavioral characteristics. These authors also recognized the probability that different factors are responsible for the initiation of smoking from those effecting its continuation.

Several studies have demonstrated that the frequency of smoking among high school students is directly related to the frequency of smoking among their parents. To most persons this has suggested the significance of imitative learning through identification, and this same mechanism has been held responsible for the initiation of various forms of drug addiction. Neurotics who become addicted to sedatives may be following the example of a parent who has done likewise, and addicts may be introduced to narcotics by older members of the same social group or by persons of the opposite sex with whom they have some kind of love relationship.

In her controlled study of childhood bereavement and adult psychiatric disorder, Dennehy included data concerning 44 males and 22 females with drug addiction. The majority of this group consisted of heroin and cocaine addicts, but a small number of barbiturate and morphine addicts were also included. In view of the small size of this sample, the author was surprised to find a significant excess of loss of both parents of female drug addicts before the age of five years. Other findings were not statistically significant, but the entire group of drug addicts appeared to suffer from a greater degree of childhood parental loss by death than any other diagnostic category in this study. It is not certain, however, to what extent these results may have been influenced by socio-economic status.

Sociocultural factors are generally held to be as significant in initiating and perpetuating drug addiction as they are believed to be in producing alcoholism. In the case of narcotics, there has been frequent reference to relatively high rates of addiction in the United States in contrast with very low rates of addiction in Britain. It has been speculated that the former rates were attributable to punitive legislation and law enforcement in the United States, whereas the latter were attributable to a benign system in England which included "registered" addicts who secured a regular maintenance dose of drugs from established clinics entirely under medical supervision. However, the different frequencies may also be interpreted on the basis of greater financial rewards in the United States, more efficient criminal organization and distribution, and less compelling cultural sanctions against narcotic addiction, leading to a need for sterner legislation and law enforcement. In an attempt to evaluate the true situation in Britain, Brill wrote as follows:*

1. There is no "registration" of addicts in England.
2. The British regulations do permit the physician to use his discretion in issuing and prescribing opiates, and some physicians apparently do issue such prescriptions although up to the present time the author has not been able to discover any published British data to describe the practice or its results in quantitative specific normal medical terms.
3. "Maintenance" actually carried out differs little from ours, and British practice also differs little from ours.
4. It is a distortion of the facts to point to any "system" since the cases are so few that any real generalizations are almost impossible.
5. The author knows of no responsible British authority who has presented a documentation of better results than ours in treatment of addiction, and informal discussion leads to the same conclusion.

---

*Reprinted by permission from H. Brill. 1963. Misapprehensions about drug addiction—some origins and repercussions. Comprehensive Psychiatry *4*, 150-159.

6. Regardless of what may be the present situation in England with regard to the handling of narcotics, there is no evidence that British regulations led to the present low statistics. Indications are that the reverse is true.

TREATMENT

As in the case of alcoholism, the treatment of patients with drug addiction consists of (1) withdrawal and disintoxication, (2) deterrent measures such as compulsory temporary confinement, (3) attempts to modify the personality vulnerability and environment stresses that led to the addiction and its perpetuation. In the case of narcotics, withdrawal may be quite abrupt, although the withdrawal symptoms may be extremely unpleasant to the addict and this procedure has sometimes been referred to as "cold turkey." More humanitarian procedures, which also increase the probability of his later involvement in therapy, consist of progressively diminishing doses of the drug, or of a substitute drug which is less addictive but controls the withdrawal symptoms. All narcotics may be totally withdrawn in this manner over a period of one to two weeks, whereas the safe withdrawal of hypnotic drugs frequently requires that the patient receive diminishing doses of sedatives and anticonvulsants over a period of three or four weeks.

Withdrawal of a narcotic may be facilitated by substitution of a less strongly addictive agent. Dole and Nyswander reported that a group of relatively nonproductive and relapse-prone heroin addicts treated with methadone showed a remarkable degree of social and vocational rehabilitation within a surprisingly short time after starting treatment. Methadone, however, is legally and pharmacologically a narcotic, with a strong potential for abuse and a monetary value in the illicit narcotics trade. Jaffe and Brill therefore preferred to employ cyclazocine in a similar program of substitution and replacement therapy, since this agent is far less addictive, and its potential for abuse considerably lower than that of most narcotic drugs. Hitherto, it has apparently had no monetary value in the illicit narcotics trade, and pilot studies suggested it could be safely administered in reducing dosage on an outpatient basis. The authors emphasized however that compulsive narcotics users form a very heterogeneous population, and that the goal of treatment is not abstinence per se, but social rehabilitation.

It is sometimes argued that a patient subjected to compulsory confinement and withdrawal will never be motivated towards a positive involvement in psychotherapy and other measures designed to prevent his returning to drugs. While voluntary cooperation is desirable, however, clinical experience indicates that compulsory withdrawal may sometimes be followed by marked changes in motivation and active involvement in therapy.

Feelings about drug addicts sometimes run high and the opinion of some law enforcement officers is reflected in a statement by an otherwise innocuous nun, who believed that the only way to deal with drug addicts was "to get them in a state of grace and shoot them." Psychologists and psychiatrists, however, are almost unanimous in regarding addicts as sick persons in need of help and treatment. According to their view, punitive action should be directed solely toward the criminals who supply the drugs and live off the misery of others. Thus, Hoch remarked that any realistic program with regard to drug addiction must embody five major points:

1. Increased law enforcement activity directed at the suppliers of narcotic drugs.

2. Educational and social efforts aimed at prevention, concentrating on those areas presenting a high risk of narcotic addiction.

3. A constructive coordinated system of in-patient and out-patient treatment and rehabilitation for addicts.

4. Greatly stepped up research to hasten the day when the means of prevention and cure for all narcotic addiction will be available.

5. Changes in the Federal and in different state laws which more clearly define the responsibilities for the various aspects of the total program.

SELECTED REFERENCES

Allentuck, S., and Bowman, K. M. 1942. The psychiatric aspects of marihuana intoxication. American Journal of Psychiatry 99, 248.

American Bar Association and American Medical Association, Joint Committee on Narcotic Drugs. 1961. *Drug Addiction: Crime or Disease?* Bloomington, Indiana, Indiana University Press.

Bell, D. S., and Trethowan, W. H. 1961. Amphetamine addiction and disturbed sexuality. AMA Archives of General Psychiatry 4, 74.

Brill, H. 1963. Misapprehensions about drug addiction—some origins and repercussions. Comprehensive Psychiatry 4, 150-159.

Brown, W. 1953. *Monkey on My Back.* Philadelphia, Chilton Books.

Chein, I., Gerard, D. L., Lee, R. S., and Rosenfeld, E. 1964. *The Road to H.* New York, Basic Books, Inc.

Clausen, J. A. 1957. Social patterns, personality, and adolescent drug use. *In Explorations in Social Psychiatry*, ed. A. H. Leighton, J. A. Clausen, and R. N. Wilson. New York, Basic Books, 230-277.

Connell, P. H. 1958. *Amphetamine Psychosis.* London, Chapman and Hall, Maudsley Monograph No. 5.

Dennehy, C. M. 1966. Childhood bereavement and psychiatric illness. British Journal of Psychiatry 112, 1049-1069.

Dole, V. P., and Nyswander, M. 1965. A medical treatment for diacetyl-morphine (heroin) addiction. Journal of the American Medical Association 193, 646-650.

Felix, R. H. 1944. An appraisal of the personality types of the addict. American Journal of Psychiatry 100, 462.

Fisher, R. A. 1958. Lung Cancer and Cigarettes. Nature 182, 108.

Gerard, D. L, and Kornetsky, C. 1954. A social and psychiatric study of adolescent opiate addicts. Psychiatric Quarterly 28, 113-125.

Glover, E. 1932. On aetiology of drug-addiction. International Journal of Psychoanalysis 13, 298.

Hoch, P. H. 1963. Comments on narcotics addiction. Comprehensive Psychiatry 4, 140-144.

Jaffe, J. H., and Brill, L. 1966. Cyclazocine, a long acting narcotic antagonist: Its voluntary acceptance as a treatment modality by narcotics abusers. The International Journal of the Addictions, 1, 99-123.

Kalinowsky, L. B. 1958. Withdrawal convulsions and withdrawal psychoses. In *Problems of Addiction and Habituation,* ed. P. H. Hoch and J. Zubin. New York, Grune & Stratton, Inc., pp. 49-56.

Knapp, P. H., Bliss, C. M., and Wells, H. 1963. Addictive aspects in heavy cigarette smoking. American Journal of Psychiatry *119,* 966-972.

Kolb, L. 1962. *Drug Addiction: A Medical Problem.* Springfield, Illinois, Charles C Thomas, Publisher.

Lehmann, H. E. 1963. Phenomenology and pathology of addiction. Comprehensive Psychiatry *4,* 168-180.

Lemere, F. 1966. The danger of amphetamine dependency. American Journal of Psychiatry *123,* 569-572.

Little, R. B., and Pearson, M. M. 1966. The management of pathologic interdependency in drug addiction. American Journal of Psychiatry *123,* 554-559.

Matarazzo, J. D., and Saslow, G. 1960. Psychological and related characteristics of smokers and non-smokers. Psychological Bulletin 57, 493-513.

Nyswander, M. 1956. *The Drug Addict as a Patient.* New York, Grune & Stratton, Inc.

Nyswander, M. 1959. Drug addictions. In *American Handbook of Psychiatry,* ed. S. Arieti. New York, Basic Books, Inc., Vol. 1, Ch. 30.

Olds, J. 1956. Pleasure centers in the brain. Scientific American *195,* October.

Pescor, M. J. 1943. A statistical analysis of the clinical records of hospitalized drug addicts. U. S. Public Health Reports, Suppl. No. 143.

Rado, S. 1958. Narcotic bondage: a general theory of the dependence on narcotic drugs. In *Problems of Addiction and Habituation.* ed. P. H. Hoch and J. Zubin. New York, Grune & Stratton, Inc., pp. 27-36.

Rasor, R. W. 1958. Narcotic addicts: Personality characteristics and hospital treatment. In *Problems of Addiction and Habituation,* ed. P. H. Hoch and J. Zubin. New York, Grune & Stratton, Inc., pp. 1-16.

Taylor, S. D., Wilbur, M., and Osnos, R. 1966. The wives of drug addicts. American Journal of Psychiatry 123, 585-591.

Vaillant, G. E. 1966. A 12-year follow-up of New York narcotic addicts. AMA Archives of General Psychiatry *15,* 599-609.

Vogel, V. H., and Vogel, V. E. 1951. *Facts About Narcotics.* Chicago, Science Research Associates, Guidance Series Booklets No. 121.

Weeks, J. R. 1962. Experimental morphine addiction: Method for automatic intravenous injections in unrestrained rats. Science *138,* 143-144.

Weeks, J. R. 1964. Experimental narcotic addiction. Scientific American *210,* 46-52.

Wikler, A. 1952. A psychodynamic study of patient during experimental self-regulated re-addiction to morphine. Psychiatric Quarterly *26,* 270.

World Health Organization. 1950-1955. Technical Report Series Nos. 57, 76, 84, 94, and 95.

CHAPTER 24

Organic Brain Disorders

Organic brain syndromes are disorders of thinking, emotion, and behavior resulting from a variety of biochemical and structural changes in the brain. *Two major groups* of organic brain syndromes are usually distinguished, according to whether the disordered brain and mental functions are temporary and reversible (i.e., *acute*), or permanent and irreversible (i.e., *chronic*).

In *both* acute and chronic brain disorders, we find *primary symptoms of intellectual impairment*, the most important of which are as follows:

1. Impairment of orientation — most marked for time, less so for place and person.
2. Impairment of memory — most marked for recent events, less so for events of the remote past.
3. Impairment of all intellectual functions — including comprehension, calculation, knowledge, learning, and others. Ideation tends to be impoverished and concrete, associated with stereotyped repetition ("perseveration"), and compensatory fabrications ("confabulation").
4. Impairment of judgment, conscience, and ability to plan for the future.
5. Shallowness or lability of affect (emotional response).

The preceding primary symptoms of organic intellectual impairment are present to some degree in all acute and chronic disorders caused by temporary or permanent damage to the brain, but they vary greatly in intensity and may be very mild or extremely severe and obvious. In addition to these primary signs of intellectual impairment, there may also be mild or severe *secondary symptoms due to accentuation or release of functional personality characteristics* that have hitherto remained latent or hidden. These secondary symptoms include the whole range of functional psychopathology such as neurotic anxiety, depressive or manic disorders, schizophrenic or paranoid manifestations, sociopathic behavior, sexual deviation, or addiction to drugs.

In every patient with an organic brain syndrome, the intellectual and behavioral changes manifested are a function of both the primary damage to the brain and the secondary functional personality characteristics. An identical type and degree of brain damage may lead to some differences in severity of primary intellectual impairment, but very marked differences in secondary manifestations due to individual vulnerability or predisposition to various forms of functional psychopathology. However, there is a tendency for most persons to react to acute brain damage with clinical syndromes of delirium or stupor, and to react to chronic brain damage with a clinical syndrome of dementia.

In the clinical syndrome of *delirium*, there is generally disordered perception with visual illusions and hallucinations, clouded consciousness, and increased or decreased psychomotor activity. These manifestations are *not* generally found in the clinical syndrome of *dementia*, in which there is more likely to be auditory hallucinations based on activation of a latent functional psychosis such as schizophrenia. The main differences between the characteristic symptoms, pathogenesis, and outcome of acute and chronic brain syndromes are summarized in Table 24-1.

Both acute reversible impairment of brain function and chronic irreversible brain damage are known to result from a tremendous variety of general infections such as malaria or pneumonia; of infections that are localized mainly within the skull such as meningitis or brain abscess; of poisons affecting the brain such as alcohol or carbon monoxide; of physical injuries that produce damage to the brain or interfere with its blood supply; of tumors that grow within the skull cavity; and of bodily illnesses that interfere with the normal nourishment and functioning of brain cells. These illnesses include any condition that reduces the normal supply of oxygen to the brain, any deficiency of certain vitamins (particularly members of the vitamin B complex), and deficiency of thyroid hormone.

All the infective, toxic, traumatic, metabolic, or other disorders that commonly cause acute reversible brain syndromes may also lead to chronic irreversible brain syndromes if the damage to brain cell function is sufficiently severe. However, chronic irreversible disorders also arise from localized intracranial lesions or de-

TABLE 24-1. Characteristics of Acute (Reversible) and Chronic (Irreversible) Brain Disorders

ACUTE REVERSIBLE BRAIN DISORDERS	CHRONIC IRREVERSIBLE BRAIN DISORDERS
Usual clinical syndrome delirium (sometimes stupor or coma).	Usual clinical syndrome dementia.
Primary impairment of orientation, memory, all intellectual functions, judgment, and affective response.	Primary impairment of orientation, memory, all intellectual functions, judgment, and affective response.
Usually associated with disordered perception (especially visual illusions and hallucinations). consciousness (e.g., stupor), and psychomotor activity (excitement or retardation).	May be prominent secondary "functional" manifestations due to release or accentuation of latent personality characteristics — psychotic, neurotic, or behavioral (e.g., depressed, paranoid, anxious, or antisocial behavior).
Due to temporary, reversible changes in brain cell function, or "biochemical lesions."	Due to permanent, irreversible damage to brain structure, or "morphological lesions."
Frequently "symptomatic" of generalized toxic, infective or metabolic disorder, also affecting other parts of the body.	May result from all the same pathogenic agents as acute (reversible) disorders; but also from insidious, localized intracranial lesion or degenerative process (sometimes hereditary).
Commonly encountered on general medical and surgical, pediatric, or obstetric wards of general hospitals.	Commonly encountered on neurological services of general hospitals or in mental hospitals.
Course brief, and may terminate in (1) death, (2) complete remission, (3) chronic (irreversible) brain disorders.	Course may be (1) chronic, or (2) progressive (with fatal termination).

generative processes with insidious onset, which are not characterized by complete reversibility and resolution. Some of these chronic disorders are hereditary, although they may not produce symptoms of abnormality until adult life, as in the case of Huntington's chorea. Others may be environmental in origin, but affect the brain of the unborn child during intrauterine life and lead to a lifelong congenital abnormality present at birth, as in the case of rubella or syphilis transmitted from the pregnant mother to her child.

If any of these disturbances in normal brain function should happen to develop prior to birth or very soon afterwards, and also be sufficiently severe to produce permanent irreversible brain damage, then they result in some degree of lifelong intellectual subnormality or *mental retardation.* In the standard nomenclature, the first category of chronic brain syndrome listed is the type associated with congenital cranial anomaly, resulting in secondary mental retardation or intellectual subnormality. However, since this type of chronic brain syndrome constitutes one of the two major varieties of mental retardation, we shall only mention it briefly here, and discuss it more fully in the next chapter. Since exactly the same pathological processes that cause acute brain syndromes may also lead to chronic brain syndromes, we shall avoid duplication in the present chapter by combining the various acute and chronic brain syndromes listed in the standard nomenclature. Table 24-2 contains a list of the main acute and chronic brain syndromes, according to the standard nomenclature.

In some cases the appearance, attitude, and behavior of the patient with an acute brain syndrome may be quite characteristic even before an attempt at verbal communication is undertaken. The usual clinical syndromes are those of either *delirium* (with illusions, hallucinations, and increased psychomotor activity) or *stupor* (with apathy and re-

tardation). In either case, the patient is apt to appear physically sick, and may be lying in bed unshaven and unkempt in appearance, with haggard or expressionless face, and often sweating profusely. Patients with active visual illusions or hallucinations may pick at imaginary objects in the air or on the bedding, and may have a worried or fearful expression. Patients with alcoholic delirium tremens have a coarse tremor of the extremities ("the shakes"), and those with increased psychomotor activity tend to be excited and sometimes aggressive, but usually their activity appears purposeless and confused.

The patient in stupor offers little or no spontaneous conversation and limited replies to direct questioning, and sometimes may be completely uncommunicative. The state of retardation and lethargy may proceed to somnolence or coma from which the patient cannot be aroused. However, when he is awake and accessible for conversation, replies to questions reveal the characteristic organic intellectual deficit that is also present in states of delirium and excitement.

In patients with *dementia* resulting from chronic brain syndromes, the severity of intellectual impairment will determine the extent of abnormality evident in their appearance, attitude, behavior, and conversation. In patients with only mild impairment, the trouble may be evident only on careful questioning or psychological testing, and not in their social behavior or casual conversation. On the other hand, in those with severe intellectual impairment, their appearance, behavior, and every attempt at conversation reflect profound confusion or dementia. In advanced cases, patients may be completely indifferent in their appearance or surroundings and regress to an infantile level, lying in bed, incontinent, and unable to feed themselves or converse.

In all cases, there is some *impairment of intellectual functions* (comprehension,

TABLE 24–2. The Main Acute and Chronic Brain Syndromes

I. *Chronic brain syndromes associated with congenital cranial anomaly, congenital spastic paraplegia, mongolism, prenatal maternal infectious disease, birth trauma*
Consists of all congenital brain disorders producing secondary or "pathological" mental deficiency

II. *Acute and chronic brain syndromes associated with infection*
  A. Intracranial infections, such as encephalitis, meningitis, brain abscess, and central nervous system syphilis.
  B. Systemic infections such as pneumonia, typhoid fever, rheumatic fever, and malaria.

III. *Acute and chronic brain syndromes associated with intoxication*
  A. Drugs (and withdrawal of drugs) generally used in medical practice, such as hypnotics and narcotics, stimulants, antibiotics, and analgesics, antihistamines, and hormones.
  B. Poisons not ordinarily used in medical practice, such as lead and other metals, carbon monoxide and other gases, and methyl alcohol ("wood alcohol or rubbing alcohol").
  C. Alcohol (ethyl alcohol) and associated vitamin deficiencies.

IV. *Acute and chronic brain syndromes associated with trauma*
Any physical brain injury, including that caused by surgical operations.

V. *Acute and chronic brain syndromes associated with circulatory disturbances*
  A. High blood pressure, heart and kidney diseases
  B. Cerebral arteriosclerosis

VI. *Acute and chronic brain syndromes associated with convulsive disorder*
Due to uncontrolled seizures caused by primary or "idiopathic" epilepsy.

VII. *Acute and chronic brain syndromes associated with disorders of metabolism*
  A. With recognized metabolic disorders, such as anoxia, anemia, vitamin deficiencies, and disorders of the thyroid or other endocrine glands.
  B. With presumed disorders of metabolism, as in senile brain disease and Alzheimer's presenile dementia.

VIII. *Acute and chronic brain syndromes associated with intracranial neoplasm*
  A. Primary tumors, originating within the skull, may be invasive (malignant) or localized (benign).
  B. Secondary (metastatic) tumors from primary cancer elsewhere in the body.

IX. *Acute and chronic brain syndromes associated with diseases of unknown or uncertain cause*
These are usually chronic degenerative diseases of the brain and nervous system whose causation is only partly established, such as multiple sclerosis, Huntington's chorea, and Pick's presenile dementia.

calculation, knowledge, learning, and the like), associated with concrete or literal thinking, impoverished ideation with a reduction of new concepts, and a tendency toward stereotyped repetition of a few thoughts or phrases. The situation in which the patient keeps answering the same word or phrase to a number of different questions is known as perseveration.

There may be impairment of *orientation* in all three spheres, but the most vulnerable is the sense of time, which is the first to be lost and the last to be restored after any acute insult to the brain. Orientation as to place also tends to be more vulnerable than for persons who have long been known to the patient, although the latter may also be lost in severe confusion.

There is impairment of *memory*, which is most marked for events of the immediate past, and in some cases there is a tendency to compensate for this deficit by confabulation or fabrication of answers with varying degrees of plausibility.

The *emotional response* associated with primary intellectual impairment tends to be shallow, inadequate, or flattened, so that the patient appears dull, listless, and apathetic. In a number of cases, however, there is a marked lability, variability, or fluctuation in response to minor external stimuli, and a "catastrophic reaction" with weeping, wailing, and agitation, may occur for no evident reason. In patients with prominent secondary symptoms of affective disorder, the predominant mood is that of either depression or euphoria, and in those with strong paranoid features the predominant mood may be one of overt hostility.

In acute brain syndromes, *illusions and hallucinations* most typically involve vision, and may consist of various moving animals and reptiles which the patient finds frightening. However, hallucinations of touch, hearing, smell, or taste are not infrequent, and transient *delusions* frequently relate to the content of these disturbances in perception. In the case of chronic brain syndromes, illusions, hallucinations, and delusions are not characteristic but may be evident in patients with prominent secondary symptoms of functional psychosis. Thus, the depressed patient may have delusions of self-accusation; the euphoric patient, delusions of grandeur; and the paranoid patient, delusions of influence or persecution, often associated with auditory hallucinations.

In acute brain syndromes, there may be considerable *fluctuation* in the mental state within quite short periods of time. During lucid intervals, judgment and insight may be fairly well preserved, but they are grossly impaired during episodes of confusion. In patients with mild degrees of chronic intellectual impairment, there may be considerable preservation of social and ethical judgment, together with partial insight into the existence of some memory deficit, but when the symptoms are severe, the patient's critical faculties of judgment and insight are absent.

We shall now present illustrative case histories of patients with a variety of acute and chronic brain syndromes, according to the standard nomenclature, as summarized in Table 24-2.

ACUTE BRAIN SYNDROME ASSOCIATED WITH INTRACRANIAL INFECTION, MENINGITIS*

In recent years, because of the widespread use of antibiotics, most acute infections are being treated early and effectively with the result that associated deliria are becoming less frequent. The following case was encountered before the introduction of antibiotics. It illustrates the difficulties which can still arise in diagnosing such an illness.

This man, aged 52, was admitted to a psychiatric hospital in a very excited, resistive condition. He tossed about violently and his conversation was incoherent. Even with heavy sedation he had very little rest. Investigation of the history indicated that he had always been a quiet, well-adjusted man, who held a responsible position as an engineer with a construction company. He was working until the day before admission, when he came home at 2 P.M. complaining of a violent headache. He lay down and slept until 6 P.M. At 9 P.M. he became restless, talked incoherently, and vomited. The family physician was called and the patient's temperature was 101 degrees F., an elevation often encountered in overactive, anxious, and disturbed patients. Although the admitting physician recognized that the patient was delirious, he did not consider that there was any immediate need to carry out special investigations. In spite of sedation, the patient remained mentally disturbed. By the following day the physical findings had altered: the right pupil was now slightly larger than the left and reacted sluggishly to light; blood pressure had risen to 190/120 mm Hg and stiffness of the neck was pronounced; the pulse varied from 64 to 120; the white blood count was 5900 per cu. mm. As a result of consultations with an internist and a neurosurgeon, the possibility of a subarachnoid hemorrhage was considered and a lumbar puncture was therefore done. Surprisingly, the cerebrospinal fluid was turbid and no blood was present. Pus cells were abundant and gram-negative diplococci were present. (These

*Reprinted by permission from J. G. Dewan, and W. B. Spaulding. 1958. *The Organic Psychoses.* Toronto, University of Toronto Press, pages 99-100.

were later identified by culture as meningococci.) The patient was at once transferred to an isolation hospital where he died four days later in spite of intensive chemotherapy with sulfonamides.

This case of meningitis is unusual because physical abnormalities were delayed in appearance, the temperature was only moderately elevated, and the white blood count was normal. However, the history of sudden onset of severe headache and delirium should have immediately raised the question of serious intracranial disease necessitating prompt, special investigation.

CHRONIC BRAIN SYNDROME ASSOCIATED WITH CENTRAL NERVOUS SYSTEM SYPHILIS (GENERAL PARESIS)

A 42-year-old married man was admitted to a state hospital with a history of a change in personality having taken place during the preceding year. The first signs of abnormality were forgetfulness and irritability. His wife noticed that he would lay things down and in a very short time would forget where he had placed them. He became very dependent on her and did not seem able to do things without her assistance. He continued to work up to the time of his admission, but was inclined to sit about and brood and became very irritable and abusive if asked to do anything. At these times he would strike his family with anything he had in his hands. On one occasion he struck his wife in the face and she called her son to come home. When the son arrived, the patient picked up his shotgun and attempted to strike the son with it. Police were called and recommended that he be committed to hospital. One of the physicians who saw him before he was admitted noted that he had expansive ideas and talked of buying a new home.

The patient was the fifth in a family of ten children and his father worked as a farmer and fisherman. He attended school until the age of 14 and completed grade eight, following which he worked in several factories. At the age of 17 he enlisted in the army and spent four years in military service, being discharged as a private. He then worked as a fisherman up to the time of his admission to hospital. At the age of 22, he married a wife six years younger than himself and they had two children, both boys. His wife described him as a good

husband and father up to the onset of his sickness. He was apparently faithful to her and never in conflict with the law.

At the time of his admission to hospital, a physician who saw him briefly noted that he had some memory loss and a slight impediment of speech, and suggested that he might have general paresis. On physical examination there were none of the neurological signs that are often present in this disease, and blood serology was negative. However, examination of his spinal fluid showed findings characteristic of neurosyphilis (elevated protein, a positive serology, and a typical colloidal gold reaction). More extensive mental examination showed varying degrees of confusion, with disorientation for time and marked impairment of memory for recent events. At times he had auditory hallucinations and delusions of reference and persecution. He thought he overheard people saying that they were going to put poison in his food and make him insane. Sometimes he thought his wife and son were in another part of the building waiting for him. His emotional reaction was labile and at times he was jovial and euphoric, laughing for no apparent reason, while on other occasions he became apprehensive or angry and aggressive.

His admission to hospital occurred some years before penicillin became available, and he received standard treatment used at that time. During a period of two months he had a total of 50 artificially induced fever treatments during each of which his temperature was raised to 105 for five hours. He also received injections of bismuth and an arsenic compound over a span of several months. Such measures were usually successful in arresting the progress of a disease that led to progressive deterioration and death within a few years, in the absence of treatment. In about a third of such cases, fever therapy was followed by considerable recovery of intellectual function and a return to former employment, but this patient was not among the lucky ones. While the disease was arrested, a great deal of permanent brain damage remained, and he continued to require long-term mental hospital care. Fifteen years after admission he still showed marked impairment of memory and other intellectual functions. Most of the time his emotional reaction was apathetic or mildly euphoric, and he expressed many delusions of grandeur, believing that he was very wealthy and rewarding everyone who asked him with automobiles and checks for several million dollars. At times, however, he became acutely hallucinated, impulsive, and violent, and required repeated suturing for cuts on the hands and forearms caused by thrusting them through windows. Following the introduction of the major tranquilizing drugs, it became possible to control much of his disturbed behavior, but there was no essential change in the symptoms of his chronic brain syndrome.

ACUTE AND RESIDUAL CHRONIC BRAIN SYNDROMES, ASSOCIATED WITH ALCOHOLISM

A 65-year-old man was admitted to the neurology service of a general hospital with a history of confused and irrational behavior for the preceding three days. He was known to be a chronic alcoholic and had been admitted to the same hospital eight years previously after vomiting large quantities of blood, due to rupture of esophageal varices caused by cirrhosis of the liver. He had also been found at about that time to have mild diabetes, but the latter had been treated by his family physician and was under control by insulin at the time of his readmission to hospital. There was a positive family history of diabetes in two of his sisters and of alcoholism in one of his brothers. Both of his parents had lived to a ripe old age, and it was never established to what extent their behavior had predisposed him to alcoholism, but his poor relationship with a neurotic wife was felt to be partly the cause and partly the outcome of his excessive drinking. About two weeks prior to his readmission to hospital she had served him with divorce papers, and this had led him to increase his alcohol consumption which was now complicated by the additional use of unknown quantities of a barbiturate (Nembutal).

At the time of his admission, it was learned that he had stopped drinking four days previously, and the following day had taken nothing until bedtime, when he had two or more Nembutal capsules. Just before he went to bed that night he began tearing up the house and furniture. The following morning he was aggressive and confused, and his wife called an ambulance to take him to a nearby hospital, but he refused to go. By that afternoon, he was running around outdoors without any clothes on and a couple of men succeeded in taking him to the local hospital where his family physician gave him a sedative (chloral hydrate) and tranquilizer (Librium), intravenous fluids, and insulin. However, he remained extremely confused and irrational. Moreover, he was found to have a large bruise on the back of his head, which raised the possibility that his organic brain syndrome might have been caused or complicated by severe head injury. He was, therefore, referred to the neurology service of a large general hospital for further evaluation.

During the first few days after his admission there, he nearly died. His diabetes was under control, and he was given fluids intravenously, but he was incontinent and semicomatose most of the time. There were variable clinical findings on neurological examination, but his spinal fluid was negative, as were skull x-rays and angiographic studies of the brain arteries. When his condition had somewhat improved an electroencephalogram was obtained, which showed mild diffuse abnormality with no focal or clearly lateralizing findings. Air studies were also undertaken and showed brain atrophy with dilatation of the lateral ventricles. These findings and his mental confusion were now attributed to his chronic alcoholism, and he was transferred to the psychiatric service.

At that time, he was correctly oriented for person and place but not for time, and he didn't even know what year it was. His memory for recent events was extremely poor and he filled the gaps with confabulation. The only positive neurological findings were those of peripheral neuritis, involving weakness and diminished sensation in both arms and legs. He was, therefore, manifesting the clinical signs of Korsakow's syndrome: polyneuritis, amnesia, and confabulation. These signs are generally attributed to deficiency of thiamin and other members of the vitamin B complex, and he was therefore given large doses of these vitamins by injection. At first, he refused to cooperate with formal psychological testing of intellectual impairment, but his level of function is illustrated by his response when asked to do serial subtractions of seven from 100. His first three answers to this simple problem were, "93, 89, 72 . . .". He maintained that there was nothing the matter with him except that he must have been hit on the head, and he denied both alcoholism and marital discord. He had no recollection of his wife having served him with divorce papers. A Minnesota Multiphasic at this time showed marked elevations on scales 4, 8, and 9 (psychopathic deviate, schizoid, and manic).

Within the next couple of weeks, however, there was considerable improvement in intellectual function, and one month after his admission to hospital it was possible to undertake formal psychological testing of his residual intellectual impairment. He had been practicing as a lawyer, but he was able to obtain a full scale IQ of only 107, with a relative preservation of vocabulary and verbal skills but impairments in other areas. (His IQ on verbal subtests was 116, and on performance subtests 94.) He was able to obtain a Wechsler Memory Quotient of only 86, indicating that his memory was relatively more affected than some other intellectual functions. On other tests, he showed evidence of concrete thinking, perseveration, and confabulation. However, a second Minnesota Multiphasic Personality Inventory administered at this time showed all clinical scales within normal limits, the two high points being on scales 2 and 4 (depression and psychopathic deviate). He continued to receive large doses of vitamin B complex and to show further gradual slight improvement in intellectual functions. His wife was very solicitous and visited him frequently, and two months after his admission to the hospital he returned home to live with her, although he did not return to work in the law firm in which he had been practicing until shortly before his admission.

CHRONIC BRAIN SYNDROME ASSOCIATED WITH BRAIN TRAUMA

A farmer was admitted to the psychiatric unit of a general hospital for the first time at the age of 69, with a history of marked personality changes following a serious automobile accident ten months previously. He was a married man with three children, and prior to the accident he had been healthy, hard working, sociable, and easy to get along with. In the automobile acci-

dent, he sustained fractures of the arm and skull with severe concussion and brain damage, so that he was unconscious for ten days afterwards.

On awakening from the coma, he had no recollection of events that had occurred immediately preceding the accident, and he continued to have difficulty in remembering certain events that happened after he recovered consciousness. What his family noticed most, however, were the marked changes in his behavior that occurred after he left the hospital and returned home to his farm. They found him extremely irritable, easily angered, and unpredictable in his behavior. He drove the chickens as though they were cows, and made then so nervous that egg production dropped drastically. He fed the cows just enough for them to stay alive. He carefully locked up empty fuel drums which he had never done previously. He wrecked some of the farm machinery so badly that his son could not repair it. He would not talk to members of his family at all except to berate and swear at them, and he threatened his wife with physical violence many times. He blamed his family for poor crops which were really due to drought, and he frequently got up at night and slammed doors.

His unusual behavior had already improved considerably by the time he was admitted to the psychiatric unit, and throughout the three weeks he remained there, he was pleasant, cooperative, and sociable, with no evidence of depression or paranoid ideation. However, he did show mild disorientation for time and impairment of memory for recent events, which remained fairly constant throughout his hospital stay and did not show the marked changes that sometimes occur in certain types of organic brain syndrome. He obtained a full scale IQ of 92, but the Graham-Kendall test of memory for designs showed slightly impaired function.

Since such organic intellectual impairment may be precipitated or aggravated by a variety of brain syndromes, he underwent extensive medical and neurological investigations. His chest x-ray showed some enlargement of the heart and arteriosclerosis of the aorta, but there was little evidence of arteriosclerosis elsewhere in the body, and he had neither high blood pressure nor impaired function of the heart, kidneys, or liver. His spinal fluid was normal, but the electroencephalogram was mildly to moderately abnormal, with intermittent irregular slowing on both sides particularly in the temporal areas. The record was considered compatible with trauma. Skull x-rays and angiographic studies of the arteries of the brain were negative. Air studies of the brain, however, showed ventricular dilatation and widening of the gyri due to cerebral atrophy. This shrinkage of the brain tissue is common in senile psychoses and other forms of chronic organic brain syndrome, but the clear history of sudden changes in intellectual function and behavior following severe head injury implicated trauma as a major precipitating factor in this man's decompensation. He continued to improve after leaving hospital, and was able to remain at home with his family, helping his son with the farm work.

ACUTE BRAIN SYNDROME ASSOCIATED WITH CIRCULATORY DISTURBANCE: SEVERE POSTPARTUM HEMORRHAGE

A 35-year-old married woman was admitted to state hospital one month after giving birth to twins. Immediately prior to delivery she had developed severe edema in both legs and lower abdomen, but there was no other evidence of toxemia, and in hospital the fluid rapidly disappeared. She had had one child seven years previously and the birth of the twins was uneventful. She remained perfectly well until one week after the delivery when she suffered a sudden severe hemorrhage from a broken blood vessel in the wall of the vagina which was sutured within a few hours. She lost a great deal of blood and received three transfusions that day (a total of 1500 cc of whole blood) but the following day her hemoglobin was still only 6.4 gm per 100 cc and she received three further transfusions (another 1500 cc of whole blood).

Immediately following the hemorrhage her blood pressure dropped very low and her pulse became almost imperceptible. She was in a state of shock and was probably unconscious for a brief time. Even after transfusions her condition remained critical and she was given oxygen and stimulants. At first she was mute and completely unresponsive to questions. She was incontinent of urine and feces, and after she became more active she smeared her feces, swore to herself, and sang hymns. For awhile she seemed suspicious, but later became friendly and smiled superficially but was otherwise apathetic. At this time she was seen in consultation by a psychiatrist, who made the mistaken diagnosis of catatonic schizophrenia, which often develops for the first time within a couple of weeks following childbirth. Unfortunately, this led to her receiving five electroshock treatments, and there was some temporary increase in her mental confusion and regressive behavior, although it is unlikely that the treatments caused any lasting increase in the brain damage that was already present. In any event, the treatments were terminated, and three weeks after her hemorrhage she was transferred to the state hospital.

On arrival she was unresponsive, wide-eyed, and seemed bewildered. She seemed unable to find words, and stopped in the middle of sentences. She sat quietly on the ward, not mixing with other patients and taking no interest in ward activities. On one occasion when the physician visited her, she was expecting her husband, and when she realized he wasn't there, she seemed upset and began to talk rapidly in a direction away from the physician. It seemed that she might have been responding to auditory hallucinations, although she denied this. As her mental confusion decreased, however, it became clear that *her vision in both eyes was very poor,* and that she had signs of clear-cut organic intellectual impairment.

She said that her vision was fine before her recent childbirth, but that now everything was dark. She was barely able to recognize the colors of clothes worn by persons standing close to her, and was unable to read large printed letters. When given a watch or pipe to identify by touch, she was unable to say what it was, but picked out the correct name when various alternatives were presented. She was unable to identify numbers printed on the palm of her hand. She could not remember how to write letters or numbers. She was disoriented as to time and place, and was four years off in giving the date of her birth.

During the next two months, however, there was gradual progressive improvement in her intellectual functions, and at the end of this time she was able to return home with her husband. There was further gradual improvement, and six months after leaving the hospital her memory and other intellectual functions appeared to be within normal limits, and quite compatible with her previous grade eight education. Her vision also improved gradually, but six months after the hemorrhage she was still only able to count fingers held two feet from her eyes. She went through a normal grief reaction to her partial loss of vision, but made a good adjustment to her disability and was able to look after her home and family.

CHRONIC BRAIN SYNDROME ASSOCIATED WITH CEREBRAL ARTERIOSCLEROSIS

An 80-year-old widow was admitted to state hospital with a history of progressive mental deterioration during the preceding seven years, of several episodes of much more severe confusion than usual, and of four "strokes" that affected her speech and paralyzed her limbs in various degrees. For two years prior to admission she had required constant nursing care, and was living in private nursing homes, but they found it increasingly difficult to care for her. For several weeks prior to her admission, she had frequently been calling out loudly at all hours of the day or night for some member of her family, often for her mother or father, both of whom had been dead for many years.

She was the eldest of four children and both her parents had lived to a ripe old age. None of her family were known to have suffered from any form of mental disorder. She was raised on a farm in no apparent financial hardship, and left school at the age of 15 after completing grade eight. She then worked as a housekeeper until the time of her marriage at the age of 23. After 40 years of marriage, her husband died from heart trouble, and she subsequently lived with one or another of her four children. They described her as having been outgoing, sociable, and active but unduly serious, conscientious, and meticulous about the cleanliness of her house. She attended church regularly and did considerable church work in her spare time. She was over 70 when her children first noticed her becoming absent-minded and forgetful. She sometimes asked the same question two or three times within half an hour, and was unable to remember when she had last eaten. She became increasingly difficult to care for at home; she was constantly packing her bags and trying to leave

the house. By the age of 78 she required constant supervision, so that the family arranged her admission to nursing home. They subsequently noted that her mental confusion would vary greatly from one time to another, and it greatly increased following each of the four "strokes" which affected her speech and paralyzed her limbs temporarily.

On arrival in mental hospital there was muscular weakness in both legs, but no complete paralysis. There was systemic arteriosclerosis, but her blood pressure was not elevated (as it often is in patients with the same type of disorder). She was, however, confined to bed at first by her weakness. She was incontinent of urine and feces and required spoon feeding by the nurses. Her manner varied considerably from time to time, and although she was pleasant and cheerful much of the time, on occasion she became quite aggressive and hostile. She talked a great deal spontaneously, but her speech was frequently unintelligible. When the physician introduced himself to her for the first time, she replied, "I thought you were Dr. X. — I knew you were. I have seen you before. I have seen you 16 times, and that lawyer who is doctoring you has seen you 16 times, and he knows you are a liar and a lawyer and a devil." Her speech at this time also showed ideas of grandeur, for example, "There is none other like us in the township of X. There is none other that can tell it like we can tell it," and so on. She also tended to perseverate on a few topics which she repeated over and over again, and to confabulate stories and events to fill in the gaps in her memory. When first asked her name, she replied, "John," and she gave her age as 36. She recalled her birthday correctly, but was 20 years off in giving the year of her birth, which she gave in response to a question as to when she had been married. She said her husband was still living and that they had six children. She was disoriented as to time, place, and person.

She remained in hospital 18 months, and recovered from one attack of pneumonia, but died during a second attack some months later. At autopsy she was found to have marked cerebral arteriosclerosis, together with several small areas of softening in different parts of the brain, which had been caused by previous thrombosis and infarction.

ACUTE BRAIN SYNDROMES ASSOCIATED WITH CONVULSIVE DISORDER, SECONDARY TO INTRACRANIAL NEOPLASM, ASTROCYTOMA

This patient was admitted to the neurology service of a general hospital at the age of 30, immediately following the sudden onset of grand mal epileptic seizures. These were rapidly controlled by means of anticonvulsant medication (Dilantin), but on awakening she was profoundly confused, with visual illusions and hallucinations, and accompanying delusions. She thought that she was in prison and that she saw Jesus on the ceiling. She thought she saw arrows pointing to Heaven and a smaller arrow pointing to Hell. She felt that her daughter must be sacrificed for her own sins, and that she herself was going to die. Within a few days, her illusions and hallucinations ceased, but she remained disoriented with gross impairment of memory. It was not until two weeks after her admission that she became completely lucid, and from this time on she had no recollection of her experiences during the time she had been acutely psychotic. It was learned that one of her sisters had had several epileptic seizures during a childhood infection, but these had not returned since, and there was no other family history of epilepsy. Extensive neurological investigations were undertaken to establish the cause of the patient's seizures, but no definite evidence of brain disease was discovered, and she was discharged from hospital on a maintenance dose of anticonvulsant medication.

Shortly after the onset of seizures, she had been divorced from her husband who was an irresponsible alcoholic and failed to provide for her and her only child. The patient now returned to work as a high school teacher to support herself and her child, and she was able to work regularly for a year, but she then had a further series of uncontrollable seizures followed by another episode of delirium, and was again admitted to the neurology service of a general hospital. Again, her acute brain syndrome cleared rapidly, and no definite evidence was found of underlying brain disease, but it was considered necessary to increase her anticonvulsant medication. She now became very sleepy at times, and had particular difficulty in waking up in the morning so that she would sleep through the ringing of her alarm clock and was frequently late for work, which led to her being fired. A third series of extensive neurological investigations were essentially negative, apart from diffuse changes on the electroencephalogram that were compatible with primary or idiopathic epilepsy.

She remained home for a further year on anticonvulsant medication, and received financial assistance from Aid to Dependent Children. Again, she had several seizures and developed an acute psychotic episode, and she was admitted to hospital for her fourth series of extensive neurological tests. On this occasion, her spinal fluid was still negative, as were angiographic studies of the brain arteries, and air studies of the ventricular system. Her electroencephalogram still showed diffuse abnormality, but her skull x-rays now showed a faint calcification in the right frontal lobe area suggesting a neoplasm. It was considered that a slow-growing tumor such as an astrocytoma was the most likely cause of this shadow, and this was confirmed at operation, when as much of the tumor was removed as possible.

Immediately following the trauma of operation, she developed another acute psychotic episode and was transferred to the psychiatric service. She had frightening hallucinations and thought that the nursing staff were going to attack and kill her. She thought she heard her daughter screaming, and misidentified a male orderly as her former husband. Later, she stated, "My husband works around here. He is one who gets rid of all the people they decide should die. He kills them by whatever means he wishes to use." She expressed other delusions of persecution and at times was quite hostile and belligerent. However, her psychotic symptoms underwent spontaneous remission two and a half weeks after her surgery, and she subsequently had no recollection of the period of her acute brain syndrome. A Minnesota Multiphasic Personality Inventory obtained during her acute psychotic episode showed a marked elevation on scale 6 (paranoid), and following remission she showed a moderate elevation on scales 9 and 4 (manic and psychopathic deviate).

During the next two years, she remained at home on anticonvulsant medications and had only occasional epileptic seizures (about 4 to 6 a year). She had some difficulty with her memory, but was able to look after her home and child. She then developed severe constant headaches which were unrelieved by medication, together with increasing weakness of the whole left side of her body. She was readmitted to hospital for a further operation, and again as much of the tumor as possible was removed surgically. On this occasion, there was no psychotic episode following the operation, and three weeks later she was able to leave hospital. At this time she showed some impairment of memory, particularly for recent events, and some residual weakness of the left side of her body, so that it was recommended she be placed in a nursing home. As time went by, her mental confusion and partial paralysis increased, and she became increasingly lethargic up till her death a couple of years later.

ACUTE BRAIN SYNDROME ASSOCIATED WITH METABOLIC DISTURBANCE, HYPOTHYROIDISM

A 39-year-old married woman was admitted to the medical service of a general hospital with a history that during the previous four or five years she had been emotionally unstable, with periodic temper outbursts against her husband and only son. It was also learned that during the preceding two years, there had been a marked change in her physical appearance and health, with gradual increase in facial puffiness and general body weight, increasing dryness of the skin and hair, coarsening of her voice, intolerance of cold, chronic fatigue with a tendency to sleep 12 hours a day, constipation, shortness of breath and dizziness, and recent tendency toward swelling of the ankles. For about a year prior to admission, her menstrual periods had been very heavy and frequent, with a seven-day flow of up to ten pads per day every two to three weeks. She also complained of frequent frontal headaches and occasional attacks of nausea and vomiting.

She had not consulted a physician for several years previously, and neither her husband nor relatives had encouraged her to do so. It was learned that her parents had separated when she was young, that she had given birth to two illegitimate children before marriage, that she was currently married to an alcoholic, and that there had been considerable marital discord during the past few years. At the time of her admission to hospital, she believed that her husband was being unfaithful to her and was the father of another woman's child. She also expressed delusions of reference and persecution by other persons, felt that everyone was watching her and at one time believed that all her family were dead. At times, she was quite agitated and depressed, and she admitted to auditory hallucinations. She spoke to one of the nurse's aides as follows, "I hear all these voices—all day I have—but you are the first voice I believe—yes, I do—I believe I can trust you. You are pure. I used to be like you—a nurse's aide helping people."

On clinical examination, it was obvious that she was suffering from hypothyroidism or myxedema, and her Basal Metabolic Rate was found to be minus 32 percent. Her protein-bound iodine was 3.6 micrograms percent (normal range four to eight micrograms) and her radioactive iodine uptake was four percent in 24 hours (normal range ten to 40 percent). Her serum cholesterol was 257 mg percent (normal range 150 to 280 mg), and she was found to have a hypochronic anemia, with a hemoglobin of 9.9 gm percent (normal range for adult women 13 to 15), and a mean corpuscular hemoglobin concentration of 29 percent (normal range 33 to 38 percent). Her electrocardiogram showed diffuse low voltage and T wave changes, consistent with the impaired function of the heart that is found in advanced hypothyroidism. She was started on small doses of thyroid extract, which were gradually increased to a maintenance dose of three grains per day.

In view of her marked mental and behavioral abnormality, psychiatric consultation was obtained immediately, and three days after her admission she was transferred to the psychiatry service. At this time she had a disheveled appearance and was in a state of great anguish. She repeatedly rubbed her forehead and said it was a way of communicating with her relatives. Her speech was repetitive and stereotyped, with much blocking. She said she frequently heard the voices of her relatives and was observed to answer them. She appeared to have hallucinations of hearing, vision, smell, and taste and she expressed delusions of reference and influence. Her emotional response was very labile, fluctuating from tears to a hostile, resentful attitude. She was orientated as to time, place, and person, and her memory for remote events was fairly well preserved, but there was marked impairment of memory for recent events. She had a short attention span and difficulty in concentration. Her abstract thinking was impaired, and she gave many inappropriate responses, with a personalistic interpretation of proverbs.

Her Minnesota Multiphasic Personality Inventory was technically invalid due to a high F score, but the elevations on scales 6 and 4 (paranoid and psychopathic deviate) were very much higher than if she had answered the questions in a completely random fashion. On formal psychological testing of intellectual function, she obtained a full scale IQ of only 73 and a Memory Quotient of 61.5, with scores on other tests that strongly suggested brain damage. After two weeks of thyroid therapy, there had been a marked improvement in her clinical condition, and a Minnesota Multiphasic Personality Inventory showed all clinical scales within normal limits except for a minor elevation on scale 9 (manic). Formal reëvaluation of her intellectual functions was deferred until six weeks after her admission at which time she obtained the full scale IQ of 93 and a Memory Quotient of 78, but still showed some evidence of brain damage on other tests of intellectual function such as the Porteus Mazes and the Graham-Kendall memory for designs. Her anemia and heart function also improved greatly, and she lost more than ten pounds of superfluous weight. Her delusions and her paranoid ideation disappeared without administration of phenothiazines or other psychoactive drugs, and she received only supportive psychotherapy and milieu therapy. Two and a half months after her admission, she was able to leave hospital on a maintenance dose of three grains of thyroid a day, and was able to look after her home and family much more adequately than for some time previously.

CHRONIC BRAIN SYNDROME ASSOCIATED WITH SENILE BRAIN DISEASE

A 73-year-old widow was admitted to a state hospital with a five-year history of gradual progressive deterioration of memory, other intellectual functions, and social behavior.

She was born and brought up in Ireland and was one of 13 children. Both her parents and several of her siblings lived to a ripe old age, but it was not known whether any of them had developed similar signs of intellectual deterioration. She obtained an elementary school education and remained home on the family farm until her marriage at the age of 28. A few years later she and her husband immigrated and he was killed in an accident when she was 50 years old. After this she continued to live with one or another of her five children until the time of her admission to the hospital. Her children reported that she was a religious person, but on the whole she was easygoing, happy, and contented. She liked to keep the home clean and tidy, but was not an exceptionally meticulous housekeeper. There was no definite history of psychopathology until she was nearly 70 years old. Prior to this she was active and had an excellent memory. The first time her family noticed anything wrong with her was on an occasion when she was given some money to visit a friend in a nearby city, but lost the money. Shortly after this she set out from her home to visit one of the other children but failed to arrive, and the police were called to help find her. Following this she lost her former interest in reading, writing letters, knitting, and other pastimes. For a year preceding her admission to hospital she had not recognized her children most of the time, and her conversation was frequently unintelligible to them. She was able to eat without assistance, but for six months prior to admission she had to be dressed and undressed, and taken to the toilet to avoid incontinence.

On arrival in hospital her manner remained pleasant and cooperative, but she showed gross impairment in comprehension. At first she could not understand that the physician wished her to accompany him for interview, but when she grasped this she came readily and walked down the hall with her arm around his waist and tickled his ribs inappropriately. During the interview she sat quietly offering little spontaneous conversation, but making some verbal response to questions. However, her replies were often inappropriate and sometimes unintelligible. She misinterpreted everyday situations and when given her first bath in the hospital, she said, "I don't want to get in the boat; the current is too swift." On another occasion her spontaneous conversation ran as follows: "Well, it is not so bad in the morning. That girl was over and she was saying that there was nothing better than the bottom one and the cows and the calves were off and she was making out that (unintelligible), but I made out I never heard her. When they go out, you see, they don't bother taking the boxes. They just take everything with them." Her memory showed gross impairment for both recent and remote events. She was able to give her name correctly but when asked her age, she replied, "I am 21 to 22 anyway, every minute." She was unable to give her birthday, the year of her birth, or any other information about her previous life. She remained a pleasant, cooperative patient in hospital until the time of her death from pneumonia six months after admission.

CHRONIC BRAIN SYNDROME ASSOCIATED WITH ALZHEIMER'S DISEASE

A 40-year-old married woman was admitted to the psychiatric unit of a general hospital with a history that during the previous three years she had been increasingly forgetful and subject to crying spells for no apparent reason. She had gradually become unable to do her housework and was neglecting her personal appearance and hygiene. Of late, she had either sat around doing nothing, or had wandered around aimlessly without accomplishing anything.

On arrival at the hospital she was asked to sign her name, but the writing was completely illegible. She appeared apathetic and made no spontaneous conversation, but attempted to answer simple questions. When asked what was the matter with her, she said she was sick and had something wrong with her thinking. She was disorientated as to time and place, but was able to recognize members of her family. She showed marked impairment of memory for both recent and remote events, gave her age as 35 and was unable to give the year of her birth. She was too confused to participate in formal psychological testing of intellectual impairment.

Her family and personal history were unremarkable, and up till three years previously, she had apparently been active, cheerful, and sociable, with no evidence of psychiatric disorder. There was no history of alcoholism or exposure to other drugs known to cause organic brain syndromes. While in hospital, she was subjected to intensive medical and neurological investiga-tions. There was no evidence of impairment of function of the heart, kidneys, liver, or metabolism, and her spinal fluid was negative. The electroencephalogram showed marked abnormality characterized by diffuse slowing, which was considered compatible with generalized brain involvement. Skull x-rays and angiographic studies of the brain arteries were negative, but air studies showed slight ventricular dilatation and definite cortical atrophy. The diagnosis of Alzheimer's disease was made, and she was committed to a state hospital where she continued to regress until the time of her death a few years later.

ACUTE BRAIN SYNDROME ASSOCIATED WITH INTRACRANIAL NEOPLASM, MENINGIOMA*

This man, aged 41, was admitted to a psychiatric hospital on a magistrate's warrant. His wife said that his manner had been peculiar for the past year and that he had finally struck her. On the advice of the family physician it was decided that a charge of assault must be laid.

On admission he appeared confused, was unsteady, and acted as if intoxicated. His memory for recent events was poor. He was untidy and would urinate on the floor. At times he complained of severe headaches, sudden in onset and of short duration. As these symptoms were strongly suggestive of organic disease of the brain, the attending physician was especially interested in learning of the onset of the mental illness with reference to previous personality and other symptoms indicative of cerebral disease. His wife stated that he had always been a well-adjusted, cheerful person who had many friends. He had worked as a florist's assistant for some years until 14 months previously when he had a difference of opinion with his employer regarding overtime, the disagreement resulting in his discharge from the job. One wonders if this dispute with his employer, which was foreign to his usual behavior, might not indeed have been the first sign of the developing mental illness. He was unable to obtain work quickly, appeared

---

*Reprinted by permission from J. G. Dewan and W. B. Spaulding. 1958. *The Organic Psychoses.* Toronto, University of Toronto Press, pages 110-112.

despondent, and would sit by himself for long periods. His behavior frequently would be facetious, he would laugh for no apparent reason, and when questioned would make irrelevant remarks. Six months previous to admission, it was noticed by the patient's family that he had a squint and the patient complained of seeing double. His mental symptoms became more pronounced, he appeared sullen and preoccupied, sitting staring into space for long periods. In the four months previous to admission he often cried out, "my head, my head," and then would laugh. The last few weeks before coming into hospital the patient stated that he expected the Devil daily at 3 P.M. He thought people were outside the window. He complained of crawling feelings up the back of his head and misidentified relatives. It was only when he struck his wife that she finally consulted a physician and this led to his admission to hospital.

The significant findings were as follows: internal strabismus of the right eye, both pupils reacted to light but the right was sluggish, a questionable weakness of the right hand grip, a tendency to fall to the right side, marked papilledema bilaterally. All other findings were negative except for a one-plus sugar reaction in the urine.

The history and mental and physical findings were in keeping with a space-occupying lesion. At operation, a large meningioma (the size of an orange and weighing 105 gm) was present in the midline, growing from the longitudinal sinus and falx and impinging on both frontal lobes. The patient did not survive the operation.

Meningioma is the most favorable type of brain tumor to remove; an early careful examination might have indicated the organic lesion. In reviewing the case it would seem that there was a wealth of signs suggesting the likelihood of an underlying organic process involving the brain: striking personality changes a year prior to admission in a man of previous stable personality; six months before admission, strabismus and double vision; complaints of sudden, severe headaches of short duration; memory defect for recent events associated with a generally confused mental state with disorientation and deterioration of finer sensibilities and personal habits; and finally the neurological findings, particularly the advanced papilledema.

CHRONIC BRAIN SYNDROME ASSOCIATED WITH HUNTINGTON'S CHOREA

This woman first consulted a psychiatrist at the age of 36, at which time she was depressed over her deteriorating relationship with her husband, who had been drinking excessively ever since his return from military service four years previously. She had completed high school and worked as a stenographer until shortly after her marriage at the age of 25. She had no previous sexual experience and felt guilty over premarital sexual relations with her husband, but she did not develop frigidity until the latter part of their marriage when he was a confirmed alcoholic. It was not until shortly after their marriage that she discovered he had been married previously, and that his first wife had committed suicide six months before he met the patient. At first, he had seemed considerate and a good provider, but on his return from military service he had become increasingly irresponsible.

She improved with supportive psychotherapy, but had several further minor episodes of depression during the next four years, at whict time she divorced her husband and continued to look after their three children with financial assistance from Aid to Dependent Children. Two years following her divorce, she again consulted a psychiatrist with symptoms of anxiety and depression that were considered of neurotic origin and intensity. She received further supportive psychotherapy with supplementary tranquilizing medication (meprobamate), and after three months she felt sufficiently improved to terminate therapy.

During the next four years, however, she developed involuntary movements of her arms and legs, which became increasingly severe and made it increasingly difficult for her to look after her home and children. She also started to become forgetful and neglected her own personal appearance and hygiene. She was now 46 years old, and the Welfare Department referred her to a psychiatrist, who recognized that she was probably suffering from Huntington's chorea and referred her to a neurologist for further evaluation. This neurologist confirmed the diagnosis and informed the patient that she had an incurable brain disease and shouldn't work or drive a car. He also told her that the disease would probably affect her children and that they should be sterilized. Not surprisingly, she reacted to this news with depression and shortly afterwards was admitted for the first time to a state hospital.

With antidepressive medication her mood improved, and after a few months she was placed in a boarding home where she could receive simple nursing care. The uncontrollable movements in her limbs increased, and she had increasing difficulty with her memory, particularly for recent events. She also became severely depressed, lost appetite and weight, and attempted suicide by drinking a cleaning fluid. She was readmitted to a state hospital and at this time she was found to be grossly delusional, believing that she had killed her children and a number of other persons, and that there were reports about her in the newspapers. She said her body was filled with germs and asked that people avoid touching her because if they did so they would die. She showed considerable impairment of intelligence, memory, and orientation, and increasing incoordination and weakness up till the time of her death a few years later.

Huntington's chorea occasionally arises as a new mutation in individuals whose parents have both been unaffected by the disease, but there is usually a history that one of the parents was similarly affected and in this case it was the patient's father. Prior to the onset of the disease, he had worked regularly as a railroad brakeman, but as the condition progressively affected his coordination and judgment, he was relegated to jobs of diminishing responsibility and then remained at home unemployed until his admission to a state hospital and death at the age of 54. Even prior to the father's sickness, it appeared that the patient's mother had been the dominant parent, and she was reported to have been strict and critical. The mother would strap the boys and shout at the girls so that the patient was afraid of her. In retrospect, it appears that the patient's predisposition to anxiety and depression was largely related to her childhood relationship with her mother. The patient was the second of five children, having three brothers and one sister. At the time of her last admission to state hospital, it was learned that one of these brothers was suffering from some form of "nervous disability," and that her youngest sister had already been admitted to another state hospital with a diagnosis of Huntington's chorea.

DEVELOPMENT AND ETIOLOGY

During the latter part of the nineteenth century, a number of pathologists and bacteriologists undertook extensive studies of the brains of persons who had died while showing evidence of mental and behavioral abnormality. Such studies have been extended during the present century by techniques that have made it possible to examine brain structure and function in persons who are still living. A great deal is now known concerning the tissue pathology and immediate or precipitating factors responsible for the development of acute and chronic brain syndromes.

The classification of these organic brain syndromes is based partly on established knowledge concerning etiology, and partly on the nature of the pathological process observed. Among the causal factors that can frequently be identified are physical, chemical, and biological agents of disease (i.e., trauma, intoxication, and infection) and biological deprivations (i.e., deficiency of oxygen, vitamins, or hormones.) Among the pathological processes for which causation is *not* clearly established are epilepsy, brain tumors, cerebral arteriosclerosis and the degenerative disorders responsible for senile and presenile psychoses. Huntington's chorea is established as due to inheritance of a single dominant autosomal gene, and certain other diseases of the brain are also hereditary, but details of the causal mechanisms involved are lacking.

Kety reviewed an interesting series of studies concerning blood flow through the brain and utilization of oxygen by the brain in normal subjects, schizophrenics, and patients with various organic brain syndromes. In patients with cerebral arteriosclerosis, and also in patients in coma due to raised intracranial pressure caused by brain tumors, there was (1) increased resistance to blood flow through the brain arteries; (2) reduced blood flow through the brain; (3) reduced consumption of oxygen by the brain. In other patients who were comatose due to either hyperglycemia (in uncontrolled diabetes) or hypoglycemia (by large doses of insulin), there was (1) no appreciable change in resistance to blood flow through brain arteries; (2) slightly increased blood flow through the brain; (3) marked reduction of oxygen consumption by the brain.

Different degrees of brain damage and behavioral abnormality may result from exposure to different degrees of a pathogenic agency or process. However, individual differences in vulnerability to identical degrees of stress have been demonstrated in experimental animals and human subjects. Windle reported changes in brain structure, memory, and learning among guinea pigs subjected to prolonged anoxia in a chamber where the atmospheric pressure could be reduced to specified levels. Such changes occurred in all animals subjected to a simulated altitude of 30,000 feet for 200 hours or more, but in only some of the animals receiving 100 to 150 hours of the same degree of decompression.

MacFarland reviewed an extensive series of observations on impairment of visual perception, intellectual functions, and behavior among humans subjected to varying degrees of anoxia. While a given degree of anoxia produced many similar changes in different individuals, it was also possible to recognize individual differences in behavioral response related to the predominant personality characteristics of the subjects. Similarly, it has been noted that sleep deprivation and administration of psychotomimetic drugs are followed by some similar and some dissimilar manifestations in different subjects (Chapter 6).

Although the *precipitating causes* of many organic brain syndromes are well recognized, these factors may be only necessary causes and not sufficient in themselves to produce all the abnormal behavior observed. Exposure to the tubercle bacillus is a necessary but not sufficient cause for the development of clinical signs of tuberculosis. Chronic syphilis is a necessary but not sufficient cause for the involvement of the brain that occurs in general paresis. Prolonged intake of alcohol and associated dietary deficiencies are necessary but not sufficient causes for the development of certain alcoholic psychoses.

It appears, then, that a number of *predisposing causes* may be necessary, in addition to the known precipitating causes, in order to permit the development of the complex intellectual and behavioral manifestations of organic brain syndromes. For convenience, these predisposing factors may be divided into three broad categories: (1) general bodily susceptibility or immunity to a specific agent (e.g., infection or intoxication), which is a function of both hereditary predisposition and lifelong environmental influence; (2) specific vulnerability of the brain to react to various insults with intellectual impairment, just as it may react to certain stimuli with epileptic seizures (the seizure threshold varying greatly in different individuals); (3) specific vulnerability of the individual to react to various biological or psychological stresses with specific forms of functional psychopathology. We shall now review some of the evidence relating to predisposition.

The increased frequency of *infectious disease* among close relatives of affected individuals is usually attributable to direct transmission from the affected person, or common exposure to the same source of infection. However, there is some indication that members of certain families are more vulnerable to developing certain infections following exposure than are members of other families. A series of twin studies has been reported in which the monozygotic cotwins were more frequently affected than the dizygotic cotwins of patients with various types of infectious disease. Since twins of the same sex frequently live in much closer proximity to

TABLE 24-3. Estimated Concordance Rates in Monozygotic and Dizygotic Cotwins of Epileptic Twins

TYPE OF EPILEPSY AND INVESTIGATOR	APPARENT ZYGOSITY OF TWINS	NUMBER OF PAIRS	ESTIMATED CONCORDANCE RATE (PER CENT)	HERITABILITY $H = \dfrac{CMZ - CDZ}{100 - CDZ}$
Unspecified Rosanoff et al., 1934	(MZ (DZ	23 84	70) 24)	0.61
Idiopathic Conrad, 1935	(MZ (DZ	22 97	86) 4)	0.85
Symptomatic Conrad, 1935	(MZ (DZ	8 34	13) 0)	0.13
Without brain damage (idiopathic) Lennox and Jolly, 1954	(MZ (DZ	51 47	88) 13)	0.86
With brain damage (symptomatic) Lennox and Jolly, 1954	(MZ (DZ	26 49	35) 12)	0.26

each other than twins of different sexes, such comparisons should be made between monozygotic twins and dizygotic twins of the same sex, and these comparisons are unfortunately lacking. Moreover, the determination of zygosity should have been undertaken with modern serological techniques; other pitfalls of twin studies have been discussed earlier, so that these results cannot be regarded as very convincing.

The twin studies of *epilepsy* appear somewhat more meaningful, even though comparisons were not made with respect to dizygotic twins of the same sex and zygosity determination did not involve modern serological techniques. These studies are summarized in Table 24-3, and may be considered somewhat more acceptable, since two different studies resulted in comparable findings that were different in each instance for two broad categories of epilepsy. Conrad found a high frequency of concordance among monozygotic twins and a low frequency of concordance among dizygotic twins with idiopathic epilepsy, together with minimal concordance among both groups of twins with epilepsy that was symptomatic of other recognized brain disease. Similarly, Lennox and Jolly

recorded a high frequency of concordance among monozygotic twins who had epilepsy without brain damage, and low frequencies of concordance among the other three groups of twins. In both of these studies, Holzinger's index of heritability is relatively high in the case of epilepsy that appears to be primary or idiopathic, but relatively low in the case of epilepsy that appears to be secondary or symptomatic of other brain disease. These findings are in keeping with clinical experience that anyone may have an epileptic seizure under sufficient provocation, that the seizure threshold varies somewhat from one person to another (and in the same individual from time to time), and that persons with primary or idiopathic epilepsy have consistently low seizure thresholds under various stimuli. It also appears probable that there is considerable individual variation in the tendency to develop confusional psychosis following a series of epileptic seizures. One factor increasing vulnerability to confusion is advancing age, and we find that elderly patients tend to become much more confused following a short course of electroshock treatments than do young adults following a longer course of the same treatments.

A few rare forms of chronic brain

disease have been found to follow a simple pattern of Mendelian inheritance. The best known of these is *Huntington's chorea*, which is transmitted by a single dominant autosomal gene and may therefore be expected to occur in about 50 percent of the parents, 50 percent of the siblings of both sexes, and 50 percent of the children of affected individuals (see Figure 24-1).

The very much more common degenerations of the brain associated with *cerebral arteriosclerosis and senile cortical atrophy* do not follow any simple Mendelian pattern of inheritance, but are found more frequently among the relatives of affected individuals than among the general population and may be partly attributable to the cumulative effects of multiple minor genes. In a study of 33 pairs of monozygotic and 75 pairs of dizygotic twins, at least one member of whom had developed a senile psychosis, Kallmann reported an age-corrected concordance rate of 43 percent among the MZ twins and only seven percent among the DZ twins, so that the Holzinger index of heritability for this series is about 0.39. With the usual reservations in mind regarding twin studies, the findings suggest a considerable heritable component, and are compatible with the hypothesis that the latter is polygenic in nature.

There is some indication that *individuals of limited intelligence and socioeconomic status* are more likely to develop organic brain syndromes than other members of the general population. Thus, Hollingshead and Redlich found frequencies of both senile psychosis and other organic psychoses inversely related to socioeconomic status. However, it is by no means clear whether the higher frequencies observed among individuals of limited socioeconomic status are due to higher frequencies of exposure, greater vulnerability to similar exposures, or less adequate medical treatment of individuals who have developed the same disorder. It has long been known that rates of mortality from many accidents and illnesses are higher throughout childhood and young adult life among those of limited socioeconomic status. Although differences in exposure and medical treatment may be partly responsible, it is probable that differences in general and specific vulnerability are also contributory.

On theoretical grounds, it is likely

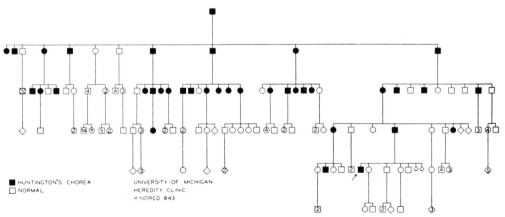

Figure 24–1. "A pedigree of Huntington's chorea. A single dominant autosomal gene is responsible for the onset at about age thirty to forty of the degeneration of various areas in the brain. In many pedigrees there appears to be a deficiency of affected persons because of the death of carriers of the gene before the age of onset." (Reprinted by permission from Neel, J. V., and Schull, W. J. 1954. *Human Heredity.* Chicago, The University of Chicago Press. Copyright © 1954, the University of Chicago.)

that the same degree of intellectual impairment will result in more complete decompensation of an individual with a limited intellectual endowment to start with. For example, a 25 percent reduction in intelligence would bring an IQ of 120 down to 90, which is still within the average range, but would bring an IQ of 80 down to 60, which is in the defective range. Moreover, the latter individual would probably be less protected by his family or economic circumstances from the social consequences of his partial incapacity. There is also evidence that those of limited intelligence and socioeconomic status are more likely to develop various forms of functional psychopathology, and we have seen that latent symptoms of this nature may be released by any organic brain syndrome.

Certain individuals develop *organic brain syndromes secondary to preëxisting functional psychiatric disorders.* Functional psychoses are apt to lead to deprivation of sleep and essential vitamins. The depressed patient may develop an organic brain syndrome from inhalation of carbon monoxide in an unsuccessful suicidal attempt. The sociopath may be more vulnerable to head injury, and the chronic alcoholic exposes himself to various factors that may contribute to the development of an organic brain syndrome. Nevertheless, a considerable proportion of patients with brain syndromes have shown no such preëxisting vulnerability, and Dewan and Spaulding remarked as follows, "A history relatively free of emotional instability in spite of considerable psychological and social stress through the years should immediately suggest the possibility of an organic factor operating in the production of the psychosis. On the other hand, a long history of emotional upsets does not automatically rule out the need to consider a physical element in the present breakdown."

There are no adequate statistics on the frequency with which organic brain syndromes complicate the illnesses of all patients treated in a given general hospital, but the relatively few studies undertaken by psychiatrists and psychologists suggest a considerably higher frequency than is generally recognized by the physicians and surgeons responsible for the patients' care (e.g., Zwerling et al.). Among patients admitted to mental hospitals, the proportion of patients with brain syndromes will depend upon such factors as the frequency of these disorders in the general population, the geographical proximity of the mental hospital to centers of population, the attitude of the public and general physicians toward the mental hospital, and the admitting policy of the mental hospital administration with respect to alcoholic psychoses and other brain syndromes.

There is a relatively high frequency of acute brain syndromes in *early childhood* associated with high fever, and in *old age* associated with the presence of degenerative changes and hitherto unrecognized mild chronic brain syndromes. At these extremes of life the *sex distribution* does not appear to differ greatly, but during the intermediate period of adult life, each sex is more vulnerable to certain hazards than the other. There is, for example, a much higher frequency of alcoholic psychoses and of psychoses resulting from industrial poisons among men, whereas women have a relatively higher frequency of brain syndromes associated with hypothyroidism. Women are also subject to brain disorders complicating pregnancy and childbirth, although the majority of postpartum psychoses are not organic brain syndromes but are affective or schizophrenic disorders.

There is considerable variation in the frequency of illnesses and intoxications responsible for brain syndromes from one geographical area to another, depending on such factors as the development of industry, sanitation, and other public health programs, the general level of nutrition, and the nature of parasitic infestations in the area. Acute and chronic brain syndromes associated with malnutrition, malaria, and trypanosomiasis are still prevalent in certain underdeveloped countries, whereas those associated with alcoholism and industrial poisons are more characteristic of countries that are technologically developed. Within these more developed countries, there is a relationship between the frequency of brain syndromes and socioeconomic status which has already been discussed.

It may therefore be concluded that intellectual and behavioral abnormality due to brain disorders depends on a variety of predisposing factors including heredity, intellectual capacity, the capacity for developing immunity to infections, resistance to the effects of vitamin deficiencies, current nutritional status, and the entire experiential background of the individual — biological, psychological, and sociocultural. The relative significance of these variables and their pattern of interaction still remains to be elucidated for many of the disorders that affect man's body, including those that have an effect upon his brain, mind, emotions, and behavior.

TREATMENT

Treatment of the wide variety of bodily diseases and intoxications that cause acute brain syndromes is too detailed for comprehensive discussion here, and is more appropriate to textbooks of medicine, neurology, and neurosurgery. For the purposes of the present chapter, such treatment may be considered as either *specific* (directed toward an established causative agent) or *supportive* (symptomatic or general measures for use in various forms of delirium or stupor).

Among the specific treatments that may be indicated are various antibiotic drugs for the elimination of infecting organisms, administration of drugs designed to help the body eliminate toxic materials present in excess (e.g., sodium chloride for bromide intoxication), brain surgery to remove a tumor or the pressure from a blood clot or fractured skull, drugs or procedures designed to increase the blood supply to the brain, administration of anticonvulsant medication, and specific measures for the correction of metabolic disorders which include the administration of fluids, minerals, vitamins, and hormones.

Supportive or general symptomatic treatment includes a variety of measures designed to minimize confusion, agitation, fever, dehydration, and malnutrition. It has long been recommended that a patient with an acute brain syndrome be treated in a quiet, cool room with constant subdued lighting (neither too bright nor total darkness), and that nursing attendants be at a minimum number, both diminishing confusion and facilitating isolation precautions in the case of infectious diseases. The patient requires sufficient supervision to protect him from self-injury, and may also require some restraint to prevent excessive agitation and aggression against others. Nowadays, restraint is usually accomplished by means of tranquilizing drugs. Phenothiazines are particularly effective, and may be given intramuscularly or intravenously for rapid action. Other supportive measures that receive consideration in all cases include the reduction of excessive fever, the maintenance of hydration, administration of supplementary vitamins (particularly members of the vitamin B complex), and attending to bowel and bladder functions and care of the skin in bed patients.

Chronic brain syndromes are those that have failed to resolve completely in spite of all currently available forms of medical and surgical treatment. In such cases, it will be necessary to reach a decision regarding the most appropriate long-term management of the patient:

whether this can be accomplished at home, or whether he requires care in a nursing home or mental hospital. In general, the patient with a chronic brain syndrome should receive a minimum of medications, particularly sedatives, since these may only increase symptoms of intellectual impairment and depression. If depression or other functional manifestations are prominent, they may be relieved by use of antidepressive or tranquilizing drugs, or occasionally by a short course of electroshock treatments. However, shock treatments tend to increase symptoms of intellectual impairment and are therefore generally contraindicated. By far the major part of the management of patients with chronic brain syndromes therefore consists of nursing care, with social, milieu, and occupational therapy.

SELECTED REFERENCES

American Psychiatric Association. 1952. *Diagnostic and Statistical Manual for Mental Disorders.* Washington, D.C., American Psychiatric Association.

Asher, R. 1949. Myxoedematous madness. British Medical Journal 2, 555-562.

Bigelow, N., Roizin, L., and Kaufman, M. A. 1959. Psychoses with Huntington's chorea. In *American Handbook of Psychiatry*, ed. S. Arieti. New York, Basic Books, Inc., Vol. 2, ch. 61.

Blachly, P. H., and Starr, A. 1964. Post-cardiotomy delirium. American Journal of Psychiatry 121, 371-375.

Brill, H. 1959. Postencephalitic psychiatric conditions. In *American Handbook of Psychiatry*, ed. S. Arieti. New York, Basic Books, Inc., Vol. 2, ch. 56.

Brosin, H. W. 1959. Psychiatric conditions following head injury. In *American Handbook of Psychiatry*, ed. S. Arieti. New York, Basic Books, Inc., Vol. 2, ch. 57.

Bruetsch, W. L. 1952. Mental disorders arising from organic disease. In *The Biology of Mental Health and Disease*. New York, Hoeber Medical Division, Harper & Row, Publishers, Inc., pp. 303-322.

Bruetsch, W. L. 1959. Neurosyphilitic conditions. In *American Handbook of Psychiatry*, ed. S. Arieti. New York, Basic Books, Inc., Vol. 2, ch. 50.

Connell, P. H. 1956. *Amphetamine Psychosis.* London, Chapman and Hall, Ltd., Maudsley Monograph No. 5.

Conrad, K. 1935. Erbanlage und Epilepsie. Z. ges. Neurol. Psychiat. *153*, 271-326.

Dewan, J. G., and Spaulding, W. B. 1958. *The Organic Psychoses.* Toronto, University of Toronto Press.

Ebaugh, F. G., and Tiffany, W. J., Jr. 1959. Infective-exhaustive psychoses. In *American Handbook of Psychiatry*, ed. S. Arieti. New York, Basic Books, Inc. Vol. 2, ch. 60.

Engel, G. L., and Romano, J. 1959. Delirium—a syndrome of cerebral insufficiency. Journal of Chronic Diseases 9, 260-277.

Ferraro, A. 1959. Senile psychoses, presenile psychoses, and psychoses with cerebral arteriosclerosis. In *American Handbook of Psychiatry*, ed. S. Arieti. New York, Basic Books, Inc. Vol. 2, ch. 51-53.

Gillies, H. 1956. Acute delirious states. British Medical Journal *1*, 623-625.

Gregory, I. 1955. The role of nicotinic acid (niacin) in mental health and disease. Journal of Mental Science *101*, 85-109.

Gregory, I. 1956. Mental disorder associated with thyroid dysfunction. Canadian Medical Association Journal *75*, 489-492.

Hare, E. H. 1959. The origin and spread of dementia paralytica. Journal of Mental Science *105*, 594-626.

Henderson, D., and Batchelor, I. R. C. 1962. *Henderson and Gillespie's Textbook of Psychiatry*, 9th edition. London, Oxford University Press, ch. 15 and 16.

Hoch, P. H., and Zubin, J., eds. 1961. *Psychopathology of Aging.* Grune & Stratton, Inc.

Hollingshead, A. B., and Redlich, F. C. 1958. *Social Class and Mental Illness.* New York, John Wiley & Sons, Inc. p. 234.

Inouye, E. 1960. Observations on forty twin index cases with chronic epilepsy and their co-twins. Journal of Nervous and Mental Disease *130*, 401-416.

Jarvie, H. F., and Hood, M. C. 1952. Acute delirious mania. American Journal of Psychiatry *108*, 758-763.

Kaelbling, R., and Patterson, R. M. 1966. *Eclectic Psychiatry.* Springfield, Illinois, Charles C Thomas, Publisher, ch. 18.

Kalinowsky, L. B. 1958. Withdrawal convulsions and withdrawal psychoses. In *Problems of Addiction and Habituation*, ed. P. H. Hoch and J. Zubin. New York, Grune & Stratton, pp. 49-56.

Kallmann, F. J. 1950. The genetics of psychoses: an analysis of 1232 twin index families. In Congrès international de psychiatrie, Paris, 1950. VI. Psychiatrie Sociale, Génétique et Eugénique. Paris, Hermann, pp. 1-27.

Kety, S. S. 1952. Cerebral circulation and metabolism. In *The Biology of Mental Health and Disease*, New York, Hoeber Medical Division, Harper & Row, Publishers, Inc., pp. 20-31.

Kral, V. A. 1955. Postischemic dementia. Journal of Nervous and Mental Disease *122*, 83-88.

Kral, V. A., Berg, I., and Pivnicki, D. 1960. Carbon monoxide dementia: a case report. Comprehensive Psychiatry *1*, 164-173.

Larsson, T., Sjogren, T., and Jacobson, G. 1963. Senile dementia. A clinical socio-medical, and genetic study. Acta Psychiatrica Scandinavica *39*, Supplementum 167.

Lennox, W. G., and Jolly, D. H. 1954. Seizures, brain waves and intelligence tests of epileptic twins. In *Genetics and the Inheritance of Integrated Neurological and Psychiatric Patterns*. Baltimore, The Williams & Wilkins, Co., Research Publications, Association for Research in Nervous and Mental Disease *33*, 325-345.

Levin, M. 1959. Toxic psychoses. In *American Handbook of Psychiatry*, ed. S. Arieti. New York, Basic Books, Inc., Vol. 2, ch. 59.

Lowy, F. 1965. The neuropsychiatric complications of viral hepatitis. Canadian Medical Association Journal *92*, 237-239.

MacFarland, R. A. 1952. Anoxia: its effects on the physiology and biochemistry on the brain and on behavior. In *The Biology of Mental Health and Disease*. New York, Hoeber Medical Division, Harper & Row, Publishers, Inc., pp. 335-355.

Mayer-Gross, W., Slater, E., and Roth, M. 1960. *Clinical Psychiatry*, 2nd edition. Baltimore, The Williams & Wilkins Co., ch. 7-11.

Meier, M. J., and French, L. A. 1965. Some personality correlates of unilateral and bilateral EEG abnormalities in psychomotor epileptics. Journal of Clinical Psychology *21*, 3-9.

Meyer, V. 1961. Psychological effects of brain damage. In *Handbook of Abnormal Psychology*, ed. H. J. Eysenck. New York, Basic Books, Inc., pp. 529-565.

Mulder, D. W. 1959. Psychoses with brain tumors and other chronic neurologic disorders. In *American Handbook of Psychiatry*, ed. S. Arieti. New York, Basic Books, Inc., Vol. 2, Ch. 55.

Kolb, L. C. 1968. *Noyes' Modern Clinical Psychiatry*, 7th edition. Philadelphia, W. B. Saunders Co., ch. 8-20.

Redlich, F. C., and Freedman, D. X. 1966. *The Theory and Practice of Psychiatry*. New York, Basic Books, Inc., ch. 16-18, 21, and 23.

Rome, H. P., and Robinson, D. B. 1959. Psychiatric conditions associated with metabolic, endocrine and nutritional disorders. In *American Handbook of Psychiatry*, ed. S. Arieti. New York, Basic Books, Inc., Vol. 2, ch. 62.

Simon, A., and Cahan, R. B. 1963. The acute brain syndrome in geriatric patients. In *Acute Psychotic Reaction*, ed. W. M. Mendel and L. J. Epstein. Washington, D. C., American Psychiatric Association, Psychiatric Reports No. 16, pp. 8-21.

Sjogren, T., Sjogren, H., and Lindgren, A. G. H. 1952. Morbus Alzheimer and Morbus Pick: A genetic, clinical and pathoanatomical study. Acta Psychiatrica et Neurologica Scandinavica, Supplementum 82.

Smith, A. D. M. 1960. Megaloblastic madness. British Medical Journal *2*, 1840-1845.

Spaulding, W. B., and Yendt, E. R. 1964. Prolonged vitamin D intoxication in a patient with hypoparathyroidism. Canadian Medical Association Journal *90*, 1049-1054.

Strauss, H. 1959. Epileptic disorders. In *American Handbook of Psychiatry*, ed. S. Arieti. New York, Basic Books, Inc., Vol. 2, ch. 54.

Thompson, G. N. 1959. Acute and chronic alcoholic conditions. In *American Handbook of Psychiatry*, ed. S. Arieti. New York, Basic Books, Inc., Vol. 2, ch. 58.

Wechsler, I. 1963. *Clinical Neurology*, 9th edition, Philadelphia, W. B. Saunders Co.

Windle, W. F. 1952. Anoxia: its effect on structure of the brain. In *The Biology of Mental Health and Disease*. New York, Hoeber Medical Division, Harper & Row, Publishers, Inc., pp. 327-334.

Young, G. G., Simson, C. B., and Frohman, C. E. 1961. Clinical and biochemical studies of an amphetamine withdrawal psychosis. Journal of Nervous and Mental Disease *132*, 234-238.

Zwerling, I., et al. 1955. Personality disorder and relationships of emotion to surgical illness in 200 surgical patients. American Journal of Psychiatry *112*, 270.

There are three kinds of brains; one understands of itself, another can be taught to understand, and the third can neither understand of itself nor be taught to understand.

Niccolo Machiavelli

Mental Retardation

Society has long recognized the slow-learning child who remains intellectually subnormal throughout life as being different from the individual whose intellectual development was normal but who subsequently becomes mentally deranged or insane. In fourteenth-century England there existed, for the management of an idiot or "born fool" (fatuus naturalis) and of his estate, legislation that distinguished between such individuals and the insane whose mental condition could fluctuate from time to time. It was not until the nineteenth century, however, that social concern and humane reform led to the widespread establishment of separate facilities for the institutional care of the mentally retarded and mentally ill.

Mental retardation is a generic term that has been applied to all degrees of intellectual subnormality present from birth or early childhood, and it has gradually come to replace the many other generic terms applied to such individuals, which include *mental deficiency, mental subnormality, amentia* and *oligophrenia*. During the early years of the present century, the development and application of standardized intelligence tests was associated with the separation of mental deficiency or retardation into three broad categories, according to the degree of subnormality present. The traditional, but now obsolescent, terms applied to these three degrees of retardation were (1) *idiot*, having an IQ of 0 to 19 and a maximum intellectual function in adult life equivalent to that of the average two-year-old child; (2) *imbecile*, having an IQ of 20 to 49 and a maximum intellectual function in adult life equivalent to that of the average seven-year-old child; (3) *moron* or *feeble-minded*, having an IQ of 50 to 69 and a maximum intellectual function in adult life equivalent to that of the average 12-year-old child.

Individuals with mental retardation are not all equally likely to be admitted to institutions, or to remain in such institutions after they have been admitted. Those with severe degrees of retardation constitute a smaller proportion of the total population than do those with mild degrees of retardation, but a much higher proportion of the mentally retarded population resident in institutions. Thus, it has been estimated that the *profoundly* retarded (idiots) number only one-tenth percent of the total population, three and one-half percent of all the mentally retarded, but 30 percent of the institutionalized retarded. *Severely* and *moderately* retarded individuals (imbeciles) number about three-tenths percent of the total population, 11 percent of the mentally retarded and 50 per cent of the total institutionalized retarded. The *mildly* retarded (morons or feeble-minded) number somewhat less than three percent of the total population, 85 percent of all mentally retarded, but only 20 percent of the institutional population of retarded individuals. These comparisons, based

TABLE 25–1. Traditional Categories of Mental Retardation,
with Percentage Representation in Population and in Institutions

TRADITIONAL CATEGORY EQUIVALENT MODERN CATEGORIES	IDIOT (PROFOUNDLY RETARDED)	IMBECILE (SEVERELY AND MODERATELY RETARDED)	MORON OR FEEBLEMINDED (MILDLY RETARDED)
IQ scores	0.0–19.0	20.0–49.0	50.0–69.0
Adult mental age in years	0.0– 2.0	3.0– 7.0	8.0–12.0
Percent of total population	0.1	0.3	3.0
Percent of retarded population	3.5	11.0	85.0
Percent of institutionalized retarded population	30.0	50.0	20.0

on traditional definitions in terms of IQ and adult mental age, are summarized in Table 25-1.

During the first half of the present century, etiological studies led to the widespread medical adoption of a simple dichotomy in classifying mental deficiency or retardation. The basis for this division of mental retardation into *two major groups* was the presence or absence of organic brain pathology. Those with recognizable brain disease were frequently described as having *"pathological"* or *"clinical"* mental deficiency, and it was found that they generally tended to be more severely retarded (i.e., at the idiot or imbecile level of intellectual function) than those without brain lesions. The group without recognizable brain pathology were frequently described as having *"physiological," "subcultural,"* or *"residual aclinical"* mental deficiency, were generally found to be mildly retarded (in the moron range of intellectual function) and hence much more numerous than those with gross brain disease.

Statistical analysis of the distribution of intelligence in the general population provides confirmation regarding the existence of these two major categories of mental retardation. The assumption has been made that tested intelligence is distributed in the general population according to the normal or Gaussian curve with a mean IQ of 100 and a standard deviation of approximately 15. Comparisons between the theoretically expected frequencies of various IQ scores and the observed IQ scores obtained on testing several large samples have indicated close correspondence except at the extreme lower end of the intelligence scale. In this lower range of tested intelligence there is an excess of observed over expected frequencies, particularly at the imbecile and idiot levels of intelligence, corresponding with those mentally retarded individuals who have gross brain pathology.

In practice, it has been found that an IQ of 50 to 55 (representing approximately three standard deviations below the mean) constitutes an approximate cutoff point of demarcation between the two major groups of mentally retarded. Below this level there is generally organic brain pathology, and above this level no gross brain pathology is usually recognizable. There are also marked differences in the extent to which hereditary and environmental factors contribute to the etiology of these two categories of mental retardation and in the nature of both hereditary and environmental factors operative. We shall return to these differences in the later section of this chapter devoted to etiology.

The standard nomenclature adopted by the American Psychiatric Association in 1952 reflected the preceding medical concern with etiology, but also resulted in an unfortunate separation of the mentally retarded within the overall framework of the classification. Those with recognizable brain pathology were considered as having *chronic brain syndromes associated with congenital cranial anomaly* and were grouped with the other chronic brain syndromes. The term *mental deficiency* was then reserved for those without recognizable brain pathology, and definition of the latter group was unfortunately expanded to include all persons found to have a tested IQ of less than 85. Since this is only one standard deviation below the population mean, it would include approximately one out of every six members of the general population, which classification does not conform with most concepts regarding mental retardation. Psychiatrists and psychologists usually prefer to reserve the term mental retardation for individuals with and without brain pathology who have a tested IQ of less than 70, and to apply the term "borderline intelligence" to those with an IQ between 70 and 80.

Many of the persons working most effectively with the mentally retarded are not medically or psychiatrically trained, and have been far less concerned with etiology than with the development of specialized programs for care, treatment, education, and rehabilitation. For most such persons, the etiological dichotomy is far less relevant than the *grouping of mentally retarded individuals according to their level of intellectual function.* For such persons, the traditional categories of idiot, imbecile, and moron have at least two major drawbacks: first, the tendency of these terms to stigmatize the retarded individual, and second, the failure to rec-

TABLE 25–2. Degrees of Mental Retardation

LEVEL	DESCRIPTIVE TERM	INTELLIGENCE QUOTIENT (IQ RANGE)
I	Profound	Below 20
II	Severe	20–35
III	Moderate	36–52
IV	Mild	53–68

ognize useful distinctions within the relatively wide imbecile range (IQ 20 to 49). In recent years, there has therefore been a widespread preference for specifying *four levels of mental retardation*, corresponding with the descriptive terms *profound, severe, moderate,* or *mild* retardation. These levels and their corresponding intelligence range are summarized in Table 25-2.

In keeping with increased interest in the problems of mental retardation, and efforts to assist the retarded in attaining their maximum potential, there have been several attempts at redefinition. The following definitions employ historical, descriptive, and etiological concepts in varying degree. First is a definition offered by a committee of the Group for the Advancement of Psychiatry (1950).

Mental retardation is a chronic condition present from birth or early childhood and characterized by impaired intellectual functioning as measured by standardized tests. It manifests itself in impaired adaptation to the daily demands of the individual's own social environment. Commonly these patients show a slow rate of maturation, physical and/or psychological, together with impaired learning capacity.

The same year, the American Association on Mental Deficiency adopted a widely accepted definition that was subsequently published in their manual on terminology and classification in mental retardation, prepared by Heber (1961). The basic definition, with a slight textual elaboration, is as follows:

Mental retardation refers to subaverage general intellectual functioning which originates during the developmental period and is associated with impairment in adaptive behavior. . . . Impaired adaptive behavior may be reflected in (1) maturation, (2) learning, and/or (3) social adjustment.

In the second edition of the *Glossary* published by the American Psychiatric Association (1964), the following definition of mental retardation appeared:

Lacking in intelligence from birth or childhood, to a degree that interferes with a reasonable adjustment in social performance. Emotional conflict often complicates the condition. The need for institutional treatment and care is proportionate to the degree of impairment and the level of emotional adjustment. There are four degrees of severity: *mild* (I.Q. 50-70); *moderate* (I.Q. 35-49); *severe* (I.Q. 20-34); *profound*, (I.Q. below 20).

The implications of these various degrees or levels of mental retardation were recognized some years ago by Sloan and Burch (1955), and are summarized in Table 25-3. At level IV (mild retardation) there is unlikely to be any history of prenatal, natal, or early postnatal abnormality. However, at levels I to III *(moderate, severe, or profound retardation)* careful inquiry will often elicit a history of significant *brain damage.* A wide variety of factors may be held responsible, but it is possible to assign presumptive etiology in only about 20 per cent of these patients. Although a probable cause may not be assigned in most instances, it is still usual to obtain a history of severe retardation in development from birth or infancy onward. By the age of five

TABLE 25-3. Adaptive Behavior Classification*

	Pre-School Age 0–5 Maturation and Development	School-Age 6–21 Training and Education	Adult 21 Social and Vocational Adequacy
Level I	Gross retardation; minimal capacity for functioning in sensori-motor areas; needs nursing care.	Some motor development present; cannot profit from training in self-help; needs total care.	Some motor and speech development; totally incapable of self-maintenance; needs complete care and supervision.
Level II	Poor motor development; speech is minimal; generally unable to profit from training in self-help; little or no communication skills.	Can talk or learn to communicate; can be trained in elemental health habits; cannot learn functional academic skills; profits from systematic habit training. ("Trainable")	Can contribute partially to self-support under complete supervision; can develop self-protection skills to a minimal useful level in controlled environment.
Level III	Can talk or learn to communicate; poor social awareness; fair motor development; may profit from self-help; can be managed with moderate supervision.	Can learn functional academic skills to approximately 4th grade level by late teens if given special education. ("Educable")	Capable of self-maintenance in unskilled or semi-skilled occupations; needs supervision and guidance when under mild social or economic stress.
Level IV	Can develop social and communication skills; minimal retardation in sensori-motor areas; rarely distinguished from normal until later age.	Can learn academic skills to approximately 6th grade level by late teens. Cannot learn general high school subjects. Needs special education, particularly at secondary school age levels. ("Educable")	Capable of social and vocational adequacy with proper education and training. Frequently needs supervision and guidance under serious social or economic stress.

*Reprinted by permission from Sloan, W., and Birch, J. W. 1955. A rationale for degrees of retardation. American Journal of Mental Deficiency *60,*258–264.

years, such subjects will not have reached the level of development greater than that of the average two-year-old. Dentition, walking, and ability to feed himself or attend to personal hygiene are correspondingly delayed and the profoundly retarded may never achieve intelligible speech. Capacity to develop resistance or immunity to infection may also be limited, resulting in frequent or severe infections and an increased mortality. *Profoundly* retarded individuals remain totally dependent on those around them for nourishment, protection, and care throughout their lifetime, but it is estimated that only 25 percent of this group are admitted to institutions in the United States. The *severely* retarded, with an IQ between 20 and 35, are regarded as "trainable" to the extent of benefitting from special programs designed to develop self-care and simple skills. The *moderately* retarded, with an IQ between 36 and 50, are regarded as "educable" to approximately the fourth grade level if given special education, and may even be able to achieve some productivity in a sheltered setting. In the United States it is estimated that only about 15 percent of this group are institutionalized.

The *mildly* retarded group, with IQs of 50 to 69, do not usually show physical stigmata of retardation (in contrast with the other more severe groups). While their development is somewhat retarded (for example by their fourth birthday they have reached a level of development typical of the average child between his second and third birthdays), it is apt to be little or no different from that of one or more other siblings, and may well pass unnoticed by parents who are themselves somewhat limited in intelligence and lacking in perception. It is therefore in school that the mildly retarded individual is apt to be first noticed as a slow learner, who is unable to keep up with the others and has to repeat early grades. Sooner or later, the learning disability is apt to result in placement in special classes or educational programs. However, such individuals are "educable" and are able to participate in elementary academic activities sufficiently to acquire vocational skills necessary for self-support. Adult occupational adjustment remains at the level of unskilled or semiskilled labor, however, and residential and socioeconomic status is apt to be marginal. Males are likely to be rejected or discharged prematurely from military service. However in the United States it is estimated that only about one percent of the mildly retarded are institutionalized.

Whereas the severely retarded do not mature sexually and remain infertile, in mild retardation sexual activity and fertility are apt to be normal or increased, particularly among the females. The males commonly have difficulty in providing themselves with a satisfactory or permanent sexual partner. They are not uncommonly involved in deviant sexual behavior with animals and sometimes direct assault on an adult female. Females with mild mental retardation do not experience the same difficulty in obtaining a sexual or marital partner. Frequently, the mildly retarded female becomes the mother of illegitimate children, and this is probably the reason that society tends to institutionalize her a little more frequently than the mildly retarded male. However, we may speculate that a number of the fathers of these children are of normal intelligence, and that this may be in part responsible for the tendency of the intelligence of these children to "regress toward the mean" (i.e., to be closer to the population mean IQ of 100 than their mothers are). There is still considerable disagreement concerning the proportion of mentally retarded among the children of the mentally retarded; and past studies of the children of the retarded, using intelligence tests, estimate between five and 30 percent of the children are also retarded.

Whether a severely retarded individual is able to remain at home depends frequently on the responsibility that his family is able and willing to undertake for his care. Whether a mildly retarded person is able to remain in the community tends to depend more on the degree of social responsibility that his family and other members of society have been able to inculcate in him during childhood and adolescence. It is more likely that he will be able to maintain an acceptable level of adjustment in the community if he is living with his family, or in a rural area, than if family ties have been broken and he is associating with delinquents in a disorganized urban area. The facts likely to precipitate residential care of mentally defective persons have been classified as follows (Group for the Advancement of Psychiatry, 1959).

1. Patient's physical status
2. Patient's psychological status
3. Family's structure, attitudes and economic status
4. Availability of community facilities and programs

5. Availability of residential facilities
6. Sociocultural attitudes

Appearance, attitude, and general behavior may be quite characteristic, particularly in severe mental retardation where the patient tends to be undersized and to show facial or bodily deformity. He may have the physical stigmata of a specific form of mental defect: for example, the facies of cretinism (Figure 25-1), mongolism (Figure 25-2), gargoylism, or hypertelorism; or the size and shape of head described as indicative of microcephaly, hydrocephaly (Figure 25-3), or acrocephaly. The profoundly retarded may be unable to feed or dress themselves, to wash, or to attend to bowel and bladder functions, so that their appearance may be very unclean and untidy unless they receive a great deal of nursing care. There may be marked disturbances of gait and involuntary movements. Sometimes such patients show relatively little interest in their immediate surroundings, but those who are not quite so severely incapacitated may remain quite active and interested in their

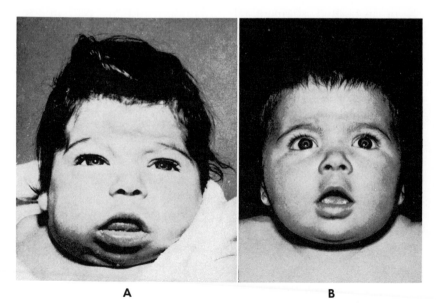

A   **B**

Figure 25-1. A, Congenitally hypothyroid infant at six months of age. B, Four months later, after treatment with thyroid medication. (From Nelson, W. E., ed. 1964. *Textbook of Pediatrics*, 8th edition. Philadelphia, W. B. Saunders Co.)

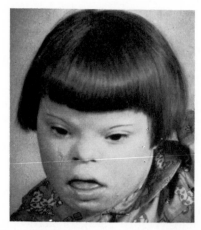

Figure 25–2. Typical facial configuration of mongolism in a 7-year-old girl. (From Nelson, W. E., ed. 1964. *Textbook of Pediatrics*, 8th edition. Philadelphia, W. B. Saunders Co.)

sation approach more closely to the norms expected of the patient's particular age and sex, but tend to resemble those of persons of limited socioeconomic status. The patient often converses spontaneously and answers simple questions relevantly and appropriately, but the conversation of the mentally retarded adult tends to show the general information, comprehension and interest pattern characteristic of the eight- to twelve-year-old child. There is a limited capacity for abstract thinking, and concepts tend to remain somewhat concrete (as in the patient with organic intellectual impairment or with schizophrenia), although there is no more evidence of magical, paralogical thinking than in the average child.

environment. In the profoundly retarded, attempts to converse may be limited to a few unintelligible sounds (either spontaneous or in response to attempts that are made by the examiner to converse), or may be limited to a few simple words or phrases.

With milder degrees of mental retardation there may be little or no physical deformity or associated stigmata, although statistically the patient still tends to be somewhat smaller than average. Appearance, behavior, and conver-

Illusions, hallucinations, and delusions are absent unless the mental retardation is complicated by a psychosis. The most common type of psychosis occurring in patients with mental retardation appears to be schizophrenia, which occurs at least as often as in the general population and may be much more frequent. There have been investigations (e.g., those by Böök, and by Larsson and Sjögren) in which there appears to have been an increased frequency of mental retardation among patients developing schizophrenia (and

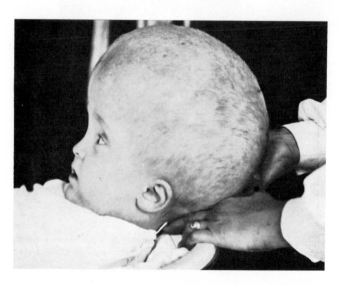

Figure 25–3. Congenital hydrocephalus. (Courtesy of Prof. Otto Marburg. From Wechsler, I. S. 1963. *Clinical Neurology*, 9th edition. Philadelphia, W. B. Saunders Co.)

possibly vice versa), and these have led to speculation concerning possible genetic connections between the two syndromes. However, most patients with mental retardation will not develop symptoms suggestive of schizophrenia or other psychosis.

Overall mood or emotional tone tends to be within normal limits, but emotional reaction tends to resemble that of the average child in being somewhat more labile than that of the typical adult.

The mental age is retarded as compared with the actual chronological age, and associated mental functions (such as orientation, memory, and judgment) tend to be roughly appropriate to the mental age of the individual. In order to assist in evaluation some of the characteristics of normal children at different ages are listed below:

At *three* years the child should be able to show his nose, eyes, ears, and so on when asked; to name a key, watch, or pencil; and to repeat three figures. At *four* years he should be able to say which of two lines is the longer, to copy a square, and to answer correctly what to do when sleepy, hungry, or cold. At *five* years he should recognize colors, be able to compare weights, and be able to give his true age. At *six* years he should know his right from left; be able to recognize a nickel, dime, or quarter; and be able to distinguish between morning and afternoon. At *seven* he should know how many fingers he has; be able to tie a bow; and be able to distinguish between fly and butterfly, stone and egg, wood and glass. At *eight* he should be able to count backward from 20 to one; to write simple phrases such as "See the little cat"; and to define such nouns as airplane, tiger, soldier, and ball. At *nine* years he should be able to give the day of the week, date, month and year; to make simple additions and subtractions using money as an example; and to make a phrase or sentence including a combination of words

such as man and work, money and box, ball and river. At *ten* years he should be able to recognize absurdities in statements made to him, repeat six figures, and repeat a 20-syllable phrase. By *twelve* years he should be able to define such concepts as revenge, charity, goodness, and justice; to interpret the meanings of fables; and to state correctly the similarity between such items as snake, cow, and sparrow; wool, cotton, and leather; rose, potato, and tree.

The development of conscience, superego, or internal control system should be appropriate to the mental age of the individual. Hence there are many mildly retarded individuals (having a mental age equivalent to that of the average eight- to twelve-year-old child) who are well able to respect the rights of others, and conform with society's expectations. However, the mentally retarded adult differs from the average eight- to twelve-year-old child in being sexually mature, while retaining some of the same impulsivity and difficulty in postponing immediate gratification (a factor accentuated by the examples of others in the limited socioeconomic circumstances in which many mature).

PROFOUND MENTAL RETARDATION, ASSOCIATED WITH EPILEPSY

An unmarried girl was first admitted to a state institution at the age of 27, with a history of mental retardation since birth, epileptic seizures since the age of five, and increasingly difficult behavior during the preceding year.

She was born the seventh of 11 children and four of her siblings had failed to progress beyond grade seven in school. Her father had left school after completing the fourth grade and her mother after completing the sixth grade, but no other member of the family had been admitted to any institution for intellectual or social abnormality.

The patient was reported to have started walking by the age of about two years and to have started talking by the age of about three years. Her parents became aware of retardation in development only following a fall at the age of five when she struck her head hard. Ever since this time she had been subject to epileptic seizures which had been largely controlled by anticonvulsant medication. The patient never attended school and remained home with her parents all her life, unable to help with household duties and requiring constant care and attention. The family regarded her as dull, quiet and good-natured, and she spent much of her time sitting and rocking in a chair and talking to herself. She was unable to dress herself or wash, and at times she laughed, cried, or became angry. It did not seem that there had been very much change in the patient's behavior during the year preceding her admission, but her mother's health was not as good as formerly so that she was less able or willing to look after the patient.

On arrival in hospital the patient was found to have some signs of brain damage. She lacked coordination, was unable to walk without assistance, and had involuntary movements of her arms. She was unable to answer anything but very simple questions, and her speech was almost unintelligible. She gave her age as five and when asked where she lived, she replied, "Mommy lives on the corner." She was able to count to eight, but was unable to recognize any letters of the alphabet. The Stanford-Binet test of intelligence showed considerable intratest variability, but her overall performance was at about the level of the average one-year-old child, giving her a formal IQ of less than 5. She made a satisfactory adjustment to long-term institutional care.

SEVERE MENTAL RETARDATION, MONGOLISM

An unmarried woman was admitted to a state institution for the first time at the age of 33. There had been no recent change in her lifelong mental retardation and associated behavior pattern, and her admission to the institution was precipitated by economic difficulties confronting her family. The elder sister who had been caring for her had four children of her own and an aged father staying with her. The sister's husband had recently had an operation and the sister had to go to work to support the family.

The patient was the third and youngest child in the family, her father being about 47 and her mother about 40 years old at the time of her birth. She was born at home with a midwife and doctor in attendance and apparently had a normal, full term delivery. However, her development was retarded from birth and she didn't begin to walk until she was nearly five years old. She didn't talk until the age of nine or ten years, and then not clearly. She was sent to school for a few weeks at the age of ten or 11, but was unable to make any progress and was sent home. She was never able to help with the housework or get outside employment and all her life was wholly dependent on her family. She remained with both parents until the death of her mother (when the patient was 27) following which she and her father stayed with one of her older sisters. She was able to dress and feed herself and her toilet habits were satisfactory. At the age of 33 she still liked to play with a doll, a guitar, and a skipping rope, and to scribble on paper. She also watched television and listened to the radio. She was good-natured, cheerful and cooperative, and there was no history of anti-social behavior.

On arrival in hospital she made no spontaneous conversation but frequently laughed for no apparent reason. She answered questions to the best of her ability, but had a marked speech defect which rendered many of her replies unintelligible. She gave her name correctly, but gave her age as three, and could not say where she lived. She said that she went to school and that she could read, but was unable to name the letters of the alphabet or any numbers that were shown to her. Formal intelligence testing by means of the Stanford-Binet test showed her to have a mental age of three years and ten months, corresponding with an IQ of 26, in the lower part of the imbecile range. Her facial appearance was characteristic of mongolism (as also was the age of her mother at the time she was born). Her family should receive every credit for her socialization, and she made an uneventful adjustment to institutional routine.

MILD MENTAL RETARDATION ASSOCIATED WITH NEUROTIC DEPRESSION

A 39-year-old unmarried woman was admitted to a state hospital with a history that during the preceding year she had become increasingly discouraged because she had been unable to obtain anything other than temporary employment. She was eating and sleeping poorly, weeping quite frequently, and stating that she didn't want to be a burden to anyone and that life wasn't worth living. On one occasion she had become sufficiently discouraged to take a few sleeping pills in an apparent suicidal attempt, but suffered no ill effects from them and was not hospitalized until a few months later.

The patient was the second of five children, but her only brother had died at the age of nine months of meningitis so she was raised in a family of four girls. Her parents were still living together at the time of her admission and her father had repaired shoes for many years but was currently working as a night watchman. He was described as quiet and stubborn but always lenient with the children. Mother, on the other hand, had a "nervous temperament," and was a chronic nagger who was always demanding, controlling, and critical.

The patient was slower in learning to talk and walk than her elder sister, and before many years it was recognized that she was retarded in comparison with all her sisters. She obtained poor grades in school and hated studying. A sister who was nearly three years younger than herself advanced beyond her while she was still in school and the patient finally left school at the age of about 14 with the equivalent of about grade six education. After leaving school she remained home for a year or two and then held a number of different jobs in domestic service, but stayed home a lot between jobs. At the age of about 19 she left home to obtain employment on her own and from the ages of 21 to 25 she was a novice in a convent. This apparently was a rigidly cloistered order, and the patient stated she left because it was too much of a strain on her. During her last year there she said that she lost forty pounds in weight and became "nervous." After leaving the convent she went to stay in a nursing home for a few days and remained there several months helping the owner who had been kind to her. During the next 14 years she had obtained a variety of jobs in factories and domestic service, but had difficulty in holding her employment, apparently because of her limited abilities. She was conscientious and religious, and denied ever having had any form of sexual experience.

On arrival in hospital she said, "I was getting along fine until five days ago when the doctor took me off night medicine and I haven't slept since. It's not the way I live, but the way I feel. I can't see anything to live for in life." She admitted that at times the future had looked hopeless and she had contemplated suicide, but that she felt this was wrong. When asked about the overdose of sleeping pills, she had taken some months previously, she replied, "I didn't really mean to do away with myself. I just meant to sleep on." There was no evidence of illusion, hallucination, or delusions. She was correctly oriented and showed no gross impairment of memory. Her intellectual function was estimated as being at the upper limit of the mentally defective range, and she obtained an IQ of 69. The following are some of her responses to a Sentence Completion test:

I always wanted to be a nun.
If I were ever in charge, I would not try to be a boss.
Most of my friends don't know that I am afraid of life.
My greatest mistake was not being educated.
My greatest weakness is not having confidence in myself.

She was also discouraged over having failed to get married and raise a family and said, "I soon won't be able to have any children. I'm too old now. My hair is growing gray. I've been teased about being 'just an old maid,' and it hurts."

However, her depression rapidly improved following a short course of electroshock treatments and she left hospital after three months to work in a nearby convent. Three months later she was again depressed and returned to hospital, but on this occasion she remained only three weeks, and again returned to work in the convent. For some time afterward she continued to receive a small dose of tranquilizing medication to relieve symptoms of anxiety and irritability, but she made a satisfactory adjustment and there was no recurrence of acute symptoms during the next five years.

MILD MENTAL RETARDATION ASSOCIATED WITH CATATONIC SCHIZOPHRENIA

This patient was the eldest of three children, having a brother one year younger and a sister five years younger than herself. The mother's pregnancy was uneventful but the labor was prolonged and terminated in a difficult instrumental delivery under deep anesthetic. It is probable that during this time the blood supply to the patient's brain contained too little oxygen, and at the time of her birth her face was badly marked by the instruments, unlike that of her two younger siblings. Some degree of mild facial deformity persisted, but her parents did not notice any retardation in her early development. She was a little slower than her younger siblings in starting to walk and talk, and her speech was more difficult to understand but there was no evidence of obvious damage to the nervous system. She commenced school at the age of six, had some difficulty in learning, particularly arithmetic, but was advanced to another grade each year until she reached grade 7 which she had to repeat. During her second year in grade 7, however, she made little further progress than the preceding year. No special instruction was available for retarded children, and her parents were advised to keep her home. Her brother and sister both went on to complete school like their parents.

After leaving school the patient remained home and never went out to work. She complained of nervousness and inability to concentrate and helped her mother very little. However, her parents did not consider her behavior abnormal until one day when she was 19, she went out and failed to return home. They found her standing in a laneway and she didn't seem to know why she was there. During the next three years she became increasingly seclusive and remained in the house most of the time. She stopped going to church and on one occasion a neighbor expressed surprise at learning there were three children in the family as he had seen only two of them. At the age of 21 her parents thought that there was an improvement in her condition since she started to become more talkative. However, her conversation soon became quite disconnected and unintelligible to them. She repeated over and over again the names of people she had known and then began to refuse her meals. She became destructive to her clothing and started to throw dishes and furniture about the house. She began screaming and shouting with no apparent reason, and moved about constantly. Suddenly her condition changed to one of stupor and withdrawal and she remained in bed for several weeks. When she again became acutely excited and disturbed, she was admitted to state hospital for the first time, at the age of 22. When asked how old she was, she replied, "I must be 99. It's my great-grandmother. I knew one in the first battalion." When asked her age again, she replied "Oh, somewhere in the millions. At the barracks. That's all I know since I died on the first of May." When asked what year it was, she said, "Leap year. I don't know. Over 99 millions. It's the boy and girl question. I think my sister is doing this. They went all through the barracks. I went to Europe."

At that time she received convulsive therapy (induced by injections of Metrazol) which controlled her episode of catatonic excitement. However, she had further episodes of both stupor and excitement and remained in hospital for over two years before she stabilized and returned home to live with her parents. During the next 13 years she remained home without outside interests or friendships, but without any recurrence of acute symptomatology. She then again became uncommunicative and inactive, spent all her time in bed, stopped eating, and lost weight so that she was readmitted to hospital at the age of 39. By this time electroshock treatments were available and her catatonic stupor responded promptly to a short course of treatment. When she was rational and had been off treatment for several weeks, a full scale IQ of 55 was obtained and it was estimated that her intellectual function had never been higher than the moron level (IQ 50 to 70). She subsequently went home with her parents but had another attack of acute excitement which was readily controlled by chlorpromazine (Thorazine) medication. However, long-term medication was unable to control the tendency to recurrent catatonic episodes, particularly states of stupor in which she would become motionless and mute and refuse nourishment. After repeated visits home with her family, she was readmitted to hospital for long-term custodial care, with periodic symptomatic treatment of her acute episodes.

DEVELOPMENT AND ETIOLOGY

HEREDITARY FACTORS

Studies on samples of the general population have shown that positive

TABLE 25-4. Estimated Concordance Rates in Monozygotic and Dizygotic Cotwins of Institutionalized Mental Defective Twins

INVESTIGATOR	APPARENT ZYGOSITY OF TWINS	NUMBER OF PAIRS	ESTIMATED CONCORDANCE RATE (PER CENT)	HERITABILITY $H = \dfrac{CMZ - CDZ}{100 - CDZ}$
Rosanoff et al. (1937)	MZ DZ	126 240	91 53	0.81
Juda (1939)	MZ DZ	71 149	97 56	0.93

correlations exist between the intelligence of normal persons and that of their close relatives. Data presented in Chapter 5 showed correlations for intelligence of about +0.5 between full siblings, and also between parents and children. Other studies of twins and foster children suggest that a considerable proportion of the variation in intelligence is determined by hereditary factors, which have been presumed *polygenic* in nature. Early studies of individuals with mental retardation also revealed high frequencies of retardation among their siblings and parents, and two large series of institutionalized twins with mental deficiency showed much higher concordance rates for monozygotic than dizygotic twins (see Table 25-4).

Wildenskov (1934) divided a series of mentally defective subjects into a mild and a severe group, and found that mental deficiency existed in 51 percent of the siblings of the mild group, but in only 26 percent of the siblings of the severe group. In an extensive study of 1280 mental defectives, Penrose (1938) reported the intelligence of their siblings according to the intelligence level of the subjects. His results were summarized by Roberts (1950) and are shown in Table 25-5. It may be seen that the mildly retarded (dull and feebleminded) subjects had a high proportion of mildly retarded siblings, whereas severely retarded subjects (imbeciles and idiots) had relatively higher proportions of siblings with severe degrees of retardation.

In a subsequent paper, Roberts (1952) presented graphically the frequency distribution of intelligence among 562 *siblings* of feebleminded and imbecile subjects falling within the IQ range 30 to 68. His findings are reproduced in Figure 25-4, which shows that the siblings of the feebleminded (mildly retarded) had a lower than average intelligence, and a high proportion of mildly retarded individuals. The siblings of the imbeciles (more severely retarded), on the other hand, more closely approached the average distribution of intelligence in the population, but had a few members in the severely retarded range.

Similarly, it has been found that the *parents* of mildly retarded patients are of lower average intelligence and more likely to be mildly retarded than are the parents of the severely retarded. Table 25-6 shows the estimates made by Penrose of the mean intelligence quotients of the parents and siblings of his large series of mentally retarded

TABLE 25-5. Percentages of Siblings of Mental Defectives, According to Level of Intelligence*

GRADE OF SUBJECT	GRADE OF SIBLINGS				
	NORMAL (OR SUPERIOR)	DULL	FEEBLE-MINDED	IMBECILE	IDIOT
Dull	77.4	16.2	4.9	1.0	0.5
Feeble-minded	76.8	11.9	8.3	2.5	0.6
Imbecile	83.5	7.6	4.6	3.5	0.7
Idiot	81.0	9.9	4.2	1.7	3.2

*Data from Penrose (1938) condensed by Roberts.
Reprinted by permission from Roberts, J. A. F. 1950. The genetics of oligophrenia. *In* Congrès International de Psychiatrie. Paris, VI. Psychiatrie Sociale. Génétique et Eugénique. Paris, Hermann, pp. 55–117.

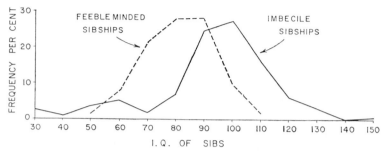

Figure 25–4. Frequency distributions of the IQ's of 562 sibs of feebleminded and imbeciles of the IQ range 30 to 68. (Reprinted by permission from Roberts, J. A. F. 1952. The genetics of mental deficiency. Eugenics Review 44, 71–83.)

patients. Penrose commented on "the noticeable tendency for the grade of the patient to have an *inverse* correspondence with the grade of the parent. When the parents have normal capacity, there is clear segregation between the patients and their relatives. In families where parental abilities are subnormal, the distinction is lessened; the patients are higher and the siblings lower. This is merely a further illustration . . . that the patients fall mainly into two biological groups: the low-grade infertile cases and the high-grade fertile types who are capable of transmitting genes tending to cause low scholastic capacity to their children."

TABLE 25-6. Estimated Mean Intelligence Quotients of Parents, Sibs and Mentally Defective Patients*

TYPE OF MATING	PARENTS	SIBS OF PATIENTS	MENTALLY DEFECTIVE PATIENTS
S × S	122	—	34.0
S × N	111	107.6	38.9
N × N	100	96.7	37.4
N × D	89	88.0	50.5
N × F or D × D	78	82.0	49.4
N × Imbecile or D × F	67	75.1	50.7
D × Imbecile or F × F	56	67.3	45.0

Superior = S = 122   Feeble-minded = F = 56
Normal = N = 100   Imbecile = 34
Defective = D = 78   Idiot = 12

*From Penrose, L. S. 1962. *The Biology of Mental Defect*, 2nd ed. New York, Grune & Stratton, Inc., p. 123.

Apart from differentiating between two broad groups of mental retardation, analysis of family data has also led to the identification of *simple Mendelian inheritance* as responsible for the development of a number of rare syndromes associated with mental retardation. The degree of retardation associated with these rare syndromes is nearly always severe, so that affected individuals do not usually reproduce and thus do not transmit their defective genes to offspring. Nevertheless, certain forms of severe mental retardation have been attributed to the presence of a single *dominant* gene, arising by new mutation: for example, epiloia (tuberous sclerosis), hypertelorism (in which the eyes are much farther apart than normal), and other syndromes associated with lesions of the skin, blood vessels, and bones. Mental retardation attributed to a single pair of *recessive* genes will be found in individuals with apparently normal parents (who are heterozygous carriers of the condition), and in 25 per cent of the siblings of affected individuals. The recessive form of inheritance has been found in the case of certain patients with microcephaly (which, however, may also be caused by infections and other environmental processes), in amaurotic familial idiocy (associated with blindness), in phenylketonuria or PKU (involving inability to metabolize phenylalanine normally), in gargoylism (a disorder of carbohydrate metabolism associated with facial and other deformities), and other forms of metabolic disturbance.

These forms of mental retardation due to simple Mendelian inheritance are not only rare (and usually associated with severe degrees of retardation), but also they constitute a minority of all mental deficiencies associated with severe retardation, which are themselves much less frequent than mild retardation. By contrast, hereditary factors are believed to make a much more significant overall contribution to the causation of *mild* or "subcultural" mental retardation, which is itself much more frequent than the severe forms of subnormality. In fact, the contribution of heredity to the causation of mild mental retardation appears to be approximately the same in degree (one-half to two-thirds of the overall variance) and in nature (polygenic transmission) as in the overall determination of intelligence in the general population.

The preceding studies of family data no longer constitute the only type of information available concerning the role of genetic factors in the causation of mental subnormality. During the past decade, advances in cytogenetic techniques have led to the discovery of several *chromosome anomalies*. It may be recalled that the normal female has two X chromosomes and 22 pairs of autosomes, whereas the normal male has one X and one Y chromosome in addition to the 22 pairs of autosomes. In the majority of persons with *Turner's syndrome* (externally females, but lacking gonads) there is only one X chromosome, while the majority of patients with *Klinefelter's syndrome* (with underdeveloped testes) have two X as well as one Y chromosome. A variety of other anomalies of the sex chromosomes have been found, the most common of which appears to be the presence of three X chromosomes. Maclean et al. (1962) found the presence of extra X chromosomes to be several times as frequent in a large

sample of both male and female mental defectives as in a large sample of the general population. The presence of extra sex chromosomes, however, is still rare among mental defectives and is usually accompanied by mild rather than severe subnormality.

The situation with respect to *mongolism* is a different one. This condition is usually associated with severe mental retardation, and the characteristic facial appearance led to its recognition nearly 100 years before the discovery of associated chromosomal anomalies. At the beginning of the present century it was observed that mongols tended to be the offspring of elderly mothers, and Penrose reported the frequency of mongolian offspring to be over 100 times as great for mothers past the age of 45 years as for mothers under the age of 20. On the other hand, a genetic basis was suggested by a very high rate of concordance in monozygotic cotwins and a very low rate of concordance in dizygotic cotwins. Moreover, the few mongolian mothers that reproduced gave birth to about 50 percent normal and 50 percent mongolian children. The latter observation was frequently interpreted as evidence of transmission by a single dominant gene, but it was established by Lejeune et al. (1959) as being due to the transmission of a whole extra chromosome (*trisomy*). This extra chromosome present in many mongols is not a sex chromosome but a small autosome, and mongolism was the first example to be discovered of an autosomal aberration in man. It was not long, however, before several mongols were discovered who did not possess the extra chromosome, and it is believed that at least certain cases of this syndrome occur as a result of *translocation* or exchange of segments between nonhomologous chromosomes. On the basis of cytogenetic studies of six families each containing more than one mongol, Shaw (1962) concluded that there are many different causes of familial mongolism, and that every family in which more than one mongol has occurred warrants careful investigation.

ENVIRONMENTAL FACTORS

Just as mild and severe mental retardation tend to be associated with different forms of genetic transmission and chromosome anomalies, they are also associated with different forms of *environmental determinants.* The mildly retarded tend to grow up in families with limited intelligence and socioeconomic status, and to experience difficulties in social adjustment in relation to developmental experiences involving emotional and social deprivation. The severely retarded, on the other hand, tend to have difficulties in learning and adaptation because their brains have been subjected to any of the tremendous variety of biological insults that may lead to a chronic brain syndrome. Such brain damage may occur during intrauterine life, during the birth process, or during early postnatal life; and may be due to infections, intoxications, physical injury, uncontrolled seizures, or deficiencies of oxygen, essential vitamins, thyroid hormone, and the like.

Wilson (1959) reviewed the extensive literature on the experimental production of *congenital deformities* in the developing embryos of chicks and various mammals. Such deformities have been produced by a variety of physical agents, maternal nutritional deficiencies, growth inhibitors and antimetabolic substances, virus infections, hormone injections, and miscellaneous drugs and chemicals. Such insults to the developing embryo frequently produce hydrocephaly, microcephaly, or other evidence of damage to the brain, and are highly relevant to the etiology of death, deformity, and "pathological" mental retardation in the human organism.

Four main types of maternal and fetal *infection* have been regarded as important causes of mental subnormality: the spirochete causing congenital syphilis, the virus causing rubella or German measles, the protozoan causing toxoplasmosis, and virus infections causing cytomegalic inclusion disease. Other infections of the brain occurring shortly after birth may also cause lifelong mental retardation.

Congenital syphilis may result in stillbirth, prematurity, bodily deformity, or brain damage, and was formerly the main intrauterine infection recognized as a cause of mental retardation. Routine serological testing of pregnant women and prompt treatment with penicillin have greatly reduced its frequency, and prompt treatment of the newborn may arrest the infection, with consequent normal intelligence or mild retardation in the child rather than severe retardation and death.

Rubella or German measles is acquired by inhalation of infected droplets and is generally a mild infection, but efforts to control it are prompted by the hazards of congenital defects in the offspring of women who acquire the disease during pregnancy. The extent of this risk is uncertain, but approximately ten to 20 percent of living infants born after maternal rubella *during the first three months of pregnancy* have anomalies. These anomalies frequently affect the eyes or heart rather than the brain, but may occasionally result in mental retardation in the child.

The protozoan responsible for toxoplasmosis has a worldwide distribution among a variety of animals, and infection probably occurs through swallowing contaminated water. Infection may be acquired prenatally from the mother and may result in a variety of brain lesions leading to hydrocephaly, microcephaly, or epilepsy associated with mental retardation. The virus infections responsible for cytomegalic inclusion disease may result in a similar variety of brain lesions with associated mental retardation.

Among the *toxic agents* responsible for mental retardation, Jervis included large doses of x-ray therapy to the abdominal region of the pregnant mother, severe jaundice caused by incompatibility between the blood of the mother and fetus, and lead poisoning which is usually acquired by ingesting paint and other substances after birth. Fetal damage due to x-ray therapy of the mother has become extremely rare since pregnancy tests have been employed routinely before such therapy is undertaken on a woman of childbearing age. In the case of hemolytic jaundice due to destruction of the infant's red blood cells by antibodies present in the serum of the mother, the damage to the brain involves the basal ganglia ("kernicterus") and apparently results from the presence of large amounts of bilirubin, a breakdown product of hemoglobin. The best-known form of this serological incompatibility is that due to the Rhesus blood group factor, but prompt exchange transfusions of affected infants appear to have prevented much of the brain damage and mental retardation attributed to this source in former years.

The term *cerebral birth injury* commonly implies two major conditions, namely mechanical trauma and brain damage due to anoxia, and the effects of these two agencies are extremely difficult to unravel. During the first half of the present century a number of ingenious experiments were performed on animals, which clearly demonstrated that the birth process obeys the physical laws of hydrodynamics, and that brain lesions could be produced by subjecting the head of an animal to a lower pressure than the rest of its body. Schwartz accomplished this by placing a suction cup on the heads of newborn animals, and was able to reproduce all cranial and cerebral changes occurring in normal and pathological births. Dekaban presented the results of an intensive study of 15 brains of human infants with acute hemorrhagic lesions related to the process of birth. He advanced the opinion that a combination of various adverse factors is responsible for the occurrence of cerebral birth injury, but that nevertheless, a particularly difficult and hasty delivery may lead to obvious mechanical injury, this being the major or sole cause of severe intracranial hemorrhage.

In his experiments on the production of *anoxia* in adult guinea pigs, Windle demonstrated changes in brain structure associated with impairment of memory and learning. He also carried out a series of experiments on infant guinea pigs subjected to varying degrees of asphyxia at birth, and found similar changes in brain structure and in learning ability at about eight weeks of age. In a subsequent series of experiments on monkeys, Windle et al. demonstrated structural changes in the central nervous system, neurological abnormalities including epileptic seizures, and behavioral deviations following asphyxia at birth.

Premature birth sometimes results from complications of pregnancy in the mother such as toxemia or bleeding, or from a variety of other conditions that may impair the health of the mother. Regardless of the origin, however, premature birth exposes the child to an increased risk of brain damage from mechanical trauma and anoxia. In a longitudinal study of 500 single-born premature infants and 492 full-term control infants, Knobloch et al. found that the frequency of neuropsychiatric abnormality increased as the birth weight of the infant decreased. When the rates in the total premature population were adjusted according to the expected weight distribution of the surviving prematures, the corrected frequency of serious neurological abnormality was 8.2 percent, as compared with 1.6 percent for the controls. The corrected frequency of mental retardation among the prematures was 2.6

percent, as compared with 1.6 percent for the full-term infants. Among those infants with a birth weight less than 1501 gm, 50.9 percent had neurological or intellectual defect, and some of these also had a major visual handicap. The adjusted percentage of premature infants who showed some departure from normal development was 25.7 percent, as compared with 12.8 percent of the full-term controls.

Postmature birth also appears to result in an increased risk of anoxia for the child, both during the later weeks of pregnancy and during the birth process. Turnbull and Baird studied the oxygen content of venous and arterial blood from the umbilical cord after 100 first deliveries. Pregnancy in all of these women had been clinically normal. However, the average oxygen saturation became less as maternal age and the length of gestation increased, and was sometimes dangerously low, especially in women giving birth to their first child after the age of 40, and after the forty-first week of pregnancy. There is a relatively high rate of death among these postmature infants born to older mothers pregnant for the first time, and it appears probable that there is also a relatively higher frequency of neurological abnormality and intellectual subnormality.

Vitamin deficiencies in experimental animals have been shown to result in infertility, and in high rates of death and deformity among the offspring of those animals that do become pregnant. Nearly all the congenital defects that occur in man have been reproduced in experimental animals maintained on a diet deficient in vitamin A. If female rabbits are given a diet deficient in vitamin A for 20 weeks before mating, the frequency of hydrocephaly in their litters is almost 100 percent. Congenital defects have also been produced by deficiencies of other vitamins as well as by an excess of vitamin A or nicotinic acid. Woollam and Millen pointed out that the relevance of these animal experiments to the human organism is still open to question. However, minor degrees of experimental vitamin deficiencies exert their effect in producing malformation *during the early months of pregnancy*, at a time when even the existence of pregnancy may not have been established. The results of these experiments therefore suggest that the only way in which the nutrition of the embryo can be safeguarded is by attention being directed toward the diet of women throughout their reproductive lives, and not simply during the few months after pregnancy has been recognized.

Deficiency or excess of certain *hormones* has been shown to produce developmental defects in experimental animals. In women certain endocrine disorders are known to result in infertility or fetal death. Uncontrolled diabetes in the mother may lead to fetal death or postmaturity, with its accompanying hazards. Several endocrine disorders in the infant may also result in mental subnormality, but by far the most frequent is hypothyroidism. In children, this is manifested as *cretinism*, and the latter may be present at birth or may become apparent only subsequently. The condition may be recognized from the facial appearance of the child, dry skin, overweight, lethargy, or developmental retardation, and the diagnosis may be confirmed by means of laboratory tests of the protein-bound iodine and the radioactive iodine uptake. Wilkins presented data indicating that in severe congenital cretinism the ultimate response to administration of thyroid hormone depends on *the age at which treatment was started*. Among 22 such cases in which treatment was started at the age of 1 to 6 months, 45 percent attained an IQ of 90 or more, 37 percent an IQ of 51 to 89; and 18 percent retained an IQ of 50 or less. Among 22 such cases starting thyroid therapy after the age of one year, none attained an IQ of 90 or more, 60 percent attained an IQ of 51 to 89, and 40 percent retained an IQ of 50 or less.

It has long been recognized that

lifelong *deafness* may result in retardation of intellectual development, and it has sometimes been thought that many children with mental retardation are also deaf. Fowler and Kastein, however, pointed out that it is necessary to distinguish carefully between true deafness due to peripheral hearing impairment or loss, and defects in language development due to central hearing impairments. Among 156 children referred for hearing tests because of impaired or absent language and speech development, they found that only 54 had peripheral hearing loss alone, and a further 27 had peripheral hearing loss combined with either brain injury, mental retardation,

or emotional disturbance. The remaining 75 were found to have central hearing impairments associated with various forms of behavior disturbance, including 23 cases with diagnosable mental retardation and 13 cases with diagnosable mental illness. While partial or total deafness may certainly cause retardation in mental development, such individuals are not inherently mentally retarded and will respond to appropriate methods of training and education.

Childhood schizophrenia leads to cognitive impairment and may result in failure of language development and other signs of mental retardation. Furthermore, a number of such

TABLE 25-7. The Two Main Groups of the Mentally Subnormal Who Require Hospital Care

	Severe	Mild
Degree of defect		
Incidence of group in population	Uncommon: $\frac{1}{4}$ per cent	Common: 2 per cent
Proportion of group in hospital	Many: 25 per cent	Few: 3 per cent
Sex incidence	Males predominate	Females predominate
Psychological classification	Low grade, imbecile or idiot (modal I.Q. about 17)	High grade, simpleton moron, feeble-minded (modal I.Q. about 57)
Predominant medical classification	Pathological, clinical, associated with physical malformations	Physiological, aclinical, residual, associated with behaviour disorders
Mental capacity in absence of disease	Normal	Subcultural
Physical measurements	Means below normal, increased variabilities	Means and variabilities within normal range
Biological classification	Non-fertile	Fertility usually normal
Traditional obsolete view on causation	Environmental, secondary, exogenous, extrinsic	Hereditary, primary, endogenous, intrinsic
Status of relatives	Parents rarely defective; brothers and sisters occasionally defective and sharply distinguished from normals	Parents, brothers and sisters rather frequently defective, but not sharply distinguished from normals
Typical hereditary causes	Rare specific genes; autosomal aberrations	Common genes: multiple additive genes: sex chromosomal aberrations
Typical environmental causes	Pre-natal maternal influences: cerebral disease or injury in very early life	Deprivation: cerebral disease or injury in childhood: antisocial environment
Treatment	Elementary training, nursing, correction of biochemical errors, cerebral surgery	Special education, socialization, physical training, psychotherapy

From Penrose, L. S. 1962. *The Biology of Mental Defect*, 2nd edition. New York, Grune & Stratton, Inc., p. 64.

children have evidence of brain pathology, and Goldfarb divided childhood schizophrenia into two groups on this basis. He postulated that in one group, organic pathology in the child plays an active role in determining the pathology in the child's ego organization; in another group of schizophrenic children there is no evidence of organic pathology, and disordered patterns of interaction within the family appear to play a crucial role in determining the child's ego deficits.

It has been widely assumed that *emotional deprivation* in infancy may result in apparent mental retardation as well as various forms of behavior disorder. Levy regarded the accumulated evidence as quite consistent in tracing a variety of deficiencies in emotional and intellectual equipment to the privations in the infantile period. There is indeed considerable evidence that emotional deprivation in infancy may lead to the subsequent development of delinquency and sociopathic personality, but it remains questionable whether such deprivation also leads to other disorders such as schizophrenia or mental retardation. Nevertheless, it appears that individuals with mild mental retardation are often raised in circumstances of emotional and economic deprivation, and that such individuals are also likely to experience difficulties in adjustment because of the sociopathic attitudes and behavior they have learned. A considerable part of the causation of social problems due to mild retardation is probably attributable to childhood experience. The main differences in etiology between mild and severe mental retardation are summarized in Table 25-7.

TREATMENT

The early diagnosis of a few forms of potentially severe mental retardation will permit specific treatment to be applied throughout the lifetime of the individual, thereby enabling the individual to attain a normal level of intellectual function, or at least preventing much more severe retardation than would otherwise develop. Phenylketonuria or PKU is an inherited metabolic defect that may be recognized by a simple blood test within the first month of life, and may be largely controlled by means of a diet relatively free of phenylalanine (which is found in most protein foods). Many of the unpleasant effects of congenital syphilis may be avoided by means of penicillin therapy, and lifelong mental retardation due to cretinism may frequently be avoided by prompt recognition and administration of thyroid hormone. Mental retardation due to deafness may be overcome by appropriate training, and retardation due to emotional deprivation may be at least partly reversible when prompt action is taken to provide adequate parental care (as by means of permanent adoptive placement).

The administration of anticonvulsant medication is an important factor in minimizing mental retardation among those subject to epileptic seizures, and the potentialities of partially paralyzed mental defectives can often be increased by active physiotherapy. Numerous nonspecific forms of medical treatment have been applied in unsuccessful attempts to increase intellectual functions, and these include the administration of vitamins, hormones, and brain stimulants. However, when mental retardation is associated with disturbed behavior, considerable benefit may result from the administration of tranquilizing drugs such as the phenothiazines.

No medical treatment is known that will consistently raise the intellectual function of the majority of mentally retarded individuals. Penrose has remarked:

> The most important work carried out in the field of training defectives is unspectacular. It is not highly technical, but requires unlimited patience, good will and common sense. The reward is to be expected not so much in scholastic im-

provement of the patient as in his personal adjustment to social life. Occupations are found for patients of all grades so that they can take part as fully and usefully as possible in human affairs. This process, which has been termed socialization, contributes greatly to the happiness not only of the patients themselves, but also of those who are responsible for their care.

Socialization programs differ according to the degree of retardation and age of the subject. In the mildly retarded, socialization involves two distinct problems, namely scholastic inefficiency and social ineptitude. The scholastic problem is a matter of teaching as much reading, writing, and arithmetic as the patient can absorb, together with speech, manual, and occupational training, and the development of vocational interests. The problem of attempting to overcome the patient's social ineptitude involves guidance and reeducation with respect to neurotic or antisocial personality characteristics that the mentally retarded are prone to develop.

SELECTED REFERENCES

Åkesson, H. O. 1961. *Epidemiology and Genetics of Mental Deficiency in a Southern Swedish Population,* tr. R. N. Elston. Uppsala, Sweden, Almqvist and Wiksells.

The American Association on Mental Deficiency. 1961. *A Manual on Terminology and Classification in Mental Retardation.* Monograph Supplement to American Journal of Mental Deficiency, 2nd edition.

American Psychiatric Association. 1952. *Diagnostic and Statistical Manual for Mental Disorders.* Washington, D.C., American Psychiatric Association.

American Psychiatric Association. 1964. *A Psychiatric Glossary,* 2nd edition, Washington, D.C., American Psychiatric Association.

Anderson, V. E. 1964. Genetics in mental retardation. In *Mental Retardation,* ed. H. A. Stevens and R. Heber. Chicago, University of Chicago Press, pp. 348-394.

Benda, C. E. 1960. *The Child with Mongolism.* New York, Grune & Stratton, Inc.

Berg, J. M., and Kirman, B. H. 1959. Some aetiological problems in mental deficiency. British Medical Journal 2, 848-852.

Boggs, E. M., and Jervis, G. A. 1966. Care and management of the retarded. In *American Handbook of* Psychiatry, ed. S. Arieti, New York, Basic Books, Inc., Vol. 3, ch. 3.

Böök, J. A. 1953. A genetic and neuropsychiatric investigation of a north-Swedish population. Acta Genetica 4, 345-414.

Brandon, M. W. G. 1957. The intellectual and social status of children of mental defectives. Journal of Mental Sciences 103, 710-738.

Cowie, V., and Slater, E. 1959. Psychiatric genetics. In *Recent Progress in Psychiatry,* Vol. III, ed. G. W. T. H. Fleming and A. Walk. New York, Grove Press, Inc., pp. 1-53.

Dekaban, A. S., 1962. Cerebral birth injury; pathology of hemorrhagic lesions. In *Mental Retardation,* ed. L. C. Kolb, R. L. Masland, and R. E. Cooke. Baltimore, The Williams & Wilkins Co., Research Publications of Association for Research in Nervous and Mental Disease, Vol. 39, pp. 196-227.

Dittmann, L. L. 1959. *The Mentally Retarded Child at Home.* Washington, D.C., U.S. Department of Health, Education and Welfare, Children's Bureau Publication No. 374.

Fowler, E. P., Jr., and Kastein, S. 1962. Hypoacusis, dysacusis and retardation. In *Mental Retardation,* ed. L. C. Kolb, R. L. Masland, and R. E. Cooke. Baltimore, The Williams & Wilkins Co., Research Publications of Association for Research in Nervous and Mental Disease, Vol. 39, pp. 270-288.

Freedman, A. M. 1962. Long-range anterospective study of premature infants. World Mental Health 14, 9-15.

Goldfarb, W. 1962. Families of schizophrenic children. In *Mental Retardation,* ed. L. C. Kolb, R. L. Masland, and R. E. Cooke. Baltimore, The Williams & Wilkins Co., Research Publication of Association for Research in Nervous and Mental Disease, Vol. 39, pp. 256-269.

Group for the Advancement of Psychiatry. 1959. *Basic Considerations in Mental Retardation: A Preliminary Report.* New York, Group for the Advancement of Psychiatry Report No. 43.

Group for the Advancement of Psychiatry. 1963. *Mental Retardation: A Family Crisis - the Therapeutic Role of the Physician.* New York, Group for the Advancement of Psychiatry Report No. 56.

Hafemeister, N. R. 1951. Development of a curriculum for the trainable child. American Journal of Mental Deficiency 55, 495-501.

Heber, R. 1961. *A Manual on Terminology and Classification in Mental Retardation.* Monograph Supplement to American Journal of Mental Deficiency, 2nd edition.

Jervis, G. A. 1959. The mental deficiencies. In *American Handbook of Psychiatry,* ed. S. Arieti. New York, Basic Books, Inc. Vol. 2, ch. 63.

Juda, A. 1939. Quoted by Shields, J., and Slater, E. 1961. Heredity and psychological abnormality. In *Handbook of Abnormal Psychology,* ed. H. J. Eysenck. New York, Basic Books, Inc. pp. 326-328.

Knobloch, H., Rider, R., Harper, P., and Pasamanick, B. 1956. Neuropsychiatric sequelae of prematurity. Journal of the American Medical Association *161*, 581-585.

Kolb, L. C., Masland, R. L., and Cooke, R. E., eds. 1962. *Mental Retardation.* Baltimore, The Williams & Wilkins Co., Research Publications for the Association for Research in Nervous and Mental Disease, Vol. 39.

Lejeune, J., Turpin, R., and Gautier, M. 1959. Quoted by Lejeune, J., and Turpin, R. 1962. Somatic chromosomes in mongolism. In *Mental Retardation,* ed. L. C. Kolb, R. L. Masland, and R. E. Cooke. Baltimore, The Williams & Wilkins Co., Research Publications of the Association for Research in Nervous and Mental Disease, Vol. 39, pp. 67-77.

Levy, D. M. 1962. Early infantile deprivation. In *Mental Retardation,* ed. L. C. Kolb, R. L. Masland, and R. E. Cooke. Baltimore, The Williams & Wilkins Co., Research Publications of the Association for Research in Nervous and Mental Disease, Vol. 39, pp. 243-255.

Maclean, N., et al. 1962. A survey of sex-chromosome abnormalities among 4,514 mental defectives. Lancet *1*, 293-296.

Masland, R. L., Sarason, S. B., and Gladwin, T. 1958. *Mental Subnormality; Biological, Psychological and Cultural Factors.* New York, Basic Books, Inc.

Medearis, D. N., Jr. 1962. Cytomegalic inclusion disease as an example of a viral infection acquired in utero which may result in mental retardation. In *Mental Retardation,* ed. L. C. Kolb, R. L. Masland, and R. E. Cooke. Baltimore, The Williams & Wilkins Co., Research Publications of the Association for Research in Nervous and Mental Disease, Vol. 39, pp. 130-140.

O'Conner, N., and Tizard, J. 1956. *The Social Problem of Mental Deficiency.* London and New York, Pergamon Press, Inc.

Pasamanick, B., and Knobloch, H. 1961. Epidemiologic studies on the complications of pregnancy and the birth process. In *Prevention of Mental Disorders in Children,* ed. G. Caplan. New York, Basic Books, Inc., pp. 74-94.

Penrose, L. S. 1962. *The Biology of Mental Defect,* 2nd edition. New York, Grune & Stratton, Inc.

Roberts, J. A. F. 1950. The genetics of oligophrenia. In *Congres International de Psychiatrie,* 1950. VI, Psychiatrie Sociale. Paris, Hermann and Cie. pp. 55-117.

Roberts, J. A. F. 1952. The genetics of mental deficiency. Eugenics Review *44*, 71-83.

Rosanoff, A. J., Handy, L. M., and Plesset, I. R. 1937. The etiology of mental deficiency. Psychological Monographs *216*, 1-137.

Sarason, S. B. 1966. Mental subnormality. In *The Theory and Practice of Psychiatry,* ed. F. C. Redlich and D. X. Freedman. New York, Basic Books, Inc., ch. 19.

Schwartz, P. 1957. *Birth Trauma as a Cause of Mental Deficiency.* Pennsylvania, Department of Welfare.

Shaw, M. W. 1962. Familial mongolism. Cytogenetics *1*, 141-179.

Sloan, W., and Birch, J. W. 1955. A rationale for degrees of retardation. American Journal of Mental Deficiency *60*, 258-264.

Stacey, C. L., and DeMartino, M. F., eds. 1957. *Counselling and Psychotherapy with the Mentally Retarded.* Glencoe, Illinois, The Free Press.

Stevens, H. A., and Heber, R., eds. 1964. *Mental Retardation.* Chicago, University of Chicago Press.

Tredgold, A. S., and Soddy, K. 1963. *A Textbook of Mental Deficiency,* 10th edition. Baltimore, The Williams & Wilkins Co.

Turnbull, E. P. N., and Baird, D. 1957. Maternal age and foetal oxygenation. British Medical Journal *2*, 1021-1024.

Wildenskov, H. O. 1934. *Investigations into the Causes of Mental Deficiency.* Copenhagen, Munksgaard; and London, Humphrey Milford.

Wilkins, L. 1962. The effects of thyroid deficiency upon the development of the brain. In *Mental Retardation,* ed. L. C. Kolb, R. L. Masland, and R. E. Cooke. Baltimore, The Williams & Wilkins Co., Research Publications of the Association for Research in Nervous and Mental Disease, Vol. 39, pp. 150-158.

Wilson, J. G. 1959. Experimental studies on congenital malformations. Journal of Chronic Diseases *10*, 111-130.

Windle, W. F. 1952. Anoxia: its effect on structure of the brain. In *The Biology of Mental Health and Disease.* New York, Hoeber Medical Division, Harper & Row, Publishers, Inc., pp. 331-334.

Windle, W. F., et al. 1962. Structural and functional sequelae of asphyxia neonatorum in monkeys. In *Mental Retardation,* ed. L. C. Kolb, R. L. Masland, and R. E. Cooke. Baltimore, The Williams & Wilkins Co., Research Publications of the Association for Research in Nervous and Mental Disease, Vol. 39, pp. 169-182.

Woollam, D. H., and Millen, J. W. 1956. Role of vitamins in embryonic development. British Medical Journal *1*:1262-1265.

World Health Organization. 1954. *The Mentally Subnormal Child.* Geneva, W.H.O. Technical Report Series No. 75.

CHAPTER 26

Disorders of Childhood

by R. Dean Coddington

One of the first descriptions of psychiatric disease in children was that of Paul Moreau in *La Folie Chez Les Enfants* published in 1888. Considerable interest in "wild boys" has been evinced throughout the ages both in literature and folk lore. The most famous being the saga of Romulus and Remus, abandoned twin boys who were nourished by a female wolf and who, according to legend, became the founders of Rome. Throughout the nineteenth century both psychologists and educators were leaders in extending our knowledge of the intellectual as well as the psychological development of children. Dietrich Tiedermann, a pediatrician, contributed the first longitudinal study of a developing child, and Charles Darwin published the biographical sketch of his son Emile in 1877.

William Healy began work with the Juvenile Court in Chicago in 1908. His book, *The Individual Delinquent*, was the product of a five-year study of a thousand troubled youths, stimulated considerable interest, and was influential in the establishment of some of the early child guidance clinics. The Commonwealth Fund became interested and contributed time, effort, and money for the organization and support of such facilities. At the time of the first White House Conference for Children in 1930, approximately 500 clinics existed in the United States. In 1943 the American Psychiatric Association established a Committee devoted to the problems of children and in 1946 the American Association of Psychiatric Clinics for Children was formed. The Group for Advancement of Psychiatry organized a Committee on Child Psychiatry in 1947 and the Academy of Child Psychiatry was formed in 1953. Representatives from the American Board of Pediatrics and the American Board of Psychiatry and Neurology agreed on the certification of Child Psychiatrists as a subspecialty of Psychiatry in 1959. The outstanding American text in the field was, and still is, Leo Kanner's *Child Psychiatry*, first published in 1935.

ETIOLOGY

Before proceeding into a discussion of the psychiatric disorders of childhood, it would seem appropriate to review the etiologic factors upon which diagnostic classifications are based. The tremendous emphasis on psychodynamic principles that followed Freud's discoveries focused much attention on early childhood development. The pendulum swung from the rather strict child rearing practices of the early part of the century to a much

607

more permissive, analytic approach in the '20s and '30s. Parents were encouraged to let their children express their creative talents even if it meant carving the legs of the dining room table. There was much disagreement and confusion among parents and those working with children. Brenneman (1933) and Kanner (1941) both came to the defense of mothers and led the way to a more rational approach. This emphasis on psychodynamic factors has resulted in the widely held view of both laymen and professionals that the existence of a normal child in a family denotes the normalcy of the parents and the home environment, and thereby argues against the diagnosis of a psychiatric disease in another child. If, on the other hand, an abnormal child is discovered in the family, the blame is commonly placed on the parents, who are then deemed to be somewhat deviant themselves. This all-or-none hypothesis is not supported by the facts.

A discussion of the genetic factors operating in the etiology of mental illness was presented in Chapter 5. In addition to the genetic factor there is a growing body of knowledge that leads us to believe that a dyadic relationship is developing in utero between mother and fetus. The work of Hooker, Sontag, Minkowski, Halverson, and Peiper, reported in Peiper (1963), indicates the development of this dyadic relationship. Mothers develop a mental representation of their unborn children which may well influence their reaction to their children postnatally. A mother described how her recently-delivered daughter reacted in utero in this manner: "I like to sleep on my side and when I got into this position she would become very active until she finally got into a comfortable position and would then settle down." Walther (in Peiper 1963) recorded the movements of the human fetus through the mother's abdominal wall and obtained continuous 24-hour graphs. He found that the greatest number of movements occurred between 5 P.M. and midnight; the period of least activity was from midnight to 6 A.M.; and most important, that the two, mother and fetus, influence each other in their waking and sleeping patterns.

Maternal psychological factors have been considered important in cases of habitual abortion. Van den Bergh (1966) has shown that the surgical prevention of abortion in such women by means of a Shirodkar operation (a purse-string suture around the cervical os) results in an increased incidence of postpartum psychoses. Davids and DeVault (1962) demonstrated a significant positive correlation between the anxiety level during pregnancy and delivery room difficulties.

A biochemical connection exists between mother and fetus. Mirsky (1953) states

Since the embryo receives its nourishment from the blood stream of the mother, any condition which affects the chemical state of the mother's blood can influence the structural development of the offspring. Thus, a nutritional inadequacy arising in the mother may affect the developing embryo irrespective of whether attributable to some emotional disturbance. The child that is born from a malnourished mother may not only be smaller at birth but may grow more slowly during the first year of life. Such children may be born with a variety of anatomical and physiological abnormalities which may not become clinically obvious until much later in life.

In a similar vein biochemical changes resulting from maternal anxiety, depression, or other psychological state may affect the fetus. Ham (1953) says

We could postulate that if a given fetus is exposed to a high level of adrenergic substances due to the mother's psychosomatic response to an external or intrapsychic conflict during the period of intense growth of the hypothalamic structures of her fetus, that this then might be the normal level of biochemical stimulus, for this fetus, for this tissue, in contrast to some other fetus whose hypothalmic structure developed in a mother and intrauterine environment of lower or higher concentration. What will be the situation and response of the required biochemical milieu for this particular fetus postnatally? Will this organism have to produce a higher level of such adrenergic substances sensitive to these factors produced in conjunction with his integrative tasks? Will this, for example, lead to chronically hyperactive function in this area, possible stimulating thyroid function in an ever increasing vicious circle of stimulation - overresponse - stimulation in the clinical syndrome of thyrotoxicosis?

Thus, by the time birth occurs, at least two etiologic factors may have already played a role in predisposing a child to mental as well as physical illness. The child psychiatrist must be concerned with the family history and with the mother's mental status before, during, and immediately after birth in addition to the interpersonal psychodynamics that exist in the extrauterine environment.

The immediate postnatal life is another period that is often overlooked in psychiatry. Levy (1959) emphasizes the importance of this early experiencing and suggests questioning the mother about her feelings when she first sees her child. The learning theory of Sears as reviewed by Maier (1965) also points out the importance of the dyadic relationship during these early weeks and months, long before any psychological value in the ordinary sense can be attributed to the infant. He points out, for instance, that a parent tends to react differently to a son from the way he would to a daughter. Therefore, each sex experiences different child rearing practices and consequently develops differently. Learning begins at birth and is based first on the reduction of inner drives such as hunger, but is carried out in a family setting and depends upon the social reinforcement associated with parental behavior.

As the infant grows the importance of other family members increases; his social environment broadens. Child psychiatrists have been aware of these complex mechanisms for many years but it remained for Ackerman (1958), Satir (1964), Lidz (1963), Brodey (1963), and others to organize various concepts into integrated systems of family psychodynamics. Such conceptual frameworks consider the psychopathology to be a part of the family constellation as a unit rather than identifying any one member of the family as a patient. So we have disease of the basic social unit, the family.

It is a simple matter to go one more step and consider the next etiologic factor, namely, the extrafamilial society. Society in its entirety, as well as each of its subgroups, its classes, gangs and groups, its cultural institutions, its problems, crises, political struggles, and its fads, affects the child in his strivings for independence, identity, and industry.

A full understanding of the child must take all these things into account. Such a model is illustrated in Figure 26-1 taken from Mutter and Schleifer (1966). The model stresses the importance of considering all three variables at all times rather than focusing exclusively on biological, social, or psychological factors in a given case.

CLASSIFICATION

The Committee on Child Psychiatry of the Group for Advancement of Psychiatry has recently published a new diagnostic classification for psychological disorders of childhood. It is more applicable to children than is similar nomenclature used elsewhere in this book, even though it is in many respects nonstandard. Consequently some of the innovations will be discussed. This classification is reproduced in Table 26-1.

HEALTHY RESPONSES

This diagnostic category was included in the classification in order to encourage the physician to think not

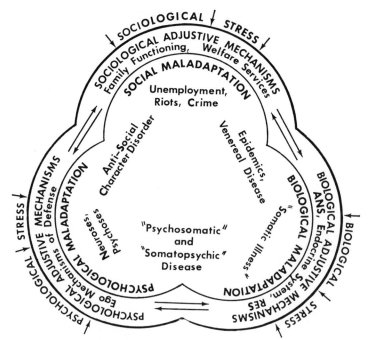

Figure 26–1. Model for multicausational concept of disease. (Reprinted by permission from Mutter, A. Z., and Schleifer, M. J. 1966. The role of psychological and social factors in the onset of somatic illness in children. Psychosomatic Medicine 28, 333–343.)

only of the exclusion of psychopathology, but also of the inclusion of the child's positive assets. The physician's orientation toward pathology that we teach so thoroughly throughout his medical education encourages him to attach undue weight to symptoms in his attempt to find a diagnosis.

Included among the developmental crises would be such things as the eighth month anxiety of infants which occurs after they have learned to differentiate themselves and their mothers from other objects. This behavior is exemplified by the behavior of infants in a pediatrician's office. They have seen the pediatrician at monthly intervals since birth and lain placidly on his examining table while he works. At around eight months of age, however, they suddenly cry in the same situation and cannot be calmed easily. This reaction is often attributed to the immunization procedures that have been used, but more careful observations will

reveal that it occurs whether or not any injections have been given. The phobias commonly seen in preschool children that are going through an identity crisis exemplify another healthy response and the compulsiveness illustrated by young school children attempting to be industrious is still another.

A grief reaction would be an example of a healthy response to a situational crisis. Bowlby has described the stages of the grief reaction consisting of protest, followed by despair, and finally by detachment. This series of events is quite consistent in children over six months of age. The child first expresses his protestations by crying, complaining, and reacting violently at times against those around him. He is protesting against the reality of the situation. The next stage following his acceptance of the reality is a period of despair or depression in which he is much quieter, sad, and less

TABLE 26–1. Classification of Psychiatric Disorders of Children*

I. Healthy Responses
   A. Development crisis
   B. Situational crisis
   C. Other responses
II. Reactive Disorders
III. Developmental Deviations
   A. Deviations in maturational patterns
   B. Deviations in specific dimensions of development
      1. Motor
      2. Sensory
      3. Speech
      4. Cognitive functions
      5. Social development
      6. Psychosexual
      7. Affective
      8. Integrative
   C. Other developmental deviation
IV. Psychoneurotic Disorders
   A. Anxiety type
   B. Phobic type
   C. Conversion type
   D. Dissociative type
   E. Obsessive-compulsive type
   F. Depressive type
   G. Other psychoneurotic disorders
V. Personality Disorders
   A. Compulsive personality
   B. Hysterical
   C. Anxious
   D. Overly dependent
   E. Oppositional
   F. Overly inhibited
   G. Overly independent
   H. Isolate
   I. Mistrustful
   J. Tension-discharge disorders

      1. Impulse-ridden personality
      2. Neurotic personality disorder
   K. Sociosyntonic personality disorder
   L. Sexual deviation
   M. Other personality disorders
VI. Psychotic Disorders
   A. Psychoses of infancy and early childhood
      1. Early infantile autism
      2. Interactional psychotic disorder
      3. Other psychoses of infancy and early childhood
   B. Psychoses of later childhood
      1. Schizophreniform psychotic disorder
      2. Other psychoses of later childhood
   C. Psychoses of adolescence
      1. Acute confusional state
      2. Schizophrenic disorder, adult type
      3. Other psychoses of adolescence
VII. Psychophysiologic Disorders
   A. Skin
   B. Musculoskeletal
   C. Respiratory
   D. Cardiovascular
   E. Hemic and lymphatic
   F. Gastrointestinal
   G. Genitourinary
   H. Endocrine
   I. Of nervous system
   J. Of organs of special sense
   K. Other psychophysiologic disorders
VIII. Brain Syndromes
   A. Acute
   B. Chronic
IX. Mental Retardation
X. Other Disorders

*Proposed by the Committee on Child Psychiatry of the Group for the Advancement of Psychiatry, 1966.

responsive than usual. The resolution of this grief comes when the mental apparatus is able to detach itself from the lost object and begin to form relationships with new objects. The stage of protest lasts a few minutes or hours, the despair days, and the period of detachment sometimes several weeks. It should be emphasized that such grief reactions can occur upon the loss of an object through death or through the hospitalization of the child or as a result of any other separations. In addition the threatened or fantasied loss of an object can produce the grief reaction. From a diagnostic point of view, then, one must determine whether the grief reaction is a healthy response to a real or seriously threatened object loss or an unhealthy response to a fantasied or otherwise unreal object loss.

REACTIVE DISORDERS

This category should be used when the child's symptom complex is the reaction to a set of events or to a situation. A reactive disorder can be superimposed upon a well-crystallized psychoneurosis, personality disorder, or psychosis, but if the reaction is a result of such internalized disorders it should be classified appropriately instead. These disorders are common in childhood particularly in children under eight or ten years of age who have developed only a limited repertoire of psychological defenses. They are relatively easy to diagnose if one is able to gather the historical data from the child since the rationale behind the disorder will be quite clear because of the fundamental principle that it is based on conscious thought processes and the child's life experiences rather than the internalized, unconscious conflicts of the neuroses, for example.

Two examples will serve to illustrate, one related to a physical illness and one to a divorce.

A ten-year-old boy was brought in with the chief complaint of a limp of two years' duration following the uncomplicated healing of a fractured femur. He had been examined by neurologists and orthopedists who could find no cause for the limp. The child explained that he had fallen from a tree while playing with friends and lay on the ground in pain. Well-meaning neighbors told him to stand up but he refused, stating that he had a "broken leg." His mother was called and wisely supported his notion that he should not be moved, and instead called an ambulance. The diagnosis was confirmed and appropriate treatment carried out. At the time of the consultation the boy was behaving differently in the vicinity of his home as compared to more distant places. That is, he would play football in front of his own home but would not play football in a school yard or his neighbors' homes. It seemed that he trusted his mother's judgment but not the judgment of other adults. When asked what he knew about the healing process of a fracture, he professed ignorance but then admitted that although he knew it wasn't true he thought maybe it took several years. He illustrated his point by telling of an aged aunt who fractured her hip seven years earlier and was still limping.

It was easy to see the genesis of his reactive disorder. Treatment consisted of a simple but honest and somewhat technical description of the healing process and his recovery confirmed the diagnosis.

A six-year-old child presented as a behavior disorder with oppositional, negativistic behavior. He seemed irritable and distraught. The mother stated that the onset of these symptoms followed by a few months her divorce from her husband. Although this action was deliberate and was considered for several months prior to the husband's leaving home, it apparently was considered impulsive by the child. The child looked very sullen and quiet as the mother discussed his problem with the physician but entered into the conversation in the latter part of the interview. He related his observation that his father left immediately after the patient had broken the knob off the father's radio. He reasoned that the father's disappearance was a result of his anger toward the boy. When one considers his developmental stage, attendant with his attempts to develop an identity of his own, one can understand the child's logic. He has, indeed, harbored hostile feelings toward his father and is not at all surprised that his father would feel angry as a consequence. The father's leaving is seen on the conscious level by the boy as a hostile act and he responds with an appropriate behavior disorder.

One can see from these case reports that a number of many diagnoses previously classed as conduct disturbances, behavior disorders, neurotic traits, habit disturbances, and certain depressions, will fall in this category of reactive disorders.

DEVELOPMENTAL DEVIATIONS

Into this category one would place all of those children who are developing in a limited, precocious, or uneven manner. Children who had delayed speech development due to deafness; children with an uncommon amount of sexual interest but who cannot be classified as having sexual inversions or perversions; retarded children who have hypo- or hyperactivity associated with their difficulty; children with markedly advanced development in one cognitive area (such as electronics at the age of ten); and children with delayed development with no apparent cause will all fall into this category.

Space does not permit examples of each of these subdivisions, but one illustration may serve the purpose.

A six-year-old boy was presented for evaluation of his behavior that had previously been diagnosed as early infantile autism. The illness had begun insidiously and was manifested by a great deal of compulsive behavior, a rather indifferent attitude toward people and rather infantile behavior. He had a tremendous interest in the shape and symmentry of buildings, streets, city blocks, and the construction materials of which they were made. He would carry around handfuls of apparently irrelevant objects such as stones to such a degree that he was unable to open doors and do other things he wished to do. He would often lie on the floor like a baby, kicking his feet contentedly for hours. The parents stated that he was not affectionate and that he refused their attentions. Indeed, he appeared very much like an autistic child, but one was forced to abandon this diagnosis of early infantile autism.

Further history revealed that four miscarriages had preceded the patient's birth and even though this last pregnancy went to term it was fraught with difficulties and the mother threatened to abort on several occasions. One got a distinct impression from this mother that she enjoyed his infantile behavior more than she enjoyed his progressive developmental steps. She played with him as with a doll, reinforcing infantile behavior. The mother, a very intelligent woman, had read about early infantile autism and had discovered that her son demonstrated many of the symptoms.

During the course of 12 psychotherapeutic visits, he at first adamantly refused to form a positive relationship with the therapist but instead threatened to hit, bite, and scratch him, saying he did not want to be friends. He seemed afraid. The therapist persisted, however, stating simply that he would not permit the child to succeed in hurting him and would see him again next week, in any event. In his play, which was largely concerned with building towers with blocks, he constantly compared the size of his towers with the towers of the therapist. Later he made the direct statement that he did not want to have a "pee wee" but wanted to be a girl. He had progressed from the concept of wanting to remain an infant into wanting to grow up to be a girl.

A few weeks later he conceded that he would be willing to become a boy. He gave up all of the hostile acting out during the sessions and formed a strong positive relationship with the therapist. It was felt that this rapid progression during a brief course of psychotherapy confirmed the diagnosis of a developmental deviation. Therapy was stopped but his progress continued.

PSYCHONEUROTIC DISORDERS

The psychoneuroses of childhood do not differ from those of adulthood as described in Chapter 15. These disorders result from intrapsychic conflict over sexual or aggressive wishes which are more or less successfully repressed. These disorders are distinct from the reactive disorders in which the conflicts are largely conscious. Neurotic conflicts may be derived from earlier conscious conflicts between the child and other persons in his environment and, indeed, almost always have their genesis in the preschool years. But well-crystallized psychoneurotic disorders do not ordinarily occur before the early school age period. When repression fails to control the unconscious sexual or aggressive wishes, anxiety or some other symptom results. Other mechanisms of defense are then called into play. Decompensation of the mental organization is not usually seen in these disorders, although some regression often takes place. Psychoneurotic disorders are rarely confused with psychotic disorders.

A 13-year-old white girl was referred to child psychiatry by an orthopedic surgeon because of a dramatic weakness of one year's duration in her left leg.

She was well until she sustained two "injuries" to her left knee, the first of which resulted from a fall while running in which she struck her left knee against the pavement. She had swelling and tenderness of the knee but did not seek medical care. Four days later she went surfing with a group of friends. She watched from the beach as one of her friends battled particularly large waves and became frightened that her turn was next. As she paddled out she saw a huge wave approaching her, hopped to her knees on the board in order to paddle faster and get through the wave before it broke, and felt sudden weakness in the quadriceps of her left leg. She was separated from the surf board and floundered in the water until rescued by one of the boys in the group. Since she complained of pain in the knee an orthopedist was consulted. Conservative treatment failed, arthrotomy was performed and a partial tear of a cruciate ligament was discovered and repaired. The weakness did not subside in spite of intensive physiotherapy and exercise. At the time of referral to psychiatry she had obvious gross atrophy of the thigh.

Psychiatric evaluation revealed an ostensibly healthy child who had a rather blase attitude about her year-long paralysis. She had always been a quiet, well-behaved girl, was quite attractive, and was not prone to neurotic complaints. She had done average work in school, although she did not like it, and was able to form adequate relationships with peers.

The one major flaw in her personality development was the complete inability to express herself when angry. She was not competitive in any way and had considerable difficulty asserting herself. The conflict which precipitated the conversion reaction had to do with aggressiveness; should she act brave and attempt to surf on this day when the ocean was particularly rough, or should she bow out and chance the ridicule of her peers? She chose to try but when overwhelmed with fear could not simply give up but was forced to develop a neurotic defense.

The neurotic symptom that was chosen was connected with the functioning of her left leg in which she had sustained an injury four days earlier. Thereafter the problem was complicated by the cosmetic defect, i.e., the surgical scar.

It should be emphasized that although this formulation is written as if it were a conscious thought process, it was certainly not so. One should be very careful not to accuse children of deliberately "faking" or "putting on" a symptom unless he is sure of his grounds. The author has seen very few children behave in such a manner. Final diagnosis of the preceding case: psychoneurotic disorder, conversion type.

PERSONALITY DISORDERS

This category should be reserved for those disturbances which are characterized by well-ingrained, pathological traits, but without the symptomatology seen in the psychoneurotic disorders. They sometimes begin with a reactive disorder of early childhood or with a psychoneurosis of later years, but become fixed and chronic and develop into a personality structure. Compulsive behavior, for example, might become an important part of the character structure of an adolescent boy, even though it began as normal compulsive behavior at eight years of age, as a result of being reinforced frequently by industrious, hard-working parents. The same character structure might also have its genesis in a conflict over sexuality that was not completely repressed, was handled in a neurotic manner with a compulsive avoidance of sexually symbolic stimuli, and was later resolved into a compulsive character disorder. In view of such diffuse etiologic factors, one can see that there will be a wide variation among persons with compulsive or any other type of personality disorders. They may range from a very mild degree of obsessiveness that will serve as an asset to a medical or engineering student, to a much more severely compulsive person who is unable to function properly because he cannot control his environment and the people in it fully enough.

Personality disorders should not really be diagnosed prior to the adolescent years since the personality structure is not well enough fixed before that time.

The Group for the Advancement of Psychiatry Committee on Child Psychiatry deviated considerably from the Standard Nomenclature of disease when developing the diagnostic schema used in this chapter. The reason they state for doing this is the shifting nature of childhood diseases and the possibility of significant change occurring during adolescence. Also conceptual problems arise when one attempts to apply the categories of the Standard Nomenclature to children. A brief definition of each subcategory will be given.

Compulsive Personality. Although these children show chronic and excessive concern with orderliness, cleanliness and conformity, they rarely decompensate in the face of increased anxiety and seldom develop crippling, neurotic symptoms. They usually perform rather well and may appear too mature.

Hysterical Personality. These children, mostly girls, appear to be very poised in social situations and seem seductive, coy, overaffective, and overdramatic, but underneath are having considerable difficulty with their sexual identification. They may develop a variety of symptoms such as hypochondriasis, conversion reactions, or dissociative reactions.

Anxious Personality. This subcategory was included in order to fit the immature child with a developmental deviation and the neurotic child with an anxiety neurosis. These children are chronically tense and apprehensive over new situations, but are often able to deal adequately with them after some initial anxiety. They seem to perceive the environment as threatening.

Overly Dependent Personality. In this category one should include the children who are chronically helpless, overdependent, and passively aggressive. Some of the children previously diagnosed as passive-aggressive personality, passive dependent type, should be included here.

Oppositional Personality. This is another new categoy. These children are characteristically oppositional and tend to answer in a negative fashion even when they have no conscious desire to do so. They sometimes present with school problems that have developed as a result of their oppositional behavior.

Overly Inhibited Personality. Here we can include children who are extremely shy and inhibited but who differ from the so-called schizoid personality by the fact that they seem to want to develop warm, meaningful relationships.

Overly Independent Personality. Children in this category are very active, demonstrating an apparent need to gain independence very rapidly, as if to cover feelings of helplessness or dependency. Children with fears of personal harm or physical inadequacies may develop this sort of independent personality.

Isolated (schizoid) Personality. In this category the children that have previously been said to have a schizoid personality are grouped. The name has been changed because only a few of these children seem to develop into a clearcut preschizophrenic picture implied by the former name which is felt to be inappropriate. The children are distant, detached, cold, or withdrawn and seen unconcerned about making friends with peers or members of their own family. They may occasionally, without provocation, demonstrate aggressive or sadistic behavior. They differ from the inhibited children previously described by virtue of their lack of desire to form meaningful relationships.

Mistrustful Personality. This category is reserved for early adolescent children who are more suspicious than is normal for that age. Projection is used as a mechanism of defense but it is felt that there is a certain group of children who do not develop into paranoid personalities.

Tension-Discharge Disorders. This is a new category that the Committee suggested largely because of the difficulty in terminology associated with such former categories as primary behavior disorders, antisocial personality, psychopathic personality, impulsive character, acting-out personality, and conduct disorders. They have then divided the category into two subcategories.

1) *Impulse-Ridden Personality.* These children seem to have a very low

frustration tolerance and shallow relationships with adults or other children. They have difficulty controlling both sexual and aggressive impulses and they have little concern about the consequences. Anxiety and guilt are not readily demonstrated and internalized conflicts are therefore not prominent. Instead they seem to have a superego defect and commonly have a history of extreme emotional deprivation during infancy and early childhood. They are often from low socioeconomic classes. Although they may have normal intelligence, they often present at the clinic with complaints of stealing, vandalism, fire setting, and the like.

2) *Neurotic Personality Disorders.* These children sometimes have the same presenting complaints, but have a greater capacity for good object relationships, have a better developed superego, and seem to be responding to internalized conflicts. Consequently, one might assume that the genetic factors, whatever they are, operated at a somewhat later age than in the case of the impulse-ridden personality disorder

Sociosyntonic Personality Disorder. This category is included in order to permit classification of children who show antisocial behavior according to the standards of the larger society but who come from subcultures in which this behavior is normal or sociosyntonic. Such an example would be a child who is behaving according to the gang mores in his isolated area of the city, or in another case, a child from a rural subculture which places a high value on magical thoughts and superstition.

Sexual Deviation. This category has been included for completeness but should rarely be used in childhood and should be reserved for a situation in which sexual deviation is regarded as the major personality disturbance. Transient homosexual behavior should not be classified here. In other words, sexual deviations should be used as a secondary diagnosis when some other

primary diagnosis is applied but should not be the primary diagnosis in and of itself.

PSYCHOTIC DISORDERS

A group of British child psychiatrists have recently established nine criteria for the diagnosis of childhood psychoses. These disorders are characterized by chronic, severe impairment of emotional relationships with others; a tendency toward preoccupation with inanimate objects; loss of speech, or failure of the development of speech; disturbance in sensory perception; bizarre or stereotyped behavior and mobility patterns; marked resistance to change in environment or in daily routine, personal identity, and uneven or fragmented intellectual development. Essentially then, this is a basic disturbance of ego function with symptoms related to all seven major areas of ego functioning: reality testing, object relations, impulse control, defensive functions, thought processes, synthetic thought, and autonomous functions of the ego.

Generally speaking, the course of childhood psychoses is chronic and relatively stable, compared to a course of adult psychoses in which one sometimes finds remissions and exacerabations.

Psychoses of Infancy and Early Childhood. In this group of psychoses we have early infantile autism, interactional psychotic disorders, and a third category in which children who do not readily fit into the first two classes can be categorized. *Early infantile autism* has its onset within the first year of life during which time the child fails to develop an attachment to its mother, remaining aloof and showing little apparent awareness of human contact. The child is much more interested in inanimate objects. Speech is usually delayed in development and, when it does develop, fails to serve the purpose of communication. Such children resist any changes in routine or in the environment and show their dissatisfaction by outbursts of temper or by acute anxiety attacks. A child often demonstrates problems in autonomous functions, feeding, and motor patterns. It is difficult to determine the intellectual capacity of such children, but their difficulty in communication through speech makes them unable to utilize what intellectual capacity they have.

A word of caution should be injected here against the use of the word autism to describe all withdrawn behavior. Autism in the sense described above is a noun. Autistic, used as a descriptive adjective, can be applied even to healthy persons who demonstrate a desire to be by themselves on occasion. One should be careful about the use of this word since the diagnosis of early infantile autism carries with it a grave prognosis.

Interactional psychotic disorder is the name applied to the second category of psychosis of infancy and early childhood which covers children with symbiotic psychoses (a term introduced by Margaret Mahler) but is not limited to this diagnosis. Many of these children seem to have developed reasonably well for the first year or two of life but then developed unusual dependency upon the mother and are apparently having considerable difficulty in developing an individual identity. One may be able to obtain a history of some real or fantasy threat to the mother-child relationship following which the child begins to regress, losing communicative speech and developing extreme anxiety and clinging behavior.

A six-year-old boy was referred with the chief complaint of alternating hyperactivity and withdrawal, and the cessation of speech. He had been the product of a full-term pregnancy, weighed ten pounds six ounces at birth, and was delivered by Caesarean section. The perinatal period and his early development were all within normal limits. He began using words at one year of age and short sentences at age two. At age two and a half he suffered several gen-

eralized convulsions during episodes of high fever and was noted to be extremely negativistic and at times withdrawn. Further development of language acquisition ceased. At age three and a half when his mother returned home from the hospital with a newborn sibling, he flew into a rage, tried to attack the baby, and ceased talking altogether. He became enuretic, stared into space for long periods of time, and developed a habit of rocking back and forth. No further development occurred in spite of participation in a special kindergarten, some family counseling, and some suggestions offered by a speech pathologist.

At six years of age he seemed to enjoy playing, but always by himself and always in a disorganized way. He was not destructive but developed some hyperactive behavior, alternating with his very withdrawn, detached behavior. He had a short attention span and although he was heard to occasionally utter short sentences to himself, he failed to develop any meaningful communication with other people. There was no family history of neurological or psychological disease and a complete physical examination including neurological evaluation failed to reveal any pathology. He was shown to have normal hearing and all observers felt that he was able to understand rather complex instructions and that he was not mentally retarded or brain damaged. Psychological testing per se could not be carried out.

The diagnosis of this child is psychosis of infancy and early childhood, interactional psychotic disorder.

Psychoses of Later Childhood. The Committee used the term *"schizophreniform psychotic disorder"* to indicate the parallels between this disorder and the adult form of schizophrenia, but to emphasize as well the developmental differences and the clinical impression that children with this disorder do not necessarily develop the later form. The disorder usually occurs in children between six and 12 years of age with either a gradual or sudden onset. They commonly develop neurotic symptoms first; then loosening of associations, hypochondriacal tendencies, temper outbursts with low frustration tolerance, withdrawal, intense involvement in fantasies; and finally a breakdown of thought processes and reality testing. When, on occasion, the disorder develops into one of the types of schizophrenia seen in adults, the appropriate diagnostic term should be used.

Psychoses of Adolescence. Adolescents may develop a schizophrenia disorder of the adult type, or an acute confusional state, a category designated by the Committee for the purpose of classifying a particular type of psychotic disorder which occurs in adolescence. The onset is often rather abrupt, with intense anxiety, depression, confusion in thinking, and depersonalization. These people seem to have a disturbed sense of identity without a true thought disorder or break with reality. The patient can sometimes maintain meaningful emotional relationships in spite of his difficulties and can also maintain, to some extent, the capacity to adapt to his environment. The prognosis is generally good for immediate recovery.

PSYCHOPHYSIOLOGIC DISORDERS

Psychophysiologic disorders have been discussed in Chapter 16, and it would be redundant to repeat this discussion here. The author would like to emphasize, however, the theory of multiple causality; emotional stress is a necessary, but not a sufficient cause for psychophysiologic disorders when the person is exposed to the emotional stress. Peptic ulcers may develop in children with high plasma pepsinogen levels (hypersecreters of hydrochloric acid) when faced with an emotional stress. Similarly, bronchial asthma is unlikely to occur in the child without a basic allergic diathesis regardless of the stress he experiences.

One must distinguish psychophysiologic disorders from reactive disorders, although the latter may predispose to the establishment of a bona fide psychophysiologic disorder at a later date. Children often suffer from separation or other emotional stresses in the course of a physical illness, and may develop a prolongation of the physical symptom as a result of the separation anxiety. A brief example will serve to illustrate this point:

A four-year-old girl was referred to the Child Psychiatry Clinic with the diagnosis of ulcerative colitis of one year duration and was successfully treated over the course of six months during which considerable attention was paid to the mother's emotional needs. This response, uncommon for ulcerative colitis, forces one to think more in terms of a reactive disorder.

At the age of three the child was suffering from a mild diarrhea which was originally diagnosed as an amoebic dysentery. She was attending nursery school at the time and it was not severe enough to cause her to miss school. After two weeks of the illness the following incident occurred: The parents and the child drove to the airport in order to say goodbye to the father who was to accept a position out of the country, from which he could return approximately once a month to see his family. On the return from the airport there was an automobile accident in which the mother and patient were run off the road, although neither was hurt. The mother became hysterical and unable to drive. A friend delivered the child to the nursery school and picked her up later that day. From this point on, the child's diarrhea became much more severe.

The diagnosis of ulcerative colitis was made and a medical regimen was instituted. During the course of psychotherapy the diarrhea was rather mild but occurred periodically, commonly during the family trips necessitating frequent stops and occasionally when the child was frustrated during psychotherapeutic sessions.

It would seem that this case would best be diagnosed as a reactive disorder but if the current remission is not maintained and exacerabations occur as the child grows, then the diagnosis should be changed to that of a psychophysiologic disorder.

There are certain types of psychophysiologic disorders that occur exclusively in children. Eczema in infants and acne in adolescents are examples of skin disorders; breath-holding spells and bronchial asthma are examples of respiratory disorders; and certain cases of paroxysmal auricular tachycardia, migraine, and certain types of syncope are examples of cardiovascular disorders. Variations in the cellular components of the hemic and lympatic system have been associated with emotional stress and may account for some decreased resistance to infectious diseases during childhood. Psychophysiologic gastrointestinal disorders peculiar to children include cardiospasm, certain types of constipation and diarrhea, certain types of pylorspasm, psychogenic megacolon (not Hirschsprung's disease), idiopathic celiac disease, certain types of polydypsia, and obesity.

Failure to thrive may be a psychologic problem of infancy as is persistent colic and certain types of recurrent vomiting. Psychophysiologic genitourinary disorders are rare in children. Some growth disturbances may be classed as psychophysiologic endocrine disorders. Other psychophysiologic disorders that one occasionally sees in children are disorders of the organs of special sense, blephrospasm, diplopia, tinnitus and hyperacusis.

The brain syndromes and mental deficiency have been dealt with in Chapters 24 and 25 respectively and will not be considered here.

THE ROLE OF PREVENTION IN CHILD PSYCHIATRY

Child psychiatry has developed a body of knowledge strong enough and broad enough to permit the application of preventive techniques and, indeed, pediatricians have been attempting to provide such aid to the parent of a young child under the term "anticipatory guidance" for many years. This is an example of primary prevention; that is, the prevention of a disease in a susceptible population. By anticipating parental concern over developmental problems, the pediatrician prevents undue concern and avoids an emotional problem. Other examples of primary prevention are intervention on behalf of the child in family crises such as separation or divorce of the parents, the birth of siblings, serious illness or death in a member of the family, and illness when it involves hospitalization or surgery for the child. A four-year-old child will be very interested in a simple explanation of the events that will surround his tonsillectomy. A pediatrician who utilizes an anesthesia mask and a surgeon's cap and mask in the course of such an explanation will find that he is able to avoid much of the Halloween-like mystery that surrounds much of our traditional medical behavior. By playing it out in the physician's office and again at home, the child is often able to work through much of the anxiety related to the surgery and sail through the surgery with no difficulty.

Secondary prevention is defined as the early diagnosis and prompt treatment of a disease so that the course of the disease can be considerably shortened. The child psychiatrist can be very effective when consulted early in the course of a disease. He should, therefore, develop a receptive attitude in his relationships with other members of the medical profession as well as with school teachers, juvenile courts, and public welfare agencies that supply services to childen. Indeed, his effectiveness is so much greater under these circumstances that it is morally mandatory for him to work closely with such community facilities. In the use of consultations alone and brief forms of psychotherapy to "nip in the bud" a developing emotional disorder, that psychiatrist is relying on the ego-strengths of the patient. He is attempting to put the patient on the right track and relying on the patient's own assets to carry on from there.

Another specific area in which the psychiatrist can be active in a preventive way entails the prevention of psychological complication which is associated with various chronic physical diseases. Rheumatoid arthritics, those with diabetes mellitus or rheumatic fever, physically handicapped children, deaf or blind children, and children who have undergone some sort of deforming surgical procedure such as colostomies might all profit tremendously by meeting, club fashion, with some child psychiatrist or a psychiatrically-oriented pediatrician in a modified form of group psychotherapy aimed at the prevention of the psychological sequelae that are prone to occur.

Tertiary prevention, that is, the treatment of advanced cases of illness in an attempt to prevent further complications and sequalae, may well involve long-term psychotherapy. The rehabilitation of institutionalized retarded children is a case in point. Continued institutionalization will separate the patient from society and yet sudden discharge from the institution often seems inappropriate. There is great need for a rehabilitative program in this area. A similar program could be devised for delinquent children.

TREATMENT

Psychiatric therapy has been the subject of public criticism on many occasions throughout history. Three types of criticisms are being heard today, and all are having an effect on child psychiatry and will continue to do so in the future. All three criticisms are justified and have been voiced by professional mental health workers as well as by the public. The length of treatment as exemplified by long-term individual psychotherapy and by psychoanalysis, although undoubtedly helpful and perhaps curative in certain instances, cannot possibly be applied to the large number of mentally ill patients. There are too few psychoanalysts, each man can treat too few patients, and the training of a psychoanalyst is too long to permit the treatment of a significant segment of the patient

population. Consequently there is a trend toward the development of briefer methods of psychotherapy, both by the psychoanalyst and psychiatrist. Since brief forms of psychotherapy are probably more effective in children than in adults, this trend is having a significant effect on child psychiatry.

The second criticism, namely, the inapplicability of psychotherapies to people in the lower socioeconomic classes, is also well taken. Workers in all mental health fields have taken in the first steps in developing new techniques applicable to all people. Since child psychiatry deals with young families who have not established economic stability, awareness of this problem applies more than it does to an older age population. Indeed, child psychiatry, in particular child guidance clinics, has pioneered in this area. Some of the techniques used in child guidance clinics for many years are now being applied in community mental health programs aimed at adults. Nevertheless, there is much to be done and this trend must go much further than it has to date.

The third major criticism, the isolation of mentally ill persons from the society and the exclusion of "identified patients" from interpersonal relationships within the society, has been longstanding. There is movement away from the establishment of residential treatment centers in the secluded countryside. To get away from the hubbub of the city life may be restful and therapeutic, but such isolation not only makes the break from previous relationships complete, it also makes it difficult to reestablish new relationships within the society. The trend toward the establishment of community mental health facilities, day care centers, night hospitals where the patient continues in his occupation or in school during the day, and short-term treatment facilities in general hospitals are all big steps in the right direction. Perhaps even more important is the sociological view that illness can occur in a family or in a group and be treated as such, rather than identifying one member of the group as a patient and isolating him from the group. This applies particularly to child psychiatry with its focus on family life.

With these trends in mind, we shall consider the various therapies available for children. One should also bear in mind another factor more explicit in the report of the Committee of Child Psychiatry of the Group for the Advancement of Psychiatry as described in the section on classification. The Committee emphasizes the assets or strengths of a child as well as the presence of psychopathology. This is most important, for in working with children one soon finds that many patients will do very well once they've been placed on the right track or, to put it another way, the parents are pathogenic only because of some misconception in respect to child rearing practices and have the ability to be very fine parents when one points out the error of their ways. The development of personalities is still in process in children and a limited amount of intervention is all that is necessary on some occasions to maintain the balance in the right direction.

Brief Psychotherapy. For our purposes brief psychotherapy is defined as therapy involving less than 12 regular visits. The diagnostic process is in itself therapeutic in many instances and it is difficult to draw the line between diagnosis and therapy. To our way of thinking the physician begins to form a diagnostic opinion in the early part of the first visit after which he obtains additional information in an attempt to confirm or reject his working diagnosis. In psychiatry, as distinct from other branches of medicine, this is a never-ending process and some have said that we should make our diagnosis after we have completed our treatment of a given case. Since this is impractical and since at some time the physician must make a statement to the patient or the family unit regarding his opinion, the author has taken the stand that the first visit is diagnostic and can be concluded by such a statement with the understanding that this working diagnosis might well require significant revision during the ensuing treatment.

Healthy responses can be diagnosed during this period of time and dealt with appropriately. Many reactive disorders can also be treated within 12 visits in a very successful manner. Acute episodes of psychoneurotic or psychophysiologic disorders might also be treated during a brief span of time even though future crises are to be expected. The author has had some success in treating children who have difficulty expressing hostility by encouraging them to experiment with different techniques in an attempt to find one that will be more adaptive than their current behavior is. This can be seen as an attempt to prevent the development of a personality disorder.

When one is undertaking brief psychotherapy he must be more active than he might be in long-term, individual psychotherapy, and he will focus on a limited number of areas of psychic functioning even to the extent of not allowing the patient to bring up other more or less irrelevant material.

Family Therapy. From the foregoing discussion it is obviously more appropriate at times to treat the entire family than any one of its members. On some occasions the identified patient presented to the child psychiatrist appears to be the healthiest member of the family group. Such cases suggest a communication problem or some sort of complex lack of understanding of feelings and needs of the various family members. Some such cases are refractory to treatment or at least require a tremendous effort on the part of the therapist while others can be managed in a relatively brief span of time. Other situations in which the treatment of the entire family would seem to be the treatment of choice would be cases of developmental deviation and in some cases of brain syndromes and mental retardation in which the family members are forced to make an adjustment to the disturbed patient. Family therapy has also been used when one member appears to be psychoneurotic and in certain cases of psychophysiologic disorders.

The reader is cautioned to distinguish between family therapy per se and psychiatric social casework of parents in conjunction with some form of psychotherapy for the child patient. Although the experienced psychiatric social worker is competent in both areas of endeavor, different techniques prevail and one is working with entirely different goals and precepts in mind. In social casework one is attempting to aid the parents to adjust to the various phases through which the child will go during the course of psychotherapy. The social caseworker is also attempting to enhance the therapy by virtue of adding additional anamnestic material and by gaining a deeper understanding into the psychodynamics of the family. One member of the family, however, has been identified as the patient and work with the other members of the family is seen as supportive and as an adjunct to the primary therapy directed toward the patient. This fundamental principle puts an entirely different focus on the therapy and thereby governs the behavior of the therapist.

Drug Therapy. The emphasis on intrapsychic, interpersonal, and family psychodynamics has resulted in a limitation of the use of pharmacologic agents in the treatment of emotional disturbances of children. But there remains a place for the use of adjunctive drug therapy. One should think of these agents as ameliorative rather than curative. Freed (1962) reports on a broad experience in this field and points out the usefulness of drugs in certain selected cases. Various phenothiazines are effective in improving the adjustment of a significant number of disturbed, mentally deficient children. Both the major and minor tranquilizers as well as some of the stimulant drugs have been found useful in the behavior disorders of children with and without brain damage. These drugs should be used only in an attempt to prevent personality disorganization or as an adjunct to some form of psychotherapy rather than to abolish anxiety. It would seem that children are less prone than adults to develop side effects from the potent tranquilizers. The most common side effect is drowsiness, which can be controlled by lowering the dosage. Basal ganglia dysfunction is the most dramatic side effect and is idiosyncratic but can also be controlled by decreasing the dosage or discontinuing the drug. The placebo effect occurs just as frequently in children as it does in adults.

Behavior Therapy. Many therapists, particularly psychologists, have emphasized recently the importance of reinforcing socially acceptable behavior in terms of the operant conditioning model. Mowrer was one of the first to point out that anxiety or fear can serve as a reinforcement or a reward. In this way neurotic symptoms are self-perpetuating because of the reinforcement which arises from their reduction of anxiety. Techniques have been developed, then, for the deconditioning of these patients, and in child psychiatry particular emphasis has been placed on the treatment of autistic children with some degree of success. Such techniques have a definite place in the armamentarium of the mental health worker who deals with children, but they are difficult for the inexperienced worker to apply. Immediate reinforcement is necessary if one is to achieve one's goal and it is difficult for the therapist to achieve such immediacy. He, in effect, reinforces the behavior that follows that which he intended to reinforce. The author used this technique briefly in the treatment of a psychotic boy whom he was trying to teach to name correctly the colors of red and blue blocks. When commanded to hand the therapist the red block, the child responded correctly in due time, but before reinforcement could be given in the form of food or social reinforcement, the child negated his correct response by saying, "It's blue." It is clear that this form of therapy lends itself to the invention of mechanical or electrically operated reinforcing machines suitable for supplying this immediate reinforcement.

Group Therapies. This form of psychotherapy has been used with children, apparently with beneficial results, but it is more efficacious for work with adults. It is difficult to collect a group of children that is homogeneous enough in age and in developmental stage to warrant treating them as a group. Adolescents lend themselves much more readily to group therapy. It would seem, however, that groups of children with similar symptoms or diseases such as diabetes mellitus, obesity, cystic fibrosis, or any other chronic disease of childhood could be treated through group work. The emphasis would at first be educational as was the case historically when Pratt used such techniques with tuberculous patients in 1905.

Long-term, Individual Psychotherapy. Long-term, psychoanalytically oriented psychotherapy has a very definite place in child psychiatry and is probably the treatment of choice in certain selected psychoneurotic patients. Classical psychoanalytic techniques are rarely used with children and it has been said that only one percent of a child analyst's time, if he is engaged in a private practice in a major eastern city in this country, is devoted to the analysis of children. Instead he uses his analytic techniques on older individuals, adolescents or adults, and is becoming more and more interested in new applications of his psychoanalytic knowledge and shorter forms of psychotherapy.

When a five- to ten-year-old child has a well-established internalized conflict and neurotic symptoms resulting from the breakdown of defensive mechanisms and when one cannot see evidence of significant pathology amongst the family members, individual psychotherapy with the child is probably indicated. This child has a psychoneurosis by definition rather than a reactive disorder and will not be likely to respond to brief psychotherapy. The therapist is forced to decide on one of two alternatives; he may help the child repress the conflict in order to alleviate the symptoms or he may set out upon a course of therapy aimed at uncovering the conflict so that it can be worked through. The theoretical danger of the former is that the conflict will reappear in later life, causing a return of these or different symptoms. Although this theoretical danger exists, the author is aware of no research designed to answer the question. On the other hand, it does not seem more logical to attempt to alleviate the neurosis itself by resolving the conflict. Well-controlled follow-up studies of long-term psychotherapy are almost nonexistent and are greatly needed.

Long-term psychotherapy may also be indicated in personality disorders and in psychophysiologic disorders. When one is faced with a latency age child who seems to be developing a personality disorder, he can often predict a very unhappy adolescence for this child unless some form of psychiatric intervention is helpful. Long-term individual psychotherapy is indicated in some of these cases with the very limited goal of attempting nothing more than enabling the child to be more flexible and hence have a greater opportunity to enjoy and to profit from the adolescent years.

Residential Treatment. When a child is too sick to attend school and when other forms of treatment seem inappropriate, residential treatment may be indicated. The form of treatment, however, should depend on the individual case since some would be able to attend a regular public school, provided they had a night hospital to turn to after school, while others would need a day care center without sleeping facilities, and still others would need either complete hospitalization or some other form of structured environment, such as a training school or even a reformatory. All of the forms of treatment previously described can be utilized within the walls of these facilities but most important is the necessity of working with the staff so that a unified approach is carried out.

Other Forms of Treatment. One should not leave the subject of therapy in child psychiatry without mentioning other community resources. The Big Brothers of America is an outstanding example. This organization was formed by a group of Presbyterian laymen in New York City who went to the Junvenile Court and offered to help delinquent boys. Their emphasis thereafter has been on predelinquent boys and they have accomplished a great deal of preventive child psychiatry. Their *modus operandi* is to hire one professional youth worker in a community whose job it is to match one young man with one fatherless boy or a boy whose father is relatively inactive in the family and agrees to his child's participation in the program. The duty of the Big Brother, then, is to see this boy at least once a week and do whatever seems appropriate, e.g., help with a school project, engage in some form of recreation, and so on. The therapist would do well to acquaint himself with YMCA, YWCA, Boy Scout, and Girl Scout programs in his community, and might refer parents of a retarded child to the local chapter of the National Association for Retarded Children. One should also be acquainted, of course, with various social agencies such as the Aid to Dependent Children Program, Foster Home Program, The Board of Child Welfare, and Homemakers Programs.

SELECTED REFERENCES

Ackerman, N. W. 1958. *The Psychodynamics of Family Life, Diagnosis and Treatment of Family Relationships.* New York, Basic Books, Inc.

Allen, L. H. 1942. *Psychotherapy with Children.* New York, W. W. Norton & Co.

Bolman, W. M., and Westman, J. C. 1967. Prevention of mental disorder: An overview of current programs. American Journal of Psychiatry *123*, 1058-1068.

Bowlby, J. 1960. Grief and mourning in infancy and early childhood. The Psychiatric Study of the Child. *15*, 9-52.

Brenneman, J. 1933. Pediatric psychology and the child guidance movement. Journal of Pediatrics *2*, 1-26.

Bridger, W. H. 1965. Individual differences in behavior and autonomic activity in newborn infants. American Journal of Public Health *55*, 1899-1901.

Brodey, W. M. 1963. On family therapy. Family Processes *2*, 280-287.

Chess, S. 1959. *An Introduction to Child Psychiatry.* New York, Grune & Stratton, Inc.

Cramer, J. B. 1959. Common neuroses of childhood. In *American Handbook of Psychiatry,* ed. S. Arieti. New York, Basic Books, Inc., pp. 797-815.

Creak, M., chairman. 1961. Schizophrenic syndrome in childhood: Progress report (April, 1961) of a working party. British Medical Journal *2*, 889-890.

Crutcher, R. 1943. Child psychiatry, A history of its development. Psychiatry *6*, 191-201.

Davids, A., and DeVault, S. 1962. Maternal anxiety during pregnancy and childbirth abnormalities. Psychosomatic Medicine *24*, 464-470.

Erikson, E. H. 1950. *Childhood and Society.* New York, W. W. Norton & Co.

Finch, S. M. 1960. *Fundamentals of Child Psychiatry.* New York, W. W. Norton & Co.

Freed, H. 1962. *The Chemistry and Therapy of Behavior Disorders in Children.* Springfield, Illinois, Charles C Thomas, Publisher.

Gardner, G. E. 1959. Psychiatric problems of adolescence. In *American Handbook of Psychiatry,* ed. S. Arieti, New York, Basic Books, Inc., pp. 870-892.

Glueck, S., and Glueck, E. 1950. *Unraveling Juvenile Delinquency.* Cambridge, Harvard University Press.

Goldfarb, W. 1961. *Childhood Schizophrenia.* Cambridge, Harvard University Press.

Group for the Advancement of Psychiatry. 1953. *Psychopathological Disorders in Childhood: Theoretical Considerations and a Proposed Classification.* New York, Group for the Advancement of Psychiatry Report No. 62.

Ham, G. C. 1953. *Twenty Years of Psychoanalysis,* ed. F. Alexander and H. Ross. New York, W. W. Norton & Co., p. 180.

Johnson, A. M. 1959. Juvenile delinquency. In *American Handbook of Psychiatry*, ed. S. Arieti. New York, Basic Books, Inc., pp. 840-856.

Kanner, L. 1941. *In Defense of Mothers: How to Bring up Children in Spite of the More Zealous Psychologists.* Springfield, Illinois, Charles C Thomas, Publisher.

Kanner, L. 1944. Early infantile autism. Journal of Pediatrics 25, 211-217.

Kanner, L. 1957. *Child Psychiatry*, 3rd edition. Springfield, Illinois, Charles C Thomas, Publisher.

Kessler, J. W. 1966. *Psychopathology of Childhood.* Englewood Cliffs, New Jersey, Prentice-Hall, Inc.

Levy, D. M. 1959. *The Demonstration Clinic for the Psychological Study and Treatment of Mother and Child in Medical Practice.* Springfield, Illinois, Charles C Thomas, Publisher.

Lidz, T. 1963. *The Family and Human Adaptation, Three Lectures.* New York, International University Press, Inc.

Lipton, E. L., Steinschneider, A., and Richmond, J. B. 1966. Autonomic function in the neonate: VII. Maturational changes in cardiac control. Child Development 37, 1-15.

Mahler, M. S., Furer, M., and Settlage, C. F. 1959. Severe emotional disturbances in childhood: Psychosis. In *American Handbook of Psychiatry*, ed. S. Arieti. New York, Basic Books, Inc., pp. 816-839.

Maier, H. W. 1965. *Three Theories of Child Development* (Erikson, Piaget and Sears). New York, Harper & Row, Publishers, Inc.

Marks, P. A. 1961. An assessment of the diagnostic process in a child guidance setting. Psychological Monographs No. 507 (Vol. 75, No. 3).

Masland, R. L., Sarason, S. B., and Gladwin, T. 1958. *Mental Subnormality: Biological, Psychological and Cultural Factors.* New York, Basic Books, Inc.

Mirsky, I. A. 1953. Psychoanalysis and the biological sciences. In *Twenty Years of Psychoanalysis*, ed. F. Alexander and H. Ross. New York, W. W. Norton & Co., p. 165.

Mirsky, I. A. 1958. Physiologic, psychologic, and social determinants in the etiology of duodenal ulcer. American Journal of Digestive Diseases, New Series 3, 285-314.

Mutter, A. Z., and Schleifer, M. J. 1966. The role of psychological and social factors in the onset of somatic illness in children. Psychosomatic Medicine 28, 333-343.

O'Neal, P., and Robins, L. N. 1958. The relation of childhood behavior problems to adult psychiatric status: A 30-year follow-up study of 150 subjects. American Journal of Psychiatry *114*, 961-969.

O'Neal, P., and Robins, L. N. 1958. Childhood patterns predictive of adult schizophrenia: A 30-year follow-up study. American Journal of Psychiatry *115*, 385-391.

Peiper, A. 1963. *Cerebral Function in Infancy and Childhood*, tr. from Nagler and Nagler the 3rd revised German edition. New York, Consultants Bureau.

Rabinovitch, R. D. 1959. Reading and learning disabilities. In *American Handbook of Psychiatry*, ed. S. Arieti. New York, Basic Books, Inc., pp. 857-869.

Ribble, M. A. 1965. *The Rights of Infants, Early Psychological Needs and Their Satisfaction*, 2nd edition. New York, Columbia University Press.

Richmond, J. B., and Lustman, S. L. 1955. Autonomic function in the neonate: 1. Implications for psychosomatic theory. Psychosomatic Medicine *17*, 269-275.

Rimland, B. 1964. *Infantile Autism; the Syndrome and Its Implications for a Neural Theory of Behavior.* New York, Appleton-Century-Crofts, Inc.

Robins, L. N. 1966. *Deviant Children Grown Up, A Sociological and Psychiatric Study of Sociopathic Personality.* Baltimore, The Williams & Wilkins Co.

Satir, V. M. 1964. *Conjoint Family Therapy; A Guide to Theory and Technique*, Palo Alto, California, Science and Behavior Books.

Soddy, K. 1960. *Clinical Child Psychiatry.* London, Bailliere, Tindall & Cox.

Spitz, R. A. 1955. The primal cavity; A contribution to the genesis of perception and its role for psychoanalytic theory. Psychoanalytic Study of the Child *10*, 215-240.

Spitz, R. A. 1965. *The First Year of Life, A Psychoanalytic Study of Normal and Deviant Development.* New York, International University Press, Inc.

Van den Bergh, R. L., Taylor, E. S., and Drose, V. 1966. Emotional illness in habitual aborters following suturing of the incompetent cervical os, Psychosomatic Medicine *28*, 257-263.

Witmer, H. L., and Kotinsky, R. 1952. *Personality in the Making, the Fact-Finding Report of the Midcentury White House Conference on Children and Youth.* New York, Harper & Row, Publishers, Inc.

Work, H. H., and Call, J. D. 1965. *A Guide to Preventive Child Psychiatry: the Art of Parenthood.* New York, Blakiston Division, McGraw-Hill Book Co., Inc.

NAME INDEX

Italicized numbers are bibliographic references.

627

SUBJECT INDEX